PUBLISHED IN GREAT BRITAIN BY

ENTHUSIASTS PUBLICATIONS
SHERINGTON,
NEWPORT PAGNELL,
BUCKS.
MK16 9PE.

PRINTED IN GREAT BRITAIN BY

WOOLNOUGH BOOKBINDING LTD.,
EXPRESS WORKS,
CHURCH STREET,
IRTHLINGBOROUGH,
NORTHANTS.
NN9 5SE.

FIRST PUBLISHED May 1987.
REPRINTED November 1987.
REPRINTED March 1989.
REPRINTED December 1989.
REPRINTED February 1990.

ISBN 0 907700 12 8

CONTENTS. PAGE.

INTRODUCTION.

MILITARY AIRFIELDS IN THE BRITISH ISLES 1939-1945.

This is an attempt to record in alphabetical order all, or the majority of the military airfields that were in use during the Second World War in the British Isles. Very little information has yet been collated on the extent and physical aspects of wartime airfields. Perhaps this summary will go some way towards rectifying this situation.

The impact of these airfields on the men and women who fought from or served on these sites, and on the local population, has been deep and long lasting. Being called to the station orderly room and handed a movement order and travel warrent could start all sorts of mixed emotions in any serving airman during the last war. If the posting was within the United Kingdom the feelings were usually pleasent; that was until a knowing look from the orderly room clerk dampened any temporary joy in the anticipation of escape from the present God-forsaken hole! Doubts were then created in the mind: could the next posting be worse? Surely that was not possible! Where was this new station? What happened there-was it an operational fighter or bomber field, of perhaps a training unit, or another back-water for the maintenance of aircraft or the storing of equipment?

How did one get there, was the accomodation in comfortable pre-war permanent buildings, or in the ubiquitous nissen or other temporary wartime huts? How far was it from the nearest railway station and the escape route away on leave? Were there any Waafs, and where was the nearest pub and dance hall?

For a small consideration the orderly room clerk would consult his book and make out a railway warrent invariably 'via London'

Until now the reference the clerk consulted has been hidden behind closed doors. Now, with the expiry of the 30-year period the information which was then available only to a few is contained in this record, together with other particulars, for the benefit of aeronautical historians and research groups. It may also recall & connect the experiences of the men and women who served with the British, Comonwealth, American and Allied Airforces & who might like to be reminded of where a tidy slice of their lives were spent.

This book does not set out to record details of operations undertaken from a particular base. This has been and is still being very carefully documented in a host of well written books and official histories. Nor does it list all units which operated from an airfield during the period of hostilities. It is simply a record of the state of the airfield at 1st. December 1944, giving details of the technical and domestic facilities available, together with its location, a lay-out plan with a sketch map of the area, and the recorded personnel strength at that date.

The 1st. December 1944 has been chosen because by then the war-time building programne for airfields was to all intents and purposes, over. Airfields still under construction or re-construction at this time included Heathrow[for Transport Command], Lakenheath[for Bomber Command], and Culdrose[for the Royal Navy]. These are a few of the airfields covered by this survey which are still in existence today.

BACKGROUND.

When military flying first started in the British Isles at the beginning of the century, any reasonable flat and level surface would suffice as a landing ground. Like the flying machines, accommodation and services were primitive, and any back-up support was usually provided by the nearest military establishment. Take-off surfaces were invariably grass, with flying restricted to daytime fine weather periods.

It was not until 1914 that the first runway was laid. This was for the use of the Royal Flying Corps at Choques in France, and consisted of railway sleepers. After the outbreak of the First World War the need for airfields increased considerably in the United Kingdom, until there were several hundred of them. They ranged in size from establishments of over one hundred aircraft to small landing grounds for aircraft in transit to and from France, manned with a minimum of men and equipment. When the war came to an end most of the fields reverted to their original owners for agriculture and other uses.

The peace-time Royal Air Force settled down to an uneasy period of contraction, consolidation and planning, with airfields and facilities just keeping pace with aircraft needs.

In 1928 an excavated and rolled limestone take-off surface was used at Cranwell, and in 1931 the first real runway was in use by the R.A.F. This was not however, in the U.K., but at Kohat in the North West frontier region of what was then the Indian Empire. The runway size was 400 yards long by 50 yards wide covered in tarmacadam.

The size of existing airfields had been specified in 1930 as an area with a diameter of 1100 yards. This was a safety distance for use when practice bombing the home aerodrome with the standard 8.5 pound practice bomb. Grass field suitability was based on the following specifications:-

Turf on clay.	- up to 25lbs. per square inch.
Good light soil.	- up to 40 " " " "
Gradients.	- not to exceed 1: 50.
Approach angles.	" " " 1: 15.

Buildings had become more permanent with hangars for aircraft and brick barracks, but some accommodation still consisted of hutted camps.

From 1934, with the commencement of the re-armament programmes, airfield construction really began to expand. A large number of new airfields had to be constructed and existing ones enlarged. This was mainly in eastern England for use against the new threat from Nazi Germany. Until then it had been considered thaf France was the only likely Continental enemy in the foreseeable future. Development of airfields had consequently taken place mainly in the south of England.

As aircraft weights increased, hardened take-off and landing strips became more necessary, with the first bitumen covered runways being built at Gosport and Odiham. This was in 1938 when it was decided that new airfields should be constructed as follows :

Class A bomber airfields [40%]	One - 1400 yard and three - 1100 yard long runways.
Class B bomber airfields [60%]	One - 1400 yard and three - 900 yard long runways.
Fighter airfields.	Two - 800 yard long runways 50 feet wide.

Runways at bomber stations were connected with a 50 feet wide perimeter track. At fighter stations this was reduced to 35 feet. In 1939 fighter runways were increased to 1000 yards in length.

By November 1940 at all new airfields the main runway length had been increased to 1400 yards, and was further increased one month later to 1600 yards. Finally, in April 1941, this was increased to 2000 yards, when secondary runways were specified at 1400 yards. The width was standardised at 50 yards. In April 1942 approach angles for all runways were fixed at 1 : 50, and gradients had not to exceed 1: 80.

When war was declared on 3rd. September 1939 many things were considered essential to achieve superiority and win the air war. The main ones probably were a high level of technical and professional skill, and a vast number of men and machines together with the airfields, buildings, storage and repair depots, flying and ground training schools, hospitals and recruit centres required to support and house the necessary personnel and equipment.

This survey only covers the locations from which military flying took place and, whilst it is appreciated it may not list every field , it does record the vast majority. The non-flying units in some cases were no more than a group of buildings, custom built, or requisitioned within a community, for headquarters or similar uses. Others were vast areas of uniform pre-fabricated buildings and nissen huts stretching into the distance.

The build-up and composition of the non-flying units and the part they played in the winning of the war in the air would be an interesting subject for research and one which has been entirely neglected.

At the beginning of the war there were about 170 airfields under R.A.F. control, with a very large construction programme under way. This reached a peak in 1941, when 125 new airfields were completed by a labour force of 60,000 men. By the end of 1944 this building programne was mainly over, bringing the total of military airfields in the British Isles to over 670[including auxiliary landing grounds and requisitioned civil airports]. 444 of these, all with runways, were completed during the period 1939-45. There were also 20 or more flying boat bases and alighting areas scattered around our coastline.

It is little wonder that Britain during this period has been referred to as an unsinkable aircraft carrier anchored off the coast of Europe, and as far as the American aircrew were concerned, usually hidden under a blanket of rain clouds.

At the end of 1944 the building programne now centred on bases for the Fleet Air Arm, which needed specialised facilities to form, work up and train the squadrons required for the carrier Task Forces of the Pacific Fleet. The Royal Navy required runway widths of only 30 yards to conform to carrier flight decks as against the 50 yard width required by the R.A.F. for their Class A operational airfields.

Some airfields, including Heathrow, Boscombe Down and Lakenheath now featured 3000 yard long runways 100 yard wide. These were constructed for the very heavy bombers planned and under construction, such as the American B29 and the British Vickers Windsor. This allowed for aircraft of up to 140,000 lbs. A.U.W. and tyre pressures of 85 P.S.I.

It is interesting to compare these runway widths with those of present day international airports, which are rarely wider than 60 metres[65 yards]

As has been stated above, the wartime construction was virtually over by December 1944. The particulars recorded here relate to the airfields as they were then. It will be appreciated that these sites were in a constant state of flux throughout the war years. Some were under construction, while others were completed only, in some cases, to be de-requisitioned. To meet operational requirements facilities were added as units were moved in and out.

It was official Air Ministry policy to name service airfields after the parish in which they were situated. They could be, and often were, known locally by one or more alternative names. This leads to misunderstanding when airfield locations are being recorded or are under discussion. Official documents compound the error by referring to the alternative names in some cases. The airfield place names in this book are those recorded in S.D.310 "R.A.F. Airfields in the United Kingdom"[1946 edition]

A large number of airfields are well known for their associations with Bomber, Fighter or Coastal Commands, and with the American Airforces, or with the operations which were mounted from them. It is , nevertheless, equally interesting to read of, and fitting to recall, the places which were less in the public eye: the air stations of Transport, Flying Training, Technical Training and Maintenance Commands, and the shore bases of the Fleet Air Arm.

Airfields were transferred from Command to Command, and within Commands from Group to Group, during the course of hostilities. This was necessary in order to meet the various operational requirements as the fortunes of war flowed and ebbed around these islands.

THE WAR YEARS.

When Britain found itself alone in 1940 after the defeat of France it was considered that the only way that victory could be achieved was through air power. Bomber Command was the obvious, and the then only, instument to fulfill this task. The British aircraft and construction industries were given the necessary directives, and access to equipment and materials to design and supply the aircraft and build the bases.

Manpower was directed into industry to meet the ever growing need for skilled labour. In fact, in the end more labour was devoted solely to the production of four engined bombers than to the production of all the equipment for the British army. To supplement home production aircraft purchasing commissions were set up in the U.S.A. to obtain further aircraft, whilst a nation wide propaganda exercise was used to sell this method of winning the war and to sustain and encourage the home front.

Although the only examples the British Government had to go by were the air policing methods used in the inter-war years in Arabia, Mesopotania and the North West frontier, it nevertheless put forward a very good case in the national press and on radio. To strengthen the message further the cinemas were used to show the full length colour cartoon "Victory Through Air Power". This was produced by the Walt Disney Organisation and was based on Sikorsky's book of the same name. However the German nation was a slightly different kettle of fish from a few thousand dissident tribesmen armed with rifles.

It was with a heartfelt sense of relief that Britain welcomed in 1941, first the Soviet Union and then the U.S.A. to its side. Other ways of winning the war then become open and the grandiose plans of victory through air power could be quietly shelved. "Victory Through Air Power" dissappeared from the screens and has not been seen since.

At the time of writing the Walt Disney Organisation can only say that there are no plans for redistribution of this film and there are no prints available in this country. It would certainly make very interesting viewing for present day aviation enthusiasts.

In 1942 R.A.F. airfields were made available to the American Airforces, units of which had begun to arrive in ever increasing numbers. 36 additional airfields were built especially for them by the Air Ministry Works Department - an example of Lend Lease in reverse [Lend Lease was an Act ot the U.S. Congress passed in March 1941 for the leasing of American arms and equipment to her allies without payment for the duration of the war]

Later the United States Army Engineer Battalions were able to make good any shortfall in British airfield construction. They completed a further 14 airfields for the American Airforces.

In order to construct each Type A or similar size wartime airfield about 600 acres had to be requisitioned, cleared and levelled, and access roads and sometimes branch railway lines built. Any existing building that could be a hazard to flying or security was demolished and compensation paid. 130,000 tons of hardcore, cement and tarmacadam were needed to lay the 40,000 square yards of runways, taxiways, hardstandings, roads and pathways. This, plus about 50 miles of pipes and conduits, went into the self contained small township that would rise out of the British countryside.

Within eighteen months, in the then usually obscure locations that the Air Ministry's Aerodromes Board had decreed must become operational airfields, prefabricated buildings for both technical and domestic use began to dot the site, with the tall steel hangars and water towers being the dominant features.

Runways were laid in the now familiar shape of a letter A, the main one being 2000 yards in length and in the direction of the prevailing wind with a subsidiary runway each side about 1400 yards long and at an angle of about 60 degrees to the main one. Even before the contractors had finished building, the R.A.F. or other service advance parties would begin to arrive in order to bring some sort of military order out of the general confusion that constituted the site.

The first tasks of these advance parties included receiving, unpacking, checking and allocating the steady stream of spare parts, ground handling and other specialised equipment, ammunition, bombs, fuel, clothing and food that began to arrive and which was needed to service the aircraft assigned to the station.

By the time the airfield had been officially taken over from the builders by the time honoured "marching in" ceremony the first aircraft had already arrived. Little time could be spared for further training before the comparitively untried unit was called upon to perform its first operational sortie.

At its peak the Eighth U.S.A.A.F., the largest of all the American Airforces, had 63 airfields mainly in East Anglia. Bomber Command had a great chain of 135 operational and non-operational airfields stretching through eastern Britain from Inverness to Cambridge. Fighter Command had 142 airfields more evenly spread over the whole country to give as wide as possible a defensive cover to centres of population, heavy industry, ports, airfields and other strategic locations.

The airfields of Coastal Command for obvious reasons were mainly located on or near our coastlines. This was to ensure that they were positioned as ideally as possible for fighting the all-important battle to secure shipping routes across the Atlantic to and from the New World. They consisted of about 45 airfields as far apart as Shetland and Cornwall. Transport Command with the airfields of the 9th U.S.A.A.F. Troop Carrier Command were mainly sited in the East Midlands and South West. Training airfields were situated through necessity in places away from probable enemy air activity and our own operational units.

Thanks to five years of combined effort British industry, by 1945 had given Bomber Command some very powerful tools to wage the war in the air. This resulted in 955,011 tons of bombs being dropped by the R.A.F. Even this staggering total of high explosives plus a further 621,830 tons unloaded by the U.S.A.A.F., and in spite of the terrible sacrifices the young aircrew were called upon to bear, still was not enough to bring Germany to its knees and sue for unconditional surrender.

By this time even the staunchest advocates of the air weapon had to admit that wars could not be won by air power alone. Before victory could be achieved the enemy had to be defeated on the field of battle and his territory occupied, a fact that is possibly not true today.

MAP REFERENCES.

Two map references are shown on the station sheets. That marked OS is the current Ordnance Survey six-figure reference. That marked AM is the 'Modified British System' introduced on military maps in 1927 and retained in use throughout the Second World War by overprinting War Office editions of Ordnance Survey maps. It should not be confused with the present National Grid. The Modified British System of reference was not used by the Royal Navy.

PREAMBLE TO THE OMNIBUS EDITION OF MILITARY AIRFIELDS 1945-1945.

When it was decided to reprint Military Airfields in response to popular demand it was considered best to amalgamate the three parts in an omnibus edition, making a more readily available source of reference with all the data between two covers only.

Although retaining the basic page layout it has been amended to give a clearer picture of the satellite features of each airfield. The 'Units in Residence' columns have been deleted and incorporated in an appendix as an Order of Battle of the R.A.F., Dominion and Allied units, U.S.A.A.F. and R.N. formations for 1st.December 1944.

Other appendices have been added including a table of geographical locations for all sites by counties. The county boundaries are as they were during the war years, and prior to the changes of 1972. Another appendix shows the established aircraft strength of Coastal Command, perhaps the cinderella of the home based operational Commands as it was starved of men and machines for much of the war years. As this table shows in the last resort it did have barely the necessary aircraft to perform the arduous tasks it was called upon to do. This appendix does show the squadrons stationed in Iceland and the Azores, and also the the U.S. Navy squadrons of PB4Y-1s' which operated from Dunkeswell. It also gives the opportunity to list the flying boat units & their bases.

Also we have featured a list of present day uses, and while it is appreciated some sites are now utilised for more than one end use, only what is considered as the main purpose is detailed. An airfield shown occupied by one or other of the armed forces does not necessarily indicate that it is used by them for flying. Help is required to complete and/or correct the information given as usages are still changing frequently.

The breakdown of the 653 sites into Commands was as follows:-

Fighter Command	142.
Bomber Command	135.
Flying Training Command	122.
8th. United States Army Air Force	63.
Coastal Command.	45.
Royal Naval Air Service	40.
Transport Command	29.
Maintenance Command	21.
Technical Training Command	13.
9th. United States Army Air Force	11.
United States Strategic Air Forces Europe	9.
R.A.F. Northern Ireland	7.
Balloon Command	5.
War Department	5.
Department of Civil Aviation	3.
United States Air Transport Command	2.
United States Naval Air Command	1.

Finally it must be noted that all military airfields are or were potentially dangerous locations. Some still come under the provisions of the Official Secrets Act and are prohibited areas. Above all none are on common land. Even those listed in this book as "Disused" belong to or are ownedby some person or body, and the rights of the owner and safe custody of his property must be respected at all times. Always obtain the owners' permission if access is required. Never pick up or disturb strange objects, but report them to a responsible person. If possible keep to hard surfaces, close all gates and leave the site as you found it. But first stand in the middle of the airfield and allow your imagination to take over, and try to cultivate the "Twelve O'clock High" syndrome. This was demonstrated in the film of that name by the retired USAAF Major who returns to his now disused wartime airfield in East Anglia, climbs through the perimeter fence onto the runway and closed his eyes and dreams. Then is nearly bowled over by the slipstreams of B 17s running up!

INDEX OF SITES BY AIRFIELD NUMBERS.

NO: 001.

AIRFIELD NAME: ABBOTS BROMLEY. OPENED : 1940.
COUNTY : Staffordshire. CLOSED : 1945.
COMMAND : Flying Training.
FORMATION : 51 Grp[Leeds] GRID REF: K533459 [62]
FUNCTION : Elementary Flying Training School[RLG] O.S.REF : SK 075253
LOCALITY : 5 miles S. of Uttoxeter.
RAILWAY STN. : Uttoxeter or Rugeley 5 miles[LMS]

LATITUDE : 52 48 38N. HEIGHT ASL : 400′ LIGHTING : None
LONGITUDE : 01 53 30W. FLYING CONTROL : None. RADIO : QDM.

LANDMARKS DAY : -

LANDMARKS NIGHT : -

OBSTRUCTIONS : -

LANDING AREA SURFACE : Grass.

QDM	LENGTH X WIDTH	Ext
N/S.	650yds.	-
E/W.	650yds.	-

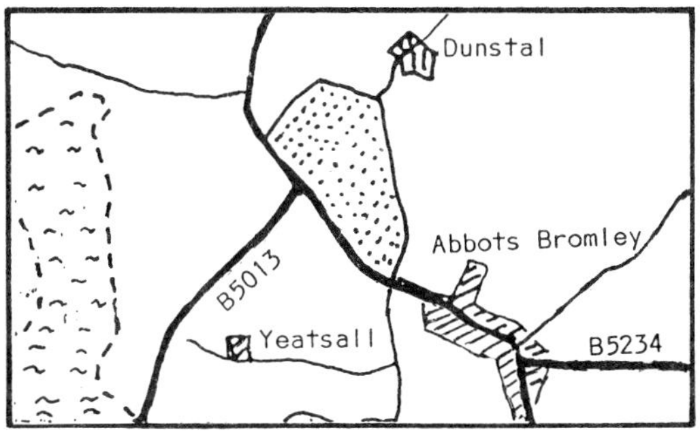

EXTENSIBILITY : 1-strip of 1600 X 200yds. Not recommended. entails road diversion.
ACCOMMODATION : Temporary
HANGARS : 9-Blisters.

HARDSTANDINGS : –

R.A.F. : OFFICERS: 1 S.N.C.O′s.: 4. O.R′s.: 70. TOTAL: 75.
W.A.A.F.: " : - " : - " : - " : -

AFFILIATED AIRFIELDS : Derby[Parent]

PRESENT USE [1985] : Agriculture.

NO: 002.

AIRFIELD NAME: ABBOTSINCH. OPENED : 1932.
COUNTY : Renfrewshire. CLOSED :
COMMAND : RN.
FORMATION : HMS Sanderling. GRID REF: S 977889[Scot]
FUNCTION : Maintenance Yard. O.S.REF : NS 479670

LOCALITY : 2.5 miles W. of Girvan.
RAILWAY STN. : Paisley[LMS]

LATITUDE : 55 52 10N. HEIGHT ASL : 18′ LIGHTING : None.
LONGITUDE : 04 25 45W. FLYING CONTROL : Yes. RADIO : QDM.

LANDMARKS DAY : Firth of Clyde with R Clyde 1.5miles NE. Glasgow & Paisley. A/F lies within fork of the Black Cart & White Cart waters which form a junction about 1000yds NE of A/F before flowing into Clyde.
LANDMARKS NIGHT : -

OBSTRUCTIONS : Mountains 1199′ 4.5miles N. Hills 749′ 3.5miles SSW. 2 pylons 218′ 1200yds ENE. 4 chimneys 450yds.from W end of runway 103-283.

LANDING AREA SURFACE : Under Re-construction.

QDM	LENGTH X WIDTH	Ext
058-238.	1400 X 50yds.	-
103-283.	1030 X 50yds.	-
173-353.	1730 X 50yds.	-

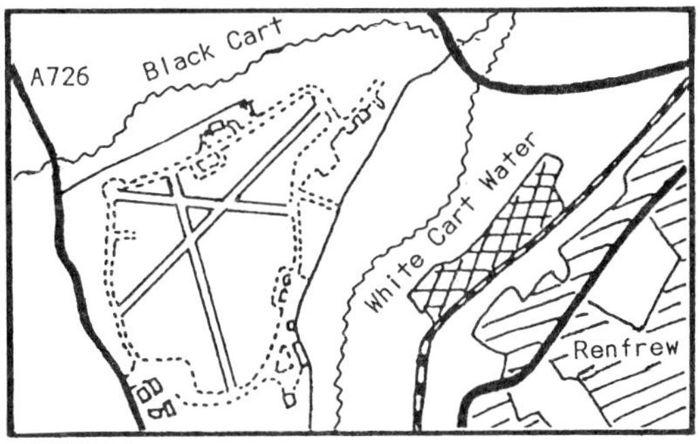

EXTENSIBILITY : -

ACCOMMODATION : Temporary.
HANGARS : Sqdn: Callendar Hamilton-180x90′-3; Bellman 187.5x105′-1; Storage: Bellman-5; 60x70′-1.
HARDSTANDINGS :

R.N. : OFFICERS: 12. Chiefs/POs/Ratings. : 1218. TOTAL: 1486.
W.R.N.S.: " : 3. " " : 309. " : 311.

AFFILIATED AIRFIELDS : -

PRESENT USE [1985] : Civil Airport[Glasgow]

NO: 003.

AIRFIELD NAME: ABERPORTH. OPENED : 1940.
COUNTY : Cardiganshire. CLOSED :
COMMAND : Fighter.
FORMATION : 70 Grp[Farnborough] GRID REF: N 702719[78]
FUNCTION : AA Co-operation Unit. O.S.REF.: SN 250494.

LOCALITY : 5.5miles NE of Cardigan.
RAILWAY STN. : Cardigan[GWR]

LATITUDE : 52 07 00N. HEIGHT ASL : 400′ LIGHTING : NONE
LONGITUDE : 04 33 15W. FLYING CONTROL : None. RADIO : QDM.

LANDMARKS DAY : Cardigan 5miles SW.

LANDMARKS NIGHT : -

OBSTRUCTIONS : Houses & chapel on SSW edge of airfield.

LANDING AREA SURFACE : Grass.

QDM	LENGTH X WIDTH	Ext
NNE-SSW.	750yds.	-
NE-SW.	966yds.	-
NW-SE.	755yds.	-

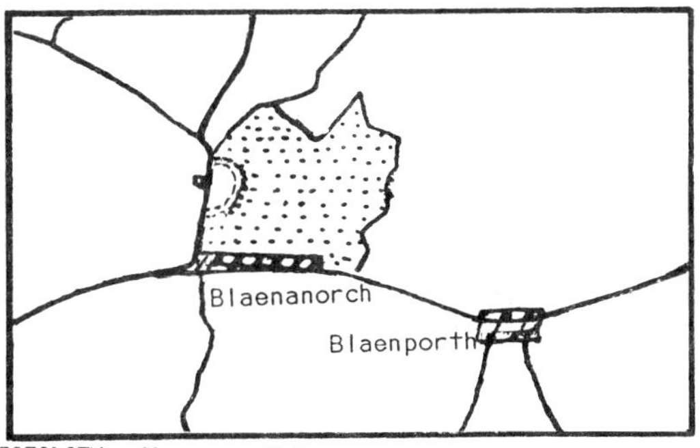

EXTENSIBILITY : None possible.

ACCOMMODATION : Temporary.
HANGARS : Bellman-2;Blister-3.

HARDSTANDINGS : -

R.A.F. : OFFICERS: 16. S.N.C.O′s.: 15. O.R′s.: 372. TOTAL: 403.
W.A.A.F.: " : 2. " : - " : 92. " : 94.

AFFILIATED AIRFIELDS : -

PRESENT USE [1985] : Royal Aircraft Establishment.

AIRFIELD NAME: ABINGDON.
COUNTY : Berkshire.
COMMAND : Bomber.
FORMATION : 91 Grp[Abingdon]
FUNCTION : Operational Training Unit.
LOCALITY : NW of Abingdon.
RAILWAY STN. : Abingdon[GWR]

OPENED : 1932.
CLOSED :

GRID REF: P 923196[105]
O.S.REF.: SU 475992

LATITUDE : 51 41 30N. HEIGHT ASL : 245′ LIGHTING : Mk2.
LONGITUDE : 01 19 00W. FLYING CONTROL : Yes. RADIO : QDM.

LANDMARKS DAY : Oxford 6miles 045degrees.

LANDMARKS NIGHT : -

OBSTRUCTIONS : Boars Head 1.5miles NE.

LANDING AREA SURFACE : Concrete.

QDM	LENGTH X WIDTH	Ext
190.	2000 x 50yds.	2500yds.
270.	1600 x 50yds.	2500yds.

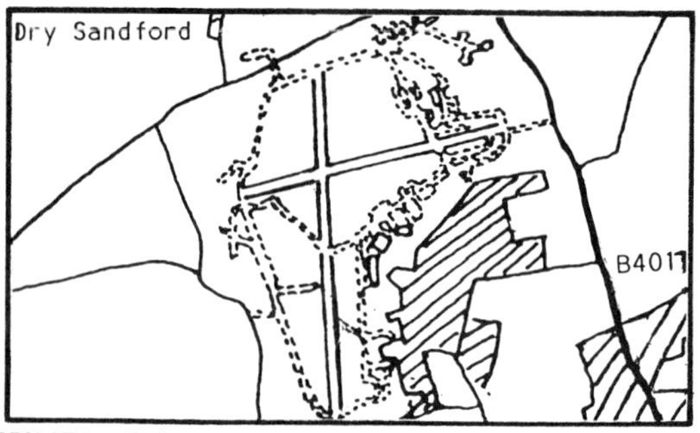

EXTENSIBILITY : Entails extensive demolition of a bungalow, 2 cottages & a small school.
ACCOMMODATION : Permanent.
HANGARS : Type C-1;Type A-4.

HARDSTANDINGS : Spectacle-6;Frying Pan-24.

R.A.F. : OFFICERS: 186.S.N.C.O′s.: 327.O.R′s.: 1237.TOTAL: 1750.
W.A.A.F.: " : 17. " : 25. " : 490. " : 532.

AFFILIATED AIRFIELDS : Stanton Harcourt[Satellite].

PRESENT USE [1985] : RAF.

NO: 005.

AIRFIELD NAME: ACASTER MALBIS.
COUNTY : Yorkshire.
COMMAND : Bomber.
FORMATION : 7 Grp[St.Vincents]
FUNCTION : Operational.

OPENED : 1942.
CLOSED : 1946.

GRID REF: A 053629[27]
O.S.REF.: SE 578430.

LOCALITY : 6miles S.of York.
RAILWAY STN. : Copmanthorpe 2.5miles[LNER]

LATITUDE : 53 52 45N. HEIGHT ASL : 30′ LIGHTING : Mk.2.
LONGITUDE : 01 06 45W. FLYING CONTROL : Yes. RADIO : QDM.

LANDMARKS DAY : Railways: York-Selby & York-Castleford. R Ouse.

LANDMARKS NIGHT : York Minster & R Ouse.

OBSTRUCTIONS : -

LANDING AREA SURFACE : Concrete.

QDM	LENGTH X WIDTH	Ext
160.	1400 x 50yds.	4000yds.
220.	2000 x 50yds.	4000yds.
290.	1400 x 50yds.	3000yds.

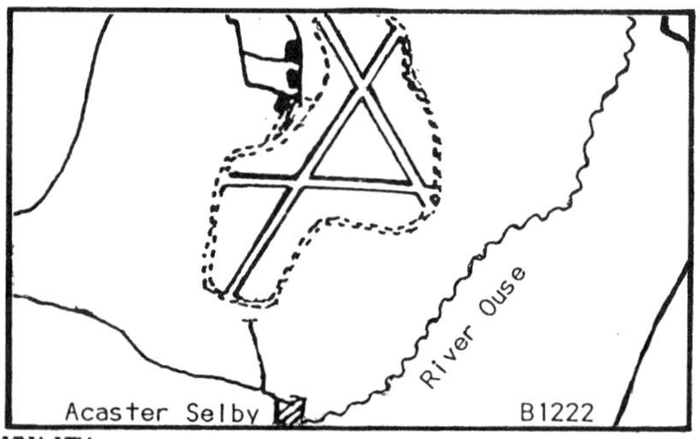

EXTENSIBILITY :

ACCOMMODATION : Temporary.
HANGARS : Type 2-2;B1-1.

HARDSTANDINGS : Spectacle 36

R.A.F. : OFFICERS: 100 S.N.C.O′s.: 242.O.R′s.: 778. TOTAL: 1120.
W.A.A.F.: " : 10. " : - " : 264. " : 274.

AFFILIATED AIRFIELDS : Marston Moor[74 Base]

PRESENT USE [1985] : Disused.

NO: 006.

AIRFIELD NAME: ACKLINGTON.
COUNTY : Northumberland.
COMMAND : Fighter.
FORMATION : 12 Grp[Watnall]
FUNCTION : Forward Airfield Night Fighter.
LOCALITY : 3miles SW of Amble.
RAILWAY STN. : Acklington 2miles[LNER]

OPENED : 1938.
CLOSED : 1972.

GRID REF: U 723210[4]
O.S.REF.: NU 230010.

LATITUDE : 55 18 00N. HEIGHT ASL : 120′ LIGHTING : Mk2.
LONGITUDE : 01 38 30W. FLYING CONTROL : Yes. RADIO : QDM.

LANDMARKS DAY : Coquet Island 5miles NE; Coquet river 2miles N & NW. Broomhill slagheap 1mile E; LNER W boundary; Amble branch junction 1.5miles S of A/F.

LANDMARKS NIGHT : Coquet Island & coasline.

OBSTRUCTIONS : -

LANDING AREA SURFACE : Tarmac & asphalt.

QDM	LENGTH X WIDTH	Ext
120.	1200 x 50yds.	1500yds.
190.	1510 x 50yds.	1700yds.
230.	1900 x 50yds.	2500yds.

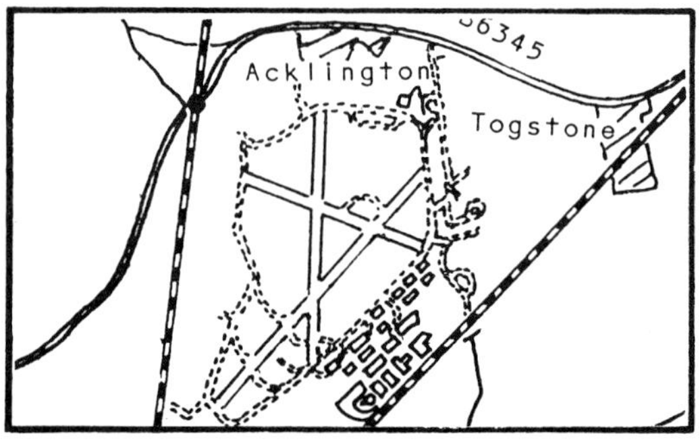

EXTENSIBILITY : Entails demolition of a farm.

ACCOMMODATION : Permanent[part]
HANGARS : Type F-2;Bellman-1;Blister-16.

HARDSTANDINGS : Punched planking:TE-6;SE-12;TE-7.

R.A.F. : OFFICERS: 124.S.N.C.O′s.: 148.O.R′s.: 1052.TOTAL: 1324.
W.A.A.F.: " : 8. " : 16. " : 369. " : 393.

AFFILIATED AIRFIELDS : Newcastle[Sector].

PRESENT USE [1985] : HM Prison.

NO: 007.

AIRFIELD NAME: AKEMAN STREET. OPENED : 1940.
COUNTY : Oxfordshire. CLOSED : 1947.
COMMAND : Flying Training.
FORMATION : 23 Grp[South Cerney] GRID REF: P 782337[93].
FUNCTION : Advanced Flying Unit [RLG] O.S.REF.: SP 332138.
LOCALITY : 3miles NNW of Witney.
RAILWAY STN. : Whitney[GWR]

LATITUDE : 51 49 15N. HEIGHT ASL : 400′ LIGHTING : None.
LONGITUDE : 01 31 00W. FLYING CONTROL : None. RADIO : QDM.

LANDMARKS DAY : Oxford wireless masts 2miles W.

LANDMARKS NIGHT : Oxford wireless masts 2miles W lit up.

OBSTRUCTIONS : -

LANDING AREA SURFACE : Grass.

QDM	LENGTH X WIDTH	Ext
N-S.	1600yds.	-
NE-SW.	950yds.	-
SE-NW.	800yds.	-

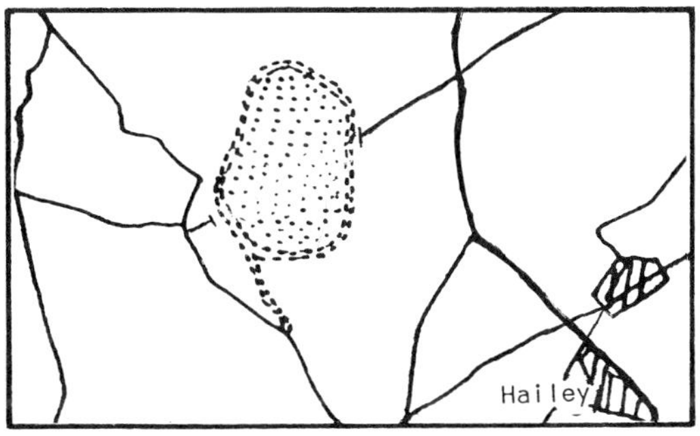

EXTENSIBILITY : None possible.

ACCOMMODATION : Temporary.
HANGARS : Bellman-1;65′ Blister-10.

HARDSTANDINGS : -

R.A.F. : OFFICERS: 1. S.N.C.O′s.: 3. O.R′s.: 15. TOTAL: 19.
W.A.A.F.: " : - " : - " : - " : -

AFFILIATED AIRFIELDS : Little Rissington[Parent]

PRESENT USE [1985] : Disused.

NO: 008.

AIRFIELD NAME: ALCONBURY. OPENED : 1938.
COUNTY : Huntingdonshire. CLOSED :
COMMAND : 8th USAAF.
FORMATION : 482nd Bomb Grp. GRID REF: L 658960[74]
FUNCTION : Operational. O.S.REF.: TL 205768.
: 240.
LOCALITY : 4miles NW of Huntingdon.
RAILWAY STN. : Huntingdon 4miles[LNER]

LATITUDE : 52 22 23N. HEIGHT ASL : 165′ LIGHTING : Mk2.
LONGITUDE : 00 13 45W. FLYING CONTROL : Yes. RADIO : QDM.

LANDMARKS DAY. : Town of Huntingdon; Ermine St. W boundary.

LANDMARKS NIGHT : -

OBSTRUCTIONS : -

LANDING AREA SURFACE : Concrete & asphalt.

QDM	LENGTH X WIDTH	Ext
180.	1400 x 50yds.	3400yds.
240.	2000 x 50yds.	2500yds.
300.	1400 x 50yds.	2200yds.

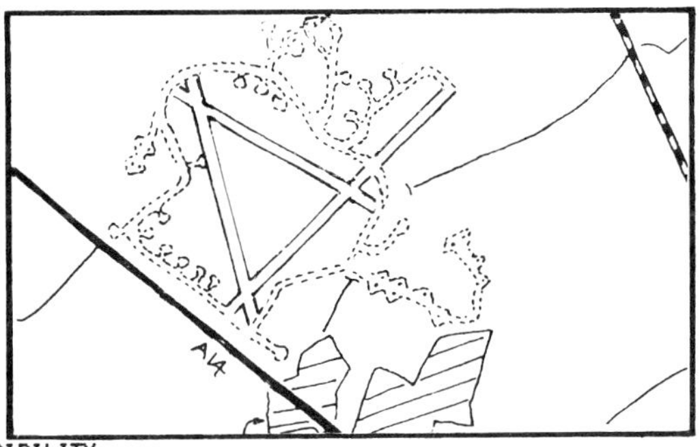

EXTENSIBILITY : -

ACCOMMODATION : Temporary.
HANGARS : T2-2.

HARDSTANDINGS : Loop-50.

USAAF.: OFFICERS: 421. Enlisted Men. : 2473.TOTAL: 2894.

AFFILIATED AIRFIELDS : -

PRESENT USE [1985] : USAFE.

NO: 009.

AIRFIELD NAME: ALDERGROVE. OPENED : 1918
COUNTY : Antrim NI. CLOSED :
COMMAND : Coastal.
FORMATION : 17 Grp[Edinburgh] GRID REF: J 145795[313NI]
FUNCTION : Heavy Conversion Unit. O.S.REF.: J 145795.

LOCALITY : 13miles NW of Belfast.
RAILWAY STN. : Aldergrove 1mile[GNI]

LATITUDE : 54 39 08N. HEIGHT ASL : 260′ LIGHTING : Mk.2.
LONGITUDE : 06 13 30W. FLYING CONTROL : Yes. RADIO : QDM.

LANDMARKS DAY : Lough Neagh 2.5miles W.

LANDMARKS NIGHT : As day.

OBSTRUCTIONS : -

LANDING AREA SURFACE : Concrete.

QDM	LENGTH X WIDTH	Ext
260.	2000 X 50yds.	-
356.	2000 X 50yds.	2400yds.

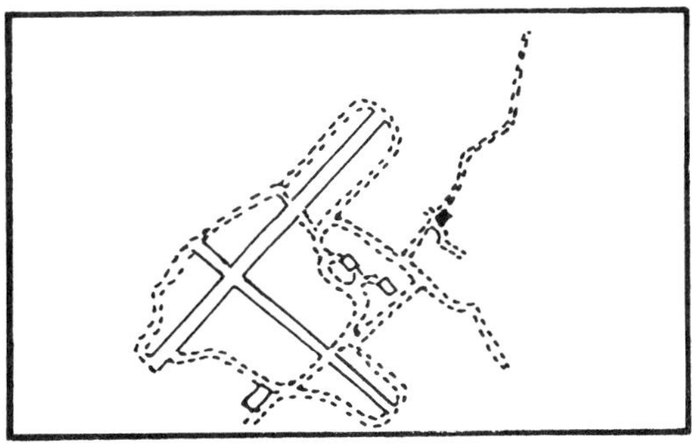

EXTENSIBILITY : Entails demolition of barn, & tree felling.

ACCOMMODATION : Permanent[Part]
HANGARS : 18 various types.

HARDSTANDINGS : Loop-30.

R.A.F. : OFFICERS: 133.S.N.C.O′s.: 219.O.R′s.: 2400.TOTAL: 2752.
W.A.A.F.: " : 8. " : 17. " : 512. " : 537.

AFFILIATED AIRFIELDS : -

PRESENT USE [1985] : Civil Airport[Aldergrove]

NO: 010.

AIRFIELD NAME: ALDERMASTON. OPENED : 1942.
COUNTY : Berkshire. CLOSED : 1950.
COMMAND : 9th USAAF.
FORMATION : 434th Troop Carrier Grp. GRID REF: Q 038835[113]
FUNCTION : Operational. O.S.REF.: SU 598635.

LOCALITY : 10miles SW of Reading.
RAILWAY STN. : Aldermaston 3miles[GWR].

LATITUDE : 51 21 53N. HEIGHT ASL : 340'.LIGHTING : Mk2.
LONGITUDE : 01 08 45W. FLYING CONTROL : Yes. RADIO : QDM.

LANDMARKS DAY : Aldermaston Court 1500' N of NE corner of A/F.

LANDMARKS NIGHT : -

OBSTRUCTIONS : Aldermaston Court tower within outer circle.
Water tower[lit] 60' high 1000' S.

LANDING AREA SURFACE : Concrete & wood chippings.

QDM	LENGTH X WIDTH	Ext
060.	2000 x 50yds.	2900yds.
170.	1400 x 50yds.	-
350.	1400 x 50yds.	-

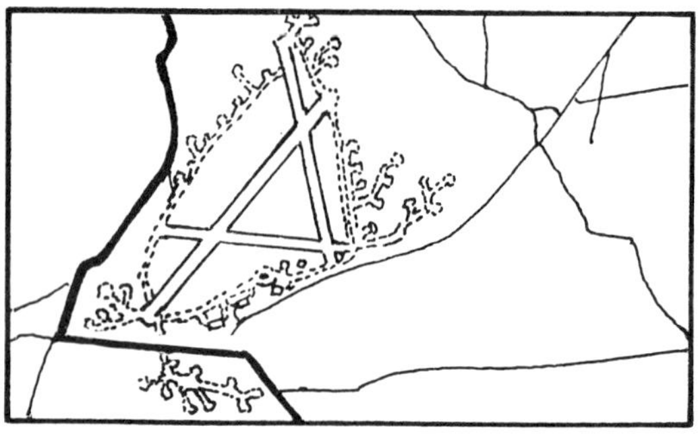

EXTENSIBILITY : Entails serious demolition & diversion.

ACCOMMODATION : Temporary.
HANGARS : T2-4;MAP-1.

HARDSTANDINGS : Concrete loop-52.

USAAF. : OFFICERS: 537. Enlisted Men. : 2280.TOTAL: 2817.

AFFILIATED AIRFIELDS : -

PRESENT USE [1985] : Atomic Weapons Research Establishment.

NO: 011.

AIRFIELD NAME: ALTON BARNES. OPENED : 1935.
COUNTY : Wiltshire. CLOSED : 1947.
COMMAND : Flying Training.
FORMATION : 50 Grp[Reading] GRID REF: U 540825[112]
FUNCTION : Elementary Flying Training School[RLG] O.S.REF.: SU 114618.
LOCALITY : 6miles E of Devizes.
RAILWAY STN. : Woodborough 7miles[GWR]

LATITUDE : 51 21 23N. HEIGHT ASL : 437' LIGHTING : None.
LONGITUDE : 01 51 23W. FLYING CONTROL : None.RADIO : QDM.

LANDMARKS DAY : Kennet & Avon canal on S side of A/F.

LANDMARKS NIGHT : -

OBSTRUCTIONS : 60' chimney adjoining SE corner of A/F.

LANDING AREA SURFACE : Grass.

QDM	LENGTH X WIDTH	Ext
N-S.	820yds	-
NE-SW.	1100yds.	-
E-W.	870yds.	-
NW-SE.	870yds.	-

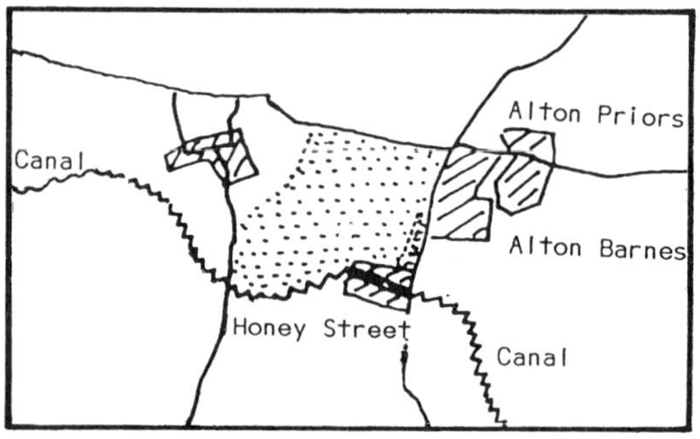

EXTENSIBILITY : None possible.

ACCOMMODATION : Temporary.
HANGARS : E.O.Blister-4;Standard Blister-6.

HARDSTANDINGS : None.

	OFFICERS	S.N.C.O's.	O.R's.	TOTAL
R.A.F.	-	-	130.	130.
W.A.A.F.	-	-	-	-

AFFILIATED AIRFIELDS : Clyffe Pypard[Parent]

PRESENT USE [1985] : Agriculture.

NO: 012.

AIRFIELD NAME: ANDOVER. OPENED : 1916.
COUNTY : Hampshire. CLOSED :
COMMAND : Fighter.
FORMATION : 70 Grp[Farnborough] GRID REF: U 769659[122]
FUNCTION : Operational Training Unit. O.S.REF.: SU 329459.
LOCALITY : 2.5miles from Andover on Amesbury Rd.
RAILWAY STN. : Andover Junction 2.5miles[SR].

LATITUDE : 51 12 30N. HEIGHT ASL : 260' LIGHTING : Mk.1.
LONGITUDE : 01 31 30W. FLYING CONTROL : Yes. RADIO : QDM.

LANDMARKS DAY : Andover town; railway Andover-Salisbury.

LANDMARKS NIGHT : Mast head lights at Wey Hill.

OBSTRUCTIONS : Wireless masts SE & 1.5miles NW of A/F.

LANDING AREA SURFACE : Grass.

QDM	LENGTH X WIDTH	Ext
ENE-WSW.	1300yds.	-
NE-SW.	1000yds.	-
SE-NW.	900yds.	-
N-S.	830yds.	-

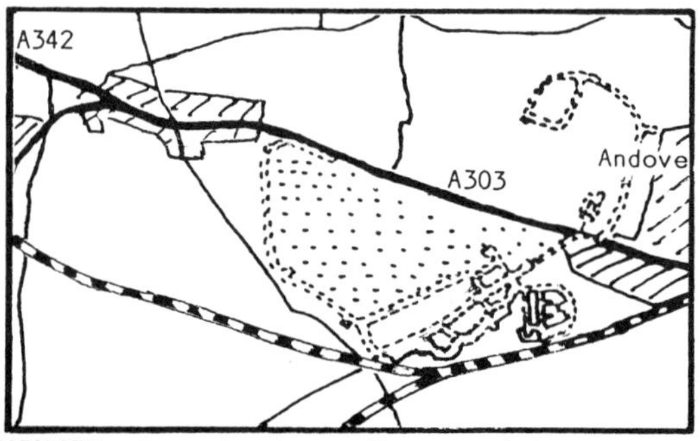

EXTENSIBILITY : Any extensions not recommended.

ACCOMMODATION : Permanent[part]
HANGARS : Blister-5;G.S.-4;Old Belfast Trussed-7.

HARDSTANDINGS : Frying pan[100' dia]-4,Temporary types-21.

	OFFICERS	S.N.C.O's.	O.R's.	TOTAL
R.A.F.	225.	148.	1284.	1657.
W.A.A.F.	18.	4.	385.	407.

AFFILIATED AIRFIELDS : -

PRESENT USE [1985] : Army.

NO: 013.

AIRFIELD NAME: ANDREAS. OPENED : 1941.
COUNTY : Isle of Man. CLOSED : 1946.
COMMAND : Flying Training.
FORMATION : 29 Grp[Dumfries] GRID REF: X 906225[17].
FUNCTION : Air Gunnery School. O.S.REF.: SC 426000.

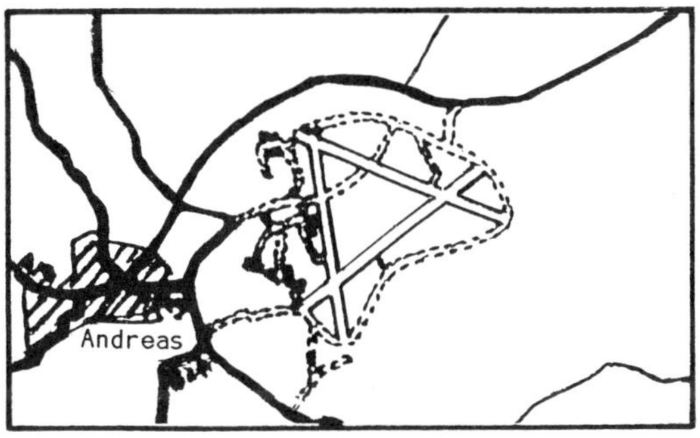

LOCALITY : 4miles NW of Ramsey.
RAILWAY STN. : Ramsey 7miles.

LATITUDE : 54 22 15N. HEIGHT ASL : 110′ LIGHTING : MK 2.
LONGITUDE : 04 25 15W. FLYING CONTROL : Yes. RADIO : QDM.

LANDMARKS DAY : W/M 375′high 3miles NE. Point of Ayr lighthouse 3.5miles NE. Snaefell 2034′ 7miles S.

LANDMARKS NIGHT : Whitstone lighthouse 4miles NE. Obstruction lights when required.

OBSTRUCTIONS : Bride Hills 320′ 1mile NE. Wireless masts 375′ 3miles NE. Snaefell 2034′ 7miles S.

LANDING AREA SURFACE : Tarmac.

QDM	LENGTH X WIDTH	Ext
060.	1350 x 50yds.	1550yds.
180.	1200 x 50yds.	1350yds.
120.	1250 x 50yds.	-

EXTENSIBILITY : Entails demolition of a farm.

ACCOMMODATION : Temporary.
HANGARS : Bellman-3;E.O.Blister-8.

HARDSTANDINGS : Octangonal[44′]-9, pens 54′wide-12, pens 75′wide-12.

	OFFICERS	S.N.C.O′s.	O.R′s.	TOTAL
R.A.F.	67.	144.	933.	1044.
W.A.A.F.	8.	7.	389.	404.

AFFILIATED AIRFIELDS : -

PRESENT USE [1985] : Agriculture.

NO: 014.

AIRFIELD NAME: ANDREWS FIELD. OPENED : 1942
COUNTY : Essex CLOSED : 1945
COMMAND : Fighter.
FORMATION : 11 Grp[Uxbridge] GRID REF: M 141435[97]
FUNCTION : Forward Airfield. O.S.REF.: TL 693250.

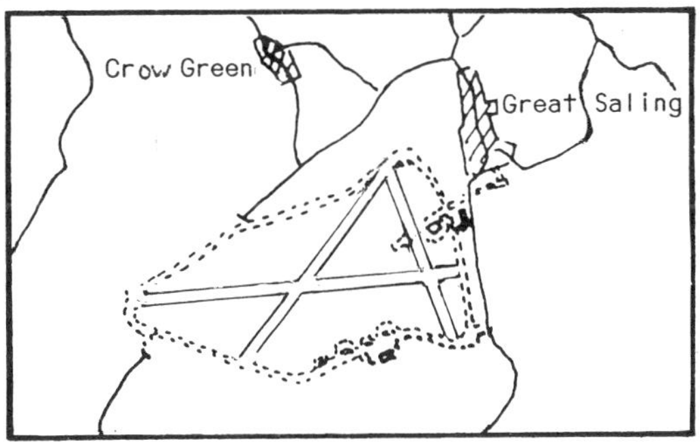

LOCALITY : 5miles W of Braintree.
RAILWAY STN. : Rayne 4miles[LNER]

LATITUDE : 51 63 45N. HEIGHT ASL : 290′ LIGHTING : MK 2.
LONGITUDE : 00 27 30E. FLYING CONTROL : Yes. RADIO : QDM.

LANDMARKS DAY : Town of Braintree, railway line Braintree-Rayne.

LANDMARKS NIGHT : Town of Braintree.

OBSTRUCTIONS : -

LANDING AREA SURFACE : Concrete, tarmac & wood chippings.

QDM	LENGTH X WIDTH	Ext
270.	2100 x 50yds.	3700yds.
020.	1400 x 50yds.	2000yds.
330.	1400 x 50yds.	2800yds.

EXTENSIBILITY : -

ACCOMMODATION : Temporary.
HANGARS : T2-2.

HARDSTANDINGS : Loop-50.

	OFFICERS	S.N.C.O′s.	O.R′s.	TOTAL
R.A.F.	200.	352.	1939.	2491.
W.A.A.F.	-	16.	240.	256.

AFFILIATED AIRFIELDS : North Weald[Sector]

PRESENT USE [1985] : Agriculture.

NO: 015.

AIRFIELD NAME: ANGLE. OPENED : 1941
COUNTY : Pembrokeshire. CLOSED : 1945.
COMMAND : Coastal
FORMATION : 19 Grp[Plymouth] GRID REF: N 304244[99].
FUNCTION : Operational. O.S.REF.: SM 858019.

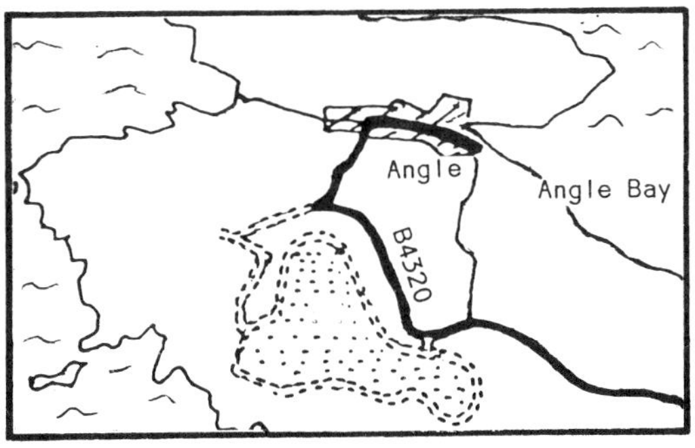

LOCALITY : 8.75miles W. of Pembroke.
RAILWAY STN. : Pembroke 8miles[LMS].

LATITUDE : 51 40 23N. HEIGHT ASL : 182′ LIGHTING : MK.2.
LONGITUDE : 05 05 45W. FLYING CONTROL : YES RADIO : QDM.

LANDMARKS DAY : Freshwater west beach, just S.

LANDMARKS NIGHT : St. Gowans lightship 8 miles S of Linney Head.

OBSTRUCTIONS : -

LANDING AREA SURFACE : Tarmac & rubber chippings.

QDM	LENGTH X WIDTH	Ext
290.	1600 x 50yds.	1800yds.
230.	1000 x 50yds.	–
162.	1200 x 50yds	–

EXTENSIBILITY : With very heavy "fill"

ACCOMMODATION : Temporary.
HANGARS : T2-1;Overblisters-4.

HARDSTANDINGS : 60′dia.[tarmac]-6.

	OFFICERS	S.N.C.O′s.	O.R′s.	TOTAL
R.A.F.	106.	126.	744.	1006.
W.A.A.F.	10.	–	50.	60.

AFFILIATED AIRFIELDS : Administered by Pembroke Dock[Parent]

PRESENT USE [1985] : Disused.

NO: 016.

AIRFIELD NAME: ANNAN. OPENED : 1942.
COUNTY : Dumfriesshire. CLOSED : 1945.
COMMAND : Maintenance.
FORMATION : 56 Wing[Carlisle] GRID REF: Y 703914[89Scot]
FUNCTION : Storage Unit. O.S.REF.: NY 218700.

LOCALITY : 2.75miles NE of Annan.
RAILWAY STN. : Annan 3miles[LMS]

LATITUDE : 55 01 00N. HEIGHT ASL : 30′ LIGHTING : Mk.2.
LONGITUDE : 03 13 45W. FLYING CONTROL : Yes. RADIO : QDM.

LANDMARKS DAY : Solway Firth 3.5miles S; Dumfries-Carlisle railway 2.5miles NE.

LANDMARKS NIGHT : Solway Firth, Rivers Nith & Annan.

OBSTRUCTIONS : Small wood situated between SE & SW runways.

LANDING AREA SURFACE : Unspecified hard surface.

QDM: 150. LENGTH X WIDTH: 1600 x 50yds. Ext: 2000yds.
: 240. : 1600 x 50yds. : 2000yds.
: : :
: : :

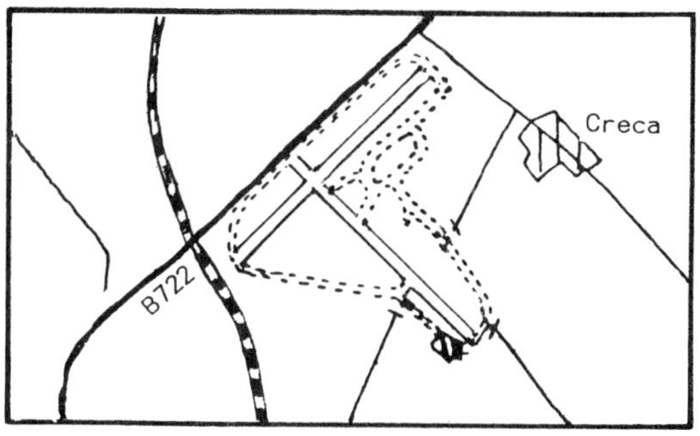

EXTENSIBILITY : -

ACCOMMODATION : Temporary.
HANGARS : T1-3;Blisters-8.

HARDSTANDINGS : 74.

R.A.F. : OFFICERS: 75. S.N.C.O′s.: 195.O.R′s.: 1630.TOTAL: 1900.
W.A.A.F.: " : 10. " : 12. " : 300. " : 322.

AFFILIATED AIRFIELDS : -

PRESENT USE [1985] : Nuclear Power Station[Chapelcross]

NO: 017.

AIRFIELD NAME: ANTHORN. OPENED : 1944.
COUNTY : Cumberland. CLOSED : 1954.
COMMAND : RN.
FORMATION : HMS Nuthatch. GRID REF: Y 665793[9]
FUNCTION : Receipt & Despatch Unit. O.S.REF.: NY 182581.
LOCALITY : 11miles NW of Carlisle.
RAILWAY STN. : Kirkbride[LNER]

LATITUDE : 54 54 35N. HEIGHT ASL : 30′ LIGHTING : Naval.
LONGITUDE : 03 16 30W. FLYING CONTROL : Yes. RADIO : QDM.

LANDMARKS DAY : Solway Firth & Morecombe Bay.

LANDMARKS NIGHT : As day.

OBSTRUCTIONS : -

LANDING AREA SURFACE : Under construction.

QDM: 035-215. LENGTH X WIDTH: 1200 x 30yds. Ext: -
: 094-274. : 1400 x 30yds. : -
: 155-335. : 1200 x 30yds. : -
: : :

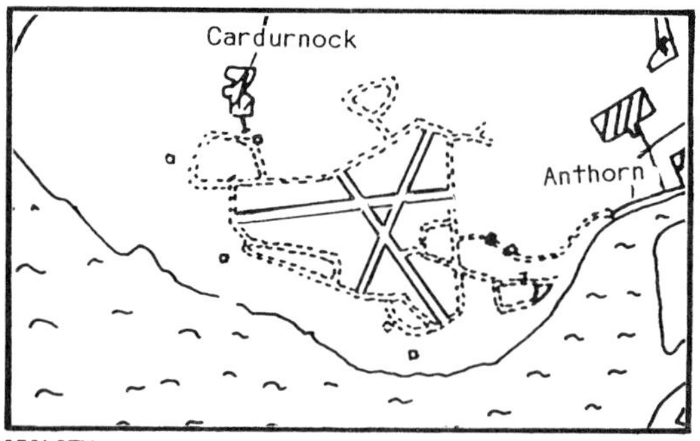

EXTENSIBILITY : -

ACCOMMODATION : Temporary.
HANGARS : Sqdn 60x84′-1;Storage 60x84′-20.

HARDSTANDINGS : Areas with A/C standings-5.

R.N. : OFFICERS: 87. Chiefs/POs/Ratings. : 906.TOTAL: 993.
W.R.N.S.: " : 13. " " : 226. " : 239.

AFFILIATED AIRFIELDS : -

PRESENT USE [1985] : Radio Research Station.

NO: 018.

AIRFIELD NAME: APPLEDRAM. OPENED : 1943.
COUNTY : Sussex. CLOSED : 1944.
COMMAND : Fighter.
FORMATION : 11 Grp[Uxbridge] GRID REF: Q 274218[133]
FUNCTION : Advanced Landing Ground O.S.REF.: SU 842023.
: 143.
LOCALITY : 1.5miles S of Chichester.
RAILWAY STN. : Chichester[SR]

LATITUDE : 50 48 38N. HEIGHT ASL : 22′ LIGHTING : None.
LONGITUDE : 00 48 45W. FLYING CONTROL : None.RADIO : QDM.

LANDMARKS DAY : Chichester cathedral 2.5miles NE of A/F.

LANDMARKS NIGHT : Chichester channel .5miles NW of A/F.

OBSTRUCTIONS : -

LANDING AREA SURFACE : Steel Matting[Sommerfeld Track]

QDM: 051. LENGTH X WIDTH: 1600yds. Ext: -
: 143. : 1400yds. : -
: : :
: : :

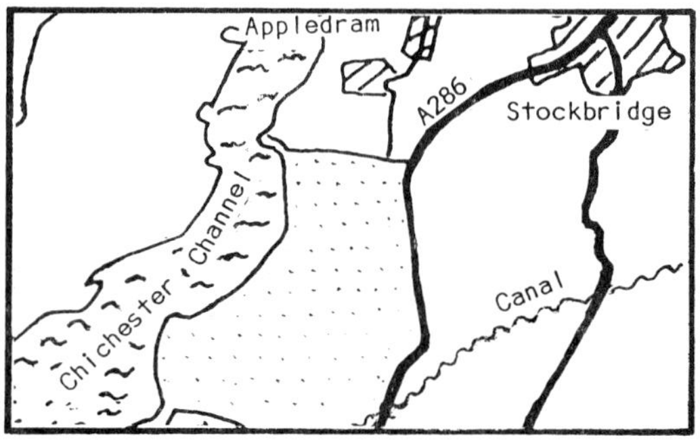

EXTENSIBILITY : -

ACCOMMODATION : Tented Camp.
HANGARS : EO Blister-1.

HARDSTANDINGS : Temporary Sommerfeld Track.

R.A.F. : OFFICERS: - S.N.C.O′s.: - O.R′s.: - TOTAL: -
W.A.A.F.: " : - " : - " : - " : -

AFFILIATED AIRFIELDS : -

PRESENT USE [1985] : Agriculture.

AIRFIELD NAME: ARBROATH.
COUNTY : Angus.
COMMAND : RN.
FORMATION : HMS Condor.
FUNCTION : Training Schools.

OPENED : 1940
CLOSED :

GRID REF: P 130645[Scot]
O.S.REF.: NO 623433.

LOCALITY : 1.5miles NW of Arbroath.
RAILWAY STN. : Arbroath[LMS]

LATITUDE : 56 34 55N. HEIGHT ASL : 160′ LIGHTING : None.
LONGITUDE : 02 37 10W. FLYING CONTROL : Yes. RADIO : QDM.

LANDMARKS DAY : Budden Ness, the N entrance point of the Firth of Tay, 8miles SSW.

LANDMARKS NIGHT : Railway NNW from Arbroath, parallel with NE boundary about 500yds.

OBSTRUCTIONS : -

LANDING AREA SURFACE : Unspecified hard surface.

QDM	LENGTH X WIDTH	Ext
034-214.	1100 x 30yds.	-
079-259.	1320 x 30yds.	-
124-304.	1130 x 30yds.	-
169-349.	1150 x 30yds.	-
079-259.	530 x 30yds.	-

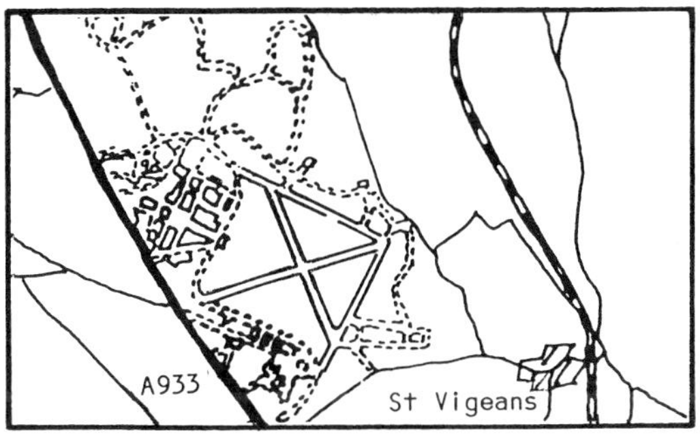

EXTENSIBILITY : 5th. R/W incorporates the dummy deck.

ACCOMMODATION : Temporary.
HANGARS : 787.5x106′:Sqdn-5;Storage-1.

HARDSTANDINGS : -

R.N. : OFFICERS: 253. Chiefs/POs/Ratings. : 1709.TOTAL: 1962.
W.R.N.S.: " : 23. " " : 538. " : 561.

AFFILIATED AIRFIELDS : -

PRESENT USE [1985] : RN.

NO: 020.

AIRFIELD NAME: ASHBOURNE.
COUNTY : Derbyshire.
COMMAND : Fighter.
FORMATION : 38 Grp[Marks Hall]
FUNCTION : Operational Training Unit.

OPENED : 1942.
CLOSED : 1954.

GRID REF: K 658660[53]
O.S.REF.: SK 198455.

LOCALITY : 9miles NW of Derby.
RAILWAY STN. : Ashbourne 1.5miles[LMS]

LATITUDE : 53 00 23N. HEIGHT ASL : 600′ LIGHTING : Mk.2.
LONGITUDE : 01 42 15W. FLYING CONTROL : Yes. RADIO : QDM.

LANDMARKS DAY : Osmaston Park & lake 1mile S.

LANDMARKS NIGHT : -

OBSTRUCTIONS : 1000′ high hills, 2miles NW & 7miles NNE.

LANDING AREA SURFACE : Concrete & wood chippings.

QDM	LENGTH X WIDTH	Ext
323.	2000 x 50yds.	2600yds.
274.	1400 x 50yds.	1600yds.
209.	1400 x 50yds.	1600yds.

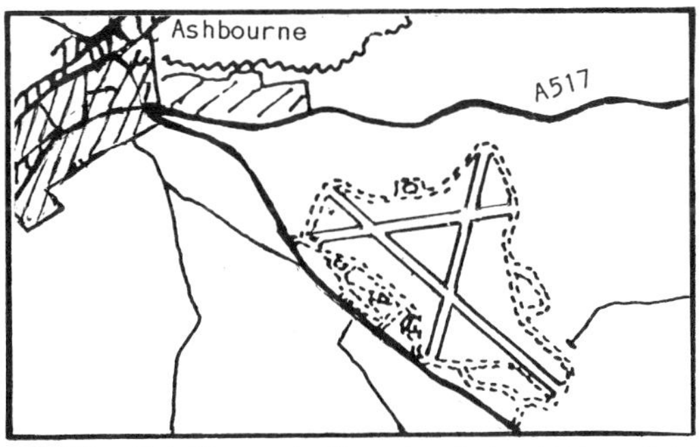

EXTENSIBILITY : Entails road diversion & demolition of 1 house.

ACCOMMODATION : Temporary.
HANGARS : T2[23 bay]-4.

HARDSTANDINGS : 125′ frying pans-30.

R.A.F. : OFFICERS: 171.S.N.C.O′s.: 454.O.R′s.: 1472.TOTAL: 2097.
W.A.A.F.: " : 10. " : 16. " : 432. " : 458.

AFFILIATED AIRFIELDS : Darley Moor[Satellite]

PRESENT USE [1985] : Industry.

NO: 021.

AIRFIELD NAME: ASHFORD.
COUNTY : Kent.
COMMAND : Maintenance.
FORMATION : 42 Grp[Reading]
FUNCTION : Fuel storage unit.

OPENED : 1943.
CLOSED : 1945.

GRID REF: R 410580[126]
O.S.REF.: TM 972405.

LOCALITY : 2.5miles SW of Ashford.
RAILWAY STN. : Ashford[SR]

LATITUDE : 51 07 15N. HEIGHT ASL : 130′ LIGHTING : None.
LONGITUDE : 00 49 00E. FLYING CONTROL : None.RADIO : QDM.

LANDMARKS DAY : -

LANDMARKS NIGHT : -

OBSTRUCTIONS : -

LANDING AREA SURFACE : Steel Matting[Sommerfield track & steel planking]

QDM	LENGTH X WIDTH	Ext
150.	1600yds.	-
040.	1250yds.	-

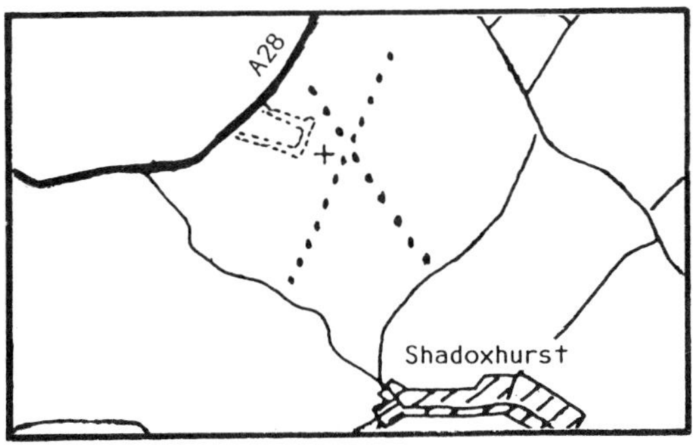

EXTENSIBILITY : -

ACCOMMODATION : Tented camp.
HANGARS : -

HARDSTANDINGS : -

R.A.F. : OFFICERS: - S.N.C.O′s.: - O.R′s.: - TOTAL: -
W.A.A.F.: " : - " : - " : - " : -

AFFILIATED AIRFIELDS : -

PRESENT USE [1985] : Agriculture.

NO: 022.

AIRFIELD NAME: ASTON DOWN. OPENED : 1938.
COUNTY : Gloucestershire. CLOSED : 1965.
COMMAND : Fighter.
FORMATION : 12 Grp[Watnall] GRID REF: P 355215[103]
FUNCTION : Tactical Exercise Unit. O.S.REF.: SO 912010.

LOCALITY : 4.5miles S of Stroud.
RAILWAY STN. : Chalford 1.5miles[GWR]

LATITUDE : 51 42 30N. HEIGHT ASL : 605' LIGHTING : None.
LONGITUDE : 02 07 45W. FLYING CONTROL : Yes. RADIO : QDM.

LANDMARKS DAY : Double loop, R Severn; Chalford Valley & canal.

LANDMARKS NIGHT : As day.

OBSTRUCTIONS : -

LANDING AREA SURFACE : Unspecified hard surface.

QDM	LENGTH X WIDTH	Ext
036.	1675 x 50yds.	2400yds.
094.	1100 x 50yds.	1150yds.
164.	1075 x 50yds.	-

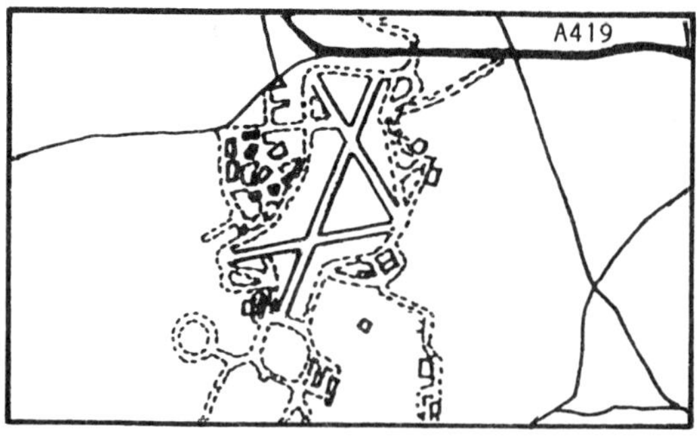

EXTENSIBILITY : Entails demolition of semi-derelict small farm & 2 small barns.
ACCOMMODATION : Permanent[part]
HANGARS : 50 of various kinds.

HARDSTANDINGS : 44.

R.A.F. : OFFICERS: 84. S.N.C.O's.: 96. O.R's.: 1734. TOTAL: 1914.
W.A.A.F.: " : 11. " : 10. " : 389. " : 410.

AFFILIATED AIRFIELDS : Chedworth[Satellite]

PRESENT USE [1985] : Home Office.

NO: 023.

AIRFIELD NAME: ATCHAM. OPENED : 1941.
COUNTY : Shropshire. CLOSED : 1946.
COMMAND : 8th USAAF.
FORMATION : 495th Fighter Train.Grp. GRID REF: K 030316[61]
FUNCTION : Crew replacement Unit. O.S.REF.: SJ 572104.

LOCALITY : 5miles E of Shrewsbury.
RAILWAY STN. : Shrewsbury [GWR]

LATITUDE : 52 41 23N. HEIGHT ASL : 200' LIGHTING : Mk.2.
LONGITUDE : 02 38 00W. FLYING CONTROL : Yes. RADIO : QDM.

LANDMARKS DAY : Wrekin 4miles ESE 1335' ASL. R Severn & Tern; Shrewsbury-Wellington railway 3.5miles S.

LANDMARKS NIGHT : R Severn.

OBSTRUCTIONS : High tension pylons running 1000yd.N of A/F. Wreken 1335' 4miles ESE.

LANDING AREA SURFACE : Tarmac & rubber chippings.

QDM	LENGTH X WIDTH	Ext
235.	1480 x 50yds.	2900/2000yds.
187.	1350 x 50yds.	1500/1400yds.
297.	1200 x 50yds.	2150/1400yds.

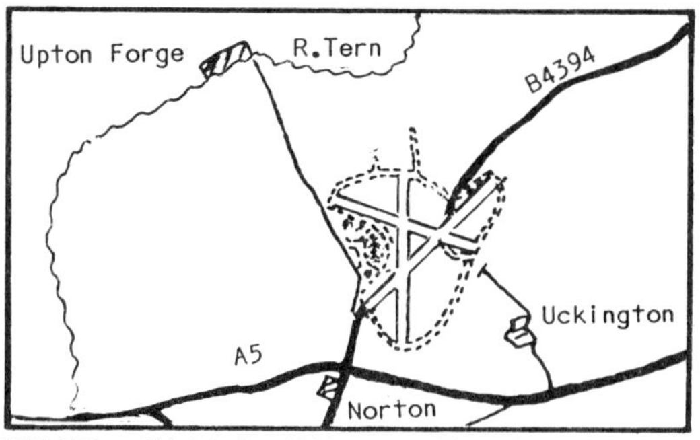

EXTENSIBILITY : Slight demolition, no diversions unless max.extension.
ACCOMMODATION : Temporary.
HANGARS : Calender Hamilton-3;O.Blister-4;EO blister-4.

HARDSTANDINGS : Banjo-26.

USAAF. : OFFICERS: 319. Enlisted Men. : 1333. TOTAL: 1652.

AFFILIATED AIRFIELDS : -

PRESENT USE [1985] : Agriculture.

NO: 024.

AIRFIELD NAME: ATTLEBRIDGE. OPENED : 1941.
COUNTY : Norfolk. CLOSED : 1959.
COMMAND : 8th USAAF.
FORMATION : 466th Bomb Grp. GRID REF: G 563333[66]
FUNCTION : Operational. O.S.REF.: TG 105150.

LOCALITY : 8miles NW of Norwich.
RAILWAY STN. : Ledwade 3miles[M&GN]

LATITUDE : 52 41 30N. HEIGHT ASL : 200' LIGHTING : Mk.2.
LONGITUDE : 01 06 45E. FLYING CONTROL : Yes. RADIO : QDM.

LANDMARKS DAY : Weston church just SE.

LANDMARKS NIGHT : -

OBSTRUCTIONS : Trees around rectory NE of A/F.

LANDING AREA SURFACE : Concrete covered with asphalt.

QDM	LENGTH X WIDTH	Ext
270.	2000 x 50yds.	3000yds.
220.	1400 x 50yds.	1800yds.
140.	1400 x 50yds.	2300yds.

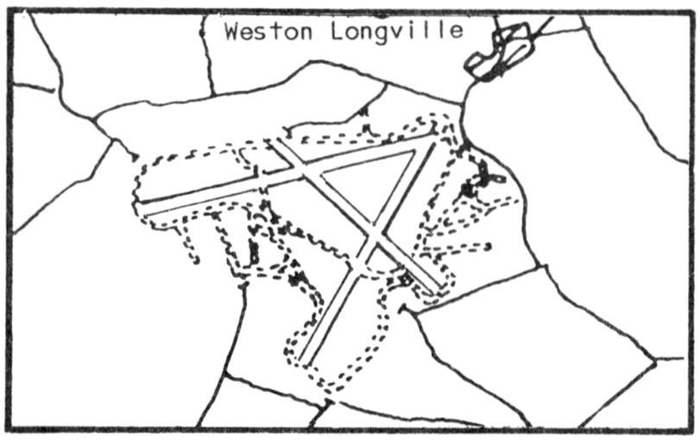

EXTENSIBILITY : -

ACCOMMODATION : Temporary.
HANGARS : T2-2.

HARDSTANDINGS : Loop-50.

USAAF. : OFFICERS: 451. Enlisted Men. : 2473. TOTAL: 2924.

AFFILIATED AIRFIELDS : -

PRESENT USE [1985] : Agriculture.

NO: 025.

AIRFIELD NAME: AYR.
COUNTY : Ayrshire.
COMMAND : RN.
FORMATION : HMS Wagtail.
FUNCTION : Disembarked Sqdns.

OPENED : 1941.
CLOSED : 1946.

GRID REF: S 855467[78Scot]
O.S.REF.: NS 358425.

LOCALITY : 4miles SSE of Troon.
RAILWAY STN. : Auchincruive .5miles[LMS]

LATITUDE : 55 28 55N. HEIGHT ASL : 50′ LIGHTING : Mk.2.
LONGITUDE : 04 35 45W. FLYING CONTROL : Yes. RADIO : QDM.

LANDMARKS DAY : Town & harbour of Troon: R Ayr 1mile S.
Ayr racecourse 1mile SSW.

LANDMARKS NIGHT : Coastline.

OBSTRUCTIONS : Chimneys 200′ 1mile S.

LANDING AREA SURFACE : Tarmac & asphalt.

QDM: 065-245. LENGTH X WIDTH: 1600 x 50yds. Ext: 2500yds.
: 004-184. : 1380 x 50yds. : -
: 131-311. : 1200 x 50yds. : 1740yds.
: : :

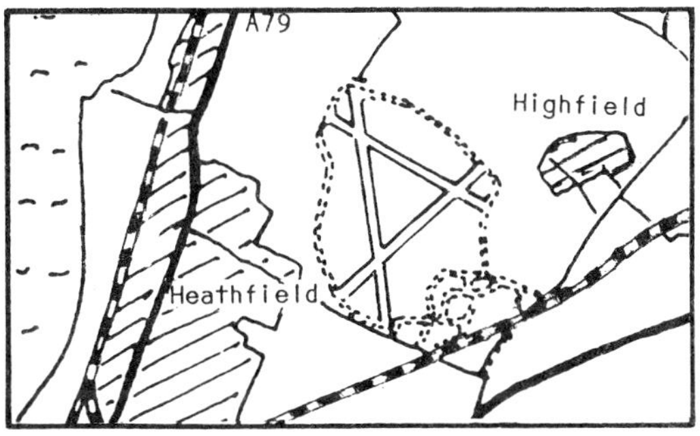

EXTENSIBILITY : -

ACCOMMODATION : Temporary.
HANGARS : 180x90′-3;Bellman-1;O Blister-17.

HARDSTANDINGS : Double Pens-16;hardstandings-6.

R.N. : OFFICERS: 132. Chiefs/POs/Ratings. : 1943.TOTAL: 2075.
W.R.N.S. : " : 8. " " : 443. " : 451.

AFFILIATED AIRFIELDS : -

PRESENT USE [1985] : Disused.

NO: 026.

AIRFIELD NAME: BABDOWN FARM.
COUNTY : Gloucestershire.
COMMAND : Flying Training.
FORMATION : 23 Grp[South Cerney]
FUNCTION : Advanced Flying Unit.

OPENED : 1940.
CLOSED : 1948.

GRID REF: P 290147[103]
O.S.REF.: ST 845936.

LOCALITY : 14miles S of Gloucester.
RAILWAY STN. : Tetbury 2.5miles[GWR].

LATITUDE : 51 38 34N. HEIGHT ASL : 580′ LIGHTING : Mk2.
LONGITUDE : 02 13 27W. FLYING CONTROL : Yes. RADIO : QDM.

LANDMARKS DAY : -

LANDMARKS NIGHT : -

OBSTRUCTIONS : -

LANDING AREA SURFACE : Steel Matting[Sommerfield Track]NW-SE grass.

QDM: 123. LENGTH X WIDTH: 1013yds. Ext: 1800yds.
: 343. : 1203yds. : -
: NW-SE. : 1000yds. : -
: : :

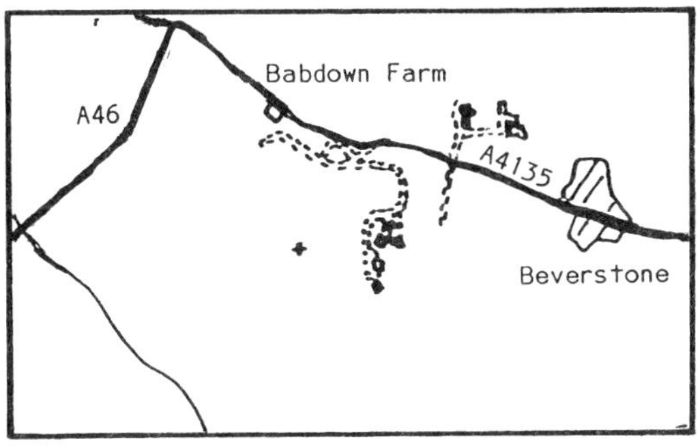

EXTENSIBILITY : Not recommended.

ACCOMMODATION : Temporary.
HANGARS : T1-3;Blisters:single-5;double-4.

HARDSTANDINGS : None.

R.A.F. : OFFICERS: 68. S.N.C.O′s.: 153.O.R′s.: 350. TOTAL: 571.
W.A.A.F.: " : 4. " : 7. " : 212. " : 223.

AFFILIATED AIRFIELDS : Castle Coome & Long Newton[Satellites]

PRESENT USE [1985] : Disused.

NO: 027.

AIRFIELD NAME: BAGINTON.
COUNTY : Warwickshire.
COMMAND : Bomber.
FORMATION : 26 Grp[Langley Hall]
FUNCTION : Operational[satellite]

OPENED : 1934.
CLOSED :

GRID REF: P 808945[72]
O.S.REF.: SP 346748.

LOCALITY : 3miles SE of Coventry.
RAILWAY STN. : Coventry 3miles[LMS]

LATITUDE : 52 21 30N. HEIGHT ASL : 270′ LIGHTING : None.
LONGITUDE : 01 28 50W. FLYING CONTROL : Yes. RADIO : QDM.

LANDMARKS DAY : Kenilworth Castle 5miles WSW; horseshoe lake
E side of Coventry.

LANDMARKS NIGHT : _

OBSTRUCTIONS : Whitley Wks SE; Alvis Wks SW.

LANDING AREA SURFACE : Grass.

QDM: NE-SW. LENGTH X WIDTH: 1730yds. Ext: 2800yds.
: N-S. : 1350yds. : 1700yds.
: NW-SE. : 1060yds. : 1500yds.
: : :

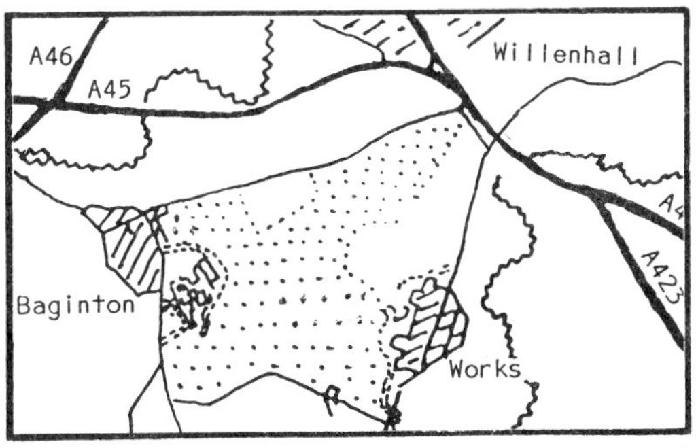

EXTENSIBILITY : Entails diversion of roads & demolition of
1 house.
ACCOMMODATION : Temporary.
HANGARS : Bellman-2.

HARDSTANDINGS : -

R.A.F. : OFFICERS: 1. S.N.C.O′s.: 5.O.R′s.: 4. TOTAL: 10.
W.A.A.F.: " : - " : 1. " : 10. " : 11.

AFFILIATED AIRFIELDS : Honiley[Parent]

PRESENT USE [1985] : Civil Airport[Coventry]

NO: 028.

AIRFIELD NAME: BALADO BRIDGE. OPENED : 1942.
COUNTY : Kinross-shire. CLOSED : 1957.
COMMAND : Fighter.
FORMATION : On loan to War Dept. GRID REF: O 596252[67Scot]
FUNCTION : On loan to War Dept. O.S.REF.: NO 095035.

LOCALITY : 2miles W of Kinross.
RAILWAY STN. : Kinross 2miles[LMS]

LATITUDE : 56 12 53N. HEIGHT ASL : 420′ LIGHTING : None.
LONGITUDE : 03 27 30W. FLYING CONTROL : Yes. RADIO : QDM.

LANDMARKS DAY : -

LANDMARKS NIGHT : -

OBSTRUCTIONS : Ochil Hills 3miles WSW 2000′,Lomand Hills 5miles E 1720′,Cleish Hills 4miles S 1250′

LANDING AREA SURFACE : Hardcore & concrete.

QDM	LENGTH X WIDTH	Ext
275.	1650 x 50yds.	2500yds.
217.	1400 x 50yds.	2500yds.

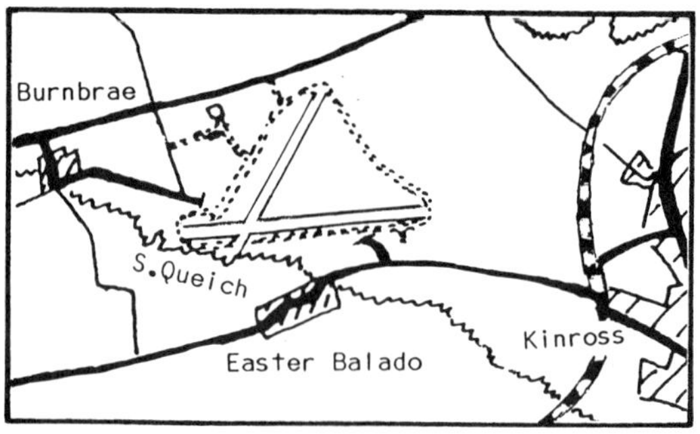

EXTENSIBILITY : Entails diversion of main road & demolition of a farm.
ACCOMMODATION : Temporary.
HANGARS : EO Blister 4;B1-1;Super Robin-1.

HARDSTANDINGS : 25.

	OFFICERS	S.N.C.O's.	O.R's.	TOTAL
R.A.F.	24.	83.	616.	723.
W.A.A.F.	2.	2.	105.	109.

AFFILIATED AIRFIELDS : -

PRESENT USE [1985] : Radio Research Station.

NO: 029.

AIRFIELD NAME: BALDERTON. OPENED : 1941.
COUNTY : Nottinghamshire. CLOSED : 1954.
COMMAND : Bomber.
FORMATION : 5 Grp[Morton Hall] GRID REF: F 280690[54]
FUNCTION : Operational. O.S.REF.: SK 816498.

LOCALITY : 2.75miles SSE of Newark on Trent.
RAILWAY STN. : Newark 4miles[LNER]

LATITUDE : 53 02 08N. HEIGHT ASL : 62′ LIGHTING : Mk.2.
LONGITUDE : 00 46 50W. FLYING CONTROL : Yes. RADIO : QDM.

LANDMARKS DAY : Gt. North Road to E & railway to W of A/F.

LANDMARKS NIGHT : -

OBSTRUCTIONS : Church 1.5miles NNE. Mental home .5miles NE.

LANDING AREA SURFACE : Tarmac.

QDM	LENGTH X WIDTH	Ext
085.	2000 x 50yds.	-
025.	1400 x 50yds.	-
146.	1400 x 50yds.	-

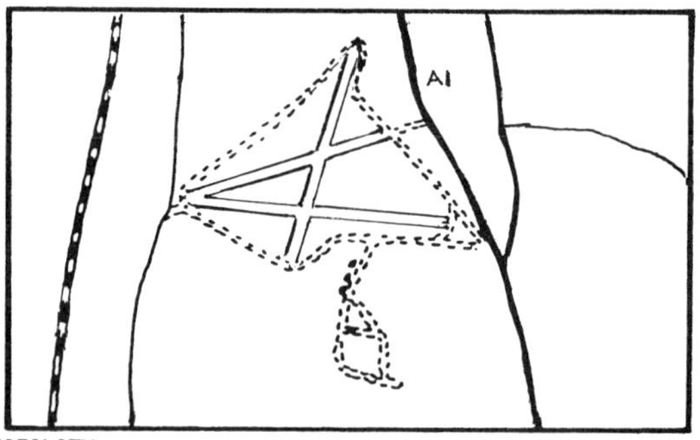

EXTENSIBILITY :

ACCOMMODATION : Temporary.
HANGARS : T2-2,Glider-2,B1-1.

HARDSTANDINGS : Heavy Bomber-50.

	OFFICERS	S.N.C.O's.	O.R's.	TOTAL
R.A.F.	69.	400.	1041.	1510.
W.A.A.F.	8.	20.	180.	208.

AFFILIATED AIRFIELDS : Syerston[56 Base]

PRESENT USE [1985] : Disused.

NO: 030.

AIRFIELD NAME: BALLYHALBERT. OPENED : 1941.
COUNTY : Down NI. CLOSED : 1946.
COMMAND : RAF NI.
FORMATION : Stormont[Belfast] GRID REF: J 640638[314NI]
FUNCTION : Training School. O.S.REF.: J 640638.

LOCALITY : 11miles SE of Newtownards.
RAILWAY STN. : Newtownards 13.5miles[B&CD]

LATITUDE : 54 29 45N. HEIGHT ASL : 26′ LIGHTING : Mk2.
LONGITUDE : 05 28 00W. FLYING CONTROL : Yes. RADIO : QDM.

LANDMARKS DAY : Coast skirts E end of A/F; Shrangford Lough 3miles W. Skulmartin lightship 4.5miles NNE of A/F.

LANDMARKS NIGHT : As day.

OBSTRUCTIONS : Hill 200′.5mile SW.Mountain of Mourne 2800′ 35miles SW.

LANDING AREA SURFACE : Tarmac & wood chippings.

QDM	LENGTH X WIDTH	Ext
025.	1147 x 50yds.	1500yds.
085.	2000 x 50yds.	-
145.	1093 x 50yds.	1700yds.

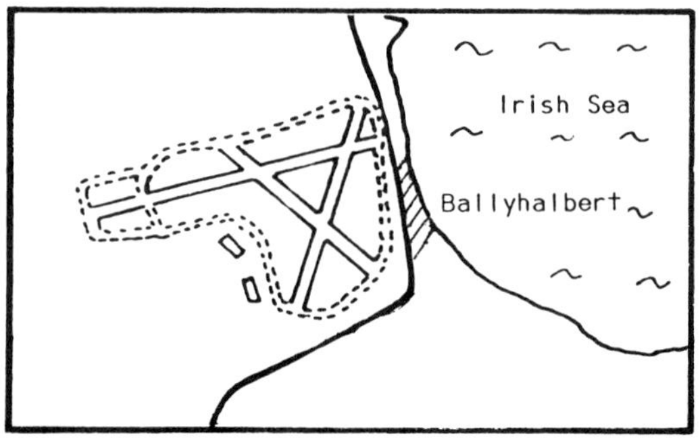

EXTENSIBILITY : Entails diversion of a minor road.

ACCOMMODATION : Temporary.
HANGARS : Transportable Bellman-2;Over blister-6; EO Blister- 6.
HARDSTANDINGS : Fighter-5;SE Twinpens-6;TE Twinpens-6.

	OFFICERS	S.N.C.O's.	O.R's.	TOTAL
R.A.F.	185.	271.	1953.	2409.
W.A.A.F.	9.	9.	309.	327.

AFFILIATED AIRFIELDS : -

PRESENT USE [1985] : Caravan site.

NO: 031.

AIRFIELD NAME: BALLYKELLY. OPENED : 1941.
COUNTY : Londonderry NI. CLOSED :
COMMAND : Coastal.
FORMATION : 15 Grp[Liverpool] GRID REF: C 632245[304NI]
FUNCTION : Operational. O.S.REF.: C 632245.

LOCALITY : 3miles W of Limavady.
RAILWAY STN. : Limavady 3miles[BNC]

LATITUDE : 55 03 45N. HEIGHT ASL : 10′ LIGHTING : Mk2.
LONGITUDE : 07 00 31W. FLYING CONTROL : Yes. RADIO : QDM.

LANDMARKS DAY : Lough Foyle just W.

LANDMARKS NIGHT : Lough Foyle, 2 steady white lights 072degrees 6miles; 092degrees 5.5miles.

OBSTRUCTIONS : Church spire 120′.75miles S,hills 1260′ NE-SW, water tower 100′high -1000′ S of N-S runway [not marked at night]

LANDING AREA SURFACE : Concrete.

QDM: 210. LENGTH X WIDTH: 2000 x 50yds. Ext: 2700yds.
: 267. : 2000 x 50yds. : 2600yds.
: 330. : 1100 x 50yds. : 1600yds.

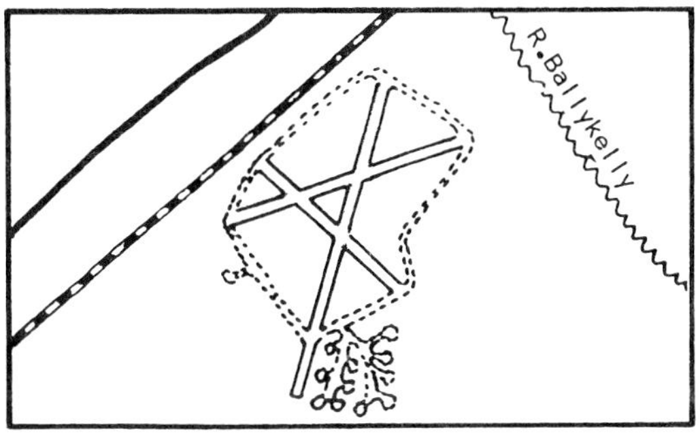

EXTENSIBILITY :

ACCOMMODATION : Temporary.
HANGARS : T2[23bay]-2;T2[13bay]-3;69′blister-8.

HARDSTANDINGS : Loop-13.

R.A.F. : OFFICERS: 183.S.N.C.O′s.: 367.O.R′s.: 1375.TOTAL: 1925.
W.A.A.F.: " : 10. " : 14. " : 378. " : 402.

AFFILIATED AIRFIELDS : -

PRESENT USE [1985] : Army.

NO: 032.

AIRFIELD NAME: BANFF. OPENED : 1943.
COUNTY : Banffshire. CLOSED : 1946.
COMMAND : Coastal.
FORMATION : 18 Grp[Pitreavie Castle] GRID REF: K 140855[30Scot]
FUNCTION : Operational. O.S.REF.: NJ 619643.

LOCALITY : 4.5miles W of Banff.
RAILWAY STN. : Portsoy 3.5miles[LMS]

LATITUDE : 57 40 00N. HEIGHT ASL : 250′ LIGHTING : Mk2.
LONGITUDE : 02 38 00W. FLYING CONTROL : Yes. RADIO : QDM.

LANDMARKS DAY : Coastline.

LANDMARKS NIGHT : Coastline.

OBSTRUCTIONS : -

LANDING AREA SURFACE : Concrete.

QDM: 180. LENGTH X WIDTH: 1400 x 50yds. Ext: -
: 236. : 1400 x 50yds. : 1700yds.
: 295. : 2000 x 50yds. : 2500yds.
: : :

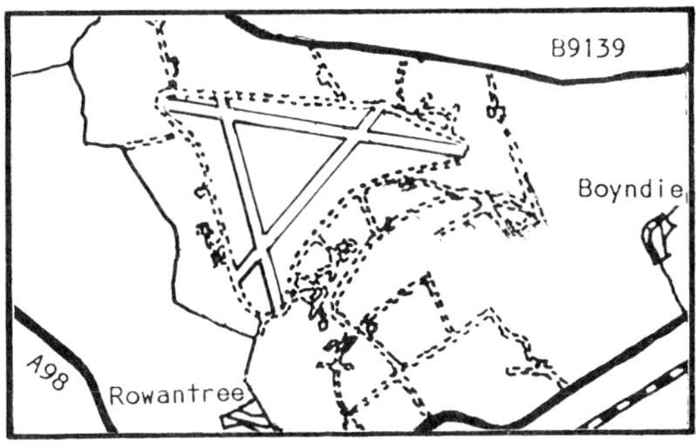

EXTENSIBILITY : -

ACCOMMODATION : Temporary.
HANGARS : T2[13 bay]-3;Double blister[69′]-13.

HARDSTANDINGS : Frying pan-36.

R.A.F. : OFFICERS: 168.S.N.C.O′s.: 279.O.R′s.: 1854.TOTAL: 2301.
W.A.A.F.: " : 10. " : 16. " : 315. " : 341.

AFFILIATED AIRFIELDS : Ballachy & Fraserburgh[Satellites]

PRESENT USE [1985] : Disused.

NO: 033.

AIRFIELD NAME: BARDNEY. OPENED : 1943.
COUNTY : Lincolnshire. CLOSED : 1963.
COMMAND : Bomber.
FORMATION : 5 Grp[Morton Hall] GRID REF: F 604904[47]
FUNCTION : Operational. O.S.REF.: TF 140712.

LOCALITY : 10miles E of Lincoln.
RAILWAY STN. : Bardney 2miles[LNER]

LATITUDE : 53 13 30N. HEIGHT ASL : 40′ LIGHTING : Mk2.
LONGITUDE : 00 17 30W. FLYING CONTROL : Yes. RADIO : QDM.

LANDMARKS DAY : Sugar beet factory in Bardney village.

LANDMARKS NIGHT : -

OBSTRUCTIONS : -

LANDING AREA SURFACE : Concrete.

QDM: 353. LENGTH X WIDTH: 2000 x 50yds. Ext: 3500yds.
: 302. : 1400 x 50yds. : 2000yds.
: 196. : 1400 x 50yds. : -
: : :

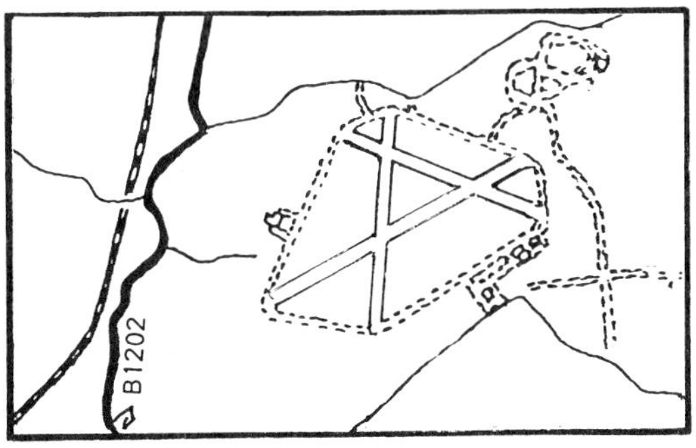

EXTENSIBILITY : -

ACCOMMODATION : Temporary.
HANGARS : T2-2;B1-1.

HARDSTANDINGS : Heavy bomber-36.

R.A.F. : OFFICERS: 87. S.N.C.O′s.: 256.O.R′s.: 799. TOTAL: 1142.
W.A.A.F.: " : 3. " : 8. " : 184. " : 195.

AFFILIATED AIRFIELDS : Waddington[53 Base]

PRESENT USE [1985] : Disused.

NO: 034.

AIRFIELD NAME: BARFORD St. JOHN. OPENED : 1941.
COUNTY : Oxfordshire. CLOSED : 1946.
COMMAND : Bomber.
FORMATION : 92 Grp[Winslow] GRID REF: P 890543[94]
FUNCTION : Operational Training Unit[satellite] O.S.REF.: SP 442341.
LOCALITY : 4.5miles SSE of Banbury.
RAILWAY STN. : Bloxham 2miles[GWR]

LATITUDE : 52 00 08N. HEIGHT ASL : 380′ LIGHTING : Mk2.
LONGITUDE : 01 21 15W. FLYING CONTROL : Yes. RADIO : QDM.

LANDMARKS DAY : -

LANDMARKS NIGHT : -

OBSTRUCTIONS : -

LANDING AREA SURFACE : Unspecified hard surface.

QDM	LENGTH X WIDTH	Ext
170.	1400 x 50yds.	-
216.	1400 x 50yds.	1600yds.
281.	2000 x 50yds.	2800yds.

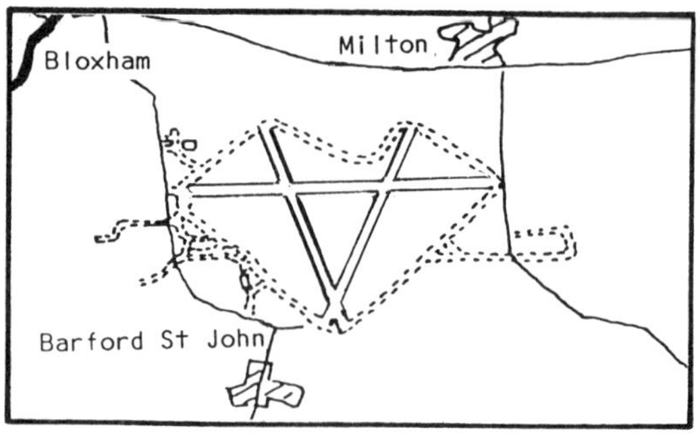

EXTENSIBILITY : -

ACCOMMODATION : Temporary.
HANGARS : T2-1;B1-1.

HARDSTANDINGS : Heavy Bomber-27.

R.A.F. : OFFICERS: 80. S.N.C.O′s.: 233.O.R′s.: 592. TOTAL: 905.
W.A.A.F.: " : 4. " : 30. " : 108. " : 142.

AFFILIATED AIRFIELDS : Upper Heyford[Parent]

PRESENT USE [1985] : Radio Research Station.

NO: 035.

AIRFIELD NAME: BARKSTON HEATH. OPENED : 1941.
COUNTY : Lincolnshire. CLOSED :
COMMAND : 9th USAAF.
FORMATION : 61st Troop Carrier Grp. GRID REF: F 432606[55]
FUNCTION : Operational. O.S.REF.: SK 970415.

LOCALITY : 5miles NNE of Grantham.
RAILWAY STN. : Ancaster 3miles[LNER]

LATITUDE : 52 57 30N. HEIGHT ASL : 350′ LIGHTING : Mk2.
LONGITUDE : 00 33 30W. FLYING CONTROL : Yes. RADIO : QDM.

LANDMARKS DAY : RAF hospital, Rauceby 4miles ENE. Water tower & chimneys 120′high. Town of Grantham 5miles SW.

LANDMARKS NIGHT : -

OBSTRUCTIONS : Low buildings on S side of landing ground.

LANDING AREA SURFACE : Concrete & wood chippings.

QDM	LENGTH X WIDTH	Ext
250.	2000 x 50yds.	3100yds.
290.	1400 x 50yds.	1900yds.
190.	1400 x 50yds.	-

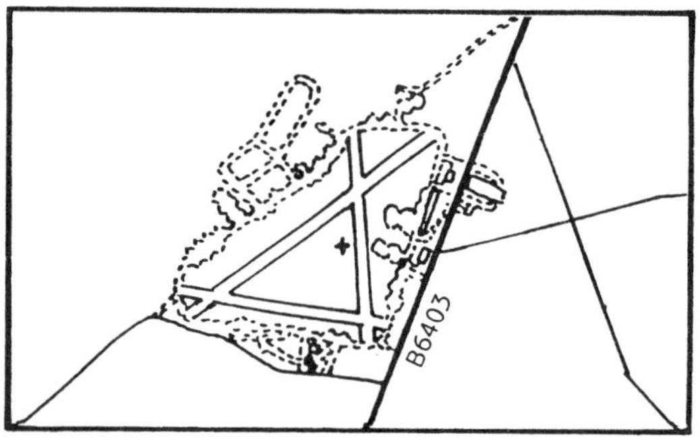

EXTENSIBILITY : Entails demolition of 1 farm & 1 lodge.

ACCOMMODATION : Temporary.
HANGARS : T2-6;B1-1.

HARDSTANDINGS : Loop-48;circular-2..

USAAF. : OFFICERS: 247. Enlisted Men. : 1140.TOTAL: 1387.

AFFILIATED AIRFIELDS : -

PRESENT USE [1985] : RAF.

NO: 036.

AIRFIELD NAME: BARROW. OPENED : 1941.
COUNTY : Lancashire. CLOSED : 1946.
COMMAND : Flying Training.
FORMATION : 25 Grp[Market Drayton] GRID REF: D 650927[24]
FUNCTION : Air Gunnery School. O.S.REF.: SD 175712.

LOCALITY : Walney Island.
RAILWAY STN. : Barrow Central[LMS]

LATITUDE : 54 07 45N. HEIGHT ASL : 25′ LIGHTING : None.
LONGITUDE : 03 16 00W. FLYING CONTROL : None.RADIO : QDM.

LANDMARKS DAY : N end of an island 1.5miles 283degrees off Barrow railway station.

LANDMARKS NIGHT : Unknown as A/F is totally unsuitable for night flying.

OBSTRUCTIONS : Slag heap 165′ high at 800yds SE of No.2 R/W.

LANDING AREA SURFACE : Tarmac.

QDM	LENGTH X WIDTH	Ext
120.	1300 x 50yds.	-
360.	1100 x 50yds.	2100yds
060.	1100 x 50yds.	-

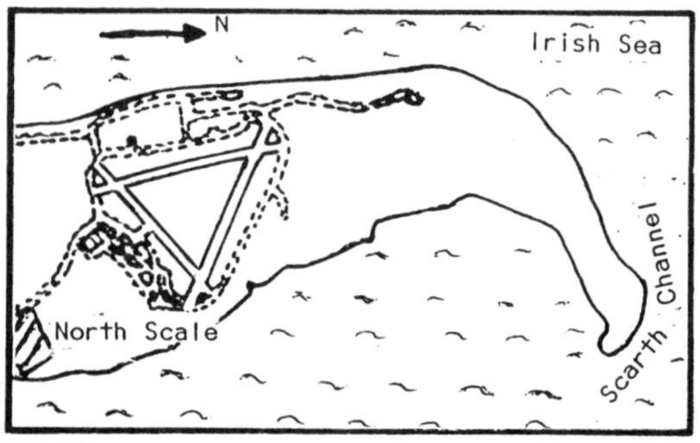

EXTENSIBILITY : -

ACCOMMODATION : Temporary.
HANGARS : Callendar Hamilton-3;E.O.Blister-15.

HARDSTANDINGS : Circular-19;Blister floors-7.

R.A.F. : OFFICERS: 80. S.N.C.O′s.: 144.O.R′s.: 1445.TOTAL: 1669.
W.A.A.F.: " : 16. " : 16. " : 370. " : 402.

AFFILIATED AIRFIELDS : -

PRESENT USE [1985] : Private Flying.

NO: 037.

AIRFIELD NAME: BASSINGBOURN. OPENED : 1938.
COUNTY : Cambridgeshire. CLOSED :
COMMAND : 8th USAAF.
FORMATION : 91st Bomb Grp. GRID REF: L 785852[85]
FUNCTION : Operational. O.S.REF.: TL 330462.

LOCALITY : 3.5miles NNW of Royston.
RAILWAY STN. : Royston 3miles[LMS]

LATITUDE : 52 05 53N. HEIGHT ASL : 78′ LIGHTING : Mk2.
LONGITUDE : 00 03 00W. FLYING CONTROL : Yes. RADIO : QDM.

LANDMARKS DAY : Avenue of trees 2.5miles long N of A/F. Roman road NNW-SSE bordering on A/F.

LANDMARKS NIGHT : R Cam running E-W 1.5miles N of A/F.

OBSTRUCTIONS : -

LANDING AREA SURFACE : Concrete covered with asphalt.

QDM	LENGTH X WIDTH	Ext
254.	2000 x 50yds.	3500yds.
308.	1400 x 50yds.	2600yds.
350.	1400 x 50yds.	2400yds.

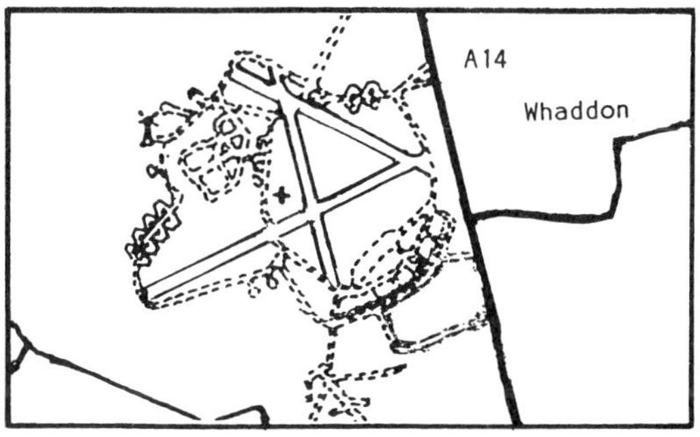

EXTENSIBILITY : 254 only recommended to 2700yds,308&350 only to 2000yds.
ACCOMMODATION : Permanent.
HANGARS : Type C-4.

HARDSTANDINGS : Loop-54.

USAAF. : OFFICERS: 443. Enlisted Men. : 2529.TOTAL: 2972.

AFFILIATED AIRFIELDS : -

PRESENT USE [1985] : Army.

NO: 038.

AIRFIELD NAME: BATTLESTEAD HILL. OPENED : 1942.
COUNTY : Staffordshire. CLOSED : 1945.
COMMAND : Flying Training.
FORMATION : 51 Grp[Leeds] GRID REF: K 673435[62]
FUNCTION : Elementary Flying Training School[RLG] O.S.REF.: SK 212232.
LOCALITY : 1.5miles W of Burton-on-Trent.
RAILWAY STN. : Burton-on-Trent[LMS]

LATITUDE : 52 48 23N. HEIGHT ASL : 300′ LIGHTING : None.
LONGITUDE : 01 41 00W. FLYING CONTROL : None.RADIO : QDM.

LANDMARKS DAY : R Trent & Burton-on-Trent 2miles SE.

LANDMARKS NIGHT : _

OBSTRUCTIONS : -

LANDING AREA SURFACE : Grass.

QDM	LENGTH X WIDTH	Ext
NE-SW.	1100yd.	-
E-W.	950yds.	-
N-S.	800yds.	-

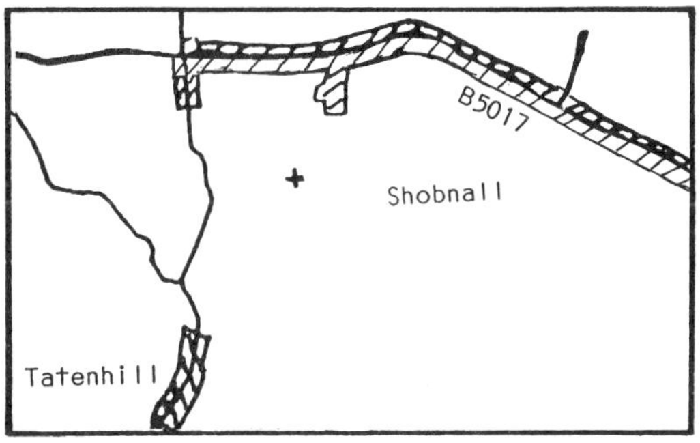

EXTENSIBILITY : -

ACCOMMODATION : Temporary.
HANGARS : Standard blister-3.

HARDSTANDINGS : None.

R.A.F. : OFFICERS: 2. S.N.C.O′s.: 4. O.R′s.: 120. TOTAL: 126.
W.A.A.F.: " : - " : - " : - " : -

AFFILIATED AIRFIELDS : -

PRESENT USE [1985] : Housing.

NO: 039.

AIRFIELD NAME: BEAULIEU. OPENED : 1942.
COUNTY : Hampshire. CLOSED : 1950.
COMMAND : Fighter.
FORMATION : 11 Grp[Uxbridge] GRID REF: U 785208[131]
FUNCTION : Forward Airfield. O.S.REF.: SU 350008.

LOCALITY : 3.5miles NNE of Lymington.
RAILWAY STN. : Brockenhurst 4.5miles[SR]

LATITUDE : 50 48 15N. HEIGHT ASL : 130′ LIGHTING : Mk2.
LONGITUDE : 01 30 15W. FLYING CONTROL : Yes. RADIO : QDM.

LANDMARKS DAY : Beaulieu Creek to SE; Sway tower to SW.

LANDMARKS NIGHT : Beaulieu Creek to SE.

OBSTRUCTIONS : -

LANDING AREA SURFACE : Tarmac.

QDM	LENGTH X WIDTH	Ext
088.	1970 x 50yds.	4700yds.
027.	1370 x 50yds.	2100yds.
151.	1370 x 50yds.	2000yds.

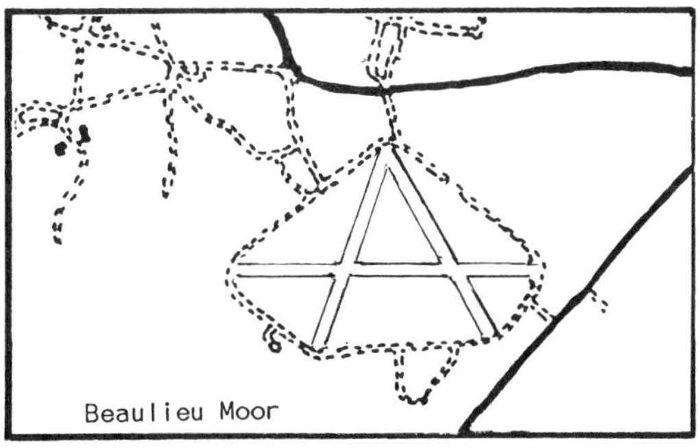

EXTENSIBILITY : Entails serious road diversions, but light demolition.
ACCOMMODATION : Temporary.
HANGARS : T2-2;Blister-1.

HARDSTANDINGS : 122′concrete-50.

R.A.F. : OFFICERS: 181.S.N.C.O′s.: 502.O.R′s.: 1436.TOTAL: 2119.
W.A.A.F.: " : 10. " : 40. " : 288. " : 338.

AFFILIATED AIRFIELDS : Middle Wallop[Sector]

PRESENT USE [1985] : Forestry Commission.

NO: 040.

AIRFIELD NAME: BECCLES.
COUNTY : Suffolk.
COMMAND : Coastal.
FORMATION : 16 Grp[Gillingham]
FUNCTION : Operational.

OPENED : 1943.
CLOSED : 1945.
GRID REF: G 910060[77]
O.S.REF.: TM 453882.

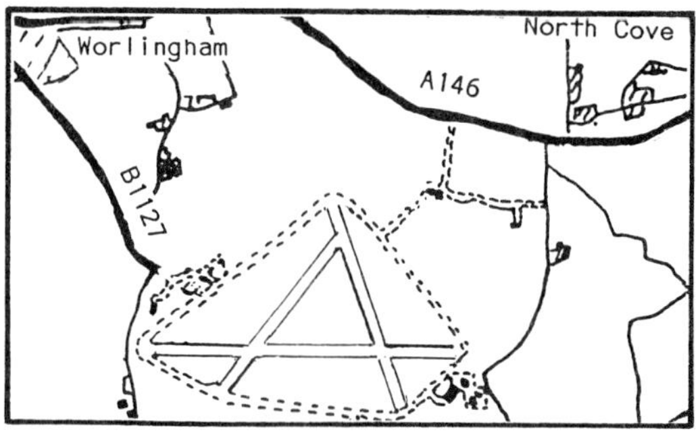

LOCALITY : 5.5miles SW of Lowestoft.
RAILWAY STN. : Beccles[LNER]

LATITUDE : 52 26 08N. HEIGHT ASL : 50′ LIGHTING : Mk2.
LONGITUDE : 01 36 30E. FLYING CONTROL : Yes. RADIO : QDM.

LANDMARKS DAY : Outer circle of A/F lighting almost touches R Waveney to the NW & Beccles church tower.

LANDMARKS NIGHT : R Waveney.

OBSTRUCTIONS : -

LANDING AREA SURFACE : Unspecified hard surface.

QDM	LENGTH X WIDTH	Ext
099.	2000 x 50yds.	2400yds.
172.	1400 x 50yds.	-
226.	1400 x 50yds.	1800yds.

EXTENSIBILITY : -

ACCOMMODATION : Temporary.
HANGARS : T2-2.

HARDSTANDINGS : Loop-50.

	OFFICERS	S.N.C.O′s.	O.R′s.	TOTAL
R.A.F.	115.	524.	2028.	2667.
W.A.A.F.	3.	-	24.	27.

AFFILIATED AIRFIELDS : -

PRESENT USE [1985] : Industry/helicopters.

NO: 041.

AIRFIELD NAME: BELFAST.
COUNTY : Down NI.
COMMAND : RN.
FORMATION : HMS Gadwall.
FUNCTION : A/C Maintenance yard.

OPENED : 1938.
CLOSED :
GRID REF: J 373764[NI]
O.S.REF.: J 373764.

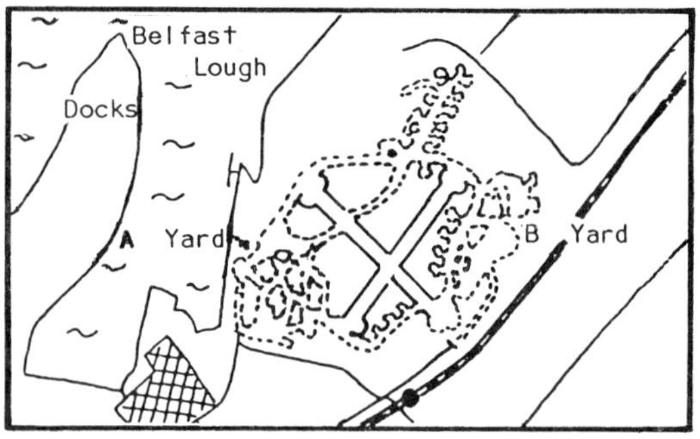

LOCALITY : E side of Belfast Docks.
RAILWAY STN. : Victoria Park .25mile[GNI]

LATITUDE : 54 36 45N. HEIGHT ASL : 19′ LIGHTING : None.
LONGITUDE : 05 52 26W. FLYING CONTROL : Yes. RADIO : Yes.

LANDMARKS DAY : Belfast Lough with harbour & city of Belfast at its head.

LANDMARKS NIGHT : -

OBSTRUCTIONS : Mountain range 1574′ 5miles W. Hills 600′ 1.5miles E.

LANDING AREA SURFACE : Concrete.

QDM	LENGTH X WIDTH	Ext
046-226.	1100 x 67yds.	-
143-323.	1100 x 67yds.	-

EXTENSIBILITY : -

ACCOMMODATION : Permanent.
HANGARS : Various-29

HARDSTANDINGS :

	OFFICERS	Chiefs/POs/Ratings.	TOTAL
R.N.	58.	440.	498.
W.R.N.S.	6.	125.	131.

AFFILIATED AIRFIELDS : -

PRESENT USE [1985] : Civil Airport[Belfast]

NO: 042.

AIRFIELD NAME: BELLASIZE.
COUNTY : Yorkshire.
COMMAND : Flying Training.
FORMATION : 51 Grp[Leeds]
FUNCTION : Elementary Flying Training School[RLG]

OPENED : 1916.
CLOSED : 1945.
GRID REF: A 288470[32]
O.S.REF.: SE 818278.

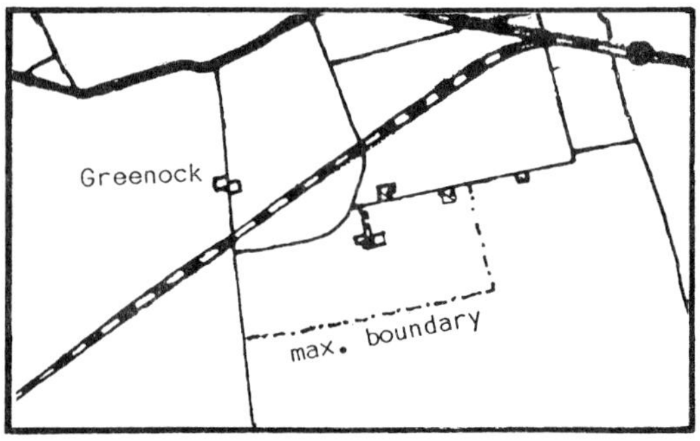

LOCALITY : 4.5miles E of Howden.
RAILWAY STN. : Straddlethorpe 1mile[LNER]

LATITUDE : 53 44 08N. HEIGHT ASL : 12′ LIGHTING : None.
LONGITUDE : 00 45 38W. FLYING CONTROL : None. RADIO : QDM.

LANDMARKS DAY : -

LANDMARKS NIGHT : -

OBSTRUCTIONS : Barrack buildings in NE corner.

LANDING AREA SURFACE : Grass.

QDM	LENGTH X WIDTH	Ext
NW-SE.	670yds.	-

EXTENSIBILITY : None recommended.

ACCOMMODATION : Temporary.
HANGARS : None.

HARDSTANDINGS : None.

	OFFICERS	S.N.C.O′s.	O.R′s.	TOTAL
R.A.F.	6.	12.	312.	330.
W.A.A.F.	-	-	-	-

AFFILIATED AIRFIELDS : Brough[Parent]

PRESENT USE [1985] : Disused.

NO: 043.

AIRFIELD NAME: BENBECULA. OPENED : 1941.
COUNTY : Hebrides. CLOSED :
COMMAND : Coastal.
FORMATION : 15 Grp[Liverpool] GRID REF: G 303802[33Scot]
FUNCTION : Operational. O.S.REF.: NF 787562.

LOCALITY : Isle of Benbecula.
RAILWAY STN. : Oban[LMS]

LATITUDE : 57 29 00N. HEIGHT ASL : 16′. LIGHTING : Mk2.
LONGITUDE : 07 21 30W. FLYING CONTROL : Yes. RADIO : QDM.

LANDMARKS DAY : Channel between N Uist & Isle of Benbecula.

LANDMARKS NIGHT : -

OBSTRUCTIONS : Mt. Eval 1138′ 11miles 060degrees T;Mt. Renval 1094′ 3miles 112degrees T.

LANDING AREA SURFACE : Bitumen on compacted sand.

QDM	LENGTH X WIDTH	Ext
111.	1990x 50yds.	2095yds.
071.	1050 x 50yds.	1900yds.
003.	1410 x 50yds.	1510yds.

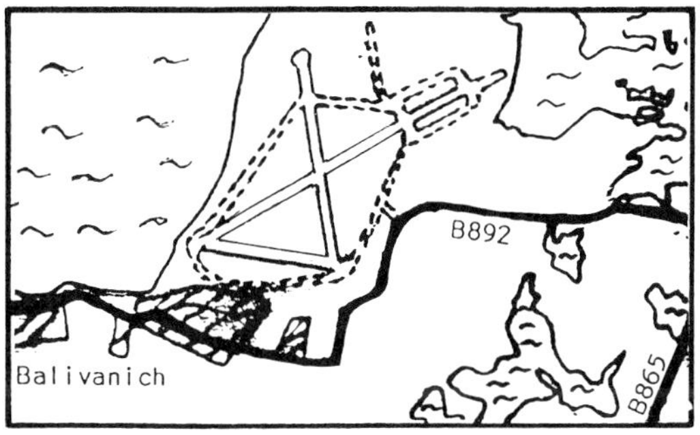

EXTENSIBILITY : Possible 4th R/W of 2000yds.

ACCOMMODATION : Temporary.
HANGARS : 1/2-T2[135x117x25′]-10.

HARDSTANDINGS : -

R.A.F. : OFFICERS: 116.S.N.C.O's.: 60. O.R's.: 2124.TOTAL: 2300.
W.A.A.F.: " : - " : 20. " : 240. " : 260.

AFFILIATED AIRFIELDS : -

PRESENT USE [1985] : Civil Airport[Western Isles]

NO: 044.

AIRFIELD NAME: BENSON. OPENED : 1939.
COUNTY : Oxfordshire. CLOSED :
COMMAND : Coastal
FORMATION : 106 Grp[Fifield House] GRID REF: L 074114[105]
FUNCTION : Photographic Recce Unit O.S.REF.: SU 628914.

LOCALITY : 1.75miles NE of Wallingford.
RAILWAY STN. : Wallingford 2.5miles[GWR]

LATITUDE : 51 37 00N. HEIGHT ASL : 200′ LIGHTING : Mk2.
LONGITUDE : 01 05 15W. FLYING CONTROL : Yes. RADIO : QDM.

LANDMARKS DAY : -

LANDMARKS NIGHT : Lights at:-1.transmitter 3off; 2.boundaries KC-B 2off; 3.hangar corners 4off; 4.top of chimney 5off; 5.fir tree. Old mansion.
OBSTRUCTIONS : Chiltern Hills 489′ 1mile 040 to 250degrees.

LANDING AREA SURFACE : Concrete & wood chippings.

QDM	LENGTH X WIDTH	Ext
069.	1990 x 50yds.	2000yds.
020.	1420 x 50yds.	2000yds.

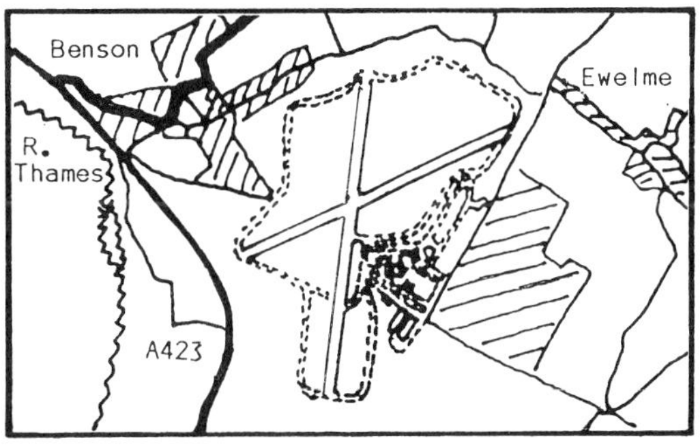

EXTENSIBILITY : Entails demolition of a sewage plant.

ACCOMMODATION : Permanent.
HANGARS : Type C-4;O.Blister-4;EO Blister-14.

HARDSTANDINGS : Concrete[120′dia]-10.

R.A.F. : OFFICERS: 182.S.N.C.O's.: 113.O.R's.: 2903.TOTAL: 3198.
W.A.A.F.: " : - " : - " : - " : -

AFFILIATED AIRFIELDS : -

PRESENT USE [1985] : RAF.

NO: 045.

AIRFIELD NAME: BENTWATERS. OPENED : 1944.
COUNTY : Suffolk. CLOSED :
COMMAND : Fighter.
FORMATION : 11 Grp[Uxbridge] GRID REF: M 800718[87]
FUNCTION : Forward Airfield. O.S.REF.: TM 353533.

LOCALITY : 4.5miles NE of Woodbridge.
RAILWAY STN. : Wickham Market[LNER]

LATITUDE : 52 07 30N. HEIGHT ASL : 80′ LIGHTING : Mk2.
LONGITUDE : 01 26 15E. FLYING CONTROL : Yes. RADIO : QDM.

LANDMARKS DAY : -

LANDMARKS NIGHT : -

OBSTRUCTIONS : -

LANDING AREA SURFACE : Concrete.

QDM	LENGTH X WIDTH	Ext
018.	1400 x 50yds.	-
315.	1400 x 50yds.	-
254.	2000 x 50yds.	-

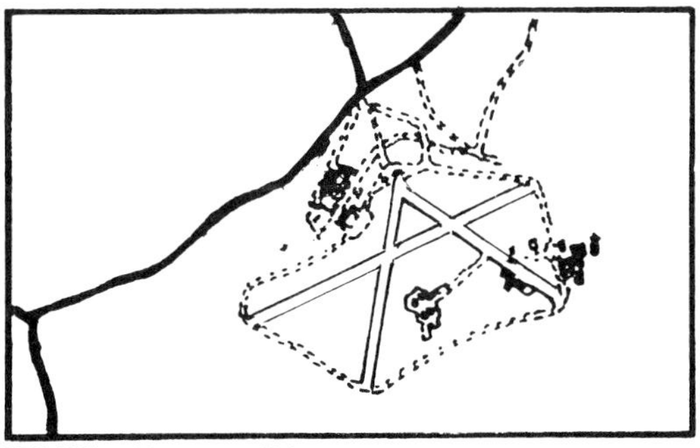

EXTENSIBILITY : None possible.

ACCOMMODATION : Temporary.
HANGARS : T2-2.

HARDSTANDINGS : Grid-50.

R.A.F. : OFFICERS: 127.S.N.C.O's.: 101.O.R's.: 1291.TOTAL: 1519.
W.A.A.F.: " : 6. " : 7. " : 256. " : 269.

AFFILIATED AIRFIELDS : -

PRESENT USE [1985] : USAFE.

NO: 046.

AIRFIELD NAME: BIBURY. OPENED : 1940.
COUNTY : Gloucestershire. CLOSED : 1945.
COMMAND : Maintenance.
FORMATION : 57 Wing[Milton] GRID REF: P 562293[104]
FUNCTION : Storage Unit. O.S.REF.: SP 115092.

LOCALITY : 6.5miles NE of Cirencester.
RAILWAY STN. : Foss Cross 1mile[GWR]

LATITUDE : 51 46 38N. HEIGHT ASL : 521′ LIGHTING : None.
LONGITUDE : 01 50 00W. FLYING CONTROL : None. RADIO : QDM.

LANDMARKS DAY : Lambrough Bank copse just NW.

LANDMARKS NIGHT : -

OBSTRUCTIONS : -

LANDING AREA SURFACE : Steel Matting[Sommerfeld Track]

QDM	LENGTH X WIDTH	Ext
040.	1145yds.	1530yds.
100.	1175yds.	-
N-W.		2000yds.

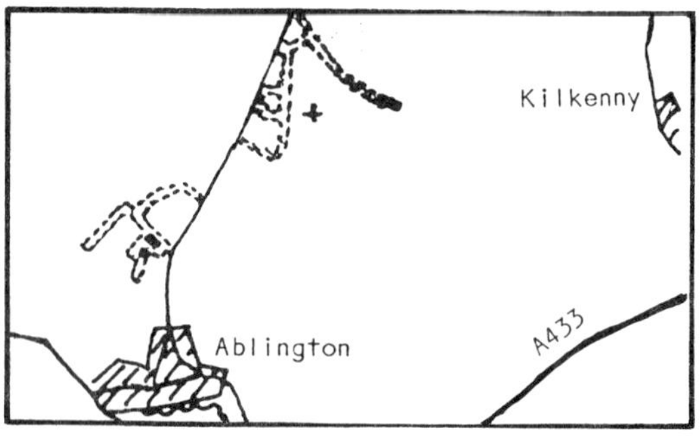

EXTENSIBILITY : Entails demolition of 2 modern cottages for NW extension
ACCOMMODATION : Temporary.
HANGARS : T1-1.

HARDSTANDINGS : -

R.A.F. : OFFICERS: 79. S.N.C.O′s.: 154. O.R′s.: 310. TOTAL: 543.
W.A.A.F.: " : 4. " : 3. " : 93. " : 100.

AFFILIATED AIRFIELDS : -

PRESENT USE [1985] : Disused.

NO: 047.

AIRFIELD NAME: BICESTER. OPENED : 1917.
COUNTY : Oxfordshire. CLOSED :
COMMAND : Fighter.
FORMATION : !2 Grp[Watnall] GRID REF: L 044450[94]
FUNCTION : Operational Training Unit[satellite] O.S.REF.: SP 598245.
LOCALITY : 1.75miles NNE of Bicester.
RAILWAY STN. : Bicester 1mile[GWR]

LATITUDE : 51 54 53N. HEIGHT ASL : 270′ LIGHTING : None.
LONGITUDE : 01 08 00W. FLYING CONTROL : Yes. RADIO : QDM.

LANDMARKS DAY : Brickwork chimneys 6miles E. Town of Bicester 1.5miles SW.

LANDMARKS NIGHT : -

OBSTRUCTIONS : -

LANDING AREA SURFACE : Grass.

QDM	LENGTH X WIDTH	Ext
NE-SW.	1250yds.	2-2700yds.
SE-NW.	1100yds.	14-2000yds.
E-W.	950yds.	14-2700yds.

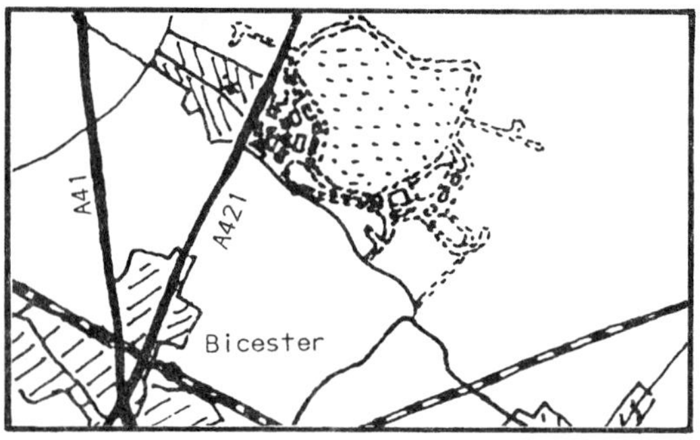

EXTENSIBILITY : The Roman Road to W of A/F is already closed & an alternative route exists.
ACCOMMODATION : Permanent.
HANGARS : Type A-2;Type C-2.

HARDSTANDINGS : Tarmac-41.

R.A.F. : OFFICERS: 172. S.N.C.O′s.: 428. O.R′s.: 1211. TOTAL: 1811.
W.A.A.F.: " : 13. " : 11. " : 576. " : 600.

AFFILIATED AIRFIELDS : Harwell[Parent]

PRESENT USE [1985] : RAF/Army/USAFE.

NO: 048.

AIRFIELD NAME: BIGGIN HILL. OPENED : 1917.
COUNTY : Kent. CLOSED :
COMMAND : Fighter.
FORMATION : 11 Grp[Uxbridge] GRID REF: Q 857794[115]
FUNCTION : Sector. O.S.REF.: TQ 415606.

LOCALITY : 5.5miles SSE of Bromley.
RAILWAY STN. : Bromley South 6.5miles[SR]

LATITUDE : 51 19 30N. HEIGHT ASL : 600′ LIGHTING : None.
LONGITUDE : 00 02 00E. FLYING CONTROL : Yes. RADIO : QDM.

LANDMARKS DAY : Addington building estate. Tatsfield BBC station.

LANDMARKS NIGHT : -

OBSTRUCTIONS : Chimney to central heating station 50′ high.

LANDING AREA SURFACE : Asphalt.

QDM	LENGTH X WIDTH	Ext
215.	1670 x 50yds.	1750yds.
235.	950 x 50yds.	1600yds.
295.	1000 x 50yds.	1400yds.
		2000yds.

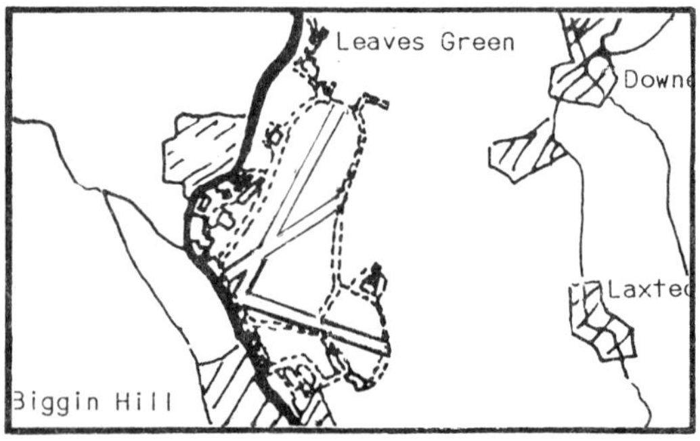

EXTENSIBILITY : 4th R/W would entail considerable expense.

ACCOMMODATION : Permanent.
HANGARS : Bessoneau-2;Blister-12.

HARDSTANDINGS : SE-19;Protected pens,SE-12,

R.A.F. : OFFICERS: 162. S.N.C.O′s.: 154. O.R′s.: 2077. TOTAL: 2393.
W.A.A.F.: " : 14. " : 8. " : 729. " : 751.

AFFILIATED AIRFIELDS : Penhurst/Detling/Kenley/Redhill/Friston/Gravesend/W.Malling/Gatwick/Hawkinge/Lympe.
PRESENT USE [1985] : RAF.

NO: 049.

AIRFIELD NAME: BINBROOK. OPENED : 1940.
COUNTY : Lincolnshire. CLOSED :
COMMAND : Bomber.
FORMATION : 1 Grp[Bawtry] GRID REF: A 660152[39]
FUNCTION : Operational[12 Base] O.S.REF.: TF 189959.
: 269.
LOCALITY : 9miles SW of Grimsby.
RAILWAY STN. : Market Rasen 9miles[LNER]

LATITUDE : 53 26 45N. HEIGHT ASL : 330' LIGHTING : Mk2.
LONGITUDE : 00 12 00W. FLYING CONTROL : Yes. RADIO : QDM.

LANDMARKS DAY : Crosby Pond & plantation approx 2miles N.
Swinhope wood .5miles E.

LANDMARKS NIGHT : 4-300' radio masts 8miles ENE[illuminated]
Subjected to enemy action.

OBSTRUCTIONS : -

LANDING AREA SURFACE : Concrete & tarmac.

QDM	LENGTH X WIDTH	Ext
217.	2000 x 50yds.	2800yds.
269.	1400 x 50yds.	2600yds.
327.	1400 x 50yds.	1450yds.
:	:	:

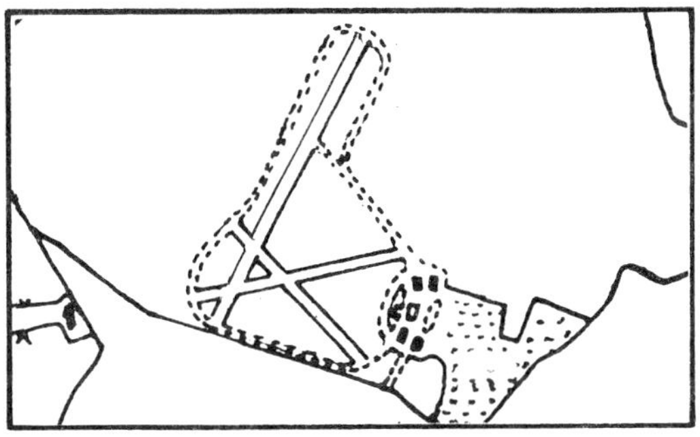

EXTENSIBILITY : Entails closure of minor roads.

ACCOMMODATION : Permanent.
HANGARS : Type C-5.

HARDSTANDINGS : Heavy bomber-36.

R.A.F. : OFFICERS: 156.S.N.C.O's.: 416.O.R's.: 1437.TOTAL: 2009.
W.A.A.F.: " : 14. " : 24. " : 350. " : 388.

AFFILIATED AIRFIELDS : Grimsby & Kelstern[Sub-stations]

PRESENT USE [1985] : RAF.

NO: 050.

AIRFIELD NAME: BIRCH. OPENED : 1944.
COUNTY : Essex. CLOSED : 1945.
COMMAND : 8th USAAF.
FORMATION : Reserve Airfield. GRID REF: M 365378[97]
FUNCTION : Reserve Airfield. O.S.REF.: TL 918915.

LOCALITY : 5miles SW of Colchester.
RAILWAY STN. : Marks Tay[LNER]

LATITUDE : 51 50 30N. HEIGHT ASL : 140' LIGHTING : Mk2.
LONGITUDE : 00 47 00E. FLYING CONTROL : Yes. RADIO : QDM.

LANDMARKS DAY : Large reservoir SE of A/F.

LANDMARKS NIGHT : -

OBSTRUCTIONS : -

LANDING AREA SURFACE : Concrete & Tarmac.

QDM	LENGTH X WIDTH	Ext
260.	2000 x 50yds.	-
200.	1400 x 50yds.	4800yds.
310.	1400 x 50yds.	2000yds.
:	:	:

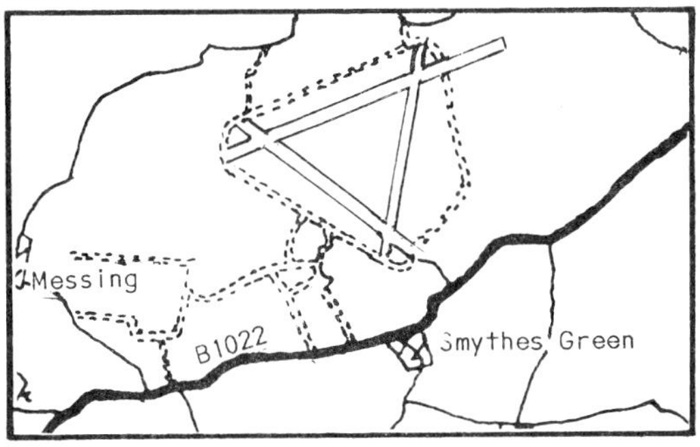

EXTENSIBILITY : Recommended to 3000&2000yds to prevent closure of a 2nd.class road.
ACCOMMODATION : Temporary.
HANGARS : T2-2.

HARDSTANDINGS : Loop-50.

USAAF. : OFFICERS: 421 Enlisted Men. : 2473.TOTAL: 2894.

AFFILIATED AIRFIELDS : -

PRESENT USE [1985] : Private flying.

NO: 051.

AIRFIELD NAME: BIRCHAM NEWTON. OPENED : 1916.
COUNTY : Norfolk. CLOSED : 1965.
COMMAND : Coastal.
FORMATION : 16 Grp[Gillingham] GRID REF: G 247528[57]
FUNCTION : Operational. O.S.REF.: TF 785345.

LOCALITY : 8miles WNW of Fakenham.
RAILWAY STN. : Docking 4miles[LNER]

LATITUDE : 52 52 23N. HEIGHT ASL : 230' LIGHTING : None.
LONGITUDE : 00 39 15E. FLYING CONTROL : Yes. RADIO : QDM.

LANDMARKS DAY : Docking railway station 2.5miles NNW.

LANDMARKS NIGHT : -

OBSTRUCTIONS : W/T masts SE corner 800yds.

LANDING AREA SURFACE : Steel Matting[BRC netting track]
Not suitable for tricycle u/c A/C.

QDM	LENGTH X WIDTH	Ext
NE-SW.	900yds.	2000yds.
:	:	1800yds.
:	:	1800yds.
:	:	:

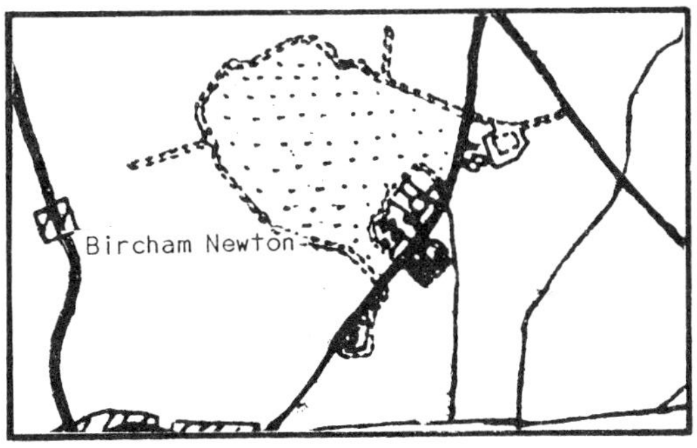

EXTENSIBILITY :

ACCOMMODATION : Permanent.
HANGARS : Type C-3;Bellman-3;Blister-10;Belfast-2.

HARDSTANDINGS : Local construction-2.

R.A.F. : OFFICERS: 263.S.N.C.O's.: 218.O.R's.: 1950.TOTAL: 2431.
W.A.A.F.: " : 10. " : 32. " : 512. " : 554.

AFFILIATED AIRFIELDS : Docking.

PRESENT USE [1985] : Industry Training Board[Construction]

NO: 052.

AIRFIELD NAME: BIRCOTES. OPENED : 1941.
COUNTY : Nottinghamshire. CLOSED : 1944.
COMMAND : Maintenance.
FORMATION : GRID REF: A 106136[38]
FUNCTION : Storage Unit. O.S.REF.: SK 642940.

LOCALITY : 1mile W of Bawtry.
RAILWAY STN. : Bawtry 2miles[LNER]

LATITUDE : 53 26 15N. HEIGHT ASL : 110′ LIGHTING : None.
LONGITUDE : 01 02 15W. FLYING CONTROL : Yes. RADIO : QDM.

LANDMARKS DAY : Great North road fork at Bawtry 1mile E. Railway running N-S 1.5miles.

LANDMARKS NIGHT : -

OBSTRUCTIONS : Colliery chimney 216′-2400yds. SE of perimeter. Water tower 530yds NE of perimeter.Brick works chimney 110′-1500yds E.

LANDING AREA SURFACE : Grass.

QDM: N-S. LENGTH X WIDTH: 1540yds. Ext: 2500yds.
: E-W. : 1980yds. : -
: NW-SE. : 1370yds. : 1900yds.

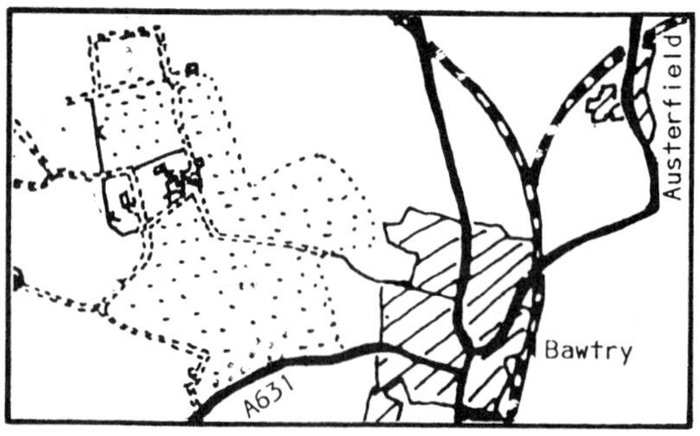

EXTENSIBILITY : SE extension entails diversion of Gainsborough-Rotherham road.
ACCOMMODATION : Temporary.
HANGARS : T2-1;B1-1;Bessoneau-1.

HARDSTANDINGS : Circular-30.

R.A.F. : OFFICERS: 84. S.N.C.O′s.: 193.O.R′s.: 487. TOTAL: 764.
W.A.A.F.: " : - " : 2. " : 78. " : 80.

AFFILIATED AIRFIELDS : -

PRESENT USE [1985] : Disused.

NO: 053.

AIRFIELD NAME: BISHOPS COURT. OPENED : 1943.
COUNTY : Down NI. CLOSED :
COMMAND : Flying Training.
FORMATION : 29 Grp[Dumfries] GRID REF: J 577425[321NI]
FUNCTION : Advanced Flying Unit. O.S.REF.: J 580425.

LOCALITY : 4miles NNE of Ardglass.
RAILWAY STN. : Ardglass[B&CD]

LATITUDE : 54 18 27N. HEIGHT ASL : 50′ LIGHTING : Mk2.
LONGITUDE : 05 34 30W. FLYING CONTROL : Yes. RADIO : QDM.

LANDMARKS DAY : Gunns Island 2miles E of A/F. Mouth of Strangford Lough N of A/F.

LANDMARKS NIGHT : -

OBSTRUCTIONS : Masts on hill 1.25miles NW.

LANDING AREA SURFACE : Concrete.

QDM: 060. LENGTH X WIDTH: 2000 x 50yds. Ext: 2500yds.
: 120. : 1400 x 50yds. : -
: 180. : 1400 x 50yds. : 2000yds.
: : :

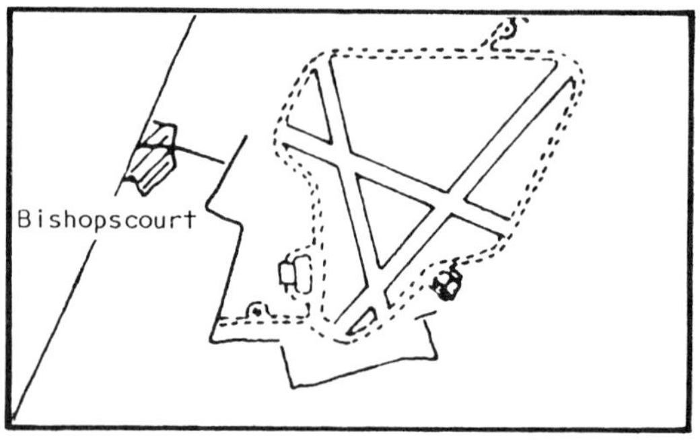

EXTENSIBILITY :

ACCOMMODATION : Temporary.
HANGARS : T2-4;EO blister-35.

HARDSTANDINGS : Circular[150′dia]-10;[125′dia]-8;Specticle-12. 800x1000′ marshalling area.
R.A.F. : OFFICERS: 147.S.N.C.O′s.: 410.O.R′s.: 1620.TOTAL: 2177.
W.A.A.F.: " : 27. " : 100. " : 457. " : 584.

AFFILIATED AIRFIELDS : -

PRESENT USE [1985] : RAF.

NO: 054.

AIRFIELD NAME: BISTERNE. OPENED : 1943.
COUNTY : Hampshire. CLOSED : 1944.
COMMAND : Fighter.
FORMATION : 11 Grp[Uxbridge] GRID REF: U 593227[147]
FUNCTION : Advanced landing groundO.S.REF.: SU 148015. [De-requisitioned]
LOCALITY : 2miles S of Ringwood.
RAILWAY STN. : Ringwood[SR]

LATITUDE : 50 49 00N. HEIGHT ASL : 55′ LIGHTING : None.
LONGITUDE : 01 46 45W. FLYING CONTROL : None.RADIO : QDM.

LANDMARKS DAY : -

LANDMARKS NIGHT : -

OBSTRUCTIONS : -

LANDING AREA SURFACE : Steel Matting[Sommerfeld Track]

QDM: 020. LENGTH X WIDTH: 1600yds. Ext: -
: : :
: : :
: : :

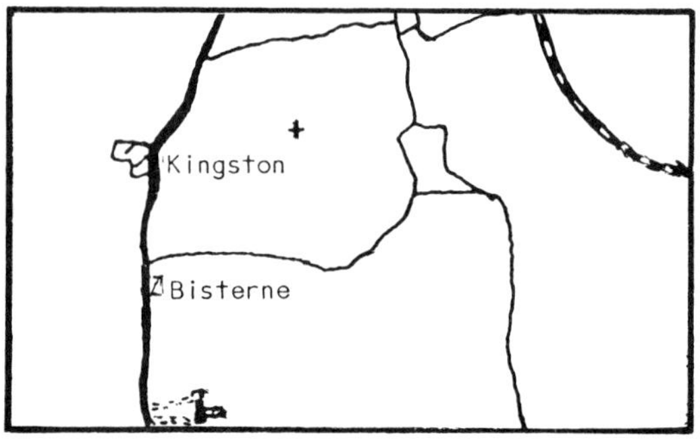

EXTENSIBILITY : -

ACCOMMODATION : Tented camp.
HANGARS : Blisters-4.

HARDSTANDINGS : Summerfeld track-80.

R.A.F. : OFFICERS: - S.N.C.O′s.: - O.R′s.: - TOTAL: -
W.A.A.F.: " : - " : - " : - " : -

AFFILIATED AIRFIELDS : -

PRESENT USE [1985] : Agriculture.

NO: 055.

AIRFIELD NAME: BITTESWELL. OPENED : 1942.
COUNTY : Leicestershire. CLOSED :
COMMAND : Transport.
FORMATION : 44 Grp[Gloucester] GRID REF: K 967045[73]
FUNCTION : Operational Training Unit[satellite] O.S.REF.: SP 514846.

LOCALITY : 6.5miles N of Rugby.
RAILWAY STN. : Lutterworth 2miles[LNER]

LATITUDE : 52 27 30N. HEIGHT ASL : 420′ LIGHTING : Mk2.
LONGITUDE : 01 14 30W. FLYING CONTROL : Yes. RADIO : QDM.

LANDMARKS DAY : W/T masts at Rugby, 8miles.

LANDMARKS NIGHT : -

OBSTRUCTIONS : Masts at Rugby: 27 up to 820′, 6miles SSE.

LANDING AREA SURFACE : Concrete & wood chippings.

QDM: 350. LENGTH X WIDTH: 1400 x 50yds. Ext: -
: 042. : 2000 x 50yds. : 2600yds.
: 108. : 1400 x 50yds. : 1550yds.
: : :

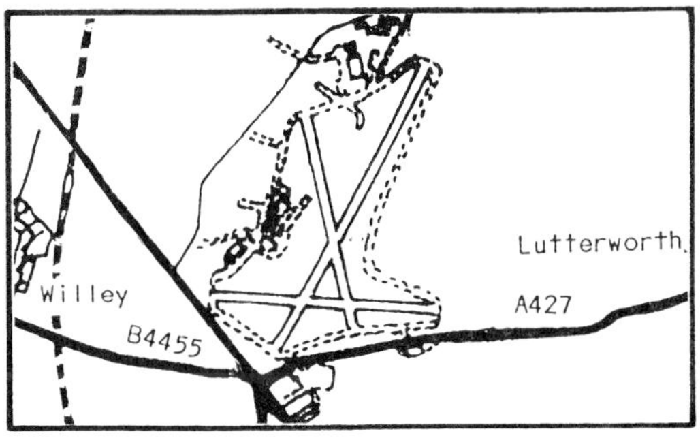

EXTENSIBILITY : Entails demolition of a house.

ACCOMMODATION : Temporary.
HANGARS : T2-1;B1-1.

HARDSTANDINGS : Spectacle-16;dispersal-11.

R.A.F. : OFFICERS: 90. S.N.C.O′s.: 353.O.R′s.: 732. TOTAL: 1175.
W.A.A.F.: " : 3. " : 16. " : 84. " : 103.

AFFILIATED AIRFIELDS : Bramcote[Parent]

PRESENT USE [1985] : Aircraft Industry[British Aerospace]

NO: 056.

AIRFIELD NAME: BLACKBUSHE. OPENED : 1943.
COUNTY : Hampshire. CLOSED : 1946.
COMMAND : Fighter.
FORMATION : 11 Grp[Uxbridge] GRID REF: Q 250788[113]
FUNCTION : Forward Airfield. O.S.REF.: SU 806595.

LOCALITY : 10miles SSE of Reading.
RAILWAY STN. : Fleet 3.25miles[SR]

LATITUDE : 51 19 30N. HEIGHT ASL : 320′ LIGHTING : Mk2.
LONGITUDE : 00 50 30W. FLYING CONTROL : Yes. RADIO : QDM.

LANDMARKS DAY : London-Basingstoke road[2miles straight] touches S boundary of A/F.

LANDMARKS NIGHT : -

OBSTRUCTIONS : -

LANDING AREA SURFACE : Concrete & wood chippings.

QDM: 262. LENGTH X WIDTH: 2000 x 50yds. Ext: 3000yds.
: 317. : 1400 x 50yds. : 1850yds.
: 011. : 1400 x 50yds. : 1500yds.
: : : 4300yds.

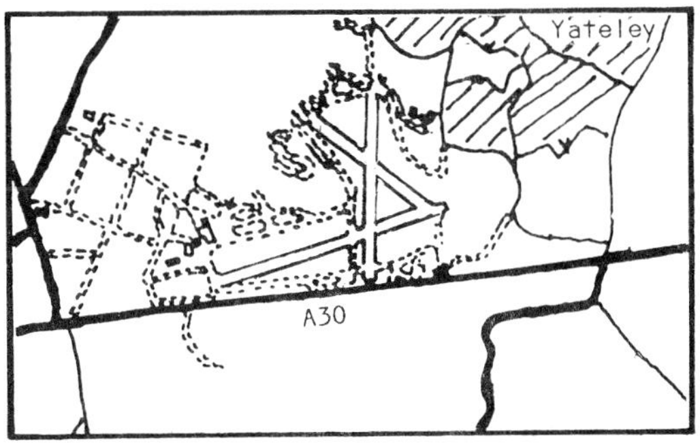

EXTENSIBILITY : Entails diversion of main London-Southampton road & demolition of 2 cottages.
ACCOMMODATION : Temporary.
HANGARS : T2[14 bay]-1[23]-2; blister-6;Bessoneau-2.

HARDSTANDINGS : Frying pan[100′]-18;special loop-50.

R.A.F. : OFFICERS: 183.S.N.C.O′s.: 414.O.R′s.: 1970.TOTAL: 2567.
W.A.A.F.: " : 6. " : 18. " : 389. " : 413.

AFFILIATED AIRFIELDS : Tangmere[Sector]

PRESENT USE [1985] : Private Flying.

NO: 057.

AIRFIELD NAME: BLAKEHILL FARM. OPENED : 1944.
COUNTY : Wiltshire. CLOSED : 1952.
COMMAND : Transport.
FORMATION : 46 Grp[Harrow Weald] GRID REF: P 522120[104]
FUNCTION : Operational. O.S.REF.: SU 078915.

LOCALITY : 2miles SW of Cricklade.
RAILWAY STN. : Cricklade[GWR]

LATITUDE : 51 37 23N. HEIGHT ASL : 305′ LIGHTING : Mk2.
LONGITUDE : 01 53 15W. FLYING CONTROL : Yes. RADIO : QDM.

LANDMARKS DAY : Cricklade church 2miles NE.

LANDMARKS NIGHT : -

OBSTRUCTIONS : -

LANDING AREA SURFACE : Tarmac.

QDM: 240. LENGTH X WIDTH: 2000 x 50yds. Ext: -
: 130. : 1400 x 50yds. : -
: 190. : 1400 x 50yds. : -
: : :

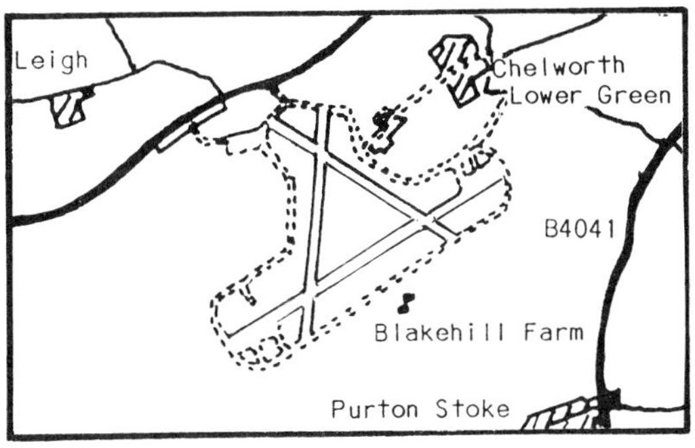

EXTENSIBILITY : –

ACCOMMODATION : Temporary.
HANGARS : T2-2.

HARDSTANDINGS : Loop-46.

R.A.F. : OFFICERS: 224.S.N.C.O′s.: 365.O.R′s.: 1990.TOTAL: 2579.
W.A.A.F.: " : 7. " : 16. " : 99. " : 122.

AFFILIATED AIRFIELDS : -

PRESENT USE [1985] : Radio Research Station.

NO: 058.

AIRFIELD NAME: BLYTON. OPENED : 1942.
COUNTY : Lincolnshire. CLOSED : 1954.
COMMAND : Bomber.
FORMATION : 7 Grp[St.Vincents] GRID REF: A 336154[39]
FUNCTION : Operational. O.S.REF.: SK 868958.

LOCALITY : 16miles NNW of Lincoln.
RAILWAY STN. : Blyton[LNER]

LATITUDE : 53 27 15N. HEIGHT ASL : 70′ LIGHTING : Mk 2.
LONGITUDE : 00 41 30W. FLYING CONTROL : Yes. RADIO : QDM.

LANDMARKS DAY : Scotton Common Woods 1.5miles N of A/F.

LANDMARKS NIGHT : R Trent 4miles W of A/F.

OBSTRUCTIONS : -

LANDING AREA SURFACE : Concrete.

QDM	LENGTH X WIDTH	Ext
212.	2000 X 50yds.	3000yds.
272.	1400 x 50yds.	2950yds.
322.	1400 x 50yds.	2000yds.

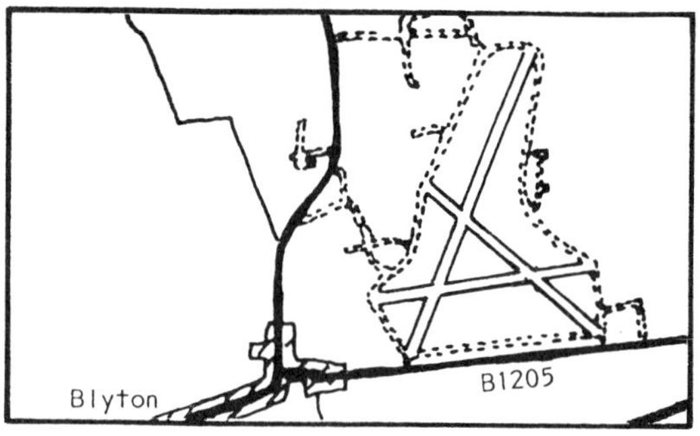

EXTENSIBILITY : Entails demolition of a farm & cottages, also of a living site.
ACCOMMODATION : Temporary.
HANGARS : T2-2;B1-1.

HARDSTANDINGS : Heavy bomber-36.

R.A.F. : OFFICERS: 148.S.N.C.O′s.: 422.O.R′s.: 1106.TOTAL: 1676.
W.A.A.F.: " : 4. " : 12. " : 348. " : 364.

AFFILIATED AIRFIELDS : Lindholme[71 Base]

PRESENT USE [1985] : Agriculture.

NO: 059.

AIRFIELD NAME: BODNEY. OPENED : 1940.
COUNTY : Norfolk. CLOSED : 1945.
COMMAND : 8th USAAF.
FORMATION : 352nd Fighter Grp. GRID REF: G 295180[66]
FUNCTION : Operational. O.S.REF.: TL 840995.

LOCALITY : 4.5miles W of Watton.
RAILWAY STN. : Watton 2miles[LNER]

LATITUDE : 52 33 38N. HEIGHT ASL : 130′ LIGHTING : Mk1.
LONGITUDE : 00 42 45E. FLYING CONTROL : Yes. RADIO : QDM.

LANDMARKS DAY : R Wissey around A/F. Woods near Thetford.

LANDMARKS NIGHT : -

OBSTRUCTIONS : -

LANDING AREA SURFACE : Grass.

QDM	LENGTH X WIDTH	Ext
NE-SW.	1000yds.	2000yds.
NW-SE.	900yds.	1400yds.
E-W.	900yds.	1400yds.

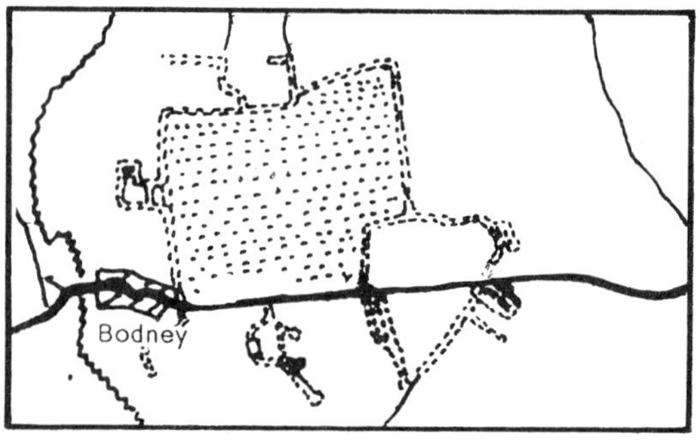

EXTENSIBILITY : Entails demolition of 3 empty farm cottages & sheds.
ACCOMMODATION : Temporary.
HANGARS : T2-2;Blister-5.

HARDSTANDINGS : Asphalt:large-15;small-12.

USAAF. : OFFICERS: 190. Enlisted Men. : 1519.TOTAL: 1709.

AFFILIATED AIRFIELDS : -

PRESENT USE [1985] : Agriculture.

NO: 060.

AIRFIELD NAME: BODORGAN. OPENED : 1940.
COUNTY : Anglesey. CLOSED : 1945.
COMMAND : Fighter.
FORMATION : 70 Grp[Farnborough] GRID REF: H 840904[41]
FUNCTION : AA Co-operation Unit. O.S.REF.: SH 375688.

LOCALITY : 12miles SE of Holyhead.
RAILWAY STN. : Bodorgan 2.5miles[LMS]

LATITUDE : 53 11 07N. HEIGHT ASL : 150′ LIGHTING : None.
LONGITUDE : 04 25 30W FLYING CONTROL : None.RADIO : QDM.

LANDMARKS DAY : Woods, lake & river estuary.

LANDMARKS NIGHT : As day.

OBSTRUCTIONS : Woods on SE side of A/F to 150′ Wireless masts near A/F buildings.

LANDING AREA SURFACE : Grass.

QDM	LENGTH X WIDTH	Ext
NNE-SSW.	1000yds.	-
E-W.	1000yds.	-
WSW-ENE.	960yds.	-

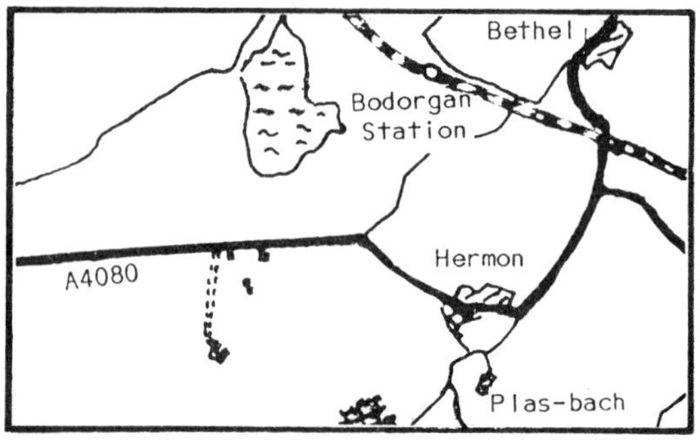

EXTENSIBILITY : None possible.

ACCOMMODATION : Temporary.
HANGARS : Bellman-2;Blister-1.

HARDSTANDINGS : None.

R.A.F. : OFFICERS: 24. S.N.C.O′s.: 23. O.R′s.: 479. TOTAL: 526.
W.A.A.F.: " : 2. " : 4. " : 124. " : 130.

AFFILIATED AIRFIELDS : -

PRESENT USE [1985] : Agriculture.

NO: 061.

AIRFIELD NAME: BOGNOR. OPENED : 1943.
COUNTY : Sussex. CLOSED : 1945.
COMMAND : Fighter.
FORMATION : 11 Grp[Uxbridge] GRID REF: Q 345198[133]
FUNCTION : Advanced Landing Ground. O.S.REF.: SU 912006.
[de-requisitioned]
LOCALITY : 2miles NW of Bognor.
RAILWAY STN. : Bognor[SR]

LATITUDE : 50 47 15N. HEIGHT ASL : 23′ LIGHTING : None.
LONGITUDE : 00 42 30W. FLYING CONTROL : None. RADIO : QDM.

LANDMARKS DAY : Gasometer 2miles SE of A/F.

LANDMARKS NIGHT : -

OBSTRUCTIONS : -

LANDING AREA SURFACE : Steel Matting[Sommerfeld track]

QDM: 072. LENGTH X WIDTH: 1600yds. Ext: -
: 151. : 1400yds. : -
: : :
: : :

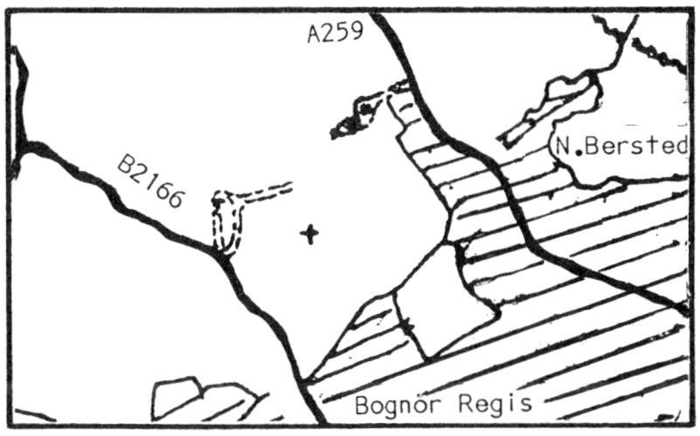

EXTENSIBILITY :

ACCOMMODATION : Tented camp.
HANGARS : EO blister-4.

HARDSTANDINGS : ST Temporary.

R.A.F. : OFFICERS: - S.N.C.O's.: - O.R's.: - TOTAL: -
W.A.A.F.: " : - " : - " : - " : -

AFFILIATED AIRFIELDS : -

PRESENT USE [1985] : Agriculture.

NO: 062.

AIRFIELD NAME: BOLT HEAD. OPENED : 1941.
COUNTY : Devonshire. CLOSED : 1947.
COMMAND : Fighter.
FORMATION : 10 Grp[Rudloe Manor] GRID REF: Y 143593[145]
FUNCTION : Operational. O.S.REF.: SX 710373.

LOCALITY : 4.5miles SSW of Kingsbridge.
RAILWAY STN. : Kingsbridge 7miles[GWR]

LATITUDE : 50 30 00N. HEIGHT ASL : 420′ LIGHTING : None.
LONGITUDE : 03 48 00W. FLYING CONTROL : Yes. RADIO : QDM.

LANDMARKS DAY : Kingsbridge estuary, Bolthead start point.

LANDMARKS NIGHT : As day.

OBSTRUCTIONS : GCI station 100yds N of E-W runway & 50yds E from NE-SW runway.

LANDING AREA SURFACE : Steel Matting[Sommerfeld Track]

QDM: 237. LENGTH X WIDTH: 1400yds. Ext: -
: 293. : 1300yds. : -
: : :
: : :

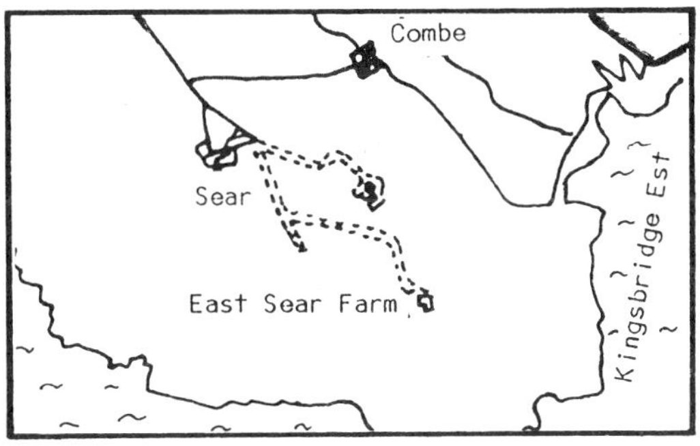

EXTENSIBILITY : -

ACCOMMODATION : Temporary.
HANGARS : Blister-2.

HARDSTANDINGS : SE-5.

R.A.F. : OFFICERS: 39. S.N.C.O's.: 60. O.R's.: 375. TOTAL: 474.
W.A.A.F.: " : 1. " : 12. " : 120. " : 133.

AFFILIATED AIRFIELDS : Exeter[Sector]

PRESENT USE [1985] : Agriculture.

NO: 063.

AIRFIELD NAME: BOOKER. OPENED : 1939.
COUNTY : Buckinghamshire. CLOSED : 1951.
COMMAND : Flying Training.
FORMATION : 50 Grp[Reading] GRID REF: L 271106[106]
FUNCTION : Elementary Flying Training School. O.S.REF.: SU 828910.
LOCALITY : 3miles SW of High Wycombe.
RAILWAY STN. : High Wycombe 3.5miles[GWR]

LATITUDE : 51 36 30N. HEIGHT ASL : 515′ LIGHTING : None.
LONGITUDE : 00 48 30W. FLYING CONTROL : None. RADIO : QDM.

LANDMARKS DAY : -

LANDMARKS NIGHT : -

OBSTRUCTIONS : Woods & buildings on E boundary.

LANDING AREA SURFACE : Grass.

QDM: N-S. LENGTH X WIDTH: 970yds. Ext: -
: NE-SW. : 1133yds. : -
: E-W. : 920yds. : -
: NW-SE. : 900yds. : -

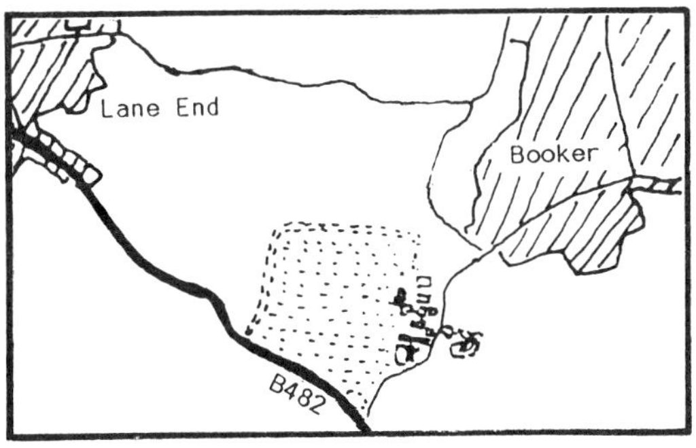

EXTENSIBILITY : -

ACCOMMODATION : Temporary.
HANGARS : Bellman[175x90x25′]-2;[175x90x71′]-2; EO blister-4.
HARDSTANDINGS : Loop-3.

R.A.F. : OFFICERS: 56. S.N.C.O's.: 88. O.R's.: 507. TOTAL: 651.
W.A.A.F.: " : - " : - " : - " : -

AFFILIATED AIRFIELDS : Denham[RLG]

PRESENT USE [1985] : Private flying.

NO: 064.

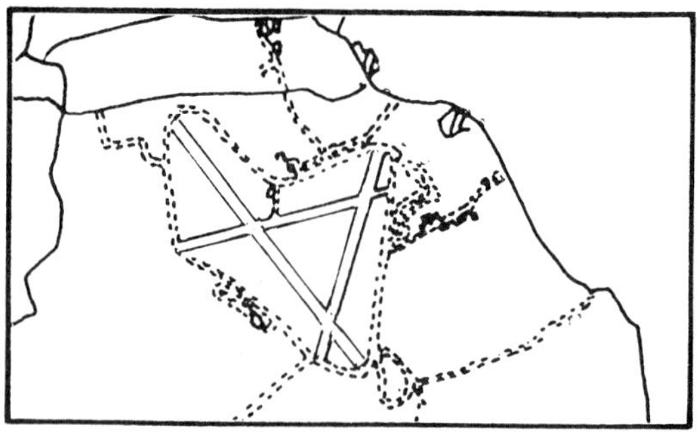

AIRFIELD NAME: BOREHAM.
COUNTY : Essex.
COMMAND : USSTAFE.
FORMATION : Air Disarmament.
FUNCTION : Operational.

OPENED : 1944.
CLOSED : 1945.
GRID REF: M 185305[97]
O.S.REF.: TL 743120.

LOCALITY : 3.5miles NE of Chelmsford.
RAILWAY STN. : Chelmsford 3.5miles[LNER]

LATITUDE : 51 46 45N. HEIGHT ASL : 170′ LIGHTING : Mk2.
LONGITUDE : 00 31 30E. FLYING CONTROL : Yes. RADIO : QDM.

LANDMARKS DAY : Hills 600′ E of A/F.

LANDMARKS NIGHT : -

OBSTRUCTIONS : -

LANDING AREA SURFACE : Concrete & tarmac.

QDM	LENGTH X WIDTH	Ext
340.	2000 x 50yds.	2600yds.
210.	1400 x 50yds.	-
270.	1400 x 50yds	-

EXTENSIBILITY : Not recommended. Entails closure of a B road.

ACCOMMODATION : Temporary.
HANGARS : T2-2.

HARDSTANDINGS : Spectacle-50.

USAAF. : OFFICERS: 417. Enlisted Men. : 2241.TOTAL: 2658.

AFFILIATED AIRFIELDS : -

PRESENT USE [1985] : Motor Industry[Ford]

NO: 065.

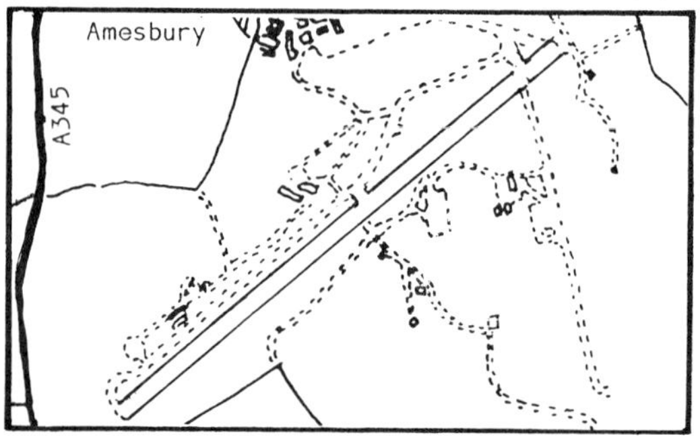

AIRFIELD NAME: BOSCOMBE DOWN.
COUNTY : Wiltshire.
COMMAND : Flying Training.
FORMATION : 23 Grp[South Cerney]
FUNCTION : Experimental Station.

OPENED : 1917.
CLOSED :
GRID REF: U 616610[122]
O.S.REF.: SU 182398.

LOCALITY : 1.5miles E of Amesbury.
RAILWAY STN. : Amesbury 2.5miles[SR]

LATITUDE : 51 09 38N. HEIGHT ASL : 377′ LIGHTING : Mk2.
LONGITUDE : 01 44 30W. FLYING CONTROL : Yes. RADIO : QDM.

LANDMARKS DAY : Beacon Hill NNE, Amesbury NW; Bulford camp N; crescent shaped wood to S of A/F

LANDMARKS NIGHT : -

OBSTRUCTIONS : Beacon Hill 668′ 1.75miles NNE of centre of A/F.

LANDING AREA SURFACE : Concrete-240, others grass.

QDM	LENGTH X WIDTH	Ext
240.	3000 x 100yds.	4000yds.
		2000yds.
WNW-ESE.	1400yds.	-
SSE-NNW.	1400yds	-

EXTENSIBILITY : -

ACCOMMODATION : Permanent.
HANGARS : Various-16.

HARDSTANDINGS : Various-17.

R.A.F. : OFFICERS: 111.S.N.C.O′s.: 202.O.R′s.: 1768.TOTAL: 2081.
W.A.A.F.: " : 7. " : 9. " : 550. " : 566.

AFFILIATED AIRFIELDS : -

PRESENT USE [1985] : RAF.

NO: 066.

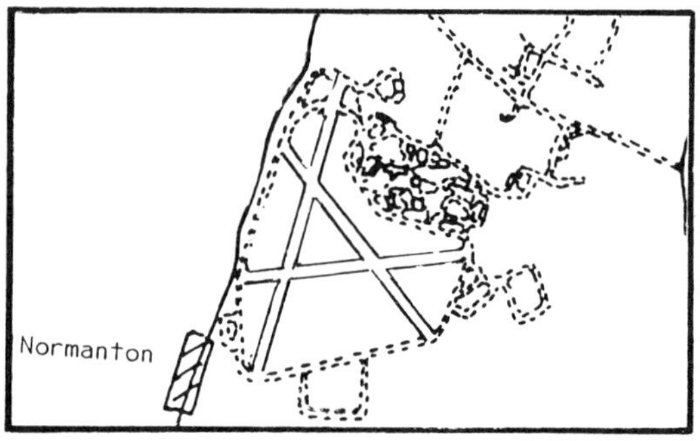

AIRFIELD NAME: BOTTESFORD.
COUNTY : Leics/Lincs.
COMMAND : Bomber.
FORMATION : 7 Grp[St.Vincents]
FUNCTION : Operational[72 Base]

OPENED : 1941.
CLOSED : 1945.
GRID REF: F 278615[54]
O.S.REF.: SK 819415.

LOCALITY : 7miles NW of Grantham.
RAILWAY STN. : Bottesford 2miles[LNER]

LATITUDE : 52 58 00N. HEIGHT ASL : 110′ LIGHTING : Mk 2.
LONGITUDE : 00 46 45W. FLYING CONTROL : Yes. RADIO : QDM.

LANDMARKS DAY : Belvoir Castle.

LANDMARKS NIGHT : Red light on church S of A/F.

OBSTRUCTIONS : Bottesford church 314′

LANDING AREA SURFACE : Concrete.

QDM	LENGTH X WIDTH	Ext
210.	1900 x 50yds.	1930yds.
277.	1400 x 50yds.	1825yds.
336.	1491 x 50yds.	2000yds.

EXTENSIBILITY : Entails closure of road from Bottesford to Great North Rd.
ACCOMMODATION : Temporary.
HANGARS : T2-6;Glider T2-3;B1-1.

HARDSTANDINGS : Heavy bomber-50.

R.A.F. : OFFICERS: 120.S.N.C.O′s.: 340.O.R′s.: 1600.TOTAL: 2060.
W.A.A.F.: " : 10. " : 8. " : 403. " : 421.

AFFILIATED AIRFIELDS : Langar & Saltby[Sub-stations]

PRESENT USE [1985] : Disused.

AIRFIELD NAME: BOTTISHAM. OPENED : 1940.
COUNTY : Cambridgeshire. CLOSED : 1946.
COMMAND : Fighter.
FORMATION : 11 Grp[Uxbridge] GRID REF: L 995786[85]
FUNCTION : Care & Maintenance. O.S.REF.: TL 540592.

LOCALITY : 5.5miles E of Cambridge.
RAILWAY STN. : Bottisham & Lode 1.5miles[LNER]

LATITUDE : 52 12 45N. HEIGHT ASL : 50′ LIGHTING : Mk2.
LONGITUDE : 00 15 23E. FLYING CONTROL : Yes. RADIO : QDM.

LANDMARKS DAY : -

LANDMARKS NIGHT : -

OBSTRUCTIONS : Control & 3 adjoining buildings inside peri-track.

LANDING AREA SURFACE : Steel Matting[Sommerfeld Track]NW-SE grass

QDM: 020. LENGTH X WIDTH: 1200 x 50yds. Ext: 3000yds.
: 090. : 1435 x 50yds. : -
: NW-SE. : 1130yds. : 1933yds.
: : :

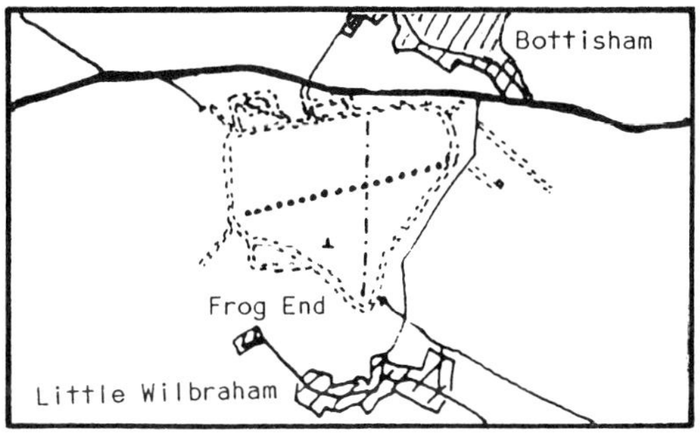

EXTENSIBILITY :

ACCOMMODATION : Temporary.
HANGARS : T2[14 bay]-1;Blister-8.

HARDSTANDINGS : Concrete-15;pierced steel matting-68.

R.A.F. : OFFICERS: - S.N.C.O's.: - O.R's.: - TOTAL: -
W.A.A.F.: " : - " : - " : - " : -

AFFILIATED AIRFIELDS : North Weald[Sector]

PRESENT USE [1985] : Motorway.

AIRFIELD NAME: BOULMER. OPENED : 1943.
COUNTY : Northumberland. CLOSED :
COMMAND : Fighter.
FORMATION : 12 Grp[Watnall] GRID REF: U 747336[4]
FUNCTION : Operational Training Unit[satellite] O.S.REF.: NU 259133.
LOCALITY : 3.75miles E of Alnwick.
RAILWAY STN. : Almouth 3.5miles[LNER]

LATITUDE : 55 24 45N. HEIGHT ASL : 44′ LIGHTING : None.
LONGITUDE : 01 35 45W. FLYING CONTROL : Yes. RADIO : QDM.

LANDMARKS DAY : LNE main railway line.

LANDMARKS NIGHT : -

OBSTRUCTIONS : -

LANDING AREA SURFACE : Hardcore tarmac & wood chippings.

QDM: 014. LENGTH X WIDTH: 1800 x 50yds. Ext: 3000yds.
: 062. : 1400 x 50yds. : -
: 152. : 1300 x 50yds. : -
: : :

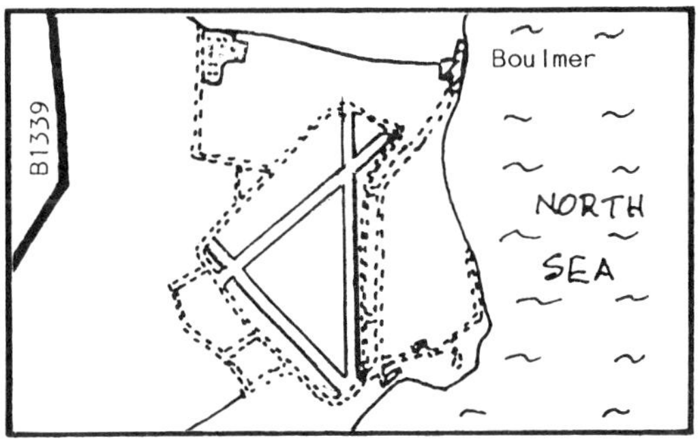

EXTENSIBILITY : Access road to village would be cut.

ACCOMMODATION : Temporary.
HANGARS : Dorman Long blister-4.

HARDSTANDINGS : SE-25.

R.A.F. : OFFICERS: 41. S.N.C.O's.: 48. O.R's.: 528. TOTAL: 617.
W.A.A.F.: " : 2. " : 4. " : 100. " : 106.

AFFILIATED AIRFIELDS : Eshott[Parent]

PRESENT USE [1985] : RAF.

AIRFIELD NAME: BOURN. OPENED : 1941.
COUNTY : Cambridgeshire. CLOSED : 1948.
COMMAND : Bomber.
FORMATION : 8 Grp[Huntingdon] GRID REF: L 793783[85]
FUNCTION : Operational. O.S.REF.: TL 341595.

LOCALITY : 7miles W of Cambridge.
RAILWAY STN. : Old North Rd. 3miles[LMS]

LATITUDE : 52 12 45N. HEIGHT ASL : 235′ LIGHTING : Mk2.
LONGITUDE : 00 02 15W. FLYING CONTROL : Yes. RADIO : QDM.

LANDMARKS DAY : Cambridge-St Neots main road forms N boundary of A/F.

LANDMARKS NIGHT : -

OBSTRUCTIONS : Barn 35′high near W side.

LANDING AREA SURFACE : Concrete.

QDM: 065. LENGTH X WIDTH: 1925 x 50yds. Ext: 2900yds.
: 007. : 1600 x 50yds. : 3000yds
: 128. : 1400 x 50yds. : 2200yds.
: : :

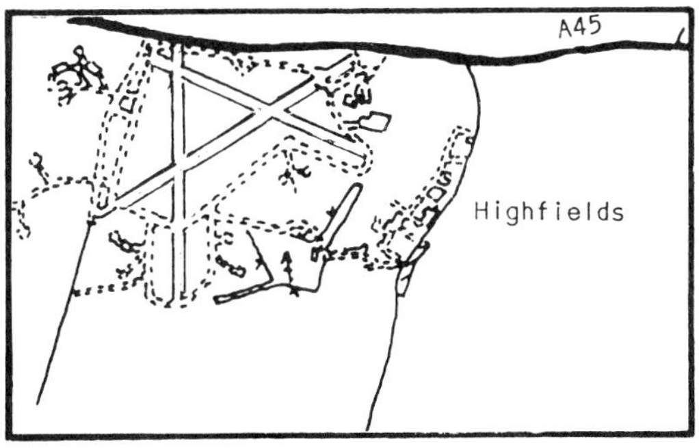

EXTENSIBILITY : Entails serious demolition of bungalow property & water reservoir.
ACCOMMODATION : Temporary.
HANGARS : T2-2;B1-1.

HARDSTANDINGS : Heavy Bomber-36.

R.A.F. : OFFICERS: 185.S.N.C.O's.: 442.O.R's.: 1200.TOTAL: 1827.
W.A.A.F.: " : 4. " : 10. " : 220. " : 234.

AFFILIATED AIRFIELDS : -

PRESENT USE [1985] : Agriculture.

NO: 070.

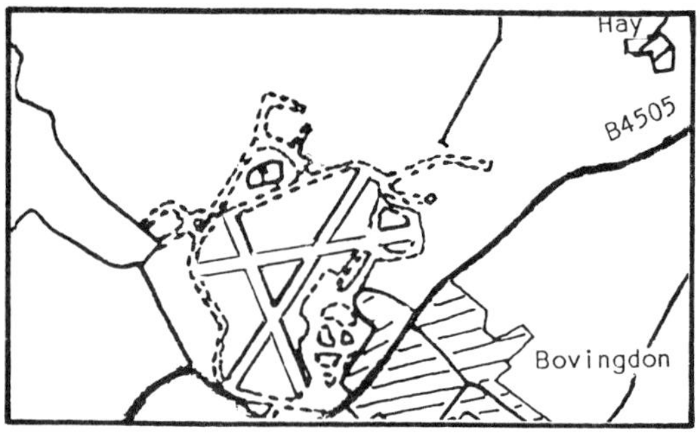

AIRFIELD NAME: BOVINGDON. OPENED : 1942.
COUNTY : Hertfordshire. CLOSED : 1972.
COMMAND : USATC.
FORMATION : European Division. GRID REF: L 452236[106]
FUNCTION : Operational. O.S.REF.: TL 005045.

LOCALITY : 7miles W of Watford.
RAILWAY STN. : Hemel Hempstead & Box Moor 3miles[LMS]

LATITUDE : 51 43 30N. HEIGHT ASL : 500′ LIGHTING : Mk2.
LONGITUDE : 00 32 30W FLYING CONTROL : Yes. RADIO : QDM.

LANDMARKS DAY : 2 tanks 2miles apart on steel towers.

LANDMARKS NIGHT : -

OBSTRUCTIONS : -

LANDING AREA SURFACE : Concrete & Asphalt.

QDM	LENGTH X WIDTH	Ext
220.	1600 x 50yds.	2750yds.
270.	1400 x 50yds.	2500yds.
350.	1300 x 50yds.	1800yds.

EXTENSIBILITY : Entails demolition of 2 houses, a farm & other houses in the approach.
ACCOMMODATION : Temporary.
HANGARS : T2-4.

HARDSTANDINGS : Loop-36.

USAAF. : OFFICERS: 635. Enlisted Men. : 2214. TOTAL: 2849.

AFFILIATED AIRFIELDS : -

PRESENT USE [1985] : Agriculture.

NO: 071.

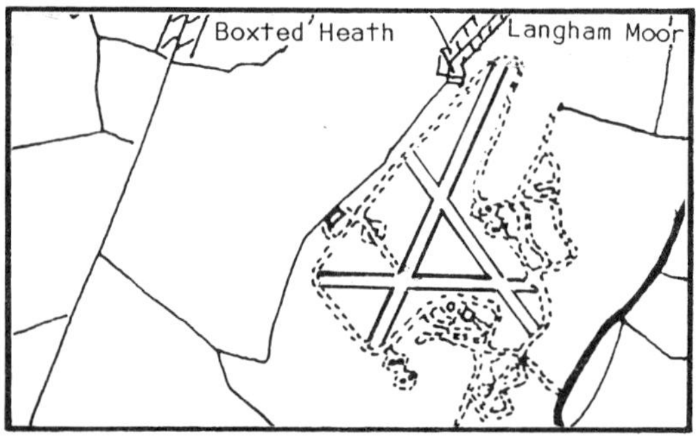

AIRFIELD NAME: BOXTED. OPENED : 1943.
COUNTY : Essex. CLOSED : 1947.
COMMAND : 8th USAAF.
FORMATION : 56th Fighter Grp. GRID REF: N 465487[97]
FUNCTION : Operational. O.S.REF.: TM 015305.

LOCALITY : 3miles N of Colchester.
RAILWAY STN. : Colchester 6miles[LNER]

LATITUDE : 51 56 58N. HEIGHT ASL : 157′ LIGHTING : Mk2.
LONGITUDE : 00 56 00E. FLYING CONTROL : Yes. RADIO : QDM.

LANDMARKS DAY : Inlet of R Stour. Radio tower due E of A/F. City of Colchester & Severalls Mental hospital SW of A/F.

LANDMARKS NIGHT : Inlet of R Stour.

OBSTRUCTIONS : -

LANDING AREA SURFACE : Concrete, tarmac & wood chippings.

QDM	LENGTH X WIDTH	Ext
220.	2000 x 50yds.	4300yds.
280.	1400 x 50yds.	2520yds.
340.	1400 x 50yds.	2920yds.

EXTENSIBILITY : Only Recommended to 3-2&2000yds as it entails closure of a road.
ACCOMMODATION : Temporary.
HANGARS : T2-2.

HARDSTANDINGS : Loop-50.

USAAF. : OFFICERS: 421. Enlisted Men. : 2473. TOTAL: 2894.

AFFILIATED AIRFIELDS : -

PRESENT USE [1985] : Agriculture.

NO: 072.

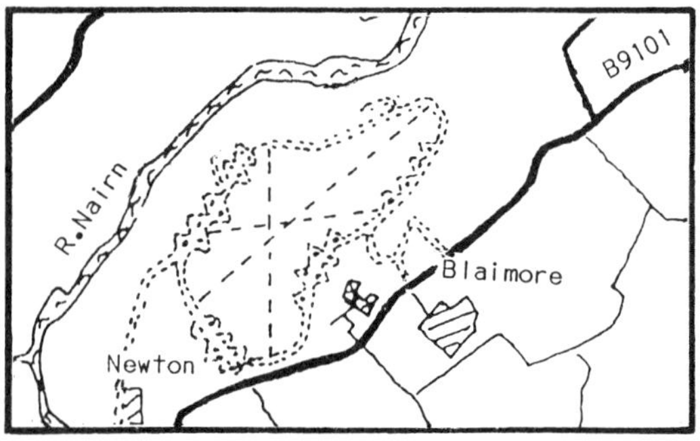

AIRFIELD NAME: BRACKLA. OPENED : 1941.
COUNTY : Nairnshire. CLOSED : 1946.
COMMAND : Flying Training.
FORMATION : 29 Grp[Dumfries] GRID REF: J 378742[28Scot]
FUNCTION : Aircrew Allocation Centre. O.S.REF.: NH 858519.
LOCALITY : 12miles NE Inverness.
RAILWAY STN. : Brackla 4miles[LMS]

LATITUDE : 57 32 30N HEIGHT ASL : 82′ LIGHTING : None.
LONGITUDE : 03 54 38W. FLYING CONTROL : None. RADIO : QDM.

LANDMARKS DAY : R Nain on N boundary; Distillery S side.

LANDMARKS NIGHT : Fort George peninsular 6.5miles NW.

OBSTRUCTIONS : Trees NW corner.

LANDING AREA SURFACE : Grass.

QDM	LENGTH X WIDTH	Ext
SW-NE.	2000yds.	3000yds.
N-S.	1450yds.	-
E-W.	1450yds.	-

EXTENSIBILITY : Entails demolition of a farm.

ACCOMMODATION : Temporary.
HANGARS : T2-4.

HARDSTANDINGS : Diamond shaped-30.

	OFFICERS	S.N.C.O's.	O.R's.	TOTAL
R.A.F.	178.	369.	1570.	2117.
W.A.A.F.	10.	22.	415.	447.

AFFILIATED AIRFIELDS : -

PRESENT USE [1985] : Disused.

NO: 073.

AIRFIELD NAME: BRADWELL BAY. OPENED : 1941.
COUNTY : Essex. CLOSED : 1946.
COMMAND : Fighter.
FORMATION : 11 Grp[Uxbridge] GRID REF: M 452263[108]
FUNCTION : Operational. O.S.REF.: TM 005082.

LOCALITY : 6miles NNE of Southminster.
RAILWAY STN. : Southminster [LNER]

LATITUDE : 51 44 04N. HEIGHT ASL : 30′ LIGHTING : Mk2.
LONGITUDE : 00 54 15E. FLYING CONTROL : Yes. RADIO : QDM.

LANDMARKS DAY : R Blackwater.

LANDMARKS NIGHT : R Blackwater.

OBSTRUCTIONS : -

LANDING AREA SURFACE : Tarmac & asphalt.

QDM	LENGTH X WIDTH	Ext
240.	1890 x 50yds	2500yds.
172.	1000 x 50yds.	1600yds.
120.	1400 x 50yds.	-

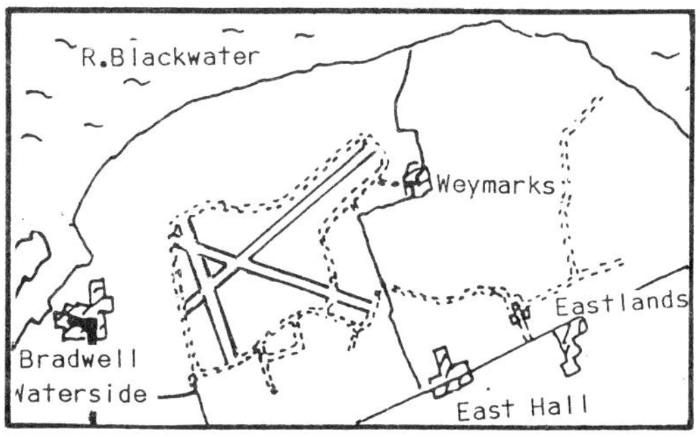

EXTENSIBILITY : Not recommended as it entails demolition of 10 cottages,2 bungalows,1 houses etc.
ACCOMMODATION : Temporary.
HANGARS : Bellman-1;Blister-12.

HARDSTANDINGS : TE-12;bomber-3;Protected pens TE-24.

R.A.F. : OFFICERS: 125.S.N.C.O′s.: 136.O.R′s.: 1390.TOTAL: 1651.
W.A.A.F.: " : 7. " : 4. " : 255. " : 266.

AFFILIATED AIRFIELDS : North Weald[Sector]

PRESENT USE [1985] : Nuclear Power Station[Bradwell Bay]

NO: 074.

AIRFIELD NAME: BRAMCOTE. OPENED : 1940.
COUNTY : Warwickshire. CLOSED :
COMMAND : Transport.
FORMATION : 44 Grp[Gloucester] GRID REF: F 863080[73]
FUNCTION : Operational Training Unit. O.S.REF.: SP 406883.
LOCALITY : 4miles SE of Nuneaton.
RAILWAY STN. : Nuneaton,Trent Valley 4.5miles[LMS]

LATITUDE : 52 29 15N. HEIGHT ASL : 378′ LIGHTING : MK1.
LONGITUDE : 01 23 45W. FLYING CONTROL : Yes. RADIO : QDM.

LANDMARKS DAY : Wireless station Dunsmore, Rugby 12miles.

LANDMARKS NIGHT : -

OBSTRUCTIONS : -

LANDING AREA SURFACE : Steel matting[Sommerfeld track]

QDM	LENGTH X WIDTH	Ext
030.	1600yds.	2300yds.
130.	1400yds.	1600yds.
090.	1400yds.	1550yds.

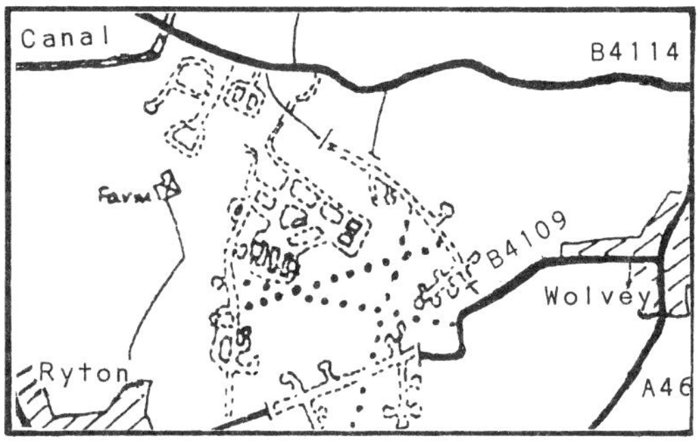

EXTENSIBILITY : Entails demolition of a cottage.

ACCOMMODATION : Permanent.
HANGARS : Type C-5.

HARDSTANDINGS : Frying pan-30.

R.A.F. : OFFICERS: 174.S.N.C.O′s.: 312.O.R′s.: 1187.TOTAL: 1673.
W.A.A.F.: " : 8. " : 8. " : 437. " : 453.

AFFILIATED AIRFIELDS : Nuneaton & Bitteswell[Satellites]

PRESENT USE [1985] : Army.

NO: 075.

AIRFIELD NAME: BRATTON. OPENED : 1940.
COUNTY : Shropshire. CLOSED : 1945.
COMMAND : Flying Training.
FORMATION : 25 Grp[Market Drayton] GRID REF: K 094357[61]
FUNCTION : Advanced Flying Unit. [RLG] O.S.REF.: SJ 635145.
LOCALITY : 2miles NNE of Wellington.
RAILWAY STN. : Crudington.5miles[GWR],Wellington 2.5miles[LMS]

LATITUDE : 52 43 45N. HEIGHT ASL : 191′ LIGHTING : None.
LONGITUDE : 02 32 15W. FLYING CONTROL : None.RADIO : QDM.

LANDMARKS DAY : Wrekin 1335′ 4miles to S.

LANDMARKS NIGHT : -

OBSTRUCTIONS : -

LANDING AREA SURFACE : Grass.

QDM	LENGTH X WIDTH	Ext
NW-SE.	900yds.	1200yds.
		1200yds.

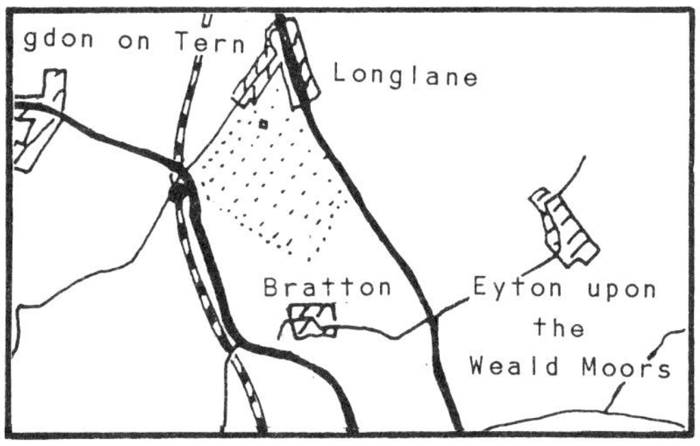

EXTENSIBILITY : Narrow strips entailing slight demolition.

ACCOMMODATION : Temporary.
HANGARS : 65′ blister-5.

HARDSTANDINGS :

R.A.F. : OFFICERS: 2. S.N.C.O′s.: 4. O.R′s.: 120. TOTAL: 126.
W.A.A.F.: " : - " : - " : - " : -

AFFILIATED AIRFIELDS : Ternhill[Parent]

PRESENT USE [1985] : Disused.

NO: 076.

AIRFIELD NAME: BRAUNSTONE. OPENED : 1935.
COUNTY : Leicestershire. CLOSED : 1945.
COMMAND : Flying Training.
FORMATION : 51 Grp[Leeds] GRID REF: K 994243[63]
FUNCTION : Elementary Flying Training School[RLG] O.S.REF.: SK 538048.
LOCALITY : 2.5miles W of Leicester.
RAILWAY STN. : Kirkby Muxloe 2miles[LMS]

LATITUDE : 52 38 00N. HEIGHT ASL : 315′ LIGHTING : None.
LONGITUDE : 01 12 15W. FLYING CONTROL : None.RADIO : QDM.

LANDMARKS DAY : Thornton lake 3.5miles NW; Croby Poole 2.5miles WNW.

LANDMARKS NIGHT : -

OBSTRUCTIONS : Factory E side;Hangar & club house W side of A/F.

LANDING AREA SURFACE : Grass.

QDM	LENGTH X WIDTH	Ext
E-W.	800yds.	1400yds.
N-S.	600yds.	1200yds.
		1100yds.

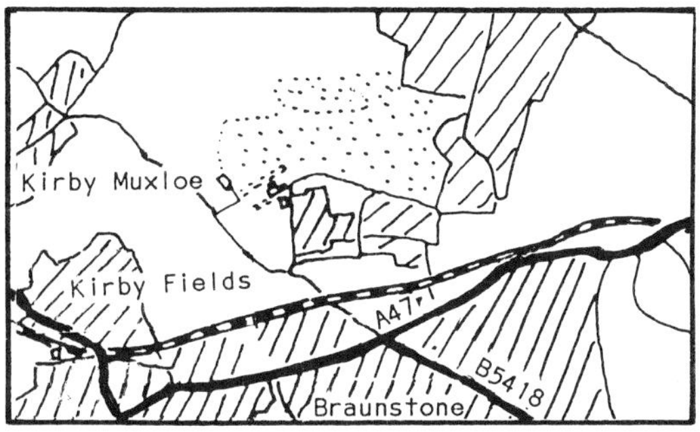

EXTENSIBILITY : Envolves heavy demolition of housing estate if extended to NE.
ACCOMMODATION : Temporary.
HANGARS : Civil-3;overblister-2.

HARDSTANDINGS : None.

	OFFICERS	S.N.C.O′s.	O.R′s.	TOTAL
R.A.F.	2.	4.	120.	126.
W.A.A.F.	-	-	-	-

AFFILIATED AIRFIELDS : Desford[Parent]

PRESENT USE [1985] : Housing.

NO: 077.

AIRFIELD NAME: BRAWDY. OPENED : 1944.
COUNTY : Pembrokeshire. CLOSED :
COMMAND : Coastal.
FORMATION : 19 Grp[Plymouth] GRID REF: N 297482[88]
FUNCTION : Operational. O.S.REF.: SM 8522552.

LOCALITY : 9miles NW of Haverfordwest.
RAILWAY STN. : Haverfordwest 9miles[GWR]

LATITUDE : 51 53 08N. HEIGHT ASL : 350′ LIGHTING : Mk2.
LONGITUDE : 05 07 23W. FLYING CONTROL : None.RADIO : QDM.

LANDMARKS DAY : Wireless masts 3miles E & 4miles ESE of A/F.

LANDMARKS NIGHT : -

OBSTRUCTIONS : Wireless masts: 725′ASL 3miles E & 580′ 4miles ESE.

LANDING AREA SURFACE : Concrete & wood chippings.

QDM	LENGTH X WIDTH	Ext
152.	2010 x 50yds.	-
086.	1420 x 50yds.	-
029.	2000 x 50yds.	2100yds.

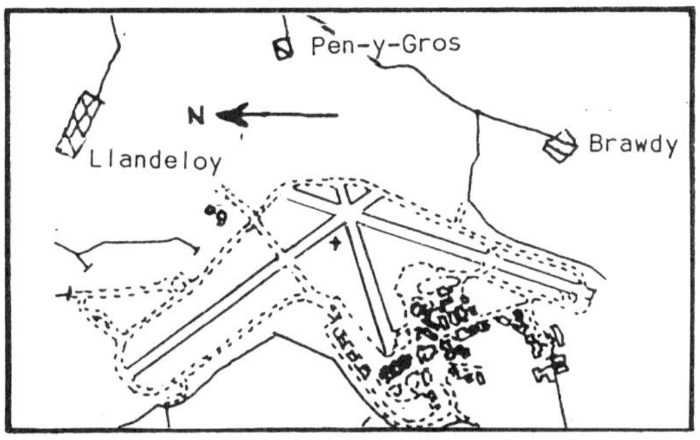

EXTENSIBILITY : -

ACCOMMODATION : Temporary.
HANGARS : T2-2.

HARDSTANDINGS : Spectacle-27.

	OFFICERS	S.N.C.O′s.	O.R′s.	TOTAL
R.A.F.	80.	280.	836.	1196.
W.A.A.F.	1.	20.	165.	186.

AFFILIATED AIRFIELDS : -

PRESENT USE [1985] : RAF.

NO: 078.

AIRFIELD NAME: BRAY. OPENED : 1941.
COUNTY : Berkshire. CLOSED : 1945.
COMMAND : Flying Training.
FORMATION : 50 Grp[Reading] GRID REF: Q 347975[114]
FUNCTION : Elementary Flying Training School[RLG] O.S.REF.: SP 905777.
LOCALITY : 3.75miles WNW of Windsor.
RAILWAY STN. : Maidenhead[GWR]

LATITUDE : 51 29 37N. HEIGHT ASL : 50′ LIGHTING : None.
LONGITUDE : 00 41 39W. FLYING CONTROL : None.RADIO : QDM.

LANDMARKS DAY : Windsor Castle, R Thames N-NE.

LANDMARKS NIGHT : -

OBSTRUCTIONS : Electric power cables & pylons approx .25miles from S boundary.

LANDING AREA SURFACE : Grass.

QDM	LENGTH X WIDTH	Ext
NE-SW.	800yds.	-
E-W.	500yds.	-

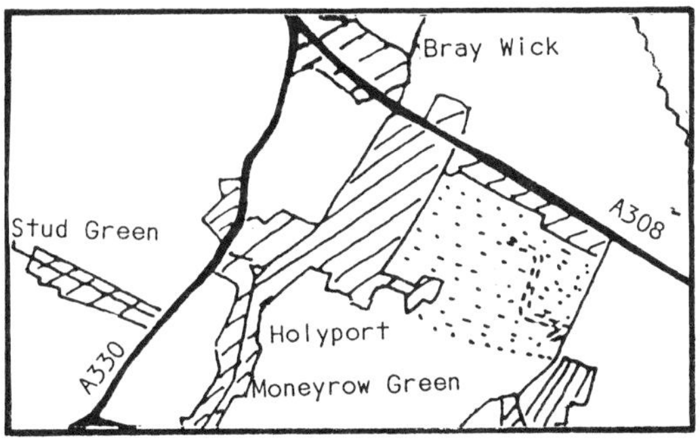

EXTENSIBILITY : -

ACCOMMODATION : None.
HANGARS : None.

HARDSTANDINGS : None.

	OFFICERS	S.N.C.O′s.	O.R′s.	TOTAL
R.A.F.	-	-	-	-
W.A.A.F.	-	-	-	-

AFFILIATED AIRFIELDS : Fairoaks[Parent]

PRESENT USE [1985] : Gravel extraction.

NO: 079.

AIRFIELD NAME: BREIGHTON. OPENED : 1942.
COUNTY : Yorkshire. CLOSED : 1946.
COMMAND : Bomber.
FORMATION : 4 Grp[York] GRID REF: A 190550[32]
FUNCTION : Operational. O.S.REF.: SE 721350.

LOCALITY : 13miles SE of York.
RAILWAY STN. : Bubwith .5miles[LNER]

LATITUDE : 53 48 15N. HEIGHT ASL : 12′ LIGHTING : Mk2.
LONGITUDE : 00 54 30W. FLYING CONTROL : Yes. RADIO : QDM.

LANDMARKS DAY : Main railway line from Selby to Market Weighton.

LANDMARKS NIGHT : R Derwent running N to S on W side of A/F.

OBSTRUCTIONS : -

LANDING AREA SURFACE : Tarmac.

QDM	LENGTH X WIDTH	Ext
087.	2000 x 50yds.	4000yds.
172.	1400 x 50yds.	3000yds.
040.	1400 x 50yds.	3000yds.

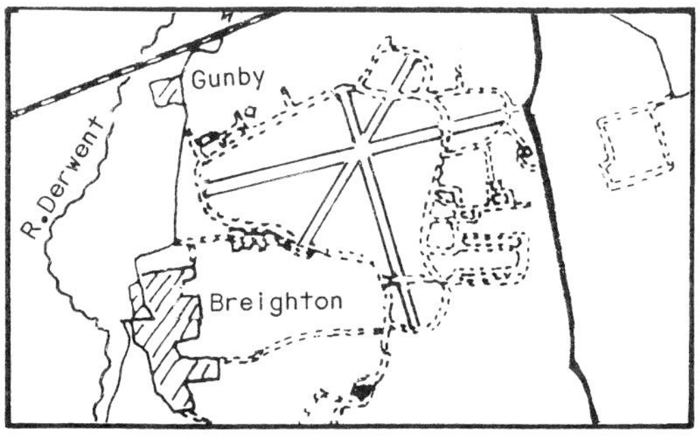

EXTENSIBILITY : Entails slight demolition.

ACCOMMODATION : Temporary.
HANGARS : T2-2;B1-1.

HARDSTANDINGS : Heavy bomber-36.

	OFFICERS	S.N.C.O′s.	O.R′s.	TOTAL
R.A.F.	153.	338.	732.	1223.
W.A.A.F.	6.	5.	180.	191.

AFFILIATED AIRFIELDS : Holme[44 Base]

PRESENT USE [1985] : Disused.

NO: 080.

AIRFIELD NAME: BRENZETT. OPENED : 1943.
COUNTY : Kent. CLOSED : 1945.
COMMAND : Fighter.
FORMATION : 11 Grp[Uxbridge] GRID REF: R 455465[126]
FUNCTION : Advanced landing Ground. O.S.REF.: TR 014281.
[de-requisitioned]
LOCALITY : 3miles NW of New Romney.
RAILWAY STN. : Brooklands 1mile[SR]

LATITUDE : 51 01 00N. HEIGHT ASL : 9′ LIGHTING : None.
LONGITUDE : 00 52 30E. FLYING CONTROL : None.RADIO : QDM.

LANDMARKS DAY : Ivychurch .25miles SE; Brenzett church .5miles SW; Shave church 1mile N.

LANDMARKS NIGHT : -

OBSTRUCTIONS : -

LANDING AREA SURFACE : Steel Matting[Sommerfeld track]

QDM	LENGTH X WIDTH	Ext
N-S.	1600yds.	-
E-W.	1400yds.	-

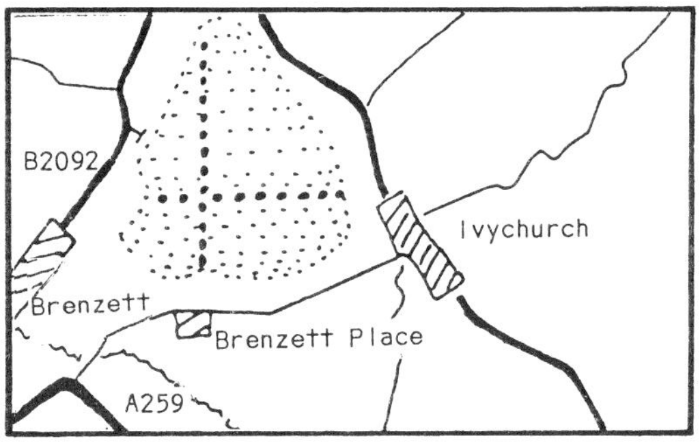

EXTENSIBILITY :

ACCOMMODATION : Tented camp.
HANGARS : None.

HARDSTANDINGS :

	OFFICERS	S.N.C.O′s.	O.R′s.	TOTAL
R.A.F.	-	-	-	-
W.A.A.F.	-	-	-	-

AFFILIATED AIRFIELDS : -

PRESENT USE [1985] : Agriculture.

NO: 081.

AIRFIELD NAME: BRIDLEWAY GATE. OPENED : 1941.
COUNTY : Shropshire. CLOSED : 1945.
COMMAND : Maintenance.
FORMATION : 42 Grp[Reading] GRID REF: K 998474[61]
FUNCTION : Relief Landing Ground. O.S.REF.: SJ 541258.

LOCALITY : 9miles NNE of Shrewsbury.
RAILWAY STN. : Wem 2.5miles[LMS]

LATITUDE : 52 49 53N. HEIGHT ASL : 310′ LIGHTING : None.
LONGITUDE : 02 41 15W. FLYING CONTROL : None.RADIO : QDM.

LANDMARKS DAY : Wem, Salop 2.5miles to NNW; Hawk lake QDM 320 degrees 3miles.

LANDMARKS NIGHT : -

OBSTRUCTIONS : -

LANDING AREA SURFACE : Grass.

QDM	LENGTH X WIDTH	Ext
N-S.	950yds.	-
NE-SW.	985yds.	-
E-W.	1030yds.	-
SE-NW.	1200yds.	-

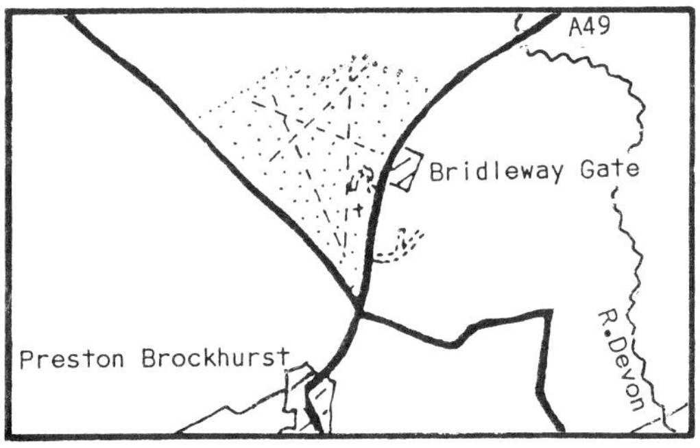

EXTENSIBILITY : None possible.

ACCOMMODATION : Temporary.
HANGARS : EO Blister-10.

HARDSTANDINGS : -

	OFFICERS	S.N.C.O′s.	O.R′s.	TOTAL
R.A.F.	2.	2.	120.	124.
W.A.A.F.	-	-	-	-

AFFILIATED AIRFIELDS : -

PRESENT USE [1985] : -

NO: 082.

AIRFIELD NAME: BRIZE NORTON. OPENED : 1937.
COUNTY : Oxfordshire. CLOSED :
COMMAND : Flying Training.
FORMATION : 23 Grp[South Cerney] GRID REF: P 737263[104]
FUNCTION : Heavy Glider Conversion Unit. O.S.REF.: SP 293058.
LOCALITY : 4miles SW of Witney.
RAILWAY STN. : Brize Norton & Bampton 3miles[GWR]

LATITUDE : 51 45 08N. HEIGHT ASL : 270′ LIGHTING : Mk2.
LONGITUDE : 01 34 30W. FLYING CONTROL : Yes. RADIO : QDM.

LANDMARKS DAY : Brampton church spire 1mile to S.

LANDMARKS NIGHT : -

OBSTRUCTIONS : Buildings NW corner.

LANDING AREA SURFACE : Concrete & wood chippings.

QDM	LENGTH X WIDTH	Ext
224.	2000 x 50yds.	-
266.	2000 x 50yds.	-

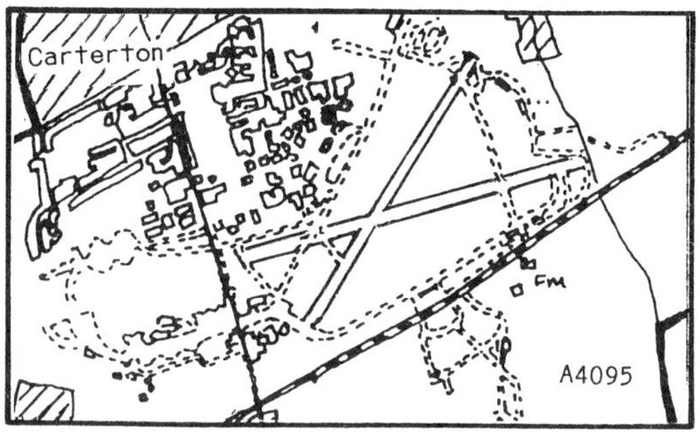

EXTENSIBILITY : None possible.

ACCOMMODATION : Permanent.
HANGARS : Various-33.

HARDSTANDINGS : None.

	OFFICERS	S.N.C.O′s.	O.R′s.	TOTAL
R.A.F.	170.	319.	1493.	1982.
W.A.A.F.	8.	9.	331.	348.

AFFILIATED AIRFIELDS : -

PRESENT USE [1985] : RAF.

NO: 083.

AIRFIELD NAME: BROADWELL. OPENED : 1943.
COUNTY : Oxfordshire. CLOSED : 1947.
COMMAND : Transport.
FORMATION : 46 Grp[Harrow Weald] GRID REF: P 694273[104]
FUNCTION : Parent. O.S.REF.: SP 248065.

LOCALITY : 3miles S of Burford.
RAILWAY STN. : Brize Norton[GWR]

LATITUDE : 51 45 30N. HEIGHT ASL : 340′ LIGHTING : Mk2.
LONGITUDE : 01 38 23W. FLYING CONTROL : Yes. RADIO : QDM.

LANDMARKS DAY : Farmhouse & windmill pump, 140yds to L of R/W 070degrees & 270yds down. Electric pylons run 2000yds from R/W 190degrees to N of A/F.

LANDMARKS NIGHT : Brize Norton outer circle intersects Broadwell outer circle.

OBSTRUCTIONS : Farmhouse with obstruction lights stands in approach to R/W 190.

LANDING AREA SURFACE : Concrete & wood chippings.

QDM	LENGTH X WIDTH	Ext
190.	2000 x 50yds.	-
170.	1400 x 50yds.	-
310.	1400 x 50yds.	-

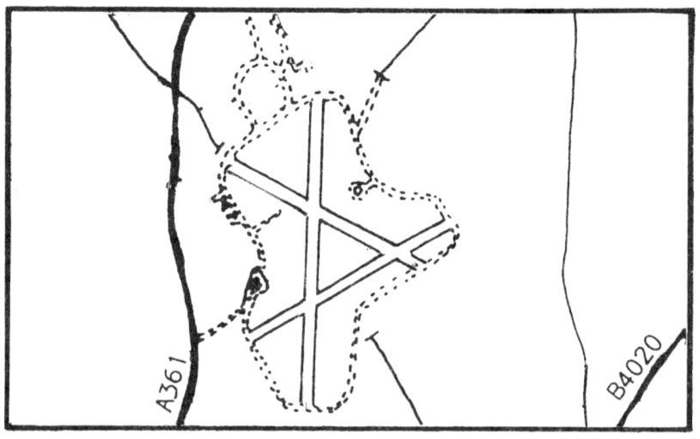

EXTENSIBILITY : None possible.

ACCOMMODATION : Temporary.
HANGARS : T2-2.

HARDSTANDINGS : 48.

	OFFICERS	S.N.C.O′s.	O.R′s.	TOTAL
R.A.F.	275.	361.	1405.	2041.
W.A.A.F.	13.	20.	220.	253.

AFFILIATED AIRFIELDS : -

PRESENT USE [1985] : Disused

NO: 084.

AIRFIELD NAME: BROUGH. OPENED : 1916.
COUNTY : Yorkshire. CLOSED :
COMMAND : Flying Training.
FORMATION : 51 Grp[Leeds] GRID REF: A 413454[33]
FUNCTION : Elementary Flying Training School. O.S.REF.: SE 948255.
LOCALITY : 7miles W of Hull.
RAILWAY STN. : Brough .25miles[LNER]

LATITUDE : 53 43 00N. HEIGHT ASL : 13′ LIGHTING : None.
LONGITUDE : 00 33 45W. FLYING CONTROL : Yes. RADIO : QDM.

LANDMARKS DAY : R Humber adjoins S boundary; cement wks 1mile E.

LANDMARKS NIGHT : R Humber adjoins S boundary.

OBSTRUCTIONS : Factory & A/F buildings N & NW corner.

LANDING AREA SURFACE : Concrete covered with tarmac.

QDM	LENGTH X WIDTH	Ext
305.	1430 x 100yds.	-

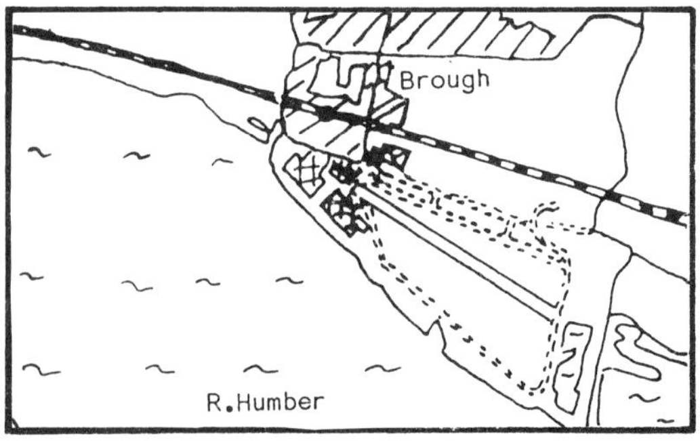

EXTENSIBILITY : Not possible NW or S, but perhaps to E with heavy fills.
ACCOMMODATION : Temporary[all RAF buildings]
HANGARS : Civil 500x175′-1;O.blister-6;DO.blister-1.

HARDSTANDINGS : Rectangular-8.

	OFFICERS	S.N.C.O′s.	O.R′s.	TOTAL
R.A.F.	98.	51.	369.	518.
W.A.A.F.	-	-	-	-

AFFILIATED AIRFIELDS : Bellasize[RLG]

PRESENT USE [1985] : Aircraft Industry[British Aerospace]

NO: 085.

AIRFIELD NAME: BRUNTINGTHORPE. OPENED : 1942.
COUNTY : Leicestershire. CLOSED : 1962.
COMMAND : Bomber.
FORMATION : 92 Grp[Winslow] GRID REF: F 046085[73]
FUNCTION : Operational Training Unit. O.S.REF.: SP 590885.
LOCALITY : 10miles S of Leicester.
RAILWAY STN. : Lutterworth[LNER]

LATITUDE : 52 29 30N. HEIGHT ASL : 450′ LIGHTING : Mk2.
LONGITUDE : 01 07 15W. FLYING CONTROL : Yes. RADIO : QDM.

LANDMARKS DAY : -

LANDMARKS NIGHT : -

OBSTRUCTIONS : -

LANDING AREA SURFACE : Concrete & wood chippings.

QDM: 246. LENGTH X WIDTH: 2000 x 50yds. Ext: 4000yds.
: 185. : 1400 x 50yds. : 1600yds.
: 132. : 1400 x 50yds. : 2700yds.
: : :

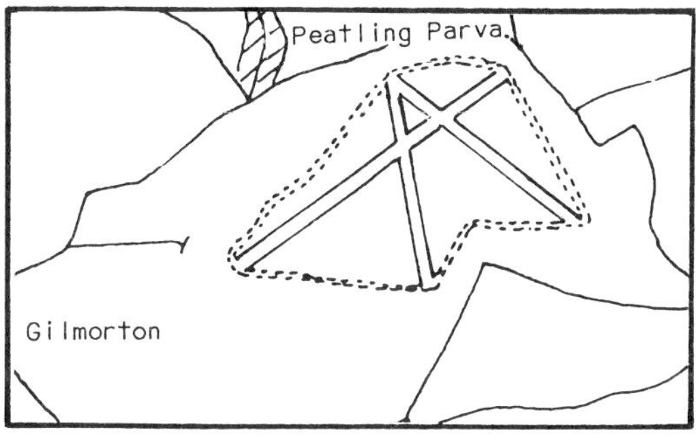

EXTENSIBILITY : Entails diversion of a minor road.

ACCOMMODATION : Temporary.
HANGARS : T2-4;B1-1.

HARDSTANDINGS : Frying pan-30.

R.A.F. : OFFICERS: 214.S.N.C.O′s.: 656.O.R′s.: 894. TOTAL: 1764.
W.A.A.F.: " : 10. " : 10. " : 420. " : 440.

AFFILIATED AIRFIELDS : -

PRESENT USE [1985] : Industry.

NO: 086.

AIRFIELD NAME: BRUNTON. OPENED : 1942.
COUNTY : Northumberland. CLOSED : 1945.
COMMAND : Fighter.
FORMATION : 12 Grp[Watnall] GRID REF: U 698463[2]
FUNCTION : Operational Training Unit[satellite] O.S.REF.: NU 205257.
LOCALITY : 9miles N of Alnwick.
RAILWAY STN. : Chathill 2.5mniles(LNER]

LATITUDE : 55 31 30N. HEIGHT ASL : 80′ LIGHTING : None.
LONGITUDE : 01 40 30W. FLYING CONTROL : Yes. RADIO : QDM.

LANDMARKS DAY : Bamburgh castle, LNE railway.

LANDMARKS NIGHT : LNE railway.

OBSTRUCTIONS : -

LANDING AREA SURFACE : Tarmac.

QDM: 030. LENGTH X WIDTH: 1600 x 50yds. Ext: 2000yds.
: 150. : 1100 x 50yds. : 1400yds.
: 079. : 1100 x 50yds. : 2000yds.
: : :

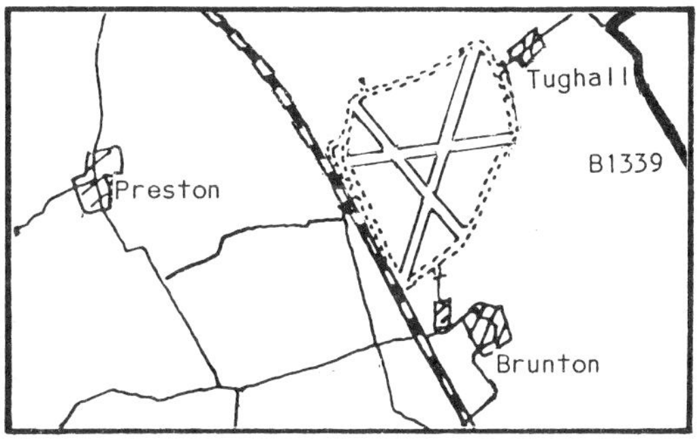

EXTENSIBILITY : 030. only effective to 1800yds.

ACCOMMODATION : Temporary.
HANGARS : Blister-4.

HARDSTANDINGS : 25.

R.A.F. : OFFICERS: 38. S.N.C.O′s.: 64. O.R′s.: 552. TOTAL: 654.
W.A.A.F.: " : 2. " : 2. " : 104. " : 108.

AFFILIATED AIRFIELDS : Milfield[Parent]

PRESENT USE [1985] : Disused.

NO: 087.

AIRFIELD NAME: BUNGAY. OPENED : 1942.
COUNTY : Suffolk. CLOSED : 1945.
COMMAND : 8th USAAF.
FORMATION : 446th Bomb Grp. GRID REF: G 778048[77]
FUNCTION : Operational. O.S.REF.: TM 323868.

LOCALITY : 6miles WSW of Beccles.
RAILWAY STN. : Beccles 2miles[LNER]

LATITUDE : 52 25 45N. HEIGHT ASL : 130′ LIGHTING : Mk2.
LONGITUDE : 01 25 15E. FLYING CONTROL : Yes. RADIO : QDM.

LANDMARKS DAY : Flixton Hall, R Waveney.

LANDMARKS NIGHT : -

OBSTRUCTIONS : White cottage approx 100yds from S end of No.2 R/W.

LANDING AREA SURFACE : Concrete, tarmac & wood chippings.

QDM: 050. LENGTH X WIDTH: 2000 x 50yds. Ext: 2600yds.
: 000. : 1480 x 50yds. : 1750yds.
: 100. : 1400 x 50yds. : -
: : :

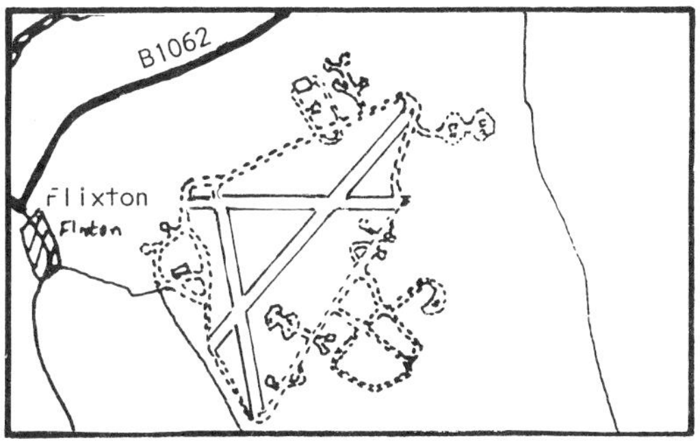

EXTENSIBILITY :

ACCOMMODATION : Temporary.
HANGARS : T2-2.

HARDSTANDINGS : Loop-50.

USAAF. : OFFICERS: 421. Enlisted Men. : 2473.TOTAL: 2894.

AFFILIATED AIRFIELDS : -

PRESENT USE [1985] : Disused.

NO: 088.

AIRFIELD NAME: BURN. OPENED : 1942.
COUNTY : Yorkshire. CLOSED : 1946.
COMMAND : Bomber.
FORMATION : 4 Grp[York] GRID REF: A 073484[32]
FUNCTION : Operational. O.S.REF.: SE 604285.

LOCALITY : 2.5miles S of Selby.
RAILWAY STN. : Selby 2.5miles[LNER]

LATITUDE : 53 44 53N. HEIGHT ASL : 20′ LIGHTING : Mk2.
LONGITUDE : 01 05 08W. FLYING CONTROL : Yes. RADIO : QDM.

LANDMARKS DAY : -

LANDMARKS NIGHT : -

OBSTRUCTIONS : Brayton Baeff hill 150′-1.5miles.

LANDING AREA SURFACE : Concrete & Tarmac.

QDM	LENGTH X WIDTH	Ext
200.	2000 x 50yds.	3000yds.
264.	1400 x 50yds.	2200yds.
335.	1400 x 50yds.	1550yds.

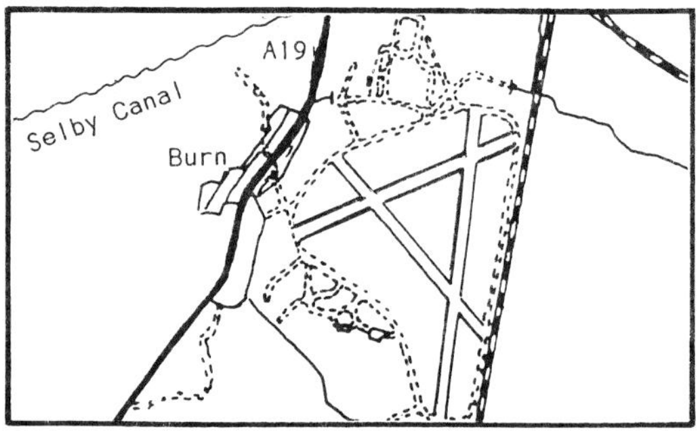

EXTENSIBILITY : Entails diversion of main York-Doncaster road.
ACCOMMODATION : Temporary.
HANGARS : T2-2;B1-1.

HARDSTANDINGS : Heavy bomber-36.

R.A.F. : OFFICERS: 129.S.N.C.O′s.: 279.O.R′s.: 1397.TOTAL: 1805.
W.A.A.F.: " : 12. " : 18. " : 246. " : 276.

AFFILIATED AIRFIELDS : Snaith.

PRESENT USE [1985] : Disused.

NO: 089.

AIRFIELD NAME: BURNFOOT. OPENED : 1940.
COUNTY : Cumberland. CLOSED : 1945.
COMMAND : Flying Training.
FORMATION : 51 Grp[Leeds] GRID REF: Y 857877[5]
FUNCTION : Elementary Flying Training School[RLG] O.S.REF.: NY 368665.
LOCALITY : 7miles NNW of Carlisle.
RAILWAY STN. : Longtown 2miles[LNER]

LATITUDE : 54 59 15N. HEIGHT ASL : 40′ LIGHTING : None.
LONGITUDE : 02 59 00W. FLYING CONTROL : None.RADIO : QDM.

LANDMARKS DAY : Solway estuary.

LANDMARKS NIGHT : -

OBSTRUCTIONS : -

LANDING AREA SURFACE : Grass.

QDM	LENGTH X WIDTH	Ext
NW-SE.	1150yds.	1900yds.
E-W.	1100yds.	1400yds.
		1600yds.

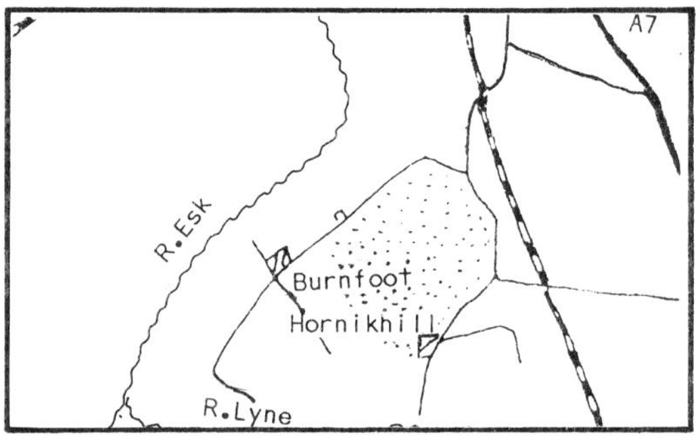

EXTENSIBILITY : Entails demolition of a derelict cottage.

ACCOMMODATION : Temporary.
HANGARS : EO blister-2;Standard blister-3.

HARDSTANDINGS : -

R.A.F. : OFFICERS: 4. S.N.C.O′s.: 6. O.R′s.: 84. TOTAL: 94.
W.A.A.F.: " : - " : - " : - " : -

AFFILIATED AIRFIELDS : Carlisle[Parent]

PRESENT USE [1985] : Agriculture.

NO: 090.

AIRFIELD NAME: BURSCOUGH. OPENED : 1943.
COUNTY : Lancashire. CLOSED : 1957.
COMMAND : RN.
FORMATION : HMS Ringtail. GRID REF: D 902323[35]
FUNCTION : Day & Night Fighter facilities. O.S.REF.: SD 425114.
LOCALITY : 1mile NE of Ormskirk.
RAILWAY STN. : Burscough Bridge 1mile[LMS]

LATITUDE : 53 35 35N. HEIGHT ASL : 78′ LIGHTING : Naval.
LONGITUDE : 02 51 35W. FLYING CONTROL : Yes. RADIO : Yes.

LANDMARKS DAY : Liverpool bay, the town of Liverpool & R Mersey.

LANDMARKS NIGHT : -

OBSTRUCTIONS : -

LANDING AREA SURFACE : Tarmac.

QDM	LENGTH X WIDTH	Ext
215.	1000 x 30yds.	-
260.	1240 x 30yds.	-
301.	1000 x 30yds.	-
350.	1000 x 30yds.	-

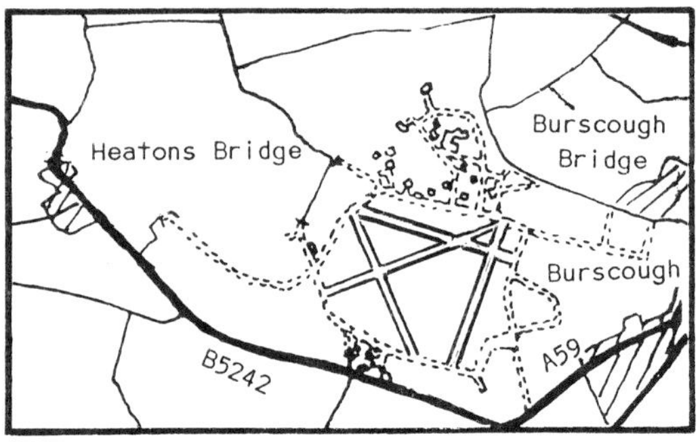

EXTENSIBILITY : -

ACCOMMODATION : Temporary.
HANGARS : 60x70′storage-14;60x70′sqdn-18.

HARDSTANDINGS : 3.

R.N. : OFFICERS: 189. Chiefs/POs/Ratings. : 1204.TOTAL: 1393.
W.R.N.S. : " : 15. " " : 355. " : 370.

AFFILIATED AIRFIELDS : -

PRESENT USE [1985] : Disused.

NO: 091.

AIRFIELD NAME: BURTONWOOD. OPENED : 1940.
COUNTY : Lancashire. CLOSED :
COMMAND : USSTAFE.
FORMATION : Air Service Command. GRID REF: E 033120[36]
FUNCTION : Base Air Depot. O.S.REF.: SJ 568910.

LOCALITY : 3miles NW of Warrington.
RAILWAY STN. : Warrington Bank Quay 3miles[LMS]

LATITUDE : 53 24 34N. HEIGHT ASL : 60′ LIGHTING : None.
LONGITUDE : 02 39 15W. FLYING CONTROL : Yes. RADIO : QDM.

LANDMARKS DAY : -

LANDMARKS NIGHT : -

OBSTRUCTIONS : A/F obstructed. A/C picketted out on A/F between runways.

LANDING AREA SURFACE : Concrete covered with asphalt.

QDM	LENGTH X WIDTH	Ext
270.	1750 x 50yds.	3000yds.
220.	1450 x 50yds.	2000yds.
150.	1450 x 50yds.	2000yds.

EXTENSIBILITY : Entails road diversion in E, & slight demolition.
ACCOMMODATION : Permanent[part]
HANGARS : 513,605sq ft storage;1,074,291sq ft shops

HARDSTANDINGS : Various-53.

USAAF. : OFFICERS: 708. Enlisted Men. 19280.TOTAL:19986.

AFFILIATED AIRFIELDS : -

PRESENT USE [1985] : USAFE.

NO: 092.

AIRFIELD NAME: BURY-St-EDMUNDS. OPENED : 1942.
COUNTY : Suffolk. CLOSED : 1948.
COMMAND : 8th USAAF.
FORMATION : 94th Bomb Grp. GRID REF: M 340830[86]
FUNCTION : Operational. O.S.REF.: TL 898644.

LOCALITY : 3miles E of Bury-St-Edmunds.
RAILWAY STN. : Thurston 1.5miles[LNER]

LATITUDE : 52 14 38N. HEIGHT ASL : 61′ LIGHTING : Mk2.
LONGITUDE : 00 46 00E. FLYING CONTROL : Yes. RADIO : QDM.

LANDMARKS DAY : Railway N of A/F running E-W, town of Bury-St-Edmunds to W.

LANDMARKS NIGHT : -

OBSTRUCTIONS : Moreton Hall.

LANDING AREA SURFACE : Concrete partially tarred, & wood chipping

QDM	LENGTH X WIDTH	Ext
275.	2000 x 50yds.	3500yds.
160.	1400 x 50yds.	-
220.	1400 x 50yds.	1700yds.

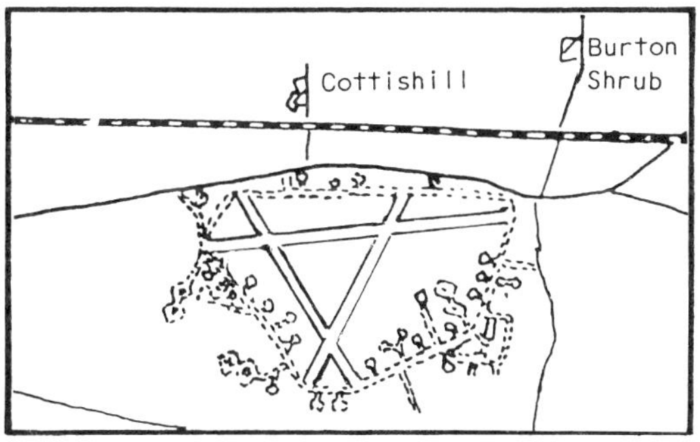

EXTENSIBILITY : -

ACCOMMODATION : Temporary.
HANGARS : T2-2.

HARDSTANDINGS : Concrete loop-50.

USAAF. : OFFICERS: 443. Enlisted Men. : 2529.TOTAL: 2972.

AFFILIATED AIRFIELDS : -

PRESENT USE [1985] : Industry.

NO: 093.

AIRFIELD NAME: BUSH BARN. OPENED : 1941.
COUNTY : Berkshire. CLOSED : 1945.
COMMAND : RN.
FORMATION : Books of HMS Kestrel. GRID REF: P 804163[104]
FUNCTION : Storage Depot. O.S.REF.: SU 360962.

LOCALITY : 10miles SW of Oxford.
RAILWAY STN. : Challow 5miles[GWR]

LATITUDE : 51 39 40N. HEIGHT ASL : 280′ LIGHTING : None.
LONGITUDE : 01 28 46W. FLYING CONTROL : None.RADIO : None.

LANDMARKS DAY : Railway 3miles S, R Thames 3miles N.

LANDMARKS NIGHT : -

OBSTRUCTIONS : Surrounded by trees with gaps on the indicated approaches.

LANDING AREA SURFACE : Grass.

QDM	LENGTH X WIDTH	Ext
263.	880yds.	-
281.	1130yds.	-
341.	980yds.	

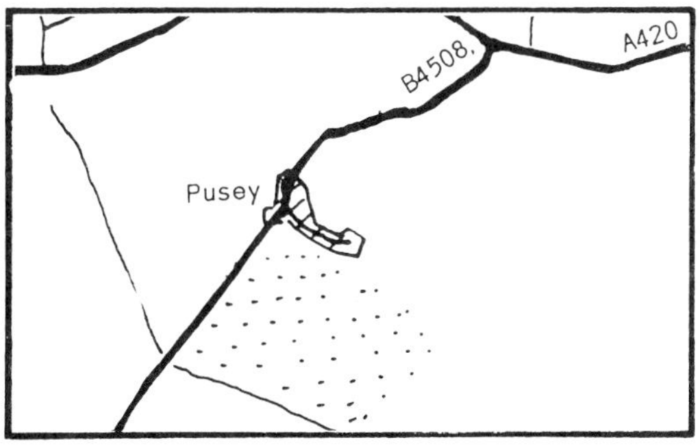

EXTENSIBILITY : -

ACCOMMODATION : -
HANGARS :

HARDSTANDINGS : -

	OFFICERS	Chiefs/POs/Ratings	TOTAL
R.N.	-	-	-
W.R.N.S.	-	-	-

AFFILIATED AIRFIELDS : -

PRESENT USE [1985] : -

NO: 094.

AIRFIELD NAME: CAISTER. OPENED : 1941.
COUNTY : Lincolnshire. CLOSED : 1963.
COMMAND : Technical Training.
FORMATION : 27 Grp[Cirencester] GRID REF: A 553215[39]
FUNCTION : Radio School. O.S.REF.: TA 086021.

LOCALITY : 5.5miles SE of Brigg.
RAILWAY STN. : Moortown 3miles[LNER]

LATITUDE : 53 30 15N. HEIGHT ASL : 100′ LIGHTING : None.
LONGITUDE : 00 21 38W. FLYING CONTROL : Yes. RADIO : Yes.

LANDMARKS DAY : Caister village[large] 1.5miles E, hills 2miles due E 460′

LANDMARKS NIGHT : Obstruction lights on hills to E.

OBSTRUCTIONS : High trees E; hill 463′ with monument approx 125′ high 2miles ENE of A/F.

LANDING AREA SURFACE : Grass.

QDM	LENGTH X WIDTH	Ext
N-E.	1100yds.	2200yds.
NE-SW.	1400yds.	-
E-W.	1200yds.	1400yds.
SE-NW.	1450yds.	-

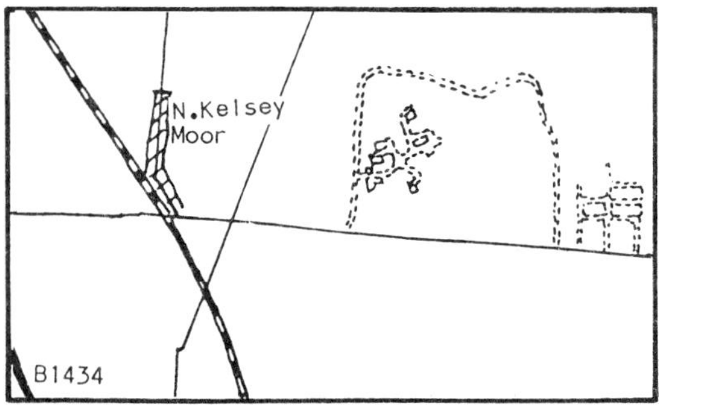

EXTENSIBILITY : Possible to subsidiaries but entails diversion to important minor road.
ACCOMMODATION : Temporary.
HANGARS : Double blister-1.

HARDSTANDINGS : Fighter-6.

R.A.F. : OFFICERS: 76. S.N.C.O's.: 41. O.R's.: 461. TOTAL: 578.
W.A.A.F.: " : - " : - " : - " : -

AFFILIATED AIRFIELDS : Cranwell[Parent]

PRESENT USE [1985] : Disused.

NO: 095.

AIRFIELD NAME: CALVELEY. OPENED : 1942.
COUNTY : Cheshire. CLOSED : 1946.
COMMAND : Flying Training.
FORMATION : 21 Grp[Spittlegate] GRID REF: K 060785[44]
FUNCTION : Advanced Flying Unit. O.S.REF.: SJ 595575.

LOCALITY : 5miles NW of Nantwich.
RAILWAY STN. : Calveley 1mile[LMS]

LATITUDE : 53 06 45N. HEIGHT ASL : 180′ LIGHTING : Mk2.
LONGITUDE : 02 36 15W. FLYING CONTROL : None. RADIO : Yes.

LANDMARKS DAY : Peckforton Hill 5miles W, Shropshire Union canal running NW-SE.

LANDMARKS NIGHT : _

OBSTRUCTIONS : -

LANDING AREA SURFACE : Concrete.

QDM	LENGTH X WIDTH	Ext
040.	1400 x 50yds.	-
110.	1300 x 50yds.	-
170.	1100 x 50yds.	-

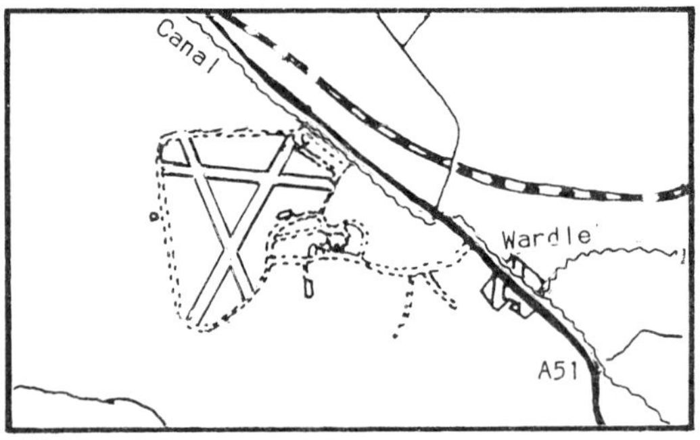

EXTENSIBILITY : Not recommended.

ACCOMMODATION : Temporary.
HANGARS : T1-1;65′blisters-4.

HARDSTANDINGS : None.

R.A.F. : OFFICERS: 96. S.N.C.O's.: 238. O.R's.: 777. TOTAL: 1111.
W.A.A.F.: " : 6. " : 88. " : 248. " : 342.

AFFILIATED AIRFIELDS : Cranage & Wrekham[Satellites]

PRESENT USE [1985] : Disused.

NO: 096.

AIRFIELD NAME: CAMBRIDGE. OPENED : 1929.
COUNTY : Cambridgeshire. CLOSED :
COMMAND : Flying Training.
FORMATION : 50 Grp[Reading] GRID REF: L 940776[85]
FUNCTION : Elementary Flying Training School. O.S.REF.: TL 486584.
LOCALITY : 2miles E of Cambridge.
RAILWAY STN. : Cambridge 3miles[LNER]

LATITUDE : 52 12 30N. HEIGHT ASL : 35′ LIGHTING : None.
LONGITUDE : 00 10 45E. FLYING CONTROL : Yes. RADIO : Yes.

LANDMARKS DAY : Chimney 150′high S of A/F, R Cam. Town of Cambridge 1mile W of A/F.

LANDMARKS NIGHT : -

OBSTRUCTIONS : Hangars NW, trees on E side. Chimney S 150′ -800 yds from perimeter.

LANDING AREA SURFACE : Grass.

QDM	LENGTH X WIDTH	Ext
N-S.	1300yds.	-
NE-SW.	1400yds.	-
E-W.	1400yds.	-
NW-SE.	1100yds.	-

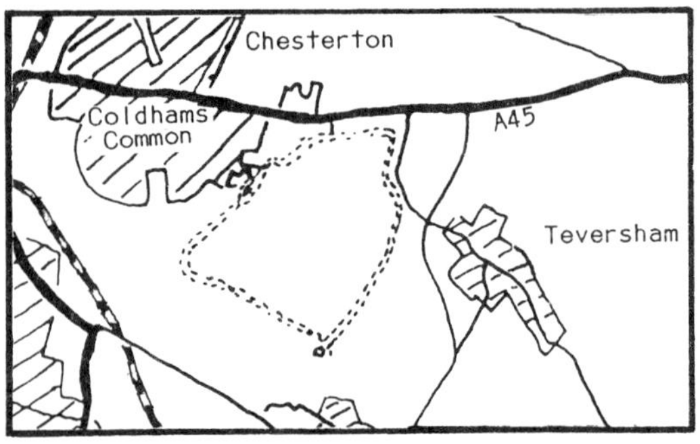

EXTENSIBILITY : Not recommended.

ACCOMMODATION : Permanent[part]
HANGARS : RAF-4 various;MAP-3 various.

HARDSTANDINGS : -

R.A.F. : OFFICERS: - S.N.C.O's.: - O.R's.: - TOTAL: -
W.A.A.F.: " : - " : - " : - " : -

AFFILIATED AIRFIELDS : Caxton Gibbet[RLG]

PRESENT USE [1985] : Aircraft Industry[Marshalls]

NO: 097.

AIRFIELD NAME: CAMMERINGHAM. OPENED : 1942.
COUNTY : Lincolnshire. CLOSED : 1945.
COMMAND : Bomber.
FORMATION : 1 Grp[Bawtry] GRID REF: A 430030[39]
FUNCTION : Operational. O.S.REF.: SK 965838.

LOCALITY : 8miles NNW of Lincoln.
RAILWAY STN. : Ingham[LNER]

LATITUDE : 52 20 30N. HEIGHT ASL : 200′ LIGHTING : None.
LONGITUDE : 00 33 15W. FLYING CONTROL : Yes. RADIO : QDM.

LANDMARKS DAY : Water tower & reservoir SW side, Farmhouse & control tower in centre of A/F.

LANDMARKS NIGHT : -

OBSTRUCTIONS : As day.

LANDING AREA SURFACE : Grass.

QDM: N-S. LENGTH X WIDTH: 1600yds. Ext: 2500yds.
: E-W. : 1200yds. : 1300yds.
: SW-NE. : 1600yds. : 2600yds.
: : :

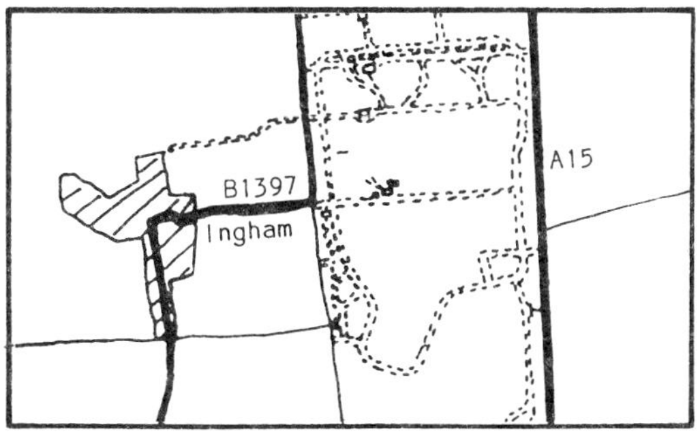

EXTENSIBILITY : Entails closure of "Middle Street" for extension SE of No.1 R/W.
ACCOMMODATION : Temporary.
HANGARS : T2-2; B1-1.

HARDSTANDINGS : Frying pan-35.

R.A.F. : OFFICERS: 95. S.N.C.O′s.: 250.O.R′s.: 922.TOTAL: 1267.
W.A.A.F.: " : 12. " : 30. " : 92. " : 134.

AFFILIATED AIRFIELDS : Hemswell.

PRESENT USE [1985] : Agriculture.

NO: 098.

AIRFIELD NAME: CAMPBELTOWN. OPENED : 1934.
COUNTY : Argyllshire. CLOSED : 1945.
COMMAND : RN.
FORMATION : HMS Landrail 11. GRID REF: S 164434[Scot]
FUNCTION : Aircraft Storage. O.S.REF.: NR 690210.

LOCALITY : 2miles W of Campbeltown.
RAILWAY STN. : No rail communications.

LATITUDE : 55 25 10N. HEIGHT ASL : 38′ LIGHTING : None.
LONGITUDE : 05 40 05W. FLYING CONTROL : None.RADIO : None.

LANDMARKS DAY : The Mull of Kintyre. Campbeltown Loch & town at its head.

LANDMARKS NIGHT : -

OBSTRUCTIONS : Mountainous country to N & S, & hills 1462′ 4.5miles SW.

LANDING AREA SURFACE : Grass.

QDM: NNW-SSE. LENGTH X WIDTH: 770yds. Ext: -
: ENE-WSW. : 850yds. : -
: : :
: : :

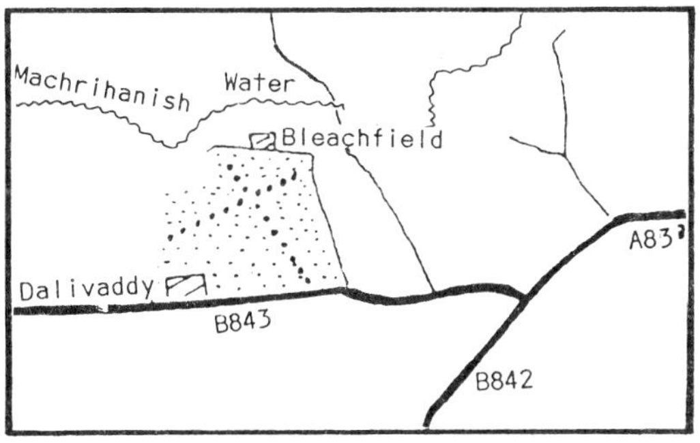

EXTENSIBILITY : -

ACCOMMODATION : None.
HANGARS : None.

HARDSTANDINGS :

R.N. : OFFICERS: - Chiefs/POs/Ratings. : - TOTAL: -
W.R.N.S.: " : - " " : - " : -

AFFILIATED AIRFIELDS : Machrihanish[Parent]

PRESENT USE [1985] : Disused.

NO: 099.

AIRFIELD NAME: CARDIFF. OPENED : 1931.
COUNTY : Glamorganshire. CLOSED : 1954.
COMMAND : Maintenance.
FORMATION : 53 Wing[Andover] GRID REF: T 657984[110]
FUNCTION : Packing Depot. O.S.REF.: ST 215770.

LOCALITY : West outskirts of Cardiff.
RAILWAY STN. : Cardiff 2.5miles[GWR]

LATITUDE : 51 29 08N. HEIGHT ASL : 23′ LIGHTING : None.
LONGITUDE : 03 07 56W. FLYING CONTROL : Yes. RADIO : Yes.

LANDMARKS DAY : Blast furnace 1mile to W. Power station .5miles to N.

LANDMARKS NIGHT : Nil except for lightship in Bristol Channel.

OBSTRUCTIONS : 2 large chimney stacks to W.

LANDING AREA SURFACE : Concrete & wood chippings.

QDM: 230. LENGTH X WIDTH: 960 x 25yds. Ext: 1500x100yds.
: - : - : 833x200yds.
: : :

EXTENSIBILITY : Entails no demolition unless in NW approach.

ACCOMMODATION : Temporary[RAF]
HANGARS : None.

HARDSTANDINGS : None.

R.A.F. : OFFICERS: 23. S.N.C.O′s.: 18. O.R′s.: 262. TOTAL: 303.
W.A.A.F.: " : 3. " : 1. " : 64. " : 68.

AFFILIATED AIRFIELDS : -

PRESENT USE [1985] : Industry.

NO: 100.

AIRFIELD NAME: CAREW CHERITON. OPENED : 1939.
COUNTY : Pembrokeshire. CLOSED : 1945.
COMMAND : Technical Training.
FORMATION : 27 Grp[Cirencester] GRID REF: N 498255[99]
FUNCTION : Radio School. O.S.REF.: SN 055026.

LOCALITY : 6miles W of Tenby.
RAILWAY STN. : Tenby 6miles[LMS]

LATITUDE : 51 41 15N. HEIGHT ASL : 100′ LIGHTING : Mk2.
LONGITUDE : 04 48 45W. FLYING CONTROL : Yes. RADIO : QDM.

LANDMARKS DAY : Carew castle; Caldy Island lighthouse; fork of R Cresswell & R Carew.

LANDMARKS NIGHT : Carew river fork & Milford Haven on all but blackest nights.

OBSTRUCTIONS : Hills surrounding up to 350′ Carew Cheriton church W of A/F approx 200′

LANDING AREA SURFACE : Concrete covered with tar & bitumen.

QDM	LENGTH X WIDTH	Ext
300.	1040 x 50yds.	2000yds.
050.	965 x 50yds.	-
340.	765 x 50yds.	-

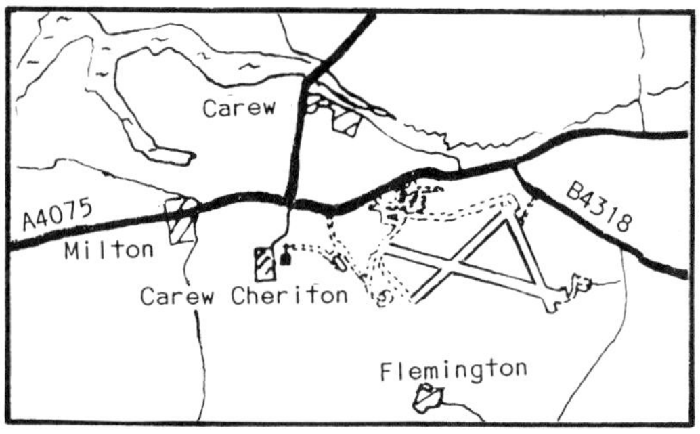

EXTENSIBILITY : Would be a major operation.

ACCOMMODATION : Temporary.
HANGARS : Bellman-2;Bessoneau-2.

HARDSTANDINGS : None.

	OFFICERS	S.N.C.O's.	O.R's.	TOTAL
R.A.F.	74.	19.	1019.	1112.
W.A.A.F.	4.	-	200.	204.

AFFILIATED AIRFIELDS : -

PRESENT USE [1985] : Disused.

NO: 101.

AIRFIELD NAME: CARK. OPENED : 1941.
COUNTY : Lancashire. CLOSED : 1945.
COMMAND : Flying Training.
FORMATION : 25 Grp[Market Drayton] GRID REF: D 850957[19]
FUNCTION : Staff Pilot Training. O.S.REF.: SD 374745.

LOCALITY : 1.75miles S of Cartmel.
RAILWAY STN. : Cark & Cartmel 1.5miles[LMS]

LATITUDE : 54 09 45N. HEIGHT ASL : 17′ LIGHTING : Mk2.
LONGITUDE : 02 57 30W. FLYING CONTROL : Yes. RADIO : QDM.

LANDMARKS DAY : Humphrey Head 200′, 2miles ESE; hills 500′ 4miles N; hills 1000′ 9miles WNW; hills 300′ 2miles NE.

LANDMARKS NIGHT : -

OBSTRUCTIONS : Tower on hill 500′ NE; Humphrey Head SE.

LANDING AREA SURFACE : Tarmac.

QDM	LENGTH X WIDTH	Ext
170.	1100 x 50yds.	1500yds.
250.	1300 x 50yds.	1800yds.
310.	1100 x 50yds.	-

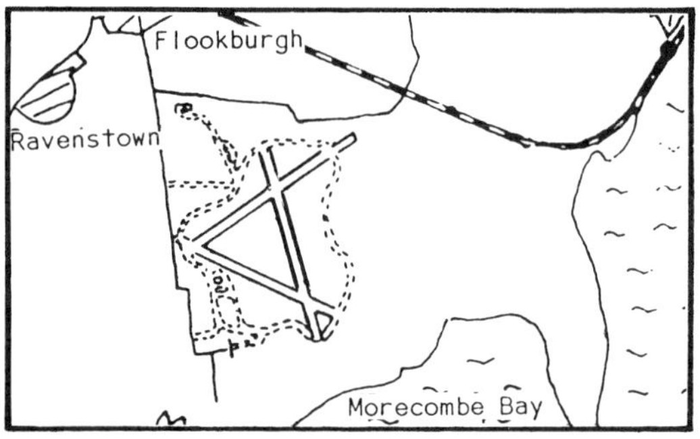

EXTENSIBILITY :

ACCOMMODATION : Temporary.
HANGARS : Bellman-1; EO blister-19.

HARDSTANDINGS : Twin fighter pens-6.

	OFFICERS	S.N.C.O's.	O.R's.	TOTAL
R.A.F.	69.	271.	518.	858.
W.A.A.F.	6.	6.	188.	200.

AFFILIATED AIRFIELDS : -

PRESENT USE [1985] : Private flying.

NO: 102.

AIRFIELD NAME: CARLISLE. OPENED : 1933.
COUNTY : Cumberland. CLOSED : 1957.
COMMAND : Flying Training.
FORMATION : 51 Grp[Leeds] GRID REF: Y 876805[5]
FUNCTION : Elementary Flying Training School. O.S.REF.: NY 390595.
LOCALITY : 2miles N of Carlisle.
RAILWAY STN. : Harker 1mile[LNER],Carlisle 2miles[LMS]

LATITUDE : 54 55 23N. HEIGHT ASL : 100′ LIGHTING : None.
LONGITUDE : 02 58 00W. FLYING CONTROL : None.RADIO : QDM.

LANDMARKS DAY : Solway area.

LANDMARKS NIGHT : -

OBSTRUCTIONS : 200′ high chimney S of SW corner of A/F.

LANDING AREA SURFACE : Grass.

QDM	LENGTH X WIDTH	Ext
NW-SE.	1000yds.	-
NE-SW.	1000yds.	-

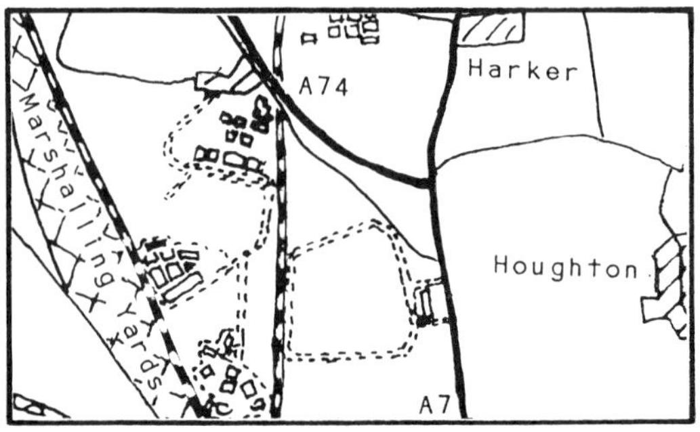

EXTENSIBILITY : None possible.

ACCOMMODATION : Communal buildings temp.1300000sq ft.perm store.
HANGARS : Various-7.

HARDSTANDINGS : –

	OFFICERS	S.N.C.O's.	O.R's.	TOTAL
R.A.F.	19.	88.	278.	385.
W.A.A.F.	-	-	-	-

AFFILIATED AIRFIELDS : Burnfoot & Kirkpatrick[RLG]

PRESENT USE [1985] : Disused.

NO: 103.

AIRFIELD NAME: CARNABY. OPENED : 1944.
COUNTY : Yorkshire. CLOSED : 1963.
COMMAND : Bomber.
FORMATION : 4 Grp[York] GRID REF: A 614837[28]
FUNCTION : Emergency Runway. O.S.REF.: TA 140640.

LOCALITY : 1.75miles SW of Bridlington.
RAILWAY STN. : Carnaby[LNER]

LATITUDE : 54 03 45N. HEIGHT ASL : 35′ LIGHTING : Mk2.
LONGITUDE : 00 15 30W. FLYING CONTROL : Yes. RADIO : QDM.

LANDMARKS DAY : Bridlington town 2.5miles NE.

LANDMARKS NIGHT : -

OBSTRUCTIONS : Farm 35′ high 50yds SE of approach.

LANDING AREA SURFACE : Bitumen,special.

QDM: 259. LENGTH X WIDTH: 3000 x 250yds Ext: 4000yds.
: : :
: : :
: : :

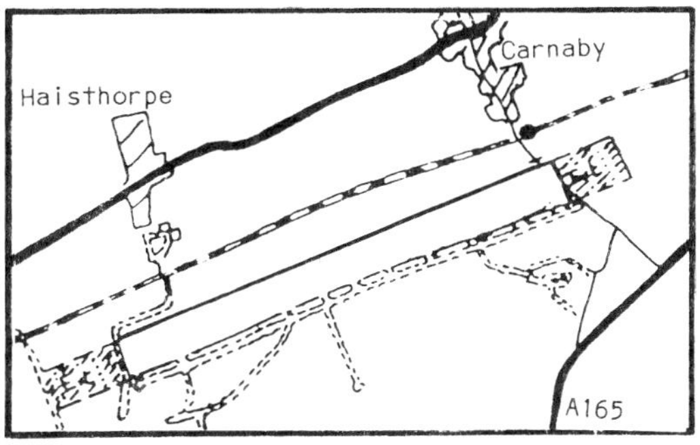

EXTENSIBILITY : 500yds at each end.

ACCOMMODATION : Temporary.[None for visiting personnel]
HANGARS : None.

HARDSTANDINGS : Dispersal loop only.

R.A.F. : OFFICERS: 18. S.N.C.O′s.: 36. O.R′s.: 494. TOTAL: 548.
W.A.A.F.: " : - " : - " : - " : -

AFFILIATED AIRFIELDS : -

PRESENT USE [1985] : Industry.

NO: 104.

AIRFIELD NAME: CASTLE BROMWICH. OPENED : 1914.
COUNTY : Warwickshire. CLOSED : 1958.
COMMAND : Fighter.
FORMATION : 70 Grp[Farnborough] GRID REF: K 598117[72]
FUNCTION : AA Co-operation Unit. O.S.REF.: SP 145915.

LOCALITY : 5miles N of Birmingham.
RAILWAY STN. : Castle Bromwich .75miles[LMS]

LATITUDE : 52 31 08N. HEIGHT ASL : 270′ LIGHTING : None.
LONGITUDE : 01 47 15W. FLYING CONTROL : Yes. RADIO : QMD.

LANDMARKS DAY : Power station 3.5miles E.

LANDMARKS NIGHT : As day.

OBSTRUCTIONS : 2 chimney stacks on E of A/F.

LANDING AREA SURFACE : Concrete.

QDM: 050. LENGTH X WIDTH: 650 x 50yds. Ext: 1400yds.
: : :
: : :
: : :

EXTENSIBILITY : Extra 1200yds in grass.

ACCOMMODATION :
HANGARS : Type C-1;obsolete wooden types-3.

HARDSTANDINGS : None.

R.A.F. : OFFICERS: 23. S.N.C.O′s.: 26. O.R′s.: 283. TOTAL: 332.
W.A.A.F.: " : 2. " : 3. " : 140. " : 145.

AFFILIATED AIRFIELDS : -

PRESENT USE [1985] : Housing.

NO: 105.

AIRFIELD NAME: CASTLE CAMPS. OPENED : 1940.
COUNTY : Essex/Cambs. CLOSED : 1946.
COMMAND : Fighter.
FORMATION : 11 Grp[Uxbridge] GRID REF: M 080605[85]
FUNCTION : Forward Airfield O.S.REF.: TL 633420.
Night Fighter.
LOCALITY : 6miles NE Saffron Walden.
RAILWAY STN. : Bartlow 4miles[LNER]

LATITUDE : 52 03 00N. HEIGHT ASL : 420′ LIGHTING : Mk2.
LONGITUDE : 00 23 00E. FLYING CONTROL : Yes. RADIO : QDM.

LANDMARKS DAY : Bendysh Woods 1mile SW.

LANDMARKS NIGHT : -

OBSTRUCTIONS : -

LANDING AREA SURFACE : Tarmac.

QDM: 063. LENGTH X WIDTH: 1950 x 50yds. Ext: 2600yds.
: 317. : 1600 x 50yds. : -
: 100. : 1070 x 50yds. : 1100yds.
: : :

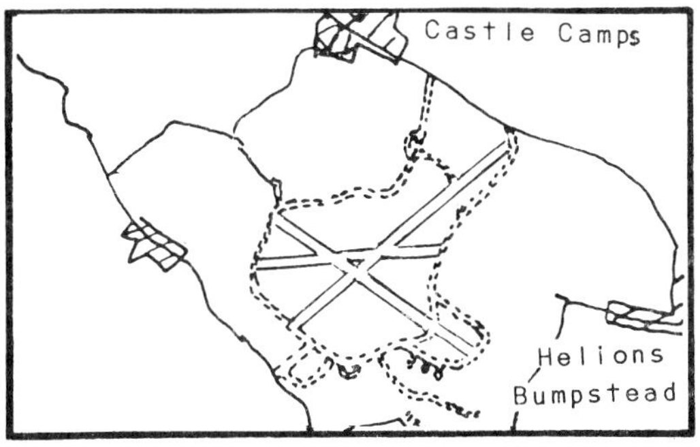

EXTENSIBILITY : Entails diversion of access road.Fourth strip of 2000yds. can be obtained after Farm demo.
ACCOMMODATION : Temporary.
HANGARS : Bellman-1;O blister-8.

HARDSTANDINGS : 16.

R.A.F. : OFFICERS: 68. S.N.C.O′s.: 101.O.R′s.: 1009.TOTAL: 1178.
W.A.A.F.: " : 4. " : 10. " : 170. " : 184.

AFFILIATED AIRFIELDS : North Weald[Sector]

PRESENT USE [1985] : Agriculture.

NO: 106.

AIRFIELD NAME: CASTLE COMBE. OPENED : 1941.
COUNTY : Wiltshire. CLOSED : 1948.
COMMAND : Flying Training.
FORMATION : 23 Grp[South Cerney] GRID REF: U 296975[111]
FUNCTION : Advanced Flying Unit. O.S.REF.: ST 854767.
[satellite]
LOCALITY : 5.5miles NW of Chippenham.
RAILWAY STN. : Chippenham 5miles[GWR]

LATITUDE : 51 29 20N. HEIGHT ASL : 430′ LIGHTING : Mk2.
LONGITUDE : 02 12 45W. FLYING CONTROL : None.RADIO : QDM.

LANDMARKS DAY : -

LANDMARKS NIGHT : -

OBSTRUCTIONS : -

LANDING AREA SURFACE : Steel Matting[Sommerfeld Track]NE-SW Grass

QDM: 313. LENGTH X WIDTH: 930yds. Ext: 1530yds.
: NE-SW. : 1085yds. : 1230yds.
: : :
: : :

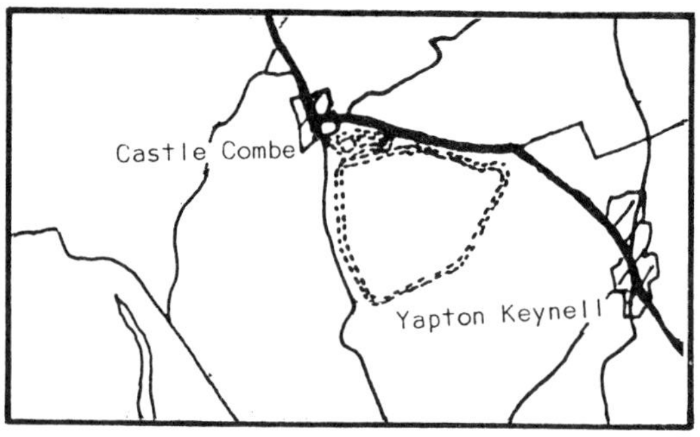

EXTENSIBILITY : -

ACCOMMODATION : Temporary.
HANGARS : T1-1; 65′Blister-5.

HARDSTANDINGS : None.

R.A.F. : OFFICERS: 105.S.N.C.O′s.: 247.O.R′s.: 454. TOTAL: 806.
W.A.A.F.: " : 4. " : 8. " : 144. " : 156.

AFFILIATED AIRFIELDS : Babdown Farm[Parent]

PRESENT USE [1985] : Disused.

NO: 107.

AIRFIELD NAME: CASTLE DONNINGTON. OPENED : 1943.
COUNTY : Leicestershire. CLOSED :
COMMAND : Transport.
FORMATION : 44 Grp[Gloucester] GRID REF: F 912460[54]
FUNCTION : Operational Training O.S.REF.: SK 454262.
Unit[satellite]
LOCALITY : 9miles SE of Derby.
RAILWAY STN. : Kegworth 3.5miles[LMS]

LATITUDE : 52 49 45N. HEIGHT ASL : 290′ LIGHTING : Mk2.
LONGITUDE : 01 19 30W FLYING CONTROL : Yes. RADIO : QDM.

LANDMARKS DAY : -

LANDMARKS NIGHT : -

OBSTRUCTIONS : -

LANDING AREA SURFACE : Concrete.

QDM: 281. LENGTH X WIDTH: 2000 x 50yds. Ext: 2400yds.
: 235. : 1400 x 50yds. : 1700yds.
: 336. : 1100 x 50yds. : -
: : :

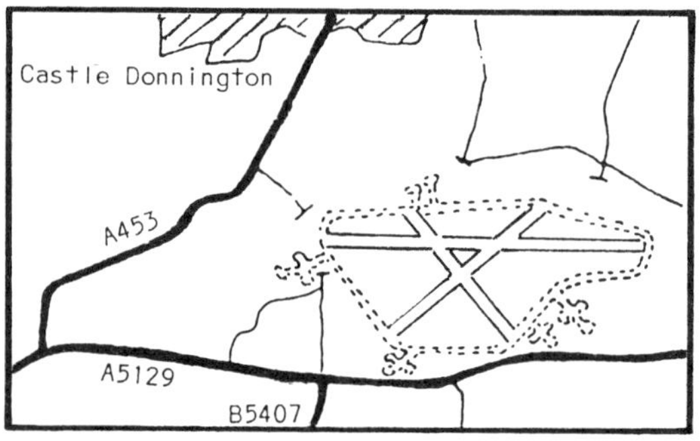

EXTENSIBILITY : Entails demolition of farm buildings.

ACCOMMODATION : Temporary.
HANGARS : T2-1, B1-1.

HARDSTANDINGS : Heavy bomber-27.

R.A.F. : OFFICERS: 60. S.N.C.O′s.: 212.O.R′s.: 644. TOTAL: 916.
W.A.A.F.: " : 2. " : 8. " : 180. " : 190.

AFFILIATED AIRFIELDS : Wymeswold[Parent]

PRESENT USE [1985] : Civil Airport[East Midlands]

NO: 108.

AIRFIELD NAME: CASTLE KENNEDY. OPENED : 1941.
COUNTY : Wigtownshire. CLOSED : 1945.
COMMAND : Flying Training.
FORMATION : 29 Grp[Dumfries] GRID REF: X 602828[90Scot]
FUNCTION : Air Gunnery School. O.S.REF.: NX 119598.

LOCALITY : 3.5miles E of Stranraer.
RAILWAY STN. : Castle Kennedy .25miles[LMS]

LATITUDE : 54 54 40N. HEIGHT ASL : 83′ LIGHTING : Mk2.
LONGITUDE : 04 56 05W. FLYING CONTROL : Yes. RADIO : QDM.

LANDMARKS DAY : 2 large lochs to N of landing area.

LANDMARKS NIGHT : -

OBSTRUCTIONS : Farm house at S side. Hills rising to 500′ NE,to 400′E.

LANDING AREA SURFACE : Concrete covered with tarmac.

QDM: 090. LENGTH X WIDTH: 1400 x 50yds. Ext: -
: 170. : 1400 x 50yds. : -
: : :
: : :

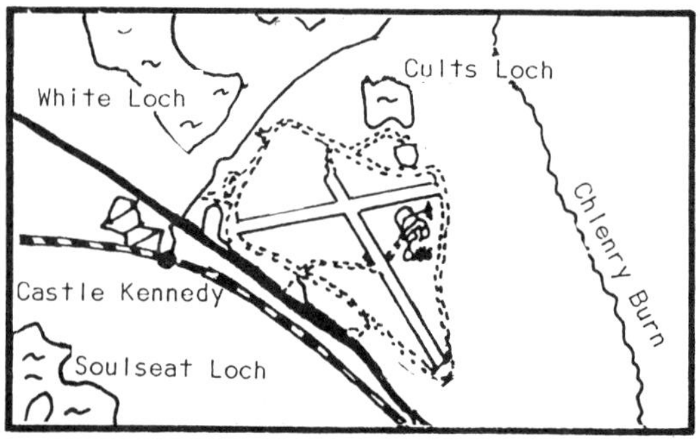

EXTENSIBILITY : -

ACCOMMODATION : Temporary.
HANGARS : Callander Hamilton-4;EO blister-9.

HARDSTANDINGS : Rectangular-10.

R.A.F. : OFFICERS: 60. S.N.C.O′s.: 201.O.R′s.: 1108.TOTAL: 1369.
W.A.A.F.: " : 19. " : 8. " : 302. " : 329.

AFFILIATED AIRFIELDS : -

PRESENT USE [1985] : Disused.

NO: 109.

AIRFIELD NAME: CASTLETOWN. OPENED : 1940.
COUNTY : Caithness. CLOSED : 1945.
COMMAND : Fighter.
FORMATION : 13 Grp[Inverness] GRID REF: D 753888[Scot]
FUNCTION : Forward Airfield. O.S.REF.: ND 215669.

LOCALITY : 5.5miles E of Thurso.
RAILWAY STN. : Thurso 6miles[LMS]

LATITUDE : 58 35 00N. HEIGHT ASL : 90′ LIGHTING : None.
LONGITUDE : 03 20 30W. FLYING CONTROL : Yes. RADIO : QDM.

LANDMARKS : -
DAY

LANDMARKS : -
NIGHT

OBSTRUCTIONS : -

LANDING AREA SURFACE : Asphalt.

QDM: 250. LENGTH X WIDTH: 1200 x 50yds. Ext: 2000yds.
: 292. : 1125 x 50yds. : 2000yds.
: 161. : 1085 x 50yds. : 1150yds.
: : :

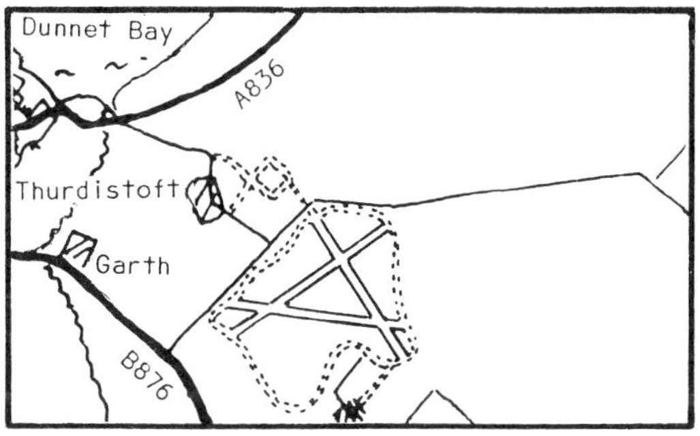

EXTENSIBILITY : Entails slight demolition.

ACCOMMODATION : Temporary.
HANGARS : Bellman-1; T3-1.

HARDSTANDINGS : S.E.-6.

R.A.F. : OFFICERS: 60. S.N.C.O's.: 113.O.R's.: 1054.TOTAL: 1227.
W.A.A.F.: " : " : " : " :

AFFILIATED AIRFIELDS : Kirkwall Operations Room[Sector]

PRESENT USE [1985] : Disused.

NO: 110.

AIRFIELD NAME: CATFOSS. OPENED : 1932.
COUNTY : Yorkshire. CLOSED : 1963.
COMMAND : Flying Training.
FORMATION : 25 Grp[Market Drayton] GRID REF: A 612675[28]
FUNCTION : Central Gunnery School.O.S.REF.: TA 135485.

LOCALITY : 4 miles W of Hornsea.
RAILWAY STN. : Hornsea Town[LNER]

LATITUDE : 53 55 15N. HEIGHT ASL : 40′ LIGHTING : Mk2.
LONGITUDE : 00 16 30W. FLYING CONTROL : Yes. RADIO : QDM.

LANDMARKS : -
DAY

LANDMARKS : -
NIGHT

OBSTRUCTIONS : Grange Farm E-end E-W runway;Manor Farm
N-end N-S runway; wireless
masts 90′ E-end of camp.
LANDING AREA SURFACE : Concrete & wood chippings.

QDM: 193. LENGTH X WIDTH: 1750 x 50yds. Ext: 2000yds.
: 240. : 1560 x 50yds. : 2000yds.
: 295. : 1710 x 50yds. : 2000yds.

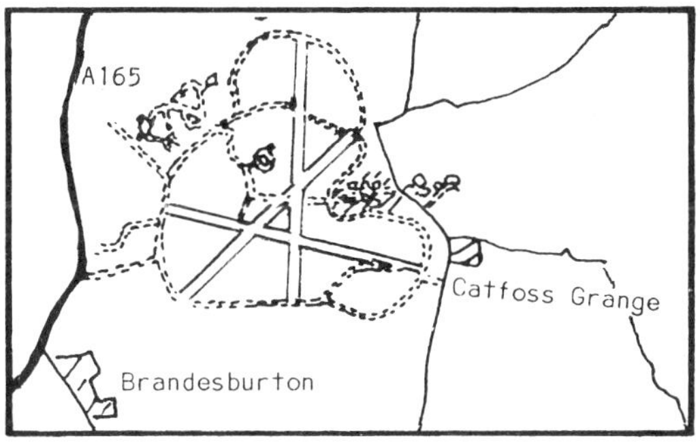

EXTENSIBILITY : Entails demolition of 3 farms.

ACCOMMODATION : Temporary,except 1 hangar & some married quarters.
HANGARS : A-1;A1-1;Bellman-2;T1-1;EO blister-15.

HARDSTANDINGS : 120′dia-25;250x150′concrete base-2;oval-13.

R.A.F. : OFFICERS: 165.S.N.C.O's.: 281.O.R's.: 1860.TOTAL: 2306.
W.A.A.F.: " : 11. " : 23. " : 392. " : 426.

AFFILIATED AIRFIELDS : -

PRESENT USE [1985] : Disused.

NO: 111.

AIRFIELD NAME: CATTERICK. OPENED : 1914.
COUNTY : Yorkshire. CLOSED :
COMMAND : Fighter.
FORMATION : 12 Grp[Watnall] GRID REF: Z 725172[21]
FUNCTION : Forward Airfield. O.S.REF.: SE 250968.

LOCALITY : 4.5miles SE of Richmond.
RAILWAY STN. : Catterick Bridge 2miles[LNER]

LATITUDE : 54 22 00N. HEIGHT ASL : 175′ LIGHTING : Mk2.
LONGITUDE : 01 37 00W. FLYING CONTROL : Yes. RADIO : QDM.

LANDMARKS : R Swale, railway, Catterick military camp.
DAY

LANDMARKS : -
NIGHT

OBSTRUCTIONS : -

LANDING AREA SURFACE : Asphalt.

QDM: 285. LENGTH X WIDTH: 1200 x 50yds. Ext: -
: : :
: : :
: : :

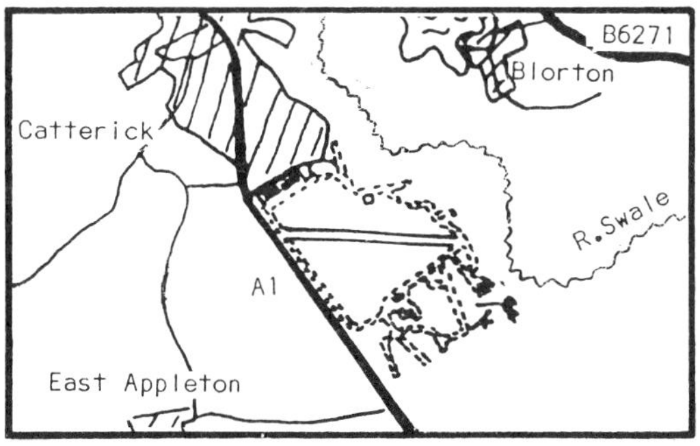

EXTENSIBILITY : None possible.

ACCOMMODATION : Permanent.
HANGARS : Type C-2;O blister-2;EO blister-6.

HARDSTANDINGS : SE-5.

R.A.F. : OFFICERS: 110.S.N.C.O's.: 110.O.R's.: 1210.TOTAL: 1430.
W.A.A.F.: " : 13. " : 10. " : 495. " : 518.

AFFILIATED AIRFIELDS : Newcastle Operations Room[Sector]

PRESENT USE [1985] : RAF.

NO: 112.

AIRFIELD NAME: CAXTON GIBBET. OPENED : 1940.
COUNTY : Cambridgeshire. CLOSED : 1945.
COMMAND : Flying Training.
FORMATION : 50 Grp[Reading] GRID REF: L 754793[85]
FUNCTION : Elementary Flying Training School[RLG] O.S.REF.: TL 754793.
LOCALITY : 9miles W of Cambridge.
RAILWAY STN. : Old North Road 5miles[LMS]

LATITUDE : 52 13 15N. HEIGHT ASL : 200′ LIGHTING : None.
LONGITUDE : 00 05 15W. FLYING CONTROL : None.RADIO : QDM.

LANDMARKS DAY : "T" shaped wood 2miles W. Papworth village 3miles N.

LANDMARKS NIGHT : -

OBSTRUCTIONS : Wood NE 30′;public house with wireless aerial NW corner 50′;farmhouse with wireless aerial E corner 40′.
LANDING AREA SURFACE : Grass.

QDM	LENGTH X WIDTH	Ext
N-E.	1100yds.	-
NE-SW.	700yds.	-
E-W.	600yds.	-
NW-SE.	1000yds.	-

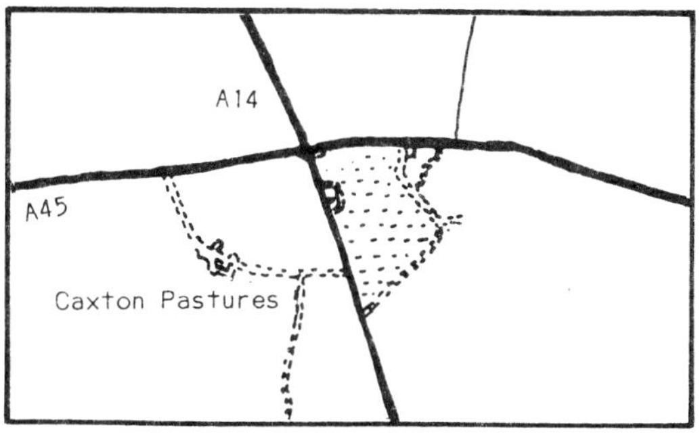

EXTENSIBILITY : Main roads on E&N, the only 2 directions in which extensions might be possible.
ACCOMMODATION : Temporary.
HANGARS : O blister-2;standard blister-5.

HARDSTANDINGS : None.

R.A.F. : OFFICERS: - S.N.C.O′s.: - O.R′s.: 78. TOTAL: 78.
W.A.A.F.: " : - " : - " : - " : -

AFFILIATED AIRFIELDS : Cambridge[Parent]

PRESENT USE [1985] : Agriculture.

NO: 113.

AIRFIELD NAME: CHAILEY. OPENED : 1944.
COUNTY : Sussex. CLOSED : 1944.
COMMAND : Fighter.
FORMATION : 11 Grp[Uxbridge] GRID REF: Q 808382[134]
FUNCTION : Advanced Landing Ground. [de-requisitioned] O.S.REF.: TQ 378205.
LOCALITY : 9miles NNW of Brighton.
RAILWAY STN. : Plumpton[SR]

LATITUDE : 50 57 15N. HEIGHT ASL : 105′ LIGHTING : None.
LONGITUDE : 00 02 45W. FLYING CONTROL : None.RADIO : QDM.

LANDMARKS DAY : White strips on edge of runway corner marking flying strip. Touchdown point of white chalk.

LANDMARKS NIGHT : -

OBSTRUCTIONS : -

LANDING AREA SURFACE : Steel Matting[Sommerfeld Track]

QDM	LENGTH X WIDTH	Ext
NW-SE.	1200yds.	-
E-W.	1500yds.	-

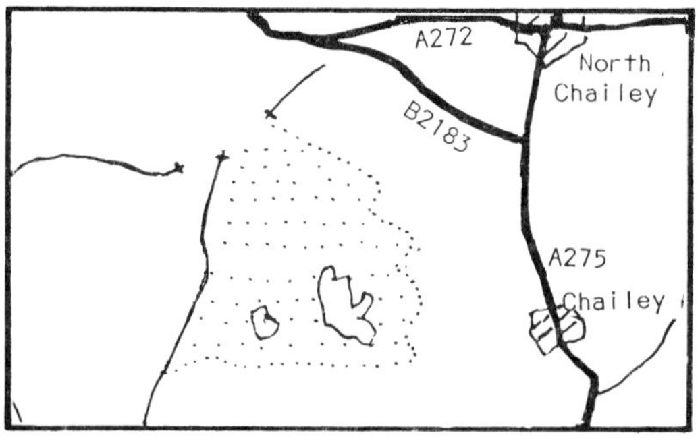

EXTENSIBILITY :

ACCOMMODATION : Tented camp.
HANGARS : Blister-4.

HARDSTANDINGS : Hardcore & ash-3.

R.A.F. : OFFICERS: - S.N.C.O′s.: - O.R′s.: - TOTAL: -
W.A.A.F.: " : - " : - " : - " : -

AFFILIATED AIRFIELDS : -

PRESENT USE [1985] : Agriculture.

NO: 114.

AIRFIELD NAME: CHALGROVE. OPENED : 1943.
COUNTY : Oxfordshire. CLOSED :
COMMAND : 9th USAAF.
FORMATION : GRID REF: L 087171[105]
FUNCTION : De-activated. O.S.REF.: SU 635977.

LOCALITY : 9miles SE of Oxford.
RAILWAY STN. : Watlington 5miles[GWR]

LATITUDE : 51 40 30N. HEIGHT ASL : 230′ LIGHTING : Mk2.
LONGITUDE : 01 04 30W. FLYING CONTROL : Yes. RADIO : QDM.

LANDMARKS DAY : -

LANDMARKS NIGHT : -

OBSTRUCTIONS : -

LANDING AREA SURFACE : Concrete & tarmac.

QDM	LENGTH X WIDTH	Ext
140.	2000 x 50yds.	3000yds.
250.	1400 x 50yds.	2000yds.
190.	1400 x 50yds.	2000yds.

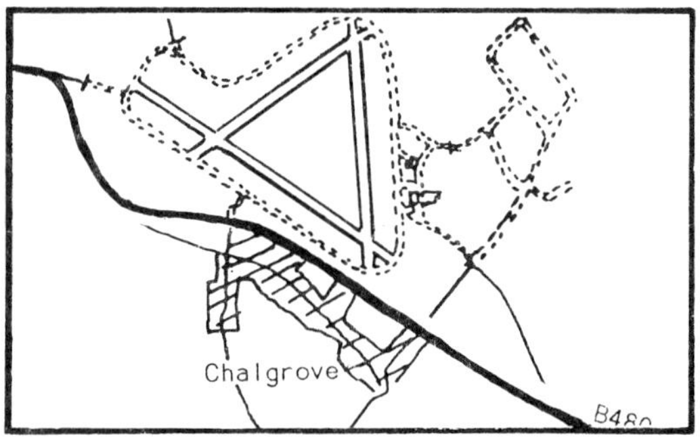

EXTENSIBILITY : Entails poss. diversion of short portion of a road, & demolition of 2 barns & a shed.
ACCOMMODATION : Temporary.
HANGARS : T2-2.

HARDSTANDINGS : Loop-50.

USAAF. : OFFICERS: 364. Enlisted Men. : 2193.TOTAL: 2557.

AFFILIATED AIRFIELDS : -

PRESENT USE [1985] : Aircraft Industry[Martin Baker]

AIRFIELD NAME: CHARLTON HORETHORNE. OPENED : 1942.
COUNTY : Dorsetshire. CLOSED : 1948.
COMMAND : RN.
FORMATION : Books of HMS Heron. GRID REF: P 452082[130]
FUNCTION : Flying Training. O.S.REF.: ST 642244.

LOCALITY : 1mile WNW of Charlton Horethorne.
RAILWAY STN. : Milborn Port 1.5miles[GWR]

LATITUDE : 51 01 05N. HEIGHT ASL : 620′ LIGHTING : None.
LONGITUDE : 02 30 30W. FLYING CONTROL : Yes. RADIO : QDM.

LANDMARKS DAY : Small lake surrounded by a wood immediately N of A/F.

LANDMARKS NIGHT : -

OBSTRUCTIONS : -

LANDING AREA SURFACE : Grass.

QDM: NE-SW. LENGTH X WIDTH: 1200yds. Ext: -
: NW-SE. : 900yds. : -
: : :
: : :

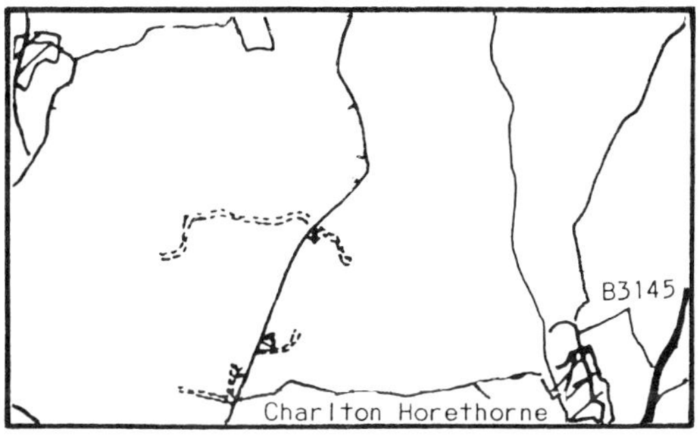

EXTENSIBILITY : -

ACCOMMODATION : Temporary.
HANGARS : 60x84′[sqdn]-2;91x45′[sqdn]-4.

HARDSTANDINGS : Double pens-6;A/C standings-5.

R.N. : OFFICERS: 62. Chiefs/POs/Ratings. : 457.TOTAL: 519.
W.R.N.S. : " : 1. " " : 73. " : 74.

AFFILIATED AIRFIELDS : -

PRESENT USE [1985] : Agriculture.

NO: 116.

AIRFIELD NAME: CHARMY DOWN. OPENED : 1940.
COUNTY : Somersetshire. CLOSED : 1946.
COMMAND : Flying Training.
FORMATION : 23 Grp[South Cerney] GRID REF: U 205906[111]
FUNCTION : Advanced Training Unit [satellite] O.S.REF.: ST 764700.
LOCALITY : 3.5miles N of Bath.
RAILWAY STN. : Bath 4miles[GWR]

LATITUDE : 51 25 38N. HEIGHT ASL : 688′ LIGHTING : Mk2.
LONGITUDE : 02 20 31W. FLYING CONTROL : Yes. RADIO : QDM.

LANDMARKS DAY : City of Bath 4miles SW.

LANDMARKS NIGHT : R Avon 2miles S.

OBSTRUCTIONS : -

LANDING AREA SURFACE : Tarmac.

QDM: 310. LENGTH X WIDTH: 1450 x 50yds. Ext: -
: 250. : 1350 x 50yds. : -
: 012. : 933 x 50yds. : 1150.
: : :

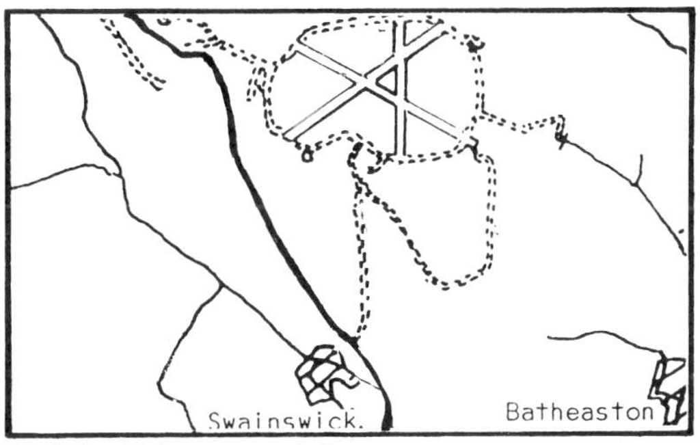

EXTENSIBILITY : Not recommended.

ACCOMMODATION : Temporary.
HANGARS : Blister-12.

HARDSTANDINGS : Dispersals-45.

R.A.F. : OFFICERS: S.N.C.O's.: O.R's.: TOTAL:
W.A.A.F.: " : " : " : " :

AFFILIATED AIRFIELDS : South Cerney[Parent]

PRESENT USE [1985] : Disused.

NO: 117.

AIRFIELD NAME: CHARTER HALL. OPENED : 1942.
COUNTY : Berwickshire. CLOSED : 1946.
COMMAND : Fighter.
FORMATION : 12 Grp[Watnall] GRID REF: U 262676[75Scot]
FUNCTION : Operational Training Unit. O.S.REF.: NT 765463.
LOCALITY : 15miles WSW of Berwick on Tweed.
RAILWAY STN. : Greenlaw 3miles[LNER]

LATITUDE : 55 42 38N. HEIGHT ASL : 350′ LIGHTING : Mk2.
LONGITUDE : 02 22 30W. FLYING CONTROL : Yes. RADIO : QDM.

LANDMARKS DAY : R Tweed 6miles SSW; R Black Adder 1mile NW.

LANDMARKS NIGHT : -

OBSTRUCTIONS : Wireless masts 60′ high, 1mile W; woods in the A/F circuit.

LANDING AREA SURFACE : Hardcore & tarmac.

QDM: 077. LENGTH X WIDTH: 1600 x 50yds. Ext: -
: 024. : 1600 x 50yds. : -
: : :
: : :

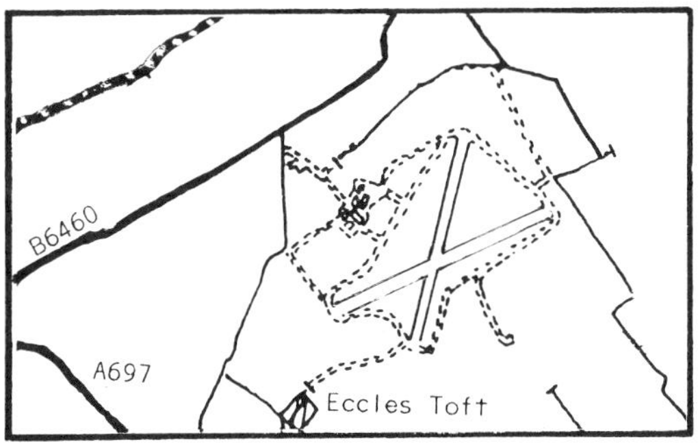

EXTENSIBILITY : -

ACCOMMODATION : Temporary.
HANGARS : Bellman-4;Blister-7.

HARDSTANDINGS : 38.

R.A.F. : OFFICERS: 106.S.N.C.O's.: 110.O.R's.: 1176.TOTAL: 1392.
W.A.A.F.: " : 20. " : 20. " : 424. " : 464.

AFFILIATED AIRFIELDS : Winfield[Satellite]

PRESENT USE [1985] : Disused.

AIRFIELD NAME: CHEDBURGH. OPENED : 1942.
COUNTY : Suffolk. CLOSED : 1952.
COMMAND : Bomber.
FORMATION : 3 Grp[Exning] GRID REF: M 243754[86]
FUNCTION : Operational. O.S.REF.: TL 790570.

LOCALITY : 6miles SW of Bury St Edmunds.
RAILWAY STN. : Bury St Edmunds[LNER]

LATITUDE : 52 10 53N. HEIGHT ASL : 410′ LIGHTING : Mk2.
LONGITUDE : 00 37 15E. FLYING CONTROL : Yes. RADIO : QDM.

LANDMARKS DAY : -

LANDMARKS NIGHT : -

OBSTRUCTIONS : -

LANDING AREA SURFACE : Concrete.

QDM	LENGTH X WIDTH	Ext
173.	1400 x 50yds.	2000yds.
231.	2000 x 50yds.	3000yds.
302.	1400 x 50yds.	2000yds.
:	:	:

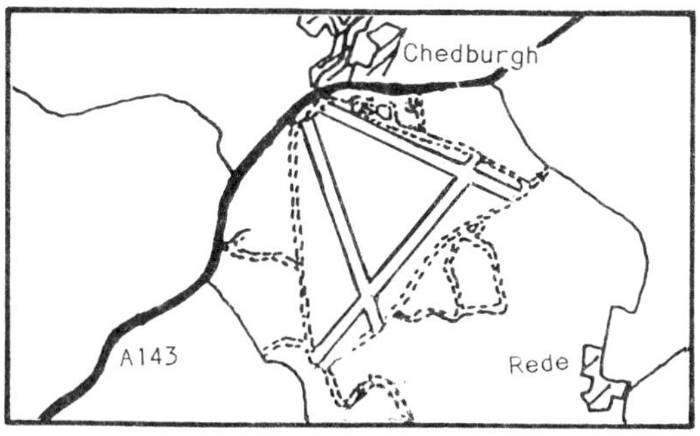

EXTENSIBILITY : Entails demolition of 4 houses & closure of main road to B-St-E.
ACCOMMODATION : Temporary.
HANGARS : T2-2;Glider-3;B1-1.

HARDSTANDINGS : Heavy bomber-36.

	OFFICERS	S.N.C.O's.	O.R's.	TOTAL
R.A.F.	161.	495.	966.	1622.
W.A.A.F.	10.	9.	222.	241.

AFFILIATED AIRFIELDS : Stradishall[31 Base]

PRESENT USE [1985] : Disused.

AIRFIELD NAME: CHEDDINGTON. OPENED : 1942.
COUNTY : Buckinghamshire. CLOSED :
COMMAND : 8th USAAF.
FORMATION : RCM&Night Leaflet Sqdns. GRID REF: L 360355[95]
FUNCTION : Operational. O.S.REF.: SP 910160.

LOCALITY : 6.75miles ENE of Aylesbury.
RAILWAY STN. : Aylesbury 2.5miles[LMS]

LATITUDE : 51 50 00N. HEIGHT ASL : 300′ LIGHTING : Mk2.
LONGITUDE : 00 40 45W. FLYING CONTROL : Yes. RADIO : QDM.

LANDMARKS DAY : Canals & reservoirs E. Chimney, Pitstone cement wks 1mile ESE. Railways E & 1mile N. 2 hills N adjoining boundary 150′ above A/F level.

LANDMARKS NIGHT : Canals & reservoirs E & S.

OBSTRUCTIONS : Hills 150′ above A/F level adjoining N boundary. Will be marked by night by obstruction lights.

LANDING AREA SURFACE : Concrete & wood chippings.

QDM	LENGTH X WIDTH	Ext
200.	1400 x 50yds.	-
140.	1400 x 50yds.	-
260.	1800 x 50yds	-

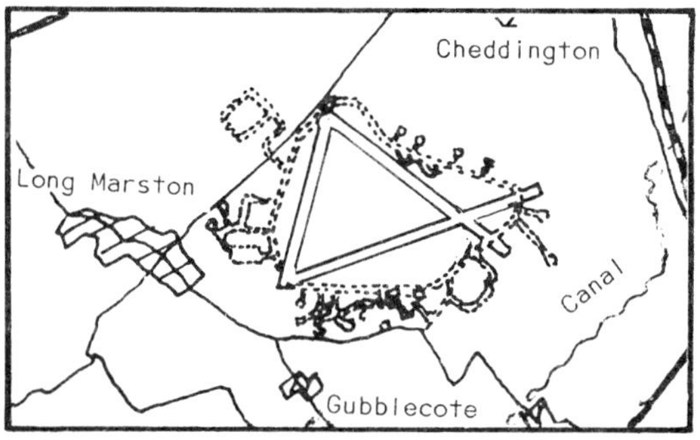

EXTENSIBILITY : None possible.

ACCOMMODATION : Temporary.
HANGARS : T2-4.

HARDSTANDINGS : Loop-37.

USAAF. : OFFICERS: 558. Enlisted Men. : 1993. TOTAL: 2551.

AFFILIATED AIRFIELDS : -

PRESENT USE [1985] : Army.

AIRFIELD NAME: CHEDWORTH. OPENED : 1942.
COUNTY : Gloucestershire. CLOSED : 1946.
COMMAND : Fighter.
FORMATION : 12 Grp[Watnall] GRID REF: P 488333[93]
FUNCTION : Tactical Exercise Unit. O.S.REF.: SP 042131.

LOCALITY : 8miles SE of Cheltenham.
RAILWAY STN. : Cheltenham 10.5miles[GWR]

LATITUDE : 51 48 53N. HEIGHT ASL : 826′ LIGHTING : None.
LONGITUDE : 01 56 23W. FLYING CONTROL : None. RADIO : QDM.

LANDMARKS DAY : Withington Woods & Chedworth Woods N of A/F.

LANDMARKS NIGHT : -

OBSTRUCTIONS : -

LANDING AREA SURFACE : Tarmac.

QDM	LENGTH X WIDTH	Ext
035.	1400 x 50yds.	-
115.	1300 x 50yds.	-
:	:	:
:	:	:

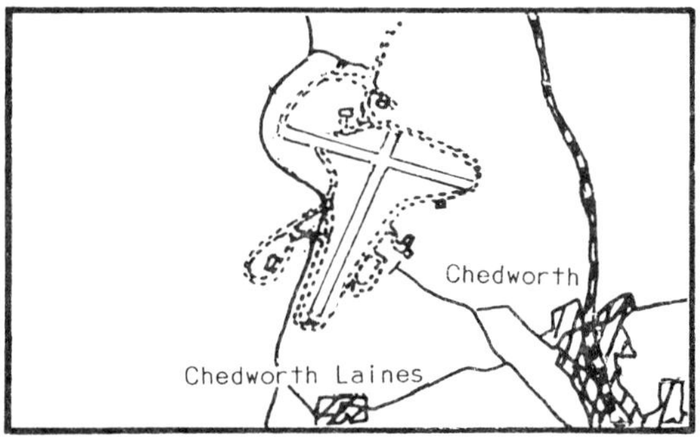

EXTENSIBILITY : None possible.

ACCOMMODATION : Temporary.
HANGARS : EO blister-2.

HARDSTANDINGS : 25.

	OFFICERS	S.N.C.O's.	O.R's.	TOTAL
R.A.F.	21.	120.	465.	606.
W.A.A.F.	1.	5.	60.	66.

AFFILIATED AIRFIELDS : Aston Down[Parent]

PRESENT USE [1985] : Agriculture.

NO: 121.

AIRFIELD NAME: CHELVESTON. OPENED : 1941.
COUNTY : Northamptonshire. CLOSED :
COMMAND : 8th USAAF.
FORMATION : 305th Bomb Group. GRID REF: L 458883[74]
FUNCTION : Operational. O.S.REF.: TL 006685.

LOCALITY : 6.5miles S of Thrapston.
RAILWAY STN. : Higham Ferrers 4miles[GWR]

LATITUDE : 52 18 15N. HEIGHT ASL : 292′ LIGHTING : Mk2.
LONGITUDE : 00 31 23W. FLYING CONTROL : Yes. RADIO : QDM.

LANDMARKS DAY : Higham Ferrers church spire 2.5miles W.

LANDMARKS NIGHT : -

OBSTRUCTIONS : -

LANDING AREA SURFACE : Concrete & tarmac.

QDM: 060. LENGTH X WIDTH: 2000 x 50yds. Ext: 4000yds.
: 180. : 1389 x 50yds. : 1600yds.
: 120. : 1200 x 50yds. : 2000yds.
: : :

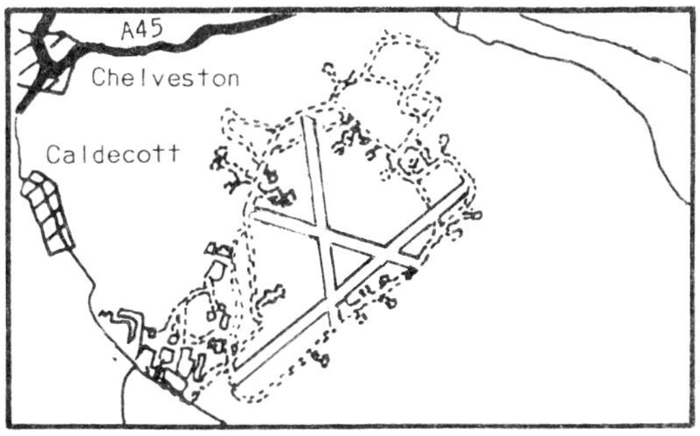

EXTENSIBILITY : Entails demolition of dispersal site & 2 water towers.
ACCOMMODATION : Temporary.
HANGARS : T2-2;Type J-1.

HARDSTANDINGS : Loop-50.

USAAF. : OFFICERS: 421. Enlisted Men. : 2473.TOTAL: 2894.

AFFILIATED AIRFIELDS : -

PRESENT USE [1985] : USAFE.

NO: 122.

AIRFIELD NAME: CHETWYND. OPENED : 1941.
COUNTY : Shropshire. CLOSED :
COMMAND : Flying Training.
FORMATION : 21 Grp[Spittlegate] GRID REF: K 185447[61]
FUNCTION : Advanced Flying Unit. O.S.REF.: SJ 725254.

LOCALITY : 2.5miles NNW of Newport.
RAILWAY STN. : Newport,Salop[LMS]

LATITUDE : 52 48 45N. HEIGHT ASL : 265′ LIGHTING : None.
LONGITUDE : 02 24 23W. FLYING CONTROL : None.RADIO : QDM.

LANDMARKS DAY : The Wrekin 10miles SE. Red warning lights 1335′

LANDMARKS NIGHT : -

OBSTRUCTIONS : H/T cables running S to E of A/F 2000yds distant.

LANDING AREA SURFACE : Grass.

QDM: N-S. LENGTH X WIDTH: 1200yds. Ext: 1600yds.
: E-W. : 1150yds. : 1300yds.
: : : 1200yds.
: : :

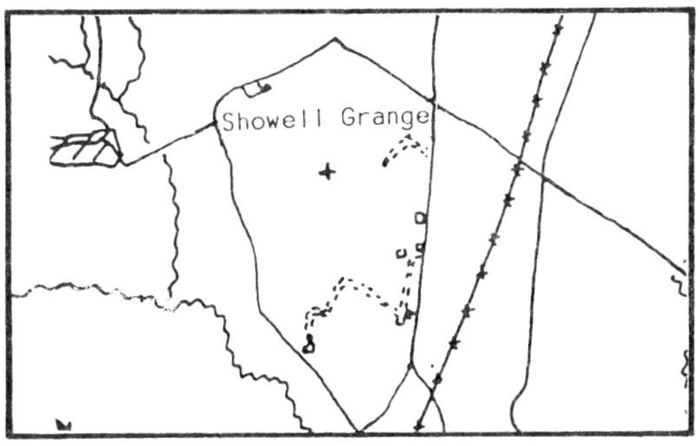

EXTENSIBILITY : Entails demolition of a farm to N.

ACCOMMODATION : Temporary.
HANGARS : 65′ Blister-7.

HARDSTANDINGS : -

R.A.F. : OFFICERS: 11. S.N.C.O′s.: 4. O.R′s.: 134. TOTAL: 149.
W.A.A.F.: " : - " : - " : - " : -

AFFILIATED AIRFIELDS : Ternhill[Parent]

PRESENT USE [1985] : Unspecified.

NO: 123.

AIRFIELD NAME: CHILBOLTON. OPENED : 1940.
COUNTY : Hampshire. CLOSED : 1961.
COMMAND : Fighter.
FORMATION : 11 Grp[Uxbridge] GRID REF: U 834584[123]
FUNCTION : Operational. O.S.REF.: SU 393385.

LOCALITY : 4miles SE of Andover.
RAILWAY STN. : Fullerton Junction 1mile[SR]

LATITUDE : 51 08 38N. HEIGHT ASL : 300′ LIGHTING : Mk2.
LONGITUDE : 01 26 08W. FLYING CONTROL : Yes. RADIO : QDM.

LANDMARKS DAY : -

LANDMARKS NIGHT : -

OBSTRUCTIONS : -

LANDING AREA SURFACE : Concrete, tarmac & wood chippings.

QDM: 200. LENGTH X WIDTH: 1800 x 50yds. Ext: -
: 300. : 1600 x 50yds. : -
: 250. : 1400 x 50yds. : -
: : :

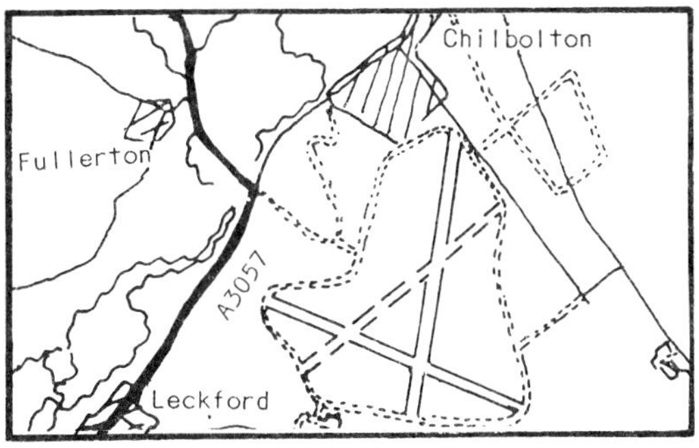

EXTENSIBILITY : None possible.

ACCOMMODATION : Temporary.
HANGARS : T2-2;blister-3.

HARDSTANDINGS : Loop-48.

R.A.F. : OFFICERS: 225.S.N.C.O′s.: 638.O.R′s.: 1937.TOTAL: 2800.
W.A.A.F.: " : - " : - " : - " : -

AFFILIATED AIRFIELDS : Middle Wallop[Sector]

PRESENT USE [1985] : Radio Research Station.

NO: 124.

AIRFIELD NAME: CHIPPING NORTON. OPENED : 1940.
COUNTY : Oxfordshire. CLOSED : 1945.
COMMAND : Flying Training.
FORMATION : 23 Grp[South Cerney] GRID REF: P 773455[93]
FUNCTION : Advanced Training Unit. [satellite] O.S.REF.: SP 325253.
LOCALITY : 1.5miles SSE of Chipping Norton.
RAILWAY STN. : Chipping Norton 2miles[GWR]

LATITUDE : 51 55 23N. HEIGHT ASL : 690′ LIGHTING : None.
LONGITUDE : 01 31 30W. FLYING CONTROL : None. RADIO : QDM.

LANDMARKS DAY : Wychurch Forest 5miles S, railway running NE 2miles NE.

LANDMARKS NIGHT : R Evantode 3miles S.

OBSTRUCTIONS : Bellman hangars NE side; farm buildings centre S side; trees NE side; buildings SE side.

LANDING AREA SURFACE : Steel Matting[Sommerfeld track]

QDM	LENGTH X WIDTH	Ext
117.	1010yds.	1800yds.
064.	973yds.	1400yds.
		1400yds.

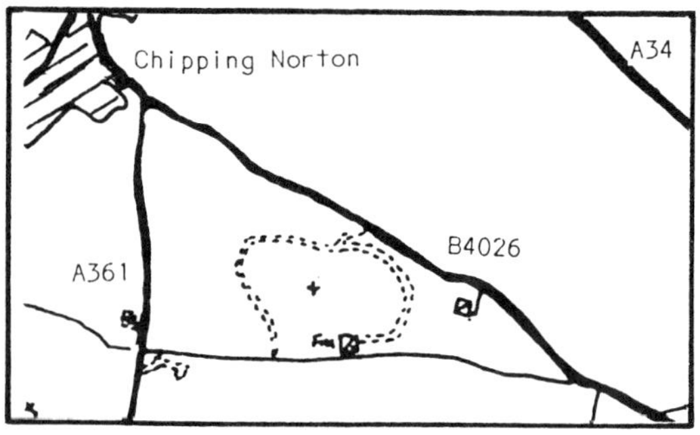

EXTENSIBILITY : -

ACCOMMODATION : Temporary.
HANGARS : Bellman-2;65′ blister-10.

HARDSTANDINGS : None.

R.A.F. : OFFICERS: 110.S.N.C.O′s.: 208.O.R′s.: 886. TOTAL: 1204.
W.A.A.F.: " : 4. " : 3. " : 180. " : 187.

AFFILIATED AIRFIELDS : Little Rissington[Parent]

PRESENT USE [1985] : Agriculture.

NO: 125.

AIRFIELD NAME: CHIPPING ONGAR. OPENED : 1943.
COUNTY : Essex. CLOSED : 1946.
COMMAND : USSTAFE.
FORMATION : Air Disarmament. GRID REF: M 030246[107]
FUNCTION : Operational. O.S.REF.: TL 582055.

LOCALITY : 2 miles NE of Chipping Ongar.
RAILWAY STN. : Ongar 2.75miles[LNER]

LATITUDE : 51 43 48N. HEIGHT ASL : 250′ LIGHTING : Mk2.
LONGITUDE : 00 17 40E. FLYING CONTROL : Yes RADIO : QDM.

LANDMARKS DAY : North Weald radio towers.

LANDMARKS NIGHT : R Roding.

OBSTRUCTIONS : -

LANDING AREA SURFACE : Concrete & wood chippings.

QDM	LENGTH X WIDTH	Ext
030.	2000 x 50yds.	-
090.	1400 x 50yds.	1800yds.
150.	1400 x 50yds.	2300yds.

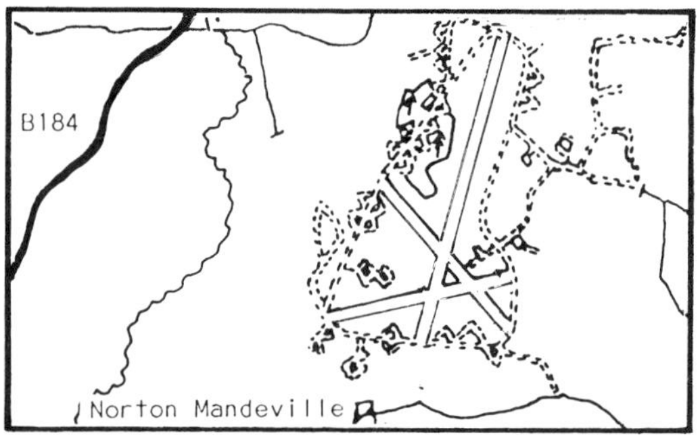

EXTENSIBILITY : Requires very heavy filling to R/W 2.

ACCOMMODATION : Temporary.
HANGARS : T2-2.

HARDSTANDINGS : Loop-50.

USAAF. : OFFICERS: 443. Enlisted Men. : 2327.TOTAL: 2770.

AFFILIATED AIRFIELDS : -

PRESENT USE [1985] : Agriculture.

NO: 126.

AIRFIELD NAME: CHIPPING WARDEN. OPENED : 1941.
COUNTY : Oxfordshire. CLOSED : 1946.
COMMAND : Bomber.
FORMATION : 92 Grp[Winslow] GRID REF: P 946697[83]
FUNCTION : Operational Training Unit. O.S.REF.: SP 495498.
LOCALITY : 6miles NNE of Banbury.
RAILWAY STN. : Banbury 7miles[LMS]

LATITUDE : 52 08 40N. HEIGHT ASL : 457′ LIGHTING : Mk2.
LONGITUDE : 01 16 30W. FLYING CONTROL : Yes. RADIO : QDM.

LANDMARKS DAY : Reservoir 2miles N.

LANDMARKS NIGHT : As day.

OBSTRUCTIONS : Hills 1200′ NNE, 624′ ASL; hills 1000′ ENE, 586′ASL

LANDING AREA SURFACE : Concrete.

QDM	LENGTH X WIDTH	Ext
133.	1100 x 50yds.	1433yds.
253.	1600 x 50yds.	2227yds.
011.	1400 x 50yds.	1466yds.

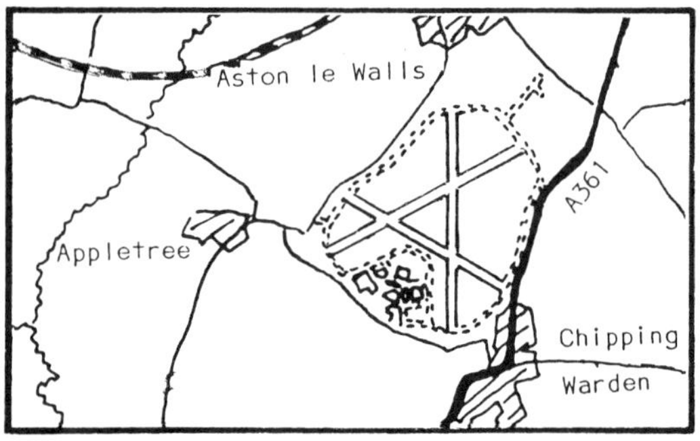

EXTENSIBILITY : Entails demolition of 2 cottages & some RAF bungalows.
ACCOMMODATION : Temporary.
HANGARS : Type J-1;T2-4.

HARDSTANDINGS : Heavy Bomber-30.

R.A.F. : OFFICERS: 171.S.N.C.O′s.: 610.O.R′s.: 1704.TOTAL: 2485.
W.A.A.F.: " : 12. " : 15. " : 417. " : 444.

AFFILIATED AIRFIELDS : Edgehill[Satellite]

PRESENT USE [1985] : Disused.

AIRFIELD NAME: CHIVENOR. OPENED : 1940.
COUNTY : Devonshire. CLOSED :
COMMAND : Coastal.
FORMATION : 19 Grp[Plymouth] GRID REF: S 930565[118]
FUNCTION : Operational. O.S.REF.: SS 492344.

LOCALITY : 4.5miles W of Barnstaple.
RAILWAY STN. : Wrafton 1mile[SR]

LATITUDE : 51 05 18N. HEIGHT ASL : 16′ LIGHTING : Mk2.
LONGITUDE : 04 09 00W. FLYING CONTROL : Yes. RADIO : QDM.

LANDMARKS DAY : Estuary.

LANDMARKS NIGHT : -

OBSTRUCTIONS : Church on hill 040degrees T, 1mile 250′; masts 235degrees T, 4miles 325′; masts on hill 320 degrees T, 3miles 500′

LANDING AREA SURFACE : Concrete covered with asphalt.

QDM: 102. LENGTH X WIDTH: 2000 x 50yds. Ext: -
: 242. : 1460 x 50yds. : -
: 162. : 1170 x 50yds. : -

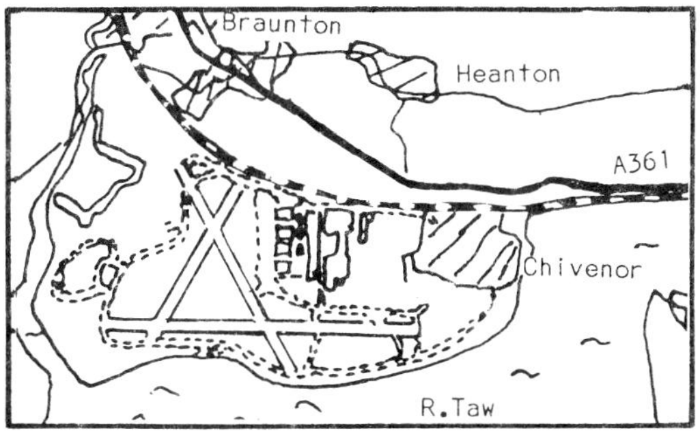

EXTENSIBILITY : None possible.

ACCOMMODATION : Temporary.
HANGARS : EO blister-1;Bellman-4;Hinaidi-4.

HARDSTANDINGS : Spectacle[concrete]-45;150′ dia-5.

R.A.F. : OFFICERS: 266.S.N.C.O′s.: 506.O.R′s.: 1906.TOTAL: 2678.
W.A.A.F.: " : 2. " : – " : 331. " : 333.

AFFILIATED AIRFIELDS : -

PRESENT USE [1985] : RAF.

AIRFIELD NAME: CHRISTCHURCH. OPENED : 1935.
COUNTY : Hampshire. CLOSED : 1967.
COMMAND : Fighter.
FORMATION : 11 Grp[Uxbridge] GRID REF: U 612131[141]
FUNCTION : Operational O.S.REF.: SZ 186933.

LOCALITY : 1.5miles E of Christchurch.
RAILWAY STN. : Christchurch[SR]

LATITUDE : 50 44 03N. HEIGHT ASL : 20′ LIGHTING : None.
LONGITUDE : 01 44 53W. FLYING CONTROL : None.RADIO : QDM.

LANDMARKS DAY : Christchurch harbour to SSW.

LANDMARKS NIGHT : As day.

OBSTRUCTIONS : -

LANDING AREA SURFACE : Steel Matting[BRC netting track], 245 concrete & grass.

QDM: 245. LENGTH X WIDTH: 1650 x 50yds. Ext: -
: N-S. : 1000yds. : -
: NE-SW. : 1000yds. : -
: E-W. : 1000yds. : -
: NW-SE. : 950yds. : -

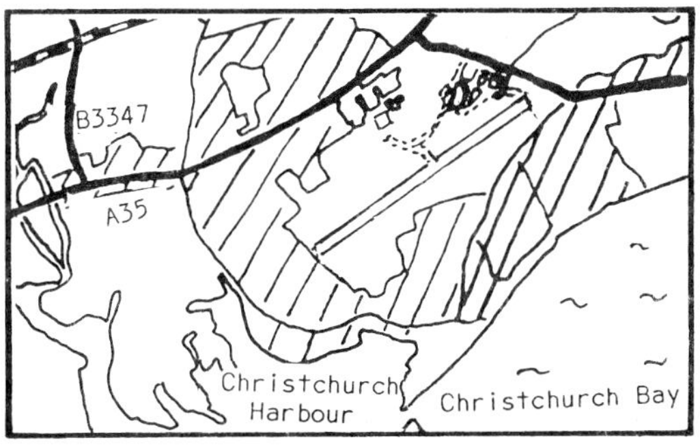

EXTENSIBILITY : Possible to obtain 2 strips of 1800 & 1400yds.

ACCOMMODATION : Temporary.
HANGARS : Bellman-1;Bessoneau-1;EO blister-3.

HARDSTANDINGS : None.

R.A.F. : OFFICERS: 4. S.N.C.O′s.: 9. O.R′s.: 236. TOTAL: 249.
W.A.A.F.: " : - " : - " : - " : -

AFFILIATED AIRFIELDS : Middle Wallop[Sector]

PRESENT USE [1985] : Industry.

AIRFIELD NAME: CHURCH BROUGHTON. OPENED : 1942.
COUNTY : Derbyshire. CLOSED : 1945.
COMMAND : Bomber.
FORMATION : 93 Grp[Egginton] GRID REF: K 665525[53]
FUNCTION : Operational Training Unit[satellite] O.S.REF.: SK 205325.
LOCALITY : 9miles W of Derby.
RAILWAY STN. : Tutbury 2miles[LMS]

LATITUDE : 52 53 08N. HEIGHT ASL : 225′ LIGHTING : Mk2.
LONGITUDE : 01 41 45W. FLYING CONTROL : Yes. RADIO : QDM.

LANDMARKS DAY : Railway adjacent to river & running parallel, S of A/F.

LANDMARKS NIGHT : River running W to E .5miles S of A/F.

OBSTRUCTIONS : Hanbury Hill 476′ 3miles SW by W.

LANDING AREA SURFACE : Concrete & tarmac.

QDM: 015. LENGTH X WIDTH: 1400 x 50yds. Ext: 2500yds.
: 064. : 1900 x 50yds. : 3000yds.
: 125. : 1350 x 50yds. : 2000yds.
: : :

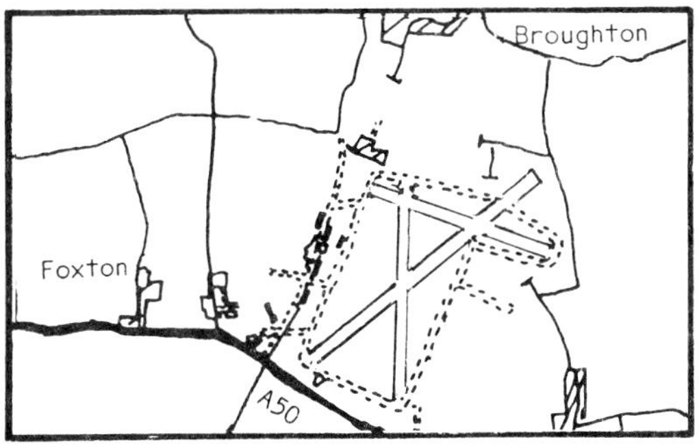

EXTENSIBILITY : Restrict to 2000,1900 & 1400yds to obviate serious demolition.
ACCOMMODATION : Temporary.
HANGARS : T2-1;B1-1.

HARDSTANDINGS : Heavy bomber-27.

R.A.F. : OFFICERS: 109.S.N.C.O′s.: 157.O.R′s.: 1008.TOTAL: 1274.
W.A.A.F.: " : 2. " : 4. " : 150. " : 156.

AFFILIATED AIRFIELDS : Lichfield[Parent]

PRESENT USE [1985] : Disused.

NO: 130.

AIRFIELD NAME: CHURCH FENTON.   OPENED : 1937.
COUNTY : Yorkshire.   CLOSED :
COMMAND : Fighter.
FORMATION : 12 Grp[Watnall]   GRID REF: E 000577[32]
FUNCTION : Operational[Sector]   O.S.REF.: SE 531378.

LOCALITY : 4miles SE of Tadcaster.
RAILWAY STN. : Church Fenton 1.5miles[LNER]

LATITUDE : 53 50 00N. HEIGHT ASL : 27′ LIGHTING : Mk2.
LONGITUDE : 01 12 00W. FLYING CONTROL : Yes. RADIO : QDM.

LANDMARKS DAY : Town of Tadcaster 4miles NW.

LANDMARKS NIGHT : River running approx W-E on N side of A/F. Railway running N-S on W side of A/F.

OBSTRUCTIONS : None.

LANDING AREA SURFACE : Concrete & tarmac.

QDM	LENGTH X WIDTH	Ext
245.	1400 x 50yds.	4000yds.
168.	1600 x 50yds.	3000yds.
		3000yds.

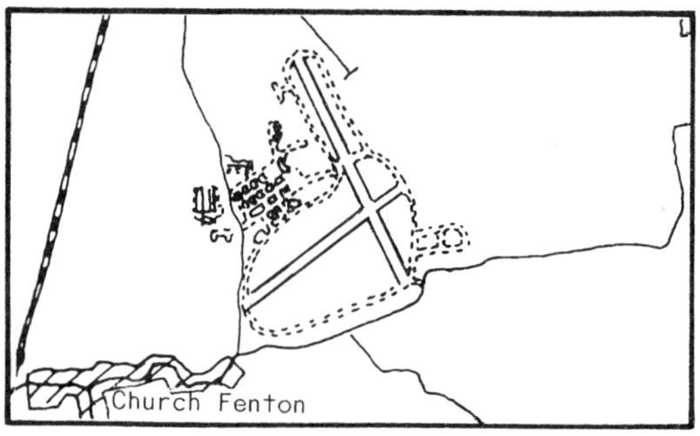

EXTENSIBILITY : Restrict to 1600, 2000 & 1600yds to obviate diversion of lanes.
ACCOMMODATION : Permanent.
HANGARS : Type C-2;EO blister-10;Bellman-1.

HARDSTANDINGS : SE-4.

	OFFICERS	S.N.C.O′s.	O.R′s.	TOTAL
R.A.F.	119.	150.	976.	1245.
W.A.A.F.	12.	10.	308.	330.

AFFILIATED AIRFIELDS : Hutton Cranswick, York[Forward A/F] Wood Vale[Night fighter F/A]
PRESENT USE [1985] : RAF.

NO: 131.

AIRFIELD NAME: CHURCH LAWFORD.   OPENED : 1941.
COUNTY : Warwickshire.   CLOSED : 1955.
COMMAND : Flying Training.
FORMATION : 23 Grp[South Cerney]   GRID REF: K 902935[73]
FUNCTION : Advanced Flying Unit.   O.S.REF.: SP 448736.

LOCALITY : 3.5miles WSW of Rugby.
RAILWAY STN. : Dunchurch 2miles[LMS]

LATITUDE : 52 21 23N. HEIGHT ASL : 366′ LIGHTING : Mk2.
LONGITUDE : 01 20 15W. FLYING CONTROL : Yes. RADIO : QDM.

LANDMARKS DAY : Wireless masts, Rugby; cement wks, Long Itchington.

LANDMARKS NIGHT : -

OBSTRUCTIONS : Rugby wireless masts.

LANDING AREA SURFACE : Concrete covered with tarmac.

QDM	LENGTH X WIDTH	Ext
355.	1420 x 50yds.	1600yds.
045.	1200 x 50yds.	3100yds.
270.	1400 x 50yds.	2500yds.

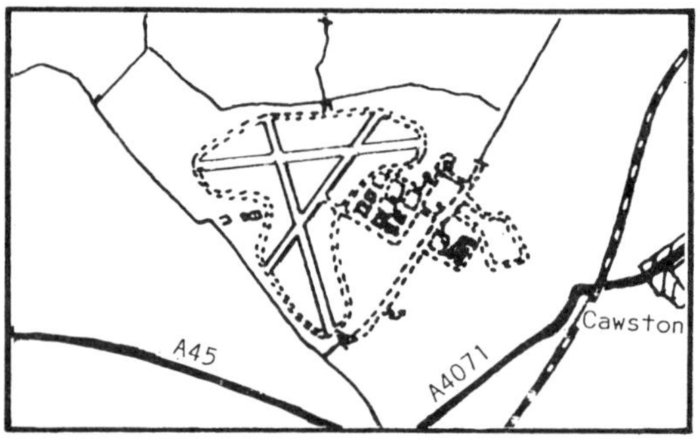

EXTENSIBILITY : Restrict to 1500, 1500 & 2100yds to obviate any diversions & demolitions.
ACCOMMODATION : Temporary.
HANGARS : Bellman-6;ARS[2bay]-1;65′ blister-10.

HARDSTANDINGS : None.

	OFFICERS	S.N.C.O′s.	O.R′s.	TOTAL
R.A.F.	203.	145.	787.	1135.
W.A.A.F.	10.	-	410.	420.

AFFILIATED AIRFIELDS : Snitterfield[Satellite], Warwick[RLG]

PRESENT USE [1985] : Disused.

NO: 132.

AIRFIELD NAME: CLEAVE.   OPENED : 1939.
COUNTY : Cornwall.   CLOSED : 1945.
COMMAND : Fighter.
FORMATION : 70 Grp[Farnborough]   GRID REF: S 640350[127]
FUNCTION : AA Co-Operation Unit.   O.S.REF.: SS 205128.

LOCALITY : 4.5miles N of Bude.
RAILWAY STN. : Bude 7.5miles[SR]

LATITUDE : 50 53 08N. HEIGHT ASL : 400′ LIGHTING : None.
LONGITUDE : 04 33 00W. FLYING CONTROL : None.RADIO : QDM.

LANDMARKS DAY : -

LANDMARKS NIGHT : -

OBSTRUCTIONS : -

LANDING AREA SURFACE : Grass.

QDM	LENGTH X WIDTH	Ext
ENE-WSW.	900yds.	1000yds.
N-S.	750yds.	800yds.
		1000yds.
		1140yds.
		1000yds.

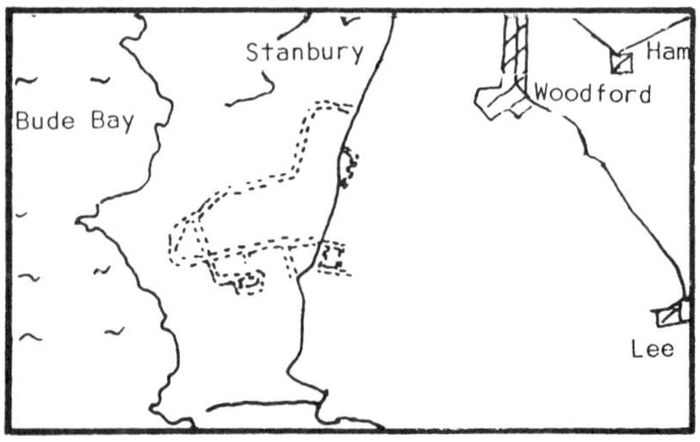

EXTENSIBILITY : -

ACCOMMODATION : Temporary.
HANGARS : Bellmen-2;Blister-1.

HARDSTANDINGS : None.

	OFFICERS	S.N.C.O′s.	O.R′s.	TOTAL
R.A.F.	11.	28.	380.	419.
W.A.A.F.	2.	4.	74.	80.

AFFILIATED AIRFIELDS : -

PRESENT USE [1985] : Radio Research Station.

NO: 133.

AIRFIELD NAME: CLUNTOE. OPENED : 1942.
COUNTY : Tyrone NI. CLOSED : 1955.
COMMAND : RAF NI.
FORMATION : Stormont[Belfast] GRID REF: 945755[313NI]
FUNCTION : Care & Maintenance. O.S.REF.: H 945755.

LOCALITY : 10miles SE of Cookstown.
RAILWAY STN. : Cookstown 10miles[NCC].

LATITUDE : 54 37 10N. HEIGHT ASL : 86′ LIGHTING : Mk 2.
LONGITUDE : 06 32 15W. FLYING CONTROL : Yes. RADIO : QDM.

LANDMARKS DAY : Slieve Galleon 1737′12miles NW, & Lough Neagh .5miles due E.

LANDMARKS NIGHT : Lough Neagh due E.

OBSTRUCTIONS : -

LANDING AREA SURFACE : Concrete & tarmac.

QDM: 240. LENGTH X WIDTH: 2000 x 50yds. Ext: 2650yds.
: 100. : 1400 x 50yds. : 2000yds
: 360. : 1400 x 50yds. : 2000yds.
: : :

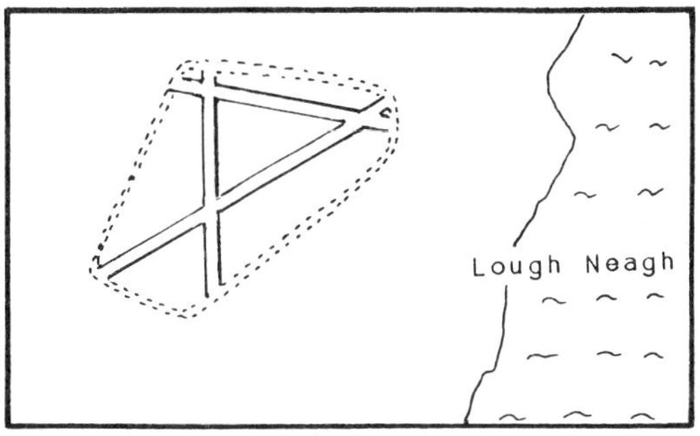

EXTENSIBILITY : Entails diversion of minor road & demo. of farm,cottage & 3 semi-derelict cottages.
ACCOMMODATION : Temporary.
HANGARS : T2-4.

HARDSTANDINGS : 125′ dia frying pan-30;fighter-50.

R.A.F. : OFFICERS: 553.S.N.C.O′s.: - O.R′s.: 1959.TOTAL: 2512.
W.A.A.F.: " : - " : - " : - " : -

AFFILIATED AIRFIELDS : -

PRESENT USE [1985] : Disused.

NO: 134.

AIRFIELD NAME: CLYFFE PYPARD. OPENED : 1941.
COUNTY : Wiltshire. CLOSED : 1947.
COMMAND : Flying Training.
FORMATION : 50 Grp[Reading] GRID REF: U 512960[112]
FUNCTION : Elementary Flying Training School. O.S.REF.: SU 070756.
LOCALITY : 3.5miles S of Wootton Bassett.
RAILWAY STN. : Swindon Junction 11miles[GWR]

LATITUDE : 51 28 45N. HEIGHT ASL : 660′ LIGHTING : None.
LONGITUDE : 01 54 00W. FLYING CONTROL : None.RADIO : QDM.

LANDMARKS DAY : Clenhill monument 3.5miles 190degrees.

LANDMARKS NIGHT : -

OBSTRUCTIONS : Bomb store in N corner of A/F.

LANDING AREA SURFACE : Grass.

QDM: N-S. LENGTH X WIDTH: 1100yds. Ext: -
: NE-SW. : 1160yds. : -
: E-W. : 1333yds. : -
: NW-ES. : 1050yds. : -

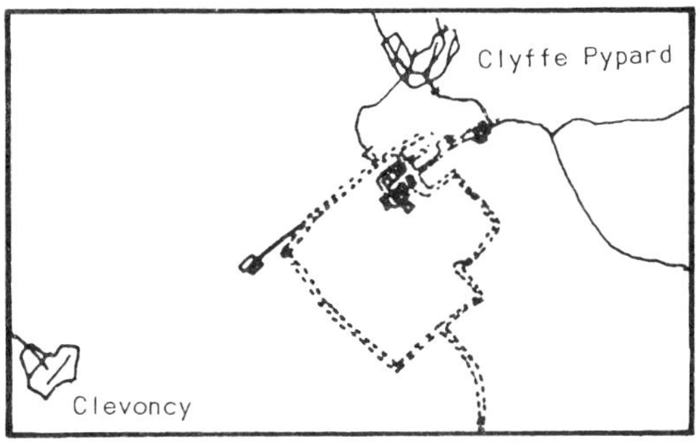

EXTENSIBILITY : None possible.

ACCOMMODATION : Temporary.
HANGARS : Bellman-4;O blister-1;Standard blister-14.

HARDSTANDINGS : None.

R.A.F. : OFFICERS: 48. S.N.C.O′s.: 98. O.R′s.: 482. TOTAL: 628.
W.A.A.F.: " : - " : - " : - " : -

AFFILIATED AIRFIELDS : Alton Barnes[RLG]

PRESENT USE [1985] : Agriculture.

NO: 135.

AIRFIELD NAME: COLEBY GRANGE. OPENED : 1940.
COUNTY : Lincolnshire. CLOSED : 1963.
COMMAND : Technical Training.
FORMATION : 27 Grp[Cirencester] GRID REF: F 470800[47]
FUNCTION : Radio School. O.S.REF.: TF 005605.

LOCALITY : 6miles S of Lincoln.
RAILWAY STN. : Lincoln 8miles[LMS & LNER]

LATITUDE : 53 07 53N. HEIGHT ASL : 200′ LIGHTING : Mk2.
LONGITUDE : 00 29 53W. FLYING CONTROL : Yes. RADIO : QDM.

LANDMARKS DAY : -

LANDMARKS NIGHT : -

OBSTRUCTIONS : -

LANDING AREA SURFACE : Grass.

QDM: NE-SW. LENGTH X WIDTH: 2000yds. Ext: -
: NW-SE. : 1400yds. : 1600yds.
: N-S. : 966yds. : 1400yds.
: : :

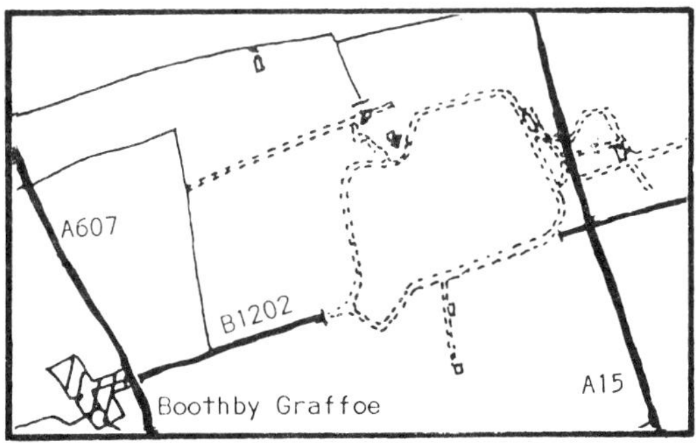

EXTENSIBILITY : Road diversion necessary if No 2 strip extended to 1600yds.
ACCOMMODATION : Temporary.
HANGARS : T1-1;Blister-1;EO blister-7.

HARDSTANDINGS : TE-7.

R.A.F. : OFFICERS: 78. S.N.C.O′s.: 102.O.R′s.: 1066.TOTAL: 1246.
W.A.A.F.: " : 2. " : 1. " : 135. " : 138.

AFFILIATED AIRFIELDS : Cranwell[Parent]

PRESENT USE [1985] : Agriculture.

AIRFIELD NAME: COLERNE. OPENED : 1940.
COUNTY : Wiltshire. CLOSED :
COMMAND : Fighter.
FORMATION : 10 Grp[Rudloe Manor] GRID REF: U 248935[111]
FUNCTION : Sector. O.S.REF.: ST 803715.

LOCALITY : 6miles NNE of Bath.
RAILWAY STN. : Box 4miles[GWR]

LATITUDE : 51 26 45N. HEIGHT ASL : 588′ LIGHTING : Mk2.
LONGITUDE : 02 16 45W. FLYING CONTROL : Yes. RADIO : QDM.

LANDMARKS DAY : -

LANDMARKS NIGHT : -

OBSTRUCTIONS : -

LANDING AREA SURFACE : Tarmac.

QDM	LENGTH X WIDTH	Ext
196.	1200 x 50yds.	2430yds.
256.	1950 x 50yds.	2040yds.
302.	1150 x 50yds.	1050yds.

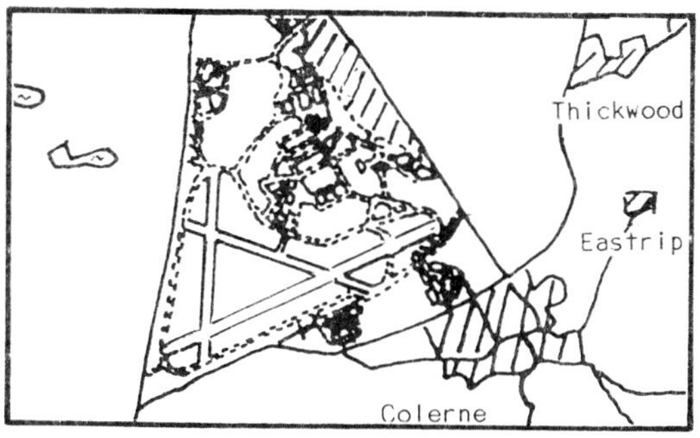

EXTENSIBILITY : Entails demolition of hangars.

ACCOMMODATION : Permanent.
HANGARS : Type J-1;O blister-1;Type K-3, Type L-5;Robin-6.
HARDSTANDINGS : TE-16;Fortress-1.

R.A.F. : OFFICERS: 143.S.N.C.O′s.: 266.O.R′s.: 2646.TOTAL: 3055.
W.A.A.F.: " : 24. " : 19. " : 242. " : 285.

AFFILIATED AIRFIELDS : Defford[FA]Fairwood Common[NF-FA]

PRESENT USE [1985] : RAF.

AIRFIELD NAME: COLLYWESTON. OPENED : 1940.
COUNTY : Northamptonshire. CLOSED :
COMMAND : Fighter.
FORMATION : 12 Grp[Watnall] GRID REF: F 468214[64]
FUNCTION : Operational. O.S.REF.: TF 015023.

LOCALITY : 3miles SSW of Stamford.
RAILWAY STN. : Ketton 1.5miles[LNER]

LATITUDE : 52 36 00N. HEIGHT ASL : 282′ LIGHTING : Mk2.
LONGITUDE : 00 30 00W. FLYING CONTROL : Yes. RADIO : QDM.

LANDMARKS DAY : Ketton cement works.

LANDMARKS NIGHT : -

OBSTRUCTIONS : -

LANDING AREA SURFACE : Grass.

QDM	LENGTH X WIDTH	Ext
N-S.	1500yds.	-
NE-SW.	1460yds.	-
E-W.	1000yds.	-
SE-NW.	1260yds.	-

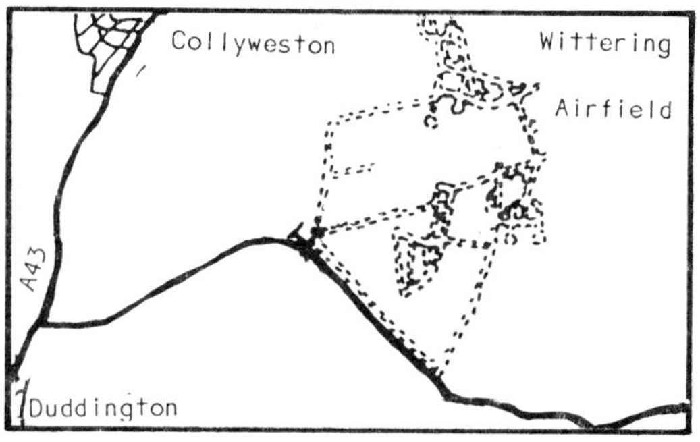

EXTENSIBILITY : -

ACCOMMODATION : Temporary.
HANGARS : O blister-4.

HARDSTANDINGS : 6.

R.A.F. : OFFICERS: 24. S.N.C.O′s.: 98. O.R′s.: 552. TOTAL: 674.
W.A.A.F.: " : 2. " : 4. " : 60. " : 66.

AFFILIATED AIRFIELDS : Digby[Sector]

PRESENT USE [1985] : RAF.

AIRFIELD NAME: COLTISHALL. OPENED : 1940.
COUNTY : Norfolk. CLOSED :
COMMAND : Fighter.
FORMATION : 12 Grp[Watnall] GRID REF: G 725407[67]
FUNCTION : Sector. O.S.REF.: TG 262225.

LOCALITY : 8miles NNE of Norwich.
RAILWAY STN. : Buxton Lomas[LNER]via Norwich.

LATITUDE : 52 45 15N. HEIGHT ASL : 57′ LIGHTING : Mk2.
LONGITUDE : 01 21 30E. FLYING CONTROL : Yes. RADIO : QDM.

LANDMARKS DAY : -

LANDMARKS NIGHT : -

OBSTRUCTIONS : None.

LANDING AREA SURFACE : Steel Matting[Sommerfeld track]

QDM	LENGTH X WIDTH	Ext
096.	2000yds.	-
050.	1600yds.	3000yds.
150.	1400yds.	2000yds.

EXTENSIBILITY : Entails very slight demolition.

ACCOMMODATION : Permanent.
HANGARS : Type C-4;O Blister-6;EO blister-2.

HARDSTANDINGS : SE-6;TE-14.

R.A.F. : OFFICERS: 137.S.N.C.O′s.: 190.O.R′s.: 1876.TOTAL: 2203.
W.A.A.F.: " : 9. " : 8. " : 488. " : 505.

AFFILIATED AIRFIELDS : Matlast.

PRESENT USE [1985] : RAF.

AIRFIELD NAME: CONDOVER. OPENED : 1942.
COUNTY : Shropshire. CLOSED : 1945.
COMMAND : Flying Training.
FORMATION : 21 Grp[Spittlegate] GRID REF: J 902255[60]
FUNCTION : Advanced Flying Unit. O.S.REF.: SJ 505045.

LOCALITY : 4.5miles S of Shrewsbury.
RAILWAY STN. : Dorrington 2miles[GWR & LMS]

LATITUDE : 52 38 08N. HEIGHT ASL : 420′ LIGHTING : Mk2.
LONGITUDE : 02 43 45W. FLYING CONTROL : Yes. RADIO : QDM.

LANDMARKS DAY : Wrekin[1335′] 081degrees 8miles.

LANDMARKS NIGHT : As day lit by 2 red obstruction lights.

OBSTRUCTIONS : -

LANDING AREA SURFACE : Concrete & wood chippings.

QDM	LENGTH X WIDTH	Ext
180.	1330 x 50yds.	1400yds.
110.	1380 x 50yds.	1650yds.
050.	1145 x 50yds.	1600yds.

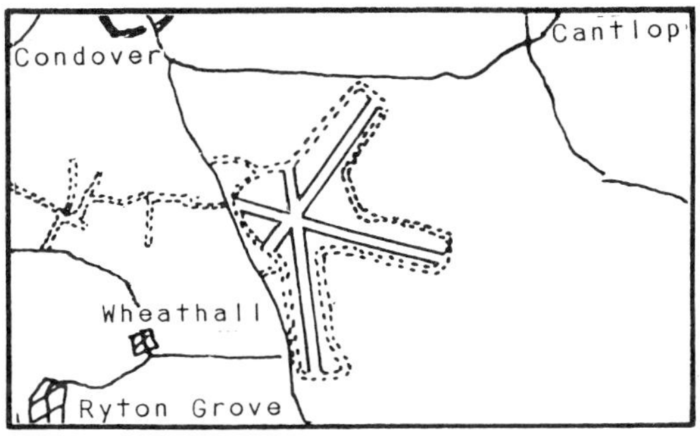

EXTENSIBILITY : Entails slight demolition.

ACCOMMODATION : Temporary.
HANGARS : T1-1;65′ blister-4;69′ blister-5.

HARDSTANDINGS : Rectangular concrete-2.

R.A.F. : OFFICERS: 67. S.N.C.O′s.: 101.O.R′s.: 493. TOTAL: 661.
W.A.A.F.: " : 8. " : 1. " : 89. " : 98.

AFFILIATED AIRFIELDS : Ternhill[Parent]

PRESENT USE [1985] : Disused.

AIRFIELD NAME: CONINGSBY. OPENED : 1940.
COUNTY : Lincolnshire. CLOSED :
COMMAND : Bomber.
FORMATION : 5 Grp[Morton Hall] GRID REF: F 688760[47]
FUNCTION : Operational[54 Base] O.S.REF.: TF 225565.

LOCALITY : 7.5miles SSW of Horncastle.
RAILWAY STN. : Horncastle 7.5miles[LNER], Boston 11miles[LNER]

LATITUDE : 53 05 30N. HEIGHT ASL : 25′ LIGHTING : Mk2.
LONGITUDE : 00 10 15W. FLYING CONTROL : Yes. RADIO : QDM.

LANDMARKS DAY : Windmill 100′, Coningsby village, Tattershall Castle.

LANDMARKS NIGHT : -

OBSTRUCTIONS : Tattershall Castle 180′-2000yds.

LANDING AREA SURFACE : Concrete & Asphalt.

QDM	LENGTH X WIDTH	Ext
217.	1400 x 50yds.	5000yds.
264.	1950 x 50yds.	2800yds.
306.	1550 x 50yds.	2600yds.

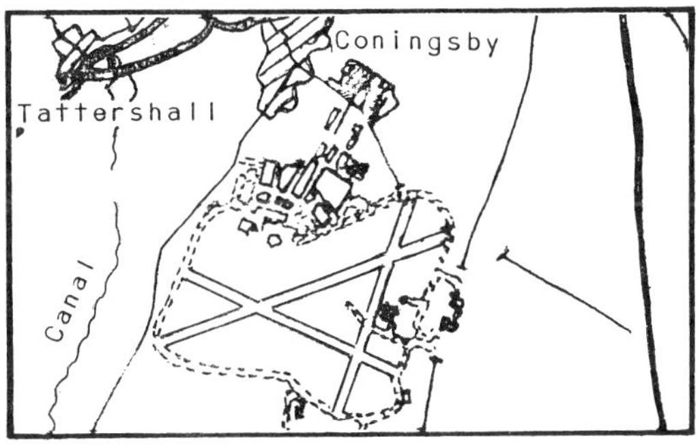

EXTENSIBILITY : Restrict to 3000, 2000 & 2000yds to obviate road closure, diversion & demolition.
ACCOMMODATION : Permanent.
HANGARS : Type J-2;T2-3;B1-1.

HARDSTANDINGS : Heavy bomber-36.

R.A.F. : OFFICERS: 122.S.N.C.O′s.: 396.O.R′s.: 1678.TOTAL: 2196.
W.A.A.F.: " : 13. " : 15. " : 356. " : 384.

AFFILIATED AIRFIELDS : Metheringham & Woodhall Spa[Sub-stations]

PRESENT USE [1985] : RAF.

AIRFIELD NAME: CONNEL. OPENED : 1942.
COUNTY : Argyllshire. CLOSED : 1945.
COMMAND : Coastal.
FORMATION : 17 Grp[Edinburgh] GRID REF: N 411563[54Scot]
FUNCTION : Satellite. O.S.REF.: NM 905351.

LOCALITY : 5miles NE of Oban.
RAILWAY STN. : North Connel Halt[LMS]

LATITUDE : 56 28 00N. HEIGHT ASL : 18′ LIGHTING : None.
LONGITUDE : 05 23 58W. FLYING CONTROL : None.RADIO : QDM.

LANDMARKS DAY : Railway bridge over Loch Ective S of A/F. Railway line adjacent to A/F. Ben Cindchen mountain.

LANDMARKS NIGHT : -

OBSTRUCTIONS : Ben Lora 1007′ 2miles. Hill 800′ NE.

LANDING AREA SURFACE : Tarmac.

QDM	LENGTH X WIDTH	Ext
202.	1400 x 50yds.	-
214.	1050 x 50yds.	-

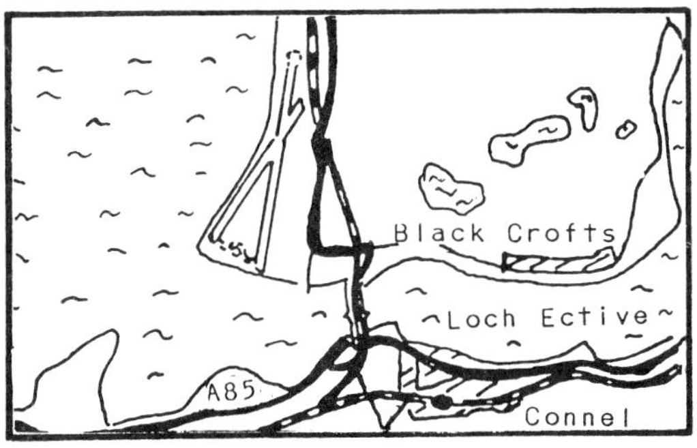

EXTENSIBILITY : None possible.

ACCOMMODATION : Temporary.
HANGARS : T3-2.

HARDSTANDINGS : None.

R.A.F. : OFFICERS: 2. S.N.C.O′s.: 16. O.R′s.: 91. TOTAL: 109.
W.A.A.F.: " : 1. " : 5. " : 25. " : 31.

AFFILIATED AIRFIELDS : Oban flying boat base[Parent]

PRESENT USE [1985] : Private flying.

NO: 142.

AIRFIELD NAME: COOLHAM. OPENED : 1944.
COUNTY : Sussex. CLOSED : 1944.
COMMAND : Fighter.
FORMATION : 11 Grp[Uxbridge] GRID REF: Q 562415[133]
FUNCTION : Advanced Landing Ground. O.S.REF.: TQ 125224.
[De-requisitioned]
LOCALITY : 6miles SSW of Horsham.
RAILWAY STN. : Southwater[SR]

LATITUDE : 50 59 15N HEIGHT ASL : 55' LIGHTING : None.
LONGITUDE : 00 23 45W. FLYING CONTROL : None.RADIO : QDM.

LANDMARKS DAY : Lake 2.5miles 100degreesT from centre of A/F.

LANDMARKS NIGHT : As day.

OBSTRUCTIONS : Hills 5-6miles.

LANDING AREA SURFACE : Steel Matting[Sommerfeld track]

QDM: 050. LENGTH X WIDTH: 1200yds. Ext: -
: 120. : 1500yds. : -
: : :
: : :

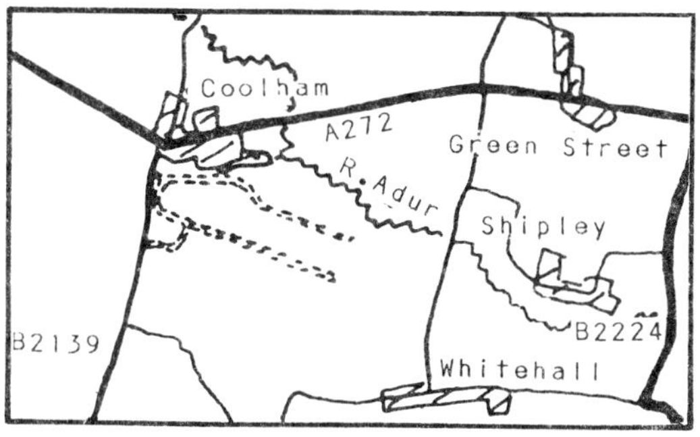

EXTENSIBILITY : -

ACCOMMODATION : Tented camp.
HANGARS : Blister-5.

HARDSTANDINGS : Sommerfeld track-50, hardcore-5.

	OFFICERS:	S.N.C.O's.:	O.R's.:	TOTAL:
R.A.F. :				
W.A.A.F.:	" :	" :	" :	" :

AFFILIATED AIRFIELDS : -

PRESENT USE [1985] : Agriculture.

NO: 143.

AIRFIELD NAME: COSFORD. OPENED : 1938.
COUNTY : Shropshire. CLOSED :
COMMAND : Technical Training.
FORMATION : 24 Grp[Hereford] GRID REF: K 248256[61]
FUNCTION : Technical Training School. O.S.REF.: SJ 792046.
LOCALITY : 8miles NW of Wolverhampton.
RAILWAY STN. : Cosford[GWR]

LATITUDE : 52 38 30N. HEIGHT ASL : 260' LIGHTING : None.
LONGITUDE : 02 18 15W. FLYING CONTROL : Yes. RADIO : QDM.

LANDMARKS DAY : Waterworks stack SW-W. Railway N perimeter.

LANDMARKS NIGHT : -

OBSTRUCTIONS : Chimney 150'-500yds NW corner.Railway embankment E-W.

LANDING AREA SURFACE : Asphalt.

QDM: 073. LENGTH X WIDTH: 1200 x 50yds. Ext: 2200yds.
: : :
: : :

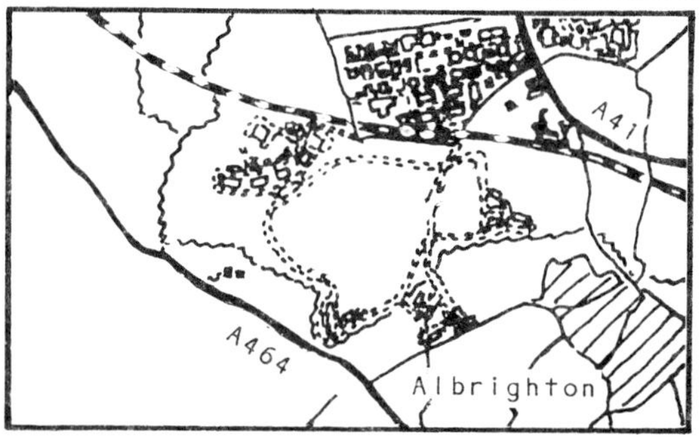

EXTENSIBILITY : Entails slight demolition.

ACCOMMODATION : Permanent.
HANGARS : Various-38.

HARDSTANDINGS : None.

	OFFICERS:	S.N.C.O's.:	O.R's.:	TOTAL:
R.A.F. :	1023.	300.	7591.	8914.
W.A.A.F.:	91.	25.	787.	903.

AFFILIATED AIRFIELDS : -

PRESENT USE [1985] : RAF.

NO: 144.

AIRFIELD NAME: COTTAM. OPENED : 1939.
COUNTY : Yorkshire. CLOSED : 1945.
COMMAND : Maintenance.
FORMATION : 42 Grp[Reading] GRID REF: A 468836[28]
FUNCTION : Storage Unit. O.S.REF.: SE 995644.

LOCALITY : 5.5miles N of Driffield.
RAILWAY STN. : Driffield[LNER]

LATITUDE : 54 03 45N. HEIGHT ASL : 485' LIGHTING : Mk2.
LONGITUDE : 00 28 45W. FLYING CONTROL : None.RADIO : QDM.

LANDMARKS DAY : -

LANDMARKS NIGHT : -

OBSTRUCTIONS : -.

LANDING AREA SURFACE : Concrete & wood chippings.

QDM: 013. LENGTH X WIDTH: 1285 x 50yds. Ext: -
: 084. : 1800 x 50yds. : -
: 126. : 1400 x 50yds : -
: : :

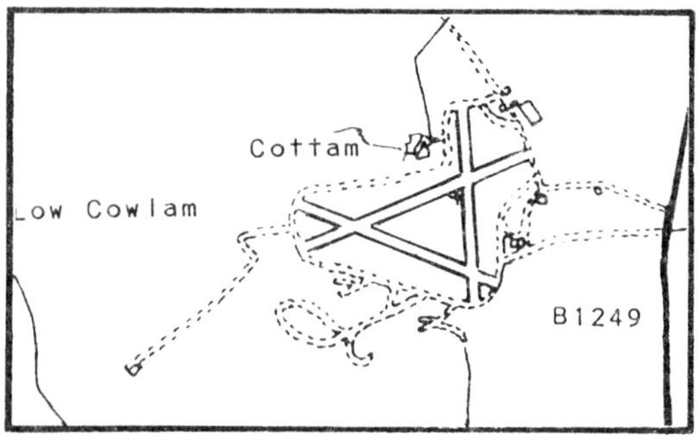

EXTENSIBILITY : None possible.

ACCOMMODATION : Temporary.
HANGARS : T2-1.

HARDSTANDINGS : 150'dia. concrete-24;tarmac-3.

	OFFICERS:	S.N.C.O's.:	O.R's.:	TOTAL:
R.A.F. :	60.	214.	783.	1057.
W.A.A.F.:	2.	8.	108.	118.

AFFILIATED AIRFIELDS : -

PRESENT USE [1985] : Disused.

NO: 145.

AIRFIELD NAME: COTTESMORE. OPENED : 1938.
COUNTY : Rutland. CLOSED :
COMMAND : 9th USAAF.
FORMATION : 316th Troop Carrier Grp. GRID REF: F 367350[64]
FUNCTION : Operational. O.S.REF.: SK 910158.

LOCALITY : 5.5miles NNE of Oakham.
RAILWAY STN. : Oakham 6miles[LMS]

LATITUDE : 52 43 45N. HEIGHT ASL : 425′ LIGHTING : Mk1.
LONGITUDE : 00 39 15W. FLYING CONTROL : Yes. RADIO : QDM.

LANDMARKS DAY : Burley House & fish ponds; Cottesmore 4miles 205degrees.

LANDMARKS NIGHT : -

OBSTRUCTIONS : Buildings on Tech site. Heath farm buildings. Cottesmore church spire.

LANDING AREA SURFACE : Tarmac.

QDM: 230. LENGTH X WIDTH: 2000 x 50yds. Ext: 2200yds.
: 280. : 1600 x 50yds. : -
: 190. : 1500 x 50yds. : 1700yds.
: : :

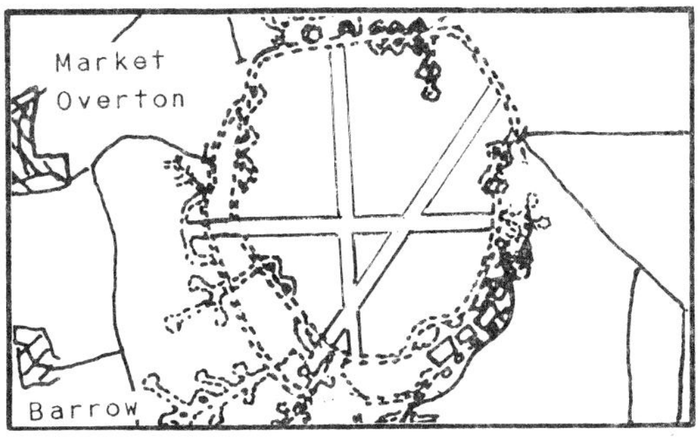

EXTENSIBILITY : Entails diversion of a minor road & demolition of 3 small barns.
ACCOMMODATION : Permanent.
HANGARS : Type C-4;T2-1.

HARDSTANDINGS : Concrete-37;Tarmac-17.

USAAF. : OFFICERS: 512. Enlisted Men. : 2253.TOTAL: 2765.

AFFILIATED AIRFIELDS : -

PRESENT USE [1985] : RAF.

NO: 146.

AIRFIELD NAME: COWDRAY PARK. OPENED : 1941.
COUNTY : Sussex. CLOSED : 1945.
COMMAND : RN.
FORMATION : Books of HMS Daedalus. GRID REF: Q 355405[133]
FUNCTION : Dispersed storage. O.S.REF.: SU 902218.

LOCALITY : 2miles E of Midhurst.
RAILWAY STN. : Midhurst[SR]

LATITUDE : 50 58 30N. HEIGHT ASL : 85′ LIGHTING : None.
LONGITUDE : 00 41 15W. FLYING CONTROL : None.RADIO : None.

LANDMARKS DAY : Selby Bill 16miles SSW. R Rother N of A/F.

LANDMARKS NIGHT : -

OBSTRUCTIONS : Rising ground S 764′ 2miles SSW. Rising ground N 626′ 2.5miles NNW.

LANDING AREA SURFACE : Grass.

QDM: N-S. LENGTH X WIDTH: 550yds. Ext: -
: E-W. : 750yds. : -
: : :
: : :

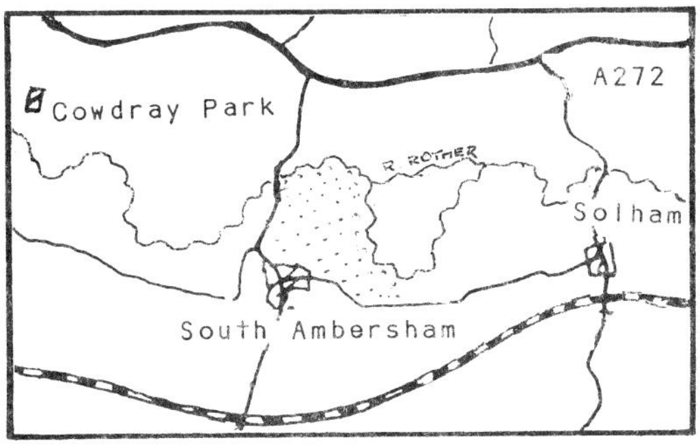

EXTENSIBILITY : -

ACCOMMODATION : Temporary.
HANGARS : Dutch barns 20x40′-25.

HARDSTANDINGS : None.

R.N. : OFFICERS: 1. Chiefs/POs/Ratings. : 43. TOTAL: 44.
W.R.N.S. : " : - " " : - " : -

AFFILIATED AIRFIELDS : -

PRESENT USE [1985] : Park land.

NO: 147.

AIRFIELD NAME: CRAIL. OPENED : 1940.
COUNTY : Fifeshire. CLOSED : 1958.
COMMAND : RN.
FORMATION : HMS Jackdaw. GRID REF: P 127299[Scot]
FUNCTION : Operational training. O.S.REF.: NO 625085.

LOCALITY : 7.5miles SE of St Andrews.
RAILWAY STN. : Crail 1mile[LNER]

LATITUDE : 56 61 20N. HEIGHT ASL : 75′ LIGHTING : Naval.
LONGITUDE : 02 36 15W. FLYING CONTROL : Yes. RADIO : QDM.

LANDMARKS DAY : Firth of Forth, Isle of May 5miles SSE.

LANDMARKS NIGHT : As day.

OBSTRUCTIONS : Crail church 1250yds 282degrees & Balcomie Castle 860yds 354degrees respectively from control buildings[with obstruction lights]

LANDING AREA SURFACE : Tarmac.
QDM: 209. LENGTH X WIDTH: 1000 x 33yds. Ext: -
: 247. : 1200 x 33yds. : -
: 297. : 1000 x 33yds. : -
: 337. : 1000 x 33yds. : -

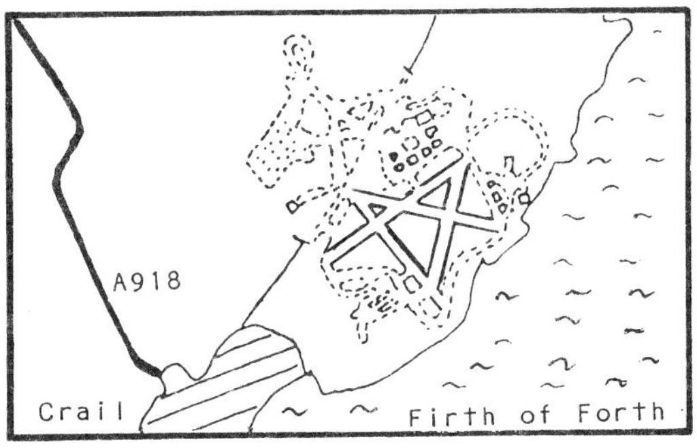

EXTENSIBILITY : -

ACCOMMODATION : Temporary.
HANGARS : 187′-6"x105′-10"[Sqdn]-7.

HARDSTANDINGS : -

R.N. : OFFICERS: 239. Chiefs/POs/Ratings. : 1208.TOTAL: 1447.
W.R.N.S. : " : 27. " " : 673. " : 700.

AFFILIATED AIRFIELDS : -

PRESENT USE [1985] : Disused.

NO: 148.

AIRFIELD NAME: CRANAGE. OPENED : 1940.
COUNTY : Cheshire. CLOSED : 1945.
COMMAND : Flying Training
FORMATION : 21 Grp[Spittlegate] GRID REF: K 197910[44]
FUNCTION : Advanced Flying Unit. O.S.REF.: SJ 730697.

LOCALITY : 2.75miles NNE of Middlewich.
RAILWAY STN. : Holmes Chapel 4.5miles[LMS]

LATITUDE : 53 13 23N. HEIGHT ASL : 150′ LIGHTING : Mk2.
LONGITUDE : 02 24 00W. FLYING CONTROL : Yes. RADIO : QDM.

LANDMARKS DAY : Vickers factory & Holmes Chapel Viaduct.

LANDMARKS NIGHT : -

OBSTRUCTIONS : Trees & woods on all sides.

LANDING AREA SURFACE : Steel Matting[American metal plank]

QDM	LENGTH X WIDTH	Ext
160.	1090yds.	2300yds.
230.	1263yds.	2090yds.
280.	1283yds.	1660yds.

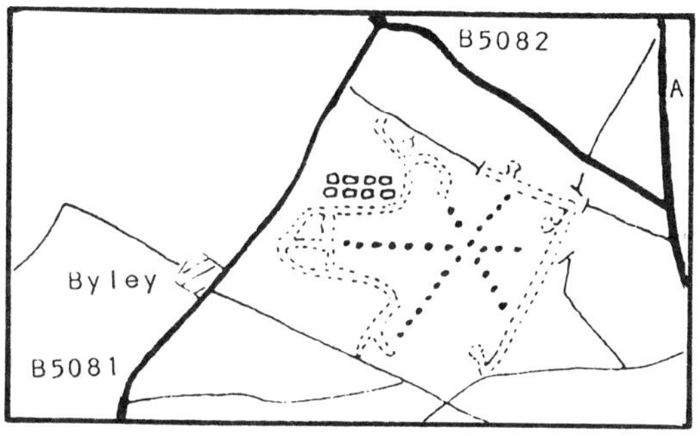

EXTENSIBILITY : Entails considerable demolition.

ACCOMMODATION : Temporary.
HANGARS : Bellman-8;Blister 69′-4.

HARDSTANDINGS : None.

R.A.F. : OFFICERS: 216.S.N.C.O′s.: 202.O.R′s.: 899. TOTAL: 1317.
W.A.A.F.: " : 8. " : 10. " : 368. " : 386.

AFFILIATED AIRFIELDS : -

PRESENT USE [1985] : Disused.

NO: 149.

AIRFIELD NAME: CRANFIELD. OPENED : 1937.
COUNTY : Bedfordshire. CLOSED : 1952.
COMMAND : Fighter.
FORMATION : 12 Grp[Watnall] GRID REF: L 396617[84]
FUNCTION : Operational Training Unit. O.S.REF.: SP 946421.
LOCALITY : 8miles SW of Bedford.
RAILWAY STN. : Woburn Sands 5.75miles[LMS]

LATITUDE : 52 04 08W. HEIGHT ASL : 336′ LIGHTING : Mk2.
LONGITUDE : 00 37 15W. FLYING CONTROL : Yes. RADIO : QDM.

LANDMARKS DAY : Brickworks[chimneys] 4miles E of Cranfield.

LANDMARKS NIGHT : -

OBSTRUCTIONS : None.

LANDING AREA SURFACE : Concrete.

QDM	LENGTH X WIDTH	Ext
265.	2000 x 50yds.	2500yds.
186.	1100 x 50yds.	2000yds.
224.	2000 x 50yds.	-

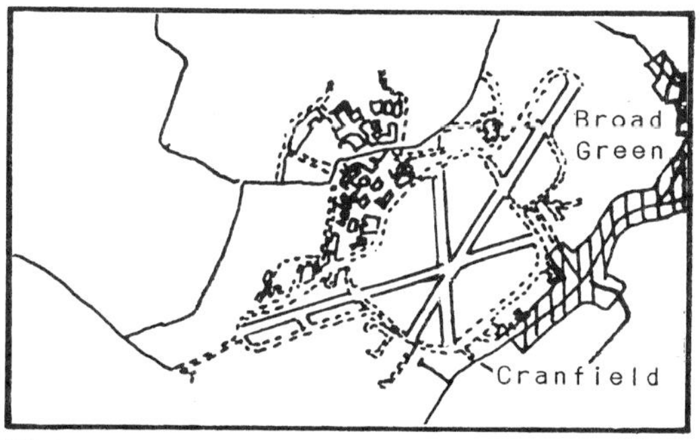

EXTENSIBILITY : Not recommended-2 road diversions would be necessary.
ACCOMMODATION : Permanent.
HANGARS : EO blister-9;Type C-4;T3-1.

HARDSTANDINGS : 25.

R.A.F. : OFFICERS: 89. S.N.C.O′s.: 187.O.R′s.: 1389.TOTAL: 1665.
W.A.A.F.: " : 6. " : 7. " : 645. " : 658.

AFFILIATED AIRFIELDS : Twinwood Farm[Satellite]

PRESENT USE [1985] : Institute of Technology.

NO: 150.

AIRFIELD NAME: CRANWELL[North] OPENED : 1916.
COUNTY : Lincolnshire. CLOSED :
COMMAND : Technical Training.
FORMATION : 27 Grp[Cirencester] GRID REF: F 467686[55]
FUNCTION : Radio School. O.S.REF.: TF 025515.

LOCALITY : 4miles NW of Sleaford.
RAILWAY STN. : Sleaford 6miles[LNER]

LATITUDE : 53 02 15N. HEIGHT ASL : 200′ LIGHTING : None.
LONGITUDE : 00 29 30W. FLYING CONTROL : Yes. RADIO : QDM.

LANDMARKS DAY : College tower on N airfield.

LANDMARKS NIGHT : -

OBSTRUCTIONS : RAF College tower 135′; W/T masts 70′; water tower 100′; Hangars & buildings along N side of South A/F & S side of North A/F.

LANDING AREA SURFACE : Grass[1100x50yds-asphalt]

QDM	LENGTH X WIDTH	Ext
E-W.	1100 x 50yds	-
E-W.	2500yds.	-
NE-SW.	1000yds.	-
SE-NW.	1200yds.	-

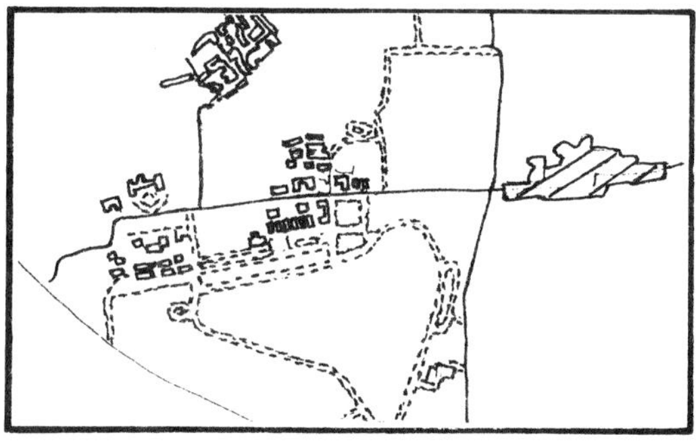

EXTENSIBILITY : -

ACCOMMODATION : Permanent[part]
HANGARS : Type C-2;Type F-8;Bellman-4;Blister-5.

HARDSTANDINGS :

R.A.F. : OFFICERS: 465.S.N.C.O′s.: 744.O.R′s.: 7720.TOTAL: 8929.
W.A.A.F.: " : 37. " : 78. " : 1720. " : 1835.

AFFILIATED AIRFIELDS : Caister, Coleby Grange & Wellingore [Satellites]
PRESENT USE [1985] : RAF.

NO: 151.

AIRFIELD NAME: CRANWELL[South] OPENED : 1916.
COUNTY : Lincolnshire. CLOSED :
COMMAND : Technical.
FORMATION : 27 Grp[Cirencester] GRID REF: F 467686[55]
FUNCTION : Radio School. O.S.REF.: TF 015488.

LOCALITY : 4miles NW of Sleaford.
RAILWAY STN. : Sleaford 6miles[LNER]

LATITUDE : 53 02 15N. HEIGHT ASL : 200′ LIGHTING : None.
LONGITUDE : 00 29 30E. FLYING CONTROL : Yes. RADIO : QDM.

LANDMARKS DAY : See Cranwell[North]

LANDMARKS NIGHT : " " "

OBSTRUCTIONS : " " "

LANDING AREA SURFACE : Grass.

QDM	LENGTH X WIDTH	Ext
N-S.	1200yds.	2000yds.
NE-SW.	1500yds.	1400yds.
E-W.	900yds.	1400yds.
SE-NW.	750yds.	-

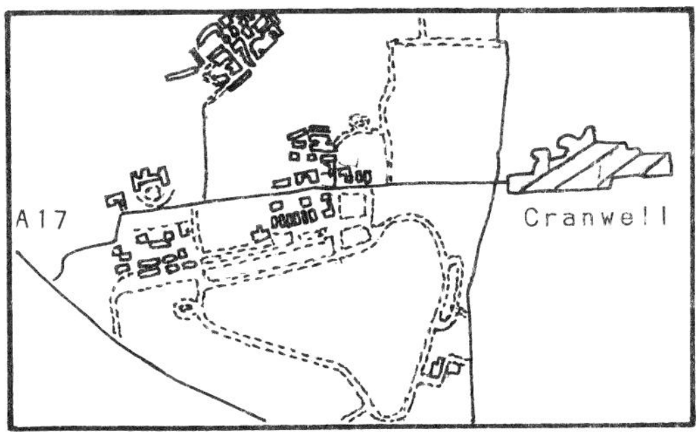

EXTENSIBILITY : -

ACCOMMODATION : See Cranwell[North]
HANGARS : " " "

HARDSTANDINGS : -

R.A.F. : OFFICERS: S.N.C.O′s.: O.R′s.: TOTAL:
W.A.A.F.: " : " : " : " :

AFFILIATED AIRFIELDS : See Cranwell[North]

PRESENT USE [1985] : RAF.

NO: 152.

AIRFIELD NAME: CRIMOND. OPENED : 1944.
COUNTY : Aberdeenshire. CLOSED : 1946.
COMMAND : RN.
FORMATION : HMS Merganser. GRID REF: K 57 [Scot]
FUNCTION : Air Observer School. O.S.REF.: NK 065580.

LOCALITY : 6miles SE of Fraserburgh.
RAILWAY STN. : Lonmay 3miles[GNS]

LATITUDE : 57 36 35N HEIGHT ASL : 40′ LIGHTING : Naval.
LONGITUDE : 01 53 20W. FLYING CONTROL : None. RADIO : QDM.

LANDMARKS DAY : Kinnairds Head, the S entrance point to the Moray Firth, town of Fraserburgh.

LANDMARKS NIGHT : -

OBSTRUCTIONS : Waughton hill 769′ 5miles S.

LANDING AREA SURFACE : Under construction.

QDM	LENGTH X WIDTH	Ext
206.	1000 x 30yds.	-
255.	1200 x 30yds.	-
300.	1200 x 30yds.	-
344.	1000 x 30yds.	-

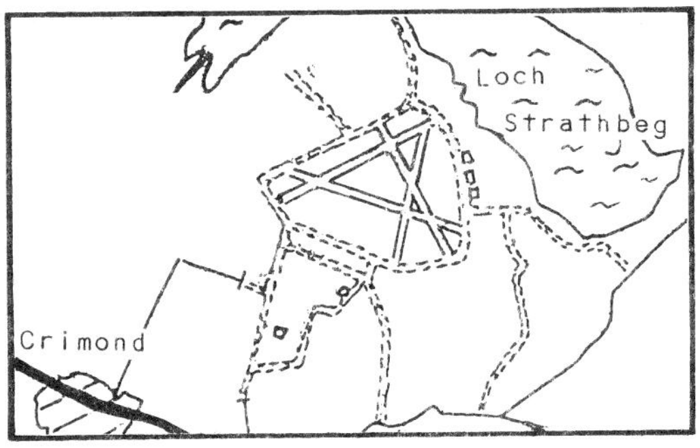

EXTENSIBILITY : -

ACCOMMODATION : Temporary.
HANGARS : Large[Sqdn]-5;Fromson[Sqdn]-6;[storage]-8.

HARDSTANDINGS : -

R.N. : OFFICERS: 361. Chiefs/POs/Ratings. : 1924.TOTAL: 2285.
W.R.N.S. : " : 18. " " : 619. " : 637.

AFFILIATED AIRFIELDS : -

PRESENT USE [1985] : Radio Research Station.

NO: 153.

AIRFIELD NAME: CROFT. OPENED : 1941.
COUNTY : Yorkshire. CLOSED : 1946.
COMMAND : Bomber.
FORMATION : 6 RCAF Grp[Allerton Pk] GRID REF: Z 764272[14]
FUNCTION : Operational. O.S.REF.: NZ 285068.

LOCALITY : 4.5miles S of Darlington.
RAILWAY STN. : Croft Spa 2miles[LNER]

LATITUDE : 54 27 15N. HEIGHT ASL : 182′ LIGHTING : Mk2.
LONGITUDE : 01 33 45W. FLYING CONTROL : Yes. RADIO : QDM.

LANDMARKS DAY : LNER main line, York to Darlington. R Tees NE of A/F.

LANDMARKS NIGHT : -

OBSTRUCTIONS : -

LANDING AREA SURFACE : Tarmac.

QDM	LENGTH X WIDTH	Ext
085.	2000 x 50yds.	-
026.	1400 x 50yds.	2500yds.
145.	1400 x 50yds.	2000yds.

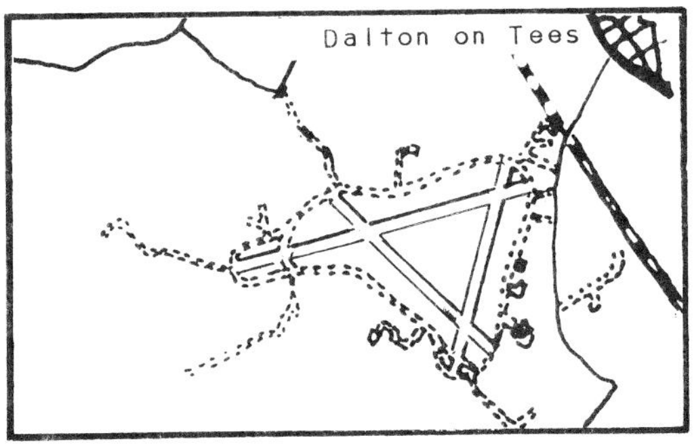

EXTENSIBILITY : Entails light demolition only, but not recommended.
ACCOMMODATION : Temporary.
HANGARS : T2-2; B1-1.

HARDSTANDINGS : Heavy bomber-36.

R.C.A.F.: OFFICERS: 199.S.N.C.O′s.: 425.O.R′s.: 1018.TOTAL: 1642.
W.A.A.F.: " : 6. " : 4. " : 240. " : 250.

AFFILIATED AIRFIELDS : Middleton-st-George[64 RCAF Base]

PRESENT USE [1985] : Disused.

NO: 154.

AIRFIELD NAME: CROSBY-on-EDEN. OPENED : 1941.
COUNTY : Cumberland. CLOSED :
COMMAND : Transport.
FORMATION : 44 Grp[Gloucester] GRID REF: Y 968820[5]
FUNCTION : Operational Training Unit. O.S.REF.: NY 482606.
LOCALITY : 6miles NE of Carlisle.
RAILWAY STN. : Carlisle[LMS]

LATITUDE : 54 56 14N. HEIGHT ASL : 155′ LIGHTING : Mk2.
LONGITUDE : 02 48 30W. FLYING CONTROL : Yes. RADIO : QDM.

LANDMARKS DAY : Solway Firth.

LANDMARKS NIGHT : Crosby.

OBSTRUCTIONS : Hill 2059′ 7miles SE. Chimney 300′ 5miles SW.

LANDING AREA SURFACE : Tarmac.

QDM	LENGTH X WIDTH	Ext
252.	2000 x 50yds.	-
192.	1400 x 50yds.	-
315.	1400 x 50yds.	1650yds.

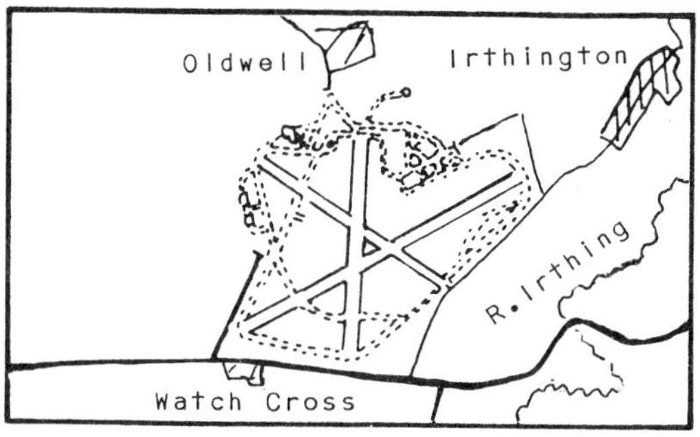

EXTENSIBILITY : Entails demolition ot a house & farm.

ACCOMMODATION : Temporary.
HANGARS : T2[12 bay]-3;Bellman-3;Blister-5.

HARDSTANDINGS : Loop type-19;150′ dia-2;100′ dia-4;fighter-33.

R.A.F. : OFFICERS: 156.S.N.C.O′s.: 339.O.R′s.: 1588.TOTAL: 2083.
W.A.A.F.: " : 8. " : 16. " : 230. " : 254.

AFFILIATED AIRFIELDS : Longtown[Satellite]

PRESENT USE [1985] : Civil Airport[Carlisle]

NO: 155.

AIRFIELD NAME: CROUGHTON. OPENED : 1941.
COUNTY : Northamptonshire. CLOSED : 1946.
COMMAND : Flying Training.
FORMATION : 23 Grp[South Cerney] GRID REF: L 013523[94]
FUNCTION : Advanced Flying Unit. O.S.REF.: SP 563225.

LOCALITY : 3miles SSW of Brackley.
RAILWAY STN. : Brackley 3miles[LMS]

LATITUDE : 51 59 15N. HEIGHT ASL : 450′ LIGHTING : Mk2.
LONGITUDE : 01 11 00W. FLYING CONTROL : Yes. RADIO : QDM.

LANDMARKS DAY : -

LANDMARKS NIGHT : -

OBSTRUCTIONS : -

LANDING AREA SURFACE : Grass.

QDM	LENGTH X WIDTH	Ext
E-W.	2000yds.	2200yds.
NE-SW.	1400yds.	1450yds.
NW-SE.	1300yds.	1670yds.

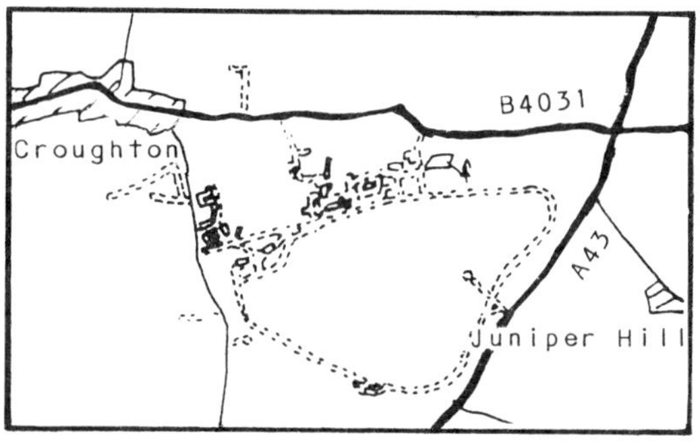

EXTENSIBILITY : Entails slight diversion of a main road.

ACCOMMODATION : Temporary.
HANGARS : T2-4;Blister[65′]-10.

HARDSTANDINGS : Circular-15;double fighter pens-6.

R.A.F. : OFFICERS: 133.S.N.C.O′s.: 300.O.R′s.: 649. TOTAL: 1082.
W.A.A.F.: " : 3. " : 6. " : 182. " : 191.

AFFILIATED AIRFIELDS : Kidlington[Parent]

PRESENT USE [1985] : Radio research station.

NO: 156.

AIRFIELD NAME: CROYDON. OPENED : 1916.
COUNTY : Surrey. CLOSED : 1955.
COMMAND : Dept of Civil Aviation.
FORMATION : 110 Wing[Croydon] GRID REF: Q 746825[115]
FUNCTION : Civil Airport. O.S.REF.: TQ 306635.

LOCALITY : 2.5miles SW of Croydon.
RAILWAY STN. : Waddon[SR]

LATITUDE : 51 21 15N. HEIGHT ASL : 217′ LIGHTING : Mk1.
LONGITUDE : 00 07 30W. FLYING CONTROL : Yes. RADIO : QDM.

LANDMARKS DAY : Gas works. Main railway line from Redhill.

LANDMARKS NIGHT : Purley Way.

OBSTRUCTIONS : Chimney 90′ 400yds. NE.

LANDING AREA SURFACE : Grass.

QDM	LENGTH X WIDTH	Ext
NW-SE.	1300yds.	2000yds.
NE-SW.	1100yds.	1400yds.
E-W.	1200yds.	1400yds.

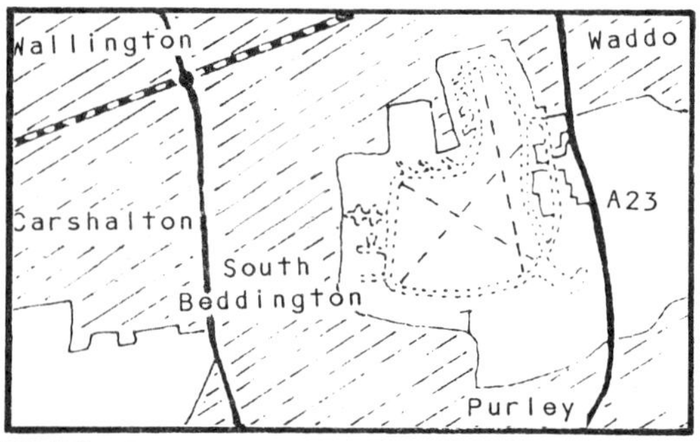

EXTENSIBILITY : Entails road diversion & very serious demolition.
ACCOMMODATION :
HANGARS : EO blister-4.

HARDSTANDINGS : TE-22.

R.A.F. : OFFICERS: 83. S.N.C.O′s.: 140.O.R′s.: 436. TOTAL: 659.
W.A.A.F.: " : 5. " : 6. " : 204. " : 215.

AFFILIATED AIRFIELDS : -

PRESENT USE [1985] : Housing.

NO: 157.

AIRFIELD NAME: CULDROSE. OPENED : Under Const.
COUNTY : Cornwall. CLOSED :
COMMAND : RN.
FORMATION : Under Construction. GRID REF: X 096492[141]
FUNCTION : Under Construction. O.S.REF.: SW 675258.

LOCALITY : 1mile SE of Helston.
RAILWAY STN. : Gwinear Road[GWR]

LATITUDE : 50 04 50N. HEIGHT ASL : 260′ LIGHTING :
LONGITUDE : 05 14 50W. FLYING CONTROL : RADIO :

LANDMARKS DAY : Lands End 17miles W & Lizard Point.

LANDMARKS NIGHT : -

OBSTRUCTIONS : -

LANDING AREA SURFACE : Under construction.

QDM	LENGTH X WIDTH	Ext
ESE-WNW.	2000 x 50yds.	-
N-S.	1100 x 50yds.	-
ENE-WSW.	1100 x 50yds.	-

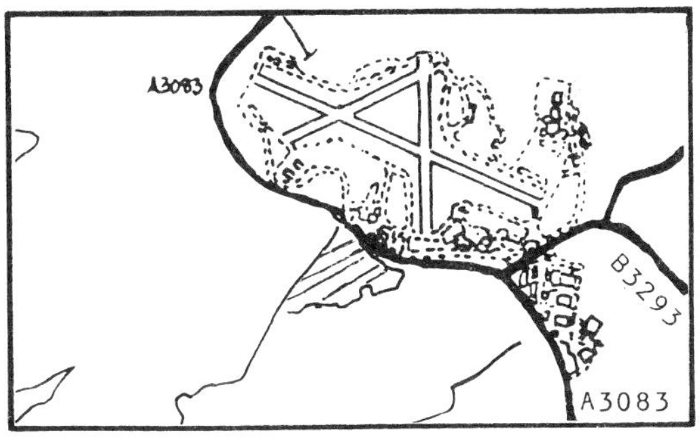

EXTENSIBILITY : -

ACCOMMODATION : -
HANGARS :

HARDSTANDINGS : -

R.N. : OFFICERS: - Chiefs/POs/Ratings. : - TOTAL: -
W.R.N.S. : " : - " " : - " : -

AFFILIATED AIRFIELDS : -

PRESENT USE [1985] : RN.

NO: 158.

AIRFIELD NAME: CULHAM. OPENED : 1944.
COUNTY : Oxfordshire. CLOSED : 1953.
COMMAND : RN.
FORMATION : HMS Hornbill. GRID REF: P 980153[105]
FUNCTION : Receipt & Despatch Unit. O.S.REF.: SU 535958.

LOCALITY : 5miles S of Oxford.
RAILWAY STN. : Culham[GWR]

LATITUDE : 51 39 35N. HEIGHT ASL : 190′ LIGHTING :
LONGITUDE : 01 13 40W. FLYING CONTROL : RADIO :

LANDMARKS DAY : Town of Oxford on R Isis.

LANDMARKS NIGHT : Didcot Junction.

OBSTRUCTIONS : -

LANDING AREA SURFACE : Under construction.

QDM	LENGTH X WIDTH	Ext
060-240.	1200 x 30yds.	-
103-283.	1400 x 30yds.	-
168-348.	1200 x 30yds.	-

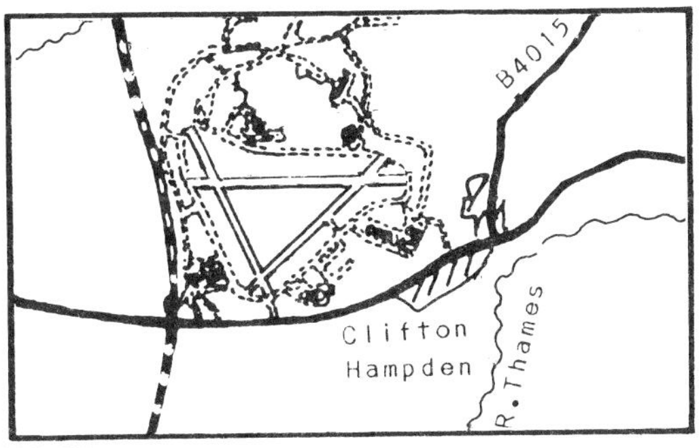

EXTENSIBILITY : -

ACCOMMODATION : Temporary.
HANGARS : 87.5x60′:Sqdn-1;Storage-20.

HARDSTANDINGS : -

R.N. : OFFICERS: - Chiefs/POs/Ratings. : - TOTAL: -
W.R.N.S. : " : - " " : - " : -

AFFILIATED AIRFIELDS : -

PRESENT USE [1985] : Atomic Energy Commission.

NO: 159.

AIRFIELD NAME: CULMHEAD. OPENED : 1941.
COUNTY : Somersetshire. CLOSED : 1946.
COMMAND : Fighter.
FORMATION : 10 Grp[Rudloe Manor] GRID REF: T 644364[129]
FUNCTION : Operational. O.S.REF.: ST 208154.

LOCALITY : 6miles S of Taunton.
RAILWAY STN. : Taunton[GWR]

LATITUDE : 50 55 45N. HEIGHT ASL : 864′ LIGHTING : None.
LONGITUDE : 03 07 45W. FLYING CONTROL : None. RADIO : QDM.

LANDMARKS DAY : Wellington Memorial.

LANDMARKS NIGHT : -

OBSTRUCTIONS : -

LANDING AREA SURFACE : Asphalt.

QDM	LENGTH X WIDTH	Ext
216.	1410 x 50yds.	2850yds.
276.	1130 x 50yds.	1350yds.
330.	1150 x 50yds.	-

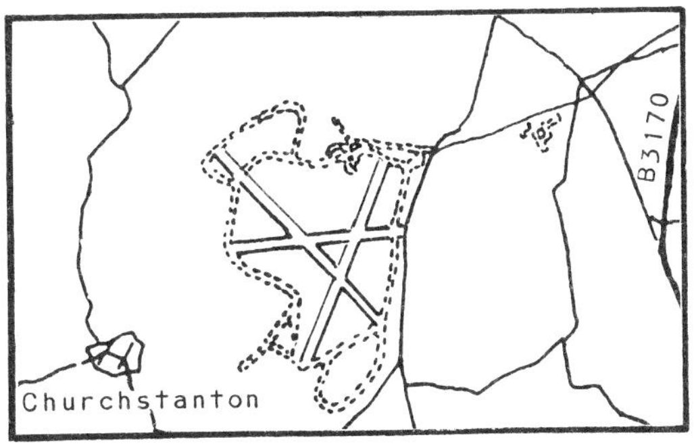

EXTENSIBILITY : Entails diversion of 2 lanes of local importance only.
ACCOMMODATION : Temporary.
HANGARS : T2-1;O blister-4;EO blister-6.

HARDSTANDINGS : TE-9, SE-27.

R.A.F. : OFFICERS: 13. S.N.C.O′s.: 100. O.R′s.: 1023. TOTAL: 1136.
W.A.A.F.: " : 10. " : - " : 291. " : 301.

AFFILIATED AIRFIELDS : Exeter[Sector]

PRESENT USE [1985] : Radio research station.

NO: 160.

AIRFIELD NAME: DALCROSS. OPENED : 1941.
COUNTY : Inverness-shire. CLOSED :
COMMAND : Flying Training.
FORMATION : 29 Grp[Dumfries] GRID REF: J 292739[28Scot]
FUNCTION : Air Gunnery School. O.S.REF.: NH 775521.

LOCALITY : 6.75miles NE of Inverness.
RAILWAY STN. : Dalcross 2miles[LMS]

LATITUDE : 57 32 32N. HEIGHT ASL : 45′ LIGHTING : Mk2.
LONGITUDE : 04 03 08W. FLYING CONTROL : Yes. RADIO : QDM.

LANDMARKS DAY : Moray Firth; Inverness-Nairn railway.

LANDMARKS NIGHT : Moray Firth W of A/F & coast.

OBSTRUCTIONS : -

LANDING AREA SURFACE : Concrete.

QDM	LENGTH X WIDTH	Ext
240.	1833 x 50yds.	4000yds.
200.	1300 x 50yds.	1400yds.
120.	1366 x 50yds.	1400yds.

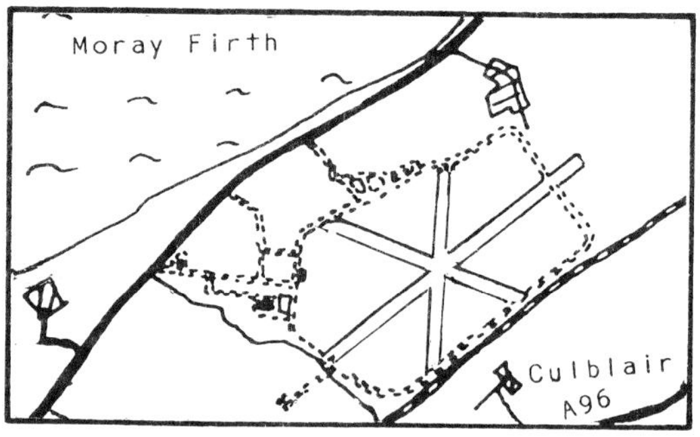

EXTENSIBILITY : No.1 runway could be extended to 5000yds.

ACCOMMODATION : Temporary.
HANGARS : AR-2; Bellman-2; EO blister-9.

HARDSTANDINGS : 300x100′ hardcore area.

R.A.F. : OFFICERS: 170.S.N.C.O′s.: 243.O.R′s.: 1218.TOTAL: 1631.
W.A.A.F.: " : 6. " : - " : 300. " : 306.

AFFILIATED AIRFIELDS : -

PRESENT USE [1985] : Civil Airport[Inverness]

NO: 161.

AIRFIELD NAME: DALE. OPENED : 1942.
COUNTY : Pembrokeshire. CLOSED : 1947.
COMMAND : RN.
FORMATION : HMS Goldcrest GRID REF: N 238297[99]
FUNCTION : Twin Engine Conversion. O.S.REF.: SM 795065.

LOCALITY : 7miles W of Milford Haven.
RAILWAY STN. : Milford Haven[GWR]

LATITUDE : 51 43 00N. HEIGHT ASL : 270′ LIGHTING : Mk2.
LONGITUDE : 05 11 30W. FLYING CONTROL : Yes. RADIO : QDM.

LANDMARKS DAY : St.Annes Head & Milford Haven. Skomer & Skokholm Islands lying 3.5miles & 2.5miles WNW.

LANDMARKS NIGHT : -

OBSTRUCTIONS : -

LANDING AREA SURFACE : Tarmac.

QDM	LENGTH X WIDTH	Ext
040.	1140 x 50yds.	1400yds.
110.	1410 x 50yds.	-
160.	1280 x 50yds.	-

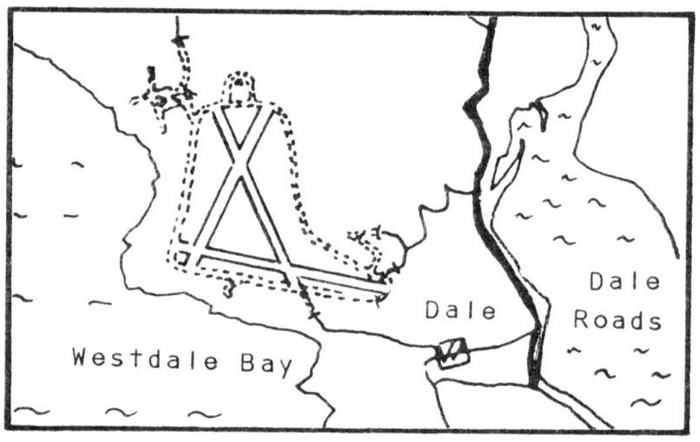

EXTENSIBILITY : Entails demolition of a water tower.

ACCOMMODATION : Temporary.
HANGARS : 185x110′[Sqdn]-5;60x84′[Sqdn]-9;[storage]-6.

HARDSTANDINGS : Large A/C standings-11.

R.N. : OFFICERS: 50. Chiefs/POs/Ratings. : 250. TOTAL: 300.
W.R.N.S.: " : 25. " " : 171. " : 196.

AFFILIATED AIRFIELDS : -

PRESENT USE [1985] : Agriculture.

NO: 162.

AIRFIELD NAME: DALLACHY. OPENED : 1943.
COUNTY : Morayshire. CLOSED : 1945.
COMMAND : Coastal.
FORMATION : 18 Grp[Pitreavie Castle] GRID REF: J 884850[29Scot]
FUNCTION : Operational[satellite] O.S.REF.: NJ 365635.

LOCALITY : 9miles E of Elgin.
RAILWAY STN. : Spey Bay[LNER]

LATITUDE : 57 39 23N. HEIGHT ASL : 250′ LIGHTING : Mk2.
LONGITUDE : 03 04 00W. FLYING CONTROL : Yes. RADIO : QDM.

LANDMARKS DAY : Coastline.

LANDMARKS NIGHT : As day.

OBSTRUCTIONS : -

LANDING AREA SURFACE : Concrete.

QDM	LENGTH X WIDTH	Ext
228.	1600 x 50yds.	3000yds.
290.	1400 x 50yds.	-

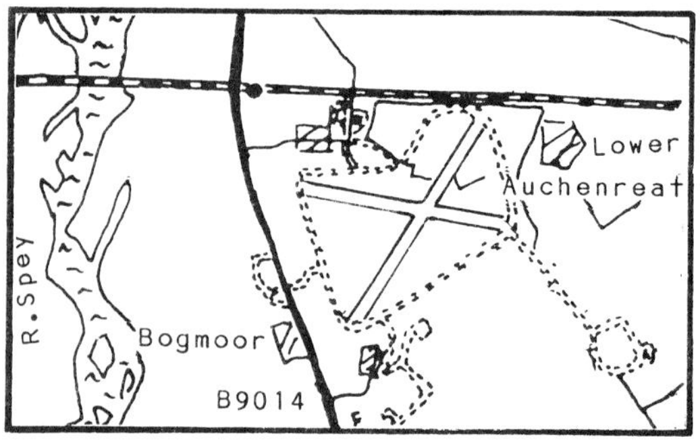

EXTENSIBILITY : Entails demolition of a farm & cottages.

ACCOMMODATION : Temporary.
HANGARS : T2-2; Double blister[69′]-5.

HARDSTANDINGS : Frying pan-1, concrete loop-36.

R.A.F. : OFFICERS: 105.S.N.C.O′s.: 305.O.R′s.: 1120.TOTAL: 1530.
W.A.A.F.: " : 10. " : 20. " : 378. " : 408.

AFFILIATED AIRFIELDS : Banff[Parent]

PRESENT USE [1985] : Disused.

NO: 163.

AIRFIELD NAME: DALTON. OPENED : 1941.
COUNTY : Yorkshire. CLOSED : 1945.
COMMAND : Bomber.
FORMATION : 7 Grp[St.Vincents] GRID REF: E 895959[22]
FUNCTION : Operational. O.S.REF.: SE 420760.

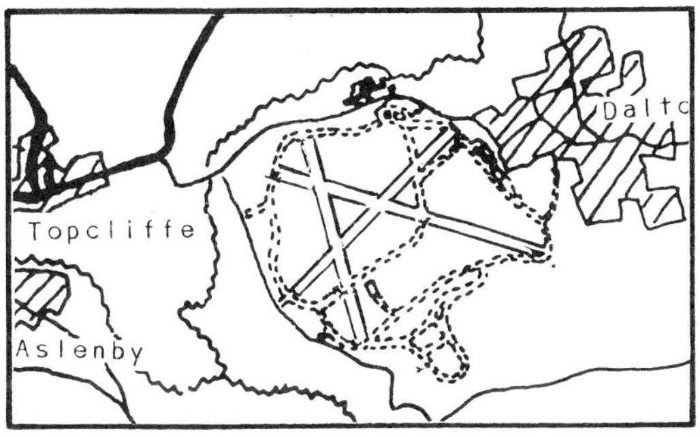

LOCALITY : 4miles S of Thirsk.
RAILWAY STN. : Thirsk[LNER]

LATITUDE : 54 10 30N. HEIGHT ASL : 73′ LIGHTING : Mk2.
LONGITUDE : 01 21 30W. FLYING CONTROL : Yes. RADIO : QDM.

LANDMARKS DAY : Topcliffe church 1mile W of A/F.

LANDMARKS NIGHT : -

OBSTRUCTIONS : High ground 100′, 1200 & 1800yds, 132 & 223degrees.

LANDING AREA SURFACE : Tarmac.

QDM: 297. LENGTH X WIDTH: 1800 x 50yds. Ext: 3200yds.
: 236. : 1560 x 50yds. : -
: 176. : 1400 x 50yds. : -
: : :

EXTENSIBILITY : Entails slight demolition.

ACCOMMODATION : Temporary.
HANGARS : T2-2; B1-1.

HARDSTANDINGS : Heavy bomber-36.

R.A.F. : OFFICERS: 60. S.N.C.O′s.: 288. O.R′s.: 787. TOTAL: 1135.
W.A.A.F.: " : 8. " : 13. " : 195. " : 216.

AFFILIATED AIRFIELDS : Topcliffe[76 RCAF Base]

PRESENT USE [1985] : Industry.

NO: 164.

AIRFIELD NAME: DARLEY MOOR. OPENED : 1942.
COUNTY : Derbyshire. CLOSED : 1945.
COMMAND : Fighter.
FORMATION : 38 Grp[Marks Hall] GRID REF: K 635625[53]
FUNCTION : Operational Training Unit[satellite] O.S.REF.: SK 175425.

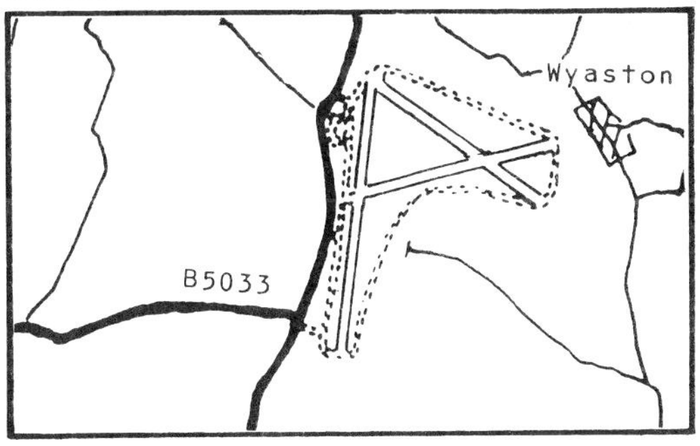

LOCALITY : 3miles S of Ashbourne.
RAILWAY STN. : Clifton 2miles[LMS]

LATITUDE : 52 58 30N. HEIGHT ASL : 580′ LIGHTING : Mk2.
LONGITUDE : 01 44 30W. FLYING CONTROL : Yes. RADIO : QDM.

LANDMARKS DAY : Osmaston park & lake, 2miles E.

LANDMARKS NIGHT : -

OBSTRUCTIONS : Wyaston village 300yds. to W of E-W runway.

LANDING AREA SURFACE : Concrete & wood chippings.

QDM: 200. LENGTH X WIDTH: 1800 x 50yds. Ext: 1900yds.
: 269. : 1400 x 50yds. : 1600yds.
: 319. : 1400 x 50yds. : 1600yds.
: : :

EXTENSIBILITY : Entails diversion of important minor road.

ACCOMMODATION : Temporary.
HANGARS : None.

HARDSTANDINGS : Frying pan 125′-27.

R.A.F. : OFFICERS: 60. S.N.C.O′s.: 267. O.R′s.: 735. TOTAL: 1062.
W.A.A.F.: " : 8. " : 40. " : 135. " : 183.

AFFILIATED AIRFIELDS : Ashbourne[Parent]

PRESENT USE [1985] : Disused.

NO: 165.

AIRFIELD NAME: DAVIDSTOW MOOR. OPENED : 1942.
COUNTY : Cornwall. CLOSED : 1945.
COMMAND : Coastal.
FORMATION : 19 Grp[Plymouth] GRID REF: S 584074[136]
FUNCTION : Operational. O.S.REF.: SX 150850.

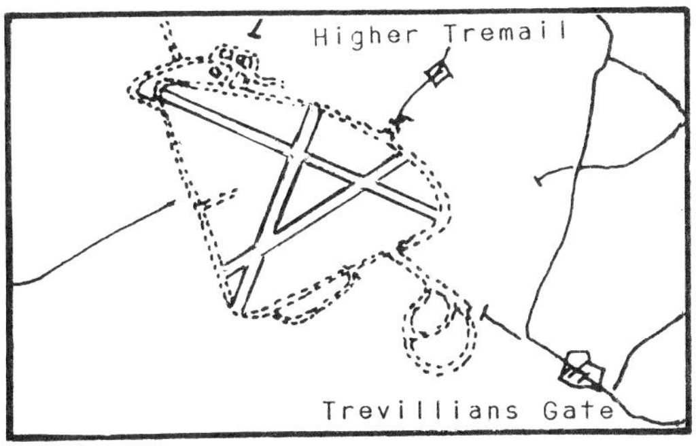

LOCALITY : 11miles W of Launceston.
RAILWAY STN. : Otterham 2.5miles[SR]

LATITUDE : 50 38 00N. HEIGHT ASL : 969′ LIGHTING : Mk2.
LONGITUDE : 04 37 15W. FLYING CONTROL : Yes. RADIO : QDM.

LANDMARKS DAY : Rough Tor 1311′ & Brown Willy 1375′ S of A/F.

LANDMARKS NIGHT : -

OBSTRUCTIONS : Rough Tor 1311′ 2.5miles, & Brown Willy 1375′ 3.5miles S.

LANDING AREA SURFACE : Concrete.

QDM: 304. LENGTH X WIDTH: 2000 x 50yds. Ext: -
: 248. : 1400 x 50yds. : 1700yds.
: 210. : 1400 x 50yds. : -

EXTENSIBILITY : Also possible: a 4th strip of 1450yds.

ACCOMMODATION : Temporary.
HANGARS : T2-3.

HARDSTANDINGS : 130′ dia concrete-50.

R.A.F. : OFFICERS: 298. S.N.C.O′s.: 718. O.R′s.: 1732. TOTAL: 2748.
W.A.A.F.: " : 4. " : 22. " : 486. " : 512.

AFFILIATED AIRFIELDS : -

PRESENT USE [1985] : Disused.

AIRFIELD NAME: DEANLAND.
COUNTY : Sussex.
COMMAND : Fighter.
FORMATION : 11 Grp[Uxbridge]
FUNCTION : Advanced Landing Ground [de-requisitioned]
LOCALITY : 4miles WNW of Hailsham.
RAILWAY STN. : Berwick[SR]

OPENED : 1944.
CLOSED : 1944.
GRID REF: Q 960305[134]
O.S.REF.: TQ 518115.

LATITUDE : 50 53 00N. HEIGHT ASL : 77′ LIGHTING : None.
LONGITUDE : 00 10 00E. FLYING CONTROL : None.RADIO : QDM.

LANDMARKS DAY : -

LANDMARKS NIGHT : -

OBSTRUCTIONS : -

LANDING AREA SURFACE : Steel Matting[Sommerfeld Track]

QDM: WSW-ENE. LENGTH X WIDTH: 1600yds. Ext: -
: SSW-NNE. : 1400yds. : -

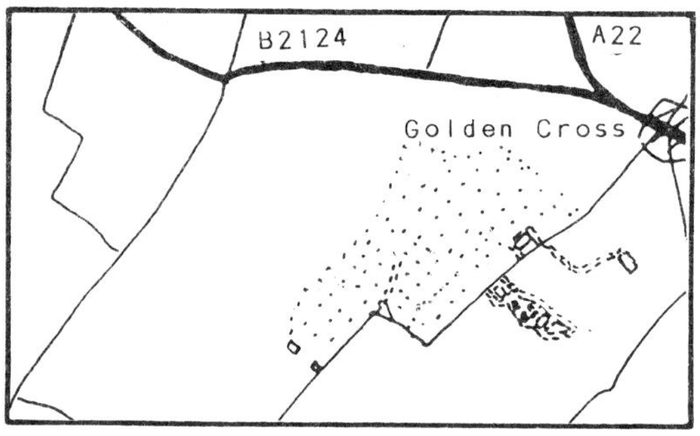

EXTENSIBILITY : -

ACCOMMODATION : Tented camp.
HANGARS : O blisters-4.

HARDSTANDINGS : 200x100′ concrete refuelling-4.

R.A.F. : OFFICERS: S.N.C.O′s.: O.R′s.: TOTAL:
W.A.A.F.: " : " : " : " :

AFFILIATED AIRFIELDS : -

PRESENT USE [1985] : Agriculture.

NO: 167.

AIRFIELD NAME: DEBACH.
COUNTY : Suffolk.
COMMAND : 8th USAAF.
FORMATION : 493rd Bomb Grp.
FUNCTION : Operational.

OPENED : 1944.
CLOSED : 1945.
GRID REF: M 691718[87]
O.S.REF.: TM 240540.

LOCALITY : 3miles NW of Woodbridge.
RAILWAY STN. : Woodbridge[LNER]

LATITUDE : 52 08 08N. HEIGHT ASL : 180′ LIGHTING : Mk2.
LONGITUDE : 01 16 23E. FLYING CONTROL : Yes. RADIO : QDM.

LANDMARKS DAY : Debach church at NE end of No. 2 R/W.

LANDMARKS NIGHT : -

OBSTRUCTIONS : -

LANDING AREA SURFACE : Concrete & Tarmac.

QDM: 180. LENGTH X WIDTH: 2000 x 50yds. Ext: 3000yds.
: 250. : 1400 x 50yds. : 2000yds.
: 310. : 1400 x 50yds. : 1600yds.

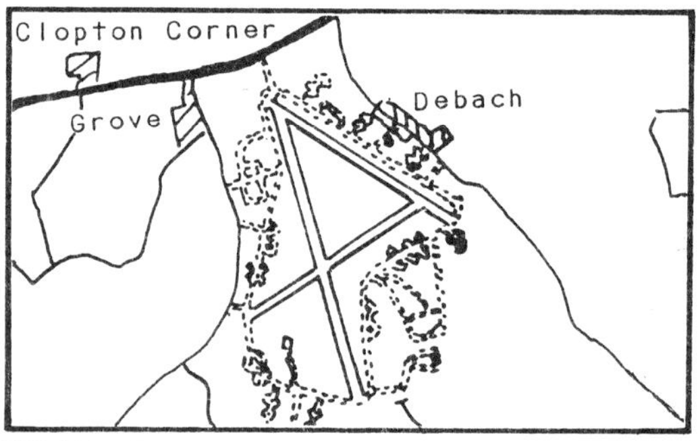

EXTENSIBILITY : Entails diversion of minor road.

ACCOMMODATION : Temporary.
HANGARS : T2-2.

HARDSTANDINGS : Spectacle-50.

USAAF. : OFFICERS: 421. Enlisted Men. : 2473.TOTAL: 2894.

AFFILIATED AIRFIELDS : -

PRESENT USE [1985] : Disused.

NO: 168.

AIRFIELD NAME: DEBDEN.
COUNTY : Essex.
COMMAND : 8th USAAF.
FORMATION : 4th Fighter Grp.
FUNCTION : Operational.
: 350.
LOCALITY : 2miles SSE of Saffron Walden.
RAILWAY STN. : Saffron Walden[LNER]

OPENED : 1937.
CLOSED : 1975.
GRID REF: M 014537[96]
O.S.REF.: TL 562351.

LATITUDE : 51 59 15N. HEIGHT ASL : 395′ LIGHTING : Mk2.
LONGITUDE : 00 16 45E. FLYING CONTROL : Yes. RADIO : QDM.

LANDMARKS DAY. : Railway line. White water tower E of A/F.
:

LANDMARKS NIGHT : -

OBSTRUCTIONS : -

LANDING AREA SURFACE : Concrete & tarmac.

QDM: 280. LENGTH X WIDTH: 1600 x 50yds. Ext: 2600yds.
: 350. : 1300 x 50yds. : 2100yds.
: : :

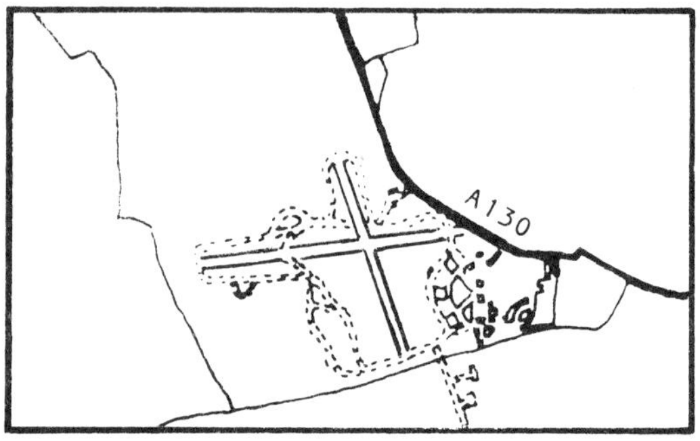

EXTENSIBILITY : Not recommended-entails demolition of 2 houses,1 garage & re-siting buildings.
ACCOMMODATION : Permanent[part]
HANGARS : Type C 225′-3;Bellman-1;Blister-11.

HARDSTANDINGS : 80.

USAAF. : OFFICERS: 190. Enlisted Men. : 1519.TOTAL: 1709.

AFFILIATED AIRFIELDS : -

PRESENT USE [1985] : Disused.

NO: 169.

AIRFIELD NAME: DEENTHORPE.　　OPENED : 1943.
COUNTY : Northamptonshire.　　CLOSED : 1946.
COMMAND : 8th USAAF.
FORMATION : 401st Bomb Grp.　　GRID REF: F 415100[74]
FUNCTION : Operational.　　O.S.REF.: SP 958902.

LOCALITY : 9miles NNE of Kettering.
RAILWAY STN. : Corby 2miles[LMS]

LATITUDE : 52 30 15N. HEIGHT ASL : 330′ LIGHTING : Mk2.
LONGITUDE : 00 35 15W. FLYING CONTROL : Yes. RADIO : QDM.

LANDMARKS DAY : Kettering SW; Oundle ESE.

LANDMARKS NIGHT : Corby ironworks W.

OBSTRUCTIONS : -

LANDING AREA SURFACE : Concrete & wood chippings.

QDM: 050. LENGTH X WIDTH: 2000 x 50yds. Ext: 2700yds.
: 100. : 1400 x 50yds. : 2200yds.
: 150. : 1400 x 50yds. : -

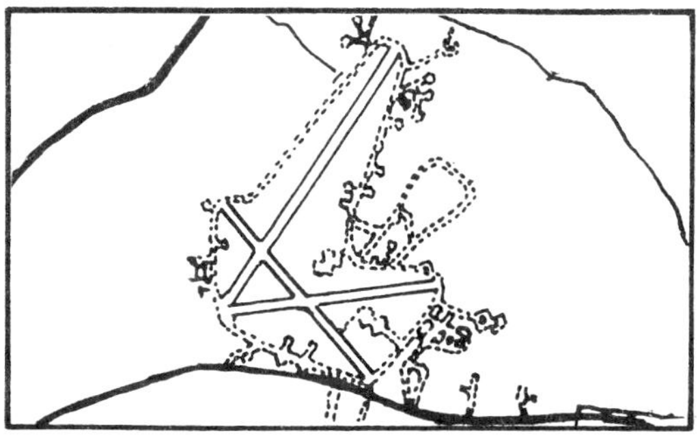

EXTENSIBILITY : -

ACCOMMODATION : Temporary.
HANGARS : T2-2.

HARDSTANDINGS : Loop-50.

USAAF. : OFFICERS: 421. Enlisted Men. : 2473.TOTAL: 2894.

AFFILIATED AIRFIELDS : -

PRESENT USE [1985] : Disused.

NO: 170.

AIRFIELD NAME: DEFFORD.　　OPENED : 1941.
COUNTY : Worcestershire.　　CLOSED : 1957.
COMMAND : Fighter.
FORMATION : 10 Grp[Rudloe Manor]　　GRID REF: P 352651[81]
FUNCTION : Forward Airfield.　　O.S.REF.: SO 903443.

LOCALITY : 7.5miles SSE of Worcester.
RAILWAY STN. : Defford 1.75miles[LMS],Pershore 6miles[GWR]

LATITUDE : 52 05 45N. HEIGHT ASL : 63′ LIGHTING : Mk2.
LONGITUDE : 02 08 30W. FLYING CONTROL : Yes. RADIO : QDM.

LANDMARKS DAY : Bredon Hills, ESE; railway SE & NW from E boundary.

LANDMARKS NIGHT : Lakes on moonlight nights. Small lakes W & NW; R Avon E.

OBSTRUCTIONS : -

LANDING AREA SURFACE : Asphalt.

QDM: 216. LENGTH X WIDTH: 2000 x 50yds. Ext: -
: 284. : 1400 x 50yds. : -
: 166. : 1350 x 50yds. : 1493yds.

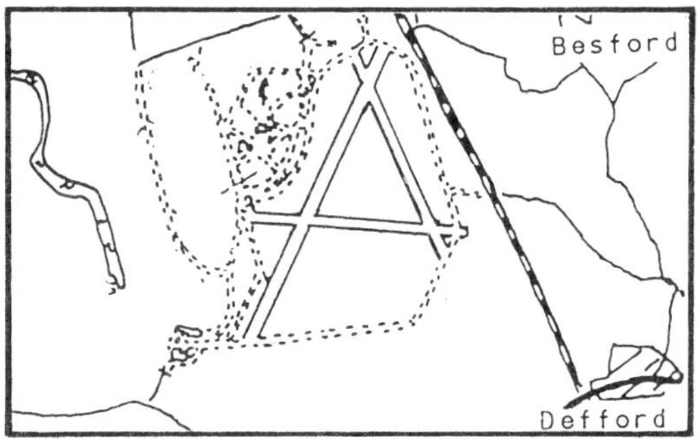

EXTENSIBILITY : -

ACCOMMODATION : Temporary.
HANGARS : T2[14bay]-2,[24bay]-4;EO blister-8.

HARDSTANDINGS : TE-53;SE-6.

R.A.F. : OFFICERS: 110.S.N.C.O′s.: 216.O.R′s.: 1738.TOTAL: 2064.
W.A.A.F.: " : 11. " : 18. " : 434. " : 463.

AFFILIATED AIRFIELDS : Colerne[Sector]

PRESENT USE [1985] : Royal Radar Establishment.

NO: 171.

AIRFIELD NAME: DENHAM.　　OPENED : 1917.
COUNTY : Buckinghamshire.　　CLOSED : 1945.
COMMAND : Flying Training.
FORMATION : 50 Grp[Reading]　　GRID REF: L 475082[106]
FUNCTION : Elementary Flying Training School[RLG]　　O.S.REF.: TQ 03086.
LOCALITY : 2miles NW of Uxbridge.
RAILWAY STN. : Denham Golf Club[GWR/LNER]

LATITUDE : 51 35 15N. HEIGHT ASL : 225′ LIGHTING : None.
LONGITUDE : 00 30 45W. FLYING CONTROL : None.RADIO : QDM.

LANDMARKS DAY : Denham film studios 1mile E.

LANDMARKS NIGHT : -

OBSTRUCTIONS : -

LANDING AREA SURFACE : Grass.

QDM: N-S. LENGTH X WIDTH: 1050yds. Ext: -
: NE-SW. : 860yds. : -
: E-W. : 1380yds. : -
: NW-SE. : 860yds. : -

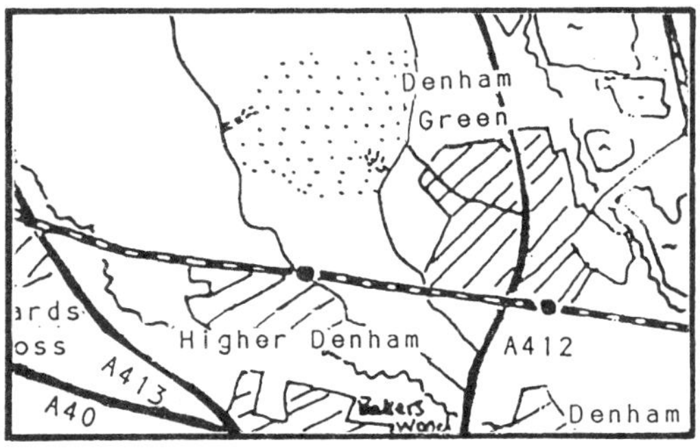

EXTENSIBILITY : None possible.

ACCOMMODATION : None.
HANGARS : Bessoneau[155x25x22′]-1,[120x50x12′]-1;
EO blister-3.
HARDSTANDINGS : 1.

R.A.F. : OFFICERS: - S.N.C.O′s.: - O.R′s.: - TOTAL: -
W.A.A.F.: " : - " : - " : - " : -

AFFILIATED AIRFIELDS : Booker[Parent]

PRESENT USE [1985] : Private flying.

NO: 172.

AIRFIELD NAME: DENTON.
COUNTY : Northamptonshire.
COMMAND : Flying Training.
FORMATION : 50 Grp[Reading]
FUNCTION : Elementary Flying Training School[RLG]
LOCALITY : 5miles SE of Northampton.
RAILWAY STN. : Piddington 2.5miles[LMS]

OPENED : 1940.
CLOSED : 1945.
GRID REF: L 274768[83]
O.S.REF.: SP 835578.

LATITUDE : 52 12 23N. HEIGHT ASL : 365′ LIGHTING : None.
LONGITUDE : 00 47 15W. FLYING CONTROL : None. RADIO : QDM.

LANDMARKS DAY : -

LANDMARKS NIGHT : -

OBSTRUCTIONS : -

LANDING AREA SURFACE : Grass.

QDM	LENGTH X WIDTH	Ext
N-S.	900yds.	-
NE-SW.	1000yds.	2000yds.
E-W.	820yds.	-
NW-SE.	880yds.	-

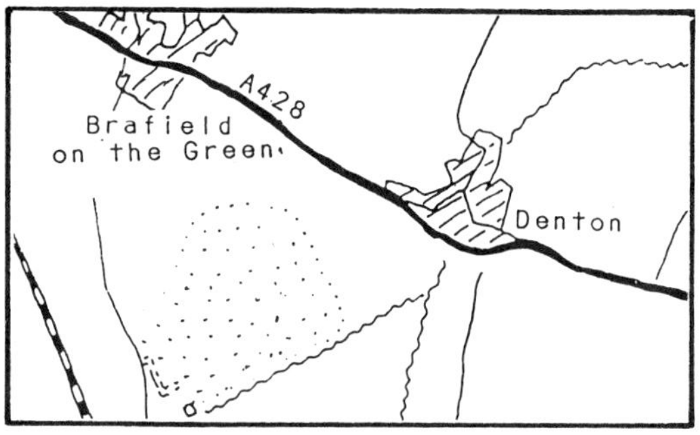

EXTENSIBILITY : Recommended to 1600yds-entails demolition of farm buildings & various RAF buildings.
ACCOMMODATION : Temporary.
HANGARS : EO blister-2; Standard Blister-8.

HARDSTANDINGS : None.

R.A.F. : OFFICERS: 2. S.N.C.O′s.: 4. O.R′s.: 120. TOTAL: 126.
W.A.A.F.: " : - " : - " : - " : -

AFFILIATED AIRFIELDS : Sywell[Parent]

PRESENT USE [1985] : Agriculture.

NO: 173.

AIRFIELD NAME: DEOPHAM GREEN.
COUNTY : Norfolk.
COMMAND : 8th USAAF.
FORMATION : 452nd Bomb Grp.
FUNCTION : Operational.

OPENED : 1944.
CLOSED : 1959.
GRID REF: G 508160[66]
O.S.REF.: TM 030990.

LOCALITY : 1.75miles N of Attleborough.
RAILWAY STN. : Attleborough[LNER]

LATITUDE : 53 33 08N. HEIGHT ASL : 185′ LIGHTING : Mk2.
LONGITUDE : 00 59 38W. FLYING CONTROL : Yes. RADIO : QDM.

LANDMARKS DAY : Sea Mere[lake] N of runway 240degrees 1mile.

LANDMARKS NIGHT : -

OBSTRUCTIONS : -

LANDING AREA SURFACE : Concrete & tarmac.

QDM	LENGTH X WIDTH	Ext
240.	2000 x 50yds.	3000yds.
110.	1400 x 50yds.	2000yds.
350.	1400 x 50yds.	1900yds.

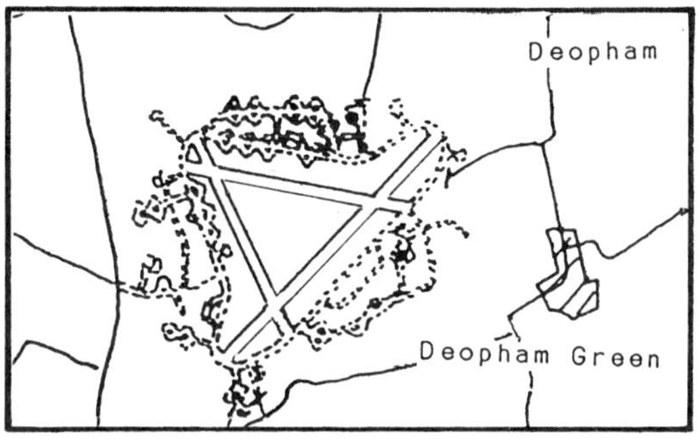

EXTENSIBILITY : Not recommended-involves demolition of a school, farm, & 10 cottages.
ACCOMMODATION : Temporary.
HANGARS : T2-2.

HARDSTANDINGS : Loop-49, frying pan-2.

USAAF. : OFFICERS: 421. Enlisted Men. : 2473. TOTAL: 2894.

AFFILIATED AIRFIELDS : -

PRESENT USE [1985] : Disused.

NO: 174.

AIRFIELD NAME: DERBY.
COUNTY : Derbyshire.
COMMAND : Flying Training.
FORMATION : 51 Grp[Leeds]
FUNCTION : Elementary Flying Training School.
LOCALITY : 5miles SW of Derby.
RAILWAY STN. : Derby[LMS]

OPENED : 1939.
CLOSED : 1963.
GRID REF: K 749508[63]
O.S.REF.: SK 290303.

LATITUDE : 52 52 15N. HEIGHT ASL : 220′ LIGHTING : None.
LONGITUDE : 01 34 00W. FLYING CONTROL : None. RADIO : QDM.

LANDMARKS DAY : -

LANDMARKS NIGHT : -

OBSTRUCTIONS : Various cottages; can be lighted at night.

LANDING AREA SURFACE : Grass.

QDM	LENGTH X WIDTH	Ext
E-W.	1170yds.	2800yds.
NE-SW.	1060yds.	1800yds.
SE-NBW.	1050yds.	1600yds.
N-S.	860yds.	

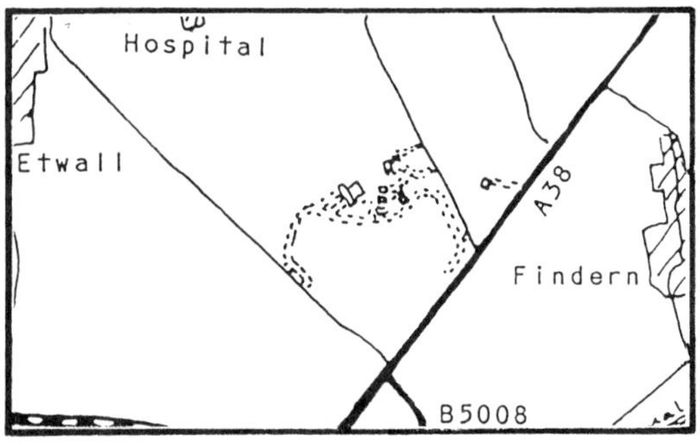

EXTENSIBILITY : Recommended to 2000&1600yds only. Entails road diversion & demo.of 2 farms,12 cottages.
ACCOMMODATION : Temporary.
HANGARS : Bellman-1;Civil[115x115′]-1,[330x250′]-1; double standard-4;EO blister-3.
HARDSTANDINGS : None.

R.A.F. : OFFICERS: 68. S.N.C.O′s.: 70. O.R′s.: 333. TOTAL: 471.
W.A.A.F.: " : - " : - " : - " : -

AFFILIATED AIRFIELDS : Abbots Bromley & Battlestead[RLG]

PRESENT USE [1985] : Disused.

NO: 175.

AIRFIELD NAME: DESBOROUGH. OPENED : 1943.
COUNTY : Northamptonshire. CLOSED : 1946.
COMMAND : Bomber.
FORMATION : 92 Grp[Winslow] GRID REF: F 270055[73]
FUNCTION : Operational Training Unit. O.S.REF.: SP 817865.
LOCALITY : 6miles NNW of Kettering.
RAILWAY STN. : Kettering[LMS]

LATITUDE : 52 28 00N. HEIGHT ASL : 460′ LIGHTING : Mk2.
LONGITUDE : 00 48 00W. FLYING CONTROL : Yes. RADIO : QDM.

LANDMARKS DAY : -

LANDMARKS NIGHT : -

OBSTRUCTIONS : -

LANDING AREA SURFACE : Tarmac & wood chippings.

QDM	LENGTH X WIDTH	Ext
201.	1400 x 50yds.	-
272.	2000 x 50yds.	-
321.	1400 x 50yds.	1600yds.

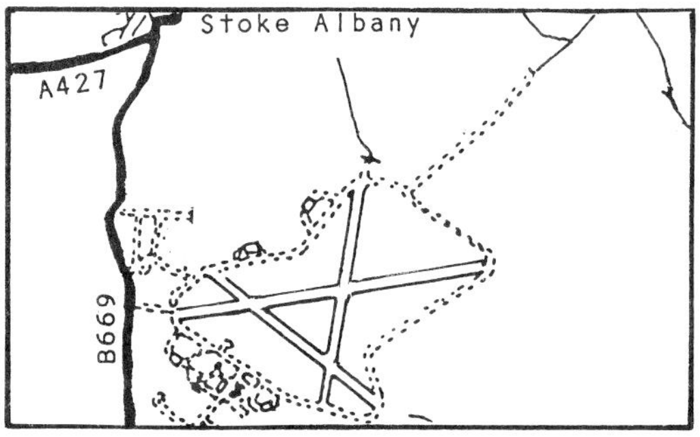

EXTENSIBILITY : Entails demolition of a farm.

ACCOMMODATION : Temporary.
HANGARS : T2-4;B1-1.

HARDSTANDINGS : Pan-29.

R.A.F. : OFFICERS: 159.S.N.C.O′s.: 394.O.R′s.: 1004.TOTAL: 1557.
W.A.A.F.: " : 8. " : 15. " : 297. " : 320.

AFFILIATED AIRFIELDS : -

PRESENT USE [1985] : Agriculture.

NO: 176.

AIRFIELD NAME: DESFORD. OPENED : 1935.
COUNTY : Leicestershire. CLOSED : 1953.
COMMAND : Flying Training.
FORMATION : 51 Grp[Leeds] GRID REF: K 935220[63]
FUNCTION : Elementary Flying Training School. O.S.REF.: SK 478020.
LOCALITY : 6.5miles WSW of Leicester.
RAILWAY STN. : Desford 1mile[LMS]

LATITUDE : 52 36 45N. HEIGHT ASL : 425′ LIGHTING : None.
LONGITUDE : 01 17 30W. FLYING CONTROL : None.RADIO : QDM.

LANDMARKS DAY : Lake at Thornton 3miles N. Croby Pool 4.5miles NE. Quarry 3miles S.

LANDMARKS NIGHT : Lake, possibly visible.

OBSTRUCTIONS : Factory S side; trees, hangars, factory near N side.

LANDING AREA SURFACE : Grass.

QDM	LENGTH X WIDTH	Ext
NE-SW.	1200yds.	1400yds.
E-W.	900yds.	1400yds.
-	-	1300yds.

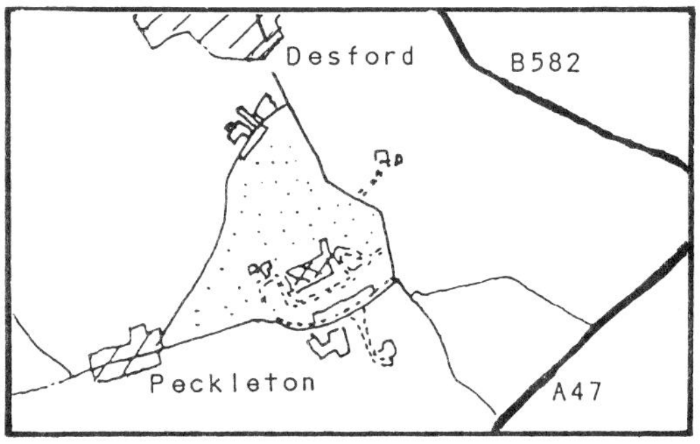

EXTENSIBILITY : Entails demolition of 1 house to NW.

ACCOMMODATION : Semi-permanent.
HANGARS : Civil-2;Bellman[MAP]-1;Blister:standard-13; O-1;EO-1.
HARDSTANDINGS : -

R.A.F. : OFFICERS: 34. S.N.C.O′s.: 69. O.R′s.: 262. TOTAL: 365.
W.A.A.F.: " : - " : - " : - " : -

AFFILIATED AIRFIELDS : Braunstone[RLG]

PRESENT USE [1985] : Industry.

NO: 177.

AIRFIELD NAME: DETLING. OPENED : 1938.
COUNTY : Kent. CLOSED : 1959.
COMMAND : Fighter.
FORMATION : 11 Grp[Uxbridge] GRID REF: R 254780[116]
FUNCTION : Forward Airfield. O.S.REF.: TQ 812595.

LOCALITY : 3.5miles NE of Maidstone.
RAILWAY STN. : Maidstone[SR]

LATITUDE : 51 18 20N. HEIGHT ASL : 600′ LIGHTING : None.
LONGITUDE : 00 36 00E. FLYING CONTROL : Yes. RADIO : QDM.

LANDMARKS DAY : Maidstone 4miles 50degrees.

LANDMARKS NIGHT : -

OBSTRUCTIONS : -

LANDING AREA SURFACE : Grass.

QDM	LENGTH X WIDTH	Ext
NE-SW.	1400yds.	2000yds.
E-W.	900yds.	1400yds.
N-S.	900yds.	1400yds.

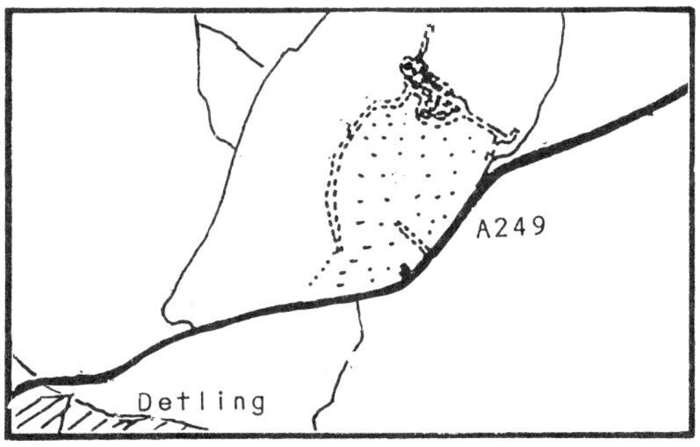

EXTENSIBILITY : Entails serious demolition of small houses & also of RAF temporary sites.
ACCOMMODATION : Permanent[part]
HANGARS : Bellman-1;Blister-14;Bessoneau-1.

HARDSTANDINGS : Spur-41;BRC fabric-23.

R.A.F. : OFFICERS: 41. S.N.C.O′s.: 79. O.R′s.: 1386.TOTAL: 1506.
W.A.A.F.: " : - " : - " : 281. " : 281.

AFFILIATED AIRFIELDS : Biggin Hill[Sector]

PRESENT USE [1985] : Industry/agriculture.

AIRFIELD NAME: DIGBY. OPENED : 1918.
COUNTY : Lincolnshire. CLOSED :
COMMAND : Fighter.
FORMATION : 12 Grp[Watnall] GRID REF: F 510760[47]
FUNCTION : Sector. O.S.REF.: TF 042570.

LOCALITY : 10miles SSE of Lincoln.
RAILWAY STN. : Digby[LNER]

LATITUDE : 53 05 53N. HEIGHT ASL : 100′ LIGHTING : Mk2.
LONGITUDE : 00 26 30W. FLYING CONTROL : Yes. RADIO : QDM.

LANDMARKS DAY : Central tower of Cranwell 4.5miles S.

LANDMARKS NIGHT : -

OBSTRUCTIONS : -

LANDING AREA SURFACE : Grass.

QDM	LENGTH X WIDTH	Ext
N-S.	1250yds.	2500yds.
E-W.	1050yds.	1700yds.
NE-SW.	1400yds.	2000yds.

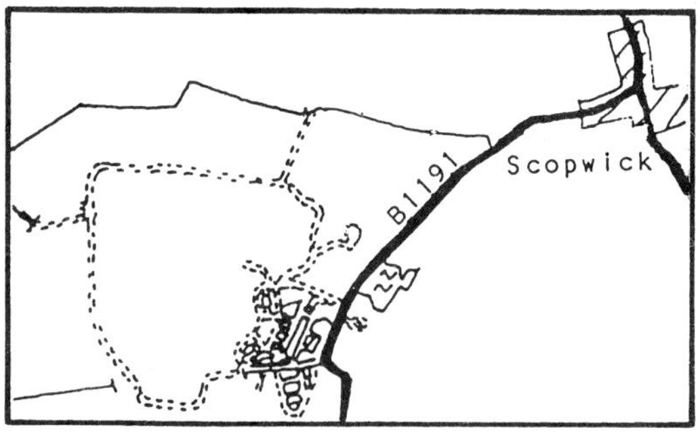

EXTENSIBILITY : Reco. to 2000-1400&1400yds only. Entails demo. of toll bar cottages & RAF huts & pens.
ACCOMMODATION : Permanent.
HANGARS : Type C-2;blister:0-6;E0-4.

HARDSTANDINGS : SE-7.

	OFFICERS	S.N.C.O's.	O.R's.	TOTAL
R.A.F.	130.	190.	1630.	1950.
W.A.A.F.	20.	10.	510.	540.

AFFILIATED AIRFIELDS : Collyweston & Wittering[N/F Forward Airfields]
PRESENT USE [1985] : RAF.

NO: 179.

AIRFIELD NAME: DISHFORTH. OPENED : 1936.
COUNTY : Yorkshire. CLOSED :
COMMAND : Bomber.
FORMATION : 7 Grp[St.Vincents] GRID REF: E 856920[21
FUNCTION : Operational. O.S.REF.: SE 381719.

LOCALITY : 4miles E of Rippon.
RAILWAY STN. : Thirsk 8miles[LNER]

LATITUDE : 54 08 15N. HEIGHT ASL : 106′ LIGHTING : Mk2.
LONGITUDE : 01 25 00W. FLYING CONTROL : Yes. RADIO : QDM.

LANDMARKS DAY : Windmill[Great North Road]

LANDMARKS NIGHT : -

OBSTRUCTIONS : D/F aerial masts 1.5miles ESE 30′ above A/F level.

LANDING AREA SURFACE : Concrete & tarmac.

QDM	LENGTH X WIDTH	Ext
220.	1400 x 50yds.	3000yds.
280.	1400 x 50yds.	2000yds.
340.	2000 x 50yds.	2000yds.

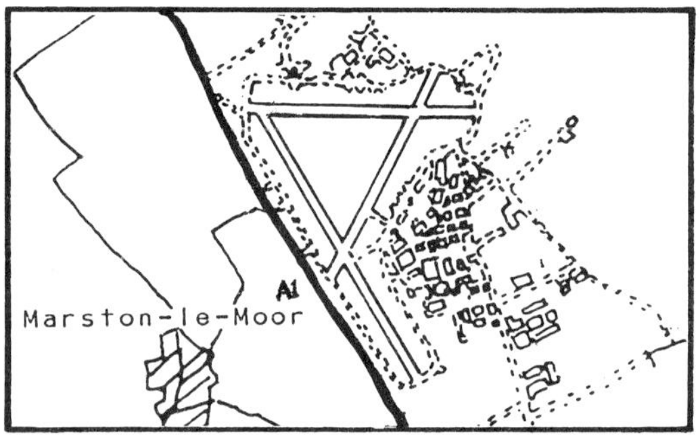

EXTENSIBILITY : Entails diversion of Gt North Road for about 4000yds.
ACCOMMODATION : Permanent.
HANGARS : Type C-5.

HARDSTANDINGS : Heavy bomber-36.

	OFFICERS	S.N.C.O's.	O.R's.	TOTAL
R.C.A.F.	260.	360.	1479.	2099.
W.A.A.F.	16.	13.	449.	478.

AFFILIATED AIRFIELDS : Topcliffe[76 RCAF Base]

PRESENT USE [1985] : RAF.

NO: 180.

AIRFIELD NAME: DOCKING. OPENED : 1940.
COUNTY : Norfolk. CLOSED : 1958.
COMMAND : Coastal.
FORMATION : 16 Grp[Gillingham] GRID REF: G 250576[56]
FUNCTION : Operational[satellite] O.S.REF.: TF 788393.

LOCALITY : 10miles NW of Fakenham.
RAILWAY STN. : Docking 2miles[LNER]

LATITUDE : 52 55 15N. HEIGHT ASL : 210′ LIGHTING : Mk2.
LONGITUDE : 00 39 45E. FLYING CONTROL : Yes. RADIO : QDM.

LANDMARKS DAY : Docking village with church 2.5miles W by S.

LANDMARKS NIGHT : -

OBSTRUCTIONS : -

LANDING AREA SURFACE : Grass.

QDM	LENGTH X WIDTH	Ext
NE-SW.	1730yds.	4000yds.
E-W.	1400yds.	2500yds.
N-S.	1100yds.	2000yds.

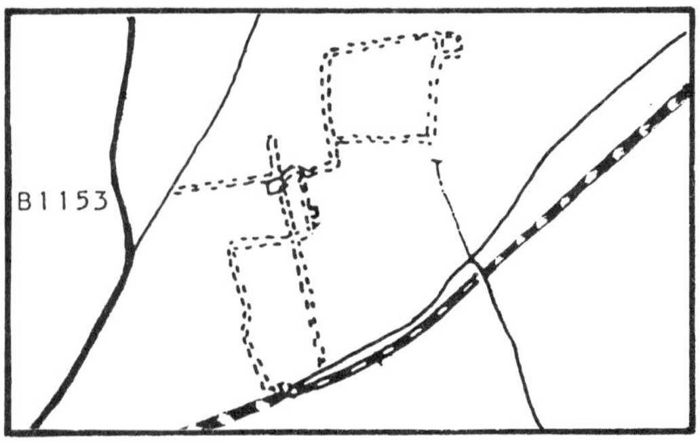

EXTENSIBILITY : N-S not recommended.

ACCOMMODATION : Temporary.
HANGARS : Blister-8;A1-1.

HARDSTANDINGS : None.

	OFFICERS	S.N.C.O's.	O.R's.	TOTAL
R.A.F.	60.	115.	615.	790.
W.A.A.F.	2.	2.	88.	92.

AFFILIATED AIRFIELDS : Bircham Newton[Parent]

PRESENT USE [1985] : Disused.

NO: 181.

AIRFIELD NAME: DONCASTER. OPENED : 1916.
COUNTY : Yorkshire. CLOSED : 1954.
COMMAND : Transport.
FORMATION : 44 Grp[Gloucester] GRID REF: A 063330[38]
FUNCTION : Care & maintenance. O.S.REF.: SE 595020.

LOCALITY : 1.25miles SE of Doncaster.
RAILWAY STN. : Doncaster Centre[LNER]

LATITUDE : 53 30 30N. HEIGHT ASL : 25′ LIGHTING : None.
LONGITUDE : 01 06 15W. FLYING CONTROL : Yes. RADIO : QDM.

LANDMARKS DAY : -

LANDMARKS NIGHT : -

OBSTRUCTIONS : Hangars & buildings outside perimeter track.

LANDING AREA SURFACE : Grass[987yds of No 3 strip Sommerfeld track]

QDM: SE-NW. LENGTH X WIDTH: 1300yds. Ext: -
: N-S. : 1350yds. : -
: NE-SW. : 1200yds. : -
: : :

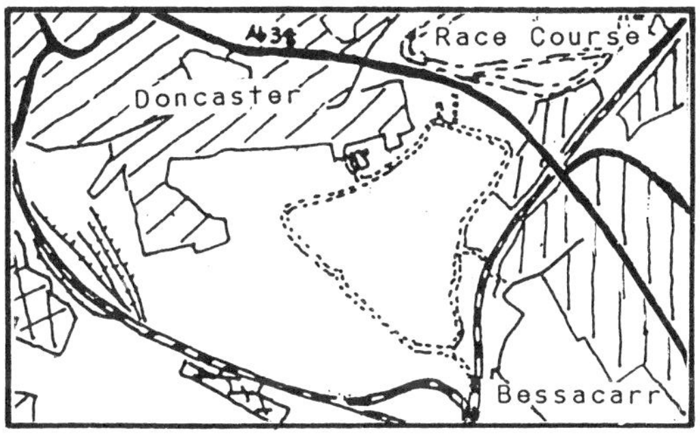

EXTENSIBILITY : -

ACCOMMODATION : Temporary.
HANGARS : Bellman-3.

HARDSTANDINGS : Frying pan-13.

R.A.F. : OFFICERS: 58. S.N.C.O′s.: 247.O.R′s.: 664. TOTAL: 969.
W.A.A.F.: " : 6. " : 6. " : 142. " : 154.

AFFILIATED AIRFIELDS : -

PRESENT USE [1985] : Private flying.

NO: 182.

AIRFIELD NAME: DONIBRISTLE. OPENED : 1917.
COUNTY : Fifeshire. CLOSED : 1959.
COMMAND : RN.
FORMATION : HMS Merlin. GRID REF: O 659059[Scot]
FUNCTION : H.Q.of Com.NAS[N] O.S.REF.: NT 155834.
Repair Yard.
LOCALITY : 2.5miles NE of Queensferry & Forth Bridge.
RAILWAY STN. : Inverkeithing[LNER]

LATITUDE : 56 02 25N. HEIGHT ASL : 125′ LIGHTING : None.
LONGITUDE : 03 21 00W. FLYING CONTROL : Yes. RADIO : QDM.

LANDMARKS DAY : Firth of Forth with Rosyth Dockyard & Forth Bridge. Donibristle & Dalgety bays S.

LANDMARKS NIGHT : As day.

OBSTRUCTIONS : Land rises to 700′ within 2.5miles NNE.

LANDING AREA SURFACE : Tarmac.

QDM: 261. LENGTH X WIDTH: 800 x 50yds. Ext: -
: 277. : 970 x 50yds. : -
: : :

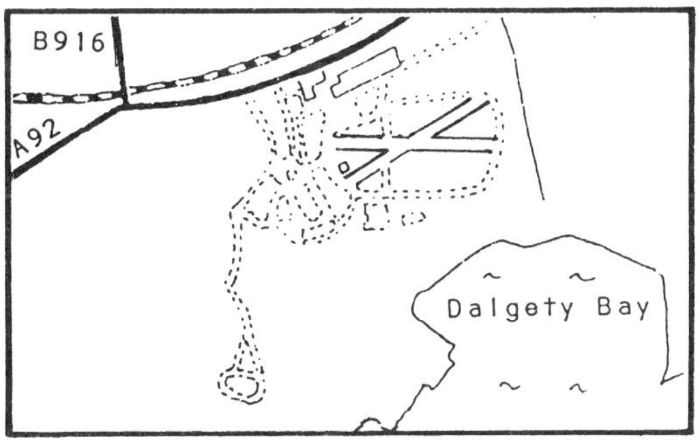

EXTENSIBILITY : -

ACCOMMODATION : Permanent.
HANGARS : 187.5x105′ Bellman[sqdn&storage]-4;
65x79′ Bessoneau[storage]-3.
HARDSTANDINGS :

R.N. : OFFICERS: 149. Chiefs/POs/Ratings. : 973. TOTAL: 1122.
W.R.N.S. : " : 29. " " : 548. " : 577.

AFFILIATED AIRFIELDS : -

PRESENT USE [1985] : Industry/Housing.

NO: 183.

AIRFIELD NAME: DONNA NOOK. OPENED : 1940.
COUNTY : Lincolnshire. CLOSED : 1945.
COMMAND : Coastal.
FORMATION : 16 Grp[Gillingham] GRID REF: A 902189[40]
FUNCTION : Operational[satellite] O.S.REF.: TF 430980.

LOCALITY : 12.5miles SE of Grimsby.
RAILWAY STN. : Lough 11miles[LNER]

LATITUDE : 53 27 30N. HEIGHT ASL : 13′ LIGHTING : Mk1.
LONGITUDE : 00 09 30E. FLYING CONTROL : Yes. RADIO : QDM.

LANDMARKS DAY : Admiralty Beacon 90′ high north of A/F 1900yds from centre.

LANDMARKS NIGHT : As day.

OBSTRUCTIONS : See permanent landmarks.

LANDING AREA SURFACE : Grass.

QDM: NE-SW. LENGTH X WIDTH: 1400yds. Ext: 2800yds.
: NW-SE. : 1600yds. : 1600yds.
: - : - : 2200yds.
: : :

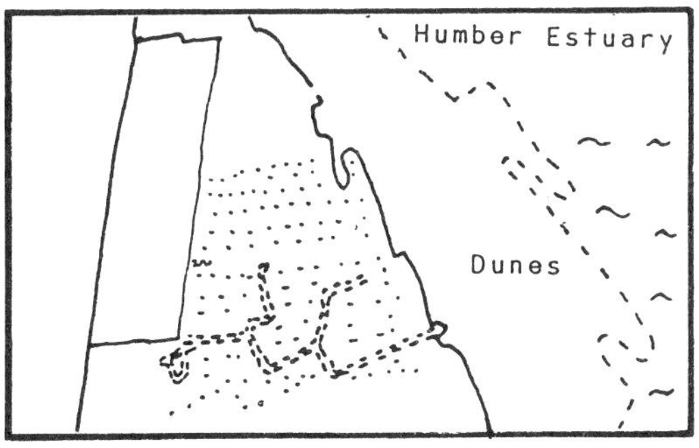

EXTENSIBILITY : Entails demolition of 1 small farm & 3 cottages.
ACCOMMODATION : Temporary.
HANGARS : T2-1;blister-2.

HARDSTANDINGS : None.

R.A.F. : OFFICERS: 67. S.N.C.O′s.: 115.O.R′s.: 1303.TOTAL: 1485.
W.A.A.F.: " : 4. " : 2. " : 98. " : 104.

AFFILIATED AIRFIELDS : North Coates.

PRESENT USE [1985] : Agriculture.

NO: 184.

AIRFIELD NAME: DOUNREAY. OPENED : Under Cons.
COUNTY : Caithness. CLOSED : 1954.
COMMAND : RN.
FORMATION : HMS Tern 11. GRID REF: D 58 [Scot]
FUNCTION : Under Construction. O.S.REF.: NC 993670.

LOCALITY : 1.5miles NE of Reay.
RAILWAY STN. : Thurso[LMS]

LATITUDE : 58 34 45N. HEIGHT ASL : 90′ LIGHTING : None.
LONGITUDE : 03 43 35W. FLYING CONTROL : None.RADIO : None.

LANDMARKS DAY : Dunnet Head 12miles ENE with Dunnet & Thurso bays, & town of Thurso.

LANDMARKS NIGHT : -

OBSTRUCTIONS : -

LANDING AREA SURFACE : Under construction.

QDM: 048-228. LENGTH X WIDTH: 2000 x 50yds. Ext: -
: 170-350. : 1100 x 50yds. : -
: 110-290. : 1100 x 50yds. : -
: : :

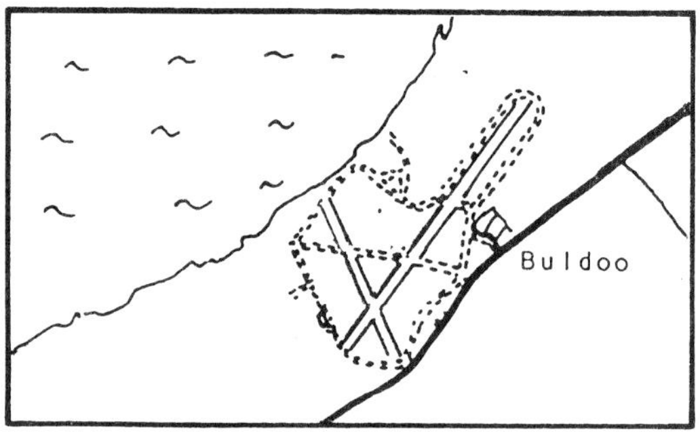

EXTENSIBILITY : -

ACCOMMODATION : Temporary.
HANGARS :

HARDSTANDINGS :

R.N. : OFFICERS: 98. Chiefs/POs/Ratings. : 640. TOTAL: 738.
W.R.N.S. : " : 7. " " : 247. " : 254.

AFFILIATED AIRFIELDS : -

PRESENT USE [1985] : Nuclear Power Station[Dounreay]

NO: 185.

AIRFIELD NAME: DOWN AMPNEY. OPENED : 1944.
COUNTY : Wiltshire. CLOSED : 1946.
COMMAND : Transport.
FORMATION : 46 Grp[Harrow Weald] GRID REF: P 558172[104]
FUNCTION : Operational. O.S.REF.: SU 112965.

LOCALITY : 7miles NNW of Swindon.
RAILWAY STN. : Cricklade[GWR]

LATITUDE : 51 40 00N. HEIGHT ASL : 265′ LIGHTING : Mk2.
LONGITUDE : 01 50 15W. FLYING CONTROL : Yes. RADIO : QDM.

LANDMARKS DAY : Town of Cricklade to SSW.

LANDMARKS NIGHT : -

OBSTRUCTIONS : -

LANDING AREA SURFACE : Concrete.

QDM: 030. LENGTH X WIDTH: 2000 x 50yds. Ext: 3600yds.
: 090. : 1400 x 50yds. : 2800yds.
: 150. : 1400 x 50yds. : 2700yds.

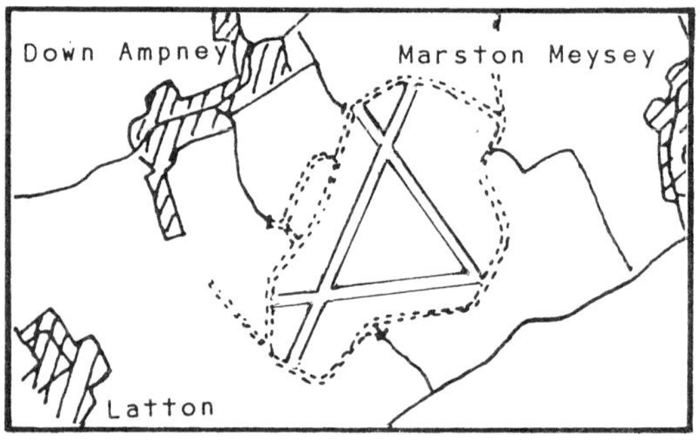

EXTENSIBILITY : Entails demolition of farm building in NW approach to No 3 R/W.
ACCOMMODATION : Temporary.
HANGARS : T2-2.

HARDSTANDINGS : Loop-50.

R.A.F. : OFFICERS: 249.S.N.C.O's.: 510.O.R's.: 1386.TOTAL: 2145.
W.A.A.F.: " : 12. " : 20. " : 252. " : 284.

AFFILIATED AIRFIELDS : -

PRESENT USE [1985] : Gravel extraction.

NO: 186.

AIRFIELD NAME: DOWNHAM MARKET. OPENED : 1942.
COUNTY : Norfolk. CLOSED : 1946.
COMMAND : Bomber.
FORMATION : 8 Grp[Huntingdon] GRID REF: G 082226[65]
FUNCTION : Operational. O.S.REF.: TF 630042.

LOCALITY : 10miles S of Kings Lynn.
RAILWAY STN. : Downham Market[LNER]

LATITUDE : 52 36 30N. HEIGHT ASL : 123′ LIGHTING : Mk2.
LONGITUDE : 00 24 30E. FLYING CONTROL : Yes. RADIO : QDM.

LANDMARKS DAY : -

LANDMARKS NIGHT : -

OBSTRUCTIONS : -

LANDING AREA SURFACE : Concrete.

QDM: 093. LENGTH X WIDTH: 1900 x 50yds. Ext: 3000yds.
: 034. : 1400 x 50yds. : 2000yds.
: 337. : 1400 x 50yds. : -
: : :

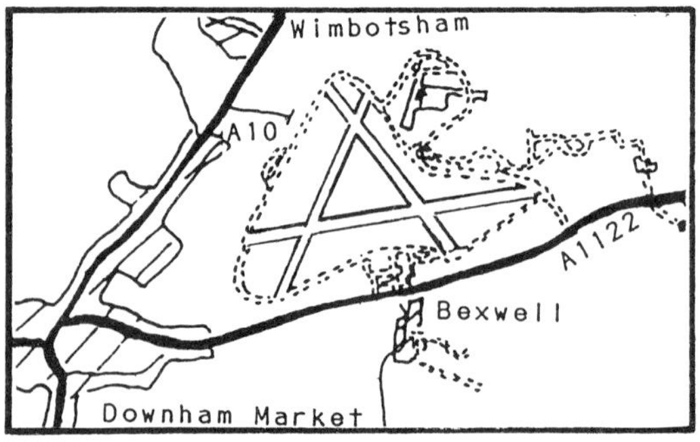

EXTENSIBILITY : Entails heavy grading & filling, diversion of a road & demolition of a farm.
ACCOMMODATION : Temporary.
HANGARS : T2-2;Glider[T2];B1-1.

HARDSTANDINGS : Frying pan-36.

R.A.F. : OFFICERS: 185.S.N.C.O's.: 262.O.R's.: 1272.TOTAL: 1719.
W.A.A.F.: " : 8. " : 8. " : 310. " : 326.

AFFILIATED AIRFIELDS : -

PRESENT USE [1985] : Disused.

NO: 187.

AIRFIELD NAME: DREM. OPENED : 1917.
COUNTY : East Lothian. CLOSED : 1946.
COMMAND : Fighter.
FORMATION : 13 Grp[Inverness] GRID REF: 0 989015[68Scot]
FUNCTION : Forward Airfield. Night Fighter. O.S.REF.: NT 505810.
LOCALITY : 4miles NNW Haddington.
RAILWAY STN. : Drem 2miles[LMS]

LATITUDE : 56 01 07N. HEIGHT ASL : 52′ LIGHTING : Mk2.
LONGITUDE : 02 48 00W. FLYING CONTROL : Yes. RADIO : QDM.

LANDMARKS DAY : Bass Rock & Berwick Law 250degrees M.

LANDMARKS NIGHT : -

OBSTRUCTIONS : -

LANDING AREA SURFACE : Grass.

QDM	LENGTH X WIDTH	Ext
E-W.	1850yds.	2300yds.
NW-SE.	1400yds.	-
NE-SW.	1400yds.	-

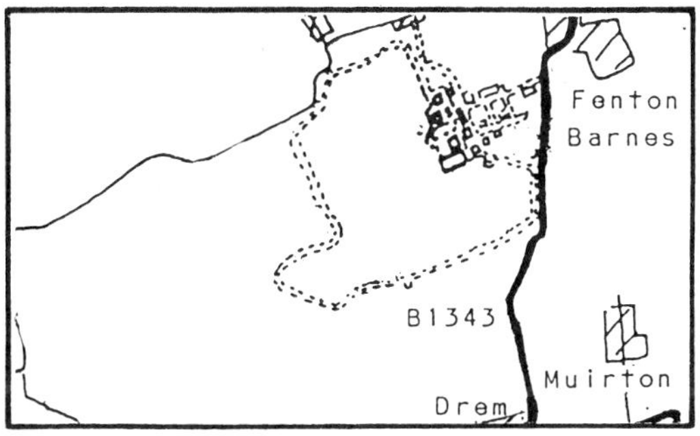

EXTENSIBILITY : -

ACCOMMODATION : Temporary.
HANGARS : Bellman-3;blister:0-10;EO-4.

HARDSTANDINGS : SE-7.

	OFFICERS	S.N.C.O's.	O.R's.	TOTAL
R.A.F.	104.	198.	1505.	1807.
W.A.A.F.	10.	8.	356.	374.

AFFILIATED AIRFIELDS : Turnhouse[Sector]

PRESENT USE [1985] : Disused.

NO: 188.

AIRFIELD NAME: DRIFFIELD. OPENED : 1936.
COUNTY : Yorkshire. CLOSED : 1977.
COMMAND : Bomber.
FORMATION : 4 Grp[York] GRID REF: A 477760[28]
FUNCTION : Operational[43 Base] O.S.REF.: SE 995565.

LOCALITY : 2miles WSW of Great Driffield.
RAILWAY STN. : Driffield[LNER]

LATITUDE : 53 59 45N. HEIGHT ASL : 65′ LIGHTING : Mk1.
LONGITUDE : 00 28 15W. FLYING CONTROL : Yes. RADIO : QDM.

LANDMARKS DAY : Great Driffield 2miles & monument 4.5miles NNW.

LANDMARKS NIGHT : Flamborough Head 18miles NNE.

OBSTRUCTIONS : -

LANDING AREA SURFACE : Concrete.

QDM	LENGTH X WIDTH	Ext
236.	2000 x 50yds.	-
281.	1400 x 50yds.	-
336.	1400 x 50yds.	-

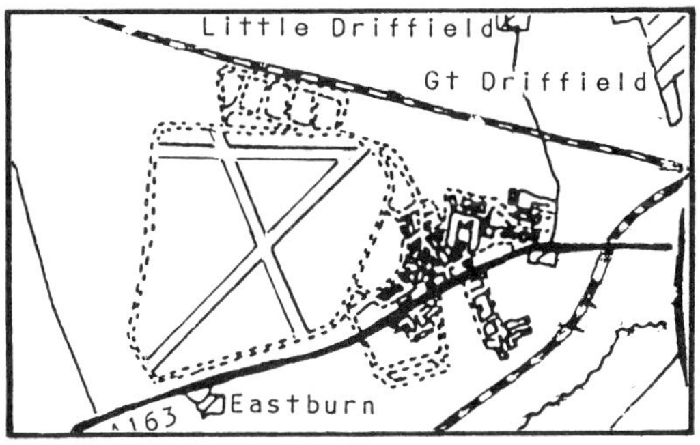

EXTENSIBILITY : None possible.

ACCOMMODATION : Permanent.
HANGARS : Type C-5.

HARDSTANDINGS : Heavy bomber-36.

	OFFICERS	S.N.C.O's.	O.R's.	TOTAL
R.A.F.	189.	373.	1322.	1884.
W.A.A.F.	20.	22.	380.	422.

AFFILIATED AIRFIELDS : Leconfield & Lissett[Sub-stations]

PRESENT USE [1985] : Agriculture.

NO: 189.

AIRFIELD NAME: DUMFRIES. OPENED : 1940.
COUNTY : Dumfriesshire. CLOSED : 1957.
COMMAND : Flying Training.
FORMATION : 29 Grp[Dumfries] GRID REF: T 484008[88Scot]
FUNCTION : Advanced Flying Unit. [parent] O.S.REF.: NX 998788.
LOCALITY : 2miles NNE of Dumfries.
RAILWAY STN. : Dumfries[LMS]

LATITUDE : 55 05 38N. HEIGHT ASL : 100′ LIGHTING : Mk2.
LONGITUDE : 03 34 15W. FLYING CONTROL : Yes. RADIO : QDM.

LANDMARKS DAY : Solway Firth, R Nith.

LANDMARKS NIGHT : As day.

OBSTRUCTIONS : -

LANDING AREA SURFACE : Concrete & tarmac.

QDM	LENGTH X WIDTH	Ext
180.	1300 x 50yds.	1400yds.
090.	1000 x 50yds.	1100yds.

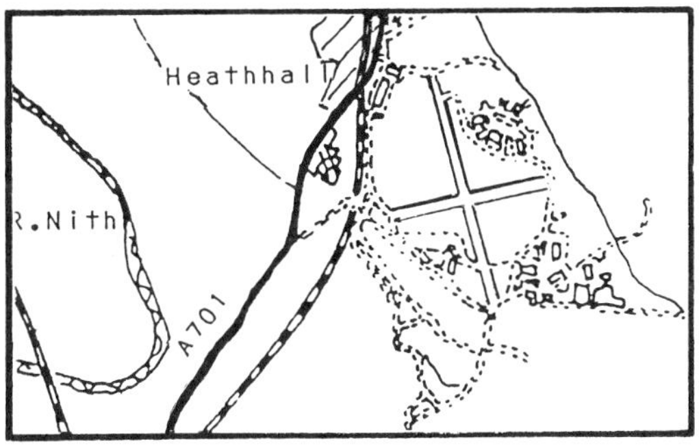

EXTENSIBILITY : -

ACCOMMODATION : Permanent[part]
HANGARS : Various-36.

HARDSTANDINGS : None.

	OFFICERS	S.N.C.O's.	O.R's.	TOTAL
R.A.F.	197.	371.	778.	1346.
W.A.A.F.	14.	8.	423.	445.

AFFILIATED AIRFIELDS : -

PRESENT USE [1985] : Industry.

NO: 190.

AIRFIELD NAME: DUNDONALD. OPENED : 1940.
COUNTY : Ayrshire. CLOSED : 1945.
COMMAND : Transport.
FORMATION : 44 Grp[Gloucester] GRID REF: S 851580[Scot]
FUNCTION : Training. O.S.REF.: NS 370362.

LOCALITY : 4.5miles SW of Kilmarnock.
RAILWAY STN. : Troon[LMS]

LATITUDE : 55 35 00N. HEIGHT ASL : 50′ LIGHTING : None.
LONGITUDE : 04 36 30W. FLYING CONTROL : None.RADIO : QDM.

LANDMARKS DAY : Railway bounding NW perimeter. High ground to S. Spot height 477′

LANDMARKS NIGHT : -

OBSTRUCTIONS : High ground to S of A/F.

LANDING AREA SURFACE : Steel Matting[Sommerfeld track]

QDM: 230. LENGTH X WIDTH: 1480yds. Ext: -
: 285. : 900yds. : -
: : :
: : :

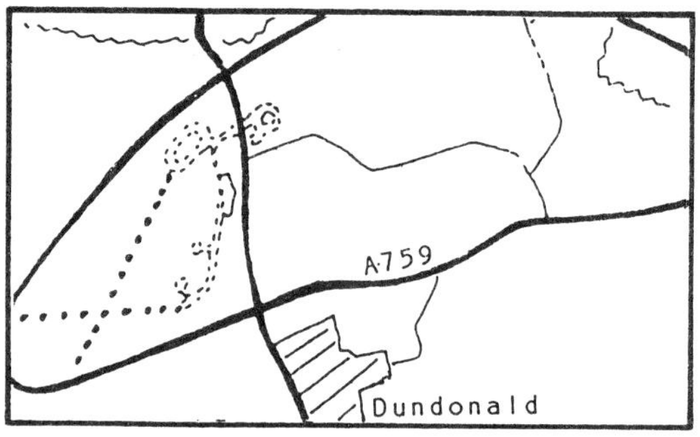

EXTENSIBILITY : None possible.

ACCOMMODATION : Temporary.
HANGARS : 0 blister-2.

HARDSTANDINGS : Concrete-5.

R.A.F. : OFFICERS: 10. S.N.C.O′s.: 33. O.R′s.: 161. TOTAL: 204.
W.A.A.F.: " : - " : - " : - " : -

AFFILIATED AIRFIELDS : -

PRESENT USE [1985] : Agriculture.

NO: 191.

AIRFIELD NAME: DUNHOLME LODGE. OPENED : 1943.
COUNTY : Lincolnshire. CLOSED : 1964.
COMMAND : Bomber.
FORMATION : 1 Grp[Bawtry] GRID REF: F 466976[47]
FUNCTION : Operational. O.S.REF.: SK 995784.

LOCALITY : 5miles NE of Lincoln.
RAILWAY STN. : Langworth 4miles[LNER]

LATITUDE : 53 17 30N. HEIGHT ASL : 100′ LIGHTING : Mk2.
LONGITUDE : 00 30 15W. FLYING CONTROL : Yes. RADIO : QDM.

LANDMARKS DAY : Wood on E side.

LANDMARKS NIGHT : -

OBSTRUCTIONS : Wood on E side.

LANDING AREA SURFACE : Concrete & tarmac.

QDM: 164. LENGTH X WIDTH: 1700 x 50yds. Ext: 2000yds.
: 220. : 2000 x 50yds. : 2500yds.
: 278. : 1400 x 50yds. : 1600yds.

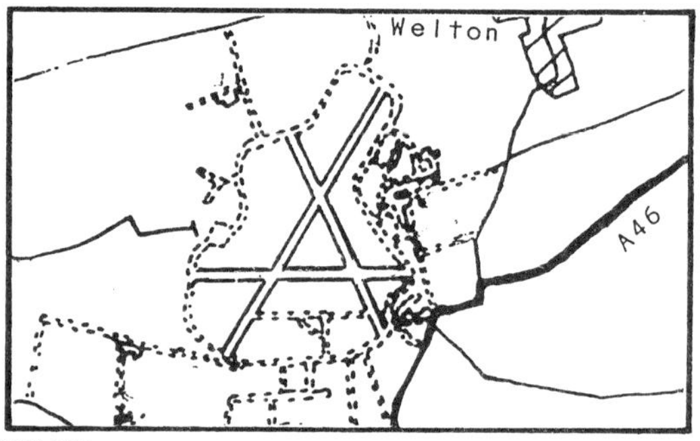

EXTENSIBILITY : -

ACCOMMODATION : Temporary.
HANGARS : T2-2;Type B-1.

HARDSTANDINGS : Heavy bomber-36.

R.A.F. : OFFICERS: 144.S.N.C.O′s.: 369.O.R′s.: 1124.TOTAL: 1637.
W.A.A.F.: " : 12. " : 24. " : 432. " : 468.

AFFILIATED AIRFIELDS : Scampton[15 Base]

PRESENT USE [1985] : Agriculture.

NO: 192.

AIRFIELD NAME: DUNINO. OPENED : 1941.
COUNTY : Fifeshire. CLOSED : 1946.
COMMAND : RN.
FORMATION : Books of HMS Jackdaw. GRID REF: P 065325[Scot]
FUNCTION : Storage[satellite] O.S.REF.: NO 565115.

LOCALITY : 4miles SE of St Andrews.
RAILWAY STN. : St Andrews & Crail[NB]

LATITUDE : 56 17 25N. HEIGHT ASL : 250′ LIGHTING : None.
LONGITUDE : 02 42 20W. FLYING CONTROL : None.RADIO : QDM.

LANDMARKS DAY : Firth of Forth with Isle of May 8.75miles SE. Coastal railway Crail-St.Andrews eastern end of A/F.

LANDMARKS NIGHT : -

OBSTRUCTIONS : -

LANDING AREA SURFACE : Grass, 051-231 Steel Matting [BRC & Sommerfeld Track]
QDM: 090-270. LENGTH X WIDTH: 1284 x 50yds. Ext: -
: 051-231. : 1200yds. : -
: 090-270. : 1400yds. : -
: 156-336. : 900yds. : -

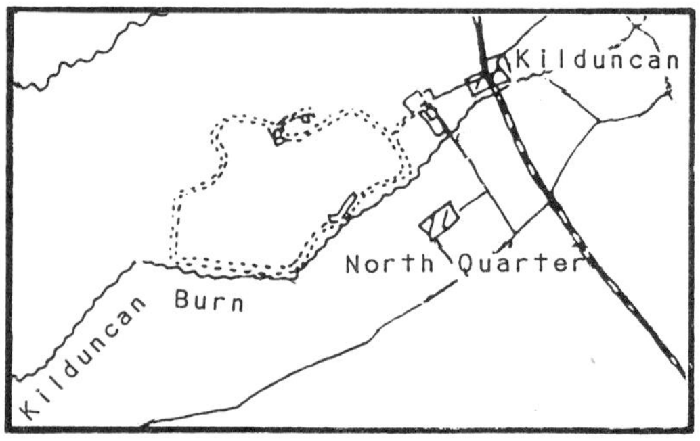

EXTENSIBILITY : -

ACCOMMODATION : Temporary.
HANGARS : Superblister 91x45′[sqdn]-8;60x70′[sqdn]-4; 60x70′[storage]-4.
HARDSTANDINGS :

R.N. : OFFICERS: 88. Chiefs/POs/Ratings. : 647. TOTAL: 735.
W.R.N.S. : " : 5. " " : 135. " : 140.

AFFILIATED AIRFIELDS : Crail[Parent]

PRESENT USE [1985] : Agriculture.

NO: 193.

AIRFIELD NAME: DUNKESWELL. OPENED : 1943.
COUNTY : Devonshire. CLOSED : 1949.
COMMAND : USNAC.
FORMATION : Fleet Air Wing 7. GRID REF: T 566290[129]
FUNCTION : Operational. O.S.REF.: ST 132079.

LOCALITY : 5miles NNW of Honiton.
RAILWAY STN. : Honiton[SR]

LATITUDE : 50 51 45N. HEIGHT ASL : 825′ LIGHTING : Mk2.
LONGITUDE : 03 14 00W. FLYING CONTROL : Yes. RADIO : QDM.

LANDMARKS DAY : Wellington monument 6miles N of A/F.

LANDMARKS NIGHT : -

OBSTRUCTIONS : -

LANDING AREA SURFACE : Concrete covered with asphalt.

QDM	LENGTH X WIDTH	Ext
230.	2000 x 50yds.	-
360.	1470 x 50yds.	-
270.	1270 x 50yds.	-

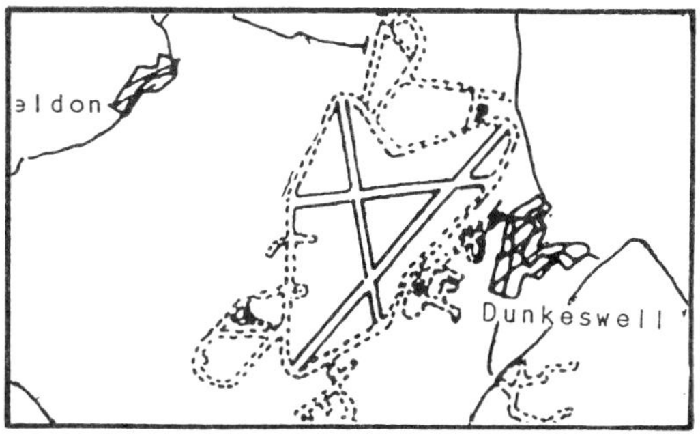

EXTENSIBILITY : -

ACCOMMODATION : Temporary.
HANGARS : T2-5.

HARDSTANDINGS : 125′dia tarmac on concrete-44;spectacle ditto-6.

USN. : OFFICERS: 252. Enlisted Men. : 2320.TOTAL: 2572.

AFFILIATED AIRFIELDS : -

PRESENT USE [1985] : Industry.

NO: 194.

AIRFIELD NAME: DUNSFOLD. OPENED : 1942.
COUNTY : Surrey. CLOSED :
COMMAND : Fighter.
FORMATION : 11 Grp[Uxbridge] GRID REF: Q 465555[124]
FUNCTION : Forward Airfield. O.S.REF.: TQ 025363.

LOCALITY : 8.5miles SSE of Guildford.
RAILWAY STN. : Cranleigh[SR]

LATITUDE : 51 06 53N. HEIGHT ASL : 168′ LIGHTING : Mk2.
LONGITUDE : 00 31 53W. FLYING CONTROL : Yes. RADIO : QDM.

LANDMARKS DAY : Town of Guildford 9miles 060degrees.

LANDMARKS NIGHT : -

OBSTRUCTIONS : -

LANDING AREA SURFACE : Concrete & wood chippings.

QDM	LENGTH X WIDTH	Ext
257.	2000 x 50yds.	2500yds.
210.	1400 x 50yds.	2000yds.
306.	1400 x 50yds.	2100yds.

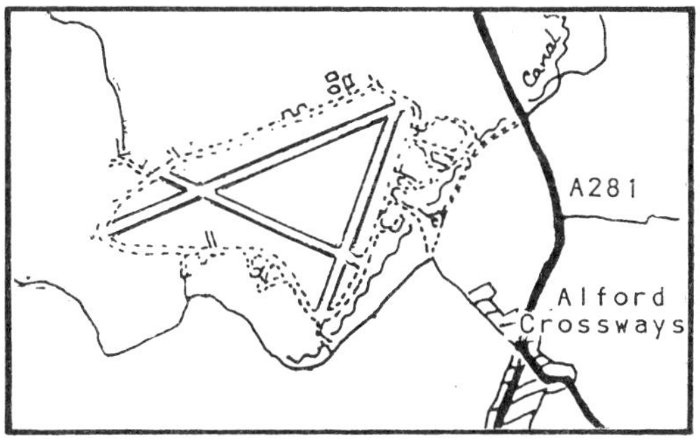

EXTENSIBILITY : Entails some demolition-recommended to 2500-1750&1750yds only.
ACCOMMODATION : Temporary.
HANGARS : T2-2;blister-11.

HARDSTANDINGS : Frying pan[100′sq]-38.

R.A.F. : OFFICERS: 102.S.N.C.O′s.: 103.O.R′s.: 825. TOTAL: 1030.
W.A.A.F.: " : 6. " : 10. " : 195. " : 211.

AFFILIATED AIRFIELDS : Tangmere[Sector]

PRESENT USE [1985] : Aircraft Industry[British Aerospace]

NO: 195.

AIRFIELD NAME: DUXFORD. OPENED : 1919.
COUNTY : Cambridgeshire. CLOSED : 1961.
COMMAND : 8th USAAF.
FORMATION : 78th Fighter Grp. GRID REF: L 916648[85]
FUNCTION : Operational. O.S.REF.: TL 464558.

LOCALITY : 8miles S of Cambridge.
RAILWAY STN. : Whittlesford 2miles[LNER]

LATITUDE : 52 05 27N. HEIGHT ASL : 97′ LIGHTING : None.
LONGITUDE : 00 08 00E. FLYING CONTROL : Yes. RADIO : QDM.

LANDMARKS DAY : LNER 2miles E. Newmarket-Royston main road N boundary.

LANDMARKS NIGHT : -

OBSTRUCTIONS : Trees 40′ high E-W approach. 2 radio masts & 4 hangars on N approach.

LANDING AREA SURFACE : Grass.

QDM	LENGTH X WIDTH	Ext
N-S.	1400yds.	400yds.
NW-SE.	1600yds.	3000yds.
NE-SW.	1800yds.	2000yds.

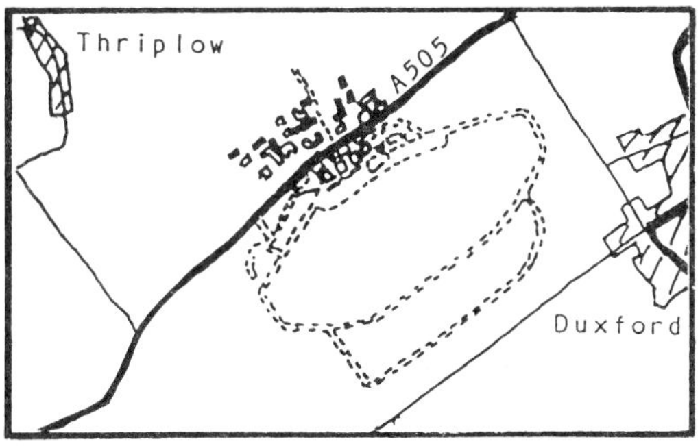

EXTENSIBILITY : Only 2 X 2000yds recommended-entails diversion & possible demolition of 14 houses.
ACCOMMODATION : Permanent.
HANGARS : Blister-8;Belfast:[double]-3;[single]-1.

HARDSTANDINGS : TE-26, steel-47.

USAAF. : OFFICERS: 190. Enlisted Men. : 1519.TOTAL: 1709.

AFFILIATED AIRFIELDS : -

PRESENT USE [1985] : Museum[Imperial War Museum]

NO: 196.

AIRFIELD NAME: DYCE. OPENED : 1934.
COUNTY : Aberdeenshire. CLOSED :
COMMAND : Coastal.
FORMATION : 106 Grp[Fifield House] GRID REF: K 395331[45Scot]
FUNCTION : Photographic Recce Unit O.S.REF.: NO 879126.
Operational Training.
LOCALITY : 5miles NNW of Aberdeen.
RAILWAY STN. : Dyce 2miles[LNER]

LATITUDE : 57 12 15N. HEIGHT ASL : 200′ LIGHTING : Mk2.
LONGITUDE : 02 12 15W. FLYING CONTROL : Yes. RADIO : QDM.

LANDMARKS DAY : R Don, NE of Aberdeen.

LANDMARKS NIGHT : -

OBSTRUCTIONS : Hill 1.5miles W 550′. Hill 2miles SW 600′

LANDING AREA SURFACE : Concrete covered with tarmac.

QDM	LENGTH X WIDTH	Ext
193.	1330 x 50yds.	1900yds.
241.	1230 x 50yds.	1900yds.
334.	1330 x 50yds.	

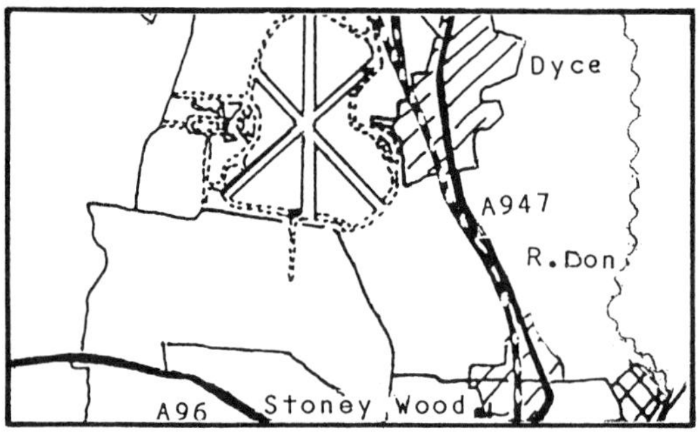

EXTENSIBILITY : -

ACCOMMODATION : Temporary.
HANGARS : Bellman-4;blister:EO-10;twin EO-2;twin T3-2.

HARDSTANDINGS : 80′dia-37.

	OFFICERS	S.N.C.O′s.	O.R′s.	TOTAL
R.A.F.	101.	152.	1089.	1342.
W.A.A.F.	6.	44.	484.	534.

AFFILIATED AIRFIELDS : -

PRESENT USE [1985] : Civil Airport[Aberdeen]

NO: 197.

AIRFIELD NAME: EARLS COLNE. OPENED : 1943.
COUNTY : Essex. CLOSED : 1947.
COMMAND : Fighter.
FORMATION : 38 Grp[Marks Hall] GRID REF: M 303447[97]
FUNCTION : Operational. O.S.REF.: TL 848270.

LOCALITY : 3miles SW of Halstead.
RAILWAY STN. : Earls Colne 1.5miles[LNER]

LATITUDE : 51 54 30N. HEIGHT ASL : 225′ LIGHTING : Mk2.
LONGITUDE : 00 41 15E. FLYING CONTROL : Yes. RADIO : QDM.

LANDMARKS DAY : Earls Colne 1mile NE; Coggeshall 2miles SE.

LANDMARKS NIGHT : -

OBSTRUCTIONS : Nil, except building marked with obstruction light.

LANDING AREA SURFACE : Concrete, tarmac & wood chippings.

QDM	LENGTH X WIDTH	Ext
192.	2000 x 50yds.	2750yds.
252.	1400 x 50yds.	3400yds.
302.	1400 x 50yds.	2100yds.

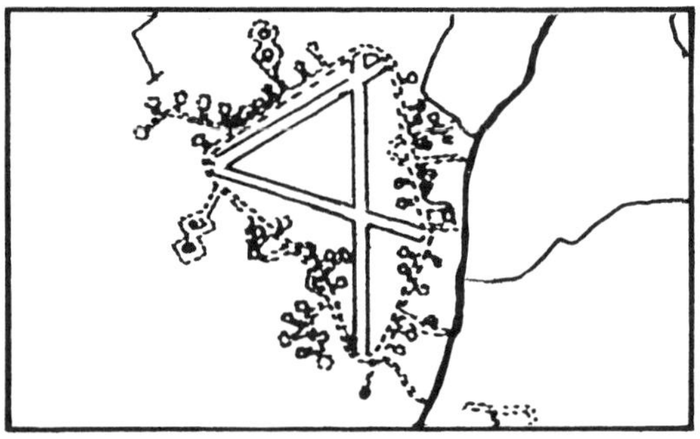

EXTENSIBILITY : Would entail demolition of farm buildings etc, & extensive tree felling.
ACCOMMODATION : Temporary.
HANGARS : T2-2.

HARDSTANDINGS : Frying pan-35.

	OFFICERS	S.N.C.O′s.	O.R′s.	TOTAL
R.A.F.	208.	501.	1304.	2013.
W.A.A.F.	10.	20.	255.	285.

AFFILIATED AIRFIELDS : -

PRESENT USE [1985] : Disused.

NO: 198.

AIRFIELD NAME: EAST FORTUNE. OPENED : 1916.
COUNTY : East Lothian. CLOSED : 1961.
COMMAND : Coastal.
FORMATION : 17 Grp[Edinburgh] GRID REF: T 055000[68Scot]
FUNCTION : Operational Training Unit[parent] O.S.REF.: NT 555786.
LOCALITY : 4miles NNE of Haddington.
RAILWAY STN. : East Fortune[LNER]

LATITUDE : 56 00 00N. HEIGHT ASL : 95′ LIGHTING : Mk2.
LONGITUDE : 02 42 45W. FLYING CONTROL : Yes. RADIO : QDM.

LANDMARKS DAY : North Berwick Law 613′ASL. 3.5miles N. Railway N & E edge.

LANDMARKS NIGHT : _

OBSTRUCTIONS : Garleton Hill 596′ ASL 250degrees T.Lammermuir to S 1500′ ASL. Chimney N side 150′

LANDING AREA SURFACE : Hardcore & Tarmac.

QDM	LENGTH X WIDTH	Ext
192.	1100 x 50yds.	1104yds.
252.	1710 x 50yds.	2000yds.
293.	1560 x 50yds.	2000yds.

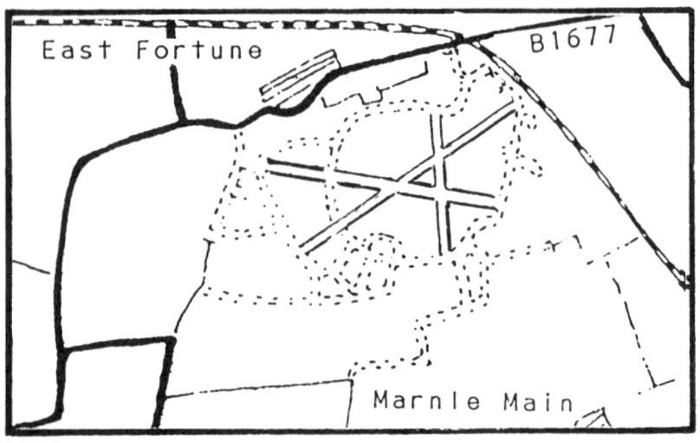

EXTENSIBILITY : -

ACCOMMODATION : Temporary.
HANGARS : Callendar Hamilton-3;blister:O[65′]-2;EO[69′]-6. T2-1.
HARDSTANDINGS : TE[hardcore]-40;[concrete on hardcore]-6.

	OFFICERS	S.N.C.O′s.	O.R′s.	TOTAL
R.A.F.	183.	236.	1082.	1501.
W.A.A.F.	12.	9.	683.	704.

AFFILIATED AIRFIELDS : -

PRESENT USE [1985] : Museum[Scottish Museum of Flight]

AIRFIELD NAME: EAST HAVEN. OPENED : 1943.
COUNTY : Angus. CLOSED : 1946.
COMMAND : RN.
FORMATION : HMS Peewit. GRID REF: P 097589[Scot]
FUNCTION : Deck landing training School. O.S.REF.: NO 595375.

LOCALITY : 3miles SW of Arbroath.
RAILWAY STN. : East Haven .5mile[DAJT]

LATITUDE : 56 31 45N. HEIGHT ASL : 75′ LIGHTING : Naval.
LONGITUDE : 02 39 55W. FLYING CONTROL : Yes. RADIO : QDM.

LANDMARKS DAY : Buddon Ness the N entrance point of Firth of Tay 4miles SW. Main road Arbroath-Dundee NW boundary. Railway 400yds. SE boundary.

LANDMARKS NIGHT : -

OBSTRUCTIONS : Rising land to N & W[600′ within 5miles]

LANDING AREA SURFACE : Tarmac.

QDM: 009-189. LENGTH X WIDTH: 1060 x 30yds. Ext: -
: 055-235.[low visibility] : 1220 x 30yds. : -
: 099-279. : 1015 x 30yds. : -
: 145-325. : 1000 x 30yds. : -

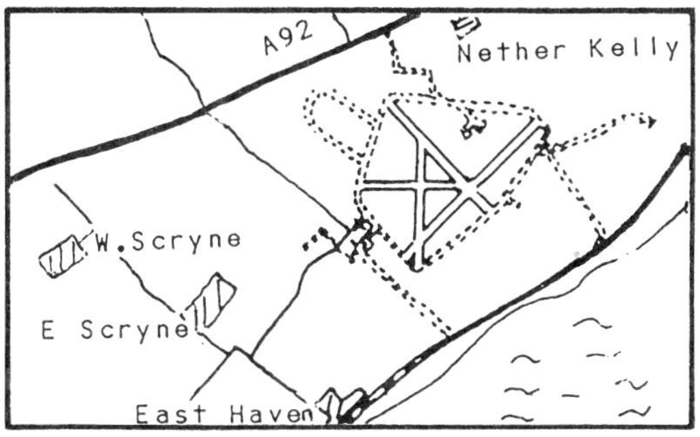

EXTENSIBILITY : -

ACCOMMODATION : Temporary.
HANGARS : 60x70′[sqdn]-12;[storage]-12.

HARDSTANDINGS : 4.

R.N. : OFFICERS: 154. Chiefs/POs/Ratings. : 1012.TOTAL: 1166.
W.R.N.S. : " : 14. " " : 364. " : 378.

AFFILIATED AIRFIELDS : -

PRESENT USE [1985] : Disused.

AIRFIELD NAME: EAST KIRKBY. OPENED : 1943.
COUNTY : Lincolnshire. CLOSED : 1970.
COMMAND : Bomber.
FORMATION : 5 Grp[Morton Hall] GRID REF: F 804807[48]
FUNCTION : Operational[55 Base] O.S.REF.: TF 342618.

LOCALITY : 4miles SW of Spilsby.
RAILWAY STN. : Stickney[LNER]

LATITUDE : 53 08 00N. HEIGHT ASL : 30′ LIGHTING : Mk2.
LONGITUDE : 00 00 15E. FLYING CONTROL : Yes. RADIO : QDM.

LANDMARKS DAY : Boston cathedral stump 12miles S of A/F.

LANDMARKS NIGHT : -

OBSTRUCTIONS : Hill 300′ 3miles 060degrees.

LANDING AREA SURFACE : Concrete.

QDM: 200. LENGTH X WIDTH: 2000 x 50yds. Ext: 2300yds.
: 263. : 1400 x 50yds. : 4000yds.
: 308. : 1400 x 50yds. : 2200yds.
: : :

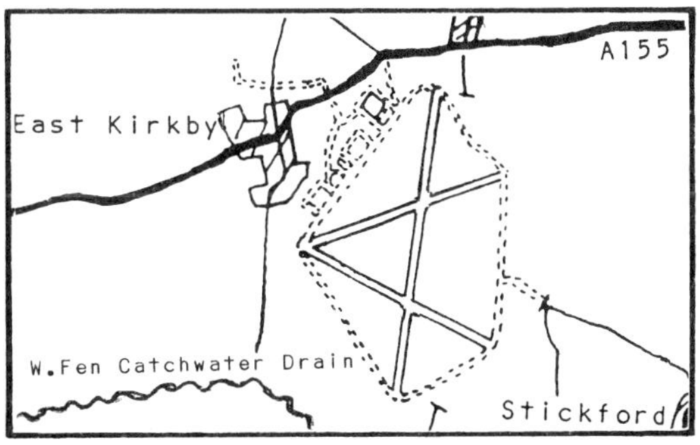

EXTENSIBILITY : -

ACCOMMODATION : Temporary.
HANGARS : T2-6;B1-1.

HARDSTANDINGS : Circular concrete-27;loop-5.

R.A.F. : OFFICERS: 196.S.N.C.O′s.: 428.O.R′s.: 1341.TOTAL: 1965.
W.A.A.F. : " : 10. " : 26. " : 456. " : 482.

AFFILIATED AIRFIELDS : Spilsby & Strubby[Sub-stations]

PRESENT USE [1985] : Agriculture.

AIRFIELD NAME: EAST MOOR. OPENED : 1942.
COUNTY : Yorkshire. CLOSED : 1946.
COMMAND : Bomber.
FORMATION : 6 RCAF Grp[Allerton Pk] GRID REF: A 075840[27]
FUNCTION : Operational. O.S.REF.: SE 600640.

LOCALITY : 7.75miles N of York.
RAILWAY STN. : York[LNER]

LATITUDE : 54 04 00N. HEIGHT ASL : 87′ LIGHTING : Mk2.
LONGITUDE : 01 05 00W. FLYING CONTROL : Yes. RADIO : QDM.

LANDMARKS DAY : Sheriff Hutton castle 3.5miles 065degrees.

LANDMARKS NIGHT : -

OBSTRUCTIONS : -

LANDING AREA SURFACE : Concrete.

QDM: 078. LENGTH X WIDTH: 1407 x 50yds. Ext: 4000yds.
: 036. : 1433 x 50yds. : 2500yds.
: 169. : 1900 x 50yds. : 3500yds.
: : :

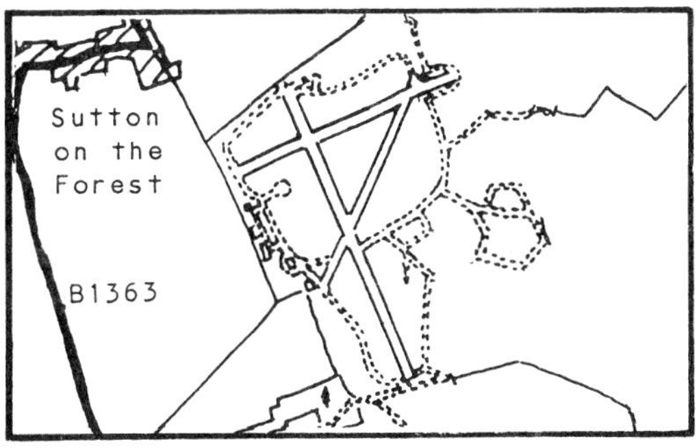

EXTENSIBILITY : Entails replacement of considerable lengths of unclassified roads.
ACCOMMODATION : Temporary.
HANGARS : T2-2;B1-1.

HARDSTANDINGS : Heavy bomber-36.

R.C.A.F. : OFFICERS: 152.S.N.C.O′s.: 387.O.R′s.: 1555.TOTAL: 2094.
W.A.A.F. : " : 4. " : 16. " : 387. " : 407.

AFFILIATED AIRFIELDS : Linton on Ouse[62 RCAF Base]

PRESENT USE [1985] : Agriculture.

AIRFIELD NAME: EAST WRETHAM. OPENED : 1940.
COUNTY : Norfolk. CLOSED : 1946.
COMMAND : 8th USAAF.
FORMATION : 359th Fighter Grp. GRID REF: G 360080[76]
FUNCTION : Operational. O.S.REF.: TL 905895.

LOCALITY : 6miles NE of Thetford.
RAILWAY STN. : Wretham & Hockham[LNER]

LATITUDE : 52 28 08N. HEIGHT ASL : 135′ LIGHTING : Mk2.
LONGITUDE : 00 48 15E. FLYING CONTROL : Yes RADIO : QDM.

LANDMARKS DAY : Plantation[Forestry Commission] & lakes.

LANDMARKS NIGHT : As day.

OBSTRUCTIONS : _

LANDING AREA SURFACE : Grass.

QDM	LENGTH X WIDTH	Ext
NE-SW.	1880yds.	4000yds.
NNW-SSE.	1400yds.	4000yds.
N-S.	1400yds.	2600yds.

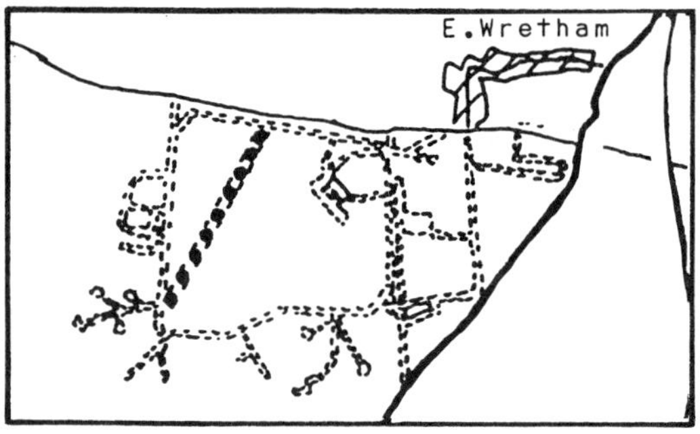

EXTENSIBILITY : -

ACCOMMODATION : Temporary.
HANGARS : Bellman-2;Blister-6;Canvas[steel frame]-1.

HARDSTANDINGS : Punched planking-12, macadem-24.

USAAF. : OFFICERS: 190. Enlisted Men. : 1519.TOTAL: 1709.

AFFILIATED AIRFIELDS : -

PRESENT USE [1985] : Disused.

NO: 203.

AIRFIELD NAME: EASTCHURCH. OPENED : 1911.
COUNTY : Kent. CLOSED : 1946.
COMMAND : Flying Training.
FORMATION : 54 Grp[Sunningdale] GRID REF: R 426880[116]
FUNCTION : Aircrew Re-selection Centre. O.S.REF.: TQ 988698.
LOCALITY : 4.5miles SE of Sheppey.
RAILWAY STN. : Eastchurch[SR]

LATITUDE : 51 23 30N. HEIGHT ASL : 47′ LIGHTING : None.
LONGITUDE : 00 51 00E. FLYING CONTROL : None.RADIO : QDM.

LANDMARKS DAY : Water tower 200′ ASL to NW inside boundary.

LANDMARKS NIGHT : R Swale & waterways to S.

OBSTRUCTIONS : Water tower 200′ ASL & hangars[35′approx]on the inside of "L" formed by the 2 landing areas 2 wireless masts 70′ high to be errected.

LANDING AREA SURFACE : Grass.

QDM	LENGTH X WIDTH	Ext
SE-NW.	1600yds.	2000x400yds.
N-S.	1200yds.	1400x200yds.
E-W.	1200yds.	1400x200yds.

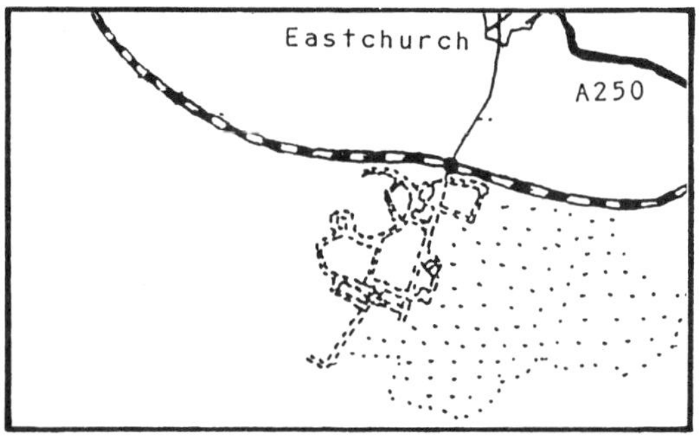

EXTENSIBILITY : -

ACCOMMODATION : Permanent[part]
HANGARS : Bellman-3.

HARDSTANDINGS : Rectangular[sommerfeld]-51.

R.A.F. : OFFICERS: 118.S.N.C.O's.: 81. O.R's.: 1809.TOTAL: 2008
W.A.A.F.: " : 16. " : - " : 294. " : 310

AFFILIATED AIRFIELDS : -

PRESENT USE [1985] : HM Prison.

NO: 204.

AIRFIELD NAME: EASTLEIGH. OPENED : 1917.
COUNTY : Hampshire. CLOSED :
COMMAND : RN.
FORMATION : HMS Raven. GRID REF: U 887372[132]
FUNCTION : Training Schools & storage Depot. O.S.REF.: SU 452168.
LOCALITY : NE outskirts of Southampton.
RAILWAY STN. : Swaythling .75miles[SR]

LATITUDE : 50 57 00N. HEIGHT ASL : 37′ LIGHTING : None.
LONGITUDE : 01 21 35W. FLYING CONTROL : Yes. RADIO : QDM.

LANDMARKS DAY : Southampton Water with Southampton at its head. Southampton-Eastleigh road & railway & Itchen navigation canal flowing past E boundary.

LANDMARKS NIGHT : -

OBSTRUCTIONS : W/T mast 240′ on a 389′ summit 5.75miles ENE. Balloon barrage in vicinity.

LANDING AREA SURFACE : Grass.

QDM	LENGTH X WIDTH	Ext
NNE-SSW.	1270yds.	-
WNW-ESE.	680yds.	-
208.	1200yds.	-

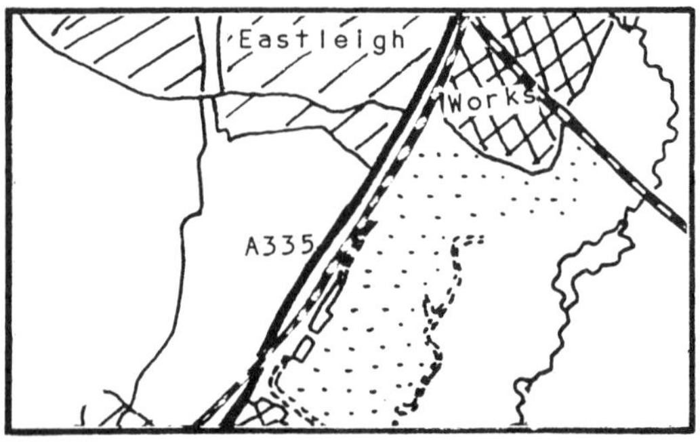

EXTENSIBILITY : -

ACCOMMODATION : Permanent[part]
HANGARS : 65x79′ Bessoneau-1.

HARDSTANDINGS :

R.N. : OFFICERS: 48. Chiefs/POs/Ratings. : 691. TOTAL: 739.
W.R.N.S. : " : 8. " " : 183. " : 191.

AFFILIATED AIRFIELDS : -

PRESENT USE [1985] : Civil Airport[Southampton]

NO: 205.

AIRFIELD NAME: EDGE HILL. OPENED : 1941.
COUNTY : Warwickshire. CLOSED : 1945.
COMMAND : Bomber.
FORMATION : 92 Grp[Winslow] GRID REF: P 812633[82]
FUNCTION : Operational Training Unit[satellite] O.S.REF.: SP 363433.
LOCALITY : 3miles SE of Kineton.
RAILWAY STN. : Banbury[GWR & LMS],Kineton[LMS]

LATITUDE : 52 05 08N. HEIGHT ASL : 628′ LIGHTING : Mk2.
LONGITUDE : 01 28 15W. FLYING CONTROL : Yes. RADIO : QDM.

LANDMARKS DAY : -

LANDMARKS NIGHT : -

OBSTRUCTIONS : Epwell hill 745′ 1mile SW. Shenlow hill 750′ .5miles from centre of A/F

LANDING AREA SURFACE : Concrete & tarmac.

QDM	LENGTH X WIDTH	Ext
172.	1540 x 50yds.	2440yds.
239.	1100 x 50yds.	1350yds.
284.	1100 x 50yds.	1315yds.

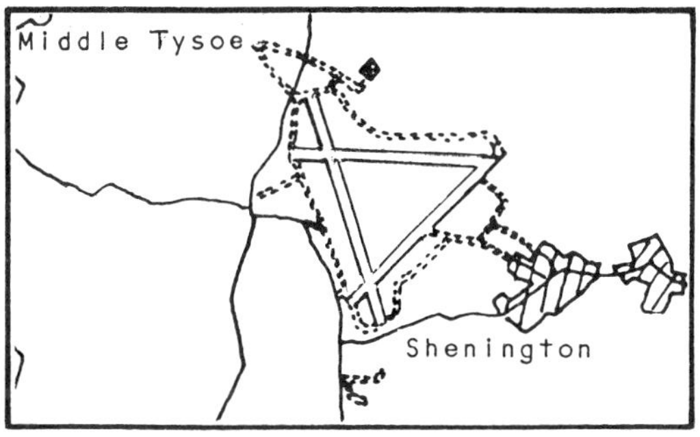

EXTENSIBILITY : Entails demolition of a barn.

ACCOMMODATION : Temporary.
HANGARS : T2-2;B1-1.

HARDSTANDINGS : Heavy bomber-27.

R.A.F. : OFFICERS: 70. S.N.C.O′s.: 291. O.R′s.: 646. TOTAL: 1007.
W.A.A.F.: " : 2. " : 5. " : 108. " : 115.

AFFILIATED AIRFIELDS : Chipping Warden[Parent]

PRESENT USE [1985] : Disused.

NO: 206.

AIRFIELD NAME: EDZELL. OPENED : 1940.
COUNTY : Forfarshire. CLOSED : 1952.
COMMAND : Maintenance.
FORMATION : 41 Grp[Andover] GRID REF: P 137902[51Scot]
FUNCTION : A/C Storage Unit. O.S.REF.: NO 632691.

LOCALITY : 6.5miles N of Brechin.
RAILWAY STN. : Montrose[LNER]

LATITUDE : 56 48 38N. HEIGHT ASL : 155′ LIGHTING : None.
LONGITUDE : 02 36 23W. FLYING CONTROL : Yes. RADIO : QDM.

LANDMARKS DAY : Pond N of boundary. North Eske river to W & S of A/F. Edzell wood 1mile SW of A/F.

LANDMARKS NIGHT : Small pond. North Eske river.

OBSTRUCTIONS : Hills 1500-300′ 3 to 5miles W & NW.

LANDING AREA SURFACE : Concrete.

QDM	LENGTH X WIDTH	Ext
243.	1600 x 50yds.	3000yds.
334.	1600 x 50yds.	3000yds.

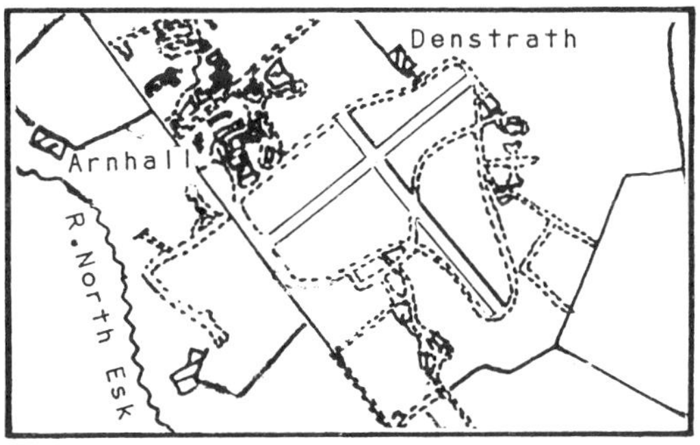

EXTENSIBILITY : Entails cutting of camp access & demolition of 2 farms.
ACCOMMODATION : Temporary.
HANGARS : Various-36.

HARDSTANDINGS : ′Y′ type 30′wide:concrete-50;tarmacadem-16.

R.A.F. : OFFICERS: 20. S.N.C.O′s.: 81. O.R′s.: 621. TOTAL: 722.
W.A.A.F.: " : 7. " : 8. " : 320. " : 335.

AFFILIATED AIRFIELDS : -

PRESENT USE [1985] : Radio Research Station.

NO: 207.

AIRFIELD NAME: EGLINTON. OPENED : 1941.
COUNTY : Londonderry NI. CLOSED : 1966.
COMMAND : RN.
FORMATION : HMS Gannet. GRID REF: C 540220[304NI]
FUNCTION : Formation & Working Up [fighters] O.S.REF.: C 540220.
LOCALITY : 7miles NE of Londonderry.
RAILWAY STN. : Eglinton 1mile[BNC]

LATITUDE : 55 02 30N. HEIGHT ASL : SL. LIGHTING : None.
LONGITUDE : 07 09 30W. FLYING CONTROL : Yes. RADIO : QDM.

LANDMARKS DAY : Lough Foyle & R Foyle, with Londonderry on its W bank.

LANDMARKS NIGHT : -

OBSTRUCTIONS : Mountain 1298′ 4miles SE. Considerable mountain ranges 5miles NW.

LANDING AREA SURFACE : Tarmac.

QDM	LENGTH X WIDTH	Ext
032-212.	1100 x 50yds.	-
088-268.	1600 x 50yds.	-
153-333.	1100 x 50yds.	-

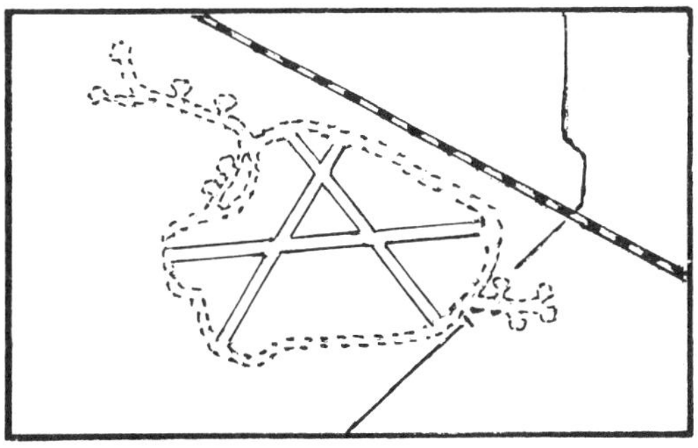

EXTENSIBILITY : None possible.

ACCOMMODATION : Temporary.
HANGARS : 70x90.5′[sqdn]-10;Blister:65x45′[sqdn]-7, 69x45′[storage]-5.
HARDSTANDINGS : A/C standings-10;pens-12;aprons:340x120′-1; 600x80′-1.
R.N. : OFFICERS: 175. Chiefs/POs/Ratings. : 1769. TOTAL: 1944.
W.R.N.S. : " : 22. " " : 343. " : 365.

AFFILIATED AIRFIELDS : -

PRESENT USE [1985] : Disused.

NO: 208.

AIRFIELD NAME: ELGIN. OPENED : 1940.
COUNTY : Morayshire. CLOSED : 1947.
COMMAND : Bomber.
FORMATION : 91 Grp[Abingdon] GRID REF: J 723814[29Scot]
FUNCTION : Operational Training Unit[satellite] O.S.REF.: NJ 200600.
LOCALITY : 1.75miles SW of Elgin.
RAILWAY STN. : Elgin[LNER]

LATITUDE : 57 37 30N. HEIGHT ASL : 100′ LIGHTING : None.
LONGITUDE : 03 20 15W. FLYING CONTROL : Yes. RADIO : QDM.

LANDMARKS DAY : Elgin town NE of A/F.

LANDMARKS NIGHT : R Lossie on E boundary of A/F.

OBSTRUCTIONS : Wooded hill 3miles WSW, 767′. Castle Hill 1mile S 364′, Hart hill 4miles SSE 902′, Brown Muir 4.5miles SE 1110′

LANDING AREA SURFACE : Grass.

QDM	LENGTH X WIDTH	Ext
N-S.	1400yds.	2000yds.
E-W.	1250yds.	1400yds.
SE-NW.	1100yds.	1200yds.

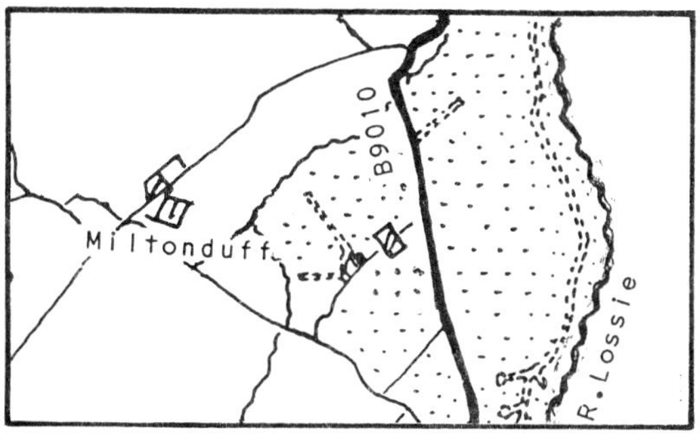

EXTENSIBILITY : -

ACCOMMODATION : Temporary.
HANGARS : T2-1;B1-1.

HARDSTANDINGS : Heavy bomber-19.

R.A.F. : OFFICERS: 66. S.N.C.O′s.: 157. O.R′s.: 864. TOTAL: 1087.
W.A.A.F.: " : 6. " : 35. " : 193. " : 234.

AFFILIATED AIRFIELDS : Lossiemouth[Parent]

PRESENT USE [1985] : Agriculture.

NO: 209.

AIRFIELD NAME: ELMDON. OPENED : 1939.
COUNTY : Warwickshire. CLOSED :
COMMAND : Flying Training.
FORMATION : 51 Grp[Leeds] GRID REF: K 625042[72]
FUNCTION : Elementary Flying Training School. O.S.REF.: SP 172840.
LOCALITY : 6.5miles SE of Birmingham.
RAILWAY STN. : Birmingham[LMS&LNER]

LATITUDE : 52 07 00N. HEIGHT ASL : 362′ LIGHTING : None.
LONGITUDE : 01 44 45W. FLYING CONTROL : None. RADIO : QDM.

LANDMARKS DAY : Hamshall power station 5.5miles to NE 42degrees.

LANDMARKS NIGHT : -

OBSTRUCTIONS : -

LANDING AREA SURFACE : Concrete.

QDM	LENGTH X WIDTH	Ext
060.	1344 x 50yds.	-
150.	1363 x 50yds.	1600yds.
		1200yds.

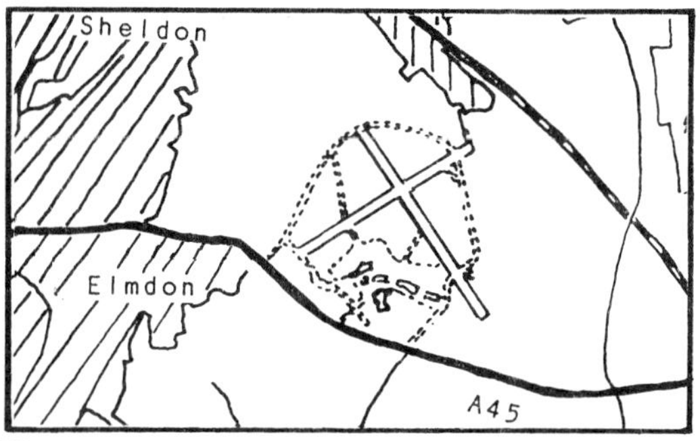

EXTENSIBILITY : Entails demolition of a cottage, house & bungalow, but not recommended.
ACCOMMODATION : Temporary[RAF]
HANGARS : Bellman[1MAP]-2;Civil[1MAP]-2;Blisters: Standard-9;EO-2.
HARDSTANDINGS : Ashes-1.

R.A.F. : OFFICERS: 28. S.N.C.O′s.: 61. O.R′s.: 251. TOTAL: 340.
W.A.A.F.: " : - " : - " : - " : -

AFFILIATED AIRFIELDS : Hockley Heath[RLG]

PRESENT USE [1985] : Civil Airport[Birmingham]

NO: 210.

AIRFIELD NAME: ELSHAM WOLDS. OPENED : 1941.
COUNTY : Lincolnshire. CLOSED : 1947.
COMMAND : Bomber.
FORMATION : 1 Grp[Bawtry] GRID REF: A 513330[33]
FUNCTION : Operational[13 Base] O.S.REF.: TA 042135.

LOCALITY : 5miles NNE of Brigg.
RAILWAY STN. : Barnetby[LNER]

LATITUDE : 53 36 30N. HEIGHT ASL : 256′ LIGHTING : Mk2.
LONGITUDE : 00 25 15W. FLYING CONTROL : Yes. RADIO : QDM.

LANDMARKS DAY : Scunthorpe ironworks 273degrees,7miles N; R Humber 6miles N.

LANDMARKS NIGHT : As day.

OBSTRUCTIONS : _

LANDING AREA SURFACE : Concrete.

QDM	LENGTH X WIDTH	Ext
198.	1400 x 50yds.	-
258.	1600 x 50yds.	2100yds.
318.	2000 x 50yds.	3000yds.

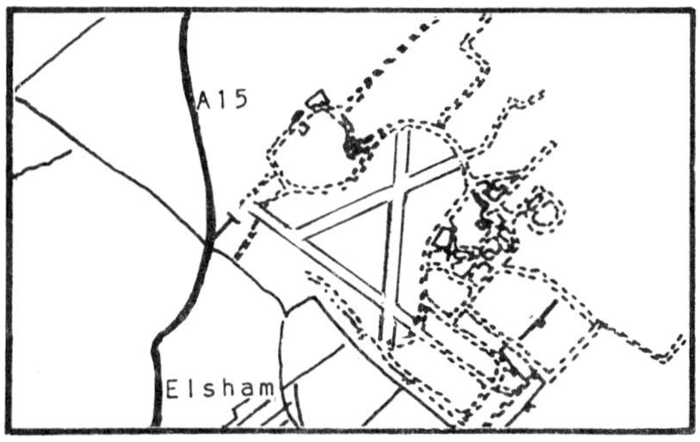

EXTENSIBILITY : Entails diversion of a main road.

ACCOMMODATION : Temporary.
HANGARS : J1-1;T2-5.

HARDSTANDINGS : Heavy bomber-36.

R.A.F. : OFFICERS: 174. S.N.C.O′s.: 480. O.R′s.: 1414. TOTAL: 2068.
W.A.A.F.: " : 13. " : 14. " : 466. " : 493.

AFFILIATED AIRFIELDS : North Killingholme&Kirmington[Sub-stations]

PRESENT USE [1985] : Motorway.

NO: 211.

AIRFIELD NAME: ELVINGTON.   OPENED : 1942.
COUNTY : Yorkshire.   CLOSED :
COMMAND : Bomber.
FORMATION : 4 Grp[York]   GRID REF: A 147683[27]
FUNCTION : Operational.   O.S.REF.: SE 665480.

LOCALITY : 5miles ESE of York.
RAILWAY STN. : York[LNER]

LATITUDE : 53 55 30N.   HEIGHT ASL : 45′   LIGHTING : Mk2.
LONGITUDE : 00 58 30W.   FLYING CONTROL : Yes.   RADIO : QDM.

LANDMARKS DAY : York 5miles NE.

LANDMARKS NIGHT : -

OBSTRUCTIONS : Overhead cables. Pylons 50-60′ 3000yds. N.

LANDING AREA SURFACE : Asphalt.

QDM	LENGTH X WIDTH	Ext
203.	1400 x 50yds.	3000yds.
263.	2000 x 50yds.	-
143.	1400 x 50yds.	2000yds.

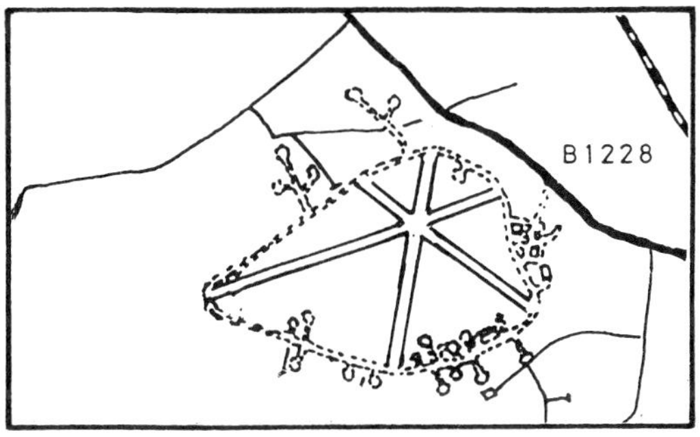

EXTENSIBILITY : -

ACCOMMODATION : Temporary.
HANGARS : T2-2;B1-1.

HARDSTANDINGS : Heavy bomber-36.

R.A.F. : OFFICERS: 123. S.N.C.O′s.: 411. O.R′s.: 1696. TOTAL: 2230.
W.A.A.F.: " : 4. " : 11. " : 363. " : 378.

AFFILIATED AIRFIELDS : Pocklington[42 Base]

PRESENT USE [1985] : RAF.

NO: 212.

AIRFIELD NAME: ENSTONE.   OPENED : 1942.
COUNTY : Oxfordshire.   CLOSED : 1947.
COMMAND : Bomber.
FORMATION : 91 Grp[Abingdon]   GRID REF: P 840455[94]
FUNCTION : Operational Training Unit[satellite]   O.S.REF.: SP 390258.
LOCALITY : 5miles E of Chipping Norton.
RAILWAY STN. : Charlbury 5miles[GWR]

LATITUDE : 51 55 45N.   HEIGHT ASL : 550′   LIGHTING : Mk2.
LONGITUDE : 01 25 45W.   FLYING CONTROL : Yes.   RADIO : QDM.

LANDMARKS DAY : Wychwood forest & R Everlode 50 51 00N, 01 31 00W.

LANDMARKS NIGHT : -

OBSTRUCTIONS : -

LANDING AREA SURFACE : Concrete.

QDM	LENGTH X WIDTH	Ext
195.	1200 x 50yds.	2000yds.
256.	2000 x 50yds.	2225yds.
329.	1325 x 50yds.	-

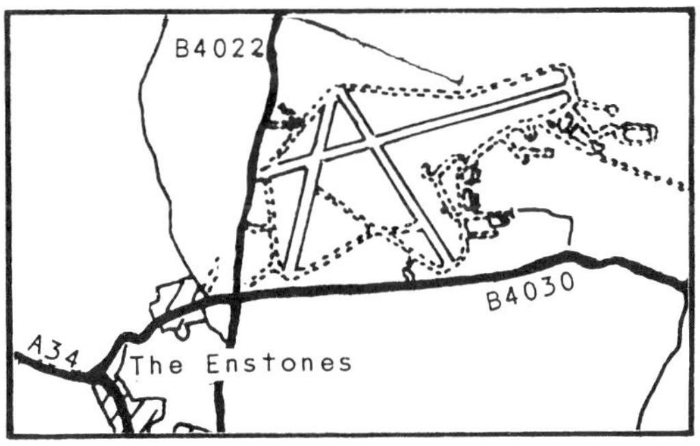

EXTENSIBILITY : Entails diversion of a main road.

ACCOMMODATION : Temporary.
HANGARS : T2-1;B1-1.

HARDSTANDINGS : Heavy bomber.

R.A.F. : OFFICERS: 72. S.N.C.O′s.: 261. O.R′s.: 450. TOTAL: 783.
W.A.A.F.: " : 2. " : 4. " : 158. " : 164.

AFFILIATED AIRFIELDS : Moreton in Marsh[Parent]

PRESENT USE [1985] : Private flying.

NO: 213.

AIRFIELD NAME: ERROL.   OPENED : 1942.
COUNTY : Perthshire.   CLOSED : 1948.
COMMAND : Flying Training.
FORMATION : 21 Grp[Spittlegate]   GRID REF: O 765458[64Scot]
FUNCTION : Advanced Flying Unit.   O.S.REF.: NO 268242.

LOCALITY : 1mile NE of Errol.
RAILWAY STN. : Errol[LMS]

LATITUDE : 56 24 10N.   HEIGHT ASL : 31′   LIGHTING : Mk2.
LONGITUDE : 03 11 00W.   FLYING CONTROL : Yes.   RADIO : QDM.

LANDMARKS DAY : A/F situated on estuary, N bank.

LANDMARKS NIGHT : As day.

OBSTRUCTIONS : 900′ hills 2.5miles S & N of A/F.

LANDING AREA SURFACE : Tarmac & wood chippings.

QDM	LENGTH X WIDTH	Ext
230.	1600 x 50yds.	-
290.	1180 x 50yds.	1400yds.
350.	1170 x 50yds.	1400yds.

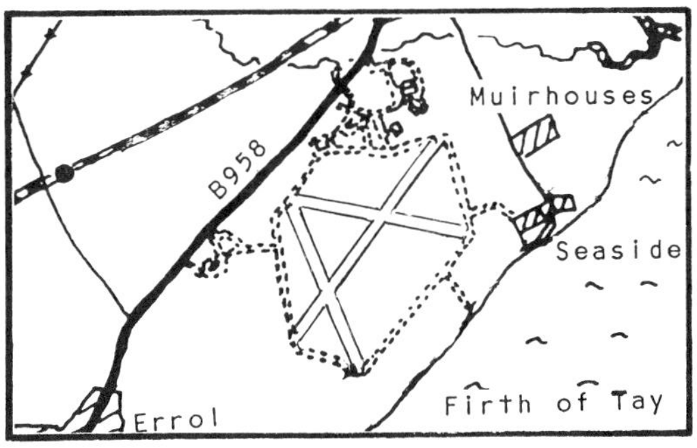

EXTENSIBILITY : Entails demolition of a farm & 2 cottages.

ACCOMMODATION : Temporary.
HANGARS : T1-6;Blister[69′]-13.

HARDSTANDINGS : Circular concrete-17.

R.A.F. : OFFICERS: 67. S.N.C.O′s.: 116. O.R′s.: 1682. TOTAL: 1865.
W.A.A.F.: " : 10. " : 15. " : 405. " : 430.

AFFILIATED AIRFIELDS : Tealing[Satellite]

PRESENT USE [1985] : Disused.

NO: 214.

AIRFIELD NAME: ESHOTT. OPENED : 1942.
COUNTY : Northumberland. CLOSED : 1945.
COMMAND : Fighter.
FORMATION : 12 Grp[Watnall] GRID REF: U 672192[4]
FUNCTION : Operational Training Unit. O.S.REF.: NZ 183984.

LOCALITY : 7.75miles NNW of Ashington.
RAILWAY STN. : Acklington 3.5miles[LNER]

LATITUDE : 55 16 45N. HEIGHT ASL : 151′ LIGHTING : None.
LONGITUDE : 01 42 45W. FLYING CONTROL : Yes. RADIO : QDM.

LANDMARKS DAY : R Coquet & Gt.North Rd.

LANDMARKS NIGHT : R Coquet.

OBSTRUCTIONS : -

LANDING AREA SURFACE : Hardcore.

QDM	LENGTH X WIDTH	Ext
264.	1900 x 50yds.	3000yds.
323.	1260 x 50yds.	2000yds.
022.	1250 x 50yds.	2000yds.

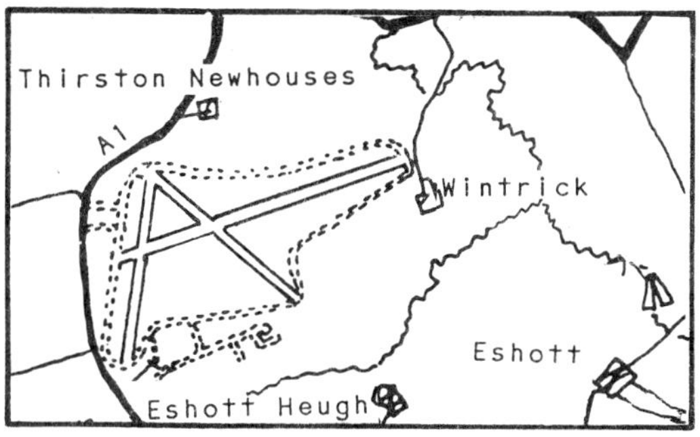

EXTENSIBILITY : Entails diversion of the Great North Road.

ACCOMMODATION : Temporary.
HANGARS : T1-1;Blister-8.

HARDSTANDINGS : SE-50.

R.A.F. : OFFICERS: 108.S.N.C.O′s.: 110.O.R′s.: 1260.TOTAL: 1478.
W.A.A.F.: " : 8. " : 18. " : 415. " : 441.

AFFILIATED AIRFIELDS : Boulmer[Satellite]

PRESENT USE [1985] : Disused.

NO: 215.

AIRFIELD NAME: EVANTON. OPENED : 1937.
COUNTY : Ross-shire. CLOSED : 1947.
COMMAND : RN.
FORMATION : HMS Fieldfare. GRID REF: J 145890[27Scot]
FUNCTION : Reserve A/C Storage. O.S.REF.: NH 625664.

LOCALITY : 6.5miles NE of Dingwall.
RAILWAY STN. : Evanton 1mile[LMS]

LATITUDE : 57 40 08N. HEIGHT ASL : 12′ LIGHTING : Mk2.
LONGITUDE : 04 18 38W. FLYING CONTROL : Yes. RADIO : QDM.

LANDMARKS DAY : Cromarty & Moray Firths.

LANDMARKS NIGHT : As day.

OBSTRUCTIONS : Mountains rising from a point 1mile NW to 2000′ within 5miles, & 3400′ within 10miles W.

LANDING AREA SURFACE : Tarmac.

QDM	LENGTH X WIDTH	Ext
043-223.	1233 x 50yds.	-
095-275.	970 x 50yds.	-

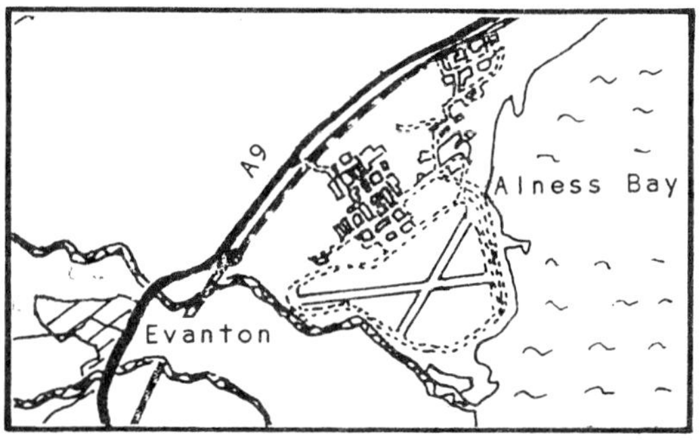

EXTENSIBILITY : None possible.

ACCOMMODATION : Permanent[part]
HANGARS : Boulton & Paul-2;bellman-4;type F-1;EO blister-6.

HARDSTANDINGS : Hangar apron 190x280′ approx.

R.N. : OFFICERS: 20. Chiefs/POs/Ratings. : 363. TOTAL: 383.
W.R.N.S.: " : 4. " : - " : 124. " : 128.

AFFILIATED AIRFIELDS : -

PRESENT USE [1985] : Industry.

NO: 216.

AIRFIELD NAME: EXETER. OPENED : 1937.
COUNTY : Devonshire. CLOSED :
COMMAND : Fighter.
FORMATION : 10 Grp[Rudloe Manor] GRID REF: T 430153[138]
FUNCTION : Sector. O.S.REF.: SY 002938.

LOCALITY : 4miles E of Exeter.
RAILWAY STN. : Exeter: Central[SR], St Davids[GWR]

LATITUDE : 50 44 00N. HEIGHT ASL : 105′ LIGHTING : Mk2.
LONGITUDE : 03 24 45W. FLYING CONTROL : Yes. RADIO : QDM.

LANDMARKS DAY : Exeter town 5miles W. Coast 8.5miles S.

LANDMARKS NIGHT : -

OBSTRUCTIONS : -

LANDING AREA SURFACE : Asphalt.

QDM	LENGTH X WIDTH	Ext
200.	900 x 50yds.	2250yds.
266.	2000 x 50yds.	-
312.	1450 x 50yds.	-

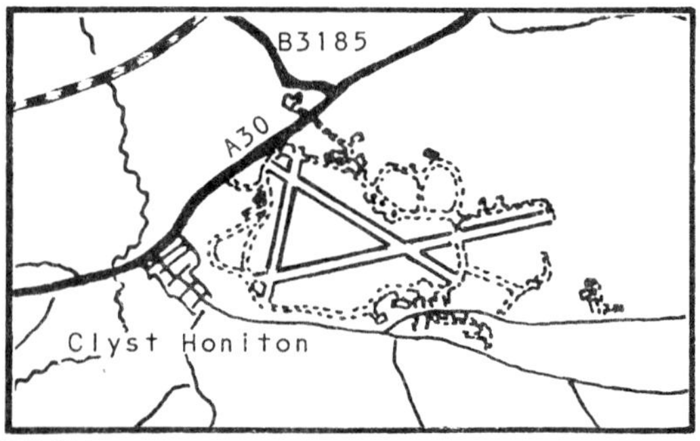

EXTENSIBILITY : -

ACCOMMODATION : Temporary.
HANGARS : RAF 7 Hinaidi-1;blister:O-6,EO-4.

HARDSTANDINGS : TE-19;SE-5.

R.A.F. : OFFICERS: 210.S.N.C.O′s.: 544.O.R′s.: 1594.TOTAL: 2348.
W.A.A.F.: " : 14. " : 8. " : 631. " : 653.

AFFILIATED AIRFIELDS : Bolt Head, Culmhead[FA], Winkleigh.

PRESENT USE [1985] : Civil Airport[Exeter]

NO: 217.

AIRFIELD NAME: EYE. OPENED : 1944.
COUNTY : Suffolk. CLOSED : 1945.
COMMAND : 8th USAAF.
FORMATION : 490th Bomb Grp. GRID REF: M 585934[76-77]
FUNCTION : Operational. O.S.REF.: TM 130750.

LOCALITY : 11miles NNE of Stowmarket.
RAILWAY STN. : Mellis 2miles[LNER]

LATITUDE : 52 20 00N. HEIGHT ASL : 150′ LIGHTING : Mk2.
LONGITUDE : 01 08 00E. FLYING CONTROL : Yes. RADIO : QDM.

LANDMARKS DAY : A/F bounded by Roman road on W, County road on E, County road & railroad on S.

LANDMARKS NIGHT : -

OBSTRUCTIONS : Eye church at S end of R/W 330. Will be marked with red light.

LANDING AREA SURFACE : Screeded finish.

QDM: 212. LENGTH X WIDTH: 2000 x 50yds. Ext: -
: 270. : 1400 x 50yds. : 2000yds.
: 328. : 1400 x 50yds. : 2000yds.
: : :

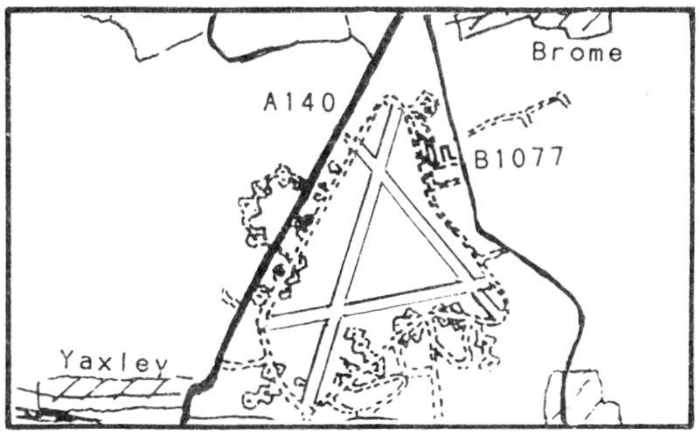

EXTENSIBILITY : Entails heavy demolition & major road diversion.

ACCOMMODATION : Temporary.
HANGARS : T2-2.

HARDSTANDINGS : Spectacle-50.

USAAF. : OFFICERS: 421. Enlisted Men. : 2473.TOTAL: 2894.

AFFILIATED AIRFIELDS : -

PRESENT USE [1985] : Agriculture.

NO: 218.

AIRFIELD NAME: FAIRFORD. OPENED : 1944.
COUNTY : Gloucestershire. CLOSED :
COMMAND : Flying Training.
FORMATION : 23 Grp[South Cerney] GRID REF: P 602184[104]
FUNCTION : Heavy Glider Con. Unit [satellite] O.S.REF.: SU 154982.
LOCALITY : 9miles N of Swindon.
RAILWAY STN. : Fairford[GWR]

LATITUDE : 51 40 53N. HEIGHT ASL : 260′ LIGHTING : Mk2.
LONGITUDE : 01 46 30W. FLYING CONTROL : Yes. RADIO : QDM.

LANDMARKS DAY. : -

LANDMARKS NIGHT : -

OBSTRUCTIONS : Kempsford church bearing 180degrees M-2300yds.

LANDING AREA SURFACE : Concrete & asphalt.
QDM: 230. LENGTH X WIDTH: 2000 x 50yds.EXT. TO: -
: 280. : 1400 x 50yds. : 2250yds.
: 330. : 1400 x 50yds. : 2150yds.
: : :

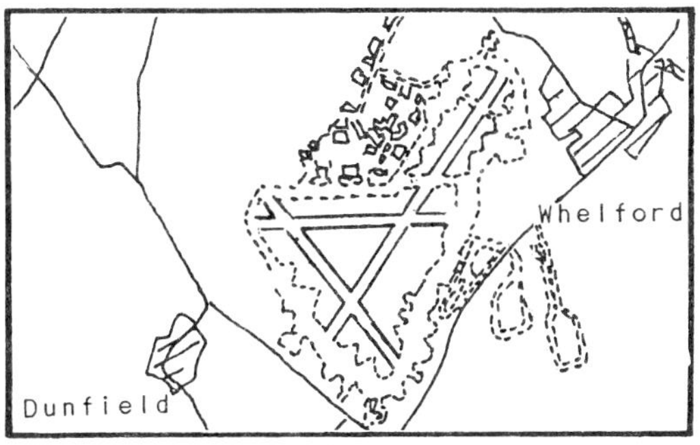

EXTENSIBILITY : R/W 280 has 200yds. extension in American track.

ACCOMMODATION : Temporary.
HANGARS : T2-2.

HARDSTANDINGS : Spectacle-52.

R.A.F. : OFFICERS: 172.S.N.C.O′s.: 648.O.R′s.: 1562.TOTAL: 2382.
W.A.A.F.: " : 8. " : 6. " : 302. " : 316.

AFFILIATED AIRFIELDS : Keevil[Parent]

PRESENT USE [1985] : USAFE.

NO: 219.

AIRFIELD NAME: FAIRLOP. OPENED : 1941.
COUNTY : Essex. CLOSED : 1946.
COMMAND : Balloon.
FORMATION : 24 Balloon Centre. GRID REF: L 905095[107]
FUNCTION : Non-operational. O.S.REF.: TQ 460905.

LOCALITY : 3miles NE of Ilford.
RAILWAY STN. : Fairlop[LNER]

LATITUDE : 51 35 30N. HEIGHT ASL : 85′ LIGHTING : Mk2.
LONGITUDE : 00 06 08E. FLYING CONTROL : Yes. RADIO : QDM.

LANDMARKS DAY. : a]Hainult Forest;b]LNER Woodford-Ilford[from W boundary of A/F;c]London-Southend double track arterial road 1mile S;d]Mental hospital , Woodford Bridge 1.5miles NW.
LANDMARKS NIGHT : -

OBSTRUCTIONS : Fairlop railway station & embankment obstructs approach to W end of E-W runway.

LANDING AREA SURFACE : Concrete & asphalt.
QDM: 205. LENGTH X WIDTH: 1100 x 50yds.EXT. TO: -
: 245. : 1600 x 50yds. : -
: 290. : 1100 x 50yds. : -
: : :

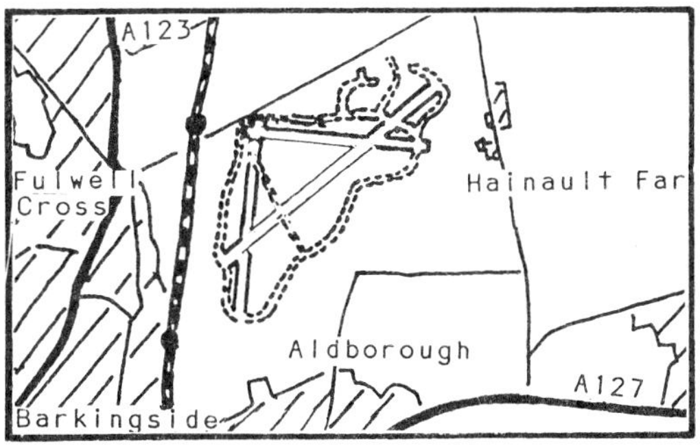

EXTENSIBILITY :

ACCOMMODATION : Temporary.
HANGARS : Blister-8.

HARDSTANDINGS : Blenheim TE-12; Frying Pan[50′]-2; hardcore & asphalt-24.
R.A.F. : OFFICERS: 45. S.N.C.O′s.: 48. O.R′s.: 958. TOTAL: 1051.
W.A.A.F.: " : 9. " : 32. " : 112. " : 153.

AFFILIATED AIRFIELDS : -

PRESENT USE [1985] : Disused.

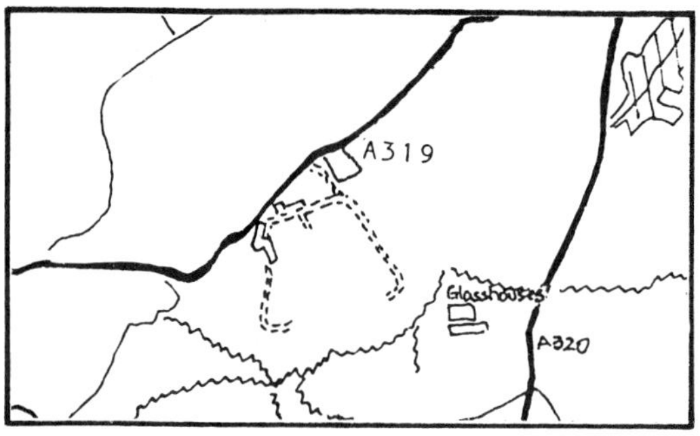

AIRFIELD NAME: FAIROAKS. OPENED : 1937.
COUNTY : Surrey. CLOSED : 1967.
COMMAND : Flying Training.
FORMATION : 50 Grp[Reading] GRID REF: Q 445815[114]
FUNCTION : Elementary Flying Training School. O.S.REF.: TQ 005623.
LOCALITY : 2miles N of Woking.
RAILWAY STN. : Woking 2miles[SR]

LATITUDE : 51 20 53N. HEIGHT ASL : 100′ LIGHTING : None.
LONGITUDE : 00 33 30W. FLYING CONTROL : None.RADIO : QDM.

LANDMARKS DAY. : Glasshouse & 65′high chimney on SE corner.

LANDMARKS NIGHT : -

OBSTRUCTIONS : Trees & buildings on N boundary & on N half of W boundary. Trees along N half of E boundary.

LANDING AREA SURFACE : Grass.

QDM	LENGTH X WIDTH	EXT. TO
N-S.	850yds.	1250yds.
NE-SW.	950yds.	-
E-W.	880yds.	-
NW-SE.	950yds.	

EXTENSIBILITY : -

ACCOMMODATION : Temporary[RAF buildings]
HANGARS : Various-15.

HARDSTANDINGS : Nil.

	OFFICERS	S.N.C.O′s.	O.R′s.	TOTAL
R.A.F.	-	39.	136.	175.
W.A.A.F.	-	-	-	-

AFFILIATED AIRFIELDS : Winkfield, Smiths Lawn & Bray[RLG]

PRESENT USE [1985] : Private flying.

NO: 221.

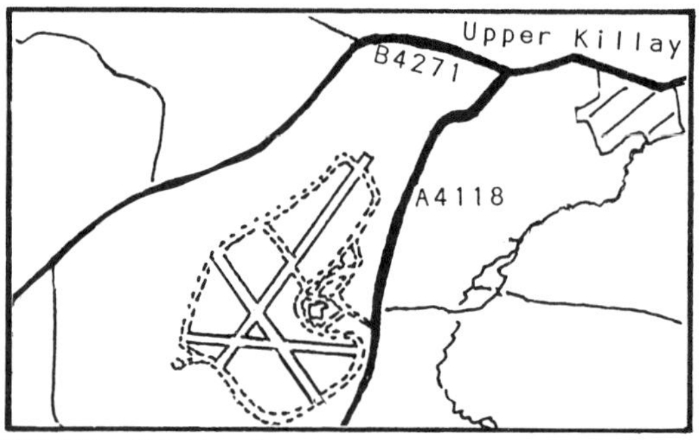

AIRFIELD NAME: FAIRWOOD COMMON. OPENED : 1941.
COUNTY : Glamorganshire. CLOSED :
COMMAND : Fighter.
FORMATION : 10 Grp[Rudloe Manor] GRID REF: O 012132[100]
FUNCTION : Armament Practice Camp. O.S.REF.: SS 568912.
LOCALITY : 5miles W of Swansea.
RAILWAY STN. : High Street[GWR]

LATITUDE : 51 36 08N. HEIGHT ASL : 272′ LIGHTING : MK2.
LONGITUDE : 04 04 08W. FLYING CONTROL : Yes. RADIO : QDM.

LANDMARKS DAY. : Coast 3.5miles S.

LANDMARKS NIGHT : As day.

OBSTRUCTIONS : None.

LANDING AREA SURFACE : Tarmac & sealed coat.

QDM	LENGTH X WIDTH	EXT. TO
231.	1650 x 50yds.	1850yds.
290.	1350 x 50yds.	1360yds.
338.	1350 x 50yds.	-

EXTENSIBILITY : Entails diversion of secondary road.

ACCOMMODATION : Temporary.
HANGARS : Bellman-3;EO blister-8.

HARDSTANDINGS : SE-24.

	OFFICERS	S.N.C.O′s.	O.R′s.	TOTAL
R.A.F.	98.	206.	1770.	2074.
W.A.A.F.	12.	8.	397.	417.

AFFILIATED AIRFIELDS : Colerne[Sector]

PRESENT USE [1985] : Civil Airport[Swansea]

NO: 222.

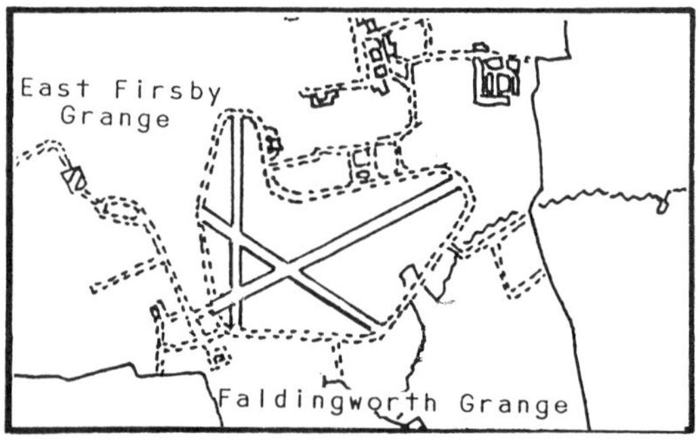

AIRFIELD NAME: FALDINGWORTH. OPENED : 1943.
COUNTY : Lincolnshire. CLOSED : 1972.
COMMAND : Bomber.
FORMATION : 1 Grp[Bawtry] GRID REF: A 505058[39]
FUNCTION : Operational. O.S.REF.: TF 037849.

LOCALITY : 5.25miles SW of Market Rasen.
RAILWAY STN. : Market Rasen[LNER]

LATITUDE : 53 21 15N. HEIGHT ASL : 50′ LIGHTING : Mk2.
LONGITUDE : 00 26 30W. FLYING CONTROL : Yes. RADIO : QDM.

LANDMARKS DAY. : -

LANDMARKS NIGHT : -

OBSTRUCTIONS : -

LANDING AREA SURFACE : Concrete & wood chippings.

QDM	LENGTH X WIDTH	EXT. TO
256.	2000 x 50yds.	-
312.	1400 x 50yds.	3500yds.
010.	1400 x 50yds.	3100yds.

EXTENSIBILITY : Entails diversion of 2 by-roads.

ACCOMMODATION : Temporary.
HANGARS : T2-2;B1-1.

HARDSTANDINGS : Loop-36.

	OFFICERS	S.N.C.O′s.	O.R′s.	TOTAL
R.A.F.	87.	358.	1512.	1957.
W.A.A.F.	10.	16.	255.	281.

AFFILIATED AIRFIELDS : Ludford Magna[14 Base]

PRESENT USE [1985] : Explosive testing & storage.

AIRFIELD NAME: FARNBOROUGH. OPENED : 1941.
COUNTY : Hampshire. CLOSED :
COMMAND : Technical Training.
FORMATION : 24 Grp[Hereford] GRID REF: Q 305740[114]
FUNCTION : Photographic School. O.S.REF.: SU 856538.

LOCALITY : 1.5miles NNE of Aldershot.
RAILWAY STN. : Farnborough 1.5miles[SR]

LATITUDE : 51 16 45N. HEIGHT ASL : 220′ LIGHTING : None.
LONGITUDE : 00 45 53W. FLYING CONTROL : None.RADIO : QMD.

LANDMARKS DAY. : Laffans Plain; Farnborough-Byfleet railway.

LANDMARKS NIGHT : -

OBSTRUCTIONS : Hangars & buildings on NE & E of A/F.

LANDING AREA SURFACE : Concrete.

QDM	LENGTH X WIDTH	EXT. TO
183.	1000 x 50yds.	-
223.5.	1360 x 50yds.	-
251.5.	2050 x 50yds.	-
300.	1000 x 50yds.	

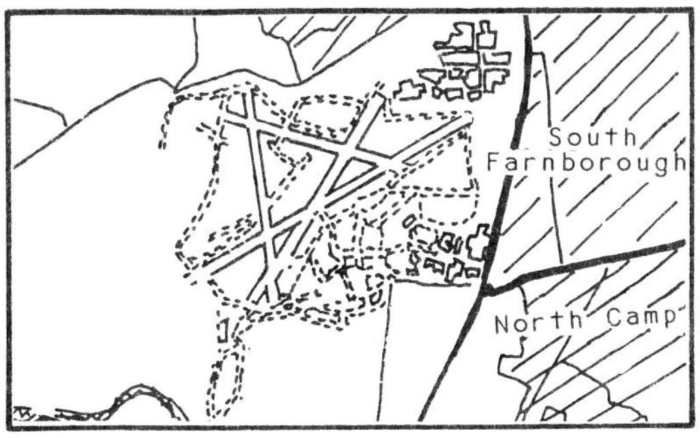

EXTENSIBILITY :

ACCOMMODATION : Permanent[part]
HANGARS : Permanent-4, blister-various.

HARDSTANDINGS : Dimond-10, circular-7.

	OFFICERS	S.N.C.O's.	O.R's.	TOTAL
R.A.F.	185.	182.	867.	1234.
W.A.A.F.	16.	23.	534.	573.

AFFILIATED AIRFIELDS : -

PRESENT USE [1985] : Royal Aircraft Establishment.

AIRFIELD NAME: FEARN. OPENED : 1941.
COUNTY : Ross-shire. CLOSED : 1946.
COMMAND : RN.
FORMATION : HMS Owl. GRID REF: J 366981[Scot]
FUNCTION : Training School. O.S.REF.: NH 842758.

LOCALITY : 8.5miles NE of Invergordon.
RAILWAY STN. : Fearn 2miles[HR]

LATITUDE : 57 45 35N. HEIGHT ASL : 25′ LIGHTING : Naval.
LONGITUDE : 03 56 10W. FLYING CONTROL : Yes. RADIO : QDM.

LANDMARKS DAY. : Tarbat Ness 8miles NE. Cromarty Firth W & SW.

LANDMARKS NIGHT : -

OBSTRUCTIONS : Hill of Nigg 666′ 2.25miles SSW.

LANDING AREA SURFACE : Tarmac.

QDM	LENGTH X WIDTH	EXT. TO
176-356.	1180 x 50yds.	-
052-232.	1475 x 50yds.	-
115-295.	1260 x 50yds.	-

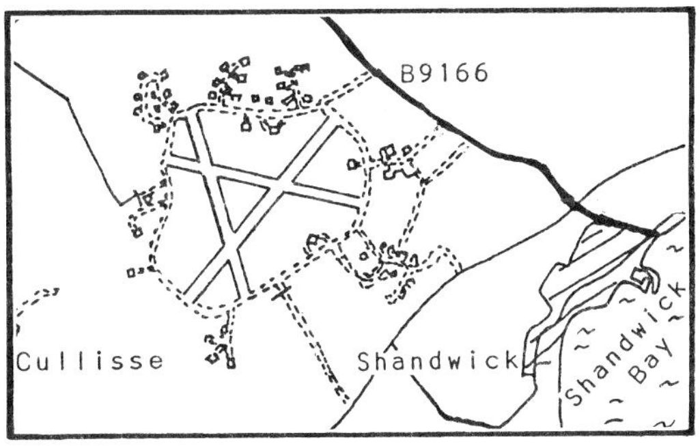

EXTENSIBILITY : -

ACCOMMODATION : Temporary.
HANGARS : Sqdn:66x75′-2;60x70′-14.Storage:60x70′-16, 125x185′-1.
HARDSTANDINGS : 7 [+6pens]

	OFFICERS	Chiefs/POs/Ratings.	TOTAL
R.N.	149.	1065.	1214.
W.R.N.S.	13.	334.	347.

AFFILIATED AIRFIELDS : -

PRESENT USE [1985] : Agriculture.

AIRFIELD NAME: FELTWELL. OPENED : 1937.
COUNTY : Norfolk. CLOSED :
COMMAND : Bomber.
FORMATION : 3 Grp[Exning] GRID REF: G 165085.
FUNCTION : Lancaster school. O.S.REF.: TL 712898.

LOCALITY : 5miles NW of Brandon.
RAILWAY STN. : Lakenheath 4miles[LNER]

LATITUDE : 52 28 45N. HEIGHT ASL : 50′ LIGHTING : Mk2.
LONGITUDE : 00 31 00E. FLYING CONTROL : Yes. RADIO : QDM.

LANDMARKS DAY. : Little Ouse river 2miles to S; large expanses of wooded area 5miles to E.

LANDMARKS NIGHT : As day.

OBSTRUCTIONS : -

LANDING AREA SURFACE : Grass.

QDM	LENGTH X WIDTH	EXT. TO
E-W.	1800yds.	3000yds.
NE-SW.	1400yds.	-
NW-SE.	1200yds.	1400yds.

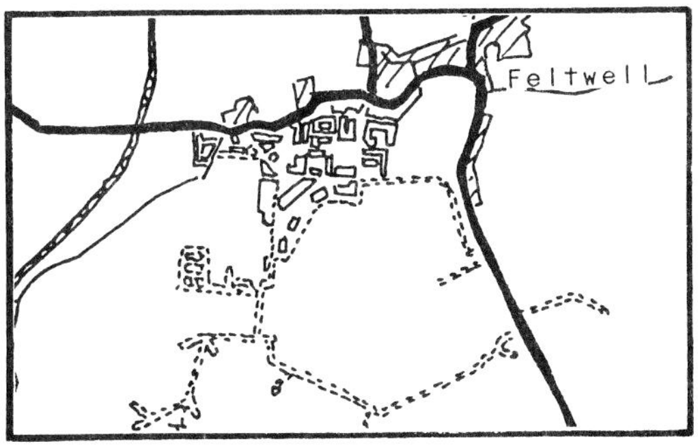

EXTENSIBILITY : Entails closure of a road.

ACCOMMODATION : Permanent.
HANGARS : Type C-5.

HARDSTANDINGS : Pan-20.

	OFFICERS	S.N.C.O's.	O.R's.	TOTAL
R.A.F.	117.	257.	1106.	1480.
W.A.A.F.	9.	17.	332.	358.

AFFILIATED AIRFIELDS : -

PRESENT USE [1985] : USAFE.

NO: 226.

AIRFIELD NAME: FERSFIELD. OPENED : 1944.
COUNTY : Norfolk. CLOSED : 1945.
COMMAND : 8th USAAF.
FORMATION : Not assigned. GRID REF: G 530033[76]
FUNCTION : Special projects. O.S.REF.: TM 080850.

LOCALITY : 16miles SW of Norwich.
RAILWAY STN. : Diss[LNER]

LATITUDE : 52 25 23N. HEIGHT ASL : 175' LIGHTING : Mk2.
LONGITUDE : 01 03 15E. FLYING CONTROL : Yes. RADIO : QDM.

LANDMARKS DAY : Diss town & Mere[in town]

LANDMARKS NIGHT : As day.

OBSTRUCTIONS : -

LANDING AREA SURFACE : Concrete.

QDM	LENGTH X WIDTH	EXT. TO
066.	2000 x 50yds.	-
186.	1400 x 50yds.	2600yds.
304.	1400 x 50yds.	2800yds.

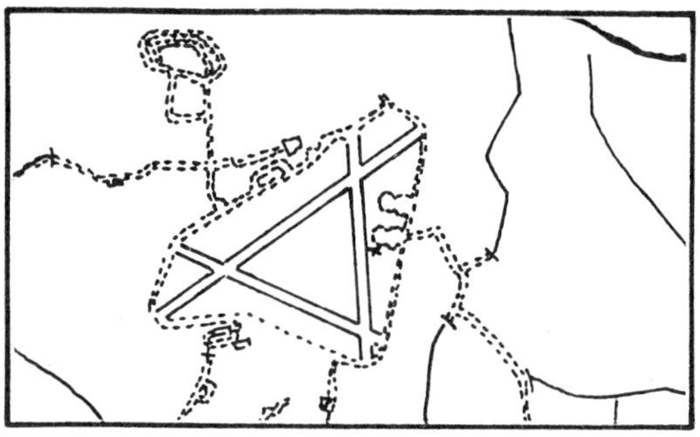

EXTENSIBILITY : 186&304 recommended to 2000yds only. Entails demolition of 1 house,3 barns & 2 cottages.
ACCOMMODATION : Temporary.
HANGARS : T2-2.

HARDSTANDINGS : Spectacle-50.

USAAF. : OFFICERS: 421. Enlisted Men. : 2473.TOTAL: 2894.

AFFILIATED AIRFIELDS : -

PRESENT USE [1985] : Disused.

NO: 227.

AIRFIELD NAME: FILTON. OPENED : 1910.
COUNTY : Gloucestershire. CLOSED :
COMMAND : Transport.
FORMATION : 44 Grp[Gloucester] GRID REF: U 042014[111]
FUNCTION : Parent. O.S.REF.: ST 600804.

LOCALITY : 4.75miles NW of Bristol.
RAILWAY STN. : Filton Junction 4miles[GWR]

LATITUDE : 51 31 11N. HEIGHT ASL : 210' LIGHTING : None.
LONGITUDE : 02 34 40W. FLYING CONTROL : Yes. RADIO : QDM.

LANDMARKS DAY : Railway Avonmouth-Bristol.

LANDMARKS NIGHT : Red obstruction lights on hangars, Filton laundry, West wks, NE & W, also manager's office. BAC operate when night flying is in progress.

OBSTRUCTIONS : Hill & wks S. Works E.

LANDING AREA SURFACE : Concrete & tarmac.

QDM	LENGTH X WIDTH	EXT. TO
101.	1500 x 50yds.	-
030.	1338 x 50yds.	-

EXTENSIBILITY : If extended to continental airport standard entails main rd closure & very heavy demo.
ACCOMMODATION : Permanent[part]
HANGARS : Old type[wood]-23; Type B:1 bay-1,4 bay-1.

HARDSTANDINGS : Aprons & new Hardstandings for 45-63 A/C.

	OFFICERS	S.N.C.O's.	O.R's.	TOTAL
R.A.F.	73.	82.	592.	747.
W.A.A.F.	4.	6.	164.	174.

AFFILIATED AIRFIELDS : -

PRESENT USE [1985] : Aircraft Industry[British Aerospace]

NO: 228.

AIRFIELD NAME: FINDO GASK. OPENED : 1941.
COUNTY : Perthshire. CLOSED : 1948.
COMMAND : Flying Training.
FORMATION : On loan to War Dept. GRID REF: O 512434[63Scot]
FUNCTION : On loan to War Dept. O.S.REF.: NO 009215.

LOCALITY : 7miles W of Perth.
RAILWAY STN. : Dunning 3miles[LMS]

LATITUDE : 56 22 30N. HEIGHT ASL : 375' LIGHTING : Mk2.
LONGITUDE : 03 36 23W. FLYING CONTROL : Yes. RADIO : QDM.

LANDMARKS DAY : R Earn & woods with Dolphin lake S of A/F.

LANDMARKS NIGHT : Town of Perth on Tay 6miles SE of A/F.

OBSTRUCTIONS : -

LANDING AREA SURFACE : Steel Matting[Sommerfeld track]

QDM	LENGTH X WIDTH	EXT. TO
010.	1100yds.	-
070.	1950yds.	1750yds.
110.	1250yds.	1400yds.

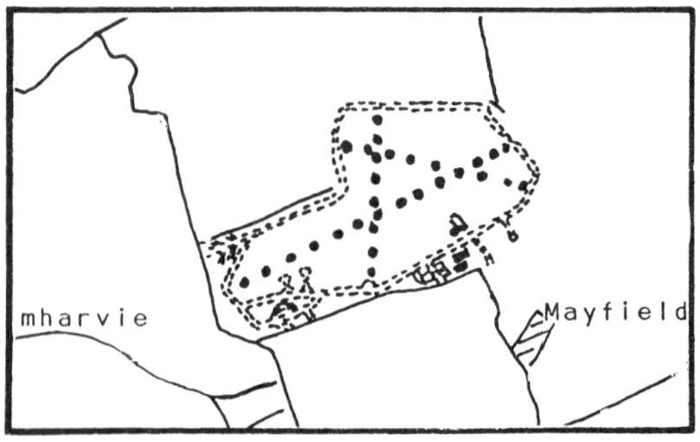

EXTENSIBILITY : Entails diversion of main rd W of A/F & demolition of barn & farm.
ACCOMMODATION : Temporary.
HANGARS : T2[13bay]-1;blister[69']-7.

HARDSTANDINGS : Circular-16.

	OFFICERS	S.N.C.O's.	O.R's.	TOTAL
R.A.F.	59.	70.	538.	667.
W.A.A.F.	3.	5.	188.	196.

AFFILIATED AIRFIELDS : -

PRESENT USE [1985] : Disused.

NO: 229.

AIRFIELD NAME: FINMERE. OPENED : 1941.
COUNTY : Buckinghamshire. CLOSED : 1945.
COMMAND : Fighter.
FORMATION : 12 Grp[Watnall] GRID REF: L 090520[94]
FUNCTION : Operational Training Unit[satellite] O.S.REF.: SP 642322.
LOCALITY : 3.5miles W of Buckingham.
RAILWAY STN. : Finmere.5miles[LNER]

LATITUDE : 51 58 46N. HEIGHT ASL : 405′ LIGHTING : Mk2.
LONGITUDE : 01 03 45W. FLYING CONTROL : Yes. RADIO : QDM.

LANDMARKS DAY : -

LANDMARKS NIGHT : -

OBSTRUCTIONS : Radio masts 51mins58secs N 06mins59secs W of Tingewyck village.

LANDING AREA SURFACE : Concrete & wood chippings.

QDM	LENGTH X WIDTH	EXT. TO
280.	2043 x 50yds.	-
230.	1535 x 50yds.	1750yds.
162.	1400 x 50yds.	-

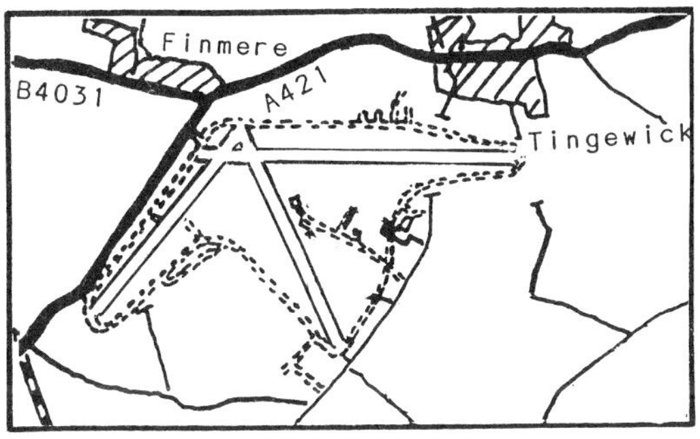

EXTENSIBILITY : Not recommended: entails diversion of main rd W of A/F, & demolition of a barn & farm.
ACCOMMODATION : Temporary.
HANGARS : T2-1;B1-1.

HARDSTANDINGS : Sausepan-27.

	OFFICERS	S.N.C.O's.	O.R's.	TOTAL
R.A.F.	92.	320.	814.	1226.
W.A.A.F.	4.	-	189.	193.

AFFILIATED AIRFIELDS : Harwell[Parent]

PRESENT USE [1985] : Private flying.

NO: 230.

AIRFIELD NAME: FINNINGLEY. OPENED : 1936.
COUNTY : Yorkshire. CLOSED :
COMMAND : Bomber.
FORMATION : 91 Grp[Abingdon] GRID REF: A 130188[38]
FUNCTION : Operational Training Unit. O.S.REF.: SK 663985.
LOCALITY : 7.5miles SE of Doncaster.
RAILWAY STN. : Finningley 1mile[LNER]

LATITUDE : 53 29 00N. HEIGHT ASL : 30′ LIGHTING : Mk2.
LONGITUDE : 01 00 15W. FLYING CONTROL : Yes. RADIO : QDM.

LANDMARKS DAY : a]Doncaster town W by N 4miles;b]Latfield Moor 4miles NE;c]Gainsborough E by S 11miles.

LANDMARKS NIGHT : Bounded by R Trent 8-10miles E; railway running E-W.

OBSTRUCTIONS : Bomb dump SW 20′; transformer SW by SSW 10′; petrol installations SW by SWW 15′

LANDING AREA SURFACE : Concrete & tarmac.

QDM	LENGTH X WIDTH	EXT. TO
209.	2000 x 50yds.	-
253.	1400 x 50yds.	2000yds.
300.	1400 x 50yds.	1550yds.

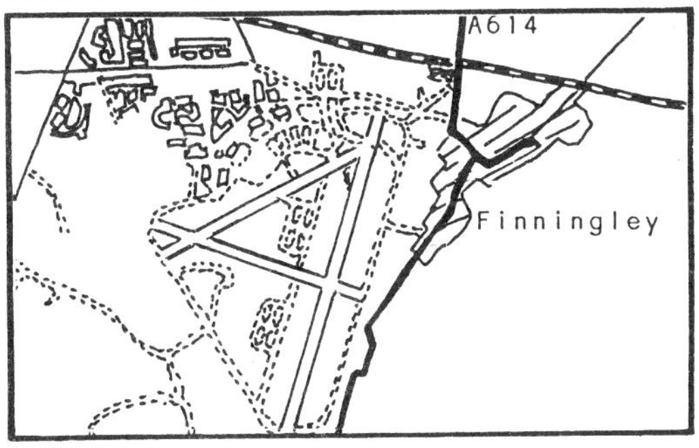

EXTENSIBILITY : Entails crossing of main rd if No 2 R/W is extended.
ACCOMMODATION : Permanent.
HANGARS : Type C-5.

HARDSTANDINGS : Circular-26; spectacle-1.

	OFFICERS	S.N.C.O's.	O.R's.	TOTAL
R.A.F.	159.	473.	1784.	2416.
W.A.A.F.	8.	8.	419.	435.

AFFILIATED AIRFIELDS : Worksop[Satellite]

PRESENT USE [1985] : RAF.

NO: 231.

AIRFIELD NAME: FIRBECK. OPENED : 1940.
COUNTY : Yorkshire. CLOSED : 1945.
COMMAND : Flying Training.
FORMATION : 21 Grp[Spittlegate] GRID REF: A 025085[38]
FUNCTION : Elementary Flying Training School[satellite] O.S.REF.: SK 555892.
LOCALITY : 6miles NNW of Worksop.
RAILWAY STN. : Worksop 6miles[LNER]

LATITUDE : 53 23 15N. HEIGHT ASL : 200′ LIGHTING : none.
LONGITUDE : 01 09 45W. FLYING CONTROL : Yes. RADIO : QDM.

LANDMARKS DAY : Firbeck Hall, lake & woods[not prominent]

LANDMARKS NIGHT : -

OBSTRUCTIONS : Wood on NW; trees & church on SE; trees E.

LANDING AREA SURFACE : Grass.

QDM	LENGTH X WIDTH	EXT. TO
E-W.	850yds.	-
	90-100acres.	-

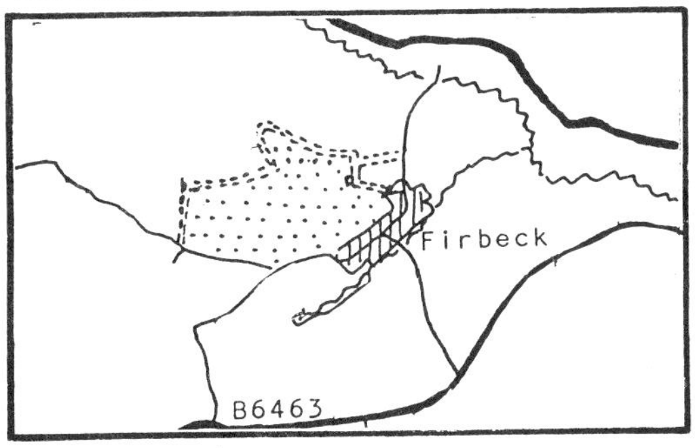

EXTENSIBILITY : None possible.

ACCOMMODATION : Temporary.
HANGARS : Blisters [69′]-2.

HARDSTANDINGS : None.

	OFFICERS	S.N.C.O's.	O.R's.	TOTAL
R.A.F.	5.	8.	270.	293.
W.A.A.F.	-	-	-	-

AFFILIATED AIRFIELDS : Hucknall[Parent]

PRESENT USE [1985] : Disused.

AIRFIELD NAME: FISKERTON. OPENED : 1943.
COUNTY : Lincolnshire. CLOSED : 1945.
COMMAND : Bomber.
FORMATION : 1 Grp[Bawtry] GRID REF: F 510923[47]
FUNCTION : Operational. O.S.REF.: TF 045730.

LOCALITY : 4.5miles E of Lincoln.
RAILWAY STN. : Reepham 1.5miles[LNER]

LATITUDE : 53 14 30N. HEIGHT ASL : 40′ LIGHTING : Mk2.
LONGITUDE : 00 25 45W. FLYING CONTROL : Yes. RADIO : QDM.

LANDMARKS DAY : Reepham church 1mile NW.

LANDMARKS NIGHT : -

OBSTRUCTIONS : -

LANDING AREA SURFACE : Concrete & tarmac.

QDM	LENGTH X WIDTH	EXT. TO
263.	2000 x 50yds.	-
311.	1400 x 50yds.	1600yds.
054.	1400 x 50yds.	2400yds.

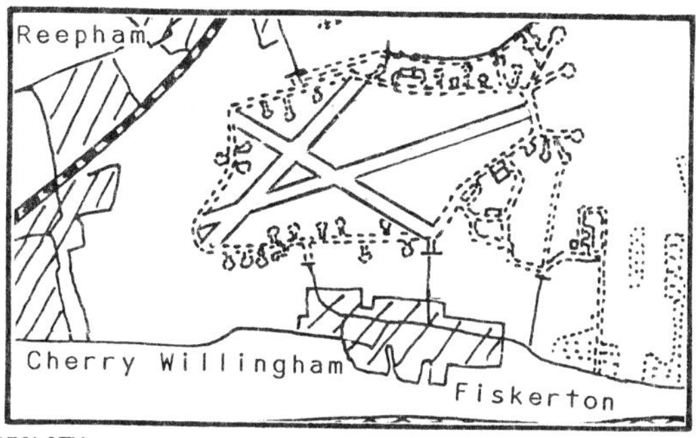

EXTENSIBILITY :

ACCOMMODATION : Temporary
HANGARS : T2-2; B1-1.

HARDSTANDINGS : Heavy bomber-36.

	OFFICERS	S.N.C.O's.	O.R's.	TOTAL
R.A.F.	102.	356.	979.	1437.
W.A.A.F.	2.	4.	192.	198.

AFFILIATED AIRFIELDS : Scampton[15 Base]

PRESENT USE [1985] : Agriculture.

NO: 233.

AIRFIELD NAME: FOLKINGHAM. OPENED : 1944.
COUNTY : Lincolnshire. CLOSED : 1963.
COMMAND : 9th USAAF.
FORMATION : 313th Troop Carrier Grp. GRID REF: F 510495[55]
FUNCTION : Operational. O.S.REF.: TF 049301.

LOCALITY : 8miles ESE of Grantham.
RAILWAY STN. : Grantham 8miles[LNER]

LATITUDE : 52 51 30N. HEIGHT ASL : 240′ LIGHTING : Mk2.
LONGITUDE : 00 26 30W. FLYING CONTROL : Yes. RADIO : QDM.

LANDMARKS DAY : -

LANDMARKS NIGHT : -

OBSTRUCTIONS : Observation post errected by War Office.

LANDING AREA SURFACE : Concrete & tarmac.

QDM	LENGTH X WIDTH	EXT. TO
020.	2000 x 50yds.	-
250.	1400 x 50yds.	2500yds.
310.	1400 x 50yds.	2000yds.

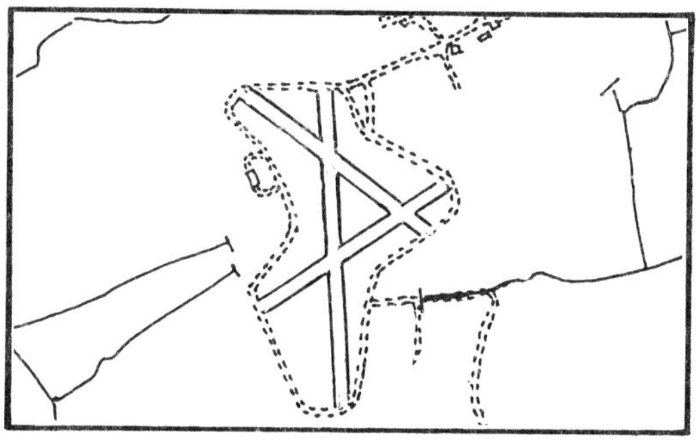

EXTENSIBILITY :

ACCOMMODATION : Temporary.
HANGARS : T2-2.

HARDSTANDINGS : Loop-50.

USAAF. : OFFICERS: 245. Enlisted Men. : 1053. TOTAL: 1298.

AFFILIATED AIRFIELDS : -

PRESENT USE [1985] : Agriculture.

NO: 234.

AIRFIELD NAME: FORD. OPENED : 1918.
COUNTY : Sussex. CLOSED : 1958.
COMMAND : Fighter.
FORMATION : 11 Grp[Uxbridge] GRID REF: Q 430222[133]
FUNCTION : Forward Airfield. Night Fighter. O.S.REF.: SU 995029.
LOCALITY : 2.25miles NW of Littlehampton.
RAILWAY STN. : Ford 1mile[SR]

LATITUDE : 50 48 53N. HEIGHT ASL : 20′ LIGHTING : Mk2.
LONGITUDE : 00 35 00W. FLYING CONTROL : Yes. RADIO : QDM.

LANDMARKS DAY : Arundel Castle 3miles N. R Arun E.

LANDMARKS NIGHT : R Arun & coastline.

OBSTRUCTIONS : Radio masts 076degrees 2.5miles.

LANDING AREA SURFACE : Tarmac & wood chippings.

QDM	LENGTH X WIDTH	EXT. TO
248.	2000 x 50yds.	-
337.	1600 x 50yds.	3100yds.

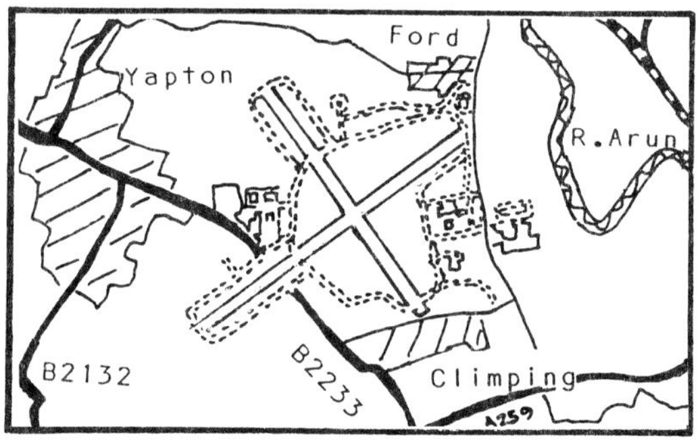

EXTENSIBILITY : Entails very slight demolition but main rd. diversion of 1000yds.
ACCOMMODATION : Temporary[permanent M.Q.]
HANGARS : Bellman-5; general purpose-1; blisters: over-4; EO-16.
HARDSTANDINGS :

	OFFICERS	S.N.C.O's.	O.R's.	TOTAL
R.A.F.	227.	356.	1959.	2542.
W.A.A.F.	-	4.	295.	299.

AFFILIATED AIRFIELDS : Tangmere[sector]

PRESENT USE [1985] : HM Prison.

NO: 235.

AIRFIELD NAME: FORDOUN. OPENED : 1942.
COUNTY : Kincardineshire. CLOSED : 1945.
COMMAND : Flying Training.
FORMATION : On loan to War Dept. GRID REF: P 265985[51Scot]
FUNCTION : On loan to War Dept. O.S.REF.: NH 755774.

LOCALITY : 9miles SW of Stonehaven.
RAILWAY STN. : Fordoun 1mile[LMS]

LATITUDE : 56 53 08N. HEIGHT ASL : 200′ LIGHTING : None.
LONGITUDE : 02 24 15W. FLYING CONTROL : None.RADIO : QDM.

LANDMARKS DAY. : Bounded by Grampian hills from ENE to WNW at approx 3-4miles. Main railway line running along SE extremity.

LANDMARKS NIGHT : -

OBSTRUCTIONS : Railway telegraph wires along SE boundary; silo & trees at Balfeith Farm 550yds SE of No 1 R/W.

LANDING AREA SURFACE : Concrete.
QDM: 170. LENGTH X WIDTH: 1100 x 50yds.EXT. TO: -
: 060. : 1500 x 50yds. : 1800yds.

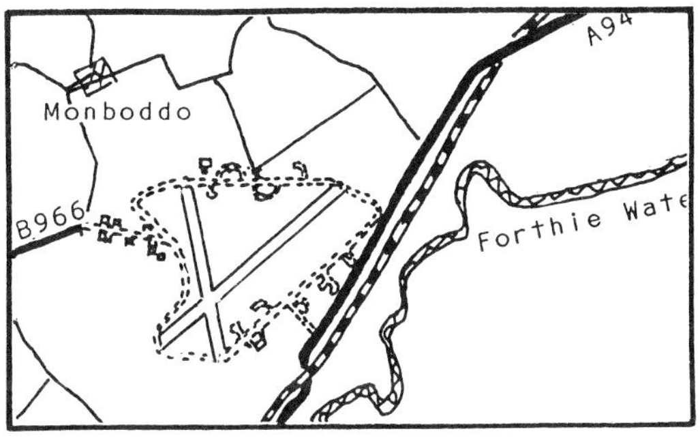

EXTENSIBILITY : Entails slight demolition.

ACCOMMODATION : Temporary.
HANGARS : 65′ blister-4.

HARDSTANDINGS : Double fighter-6.

R.A.F. : OFFICERS: 29. S.N.C.O′s.: 40. O.R′s.: 405. TOTAL: 474.
W.A.A.F.: " : - " : 16. " : 45. " : 61.

AFFILIATED AIRFIELDS : -

PRESENT USE [1985] : Private flying.

NO: 236.

AIRFIELD NAME: FORRES. OPENED : 1940.
COUNTY : Morayshire. CLOSED : 1946.
COMMAND : Bomber.
FORMATION : On loan to War Dept. GRID REF: J 540798[28Scot]
FUNCTION : On loan to War Dept. O.S.REF.: NJ 019578.

LOCALITY : 13miles WSW of Elgin.
RAILWAY STN. : Forres 13miles[LMS]

LATITUDE : 57 35 53N. HEIGHT ASL : 50′ LIGHTING : None.
LONGITUDE : 03 38 30W. FLYING CONTROL : None.RADIO : QDM.

LANDMARKS DAY. : Forrestown & R Findhorn.

LANDMARKS NIGHT : R Findhorn. BBC masts 10miles ENE 670′MSL. 5 spaced red lights.

OBSTRUCTIONS : Cluny hill & tower 1mile E. Findhorn bridge NW. Burgh head radio masts 650′ 9miles NE.

LANDING AREA SURFACE : Grass.
QDM: NE-SW. LENGTH X WIDTH: 1700yds. EXT. TO: -
: NW-SE. : 1100yds. : -
: : : 600yds.
: : :

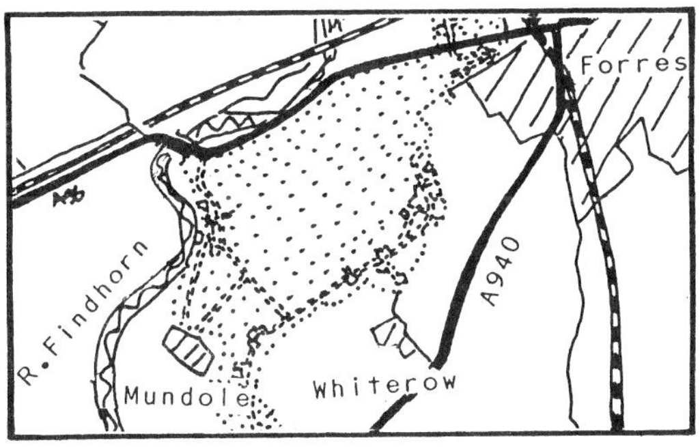

EXTENSIBILITY : Entails demolition of a farm, house & 2 cottages.

ACCOMMODATION : Temporary.
HANGARS : T2-1.

HARDSTANDINGS : Fryingpan-22; also 2 too close to railway for safety.

R.A.F. : OFFICERS: 89. S.N.C.O′s.: 236.O.R′s.: 509. TOTAL: 834.
W.A.A.F.: " : 1. " : 2. " : 170. " : 173.

AFFILIATED AIRFIELDS : -

PRESENT USE [1985] : Disused.

NO: 237.

AIRFIELD NAME: FOULSHAM. OPENED : 1942.
COUNTY : Norfolk. CLOSED : 1945.
COMMAND : Bomber.
FORMATION : 100 Grp[Bylaugh Hall] GRID REF: G 488449[57]
FUNCTION : Operational. O.S.REF.: TG 028269.

LOCALITY : 8.5miles NNE of Dereham.
RAILWAY STN. : Foulsham 1.5miles[LNER]

LATITUDE : 52 48 00N. HEIGHT ASL : 190′ LIGHTING : MK2.
LONGITUDE : 01 00 30E. FLYING CONTROL : Yes. RADIO : QDM.

LANDMARKS DAY. : Water tower.

LANDMARKS NIGHT : -

OBSTRUCTIONS : Hindel Weston & Foulsham churches.Water tower 60′ on technical site.

LANDING AREA SURFACE : Tar & wood chippings.
QDM: 190. LENGTH X WIDTH: 1900 x 50yds.EXT. TO: -
: 260. : 1400 x 50yds. : 2000yds.
: 326. : 1350 x 50yds. : 2000yds.
: : :

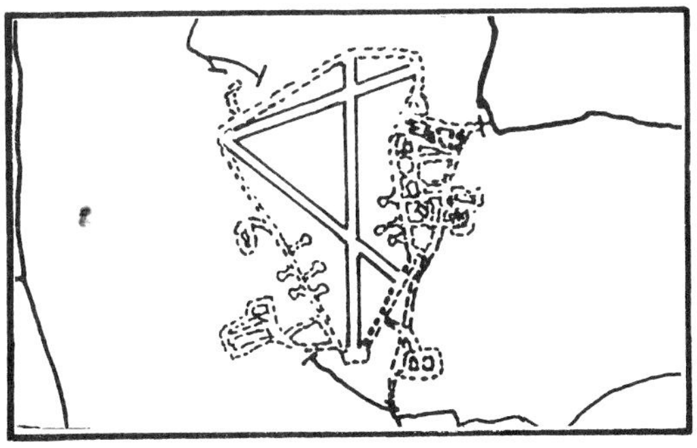

EXTENSIBILITY : Entails closure/diversion of 2 secondary rds, & demo. of Morton Hall & ruins of St Georges church.
ACCOMMODATION : Temporary.
HANGARS : T2-9; B1-1.

HARDSTANDINGS : Heavy bomber-36.

R.A.F. : OFFICERS: 101.S.N.C.O′s.: 330.O.R′s.: 1704.TOTAL: 2135.
W.A.A.F.: " : 9. " : 10. " : 336. " : 355.

AFFILIATED AIRFIELDS : -

PRESENT USE [1985] : Disused.

NO: 238.

AIRFIELD NAME: FOWLMERE. OPENED : 1940.
COUNTY : Cambridgeshire. CLOSED : 1945.
COMMAND : 8th USAAF.
FORMATION : 339th Fighter Grp. GRID REF: L 862629[85]
FUNCTION : Operational. O.S.REF.: TL 415446.

LOCALITY : 3.5miles NE of Royston.
RAILWAY STN. : Shepreth 3miles[LNER]

LATITUDE : 52 04 30N. HEIGHT ASL : 100′ LIGHTING : None.
LONGITUDE : 00 03 45E. FLYING CONTROL : Yes. RADIO : QDM.

LANDMARKS DAY. : Main Newmarket-Royston road 500yds S of A/F.

LANDMARKS NIGHT : -

OBSTRUCTIONS : -

LANDING AREA SURFACE : Steel Matting[Sommerfeld Track]

QDM: 110. LENGTH X WIDTH: 1400 x 50yds.EXT. TO: -
: 050. : 1600 x 50yds. : -
: : :
: : :

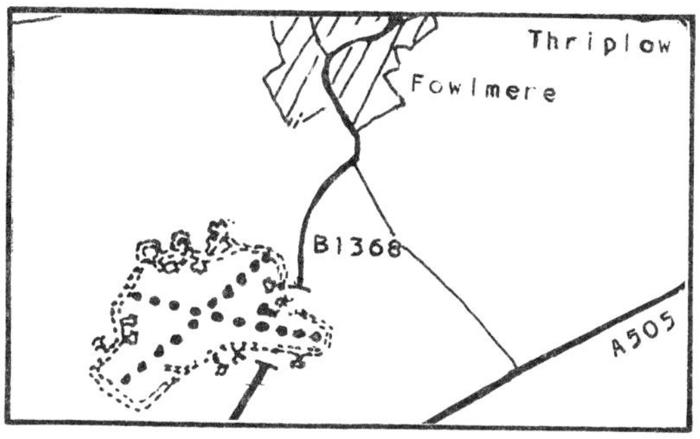

EXTENSIBILITY : Not recommended; entails demolition of a farm.

ACCOMMODATION : Temporary.
HANGARS : T2-1;blister-7.

HARDSTANDINGS : Concrete-80.

USAAF. : OFFICERS: 190. Enlisted Men. : 1519.TOTAL: 1709.

AFFILIATED AIRFIELDS : -

PRESENT USE [1985] : Agriculture.

NO: 239.

AIRFIELD NAME: FRAMLINGHAM. OPENED : 1943.
COUNTY : Suffolk. CLOSED : 1945.
COMMAND : 8th USAAF.
FORMATION : 390th Bomb Grp. GRID REF: M 785787[87]
FUNCTION : Operational. O.S.REF.: TM 330608.

LOCALITY : 3miles SE of Framlingham.
RAILWAY STN. : Parham 2miles[LNER]

LATITUDE : 52 11 38N. HEIGHT ASL : 140′ LIGHTING : Mk2.
LONGITUDE : 01 24 30E. FLYING CONTROL : Yes. RADIO : QDM.

LANDMARKS DAY. : Windmill of North Green. Water tower.

LANDMARKS NIGHT : -

OBSTRUCTIONS : -

LANDING AREA SURFACE : Concrete & wood chippings.

QDM: 282. LENGTH X WIDTH: 2000 x 50yds.EXT. TO: -
: 173. : 1400 x 50yds. : 1800yds.
: 234. : 1400 x 50yds. : 2000yds.
: : :

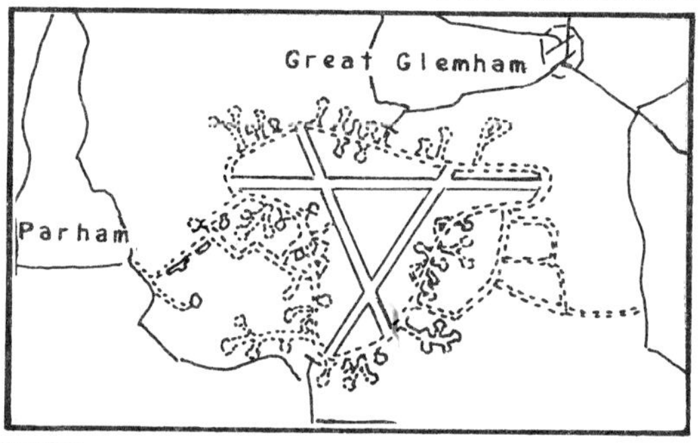

EXTENSIBILITY :

ACCOMMODATION : Temporary.
HANGARS : T2-2.

HARDSTANDINGS : Loop-50.

USAAF. : OFFICERS: 421. Enlisted Men. : 2473.TOTAL: 2894.

AFFILIATED AIRFIELDS : -

PRESENT USE [1985] : Agriculture.

NO: 240.

AIRFIELD NAME: FRASERBURGH. OPENED : 1941.
COUNTY : Aberdeenshire. CLOSED : 1945.
COMMAND : Coastal.
FORMATION : 18 Grp[Pitreavie Castle] GRID REF: K 560850[31Scot]
FUNCTION : Operational. O.S.REF.: NK 040645.

LOCALITY : 17.5miles NW of Peterhead.
RAILWAY STN. : Fraserburgh .5miles[LNER]

LATITUDE : 57 40 08N. HEIGHT ASL : 52′ LIGHTING : Mk2.
LONGITUDE : 01 56 00W. FLYING CONTROL : Yes. RADIO : QDM.

LANDMARKS DAY. : -

LANDMARKS NIGHT : -

OBSTRUCTIONS : -

LANDING AREA SURFACE : Tarmac.

QDM: 170. LENGTH X WIDTH: 1100 x 50yds.EXT. TO: -
: 236. : 1350 x 50yds. : -
: 304. : 1000 x 50yds. : 2000yds.
: : :

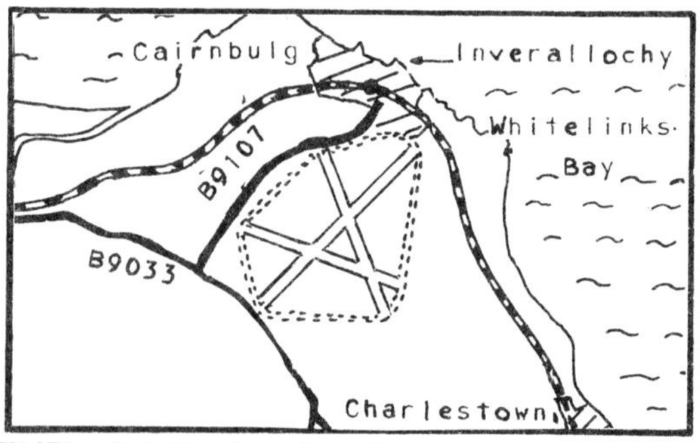

EXTENSIBILITY : Entails diversion of only access road to Inverallochy & light demolition.
ACCOMMODATION : Temporary.
HANGARS : T2-1; double blister-6.

HARDSTANDINGS : Loop-3; frying pan-18.

R.A.F. : OFFICERS: 97. S.N.C.O′s.: 60. O.R′s.: 830. TOTAL: 987.
W.A.A.F.: " : 14. " : 5. " : 208. " : 227.

AFFILIATED AIRFIELDS : Banff[Parent]

PRESENT USE [1985] : Agriculture.

NO: 241.

AIRFIELD NAME: FRISTON.
COUNTY : Sussex.
COMMAND : Fighter.
FORMATION : 11 Grp[Uxbridge]
FUNCTION : Operational.

OPENED : 1940.
CLOSED : 1946.

GRID REF: Q 966167[134]
O.S.REF.: TV 555989.

LOCALITY : 5miles WSW of Eastbourne.
RAILWAY STN. : Eastbourne 5miles[SR]

LATITUDE : 50 45 43N. HEIGHT ASL : 355′ LIGHTING : None.
LONGITUDE : 00 10 15E. FLYING CONTROL : Yes. RADIO : QDM.

LANDMARKS DAY. : Beachy Head to E. Water tower, East Dean 1mile. Cuckmere river & valley to W.

LANDMARKS NIGHT : -

OBSTRUCTIONS : -

LANDING AREA SURFACE : Grass.

QDM	LENGTH X WIDTH	EXT. TO
NE-SW.	1675yds.	-
N-S.	950yds.	1000yds.
		-

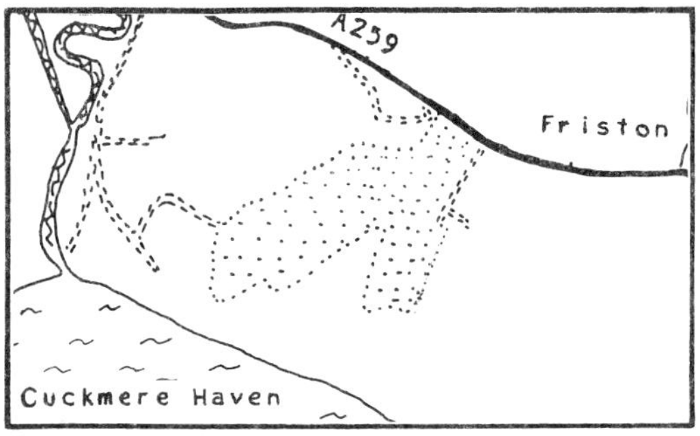

EXTENSIBILITY : -

ACCOMMODATION : Temporary.
HANGARS : 0 blister-2.

HARDSTANDINGS : None.

R.A.F. : OFFICERS: 96. S.N.C.O′s.: 175.O.R′s.: 977. TOTAL: 1248.
W.A.A.F.: " : 3. " : 3. " : 146. " : 152.

AFFILIATED AIRFIELDS : Biggin Hill[Sector]

PRESENT USE [1985] : Agriculture.

NO: 242.

AIRFIELD NAME: FULBECK.
COUNTY : Lincolnshire.
COMMAND : Bomber.
FORMATION : 5 Grp[Morton Hall]
FUNCTION : Operational.

OPENED : 1940.
CLOSED : 1970.

GRID REF: F 365706[55]
O.S.REF.: SK 900510.

LOCALITY : 6.5miles ESE of Newark on Trent.
RAILWAY STN. : Leadenham 3miles[LNER]

LATITUDE : 53 03 00N. HEIGHT ASL : 50′ LIGHTING : Mk2.
LONGITUDE : 00 39 30W. FLYING CONTROL : Yes. RADIO : QDM.

LANDMARKS DAY. : -

LANDMARKS NIGHT : -

OBSTRUCTIONS : Masts E end of W runway.

LANDING AREA SURFACE : Concrete & tarmac.

QDM	LENGTH X WIDTH	EXT. TO
233.	2000 x 50yds.	-
297.	1400 x 50yds.	2030yds.
007.	1400 x 50yds.	2400yds.

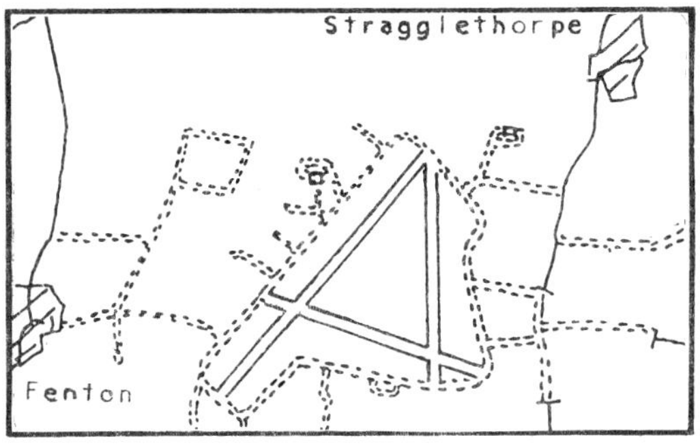

EXTENSIBILITY :

ACCOMMODATION : Temporary.
HANGARS : T2-2; glider[T2]-3.

HARDSTANDINGS : Heavy bomber-50.

R.A.F. : OFFICERS: 517.S.N.C.O′s.: 33. O.R′s.: 2285.TOTAL: 2835.
W.A.A.F.: " : - " : - " : - " : -

AFFILIATED AIRFIELDS : Syerston[56 base]

PRESENT USE [1985] : Disused.

NO: 243.

AIRFIELD NAME: FULL SUTTON.
COUNTY : Yorkshire.
COMMAND : Bomber.
FORMATION : 4 Grp[York]
FUNCTION : Operational.

OPENED : 1944.
CLOSED : 1963.

GRID REF: A 218739[27]
O.S.REF.: SE 745545.

LOCALITY : 8miles E of York.
RAILWAY STN. : Fangfoss 1.5miles[LNER]

LATITUDE : 53 58 45N. HEIGHT ASL : 50′ LIGHTING : Mk2.
LONGITUDE : 00 52 00W. FLYING CONTROL : Yes. RADIO : QDM.

LANDMARKS DAY. : -

LANDMARKS NIGHT : -

OBSTRUCTIONS : Water tower 700yds NE 115′. Farm 880 yds NNE 115′.Railway gate. House 1650yds WSW 35′

LANDING AREA SURFACE : Concrete & tarmac.

QDM	LENGTH X WIDTH	EXT. TO
162.	2000 x 50yds.	-
046.	1600 x 50yds.	1900yds.
291.	1400 x 50yds.	2000yds.

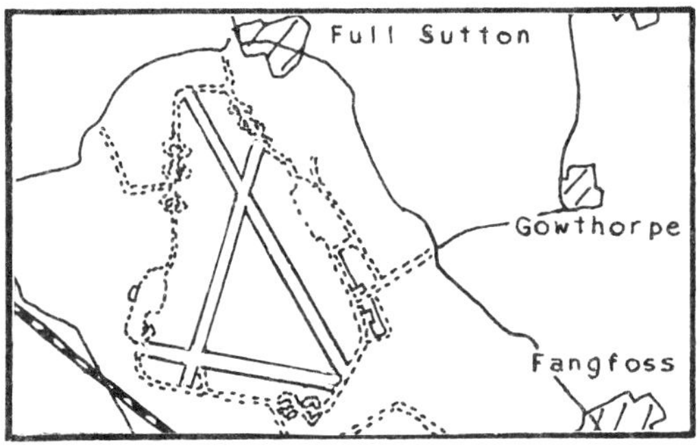

EXTENSIBILITY : -

ACCOMMODATION : Temporary.
HANGARS : T2-2; B1-1.

HARDSTANDINGS : Loop-36.

R.A.F. : OFFICERS: 183.S.N.C.O′s.: 410.O.R′s.: 850. TOTAL: 1443.
W.A.A.F.: " : 10. " : 20. " : 337. " : 367.

AFFILIATED AIRFIELDS : Pocklington[42 base]

PRESENT USE [1985] : Disused.

NO: 244.

AIRFIELD NAME: FUNTINGTON. OPENED : 1943.
COUNTY : Sussex. CLOSED : 1944.
COMMAND : Fighter.
FORMATION : 11 Grp[Uxbridge] GRID REF: Q 220279[132]
FUNCTION : Advanced Landing Ground. O.S.REF.: SU 790083.
[De-requisitioned]
LOCALITY : 5miles W of Chichester.
RAILWAY STN. : Nutbourne[SR]

LATITUDE : 50 52 00N. HEIGHT ASL : 115′ LIGHTING : None.
LONGITUDE : 00 52 45W. FLYING CONTROL : None.RADIO : QDM.

LANDMARKS DAY. : Railway running N-S 1.5miles W of A/F.

LANDMARKS NIGHT : -

OBSTRUCTIONS : -

LANDING AREA SURFACE : Steel Matting[Sommerfeld track]
QDM: 083. LENGTH X WIDTH: 1600yds. EXT. TO: -
: 343. : 1200yds. : -
: : :
: : :

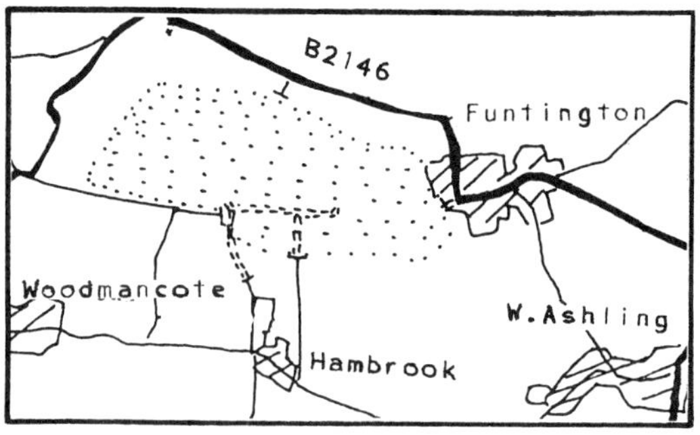

EXTENSIBILITY : -

ACCOMMODATION : Tented camp.
HANGARS : EO blister-4.

HARDSTANDINGS : Somerfeld track.

R.A.F. : OFFICERS: - S.N.C.O′s.: - O.R′s.: - TOTAL: -
W.A.A.F.: " : - " : - " : - " : -

AFFILIATED AIRFIELDS : -

PRESENT USE [1985] : Agriculture.

NO: 245.

AIRFIELD NAME: GAMSTON. OPENED : 1942.
COUNTY : Nottinghamshire. CLOSED : 1957.
COMMAND : Bomber.
FORMATION : 7 Grp[St.Vincents] GRID REF: F 159960[46]
FUNCTION : Operational. O.S.REF.: SK 693762.

LOCALITY : 3miles S of East Retford.
RAILWAY STN. : Retford [LNER]

LATITUDE : 53 16 45N. HEIGHT ASL : 90′ LIGHTING : Mk2.
LONGITUDE : 00 57 30W. FLYING CONTROL : Yes. RADIO : QDM.

LANDMARKS DAY. : -

LANDMARKS NIGHT : -

OBSTRUCTIONS : Water tower WNW.

LANDING AREA SURFACE : Concrete & tarmac.
QDM: 216. LENGTH X WIDTH: 2000 x 50yds.EXT. TO: -
: 270. : 1400 x 50yds. : -
: 332. : 1400 x 50yds. : -
: : :

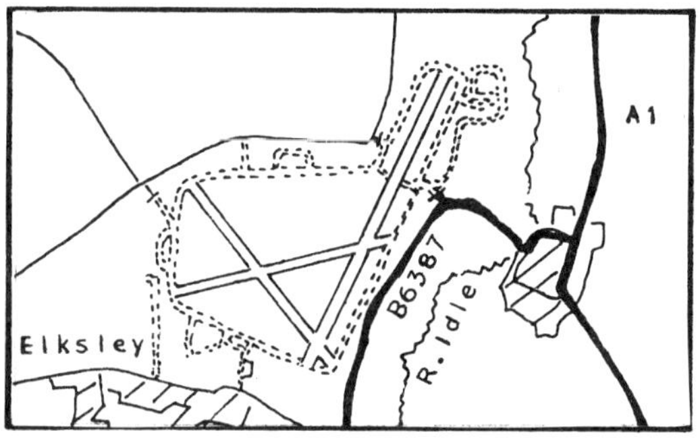

EXTENSIBILITY : None possible.

ACCOMMODATION : Temporary.
HANGARS : T2-4; B1-1.

HARDSTANDINGS : Heavy bomber-30.

R.A.F. : OFFICERS: 131.S.N.C.O′s.: 240.O.R′s.: 594. TOTAL: 965.
W.A.A.F.: " : 4. " : 16. " : 287. " : 307.

AFFILIATED AIRFIELDS : Topcliffe[76 RCAF base]

PRESENT USE [1985] : Disused.

NO: 246.

AIRFIELD NAME: GATWICK. OPENED : 1930.
COUNTY : Surrey. CLOSED :
COMMAND : Fighter.
FORMATION : 11 Grp[Uxbridge] GRID REF: Q 724597[125]
FUNCTION : Forward Airfield. O.S.REF.: TQ 270404.

LOCALITY : 6miles SSE of Reigate.
RAILWAY STN. : Gatwick Airport[SR]

LATITUDE : 51 09 00N. HEIGHT ASL : 200′ LIGHTING : Mk2.
LONGITUDE : 00 10 00W. FLYING CONTROL : Yes. RADIO : QDM.

LANDMARKS DAY. : London-Brighton railway. Crawley by-pass.

LANDMARKS NIGHT : As above on moonlit nights.

OBSTRUCTIONS : Railway embankment on E side.

LANDING AREA SURFACE : Steel Matting[Army track.NW-SE Grass]
QDM: 238. LENGTH X WIDTH: 1400yds. EXT. TO: -
: 277. : 1200yds. : -
: NW-SE. : 1000yds. : -
: : :

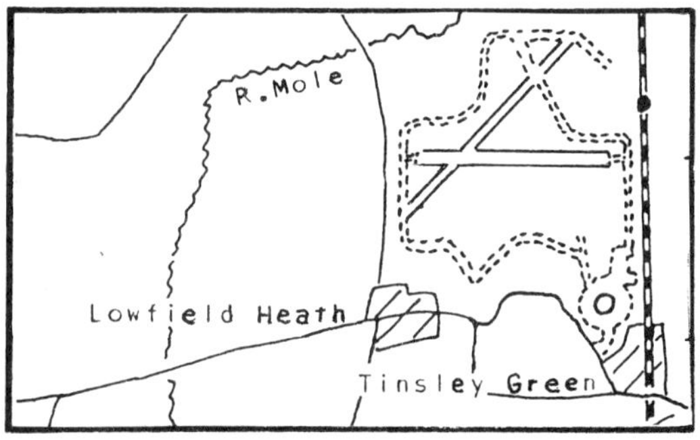

EXTENSIBILITY : New strips of 1600-2100-1200-2000-1150-1550yds. entail fairly heavy demolition.
ACCOMMODATION : Temporary [civil airport buildings permanent]
HANGARS : Bellman-1;Blister-6.

HARDSTANDINGS : Blenheim-12;frypan:50′-3;100′-17.

R.A.F. : OFFICERS: 79. S.N.C.O′s.: 111.O.R′s.: 720. TOTAL: 910.
W.A.A.F.: " : 6. " : 4. " : 202. " : 212.

AFFILIATED AIRFIELDS : Biggin Hill[Sector]

PRESENT USE [1985] : Civil Airport[London Gatwick]

NO: 247.

AIRFIELD NAME: GAYDON. OPENED : 1942.
COUNTY : Warwickshire. CLOSED : 1974.
COMMAND : Bomber.
FORMATION : 91 Grp[Abingdon] GRID REF: P 805749[82]
FUNCTION : Operational Training Unit[satellite] O.S.REF.: SP 353458.
LOCALITY : 7.5miles SSE of Leamington.
RAILWAY STN. : Kineton 4miles[LMS]

LATITUDE : 52 11 15N. HEIGHT ASL : 410′ LIGHTING : Mk2.
LONGITUDE : 01 29 00W. FLYING CONTROL : Yes. RADIO : QDM.

LANDMARKS DAY : Rolling country; no outstanding features.

LANDMARKS NIGHT : -

OBSTRUCTIONS : -

LANDING AREA SURFACE : Concrete covered with tar & sand.

QDM	LENGTH X WIDTH	EXT. TO
178.	1400 x 50yds.	-
248.	1600 x 50yds.	3200yds.
316.	1400 x 50yds.	-

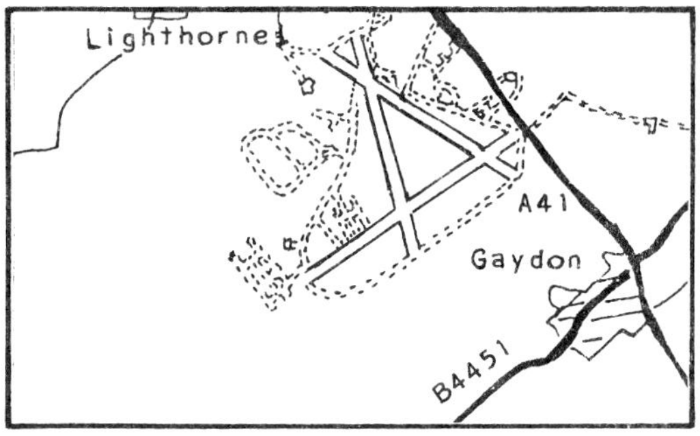

EXTENSIBILITY : -

ACCOMMODATION : Temporary.
HANGARS : T2-1; B1-1.

HARDSTANDINGS : Heavy bomber-27.

R.A.F. : OFFICERS: 87. S.N.C.O′s.: 340. O.R′s.: 1224. TOTAL: 1651.
W.A.A.F.: " : 2. " : 8. " : 186. " : 196.

AFFILIATED AIRFIELDS : Wellesbourne Mountford[Parent]

PRESENT USE [1985] : Industry.

NO: 248.

AIRFIELD NAME: GLATTON. OPENED : 1943.
COUNTY : Huntingdonshire. CLOSED : 1946.
COMMAND : 8th USAAF.
FORMATION : 457th Bomb Grp. GRID REF: F 640060[74]
FUNCTION : Operational. O.S.REF.: TL 186868.

LOCALITY : 10miles N of Huntingdon.
RAILWAY STN. : Holme 1mile[LNER]

LATITUDE : 52 27 53N. HEIGHT ASL : 20′ LIGHTING : Mk2.
LONGITUDE : 00 15 00W. FLYING CONTROL : Yes. RADIO : QDM.

LANDMARKS DAY : Railway line running N-S at E edge of A/F.

LANDMARKS NIGHT : Illuminated chimney 7miles N of A/F.

OBSTRUCTIONS : Farm buildings at centre of A/F but none within approach angles.

LANDING AREA SURFACE : Tarmac & wood chippings.

QDM	LENGTH X WIDTH	EXT. TO
140.	2000 x 50yds.	-
160.	1400 x 50yds.	2000yds.
235.	1400 x 50yds.	2200yds.

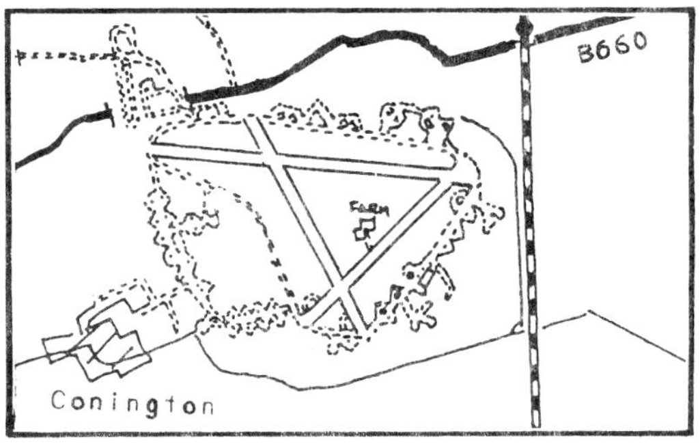

EXTENSIBILITY : -

ACCOMMODATION : Temporary.
HANGARS : T2-2.

HARDSTANDINGS : Loop-50.

USAAF. : OFFICERS: 421. Enlisted Men. : 2473. TOTAL: 2894.

AFFILIATED AIRFIELDS : -

PRESENT USE [1985] : Private flying.

NO: 249.

AIRFIELD NAME: GOSFIELD. OPENED : 1943.
COUNTY : Essex. CLOSED : 1945.
COMMAND : Bomber.
FORMATION : 3 Grp[Exning] GRID REF: M 225495[97]
FUNCTION : Care & Maintenance. O.S.REF.: TL 778312.

LOCALITY : 2miles W of Halstead.
RAILWAY STN. : Halstead 2miles[LNER]

LATITUDE : 51 57 00N. HEIGHT ASL : 285′ LIGHTING : Mk2.
LONGITUDE : 00 35 00E. FLYING CONTROL : Yes. RADIO : QDM.

LANDMARKS DAY : Gosfield Lake 1mile S. Headingham Castle 3.5miles NNE

LANDMARKS NIGHT : Braintree town 6miles S.

OBSTRUCTIONS : -

LANDING AREA SURFACE : Concrete & wood chippings.

QDM	LENGTH X WIDTH	EXT. TO
317.	2000 x 50yds.	-
019.	1400 x 50yds.	-
084.	1400 x 50yds.	2000yds.

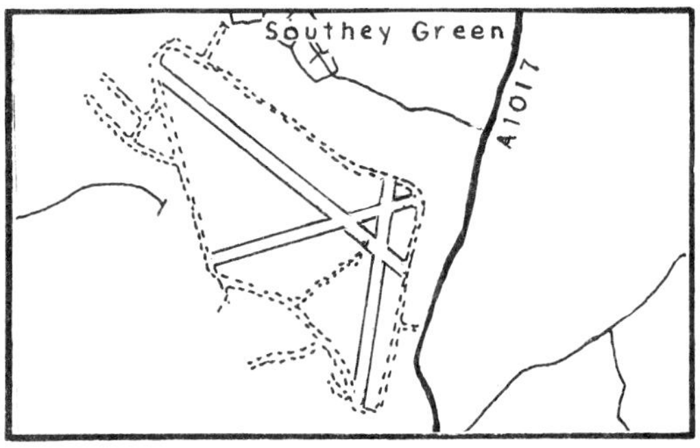

EXTENSIBILITY : Not recommended-entails diversion of a road & demolition of 6 bungalows.
ACCOMMODATION : Temporary.
HANGARS : T2-2.

HARDSTANDINGS : Spectacle-50.

R.A.F. : OFFICERS: 7. S.N.C.O′s.: 21. O.R′s.: 742. TOTAL: 840.
W.A.A.F.: " : " : " : " :

AFFILIATED AIRFIELDS : Stradishall[31 base]

PRESENT USE [1985] : Consumer′s Association.

NO: 250.

AIRFIELD NAME: GOSPORT. OPENED : 1914.
COUNTY : Hampshire CLOSED : 1956.
COMMAND : Coastal.
FORMATION : 16 Grp[Gillingham] GRID REF: Q 024207[132]
FUNCTION : Development Unit. O.S.REF.: SU 586010.

LOCALITY : 4miles W of Portsmouth.
RAILWAY STN. : Portsmouth Harbour.

LATITUDE : 51 57 00N. HEIGHT ASL : 24′ LIGHTING : None.
LONGITUDE : 00 35 00E. FLYING CONTROL : Yes. RADIO : QDM.

LANDMARKS DAY. : Fareham-Gosport railway E boundary.

LANDMARKS NIGHT : _

OBSTRUCTIONS : -

LANDING AREA SURFACE : Tarmac[N-S & NW-SE grass]
QDM: NNW-SSE. LENGTH X WIDTH: 533 x 50yds.EXT. TO: -
: NE-SW. : 600 x 50yds. : -
: N-S. : 1500yds. : -
: NW-SE. : 1250yds. : -

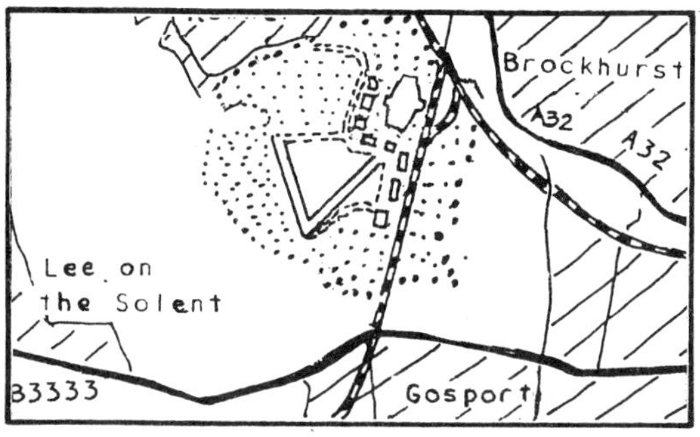

EXTENSIBILITY : Two other grass R/W; NE-SW=1500yds; E-W 850yds.
ACCOMMODATION : Permanent.
HANGARS : Types C-1;A-4[1 U/S];Bellman-2;Bessoneau-1; EO blister-5.
HARDSTANDINGS : BRC fabric-23.

R.A.F. : OFFICERS: 131.S.N.C.O′s.: 166.O.R′s.: 2307.TOTAL: 2604.
W.A.A.F.: " : 16. " : 10. " : 704. " : 730.

AFFILIATED AIRFIELDS : -

PRESENT USE [1985] : Housing.

NO: 251.

AIRFIELD NAME: GOXHILL. OPENED : 1941.
COUNTY : Lincolnshire. CLOSED : 1953.
COMMAND : 8th USAAF.
FORMATION : 496th Fighter Grp. GRID REF: A 583408[33]
FUNCTION : Combat Crew Replace-ment Centre. O.S.REF.: TA 115218.
LOCALITY : 5miles E of Barrow on Humber.
RAILWAY STN. : Goxhill 1.5miles[LNER]

LATITUDE : 53 40 38N. HEIGHT ASL : 20′ LIGHTING : Mk2.
LONGITUDE : 00 18 53W. FLYING CONTROL : Yes. RADIO : QDM.

LANDMARKS DAY. : Goxhill church steeple; Greenhouse N end of A/F.

LANDMARKS NIGHT : R Humber 2miles N of A/F.

OBSTRUCTIONS : Trees surrounding A/F.

LANDING AREA SURFACE : Tarmac.
QDM: 070. LENGTH X WIDTH: 1600 x 50yds.EXT. TO: -
: 010. : 1100 x 50yds. : 1500yds.
: 130. : 1100 x 50yds. : 2000yds.
: : :

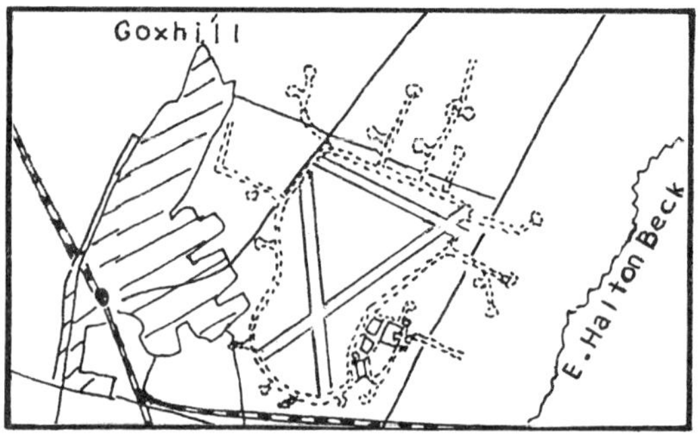

EXTENSIBILITY : Entails fairly heavy demolition.

ACCOMMODATION : Temporary.
HANGARS : Type J-1; T2-2; blister-4.

HARDSTANDINGS : Pen-50.

USAAF. : OFFICERS: 190. Enlisted Men. : 1519.TOTAL: 1709.

AFFILIATED AIRFIELDS : -

PRESENT USE [1985] : Disused.

NO: 252.

AIRFIELD NAME: GRAFTON UNDERWOOD. OPENED : 1942.
COUNTY : Northamptonshire. CLOSED : 1959.
COMMAND : 8th USAAF.
FORMATION : 384th Bomb Grp. GRID REF: F 377007[74]
FUNCTION : Operational. O.S.REF.: SP 923813.

LOCALITY : 3.75miles ENE of Kettering.
RAILWAY STN. : Cranford 3miles[LMS]

LATITUDE : 52 25 15N. HEIGHT ASL : 338′ LIGHTING : Mk2.
LONGITUDE : 00 38 45W. FLYING CONTROL : Yes. RADIO : QDM.

LANDMARKS DAY. : Steel wks Corby; Iron foundary Thrapston; Iron ore pits Cranford; Kettering town.

LANDMARKS NIGHT : As day.

OBSTRUCTIONS : Water tower with red light.

LANDING AREA SURFACE : Asphalt & wood chippings.
QDM: 045. LENGTH X WIDTH: 2000 x 50yds.EXT. TO: -
: 358. : 1400 x 50yds. : 1650yds.
: 293. : 1400 x 50yds. : -
: : :

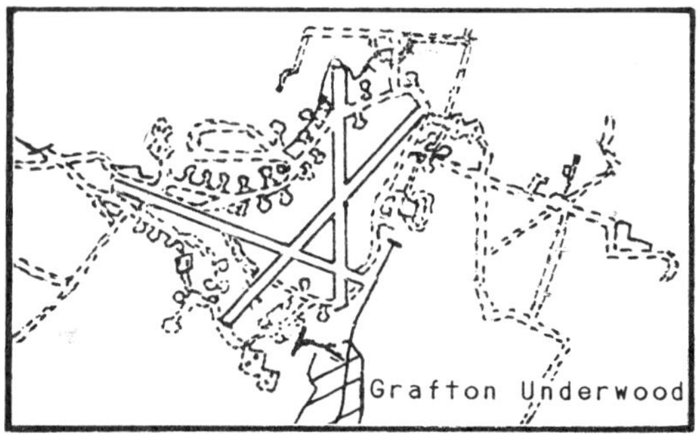

EXTENSIBILITY : Not recommended.

ACCOMMODATION : Temporary.
HANGARS : T2-2.

HARDSTANDINGS : Loop-50.

USAAF. : OFFICERS: 421. Enlisted Men. : 2473.TOTAL: 2894.

AFFILIATED AIRFIELDS : -

PRESENT USE [1985] : Disused.

NO: 253.

AIRFIELD NAME: GRANGEMOUTH. OPENED : 1939.
COUNTY : Stirlingshire. CLOSED : 1945.
COMMAND : Maintenance.
FORMATION : 56 Wing[Carlisle] GRID REF: 0 436031[67Scot]
FUNCTION : Storage Unit. O.S.REF.: NS 946820.

LOCALITY : 3miles NE of Falkirk.
RAILWAY STN. : Grangemouth 1mile[LMS]

LATITUDE : 56 00 27N. HEIGHT ASL : 12′ LIGHTING : None.
LONGITUDE : 03 42 00W. FLYING CONTROL : None. RADIO : QDM.

LANDMARKS DAY. : Grangemouth harbour projects from S bank; Firth of Forth.

LANDMARKS NIGHT : Firth of Forth.

OBSTRUCTIONS : -

LANDING AREA SURFACE : Tarmac.

QDM: 278. LENGTH X WIDTH: 1400 x 50yds. EXT. TO: 2400yds.
: 222. : 1100 x 50yds. : -
: : :
: : :

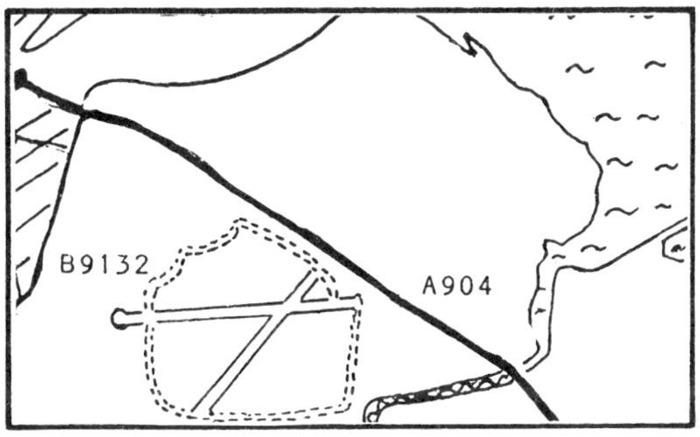

EXTENSIBILITY : Entails diversion of important Grangemouth-Edinburgh main road.
ACCOMMODATION : Temporary.
HANGARS : Civil airport-2; blister-8.

HARDSTANDINGS : 20.

R.A.F. : OFFICERS: 10. S.N.C.O′s.: 22. O.R′s.: 356. TOTAL: 388.
W.A.A.F.: " : 10. " : 5. " : 191. " : 206.

AFFILIATED AIRFIELDS : -

PRESENT USE [1985] : Industry.

NO: 254.

AIRFIELD NAME: GRANSDEN LODGE. OPENED : 1942.
COUNTY : Bedfordshire. CLOSED : 1955.
COMMAND : Bomber.
FORMATION : 8 Grp[Huntingdon] GRID REF: L 740740[85]
FUNCTION : Operational. O.S.REF.: TL 290555.

LOCALITY : 10miles W of Cambridge.
RAILWAY STN. : Gamlingay 3miles[LMS]

LATITUDE : 52 10 45N. HEIGHT ASL : 248′ LIGHTING : Mk2.
LONGITUDE : 00 07 00W. FLYING CONTROL : Yes. RADIO : QDM.

LANDMARKS DAY. : Windmill .75miles W of A/F.

LANDMARKS NIGHT : -

OBSTRUCTIONS : -

LANDING AREA SURFACE : Concrete.

QDM: 036. LENGTH X WIDTH: 2000 x 50yds. EXT. TO: -
: 351. : 1400 x 50yds. : 2000yds.
: 100. : 1400 x 50yds. : 2000yds.
: : :

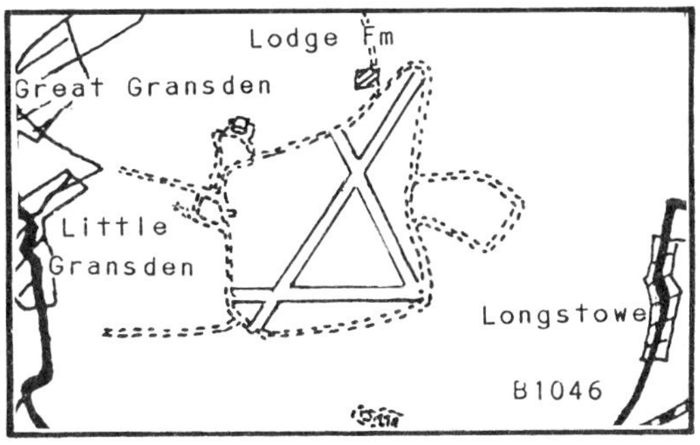

EXTENSIBILITY : Entails demolition of Gransden Lodge & Hill Farm.
ACCOMMODATION : Temporary.
HANGARS : T2-2; B1-1.

HARDSTANDINGS : Heavy bomber-36.

R.A.F. : OFFICERS: 86. S.N.C.O′s.: 196. O.R′s.: 829. TOTAL: 1111.
W.A.A.F.: " : 7. " : 6. " : 262. " : 275.

AFFILIATED AIRFIELDS : -

PRESENT USE [1985] : Agriculture.

NO: 255.

AIRFIELD NAME: GRAVELEY. OPENED : 1942.
COUNTY : Huntingdonshire. CLOSED : 1968.
COMMAND : Bomber.
FORMATION : 8 Grp[Huntingdon] GRID REF: L 690833[84]
FUNCTION : Operational. O.S.REF.: TL 290555.

LOCALITY : 5miles S of Huntingdon.
RAILWAY STN. : Buckden 3.5miles[LNER]

LATITUDE : 52 15 45N. HEIGHT ASL : 177′ LIGHTING : Mk2.
LONGITUDE : 00 11 00W. FLYING CONTROL : Yes. RADIO : QDM.

LANDMARKS DAY. : -

LANDMARKS NIGHT : -

OBSTRUCTIONS : -

LANDING AREA SURFACE : Concrete.

QDM: 209. LENGTH X WIDTH: 1400 x 50yds. EXT. TO: 2700yds.
: 269. : 2000 x 50yds. : 2700yds.
: 330. : 1400 x 50yds. : 3800yds.
: : :

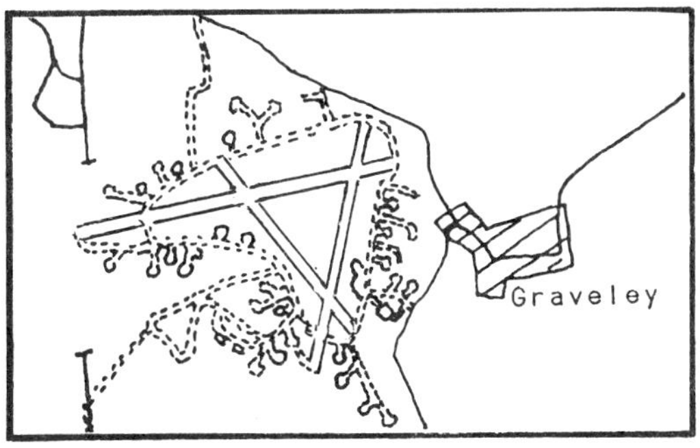

EXTENSIBILITY : Entails closure of 2-′B′ roads & demolition of 2 buildings & removal of dispersed site.
ACCOMMODATION : Temporary.
HANGARS : T2-3; B1-1.

HARDSTANDINGS : Heavy bomber-36.

R.A.F. : OFFICERS: 159. S.N.C.O′s.: 386. O.R′s.: 1755. TOTAL: 2300.
W.A.A.F.: " : 7. " : 20. " : 272. " : 299.

AFFILIATED AIRFIELDS : -.

PRESENT USE [1985] : Agriculture.

NO: 256.

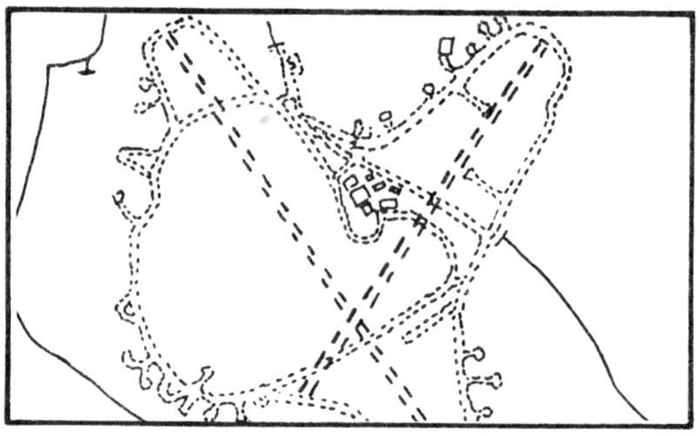

AIRFIELD NAME: GRAVESEND. OPENED : 1932.
COUNTY : Kent. CLOSED : 1956.
COMMAND : Fighter.
FORMATION : 11 Grp[Uxbridge] GRID REF: R 106903[115]
FUNCTION : Operational. O.S.REF.: TQ 675720.

LOCALITY : 2 miles SE of Gravesend.
RAILWAY STN. : Gravesend Central[SR]

LATITUDE : 51 25 00N. HEIGHT ASL : 240′ LIGHTING : Mk2.
LONGITUDE : 00 23 47E. FLYING CONTROL : Yes. RADIO : QDM.

LANDMARKS DAY. : Gravesend Reach[R Thames] 1.75miles N.

LANDMARKS NIGHT : As day.

OBSTRUCTIONS : -

LANDING AREA SURFACE : Grass.

QDM	LENGTH X WIDTH	EXT. TO
W-S.	1420yds.	1800yds.
ENE-WSW.	1480yds.	1760yds.

EXTENSIBILITY : -

ACCOMMODATION : Temporary[part]
HANGARS : Blister-8; T1-1.

HARDSTANDINGS : Blenheim TE-6; Frypan[65′]-30.

	OFFICERS	S.N.C.O′s.	O.R′s.	TOTAL
R.A.F.	42.	71.	1197.	1310.
W.A.A.F.	6.	12.	200.	218.

AFFILIATED AIRFIELDS : Biggin Hill[Sector]

PRESENT USE [1985] : Housing.

NO: 257.

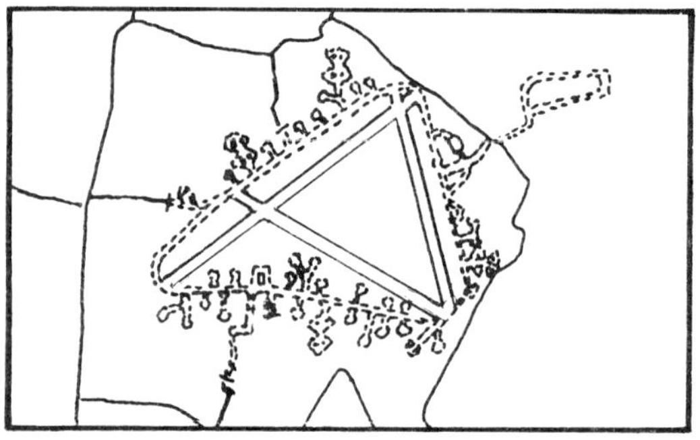

AIRFIELD NAME: GREAT ASHFIELD. OPENED : 1943.
COUNTY : Suffolk. CLOSED : 1960.
COMMAND : 8th USAAF.
FORMATION : 385th Bomb Grp. GRID REF: M 464842[86]
FUNCTION : Operational. O.S.REF.: TM 010663.

LOCALITY : 10miles E of Bury St. Edmunds.
RAILWAY STN. : Elmswell 2.5miles[LNER]

LATITUDE : 52 15 15N. HEIGHT ASL : 200′ LIGHTING : Mk2.
LONGITUDE : 00 56 45E. FLYING CONTROL : Yes. RADIO : QDM.

LANDMARKS DAY. : Railway Bury-St-Edmunds/Ipswich 1mile W. Tall chimney 2miles to SW near railway.

LANDMARKS NIGHT : -

OBSTRUCTIONS : -

LANDING AREA SURFACE : Concrete & wood chippings.

QDM	LENGTH X WIDTH	EXT. TO
068.	2000 x 50yds.	3000yds.
360.	1400 x 50yds.	2000yds.
132.	1500 x 50yds.	2000yds.

EXTENSIBILITY : Entails diversion of 2 minor roads & demolition of a cottage.
ACCOMMODATION : Temporary.
HANGARS : T2-2.

HARDSTANDINGS : Spectacle-17; Frypan-33.

USAAF. : OFFICERS: 421. Enlisted Men. : 2473.TOTAL: 2894.

AFFILIATED AIRFIELDS : -

PRESENT USE [1985] : Agriculture.

NO: 258.

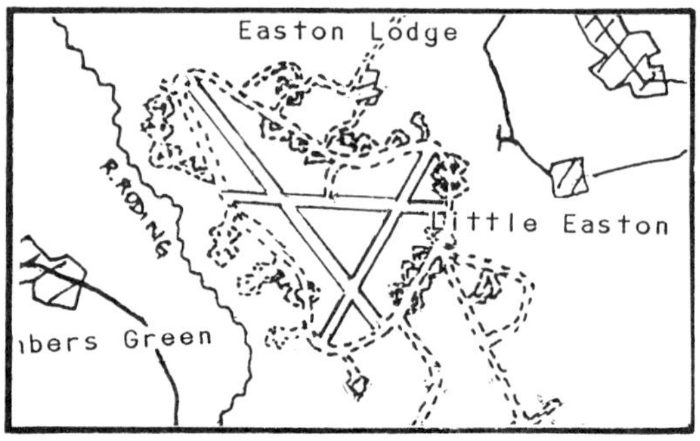

AIRFIELD NAME: GREAT DUNMOW. OPENED : 1943.
COUNTY : Essex. CLOSED : 1958.
COMMAND : Fighter.
FORMATION : 38 Grp[Marks Hall] GRID REF: M 041418[96]
FUNCTION : Operational. O.S.REF.: TL 592235.

LOCALITY : 6.5miles E of Bishops Stortford.
RAILWAY STN. : Easton Lodge 1mile[LNER]

LATITUDE : 51 53 00N. HEIGHT ASL : 325′ LIGHTING : Mk2.
LONGITUDE : 00 18 45E. FLYING CONTROL : Yes. RADIO : QDM.

LANDMARKS DAY. : Easton Lodge 300yds NNE of A/F.

LANDMARKS NIGHT : -

OBSTRUCTIONS : -

LANDING AREA SURFACE : Concrete & wood chippings.

QDM	LENGTH X WIDTH	EXT. TO
150.	2000 x 50yds.	-
110.	1400 x 50yds.	1750yds.
040.	1400 x 50yds.	1600yds.

EXTENSIBILITY : Not recommended.

ACCOMMODATION : Temporary.
HANGARS : T2-2;Blister-1.

HARDSTANDINGS : Spectacle-50.

	OFFICERS	S.N.C.O′s.	O.R′s.	TOTAL
R.A.F.	187.	513.	1533.	2233.
W.A.A.F.	-	12.	308.	320.

AFFILIATED AIRFIELDS : -

PRESENT USE [1985] : Agriculture.

NO: 259.

AIRFIELD NAME: GREAT MASSINGHAM. OPENED : 1940.
COUNTY : Norfolk. CLOSED : 1958.
COMMAND : Bomber.
FORMATION : 100 Grp[Bylaugh Hall] GRID REF: G 268426[57]
FUNCTION : Operational. O.S.REF.: TF 805236.

LOCALITY : 7.5miles WSW of Fakenham.
RAILWAY STN. : Massingham 1mile[M&GM]

LATITUDE : 52 46 53N. HEIGHT ASL : 295′ LIGHTING : Mk2.
LONGITUDE : 00 40 45E. FLYING CONTROL : Yes. RADIO : QDM.

LANDMARKS DAY : -

LANDMARKS NIGHT : -

OBSTRUCTIONS : -

LANDING AREA SURFACE : Concrete.

QDM	LENGTH X WIDTH	EXT. TO
100.	2000 x 50yds.	3000yds.
040.	1400 x 50yds.	-
150.	1400 x 50yds.	-

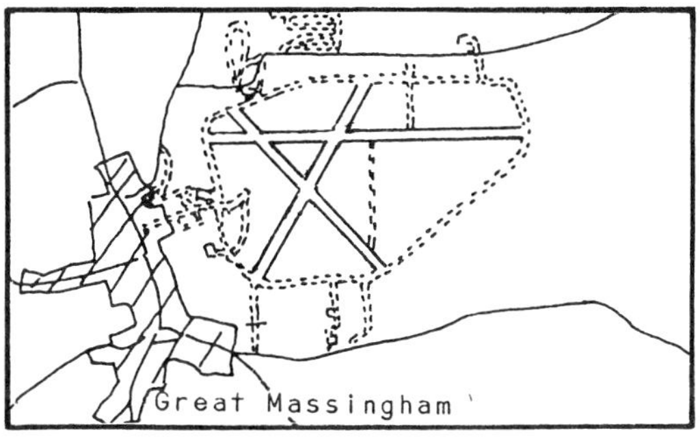

EXTENSIBILITY : -

ACCOMMODATION : Temporary.
HANGARS : T2-4; B1-1.

HARDSTANDINGS : Spectacle-21; pan-15.

	OFFICERS	S.N.C.O′s.	O.R′s.	TOTAL
R.A.F.	91.	260.	846.	1197.
W.A.A.F.	6.	8.	112.	126.

AFFILIATED AIRFIELDS : -

PRESENT USE [1985] : Agriculture.

NO: 260.

AIRFIELD NAME: GREAT ORTON. OPENED : 1943.
COUNTY : Cumberland. CLOSED : 1952.
COMMAND : Coastal.
FORMATION : 17 Grp[Edinburgh] GRID REF: Y 794753[9]
FUNCTION : Operational Training Unit[satellite] O.S.REF.: NY 310538.
LOCALITY : 1.25miles S of Kirkbampton.
RAILWAY STN. : Carlisle 6.5miles[LMS]

LATITUDE : 54 52 30N. HEIGHT ASL : 241′ LIGHTING : Mk2.
LONGITUDE : 03 04 30W. FLYING CONTROL : Yes. RADIO : QDM.

LANDMARKS DAY : -

LANDMARKS NIGHT : -

OBSTRUCTIONS : -

LANDING AREA SURFACE : Concrete covered with tar.

QDM	LENGTH X WIDTH	EXT. TO
082.	1990 x 50yds.	3000yds.
130.	1410 x 50yds.	2500yds.
024.	1400 x 50yds.	-

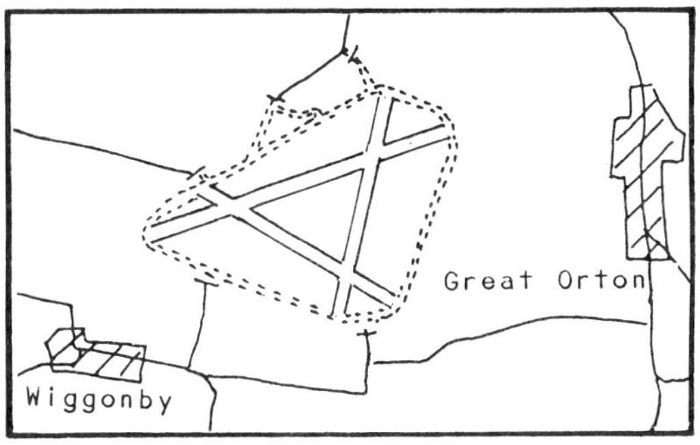

EXTENSIBILITY : Entails demolition of a cottage & probably 2 houses.
ACCOMMODATION : Temporary.
HANGARS : Blister-3.

HARDSTANDINGS : Loop-20; Frypan-1.

	OFFICERS	S.N.C.O′s.	O.R′s.	TOTAL
R.A.F.	84.	160.	738.	982.
W.A.A.F.	2.	10.	90.	102.

AFFILIATED AIRFIELDS : Silloth[Parent]

PRESENT USE [1985] : Disused.

NO: 261.

AIRFIELD NAME: GREAT SAMPFORD. OPENED : 1942.
COUNTY : Essex. CLOSED : 1945.
COMMAND : Balloon.
FORMATION : 24 Balloon Centre. GRID REF: M 060534[96]
FUNCTION : Storage. O.S.REF.: TL 616350.

LOCALITY : 7miles SE of Saffron Walden.
RAILWAY STN. : Saffron Walden[LNER]

LATITUDE : 51 59 23N. HEIGHT ASL : 342′ LIGHTING : None.
LONGITUDE : 00 21 15E. FLYING CONTROL : None. RADIO : QDM.

LANDMARKS DAY : Large wooded area to NW of A/F. Water towers: 1mile N, & 2miles NNW. Thaxted church steeple S. Redwinter church steeple N.

LANDMARKS NIGHT : -

OBSTRUCTIONS : High trees & water tower on starboard side of SE-NW R/W.

LANDING AREA SURFACE : Steel Matting[Sommerfeld track]

QDM	LENGTH X WIDTH	EXT. TO
230.	1600yds.	2000yds.
127.	1050yds.	1400yds.

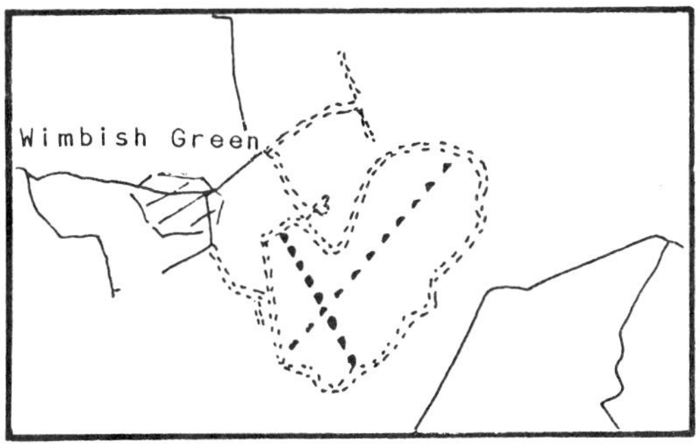

EXTENSIBILITY : -

ACCOMMODATION : Temporary.
HANGARS : 0 blister-4.

HARDSTANDINGS : SE-6;concrete-9.

	OFFICERS	S.N.C.O′s.	O.R′s.	TOTAL
R.A.F.	34.	106.	669.	809.
W.A.A.F.	-	5.	60.	65.

AFFILIATED AIRFIELDS : Fairlop[24 Balloon Centre]

PRESENT USE [1985] : Disused.

NO: 262.

AIRFIELD NAME: GREENCASTLE. OPENED : 1942.
COUNTY : Down NI. CLOSED : 1945.
COMMAND : USSTAFE.
FORMATION : Air Service Command. GRID REF: J 285118[327NI]
FUNCTION : Air Depot. O.S.REF.: J 285115.

LOCALITY : 2miles SW of Kinkeel.
RAILWAY STN. : Newcastle 14miles[B&CD]

LATITUDE : 54 02 15N. HEIGHT ASL : 50′ LIGHTING : Mk2.
LONGITUDE : 06 02 08W. FLYING CONTROL : Yes. RADIO : QDM.

LANDMARKS DAY. : Kilkeel 1.5miles S on edge of sea. Mourne Mountains approx 8miles to W.

LANDMARKS NIGHT : Sea.

OBSTRUCTIONS : W/T masts 250′ high approx 3miles W.

LANDING AREA SURFACE : Concrete & wood chippings.

QDM	LENGTH X WIDTH	EXT. TO
080.	2000 x 50yds.	2700yds.
030.	1400 x 50yds.	-
140.	1400 x 50yds.	-

EXTENSIBILITY : Entails considerable demolition for NE extension.

ACCOMMODATION : Temporary.
HANGARS : T2-4.

HARDSTANDINGS : Loop-30; Y type[for bombers]-100.

USAAF. : OFFICERS: 553. Enlisted Men. : 1959.TOTAL: 2512.

AFFILIATED AIRFIELDS : -

PRESENT USE [1985] : Industry.

NO: 263.

AIRFIELD NAME: GREENHAM COMMON. OPENED : 1942.
COUNTY : Berkshire. CLOSED :
COMMAND : 9th USAAF.
FORMATION : 438th Troop Carrier Grp. GRID REF: U 934855[113]
FUNCTION : Operational. O.S.REF.: SU 502646.

LOCALITY : 2miles SE of Newbury.
RAILWAY STN. : Newbury Town 1.5miles[GWR]

LATITUDE : 51 22 38N. HEIGHT ASL : 381′ LIGHTING : Mk2.
LONGITUDE : 01 17 15W. FLYING CONTROL : Yes. RADIO : QDM.

LANDMARKS DAY. : GWR main line Reading-Newbury-Westbury, direction E-W. R Kennet bends NW-SE opposite NE corner of A/F. Thatcham village NE. Headley village SE.

LANDMARKS NIGHT : R Kennet.

OBSTRUCTIONS : 50′ water tower 200yds NE end of No. 1 R/W.
25′ water tower 700yds W of No 2 R/W.

LANDING AREA SURFACE : Concrete & tarmac.

QDM	LENGTH X WIDTH	EXT. TO
110.	2000 x 50yds.	2750yds.
140.	1400 x 50yds.	1750yds.
030.	1100 x 50yds.	1110yds.

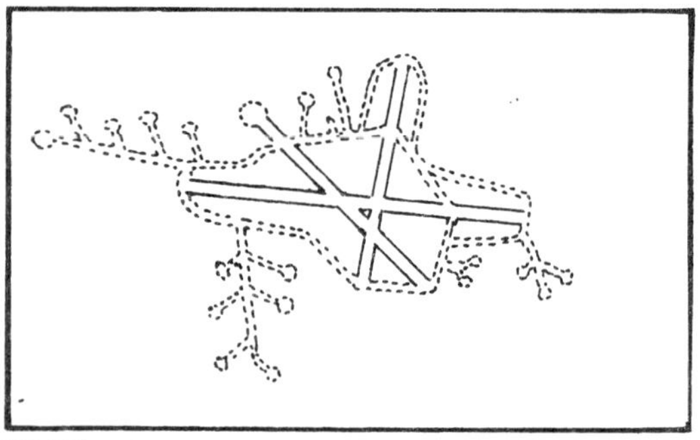

EXTENSIBILITY : With great difficulty as main Newbury-Basingstoke road runs through the technical site.
ACCOMMODATION : Temporary.
HANGARS : T2-2.

HARDSTANDINGS : Multi engined-50.

USAAF. : OFFICERS: 470. Enlisted Men. 1898.TOTAL: 2368.

AFFILIATED AIRFIELDS : -

PRESENT USE [1985] : USAFE.

NO: 264.

AIRFIELD NAME: GRIMSBY. OPENED : 1941.
COUNTY : Lincolnshire. CLOSED : 1946.
COMMAND : Bomber.
FORMATION : 1 Grp[Bawtry] GRID REF: A 750217[40]
FUNCTION : Operational O.S.REF.: TA 279025.

LOCALITY : 9miles S of Grimsby.
RAILWAY STN. : Waltham 3miles[LNER]

LATITUDE : 53 30 15N. HEIGHT ASL : 350′ LIGHTING : Mk2.
LONGITUDE : 00 04 23W. FLYING CONTROL : Yes. RADIO : QDM.

LANDMARKS DAY. : Mouth of Humber 4miles NE.

LANDMARKS NIGHT : Humberstone masts 340′ high showing obstruction lights.

OBSTRUCTIONS : As above.

LANDING AREA SURFACE : Concrete & tarmac.

QDM	LENGTH X WIDTH	EXT. TO
181.	2000 x 50yds.	2800yds.
241.	1400 x 50yds.	1450yds.
301.	1100 x 50yds.	1800yds.

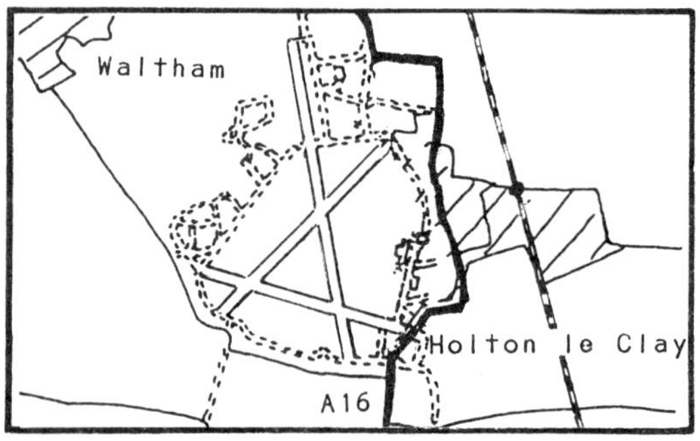

EXTENSIBILITY : Entails diversion of Grimsby-Lough road[already controlled]
ACCOMMODATION : Temporary.
HANGARS : T2-2; B1-1.

HARDSTANDINGS : Heavy bomber-36.

R.A.F. : OFFICERS: 110.S.N.C.O′s.: 319.O.R′s.: 967. TOTAL: 1396.
W.A.A.F.: " : 2. " : 8. " : 276. " : 286.

AFFILIATED AIRFIELDS : Binbrook[12 base]

PRESENT USE [1985] : Disused.

NO: 265.

AIRFIELD NAME: GRIMSETTER. OPENED : 1940.
COUNTY : Orkneys. CLOSED :
COMMAND : RN.
FORMATION : HMS Robin. GRID REF: Z 020297[Scot]
FUNCTION : Disembarked Sqdns. O.S.REF.: HY 481083.

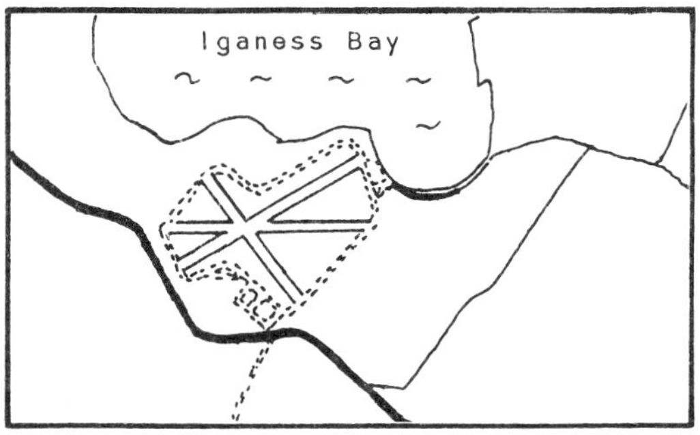

LOCALITY : SE portion of mainland Orkney.
RAILWAY STN. : Thurso[LMS]

LATITUDE : 58 57 15N. HEIGHT ASL : 30′ LIGHTING :
LONGITUDE : 02 54 00W. FLYING CONTROL : RADIO :

LANDMARKS DAY. : Scapa Flow 2.5miles SW.

LANDMARKS NIGHT : As day.

OBSTRUCTIONS : Tower hill 279′ with 4 W/T masts 100′ 1800yds. NW & ground rising 220′ 1600yds SW.

LANDING AREA : Under construction.
SURFACE :
QDM: 071-250. LENGTH X WIDTH: 1310 x 50yds.EXT. TO: -
: 101-281. : 1240 x 50yds. : -
: 154-334. : 970 x 50yds. : -

EXTENSIBILITY : -

ACCOMMODATION : Temporary.
HANGARS : Sqdn: 60x84′-6; 185x105′-1. Storage 60x84′-7.

HARDSTANDINGS : -

R.N. : OFFICERS: 45. Chiefs/POs/Ratings. : 390. TOTAL: 435.
W.R.N.S. : " : 9. " - : 165. " : 174.

AFFILIATED AIRFIELDS : -

PRESENT USE [1985] : Civil Airport[Kirkwall]

NO: 266.

AIRFIELD NAME: GROVE. OPENED : 1942.
COUNTY : Berkshire. CLOSED : 1946.
COMMAND : USSTAFE.
FORMATION : Air Service Command. GRID REF: P 833094[105]
FUNCTION : 3rd Tactical Air Depot. O.S.REF.: SU 389898.

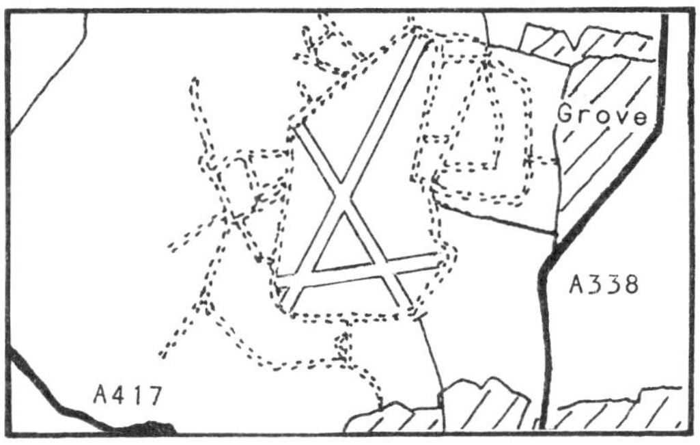

LOCALITY : 1.5miles NW of Wantage.
RAILWAY STN. : Wantage Road 1.25miles[GWR]

LATITUDE : 51 36 08N. HEIGHT ASL : 275′ LIGHTING : Mk2.
LONGITUDE : 01 26 15W. FLYING CONTROL : Yes. RADIO : QDM.

LANDMARKS DAY. : -

LANDMARKS NIGHT : -

OBSTRUCTIONS : -

LANDING AREA : Concrete.
SURFACE :
QDM: 220. LENGTH X WIDTH: 2000 x 50yds.EXT. TO: -
: 340. : 1400 x 50yds. : -
: 270. : 1200 x 50yds. : -

EXTENSIBILITY : No extension possible.

ACCOMMODATION : Temporary.
HANGARS : T2-6.

HARDSTANDINGS : Frypan-24; Spectacle-26.

USAAF. : OFFICERS: 214. Enlisted Men. .: 3188.TOTAL: 3402.

AFFILIATED AIRFIELDS : -

PRESENT USE [1985] : Housing.

NO: 267.

AIRFIELD NAME: HALDON. OPENED : 1929.
COUNTY : Devon. CLOSED : 1946.
COMMAND : RN.
FORMATION : HMS Heron. GRID REF: Y 348984[138]
FUNCTION : ATC Glider Training. O.S.REF.: SX 884812.

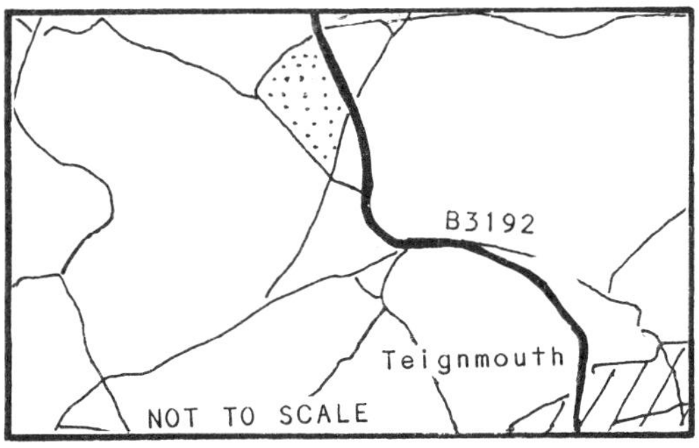

LOCALITY : 2miles NW of Teignmouth.
RAILWAY STN. : Teignmouth[GWR]

LATITUDE : 50 34 40N. HEIGHT ASL : 770′ LIGHTING : None.
LONGITUDE : 03 31 50W. FLYING CONTROL : None.RADIO : None.

LANDMARKS DAY. : R Exe with Exmouth at its E entrance point.

LANDMARKS NIGHT : -

OBSTRUCTIONS : -

LANDING AREA : Grass.
SURFACE :
QDM: 002/182. LENGTH X WIDTH: 900 x 145yds.EXT. TO: -
: 047/227. : 694 x 150yds. : -
: 137/317. : 500 x 150yds. : -

EXTENSIBILITY : -

ACCOMMODATION : None.
HANGARS : None.

HARDSTANDINGS : None.

R.N. : OFFICERS: - Chiefs/POs/Ratings. : - TOTAL: -
W.R.N.S. : " : - " " : - " : -

AFFILIATED AIRFIELDS : -

PRESENT USE [1985] : Disused.

NO: 268.

AIRFIELD NAME: HALESWORTH. OPENED : 1942
COUNTY : Suffolk. CLOSED : 1946.
COMMAND : 8th USAAF.
FORMATION : De-activated. GRID REF: M 860975[77]
FUNCTION : De-activated. O.S.REF.: TM 402798.

LOCALITY : 7.5miles W of Southwold.
RAILWAY STN. : Halesworth 2miles[LNER]

LATITUDE : 52 21 45N. HEIGHT ASL : 120′ LIGHTING : Mk2.
LONGITUDE : 01 32 00E. FLYING CONTROL : Yes. RADIO : QDM.

LANDMARKS DAY. : Wireless masts at Dersham, approx 5miles due S of Halesworth water tower, approx 1000yds. SW of S end of no.2 R/W.

LANDMARKS NIGHT : R Blythe by moonlight.

OBSTRUCTIONS : -

LANDING AREA SURFACE : Concrete & wood chippings.

QDM	LENGTH X WIDTH	EXT. TO
240.	2000 x 50yds.	-
190.	1400 x 50yds.	2250yds.
290.	1400 x 50yds.	2050yds.

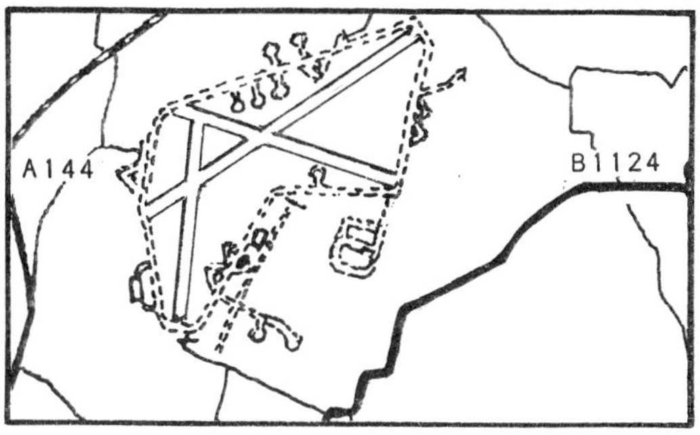

EXTENSIBILITY : -

ACCOMMODATION : Temporary.
HANGARS : T2-2.

HARDSTANDINGS : Loop-50.

USAAF. : OFFICERS: 443.S.N. Enlisted Men. : 2529.TOTAL: 2972.

AFFILIATED AIRFIELDS : -

PRESENT USE [1985] : Agriculture.

NO: 269.

AIRFIELD NAME: HALFPENNY GREEN. OPENED : 1941.
COUNTY : Worcestershire. CLOSED : 1953.
COMMAND : Flying Training.
FORMATION : 25 Grp[Market Drayton] GRID REF: K 279118[71]
FUNCTION : Advanced Flying Unit [Observer] O.S.REF.: SO 824912.
LOCALITY : 7miles SW of Wolverhampton.
RAILWAY STN. : Wolverhampton 7miles[GWR & LMS]

LATITUDE : 53 30 53N. HEIGHT ASL : 270′ LIGHTING : Mk2.
LONGITUDE : 02 15 38W. FLYING CONTROL : Yes. RADIO : QDM.

LANDMARKS DAY. : Bridgenorth on R Severn 28degrees 6miles.

LANDMARKS NIGHT : -

OBSTRUCTIONS : -

LANDING AREA SURFACE : Concrete covered with tarmac.

QDM	LENGTH X WIDTH	EXT. TO
166.	1238 x 50yds.	2100yds.
228.	1200 x 50yds.	2100yds.
288.	1150 x 50yds.	1900yds.

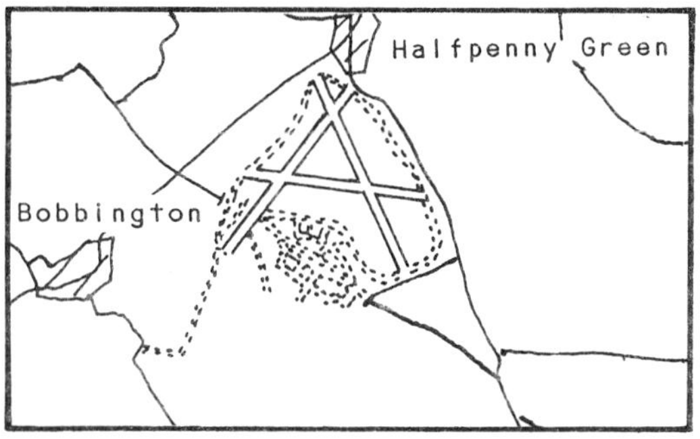

EXTENSIBILITY : Recommended to 1600-1900&1500yds respectively.Entails diversion of several minor rds & heavy demo.
ACCOMMODATION : Temporary.
HANGARS : Bellman-7; EO blister-16.

HARDSTANDINGS : None.

	OFFICERS	S.N.C.O′s.	O.R′s.	TOTAL
R.A.F.	229.	524.	832.	1585.
W.A.A.F.	6.	6.	281.	293.

AFFILIATED AIRFIELDS : -

PRESENT USE [1985] : Private flying.

NO: 270.

AIRFIELD NAME: HALTON. OPENED : 1917.
COUNTY : Buckinghamshire. CLOSED :
COMMAND : Technical Training.
FORMATION : 24 Grp[Hereford] GRID REF: L 316306[95]
FUNCTION : Tech.Training School. O.S.REF.: SP 870112.

LOCALITY : 4miles SE of Aylesbury.
RAILWAY STN. : Wendover 1.5miles[Metro&LNER]

LATITUDE : 51 46 53N. HEIGHT ASL : 360′ LIGHTING : None.
LONGITUDE : 00 43 30W. FLYING CONTROL : None.RADIO : QDM.

LANDMARKS DAY. : Weston Turville reservoir & Wiltshire reservoir 2.5 & 3.5miles NE.

LANDMARKS NIGHT : -

OBSTRUCTIONS : Chiltern hills 800′ SE of A/F. Trees on all boundaries[except SW]

LANDING AREA SURFACE : Grass.

QDM	LENGTH X WIDTH	EXT. TO
N-S.	1000yds.	2350yds.
NE-SW.	620yds.	3000yds.
E-W.	690yds.	1400yds.
SE-NW.	690yds.	-

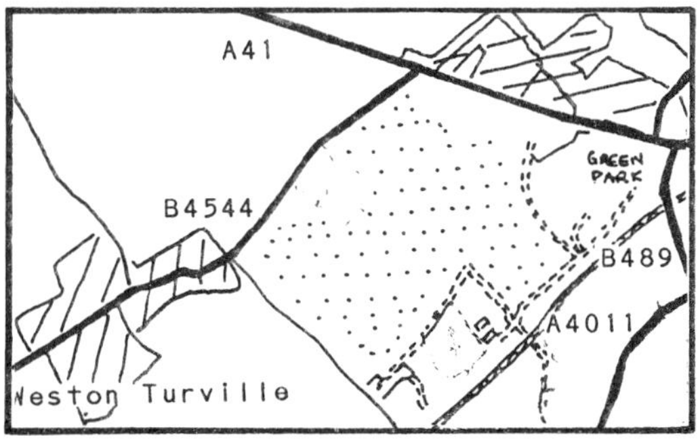

EXTENSIBILITY : Recommended to 2000-1200&1150yds. only. Entails demolition of a bungalow.
ACCOMMODATION : Permanent.
HANGARS :

HARDSTANDINGS :

	OFFICERS	S.N.C.O′s.	O.R′s.	TOTAL
R.A.F.	184.	383.	8326.	8893.
W.A.A.F.	134.	71.	1770.	1975.

AFFILIATED AIRFIELDS : -

PRESENT USE [1985] : RAF.

NO: 271.

AIRFIELD NAME: HAMPSTEAD NORRIS. OPENED : 1940.
COUNTY : Berkshire. CLOSED : 1945.
COMMAND : Fighter.
FORMATION : 12 Grp[Watnall] GRID REF: U 990975[113]
FUNCTION : Operational Training Unit[satellite] O.S.REF.: SU 545773.
LOCALITY : 11miles WNW of Reading.
RAILWAY STN. : Hampstead Norris 2miles[GWR]

LATITUDE : 51 46 53N. HEIGHT ASL : 376′ LIGHTING : Mk2.
LONGITUDE : 00 43 30W. FLYING CONTROL : Yes. RADIO : QDM.

LANDMARKS DAY. : Single line railway N-S 1.5miles to W. Large wood to SW.

LANDMARKS NIGHT : R Thames 4miles ENE. Weir at Goring.

OBSTRUCTIONS : -

LANDING AREA SURFACE : Concrete & Tarmac.

QDM	LENGTH X WIDTH	EXT. TO
140.	1100 x 50yds.	1400yds.
230.	1600 x 50yds.	-
276.	1100 x 50yds.	1200yds.

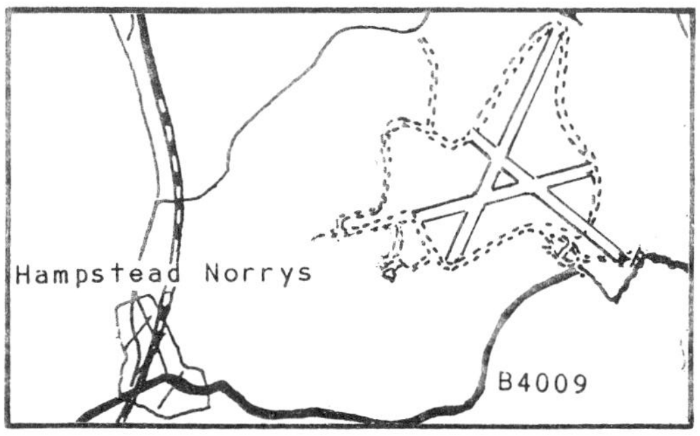

EXTENSIBILITY : –

ACCOMMODATION : Temporary.
HANGARS : T2-1; B1-1; Bessoneau-1.

HARDSTANDINGS : Circular tarmac-28.

R.A.F. : OFFICERS: 64. S.N.C.O′s.: 100. O.R′s.: 528. TOTAL: 692.
W.A.A.F.: " : 4. " : - " : 156. " : 160.

AFFILIATED AIRFIELDS : Harwell[Parent]

PRESENT USE [1985] : Disused.

NO: 272.

AIRFIELD NAME: HARDWICK. OPENED : 1942.
COUNTY : Norfolk. CLOSED : 1962.
COMMAND : 8th USAAF.
FORMATION : 93rd Bomb Grp. GRID REF: M 705085[77]
FUNCTION : Operational. O.S.REF.: TM 248906.

LOCALITY : 5.5miles W of Bungay.
RAILWAY STN. : Hammersfield 4miles[LNER]

LATITUDE : 52 28 08N. HEIGHT ASL : 170′ LIGHTING : Mk2.
LONGITUDE : 01 18 45E. FLYING CONTROL : Yes. RADIO : QDM.

LANDMARKS DAY. : Wireless masts of Stoke Holy Cross & Pulham W/T station.

LANDMARKS NIGHT : -

OBSTRUCTIONS : -

LANDING AREA SURFACE : Concrete & tarmac.

QDM	LENGTH X WIDTH	EXT. TO
020.	2000 x 50yds.	4500yds.
080.	1400 x 50yds.	2500yds.
140.	1400 x 50yds.	2000yds.

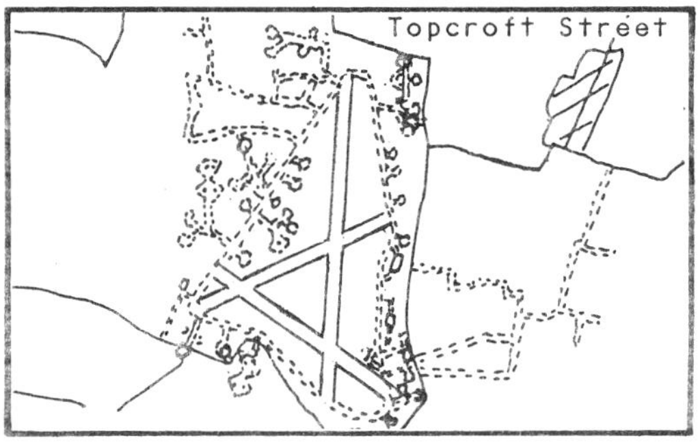

EXTENSIBILITY : Recommended to 3000-2000&2000yds only; otherwise very heavy demolition.
ACCOMMODATION : Temporary.
HANGARS : T2-3.

HARDSTANDINGS : Loop-50.

USAAF. : OFFICERS: 443. Enlisted Men. : 2529. TOTAL: 2972.

AFFILIATED AIRFIELDS : -

PRESENT USE [1985] : Agriculture.

NO: 273.

AIRFIELD NAME: HARLAXTON. OPENED : 1942.
COUNTY : Lincolnshire. CLOSED : 1945.
COMMAND : Flying Training.
FORMATION : 21 Grp[Spittlegate] GRID REF: F 368520[55]
FUNCTION : Advanced Flying Unit. [RLG] O.S.REF.: SX 902325.
LOCALITY : 2miles S of Grantham.
RAILWAY STN. : Grantham 2miles[LNER]

LATITUDE : 52 53 00N. HEIGHT ASL : 425′ LIGHTING : Mk2.
LONGITUDE : 00 39 15W. FLYING CONTROL : Yes. RADIO : QDM.

LANDMARKS DAY. : Belvoir Castle 6miles SW.

LANDMARKS NIGHT : Grantham station & marshalling yards LNER.

OBSTRUCTIONS : 50′ trees 200yds. W.

LANDING AREA SURFACE : Grass.

QDM	LENGTH X WIDTH	EXT. TO
NNW-SSE.	1300yds.	2000yds.
WSW-ENE.	1300yds.	1400yds.
SW-NE.	1300yds.	1400yds.

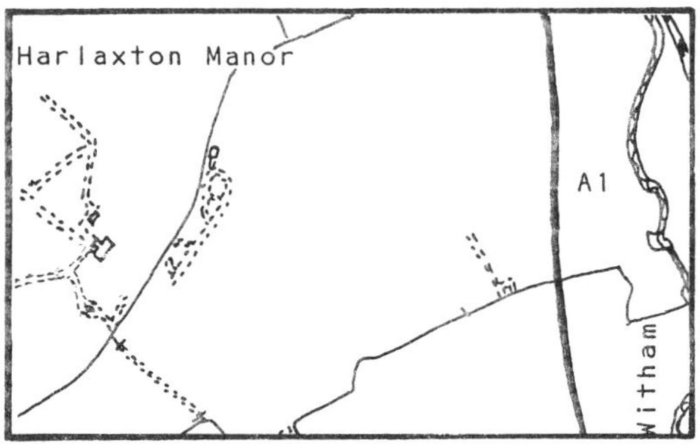

EXTENSIBILITY : Entails diversion of a minor road, but not demolition, except RAF blister hangars.
ACCOMMODATION : Temporary.
HANGARS : Blister: 69′-14; 65′-4.

HARDSTANDINGS : -

R.A.F. : OFFICERS: 1. S.N.C.O′s.: 16. O.R′s.: 219. TOTAL: 236.
W.A.A.F.: " : - " : - " : - " : -

AFFILIATED AIRFIELDS : Spittlegate[Parent]

PRESENT USE [1985] : Disused.

NO: 274.

AIRFIELD NAME: HARRINGTON. OPENED : 1943.
COUNTY : Northamptonshire. CLOSED : 1963.
COMMAND : 8th USAAF.
FORMATION : 492nd Bomb Grp. GRID REF: L 230975[73]
FUNCTION : Operational. O.S.REF.: SP 775778.

LOCALITY : 5miles W of Kettering.
RAILWAY STN. : Lamport 3miles[LMS]

LATITUDE : 52 23 30N. HEIGHT ASL : 520′ LIGHTING : Mk2.
LONGITUDE : 00 51 30W. FLYING CONTROL : Yes. RADIO : QDM.

LANDMARKS DAY. : -

LANDMARKS NIGHT : -

OBSTRUCTIONS : -

LANDING AREA SURFACE : Concrete.

QDM	LENGTH X WIDTH	EXT. TO
184.	2000 x 50yds.	3000yds.
230.	1400 x 50yds.	1600yds.
298.	1400 x 50yds.	2000yds.

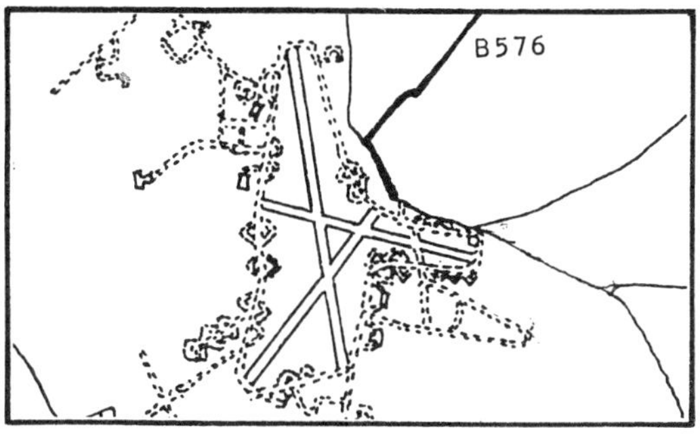

EXTENSIBILITY : Entails diversion of a minor road.

ACCOMMODATION : Temporary.
HANGARS : T2-4.

HARDSTANDINGS : Spectacle-36.

USAAF. : OFFICERS: 229. Enlisted Men. : 1553.TOTAL: 1782.

AFFILIATED AIRFIELDS : -

PRESENT USE [1985] : Agriculture.

NO: 275.

AIRFIELD NAME: HARROWBEER. OPENED : 1941.
COUNTY : Devon. CLOSED : 1950.
COMMAND : Fighter.
FORMATION : 10 Grp[Rudloe Manor] GRID REF: X 944899[137]
FUNCTION : Care & Maintenance. O.S.REF.: SX 513680.

LOCALITY : 9miles NNE of Plymouth.
RAILWAY STN. : Harrabridge .5miles[GWR]

LATITUDE : 50 29 30N. HEIGHT ASL : 650′ LIGHTING : None.
LONGITUDE : 04 05 45W. FLYING CONTROL : Yes. RADIO : QDM.

LANDMARKS DAY. : Dartmoor on E. Saltash estuary & bridge SSW.

LANDMARKS NIGHT : Saltash estuary & R Tavy SSW. Burratoo reser-voir E. Calstock bridge over R Tamar W.

OBSTRUCTIONS : Dartmoor E. Roborough Down & Yelverton Rock SSE. Yelverton village & church at NE corner of A/F.

LANDING AREA SURFACE : Asphalt.

QDM	LENGTH X WIDTH	EXT. TO
110.	1300 x 50yds.	1450yds.
166.	1100 x 50yds.	1450yds.
229.	900 x 50yds.	-

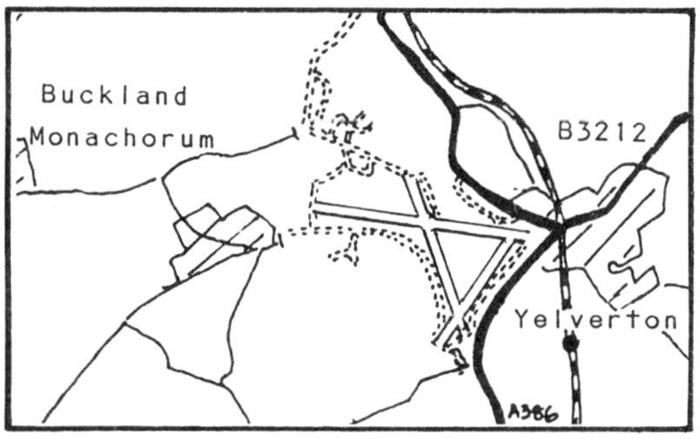

EXTENSIBILITY : Entails light demolition.

ACCOMMODATION : Temporary.
HANGARS : Bellman-2; O blister-8.

HARDSTANDINGS : TE-18.

R.A.F. : OFFICERS: 69. S.N.C.O′s.: 139.O.R′s.: 1260.TOTAL: 1468.
W.A.A.F.: " : 7. " : - " : 224. " : 231.

AFFILIATED AIRFIELDS : -

PRESENT USE [1985] : Disused.

NO: 276.

AIRFIELD NAME: HARWELL. OPENED : 1937.
COUNTY : Berkshire. CLOSED : 1945.
COMMAND : Fighter.
FORMATION : 12 Grp[Watnall] GRID REF: P 923067[105]
FUNCTION : Operational Training Unit. O.S.REF.: SU 475865.

LOCALITY : 6miles S of Abingdon.
RAILWAY STN. : Didcot[GWR]

LATITUDE : 51 34 30N. HEIGHT ASL : 375. LIGHTING : Mk2.
LONGITUDE : 01 18 30W. FLYING CONTROL : Yes. RADIO : QDM.

LANDMARKS DAY. : -

LANDMARKS NIGHT : -

OBSTRUCTIONS : High ground S-SW, extending 2.5miles 648′ marked by 3 red lights.

LANDING AREA SURFACE : Concrete.

QDM	LENGTH X WIDTH	EXT. TO
151.	1300 x 50yds.	-
258.	1400 x 50yds.	3000yds.
295.	2000 x 50yds.	-

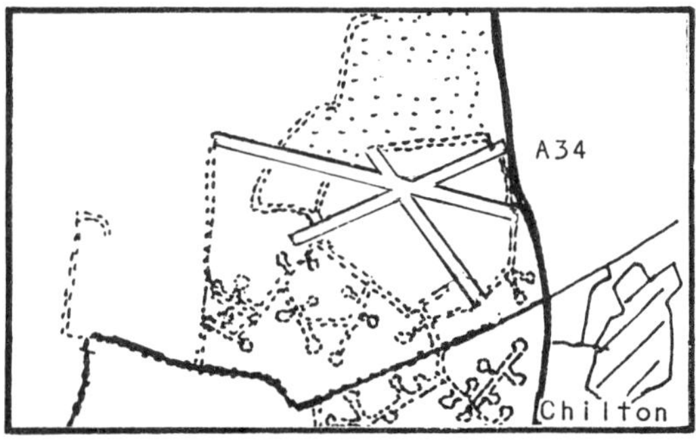

EXTENSIBILITY : Entails diversion of main road & demolition of barns & RAF buildings.
ACCOMMODATION : Permanent.
HANGARS : Type C-4.

HARDSTANDINGS : Tarmac-10; concrete-45.

R.A.F. : OFFICERS: 284.S.N.C.O′s.: 464.O.R′s.: 1606.TOTAL: 2354.
W.A.A.F.: " : 8. " : 5. " : 307. " : 320.

AFFILIATED AIRFIELDS : Hampstead Norris-Bicester-Finmere [Satellites]
PRESENT USE [1985] : Atomic Energy Commission.

NO: 277.

AIRFIELD NAME: HATFIELD. OPENED : 1930.
COUNTY : Hertfordshire. CLOSED :
COMMAND : Flying Training.
FORMATION : 50 Grp[Reading] GRID REF: L 660279[106]
FUNCTION : Elementary Flying Training School[RLG] O.S.REF.: TL 206090.
LOCALITY : 6miles SSW of Hertford.
RAILWAY STN. : Hatfield 1.25miles[LNER]

LATITUDE : 51 45 53N. HEIGHT ASL : 250′ LIGHTING : None.
LONGITUDE : 00 14 45W. FLYING CONTROL : None. RADIO : QDM.

LANDMARKS DAY. : Barnet by-pass & North orbital road. 2 wireless stations SW & W of A/F approx 1.5miles.

LANDMARKS NIGHT : -

OBSTRUCTIONS : Hangars & factory on E & NE side of A/F.

LANDING AREA SURFACE : Grass.

QDM	LENGTH X WIDTH	EXT. TO
N-S.	1250yds.	2000yds.
NE-SW.	1250yds.	1750yds.
E-W.	1000yds.	1400yds.
SE-NW.	1050yds.	-

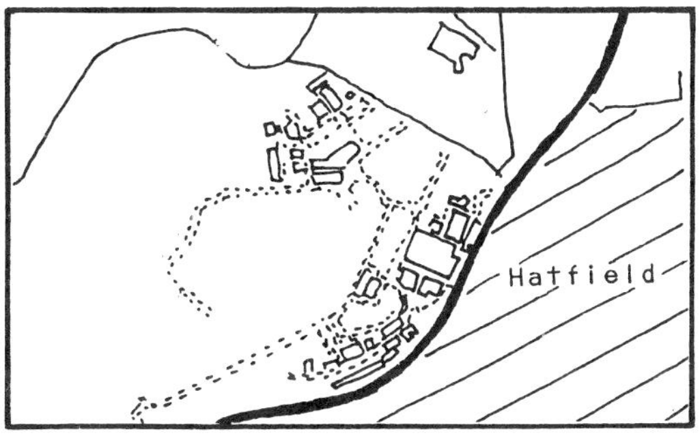

EXTENSIBILITY : Entails slight demolition.

ACCOMMODATION : Temporary[RAF buildings]
HANGARS : None.

HARDSTANDINGS : None.

R.A.F. : OFFICERS: 85. S.N.C.O′s.: 22. O.R′s.: 88. TOTAL: 195.
W.A.A.F.: " : - " : - " : - " : -

AFFILIATED AIRFIELDS : Panshanger[Parent]

PRESENT USE [1985] : Aircraft Industry[British Aerospace]

NO: 278.

AIRFIELD NAME: HATSTON. OPENED : 1940.
COUNTY : Orkneys. CLOSED : 1945.
COMMAND : RN.
FORMATION : HMS Sparrowhawk. GRID REF: Y 976340[Scot]
FUNCTION : 1st. line & disembarked facilities. O.S.REF.: NY 435123.
LOCALITY : N coast of mainland Orkney.
RAILWAY STN. : Thurso[LMS]

LATITUDE : 58 59 30W. HEIGHT ASL : 35′ LIGHTING : None.
LONGITUDE : 02 58 40W. FLYING CONTROL : Yes. RADIO : QDM.

LANDMARKS DAY. : Scapa Flow on S side of mainland.

LANDMARKS NIGHT : As day.

OBSTRUCTIONS : Wideford Hill 741′1.5miles W. W/T masts 360′on hill 180′ 4miles SSE.

LANDING AREA SURFACE : Tarmac.

QDM	LENGTH X WIDTH	EXT. TO
015-195.	780 x 17yds.	
069-249.	810 x 17yds.	
121-301.	790 x 50yds.	
150-330.	1000 x 17yds.	

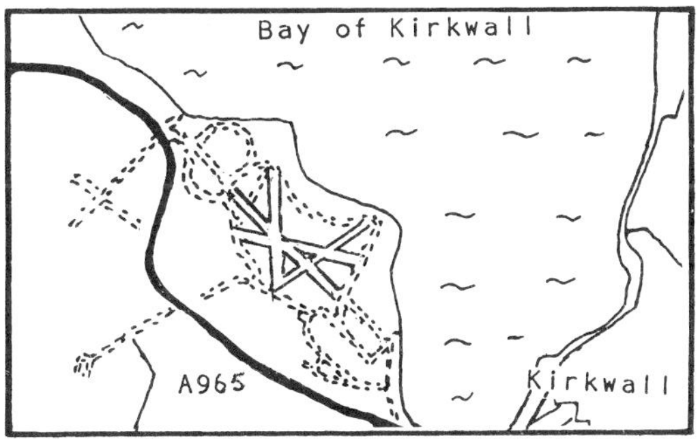

EXTENSIBILITY : -

ACCOMMODATION : Temporary.
HANGARS : Sqdn: 175x95′-1; 187.5x106′-4; Storage: 175x95′-2; 60x70′-7.
HARDSTANDINGS : Pens-9; standings-2.

R.N. : OFFICERS: 180. Chiefs/POs/Ratings. : 1260. TOTAL: 1440.
W.R.N.S. : " : 15. " " : 224. " : 239.

AFFILIATED AIRFIELDS : -

PRESENT USE [1985] : Disused.

NO: 279.

AIRFIELD NAME: HAVERFORDWEST. OPENED : 1943.
COUNTY : Pembrokeshire. CLOSED : 1945.
COMMAND : Coastal.
FORMATION : 17 Grp[Edinburgh] GRID REF: N 405417.
FUNCTION : Care & Maintenance. O.S.REF.: SM 958192.

LOCALITY : 2miles N of Haverfordwest.
RAILWAY STN. : Haverfordwest 2miles[GWR]

LATITUDE : 51 49 53N. HEIGHT ASL : 163′ LIGHTING : Mk2.
LONGITUDE : 04 57 45W. FLYING CONTROL : Yes. RADIO : QDM.

LANDMARKS DAY. : Gt.Treffgarne mountain 542′ 3.5miles N by W of A/F. Western Cleddan R running N to S on W side of A/F 1.25miles. Hays Castle cross W/T masts 386′ 5miles NNW.
LANDMARKS NIGHT : R Cleddan.

OBSTRUCTIONS : See above.

LANDING AREA SURFACE : Concrete & tarmac.

QDM	LENGTH X WIDTH	EXT. TO
044.	1700 x 50yds.	1900yds.
101.	1200 x 50yds.	1460yds.
173.	1260 x 50yds.	1400yds.

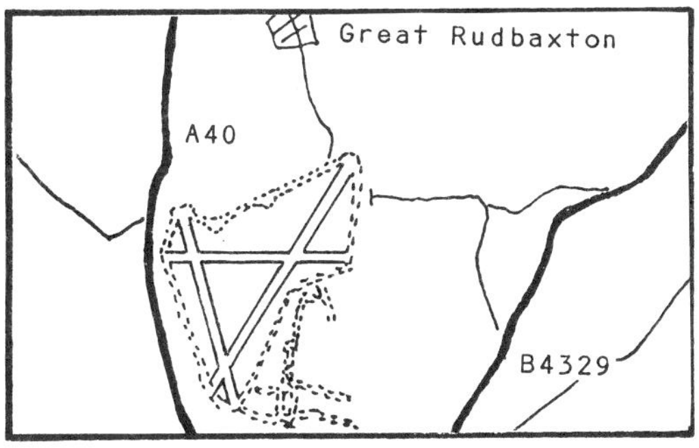

EXTENSIBILITY : The 1900yd. R/W is not recommended.

ACCOMMODATION : Temporary.
HANGARS : T2-2.

HARDSTANDINGS : 125′ dia. concrete-32.

R.A.F. : OFFICERS: 220. S.N.C.O′s.: 316. O.R′s.: 1035. TOTAL: 1571.
W.A.A.F.: " : 12. " : 14. " : 352. " : 378.

AFFILIATED AIRFIELDS : Templeton[Parent]

PRESENT USE [1985] : Private flying.

NO: 280.

AIRFIELD NAME: HAWARDEN. OPENED : 1939.
COUNTY : Flintshire. CLOSED :
COMMAND : Fighter.
FORMATION : 12 Grp[Watnall] GRID REF: J 813864[43]
FUNCTION : Operational Training Unit. O.S.REF.: SJ 345651.
LOCALITY : 4.5miles WSW of Chester.
RAILWAY STN. : Sandy Croft 2miles[GWR]

LATITUDE : 53 10 45N. HEIGHT ASL : 15′ LIGHTING : Mk2.
LONGITUDE : 02 58 45W. FLYING CONTROL : Yes. RADIO : QDM.

LANDMARKS DAY. : Coast.

LANDMARKS NIGHT : Coast.

OBSTRUCTIONS : Hills up to 1800′ NW, W & S beyond 5miles.

LANDING AREA SURFACE : Concrete & wood chippings.

QDM	LENGTH X WIDTH	EXT. TO
235.	1576 x 50yds.	2200yds.
325.	1116 x 50yds.	2650yds.
195.	1100 x 50yds.	1800yds.
:	:	:

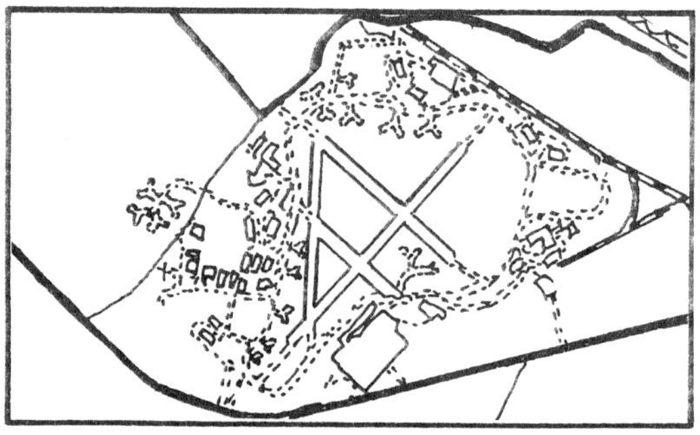

EXTENSIBILITY : Recommended to 2000-1400 & 1400yds. with possible slight demolition.
ACCOMMODATION : Permanent[part]
HANGARS : T2[23 bay]-6; Types J-1; K-3; L-6.

HARDSTANDINGS : Frypan 50′-50.

	OFFICERS	S.N.C.O′s.	O.R′s.	TOTAL
R.A.F.	304.	352.	1632.	2288.
W.A.A.F.	-	-	364.	364.

AFFILIATED AIRFIELDS : Poulton[Satellite]

PRESENT USE [1985] : Aircraft Industry[British Aerospace]

NO: 281.

AIRFIELD NAME: HAWKINGE. OPENED : 1915.
COUNTY : Kent. CLOSED : 1962.
COMMAND : Fighter.
FORMATION : 11 Grp[Uxbridge] GRID REF: R 647575[117]
FUNCTION : Forward Airfield. O.S.REF.: TR 211395.

LOCALITY : 2miles N of Folkestone.
RAILWAY STN. : Folkestone Central[SEC]

LATITUDE : 51 06 40N. HEIGHT ASL : 540′ LIGHTING : None.
LONGITUDE : 01 09 30E. FLYING CONTROL : Yes. RADIO : QDM.

LANDMARKS DAY. : Folkestone harbour.

LANDMARKS NIGHT : Reservoir.

OBSTRUCTIONS : -

LANDING AREA SURFACE : Grass.

QDM	LENGTH X WIDTH	EXT. TO
NE-SW.	1100yds.	1700yds.
N-S.	900yds.	1100yds.
E-W.	1100yds.	-
:	:	:

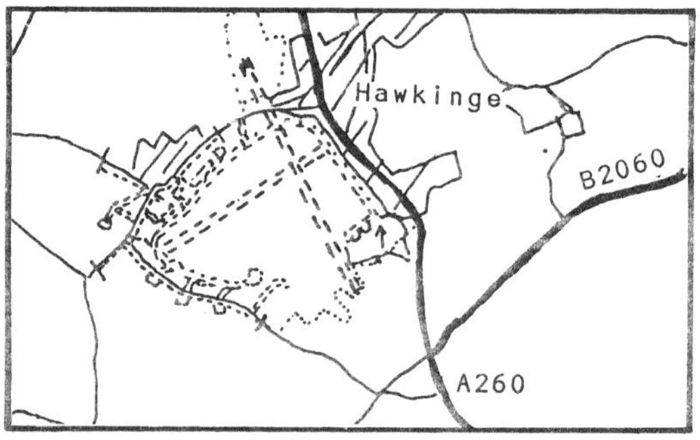

EXTENSIBILITY : Entails road diversion & demolition of 30 buildings & a small church.
ACCOMMODATION : Permanent[part]
HANGARS : Blisters: O-2; EO-4; GS-4.

HARDSTANDINGS : TE-9.

	OFFICERS	S.N.C.O′s.	O.R′s.	TOTAL
R.A.F.	102.	157.	1034.	1293.
W.A.A.F.	-	3.	199.	202.

AFFILIATED AIRFIELDS : Biggin Hill[Sector]

PRESENT USE [1985] : Housing.

NO: 282.

AIRFIELD NAME: HEADCORN. OPENED : 1943.
COUNTY : Kent. CLOSED : 1944.
COMMAND : Fighter.
FORMATION : 11 Grp[Uxbridge] GRID REF: R 320645[126]
FUNCTION : Advanced Landing Ground. [De-requisitioned] O.S.REF.: TQ 878460.
LOCALITY : 8miles WSW of Ashford.
RAILWAY STN. : Headcorn[SR]

LATITUDE : 51 10 53N. HEIGHT ASL : 107′ LIGHTING : None.
LONGITUDE : 00 41 23E. FLYING CONTROL : None. RADIO : QDM.

LANDMARKS DAY. : -

LANDMARKS NIGHT : -

OBSTRUCTIONS : -

LANDING AREA SURFACE : Steel Matting[U.S steel planking]

QDM	LENGTH X WIDTH	EXT. TO
090.	1600yds.	
180.	1300yds.	:
:	:	:
:	:	:

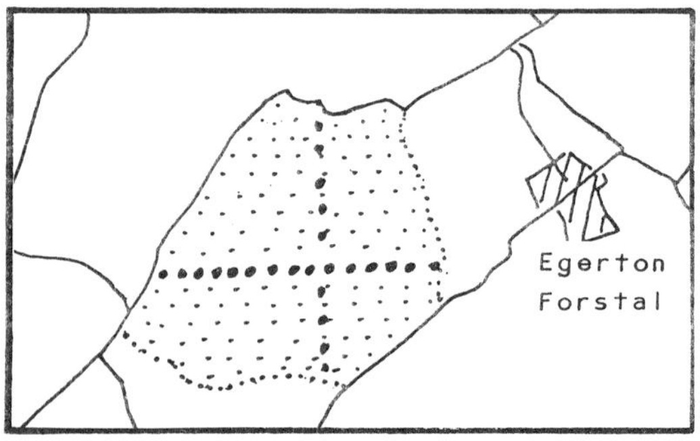

EXTENSIBILITY : -

ACCOMMODATION : Tented camp.
HANGARS : None.

HARDSTANDINGS : Sommerfeld track-70.

	OFFICERS	S.N.C.O′s.	O.R′s.	TOTAL
R.A.F.	-	-	-	-
W.A.A.F.	-	-	-	-

AFFILIATED AIRFIELDS : -

PRESENT USE [1985] : Agriculture.

NO: 283.

AIRFIELD NAME: HEATHROW. OPENED : 1945.
COUNTY : Middlesex. CLOSED :
COMMAND : Transport.
FORMATION : Under construction. GRID REF: Q 520953[114]
FUNCTION : Transport Terminal O.S.REF.: TQ 075755.

LOCALITY : 3.25miles NE of Staines.
RAILWAY STN. : Hayes & Harlington[GWR]

LATITUDE : 51 28 15N. HEIGHT ASL : 80′ LIGHTING : None.
LONGITUDE : 00 27 00W. FLYING CONTROL : None. RADIO : QDM.

LANDMARKS DAY. : -

LANDMARKS NIGHT : -

OBSTRUCTIONS : -

LANDING AREA : Under construction.
SURFACE :
QDM: 280. LENGTH X WIDTH: 3000 x 100ydsEXT. TO: -
: 156. : 2000 x 100yds. : -
: 232. : 2000 x 100yds. : -
: : :

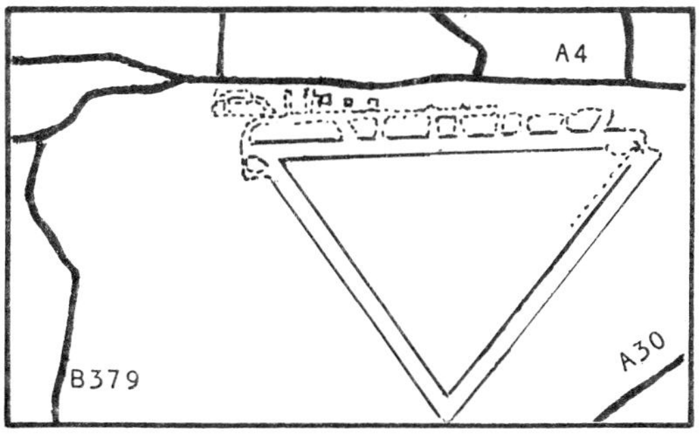

EXTENSIBILITY : -

ACCOMMODATION : -
HANGARS : -

HARDSTANDINGS : Parking Area-75000sq.ft.

R.A.F. : OFFICERS: - S.N.C.O′s.: - O.R′s.: - TOTAL: -
W.A.A.F.: " : - " : - " : - " : -

AFFILIATED AIRFIELDS : -

PRESENT USE [1985] : Civil Airport[London Heathrow]

NO: 284.

AIRFIELD NAME: HEMSWELL. OPENED : 1937.
COUNTY : Lincolnshire. CLOSED : 1967.
COMMAND : Bomber.
FORMATION : 1 Grp[Bawtry] GRID REF: A 411098[39]
FUNCTION : Operational. O.S.REF.: SK 941908.

LOCALITY : 7miles E of Gainsborough.
RAILWAY STN. : Gainsborough[LNER]

LATITUDE : 53 24 08N. HEIGHT ASL : 200′ LIGHTING : Mk2.
LONGITUDE : 00 34 53W. FLYING CONTROL : Yes. RADIO : QDM.

LANDMARKS DAY. : Bounded on all sides by roads.

LANDMARKS NIGHT : Red obstruction lights on 2 end hangars in direction NNE-SSW.

OBSTRUCTIONS : -

LANDING AREA : Concrete & tarmac.
SURFACE :
QDM: 170. LENGTH X WIDTH: 2000 x 50yds.EXT. TO: 3300yds.
: 239. : 1700 x 50yds. : -
: 281. : 1700 x 50yds. : -
: : :

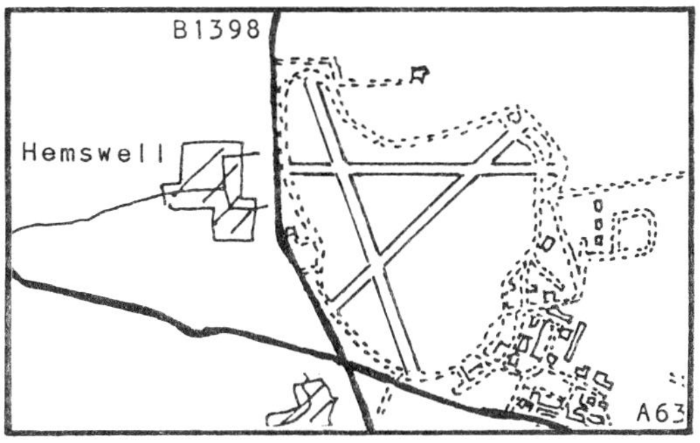

EXTENSIBILITY : Recommended to 2600yds only; entails some road diversions.
ACCOMMODATION : Permanent.
HANGARS : Type C-4; T2-1.

HARDSTANDINGS : Loop-17; Frypan-19.

R.A.F. : OFFICERS: 240.S.N.C.O′s.: 566.O.R′s.: 1220.TOTAL: 2026.
W.A.A.F.: " : 10. " : 14. " : 232. " : 256.

AFFILIATED AIRFIELDS : Ingham & Sturgate[Sub-stations.]

PRESENT USE [1985] : Disused.

NO: 285.

AIRFIELD NAME: HENDON. OPENED : 1910.
COUNTY : Middlesex. CLOSED : 1957.
COMMAND : Transport.
FORMATION : 116 Wing[Hendon] GRID REF: L 661098[106]
FUNCTION : Airport. O.S.REF.: TQ 215905.

LOCALITY : 8miles NW of St.Pauls.
RAILWAY STN. : Colindale[LPTB], Hendon 3miles[LMS]

LATITUDE : 51 36 00N. HEIGHT ASL : 160′ LIGHTING : None.
LONGITUDE : 00 14 42W. FLYING CONTROL : Yes. RADIO : QDM.

LANDMARKS DAY. : Welsh Harp. Edgeware Road, LMS railway.

LANDMARKS NIGHT : Welsh Harp & LMS railway.

OBSTRUCTIONS : Colindale hospital chimney. Lymph Institute chimney.

LANDING AREA : Tarmac.
SURFACE :
QDM: 339. LENGTH X WIDTH: 1325 x 50yds.EXT. TO: -
: 280. : 1000 x 50yds. : 1450yds.
: 014. : 1020 x 50yds. : -
: : :

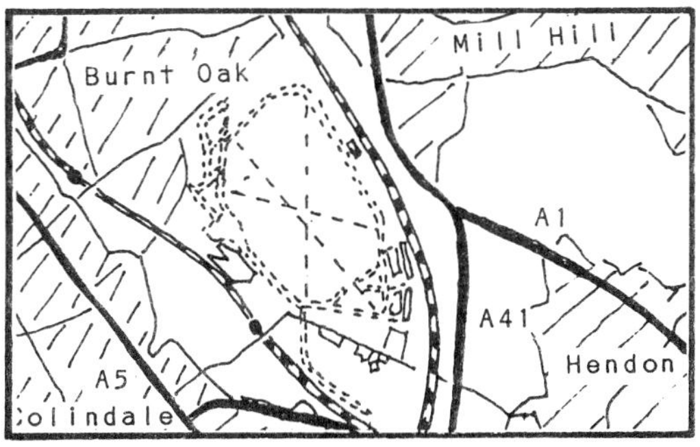

EXTENSIBILITY : –

ACCOMMODATION : Permanent[part]
HANGARS : Belfast roof -2; steel trusses & brick con.-1; sheds[3 hangars]-1; Bellman-12.
HARDSTANDINGS : Banjo-12.

R.A.F. : OFFICERS: 80. S.N.C.O′s.: 246.O.R′s.: 911. TOTAL: 1237.
W.A.A.F.: " : 15. " : 10. " : 399. " : 424.

AFFILIATED AIRFIELDS : -

PRESENT USE [1985] : Museum[Royal Air Force]

AIRFIELD NAME: HENLEY. OPENED : 1940.
COUNTY : Berkshire. CLOSED : 1945.
COMMAND : Flying Training.
FORMATION : 50 Grp[Reading] GRID REF: L 239017[105]
FUNCTION : Elementary Flying Training School[RLG] O.S.REF.: SU 795824.
LOCALITY : 6miles NNE of Reading.
RAILWAY STN. : Henley on Thames[GWR]

LATITUDE : 51 31 45N. HEIGHT ASL : 180′ LIGHTING : None.
LONGITUDE : 00 51 15W. FLYING CONTROL : None. RADIO : QDM.

LANDMARKS DAY. : -

LANDMARKS NIGHT : _

OBSTRUCTIONS : _

LANDING AREA SURFACE : Grass.

QDM	LENGTH X WIDTH	EXT. TO
SSW-NNE.	700-800yds.	1700yds.
:	:	: 1400yds.
:	:	:
:	:	:

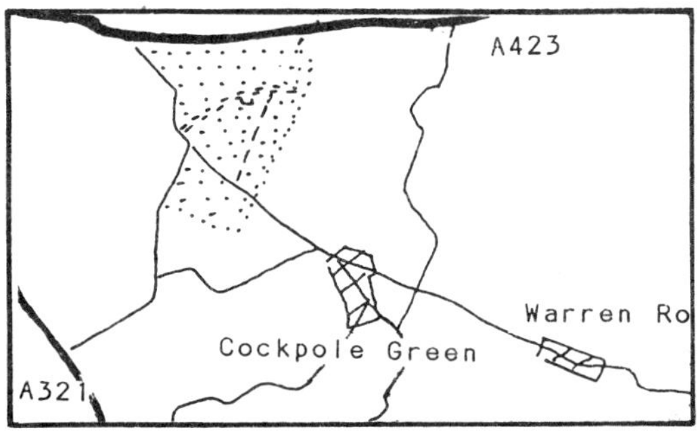

EXTENSIBILITY : Recommended to 1600yds. Entails diversion of Henley-Marlow road & demolition of a cottage.
ACCOMMODATION : Temporary.
HANGARS : Standard robin-3; Blisters:Double standard -2; standard-1.
HARDSTANDINGS : None.

	OFFICERS	S.N.C.O′s.	O.R′s.	TOTAL
R.A.F.	-	-	70.	70.
W.A.A.F.	-	-	-	-

AFFILIATED AIRFIELDS : Woodley[Parent]

PRESENT USE [1985] : Unspecified.

AIRFIELD NAME: HENLOW. OPENED : 1918.
COUNTY : Bedfordshire. CLOSED :
COMMAND : Maintenance.
FORMATION : 43 Grp[Oxford] GRID REF: L 618554[95]
FUNCTION : Repair Depot. O.S.REF.: TL 165370.

LOCALITY : 5.5miles N of Hitchin.
RAILWAY STN. : Henlow Camp[LMS]via Hitchin[LNER]

LATITUDE : 52 01 00N. HEIGHT ASL : 150′ LIGHTING : None.
LONGITUDE : 00 18 15W. FLYING CONTROL : Yes. RADIO : QDM.

LANDMARKS DAY. : Single track railway SE to NW[Hitchin-Bedford line] Arlesey Brick wks 125degrees T of landing ground. Glass hot-houses situated on S side.

LANDMARKS NIGHT : None.

OBSTRUCTIONS : 6 brick chimneys at Arlesey Brick wks 250′, 125degrees T.

LANDING AREA SURFACE : Steel Matting[Sommerfeld track]

QDM	LENGTH X WIDTH	EXT. TO
210.	1550 x 50yds.	1600yds.
: 280.	: 1150 x 50yds.	: -
: 330.	: 1300 x 50yds.	: -
:	:	: 3800yds.

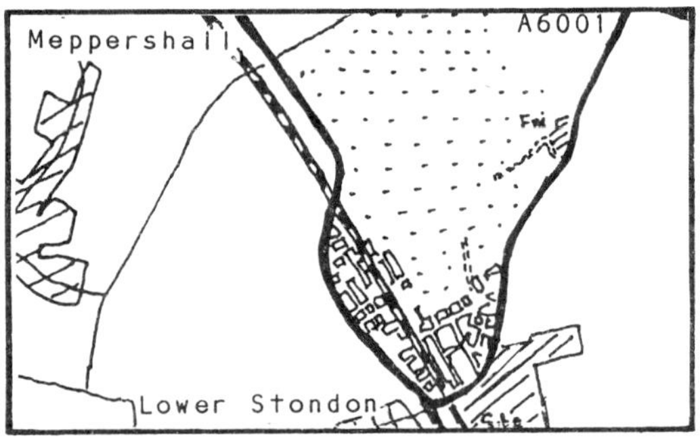

EXTENSIBILITY : Entails road diversion for the new 3800yd.strip & slight demolition.
ACCOMMODATION : Permanent.
HANGARS : Bellman-6;G.S.-6; blister-7;T2-1.

HARDSTANDINGS : Chevron-13.

	OFFICERS	S.N.C.O′s.	O.R′s.	TOTAL
R.A.F.	282.	560.	7317.	8159.
W.A.A.F.	18.	28.	957.	1003.

AFFILIATED AIRFIELDS : -

PRESENT USE [1985] : RAF.

NO: 288.

AIRFIELD NAME: HENSTRIDGE. OPENED : 1943.
COUNTY : Somersetshire. CLOSED : 1957.
COMMAND : RN.
FORMATION : HMS Dipper. GRID REF: U 1884[illegible] [130]
FUNCTION : Flying Training. O.S.REF.: ST 752205.

LOCALITY : 10miles NE of Yeovil.
RAILWAY STN. : Henstridge[S&D joint line]

LATITUDE : 50 58 50N. HEIGHT ASL : 184′ LIGHTING : Mk2.
LONGITUDE : 02 21 25W. FLYING CONTROL : Yes. RADIO : QDM.

LANDMARKS DAY. : Junction of railways 2.5miles WNW. Junction of R Cale & R Stour SE.

LANDMARKS NIGHT : As day.

OBSTRUCTIONS : W/T masts 150′ on elevation 450′ 3miles W.

LANDING AREA SURFACE : Tarmac.

QDM	LENGTH X WIDTH	EXT. TO
029-209.	1000 x 30yds.	
: 075-255.	: 1000 x 30yds.	:
: 114-294.	: 1200 x 30yds.	: No wind R/W.
: 160-340.	: 1000 x 30yds.	:
: 075-255.	: 1000 x 30yds.	: Dummy deck.

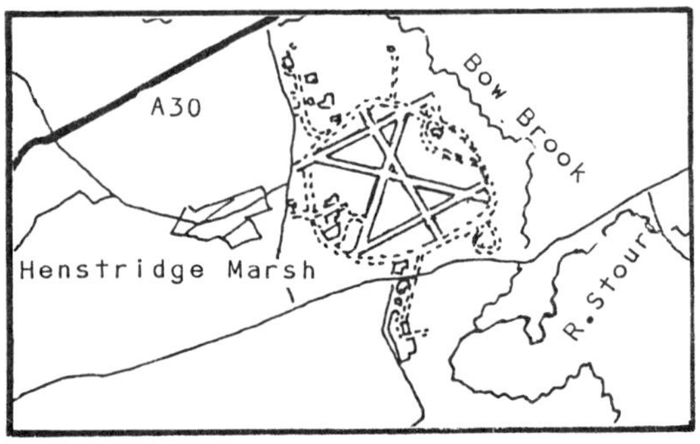

EXTENSIBILITY : –

ACCOMMODATION : Temporary.
HANGARS : 60x70′: Sqdn-16; Storage-12.

HARDSTANDINGS : 3.

	OFFICERS	Chiefs/POs/Ratings.	TOTAL
R.N.	211.	1232.	1443.
W.R.N.S.	13.	440.	453.

AFFILIATED AIRFIELDS : -

PRESENT USE [1985] : Private flying.

NO: 289.

AIRFIELD NAME: HESTON. OPENED : 1929.
COUNTY : Middlesex. CLOSED : 1947.
COMMAND : Fighter.
FORMATION : 11 Grp[Uxbridge] GRID REF: Q 558972[114]
FUNCTION : Operational. O.S.REF.: TQ 118781.

LOCALITY : 1.25miles SSW of Southall.
RAILWAY STN. : Hounslow West[LPTB]

LATITUDE : 51 29 15N. HEIGHT ASL : 100′ LIGHTING : None.
LONGITUDE : 00 23 52W. FLYING CONTROL : Yes. RADIO : QDM.

LANDMARKS DAY : Reservoirs-gas holder.

LANDMARKS NIGHT : Reservoirs.

OBSTRUCTIONS : Gasometer N of A/F.

LANDING AREA SURFACE : Grass.

QDM	LENGTH X WIDTH	EXT. TO
E-W.	1525yds.	2000yds.
NW-SE.	1517yds.	1400yds.
		1400yds.

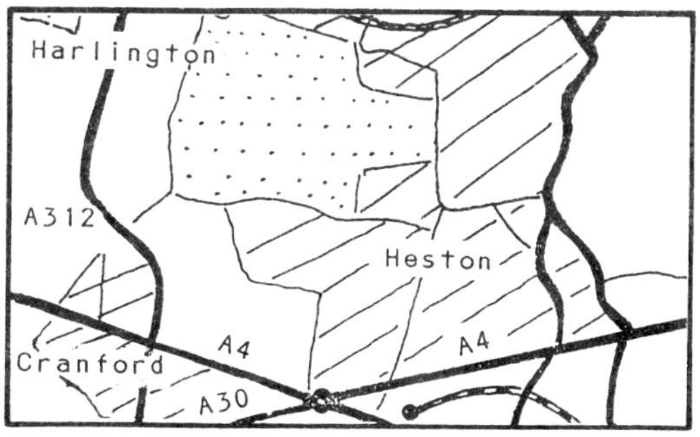

EXTENSIBILITY : Entails medium demolition unless the approaches are cleared, in which case it would be very heavy.
ACCOMMODATION : Temporary.
HANGARS : T2-6; blister-6.

HARDSTANDINGS : Blenheim[TE]-6; Frypan[100′dia]-1; Sommerfeld track 60′sq.-33.

	OFFICERS	S.N.C.O's.	O.R's.	TOTAL
R.A.F.	69.	-	340.	409.
W.A.A.F.	8.	-	181.	189.

AFFILIATED AIRFIELDS : Tangmere[Sector]

PRESENT USE [1985] : Industry/Housing.

NO: 290.

AIRFIELD NAME: HETHEL. OPENED : 1942.
COUNTY : Norfolk. CLOSED : 1947.
COMMAND : 8th USAAF.
FORMATION : 389th Bomb Grp. GRID REF: G 610188[67]
FUNCTION : Operational. O.S.REF.: TG 155008.

LOCALITY : 5miles SW of Norwich.
RAILWAY STN. : Wymondham 3.25miles[LNER]

LATITUDE : 52 33 38N. HEIGHT ASL : 160′ LIGHTING : Mk2.
LONGITUDE : 01 10 30E. FLYING CONTROL : Yes. RADIO : QDM.

LANDMARKS DAY : Abbey at Wymondham.

LANDMARKS NIGHT : -

OBSTRUCTIONS : -

LANDING AREA SURFACE : Concrete & wood chippings.

QDM	LENGTH X WIDTH	EXT. TO
240.	2000 x 50yds.	3000yds.
300.	1400 x 50yds.	2000yds.
350.	1400 x 50yds.	2000yds.

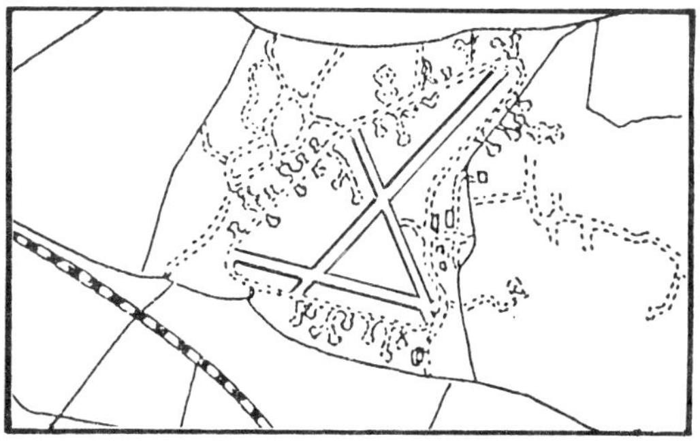

EXTENSIBILITY : Entails considerable works services & diversion of 3 minor roads & demolition of 2 farm houses.
ACCOMMODATION : Temporary.
HANGARS : T2-3.

HARDSTANDINGS : Loop-50.

USAAF. : OFFICERS: 443. Enlisted Men. : 2529.TOTAL: 2972.

AFFILIATED AIRFIELDS : -

PRESENT USE [1985] : Car Industry[Lotus]

NO: 291.

AIRFIELD NAME: HIBALDSTOW. OPENED : 1941.
COUNTY : Lincolnshire. CLOSED : 1945.
COMMAND : Fighter.
FORMATION : 12 Grp[Watnall] GRID REF: A 450205[33]
FUNCTION : Operational Training Unit[satellite] O.S.REF.: SE 982010.
LOCALITY : 3miles SW of Brigg.
RAILWAY STN. : Scawby & Hibaldstow 1.5miles[LNER]

LATITUDE : 53 29 45N. HEIGHT ASL : 25′ LIGHTING : Mk2.
LONGITUDE : 00 31 00W. FLYING CONTROL : Yes. RADIO : QDM.

LANDMARKS DAY : Ancholme canel E. Cement wks W.

LANDMARKS NIGHT : -

OBSTRUCTIONS : -

LANDING AREA SURFACE : Tarmac.

QDM	LENGTH X WIDTH	EXT. TO
084.	1600 x 50yds.	2000yds.
155.	1475 x 50yds.	2250yds.
200.	1300 x 50yds.	1800yds.

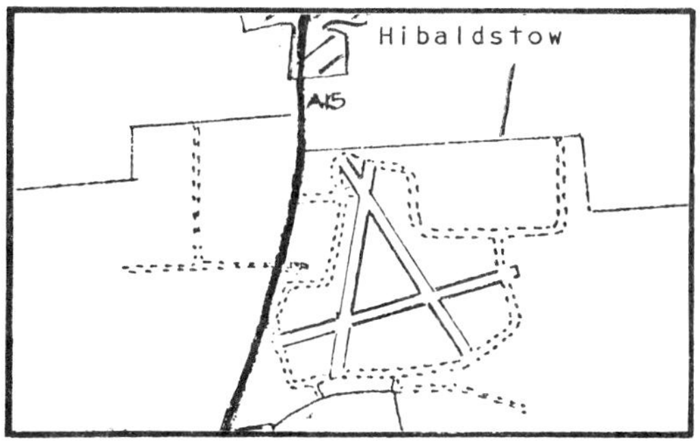

EXTENSIBILITY :

ACCOMMODATION : Temporary.
HANGARS : Blisters: O-8; EO-4; bellman-1.

HARDSTANDINGS : 12.

	OFFICERS	S.N.C.O's.	O.R's.	TOTAL
R.A.F.	112.	70.	884.	1066.
W.A.A.F.	8.	8.	189.	205.

AFFILIATED AIRFIELDS : Kirton-in-Lindsey[Parent]

PRESENT USE [1985] : Disused.

NO: 292.

AIRFIELD NAME: HIGH ERCALL.   OPENED : 1941.
COUNTY : Shropshire.   CLOSED : 1962.
COMMAND : Fighter.
FORMATION : 12 Grp[Watnall]   GRID REF: K 062393[61]
FUNCTION : Operational Training Unit.   O.S.REF.: SJ 608186.
LOCALITY : 5.25miles NNW of Wellington.
RAILWAY STN. : Crudington 2.25miles[GWR]

LATITUDE : 52 45 45W.   HEIGHT ASL : 220′   LIGHTING : Mk2.
LONGITUDE : 02 35 15W.   FLYING CONTROL : Yes.   RADIO : QDM.

LANDMARKS DAY. : The Wrekin 6miles S 1350′ ASL.

LANDMARKS NIGHT : -

OBSTRUCTIONS : -

LANDING AREA SURFACE : Concrete.

QDM	LENGTH X WIDTH	EXT. TO
110.	1612 x 50yds.	2500yds.
050.	1377 x 50yds.	1900yds.
170.	1251 x 50yds.	2200yds.

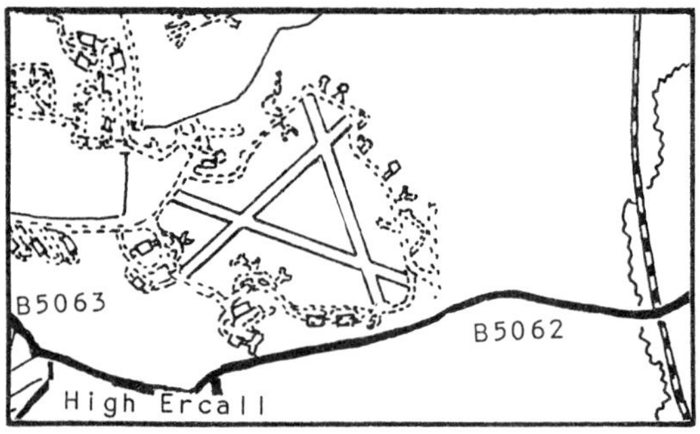

EXTENSIBILITY : Recommended to 2000-1400&1400yds.only. Entails slight demolition & diversion of a big minor rd.
ACCOMMODATION : Permanent[part]
HANGARS : T2-2; Blisters: O-4; EO-8; J-1; K-3; L-8.

HARDSTANDINGS : SE-23.

R.A.F. : OFFICERS: 140. S.N.C.O's.: 80. O.R's.: 1384. TOTAL: 1604.
W.A.A.F.: " : 8. " : 32. " : 351. " : 391.

AFFILIATED AIRFIELDS : -

PRESENT USE [1985] : Industry Training Board[Road Transport]

NO: 293.

AIRFIELD NAME: HIGH HALDON.   OPENED : 1943.
COUNTY : Kent.   CLOSED : 1644.
COMMAND : Fighter.
FORMATION : 11 Grp[Uxbridge]   GRID REF: R 330580[126]
FUNCTION : Advanced Landing Ground. [De-requisitioned]   O.S.REF.: TQ 893391.
LOCALITY : 6.5miles WSW of Ashford.
RAILWAY STN. : High Haldon Road[SR]

LATITUDE : 51 07 19N.   HEIGHT ASL : 115′   LIGHTING : None.
LONGITUDE : 00 42 15E.   FLYING CONTROL : None.   RADIO : QDM.

LANDMARKS DAY. : -

LANDMARKS NIGHT : -

OBSTRUCTIONS : -

LANDING AREA SURFACE : Steel Matting[U.S. steel planking]

QDM	LENGTH X WIDTH	EXT. TO
040.	1800yds.	
110.	1400yds.	

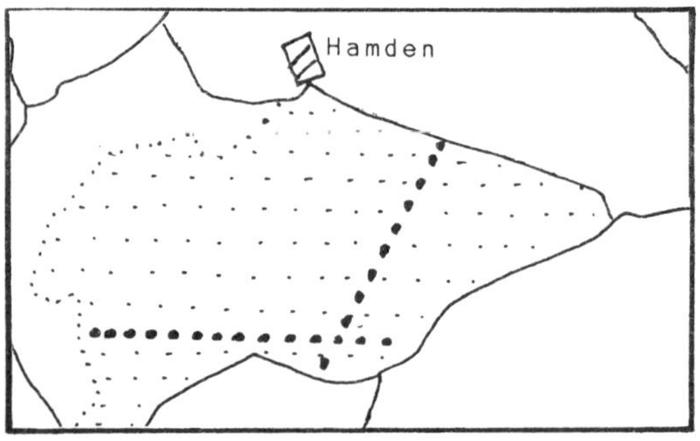

EXTENSIBILITY : —

ACCOMMODATION : Tented camp.
HANGARS : None.

HARDSTANDINGS : Sommerfeld track-70.

R.A.F. : OFFICERS: - S.N.C.O's.: - O.R's.: - TOTAL: -
W.A.A.F.: " : - " : - " : - " : -

AFFILIATED AIRFIELDS : -

PRESENT USE [1985] : Unspecified.

NO: 294.

AIRFIELD NAME: HINSTOCK.   OPENED : 1941.
COUNTY : Shropshire.   CLOSED : 1947.
COMMAND : RN.
FORMATION : HMS Godwit.   GRID REF: K 100462[60]
FUNCTION : Instrument flying training.   O.S.REF.: SJ 660265.
LOCALITY : 4miles SW of Market Drayton.
RAILWAY STN. : Hodnet 2.25miles[GWR]

LATITUDE : 52 50 05N.   HEIGHT ASL : 265′   LIGHTING : Mk2.
LONGITUDE : 02 30 20W.   FLYING CONTROL : Yes.   RADIO : QDM.

LANDMARKS DAY. : Shropshire Union canal 2.5miles NE. Railway to Market Drayton 2miles W.

LANDMARKS NIGHT : -

OBSTRUCTIONS : -

LANDING AREA SURFACE : Steel Matting[Heavy steel track]

QDM	LENGTH X WIDTH	EXT. TO
037-217.	1400 x 50yds.	-

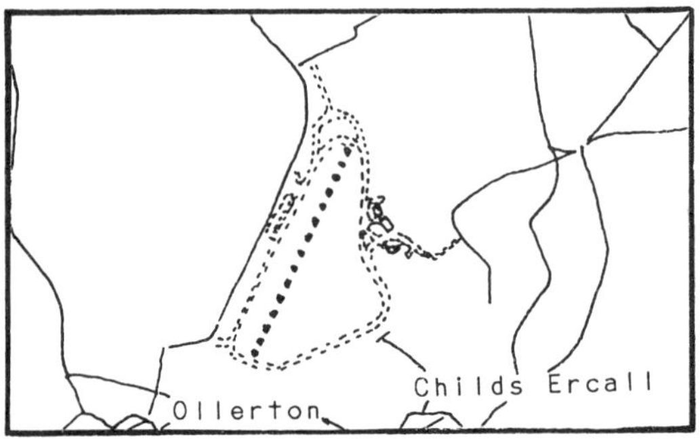

EXTENSIBILITY : -

ACCOMMODATION : Temporary.
HANGARS : Sqdn:185x110′-2;91x67.5′-5;60x70′-1;60x84′-2.

HARDSTANDINGS : Bomber-5.

R.N. : OFFICERS: 130. Chiefs/POs/Ratings.: 363. TOTAL: 493.
W.R.N.S.: " : 7. " : 144. " : 151.

AFFILIATED AIRFIELDS : _

PRESENT USE [1985] : Disused.

AIRFIELD NAME: HINTON-in-the-HEDGES. OPENED : 1940.
COUNTY : Northamptonshire. CLOSED : 1945.
COMMAND : Bomber.
FORMATION : 26 Grp[Langley Hall] GRID REF: P 995572[94]
FUNCTION : Radio Storage Unit. O.S.REF.: SP 545371.

LOCALITY : 6miles ESE of Banbury.
RAILWAY STN. : Kings Sutton2.5miles[GWR]

LATITUDE : 52 01 38N. HEIGHT ASL : 470′ LIGHTING : Mk2.
LONGITUDE : 01 12 30W. FLYING CONTROL : Yes. RADIO : QDM.

LANDMARKS DAY. : Brackley town 4miles E.

LANDMARKS NIGHT : -

OBSTRUCTIONS : Permanent building on W side of landing ground.

LANDING AREA SURFACE : Concrete & tarmac.

QDM	LENGTH X WIDTH	EXT. TO
244.	1900 x 50yds.	-
326.	1100 x 50yds.	1350yds.
280.	1100 x 50yds.	1700yds.

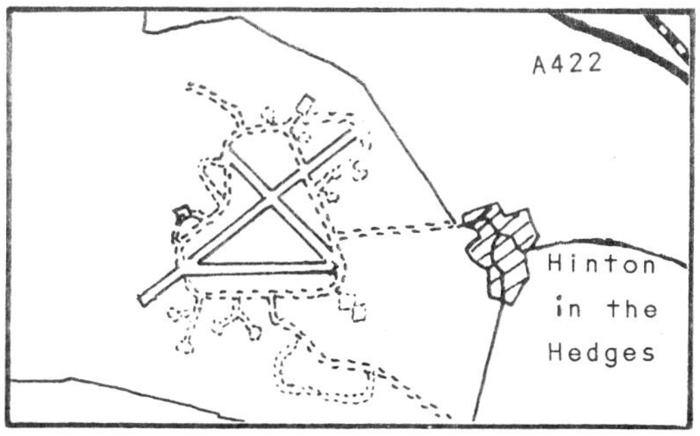

EXTENSIBILITY : –

ACCOMMODATION : Temporary.
HANGARS : B1-1; T1-1; blister-1.

HARDSTANDINGS : Pan-23.

R.A.F. : OFFICERS: 56. S.N.C.O′s.: 95. O.R′s.: 594. TOTAL: 745.
W.A.A.F.: " : 2. " : 8. " : 200. " : 210.

AFFILIATED AIRFIELDS : -

PRESENT USE [1985] : Agriculture.

NO: 296.

AIRFIELD NAME: HIXON. OPENED : 1942.
COUNTY : Staffordshire. CLOSED : 1957.
COMMAND : Bomber.
FORMATION : 93 Grp[Egginton] GRID REF: K 455470[53]
FUNCTION : Operational Training Unit. O.S.REF.: SJ 993266.
LOCALITY : 7miles NE of Stafford.
RAILWAY STN. : Stafford[LMS]

LATITUDE : 52 50 08N. HEIGHT ASL : 267′ LIGHTING : Mk2.
LONGITUDE : 02 00 23W. FLYING CONTROL : Yes. RADIO : QDM.

LANDMARKS DAY. : Bounded on NW by main LMS railway London-Manchester via Colwick. Bounded on SW by LNE Railway Stafford-Uttoxeter.

LANDMARKS NIGHT : -

OBSTRUCTIONS : Hills due E 360′ ASL. Hills W-SW 407′

LANDING AREA SURFACE : Concrete & tarmac.

QDM	LENGTH X WIDTH	EXT. TO
035.	1650 x 50yds.	-
090.	1400 x 50yds.	-
335.	1200 x 50yds.	1400yds.

EXTENSIBILITY : Entails diversion of important access road.

ACCOMMODATION : Temporary.
HANGARS : T2-4; B1-1.

HARDSTANDINGS : Heavy bomber-30.

R.A.F. : OFFICERS: 204.S.N.C.O′s.: 510.O.R′s.: 1679.TOTAL: 2393.
W.A.A.F.: " : 10. " : - " : 435. " : 445.

AFFILIATED AIRFIELDS : -

PRESENT USE [1985] : Agriculture.

NO: 297.

AIRFIELD NAME: HOCKLEY HEATH. OPENED : 1941.
COUNTY : Warwickshire. CLOSED : 1945.
COMMAND : Flying Training.
FORMATION : 51 Grp[Leeds] GRID REF: P 598947[72]
FUNCTION : Elementary Flying Training School[RLG] O.S.REF.: SK 147743.
LOCALITY : 9miles SW of Birmingham.
RAILWAY STN. : Knowle & Dorridge 2.25miles[GWR]

LATITUDE : 52 21 38N. HEIGHT ASL : 450′ LIGHTING : None.
LONGITUDE : 01 47 08W. FLYING CONTROL : None.RADIO : QDM.

LANDMARKS DAY. : -

LANDMARKS NIGHT : –

OBSTRUCTIONS : -

LANDING AREA SURFACE : Grass.

QDM	LENGTH X WIDTH	EXT. TO
SE-NW.	1250yds.	1700yds.
E-W.	800yds.	1300yds.
		1200yds.

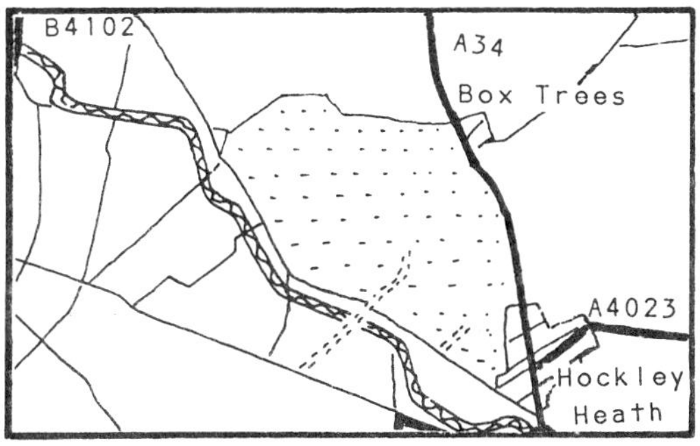

EXTENSIBILITY : Entails 3 road diversions, & demolition of 8 houses, 2 bungalows, 6 hangars & 5 huts.
ACCOMMODATION : Temporary.
HANGARS : Blisters: 0-3; double E0-1.

HARDSTANDINGS : Hardcore-1.

R.A.F. : OFFICERS: - S.N.C.O′s.: 2. O.R′s.: 73. TOTAL: 75.
W.A.A.F.: " : - " : - " : - " : -

AFFILIATED AIRFIELDS : Elmdon[Parent]

PRESENT USE [1985] : Unspecified.

NO: 298.

AIRFIELD NAME: HOLME. OPENED : 1941.
COUNTY : Yorkshire. CLOSED :
COMMAND : Bomber.
FORMATION : 4 Grp[York] GRID REF: A 302549[32]
FUNCTION : Operational[44 Base] O.S.REF.: SE 829351.

LOCALITY : 5miles SW of Market Weighton.
RAILWAY STN. : Market Weighton[LNER]

LATITUDE : 53 48 23N. HEIGHT ASL : 12′ LIGHTING : Mk2.
LONGITUDE : 00 44 23W. FLYING CONTROL : Yes. RADIO : QDM.

LANDMARKS DAY. : Market Weighton canal running N-S on E side of A/F.

LANDMARKS NIGHT : R Humber running E-W to S of A/F.

OBSTRUCTIONS : Farm on approach to No.1 runway.

LANDING AREA SURFACE : Tarmac.

QDM	LENGTH X WIDTH	EXT. TO
215.	1400 x 50yds.	4000yds.
260.	1400 x 50yds.	3000yds.
305.	2000 x 50yds.	3000yds.

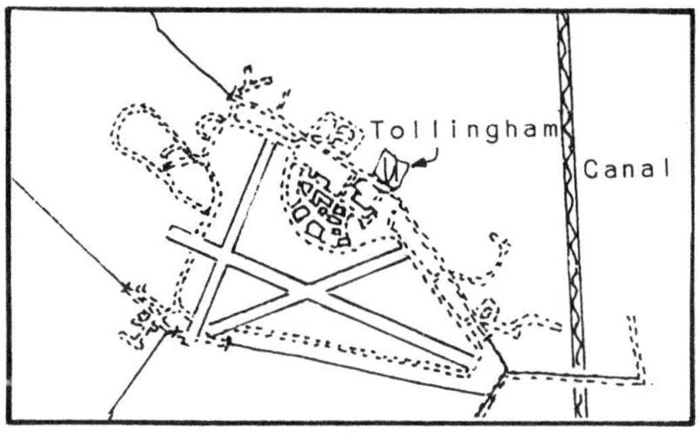

EXTENSIBILITY : Recommended to 3000-2000&2000yds only. Entails very slight demolition.
ACCOMMODATION : Temporary.
HANGARS : Type J-1; T2-5.

HARDSTANDINGS : Heavy bomber-36.

R.A.F. : OFFICERS: 134.S.N.C.O′s.: 402.O.R′s.: 1405.TOTAL: 1941.
W.A.A.F.: " : 14. " : 12. " : 355. " : 381.

AFFILIATED AIRFIELDS : Breighton & Melbourne[Sub-stations]

PRESENT USE [1985] : Aircraft Industry[British Aerospace]

NO: 299.

AIRFIELD NAME: HOLMSLEY SOUTH. OPENED : 1942
COUNTY : Hampshire. CLOSED : 1946.
COMMAND : Transport.
FORMATION : 116 Wing[Hendon] GRID REF: U 649190[131]
FUNCTION : Parent. O.S.REF.: SZ 215988.

LOCALITY : 6miles NE of Christchurch.
RAILWAY STN. : Hinton Admiral 2miles[SR]

LATITUDE : 50 47 15N. HEIGHT ASL : LIGHTING : Mk2.
LONGITUDE : 01 42 00W. FLYING CONTROL : Yes. RADIO : QDM.

LANDMARKS DAY. : Christchurch Bay. Two high W/T masts, W side of landing area.Isle of Wight.

LANDMARKS NIGHT : -

OBSTRUCTIONS : -

LANDING AREA SURFACE : Tarmac.

QDM	LENGTH X WIDTH	EXT. TO
247.	1970 x 50yds.	
302.	1400 x 50yds.	
358.	1370 x 50yds.	

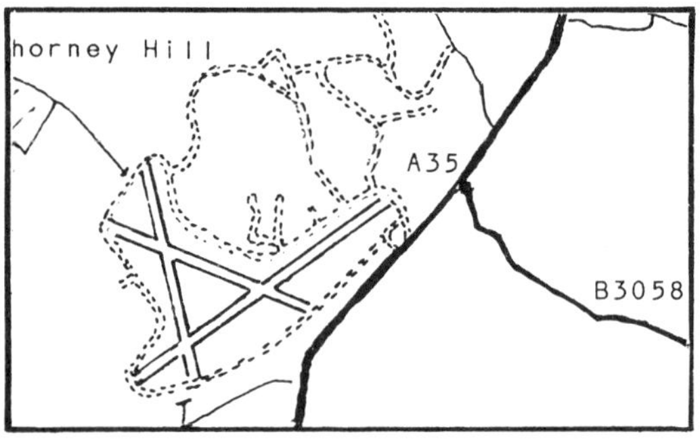

EXTENSIBILITY : None.

ACCOMMODATION : Temporary.
HANGARS : T2-5.

HARDSTANDINGS : Concrete-38.

R.A.F. : OFFICERS: 177.S.N.C.O′s.: 522.O.R′s.: 1926.TOTAL: 2625.
W.A.A.F.: " : 10. " : 16. " : 312. " : 338.

AFFILIATED AIRFIELDS : -

PRESENT USE [1985] : Forestry Commission.

NO: 300.

AIRFIELD NAME: HONEYBOURNE. OPENED : 1941.
COUNTY : Worcestershire. CLOSED : 1946.
COMMAND : Bomber.
FORMATION : 91 Grp[Abingdon] GRID REF: P 562632[82]
FUNCTION : Operational Training Unit. O.S.REF.: SP 112426.
LOCALITY : 4.75miles E of Evesham.
RAILWAY STN. : Weston-sub-Edge .25miles[GWR]

LATITUDE : 52 04 45N. HEIGHT ASL : 178′ LIGHTING : Mk2.
LONGITUDE : 01 50 00W. FLYING CONTROL : Yes. RADIO : QDM.

LANDMARKS DAY. : Broadway Hill S. Triangle Honeybourne Junction N. Bedon Hill SW.

LANDMARKS NIGHT : -

OBSTRUCTIONS : Hills 3miles S & SE 800-1000′

LANDING AREA SURFACE : Concrete.

QDM	LENGTH X WIDTH	EXT. TO
233.	1400 x 50yds.	2400yds.
292.	1300 x 50yds.	1330yds.
171.	1100 x 50yds.	1450yds.

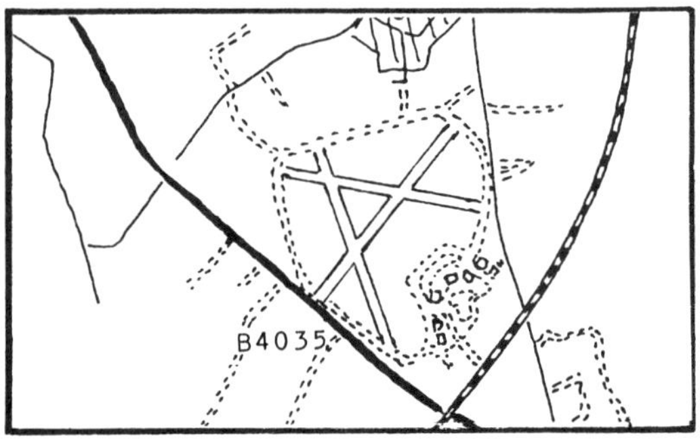

EXTENSIBILITY : Entails diversion of a road.

ACCOMMODATION : Temporary.
HANGARS : Type J-1; T2-4.

HARDSTANDINGS : Heavy bomber-30.

R.A.F. : OFFICERS: 268.S.N.C.O′s.: 389.O.R′s.: 1216.TOTAL: 1873.
W.A.A.F.: " : 10. " : 9. " : 363. " : 382.

AFFILIATED AIRFIELDS : Long Marston[Satellite]

PRESENT USE [1985] : Unspecified.

AIRFIELD NAME: HONILEY. OPENED : 1941.
COUNTY : Warwickshire. CLOSED : 1958.
COMMAND : Bomber.
FORMATION : 26 Grp[Langley Hall] GRID REF: P 685938[72]
FUNCTION : Station. O.S.REF.: SP 233736.

LOCALITY : 7miles SW of Coventry.
RAILWAY STN. : Berskwell & Balsall 3miles[LMS]

LATITUDE : 52 21 30N. HEIGHT ASL : 426′ LIGHTING : Mk2.
LONGITUDE : 01 39 30W. FLYING CONTROL : Yes. RADIO : QDM.

LANDMARKS DAY. : Big wood SW. Kenilworth 3miles E. Warwick Castle 7.5miles S. Big system of lock gates on Grand Union canals.

LANDMARKS NIGHT : -

OBSTRUCTIONS : -

LANDING AREA SURFACE : Tarmac.

QDM: 057. LENGTH X WIDTH: 2000 x 50yds.EXT. TO: 2350yds.
: 115. : 1150 x 50yds. : 1350yds.
: 167. : 1400 x 50yds. : 1900yds.
: : :

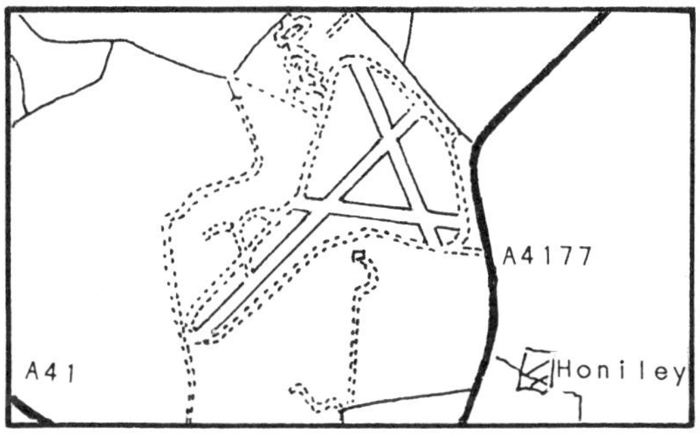

EXTENSIBILITY : Entails diversion of a secondary road, & demolition of 4 houses, an inn, & 7 cottages.
ACCOMMODATION : Temporary.
HANGARS : Blisters: O-8; EO-4; Bellman-3.

HARDSTANDINGS : -

R.A.F. : OFFICERS: 96. S.N.C.O's.: 90. O.R's.: 1397.TOTAL: 1583.
W.A.A.F.: " : 13. " : 3. " : 551. " : 567.

AFFILIATED AIRFIELDS : Baginton[Satellite]

PRESENT USE [1985] : Unspecified.

AIRFIELD NAME: HONINGTON. OPENED : 1937.
COUNTY : Suffolk. CLOSED :
COMMAND : 8th USAAF.
FORMATION : 364th Fighter Grp. GRID REF: M 346935[76]
FUNCTION : Operational. O.S.REF.: TL 891754.

LOCALITY : 7miles NNE of Bury St.Edmunds.
RAILWAY STN. : Bury St.Edmunds[LNER]

LATITUDE : 52 20 38N. HEIGHT ASL : 174. LIGHTING : Mk1.
LONGITUDE : 00 46 30E. FLYING CONTROL : Yes. RADIO : QDM.

LANDMARKS DAY. : 2 lakes 2-3miles S. Woods to N&W.

LANDMARKS NIGHT : 2 lakes 2-3miles S.

OBSTRUCTIONS : Gibbet Covert on W side.

LANDING AREA SURFACE : Grass[280-steel matting].

QDM: 280. LENGTH X WIDTH: 2000 x 40yds.EXT. TO: 3000yds.
: NE-SW. : 1400yds. : 2000yds.
: SE-NW. : 1400yds. : 2000yds.
: : :

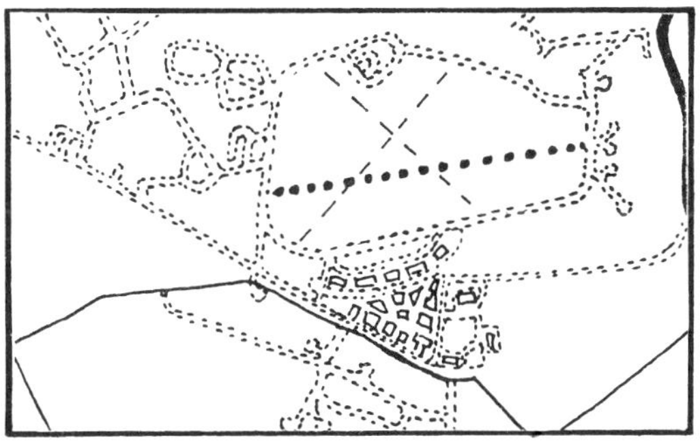

EXTENSIBILITY : Entails diversion of a road to store depot & demolition of temporary RAF buildings.
ACCOMMODATION : Permanent.
HANGARS : Type C-4; blister-9.

HARDSTANDINGS : Concrete & cement.

USAAF. : OFFICERS: 190. Enlisted Men. : 1519.TOTAL: 1709.

AFFILIATED AIRFIELDS : -

PRESENT USE [1985] : RAF.

AIRFIELD NAME: HOOTON PARK. OPENED : 1917.
COUNTY : Cheshire. CLOSED : 1957.
COMMAND : Maintenance.
FORMATION : 56 Wing[Carlisle] GRID REF: D 840002[43]
FUNCTION : Storage Unit. O.S.REF.: SJ 375792.

LOCALITY : 7miles SE of Birkenhead.
RAILWAY STN. : Hooton 1.5miles[joint LMS & GWR]

LATITUDE : 53 18 15N. HEIGHT ASL : 95′ LIGHTING : None.
LONGITUDE : 02 56 15W. FLYING CONTROL : Yes. RADIO : QDM.

LANDMARKS DAY. : Bowaters towers E. Manisty Mount E. Manchester ship canal.

LANDMARKS NIGHT : Obstruction lights on Bowaters towers & all south hangars.

OBSTRUCTIONS : Bowaters towers 200′ 1mile E.

LANDING AREA SURFACE : Tarmac.

QDM: 329. LENGTH X WIDTH: 1500 x 50yds.EXT. TO: 2500yds.
: 042. : 1100 x 50yds. : 1800yds.
: : : 1600yds.
: : :

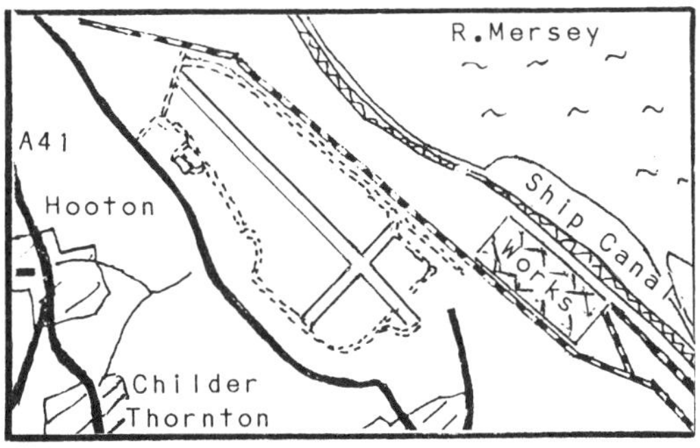

EXTENSIBILITY : Entails major road diversion & moderate demolition.
ACCOMMODATION : Temporary.
HANGARS : B1-1;Bellman-2;Robin-2; Blisters:O-4;triple O-1.

HARDSTANDINGS : -

R.A.F. : OFFICERS: - S.N.C.O's.: 90. O.R's.: 456. TOTAL: 546.
W.A.A.F.: " : - " : - " : - " : -

AFFILIATED AIRFIELDS : -

PRESENT USE [1985] : Car Industry[GM]

NO: 304.

AIRFIELD NAME: HORHAM. OPENED : 1942.
COUNTY : Suffolk. CLOSED : 1963.
COMMAND : 8th USAAF.
FORMATION : 95th Bomb Grp. GRID REF: M 655908[77]
FUNCTION : Operational. O.S.REF.: TM 205735.

LOCALITY : 4miles ESE of Eye.
RAILWAY STN. : Horham 2miles[LNER]

LATITUDE : 52 18 35N. HEIGHT ASL : 180′ LIGHTING : Mk2.
LONGITUDE : 01 14 00E. FLYING CONTROL : Yes. RADIO : QDM.

LANDMARKS DAY. : Single track railway to Horham station.

LANDMARKS NIGHT : -

OBSTRUCTIONS : -

LANDING AREA SURFACE : Concrete.

QDM: 074. LENGTH X WIDTH: 2000 x 50yds. EXT. TO: -
: 190. : 1400 x 50yds. : 2400yds.
: 310. : 1400 x 50yds. : 3100yds.

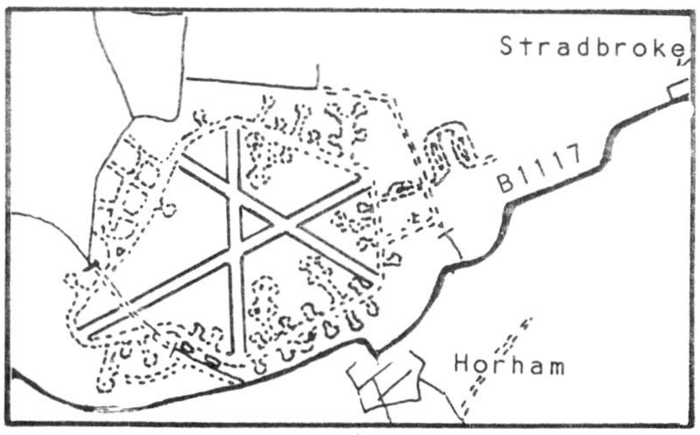

EXTENSIBILITY : Entails minor road diversion.

ACCOMMODATION : Temporary.
HANGARS : T2-2.

HARDSTANDINGS : Loop-50.

USAAF. : OFFICERS: 443. Enlisted Men. : 2529. TOTAL: 2972.

AFFILIATED AIRFIELDS : -

PRESENT USE [1985] : Unspecified.

NO: 305.

AIRFIELD NAME: HORNCHURCH. OPENED : 1928.
COUNTY : Essex. CLOSED : 1962.
COMMAND : Fighter.
FORMATION : 11 Grp[Uxbridge] GRID REF: L 975033[107]
FUNCTION : Forward Airfield. O.S.REF.: TQ 530845.

LOCALITY : 2miles SE of Romford.
RAILWAY STN. : Elm Park[District Railway] Dagenham[LMS]

LATITUDE : 51 32 15N. HEIGHT ASL : 36′ LIGHTING : None.
LONGITUDE : 00 12 45E. FLYING CONTROL : Yes. RADIO : QDM.

LANDMARKS DAY. : Factory[Fords] with 3 chimneys 3miles S; Romford -Southend arterial road N of A/F running W-E.

LANDMARKS NIGHT : -

OBSTRUCTIONS : Chimney 100′ approx, on NE boundary.

LANDING AREA SURFACE : Grass.

QDM: N-S. LENGTH X WIDTH: 1600yds. EXT. TO: 2000yds.
: NE-SW. : 1600yds. : 2000yds.
: E-W. : 1600yds. : 2000yds.

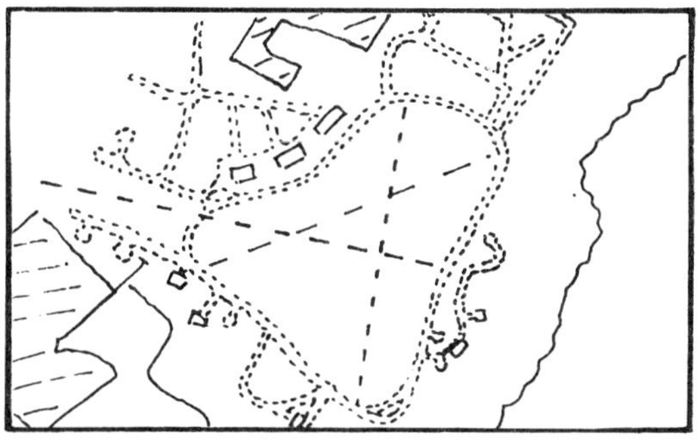

EXTENSIBILITY : Entails diversion of a minor road & demolition of farms & a bungalow.
ACCOMMODATION : Permanent.
HANGARS : Type A-2;Type C[225′]-1; Blister-12.

HARDSTANDINGS : Spitfire-10;Blenheim-2;Frypan-7; 30′sq.Sommerfeld track-7.

R.A.F. : OFFICERS: 192. S.N.C.O′s.: 290. O.R′s.: 592. TOTAL: 1074.
W.A.A.F.: " : 24. " : 38. " : 728. " : 790.

AFFILIATED AIRFIELDS : North Weald[Sector]

PRESENT USE [1985] : Housing.

NO: 306.

AIRFIELD NAME: HORNE. OPENED : 1944.
COUNTY : Surrey. CLOSED : 1944.
COMMAND : Fighter.
FORMATION : 11 Grp[Uxbridge] GRID REF: Q 782620[125]
FUNCTION : Advanced Landing Ground. [De-requisitioned] O.S.REF.: TQ 332435.
LOCALITY : 6.5miles SE of Redhill.
RAILWAY STN. : Gatwick[SR]

LATITUDE : 51 10 23N. HEIGHT ASL : 190′ LIGHTING : None.
LONGITUDE : 00 04 38W. FLYING CONTROL : None. RADIO : QDM.

LANDMARKS DAY. : -

LANDMARKS NIGHT : -

OBSTRUCTIONS : -

LANDING AREA SURFACE : Steel Matting[Sommerfeld track]

QDM: NE-SW. LENGTH X WIDTH: 1600yds. EXT. TO: -
: NW-SE. : 1600yds. : -

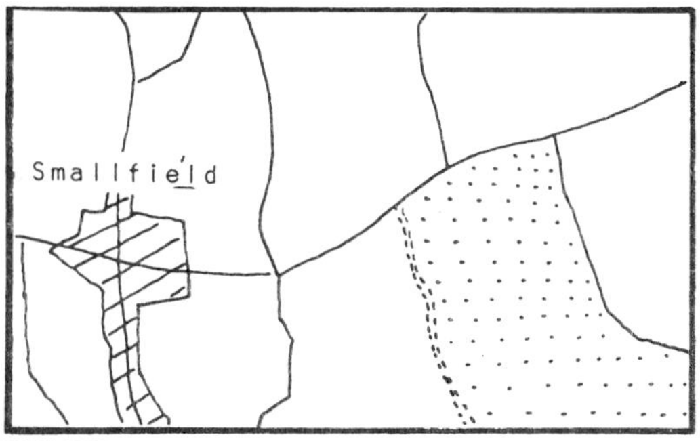

EXTENSIBILITY : -

ACCOMMODATION : Tented camp.
HANGARS : Blister-4.

HARDSTANDINGS : Sommerfeld track-32.

R.A.F. : OFFICERS: - S.N.C.O′s.: - O.R′s.: - TOTAL: -
W.A.A.F.: " : - " : - " : - " : -

AFFILIATED AIRFIELDS : -

PRESENT USE [1985] : Unspecified.

NO: 307.

AIRFIELD NAME: HORSHAM-St-FAITH. OPENED : 1940.
COUNTY : Norfolk. CLOSED :
COMMAND : 8th USAAF.
FORMATION : 458th Bomb Grp. GRID REF: G 677315[67]
FUNCTION : Operational. O.S.REF.: TG 221137.

LOCALITY : 4miles N of Norwich.
RAILWAY STN. : Norwich Thorpe 4miles[LNER]

LATITUDE : 52 40 23N. HEIGHT ASL : 120′ LIGHTING : Mk2.
LONGITUDE : 01 17 00E. FLYING CONTROL : Yes. RADIO : QDM.

LANDMARKS DAY. : S boundary bordering Norwich, which is chief permanent landmark by day & night.

LANDMARKS NIGHT : -

OBSTRUCTIONS : -

LANDING AREA SURFACE : Concrete.

QDM	LENGTH X WIDTH	EXT. TO
280.	1400 x 50yds.	2000yds.
230.	2000 x 50yds.	3870yds.
350.	1400 x 50yds.	2000yds.

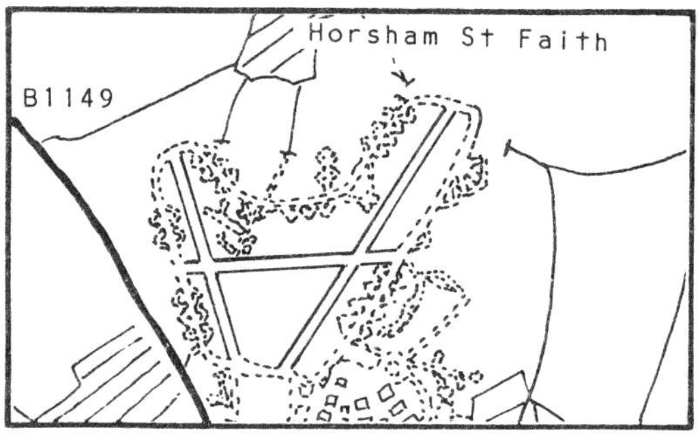

EXTENSIBILITY : Recommended to 2-3 & 2000yds. only.Entails diversion of 2 roads & isolation of houses.
ACCOMMODATION : Permanent.
HANGARS : Type C-5.

HARDSTANDINGS : Loop[4-engine]-50;fighter-6.

USAAF. : OFFICERS: 443. Enlisted Men. : 2529.TOTAL: 2972.

AFFILIATED AIRFIELDS : -

PRESENT USE [1985] : Civil Airport[Norwich]

NO: 308.

AIRFIELD NAME: HUCKNALL. OPENED : 1916.
COUNTY : Nottinghamshire. CLOSED : 1971.
COMMAND : Flying Training.
FORMATION : 21 Grp[Spittlegate] GRID REF: K 982668[54]
FUNCTION : Elementary Flying Training School. O.S.REF.: SK 526470.
LOCALITY : 8miles NW of Nottingham.
RAILWAY STN. : Hucknall Byron 2miles[LMS]

LATITUDE : 53 01 00N. HEIGHT ASL : 300′ LIGHTING : None.
LONGITUDE : 01 13 00W. FLYING CONTROL : None.RADIO : QDM.

LANDMARKS DAY. : R Trent 8miles S.

LANDMARKS NIGHT : As day.

OBSTRUCTIONS : Colliery slagheap at NE side.

LANDING AREA SURFACE : Grass.

QDM	LENGTH X WIDTH	EXT. TO
ENE-WSW.	1200yds.	
W-E.	1200yds.	

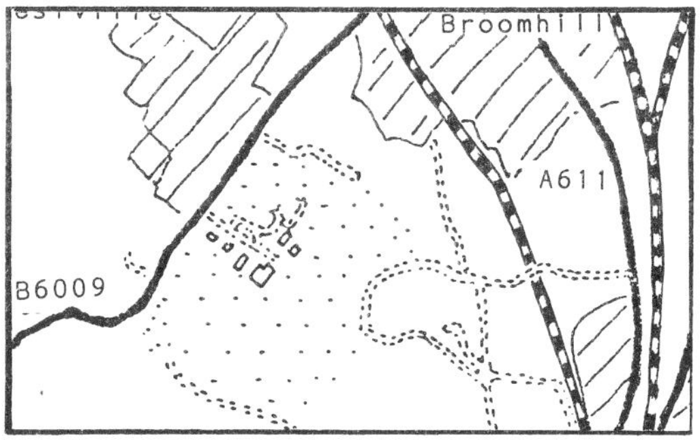

EXTENSIBILITY : None possible.

ACCOMMODATION : Permanent[part]
HANGARS : MAP:Bellman-2;200x172x25′-1;100x172x25′-1; GS:200x172x25′-2;blister 69′-5.
HARDSTANDINGS : -

	OFFICERS	S.N.C.O′s.	O.R′s.	TOTAL
R.A.F.	137.	118.	1509.	1764.
W.A.A.F.	13.	-	215.	228.

AFFILIATED AIRFIELDS : Firbeck[Satellite]; Papplewick[RLG]

PRESENT USE [1985] : Industry.

NO: 309.

AIRFIELD NAME: HULLAVINGTON. OPENED : 1937.
COUNTY : Wiltshire. CLOSED :
COMMAND : Flying Training.
FORMATION : 23 Grp[South Cerney] GRID REF: U 350015[111]
FUNCTION : Empire Central Flying School. O.S.REF.: ST 900810.
LOCALITY : 5miles N of Chippenham.
RAILWAY STN. : Chippenham[GWR]

LATITUDE : 51 31 30N. HEIGHT ASL : 340′ LIGHTING : Mk2.
LONGITUDE : 02 08 00W. FLYING CONTROL : Yes. RADIO : QDM.

LANDMARKS DAY. : Foss Way. Intersected by railway line 2miles W & 1mile N of A/F.

LANDMARKS NIGHT : -

OBSTRUCTIONS : -

LANDING AREA SURFACE : Concrete covered with tarmac.

QDM	LENGTH X WIDTH	EXT. TO
235.	1350 x 50yds.	1750yds.
140.	1130 x 50yds.	1380yds.
		2000yds.

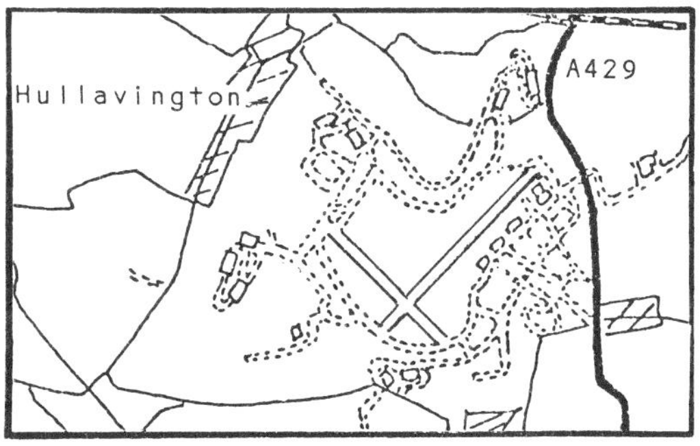

EXTENSIBILITY : -

ACCOMMODATION : Permanent.
HANGARS : C-4;Bellman-1;ARS-1;E-6;L-2;D-2;B1-1; blister-11.
HARDSTANDINGS : -

	OFFICERS	S.N.C.O′s.	O.R′s.	TOTAL
R.A.F.	178.	98.	853.	1129.
W.A.A.F.	14.	8.	340.	362.

AFFILIATED AIRFIELDS : -

PRESENT USE [1985] : RAF.

NO: 310.

AIRFIELD NAME: HUNSDON. OPENED : 1941.
COUNTY : Hertfordshire. CLOSED : 1947.
COMMAND : Fighter.
FORMATION : 11 Grp[Uxbridge] GRID REF: L 865329[96]
FUNCTION : Forward Airfield. Night Fighter. O.S.REF.: TL 426138.
LOCALITY : 4miles ESE of Ware.
RAILWAY STN. : St Margarets[LNER]

LATITUDE : 51 48 00N. HEIGHT ASL : 254′ LIGHTING : Mk2.
LONGITUDE : 00 03 00E. FLYING CONTROL : Yes. RADIO : QDM.

LANDMARKS DAY : -

LANDMARKS NIGHT : -

OBSTRUCTIONS : -

LANDING AREA SURFACE : Asphalt.

QDM: 086. LENGTH X WIDTH: 1750 x 50yds. EXT. TO: -
: 214. : 1450 x 50yds. : 3200yds.

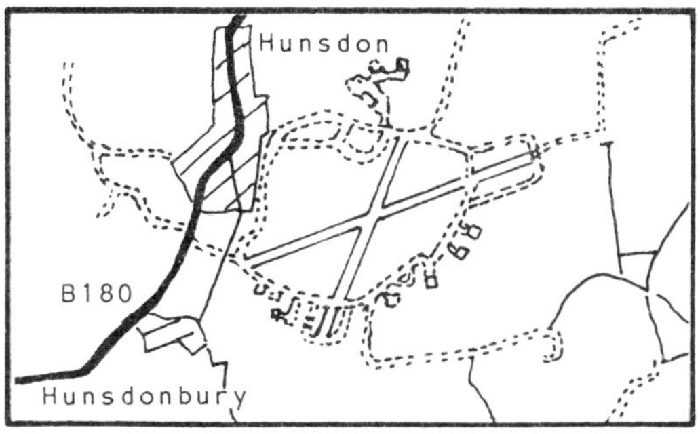

EXTENSIBILITY : -

ACCOMMODATION : Temporary.
HANGARS : Bellman-1;Blister: 0-4;E0-12.

HARDSTANDINGS : Twin engined-18.

R.A.F. : OFFICERS: 100. S.N.C.O's.: 140. O.R's.: 2000. TOTAL: 2240.
W.A.A.F.: " : 5. " : 3. " : 268. " : 276.

AFFILIATED AIRFIELDS : North Weald[Sector]

PRESENT USE [1985] : Disused.

NO: 311.

AIRFIELD NAME: HURN. OPENED : 1941.
COUNTY : Hampshire. CLOSED :
COMMAND : Fighter.
FORMATION : On loan to D.G.C.A. GRID REF: U 546183[141]
FUNCTION : On loan to D.G.C.A. O.S.REF.: SU 115980.

LOCALITY : 4miles NE of Christchurch.
RAILWAY STN. : Christchurch[SR]

LATITUDE : 50 47 00N. HEIGHT ASL : 34′ LIGHTING : Mk2.
LONGITUDE : 01 50 18W. FLYING CONTROL : Yes. RADIO : QDM.

LANDMARKS DAY : R Avon to E. R Stour to S. Bournemouth & Christchurch to S & SE.

LANDMARKS NIGHT : As day.

OBSTRUCTIONS : Nil in line with R/Ws. St Catherines Hill with 2-90′ towers, 170′ above SL 4000yds 132degrees T from con.tower. Ramsbury plantation 2300yds.

LANDING AREA SURFACE : Concrete.

QDM: 265. LENGTH X WIDTH: 2000 x 50yds. EXT. TO: 3000yds.
: 174. : 1600 x 50yds. : 2400yds.
: 309. : 1130 x 50yds. : 2400yds.

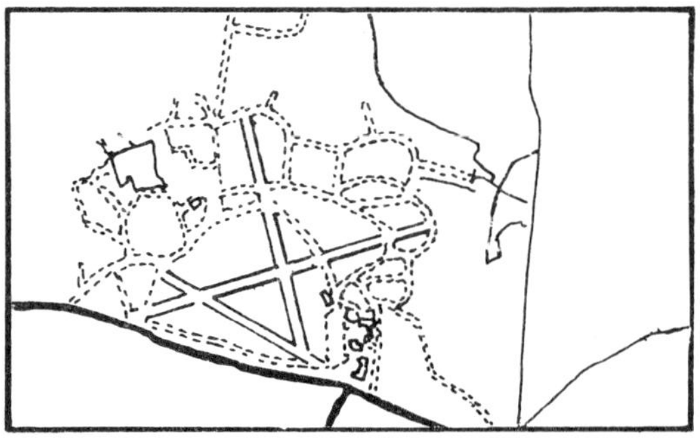

EXTENSIBILITY : Entails diversion of fairly important Hurn-Wimbourne road.
ACCOMMODATION : Temporary.
HANGARS : T2-4;Bellman-3;Blister-10.

HARDSTANDINGS : Frypan:90′-20;100′-10;special loop-46.

R.A.F. : OFFICERS: 166. S.N.C.O's.: 273. O.R's.: 1549. TOTAL: 1988.
W.A.A.F.: " : 8. " : 10. " : 444. " : 462.

AFFILIATED AIRFIELDS : -

PRESENT USE [1985] : Aircraft Industry[British Aerospace]

NO: 312.

AIRFIELD NAME: HUSBANDS BOSWORTH. OPENED : 1943.
COUNTY : Leicestershire. CLOSED : 1956.
COMMAND : Bomber.
FORMATION : 92 Grp[Winslow] GRID REF: F 105024[73]
FUNCTION : Operational Training Unit. O.S.REF.: SP 653825.
LOCALITY : 10miles NE of Rugby.
RAILWAY STN. : Welford & Kilworth[LMS]

LATITUDE : 52 26 00N. HEIGHT ASL : 505′ LIGHTING : Mk2.
LONGITUDE : 01 02 30W. FLYING CONTROL : Yes. RADIO : QDM.

LANDMARKS DAY : 2 large reservoirs, one 1mile WSW, other 1mile S of A/F.

LANDMARKS NIGHT : _

OBSTRUCTIONS : Rugby wireless masts 8miles SW of A/F [all illuminated]

LANDING AREA SURFACE : Concrete & wood chippings.

QDM: 223. LENGTH X WIDTH: 1400 x 50yds. EXT. TO: 1600yds.
: 343. : 1400 x 50yds. : 1800yds.
: 273. : 2000 x 50yds. : 2300yds.

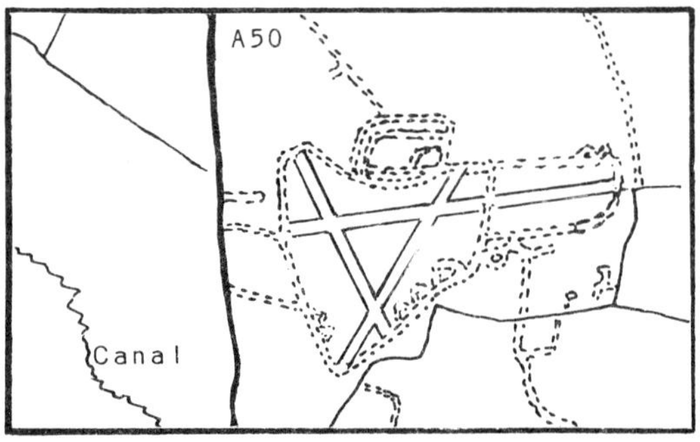

EXTENSIBILITY : Entails control of main road & demolition of a pair of cottages & farm buildings.
ACCOMMODATION : Temporary.
HANGARS : T2-4.

HARDSTANDINGS : Spectacle-36.

R.A.F. : OFFICERS: 213. S.N.C.O's.: 469. O.R's.: 854. TOTAL: 1536.
W.A.A.F.: " : 10. " : 48. " : 300. " : 358.

AFFILIATED AIRFIELDS : -

PRESENT USE [1985] : Gliding.

NO: 313.

AIRFIELD NAME: HUTTON CRANSWICK. OPENED : 1942.
COUNTY : Yorkshire. CLOSED : 1946.
COMMAND : Fighter.
FORMATION : 12 Grp[Watnall] GRID REF: A 485710[28]
FUNCTION : Operational. O.S.REF.: TA 008514.

LOCALITY : 4miles SSW of Driffield.
RAILWAY STN. : Hutton Cranswick 1mile[LNER]

LATITUDE : 53 57 00N. HEIGHT ASL : 107. LIGHTING : Mk2.
LONGITUDE : 00 27 30W. FLYING CONTROL : Yes. RADIO : QDM.

LANDMARKS DAY. : Beverley Minster.

LANDMARKS NIGHT : Hornsea Mere.

OBSTRUCTIONS : -

LANDING AREA SURFACE : Tarmac.

QDM: 279. LENGTH X WIDTH: 1580 x 50yds.EXT. TO: 2500yds.
: 041. : 1317 x 50yds. : -
: 340. : 1166 x 50yds. : 1800yds.
: : :

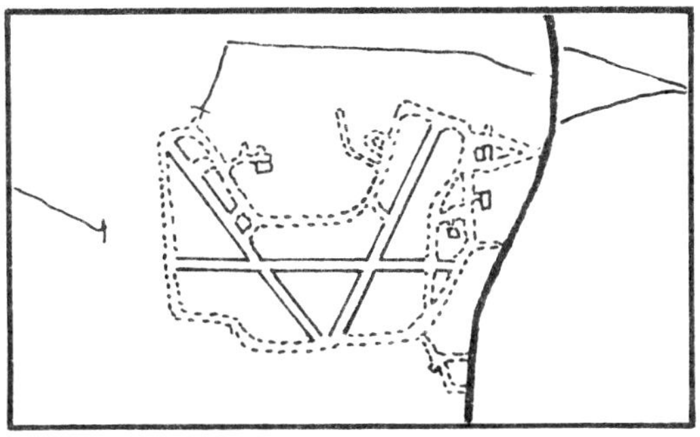

EXTENSIBILITY : -

ACCOMMODATION : Temporary.
HANGARS : T-1;Blisters:E0-4;0-4.

HARDSTANDINGS : SE-7.

R.A.F. : OFFICERS: 122.S.N.C.O's.: 114.O.R's.: 1236.TOTAL: 1472.
W.A.A.F.: " : 10. " : 10. " : 255. " : 275.

AFFILIATED AIRFIELDS : Church Fenton[Sector]

PRESENT USE [1985] : Industry.

NO: 314.

AIRFIELD NAME: IBSLEY. OPENED : 1941.
COUNTY : Hampshire. CLOSED : 1947.
COMMAND : Fighter.
FORMATION : 11 Grp[Uxbridge] GRID REF: U 588292[131]
FUNCTION : Forward Airfield. O.S.REF.: SU 153087.

LOCALITY : 3miles N of Ringwood.
RAILWAY STN. : Ringwood[SR]

LATITUDE : 50 52 30N. HEIGHT ASL : 80' LIGHTING : Mk2.
LONGITUDE : 01 46 53W. FLYING CONTROL : Yes. RADIO : QDM.

LANDMARKS DAY. : Coast & river.

LANDMARKS NIGHT : As day.

OBSTRUCTIONS : -

LANDING AREA SURFACE : Tarmac.

QDM: 010. LENGTH X WIDTH: 1600 x 50yds.EXT. TO: 3600yds.
: 050. : 1350 x 50yds. : 1500yds.
: 320. : 1400 x 50yds. : 1700yds.
: : :

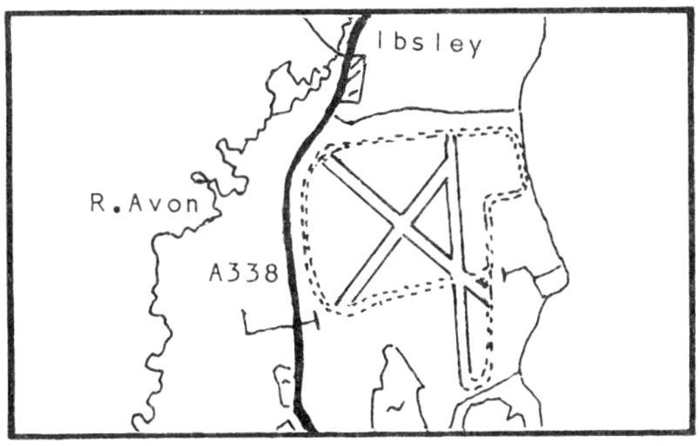

EXTENSIBILITY : Entails road diversion & slight diversion.

ACCOMMODATION : Temporary.
HANGARS : Bellman-2;blister-12.

HARDSTANDINGS : Tarmac[circular & pen type]-36.

R.A.F. : OFFICERS: 170.S.N.C.O's.: 149.O.R's.: 1492.TOTAL: 1811.
W.A.A.F.: " : 7. " : 16. " : 365. " : 388.

AFFILIATED AIRFIELDS : Middle Wallop[sector]

PRESENT USE [1985] : Gravel extraction.

NO: 315.

AIRFIELD NAME: INSKIP. OPENED : 1943.
COUNTY : Lancashire. CLOSED : 1946.
COMMAND : RN.
FORMATION : HMS Nightjar. GRID REF: D 920580[29]
FUNCTION : Night & day anti-sub. OTU. O.S.REF.: SD 451371.
LOCALITY : 7.5miles E of Blackpool.
RAILWAY STN. : Kirkham & Wesham 3miles[LMS]

LATITUDE : 53 49 35N. HEIGHT ASL : 46' LIGHTING : Naval.
LONGITUDE : 02 49 40W. FLYING CONTROL : Yes. RADIO : QDM.

LANDMARKS DAY. : R Ribble with Blackpool N & Southport S of entrance.

LANDMARKS NIGHT : Coastline.

OBSTRUCTIONS : Blackpool Tower 550' 7miles 265 degrees.

LANDING AREA SURFACE : Tarmac.

QDM: 005-185. LENGTH X WIDTH: 1000 x 30yds.EXT. TO: -
: 048-228. : 1000 x 30yds. : -
: 094-274. : 1200 x 30yds. : -
: 141-322. : 1030 x 30yds. : -

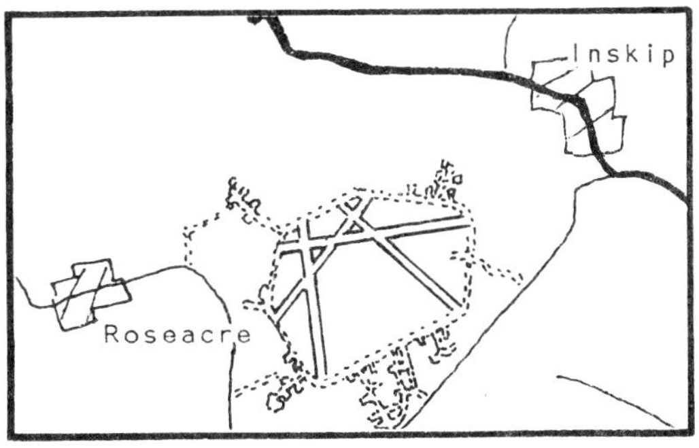

EXTENSIBILITY : -

ACCOMMODATION : Temporary.
HANGARS : 60x70': Sqdn-16;storage-16.

HARDSTANDINGS : 3.

R.N. : OFFICERS: 171. Chiefs/POs/Ratings. : 954.TOTAL: 1125.
W.R.N.S. : " : 16. " : 425. " : 441.

AFFILIATED AIRFIELDS : -

PRESENT USE [1985] : Radio Research Station.

AIRFIELD NAME: INVERNESS. OPENED : 1933.
COUNTY : Inverness-shire. CLOSED : 1947.
COMMAND : Fighter.
FORMATION : 13 Grp[Inverness] GRID REF: S 188689[37Scot]
FUNCTION : Non-operational. O.S.REF.: NH 670465.

LOCALITY : .75miles N of Inverness.
RAILWAY STN. : Inverness 1mile[LMS]

LATITUDE : 57 28 00N. HEIGHT ASL : 8′ LIGHTING : None.
LONGITUDE : 01 14 00W. FLYING CONTROL : Yes. RADIO : QDM.

LANDMARKS DAY. : Gasometer SW; R Ness. Loch Ness lying 6-7miles SW.

LANDMARKS NIGHT : -

OBSTRUCTIONS : -

LANDING AREA SURFACE : Grass.
QDM: NE-SW. LENGTH X WIDTH: 1260yds. EXT. TO: 2550yds.
: E-W. : 1468yds. : 1800yds.
: : :
: : :

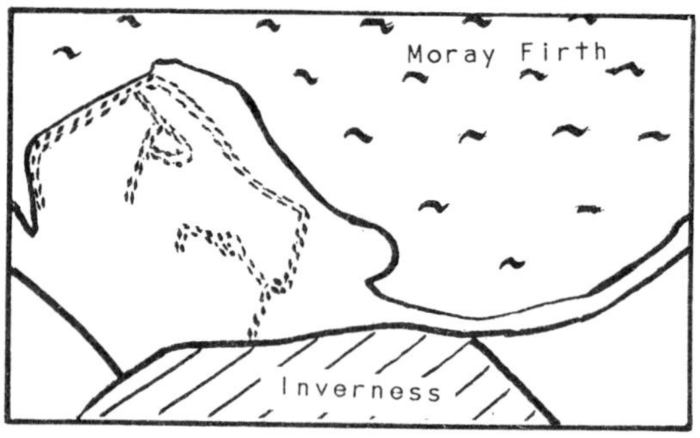

EXTENSIBILITY : -

ACCOMMODATION : Permanent[part]
HANGARS : Bessoneau-2;T1-1;Bellman-1;Super Robin-1; Blister-1;civil airport-1.
HARDSTANDINGS : -

R.A.F. : OFFICERS: - S.N.C.O′s.: 40.O.R′s.: 234.TOTAL: 274.
W.A.A.F.: " : - " : 3. " : 52. " : 55.

AFFILIATED AIRFIELDS : Lerwick operations room[Sector]

PRESENT USE [1985] : Industry.

NO: 317.

AIRFIELD NAME: IPSWICH. OPENED : 1930.
COUNTY : Suffolk. CLOSED :
COMMAND : Fighter.
FORMATION : 70 Grp[Farnborough] GRID REF: M 642597[87]
FUNCTION : AA Co-operation Unit. O.S.REF.: TM 190410.

LOCALITY : SE boundary of Ipswich.
RAILWAY STN. : Ipswich[LNER]

LATITUDE : 52 01 38N. HEIGHT ASL : 123′ LIGHTING : None.
LONGITUDE : 01 11 45E. FLYING CONTROL : None.RADIO : QDM.

LANDMARKS DAY. : Factory with tall metal chimney 440yds away.

LANDMARKS NIGHT : R Orwell .5miles SW.

OBSTRUCTIONS : -

LANDING AREA SURFACE : Grass.
QDM: NE-SW. LENGTH X WIDTH: 1250yds. EXT. TO: 2000yds.
: NW-SE. : 1250yds. : 1600yds.
: : :
: : :

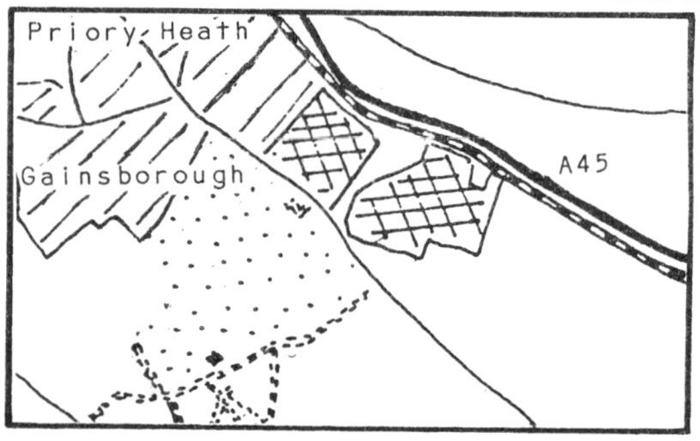

EXTENSIBILITY : Entails closure of a road & demolition of 2 houses.
ACCOMMODATION : Temporary.
HANGARS : Civil airport hangar-4.

HARDSTANDINGS : -

R.A.F. : OFFICERS: 13.S.N.C.O′s.: 38.O.R′s.: 292.TOTAL: 343.
W.A.A.F.: " : - " : - " : - " : -

AFFILIATED AIRFIELDS : -

PRESENT USE [1985] : Civil Airport[Ipswich]

NO: 318.

AIRFIELD NAME: JURBY. OPENED : 1939.
COUNTY : Isle of Man. CLOSED : 1972.
COMMAND : Flying Training.
FORMATION : 29 Grp[Dumfries] GRID REF: X 842209[17]
FUNCTION : Air Navigation & Bombing School. O.S.REF.: SC 361983.

LOCALITY : 6miles WNW of Ramsey.
RAILWAY STN. : Sulby Glen 3miles[IMR]

LATITUDE : 54 21 15N. HEIGHT ASL : 84′ LIGHTING : Mk2.
LONGITUDE : 04 31 15W. FLYING CONTROL : Yes. RADIO : QDM.

LANDMARKS DAY. : Coastline.

LANDMARKS NIGHT : As day.

OBSTRUCTIONS : Range of hills 3miles S from SSW to SE capped by Snaefel 2030′

LANDING AREA SURFACE : Tarmac.
QDM: 260. LENGTH X WIDTH: 1200 x 50yds.EXT. TO: -
: 340. : 1000 x 50yds. : -
: : :
: : :

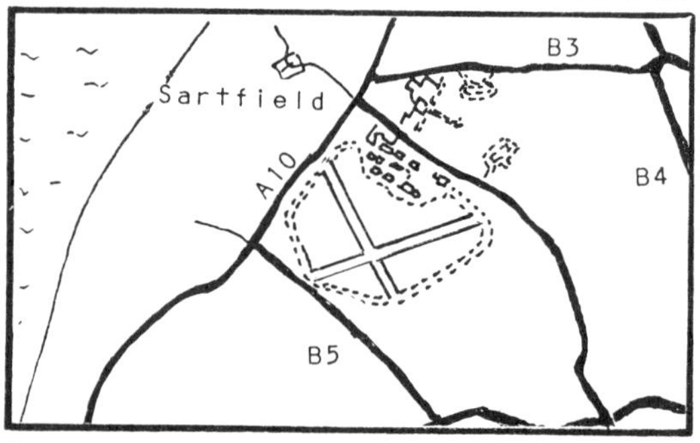

EXTENSIBILITY : Would necessitate road closure.

ACCOMMODATION : Temporary[except MQ]
HANGARS : Bellman-4;VR-2;F-1;EO blister-19.

HARDSTANDINGS : Hangar apron 200x180′

R.A.F. : OFFICERS: 141.S.N.C.O′s.: 347.O.R′s.: 1666.TOTAL: 2154.
W.A.A.F.: " : 2. " : 5. " : 187. " : 194.

AFFILIATED AIRFIELDS : -

PRESENT USE [1985] : Disused.

NO: 319.

AIRFIELD NAME: KEEVIL. OPENED : 1942.
COUNTY : Wiltshire. CLOSED : 1965.
COMMAND : Flying Training.
FORMATION : 23 Grp[South Cerney] GRID REF: U 363774[111]
FUNCTION : Heavy Glider Con. Unit. O.S.REF.: ST 922571.

LOCALITY : 4.5miles E of Trowbridge.
RAILWAY STN. : Edington & Bratton 1.5miles[GWR]

LATITUDE : 51 18 45N. HEIGHT ASL : 188′ LIGHTING : Mk2.
LONGITUDE : 02 06 45W. FLYING CONTROL : Yes. RADIO : QDM.

LANDMARKS DAY. : -

LANDMARKS NIGHT : -

OBSTRUCTIONS : Hangars: near approach to R/W 024. height 39′, to R/W 075. height 30′. Barns height 30′, near approach to 312. & 1mile on approach to 255.

LANDING AREA SURFACE : Concrete & wood chippings.

QDM	LENGTH X WIDTH	EXT. TO
075.	2000 x 50yds.	2500yds.
132.	1400 x 50yds.	2600yds.
204.	1400 x 50yds.	3500yds.

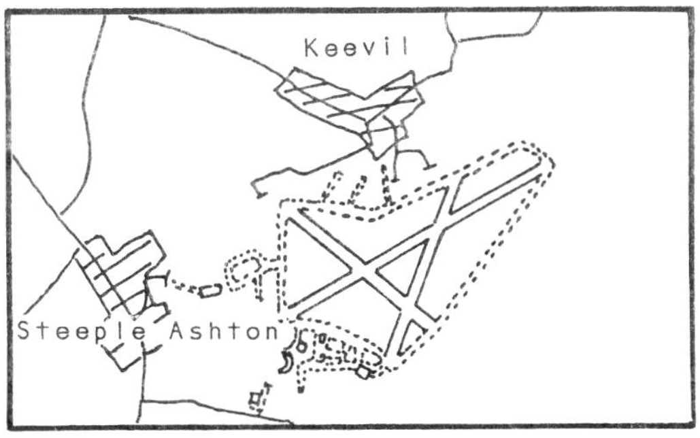

EXTENSIBILITY : Not recommended owing to wet site & poor bedding soil making extensions speculative.
ACCOMMODATION : Temporary.
HANGARS : T2-2;EO blister-9.

HARDSTANDINGS : 150′ dia.-9;125′ dia.-41;75′ dia.-1.

	OFFICERS	S.N.C.O′s.	O.R′s.	TOTAL
R.A.F.	155.	504.	1434.	2093.
W.A.A.F.	10.	19.	420.	449.

AFFILIATED AIRFIELDS : Fairford[Satellite]

PRESENT USE [1985] : Disused.

NO: 320.

AIRFIELD NAME: KELMSCOTT. OPENED : 1942.
COUNTY : Oxfordshire. CLOSED : 1946.
COMMAND : Flying Training.
FORMATION : 50 Grp[Reading] GRID REF: P 696205[104]
FUNCTION : Beam Approach School. O.S.REF.: SU 243998.

LOCALITY : 2.5miles ENE of Lechlade.
RAILWAY STN. : Kelmscott & Langford[GWR]

LATITUDE : 51 41 53N. HEIGHT ASL : 230′ LIGHTING : Mk2.
LONGITUDE : 01 39 00W. FLYING CONTROL : None. RADIO : QDM.

LANDMARKS DAY. : Lechlade church spire. R Thames 1mile to S.

LANDMARKS NIGHT : R Thames.

OBSTRUCTIONS : Telephone wires to S.

LANDING AREA SURFACE : Grass.

QDM	LENGTH X WIDTH	EXT. TO
E-W.	1400yds.	2700yds.
NW-SE.	1000yds.	1400yds.
		1450yds.

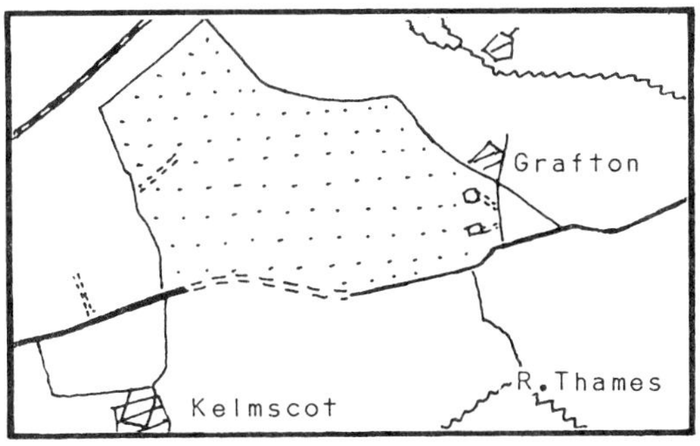

EXTENSIBILITY : Entails diversion of a road.

ACCOMMODATION : Temporary.
HANGARS : EO blister[temporary]-1.

HARDSTANDINGS : -

	OFFICERS	S.N.C.O′s.	O.R′s.	TOTAL
R.A.F.	21.	36.	647.	704.
W.A.A.F.	-	-	-	-

AFFILIATED AIRFIELDS : Watchfield[Parent]

PRESENT USE [1985] : Agriculture.

NO: 321.

AIRFIELD NAME: KELSTERN. OPENED : 1943.
COUNTY : Lincolnshire. CLOSED : 1945.
COMMAND : Bomber.
FORMATION : 1 Grp[Bawtry] GRID REF: A 730115[39]
FUNCTION : Operational. O.S.REF.: TF 262922.

LOCALITY : 5miles NW of Lough.
RAILWAY STN. : Ludborough 5.5miles[LNER]

LATITUDE : 53 24 38N. HEIGHT ASL : 410′ LIGHTING : Mk2.
LONGITUDE : 00 06 00W. FLYING CONTROL : Yes. RADIO : QDM.

LANDMARKS DAY. : -

LANDMARKS NIGHT : -

OBSTRUCTIONS : -

LANDING AREA SURFACE : Concrete & tarmac.

QDM	LENGTH X WIDTH	EXT. TO
242.	2000 x 50yds.	4200yds.
191.	1400 x 50yds.	2400yds.
308.	1400 x 50yds.	2200yds.

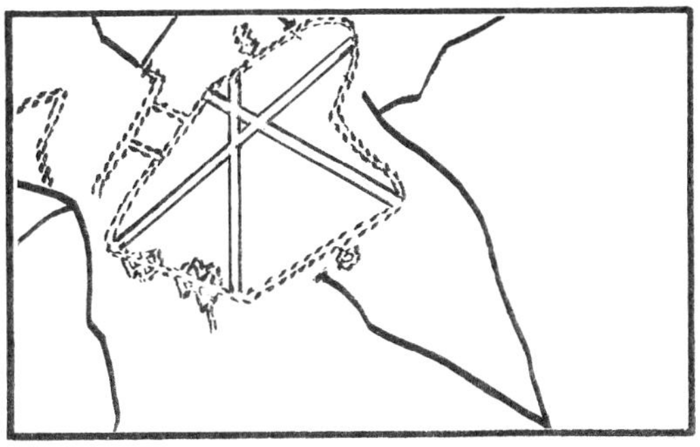

EXTENSIBILITY : Entails demolition of a small farm.

ACCOMMODATION : Temporary.
HANGARS : T2-2;B1-1.

HARDSTANDINGS : Spectacle-36.

	OFFICERS	S.N.C.O′s.	O.R′s.	TOTAL
R.A.F.	100.	296.	1189.	1585.
W.A.A.F.	10.	24.	312.	346.

AFFILIATED AIRFIELDS : Binbrook[12 Base]

PRESENT USE [1985] : Agriculture.

NO: 322.

AIRFIELD NAME: KEMBLE.
COUNTY : Gloucestershire.
COMMAND : Transport.
FORMATION : 116 Wing[Hendon]
FUNCTION : Parent.

OPENED : 1938.
CLOSED : 1984.

GRID REF: P 407173[104]
O.S.REF.: ST 960965.

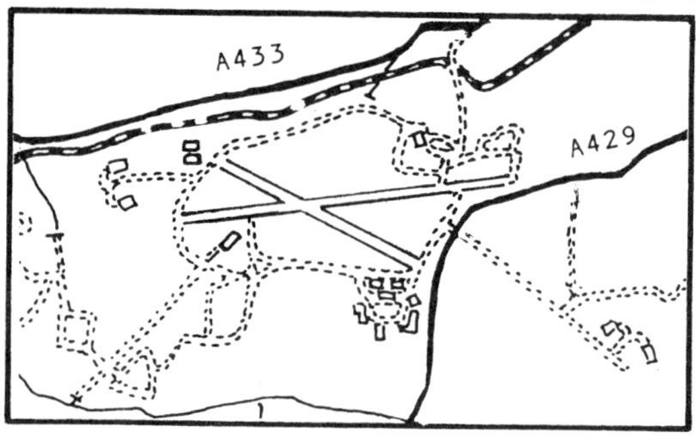

LOCALITY : 4.5miles SW of Cirencester.
RAILWAY STN. : Kemble 2miles[GWR]

LATITUDE : 51 40 00N. HEIGHT ASL : 425′ LIGHTING : None.
LONGITUDE : 02 03 15W. FLYING CONTROL : Yes. RADIO : QDM.

LANDMARKS DAY. : -

LANDMARKS NIGHT : -

OBSTRUCTIONS : -

LANDING AREA SURFACE : Concrete covered with asphalt.

QDM: 270. LENGTH X WIDTH: 2000 x 50yds.EXT. TO: 3000yds.
: 320. : 1300 x 50yds. : -
: : : 1400yds.
: : :

EXTENSIBILITY : –

ACCOMMODATION : Permanent.
HANGARS : Types:C-1;D-4;E-2;L-4;T2-2;Lammella-4; Robin-8;Super Robin-4;blister-2.
HARDSTANDINGS : Spectacle-20.

	OFFICERS	S.N.C.O′s.	O.R′s.	TOTAL
R.A.F.	36.	89.	897.	1022.
W.A.A.F.	4.	6.	166.	176.

AFFILIATED AIRFIELDS : -

PRESENT USE [1985] : Disused.

NO: 323.

AIRFIELD NAME: KENLEY.
COUNTY : Surrey.
COMMAND : Fighter.
FORMATION : 11 Grp[Uxbridge]
FUNCTION : Forward Airfield.

OPENED : 1917.
CLOSED :

GRID REF: Q 774769[115]
O.S.REF.: TQ 328580.

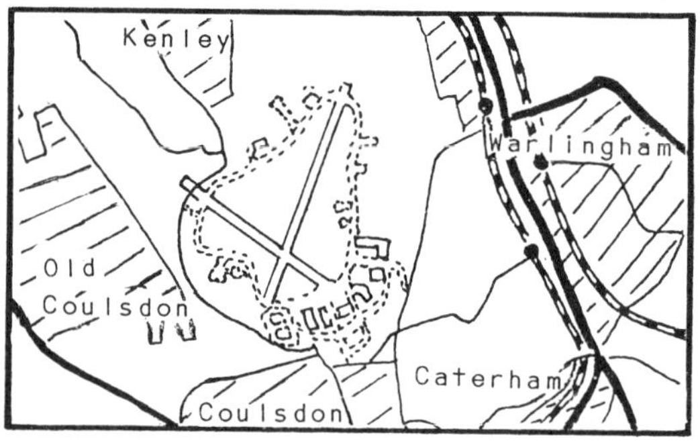

LOCALITY : 4miles S of Croydon.
RAILWAY STN. : Whyteleafe 1mile[SR]

LATITUDE : 51 18 15N. HEIGHT ASL : 557′ LIGHTING : None.
LONGITUDE : 00 05 18W. FLYING CONTROL : Yes. RADIO : QDM.

LANDMARKS DAY. : Chalk pits 5miles to SE.

LANDMARKS NIGHT : -

OBSTRUCTIONS : -

LANDING AREA SURFACE : Concrete.

QDM: 212. LENGTH X WIDTH: 1200 x 50yds.EXT. TO: 1285yds.
: 312. : 1000 x 50yds. : -
: : :
: : :

EXTENSIBILITY : -

ACCOMMODATION : Permanent.
HANGARS : Belfast Truss[2 bay]-1;blister:O-4;EO-4.

HARDSTANDINGS : SE-18.

	OFFICERS	S.N.C.O′s.	O.R′s.	TOTAL
R.A.F.	142.	2.	478.	622.
W.A.A.F.	-	3.	122.	125.

AFFILIATED AIRFIELDS : Biggin Hill[Sector]

PRESENT USE [1985] : Army.

NO: 324.

AIRFIELD NAME: KIDDINGTON.
COUNTY : Oxfordshire.
COMMAND : Flying Training.
FORMATION : 23 Grp[South Cerney]
FUNCTION : Advanced Flying Unit. [RLG]

OPENED : 1940.
CLOSED : 1945.

GRID REF: P 885430[94]
O.S.REF.: SP 424230.

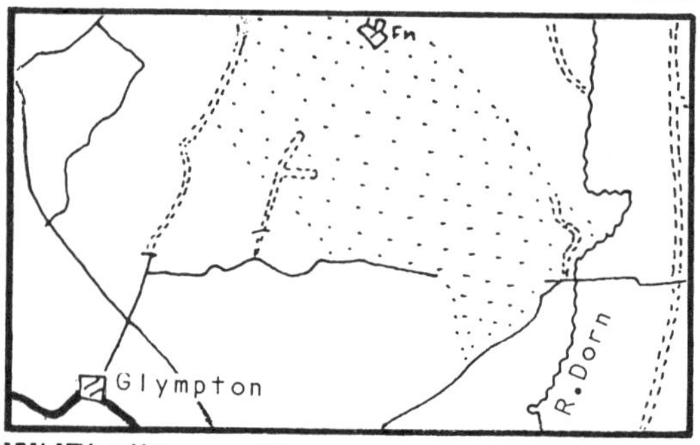

LOCALITY : 9miles NW of Oxford.
RAILWAY STN. : Woodstock 6miles[GWR]

LATITUDE : 51 54 15N. HEIGHT ASL : 450′ LIGHTING : None.
LONGITUDE : 01 22 00W. FLYING CONTROL : None.RADIO : QDM.

LANDMARKS DAY. : Cement wks. chimney 4miles SE.

LANDMARKS NIGHT : Blenheim Palace 4.5miles S.

OBSTRUCTIONS : Depression 300′N of S boundary. Ground slopes away very steeply for last 200yds. at N end.

LANDING AREA SURFACE : Grass.

QDM: N-S. LENGTH X WIDTH: 1026yds. EXT. TO: -
: : :
: : :
: : :

EXTENSIBILITY : None possible.

ACCOMMODATION : -
HANGARS : -

HARDSTANDINGS : -

	OFFICERS	S.N.C.O′s.	O.R′s.	TOTAL
R.A.F.	-	-	-	-
W.A.A.F.	-	-	-	-

AFFILIATED AIRFIELDS : Kidlington[Parent]

PRESENT USE [1985] : Parkland.

AIRFIELD NAME: KIDLINGTON. OPENED : 1938.
COUNTY : Oxfordshire. CLOSED :
COMMAND : Flying Training.
FORMATION : 23 Grp[South Cerney] GRID REF: P 913359[94]
FUNCTION : Advanced Flying Unit. O.S.REF.: SP 468156.

LOCALITY : 5miles N of Oxford.
RAILWAY STN. : Kidlington .5miles[GWR]

LATITUDE : 51 50 00N. HEIGHT ASL : 272′ LIGHTING : None.
LONGITUDE : 01 19 00W. FLYING CONTROL : None.RADIO : QDM.

LANDMARKS DAY. : Lake at Woodstock 2miles W. Cement wks 1.5miles N.

LANDMARKS NIGHT : As above in moonlight.

OBSTRUCTIONS : -

LANDING AREA SURFACE : Steel Matting[Army track]

QDM	LENGTH X WIDTH	EXT. TO
024.	1140yds.	2000yds.
351.	1140yds.	2500yds.
286.	1312yds.	1400yds.

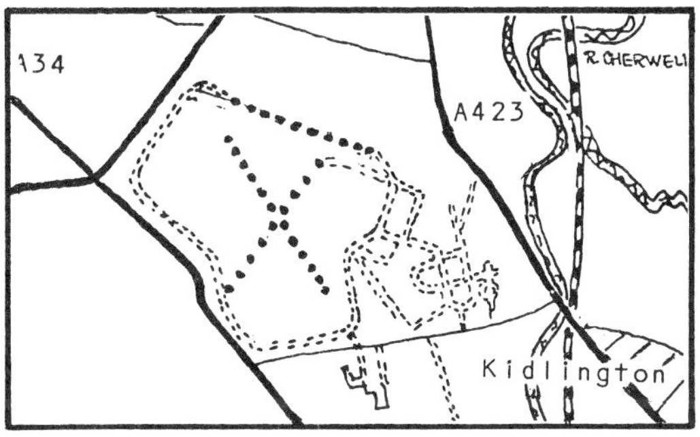

EXTENSIBILITY : Entails diversion of a main & 2 minor roads, also demolition of a cottage.
ACCOMMODATION : Temporary.
HANGARS : Bellman-7;Horace-1;65′ blister-10.

HARDSTANDINGS : Rectangular-4.

R.A.F. : OFFICERS: 140.S.N.C.O′s.: 310.O.R′s.: 980.TOTAL: 1430.
W.A.A.F.: " : 8. " : 6. " : 454. " : 468.

AFFILIATED AIRFIELDS : Croughton & Weston-on-the-Green[Satellites]

PRESENT USE [1985] : Civil Airport[Oxford]

AIRFIELD NAME: KIMBOLTON. OPENED : 1941.
COUNTY : Huntingdonshire. CLOSED : 1946.
COMMAND : 8th USAAF.
FORMATION : 379th Bomb Grp. GRID REF: L 555893[74]
FUNCTION : Operational. O.S.REF.: TL 102701.

LOCALITY : 8miles W of Huntingdon.
RAILWAY STN. : Kimbolton 5miles[LMS]

LATITUDE : 52 19 00N. HEIGHT ASL : 241′ LIGHTING : Mk2.
LONGITUDE : 00 23 00W. FLYING CONTROL : Yes. RADIO : QDM.

LANDMARKS DAY. : LMS railway[Kettering-Thrapston-Huntingdon branch]

LANDMARKS NIGHT : -

OBSTRUCTIONS : -

LANDING AREA SURFACE : Concrete covered with asphalt.

QDM	LENGTH X WIDTH	EXT. TO
330.	2000 x 50yds.	4000yds.
210.	1400 x 50yds.	-
270.	1400 x 50yds.	-

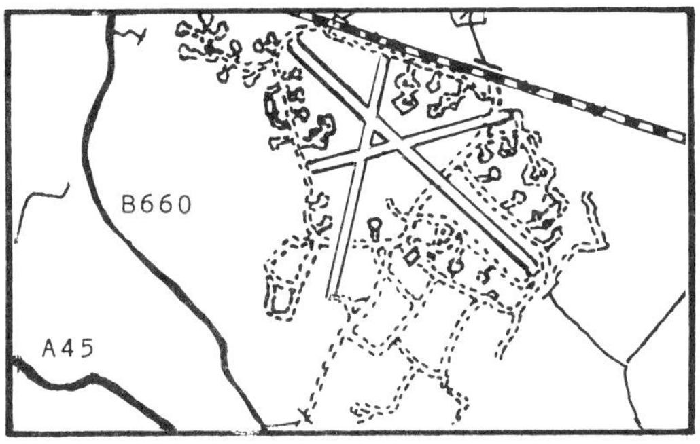

EXTENSIBILITY : Entails demolition of a farm & villa & closure of a minor road.
ACCOMMODATION : Temporary.
HANGARS : T2-2.

HARDSTANDINGS : Loop-50.

USAAF.: OFFICERS: 421. Enlisted Men. : 2473.TOTAL: 2894.

AFFILIATED AIRFIELDS : -

PRESENT USE [1985] : Agriculture.

AIRFIELD NAME: KINGSCLIFFE. OPENED : 1941.
COUNTY : Northamptonshire. CLOSED : 1959.
COMMAND : 8th USAAF.
FORMATION : 20th Fighter Grp. GRID REF: F 485172[64]
FUNCTION : Operational. O.S.REF.: TL 028978.

LOCALITY : 12miles W of Peterborough.
RAILWAY STN. : Kingscliffe 1mile[LMS]

LATITUDE : 52 34 00N. HEIGHT ASL : 251′ LIGHTING : Mk2.
LONGITUDE : 00 29 15W. FLYING CONTROL : Yes. RADIO : QDM.

LANDMARKS DAY. : Ketton cement wks. NE. Railway to S of A/F R Nene S.

LANDMARKS NIGHT : Obstruction light on Ketton cement wks.

OBSTRUCTIONS : Control tower & farmhouse adjacent to R/W 260[marked by obstruction lights controlled by tower]

LANDING AREA SURFACE : Unspecified Hard surface.

QDM	LENGTH X WIDTH	EXT. TO
260.	1700 x 50yds.	1800yds.
210.	1325 x 50yds.	2000yds.
350.	1100 x 50yds.	1260yds.

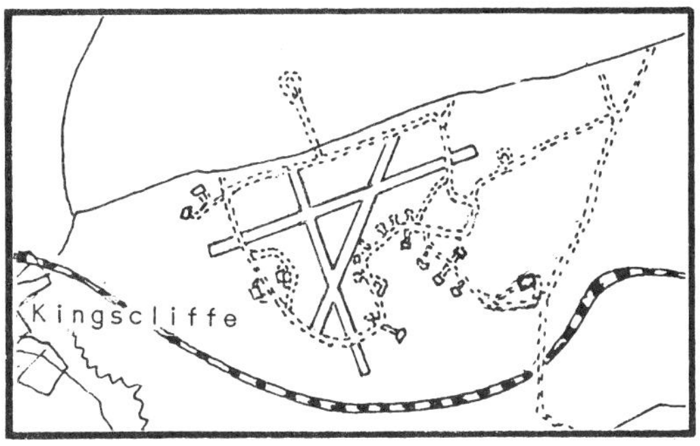

EXTENSIBILITY : Entails closure of main E-W road to N of A/F & demolition of a farm.
ACCOMMODATION : Temporary.
HANGARS : T2-2;blister-4;"55"special-8.

HARDSTANDINGS : Cement-11;single pierced steel-14; revetments-13.

USAAF.: OFFICERS: 151. Enlisted Men. : 1267.TOTAL: 1418.

AFFILIATED AIRFIELDS : -

PRESENT USE [1985] : Agriculture.

NO: 328.

AIRFIELD NAME: KINGSNORTH. OPENED : 1943.
COUNTY : Kent. CLOSED : 1945.
COMMAND : Fighter.
FORMATION : 11 Grp[Uxbridge] GRID REF: R 463560[126]
FUNCTION : Advanced Landing Ground. O.S.REF.: TR 025381.
[De-requisitioned]
LOCALITY : 2miles S of Ashford.
RAILWAY STN. : Ashford[SR]

LATITUDE : 51 06 12N. HEIGHT ASL : 125' LIGHTING : None.
LONGITUDE : 00 53 30E FLYING CONTROL : None.RADIO : QDM.

LANDMARKS DAY. : Large wood 1mile S of Ashford.

LANDMARKS NIGHT : -

OBSTRUCTIONS : -

LANDING AREA SURFACE : Steel Matting[Pierced planking & Sommerfeld track]
QDM: 130. LENGTH X WIDTH: 1500yds. EXT. TO: -
: 040. : 1575yds. :

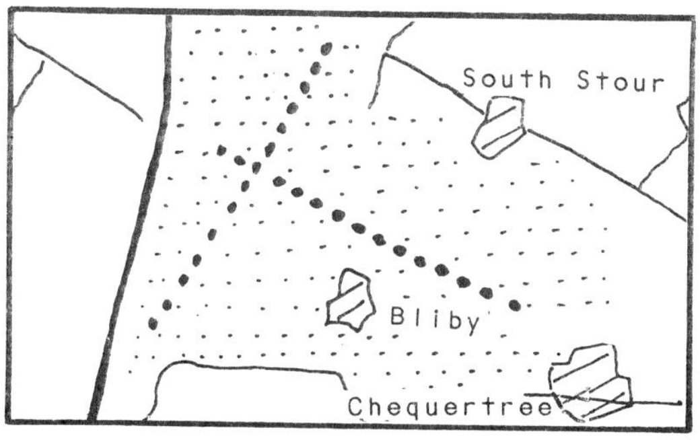

EXTENSIBILITY : -

ACCOMMODATION : Tented camp.
HANGARS : -

HARDSTANDINGS : Sommerfeld track-70.

R.A.F. : OFFICERS: - S.N.C.O's.: - O.R's.: - TOTAL: -
W.A.A.F.: " : - " : - " : - " : -

AFFILIATED AIRFIELDS : -

PRESENT USE [1985] : Agriculture.

NO: 329.

AIRFIELD NAME: KINGSTON BAGPUIZE. OPENED : 1942.
COUNTY : Berkshire. CLOSED : 1954.
COMMAND : Fighter.
FORMATION : 12 Grp[Watnall] GRID REF: P 856175[105]
FUNCTION : Operational Training Unit[satellite] O.S.REF.: SU 410974.
LOCALITY : 5miles W of Abingdon.
RAILWAY STN. : Abingdon[GWR]

LATITUDE : 51 40 15N. HEIGHT ASL : 300' LIGHTING : None.
LONGITUDE : 01 24 30W. FLYING CONTROL : None.RADIO : QDM.

LANDMARKS DAY. : -

LANDMARKS NIGHT : -

OBSTRUCTIONS : A/F buildings on E side. HT electrical power wires NE of A/F .25miles from perimeter.

LANDING AREA SURFACE : Steel Matting[Pierced steel planking]
QDM: 020. LENGTH X WIDTH: 2000 x 50yds.EXT. TO: 2400yds.
: 080. : 1400 x 50yds. : 2000yds.
: : : 2000yds.

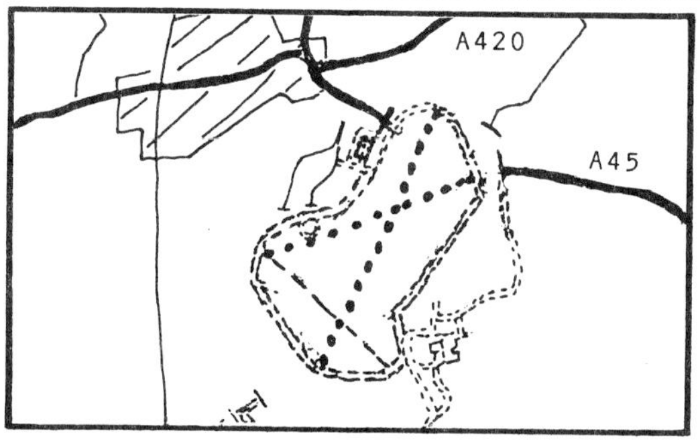

EXTENSIBILITY : Entails closure or diversion of minor roads only.
ACCOMMODATION : Temporary.
HANGARS : Butler-2;T2-2;blisters:large-2;small-1.

HARDSTANDINGS : Pierced steel planking-50.

R.A.F. : OFFICERS: 26. S.N.C.O's.: 54.O.R's.: 585.TOTAL: 667.
W.A.A.F.: " : 1. " : 4. " : 60. " : 65.

AFFILIATED AIRFIELDS : Harwell[Parent]

PRESENT USE [1985] : Disused.

NO: 330.

AIRFIELD NAME: KINLOSS. OPENED : 1939.
COUNTY : Morrayshire. CLOSED :
COMMAND : Bomber.
FORMATION : 91 Grp[Abingdon] GRID REF: J 585844[28Scot]
FUNCTION : Operational Training Unit. O.S.REF.: NJ 065536.
LOCALITY : 9miles W of Elgin.
RAILWAY STN. : Kinloss 1.5miles[LMS]

LATITUDE : 57 38 45N. HEIGHT ASL : 19' LIGHTING : Mk2.
LONGITUDE : 03 33 45N. FLYING CONTROL : Yes. RADIO : QDM.

LANDMARKS DAY. : Coast & Findhorn bay N & NW.

LANDMARKS NIGHT : As day.

OBSTRUCTIONS : BBC masts 670' 5miles NE. Hills 1000-1200' 6miles S & SE.

LANDING AREA SURFACE : Concrete & tarmac.
QDM: 263. LENGTH X WIDTH: 2000 x 50yds.EXT. TO: 5000yds.
: 208. : 1400 x 50yds. : 2600yds.
: 321. : 1400 x 50yds. : 2000yds.

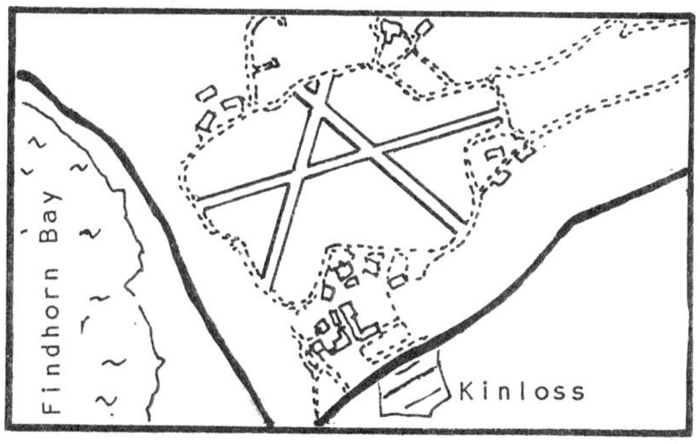

EXTENSIBILITY : Entails slight demolition.

ACCOMMODATION : Permanent[part]
HANGARS : Type L-9;Type K-2;Bellman-2.

HARDSTANDINGS : Heavy bomber-42.

R.A.F. : OFFICERS: 147.S.N.C.O's.: 527.O.R's.: 1711.TOTAL: 2385.
W.A.A.F.: " : 16. " : 10. " : 528. " : 554.

AFFILIATED AIRFIELDS : -

PRESENT USE [1985] : RAF.

NO: 331.

AIRFIELD NAME: KINNELL.
COUNTY : Angus.
COMMAND : Flying Training.
FORMATION : 21 Grp[Spittlegate]
FUNCTION : Flying Instructors School[satellite]
LOCALITY : 5.5miles S of Brechin.
RAILWAY STN. : Glasterlaw 1mile[LMS]

OPENED : 1942.
CLOSED : 1945.
GRID REF: P 118724[58Scot]
O.S.REF.: NO 610510.

LATITUDE : 56 39 00N. HEIGHT ASL : 150′ LIGHTING : Mk2.
LONGITUDE : 02 38 15W. FLYING CONTROL : Yes. RADIO : QDM.

LANDMARKS DAY : -

LANDMARKS NIGHT : -

OBSTRUCTIONS : -

LANDING AREA SURFACE : Asphalt.

QDM	LENGTH X WIDTH	EXT. TO
153.	1400 x 50yds.	1700yds.
108.	1100 x 50yds.	-

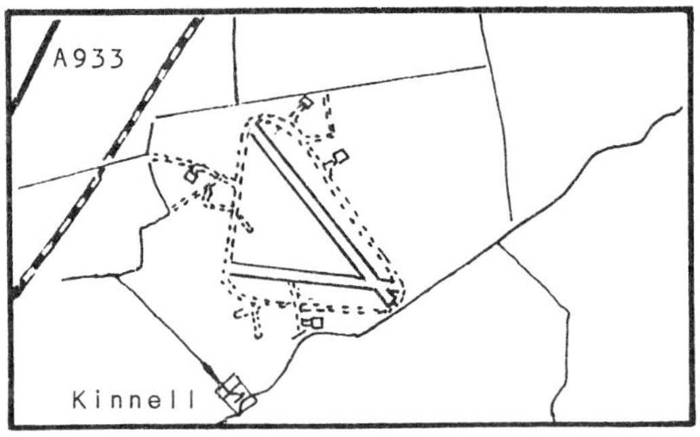

EXTENSIBILITY : Entails slight demolition.

ACCOMMODATION : EO blister-4.
HANGARS : -

HARDSTANDINGS : 25.

	OFFICERS	S.N.C.O′s.	O.R′s.	TOTAL
R.A.F.	26.	56.	585.	667.
W.A.A.F.	1.	4.	60.	65.

AFFILIATED AIRFIELDS : Montrose[Parent]

PRESENT USE [1985] : Agriculture.

NO: 332.

AIRFIELD NAME: KIRKBRIDE.
COUNTY : Cumberland.
COMMAND : Maintenance.
FORMATION : 41 Grp[Andover]
FUNCTION : Parent.

OPENED : 1939.
CLOSED : 1960.
GRID REF: Y 713764[9]
O.S.REF.: NY 229548.

LOCALITY : 12miles W of Carlisle.
RAILWAY STN. : Kirkbride 2miles[LNER]

LATITUDE : 54 52 45N. HEIGHT ASL : 28′ LIGHTING : None.
LONGITUDE : 03 12 15W. FLYING CONTROL : Yes. RADIO : QDM.

LANDMARKS DAY : Skiddaw 15miles S. Cappell 18miles W. Solway Firth Moss S & W.

LANDMARKS NIGHT : Solway Firth Dampole estuary 3miles W by N.

OBSTRUCTIONS : Airfield buildings. 5 radio masts 105′high 1mile from NW boundary. This A/F is scheduled as totally unfit for night flying.

LANDING AREA SURFACE : Concrete & tarmac.

QDM	LENGTH X WIDTH	EXT. TO
281.	1400 x 50yds.	-
232.	1000 x 50yds.	1500yds.
165.	1250 x 50yds.	1900yds.

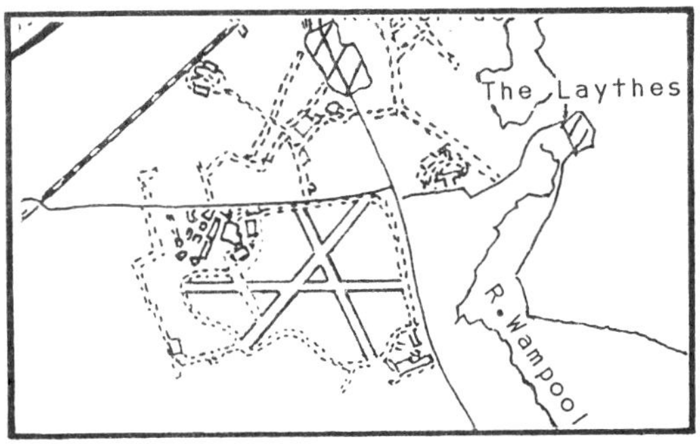

EXTENSIBILITY : Entails diversion of 2 secondary roads.

ACCOMMODATION : Permanent[part]
HANGARS : Types D-4;C-1;E-6;L-4;Robin-23.

HARDSTANDINGS : Gridiron-20;pancake-1;8 dispersal areas with a total of 94 rectangular hardstandings.

	OFFICERS	S.N.C.O′s.	O.R′s.	TOTAL
R.A.F.	-	10.	226.	236.
W.A.A.F.	-	-	-	-

AFFILIATED AIRFIELDS : -

PRESENT USE [1985] : Private flying.

NO: 333.

AIRFIELD NAME: KIRKISTOWN.
COUNTY : Down NI.
COMMAND : RAF NI.
FORMATION : Stormont[Belfast]
FUNCTION : Care & Maintenance.

OPENED : 1941.
CLOSED : 1952.
GRID REF: J 642588[321NI]
O.S.REF.: J 645595.

LOCALITY : 2.5miles S of Ballyhalbert.
RAILWAY STN. : Newtownards[B & CDR]

LATITUDE : 54 27 03N. HEIGHT ASL : 20′ LIGHTING : None.
LONGITUDE : 05 27 53W. FLYING CONTROL : None. RADIO : QDM.

LANDMARKS DAY : Strangford Lough. A/F situated on peninsular E of same.

LANDMARKS NIGHT : As above in moonlight conditions.

OBSTRUCTIONS : -

LANDING AREA SURFACE : Tarmac.

QDM	LENGTH X WIDTH	EXT. TO
222.	1300 x 50yds.	1320yds.
280.	1160 x 50yds.	-
341.	1000 x 50yds.	1700yds.

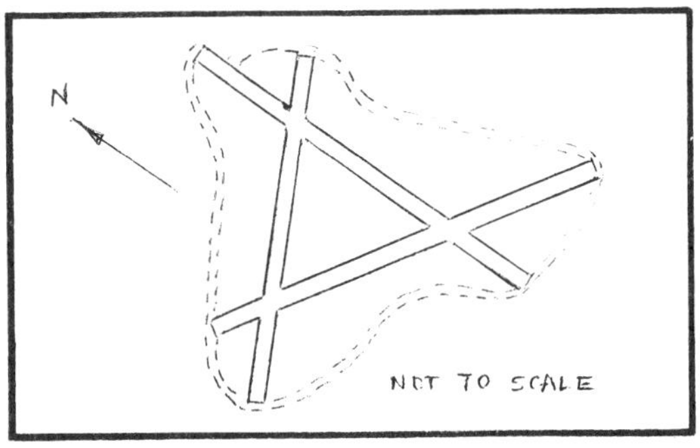

EXTENSIBILITY : -

ACCOMMODATION : Temporary.
HANGARS : Blister-4.

HARDSTANDINGS : Frying pan[fighter]-34;double dispersal pens-6.

	OFFICERS	S.N.C.O′s.	O.R′s.	TOTAL
R.A.F.	136.	168.	1015.	1319.
W.A.A.F.	-	-	-	-

AFFILIATED AIRFIELDS : -

PRESENT USE [1985] : Recreation.

NO: 334.

AIRFIELD NAME: KIRKNEWTON.
COUNTY : Midlothian.
COMMAND : Maintenance.
FORMATION : 42 Grp[Reading]
FUNCTION : Storage Unit.

OPENED : 1941.
CLOSED : 1952.

GRID REF: T 621871[73Scot]
O.S.REF.: NT 125655.

LOCALITY : 9miles SW of Edinburgh.
RAILWAY STN. : Mid Calder[LMS]

LATITUDE : 55 52 27N. HEIGHT ASL : 652′ LIGHTING : None.
LONGITUDE : 03 24 00W. FLYING CONTROL : None.RADIO : QDM.

LANDMARKS DAY. : Kaimes Hill. Harperrig & Cobbinshaw reservoirs.

LANDMARKS NIGHT : -

OBSTRUCTIONS : Kaimes Hill 400′ 800yds. NE. Stacked bombs on R/W.

LANDING AREA SURFACE : Tarmac.

QDM	LENGTH X WIDTH	EXT. TO
182.	1100 x 50yds.	-
060.	1100 x 50yds.	-
002.	945 x 50yds.	-

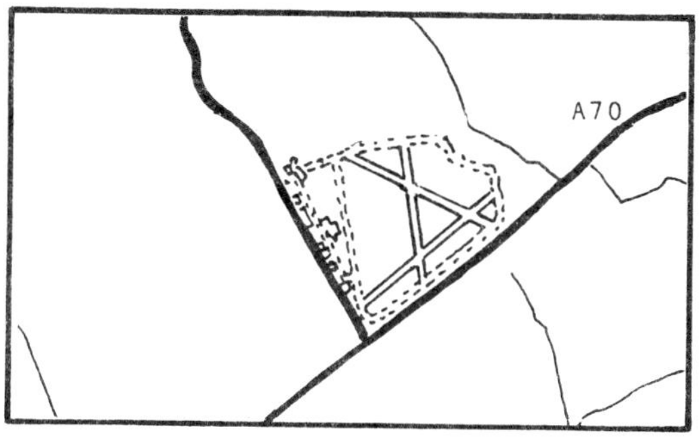

EXTENSIBILITY : -

ACCOMMODATION : Temporary.
HANGARS : Bellman-1;Blister-4.

HARDSTANDINGS : -

	OFFICERS	S.N.C.O′s.	O.R′s.	TOTAL
R.A.F.	2.	10.	156.	168.
W.A.A.F.	-	-	-	-

AFFILIATED AIRFIELDS : -

PRESENT USE [1985] : Gliding.

NO: 335.

AIRFIELD NAME: KIRKPATRICK.
COUNTY : Dumfriesshire.
COMMAND : Flying Training.
FORMATION : 51 Grp[Leeds]
FUNCTION : Elementary Flying Training School[RLG]

OPENED : 1940.
CLOSED : 1945.

GRID REF: Y 741916[89Scot]
O.S.REF.: NY 255702.

LOCALITY : 13miles NW of Carlisle.
RAILWAY STN. : Kirkpatrick 2miles[LMS]

LATITUDE : 55 01 15N. HEIGHT ASL : 150′ LIGHTING : None.
LONGITUDE : 03 10 15W. FLYING CONTROL : None.RADIO : QDM.

LANDMARKS DAY. : Solway area.

LANDMARKS NIGHT : -

OBSTRUCTIONS : -

LANDING AREA SURFACE : Grass.

QDM	LENGTH X WIDTH	EXT. TO
NW-SE.	1200yds.	1400yds.
SW-NE.	1200yds.	-

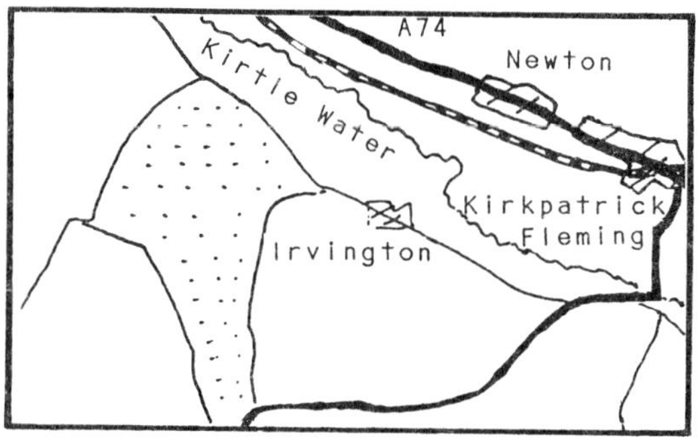

EXTENSIBILITY : -

ACCOMMODATION : Temporary.
HANGARS : Blisters:standard-3;EO-2.

HARDSTANDINGS : -

	OFFICERS	S.N.C.O′s.	O.R′s.	TOTAL
R.A.F.	2.	4.	120.	126.
W.A.A.F.	-	-	-	-

AFFILIATED AIRFIELDS : Carlisle[Parent]

PRESENT USE [1985] : Disused.

NO: 336.

AIRFIELD NAME: KIRMINGTON.
COUNTY : Lincolnshire.
COMMAND : Bomber.
FORMATION : 1 Grp[Bawtry]
FUNCTION : Operational.

OPENED : 1942.
CLOSED :

GRID REF: A 565298[39]
O.S.REF.: TA 095103.

LOCALITY : 6miles NE of Brigg.
RAILWAY STN. : Barnetby 3miles[LNER]

LATITUDE : 53 34 45N. HEIGHT ASL : 86′ LIGHTING : Mk2.
LONGITUDE : 00 20 45W. FLYING CONTROL : Yes. RADIO : QDM.

LANDMARKS DAY. : Humber. Village church spire[Green spire]

LANDMARKS NIGHT : Humber.

OBSTRUCTIONS : -

LANDING AREA SURFACE : Concrete & tarmac.

QDM	LENGTH X WIDTH	EXT. TO
217.	2000 x 50yds.	2500yds.
326.	1400 x 50yds.	1800yds.
272.	1400 x 50yds.	-

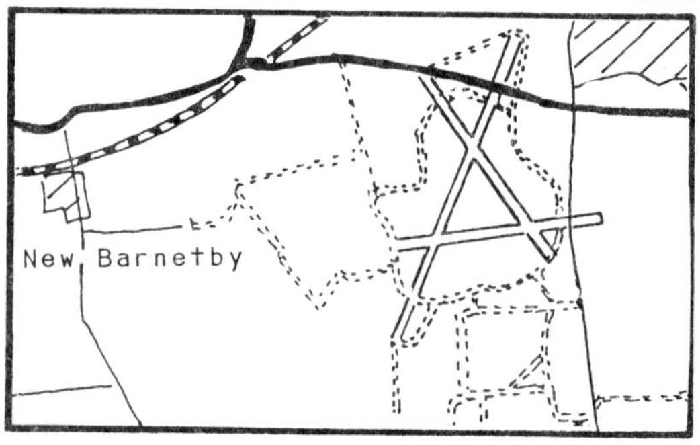

EXTENSIBILITY : Entails dversion of Brigg-Grimsby road. [which is already controlled.

ACCOMMODATION : Temporary.
HANGARS : T2-2;B1-1.

HARDSTANDINGS : Heavy bomber-36.

	OFFICERS	S.N.C.O′s.	O.R′s.	TOTAL
R.A.F.	162.	332.	940.	1434.
W.A.A.F.	6.	12.	192.	210.

AFFILIATED AIRFIELDS : Elsham Wolds[13 Base]

PRESENT USE [1985] : Civil Airport[Humberside]

AIRFIELD NAME: KIRTON-in-LINDSEY. OPENED : 1940.
COUNTY : Lincolnshire. CLOSED :
COMMAND : Fighter.
FORMATION : 12 Grp[Watnall] GRID REF: A 414166[39]
FUNCTION : Operational Training Unit. O.S.REF.: SK 945972.
LOCALITY : 16miles N of Lincoln.
RAILWAY STN. : Kirton-in-Lindsey 1.5miles[LNER]

LATITUDE : 53 27 45N. HEIGHT ASL : 200′ LIGHTING : None.
LONGITUDE : 00 34 30W. FLYING CONTROL : Yes. RADIO : QDM.

LANDMARKS DAY. : Cement wks 2.5miles 24degrees.

LANDMARKS NIGHT : -

OBSTRUCTIONS : -

LANDING AREA : Grass.
SURFACE :
QDM: N-S. LENGTH X WIDTH: 1100yds. EXT. TO: 2000yds.
: E-W. : 1100yds. : 1800yds.

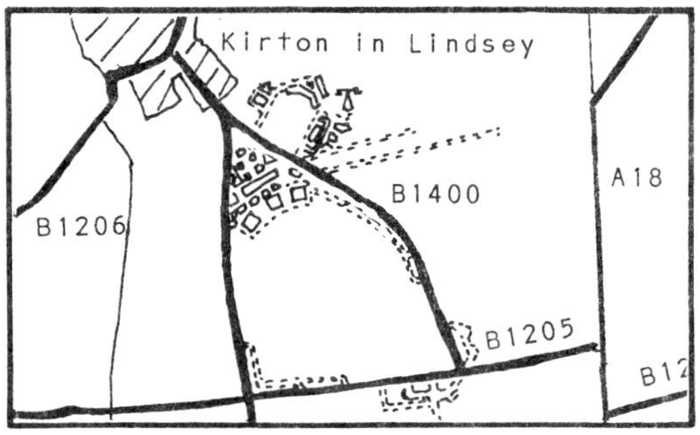

EXTENSIBILITY : -

ACCOMMODATION : Permanent.
HANGARS : Type C[225′]-3;Overblister-4.

HARDSTANDINGS : 10.

R.A.F. : OFFICERS: 89.S.N.C.O′s.: 102.O.R′s.: 1146.TOTAL: 1337.
W.A.A.F.: " : 10. " : 9. " : 512. " : 531.

AFFILIATED AIRFIELDS : Hibaldstow[Satellite]

PRESENT USE [1985] : Army.

NO: 338.

AIRFIELD NAME: KNETTISHALL. OPENED : 1943.
COUNTY : Suffolk. CLOSED : 1957.
COMMAND : 8th USAAF.
FORMATION : 388th Bomb Grp. GRID REF: M 424976[76]
FUNCTION : Operational. O.S.REF.: TL 968795.

LOCALITY : 6miles SE of Thetford.
RAILWAY STN. : Harling Road[LNER]

LATITUDE : 52 22 30N. HEIGHT ASL : 130′ LIGHTING : Mk2.
LONGITUDE : 00 53 30E. FLYING CONTROL : Yes. RADIO : QDM.

LANDMARKS DAY. : St Mary church Coney Weston.

LANDMARKS NIGHT : -

OBSTRUCTIONS : -

LANDING AREA : Concrete & wood chippings.
SURFACE :
QDM: 220. LENGTH X WIDTH: 2000 x 50yds.EXT. TO: 3800yds.
: 270. : 1400 x 50yds. : 1650yds.
: 330. : 1400 x 50yds. : 1650yds.

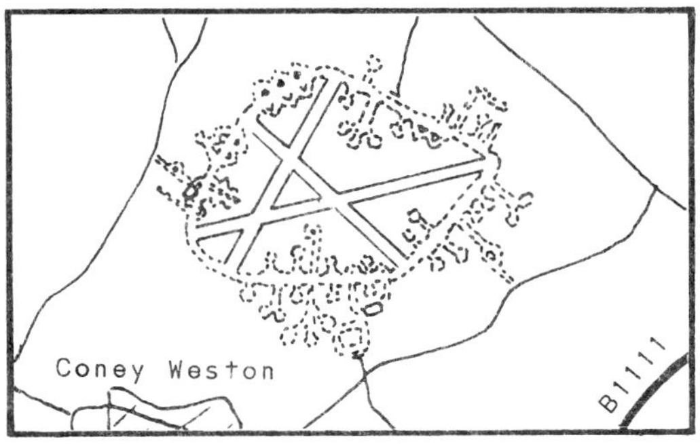

EXTENSIBILITY : -

ACCOMMODATION : Temporary.
HANGARS : T2-1.

HARDSTANDINGS : Loop-50.

USAAF. : OFFICERS: 421. Enlisted Men. : 2473.TOTAL: 2894.

AFFILIATED AIRFIELDS : -

PRESENT USE [1985] : Disused.

NO: 339.

AIRFIELD NAME: LAKENHEATH. OPENED : 1941.
COUNTY : Suffolk. CLOSED :
COMMAND : Bomber.
FORMATION : Under re-construction. GRID REF: G 192000[76]
FUNCTION : Under re-construction. O.S.REF.: TL 740820.

LOCALITY : 4.5miles SW of Brandon.
RAILWAY STN. : Brandon 6miles[LNER]

LATITUDE : 52 24 15N. HEIGHT ASL : 28′ LIGHTING : Mk2.
LONGITUDE : 00 33 15E. FLYING CONTROL : Yes. RADIO : QDM.

LANDMARKS DAY. : -

LANDMARKS NIGHT : -

OBSTRUCTIONS : Hill 96′ at end of SE-NW runway.

LANDING AREA : Under re-construction.
SURFACE : Concrete-estimated date of completion 8/45.
QDM: 186. LENGTH X WIDTH: 2000 x 100ydsEXT. TO: -
: 246. : 3000 x 100yds : -
: 322. : 2000 x 100yds. : 2200yds.

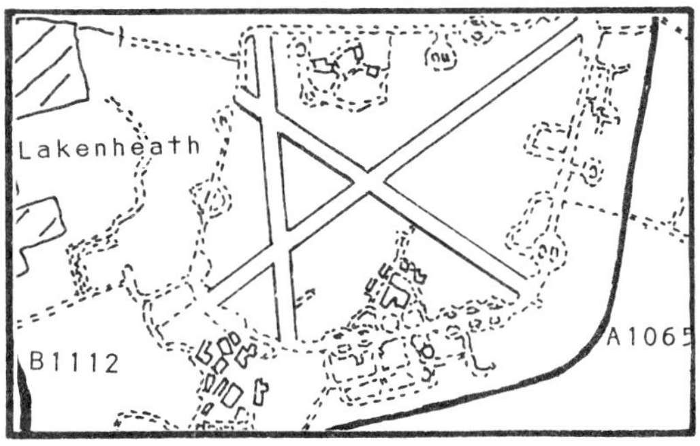

EXTENSIBILITY : Entails diversion of London-Kings Lynn road & 2 minor roads.
ACCOMMODATION : Temporary.
HANGARS : T2-2;Glider-3;B1-1.

HARDSTANDINGS : Very heavy bomber-12.

R.A.F. : OFFICERS: 144.S.N.C.O′s.: 513.O.R′s.: 1048.TOTAL: 1705.
W.A.A.F.: " : 6. " : 11. " : 228. " : 245.

AFFILIATED AIRFIELDS : -

PRESENT USE [1985] : USAFE.

NO: 340.

AIRFIELD NAME: LANGAR. OPENED : 1941.
COUNTY : Nottinghamshire. CLOSED : 1968.
COMMAND : Bomber.
FORMATION : 7 Grp[St.Vincents] GRID REF: F 200530[54]
FUNCTION : Operational. O.S.REF.: SK 740335.

LOCALITY : 9miles SE of Nottingham.
RAILWAY STN. : Harley & Stathern 3miles[LNER & LMS]

LATITUDE : 52 53 30N. HEIGHT ASL : 106. LIGHTING : Mk2.
LONGITUDE : 00 54 00W. FLYING CONTROL : Yes. RADIO : QDM.

LANDMARKS DAY. : Cement wks.

LANDMARKS NIGHT : -

OBSTRUCTIONS : Hills 400′ SE & S.

LANDING AREA SURFACE : Concrete & tarmac.

QDM: 194. LENGTH X WIDTH: 2000 x 50yds.EXT. TO: 3000yds.
: 252. : 1400 x 50yds. : 2130yds.
: 315. : 1400 x 50yds. : 1433yds.
: : :

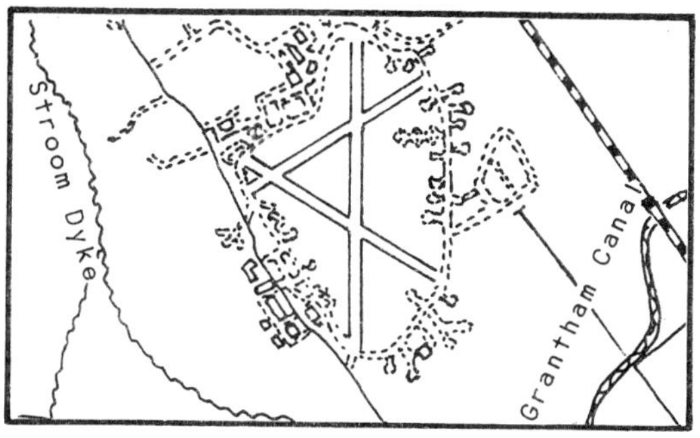

EXTENSIBILITY : Entails closure of main access road to A/F & demolition of dis-used windmill.
ACCOMMODATION : Temporary.
HANGARS : T2-2;Glider-2.

HARDSTANDINGS : Heavy bomber-50.

R.A.F. : OFFICERS: 163.S.N.C.O′s.: 342.O.R′s.: 1689.TOTAL: 2194.
W.A.A.F.: " : 3. " : 9. " : 88. " : 100.

AFFILIATED AIRFIELDS : Bottesford[72 Base]

PRESENT USE [1985] : Disused.

NO: 341.

AIRFIELD NAME: LANGFORD LODGE. OPENED : 1942.
COUNTY : Antrim NI. CLOSED : 1946.
COMMAND : USSTAFE.
FORMATION : Air Service Command. GRID REF: J 100756[313NI]
FUNCTION : 3rd Base Air Depot. O.S.REF.: J 100756.

LOCALITY : 4miles W of Crumlin.
RAILWAY STN. : Antrim[BNC]

LATITUDE : 54 37 23N. HEIGHT ASL : 100′ LIGHTING : None.
LONGITUDE : 06 18 00W. FLYING CONTROL : Yes. RADIO : QDM.

LANDMARKS DAY. : Lough Neagh & jutting peninsula.

LANDMARKS NIGHT : -

OBSTRUCTIONS : -

LANDING AREA SURFACE : Asphalt & tarmac.

QDM: 022. LENGTH X WIDTH: 2000 x 50yds.EXT. TO: 2700yds.
: 066. : 1530 x 50yds. : 2100yds.
: : :
: : :

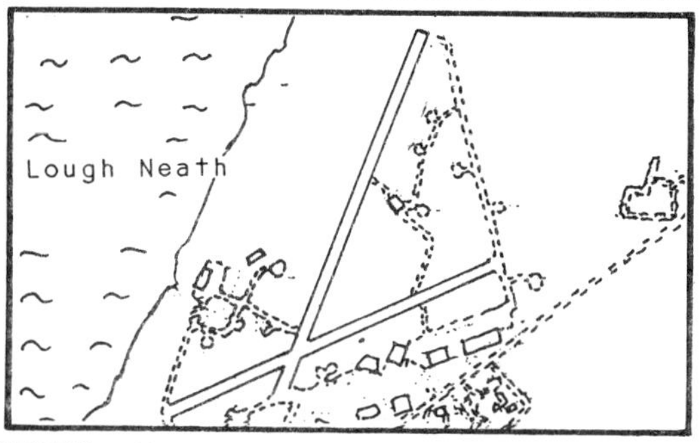

EXTENSIBILITY : Also possible new R/W of 1700yds.

ACCOMMODATION : Temporary.
HANGARS : T2[110x220′]-9;232328 sq.ft.storage.

HARDSTANDINGS : Cement-126.

USAAF. : OFFICERS: 500. ENLISTED MEN: 3000. CIVILIANS: 1500. TOTAL: 5000.

AFFILIATED AIRFIELDS : -

PRESENT USE [1985] : Unspecified.

NO: 342.

AIRFIELD NAME: LANGHAM. OPENED : 1940.
COUNTY : Norfolk. CLOSED : 1961.
COMMAND : Coastal.
FORMATION : 16 Grp[Gillingham] GRID REF: G 456605[57]
FUNCTION : Operational. O.S.REF.: TF 988420.

LOCALITY : 5.5miles NW of Holt.
RAILWAY STN. : Thursford 5miles[LNER]

LATITUDE : 52 56 23N. HEIGHT ASL : 60′ LIGHTING : Mk2.
LONGITUDE : 00 58 00E. FLYING CONTROL : Yes. RADIO : QDM.

LANDMARKS DAY. : Blakeney Point, a sand spit extending in a westerly direction from Blakeney harbour.

LANDMARKS NIGHT : -

OBSTRUCTIONS : -

LANDING AREA SURFACE : Concrete covered with tar.

QDM: 253. LENGTH X WIDTH: 2000 x 50yds.EXT. TO: 2800yds.
: 202. : 1400 x 50yds. : 1800yds.
: 305. : 1400 x 50yds. : 2400yds.
: : :
: : :

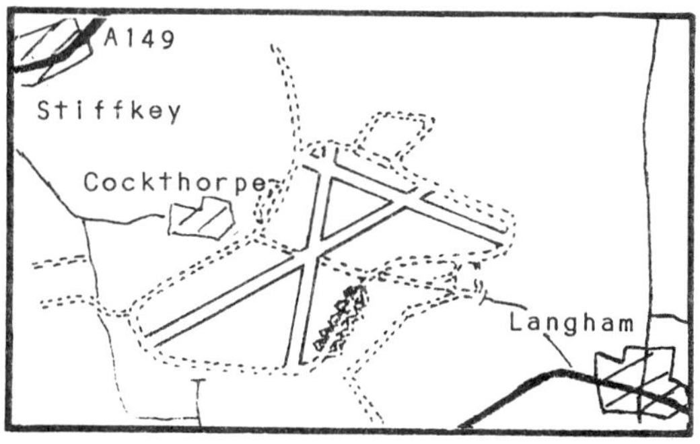

EXTENSIBILITY : Entails diversion of important minor road.

ACCOMMODATION : Temporary.
HANGARS : T2-3;blister-4.

HARDSTANDINGS : Spectacle-36.

R.A.F. : OFFICERS: 147.S.N.C.O′s.: 434.O.R′s.: 1440.TOTAL: 2021.
W.A.A.F.: " : 14. " : 20. " : 360. " : 394.

AFFILIATED AIRFIELDS : -

PRESENT USE [1985] : Agriculture.

NO: 343.

AIRFIELD NAME: LASHAM. OPENED : 1942.
COUNTY : Hampshire. CLOSED : 1948.
COMMAND : Fighter.
FORMATION : 11 Grp[Uxbridge] GRID REF: Q 118630[123]
FUNCTION : Forward Airfield. O.S.REF.: SU 675435.

LOCALITY : 6miles SSE of Basingstoke.
RAILWAY STN. : Alton 4miles[SR]

LATITUDE : 51 11 00N. HEIGHT ASL : 600′ LIGHTING : Mk2.
LONGITUDE : 01 01 45W. FLYING CONTROL : Yes. RADIO : QDM.

LANDMARKS DAY. : -

LANDMARKS NIGHT : -

OBSTRUCTIONS : -

LANDING AREA SURFACE : Concrete & wood chippings.

QDM	LENGTH X WIDTH	EXT. TO
095.	1900 x 50yds.	1960yds.
175.	1200 x 50yds.	-
063.	1400 x 50yds.	2300yds.

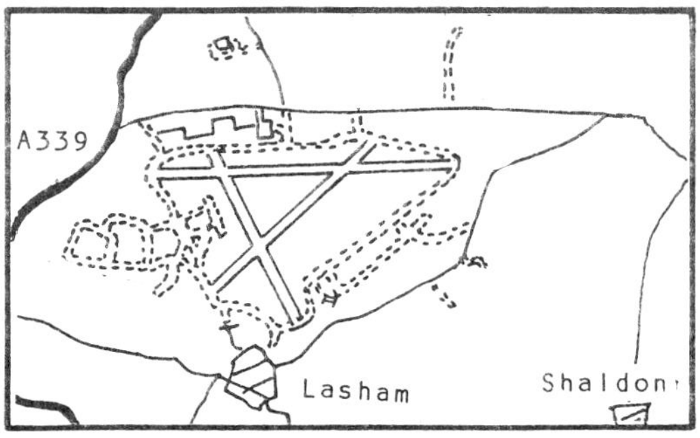

EXTENSIBILITY : Entails demolition of 3 cottages.

ACCOMMODATION : Temporary.
HANGARS : T2-4.

HARDSTANDINGS : Frypan[125′]-52.

	OFFICERS	S.N.C.O's.	O.R's.	TOTAL
R.A.F.	142.	407.	1305.	1854.
W.A.A.F.	10.	20.	390.	420.

AFFILIATED AIRFIELDS : Tangmere[Sector]

PRESENT USE [1985] : Private flying.

NO: 344.

AIRFIELD NAME: LASHENDEN. OPENED : 1943.
COUNTY : Kent. CLOSED : 1945.
COMMAND : Fighter.
FORMATION : 11 Grp[Uxbridge] GRID REF: R 294613[126]
FUNCTION : Advanced Landing Ground. [De-requisitioned] O.S.REF.: TQ 855429.
LOCALITY : 9miles SE of Maidstone.
RAILWAY STN. : Frittenden Road[SR]

LATITUDE : 51 09 15N. HEIGHT ASL : 72′ LIGHTING : None.
LONGITUDE : 00 39 00E. FLYING CONTROL : None. RADIO : None.

LANDMARKS DAY. : -

LANDMARKS NIGHT : -

OBSTRUCTIONS : -

LANDING AREA SURFACE : Steel Matting[Sommerfeld track]

QDM	LENGTH X WIDTH	EXT. TO
010.	1600yds.	-
110.	1400yds.	-

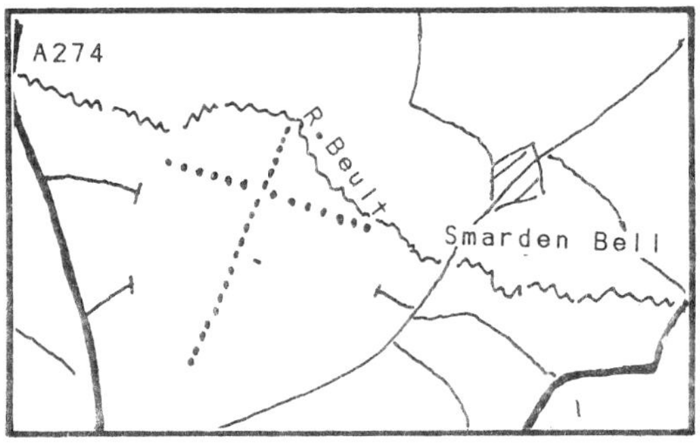

EXTENSIBILITY : -

ACCOMMODATION : Tented camp.
HANGARS : -

HARDSTANDINGS : Sommerfeld track-70.

	OFFICERS	S.N.C.O's.	O.R's.	TOTAL
R.A.F.	-	-	-	-
W.A.A.F.	-	-	-	

AFFILIATED AIRFIELDS : -

PRESENT USE [1985] : Private flying.

NO: 345.

AIRFIELD NAME: LAVENHAM. OPENED : 1943.
COUNTY : Suffolk. CLOSED : 1948.
COMMAND : 8th USAAF.
FORMATION : 487th Bomb Grp. GRID REF: M 347708[86]
FUNCTION : Operational. O.S.REF.: TL 895524.

LOCALITY : 7miles N of Sudbury.
RAILWAY STN. : Lavenham[GE]

LATITUDE : 52 08 04N. HEIGHT ASL : 290′ LIGHTING : Mk2.
LONGITUDE : 00 46 15E. FLYING CONTROL : Yes. RADIO : QDM.

LANDMARKS DAY. : Lavenham church tower 2miles SE. "A" shaped runways.

LANDMARKS NIGHT : -

OBSTRUCTIONS : -

LANDING AREA SURFACE : Concrete.

QDM	LENGTH X WIDTH	EXT. TO
270.	2000 x 50yds.	-
220.	1400 x 50yds.	-
330.	1400 x 50yds.	-

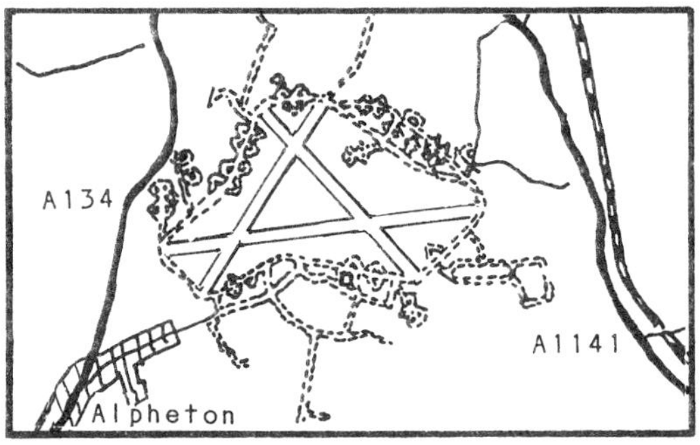

EXTENSIBILITY : None possible.

ACCOMMODATION : Temporary.
HANGARS : T2-2.

HARDSTANDINGS : Concrete-50.

USAAF. : OFFICERS: 421. Enlisted Men. : 2473. TOTAL: 2894.

AFFILIATED AIRFIELDS : -

PRESENT USE [1985] : Agriculture.

NO: 346.

AIRFIELD NAME: LECONFIELD. OPENED : 1936.
COUNTY : Yorkshire. CLOSED :
COMMAND : Bomber.
FORMATION : 4 Grp[York] GRID REF: A 502630[28]
FUNCTION : Operational. O.S.REF.: TA 030435.

LOCALITY : 2.75miles N of Beverley.
RAILWAY STN. : Beverley[LNER]

LATITUDE : 53 52 45N. HEIGHT ASL : 25′ LIGHTING : Mk2.
LONGITUDE : 00 26 00W. FLYING CONTROL : Yes. RADIO : QDM.

LANDMARKS DAY : Beverley town & Minster.

LANDMARKS NIGHT : -

OBSTRUCTIONS : -

LANDING AREA SURFACE : Concrete.

QDM	LENGTH X WIDTH	EXT. TO
190.	2000 x 50yds.	3000yds.
050.	1400 x 50yds.	2000yds.
140.	1400 x 50yds.	1600yds.

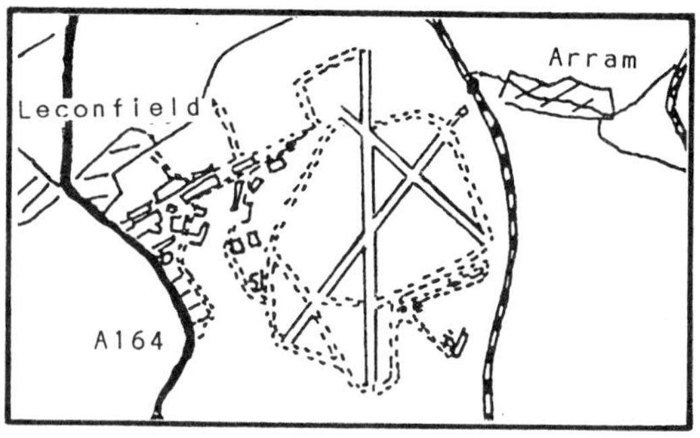

EXTENSIBILITY : Additional R/W of 1600yds possible into prevailing wind:entails demolition of a farm.
ACCOMMODATION : Permanent.
HANGARS : Type C-5.

HARDSTANDINGS : Heavy bomber-36.

	OFFICERS	S.N.C.O′s.	O.R′s.	TOTAL
R.A.F.	120.	392.	1231.	1743.
W.A.A.F.	5.	10.	234.	249.

AFFILIATED AIRFIELDS : Driffield[43 Base]

PRESENT USE [1985] : RAF.

NO: 347.

AIRFIELD NAME: LEE-on-SOLENT. OPENED : 1917.
COUNTY : Hampshire. CLOSED :
COMMAND : RN.
FORMATION : On books of Daedalus. GRID REF: U 995205[132]
FUNCTION : HQ Flag Officer NAS. O.S.REF.: SU 562020.

LOCALITY : 4miles WNW of Portsmouth.
RAILWAY STN. : Gosport 2.5miles[SR]

LATITUDE : 50 48 35N. HEIGHT ASL : 30. LIGHTING : Mk2.
LONGITUDE : 01 12 25W. FLYING CONTROL : Yes. RADIO : QDM.

LANDMARKS DAY : Isle of White 3.5miles SW.

LANDMARKS NIGHT : Coastline.

OBSTRUCTIONS : W/T masts 152′ on Horsea Island in Portsmouth Harbour 4miles ENE.

LANDING AREA SURFACE : Unspecified Hard Surface.

QDM	LENGTH X WIDTH	EXT. TO
178-358.	975 x 50yds.	-
056-236.	1420 x 50yds.	-
107-287.	1100 x 50yds.	

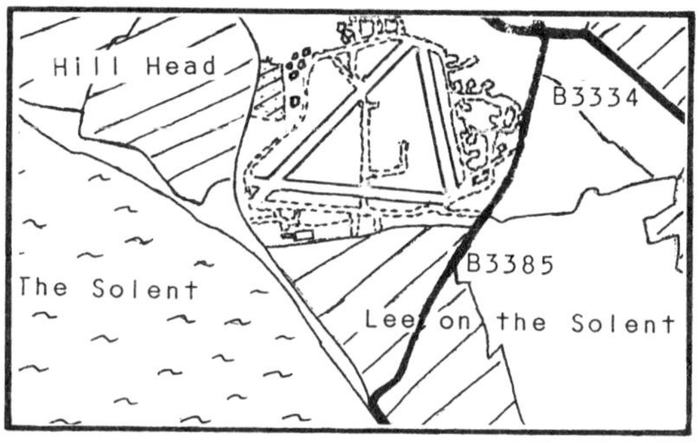

EXTENSIBILITY : -

ACCOMMODATION : Permanent[WRNS in requisitioned property in LonS]
HANGARS : Sqdn:300x150′-1;250x120′-1;Bellman 187x105′-3; Main type 60x70′-12;Fromson 60x70′-8.
HARDSTANDINGS : 12.

	OFFICERS	Chiefs/POs/Ratings.	TOTAL
R.N.	277.	4502.	4779.
W.R.N.S.	50.	892.	942.

AFFILIATED AIRFIELDS : -

PRESENT USE [1985] : RN.

NO: 348.

AIRFIELD NAME: LEEMING. OPENED : 1940.
COUNTY : Yorkshire. CLOSED :
COMMAND : Bomber.
FORMATION : 6 RCAF Grp[Allerton Pk] GRID REF: Z 780095[21]
FUNCTION : Operational[63 Base] O.S.REF.: SE 305892.

LOCALITY : 7miles SW of Northallerton.
RAILWAY STN. : Leeming Bar 2miles[LNER]

LATITUDE : 54 18 00N. HEIGHT ASL : 109′ LIGHTING : Mk2.
LONGITUDE : 01 32 00W. FLYING CONTROL : Yes. RADIO : QDM.

LANDMARKS DAY : R Swale. LNER. Gt North Road.

LANDMARKS NIGHT : -

OBSTRUCTIONS : -

LANDING AREA SURFACE : Concrete & tarmac.

QDM	LENGTH X WIDTH	EXT. TO
347.5.	1950 x 50yds.	4000yds.
220.	1650 x 50yds.	2000yds.
305.	1400 x 50yds.	2000yds.

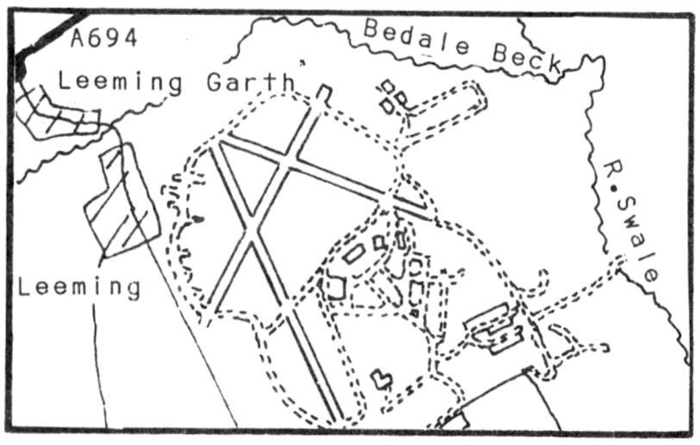

EXTENSIBILITY : 4th R/W of 2000yds possible-entails diversion of Gt North Rd for 5000yds.
ACCOMMODATION : Permanent.
HANGARS : Type C-5.

HARDSTANDINGS : Frying pan-36.

	OFFICERS	S.N.C.O′s.	O.R′s.	TOTAL
R.C.A.F.	194.	664.	1534.	2392.
W.A.A.F.	8.	10.	299.	317.

AFFILIATED AIRFIELDS : Skipton-on-Swale[Sub-station]

PRESENT USE [1985] : RAF.

NO: 349.

AIRFIELD NAME: LEICESTER EAST. OPENED : 1943.
COUNTY : Leicestershire. CLOSED :
COMMAND : Transport.
FORMATION : 46 Grp[Harrow Weald] GRID REF: F 108212[63]
FUNCTION : Operational Training Unit. O.S.REF.: SK 656015.

LOCALITY : 4miles SE of Leicester.
RAILWAY STN. : Leicester[LMS & LNER]

LATITUDE : 52 36 23N. HEIGHT ASL : 455′ LIGHTING : Mk2.
LONGITUDE : 01 02 00W. FLYING CONTROL : Yes. RADIO : QDM.

LANDMARKS DAY. : Leicester city.

LANDMARKS NIGHT : -

OBSTRUCTIONS : Haughton-on-the-Hill church steeple on approach to R/W 231.

LANDING AREA SURFACE : Concrete.

QDM	LENGTH X WIDTH	EXT. TO
107.	2000 x 50yds.	-
051.	1400 x 50yds.	-
165.	1400 x 50yds.	1500yds.

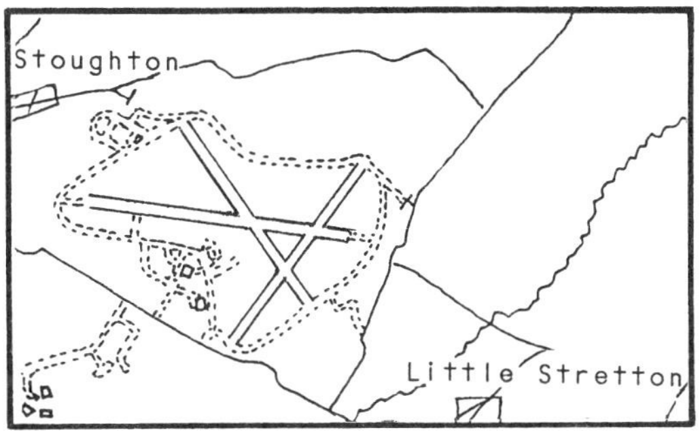

EXTENSIBILITY : Entails diversion of Roman road.

ACCOMMODATION : Temporary.
HANGARS : T2-4.

HARDSTANDINGS : Spectacle-48.

	OFFICERS	S.N.C.O′s.	O.R′s.	TOTAL
R.A.F.	116.	283.	1152.	1551.
W.A.A.F.	10.	16.	340.	366.

AFFILIATED AIRFIELDS : -

PRESENT USE [1985] : Civil Airport[Leicester]

NO: 350.

AIRFIELD NAME: LEISTON. OPENED : 1943.
COUNTY : Suffolk. CLOSED : 1953.
COMMAND : 8th USAAF.
FORMATION : 357th Fighter Grp. GRID REF: M 883821[87]
FUNCTION : Operational. O.S.REF.: TM 430645.

LOCALITY : 3miles E of Saxmundham.
RAILWAY STN. : Leiston 1mile[LNER]

LATITUDE : 52 13 23N. HEIGHT ASL : 75′ LIGHTING : Mk2.
LONGITUDE : 01 33 38E. FLYING CONTROL : Yes. RADIO : QDM.

LANDMARKS DAY. : Trees on boundary of peri track.

LANDMARKS NIGHT : -

OBSTRUCTIONS : Factory chimney at Leiston 165′high SE of A/F 3000yds.

LANDING AREA SURFACE : Concrete & tarmac.

QDM	LENGTH X WIDTH	EXT. TO
060.	2000 x 50yds.	-
130.	1400 x 50yds.	3200yds.
180.	1400 x 50yds.	2000yds.

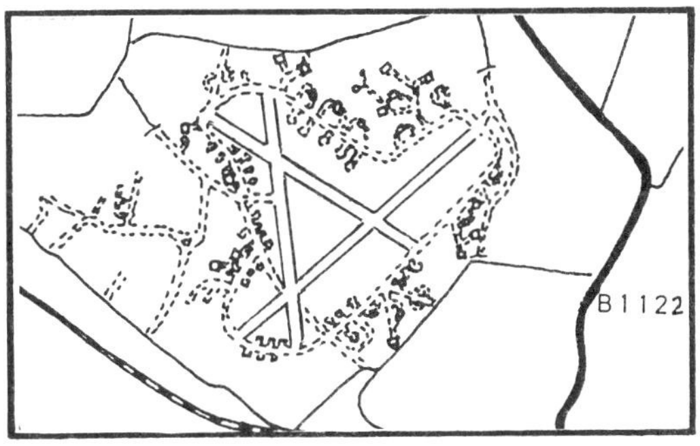

EXTENSIBILITY : Entails slight demolition, but not recommended.

ACCOMMODATION : Temporary.
HANGARS : T2-2;blister-12.

HARDSTANDINGS : Frypan-38;fighter pens[24 A/C]-12; pierced steel planking-17.

USAAF. : OFFICERS: 215. Enlisted Men. : 1799. TOTAL: 2014.

AFFILIATED AIRFIELDS : -

PRESENT USE [1985] : Agriculture.

NO: 351.

AIRFIELD NAME: LEUCHARS. OPENED : 1918.
COUNTY : Fife. CLOSED :
COMMAND : Coastal
FORMATION : 18 Grp[Pitreavie Castle] GRID REF: O 960419[64Scot]
FUNCTION : Operational. O.S.REF.: NO 467205.

LOCALITY : 4miles NW of St Andrews.
RAILWAY STN. : Leuchars Junction[LNER]

LATITUDE : 56 22 23N. HEIGHT ASL : 36′ LIGHTING : Mk1.
LONGITUDE : 02 52 15W. FLYING CONTROL : Yes. RADIO : QDM.

LANDMARKS DAY. : Coast.

LANDMARKS NIGHT : R Eden.

OBSTRUCTIONS : Trees 50′high W & NW boundaries. Hills 630′ 2.5miles W.

LANDING AREA SURFACE : Concrete & wood chippings.

QDM	LENGTH X WIDTH	EXT. TO
275.	2020 x 50yds.	4000yds.
228.	2000 x 50yds.	6000yds.
		4000yds.

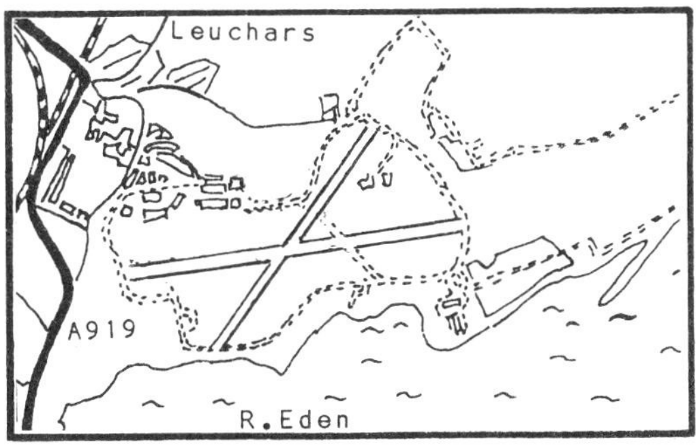

EXTENSIBILITY : Entails demolition of 2 bungalows, 1 old cottage, & a group of farm building.
ACCOMMODATION : Permanent.
HANGARS : Type C-4;bellman-2;aircraft sheds-4; EO blister-9.
HARDSTANDINGS : 100′ diameter:concrete-6;BRC fabric-44.

	OFFICERS	S.N.C.O′s.	O.R′s.	TOTAL
R.A.F.	192.	262.	1016.	1470.
W.A.A.F.	13.	7.	361.	381.

AFFILIATED AIRFIELDS : -

PRESENT USE [1985] : RAF.

NO: 352.

AIRFIELD NAME: LICHFIELD. OPENED : 1940.
COUNTY : Staffordshire. CLOSED : 1958.
COMMAND : Bomber.
FORMATION : 93 Grp[Egginton] GRID REF: K 605333[62]
FUNCTION : Operational Training Unit. O.S.REF.: SK 146131.
LOCALITY : 3miles NE of Lichfield.
RAILWAY STN. : Lichfield City[LMS]

LATITUDE : 52 42 45N. HEIGHT ASL : 220′ LIGHTING : Mk2.
LONGITUDE : 01 47 00W. FLYING CONTROL : Yes. RADIO : QDM.

LANDMARKS DAY. : Canal along NE & NW edge.

LANDMARKS NIGHT : -

OBSTRUCTIONS : Fradley church on approach to R/W 260.

LANDING AREA : Tarmac.
SURFACE :

QDM: 170. LENGTH X WIDTH: 1100 x 50yds.EXT. TO: 2000yds.
: 216. : 1100 x 50yds. : 1600yds.
: 260. : 1600 x 50yds. : 2450yds.
: : :

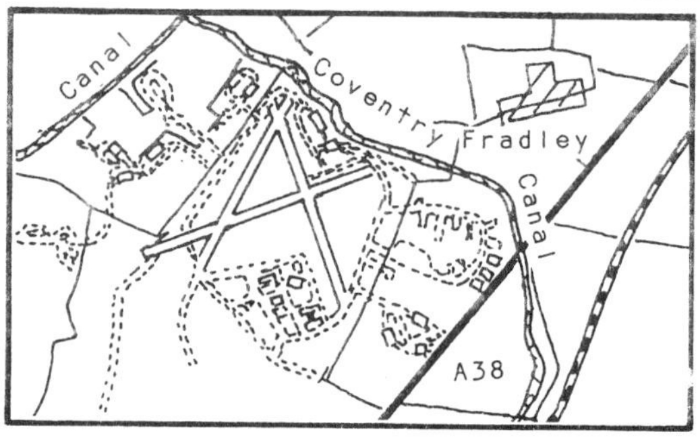

EXTENSIBILITY : Recommended to 1400-1400 & 2000yds only.

ACCOMMODATION : Permanent[part]
HANGARS : Type J-3;T2-2;B1-1;K-4;L-8.

HARDSTANDINGS : Heavy bomber-25.

R.A.F. : OFFICERS: 166.S.N.C.O′s.: 542.O.R′s.: 2536.TOTAL: 3244.
W.A.A.F.: " : 8. " : 14. " : 595. " : 617.

AFFILIATED AIRFIELDS : Church Broughton[Satellite]

PRESENT USE [1985] : Disused.

NO: 353.

AIRFIELD NAME: LIMAVADY. OPENED : 1940.
COUNTY : Londonderry NI. CLOSED : 1945.
COMMAND : Coastal.
FORMATION : 15 Grp[Liverpool] GRID REF: C 677255[304NI]
FUNCTION : Operational. O.S.REF.: C 677255.

LOCALITY : 2miles N of Limavady.
RAILWAY STN. : Limavady 2miles[BNC]

LATITUDE : 55 04 23N. HEIGHT ASL : 65′ LIGHTING : Mk2.
LONGITUDE : 06 56 15W. FLYING CONTROL : Yes. RADIO : QDM.

LANDMARKS DAY. : Lough Foyle, hills NE & E.

LANDMARKS NIGHT : Lough Foyle.

OBSTRUCTIONS : Hills 1260′ 2miles NE, 1100 3miles SE, & 1298′ 8miles SW.

LANDING AREA : Concrete & tarmac.
SURFACE :

QDM: 178. LENGTH X WIDTH: 1690 x 50yds.EXT. TO: -
: 269. : 1530 x 50yds. : -
: 313. : 1370 x 50yds. : 1500yds.
: : :

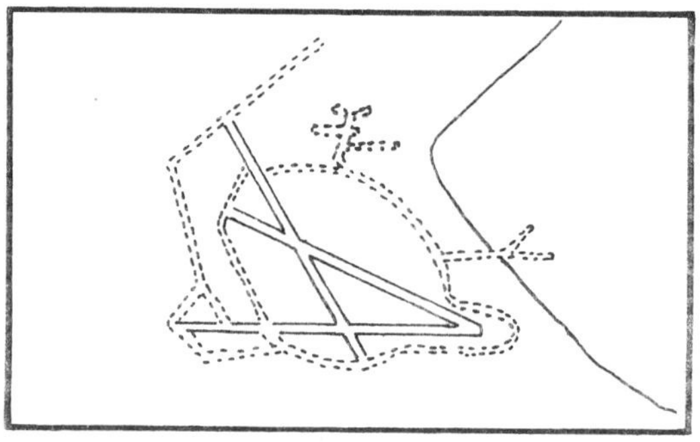

EXTENSIBILITY : Entails demolition of 1 small farm.

ACCOMMODATION : Temporary.
HANGARS : T2-2;bellman-3;Blister-6.

HARDSTANDINGS : Dia:125′concrete-24;100′tarmac-1;75′tarmac-24; 60′tarmac-4;double standing-3.

R.A.F. : OFFICERS: 136.S.N.C.O′s.: 320.O.R′s.: 1659.TOTAL: 2115.
W.A.A.F.: " : 10. " : 14. " : 330. " : 354.

AFFILIATED AIRFIELDS : -

PRESENT USE [1985] : Disused.

NO: 354.

AIRFIELD NAME: LINDHOLME. OPENED : 1940.
COUNTY : Yorkshire. CLOSED :
COMMAND : Bomber.
FORMATION : 7 Grp[St.Vincents] GRID REF: A 154260[38]
FUNCTION : Operational[71 Base] O.S.REF.: SK 685065.

LOCALITY : 7miles ENE of Doncaster.
RAILWAY STN. : Doncaster[LNER]

LATITUDE : 53 33 00N. HEIGHT ASL : 20′ LIGHTING : Mk2.
LONGITUDE : 00 58 00W. FLYING CONTROL : Yes. RADIO : QDM.

LANDMARKS DAY. : Armthorpe colliery chimney 4.5miles W.

LANDMARKS NIGHT : Lindholme lake 3miles E.

OBSTRUCTIONS : -

ANDING AREA : Concrete & tarmac.
FACE :

2. LENGTH X WIDTH: 2000 x 50yds.EXT. TO: 3000yds.
: 1400 x 50yds. : 2000yds.
: : 2000yds.
: :

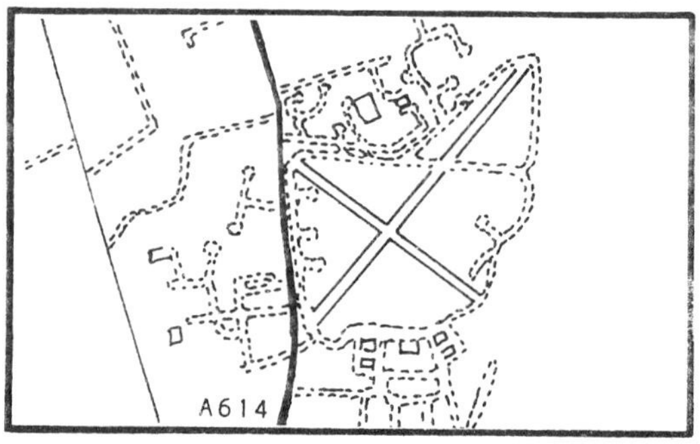

EXTENSIBILITY : Entails possible road diversion & demolition of 45 married quarters.
ACCOMMODATION : Permanent.
HANGARS : Type C-5.

HARDSTANDINGS : Heavy bomber-36.

R.A.F. : OFFICERS: 204.S.N.C.O′s.: 681.O.R′s.: 1307.TOTAL: 2192.
W.A.A.F.: " : 8. " : 17. " : 340. " : 365.

AFFILIATED AIRFIELDS : Blyton & Sandtoft[Sub-stations]

PRESENT USE [1985] : HM Prison.

NO: 355.

AIRFIELD NAME: LINTON-on-OUSE. OPENED : 1937.
COUNTY : Yorkshire. CLOSED :
COMMAND : Bomber.
FORMATION : 6 RCAF Grp[Allerton Pk] GRID REF: E 965815[27]
FUNCTION : Operational[62 Base] O.S.REF.: SE 490618.

LOCALITY : 8.75miles NW of York.
RAILWAY STN. : York[LNER]

LATITUDE : 54 02 45N. HEIGHT ASL : 43′ LIGHTING : Mk2.
LONGITUDE : 01 15 00W. FLYING CONTROL : Yes. RADIO : QDM.

LANDMARKS DAY. : R Ouse running NW-SE.

LANDMARKS NIGHT : As day.

OBSTRUCTIONS : Water tower 130′ high.

LANDING AREA SURFACE : Concrete.
QDM: 179. LENGTH X WIDTH: 1400 x 50yds.EXT. TO: 2500yds.
: 223. : 2000 x 50yds. : 3000yds.
: 287. : 1400 x 50yds. : 2500yds.
: : :

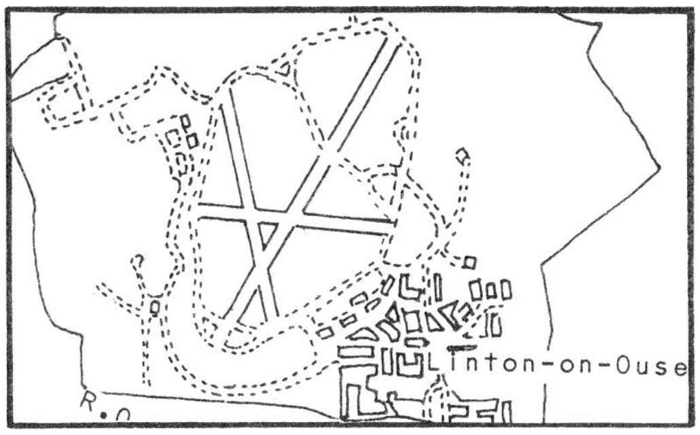

EXTENSIBILITY : Site is liable to flooding.

ACCOMMODATION : Permanent.
HANGARS : Type C-5.

HARDSTANDINGS : Heavy bomber-36.

R.C.A.F.: OFFICERS: 258.S.N.C.O′s.: 552.O.R′s.: 1596.TOTAL: 2406.
W.A.A.F.: " : 14. " : 24. " : 368. " : 406.

AFFILIATED AIRFIELDS : East Moor & Tholthorpe[Sub-stations]

PRESENT USE [1985] : RAF.

NO: 356.

AIRFIELD NAME: LISSETT. OPENED : 1943.
COUNTY : Yorkshire. CLOSED : 1945.
COMMAND : Bomber.
FORMATION : 4 Grp[York] GRID REF: A 607775[28]
FUNCTION : Operational. O.S.REF.: TA 135582.

LOCALITY : 6miles SSW of Bridlington.
RAILWAY STN. : Bridlington[LNER]

LATITUDE : 54 00 15N. HEIGHT ASL : 47′ LIGHTING : Mk2.
LONGITUDE : 00 16 30W. FLYING CONTROL : Yes. RADIO : QDM.

LANDMARKS DAY. : Lissett 048degreesT 12miles Flamborough Head.

LANDMARKS NIGHT : Hornsea Mere 155degreesT 7.5miles.

OBSTRUCTIONS : -

LANDING AREA SURFACE : Concrete.
QDM: 092. LENGTH X WIDTH: 2000 x 50yds.EXT. TO: 3000yds.
: 028. : 1400 x 50yds. : 2000yds.
: 150. : 1400 x 50yds. : 2000yds.
: : :

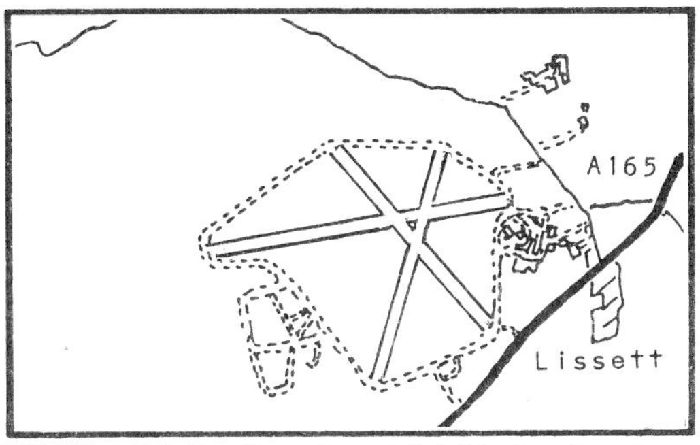

EXTENSIBILITY : Entails diversion of Bridlington-Beverley road & complete reconstruction of existing railway.
ACCOMMODATION : Temporary.
HANGARS : T2-2.

HARDSTANDINGS : Heavy bomber-36.

R.A.F. : OFFICERS: 110.S.N.C.O′s.: 310.O.R′s.: 1310.TOTAL: 1730.
W.A.A.F.: " : 3. " : 10. " : 351. " : 364.

AFFILIATED AIRFIELDS : Driffield[43 Base]

PRESENT USE [1985] : Agriculture.

NO: 357.

AIRFIELD NAME: LITTLE HORWOOD. OPENED : 1942.
COUNTY : Buckinghamshire. CLOSED : 1946.
COMMAND : Bomber.
FORMATION : 92 Grp[Winslow] GRID REF: L 226495[94]
FUNCTION : Operational Training Unit[satellite] O.S.REF.: SP 777298.
LOCALITY : 2.5miles NE of Winslow.
RAILWAY STN. : Winslow 2.5miles[LMS]

LATITUDE : 51 57 38N. HEIGHT ASL : 385. LIGHTING : Mk2.
LONGITUDE : 00 52 00W. FLYING CONTROL : Yes. RADIO : QDM.

LANDMARKS DAY. : Great Horwood church tower; water tower; LMS railway on S side of A/F.

LANDMARKS NIGHT : -

OBSTRUCTIONS : -

LANDING AREA SURFACE : Concrete.
QDM: 170. LENGTH X WIDTH: 1400 x 50yds.EXT. TO: -
: 236. : 1400 x 50yds. : -
: 295. : 2000 x 50yds. : 2450yds.
: : :

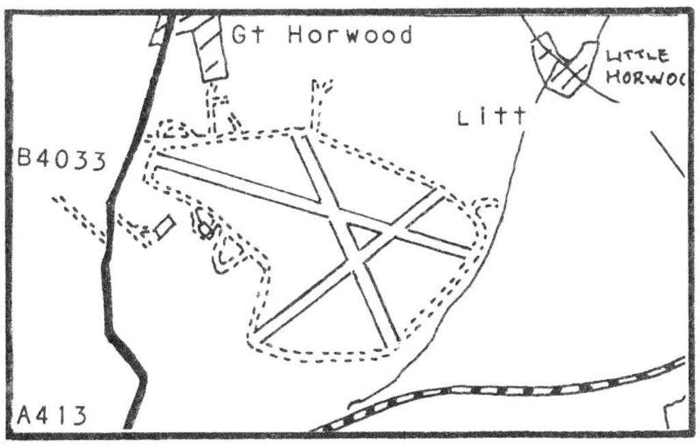

EXTENSIBILITY : Entails closure of both access roads to A/F.

ACCOMMODATION : Temporary.
HANGARS : T2-1;B1-1.

HARDSTANDINGS : Heavy bomber-30.

R.A.F. : OFFICERS: 124.S.N.C.O′s.: 304.O.R′s.: 802.TOTAL: 1230.
W.A.A.F.: " : 2. " : 3. " : 293. " : 298.

AFFILIATED AIRFIELDS : Wing[Parent]

PRESENT USE [1985] : Agriculture.

NO: 358.

AIRFIELD NAME: LITTLE RISSINGTON. OPENED : 1938.
COUNTY : Gloucestershire. CLOSED :
COMMAND : Flying Training.
FORMATION : 23 Grp[South Cerney] GRID REF: P 658390[93]
FUNCTION : Advanced Flying Unit [Pilot] O.S.REF.: SP 210188.
LOCALITY : 4.5miles NE of Burford.
RAILWAY STN. : Kingham 6miles[GWR]

LATITUDE : 51 52 00N. HEIGHT ASL : 750′ LIGHTING : Mk2.
LONGITUDE : 01 41 45W. FLYING CONTROL : Yes. RADIO : QDM.

LANDMARKS DAY. : R Windrush 2miles W running 3.5miles S; contour 816′ .5mile; North Kingham junction 4miles NE.

LANDMARKS NIGHT : R Windrush.

OBSTRUCTIONS : 2 wireless masts 84′high .5mile N; wood .5mile end of SE runway; hut at end of SE runway.

LANDING AREA SURFACE : Concrete covered with tarmac.

QDM	LENGTH X WIDTH	EXT. TO
050.	1565 x 50yds.	1600yds.
100.	1150 x 50yds.	1350yds.
140.	1035 x 50yds.	1330yds.

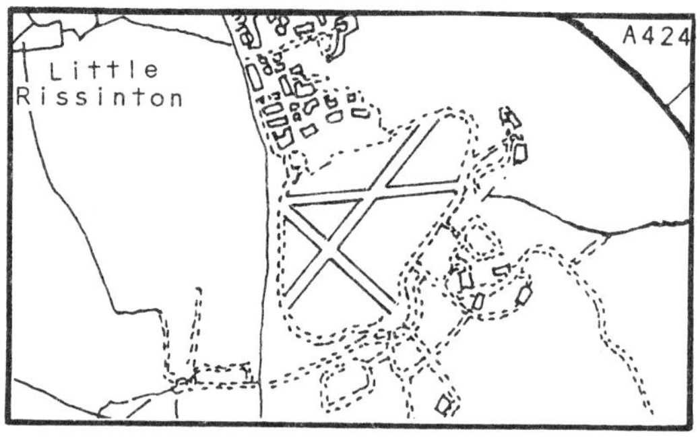

EXTENSIBILITY : -

ACCOMMODATION : Permanent.
HANGARS : Various-44.

HARDSTANDINGS : -

	OFFICERS	S.N.C.O′s.	O.R′s.	TOTAL
R.A.F.	151.	250.	916.	1317.
W.A.A.F.	9.	2.	362.	373.

AFFILIATED AIRFIELDS : Chipping Norton & Windrush[Satellites]

PRESENT USE [1985] : Army.

NO: 359.

AIRFIELD NAME: LITTLE SNORING. OPENED : 1943.
COUNTY : Norfolk. CLOSED : 1958.
COMMAND : Bomber.
FORMATION : 100 Grp[Bylaugh Hall] GRID REF: G 419517[57]
FUNCTION : Operational. O.S.REF.: TF 963334.

LOCALITY : 3.5miles NE of Fakenham.
RAILWAY STN. : Fakenham[M&GM & LNER]

LATITUDE : 52 51 38N. HEIGHT ASL : 195′ LIGHTING : Mk2.
LONGITUDE : 00 54 45E. FLYING CONTROL : Yes. RADIO : QDM.

LANDMARKS DAY. : Great Snoring church. Littleston church. Hinderingham.

LANDMARKS NIGHT : -

OBSTRUCTIONS : -

LANDING AREA SURFACE : Concrete.

QDM	LENGTH X WIDTH	EXT. TO
250.	2000 x 50yds.	2500yds.
130.	1400 x 50yds.	2700yds.
190.	1400 x 50yds.	2450yds.

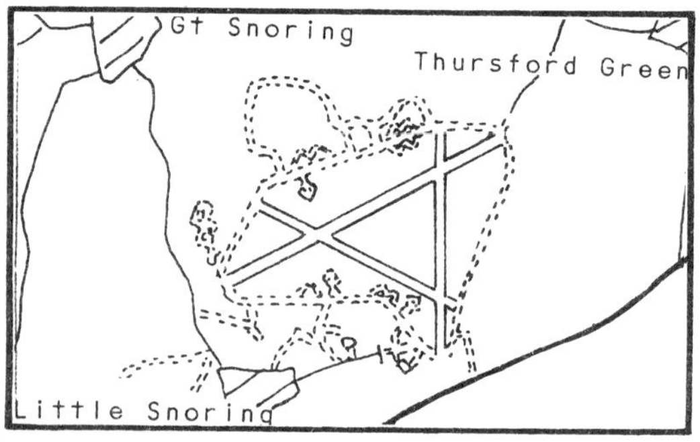

EXTENSIBILITY : Entails road diversion & straightening but negligible demolition.
ACCOMMODATION : Temporary.
HANGARS : T2-2;Glider-2;B1-1.

HARDSTANDINGS : Loop-36.

	OFFICERS	S.N.C.O′s.	O.R′s.	TOTAL
R.A.F.	155.	362.	1290.	1807.
W.A.A.F.	10.	24.	327.	361.

AFFILIATED AIRFIELDS : -

PRESENT USE [1985] : Disused.

NO: 360.

AIRFIELD NAME: LITTLE STAUGHTON. OPENED : 1942.
COUNTY : Huntingdonshire. CLOSED : 1945.
COMMAND : Bomber.
FORMATION : 8 Grp[Huntingdon] GRID REF: L 570808[84]
FUNCTION : Operational. O.S.REF.: TL 116615.

LOCALITY : 8.5miles NNE of Bedford.
RAILWAY STN. : St.Neots 6miles[LNER]

LATITUDE : 52 14 27N. HEIGHT ASL : 225′ LIGHTING : Mk2.
LONGITUDE : 00 21 45W. FLYING CONTROL : Yes. RADIO : QDM.

LANDMARKS DAY. : Church 1.5miles NW by W.

LANDMARKS NIGHT : Junction of R Ouse & R Kym 4miles E.

OBSTRUCTIONS : Buildings E & SE of A/F.

LANDING AREA SURFACE : Concrete & tarmac.

QDM	LENGTH X WIDTH	EXT. TO
250.	1920 x 50yds.	2600yds.
310.	1340 x 50yds.	1600yds.
010.	1000 x 50yds.	1200yds.

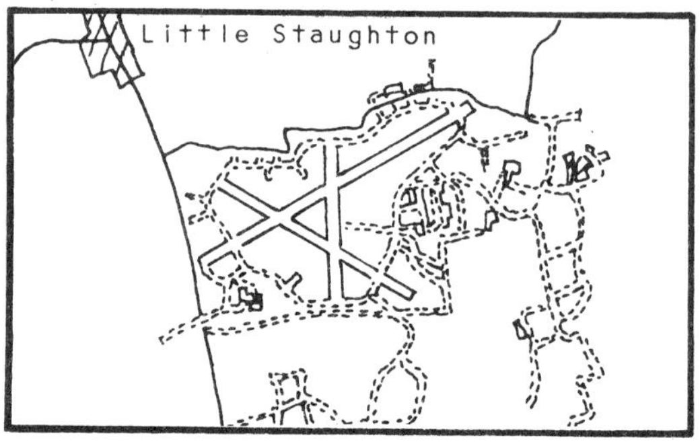

EXTENSIBILITY : Entails demolition of a cottage & buildings.

ACCOMMODATION : Temporary.
HANGARS : T2-3;Robin-8.

HARDSTANDINGS : Frypan & loop-50.

	OFFICERS	S.N.C.O′s.	O.R′s.	TOTAL
R.A.F.	213.	600.	1415.	2228.
W.A.A.F.	5.	-	120.	125.

AFFILIATED AIRFIELDS : -

PRESENT USE [1985] : Private flying.

NO: 361.

AIRFIELD NAME: LITTLE SUTTON. OPENED : 1941.
COUNTY : Cheshire. CLOSED : 1946.
COMMAND : Maintenance.
FORMATION : 43 Grp[Oxford] GRID REF: J 830970[43]
FUNCTION : Satellite. O.S.REF.: SJ 358774.

LOCALITY : 6miles NW of Chester.
RAILWAY STN. : Ledsham .25miles[GWR & LMS]

LATITUDE : 53 16 42N. HEIGHT ASL : 200′ LIGHTING : None.
LONGITUDE : 02 56 57W. FLYING CONTROL : None.RADIO : QDM.

LANDMARKS DAY. : Ellesmere Port on R Mersey 2miles E of A/F.

LANDMARKS NIGHT : R Mersey 2.5miles NE of A/F.

OBSTRUCTIONS : Overhead electricity cables running NW & SW of A/F 1000yds.

LANDING AREA SURFACE : Grass.

QDM	LENGTH X WIDTH	EXT. TO
WSW-ENE.	1000yds.	-
WNW-ESE.	700yds.	-

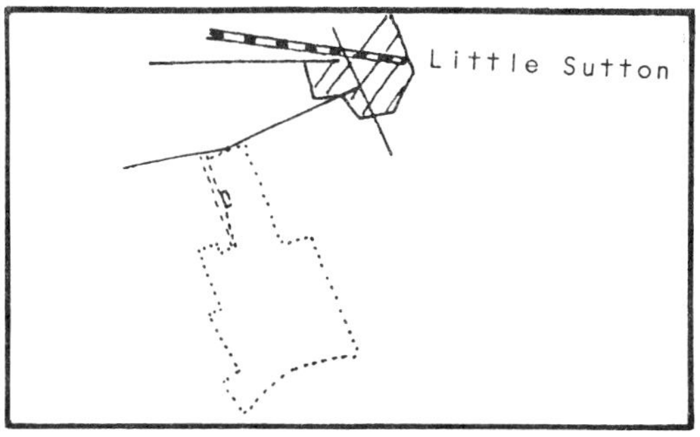

EXTENSIBILITY : Only possible to SSE along top of ridge.

ACCOMMODATION : Temporary.
HANGARS : Blister-3.

HARDSTANDINGS : -

R.A.F. : OFFICERS: - S.N.C.O′s.: - O.R′s.: - TOTAL: -
W.A.A.F.: " : - " : - " : - " : -

AFFILIATED AIRFIELDS : Sealand[Parent]

PRESENT USE [1985] : Unspecified.

NO: 362.

AIRFIELD NAME: LITTLE WALDEN. OPENED : 1944.
COUNTY : Essex. CLOSED : 1946.
COMMAND : 8th USAAF.
FORMATION : 361st Fighter Grp. GRID REF: M 005623[85]
FUNCTION : Operational. O.S.REF.: TL 558435.

LOCALITY : 3.5miles NNE of Saffron Walden.
RAILWAY STN. : Linton 2.5miles[LNER]

LATITUDE : 52 04 00N. HEIGHT ASL : 365′ LIGHTING : Mk2.
LONGITUDE : 00 16 15E. FLYING CONTROL : Yes. RADIO : QDM.

LANDMARKS DAY. : Cambridge 10miles to NW. Saffron Walden 2miles to S.

LANDMARKS NIGHT : -

OBSTRUCTIONS : 2 hangars situated on field [70′], 1 on E side, 1 on N side.

LANDING AREA SURFACE : Concrete & wood chippings.

QDM	LENGTH X WIDTH	EXT. TO
160.	1900 x 50yds.	2200yds.
100.	1400 x 50yds.	2000yds.
040.	1400 x 50yds.	1500yds.

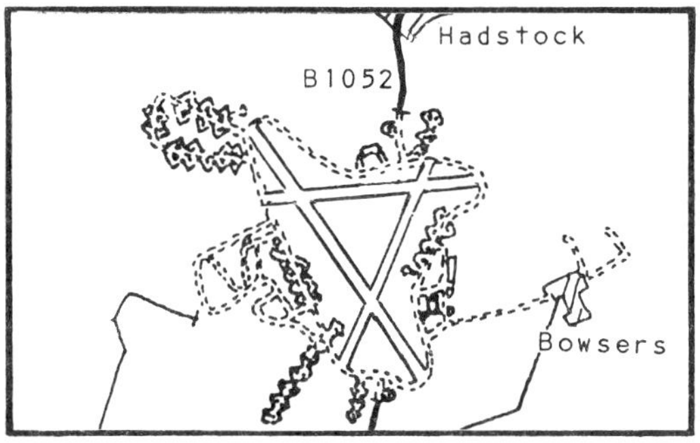

EXTENSIBILITY : Entails demolition of buildings.

ACCOMMODATION : Temporary.
HANGARS : T2-2.

HARDSTANDINGS : Spectacle-50[5 reserved for transients]

USAAF. : OFFICERS: 421. Enlisted Men. : 2473.TOTAL: 2894.

AFFILIATED AIRFIELDS : -

PRESENT USE [1985] : Unspecified.

NO: 363.

AIRFIELD NAME: LLANBEDR. OPENED : 1941.
COUNTY : Merioneth. CLOSED :
COMMAND : Fighter.
FORMATION : 12 Grp[Watnall] GRID REF: J 026480[49]
FUNCTION : Non-operational. O.S.REF.: SH 569258.

LOCALITY : 3miles SSW of Harlech
RAILWAY STN. : Talwrn Bach Halt[GWR]

LATITUDE : 52 48 45N. HEIGHT ASL : 18′ LIGHTING : None.
LONGITUDE : 04 07 15W. FLYING CONTROL : Yes. RADIO : QDM.

LANDMARKS DAY. : Harlech Castle 3miles NNE.

LANDMARKS NIGHT : -

OBSTRUCTIONS : -

LANDING AREA SURFACE : Concrete.

QDM	LENGTH X WIDTH	EXT. TO
058.	1540 x 50yds.	-
160.	1440 x 50yds.	-

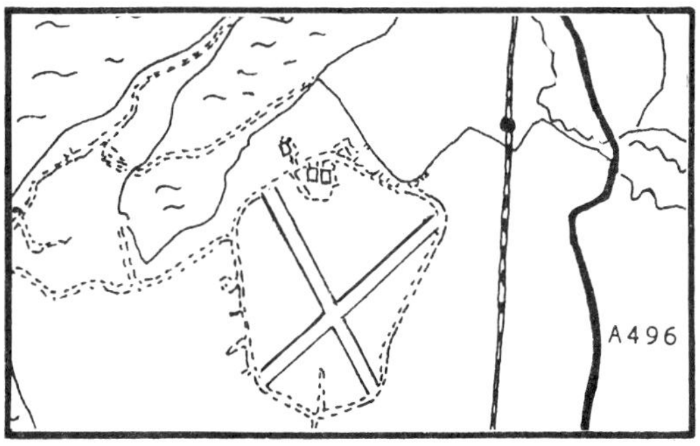

EXTENSIBILITY : None possible.

ACCOMMODATION : Temporary.
HANGARS : T2-2;0 blister-4.

HARDSTANDINGS : SE-6.

R.A.F. : OFFICERS: 85.S.N.C.O′s.: 84.O.R′s.: 762.TOTAL: 931.
W.A.A.F.: " : 4. " : 13. " : 182. " : 199.

AFFILIATED AIRFIELDS : -

PRESENT USE [1985] : Royal Aircraft Establishment.

NO: 364.

AIRFIELD NAME: LLANDOW. OPENED : 1937.
COUNTY : Glamorganshire. CLOSED : 1957.
COMMAND : Transport.
FORMATION : 44 Grp[Gloucester] GRID REF: T 402935[109]
FUNCTION : Parent. O.S.REF.: SS 959716.

LOCALITY : 14miles WSW of Cardiff.
RAILWAY STN. : Llandow[Wick Road]Halt[GWR]

LATITUDE : 51 26 00N. HEIGHT ASL : 290′ LIGHTING : None.
LONGITUDE : 03 29 45W. FLYING CONTROL : Yes. RADIO : QDM.

LANDMARKS DAY. : Twin light houses, Nash Point.

LANDMARKS NIGHT : -

OBSTRUCTIONS : -

LANDING AREA SURFACE : Tarmac.

QDM	LENGTH X WIDTH	EXT. TO
280.	1600 x 50yds.	2000yds.
240.	1000 x 50yds.	1600yds.
330.	1000 x 50yds.	1600yds.

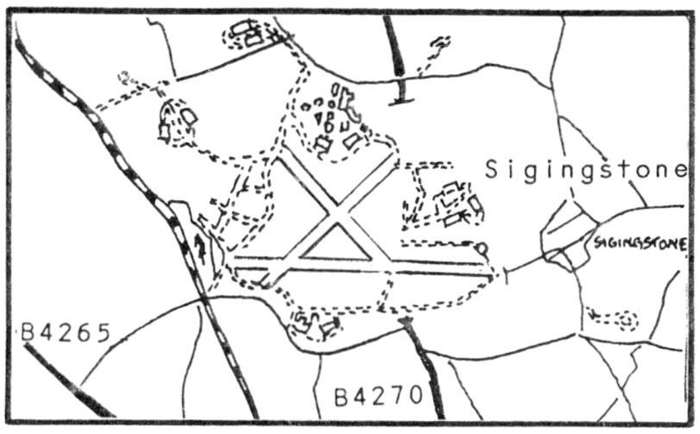

EXTENSIBILITY : Entails diversion of 2 secondary roads & extensive demolition.
ACCOMMODATION : Permanent[part]
HANGARS : Various-38.

HARDSTANDINGS : Frypan-40;loop-5.

	OFFICERS	S.N.C.O′s.	O.R′s.	TOTAL
R.A.F.	95.	320.	1208.	1623.
W.A.A.F.	18.	29.	262.	309.

AFFILIATED AIRFIELDS : -

PRESENT USE [1985] : Home Office.

NO: 365.

AIRFIELD NAME: LLANDWROG. OPENED : 1941.
COUNTY : Caernarvonshire. CLOSED : 1945.
COMMAND : Flying Training.
FORMATION : 25 Grp[Market Drayton] GRID REF: H 900815[41]
FUNCTION : Advanced Training Unit. O.S.REF.: SH 434590.

LOCALITY : 4miles SE of Caernarvon.
RAILWAY STN. : Caernarvon[GWR]

LATITUDE : 53 06 15N. HEIGHT ASL : 10′ LIGHTING : Mk2.
LONGITUDE : 04 20 00W. FLYING CONTROL : Yes. RADIO : QDM.

LANDMARKS DAY. : Coast.

LANDMARKS NIGHT : As day.

OBSTRUCTIONS : Snowden range up to 3560′ 8miles SE.

LANDING AREA SURFACE : Tarmac.

QDM	LENGTH X WIDTH	EXT. TO
226.	1100 x 50yds.	2100yds.
335.	1000 x 50yds.	1300yds.
277.	1000 x 50yds.	1400yds.

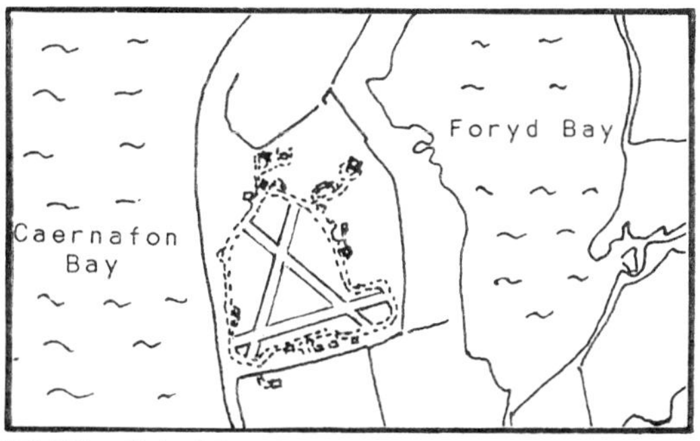

EXTENSIBILITY : Main R/W only recommended to 2000yds. Entails moderate demolition.
ACCOMMODATION : Temporary.
HANGARS : T2-2;Bellman-1;EO blister-7.

HARDSTANDINGS : -

	OFFICERS	S.N.C.O′s.	O.R′s.	TOTAL
R.A.F.	134.	298.	713.	1145.
W.A.A.F.	4.	5.	159.	168.

AFFILIATED AIRFIELDS : Penrhos[Parent]

PRESENT USE [1985] : Private flying.

NO: 366.

AIRFIELD NAME: LONG KESH. OPENED : 1941.
COUNTY : Down NI. CLOSED : 1948.
COMMAND : RAF NI.
FORMATION : Stormont[Belfast] GRID REF: J 230615[313NI]
FUNCTION : Parent. O.S.REF.: J 230615.

LOCALITY : 2.5miles SW of Lisburn.
RAILWAY STN. : Hillsborough 2miles[GNI]

LATITUDE : 54 29 15N. HEIGHT ASL : 125′ LIGHTING : Mk2.
LONGITUDE : 06 06 00W. FLYING CONTROL : Yes. RADIO : QDM.

LANDMARKS DAY. : Lagen canal on S boundary. R Lagen on N boundary. BBC masts at Blaris, 640′ASL 1.5miles E

LANDMARKS NIGHT : Illuminated BBC masts E of A/F.

OBSTRUCTIONS : Illuminated BBC masts 640′ ASL 1.5miles E.

LANDING AREA SURFACE : Tarmac.

QDM	LENGTH X WIDTH	EXT. TO
270.	1550 x 50yds.	-
340.	1190 x 50yds.	-
020.	1100 x 50yds.	1350yds.

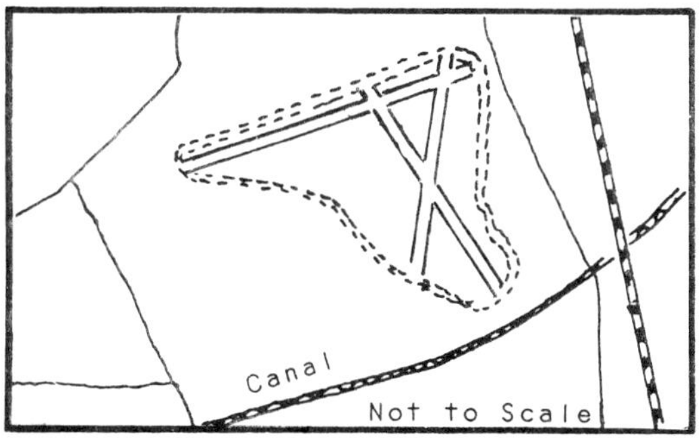

EXTENSIBILITY : -

ACCOMMODATION : Temporary.
HANGARS : T2-2;Bellman-2;Blister-5.

HARDSTANDINGS : Concrete:150′ dia-29;125′ dia-2.

	OFFICERS	S.N.C.O′s.	O.R′s.	TOTAL
R.A.F.	67.	191.	3580.	3838.
W.A.A.F.	10.	48.	331.	389.

AFFILIATED AIRFIELDS : -

PRESENT USE [1985] : HM Prison.

NO: 367.

AIRFIELD NAME: LONG MARSTON. OPENED : 1941.
COUNTY : Gloucestershire. CLOSED : 1954.
COMMAND : Bomber.
FORMATION : 91 Grp[Abingdon] GRID REF: P 620694[82]
FUNCTION : Operational Training Unit[satellite] O.S.REF.: TL 170490.
LOCALITY : 3.5miles SSW of Stratford on Avon..
RAILWAY STN. : Long Marston 2.5miles[GWR]

LATITUDE : 52 08 08N. HEIGHT ASL : 145' LIGHTING : Mk2.
LONGITUDE : 01 45 15W. FLYING CONTROL : Yes. RADIO : QDM.

LANDMARKS DAY. : Meon Hill 637' ASL 1.75miles S of A/F.

LANDMARKS NIGHT : -

OBSTRUCTIONS : Meon Hill 637' ASL 1.75miles S of A/F.

LANDING AREA SURFACE : Tarmac.

QDM	LENGTH X WIDTH	EXT. TO
050.	1500 x 50yds.	2100yds.
121.	1100 x 50yds.	2400yds.
173.	1100 x 50yds.	1500yds.
:	:	:

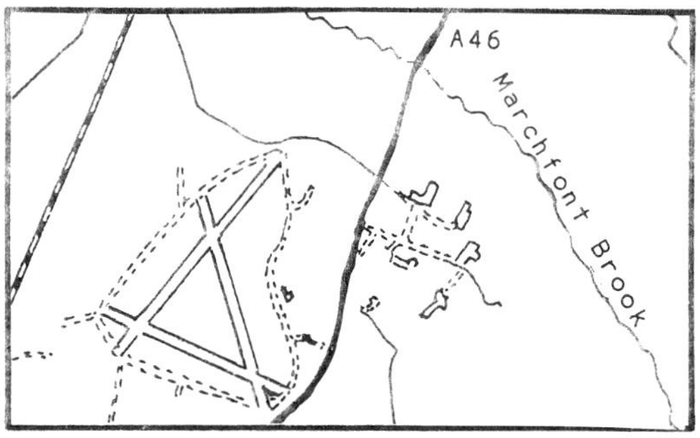

EXTENSIBILITY : Entails diversion of main Stratford-Cheltenham road & demolition of a farm & 2 barns.
ACCOMMODATION : Temporary.
HANGARS : T2-2;B1-1.

HARDSTANDINGS : Heavy bomber-27.

	OFFICERS:	S.N.C.O's.:	O.R's.:	TOTAL:
R.A.F. :	142.	165.	612.	919.
W.A.A.F.:	2.	-	105.	107.

AFFILIATED AIRFIELDS : Honeybourne[Parent]

PRESENT USE [1985] : Private flying.

NO: 368.

AIRFIELD NAME: LONG NEWNTON. OPENED : 1940.
COUNTY : Wiltshire. CLOSED : 1950.
COMMAND : Flying Training.
FORMATION : 23 Grp[South Cerney] GRID REF: P 374125[103]
FUNCTION : Advanced Flying Unit. [satellite] O.S.REF.: ST 929920.
LOCALITY : 2miles SE of Tetbury.
RAILWAY STN. : Tetbury 2miles[GWR]

LATITUDE : 51 37 30N. HEIGHT ASL : 400' LIGHTING : Mk2.
LONGITUDE : 02 06 00W. FLYING CONTROL : Yes. RADIO : QDM.

LANDMARKS DAY. : -

LANDMARKS NIGHT : -

OBSTRUCTIONS : -

LANDING AREA SURFACE : Steel matting[Sommerfeld track]

QDM	LENGTH X WIDTH	EXT. TO
214.	1140yds.	1440yds.
272.	1185yds.	2050yds.
:	:	2460yds.
:	:	:

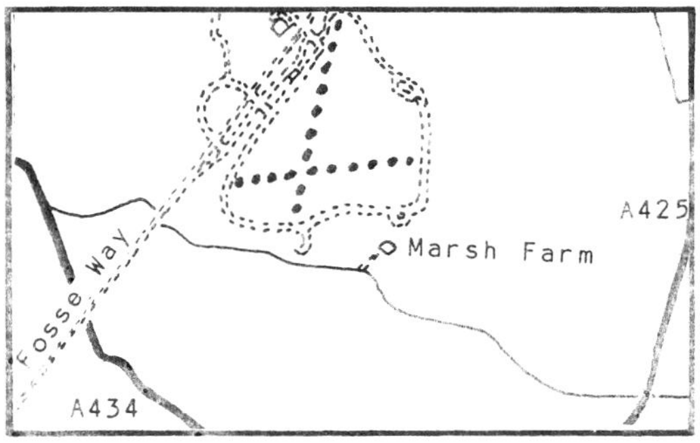

EXTENSIBILITY : Entails demolition of a farm to NW.

ACCOMMODATION : Temporary.
HANGARS : T1-1;Blister:69'-6;65'-4.

HARDSTANDINGS : -

	OFFICERS:	S.N.C.O's.:	O.R's.:	TOTAL:
R.A.F. :	83.	180.	360.	623.
W.A.A.F.:	3.	-	140.	143.

AFFILIATED AIRFIELDS : Babdown Farm[Parent]

PRESENT USE [1985] : Agriculture.

NO: 369.

AIRFIELD NAME: LONGTOWN. OPENED : 1941.
COUNTY : Cumberland. CLOSED : 1946.
COMMAND : Transport.
FORMATION : 44 Grp[Gloucester] GRID REF: Y 896896[5]
FUNCTION : Operational Training Unit[satellite] O.S.REF.: NY 411681.
LOCALITY : 8miles N of Carlisle.
RAILWAY STN. : Carlisle[LMS]

LATITUDE : 55 00 15N. HEIGHT ASL : 100' LIGHTING : Mk2.
LONGITUDE : 02 55 30W. FLYING CONTROL : Yes. RADIO : QDM.

LANDMARKS DAY. : Solway Firth.

LANDMARKS NIGHT : As day.

OBSTRUCTIONS : HT cables on pylons 75' high 2miles W.

LANDING AREA SURFACE : Concrete.

QDM	LENGTH X WIDTH	EXT. TO
209.	1380 x 50yds.	4000yds.
330.	1150 x 50yds.	4000yds.
267.	2000 x 50yds.	4000yds.
:	:	:

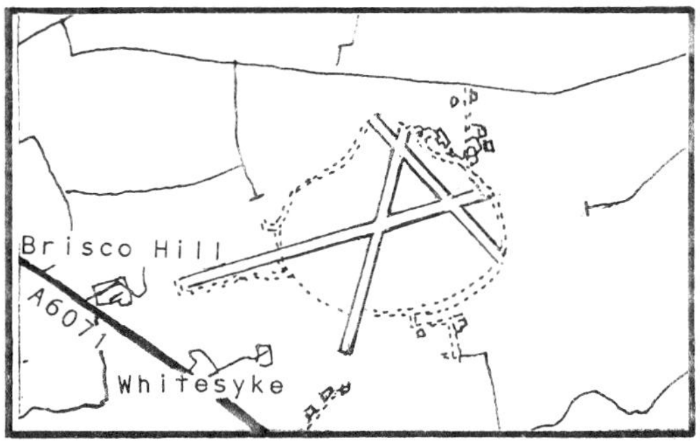

EXTENSIBILITY : Would not be to same alignment as existing R/W
ACCOMMODATION : Temporary.
HANGARS : T2-1;blister-2.

HARDSTANDINGS : Loop-5;125' dia-2;small fighter-28.

	OFFICERS:	S.N.C.O's.:	O.R's.:	TOTAL:
R.A.F. :	62.	142.	693.	897.
W.A.A.F.:	2.	15.	78.	95.

AFFILIATED AIRFIELDS : Crosby-on-Eden[Parent]

PRESENT USE [1985] : Disused.

NO: 370.

AIRFIELD NAME: LOSSIEMOUTH. OPENED : 1939.
COUNTY : Morayshire. CLOSED :
COMMAND : Bomber.
FORMATION : 91 Grp[Abingdon] GRID REF: J 735914[29Scot]
FUNCTION : Operational Training Unit. O.S.REF.: NJ 210695.

LOCALITY : 4.5miles N of Elgin.
RAILWAY STN. : Elgin 4.5miles[LNER]

LATITUDE : 57 42 38N. HEIGHT ASL : 19′ LIGHTING : Mk2.
LONGITUDE : 03 19 30W. FLYING CONTROL : Yes. RADIO : QDM.

LANDMARKS DAY. : Covesea Skerries lighthouse 1.5miles N.

LANDMARKS NIGHT : Findhorn Bay 2miles across, 13miles 240degrees.

OBSTRUCTIONS : Masts 650′ high 4miles W.

LANDING AREA SURFACE : Concrete & tarmac.

QDM	LENGTH X WIDTH	EXT. TO
190.	1400 x 50yds.	3000yds.
236.	2000 x 50yds.	3000yds.
268.	1500 x 50yds.	3000yds.
:	:	:

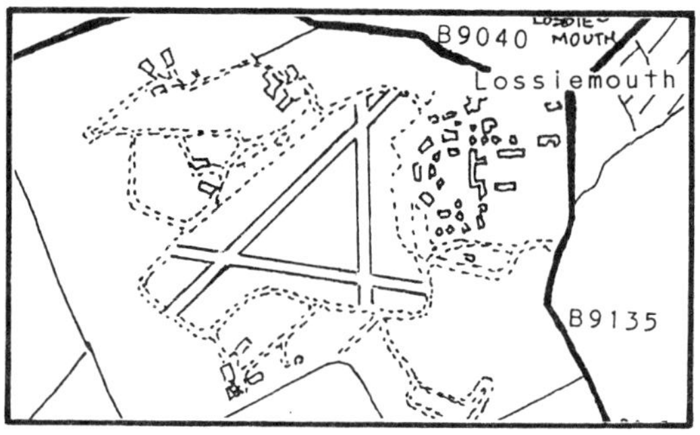

EXTENSIBILITY : Entails slight demolition.

ACCOMMODATION : Permanent[part]
HANGARS : Types:C-3;J-1;L-7;K-4.

HARDSTANDINGS : Heavy bomber-42.

	OFFICERS	S.N.C.O′s.	O.R′s.	TOTAL
R.A.F.	262.	611.	2443.	3316.
W.A.A.F.	13.	21.	797.	831.

AFFILIATED AIRFIELDS : Elgin & Milltown[Satellites]

PRESENT USE [1985] : RAF.

NO: 371.

AIRFIELD NAME: LUDFORD MAGNA. OPENED : 1943.
COUNTY : Lincolnshire. CLOSED : 1963.
COMMAND : Bomber.
FORMATION : 1 Grp[Bawtry] GRID REF: A 668073[39]
FUNCTION : Operational[14 Base] O.S.REF.: TF 201879.

LOCALITY : 6miles E of Market Rasen.
RAILWAY STN. : Market Rasen 6miles[LNER]

LATITUDE : 53 22 30N. HEIGHT ASL : 428′ LIGHTING : Mk2.
LONGITUDE : 00 11 30W. FLYING CONTROL : Yes. RADIO : QDM.

LANDMARKS DAY. : Main road Louth-Market Rasin running E-W 1mile N of A/F.

LANDMARKS NIGHT : -

OBSTRUCTIONS : Masts 4miles 850′high.

LANDING AREA SURFACE : Concrete & wood chippings.

QDM	LENGTH X WIDTH	EXT. TO
196.	2000 x 50yds.	2300yds.
286.	1400 x 50yds.	2150yds.
329.	1400 x 50yds.	1900yds.
:	:	:

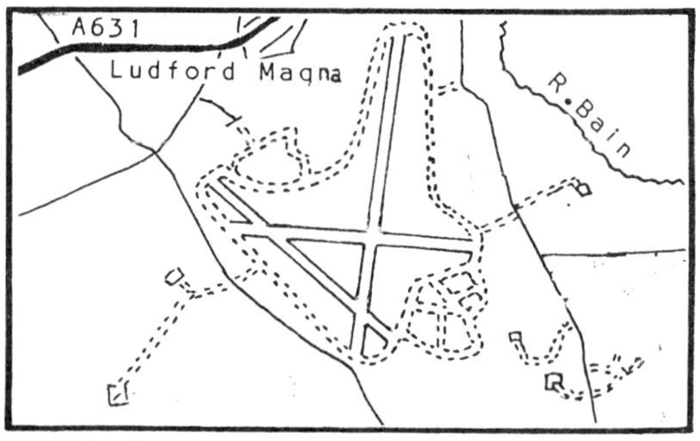

EXTENSIBILITY : Entails diversion of 2nd class road & demolition of a farm[if No.3 R/W is extended]
ACCOMMODATION : Temporary.
HANGARS : T2-6;B1-1.

HARDSTANDINGS : Frying pan/spectacle-36.

	OFFICERS	S.N.C.O′s.	O.R′s.	TOTAL
R.A.F.	167.	450.	1336.	1953.
W.A.A.F.	12.	18.	275.	305.

AFFILIATED AIRFIELDS : Faldingworth & Wickenby[Sub-stations]

PRESENT USE [1985] : Agriculture.

NO: 372.

AIRFIELD NAME: LUDHAM. OPENED : 1941.
COUNTY : Norfolk. CLOSED : 1945.
COMMAND : RN.
FORMATION : HMS Flycatcher. GRID REF: G 857375[67]
FUNCTION : HQ Mobile Naval A/F. O.S.REF.: TG 400195.

LOCALITY : 11miles NE of Norwich.
RAILWAY STN. : Potter Heigham 2.25miles[M & GN]

LATITUDE : 52 43 15N. HEIGHT ASL : 40′ LIGHTING : None.
LONGITUDE : 01 32 50E. FLYING CONTROL : None. RADIO : QDM.

LANDMARKS DAY. : Gt Yarmouth & coast. Lies between Barton Broad NW 1mile,Hickling Broad NE 1mile & R Thurne SE 1mile.

LANDMARKS NIGHT : -

OBSTRUCTIONS : -

LANDING AREA SURFACE : Concrete covered with tarmac.

QDM	LENGTH X WIDTH	EXT. TO
078-258.	1400 x 50yds.	-
018-198.	1100 x 50yds.	-
142-322.	1100 x 50yds.	-
:	:	:

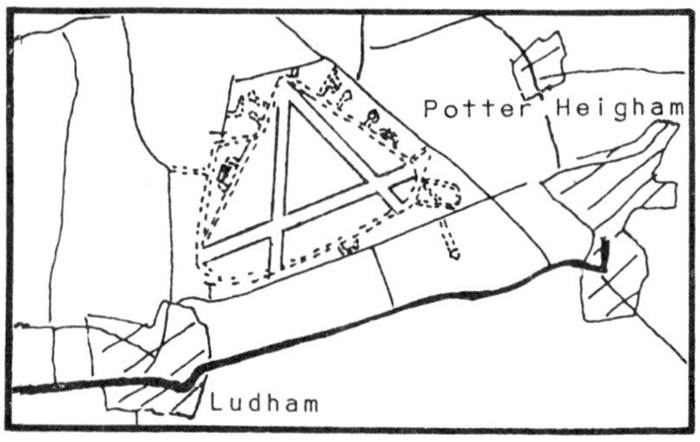

EXTENSIBILITY : -

ACCOMMODATION : Temporary.
HANGARS : T2-1;blister-4.

HARDSTANDINGS : Pens-12;hardstandings-9;USAAF type: 18 single & 17 double pierced metal.

	OFFICERS	Chiefs/POs/Ratings.	TOTAL
R.N.	190.	1519.	1709.
W.R.N.S.	"	"	"

AFFILIATED AIRFIELDS : -

PRESENT USE [1985] : Agriculture.

NO: 373.

AIRFIELD NAME: LULSGATE BOTTOM. OPENED : 1940.
COUNTY : Somersetshire. CLOSED :
COMMAND : Flying Training.
FORMATION : 23 Grp[South Cerney] GRID REF: T 945861[110]
FUNCTION : Flying Instructor's School. O.S.REF.: ST 504651.
LOCALITY : 7miles SW of Bristol.
RAILWAY STN. : Yatton 7miles[GWR]

LATITUDE : 52 43 23N. HEIGHT ASL : 692' LIGHTING : Mk2.
LONGITUDE : 01 33 15W. FLYING CONTROL : Yes. RADIO : QDM.

LANDMARKS DAY : Reservoirs N & S.

LANDMARKS NIGHT : As day.

OBSTRUCTIONS : -

LANDING AREA SURFACE : Tarmac.

QDM	LENGTH X WIDTH	EXT. TO
030.	1100 x 50yds.	1500yds.
100.	1300 x 50yds.	2500yds.
160.	1100 x 50yds.	1200yds.

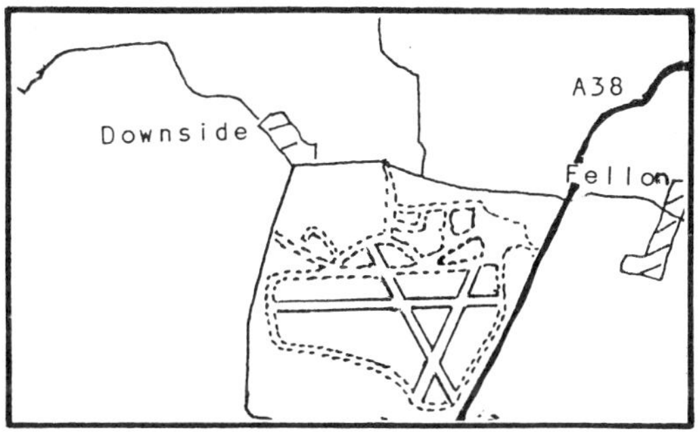

EXTENSIBILITY : Entails diversion of Bridgewater road & heavy grading.
ACCOMMODATION : Temporary.
HANGARS : Bellman-1;blisters:double 69'-3; single 69'-4.
HARDSTANDINGS : Double fighter pens-6;circular 20' dia-3.

	OFFICERS	S.N.C.O's.	O.R's.	TOTAL
R.A.F.	128.	125.	572.	825.
W.A.A.F.	4.	10.	204.	218.

AFFILIATED AIRFIELDS : -

PRESENT USE [1985] : Civil Airport[Bristol]

NO: 374.

AIRFIELD NAME: LYDD. OPENED : 1943.
COUNTY : Kent. CLOSED : 1945.
COMMAND : Fighter.
FORMATION : 11 Grp[Uxbridge] GRID REF: R 450413[135]
FUNCTION : Advanced Landing Ground. [De-requisitioned] O.S.REF.: TR 011033.
LOCALITY : 5.5miles NW of Dungeness.
RAILWAY STN. : Lydd Town[SR]

LATITUDE : 50 58 17N. HEIGHT ASL : 0' LIGHTING : None.
LONGITUDE : 00 51 53E. FLYING CONTROL : None. RADIO : QDM.

LANDMARKS DAY : Dungeness.

LANDMARKS NIGHT : As day.

OBSTRUCTIONS : -

LANDING AREA SURFACE : Steel Matting[Sommerfeld track]

QDM	LENGTH X WIDTH	EXT. TO
SE-NW.	1600 x 50yds.	-
SW-NE.	1400 x 50yds.	-

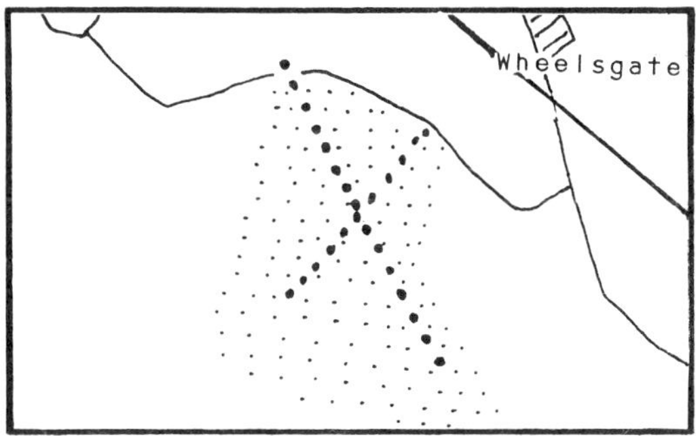

EXTENSIBILITY : -

ACCOMMODATION : Tented camp.
HANGARS : Blister-5.

HARDSTANDINGS : Hardcore-3.

	OFFICERS	S.N.C.O's.	O.R's.	TOTAL
R.A.F.	-	-	-	-
W.A.A.F.	-	-	-	-

AFFILIATED AIRFIELDS : -

PRESENT USE [1985] : Agriculture.

NO: 375.

AIRFIELD NAME: LYMINGTON. OPENED : 1944.
COUNTY : Hampshire. CLOSED : 1945.
COMMAND : Fighter.
FORMATION : 11 Grp[Uxbridge] GRID REF: U 783160[131]
FUNCTION : Advanced Landing Ground. [De-requisitioned] O.S.REF.: SZ 343960.
LOCALITY : 1mile E of Lymington.
RAILWAY STN. : Lymington 1mile[SR]

LATITUDE : 50 45 40N. HEIGHT ASL : 45' LIGHTING : None.
LONGITUDE : 01 30 15W. FLYING CONTROL : None. RADIO : QDM.

LANDMARKS DAY : Sway tower. Isle of Wight.

LANDMARKS NIGHT : -

OBSTRUCTIONS : -

LANDING AREA SURFACE : Steel Matting[E-W=American;S-N=British]

QDM	LENGTH X WIDTH	EXT. TO
E-W.	1600yds.	
S-N.	1400yds.	

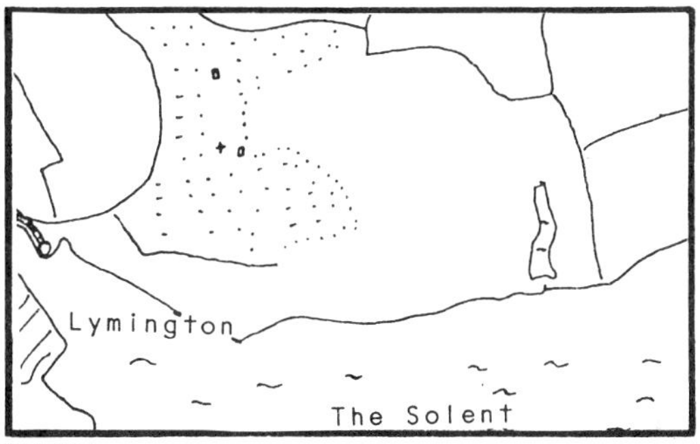

EXTENSIBILITY : -

ACCOMMODATION : Tented camp.
HANGARS : Blister-4.

HARDSTANDINGS : Sommerfeld track-75.

	OFFICERS	S.N.C.O's.	O.R's.	TOTAL
R.A.F.	-	-	-	-
W.A.A.F.	-	-	-	

AFFILIATED AIRFIELDS : -

PRESENT USE [1985] : Agriculture.

NO: 376.

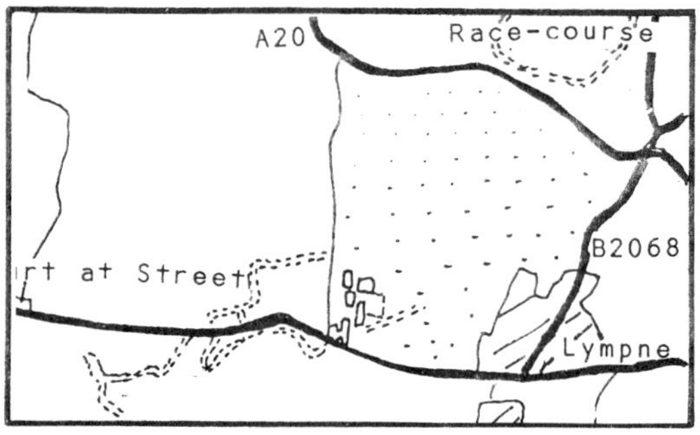

AIRFIELD NAME: LYMPNE. OPENED : 1916.
COUNTY : Kent. CLOSED : 1945.
COMMAND : Fighter.
FORMATION : 11 Grp[Uxbridge] GRID REF: R 555538[126]
FUNCTION : Operational[satellite] O.S.REF.: TR 110355.

LOCALITY : 2.5miles W of Hythe.
RAILWAY STN. : Westonhangar 2miles[SR]

LATITUDE : 51 04 38N. HEIGHT ASL : 340′ LIGHTING : None.
LONGITUDE : 01 01 00E. FLYING CONTROL : None.RADIO : QDM.

LANDMARKS : -
DAY.

LANDMARKS : -
NIGHT

OBSTRUCTIONS : -

LANDING AREA : Grass.
SURFACE :

QDM	LENGTH X WIDTH	EXT. TO
NW-SE.	1400yds.	1700yds.
NNE-SSW.	900yds.	1200yds.
NNW-SSE.	1000yds.	1100yds.
		2000yds.

EXTENSIBILITY : Would entail serious demolition & road diversion.
ACCOMMODATION : Temporary.
HANGARS : Blister-4.

HARDSTANDINGS : SE-1.

	OFFICERS	S.N.C.O's.	O.R's.	TOTAL
R.A.F.	70.	123.	847.	1040.
W.A.A.F.	3.	2.	88.	93.

AFFILIATED AIRFIELDS : Biggin Hill[Sector]

PRESENT USE [1985] : Private flying.

NO: 377.

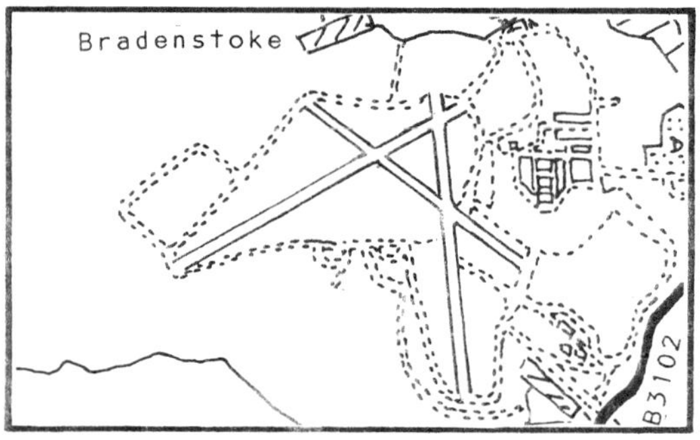

AIRFIELD NAME: LYNEHAM. OPENED : 1940.
COUNTY : Wiltshire. CLOSED :
COMMAND : Transport.
FORMATION : 116 Wing[Hendon] GRID REF: U 457987[112]
FUNCTION : Airport. O.S.REF.: SU 004788.

LOCALITY : 6.5miles NE of Chippenham.
RAILWAY STN. : Dauntsey 2miles[GWR]

LATITUDE : 51 30 23N. HEIGHT ASL : 440′ LIGHTING : Mk2.
LONGITUDE : 01 59 30W. FLYING CONTROL : Yes. RADIO : QDM.

LANDMARKS : Yatesbury tower 8miles SSE. Swindon-Chippenham mainline railway.
DAY.

LANDMARKS : Clyff Pypard tower obstruction light 3miles to SE.
NIGHT

OBSTRUCTIONS : -

LANDING AREA : Concrete covered with tarmac.
SURFACE :

QDM	LENGTH X WIDTH	EXT. TO
252.	2000 x 50yds.	2250yds.
135.	1600 x 50yds.	2400yds.
006.	2000 x 50yds.	-

EXTENSIBILITY : -

ACCOMMODATION : Permanent[part]
HANGARS : Types:J-4;K-2;L-8;Blister-30.

HARDSTANDINGS : Frypan-32;diamond-1;concrete apron for 80 A/C.

	OFFICERS	S.N.C.O's.	O.R's.	TOTAL
R.A.F.	290.	263.	2196.	2749.
W.A.A.F.	11.	6.	286.	303.

AFFILIATED AIRFIELDS : -

PRESENT USE [1985] : RAF.

NO: 378.

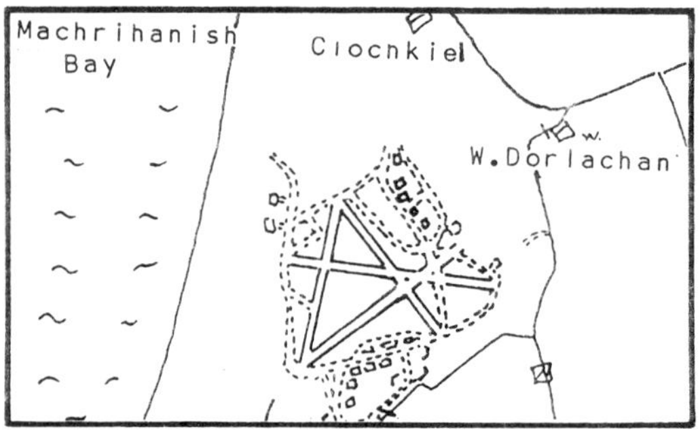

AIRFIELD NAME: MACHRIHANISH. OPENED : 1941.
COUNTY : Argyllshire. CLOSED :
COMMAND : RN.
FORMATION : HMS Landrail. GRID REF: S 153458[Scot]
FUNCTION : Disembarked Sqdns. O.S.REF.: NR 660233.

LOCALITY : Campbeltown 3.25miles ESE.
RAILWAY STN. : Glasgow[LMS & LNER]

LATITUDE : 55 26 30N. HEIGHT ASL : 30′ LIGHTING : Naval.
LONGITUDE : 05 41 55W. FLYING CONTROL : Yes. RADIO : QDM.

LANDMARKS : The Mull of Kintyre. Campbeltown lock & town.
DAY.

LANDMARKS : -
NIGHT

OBSTRUCTIONS : Mountainous country to N & S with summit 1462′ 6miles SSW. Hills 706′ 1.75miles NE & 853′ 2.5miles S. W/T masts 90′ on hill 334′ 2miles S.

LANDING AREA : Unspecified Hard Surface.
SURFACE :

QDM	LENGTH X WIDTH	EXT. TO
030-210.	1030 x 30yds.	-
075-255.	1030 x 30yds.	-
119-299.	1190 x 30yds.	-
165-345.	1000 x 30yds.	-

EXTENSIBILITY : -

ACCOMMODATION : Temporary.
HANGARS : 60x70′:Sqdn-17;storage-8;Workshop 185x105′-3.

HARDSTANDINGS : TE-6.

	OFFICERS	Chiefs/POs/Ratings.	TOTAL
R.N.	280.	1556.	1836.
W.R.N.S.	30.	662.	692.

AFFILIATED AIRFIELDS : -

PRESENT USE [1985] : USN/NATO.

NO: 379.

AIRFIELD NAME: MACMERRY. OPENED : 1929.
COUNTY : East Lothian. CLOSED : 1953.
COMMAND : Fighter.
FORMATION : 13 Grp[Inverness] GRID REF: T 935945[68Scot]
FUNCTION : Operational. O.S.REF.: NT 445734.

LOCALITY : 14miles E of Edinburgh.
RAILWAY STN. : Longniddry 2miles[LNER]

LATITUDE : 55 57 00N. HEIGHT ASL : 300′ LIGHTING : Mk2.
LONGITUDE : 02 53 45W. FLYING CONTROL : None.RADIO : QDM.

LANDMARKS DAY. : Hopetown monument. Firth of Forth.

LANDMARKS NIGHT : Firth of Forth 2miles N.

OBSTRUCTIONS : -

LANDING AREA SURFACE : Grass.

QDM: WSW-ENE. LENGTH X WIDTH: 1500yds. EXT. TO: -
: NW-SE. : 1200yds. : -
: NNW-SSE. : 1200yds. : -
: : :

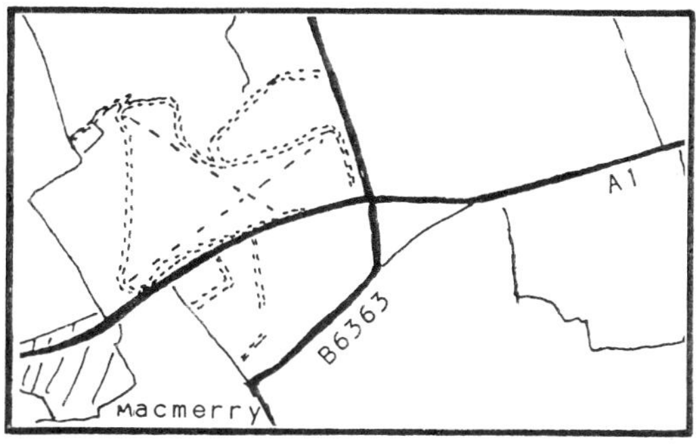

EXTENSIBILITY : None possible.

ACCOMMODATION : Temporary.
HANGARS : T2-1;civil hangar-1;blister-8.

HARDSTANDINGS : Blenheim-6.

R.A.F. : OFFICERS: 56.S.N.C.O′s.: 56.O.R′s.: 775.TOTAL: 887.
W.A.A.F.: " : 6. " : 4. " : 168. " : 178.

AFFILIATED AIRFIELDS : Turnhouse[Sector]

PRESENT USE [1985] : Agriculture.

NO: 380.

AIRFIELD NAME: MADLEY. OPENED : 1941.
COUNTY : Herefordshire. CLOSED : 1946.
COMMAND : Technical Training.
FORMATION : 27 Grp[Cirencester] GRID REF: O 866586[91]
FUNCTION : Radio School. O.S.REF.: SO 418374.

LOCALITY : 6.5miles W of Hereford.
RAILWAY STN. : Hereford[GWR]

LATITUDE : 52 01 50N. HEIGHT ASL : 265′ LIGHTING : None.
LONGITUDE : 02 51 00W. FLYING CONTROL : Yes. RADIO : QDM.

LANDMARKS DAY. : 3.5miles S of R Wye.

LANDMARKS NIGHT : As day.

OBSTRUCTIONS : Hills 905′ ASL within radius of 5miles.

LANDING AREA SURFACE : Concrete[part] & tarmac covering.

QDM: 160. LENGTH X WIDTH: 1100+100yds. EXT. TO: -
: 250. : 1100+ 70yds. : 2400yds.
: 290. : 1400+380yds. : 2000yds.
: : [+ are bottlenecks] : 1150yds.

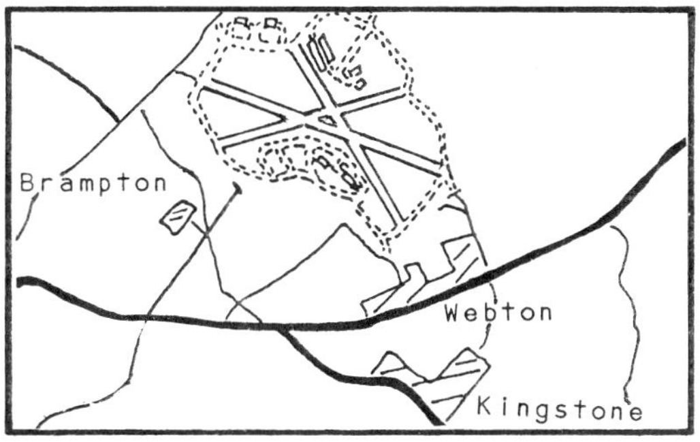

EXTENSIBILITY : Reccommended to 2000&1580yds. only.
Entails demolition of a barn & Farmhouse.
ACCOMMODATION : Temporary.
HANGARS : Hinaidi-2;Callendar-3;blister-13.

HARDSTANDINGS : Sommerfeld track-4.

R.A.F. : OFFICERS: 116.S.N.C.O′s.: 195.O.R′s.: 5982.TOTAL: 6293.
W.A.A.F.: " : 15. " : 16. " : 670. " : 701.

AFFILIATED AIRFIELDS : -

PRESENT USE [1985] : Agriculture.

NO: 381.

AIRFIELD NAME: MAGHABERRY. OPENED : 1941.
COUNTY : Antrim NI. CLOSED : 1946.
COMMAND : RAF NI.
FORMATION : Stormont[Belfast] GRID REF: J 180645[313NI]
FUNCTION : Parent. O.S.REF.: J 180645.

LOCALITY : 5miles W of Lisburn.
RAILWAY STN. : Moira 2miles[GNR]

LATITUDE : 54 30 53N. HEIGHT ASL : 300′ LIGHTING : Mk2.
LONGITUDE : 06 10 38W. FLYING CONTROL : None.RADIO : QDM.

LANDMARKS DAY. : Southend of Lough Neagh 6miles due W;
BBC wireless masts 5miles ESE.

LANDMARKS NIGHT : Outer circle lights overlap with those
of Long Kesh.

OBSTRUCTIONS : House at N end of NE-SW runway. T2 hangar
at SW edge of A/F.

LANDING AREA SURFACE : Concrete.

QDM: 032. LENGTH X WIDTH: 1100 x 50yds.EXT. TO: 1400yds.
: 106. : 1500 x 50yds. : -
: 156. : 1070 x 50yds. : -
: : :

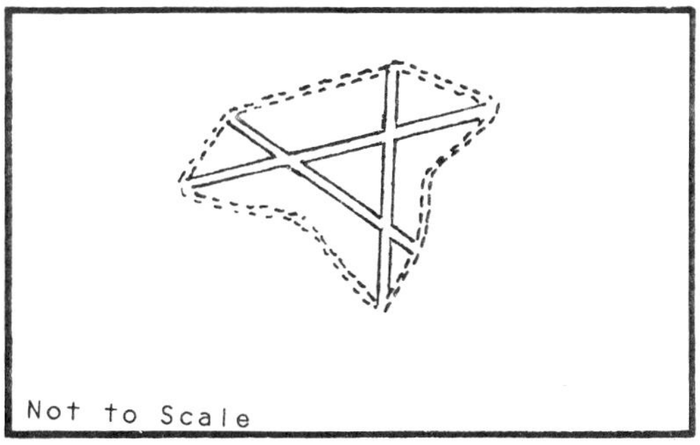

EXTENSIBILITY : -

ACCOMMODATION : Temporary.
HANGARS : T2-2.

HARDSTANDINGS : Frying pan-17;Spectacle-14.

R.A.F. : OFFICERS: 123.S.N.C.O′s.: 336.O.R′s.: 1500.TOTAL: 1959.
W.A.A.F.: " : 20. " : 80. " : 228. " : 328.

AFFILIATED AIRFIELDS : -

PRESENT USE [1985] : HM Prison.

AIRFIELD NAME: MANBY. OPENED : 1938.
COUNTY : Lincolnshire. CLOSED : 1974.
COMMAND : Flying Training.
FORMATION : 25 Grp[Market Drayton] GRID REF: A 857057[40]
FUNCTION : Empire Air Armament School. O.S.REF.: TF 385866.
LOCALITY : 4miles E of Louth.
RAILWAY STN. : Grimoldby .5miles[LNER]

LATITUDE : 52 21 30N. HEIGHT ASL : 51′ LIGHTING : Mk2.
LONGITUDE : 00 05 15E. FLYING CONTROL : None.RADIO : QDM.

LANDMARKS DAY : Louth church.

LANDMARKS NIGHT : -

OBSTRUCTIONS : -

LANDING AREA SURFACE : Concrete & wood chippings.

QDM	LENGTH X WIDTH	EXT. TO
290.	1400 x 50yds.	2000yds.
220.	1250 x 50yds.	2200yds.
		1700yds.

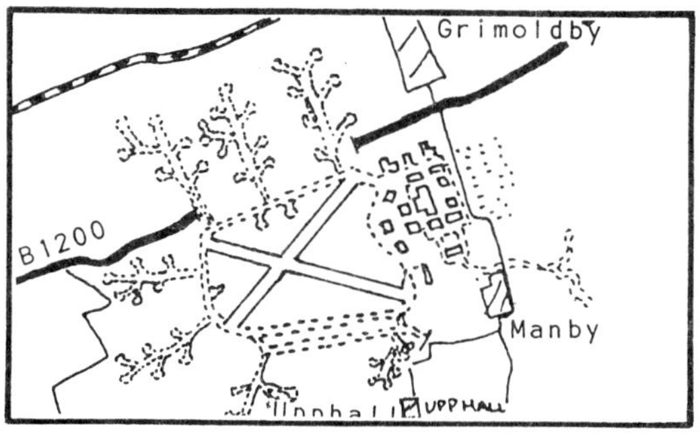

EXTENSIBILITY : Entails diversion of a second class road.

ACCOMMODATION : Permanent.
HANGARS : Type C[225′]-4;special-1;EO blister-17.

HARDSTANDINGS : Circular 125′-51.

	OFFICERS	S.N.C.O′s.	O.R′s.	TOTAL
R.A.F.	193.	254.	1062.	1509.
W.A.A.F.	8.	6.	588.	602.

AFFILIATED AIRFIELDS : -

PRESENT USE [1985] : Disused.

AIRFIELD NAME: MANORBIER. OPENED : 1935.
COUNTY : Pembrokeshire. CLOSED : 1946.
COMMAND : Fighter.
FORMATION : 70 Grp[Farnborough] GRID REF: N 522203[99]
FUNCTION : AA Co-operation Unit. O.S.REF.: SS 075990.

LOCALITY : 4miles SW of Tenby.
RAILWAY STN. : Tenby 1.25miles[GWR]

LATITUDE : 51 38 38N. HEIGHT ASL : 194′ LIGHTING : None.
LONGITUDE : 04 46 45W. FLYING CONTROL : None.RADIO : QDM.

LANDMARKS DAY : Caldy Island 3.5miles E.

LANDMARKS NIGHT : As day.

OBSTRUCTIONS : 2x100′ high W/T masts.

LANDING AREA SURFACE : Grass.

QDM	LENGTH X WIDTH	EXT. TO
NE-SW.	750yds.	-
NW-SE.	500yds.	-
E-W.	800yds.	-

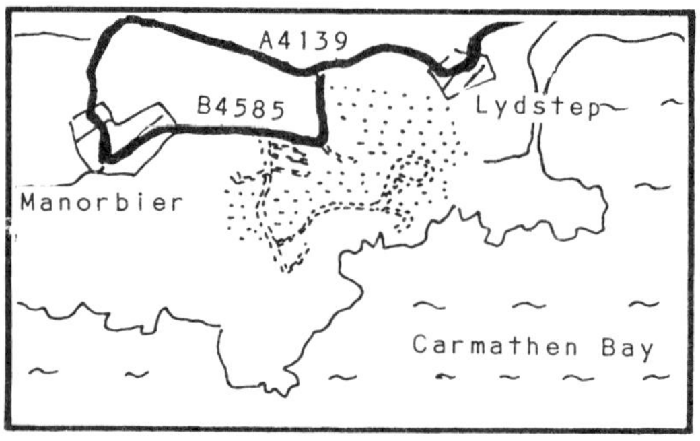

EXTENSIBILITY : None possible.

ACCOMMODATION : Temporary.
HANGARS : Bellman-1.

HARDSTANDINGS : -

	OFFICERS	S.N.C.O′s.	O.R′s.	TOTAL
R.A.F.	8.	20.	160.	188.
W.A.A.F.	-	-	-	-

AFFILIATED AIRFIELDS : -

PRESENT USE [1985] : Disused.

AIRFIELD NAME: MANSTON. OPENED : 1916.
COUNTY : Kent. CLOSED :
COMMAND : Fighter.
FORMATION : 11 Grp[Uxbridge] GRID REF: R 776844[117]
FUNCTION : Forward Airfield. [Also BC emergency R/W] O.S.REF.: TR 332599.
LOCALITY : 2.75miles WNW of Ramsgate.
RAILWAY STN. : Westgate[SR]

LATITUDE : 51 20 45N. HEIGHT ASL : 150′ LIGHTING : Mk2.
LONGITUDE : 01 21 00E. FLYING CONTROL : Yes. RADIO : QDM.

LANDMARKS DAY : Steeple, Quex Park 1mile. Chimney .75miles SE.

LANDMARKS NIGHT : -

OBSTRUCTIONS : -

LANDING AREA SURFACE : Concrete & tarmac with 500yd grass extension at each end.

QDM	LENGTH X WIDTH	EXT. TO
245.	3000yds.	4500yds.
		2500yds.
		2600yds.

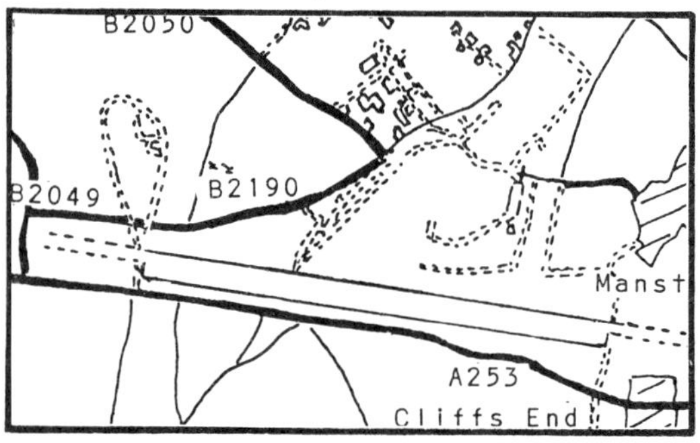

EXTENSIBILITY : Would entail serious demolition.

ACCOMMODATION : Semi-permanent[part]
HANGARS : Callendar portable-1;old type[1916]-2; EO blister-7.
HARDSTANDINGS : SE-26.

	OFFICERS	S.N.C.O′s.	O.R′s.	TOTAL
R.A.F.	150.	283.	3126.	3559.
W.A.A.F.	7.	6.	414.	427.

AFFILIATED AIRFIELDS : North Weald[Sector]

PRESENT USE [1985] : RAF.

NO: 385.

AIRFIELD NAME: MARHAM. OPENED : 1937.
COUNTY : Norfolk. CLOSED :
COMMAND : Bomber.
FORMATION : Under re-construction. GRID REF: G 186280[66]
FUNCTION : Under re-construction. O.S.REF.: TF 725084.

LOCALITY : 10miles SE of Kings Lynn.
RAILWAY STN. : Narborough & Pentney 3miles[LNER]

LATITUDE : 52 39 08N. HEIGHT ASL : 80′ LIGHTING : Mk1.
LONGITUDE : 00 33 00E. FLYING CONTROL : Yes. RADIO : QDM.

LANDMARKS DAY : Ladys Wood.

LANDMARKS NIGHT : -

OBSTRUCTIONS : Ladys wood in NE corner of A/F.

LANDING AREA : Under re-construction.
SURFACE : Concrete[estimated date of completion 8/45]

QDM	LENGTH X WIDTH	EXT. TO
245.	3000 x 100yds	4000yds.
293.	2000 x 100yds.	-
335.	2000 x 100yds.	-

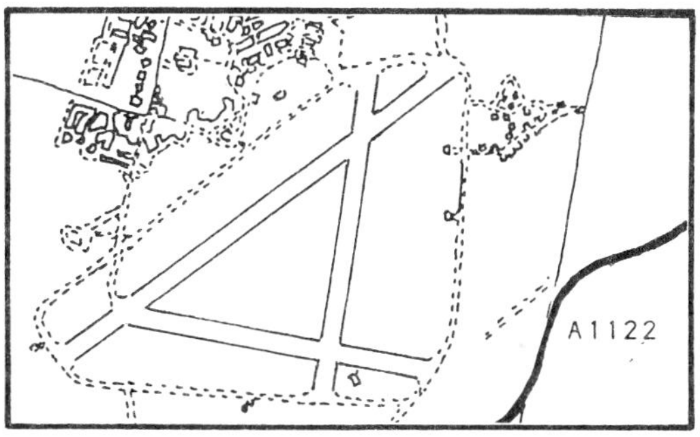

EXTENSIBILITY : Entails diversion of main road & demolition of 2 farms & RAF buildings.
ACCOMMODATION : Permanent.
HANGARS : Type C-5.

HARDSTANDINGS : Heavy bomber-36.

	OFFICERS	S.N.C.O′s.	O.R′s.	TOTAL
R.A.F.	139.	296.	1893.	2328.
W.A.A.F.	10.	16.	318.	344.

AFFILIATED AIRFIELDS : -

PRESENT USE [1985] : RAF.

NO: 386.

AIRFIELD NAME: MARKET HARBOROUGH. OPENED : 1943.
COUNTY : Leicestershire. CLOSED : 1947.
COMMAND : Bomber.
FORMATION : 92 Grp[Winslow] GRID REF: F 170088[73]
FUNCTION : Operational Training Unit. O.S.REF.: SP 712887.
LOCALITY : 2miles NW of Market Harborough.
RAILWAY STN. : Market Harborough 3miles[LMS]

LATITUDE : 52 29 30N. HEIGHT ASL : 360′ LIGHTING : Mk2.
LONGITUDE : 00 57 00W. FLYING CONTROL : Yes. RADIO : QDM.

LANDMARKS DAY : Town of Market Harborough.

LANDMARKS NIGHT : Rugby W/T masts 17miles NE.

OBSTRUCTIONS : -

LANDING AREA : Concrete & tarmac.
SURFACE :

QDM	LENGTH X WIDTH	EXT. TO
180.	1400 x 50yds.	1600yds.
140.	1900 x 50yds.	2000yds.
290.	1400 x 50yds.	-

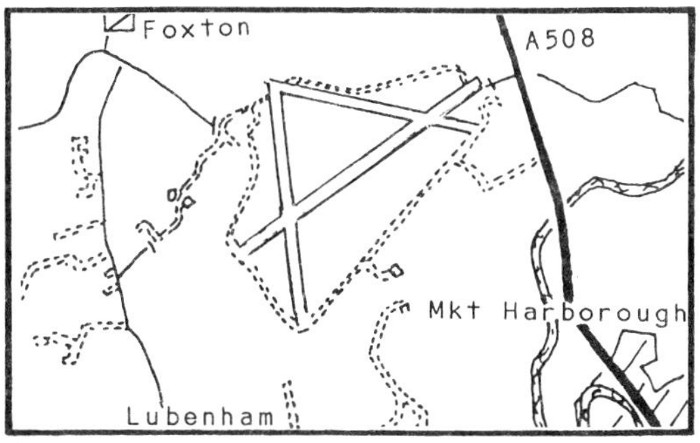

EXTENSIBILITY : -

ACCOMMODATION : Temporary.
HANGARS : T2-4;B1-1.

HARDSTANDINGS : Loop-11;Spectacle-19.

	OFFICERS	S.N.C.O′s.	O.R′s.	TOTAL
R.A.F.	171.	628.	892.	1691.
W.A.A.F.	10.	15.	427.	452.

AFFILIATED AIRFIELDS : -

PRESENT USE [1985] : HM Prison.

NO: 387.

AIRFIELD NAME: MARSTON MOOR. OPENED : 1941.
COUNTY : Yorkshire. CLOSED : 1945.
COMMAND : Bomber.
FORMATION : 7 Grp[St.Vincents] GRID REF: E 934725[27]
FUNCTION : Operational[74 Base] O.S.REF.: SE 460520.

LOCALITY : 8.5miles W of York.
RAILWAY STN. : Cattal via York 2miles[LNER]

LATITUDE : 53 57 45N. HEIGHT ASL : 68′ LIGHTING : Mk2.
LONGITUDE : 01 18 00W. FLYING CONTROL : Yes. RADIO : QDM.

LANDMARKS DAY : R Nidd. Royal Ordnance factory, Thorpe Arch.

LANDMARKS NIGHT : -

OBSTRUCTIONS : Water tower & hangars marked with obstruction lights.

LANDING AREA : Concrete.
SURFACE :

QDM	LENGTH X WIDTH	EXT. TO
226.	2000 x 50yds.	2800yds.
353.	1400 x 50yds.	2000yds.
286.	1400 x 50yds.	2000yds.

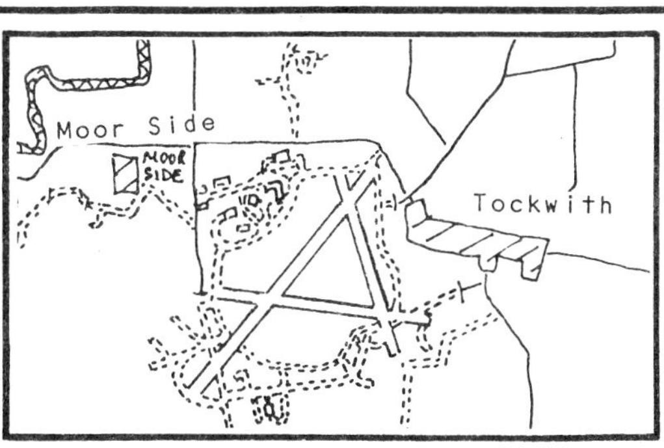

EXTENSIBILITY : Entails cutting of 2 access roads.

ACCOMMODATION : Temporary.
HANGARS : T2-6;B1-1.

HARDSTANDINGS : Heavy bomber-36.

	OFFICERS	S.N.C.O′s.	O.R′s.	TOTAL
R.A.F.	206.	744.	1164.	2114.
W.A.A.F.	12.	20.	326.	358.

AFFILIATED AIRFIELDS : Acaster Malbis & Rufforth[Sub-stations]

PRESENT USE [1985] : Home Office.

NO: 388.

AIRFIELD NAME: MARTLESHAM HEATH. OPENED : 1917.
COUNTY : Suffolk. CLOSED : 1963.
COMMAND : 8th USAAF.
FORMATION : 356th Fighter Grp. GRID REF: M 694638[87]
FUNCTION : Operational. O.S.REF.: TM 242454.

LOCALITY : 1.5miles SW of Woodbridge.
RAILWAY STN. : Woodbridge 2miles[LNER]

LATITUDE : 52 03 30N. HEIGHT ASL : 90′ LIGHTING : Mk2.
LONGITUDE : 01 16 30E. FLYING CONTROL : Yes. RADIO : QDM.

LANDMARKS DAY. : R Debden & Orwell 2.5miles E & 4.5miles S respectively.

LANDMARKS NIGHT : As day.

OBSTRUCTIONS : E & NE sides trees. W & NW hangars. S & SW open heath & good approaches.

LANDING AREA SURFACE : Unspecified hard surface.

QDM	LENGTH X WIDTH	EXT. TO
220.	1650 x 50yds.	2000yds.
040.	1700 x 50yds.	2950yds.

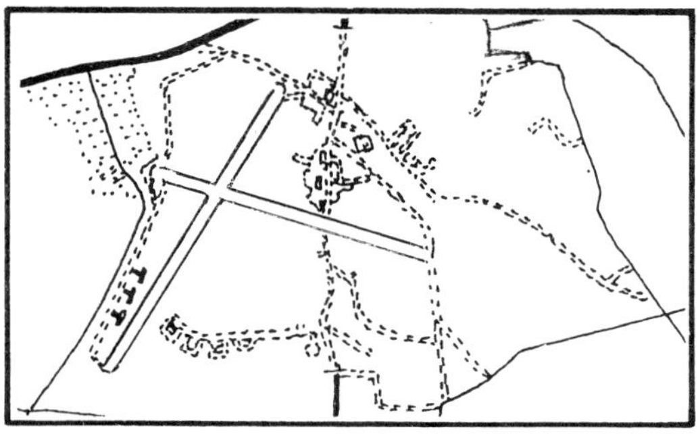

EXTENSIBILITY : Effectively only to 2000 & 2600yds. Demolition possible in approaches.
ACCOMMODATION : Permanent[part]
HANGARS : Blister-3;Types:A-1;G-1;GS-1.

HARDSTANDINGS : Steel mats-20.

USAAF. : OFFICERS: 190. Enlisted Men. : 1519. TOTAL: 1709.

AFFILIATED AIRFIELDS : -

PRESENT USE [1985] : Industry.

NO: 389.

AIRFIELD NAME: MATCHING. OPENED : 1943.
COUNTY : Essex. CLOSED : 1945.
COMMAND : Bomber.
FORMATION : 3 Grp[Exning] GRID REF: L 995306[96]
FUNCTION : Care & Maintenance. O.S.REF.: TL 550120.

LOCALITY : 5miles E of Harlow.
RAILWAY STN. : Sawbridgeworth 4miles[LNER]

LATITUDE : 51 46 53N. HEIGHT ASL : 275′ LIGHTING : Mk2.
LONGITUDE : 00 14 45E. FLYING CONTROL : Yes. RADIO : QDM.

LANDMARKS DAY. : Windmill & church 2500yds NE of A/F. Arial masts 4miles S of A/F.

LANDMARKS NIGHT : Arial masts 400′high with obstruction light.

OBSTRUCTIONS : -

LANDING AREA SURFACE : Concrete & wood chippings.

QDM	LENGTH X WIDTH	EXT. TO
200.	2000 x 50yds.	3000yds.
270.	1400 x 50yds.	3000yds.
140.	1400 x 50yds.	2000yds.

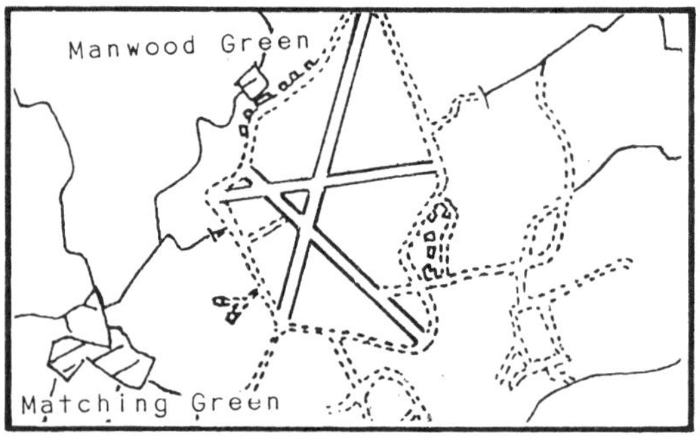

EXTENSIBILITY : Entails very serious demolition of RAF bulidings.
ACCOMMODATION : Temporary.
HANGARS : T2-2.

HARDSTANDINGS : Loop-50.

	OFFICERS	S.N.C.O′s.	O.R′s.	TOTAL
R.A.F.	-	-	-	-
W.A.A.F.	-	-	-	-

AFFILIATED AIRFIELDS : -

PRESENT USE [1985] : Unspecified.

NO: 390.

AIRFIELD NAME: MATLASK. OPENED : 1940.
COUNTY : Norfolk. CLOSED : 1945.
COMMAND : Fighter.
FORMATION : 12 Grp[Watnall] GRID REF: G 610523[58]
FUNCTION : Operational. O.S.REF.: TG 145340.

LOCALITY : 5.5miles SE of Holt.
RAILWAY STN. : Corpusty 4miles[LNER]

LATITUDE : 52 51 38N. HEIGHT ASL : 165′ LIGHTING : None.
LONGITUDE : 01 11 30E. FLYING CONTROL : None. RADIO : QDM.

LANDMARKS DAY. : West Beckham W/T masts 3miles N.

LANDMARKS NIGHT : Blickling Lake 3miles SSE.

OBSTRUCTIONS : -

LANDING AREA SURFACE : Grass.

QDM	LENGTH X WIDTH	EXT. TO
NW-SE.	1600yds.	2600yds.
SW-NE.	1300yds.	1800yds.
		1500yds.

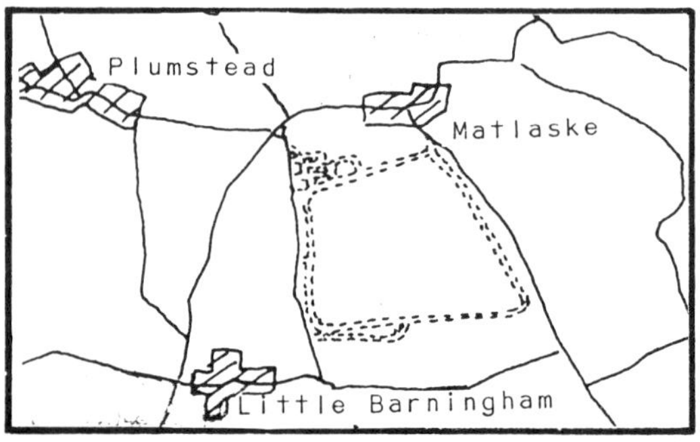

EXTENSIBILITY : -

ACCOMMODATION : Temporary.
HANGARS : D2-1;blister-5.

HARDSTANDINGS : Concrete-21.

	OFFICERS	S.N.C.O′s.	O.R′s.	TOTAL
R.A.F.	108.	105.	2330.	2543.
W.A.A.F.	2.	2.	130.	134.

AFFILIATED AIRFIELDS : Coltishall[Sector]

PRESENT USE [1985] : Disused.

NO: 391.

AIRFIELD NAME: MAYDOWN. OPENED : 1942.
COUNTY : Londonderry NI. CLOSED : 1949.
COMMAND : RN.
FORMATION : HMS Shrike. GRID REF: C 487208[304NI]
FUNCTION : Formation & working up TBR Sqdns. O.S.REF.: C 487208.
LOCALITY : 3miles NE of Londonderry.
RAILWAY STN. : Culmore.25miles[MNCI]

LATITUDE : 55 02 00N. HEIGHT ASL : 50′ LIGHTING : None.
LONGITUDE : 07 14 25W. FLYING CONTROL : Yes. RADIO : QDM.

LANDMARKS DAY. : Lough Foyle & R Foyle & Faughan. City of Londonderry.

LANDMARKS NIGHT : -

OBSTRUCTIONS : Mountains NW 1589′ 5miles. Land rises to 800′ SE & SW 5miles.

LANDING AREA SURFACE : Concrete.

QDM	LENGTH X WIDTH	EXT. TO
002-182.	1350 x 50yds.	1350yds.
069-249.	1650 x 50yds.	1920yds.

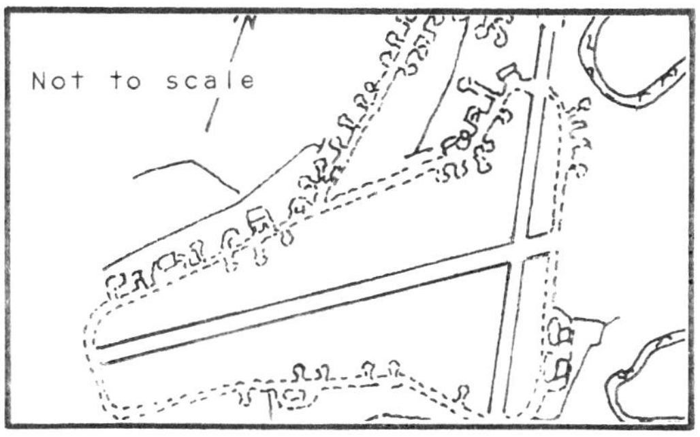

EXTENSIBILITY : -

ACCOMMODATION : Temporary.
HANGARS : Super blister[sqdn]-9;T1-1; Workshop 175x90′-1.
HARDSTANDINGS : A/C standinge-37;double pens-6.

R.N. : OFFICERS: 218. Chiefs/POs/Ratings.: 1103.TOTAL: 1321.
W.R.N.S. : " : 13. " " : 338. " : 351.

AFFILIATED AIRFIELDS : -

PRESENT USE [1985] : Disused.

NO: 392.

AIRFIELD NAME: MELBOURNE. OPENED : 1940.
COUNTY : Yorkshire. CLOSED : 1945.
COMMAND : Bomber.
FORMATION : 4 Grp[York] GRID REF: A 237618[27]
FUNCTION : Operational. O.S.REF.: SE 766421.

LOCALITY : 12miles SE of York.
RAILWAY STN. : Pocklington[LNER]

LATITUDE : 53 52 15N. HEIGHT ASL : 25′ LIGHTING : Mk2.
LONGITUDE : 00 50 15W. FLYING CONTROL : Yes. RADIO : QDM.

LANDMARKS DAY. : York 11miles NW. Line of hills running 340-160 degrees to E & NE. Windmill 100degrees 1100yds from watch tower. Melbourne village, 320degrees 1.5miles from watch tower.
LANDMARKS NIGHT : R Humber.

OBSTRUCTIONS : -

LANDING AREA SURFACE : Concrete & tarmac.

QDM	LENGTH X WIDTH	EXT. TO
193.	1350 x 50yds.	4000yds.
242.	1900 x 50yds.	4000yds.
326.	1400 x 50yds.	3000yds.

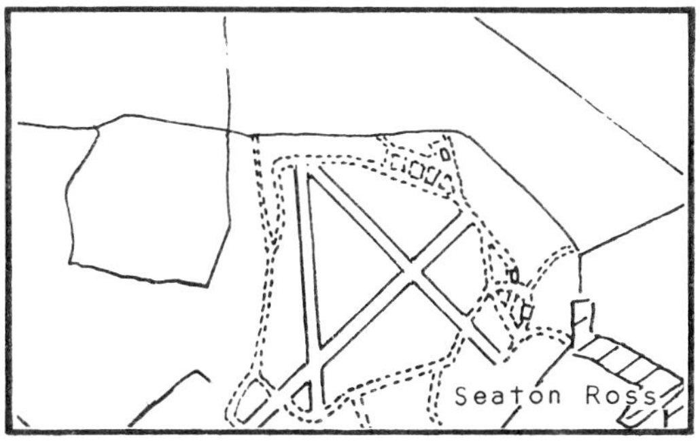

EXTENSIBILITY : -

ACCOMMODATION : Temporary.
HANGARS : T2-2;B1-1.

HARDSTANDINGS : Heavy bomber-36.

R.A.F. : OFFICERS: 155.S.N.C.O's.: 287.O.R's.: 1337.TOTAL: 1779.
W.A.A.F.: " : 4. " : 17. " : 267. " : 288.

AFFILIATED AIRFIELDS : Holme[44 Base]

PRESENT USE [1985] : Disused.

NO: 393.

AIRFIELD NAME: MELTON MOWBRAY. OPENED : 1943.
COUNTY : Leicestershire. CLOSED : 1964.
COMMAND : Transport.
FORMATION : 44 Grp[Gloucester] GRID REF: F 209355[63]
FUNCTION : Parent. O.S.REF.: SK 750158.

LOCALITY : 2miles S of Melton Mowbray.
RAILWAY STN. : Melton Mowbray[LMS]

LATITUDE : 52 44 00N. HEIGHT ASL : 400′ LIGHTING : Mk2.
LONGITUDE : 00 53 30W. FLYING CONTROL : Yes. RADIO : QDM.

LANDMARKS DAY. : Melton Mowbray 1mile N.

LANDMARKS NIGHT : -

OBSTRUCTIONS : -

LANDING AREA SURFACE : Concrete.

QDM	LENGTH X WIDTH	EXT. TO
157.	2000 x 50yds.	2500yds.
296.	1400 x 50yds.	-
035.	1300 x 50yds.	-

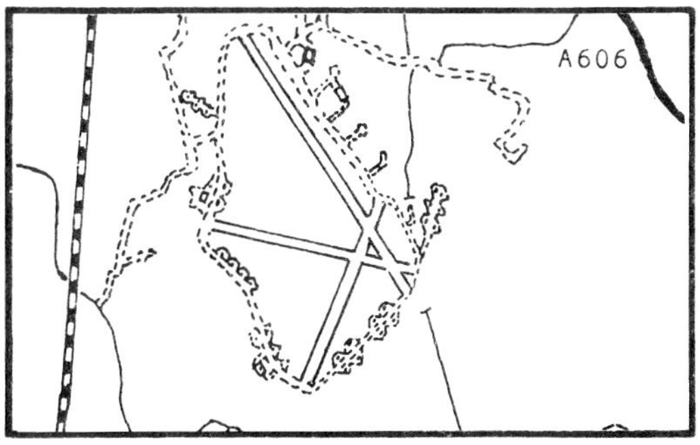

EXTENSIBILITY : Not recommended.

ACCOMMODATION : Temporary.
HANGARS : T2-4.

HARDSTANDINGS : Spectacle-12;apron-18.

R.A.F. : OFFICERS: 115.S.N.C.O's.: 414.O.R's.: 1472.TOTAL: 2001.
W.A.A.F.: " : 10. " : 24. " : 288. " : 322.

AFFILIATED AIRFIELDS : -

PRESENT USE [1985] : Industry.

NO: 394.

AIRFIELD NAME: MEMBURY.
COUNTY : Berkshire.
COMMAND : 9th USAAF.
FORMATION : 436th Troop Carrier Grp.
FUNCTION : Operational.

OPENED : 1942.
CLOSED : 1947.
GRID REF: U 750952[112]
O.S.REF.: SU 308754.

LOCALITY : 3miles SE of Lambourn.
RAILWAY STN. : Lambourn[GWR]

LATITUDE : 51 28 38N. HEIGHT ASL : 667′ LIGHTING : Mk2.
LONGITUDE : 01 33 23W. FLYING CONTROL : Yes. RADIO : QDM.

LANDMARKS DAY : -

LANDMARKS NIGHT : -

OBSTRUCTIONS : -

LANDING AREA SURFACE : Concrete & wood chippings.

QDM	LENGTH X WIDTH	EXT. TO
220.	1518 x 50yds.	1527yds.
170.	2000 x 50yds.	2593yds.
270.	1100 x 50yds.	1120yds.

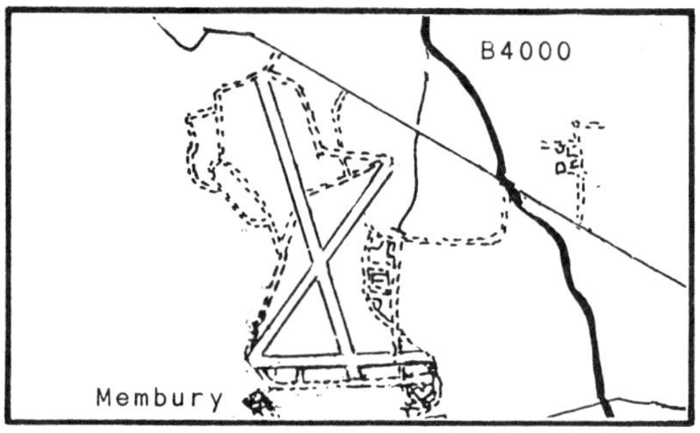

EXTENSIBILITY : Entails diversion of Roman road & demolition old house & cottages.
ACCOMMODATION : Temporary.
HANGARS : T2-4.

HARDSTANDINGS : Dispersed concrete-59.

USAAF. : OFFICERS: 470. Enlisted Men. : 1898.TOTAL: 2368.

AFFILIATED AIRFIELDS : -

PRESENT USE [1985] : Private flying.

NO: 395.

AIRFIELD NAME: MENDLESHAM.
COUNTY : Suffolk.
COMMAND : 8th USAAF.
FORMATION : 34th Bomb Grp.
FUNCTION : Operational.

OPENED : 1943.
CLOSED : 1954.
GRID REF: M 585817[87]
O.S.REF.: TM 130638.

LOCALITY : 5.5miles NE of Stowmarket.
RAILWAY STN. : Mendlesham 2miles[LNER]

LATITUDE : 52 13 53N. HEIGHT ASL : 210′ LIGHTING : Mk2.
LONGITUDE : 01 07 15E. FLYING CONTROL : Yes. RADIO : QDM.

LANDMARKS DAY : -

LANDMARKS NIGHT : -

OBSTRUCTIONS : -

LANDING AREA SURFACE : Concrete & tarmac.

QDM	LENGTH X WIDTH	EXT. TO
010.	2000 x 50yds.	3500yds.
160.	1400 x 50yds.	2250yds.
220.	1400 x 50yds.	2100yds.

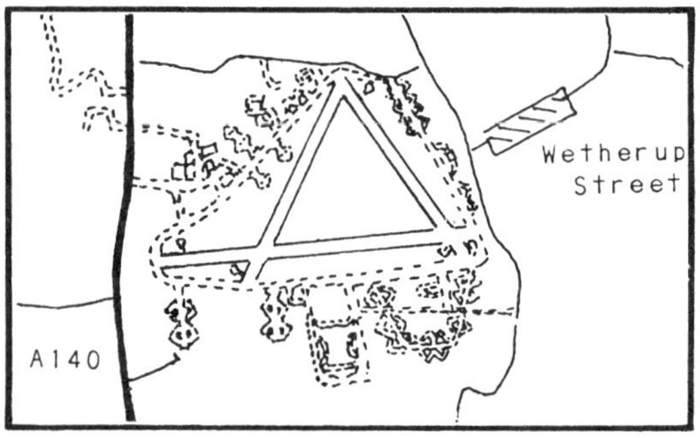

EXTENSIBILITY : Entails closure of main road.

ACCOMMODATION : Temporary.
HANGARS : T2-2.

HARDSTANDINGS : Loop-48;frypan-2.

USAAF. : OFFICERS: 443. Enlisted Men. : 2529.TOTAL: 2972.

AFFILIATED AIRFIELDS : -

PRESENT USE [1985] : Industry.

NO: 396.

AIRFIELD NAME: MEPAL.
COUNTY : Cambridgeshire.
COMMAND : Bomber.
FORMATION : 3 Grp[Exning]
FUNCTION : Operational.

OPENED : 1943.
CLOSED : 1963.
GRID REF: F 900987[75]
O.S.REF.: TL 445796.

LOCALITY : 6miles W of Ely.
RAILWAY STN. : Ely 6miles[LNER]

LATITUDE : 52 23 38N. HEIGHT ASL : 80′ LIGHTING : Mk2.
LONGITUDE : 00 07 30E. FLYING CONTROL : Yes. RADIO : QDM.

LANDMARKS DAY : Sutton church & Ely cathedrel.

LANDMARKS NIGHT : Sutton church, railway, river & dyke.

OBSTRUCTIONS : Sutton church S. Park cottages.
Sutton water tower.

LANDING AREA SURFACE : Concrete.

QDM	LENGTH X WIDTH	EXT. TO
225.	1400 x 50yds.	2500yds.
259.	2000 x 50yds.	-
319.	1400 x 50yds.	-

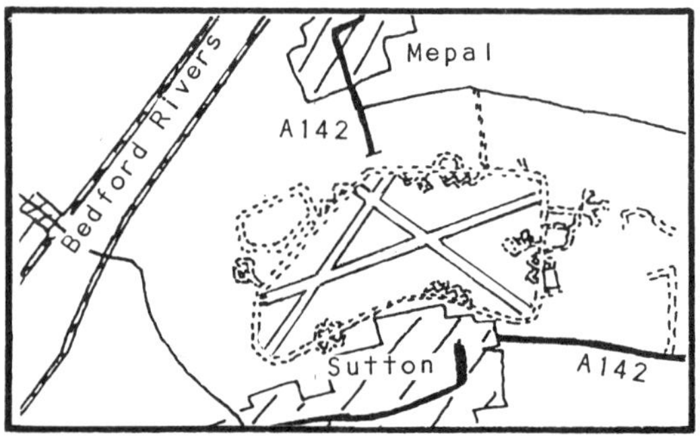

EXTENSIBILITY : Entails diversion of Ely road & demolition of possibly several council houses.
ACCOMMODATION : Temporary.
HANGARS : T2-2;B1-1.

HARDSTANDINGS : Loop-36.

	OFFICERS	S.N.C.O's.	O.R's.	TOTAL
R.A.F.	87.	295.	745.	1127.
W.A.A.F.	9.	10.	177.	196.

AFFILIATED AIRFIELDS : Waterbeach[33 Base]

PRESENT USE [1985] : Agriculture.

NO: 397.

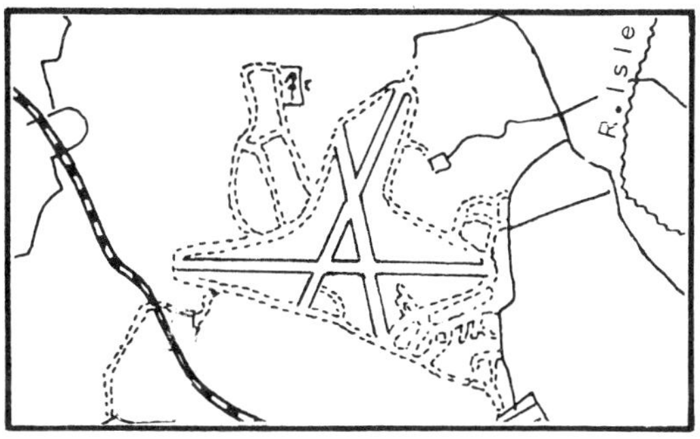

AIRFIELD NAME: MERRYFIELD.
COUNTY : Somersetshire.
COMMAND : Fighter.
FORMATION : 70 Grp[Farnborough]
FUNCTION : Care & Maintenance.

OPENED : 1943.
CLOSED :
GRID REF: T 775400[129]
O.S.REF.: ST 342186.

LOCALITY : 8miles SE of Taunton.
RAILWAY STN. : Ilminster 3.5miles[GWR]

LATITUDE : 50 57 45N. HEIGHT ASL : 110′ LIGHTING : Mk2.
LONGITUDE : 02 56 15W. FLYING CONTROL : Yes. RADIO : QDM

LANDMARKS DAY. : -

LANDMARKS NIGHT : -

OBSTRUCTIONS : -

LANDING AREA SURFACE : Concrete covered with bitumen.

QDM	LENGTH X WIDTH	EXT. TO
280.	2000 x 50yds.	2300yds.
350.	1400 x 50yds.	-
040.	1220 x 50yds.	1300yds.

EXTENSIBILITY : Entails closure of a lane.

ACCOMMODATION : Temporary.
HANGARS : T2-2.

HARDSTANDINGS : Spectacle-50.

	OFFICERS	S.N.C.O's.	O.R's.	TOTAL
R.A.F.	124.	825.	2130.	3079.
W.A.A.F.	-	-	216.	216.

AFFILIATED AIRFIELDS : Weston Zoyland[Sector]

PRESENT USE [1985] : RN.

NO: 398.

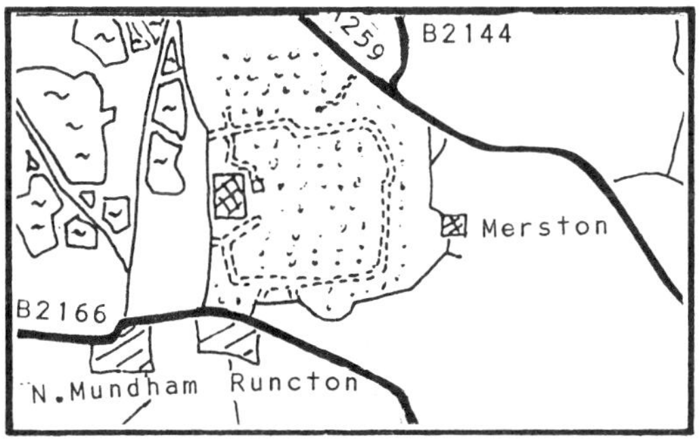

AIRFIELD NAME: MERSTON.
COUNTY : Sussex.
COMMAND : Fighter.
FORMATION : 11 Grp[Uxbridge]
FUNCTION : Operational[satellite]

OPENED : 1941.
CLOSED : 1945.
GRID REF: Q 321225[133]
O.S.REF.: SU 885031.

LOCALITY : 2.5miles SE of Chichester.
RAILWAY STN. : Chichester 2.5miles[SR]

LATITUDE : 50 49 08N. HEIGHT ASL : 50′ LIGHTING : None.
LONGITUDE : 00 44 30W. FLYING CONTROL : Yes. RADIO : QDM.

LANDMARKS DAY. : Greenhouse & chimney, W side of A/F.

LANDMARKS NIGHT : -

OBSTRUCTIONS : -

LANDING AREA SURFACE : Steel Matting[Sommerfeld track]

QDM	LENGTH X WIDTH	EXT. TO
045.	1592yds.	-
135.	1400yds.	-
		-

EXTENSIBILITY : -

ACCOMMODATION : Temporary.
HANGARS : O blister-6.

HARDSTANDINGS : SE-20.

	OFFICERS	S.N.C.O's.	O.R's.	TOTAL
R.A.F.	78.	106.	955.	1139.
W.A.A.F.	1.	-	60.	61.

AFFILIATED AIRFIELDS : Tangmere[Sector]

PRESENT USE [1985] : Agriculture.

NO: 399.

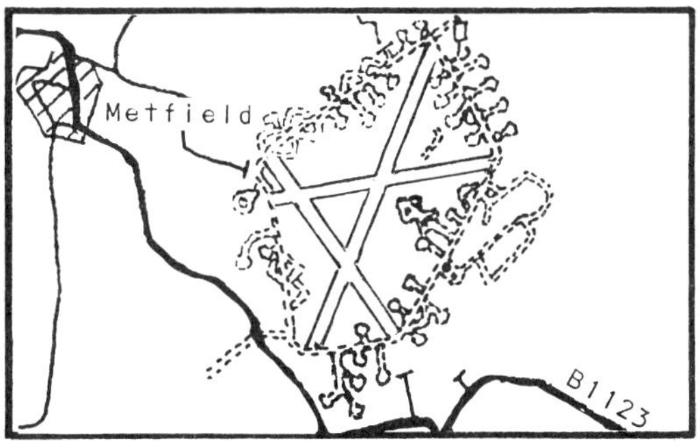

AIRFIELD NAME: METFIELD.
COUNTY : Suffolk.
COMMAND : USATC.
FORMATION : European Division.
FUNCTION : Operational.

OPENED : 1943.
CLOSED : 1945.
GRID REF: M 765970[77]
O.S.REF.: TM 311789.

LOCALITY : 5miles SE of Harleston.
RAILWAY STN. : Harleston 5miles[LNER]

LATITUDE : 52 21 40N. HEIGHT ASL : 177′ LIGHTING : Mk2.
LONGITUDE : 01 23 45E. FLYING CONTROL : Yes. RADIO : QDM.

LANDMARKS DAY. : Metfield church to N.

LANDMARKS NIGHT : Pylons to SE.

OBSTRUCTIONS : -

LANDING AREA SURFACE : Concrete & wood chippings.

QDM	LENGTH X WIDTH	EXT. TO
210.	2000 x 50yds.	4250yds.
270.	1400 x 50yds.	2500yds.
330.	1400 x 50yds.	2000yds.

EXTENSIBILITY : Recommended to 3000-2000&2000yds only. Entails demolition of a cottage.
ACCOMMODATION : Temporary.
HANGARS : T2-2.

HARDSTANDINGS : Loop-50.

USAAF. : OFFICERS: 421. Enlisted Men. : 2473. TOTAL: 2894.

AFFILIATED AIRFIELDS : -

PRESENT USE [1985] : Unspecified.

NO: 400.

AIRFIELD NAME: METHERINGHAM. OPENED : 1943.
COUNTY : Lincolnshire. CLOSED : 1946.
COMMAND : Bomber.
FORMATION : 5 Grp[Morton Hall] GRID REF: F 570803[47]
FUNCTION : Operational. O.S.REF.: TF 105610.

LOCALITY : 10miles SE of Lincoln.
RAILWAY STN. : Blankney & Metheringham 2miles[LNER]

LATITUDE : 53 08 00N. HEIGHT ASL : 60′ LIGHTING : Mk2.
LONGITUDE : 00 20 45W. FLYING CONTROL : Yes. RADIO : QDM.

LANDMARKS DAY. : -

LANDMARKS NIGHT : -

OBSTRUCTIONS : -

LANDING AREA SURFACE : Concrete.

QDM: 015. LENGTH X WIDTH: 2000 x 50yds.EXT. TO: 3000yds.
: 246. : 1400 x 50yds. : 2000yds.
: 128. : 1400 x 50yds. : 2000yds.

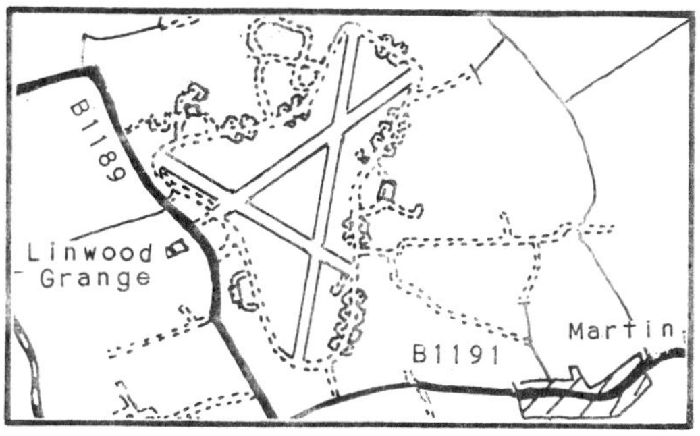

EXTENSIBILITY : Entails diversion of main access road & demolition of a farm.
ACCOMMODATION : Temporary.
HANGARS : T2-2;B1-1.

HARDSTANDINGS : Loop-36.

R.A.F. : OFFICERS: 91.S.N.C.O′s.: 200.O.R′s.: 561.TOTAL: 852.
W.A.A.F.: " : 10. " : 16. " : 316. " : 342.

AFFILIATED AIRFIELDS : Coningsby[54 Base]

PRESENT USE [1985] : Disused.

NO: 401.

AIRFIELD NAME: METHWOLD. OPENED : 1939.
COUNTY : Norfolk. CLOSED : 1958.
COMMAND : Bomber.
FORMATION : 3 Grp[Exning] GRID REF: G 189123[76]
FUNCTION : Operational. O.S.REF.: TL 730935.

LOCALITY : 5miles NW of Brandon.
RAILWAY STN. : Brandon 5miles[LNER]

LATITUDE : 52 30 45N. HEIGHT ASL : 50′ LIGHTING : Mk2.
LONGITUDE : 00 33 00E. FLYING CONTROL : Yes. RADIO : QDM.

LANDMARKS DAY. : Methwold village & church N of A/F. Large wooded area on W edge of flying field.

LANDMARKS NIGHT : 4 obstruction lights on church steeple.

OBSTRUCTIONS : -

LANDING AREA SURFACE : Concrete.

QDM: 237. LENGTH X WIDTH: 2000 x 50yds.EXT. TO: 3800yds.
: 294. : 1400 x 50yds. : 2000yds.
: 168. : 1400 x 50yds. : -

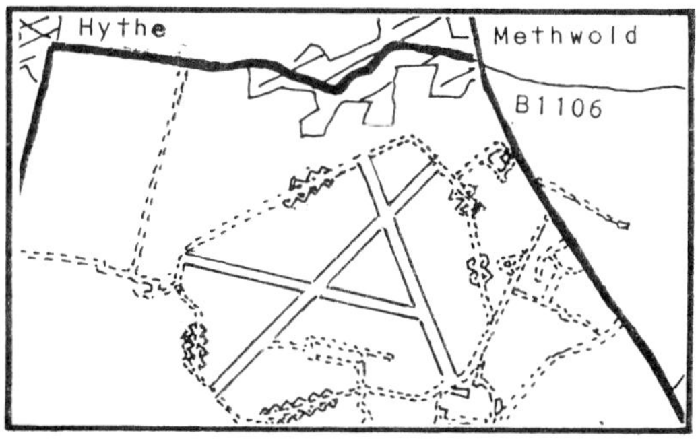

EXTENSIBILITY : Main R/W recommended to 3000yds only. Entails demolition of 3/4houses & garages.
ACCOMMODATION : Temporary.
HANGARS : T2-2;Glider T2-2;B1-1.

HARDSTANDINGS : Loop-35;pan-1.

R.A.F. : OFFICERS: 164.S.N.C.O′s.: 608.O.R′s.: 578.TOTAL: 1350.
W.A.A.F.: " : 2. " : 4. " : 60. " : 66.

AFFILIATED AIRFIELDS : Feltwell.

PRESENT USE [1985] : Agriculture.

NO: 402.

AIRFIELD NAME: MIDDLE WALLOP. OPENED : 1940.
COUNTY : Hampshire. CLOSED :
COMMAND : Fighter.
FORMATION : 11 Grp[Uxbridge] GRID REF: U 739586[122]
FUNCTION : Sector. O.S.REF.: SU 303385.

LOCALITY : 6miles SW of Andover.
RAILWAY STN. : Andover Junction[SR]

LATITUDE : 51 08 45N. HEIGHT ASL : 286′ LIGHTING : Mk2.
LONGITUDE : 01 34 07W. FLYING CONTROL : Yes. RADIO : QDM.

LANDMARKS DAY. : Denebury Hill 2600yds 121degrees magnetic from A/F.

LANDMARKS NIGHT : -

OBSTRUCTIONS : W/T masts 150′ 2100yds 357degrees magnetic from centre of landing area. Denebury Hill 2600yds 121degrees magnetic.

LANDING AREA SURFACE : Steel Matting[Sommerfeld track]

QDM: 242. LENGTH X WIDTH: 1780 x 50yds.EXT. TO: 1930yds.
: 185. : 1600 x 50yds. : 1800yds.

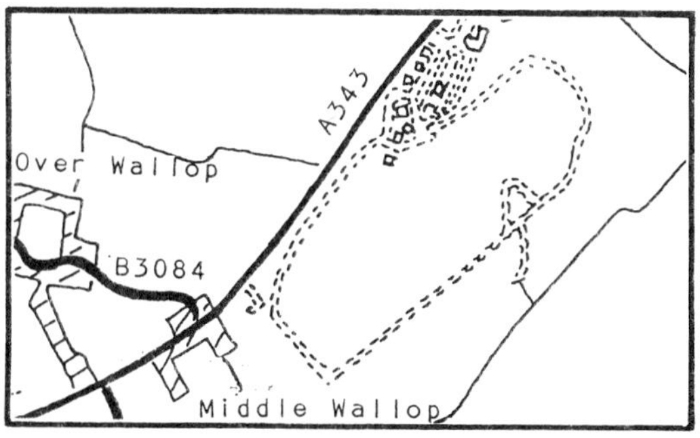

EXTENSIBILITY :

ACCOMMODATION : Permanent.
HANGARS : Type C-5;blister-4.

HARDSTANDINGS : Standard twin-8.

R.A.F. : OFFICERS: 93.S.N.C.O′s.: 262.O.R′s.: 1598.TOTAL: 1953.
W.A.A.F.: " : 17. " : 18. " : 264. " : 299.

AFFILIATED AIRFIELDS : Beaulieu[F.A/F],Christchurch[satellite], Chilbolton Ibsley & Warmwell[F.A/F]
PRESENT USE [1985] : Army.

AIRFIELD NAME: MIDDLETON-St-GEORGE. OPENED : 1941.
COUNTY : Durham. CLOSED :
COMMAND : Bomber.
FORMATION : 6 RCAF Grp[Allerton Pk] GRID REF: Z 854335[14]
FUNCTION : Operational[64 Base] O.S.REF.: NZ 375131.

LOCALITY : 5miles E of Darlington.
RAILWAY STN. : Dinsdale 1.5miles[LNER]

LATITUDE : 54 30 45N. HEIGHT ASL : 115′ LIGHTING : Mk2.
LONGITUDE : 01 25 30W. FLYING CONTROL : Yes. RADIO : QDM.

LANDMARKS DAY. : Reservoir bearing 343degrees. Darlington-Stockton railway N boundary.

LANDMARKS NIGHT : 15miles Tees Bay. R Tees winding S of A/F.

OBSTRUCTIONS : -

LANDING AREA SURFACE : Tarmac.

QDM	LENGTH X WIDTH	EXT. TO
195.	1400 x 50yds.	3000yds.
059.	2000 x 50yds.	2400yds.
283.	1400 x 50yds.	2200yds.

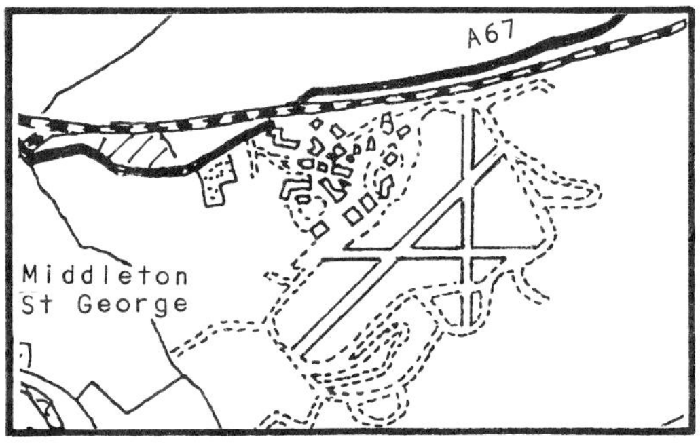

EXTENSIBILITY : But 3rd strip only effective to 2000 yds.

ACCOMMODATION : Permanent[part]
HANGARS : Types:C-1;J-1;T2-2;B1-1.

HARDSTANDINGS : Heavy bomber-36.

	OFFICERS	S.N.C.O′s.	O.R′s.	TOTAL
R.C.A.F.	140.	504.	1728.	2372.
W.A.A.F.	10.	18.	353.	381.

AFFILIATED AIRFIELDS : Croft[Sub-station]

PRESENT USE [1985] : Civil Airport[Tees-side]

NO: 404.

AIRFIELD NAME: MILDENHALL. OPENED : 1934.
COUNTY : Suffolk. CLOSED :
COMMAND : Bomber.
FORMATION : 3 Grp[Exning] GRID REF: M 143958[75]
FUNCTION : Operational[32 Base] O.S.REF.: TL 690767.

LOCALITY : 12miles NW of Bury St.Edmunds.
RAILWAY STN. : Shippen Hill 4.5miles[LNER]

LATITUDE : 52 21 45N. HEIGHT ASL : 28′ LIGHTING : Mk2.
LONGITUDE : 00 28 45E. FLYING CONTROL : Yes. RADIO : QDM.

LANDMARKS DAY. : Chalk pit 3miles 166degrees. Ely cathedral 9.5miles 294degrees.

LANDMARKS NIGHT : -

OBSTRUCTIONS : -

LANDING AREA SURFACE : Concrete.

QDM	LENGTH X WIDTH	EXT. TO
113.	2000 x 50yds.	4000yds.
040.	1400 x 50yds.	2600yds.
159.	1400 x 50yds.	2000yds.

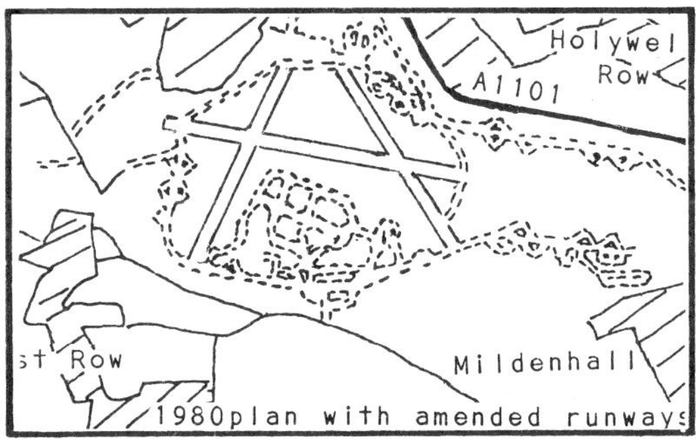

EXTENSIBILITY : Entails fairly extensive demolition by No.3 strip & re-alignment of subsidiary R/W.
ACCOMMODATION : Permanent.
HANGARS : Types:C-3;A-2;T2[glider]-2.

HARDSTANDINGS : Heavy bomber-36.

	OFFICERS	S.N.C.O′s.	O.R′s.	TOTAL
R.A.F.	189.	61.	1816.	2066.
W.A.A.F.	15.	11.	327.	353.

AFFILIATED AIRFIELDS : Newmarket & Tuddenham[Sub-stations]

PRESENT USE [1985] : USAFE.

NO: 405.

AIRFIELD NAME: MILFIELD. OPENED : 1944.
COUNTY : Northumberland. CLOSED : 1946.
COMMAND : Fighter.
FORMATION : 12 Grp[Watnall] GRID REF: U 440537[1]
FUNCTION : Operational Training Unit. O.S.REF.: NU 945330.
LOCALITY : 4miles NW of Wooler.
RAILWAY STN. : Berwick-on-Tweed 15miles[LNER]

LATITUDE : 55 35 30N. HEIGHT ASL : 150′ LIGHTING : None.
LONGITUDE : 02 05 00W. FLYING CONTROL : Yes. RADIO : QDM.

LANDMARKS DAY. : Monument on hill 600′ 1.5miles W.

LANDMARKS NIGHT : -

OBSTRUCTIONS : -

LANDING AREA SURFACE : Concrete & wood chippings.

QDM	LENGTH X WIDTH	EXT. TO
058.	1100 x 50yds.	-
357.	1400 x 50yds.	1800yds.
298.	1100 x 50yds.	1300yds.

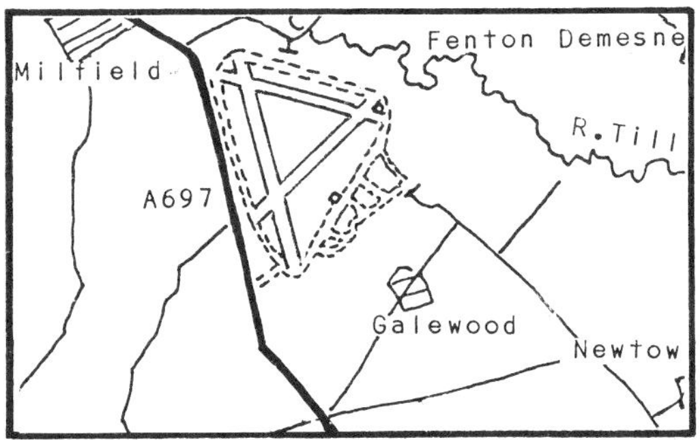

EXTENSIBILITY : Entails cutting new by pass road.

ACCOMMODATION : Temporary.
HANGARS : T2-2; EO blister-8.

HARDSTANDINGS : SE-44;TE-6.

	OFFICERS	S.N.C.O′s.	O.R′s.	TOTAL
R.A.F.	110.	265.	762.	1137.
W.A.A.F.	10.	10.	501.	521.

AFFILIATED AIRFIELDS : Brunton[Satellite]

PRESENT USE [1985] : Disused.

AIRFIELD NAME: MILLOM. OPENED : 1941.
COUNTY : Cumberland. CLOSED : 1945.
COMMAND : Flying Training.
FORMATION : 25 Grp[Market Drayton] GRID REF: Y 617008[18]
FUNCTION : Advanced Flying Unit. [Observers] O.S.REF.: SD 138790.
LOCALITY : 2miles WSW of Millom.
RAILWAY STN. : Millom 2miles[LMS]

LATITUDE : 54 12 00N. HEIGHT ASL : 0′ LIGHTING : Mk2.
LONGITUDE : 03 19 00W. FLYING CONTROL : Yes. RADIO : QDM.

LANDMARKS DAY. : Black Coombe[round hill] 1969′ 4miles N. Walney Island, long & narrow 4miles SSE.

LANDMARKS NIGHT : Blast furnaces & slag tips at Millom & Barrow district.

OBSTRUCTIONS : Hill 600′ 2miles N, hill 1969′ 4miles N.

LANDING AREA SURFACE : Hardcore & tarmac.

QDM	LENGTH X WIDTH	EXT. TO
124.	1000 x 50yds.	1970yds.
169.	1000 x 50yds.	1500yds.
079.	1000 x 50yds.	1610yds.

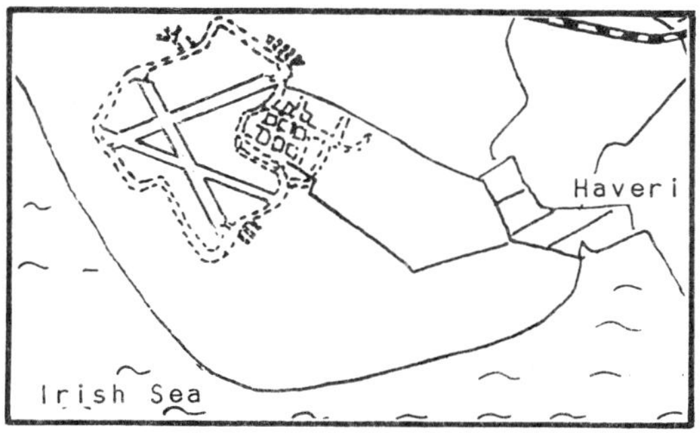

EXTENSIBILITY : -

ACCOMMODATION : Temporary.
HANGARS : Bellman-8;EO blister-13.

HARDSTANDINGS : 50-"Fingers" around peritrack approx 20′wide between 50-250′ long.

	OFFICERS	S.N.C.O′s.	O.R′s.	TOTAL
R.A.F.	178.	550.	1209.	1937.
W.A.A.F.	14.	9.	390.	413.

AFFILIATED AIRFIELDS : -

PRESENT USE [1985] : HM Prison.

AIRFIELD NAME: MILLTOWN. OPENED : 1943.
COUNTY : Morayshire. CLOSED : 1977.
COMMAND : Coastal.
FORMATION : 18 Grp[Pitreavie Castle] GRID REF: J 784874[29Scot]
FUNCTION : Operational. O.S.REF.: NJ 265655.

LOCALITY : 4miles NE of Elgin.
RAILWAY STN. : Calcots 1mile[LNER]

LATITUDE : 57 40 38N. HEIGHT ASL : 12′ LIGHTING : Mk2.
LONGITUDE : 03 13 38W. FLYING CONTROL : Yes. RADIO : QDM.

LANDMARKS DAY. : Mouth of R Spey.

LANDMARKS NIGHT : As day.

OBSTRUCTIONS : Buiin Hill, wooded, 2miles E 223′

LANDING AREA SURFACE : Concrete & tarmac.

QDM	LENGTH X WIDTH	EXT. TO
054.	1900 x 50yds.	4000yds.
114.	1540 x 50yds.	2700yds.
175.	1400 x 50yds.	1700yds.

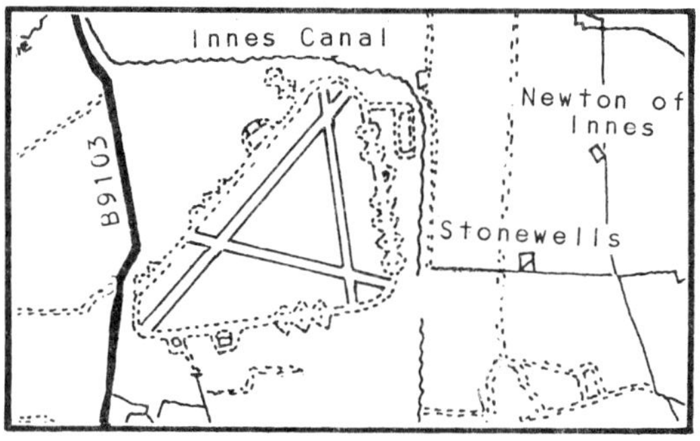

EXTENSIBILITY : Entails light demolition.

ACCOMMODATION : Temporary.
HANGARS : T2-2;B1-1.

HARDSTANDINGS : Spectacle-27.

	OFFICERS	S.N.C.O′s.	O.R′s.	TOTAL
R.A.F.	154.	270.	1214.	1638.
W.A.A.F.	6.	10.	129.	145.

AFFILIATED AIRFIELDS : -

PRESENT USE [1985] : Radio Research Station

AIRFIELD NAME: MOLESWORTH. OPENED : 1941.
COUNTY : Huntingdonshire. CLOSED :
COMMAND : 8th USAAF.
FORMATION : 303rd Bomb Grp. GRID REF: L 528970[74]
FUNCTION : Operational. O.S.REF.: TL 078774.

LOCALITY : 10.5miles WNW of Huntingdon.
RAILWAY STN. : Thrapston 9miles[LMS]

LATITUDE : 52 23 06N. HEIGHT ASL : 240′ LIGHTING : Mk2.
LONGITUDE : 00 25 15W. FLYING CONTROL : Yes. RADIO : QDM.

LANDMARKS DAY. : Old Weston church 1.25miles 098degrees.

LANDMARKS NIGHT : Thrapston ironworks 6.25miles W 270degrees.

OBSTRUCTIONS : Hangars etc marked with obstruction lights.

LANDING AREA SURFACE : Unspecified Hard Surface.

QDM	LENGTH X WIDTH	EXT. TO
191.	2000 x 50yds.	4000yds.
255.	1400 x 50yds.	2000yds.
309.	1400 x 50yds.	2000yds.

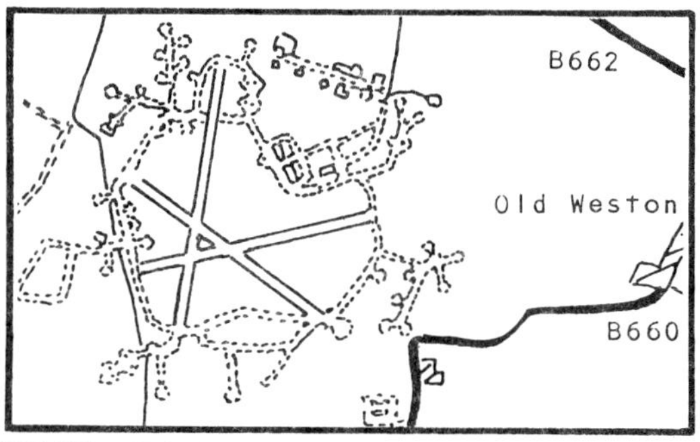

EXTENSIBILITY : Entails demolition of a farm & possible diversion of a grid.
ACCOMMODATION : Temporary.
HANGARS : T2-2.

HARDSTANDINGS : Loop-50.

USAAF. : OFFICERS: 443. Enlisted Men. : 2529.TOTAL: 2972.

AFFILIATED AIRFIELDS : -

PRESENT USE [1985] : USAFE.

NO: 409.

AIRFIELD NAME: MONA. OPENED : 1942.
COUNTY : Anglesey. CLOSED :
COMMAND : Flying Training.
FORMATION : 25 Grp[Market Drayton] GRID REF: H 877985[41]
FUNCTION : Advanced Flying Unit [Observers] O.S.REF.: SH 415760.
LOCALITY : 3miles W of Llangefni.
RAILWAY STN. : Bangor 4miles[LMS]

LATITUDE : 53 15 30N. HEIGHT ASL : 185' LIGHTING : Mk2.
LONGITUDE : 04 22 38W. FLYING CONTROL : Yes. RADIO : QDM.

LANDMARKS DAY. : Small lake 1mile W of A/F.

LANDMARKS NIGHT : -

OBSTRUCTIONS : -

LANDING AREA SURFACE : Concrete.
QDM: 230. LENGTH X WIDTH: 1800 x 50yds.EXT. TO: -
: 184. : 1100 x 50yds. : -
: 315. : 1100 x 50yds. : -
: : :

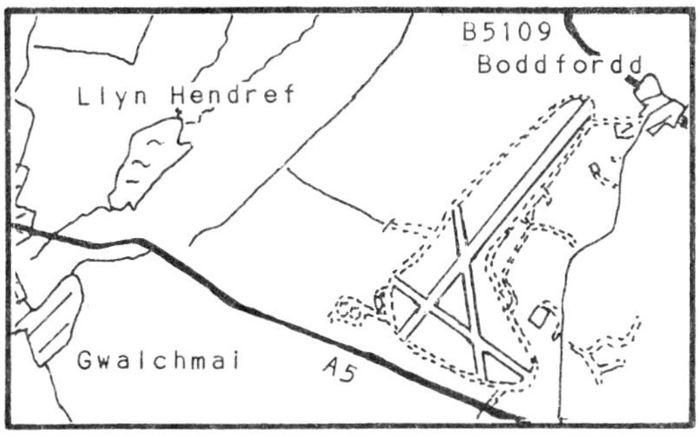

EXTENSIBILITY : None possible.

ACCOMMODATION : Temporary.
HANGARS : T1-1;EO blister-17.

HARDSTANDINGS : 900x100' approx sommerfeld track.

R.A.F. : OFFICERS: 110.S.N.C.O's.: 220.O.R's.: 1048.TOTAL: 1378.
W.A.A.F.: " : 8. " : 10. " : 390. " : 408.

AFFILIATED AIRFIELDS : -

PRESENT USE [1985] : RAF.

NO: 410.

AIRFIELD NAME: MONTFORD BRIDGE. OPENED : 1942.
COUNTY : Shropshire. CLOSED : 1945.
COMMAND : Fighter.
FORMATION : 12 Grp[Watnall] GRID REF: J 886384[60]
FUNCTION : Operational Training Unit[satellite] O.S.REF.: SJ 430170.
LOCALITY : 4.5miles WNW Shrewsbury.
RAILWAY STN. : Shrewsbury 4.5miles[LMS & GWR]

LATITUDE : 52 44 52N. HEIGHT ASL : 265' LIGHTING : None.
LONGITUDE : 02 51 45W. FLYING CONTROL : Yes. RADIO : QDM.

LANDMARKS DAY. : R Severn 600yds SE. The Wrekin 15miles SE.

LANDMARKS NIGHT : R Severn.

OBSTRUCTIONS : -

LANDING AREA SURFACE : Tarmac & rubber chippings.
QDM: 250. LENGTH X WIDTH: 1470 x 50yds.EXT. TO: 1600yds.
: 020. : 1300 x 50yds. : 1500yds.
: 330. : 1000 x 50yds. : 1700yds.
: : :

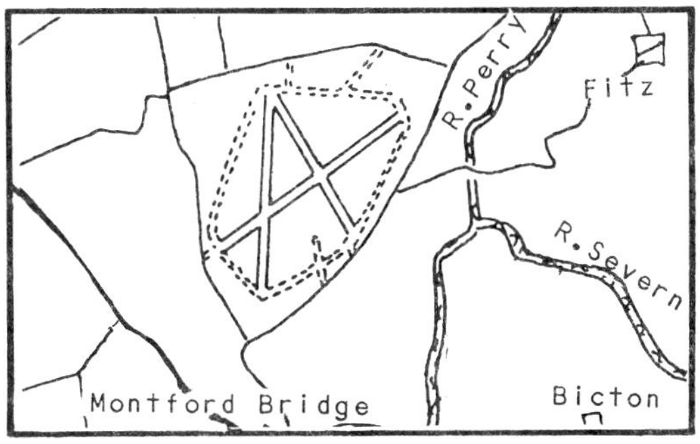

EXTENSIBILITY : Entails slight demolition & diversion of 3 minor roads.
ACCOMMODATION : Temporary.
HANGARS : O blister-4;Bessoneau:3 bay-1;6 bay-1..

HARDSTANDINGS : 27.

R.A.F. : OFFICERS: 24.S.N.C.O's.: 60.O.R's.: 616.TOTAL: 700.
W.A.A.F.: " : 2. " : 1. " : 60. " : 63.

AFFILIATED AIRFIELDS : Rednal[Parent]

PRESENT USE [1985] : Private flying.

NO: 411.

AIRFIELD NAME: MONTROSE. OPENED : 1912.
COUNTY : Angus. CLOSED : 1980.
COMMAND : Flying Training.
FORMATION : 21 Grp[Spittlegate] GRID REF: P 233809[58Scot]
FUNCTION : Flying Instructors School. O.S.REF.: NO 725598.
LOCALITY : 1mile N of Montrose.
RAILWAY STN. : Montrose[LNER]

LATITUDE : 56 43 40N. HEIGHT ASL : 30' LIGHTING : None.
LONGITUDE : 02 27 15W. FLYING CONTROL : Yes. RADIO : QDM.

LANDMARKS DAY. : Montrose Basin.

LANDMARKS NIGHT : As day.

OBSTRUCTIONS : Chimney 150' just outside SW corner.

LANDING AREA SURFACE : Steel matting[Sommerfeld track]
QDM: 040. LENGTH X WIDTH: 1325yds. EXT. TO: -
: 070. : 1000yds. : -
: 170. : 766yds. : -
: : :

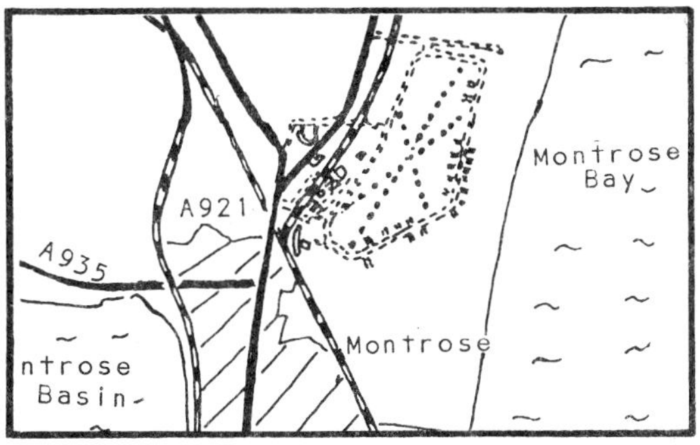

EXTENSIBILITY : -

ACCOMMODATION : Temporary[MQ permanent]
HANGARS : Bellman-4;Bessoneau-3;wooden type-3; 73x82x24'-1;wooden type 211x65x22'-2.
HARDSTANDINGS : Somerfeld track-45[light A/C only]

R.A.F. : OFFICERS: 139.S.N.C.O's.: 203.O.R's.: 1202.TOTAL: 1544.
W.A.A.F.: " : 6. " : 5. " : 240. " : 251.

AFFILIATED AIRFIELDS : Kinnel & Stracathro[Satellites]

PRESENT USE [1985] : Industry.

AIRFIELD NAME: MORETON-in-MARSH. OPENED : 1941.
COUNTY : Gloucestershire. CLOSED : 1955.
COMMAND : Bomber.
FORMATION : 91 Grp[Abingdon] GRID REF: P 667533[93]
FUNCTION : Operational Training Unit. O.S.REF.: SP 218329.
LOCALITY : 14miles S of Stratford on Avon.
RAILWAY STN. : Moreton-in-Marsh[GWR]

LATITUDE : 51 59 38N. HEIGHT ASL : 420′ LIGHTING : Mk2.
LONGITUDE : 01 41 00W. FLYING CONTROL : Yes. RADIO : QDM.

LANDMARKS DAY. : Shape of hill formation. Tower on hill NW of A/F.

LANDMARKS NIGHT : -

OBSTRUCTIONS : Hill 846′ 2.5miles WNW.

LANDING AREA SURFACE : Concrete & tarmac.

QDM	LENGTH X WIDTH	EXT. TO
157.	1100 x 50yds.	2300yds.
218.	1600 x 50yds.	3000yds.
277.	1100 x 50yds.	1400yds.

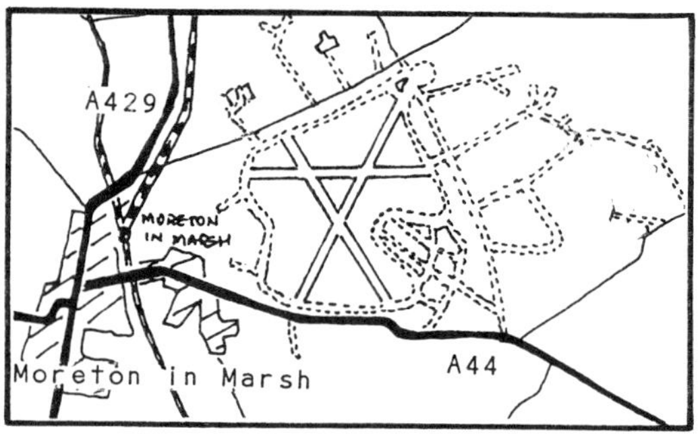

EXTENSIBILITY : Entails diversion of main road & demolition of a bungalow.
ACCOMMODATION : Temporary.
HANGARS : Type J-1;T2-4.

HARDSTANDINGS : Heavy bomber-30.

	OFFICERS	S.N.C.O′s.	O.R′s.	TOTAL
R.A.F.	150.	477.	1460.	2087.
W.A.A.F.	12.	24.	400.	436.

AFFILIATED AIRFIELDS : Enstone[Satellite]

PRESENT USE [1985] : Home Office.

NO: 413.

AIRFIELD NAME: MORETON VALENCE. OPENED : 1939.
COUNTY : Gloucestershire. CLOSED : 1962.
COMMAND : Flying Training.
FORMATION : 25 Grp[Market Drayton] GRID REF: P 242309[103]
FUNCTION : Advanced Flying Unit. [satellite] O.S.REF.: SO 796100.
LOCALITY : 6miles SSE of Gloucester.
RAILWAY STN. : Gloucester[LMS&LNER]

LATITUDE : 51 47 23N. HEIGHT ASL : 44′ LIGHTING : Mk2.
LONGITUDE : 02 17 38W. FLYING CONTROL : Yes. RADIO : QDM.

LANDMARKS DAY. : Railway to E. R Severn to W. Gloucester to N.

LANDMARKS NIGHT : -

OBSTRUCTIONS : Pitchcombe Hill 1mile due E 350′ above A/F level. A/F surrounded by trees.

LANDING AREA SURFACE : Concrete.

QDM	LENGTH X WIDTH	EXT. TO
223.	2100 x 50yds.	2400yds.
162.	1000 x 50yds.	1400yds.
101.	1000 x 50yds.	1300yds.

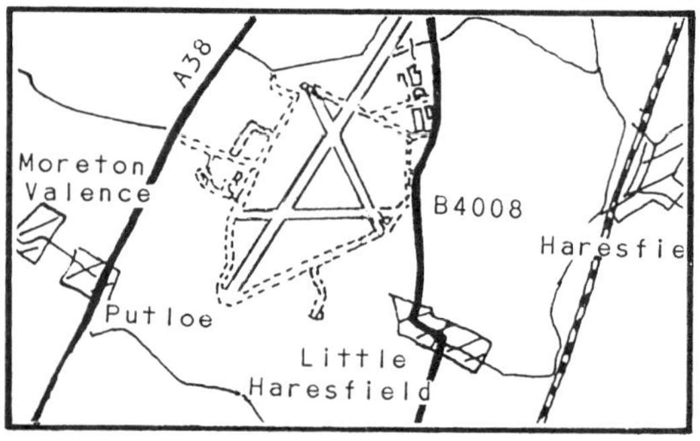

EXTENSIBILITY : Entails demolition of a farm, cottage & a bungalow.
ACCOMMODATION : Temporary.
HANGARS : A1-1;EO blister-8;MAP:B1-1;B2-4.

HARDSTANDINGS : -

	OFFICERS	S.N.C.O′s.	O.R′s.	TOTAL
R.A.F.	91.	308.	-	399.
W.A.A.F.	4.	-	43.	47.

AFFILIATED AIRFIELDS : Staverton[Parent]

PRESENT USE [1985] : Industry.

NO: 414.

AIRFIELD NAME: MORPETH. OPENED : 1942.
COUNTY : Northumberland. CLOSED : 1948.
COMMAND : Flying Training.
FORMATION : 29 Grp[Dumfries] GRID REF: U 659024[7]
FUNCTION : Air Gunnery School. O.S.REF.: NZ 169818.

LOCALITY : 3miles SW of Morpeth.
RAILWAY STN. : Morpeth[LNER]

LATITUDE : 55 07 45N. HEIGHT ASL : 363′ LIGHTING : Mk2.
LONGITUDE : 01 43 45W. FLYING CONTROL : Yes. RADIO : QDM.

LANDMARKS DAY. : Morpeth town 3miles NE. Mental hospital 1mile SE.

LANDMARKS NIGHT : -

OBSTRUCTIONS : -

LANDING AREA SURFACE : Tarmac.

QDM	LENGTH X WIDTH	EXT. TO
230.	1400 x 50yds.	1800yds.
290.	1100 x 50yds.	1500yds.
350.	1100 x 50yds.	1600yds.

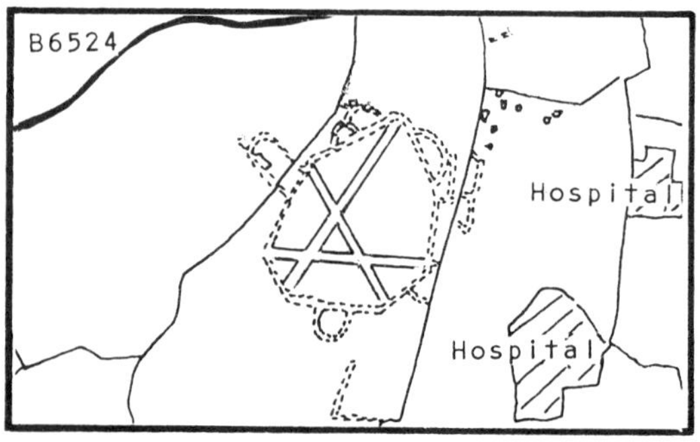

EXTENSIBILITY : -

ACCOMMODATION : Temporary.
HANGARS : T1-3;EO blister-17.

HARDSTANDINGS : Circular[50′dia]-36; marshalling area 300x100′approx.

	OFFICERS	S.N.C.O′s.	O.R′s.	TOTAL
R.A.F.	58.	153.	1038.	1249.
W.A.A.F.	10.	13.	414.	437.

AFFILIATED AIRFIELDS : -

PRESENT USE [1985] : Forestry Commission.

NO: 415.

AIRFIELD NAME: MOUNT FARM. OPENED : 1940.
COUNTY : Oxfordshire. CLOSED : 1946.
COMMAND : 8th USAAF.
FORMATION : 7th Photographic Grp. GRID REF: L 027165[105]
FUNCTION : Photo Recconaisance. O.S.REF.: SU 583965.

LOCALITY : 8miles SE of Oxford.
RAILWAY STN. : Culham 4miles[GWR]

LATITUDE : 51 39 50N. HEIGHT ASL : 139. LIGHTING : Mk2.
LONGITUDE : 01 09 30W. FLYING CONTROL : Yes. RADIO : QDM.

LANDMARKS DAY. : Witenham Clumps[hills 500′] 2.5miles S.

LANDMARKS NIGHT : R Thames 2miles S.

OBSTRUCTIONS : -

LANDING AREA SURFACE : Concrete.

QDM: 170. LENGTH X WIDTH: 1100 x 50yds. EXT. TO: 1900yds.
: 120. : 1100 x 50yds. : 2400yds.
: 240. : 1600 x 50yds. : 3000yds.

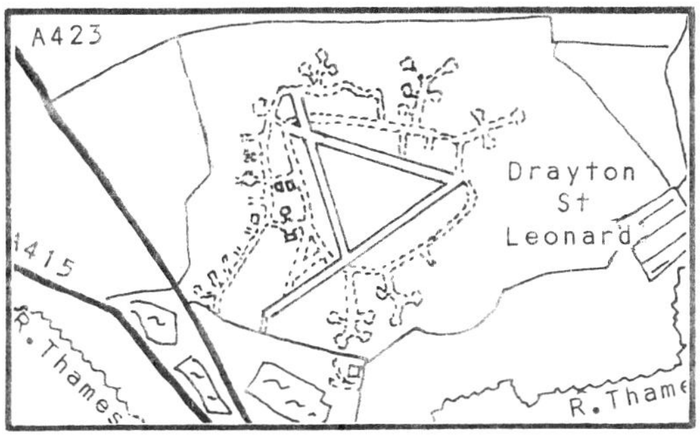

EXTENSIBILITY : Entails diversion of a minor road & demolition of 2 barns.
ACCOMMODATION : Temporary.
HANGARS : Blisters:69′-4;65′-4.

HARDSTANDINGS : Loop-24.

USAAF. : OFFICERS: 206. Enlisted Men. : 1617. TOTAL: 1823.

AFFILIATED AIRFIELDS : -

PRESENT USE [1985] : Agriculture.

NO: 416.

AIRFIELD NAME: MULLAGHMORE. OPENED : 1942.
COUNTY : Londonderry NI. CLOSED : 1945.
COMMAND : Coastal.
FORMATION : 15 Grp[Liverpool] GRID REF: C 898212[304NI]
FUNCTION : Parent. O.S.REF.: C 898212.

LOCALITY : 4miles SW of Ballymorey.
RAILWAY STN. : Aghadowey 3miles[NCC]

LATITUDE : 55 01 53N. HEIGHT ASL : 42′ LIGHTING : Mk2.
LONGITUDE : 06 35 38W. FLYING CONTROL : Yes. RADIO : QDM.

LANDMARKS DAY. : Bounded on W & N by R Agivey, & E by R Bann.
As day

LANDMARKS NIGHT : 1]2 hangars E of peritrack; 1 N & 1 W.
OBSTRUCTIONS : [obstruction lights fitted] 2]"Glenkeen" trees & house on hill, in funnels approach-ing R/W QDM090/270 1500yds out 100′AFL. [obs lights fitted] 3]"Claggan" trees & house on hill in funnels approaching R/W QDM101/190 1500yds out. 100′AFL[obs lights]

LANDING AREA SURFACE : Concrete covered with asphalt.

QDM: 190. LENGTH X WIDTH: 2000 x 50yds. EXT. TO: -
: 270. : 1421 x 50yds. : -

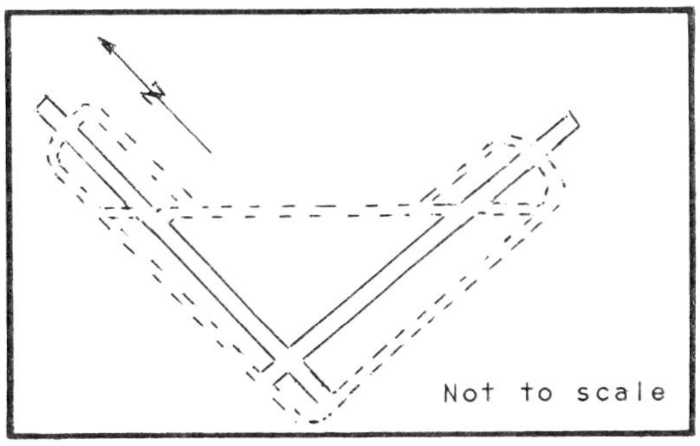

EXTENSIBILITY : None possible.

ACCOMMODATION : Temporary.
HANGARS : T2-4.

HARDSTANDINGS : Circular:150′dia-3;125′-27; "fingers" 40′wide-50.

R.A.F. : OFFICERS: 293. S.N.C.O′s.: 262. O.R′s.: 2749. TOTAL: 3304.
W.A.A.F.: " : - " : - " : - " : -

AFFILIATED AIRFIELDS : -

PRESENT USE [1985] : Disused.

NO: 417.

AIRFIELD NAME: NEEDS OAR POINT. OPENED : 1944.
COUNTY : Hampshire. CLOSED : 1944.
COMMAND : Fighter.
FORMATION : 11 Grp[Uxbridge] GRID REF: U 835175[132]
FUNCTION : Advanced Landing Ground. [De-requisitioned] O.S.REF.: SZ 410975.

LOCALITY : 5miles E of Lymington.
RAILWAY STN. : Lymington[SR]

LATITUDE : 50 46 23N. HEIGHT ASL : 30′ LIGHTING : None.
LONGITUDE : 01 23 53W. FLYING CONTROL : None. RADIO : QDM.

LANDMARKS DAY. : Sway tower. Isle of Wight.

LANDMARKS NIGHT : -

OBSTRUCTIONS : -

LANDING AREA SURFACE : Steel Matting[Sommerfeld track]

QDM: E-W. LENGTH X WIDTH: 1500yds. EXT. TO: -
: N-S. : 1600yds. : -

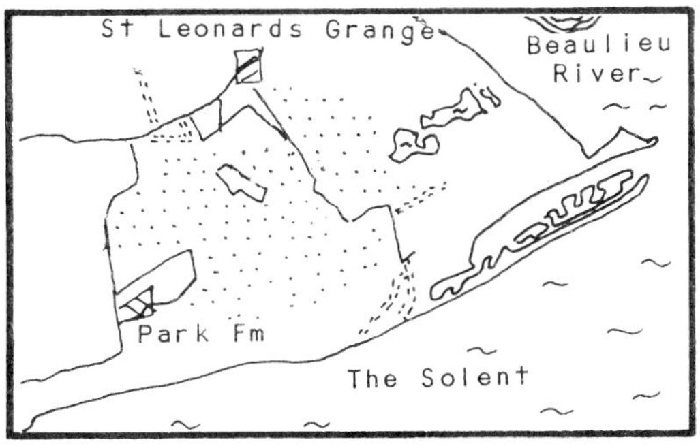

EXTENSIBILITY : -

ACCOMMODATION : Tented camp.
HANGARS : Blister-4.

HARDSTANDINGS : Somerfeld track-36.

R.A.F. : OFFICERS: - S.N.C.O′s.: - O.R′s.: - TOTAL: -
W.A.A.F.: " : - " : - " : - " : -

AFFILIATED AIRFIELDS : -

PRESENT USE [1985] : Agriculture.

NO: 418.

AIRFIELD NAME: NETHERAVON.
COUNTY : Wiltshire.
COMMAND : Fighter.
FORMATION : 38 Grp[Marks Hall]
FUNCTION : Operational[parent]

OPENED : 1913.
CLOSED :
GRID REF: U 600696[122]
O.S.REF.: SU 165490.

LOCALITY : 6miles N of Amesbury.
RAILWAY STN. : Salisbury 15miles[SR]

LATITUDE : 51 14 23N. HEIGHT ASL : 400′ LIGHTING : None.
LONGITUDE : 01 46 00W. FLYING CONTROL : Yes. RADIO : QDM.

LANDMARKS DAY. : R Avon .5miles W.

LANDMARKS NIGHT : -

OBSTRUCTIONS : -

LANDING AREA : Grass.
SURFACE :

QDM	LENGTH X WIDTH	EXT. TO
E-W.	2000yds.	-
NE-SW.	1400yds.	-
SE-NW.	1500yds.	-

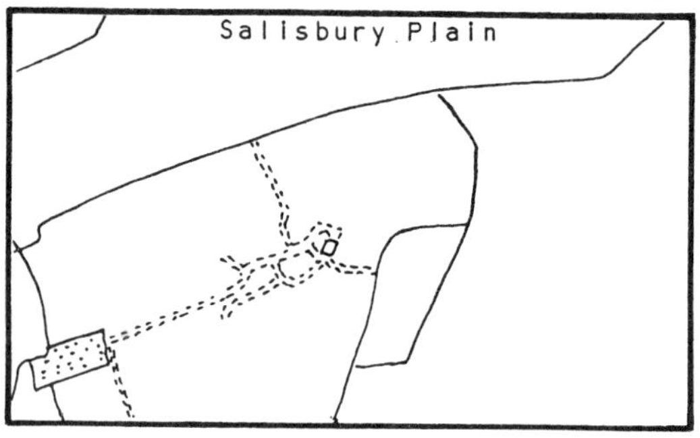

EXTENSIBILITY : None possible.

ACCOMMODATION : Permanent[part]
HANGARS : A[250x120′]-2;Bessoneau-1; Cathedral-2;Flt sheds-3.
HARDSTANDINGS : -

	OFFICERS	S.N.C.O′s.	O.R′s.	TOTAL
R.A.F.	142.	152.	1050.	1344.
W.A.A.F.	10.	13.	362.	385.

AFFILIATED AIRFIELDS : Shrewton[RLG]

PRESENT USE [1985] : Army.

NO: 419.

AIRFIELD NAME: NEW ROMNEY.
COUNTY : Kent.
COMMAND : Fighter.
FORMATION : 11 Grp[Uxbridge]
FUNCTION : Advanced Landing Ground. [De-requisitioned]

OPENED : 1943.
CLOSED : 1944.
GRID REF: R 500452[135]
O.S.REF.: TR 061269.

LOCALITY : 1.5miles N of New Romney.
RAILWAY STN. : New Romney[SR]

LATITUDE : 51 00 15N. HEIGHT ASL : 10′ LIGHTING : None.
LONGITUDE : 00 56 15E. FLYING CONTROL : None.RADIO : QDM.

LANDMARKS DAY. : St Marys in the Marsh church,approx .5miles NE of A/F.Water tower E of A/F.

LANDMARKS NIGHT : -

OBSTRUCTIONS : -

LANDING AREA : Steel Matting[Sommerfeld track]
SURFACE :

QDM	LENGTH X WIDTH	EXT. TO
NW-SE.	1375 x 50yds.	-
NE-SW.	1600 x 50yds.	-

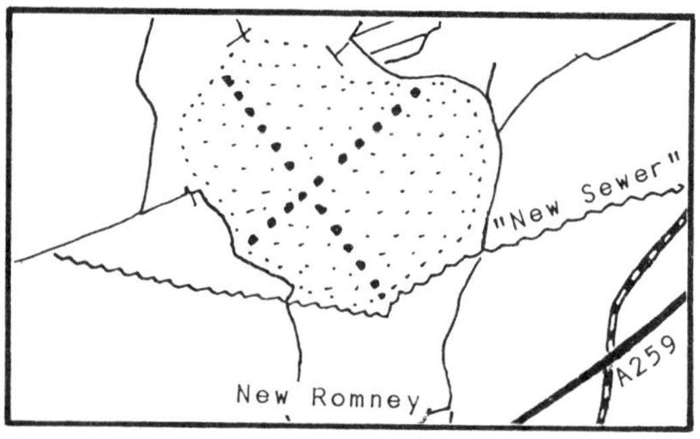

EXTENSIBILITY : -

ACCOMMODATION : Tented camp.
HANGARS : Blister-4.

HARDSTANDINGS : MT-1;refuelling-3.

	OFFICERS	S.N.C.O′s.	O.R′s.	TOTAL
R.A.F.	-	-	-	-
W.A.A.F.	-	-	-	

AFFILIATED AIRFIELDS : -

PRESENT USE [1985] : Agriculture.

NO: 420.

AIRFIELD NAME: NEWCHURCH.
COUNTY : Kent.
COMMAND : Fighter.
FORMATION : 11 Grp[Uxbridge]
FUNCTION : Advanced Landing Ground. [De-requisitioned]

OPENED : 1943.
CLOSED : 1945.
GRID REF: R 485500[126]
O.S.REF.: TR 048314.

LOCALITY : 7miles SSE of Ashford.
RAILWAY STN. : Hamstreet[SR]

LATITUDE : 51 02 45N. HEIGHT ASL : 0′ LIGHTING : None.
LONGITUDE : 00 55 15E. FLYING CONTROL : None.RADIO : QDM.

LANDMARKS DAY. : Church tower SE corner of A/F. 2 radio pylons 2miles SE.

LANDMARKS NIGHT : -

OBSTRUCTIONS : -

LANDING AREA : Steel Matting[Sommerfeld track]
SURFACE :

QDM	LENGTH X WIDTH	EXT. TO
350.	1400yds.	-
260.	1600yds.	-

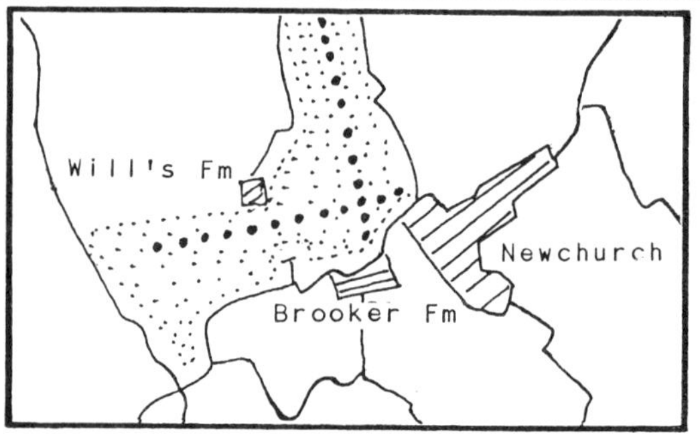

EXTENSIBILITY : -

ACCOMMODATION : Tented camp.
HANGARS : EO blister-4.

HARDSTANDINGS : -

	OFFICERS	S.N.C.O′s.	O.R′s.	TOTAL
R.A.F.	-	-	-	-
W.A.A.F.	-	-	-	-

AFFILIATED AIRFIELDS : -

PRESENT USE [1985] : Agriculture.

NO: 421.

AIRFIELD NAME: NEWMARKET. OPENED : 1939.
COUNTY : Suffolk. CLOSED : 1945.
COMMAND : Bomber.
FORMATION : 3 Grp[Exning] GRID REF: M 075819[85]
FUNCTION : Operational. O.S.REF.: TL 620630.

LOCALITY : 1.25miles W of Newmarket.
RAILWAY STN. : Newmarket[LNER]

LATITUDE : 52 14 30N. HEIGHT ASL : 96′ LIGHTING : Mk2.
LONGITUDE : 00 22 00E. FLYING CONTROL : Yes. RADIO : QDM.

LANDMARKS DAY. : Newmarket town, railway loop, golf course.

LANDMARKS NIGHT : Newmarket town, heath & railway.

OBSTRUCTIONS : -

LANDING AREA : Grass.
SURFACE :

QDM	LENGTH X WIDTH	EXT. TO
E-W.	2500yds.	-
SE-NW.	1800yds.	-
NE-SW.	1600yds.	-

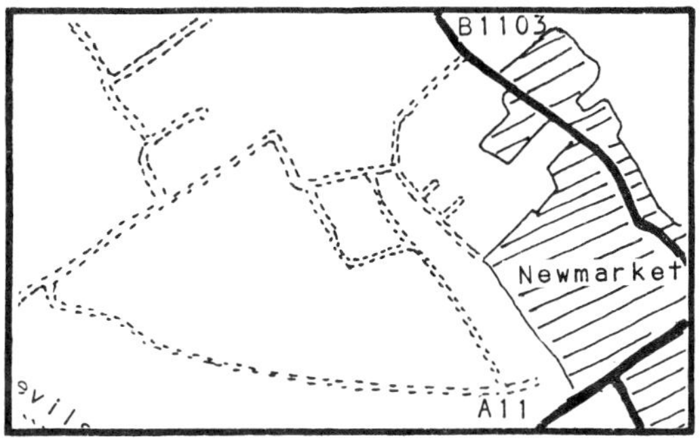

EXTENSIBILITY : No.3 strip could be extended to 2300yds.

ACCOMMODATION : Temporary.
HANGARS : T2-3;B1-3;Blister-2;double blister-1.

HARDSTANDINGS : Clock-24.

	OFFICERS	S.N.C.O′s.	O.R′s.	TOTAL
R.A.F.	105.	230.	818.	1153.
W.A.A.F.	3.	3.	138.	144.

AFFILIATED AIRFIELDS : Mildenhall[32 Base]

PRESENT USE [1985] : Race Course.

NO: 422.

AIRFIELD NAME: NEWTON. OPENED : 1937.
COUNTY : Nottinghamshire. CLOSED :
COMMAND : Flying Training.
FORMATION : 21 Grp[Spittlegate] GRID REF: F 145610[54]
FUNCTION : Service Flying Training School. O.S.REF.: SK 680415.
LOCALITY : 7miles E of Nottingham.
RAILWAY STN. : Bingham 1.75miles[LNER]

LATITUDE : 52 57 38N. HEIGHT ASL : 150′ LIGHTING : None.
LONGITUDE : 00 59 15W. FLYING CONTROL : Yes. RADIO : QDM.

LANDMARKS DAY. : R Trent. Saxondale railway junction E, Fosseway.

LANDMARKS NIGHT : R Trent running NE-SW.

OBSTRUCTIONS : Technical buildings up to 60′.
Church spire 1.5miles SE.

LANDING AREA : Grass.
SURFACE :

QDM	LENGTH X WIDTH	EXT. TO
NW-SE.	1010yds.	2600yds.
N-S.	1030yds.	1400yds.
NE-SW.	1300yds.	1400yds.

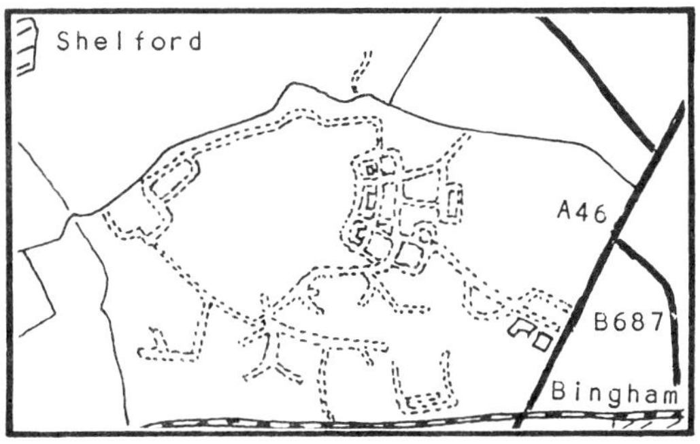

EXTENSIBILITY : Entails slight demolition.

ACCOMMODATION : Permanent.
HANGARS : Type C-5;Blisters:69′-5;65′-11.

HARDSTANDINGS : Circular-35.

	OFFICERS	S.N.C.O′s.	O.R′s.	TOTAL
R.A.F.	153.	172.	1448.	1773.
W.A.A.F.	-	16.	288.	304.

AFFILIATED AIRFIELDS : Tollerton[Satellite]Orston[RLG]

PRESENT USE [1985] : RAF.

NO: 423.

AIRFIELD NAME: NEWTOWNARDS. OPENED : 1934.
COUNTY : Down NI. CLOSED : 1945.
COMMAND : RAF NI.
FORMATION : Stormont[Belfast] GRID REF: J 494730[314NI]
FUNCTION : Parent. O.S.REF.: J 495725.

LOCALITY : 10miles E of Belfast.
RAILWAY STN. : Newtownards[B&CD]

LATITUDE : 54 35 00N. HEIGHT ASL : 0′ LIGHTING : None.
LONGITUDE : 05 41 30W. FLYING CONTROL : None. RADIO : QDM.

LANDMARKS DAY. : Scrabo Tower.

LANDMARKS NIGHT : -

OBSTRUCTIONS : Scrabo Tower. Walkers mill chimney.

LANDING AREA : Concrete & tarmac with grass extension.
SURFACE :

QDM	LENGTH X WIDTH	EXT. TO
090.	364+550yds.	914yds.
040.	1287+ 50yds.	2000yds.
160.	667+ 50yds.	717yds.

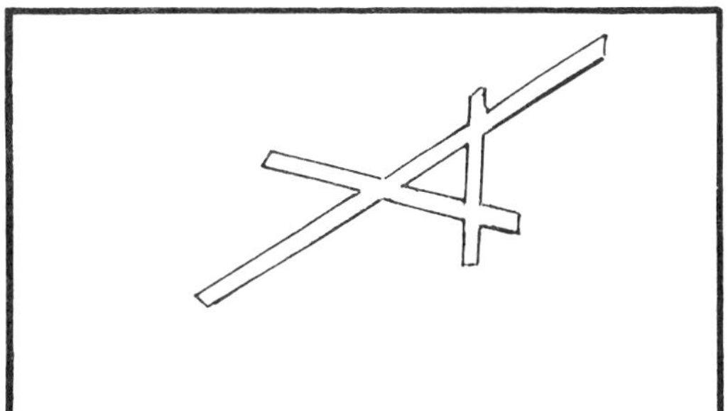
Not to scale

EXTENSIBILITY : Entails diversion of a road for SW extension & demolition of 3 small farms & camp buidings.
ACCOMMODATION : Temporary.
HANGARS : Blister-4;airport-1.

HARDSTANDINGS : -

	OFFICERS	S.N.C.O′s.	O.R′s.	TOTAL
R.A.F.	48.	117.	1006.	1171.
W.A.A.F.	-	-	-	-

AFFILIATED AIRFIELDS : -

PRESENT USE [1985] : Housing.

NO: 424.

AIRFIELD NAME: NORTH COATES. OPENED : 1935.
COUNTY : Lincolnshire. CLOSED :
COMMAND : Coastal.
FORMATION : 16 Grp[Gillingham] GRID REF: A 842213[40]
FUNCTION : Operational. O.S.REF.: TA 372028.

LOCALITY : 5miles SE of Grimsby.
RAILWAY STN. : North Thorsby 6miles[LNER]

LATITUDE : 53 30 15N. HEIGHT ASL : 12′ LIGHTING : None.
LONGITUDE : 00 04 00E. FLYING CONTROL : Yes. RADIO : QDM.

LANDMARKS : Fort at mouth of R Humber.
DAY.

LANDMARKS : -
NIGHT

OBSTRUCTIONS : Humberston W/M 5miles N. Waltham W/M 8miles NW.

LANDING AREA : Concrete[NW-SE Grass]
SURFACE :
QDM: 248. LENGTH X WIDTH: 1420 x 50yds.EXT. TO: 2000yds.
: NW-SE. : 1460 x 50yds. : 1480yds.
: : :
: : :

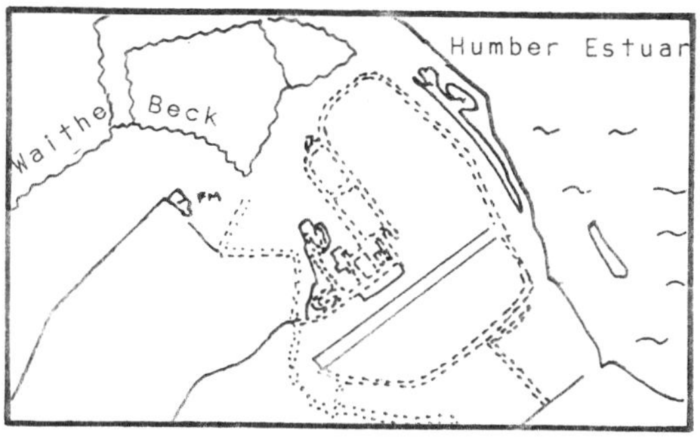

EXTENSIBILITY : -

ACCOMMODATION : Permanent[part]
HANGARS : Bellman-4;Type F-4.

HARDSTANDINGS : 125′dia-7;loop-6;modified frypan-1.

R.A.F. : OFFICERS: 116.S.N.C.O′s.: 256.O.R′s.: 1769.TOTAL: 2141.
W.A.A.F.: " : 6. " : 3. " : 448. " : 457.

AFFILIATED AIRFIELDS : Donna Nook[Satellite]

PRESENT USE [1985] : RAF.

NO: 425.

AIRFIELD NAME: NORTH CREAKE. OPENED : 1943.
COUNTY : Norfolk. CLOSED : 1947.
COMMAND : Bomber.
FORMATION : 100 Grp[Bylaugh Hall] GRID REF: G 360570[57]
FUNCTION : Operational. O.S.REF.: TA 131169.

LOCALITY : 2miles NW of Little Walsingham.
RAILWAY STN. : Wells-on-Sea 4.5miles[LNER]

LATITUDE : 52 54 38N. HEIGHT ASL : 240′ LIGHTING : Mk2.
LONGITUDE : 00 49 15E. FLYING CONTROL : Yes. RADIO : QDM.

LANDMARKS : Holkham Hall woods to NW.
DAY. Wells quay 3.5miles due N

LANDMARKS : -
NIGHT

OBSTRUCTIONS : -

LANDING AREA : Concrete.
SURFACE :
QDM: 240. LENGTH X WIDTH: 2000 x 50yds.EXT. TO: 3000yds.
: 310. : 1400 x 50yds. : 2000yds.
: 190. : 1400 x 50yds. : 2500yds.
: : :

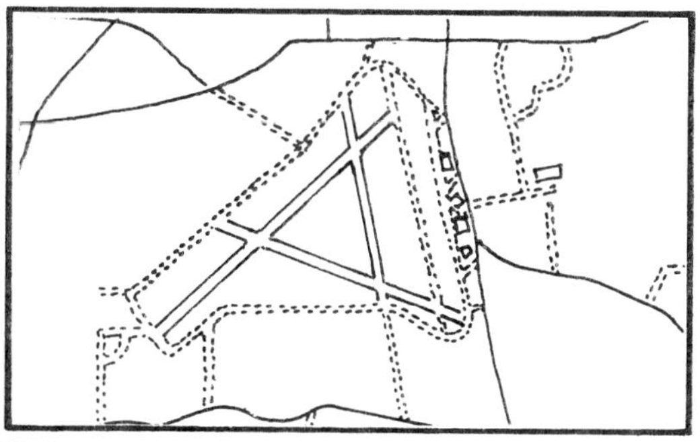

EXTENSIBILITY : -

ACCOMMODATION : Temporary.
HANGARS : T2-2;B1-1.

HARDSTANDINGS : Loop-36.

R.A.F. : OFFICERS: 108.S.N.C.O′s.: 255.O.R′s.: 985.TOTAL: 1348.
W.A.A.F.: " : 8. " : 16. " : 312. " : 336.

AFFILIATED AIRFIELDS : -

PRESENT USE [1985] : Agriculture.

NO: 426.

AIRFIELD NAME: NORTH KILLINGHOLME. OPENED : 1943.
COUNTY : Lincolnshire. CLOSED : 1945.
COMMAND : Bomber.
FORMATION : 1 Grp[Bawtry] GRID REF: A 600360[33]
FUNCTION : Operational. O.S.REF.: TA 131169.

LOCALITY : 10miles NW of Grimsby.
RAILWAY STN. : Halbrough 3miles[LNER]

LATITUDE : 53 38 15N. HEIGHT ASL : 31′ LIGHTING : Mk2.
LONGITUDE : 00 17 15W. FLYING CONTROL : Yes. RADIO : QDM.

LANDMARKS : R Humber. Towns of Grimsby & Hull.
DAY.

LANDMARKS : R Humber.
NIGHT

OBSTRUCTIONS : -

LANDING AREA : Concrete.
SURFACE :
QDM: 216. LENGTH X WIDTH: 2000 x 50yds.EXT. TO: 3000yds.
: 272. : 1400 x 50yds. : -
: 328. : 1400 x 50yds. : -
: : :

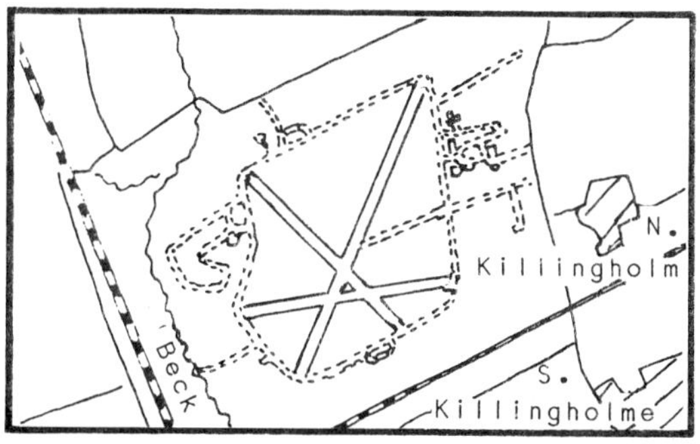

EXTENSIBILITY : Entails slight demolition only.

ACCOMMODATION : Temporary.
HANGARS : T2-2;B1-1.

HARDSTANDINGS : Loop-36.

R.A.F. : OFFICERS: 112.S.N.C.O′s.: 322.O.R′s.: 1250.TOTAL: 1684.
W.A.A.F.: " : 9. " : 18. " : 308. " : 335.

AFFILIATED AIRFIELDS : Elsham Wolds[13 Base]

PRESENT USE [1985] : Industry.

NO: 427.

AIRFIELD NAME: NORTH LUFFENHAM. OPENED : 1940.
COUNTY : Rutland. CLOSED :
COMMAND : Bomber.
FORMATION : 7 Grp[St.Vincents] GRID REF: P 395240[64]
FUNCTION : Operational[73 Base] O.S.REF.: SK 941098.

LOCALITY : 6miles SW of Oakham.
RAILWAY STN. : Luffenham 2.5miles[LMS]

LATITUDE : 52 37 53N. HEIGHT ASL : 350′ LIGHTING : Mk2.
LONGITUDE : 00 36 15W. FLYING CONTROL : Yes. RADIO : QDM.

LANDMARKS DAY. : Ketton chimney.

LANDMARKS NIGHT : -

OBSTRUCTIONS : Ketton chimney 350′

LANDING AREA SURFACE : Concrete.

QDM: 190. LENGTH X WIDTH: 1400 x 50yds.EXT. TO: 2000yds.
: 260. : 2000 x 50yds. : 2050yds.
: 320. : 1400 x 50yds. : 2500yds.
: : :

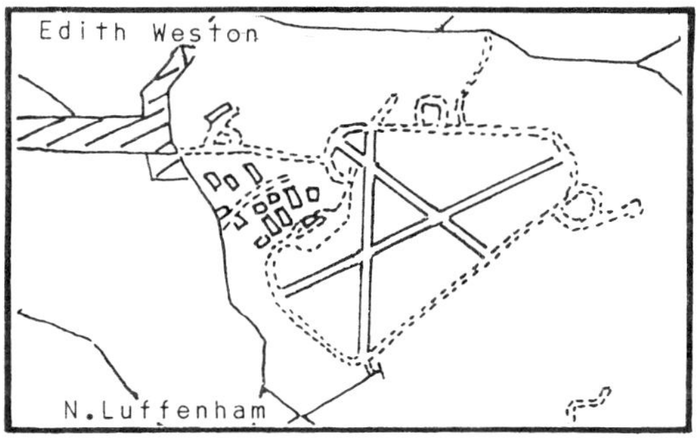

EXTENSIBILITY : Entails demolition of 2 huts & diversion of a road.
ACCOMMODATION : Permanent.
HANGARS : Type J-2;T2-3;B1-1.

HARDSTANDINGS : Loop-32;frying pan-18.

R.A.F. : OFFICERS: 108.S.N.C.O′s.: 182.O.R′s.: 1828.TOTAL: 2118.
W.A.A.F.: " : 11. " : 10. " : 290. " : 311.

AFFILIATED AIRFIELDS : Spanhoe & Woolfox Lodge[Sub-stations]

PRESENT USE [1985] : RAF.

NO: 428.

AIRFIELD NAME: NORTH PICKENHAM. OPENED : 1944.
COUNTY : Norfolk. CLOSED : 1965.
COMMAND : 8th USAAF.
FORMATION : 491st Bomb Grp. GRID REF: G 306253[66]
FUNCTION : Operational. O.S.REF.: TF 849068.

LOCALITY : 2.5miles SE of Swaffham.
RAILWAY STN. : Holme Hale 2miles[LNER]

LATITUDE : 52 37 30N. HEIGHT ASL : 190′ LIGHTING : Mk2.
LONGITUDE : 00 44 00E. FLYING CONTROL : Yes. RADIO : QDM.

LANDMARKS DAY. : Swaffham 2.5miles 330degrees.

LANDMARKS NIGHT : -

OBSTRUCTIONS : -

LANDING AREA SURFACE : Concrete & tarmac.

QDM: 240. LENGTH X WIDTH: 1900 x 50yds.EXT. TO: 4000yds.
: 190. : 1400 x 50yds. : 2000yds.
: 320. : 1400 x 50yds. : 2000yds.
: : :

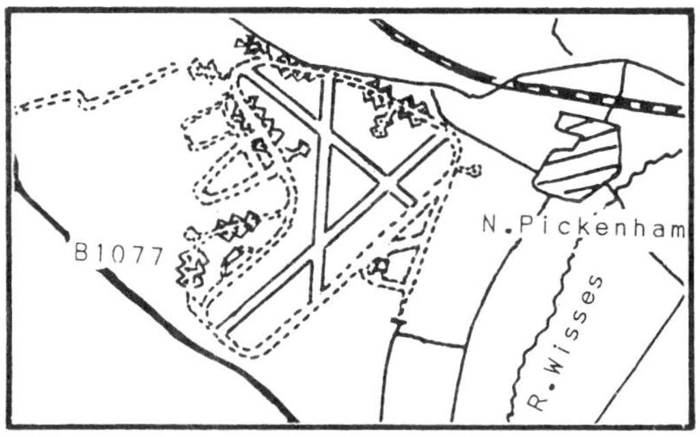

EXTENSIBILITY : Main R/W only recommended to 3000yds.

ACCOMMODATION : Temporary.
HANGARS : T2-2.

HARDSTANDINGS : Concrete-50.

USAAF. : OFFICERS: 421. Enlisted Men. : 2473.TOTAL: 2894.

AFFILIATED AIRFIELDS : -

PRESENT USE [1985] : Industry.

NO: 429.

AIRFIELD NAME: NORTH WEALD. OPENED : 1916.
COUNTY : Essex. CLOSED : 1964.
COMMAND : Fighter.
FORMATION : 11 Grp[Uxbridge] GRID REF: L 936229[107]
FUNCTION : Sector Station. O.S.REF.: TL 488044.

LOCALITY : 2.5miles NE of Epping.
RAILWAY STN. : North Weald .25miles[LNER]

LATITUDE : 51 43 00N. HEIGHT ASL : 270′ LIGHTING : See *
LONGITUDE : 00 09 15E. FLYING CONTROL : Yes. RADIO : QDM.

LANDMARKS DAY. : W/T masts.

LANDMARKS NIGHT : * Spitfire curved approach lights.

OBSTRUCTIONS : -

LANDING AREA SURFACE : Tarmac & wood chippings.

QDM: 314. LENGTH X WIDTH: 1600 x 50yds.EXT. TO: -
: 027. : 1400 x 50yds. : -
: : :
: : :

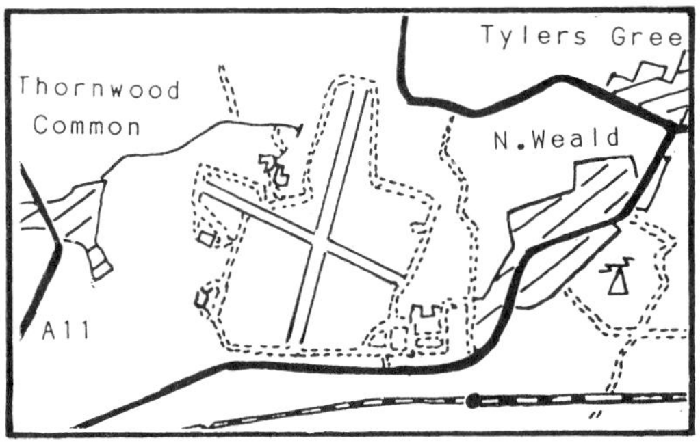

EXTENSIBILITY : -

ACCOMMODATION : Permanent.
HANGARS : Type A[250x120′]-2;blister-12.

HARDSTANDINGS : SE-11;TE-2;Frying pan[65′]-21.

R.A.F. : OFFICERS: 156.S.N.C.O′s.: 284.O.R′s.: 2795.TOTAL: 3235.
W.A.A.F.: " : 36. " : 52. " : 537. " : 625.

AFFILIATED AIRFIELDS : Hornchurch,Castle Camps,Manston etc.

PRESENT USE [1985] : Industry.

NO: 430.

AIRFIELD NAME: NORTH WITHAM.   OPENED : 1942.
COUNTY : Lincolnshire.   CLOSED : 1948.
COMMAND : USSTAFE.
FORMATION : Air Service Command.   GRID REF: F 403416[64]
FUNCTION : 1st Tactical Air Depot.   O.S.REF.: SK 946225.

LOCALITY : 8.5miles S of Grantham.
RAILWAY STN. : South Witham 3miles[LMS]

LATITUDE : 52 47 15N.   HEIGHT ASL : 390′   LIGHTING : Mk2.
LONGITUDE : 00 36 00W.   FLYING CONTROL : Yes.   RADIO : QDM.

LANDMARKS DAY. : Patch of trees between N perimeter & R/W QDM 020.

LANDMARKS NIGHT : -

OBSTRUCTIONS : -

LANDING AREA SURFACE : Concrete.

QDM	LENGTH X WIDTH	EXT. TO
020.	2000 x 50yds.	3000yds.
240.	1400 x 50yds.	1800yds.
300.	1400 x 50yds.	-

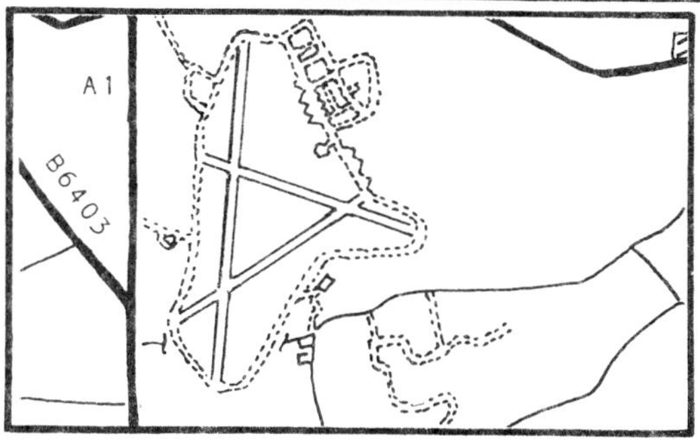

EXTENSIBILITY : To 2350&1650yds. without road closure.Also Gt N.Road might have to be controlled.
ACCOMMODATION : Temporary.
HANGARS : T2-2;Butler-6.

HARDSTANDINGS : Spectacle-50.

USAAF. : OFFICERS: 218.   Enlisted Men. : 3420.TOTAL: 3638.

AFFILIATED AIRFIELDS : -

PRESENT USE [1985] : Forestry Commission.

NO: 431.

AIRFIELD NAME: NORTHLEACH.   OPENED : 1942.
COUNTY : Gloucestershire.   CLOSED : 1945.
COMMAND : Flying Training.
FORMATION : 23 Grp[South Cerney]   GRID REF: P 556361[93]
FUNCTION : Glider Training School [satellite]   O.S.REF.: SP 103148.
LOCALITY : 12miles E of Cheltenham.
RAILWAY STN. : Andoversford Junction 7miles[GWR]

LATITUDE : 51 50 19N.   HEIGHT ASL : 682′   LIGHTING : None.
LONGITUDE : 01 50 30W.   FLYING CONTROL : None.   RADIO : QDM.

LANDMARKS DAY. : Road junctions:Cirencester-Stow on the Wolds & Cheltenham-Oxford .5miles S of A/F.

LANDMARKS NIGHT : -

OBSTRUCTIONS : Blister hangar & nissen huts on boundary.

LANDING AREA SURFACE : Grass.

QDM	LENGTH X WIDTH	EXT. TO
NE-SW.	750yds.	-
E-W.	1050yds.	-

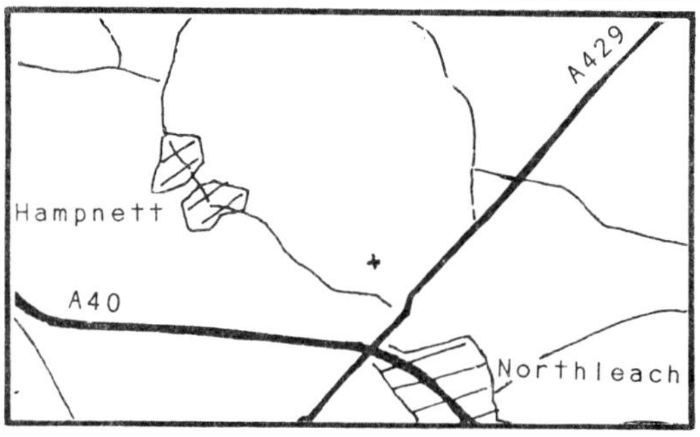

EXTENSIBILITY : One strip of restricted width of 3000yds length.
ACCOMMODATION : Temporary.
HANGARS : Blister 65′-2.

HARDSTANDINGS : -

	OFFICERS	S.N.C.O′s.	O.R′s.	TOTAL
R.A.F.	14.	23.	66.	103.
W.A.A.F.	-	-	-	-

AFFILIATED AIRFIELDS : Stoke Orchard[Parent]

PRESENT USE [1985] : Unspecified.

NO: 432.

AIRFIELD NAME: NORTHOLT.   OPENED : 1915.
COUNTY : Middlesex.   CLOSED :
COMMAND : Fighter.
FORMATION : 11 Grp[Uxbridge]   GRID REF: Q 545045[106]
FUNCTION : Forward Airfield.   O.S.REF.: TQ 098850.

LOCALITY : 3miles E of Uxbridge.
RAILWAY STN. : Ruislip Gardens[joint GWR & LNER]

LATITUDE : 51 33 15N.   HEIGHT ASL : 120′   LIGHTING : Mk2.
LONGITUDE : 00 24 38W.   FLYING CONTROL : Yes.   RADIO : QDM.

LANDMARKS DAY. : Welsh Harp, Hendon. South Harrow & Southall Gasometers.

LANDMARKS NIGHT : Ruislip reservoir. Welsh Harp.

OBSTRUCTIONS : -

LANDING AREA SURFACE : Asphalt[308-Sommerfeld track]

QDM	LENGTH X WIDTH	EXT. TO
205.	980 x 50yds.	-
260.	1800 x 50yds.	-
308.	1600 x 50yds.	-

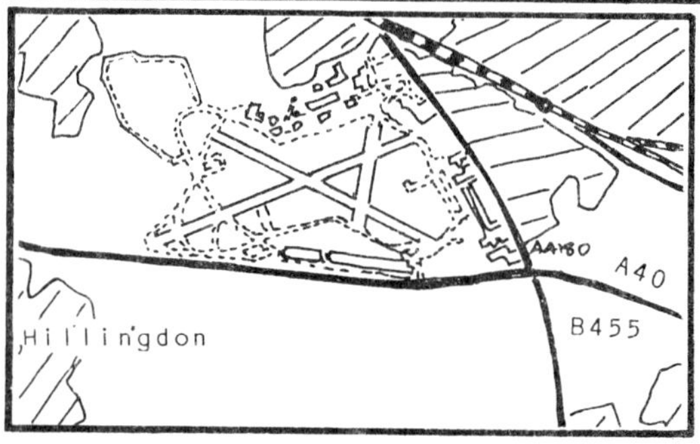

EXTENSIBILITY : None, possible but a new strip of 1700yds could be obtained involving slight demolition.
ACCOMMODATION : Permanent.
HANGARS : A1 Belfast truss-1;C1-2.

HARDSTANDINGS : TE-2;SE-30.

	OFFICERS	S.N.C.O′s.	O.R′s.	TOTAL
R.A.F.	145.	203.	1405.	1753.
W.A.A.F.	14.	13.	496.	523.

AFFILIATED AIRFIELDS : Tangmere[Sector]

PRESENT USE [1985] : RAF.

NO: 433.

AIRFIELD NAME: NUNEATON.
COUNTY : Leicestershire.
COMMAND : Transport.
FORMATION : 44 Grp[Gloucester]
FUNCTION : Operational Training Unit[satellite]
LOCALITY : 4.5miles NNE of Nuneaton.
RAILWAY STN. : Nuneaton,Trent Valley 2miles[LMS]

OPENED : 1943.
CLOSED : 1946.
GRID REF: F 830165[72]
O.S.REF.: SP 375963.

LATITUDE : 52 33 45N. HEIGHT ASL : 378′ LIGHTING : Mk2.
LONGITUDE : 01 26 45W. FLYING CONTROL : Yes. RADIO : QDM.

LANDMARKS DAY : Slagheap 2.5miles SSW.

LANDMARKS NIGHT : -

OBSTRUCTIONS : Church tower in circuit.

LANDING AREA SURFACE : Concrete.

QDM	LENGTH X WIDTH	EXT. TO
130.	1400 x 50yds.	2200yds.
240.	2000 x 50yds.	2700yds.
180.	1400 x 50yds.	2200yds.

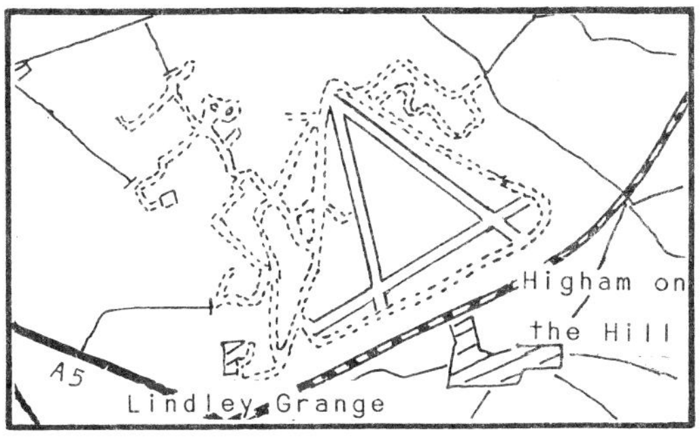

EXTENSIBILITY : Entails demolition of 2 houses & 4 cottages & diversion of a secondary road.
ACCOMMODATION : Temporary.
HANGARS : T2-1.

HARDSTANDINGS : Spectacle-27.

	OFFICERS	S.N.C.O's.	O.R's.	TOTAL
R.A.F.	87.	286.	928.	1301.
W.A.A.F.	2.	18.	140.	160.

AFFILIATED AIRFIELDS : Bramcote[Parent]

PRESENT USE [1985] : Car Industry[Research Association]

NO: 434.

AIRFIELD NAME: NUTHAMPSTEAD.
COUNTY : Hertfordshire.
COMMAND : 8th USAAF.
FORMATION : 398th Bomb Grp.
FUNCTION : Operational.
LOCALITY : 5.5miles SE of Royston.
RAILWAY STN. : Royston[LNER]

OPENED : 1943.
CLOSED : 1954.
GRID REF: L 865534[96]
O.S.REF.: TL 420346.

LATITUDE : 51 59 30N. HEIGHT ASL : 460′ LIGHTING : Mk2.
LONGITUDE : 00 04 00E. FLYING CONTROL : Yes. RADIO : QDM.

LANDMARKS DAY : Barkway Towers 243degrees.

LANDMARKS NIGHT : -

OBSTRUCTIONS : -

LANDING AREA SURFACE : Concrete covered with tarmac.

QDM	LENGTH X WIDTH	EXT. TO
230.	2000 x 50yds.	2430yds.
350.	1400 x 50yds.	2015yds.
290.	1400 x 50yds.	2200yds.

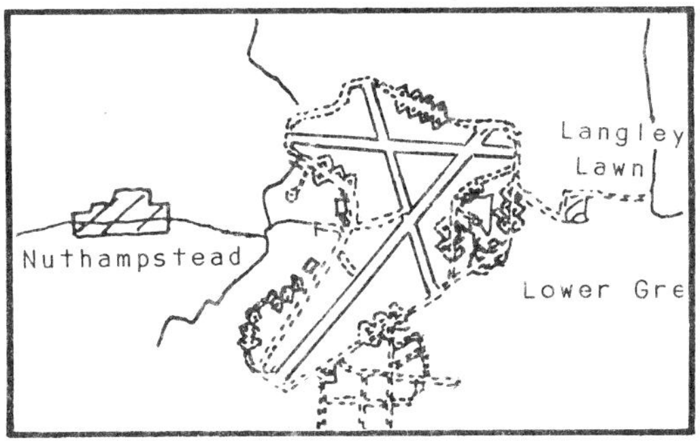

EXTENSIBILITY : Entails very heavy grading fill.

ACCOMMODATION : Temporary.
HANGARS : T2-2.

HARDSTANDINGS : Spectacle-50.

USAAF. : OFFICERS: 421. Enlisted Men. : 2473. TOTAL: 2894.

AFFILIATED AIRFIELDS : -

PRESENT USE [1985] : Agriculture.

NO: 435.

AIRFIELD NAME: NUTTS CORNER.
COUNTY : Antrim NI.
COMMAND : Transport.
FORMATION : 44 Grp[Gloucester]
FUNCTION : Airport.
LOCALITY : 2.5miles ENE of Crumlin.
RAILWAY STN. : Crumlin 2.5miles[GNI]

OPENED : 1941.
CLOSED : 1963.
GRID REF: J 190775[313NI]
O.S.REF.: J 190775.

LATITUDE : 54 37 45N. HEIGHT ASL : 350′ LIGHTING : Mk2.
LONGITUDE : 06 09 00W. FLYING CONTROL : Yes. RADIO : QDM.

LANDMARKS DAY : Lough Neagh 6miles E. Divis hill 5.5miles SE.

LANDMARKS NIGHT : As day.

OBSTRUCTIONS : Divis peak 1574′ 5miles ESE.

LANDING AREA SURFACE : Tarmac.

QDM	LENGTH X WIDTH	EXT. TO
280.	2000 x 50yds.	2800yds.
222.	1600 x 50yds.	2200yds.
158.	1200 x 50yds.	1750yds.

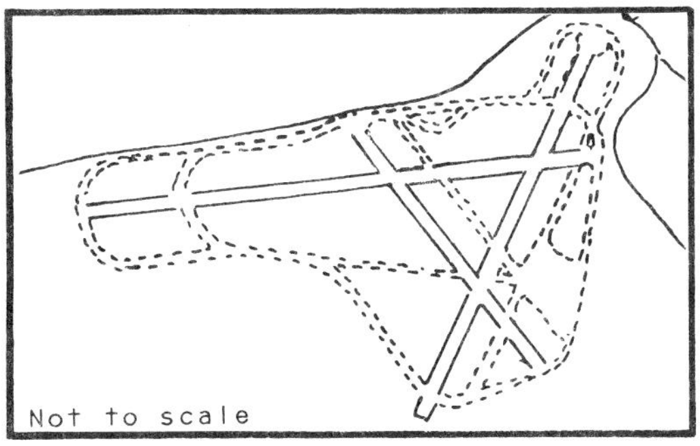

EXTENSIBILITY : Entails diversion of a road to N & demolition of a barn & 3 cottages.
ACCOMMODATION : Temporary.
HANGARS : T1-2;T2-2.

HARDSTANDINGS : Loop-50.

	OFFICERS	S.N.C.O's.	O.R's.	TOTAL
R.A.F.	546.	236.	1311.	2093.
W.A.A.F.	18.	40.	260.	318.

AFFILIATED AIRFIELDS : -

PRESENT USE [1985] : Disused.

NO: 436.

AIRFIELD NAME: OAKINGTON. OPENED : 1940.
COUNTY : Cambridgeshire. CLOSED :
COMMAND : Bomber.
FORMATION : 8 Grp[Huntingdon] GRID REF: L 864846[85]
FUNCTION : Operational. O.S.REF.: TL 412654.

LOCALITY : 5miles NW of Cambridge.
RAILWAY STN. : Longstanton 2.5miles[LNER]

LATITUDE : 52 16 08N. HEIGHT ASL : 40′ LIGHTING : Mk2.
LONGITUDE : 00 04 00E. FLYING CONTROL : Yes. RADIO : QDM.

LANDMARKS DAY. : Old & New Bedford rivers 5.5miles N. Double track Cambridge-Huntingdon R/W forms E boundary running N-S.

LANDMARKS NIGHT : Old & New Bedford rivers 5.5miles N..

OBSTRUCTIONS : Church near approach to R/W 190.

LANDING AREA : Concrete covered with tar.
SURFACE :

QDM	LENGTH X WIDTH	EXT. TO
230.	2000 x 50yds.	2750yds.
275.	1400 x 50yds.	2400yds.
190.	1400 x 50yds.	2050yds.

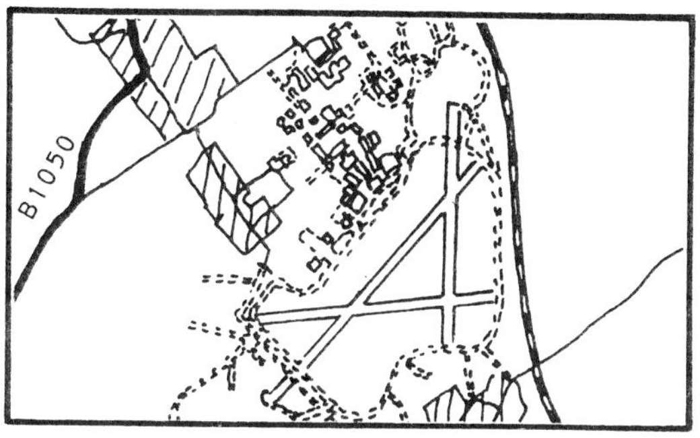

EXTENSIBILITY : Entails slight road diversion only.

ACCOMMODATION : Permanent.
HANGARS : Type J-2;T2-2;B1-1.

HARDSTANDINGS : Heavy bomber-36.

	OFFICERS	S.N.C.O's.	O.R's.	TOTAL
R.A.F.	181.	306.	1104.	1591.
W.A.A.F.	12.	22.	315.	349.

AFFILIATED AIRFIELDS : -

PRESENT USE [1985] : Army.

NO: 437.

AIRFIELD NAME: OAKLEY. OPENED : 1942.
COUNTY : Buckinghamshire. CLOSED : 1945.
COMMAND : Bomber.
FORMATION : 92 Grp[Winslow] GRID REF: L 084297[94]
FUNCTION : Operational Training Unit[satellite] O.S.REF.: SP 638103.
LOCALITY : 11.5miles WSW of Aylesbury.
RAILWAY STN. : Tiddington 3.5miles[GWR]

LATITUDE : 51 47 00N. HEIGHT ASL : 233′ LIGHTING : Mk2.
LONGITUDE : 01 04 30W. FLYING CONTROL : Yes. RADIO : QDM.

LANDMARKS DAY. : A large wood[Shabbington Wood]on NE side of A/F.

LANDMARKS NIGHT : -

OBSTRUCTIONS : Brill Hill 3miles N.

LANDING AREA : Concrete.
SURFACE :

QDM	LENGTH X WIDTH	EXT. TO
209.	2000 x 50yds.	-
249.	1400 x 50yds.	1457yds.
298.	1700 x 50yds.	2000yds.

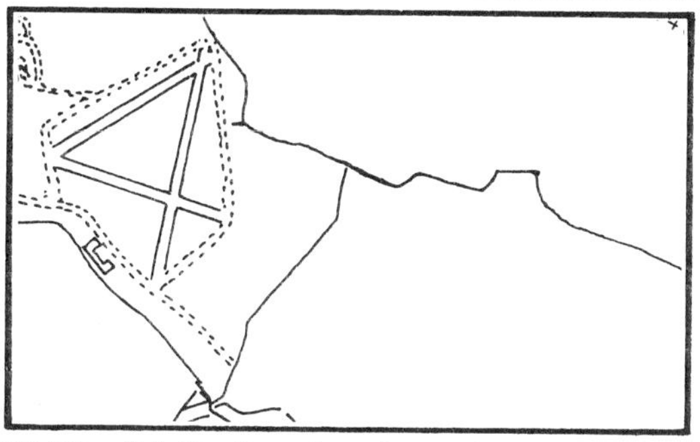

EXTENSIBILITY : Entails diversion of a road.

ACCOMMODATION : Temporary.
HANGARS : T2-1;B1-1.

HARDSTANDINGS : Heavy bomber-27.

	OFFICERS	S.N.C.O's.	O.R's.	TOTAL
R.A.F.	82.	300.	846.	1228.
W.A.A.F.	4.	8.	225.	237.

AFFILIATED AIRFIELDS : Westcott[Parent]

PRESENT USE [1985] : Disused.

NO: 438.

AIRFIELD NAME: OATLANDS HILL. OPENED : 1941.
COUNTY : Wiltshire. CLOSED : 1946.
COMMAND : Fighter.
FORMATION : 70 Grp[Farnborough] GRID REF: U 531611[122]
FUNCTION : Satellite. O.S.REF.: SU 090405.

LOCALITY : 7miles NNW of Salisbury.
RAILWAY STN. : Salisbury 7.5miles[SR & GWR]

LATITUDE : 51 09 53N. HEIGHT ASL : 423′ LIGHTING : None.
LONGITUDE : 01 52 00W. FLYING CONTROL : None. RADIO : QDM.

LANDMARKS DAY. : Trees forming a hollow square on SE perimeter of A/F. R Till 1mile W. Druids Lodge Park S boundary.

LANDMARKS NIGHT : -

OBSTRUCTIONS : -

LANDING AREA : Grass.
SURFACE :

QDM	LENGTH X WIDTH	EXT. TO
NE-SW.	1600yds.	-
E-W.	1200yds.	-
N-S.	1400yds.	-

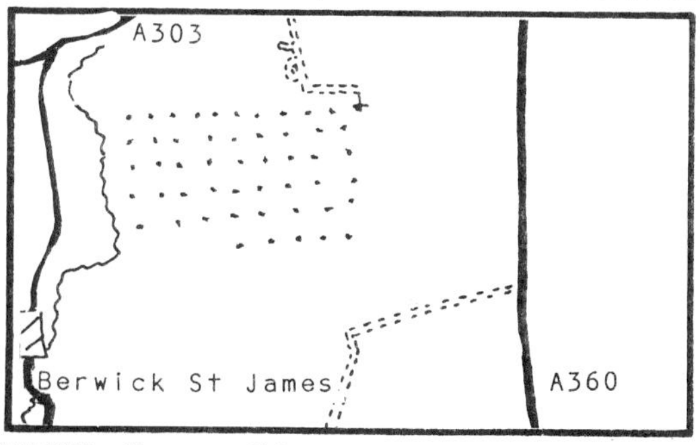

EXTENSIBILITY : None possible.

ACCOMMODATION : Temporary.
HANGARS : Blister-4.

HARDSTANDINGS : -

	OFFICERS	S.N.C.O's.	O.R's.	TOTAL
R.A.F.	5.	7.	183.	195.
W.A.A.F.	-	-	-	-

AFFILIATED AIRFIELDS : Old Sarum[Parent]

PRESENT USE [1985] : Agriculture.

AIRFIELD NAME: ODIHAM. OPENED : 1936.
COUNTY : Hampshire. CLOSED :
COMMAND : Fighter.
FORMATION : 11 Grp[Uxbridge] GRID REF: Q 175687[123]
FUNCTION : Forward Airfield. O.S.REF.: SU 738492.

LOCALITY : 6.5miles ESE of Basingstoke.
RAILWAY STN. : Hook 3.25miles[SR]

LATITUDE : 51 14 00N. HEIGHT ASL : 400′ LIGHTING : Mk2.
LONGITUDE : 00 56 45W. FLYING CONTROL : Yes. RADIO : QDM.

LANDMARKS DAY : Odiham chalk pit. Greywell waterworks.

LANDMARKS NIGHT : -

OBSTRUCTIONS : -

LANDING AREA SURFACE : Concrete & wood chippings.

QDM	LENGTH X WIDTH	EXT. TO
102.	1700 x 50yds.	-
045.	1400 x 50yds.	-

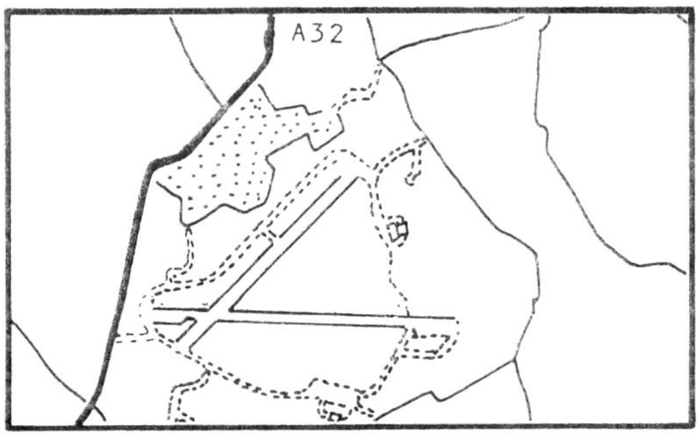

EXTENSIBILITY : None possible, but a new strip of 1400yds. might be obtainable, but would entail demolition of MQ.
ACCOMMODATION : Permanent.
HANGARS : Type C-3; blister-6.

HARDSTANDINGS : Blenheim-6;frying pan-5;spectacle-29.

	OFFICERS	S.N.C.O's.	O.R's.	TOTAL
R.A.F.	193.	167.	1368.	1728.
W.A.A.F.	7.	3.	62.	72.

AFFILIATED AIRFIELDS : Tangmere[Sector]

PRESENT USE [1985] : RAF.

AIRFIELD NAME: OKEHAMPTON. OPENED : 1928.
COUNTY : Devon. CLOSED : 1945.
COMMAND : Maintenance.
FORMATION : 57 Wing[Milton] GRID REF: T 015194[137]
FUNCTION : Storage Unit. O.S.REF.: SX 575974.

LOCALITY : 1mile N of Okehampton.
RAILWAY STN. : Okehampton 2.5miles[SR]

LATITUDE : 50 45 08N. HEIGHT ASL : 780′ LIGHTING : None.
LONGITUDE : 04 01 08W. FLYING CONTROL : None. RADIO : QDM.

LANDMARKS DAY : "Yes Tor", Dartmoor 2039′

LANDMARKS NIGHT : -

OBSTRUCTIONS : -

LANDING AREA SURFACE : Grass.

QDM	LENGTH X WIDTH	EXT. TO
N-S.	840yds.	-
NE-SW.	840yds.	-
E-W.	830yds.	-
SE-NW.	840yds.	-

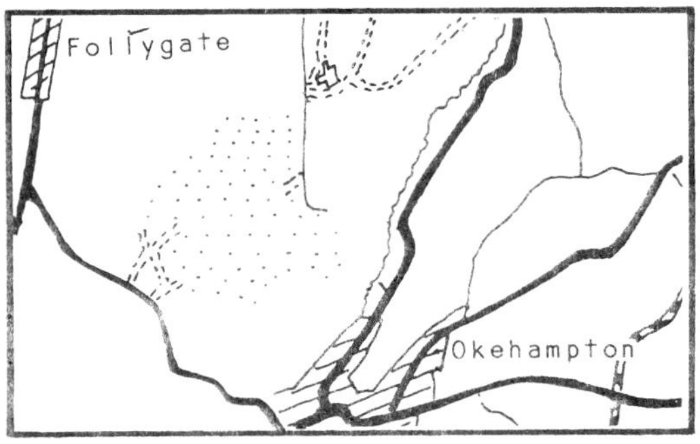

EXTENSIBILITY : -

ACCOMMODATION : Temporary.
HANGARS : -

HARDSTANDINGS : -

	OFFICERS	S.N.C.O's.	O.R's.	TOTAL
R.A.F.	-	7.	81.	88.
W.A.A.F.	2.	2.	64.	68.

AFFILIATED AIRFIELDS : -

PRESENT USE [1985] : Forestry Commission.

AIRFIELD NAME: OLD BUCKENHAM. OPENED : 1943.
COUNTY : Norfolk. CLOSED : 1945.
COMMAND : 8th USAAF.
FORMATION : 453rd Bomb Grp. GRID REF: G 535120[76]
FUNCTION : Operational. O.S.REF.: TM 078936.

LOCALITY : 2miles SE of Attleborough.
RAILWAY STN. : Attleborough 2miles[LNER]

LATITUDE : 52 30 00N. HEIGHT ASL : 195′ LIGHTING : Mk2.
LONGITUDE : 01 03 45E. FLYING CONTROL : Yes. RADIO : QDM.

LANDMARKS DAY : -

LANDMARKS NIGHT : -

OBSTRUCTIONS : -

LANDING AREA SURFACE : Concrete & wood chippings.

QDM	LENGTH X WIDTH	EXT. TO
075.	2000 x 50yds.	-
027.	1400 x 50yds.	3000yds.
130.	1400 x 50yds.	1800yds.

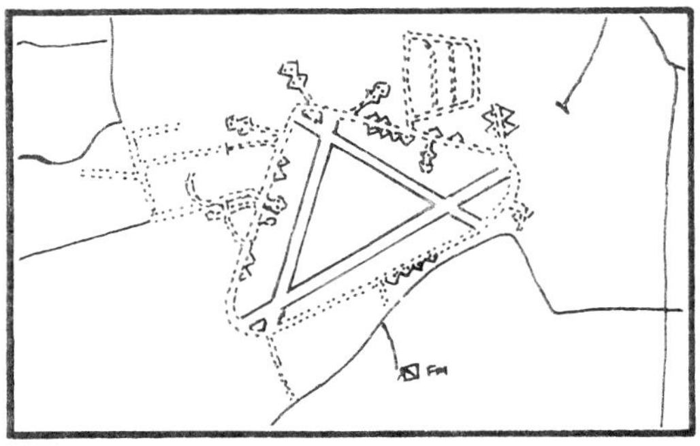

EXTENSIBILITY : Not recommended as it entails diversion of 2 roads & extensive demolition.
ACCOMMODATION : Temporary.
HANGARS : T2-2.

HARDSTANDINGS : Concrete-50.

USAAF. : OFFICERS: 421. Enlisted Men. : 2473.TOTAL: 2894.

AFFILIATED AIRFIELDS : -

PRESENT USE [1985] : Disused.

NO: 442.

AIRFIELD NAME: OLD SARUM. OPENED : 1917.
COUNTY : Wiltshire. CLOSED :
COMMAND : Fighter.
FORMATION : 70 Grp[Farnborough] GRID REF: U 587535[122]
FUNCTION : Operational Training Unit. O.S.REF.: SU 155355.
LOCALITY : 1.5miles N of Salisbury.
RAILWAY STN. : Salisbury 1.5miles[SR]

LATITUDE : 51 05 53N. HEIGHT ASL : 270′ LIGHTING : Mk1.
LONGITUDE : 01 47 00W. FLYING CONTROL : None.RADIO : QDM.

LANDMARKS DAY. : Old Sarum castle, Salisbury, Figsbury Rings 2miles E.

LANDMARKS NIGHT : -

OBSTRUCTIONS : Old Sarum castle .5miles SE, Bishopsdown Ridge S boundary.

LANDING AREA SURFACE : Grass.

QDM:	LENGTH X WIDTH:	EXT. TO:
NE-SW.	1200yds.	-
:	:	:
:	:	:
:	:	:

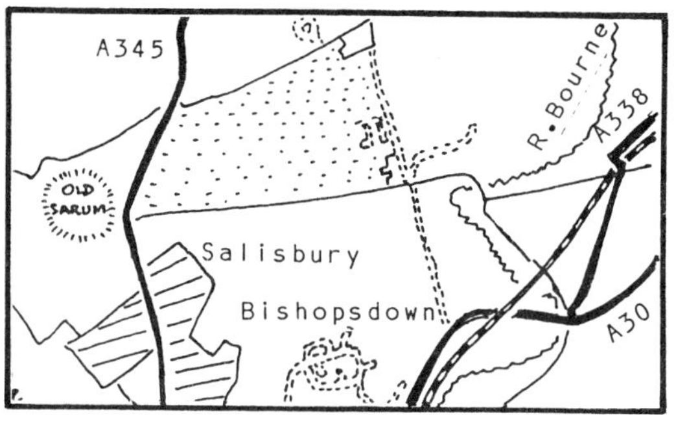

EXTENSIBILITY : None possible.

ACCOMMODATION : Permanent.
HANGARS : GS Type164x170′-3;80x170′-1;blister-2.

HARDSTANDINGS : Sommerfeld track-18.

	OFFICERS	S.N.C.O′s.	O.R′s.	TOTAL
R.A.F.	172.	84.	1131.	1387.
W.A.A.F.	7.	3.	258.	268.

AFFILIATED AIRFIELDS : Oatlands Hill[Satellite]

PRESENT USE [1985] : Aircraft Industry[Edgley Aircraft]

NO: 443.

AIRFIELD NAME: ORSTON. OPENED : 1941.
COUNTY : Nottinghamshire. CLOSED : 1945.
COMMAND : Flying Training.
FORMATION : 21 Grp[Spittlegate] GRID REF: F 244608[54]
FUNCTION : Service Flying Training School[RLG] O.S.REF.: SK 780413.
LOCALITY : 4.5miles E of Bingham.
RAILWAY STN. : Elston & Orston 1mile[LNER]

LATITUDE : 52 57 30N. HEIGHT ASL : 100′ LIGHTING : None.
LONGITUDE : 00 50 15W. FLYING CONTROL : None.RADIO : QDM.

LANDMARKS DAY. : -

LANDMARKS NIGHT : -

OBSTRUCTIONS : -

LANDING AREA SURFACE : Grass.

QDM:	LENGTH X WIDTH:	EXT. TO:
N-S.	1000yds.	2000yds.
E-W.	1200yds.	1400yds.
NW-SE.	1000yds.	1400yds.
:	:	:

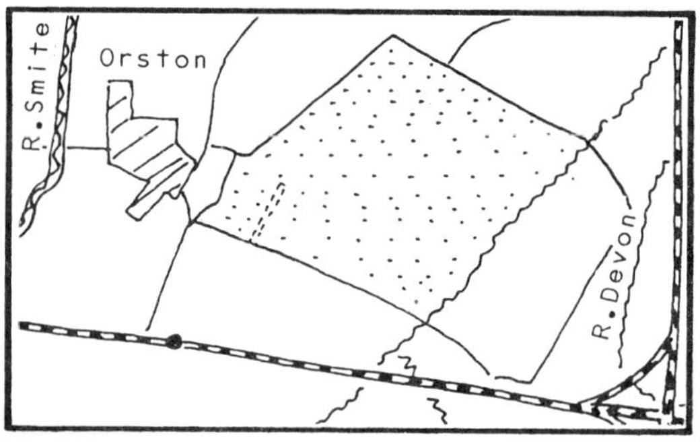

EXTENSIBILITY : -

ACCOMMODATION : Temporary.
HANGARS : 65′ blister-9.

HARDSTANDINGS : -

	OFFICERS	S.N.C.O′s.	O.R′s.	TOTAL
R.A.F.	2.	4.	120.	126.
W.A.A.F.	-	-	-	-

AFFILIATED AIRFIELDS : Newton[Parent]

PRESENT USE [1985] : Agriculture.

NO: 444.

AIRFIELD NAME: OSSINGTON. OPENED : 1942.
COUNTY : Nottinghamshire. CLOSED : 1946.
COMMAND : Bomber.
FORMATION : 93 Grp[Egginton] GRID REF: F 208846[46]
FUNCTION : Operational Training Unit. O.S.REF.: SK 780413.
LOCALITY : 8miles NNW of Newark-on-Trent.
RAILWAY STN. : Newark-on-Trent 8miles[LNER & LMS]

LATITUDE : 53 10 30N. HEIGHT ASL : 211′ LIGHTING : Mk2.
LONGITUDE : 00 53 00W. FLYING CONTROL : Yes. RADIO : QDM.

LANDMARKS DAY. : R Trent about 4miles.

LANDMARKS NIGHT : As day.

OBSTRUCTIONS : Trees on approach to QDM 240&268 R/W.

LANDING AREA SURFACE : Concrete.

QDM:	LENGTH X WIDTH:	EXT. TO:
240.	2000 x 50yds.	-
268.	1400 x 50yds.	-
318.	1400 x 50yds.	-
:	:	:

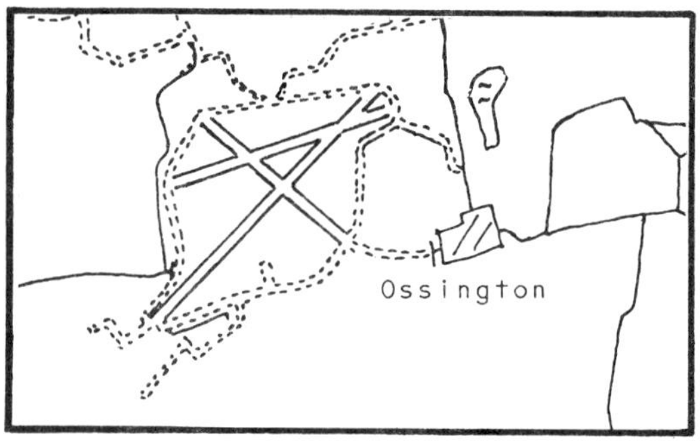

EXTENSIBILITY : None possible except 200yds. to SW.

ACCOMMODATION : Temporary.
HANGARS : T2-4.

HARDSTANDINGS : Heavy bomber-30.

	OFFICERS	S.N.C.O′s.	O.R′s.	TOTAL
R.A.F.	205.	456.	1461.	2122.
W.A.A.F.	9.	5.	327.	341.

AFFILIATED AIRFIELDS : -

PRESENT USE [1985] : Agriculture.

NO: 445.

AIRFIELD NAME: OULTON. OPENED : 1940.
COUNTY : Norfolk. CLOSED : 1947.
COMMAND : Bomber.
FORMATION : 100 Grp[Bylaugh Hall] GRID REF: G 606455[58]
FUNCTION : Operational. O.S.REF.: TG 145275.

LOCALITY : 3miles W of Aylsham.
RAILWAY STN. : Aylsham 3miles[LNER]

LATITUDE : 52 48 00N. HEIGHT ASL : 157′ LIGHTING : Mk2.
LONGITUDE : 01 11 00E. FLYING CONTROL : Yes. RADIO : QDM.

LANDMARKS DAY. : Railway running whole length of S perimeter.

LANDMARKS NIGHT : -

OBSTRUCTIONS : -

LANDING AREA SURFACE : Concrete.

QDM	LENGTH X WIDTH	EXT. TO
120.	2000 x 50yds.	3000yds.
070.	1400 x 50yds.	1750yds.
170.	1400 x 50yds.	2200yds.

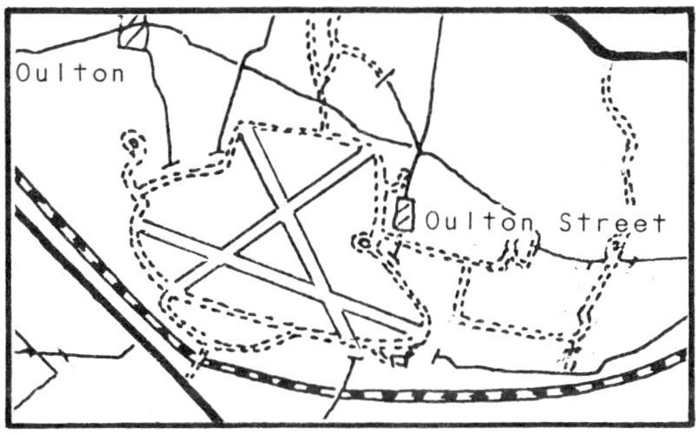

EXTENSIBILITY : Entails serious demolition & minor road diversion.
ACCOMMODATION : Temporary.
HANGARS : T2-4.

HARDSTANDINGS : Spectacle-36.

	OFFICERS	S.N.C.O′s.	O.R′s.	TOTAL
R.A.F.	104.	233.	937.	1274.
W.A.A.F.	6.	9.	196.	211.

AFFILIATED AIRFIELDS : -

PRESENT USE [1985] : Disused.

NO: 446.

AIRFIELD NAME: OUSTON. OPENED : 1941.
COUNTY : Northumberland. CLOSED :
COMMAND : Fighter.
FORMATION : 12 Grp[Watnall] GRID REF: Z 569905[7]
FUNCTION : Operational Training Unit. O.S.REF.: NZ 082700.
LOCALITY : 1mile S of Stamfordham.
RAILWAY STN. : Newcastle Central 6miles[LNER]

LATITUDE : 55 01 15N. HEIGHT ASL : 450′ LIGHTING : Mk2.
LONGITUDE : 01 52 15W. FLYING CONTROL : Yes. RADIO : QDM.

LANDMARKS DAY. : Reservoir. Whittledene. Wagshaw mast. Norlow Hill.

LANDMARKS NIGHT : Reservoir. Whittledene.

OBSTRUCTIONS : -

LANDING AREA SURFACE : Tarmac.

QDM	LENGTH X WIDTH	EXT. TO
090.	1250 x 50yds.	1600yds.
050.	1200 x 50yds.	1600yds.
140.	1400 x 50yds.	1407yds.

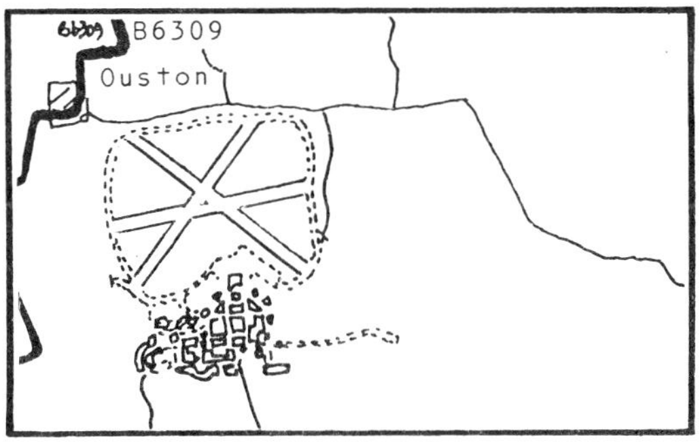

EXTENSIBILITY : -

ACCOMMODATION : Permanent.
HANGARS : Type J-1;blisters:O-6;EO-2.

HARDSTANDINGS : SE-4.

	OFFICERS	S.N.C.O′s.	O.R′s.	TOTAL
R.A.F.	113.	281.	806.	1200.
W.A.A.F.	13.	6.	563.	582.

AFFILIATED AIRFIELDS : -

PRESENT USE [1985] : Army.

NO: 447.

AIRFIELD NAME: OVERTON HEATH. OPENED : 1941.
COUNTY : Wiltshire. CLOSED : 1945.
COMMAND : Flying Training.
FORMATION : 23 Grp[South Cerney] GRID REF: U 620860[112]
FUNCTION : Flying Instructers School[RLG] O.S.REF.: SU 168655.
LOCALITY : 1.5miles S of Marlborough.
RAILWAY STN. : Savernake 5mile[GWR]

LATITUDE : 51 23 19N. HEIGHT ASL : 613′ LIGHTING : None.
LONGITUDE : 01 44 40W. FLYING CONTROL : None. RADIO : QDM.

LANDMARKS DAY. : Savernake Forest 2.5miles NE. Martinsell Hill .75miles S.

LANDMARKS NIGHT : Savernake Forest 2.5miles NE.

OBSTRUCTIONS : Martinsell Hill 350′ above A/F level, .75miles S 1220yds. SSW of A/F boundary.

LANDING AREA SURFACE : Steel Matting[Sommerfeld track]

QDM	LENGTH X WIDTH	EXT. TO
110.	1750yds.	-
060.	1500yds.	-

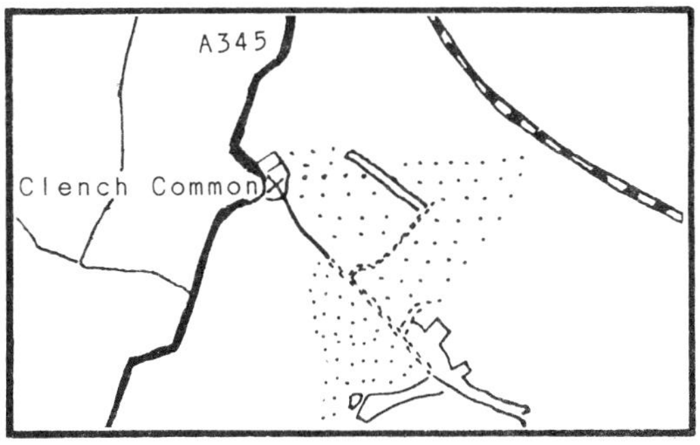

EXTENSIBILITY : -

ACCOMMODATION : Temporary.
HANGARS : Blisters:45′-2;65′-4;69′-1.

HARDSTANDINGS : -

	OFFICERS	S.N.C.O′s.	O.R′s.	TOTAL
R.A.F.	2.	3.	80.	85.
W.A.A.F.	-	-	-	-

AFFILIATED AIRFIELDS : Upavon[Parent]

PRESENT USE [1985] : Agriculture.

NO: 448.

AIRFIELD NAME: PANSHANGAR.   OPENED : 1941.
COUNTY : Hertfordshire.   CLOSED : 1953.
COMMAND : Flying Training.
FORMATION : 50 Grp[Reading]   GRID REF: L 715323[96]
FUNCTION : Elementary Flying Training School.   O.S.REF.: TL 266128.
LOCALITY : 3.5miles N of Hitchin.
RAILWAY STN. : Welwyn North 2miles[LNER]

LATITUDE : 51 48 04N. HEIGHT ASL : 250′ LIGHTING : None.
LONGITUDE : 00 09 45W. FLYING CONTROL : None. RADIO : QDM.

LANDMARKS DAY. : Viaduct.

LANDMARKS NIGHT : -

OBSTRUCTIONS : -

LANDING AREA SURFACE : Grass.

QDM	LENGTH X WIDTH	EXT. TO
N-S.	1000yds.	1800yds.
NE-SW.	1033yds.	1900yds.
E-W.	1166yds.	1400yds.
NW-SE.	1033yds.	-

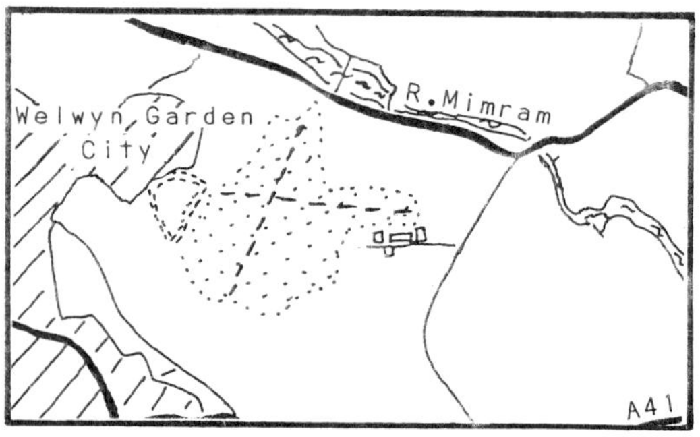

EXTENSIBILITY : By re-stripping.

ACCOMMODATION : Temporary.
HANGARS : Blisters:double EO-2;EOB-2;triple standard-1; double-1;standard-1.
HARDSTANDINGS : -

	OFFICERS	S.N.C.O′s.	O.R′s.	TOTAL
R.A.F.	-	3.	40.	43.
W.A.A.F.	-	-	-	-

AFFILIATED AIRFIELDS : Hatfield[RLG]

PRESENT USE [1985] : Private flying.

NO: 449.

AIRFIELD NAME: PAPPLEWICK MOOR.   OPENED : 1941.
COUNTY : Nottinghamshire.   CLOSED : 1945.
COMMAND : Flying Training.
FORMATION : 21 Grp[Spittlegate]   GRID REF: F 020705[54]
FUNCTION : Elementary Flying Training School[RLG]   O.S.REF.: SK 550510.
LOCALITY : 6miles N of Nottingham.
RAILWAY STN. : Hucknall 2miles[LMS]

LATITUDE : 53 02 45N. HEIGHT ASL : 220′ LIGHTING : None.
LONGITUDE : 01 10 15W. FLYING CONTROL : None. RADIO : QDM.

LANDMARKS DAY. : Hucknall town 210degrees.

LANDMARKS NIGHT : -

OBSTRUCTIONS : Electric cable near E boundary. Trees all along S boundary.

LANDING AREA SURFACE : Grass.

QDM: LENGTH X WIDTH: EXT. TO:
: Grass emergency landing ground & low flying area only.
:

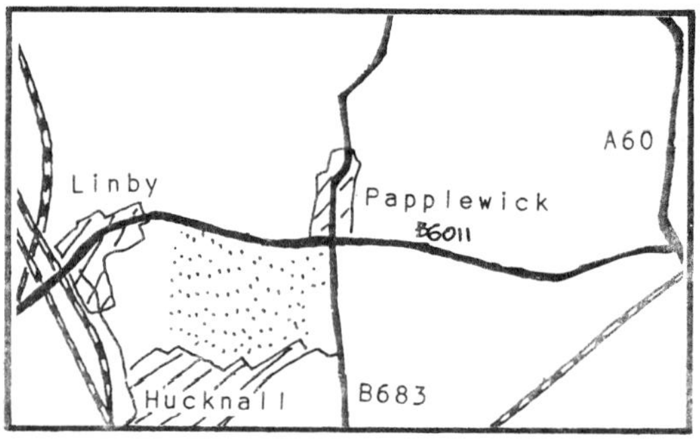

EXTENSIBILITY : None possible.

ACCOMMODATION : -
HANGARS : -

HARDSTANDINGS : -

	OFFICERS	S.N.C.O′s.	O.R′s.	TOTAL
R.A.F.	-	-	-	-
W.A.A.F.	-	-	-	-

AFFILIATED AIRFIELDS : Hucknall[Parent]

PRESENT USE [1985] : Agriculture.

NO: 450.

AIRFIELD NAME: PEMBREY.   OPENED : 1940.
COUNTY : Carmarthenshire.   CLOSED :
COMMAND : Flying Training.
FORMATION : 25 Grp[Market Drayton]   GRID REF: N 844260[100]
FUNCTION : Air Gunnery School.   O.S.REF.: SN 401035.
LOCALITY : 5miles W of Llanelly.
RAILWAY STN. : Kidwelly Flats Halt-adjoins unit[GWR]

LATITUDE : 51 42 30N. HEIGHT ASL : 17′ LIGHTING : Mk2.
LONGITUDE : 04 18 45W. FLYING CONTROL : Yes. RADIO : QDM.

LANDMARKS DAY. : Estuary of R Burry to SE. Estuary of R Towey to NE.

LANDMARKS NIGHT : -

OBSTRUCTIONS : -

LANDING AREA SURFACE : Concrete covered with tarmac & wood chippings.

QDM	LENGTH X WIDTH	EXT. TO
220.	1740 x 50yds.	4000yds.
270.	1340 x 50yds.	3500yds.
340.	1180 x 50yds.	4000yds.
		4000yds.

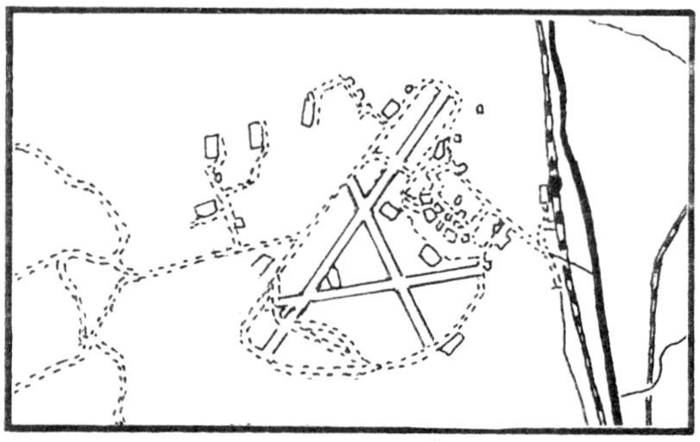

EXTENSIBILITY : No major demolition involved, but area not sufficiently mapped to be certain.
ACCOMMODATION : Temporary.
HANGARS : VR1-3;Cranwell-2;Type F-4; EO blister-13.

HARDSTANDINGS : Circular-27;twin fighter pens-3; hangar apron 1500x90′ approx.

	OFFICERS	S.N.C.O′s.	O.R′s.	TOTAL
R.A.F.	86.	180.	1263.	1529.
W.A.A.F.	5.	4.	234.	243.

AFFILIATED AIRFIELDS : -

PRESENT USE [1985] : RAF.

NO: 451.

AIRFIELD NAME: PENKRIDGE. OPENED : 1942.
COUNTY : Staffordshire. CLOSED : 1945.
COMMAND : Flying Training.
FORMATION : 51 Grp[Leeds] GRID REF: K 394335[61]
FUNCTION : Elementary Flying O.S.REF.: SJ 935137/127.
: Training School[Satellite]
LOCALITY : 6miles S of Stafford.
RAILWAY STN. : Penkridge 1.25miles[LMS]

LATITUDE : 52 42 30N. HEIGHT ASL : 340′ LIGHTING : None.
LONGITUDE : 02 05 30W. FLYING CONTROL : None.RADIO : QDM.

LANDMARKS DAY. : Gailey reservoir S of A/F.

LANDMARKS NIGHT : -

OBSTRUCTIONS : -

LANDING AREA SURFACE : Grass.

QDM:	LENGTH X WIDTH:	EXT. TO:
E-W.	950yds.	1400yds.
:	:	: 800yds.
:	:	:
:	:	:

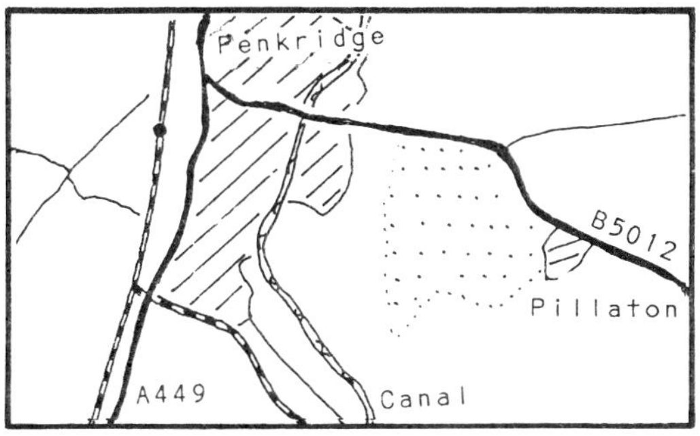

EXTENSIBILITY : -

ACCOMMODATION : Temporary.
HANGARS : Double standard-1;EO blister-1.

HARDSTANDINGS : -

	OFFICERS:	S.N.C.O's.:	O.R's.:	TOTAL:
R.A.F. :	2.	4.	120.	126.
W.A.A.F.:	-	-	-	-

AFFILIATED AIRFIELDS : Wolverhampton[Parent]

PRESENT USE [1985] : Unspecified.

NO: 452.

AIRFIELD NAME: PENRHOS. OPENED : 1937.
COUNTY : Caernarvonshire. CLOSED : 1946.
COMMAND : Flying Training.
FORMATION : 25 Grp[Market Drayton] GRID REF: H 795560[49]
FUNCTION : Advanced flying Unit. O.S.REF.: SO 975495/150.
: [Observer]
LOCALITY : 2.5miles SW of Pwllheli.
RAILWAY STN. : Pwllheli 3miles[GWR]

LATITUDE : 52 52 23N. HEIGHT ASL : 40-70LIGHTING : None.
LONGITUDE : 04 28 23W. FLYING CONTROL : Yes. RADIO : QDM.

LANDMARKS DAY. : St.Tudwal's Islands 5miles S.

LANDMARKS NIGHT : -

OBSTRUCTIONS : Hills running NW along edge of A/F 100′ 400yds.from perimeter.

LANDING AREA SURFACE : Grass.

QDM:	LENGTH X WIDTH:	EXT. TO:
NE-SW.	860yds.	-
NW-SE.	700yds.	-
E-W.	700yds.	-

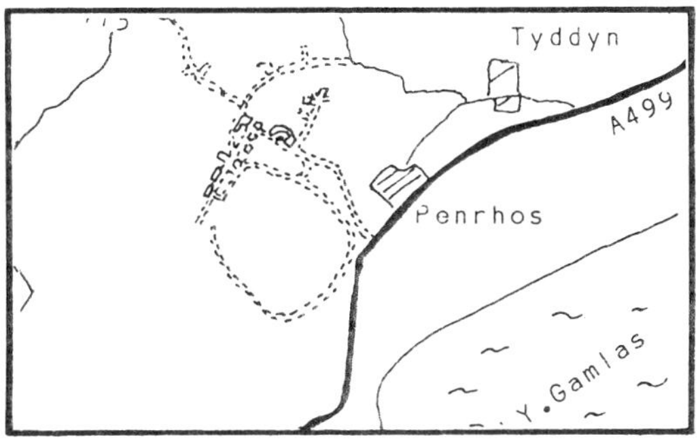

EXTENSIBILITY : None possible.

ACCOMMODATION : Permanent[part]
HANGARS : Bellman-3; Type F-1;EO blister-9.

HARDSTANDINGS : Hangar apron 300x100′

	OFFICERS:	S.N.C.O's.:	O.R's.:	TOTAL:
R.A.F. :	106.	226.	663.	995.
W.A.A.F.:	11.	3.	242.	256.

AFFILIATED AIRFIELDS : Llandwrog[satellite]

PRESENT USE [1985] : Caravan site.

NO: 453.

AIRFIELD NAME: PENSHURST. OPENED : 1942.
COUNTY : Kent. CLOSED : 1945.
COMMAND : Fighter.
FORMATION : 11 Grp[Uxbridge] GRID REF: Q 975661[125]
FUNCTION : Landing Ground. O.S.REF.: TQ 518468/188.
:
LOCALITY : 4miles SW of Tonbridge.
RAILWAY STN. : Penhurst[SR]

LATITUDE : 51 12 00N. HEIGHT ASL : 152′ LIGHTING : None.
LONGITUDE : 00 10 53E. FLYING CONTROL : None.RADIO : QDM.

LANDMARKS DAY. : Railway. Penhurst station. Church.

LANDMARKS NIGHT : Railway signal lights.

OBSTRUCTIONS : Church.

LANDING AREA SURFACE : Grass.

QDM:	LENGTH X WIDTH:	EXT. TO:
N-S.	800yds.	850yds.
E-W.	400yds.	1250yds.
:	:	850x100yds.
:	:	:

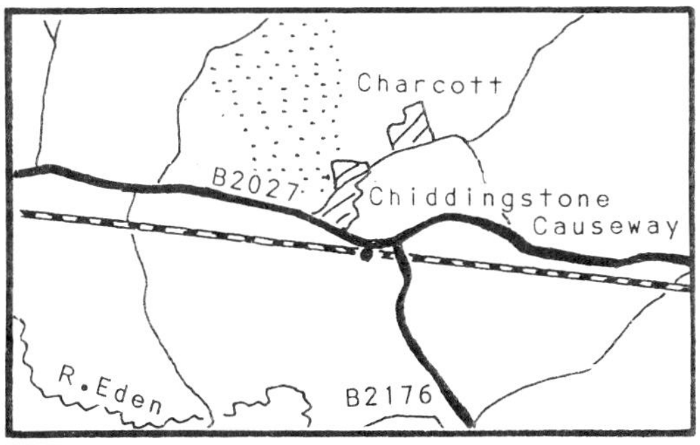

EXTENSIBILITY : -

ACCOMMODATION : Temporary.
HANGARS : -

HARDSTANDINGS : -

	OFFICERS:	S.N.C.O's.:	O.R's.:	TOTAL:
R.A.F. :	26.	10.	156.	192.
W.A.A.F.:	-	-	-	-

AFFILIATED AIRFIELDS : Biggin Hill[Sector]

PRESENT USE [1985] : Unspecified.

NO: 454.

AIRFIELD NAME: PEPLOW. OPENED : 1941.
COUNTY : Shropshire. CLOSED : 1949.
COMMAND : Flying Training.
FORMATION : 23 Grp[South Cerney] GRID REF: K 123443[61]
FUNCTION : Heavy Glider Conversion O.S.REF.: SJ 661233.
: Unit.
LOCALITY : 7miles S of Market Drayton.
RAILWAY STN. : Peplow[GWR]

LATITUDE : 52 48 30N. HEIGHT ASL : 230′ LIGHTING : None.
LONGITUDE : 02 30 00W. FLYING CONTROL : Yes. RADIO : QDM.

LANDMARKS DAY. : The Wrekin.

LANDMARKS NIGHT : As day.

OBSTRUCTIONS : -

LANDING AREA SURFACE : Concrete & wood chippings.

QDM	LENGTH X WIDTH	EXT. TO
183.	1400 x 50yds.	2000yds.
223.	2000 x 50yds.	2700yds.
300.	1400 x 50yds.	1600yds.

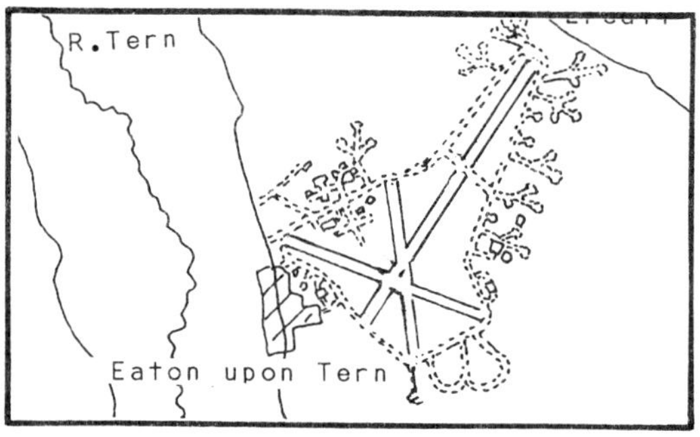

EXTENSIBILITY : Entails slight demolition.

ACCOMMODATION : Temporary.
HANGARS : T2-4;B1-1.

HARDSTANDINGS : Heavy Bomber-30.

R.A.F. : OFFICERS: 222.S.N.C.O′s.: 590.O.R′s.: 879.TOTAL: 1691.
W.A.A.F.: " : 6. " : 4. " : 344. " : 354.

AFFILIATED AIRFIELDS : Seighford[Satellite]

PRESENT USE [1985] : Agriculture.

NO: 455.

AIRFIELD NAME: PERRANPORTH. OPENED : 1941.
COUNTY : Cornwall. CLOSED : 1946.
COMMAND : Transport.
FORMATION : 46 Grp[Harrow Weald] GRID REF: W 168756[143]
FUNCTION : Parent. O.S.REF.: SW 740528/204.
:
LOCALITY : 7miles SSW of Newquay.
RAILWAY STN. : Perranporth 2miles[GWR]

LATITUDE : 50 19 40N. HEIGHT ASL : 320′ LIGHTING : None.
LONGITUDE : 05 10 45W. FLYING CONTROL : Yes. RADIO : QDM.

LANDMARKS DAY. : St.Agnes Head 3.5miles SW of. Coast N.

LANDMARKS NIGHT : As day.

OBSTRUCTIONS : -

LANDING AREA SURFACE : Tarmac.

QDM	LENGTH X WIDTH	EXT. TO
058.	1400 x 50yds.	1700yds.
100.	1100 x 50yds.	1120yds
198.	1100 x 50yds.	1120yds.

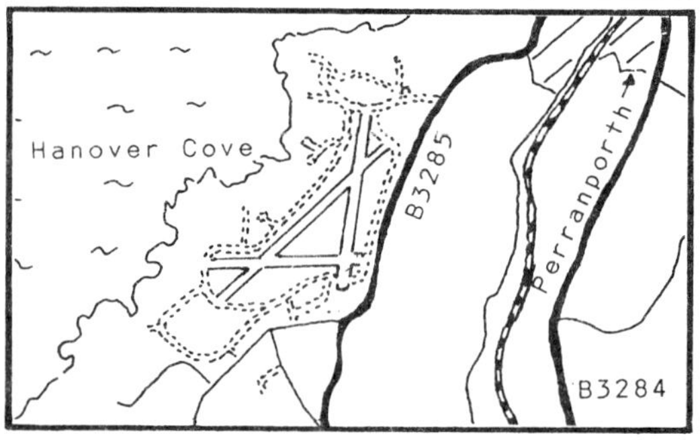

EXTENSIBILITY : -

ACCOMMODATION : Temporary.
HANGARS : Teeside-1;Blisters:O-4;EO-2.

HARDSTANDINGS : SE-20.

R.A.F. : OFFICERS: 48.S.N.C.O′s.: 69.O.R′s.: 917.TOTAL: 1034.
W.A.A.F.: " : 1. " : 1. " : 40. " : 42.

AFFILIATED AIRFIELDS : -

PRESENT USE [1985] : Disused.

NO: 456.

AIRFIELD NAME: PERSHORE. OPENED : 1941.
COUNTY : Worcestershire. CLOSED : 1978.
COMMAND : Transport.
FORMATION : 44 Grp[Gloucester] GRID REF: P 423702[82]
FUNCTION : Parent. O.S.REF.: SO 975495/150.
:
LOCALITY : 8miles ESE of Worcester.
RAILWAY STN. : Pershore 3miles[GWR]

LATITUDE : 52 08 30N. HEIGHT ASL : 123′ LIGHTING : Mk2.
LONGITUDE : 02 02 15W. FLYING CONTROL : Yes. RADIO : QDM.

LANDMARKS DAY. : Malvern Hills 12miles W. Bredon Hills 6miles S. Droitwich. W/T masts & lake.

LANDMARKS NIGHT : -

OBSTRUCTIONS : -

LANDING AREA SURFACE : Concrete & asphalt.

QDM	LENGTH X WIDTH	EXT. TO
217.	2000 x 50yds.	2800yds.
275.	1500 x 50yds.	1530yds.
336.	1400 x 50yds.	

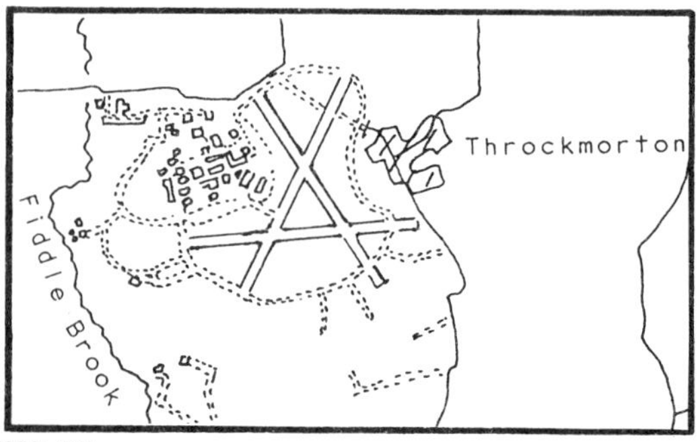

EXTENSIBILITY :

ACCOMMODATION : Temporary.
HANGARS : Type J-1;T2-4.

HARDSTANDINGS : Pans-31.

R.A.F. : OFFICERS: 214.S.N.C.O′s.: 448.O.R′s.: 1275.TOTAL: 1937.
W.A.A.F.: " : 10. " : 6. " : 396. " : 412.

AFFILIATED AIRFIELDS : -

PRESENT USE [1985] : Radio Research Station.

NO: 457.

AIRFIELD NAME: PERTH. OPENED : 1936.
COUNTY : Perthshire. CLOSED :
COMMAND : Flying Training.
FORMATION : 51 Grp[Leeds] GRID REF: O 654498[64Scot]
FUNCTION : Elementary Flying Training School. O.S.REF.: NO 156285/53.
LOCALITY : 3.5miles NE of Perth.
RAILWAY STN. : Perth 4.5miles[LMS]

LATITUDE : 56 26 23N. HEIGHT ASL : 385′ LIGHTING : None.
LONGITUDE : 03 22 08W. FLYING CONTROL : None.RADIO : QDM.

LANDMARKS DAY. : R Tay 4miles S.

LANDMARKS NIGHT : As day.

OBSTRUCTIONS : -

LANDING AREA SURFACE : Grass.

QDM	LENGTH X WIDTH	EXT. TO
NE-SW.	1300yds.	2000yds.
:	:	: 1500yds.
:	:	: 1100yds.
:	:	:

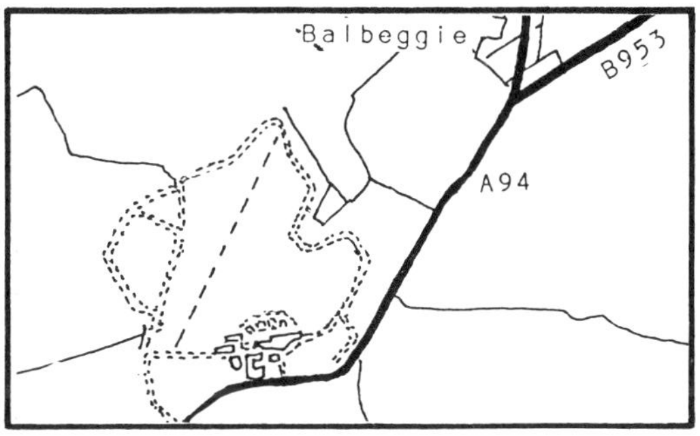

EXTENSIBILITY : Entails demolition of a farm & 2 buildings.

ACCOMMODATION : Temporary.
HANGARS : Civil:160x90′-1;120x110′-1;EO blister-6.

HARDSTANDINGS : -

	OFFICERS	S.N.C.O′s.	O.R′s.	TOTAL
R.A.F.	28.	37.	326.	391.
W.A.A.F.	-	-	-	-

AFFILIATED AIRFIELDS : Whitefield[RLG]

PRESENT USE [1985] : Aircraft Industry[Airwork]

NO: 458.

AIRFIELD NAME: PERTON. OPENED : 1941.
COUNTY : Staffordshire. CLOSED : 1945.
COMMAND : Flying Training.
FORMATION : 21 Grp[Spittlegate] GRID REF: K 317206[61]
FUNCTION : Advanced Flying Unit Unit[Satellite] O.S.REF.: SJ 865000/139.
LOCALITY : 3.5miles W of Wolverhampton.
RAILWAY STN. : Godsall 3miles[GWR]

LATITUDE : 52 35 45N. HEIGHT ASL : 400′ LIGHTING : None.
LONGITUDE : 02 12 15W. FLYING CONTROL : None.RADIO : QDM.

LANDMARKS DAY. : Wolverhampton 3.5miles E.

LANDMARKS NIGHT : -

OBSTRUCTIONS : -

LANDING AREA SURFACE : Tarmac.

QDM	LENGTH X WIDTH	EXT. TO
220.	1400 x 50yds.	1800yds.
: 160.	: 1100 x 50yds.	: 1400yds.
: 280.	: 1100 x 50yds.	: 1400yds.
:	:	:

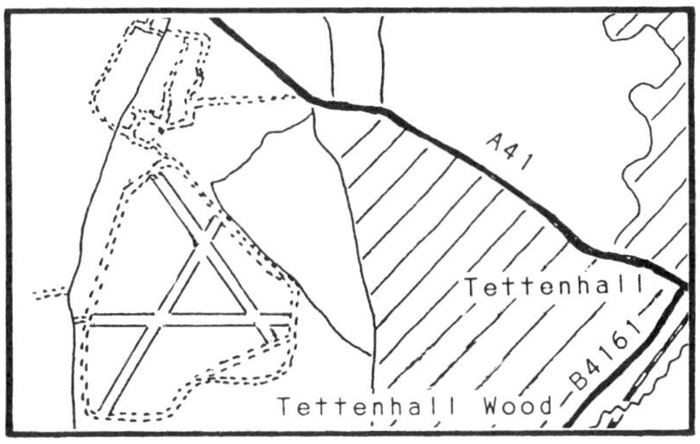

EXTENSIBILITY : Entails slight demolition.

ACCOMMODATION : Temporary.
HANGARS : T2[14bays]-1.

HARDSTANDINGS : Loop[concrete]-3

	OFFICERS	S.N.C.O′s.	O.R′s.	TOTAL
R.A.F.	39.	78.	600.	717.
W.A.A.F.	6.	7.	188.	201.

AFFILIATED AIRFIELDS : Wheaton Aston[Parent]

PRESENT USE [1985] : Agriculture.

NO: 459.

AIRFIELD NAME: PETERBOROUGH. OPENED : 1932.
COUNTY : Northamptonshire. CLOSED : 1964.
COMMAND : Flying Training.
FORMATION : 21 Grp[Spittlegate] GRID REF: F 630200[64]
FUNCTION : Advanced Flying Unit [Pilot] O.S.REF.: TF 174005/152.
LOCALITY : 1.5miles NNW of Peterborough.
RAILWAY STN. : Peterborough 2miles[LMS & LNER]

LATITUDE : 52 35 15N. HEIGHT ASL : 58′ LIGHTING : None.
LONGITUDE : 00 16 00W. FLYING CONTROL : Yes. RADIO : QDM.

LANDMARKS DAY. : Railway marshalling yards & City of Peterborough.

LANDMARKS NIGHT : -

OBSTRUCTIONS : -

LANDING AREA SURFACE : Grass.

QDM	LENGTH X WIDTH	EXT. TO
NNE-SSW.	1200yds.	2000yds.
: NE-SW.	: 1020yds.	: 1600yds.
: ENE-WSW.	: 780yds.	: 1400yds.
: SSE-NNW.	: 780yds.	: -

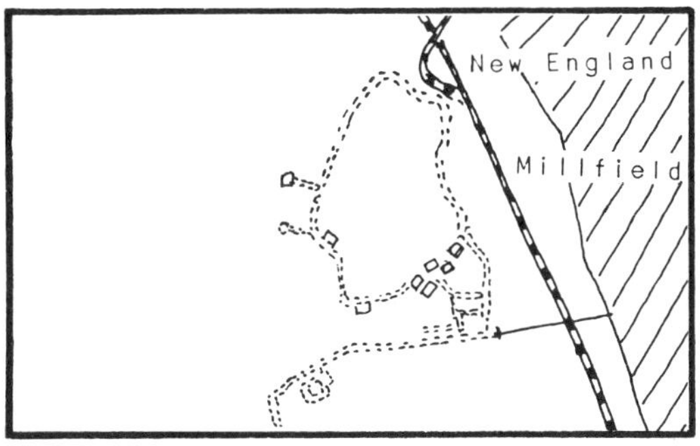

EXTENSIBILITY : Not recommended.

ACCOMMODATION : Permanent[part]
HANGARS : Type A-1;Bellman-5;
65′Blisters:treble-1;double-2;single-1.
HARDSTANDINGS : Loop-3.

	OFFICERS	S.N.C.O′s.	O.R′s.	TOTAL
R.A.F.	98.	152.	590.	840.
W.A.A.F.	5.	8.	202.	215.

AFFILIATED AIRFIELDS : Sutton Bridge[Satellite] Sibson[RLG]

PRESENT USE [1985] : Housing.

NO: 460.

AIRFIELD NAME: PETERHEAD. OPENED : 1941.
COUNTY : Aberdeenshire. CLOSED : 1945.
COMMAND : Fighter.
FORMATION : 13 Grp[Inverness] GRID REF: K 595679[31Scot]
FUNCTION : Forward Airfield O.S.REF.: NK 079473/30.
: [nightfighter]
LOCALITY : 3miles W of Peterhead.
RAILWAY STN. : Inverugie[LNER]

LATITUDE : 57 30 53N. HEIGHT ASL : 150′ LIGHTING : Mk2.
LONGITUDE : 01 52 15W. FLYING CONTROL : Yes. RADIO : QDM.

LANDMARKS DAY. : Peterhead harbour. Reservoir 1mile E. Railway 300yds N.

LANDMARKS NIGHT : Reservoir.

OBSTRUCTIONS : -

LANDING AREA SURFACE : Tarmac.

QDM	LENGTH X WIDTH	EXT. TO
231.	1500 x 50yds.	-
290.	1465 x 50yds.	-
171.	1772 x 50yds.	-

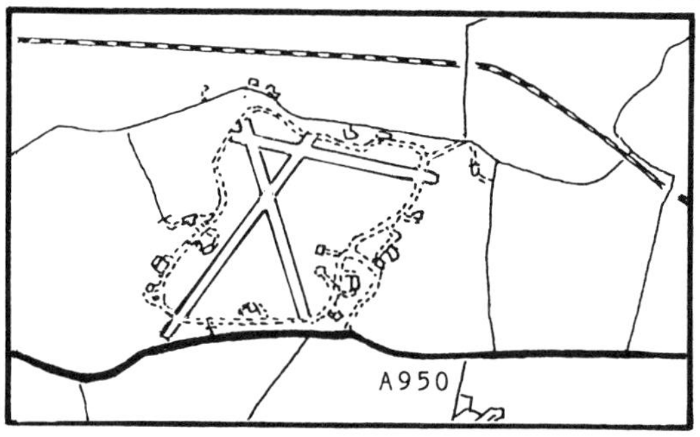

EXTENSIBILITY : None possible.

ACCOMMODATION : Temporary.
HANGARS : Teeside-5;O Blister-8.

HARDSTANDINGS : SE-4;TE-5.

	OFFICERS	S.N.C.O's.	O.R's.	TOTAL
R.A.F.	96.	120.	1360.	1576.
W.A.A.F.	14.	18.	357.	389.

AFFILIATED AIRFIELDS : Turnhouse[Sector]

PRESENT USE [1985] : Private flying.

NO: 461.

AIRFIELD NAME: POCKLINGTON. OPENED : 1941.
COUNTY : Yorkshire. CLOSED : 1946.
COMMAND : Bomber.
FORMATION : 4 Grp[York] GRID REF: A 260684[27]
FUNCTION : Operational[42 Base] O.S.REF.: SE 790485/106.
:
LOCALITY : 12miles ESE of York.
RAILWAY STN. : Pocklington .5miles[LNER]

LATITUDE : 53 55 45N. HEIGHT ASL : 84′ LIGHTING : Mk2.
LONGITUDE : 00 48 00W. FLYING CONTROL : Yes. RADIO : QDM.

LANDMARKS DAY. : Church. LNER running NW-SE to N of A/F.

LANDMARKS NIGHT : -

OBSTRUCTIONS : Hills up to 800′ approx.3.5miles NE.

LANDING AREA SURFACE : Concrete & tarmac.

QDM	LENGTH X WIDTH	EXT. TO
320.	1800 x 50yds.	3000yds.
352.	1300 x 50yds.	1400yds.
191.	1300 x 50yds.	1400yds.

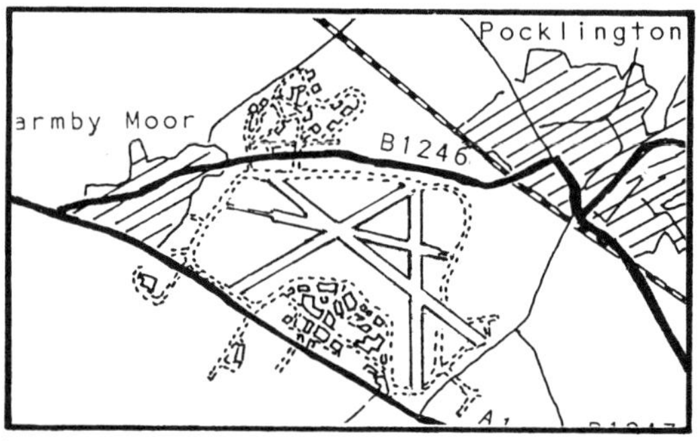

EXTENSIBILITY : -

ACCOMMODATION : Temporary.
HANGARS : Type J-1;T2-4;B1-1.

HARDSTANDINGS : Heavy bomber-36.

	OFFICERS	S.N.C.O's.	O.R's.	TOTAL
R.A.F.	166.	421.	1108.	1695.
W.A.A.F.	13.	7.	303.	323.

AFFILIATED AIRFIELDS : Elvington & Full Sutton[Sub-stations]

PRESENT USE [1985] : Agriculture.

NO: 462.

AIRFIELD NAME: PODINGTON. OPENED : 1942.
COUNTY : Bedfordshire. CLOSED : 1946.
COMMAND : 8th USAAF.
FORMATION : 92nd Bomb Grp. GRID REF: L 405795[84]
FUNCTION : Operational. O.S.REF.: SP 953603/153.
:
LOCALITY : 6miles SE of Wellingborough.
RAILWAY STN. : Wellingborough Midland Road 5miles[LMS]

LATITUDE : 52 13 53N. HEIGHT ASL : 330′ LIGHTING : Mk2.
LONGITUDE : 00 36 10W. FLYING CONTROL : Yes. RADIO : QDM.

LANDMARKS DAY. : Wellingborough-Bedford double track railway line.

LANDMARKS NIGHT : -

OBSTRUCTIONS : Trees completely surrounding A/F 50-70′

LANDING AREA SURFACE : Concrete & tarmac.

QDM	LENGTH X WIDTH	EXT. TO
050.	2000 x 50yds.	2900yds.
350.	1130 x 50yds.	-
290.	1400 x 50yds.	1700yds.

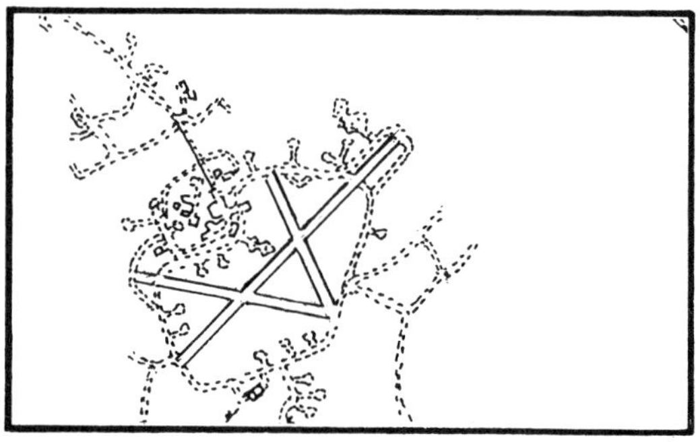

EXTENSIBILITY : Not recommended.

ACCOMMODATION : Temporary.
HANGARS : T2-2.

HARDSTANDINGS : Frying pan loop-50.

USAAF. : OFFICERS: 421. Enlisted Men. : 2473.TOTAL: 2894.

AFFILIATED AIRFIELDS : -

PRESENT USE [1985] : Race track.

NO: 463.

AIRFIELD NAME: POLEBROOK. OPENED : 1941.
COUNTY : Northamptonshire. CLOSED : 1963.
COMMAND : 8th USAAF.
FORMATION : 351st Bomb Grp. GRID REF: F 547057[74]
FUNCTION : Operational. O.S.REF.: TL 093863/142.
:
LOCALITY : 3.5miles ESE of Oundle.
RAILWAY STN. : Oundle 3miles[LMS]

LATITUDE : 52 27 57N. HEIGHT ASL : 230′ LIGHTING : Mk2.
LONGITUDE : 00 23 30W. FLYING CONTROL : Yes. RADIO : QDM.

LANDMARKS DAY. : R Nene. Oundle church. Ashton Wold wood.

LANDMARKS NIGHT : -

OBSTRUCTIONS : -

LANDING AREA SURFACE : Concrete covered with tarmac.
QDM: 250. LENGTH X WIDTH: 1950 x 50yds.EXT. TO: 4000yds.
: 190. : 1400 x 50yds. : 2000yds.
: 310. : 1400 x 50yds. : 2000yds.
: : :

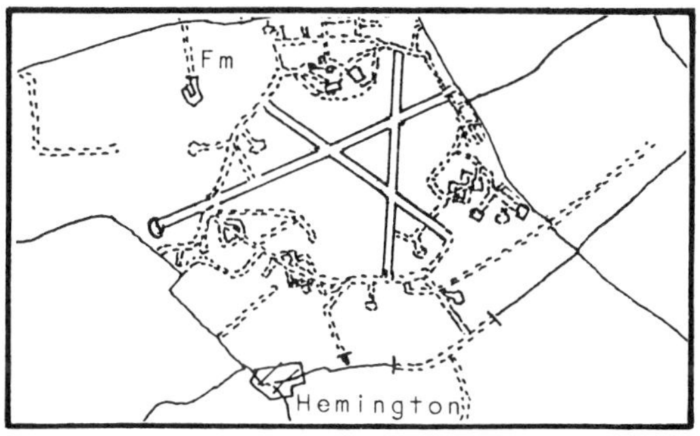

EXTENSIBILITY : No.2 R/W could be extended to 3000yds. or even further, but envolves demolition of a camp site.
ACCOMMODATION : Temporary.
HANGARS : T2-1;Type J-1.

HARDSTANDINGS : Loop-50.

USAAF. : OFFICERS: 443. Enlisted Men. : 2529.TOTAL: 2972.

AFFILIATED AIRFIELDS : -

PRESENT USE [1985] : Agriculture.

NO: 464.

AIRFIELD NAME: PORT ELLEN. OPENED : 1940.
COUNTY : Argyllshire. CLOSED : 1947.
COMMAND : Coastal.
FORMATION : 15 Grp[Liverpool] GRID REF: R 823753[69Scot]
FUNCTION : Operational. O.S.REF.: NR 325515/60.
:
LOCALITY : Isle of Islay.
RAILWAY STN. : Glasgow[LMS & LNER]

LATITUDE : 55 40 58N. HEIGHT ASL : 46′ LIGHTING : None.
LONGITUDE : 06 15 03W. FLYING CONTROL : Yes. RADIO : QDM.

LANDMARKS DAY. : Loch Indaal. A/F lies on E shore.

LANDMARKS NIGHT : Rhinns of Islay Point[Orsay Island]Lighthouse. Ardmor Lighthouse.

OBSTRUCTIONS : Hills ENE rising to 1600′ at 5miles, & to ESE rising to 1136′at 4miles.

LANDING AREA SURFACE : Bitumen & sand.
QDM: 226. LENGTH X WIDTH: 1760 x 50yds.EXT. TO: -
: 266. : 1366 x 50yds. : -
: 135. : 1630 x 50yds. : -

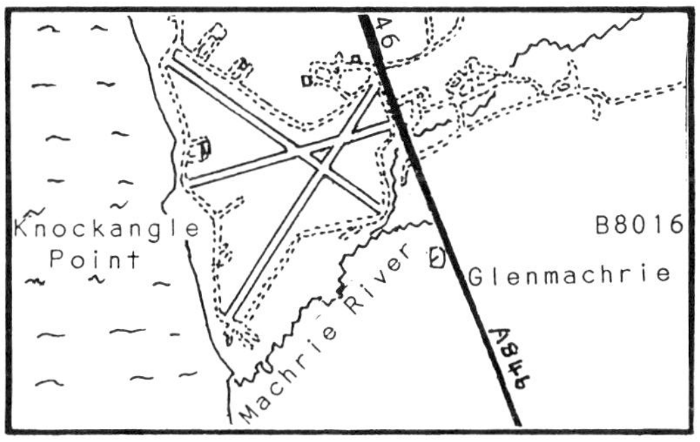

EXTENSIBILITY : Only for a 4th. R/W of 2000yds.

ACCOMMODATION : Temporary.
HANGARS : 1/2 of T2-5;Callendar Hamilton-1.

HARDSTANDINGS : -

R.A.F. :	OFFICERS: 66.	S.N.C.O's.: 92.	O.R's.: 955.	TOTAL: 1113.
W.A.A.F.:	" : 8.	" : 8.	" : 250.	" : 266.

AFFILIATED AIRFIELDS : -

PRESENT USE [1985] : Private flying.

NO: 465.

AIRFIELD NAME: PORTREATH. OPENED : 1941.
COUNTY : Cornwall. CLOSED :
COMMAND : Fighter.
FORMATION : 10 Grp[Rudloe Manor] GRID REF: X 096694[146]
FUNCTION : Sector station. O.S.REF.: SW 672465/203.
:
LOCALITY : 3.5miles N of Redruth.
RAILWAY STN. : Redruth[GWR]

LATITUDE : 50 16 00N. HEIGHT ASL : 295′ LIGHTING : Mk2.
LONGITUDE : 05 16 00W. FLYING CONTROL : Yes. RADIO : QDM.

LANDMARKS DAY. : Coast. Carnbrea Hill 738′ 3.5miles S.

LANDMARKS NIGHT : Coast W.

OBSTRUCTIONS : -

LANDING AREA SURFACE : Asphalt.
QDM: 194. LENGTH X WIDTH: 1350 x 50yds.EXT. TO: -
: 283. : 1800 x 50yds. : -
: 336. : 1150 x 50yds. : -
: 242. : 1350 x 50yds. : -

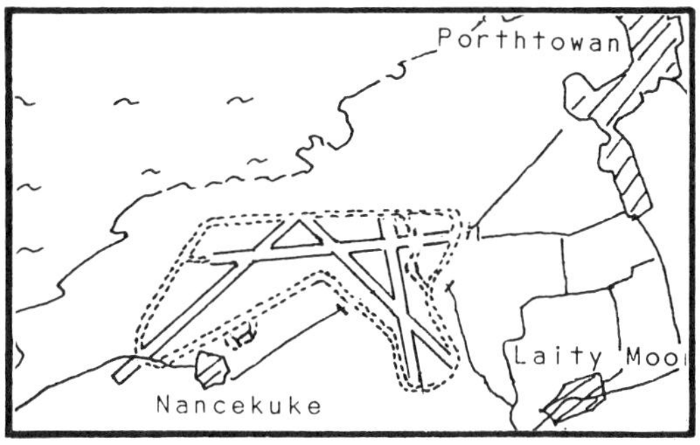

EXTENSIBILITY : None possible to existing strips.

ACCOMMODATION : Temporary.
HANGARS : Teesside-4;EO Blister-8.

HARDSTANDINGS : SE-22.

R.A.F. :	OFFICERS: 159.	S.N.C.O's.: 171.	O.R's.: 1896.	TOTAL: 2226.
W.A.A.F.:	" : 10.	" : 8.	" : 487.	" : 505.

AFFILIATED AIRFIELDS : Predannack[forward A/F, nightfighter]

PRESENT USE [1985] : RAF.

NO: 466.

AIRFIELD NAME: POULTON. OPENED : 1943.
COUNTY : Denbighshire. CLOSED : 1945.
COMMAND : Flying Training.
FORMATION : 12 Grp[Watnall] GRID REF: J 865807[43]
FUNCTION : Operational Training Unit[satellite] O.S.REF.: SJ 402595/117.
LOCALITY : 4.5miles S of Chester.
RAILWAY STN. : Rossett[GWR]

LATITUDE : 53 07 38N. HEIGHT ASL : 50′ LIGHTING : Mk2.
LONGITUDE : 02 53 45W. FLYING CONTROL : Yes. RADIO : QDM.

LANDMARKS DAY. : Eaton Hall. R Dee.

LANDMARKS NIGHT : R Dee.

OBSTRUCTIONS : Eaton Hall tower[150′ high] but not in line with any R/W.

LANDING AREA SURFACE : Concrete & wood chippings.

QDM	LENGTH X WIDTH	EXT. TO
020.	2000 x 50yds.	3600yds.
065.	1400 x 50yds.	3400yds.
140.	1400 x 50yds.	2500yds.

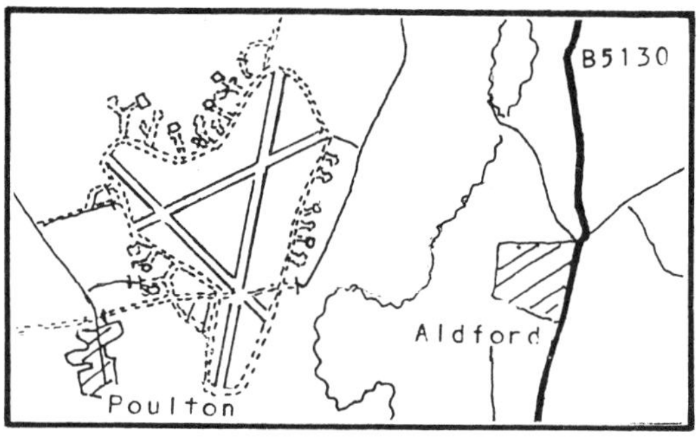

EXTENSIBILITY : Entails demolishing of 12 houses & lowering of church spire.
ACCOMMODATION : Temporary.
HANGARS : Blister-8;Bessoneau-1.

HARDSTANDINGS : Frying pan[100′]-24.

	OFFICERS	S.N.C.O′s.	O.R′s.	TOTAL
R.A.F.	79.	178.	720.	977.
W.A.A.F.	2.	8.	90.	100.

AFFILIATED AIRFIELDS : Harwarden[Parent]

PRESENT USE [1985] : Disused.

NO: 467.

AIRFIELD NAME: PREDANNACK. OPENED : 1941.
COUNTY : Cornwall. CLOSED :
COMMAND : Fighter.
FORMATION : 10 Grp[Rudloe Manor] GRID REF: X 106390[146]
FUNCTION : Forward Airfield. Night fighter. O.S.REF.: SW 468164/203.
LOCALITY : 7.5miles S of Helston.
RAILWAY STN. : Helston[GWR]

LATITUDE : 50 00 00N. HEIGHT ASL : LIGHTING : Mk2.
LONGITUDE : 05 13 45W. FLYING CONTROL : Yes. RADIO : QDM.

LANDMARKS DAY. : Tregonning Hill 635′ 10miles NNW.

LANDMARKS NIGHT : Coastline.

OBSTRUCTIONS : Mullion experimental balloon station 3miles NNE. W/T masts 3.5miles 035degreesT.

LANDING AREA SURFACE : Tarmac.

QDM	LENGTH X WIDTH	EXT. TO
012.	1360 x 50yds.	2700yds.
238.	1701 x 50yds.	2500yds.
282.	1441 x 50yds.	2300yds.
322.	1005 x 50yds.	2700yds.

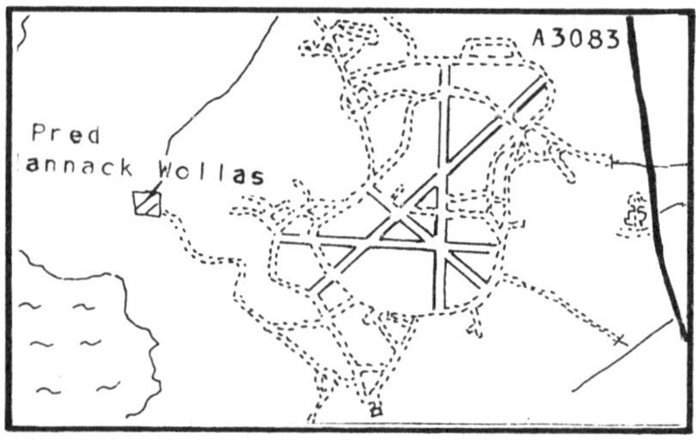

EXTENSIBILITY : Entails fairly light demolition.

ACCOMMODATION : Temporary.
HANGARS : Blisters:O-6;EO-6;Bellman-1.

HARDSTANDINGS : SE-7;TE-11.

	OFFICERS	S.N.C.O′s.	O.R′s.	TOTAL
R.A.F.	118.	213.	1577.	1908.
W.A.A.F.	3.	2.	240.	245.

AFFILIATED AIRFIELDS : Portreath[Sector]

PRESENT USE [1985] : RN.

NO: 468.

AIRFIELD NAME: PRESTWICK. OPENED : 1936.
COUNTY : Ayrshire. CLOSED :
COMMAND : Transport.
FORMATION : 44 Grp[Gloucester] GRID REF: S 855494[78Scot]
FUNCTION : Airport. O.S.REF.: NS 365268/70.
LOCALITY : 3miles NNE of Ayr.
RAILWAY STN. : Prestwick 1mile[LMS]

LATITUDE : 55 30 30N. HEIGHT ASL : 35′ LIGHTING : Mk2.
LONGITUDE : 04 35 30W. FLYING CONTROL : Yes. RADIO : QDM.

LANDMARKS DAY. : Coast W. Lady Isle 5.5miles WNW. Town & harbour of Ayr & Troon, 3.5miles SSW & 4.5miles NW respectively.

LANDMARKS NIGHT : Coast & marine lights, A/F observation lighte etc.

OBSTRUCTIONS : Church 130′ SW. Hangars 70′ NW. Terminal buildings with control tower on roof. Radio masts 50yds S.

LANDING AREA SURFACE : Concrete.

QDM	LENGTH X WIDTH	EXT. TO
315.	2200 x 50yds.	-
256.	1500 x 50yds.	-

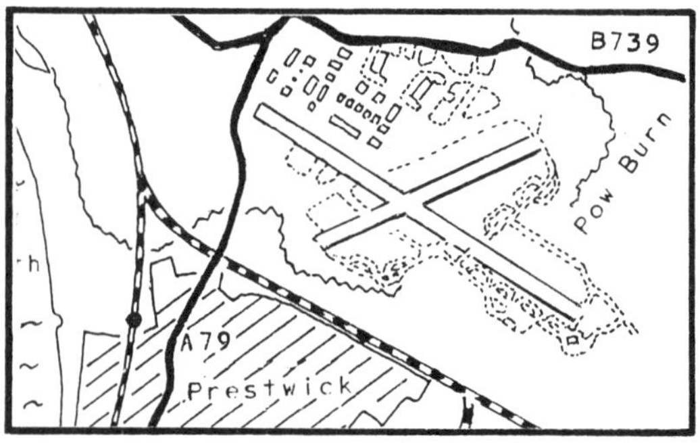

EXTENSIBILITY : 3000x1500yds. Entaild diversion of Ayr-Kilmarnock-Glasgow road & demolition.
ACCOMMODATION : Temporary.
HANGARS : Bellman-3;B1-2;freight[150x50′]-2.

HARDSTANDINGS : Loop type for 3 & 4 engined A/C. Aprons: 59200,227500 & 68444 sq.yds.

	OFFICERS	S.N.C.O′s.	O.R′s.	TOTAL
R.A.F.	83.	83.	385.	551.
W.A.A.F.	22.	8.	286.	316.

AFFILIATED AIRFIELDS : -

PRESENT USE [1985] : Civil Airport[Prestwick]

NO: 469.

AIRFIELD NAME: RACKHEATH. OPENED : 1943.
COUNTY : Norfolk. CLOSED : 1945.
COMMAND : 8th USAAF.
FORMATION : 467th Bomb Grp. GRID REF: G 749322[67]
FUNCTION : Operational. O.S.REF.: SU 270703/174.
:
LOCALITY : 5miles NE of Norwich.
RAILWAY STN. : Salhouse[LNER]

LATITUDE : 52 40 30N. HEIGHT ASL : 100' LIGHTING : Mk2.
LONGITUDE : 01 23 00E. FLYING CONTROL : Yes. RADIO : QDM.

LANDMARKS DAY. : Salhouse church. Railway station & Rackheath village hall.

LANDMARKS NIGHT : -

OBSTRUCTIONS : -

LANDING AREA SURFACE : Concrete.
:
QDM: 210. LENGTH X WIDTH: 2000 x 50yds.EXT. TO: 2350yds.
: 320. : 1400 x 50yds. : 1900yds.
: 260. : 1400 x 50yds. : -
: : :

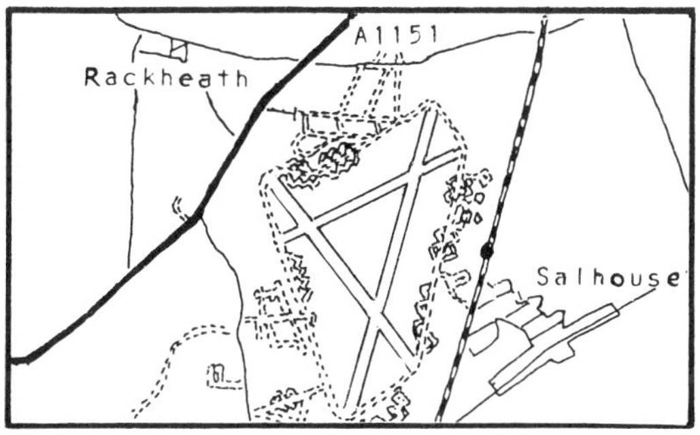

EXTENSIBILITY : -

ACCOMMODATION : Temporary.
HANGARS : T2-2.

HARDSTANDINGS : Eyeglass[concrete]-50.

USAAF. : OFFICERS: 421. Enlisted Men. : 2473.TOTAL: 2894.

AFFILIATED AIRFIELDS : -

PRESENT USE [1985] : Industry.

NO: 470.

AIRFIELD NAME: RAMSBURY. OPENED : 1942.
COUNTY : Wiltshire. CLOSED : 1946.
COMMAND : 9th USAAF.
FORMATION : 437th Troop Carrier Grp.GRID REF: U 709906[112]
FUNCTION : Operational. O.S.REF.: SU 270703/174.
:
LOCALITY : 4.5miles E of Marlborough.
RAILWAY STN. : Hungerford[GWR]

LATITUDE : 51 25 45N. HEIGHT ASL : 500' LIGHTING : Mk2.
LONGITUDE : 01 36 53W. FLYING CONTROL : Yes. RADIO : QDM.

LANDMARKS DAY. : Ramsbury town & R Kennet 1mile N.

LANDMARKS NIGHT : -

OBSTRUCTIONS : 2 water towers 57'high 350yds NE of SE end of NW-SE R/W.

LANDING AREA SURFACE : Concrete & tarmac.
:
QDM: 260. LENGTH X WIDTH: 2000 x 50yds.EXT. TO: 2800yds.
: 200. : 1100 x 50yds. : 1200yds.
: 320. : 1100 x 50yds. : 1500yds.
: : :

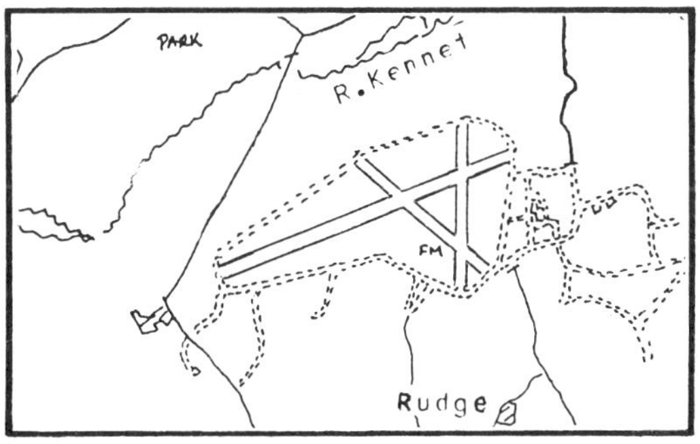

EXTENSIBILITY : Entails demolition of a farm.

ACCOMMODATION : Temporary.
HANGARS : T2-2.

HARDSTANDINGS : Concrete-50;steel planking-2.

USAAF. : OFFICERS: 470. Enlisted Men. : 1898.TOTAL: 2368.

AFFILIATED AIRFIELDS : -

PRESENT USE [1985] : Agriculture.

NO: 471.

AIRFIELD NAME: RATTLESDEN. OPENED : 1942.
COUNTY : Suffolk. CLOSED : 1945.
COMMAND : 8th USAAF.
FORMATION : 447th Bomb Grp. GRID REF: M 415745[86]
FUNCTION : Operational. O.S.REF.: TL 961560/155.
:
LOCALITY : 9miles SE of Bury St. Edmunds.
RAILWAY STN. : Stowmarket 6miles[LNER]

LATITUDE : 52 10 00N. HEIGHT ASL : 300' LIGHTING : Mk2.
LONGITUDE : 00 52 15E. FLYING CONTROL : Yes. RADIO : QDM.

LANDMARKS DAY. : Electricity grid. Windmills-2.

LANDMARKS NIGHT : -

OBSTRUCTIONS : -

LANDING AREA SURFACE : Concrete & tarmac.
:
QDM: 243. LENGTH X WIDTH: 2000 x 50yds.EXT. TO: 3000yds.
: 177. : 1400 x 50yds. : 2300yds.
: 310. : 1400 x 50yds. : 3000yds.
: : :

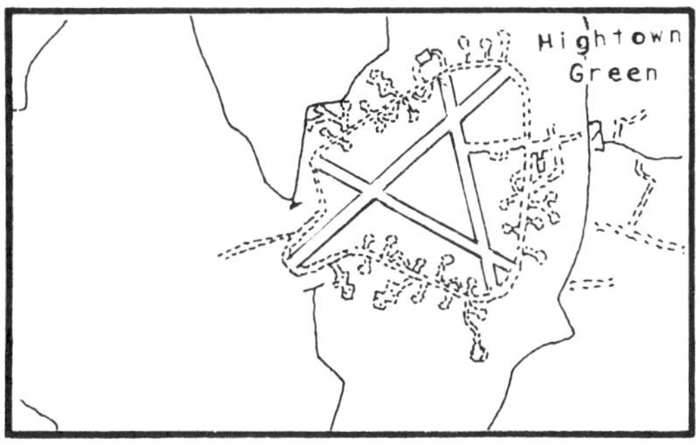

EXTENSIBILITY : -

ACCOMMODATION : Temporary.
HANGARS : T2-2.

HARDSTANDINGS : Loop-50.

USAAF. : OFFICERS: 421. Enlisted Men. : 2473.TOTAL: 2894.

AFFILIATED AIRFIELDS : -

PRESENT USE [1985] : Disused.

NO: 472.

AIRFIELD NAME: RAYDON. OPENED : 1943.
COUNTY : Suffolk. CLOSED : 1958.
COMMAND : 8th USAAF.
FORMATION : 353rd Fighter Grp. GRID REF: M 509577[86]
FUNCTION : Operational. O.S.REF.: TM 060390/155.
:
LOCALITY : 3miles SE of Hadleigh.
RAILWAY STN. : Raydon Wood[LNER]

LATITUDE : 52 00 45N. HEIGHT ASL : 170′ LIGHTING : Mk2.
LONGITUDE : 01 00 15E. FLYING CONTROL : Yes. RADIO : QDM.

LANDMARKS DAY. : A/F lies between R Orwell & R Stour.

LANDMARKS NIGHT : -

OBSTRUCTIONS : -

LANDING AREA SURFACE : Concrete.
:
QDM: 270. LENGTH X WIDTH: 2000 x 50yds.EXT. TO: -
: 170. : 1400 x 50yds. : 2600yds.
: 230. : 1400 x 50yds. : 2500yds.
: : :

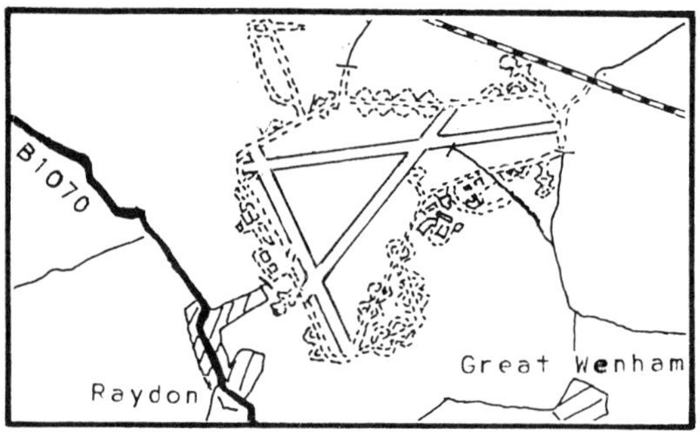

EXTENSIBILITY : Main R/W can be widened to 400yds; others to 250yds.
ACCOMMODATION : Temporary.
HANGARS : T2-2.

HARDSTANDINGS : Loop-50.

USAAF. : OFFICERS: 364. Enlisted Men. : 2478.TOTAL: 2842.

AFFILIATED AIRFIELDS : -

PRESENT USE [1985] : Disused.

NO: 473.

AIRFIELD NAME: REDHILL. OPENED : 1937.
COUNTY : Surrey. CLOSED : 1954.
COMMAND : Fighter.
FORMATION : 11 Grp[Uxbridge] GRID REF: Q 743668[125]
FUNCTION : Operational. O.S.REF.: TQ 298476/187.
:
LOCALITY : 2miles SE of Redhill.
RAILWAY STN. : Nutfield 1.25miles[SR]

LATITUDE : 51 12 53N. HEIGHT ASL : 205′ LIGHTING : Mk2.
LONGITUDE : 00 08 15W. FLYING CONTROL : Yes. RADIO : QDM.

LANDMARKS DAY. : The Priory, a large storehouse N. Canadian road running E-W N of A/F 1.125miles long. Railway running E to W, N of A/F.

LANDMARKS NIGHT : -

OBSTRUCTIONS : -

LANDING AREA SURFACE : Steel Matting[Army track]
:
QDM: 087. LENGTH X WIDTH: 1567yds. EXT. TO: 2100yds.
: 019. : 1057yds. : 1200yds.
: : :
: : :

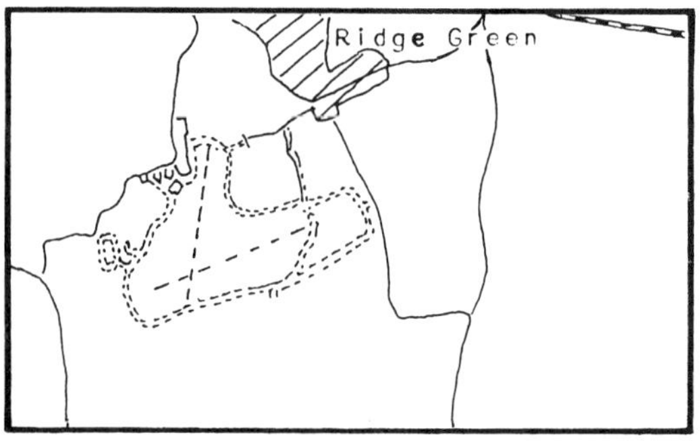

EXTENSIBILITY : On slightly different alignment[or 1600yds with very heavy fill]
ACCOMMODATION : Temporary[except for civil airport buildings]
HANGARS : Blister-8;Civil-1.

HARDSTANDINGS : Blenheim TE-12;Frying pan-12.

R.A.F. : OFFICERS: 30.S.N.C.O′s.: - O.R′s.: 333.TOTAL: 363.
W.A.A.F.: " : - " : - " : - " : -

AFFILIATED AIRFIELDS : Biggin Hill[Sector]

PRESENT USE [1985] : Helicopters.

NO: 474.

AIRFIELD NAME: REDNAL. OPENED : 1942.
COUNTY : Shropshire. CLOSED : 1945.
COMMAND : Fighter.
FORMATION : 12 Grp[Watnall] GRID REF: J 830489[51]
FUNCTION : Operational Training O.S.REF.: SJ 373275/126.
: Unit.
LOCALITY : 12miles NW of Shrewsbury.
RAILWAY STN. : Rednal & West Felton1.25miles[GWR]

LATITUDE : 52 50 30N. HEIGHT ASL : 300′ LIGHTING : None.
LONGITUDE : 02 56 00W. FLYING CONTROL : Yes. RADIO : QDM.

LANDMARKS DAY. : Ellesmere Lakes 5miles NNE; railway; disused canals.

LANDMARKS NIGHT : As day.

OBSTRUCTIONS : Hill at end of No.1 R/W 70′high.

LANDING AREA SURFACE : Tarmac.
:
QDM: 280. LENGTH X WIDTH: 1600 x 50yds.EXT. TO: -
: 130. : 1100 x 50yds. : 2000yds.
: 160. : 1100 x 50yds. : 1400yds.
: : :

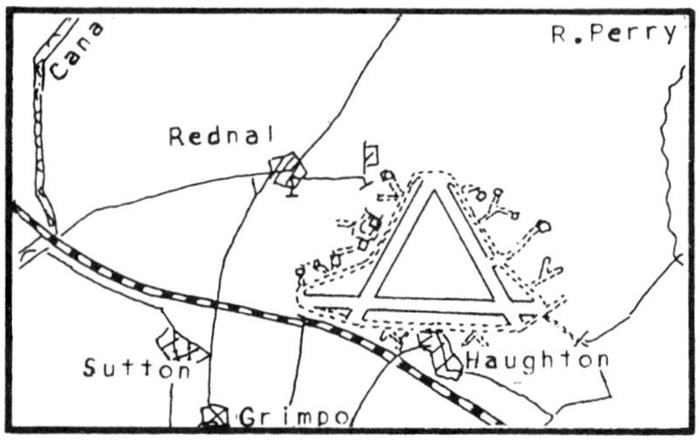

EXTENSIBILITY : Entails slight demolition.

ACCOMMODATION : Temporary.
HANGARS : Bellman-3;Blister-8.

HARDSTANDINGS : 50.

R.A.F. : OFFICERS: 98.S.N.C.O′s.: 130.O.R′s.: 1126.TOTAL: 1354.
W.A.A.F.: " : 22. " : 20. " : 252. " : 294.

AFFILIATED AIRFIELDS : Montford Bridge[Satellite]

PRESENT USE [1985] : Disused.

AIRFIELD NAME: RHOOSE. OPENED : 1942.
COUNTY : Glamorganshire. CLOSED :
COMMAND : Maintenance.
FORMATION : 57 Wing[Milton] GRID REF: T 505888[109]
FUNCTION : Storage Unit. O.S.REF.: ST 064675/170.
:
LOCALITY : 3miles W of Barry.
RAILWAY STN. : Rhoose .5mile[GWR]

LATITUDE : 51 23 45N. HEIGHT ASL : 200' LIGHTING : None.
LONGITUDE : 03 20 45W. FLYING CONTROL : None. RADIO : QDM.

LANDMARKS DAY. : Barry docks. Rhoose cement works.

LANDMARKS NIGHT : Barry docks.

OBSTRUCTIONS : -

LANDING AREA SURFACE : Tarmac.

QDM	LENGTH X WIDTH	EXT. TO
216.	1475 x 50yds.	-
126.	1066 x 50yds.	1500yds.

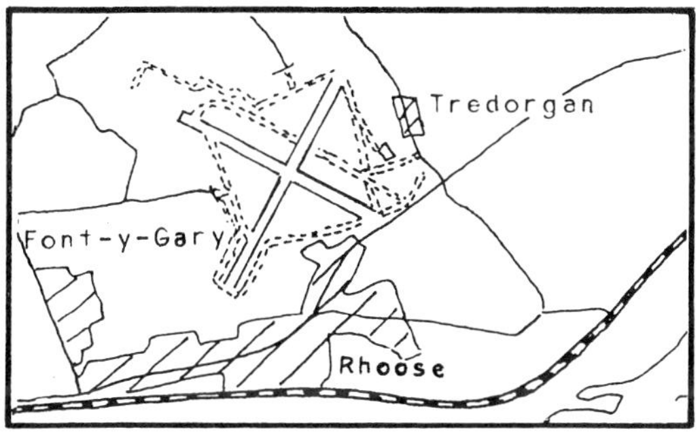

EXTENSIBILITY : Only one R/W is capable of extension on account of new road.
ACCOMMODATION : Temporary.
HANGARS : EO Blisters-4.

HARDSTANDINGS : Circular[40']-25.

	OFFICERS	S.N.C.O's.	O.R's.	TOTAL
R.A.F.	24.	64.	450.	538.
W.A.A.F.	2.	5.	105.	112.

AFFILIATED AIRFIELDS : -

PRESENT USE [1985] : Civil Airport[Cardiff]

NO: 476.

AIRFIELD NAME: RICCALL. OPENED : 1942.
COUNTY : Yorkshire. CLOSED : 1946.
COMMAND : Bomber.
FORMATION : 7 Grp[St.Vincents] GRID REF: A 108563[32]
FUNCTION : Operational. O.S.REF.: SE 636365/105.
:
LOCALITY : 10miles S of York.
RAILWAY STN. : Riccall[LNER]

LATITUDE : 53 49 08N. HEIGHT ASL : 35' LIGHTING : Mk2.
LONGITUDE : 01 01 45W. FLYING CONTROL : Yes. RADIO : QDM.

LANDMARKS DAY. : Selby oil mills.

LANDMARKS NIGHT : -

OBSTRUCTIONS : -

LANDING AREA SURFACE : Concrete & asphalt.

QDM	LENGTH X WIDTH	EXT. TO
172.	1400 x 50yds.	2400yds.
232.	2000 x 50yds.	3000yds.
292.	1400 x 50-yds.	2000yds.

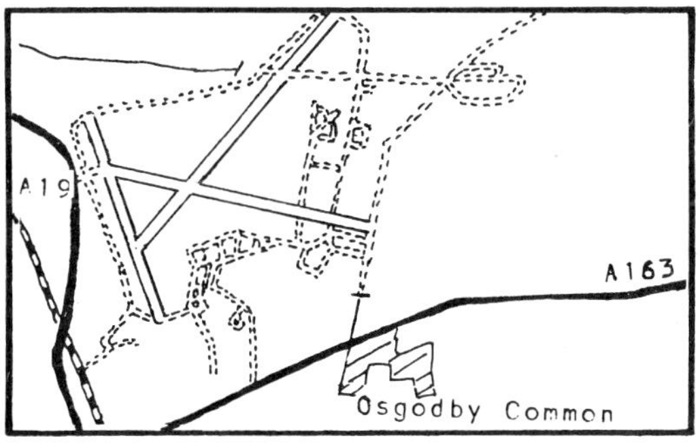

EXTENSIBILITY : -

ACCOMMODATION : Temporary.
HANGARS : T2-6;B1-1.

HARDSTANDINGS : Heavy bomber-36.

	OFFICERS	S.N.C.O's.	O.R's.	TOTAL
R.A.F.	165.	520.	761.	1446.
W.A.A.F.	6.	11.	324.	341.

AFFILIATED AIRFIELDS : Marston Moor[74 Base]

PRESENT USE [1985] : Agriculture.

NO: 477.

AIRFIELD NAME: RIDGEWELL. OPENED : 1942.
COUNTY : Essex. CLOSED : 1957.
COMMAND : 8th USAAF.
FORMATION : 381st Bomb Grp. GRID REF: M 209601[86]
FUNCTION : Operational. O.S.REF.: TL 756416/155.
:
LOCALITY : 7.5miles NNW of Halstead.
RAILWAY STN. : Yeldham 1.5miles[LNER]

LATITUDE : 52 02 38N. HEIGHT ASL : 260' LIGHTING : Mk2.
LONGITUDE : 00 33 30E. FLYING CONTROL : Yes. RADIO : QDM

LANDMARKS DAY. : -

LANDMARKS NIGHT : -

OBSTRUCTIONS : -

LANDING AREA SURFACE : Concrete & wood chippings.

QDM	LENGTH X WIDTH	EXT. TO
100.	2000 x 50yds.	3800yds.
060.	1400 x 50yds.	1600yds.
170.	1400 x 50yds.	1500yds.

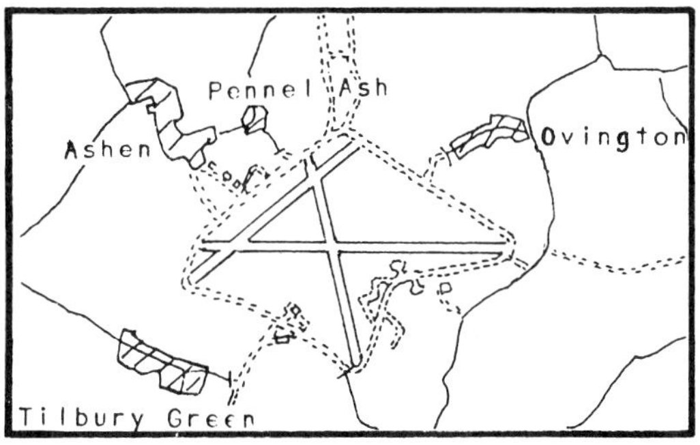

EXTENSIBILITY : Entails demolition of one farm & two cottages.

ACCOMMODATION : Temporary.
HANGARS : T2-2.

HARDSTANDINGS : Loop-50.

USAAF. : OFFICERS: 421. Enlisted Men. : 2473. TOTAL: 2894.

AFFILIATED AIRFIELDS : -

PRESENT USE [1985] : Agriculture.

NO: 478.

AIRFIELD NAME: RINGWAY. OPENED : 1938.
COUNTY : Cheshire. CLOSED :
COMMAND : Fighter.
FORMATION : 38 Grp[Marks Hall] GRID REF: E 284050[44]
FUNCTION : Parachute Training O.S.REF.: SJ 816843/109.
: School[parent]
LOCALITY : 3.5miles SE of Altrincham.
RAILWAY STN. : Heald Green 2miles[LMS]

LATITUDE : 53 21 15N. HEIGHT ASL : 235′ LIGHTING : Mk2.
LONGITUDE : 02 16 30W. FLYING CONTROL : Yes. RADIO : QDM.

LANDMARKS DAY. : Mainline railway 1.5miles E.

LANDMARKS NIGHT : -

OBSTRUCTIONS : Radio mast on control tower 80′.
Chimney 105′

LANDING AREA : Concrete & tarmac.
SURFACE :

QDM	LENGTH X WIDTH	EXT. TO
240.	1400 x 50yds.	2200yds.
200.	1100 x 50yds.	1400yds.
280.	1000 x 50yds.	2500yds.

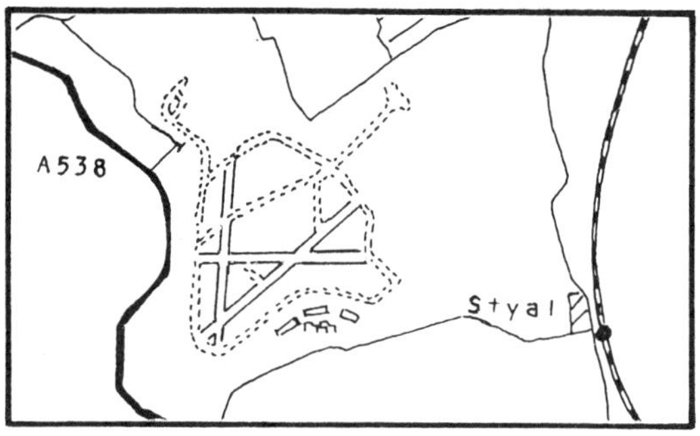

EXTENSIBILITY : Entails diversion of 2nd.class road & considerable demolition.
ACCOMMODATION : Temporary[except for civil airport buildings.
HANGARS : Bellman-4;A1-1;VR-1;AAF-1.

HARDSTANDINGS : Frying pan[50′]-20′

	OFFICERS	S.N.C.O's.	O.R's.	TOTAL
R.A.F.	40.	36.	1845.	1921.
W.A.A.F.	-	-	-	-

AFFILIATED AIRFIELDS : Tatton Park[RLG]

PRESENT USE [1985] : Civil Airport[Manchester]

NO: 479.

AIRFIELD NAME: RIVENHALL. OPENED : 1943.
COUNTY : Essex. CLOSED : 1945.
COMMAND : Fighter.
FORMATION : 38 Grp[Marks Hall] GRID REF: M 270390[97]
FUNCTION : Operational. O.S.REF.: TL 820206/168.
:
LOCALITY : 1.75miles N of Witham.
RAILWAY STN. : Kelvedon 2.25miles[LNER]

LATITUDE : 51 51 15N. HEIGHT ASL : 168′ LIGHTING : Mk2.
LONGITUDE : 00 38 30E. FLYING CONTROL : Yes. RADIO : QDM.

LANDMARKS DAY. : Large pond to W side of A/F.

LANDMARKS NIGHT : -

OBSTRUCTIONS : -

LANDING AREA : Concrete & tarmac.
SURFACE :

QDM	LENGTH X WIDTH	EXT. TO
280.	2000 x 50yds.	3000yds.
220.	1400 x 50yds.	2500yds.
340.	1400 x 50yds.	1800yds.

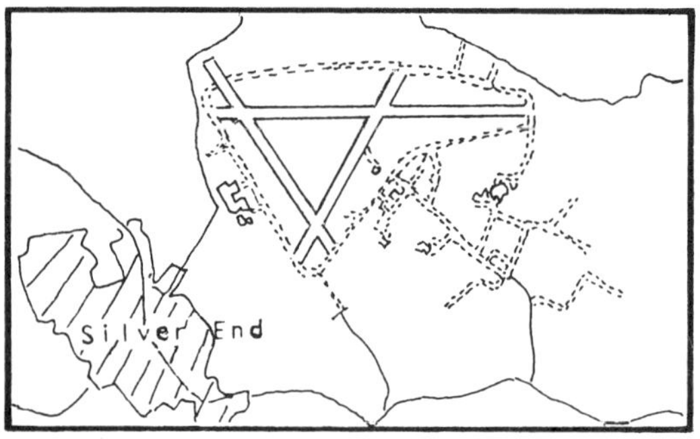

EXTENSIBILITY : -

ACCOMMODATION : Temporary.
HANGARS : T2-2;Blister-1.

HARDSTANDINGS : Spectacle-50.

	OFFICERS	S.N.C.O's.	O.R's.	TOTAL
R.A.F.	421.		2473.	2894.
W.A.A.F.	"	"	"	"

AFFILIATED AIRFIELDS : -

PRESENT USE [1985] : Industry.

NO: 480.

AIRFIELD NAME: ROBOROUGH. OPENED : 1931.
COUNTY : Devon. CLOSED :
COMMAND : Coastal.
FORMATION : 19 Grp[Plymouth] GRID REF: X 930825[144]
FUNCTION : Satellite. O.S.REF.: SX 503605/201.
:
LOCALITY : 4miles NNE of Plymouth.
RAILWAY STN. : Plymouth North Road[GWR]

LATITUDE : 50 26 00N. HEIGHT ASL : 488′ LIGHTING : None.
LONGITUDE : 04 07 00W. FLYING CONTROL : None. RADIO : QDM.

LANDMARKS DAY. : Kit Hill chimney 318degreesT, 12miles. City of Plymouth 180degreesT 4miles. White clay mounds 82degreesT 8miles.

LANDMARKS NIGHT : Plymouth Sound 180degreesT 5miles.

OBSTRUCTIONS : Woods at S & SW boundaries of A/F.

LANDING AREA : Grass.
SURFACE :

QDM	LENGTH X WIDTH	EXT. TO
NW-SE.	800 X 100yds.	-
NE-SW.	900 X 100yds.	-
E-W.	600 x 100yds.	

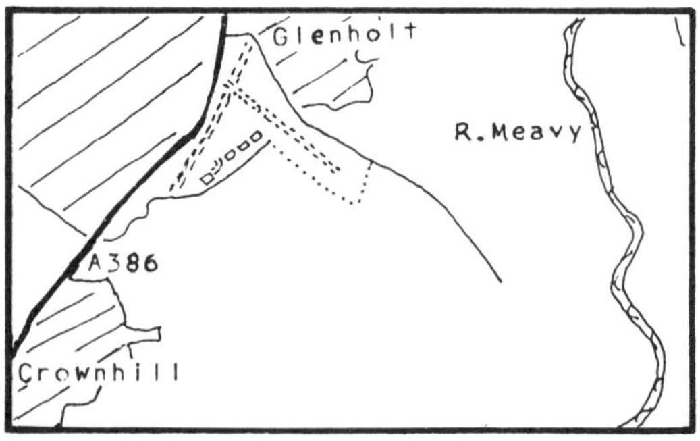

EXTENSIBILITY : None possible.

ACCOMMODATION : Temporary.
HANGARS : Blister-1;
Civil flying club[4 x S/E aircraft in each.
HARDSTANDINGS : Concrete with brick walls[3bays] holds one S/E aircraft in each bay.

	OFFICERS	S.N.C.O's.	O.R's.	TOTAL
R.A.F.	-	16.	320.	336.
W.A.A.F.	-	16.	50.	66.

AFFILIATED AIRFIELDS : Mount Batten[Parent]

PRESENT USE [1985] : Civil Airport[Plymouth]

NO: 481.

AIRFIELD NAME: RONALDSWAY.
COUNTY : Isle of Man.
COMMAND : RN.
FORMATION : HMS Urley.
FUNCTION : Torpedo working up
: station.
LOCALITY : 7miles SW of Douglas.
RAILWAY STN. : -

OPENED : 1929.
CLOSED :

GRID REF: C 758912[17]
O.S.REF.: SC 285685/95.

LATITUDE : 54 05 10N. HEIGHT ASL : 32' LIGHTING : Naval.
LONGITUDE : 04 37 50W. FLYING CONTROL : Yes. RADIO : QDM.

LANDMARKS DAY. : Calf of Man 6miles WSW. Town & harbour of Douglas.

LANDMARKS NIGHT : Coastline.

OBSTRUCTIONS : Rising ground N&W 1585' 4miles. King William College Tower 115' 300yds. W of SW end of R/W 04-22.

LANDING AREA SURFACE : Tarmac.

QDM	LENGTH X WIDTH	EXT. TO
360-180.	1000 x 30yds.	-
041-221.	1000 x 30yds.	-
090-270.	1400 x 30yds.	-
129-309.	1000 x 30yds.	-

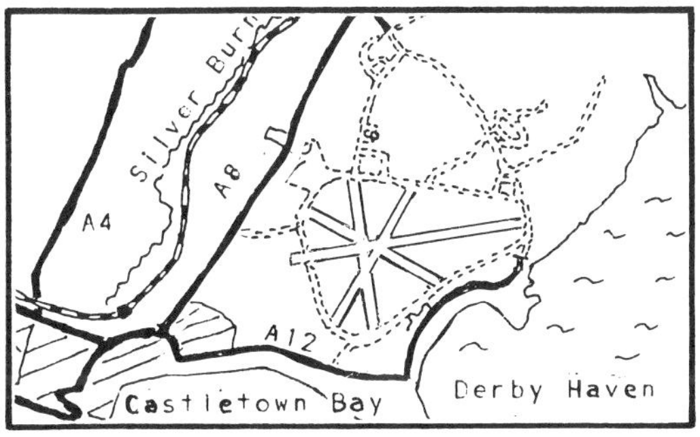

EXTENSIBILITY : -

ACCOMMODATION : Temporary.
HANGARS : Sqdn:185x105'-5;60x70'-2;200x70'-1;
Storage: 185x105'-2.
HARDSTANDINGS : 3 large aprons-450'

R.N. : OFFICERS: 267. Chiefs/POs/Ratings.: 1377.TOTAL: 1644.
W.R.N.S.: " : 17. " : - " : 463. " : 480.

AFFILIATED AIRFIELDS : -

PRESENT USE [1985] : Civil Airport[Isle of Man]

NO: 482.

AIRFIELD NAME: RUFFORTH.
COUNTY : Yorkshire.
COMMAND : Bomber.
FORMATION : 7 Grp[St.Vincents]
FUNCTION : Operational.
:
LOCALITY : 3.5miles W of York.
RAILWAY STN. : York[LNER]

OPENED : 1942.
CLOSED : 1954.

GRID REF: A 009705[27]
O.S.REF.: SE 535505/105.

LATITUDE : 53 56 45N. HEIGHT ASL : 64' LIGHTING : Mk2.
LONGITUDE : 01 11 00W. FLYING CONTROL : Yes. RADIO : QDM.

LANDMARKS DAY. : York Minster 4miles E.

LANDMARKS NIGHT : -

OBSTRUCTIONS : -

LANDING AREA SURFACE : Tarmac.

QDM	LENGTH X WIDTH	EXT. TO
181.	1400 x 50yds.	3000yds.
240.	2000 x 50yds.	4000yds.
294.	1350 x 50yds.	3000yds.

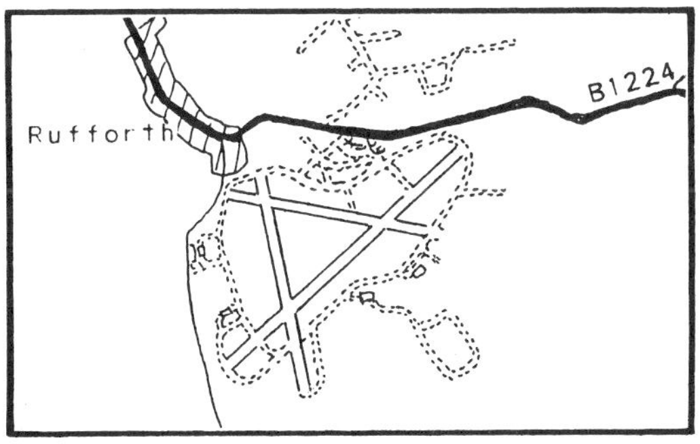

EXTENSIBILITY : Entails diversion of a road.

ACCOMMODATION : Temporary.
HANGARS : T2-2;B1-1.

HARDSTANDINGS : Heavy bomber-36.

R.A.F. : OFFICERS: 124.S.N.C.O's.: 568.O.R's.: 839.TOTAL: 1531.
W.A.A.F.: " : 2. " : 10. " : 239. " : 251.

AFFILIATED AIRFIELDS : Marston Moor[74 Base]

PRESENT USE [1985] : Agriculture.

NO: 483.

AIRFIELD NAME: SALTBY.
COUNTY : Leicestershire.
COMMAND : 9th USAAF.
FORMATION : 314th Troop Carrier Grp.
FUNCTION : Operational.
:
LOCALITY : 8miles NE of Melton Mowbray.
RAILWAY STN. : Great Ponton 5miles[LNER]

OPENED : 1943.
CLOSED : 1955.

GRID REF: F 330458[55]
O.S.REF.: SK 868265/130.

LATITUDE : 52 49 45N. HEIGHT ASL : 475' LIGHTING : Mk2.
LONGITUDE : 00 42 30W. FLYING CONTROL : Yes. RADIO : QDM.

LANDMARKS DAY. : Kimpton reservoir,Saltby 300degrees 3miles.

LANDMARKS NIGHT : -

OBSTRUCTIONS : House on NE side of A/F.

LANDING AREA SURFACE : Tarmac.

QDM	LENGTH X WIDTH	EXT. TO
196.	1400 x 50yds.	2000yds.
255.	2000 x 50yds.	-
314.	1400 x 50yds.	2100yds.

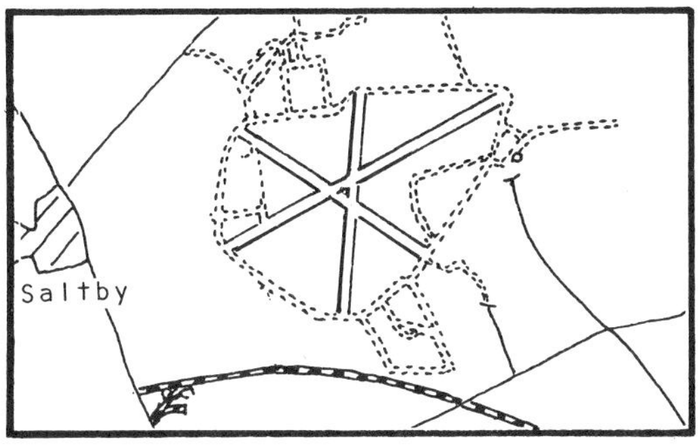

EXTENSIBILITY : -

ACCOMMODATION : Temporary.
HANGARS : T2-4;B1-1.

HARDSTANDINGS : Heavy bomber-50.

USAAF. : OFFICERS: 397. Enlisted Men. : 2378.TOTAL: 2775.

AFFILIATED AIRFIELDS : -

PRESENT USE [1985] : Agriculture.

NO: 484.

AIRFIELD NAME: SANDTOFT. OPENED : 1943.
COUNTY : Lincolnshire. CLOSED : 1955.
COMMAND : Bomber.
FORMATION : 7 Grp[St.Vincents] GRID REF: A 223278[38]
FUNCTION : Operational. O.S.REF.: SK 750075/112.

LOCALITY : 11.75miles NE of Doncaster.
RAILWAY STN. : Crowle Central 4miles[LNER]

LATITUDE : 52 49 45N. HEIGHT ASL : 8′ LIGHTING : Mk2.
LONGITUDE : 00 42 30W. FLYING CONTROL : Yes. RADIO : QDM.

LANDMARKS DAY. : Crowle chimneys 043degrees from A/F, 400yds 120′high;Haxey water tower 179degrees from A/F 5miles.

LANDMARKS NIGHT : Crowle chimneys[lighted with obstruction lights]

OBSTRUCTIONS : Crowle chimneys.

LANDING AREA SURFACE : Concrete[tarmac at each end for touchdown]

QDM	LENGTH X WIDTH	EXT. TO
240.	2000 x 50yds.	3500yds.
120.	1400 x 50yds.	1700yds.
170.	1400 x 50yds.	2000yds.

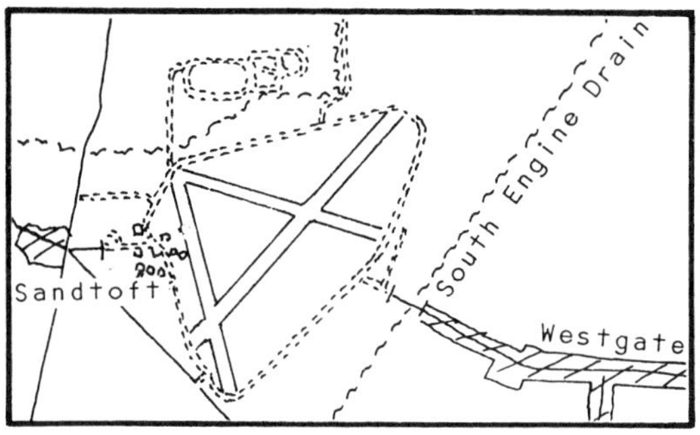

EXTENSIBILITY : Entails diversion of a road.

ACCOMMODATION : Temporary.
HANGARS : T2-2;B1-1.

HARDSTANDINGS : Spectacle-36.

	OFFICERS	S.N.C.O′s.	O.R′s.	TOTAL
R.A.F.	249.	160.	1512.	1921.
W.A.A.F.	10.	16.	336.	362.

AFFILIATED AIRFIELDS : Lindholme[71 Base]

PRESENT USE [1985] : Private flying.

NO: 485.

AIRFIELD NAME: SAWBRIDGEWORTH. OPENED : 1943.
COUNTY : Hertfordshire. CLOSED :
COMMAND : Maintenance.
FORMATION : Miscellaneous A/F. GRID REF: L 906365[96]
FUNCTION : Storage Unit. O.S.REF.: TL 464178/167.

LOCALITY : 3miles SW of Bishops Stortford.
RAILWAY STN. : Sawbridgeworth[LNER]

LATITUDE : 51 50 08N. HEIGHT ASL : 320′ LIGHTING : Mk2.
LONGITUDE : 00 07 15E. FLYING CONTROL : Yes. RADIO : QDM.

LANDMARKS DAY. : Mathams Wood N. Thorley church.

LANDMARKS NIGHT : -

OBSTRUCTIONS : -

LANDING AREA SURFACE : Steel Matting[Sommerfeld track]

QDM	LENGTH X WIDTH	EXT. TO
306.	1700yds.	-
244.	1400yds.	1700yds.
188.	1350yds.	1900yds.

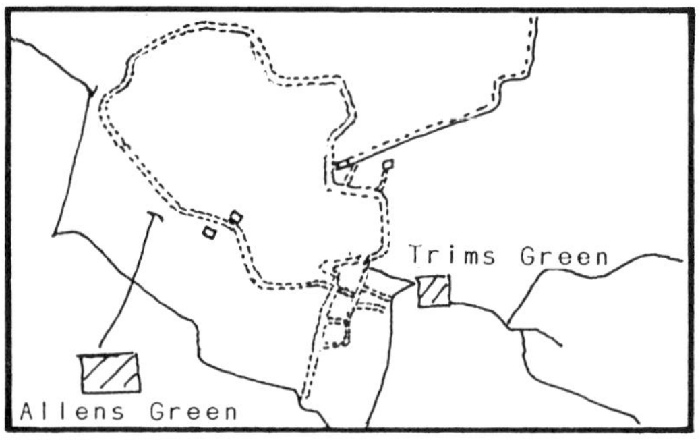

EXTENSIBILITY : Entails closure of a road & demolition of 3 houses & a cottage[if No.3 R/W extended]
ACCOMMODATION : Temporary.
HANGARS : T2-1;Blister-11.

HARDSTANDINGS : Blenheim-13;frying pan[50′]-15.

	OFFICERS	S.N.C.O′s.	O.R′s.	TOTAL
R.A.F.	69.	87.	840.	996.
W.A.A.F.	4.	10.	120.	134.

AFFILIATED AIRFIELDS : -

PRESENT USE [1985] : Unspecified.

NO: 486.

AIRFIELD NAME: SCAMPTON. OPENED : 1916.
COUNTY : Lincolnshire. CLOSED :
COMMAND : Bomber.
FORMATION : 1 Grp[Bawtry] GRID REF: F 430990[47]
FUNCTION : Operational[15 Base] O.S.REF.: SK 965798/121.

LOCALITY : 5.5miles N of Lincoln.
RAILWAY STN. : Lincoln[LNER & LMS]

LATITUDE : 53 18 15N. HEIGHT ASL : 195′ LIGHTING : Mk1.
LONGITUDE : 00 33 00W. FLYING CONTROL : Yes. RADIO : QDM.

LANDMARKS DAY. : Lincoln cathedral 5miles S of A/F.

LANDMARKS NIGHT : -

OBSTRUCTIONS : SE side of A/F, buildings. E side telephone wires 20′ high along road.

LANDING AREA SURFACE : Concrete & tarmac.

QDM	LENGTH X WIDTH	EXT. TO
230.	2000 x 50yds.	3200yds.
190.	1400 x 50yds.	2500yds.
290.	1400 x 50yds.	2600yds.

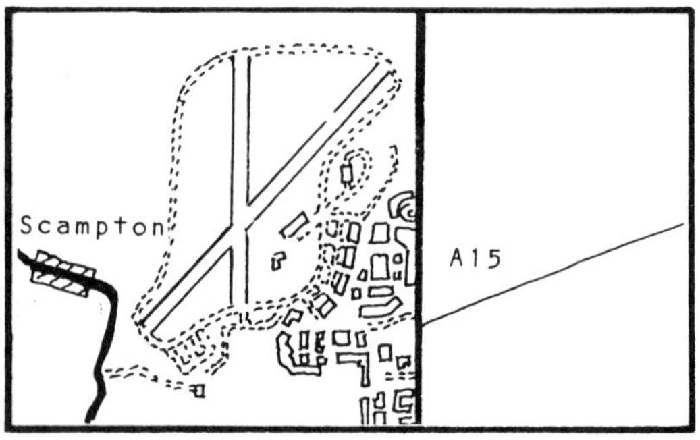

EXTENSIBILITY : Entails diversion of Lincoln-Brigg road.

ACCOMMODATION : Permanent.
HANGARS : Type C2-4;T1-1.

HARDSTANDINGS : Heavy bomber-36.

	OFFICERS	S.N.C.O′s.	O.R′s.	TOTAL
R.A.F.	198.	1044	1084.	2326.
W.A.A.F.	17.	14.	237.	268.

AFFILIATED AIRFIELDS : Dunholme Lodge & Fiskerton[Sub-stations]

PRESENT USE [1985] : RAF.

NO: 487.

AIRFIELD NAME: SCATSTA. OPENED : 1940.
COUNTY : Shetlands. CLOSED : 1946.
COMMAND : Coastal.
FORMATION : 18 Grp[Pitreavie Castle] GRID REF: U 945932[2Scot]
FUNCTION : Satellite. O.S.REF.: HU 388725/3.
:
LOCALITY : 20miles N of Lerwick.
RAILWAY STN. : Aberdeen[LMS & LNER]

LATITUDE : 60 26 00N. HEIGHT ASL : 20′ LIGHTING : None.
LONGITUDE : 01 17 45W. FLYING CONTROL : None. RADIO : QDM.

LANDMARKS DAY. : RAF Sullom Voe, moorings,pier,hangars, & road alongside runways.

LANDMARKS NIGHT : Shape of Garth Voe of Scatsta. Separated by peninsular of Sella Ness.

OBSTRUCTIONS : Hill of Graven 400′ 2000yds. due SE of longer R/W.
Frawhoull 190′ 500yds. W of SW end of shorter R/W.
Verges on either side R/Ws are dangerous.

LANDING AREA SURFACE : Tarmac.
:
QDM: 130. LENGTH X WIDTH: 1400 x 50yds. EXT. TO: -
: 250. : 1510 x 50yds. : -
: : :

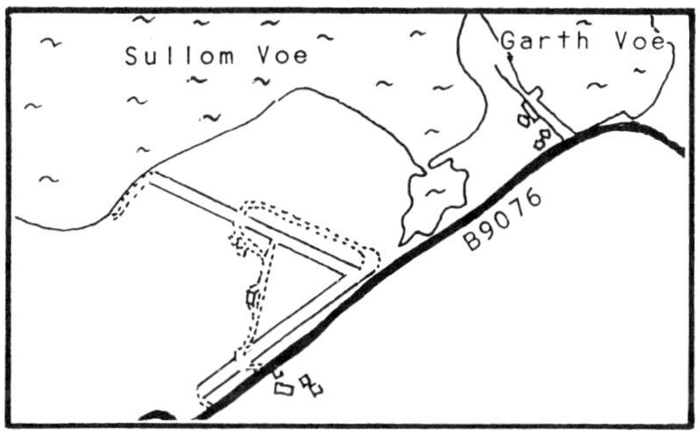

EXTENSIBILITY : None possible.

ACCOMMODATION : Temporary.
HANGARS : T1[10 bay]-1.

HARDSTANDINGS : Floor & aprons for hangars;T1-1;T2-1.

	OFFICERS	S.N.C.O′s.	O.R′s.	TOTAL
R.A.F.	4.	25.	333.	362.
W.A.A.F.	–	–	–	–

AFFILIATED AIRFIELDS : Sullom Voe flyingboat base[Parent]

PRESENT USE [1985] : Private flying.

NO: 488.

AIRFIELD NAME: SCORTON. OPENED : 1939.
COUNTY : Yorkshire. CLOSED : 1945.
COMMAND : Balloon.
FORMATION : GRID REF: Z 717207[14]
FUNCTION : Storage. O.S.REF.: NZ 240003/88.
:
LOCALITY : 9miles SSW of Darlington.
RAILWAY STN. : Scorton 1mile[LNER]

LATITUDE : 54 23 45N. HEIGHT ASL : 200′ LIGHTING : Mk2.
LONGITUDE : 01 37 45W. FLYING CONTROL : Yes. RADIO : QDM.

LANDMARKS DAY. : R Swale S of A/F. Railway N side running NE-SW.

LANDMARKS NIGHT : -

OBSTRUCTIONS : -

LANDING AREA SURFACE : Tarmac.
:
QDM: 220. LENGTH X WIDTH: 1200 x 50yds. EXT. TO: 1230yds.
: 351. : 1200 x 50yds. : 1230yds.
: 258. : 1600 x 50yds. : 2000yds.
: : :

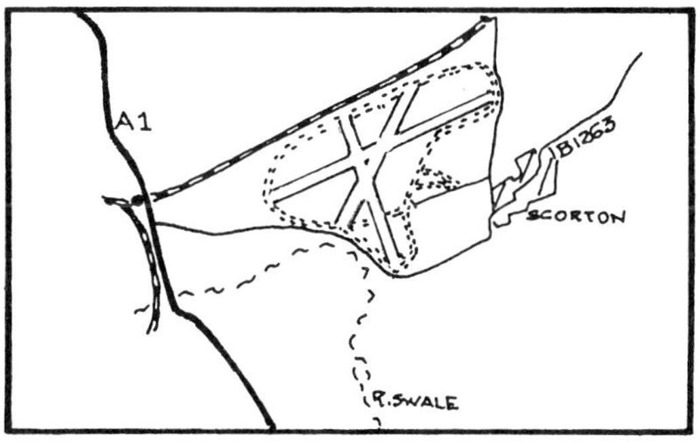

EXTENSIBILITY : Entails slight demolition.

ACCOMMODATION : Temporary.
HANGARS : Blisters:O-4;EO-8.

HARDSTANDINGS : SE-4;TE-6.

	OFFICERS	S.N.C.O′s.	O.R′s.	TOTAL
R.A.F.	110.	100.	980.	1190.
W.A.A.F.	–	1.	157.	158.

AFFILIATED AIRFIELDS : -

PRESENT USE [1985] : Agriculture.

NO: 489.

AIRFIELD NAME: SCULTHORPE. OPENED : 1943.
COUNTY : Norfolk. CLOSED :
COMMAND : Bomber.
FORMATION : Under re-construction. GRID REF: G 320498[57]
FUNCTION : Under re-construction. O.S.REF.: TF 862313/132.
:
LOCALITY : 4miles WNW of Fakenham.
RAILWAY STN. : Fakenham 5miles[M & GN]

LATITUDE : 52 50 45N. HEIGHT ASL : 200′ LIGHTING : Mk2.
LONGITUDE : 00 45 45W. FLYING CONTROL : Yes. RADIO : QDM.

LANDMARKS DAY. : Water tank 50′ high NW of watch tower.

LANDMARKS NIGHT : -

OBSTRUCTIONS : -

LANDING AREA : Under re-construction.
SURFACE : Concrete[estimated date of completion 8/45]
QDM: 182. LENGTH X WIDTH: 2000 x 100yds EXT. TO: -
: 243. : 3000 x 100yds. : -
: 131. : 2000 x 100yds. : -
: : :

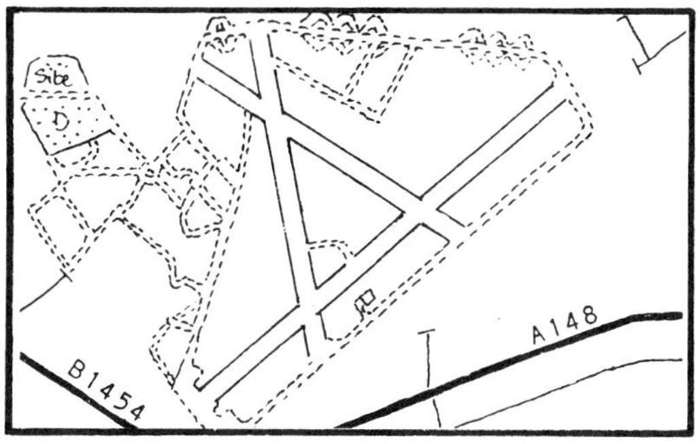

EXTENSIBILITY : None possible after re-construction.

ACCOMMODATION : Temporary.
HANGARS : T2-4;B1-1.

HARDSTANDINGS : Very heavy bomber-12.

	OFFICERS	S.N.C.O′s.	O.R′s.	TOTAL
R.A.F.	139.	434.	1200.	1773.
W.A.A.F.	9.	22.	378.	409.

AFFILIATED AIRFIELDS : -

PRESENT USE [1985] : USAFE.

NO: 490.

AIRFIELD NAME: SEALAND. OPENED : 1917.
COUNTY : Flintshire. CLOSED :
COMMAND : Maintenance.
FORMATION : 43 Grp[Oxford] GRID REF: J 797920[43]
FUNCTION : Parent station. O.S.REF.: SJ 331709/117.
:
LOCALITY : 5miles NW of Chester.
RAILWAY STN. : Sealand via Chester[LNER]

LATITUDE : 53 13 30N. HEIGHT ASL : 15′ LIGHTING : None.
LONGITUDE : 03 00 15W. FLYING CONTROL : Yes. RADIO : QDM.

LANDMARKS DAY. : Steel wks. 2000yds. W of A/F. Dee Estuary 2000yds.NW of A/F.

LANDMARKS NIGHT : Dee Estuary 2000yds. N/W.

OBSTRUCTIONS : Chimneys 150′ 2000yds. W of A/F. Water tower 80′ 1000yds. S of A/F.

LANDING AREA : Grass[Tarmac-310]
SURFACE : First 3 R/Ws are North site, others South site.
QDM: 310. LENGTH X WIDTH: 1270 x 50yds.EXT. TO: 2200yds.
: NE-SW. : 1300yds. : 1400yds.
: E-W. : 1000yds. : -
: N-S. : 1330yds. : -
: E-W. : 1030yds. : -

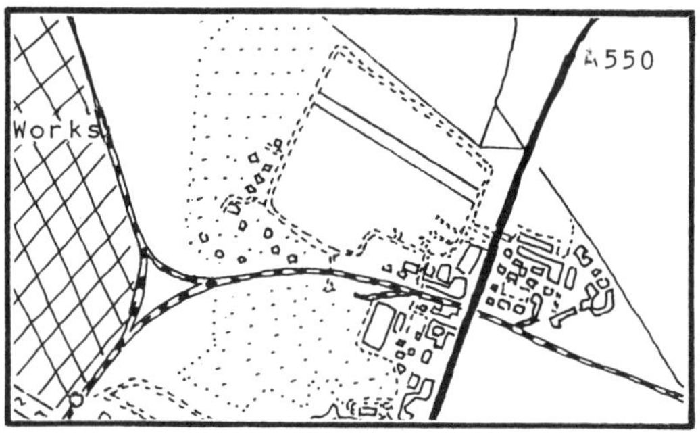

EXTENSIBILITY : Entails diversion of a minor road.

ACCOMMODATION : Permanent.
HANGARS : Blister-18;Bellman-4;Type C-3;A/C sheds-6; A.1.-1;"L"type sheds-2.
HARDSTANDINGS : -

R.A.F. : OFFICERS: 124.S.N.C.O′s.: 438.O.R′s.: 2600.TOTAL: 3162.
W.A.A.F.: " : 15. " : 19. " : 885. " : 919.

AFFILIATED AIRFIELDS : Little Sutton[Satellite]

PRESENT USE [1985] : RAF.

NO: 491.

AIRFIELD NAME: SEETHING. OPENED : 1943.
COUNTY : Norfolk. CLOSED : 1945.
COMMAND : 8th USAAF.
FORMATION : 448th Bomb Grp. GRID REF: G 768137[67]
FUNCTION : Operational. O.S.REF.: TM 315955/134.
:
LOCALITY : 9.5miles SE of Norwich.
RAILWAY STN. : Ditchingham 6miles[LNER]

LATITUDE : 52 30 30N. HEIGHT ASL : 130′ LIGHTING : Mk2.
LONGITUDE : 01 24 45E. FLYING CONTROL : Yes. RADIO : QDM.

LANDMARKS DAY. : -

LANDMARKS NIGHT : -

OBSTRUCTIONS : -

LANDING AREA : Concrete.
SURFACE :
QDM: 070. LENGTH X WIDTH: 2000 x 50yds.EXT. TO: 3000yds.
: 010. : 1400 x 50yds. : 2000yds.
: 300. : 1400 x 50yds. : 2000yds.
: : :

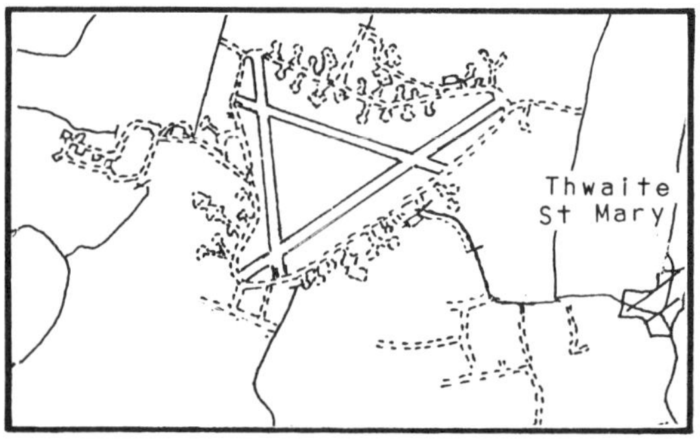

EXTENSIBILITY : Entails demolition of a cottage.

ACCOMMODATION : Temporary.
HANGARS : T2-2.

HARDSTANDINGS : Communal & pans-51.

USAAF. : OFFICERS: 421. Enlisted Men. : 2473.TOTAL: 2894.

AFFILIATED AIRFIELDS : -

PRESENT USE [1985] : Disused.

NO: 492.

AIRFIELD NAME: SELSEY. OPENED : 1943.
COUNTY : Sussex. CLOSED : 1945.
COMMAND : Fighter.
FORMATION : 11 Grp[Uxbridge] GRID REF: Q 300150[133]
FUNCTION : Advanced Landing Ground.O.S.REF.: SZ 865985/197.
:
LOCALITY : 5miles S of Chichester.
RAILWAY STN. : Ferry Halt[SR]

LATITUDE : 50 45 15N. HEIGHT ASL : 20′ LIGHTING : None.
LONGITUDE : 00 46 30W. FLYING CONTROL : None.RADIO : QDM.

LANDMARKS DAY. : Pagham harbour 1.5miles S.

LANDMARKS NIGHT : As day.

OBSTRUCTIONS : -

LANDING AREA : Steel Matting[Sommerfeld track]
SURFACE :
QDM: 045. LENGTH X WIDTH: 1400yds. EXT. TO: -
: 135. : 1250yds. : -
: : :
: : :

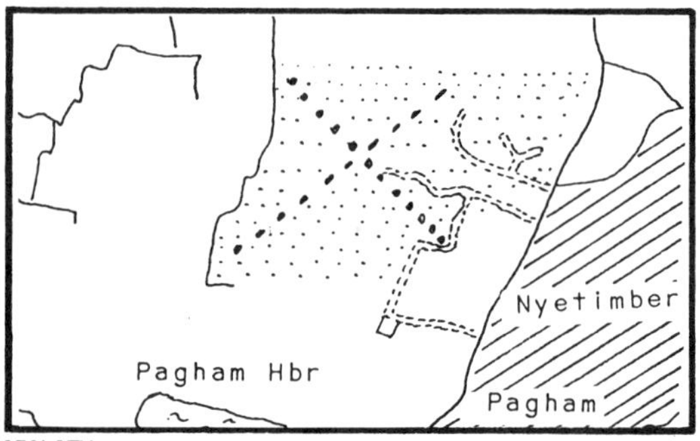

EXTENSIBILITY : -

ACCOMMODATION : Tented camp.
HANGARS : EO Blister-4.

HARDSTANDINGS : Sommerfeld track.

R.A.F. : OFFICERS: - S.N.C.O′s.: - O.R′s.: - TOTAL: -
W.A.A.F.: " : - " : - " : - " : -

AFFILIATED AIRFIELDS : -

PRESENT USE [1985] : Agriculture.

AIRFIELD NAME: SHAWBURY. OPENED : 1917.
COUNTY : Shropshire. CLOSED :
COMMAND : Flying Training.
FORMATION : 25 Grp[Market Drayton] GRID REF: K 013435[61]
FUNCTION : Empire Air Navigation School. O.S.REF.: SJ 550220/126.
LOCALITY : 6.5miles NE of Shrewsbury.
RAILWAY STN. : Shrewsbury[GWR]

LATITUDE : 52 47 45N. HEIGHT ASL : 245′ LIGHTING : Mk2.
LONGITUDE : 02 40 00W. FLYING CONTROL : Yes. RADIO : QDM.

LANDMARKS DAY. : Grinshill 629′ 4000yds.WNW. The Wrekin 1335′ 10miles SSE.

LANDMARKS NIGHT : -

OBSTRUCTIONS : Grinshill 1.5miles W.

LANDING AREA SURFACE : Tarmac.

QDM	LENGTH X WIDTH	EXT. TO
192.	1400 x 50yds.	3500yds.
237.	1500 x 50yds.	3000yds.
		3000yds.

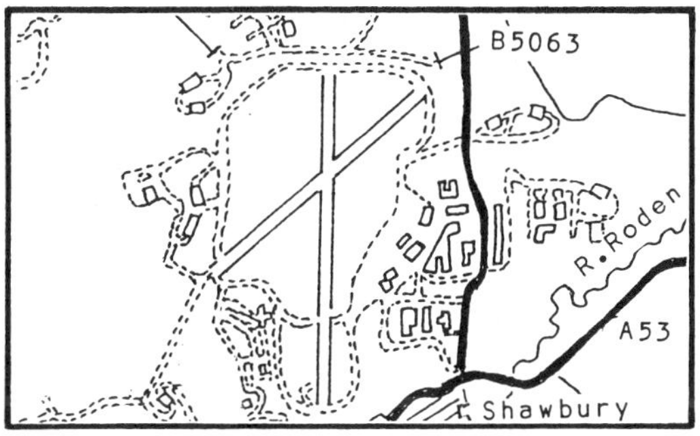

EXTENSIBILITY : Entails slight demolition.

ACCOMMODATION : Permanent.
HANGARS : Types:C-1;D-2;L-4;AR-1;Lamella-6;T2-2; Bellman-2;EO Blister-16.
HARDSTANDINGS : Oblong-70;hangar apron 1200x100′.

	OFFICERS	S.N.C.O′s.	O.R′s.	TOTAL
R.A.F.	244.	298.	848.	1390.
W.A.A.F.	11.	7.	491.	509.

AFFILIATED AIRFIELDS :

PRESENT USE [1985] : RAF.

NO: 494.

AIRFIELD NAME: SHELLINGFORD. OPENED : 1941.
COUNTY : Berkshire. CLOSED : 1948.
COMMAND : Flying Training.
FORMATION : 50 Grp[Reading] GRID REF: P 770134[104]
FUNCTION : Elementary Flying Training School. O.S.REF.: SU 328925/174.
LOCALITY : 2.75miles SE of Farringdon.
RAILWAY STN. : Challow 2.5miles[GWR]

LATITUDE : 51 38 15N. HEIGHT ASL : 275. LIGHTING : None.
LONGITUDE : 01 31 30W. FLYING CONTROL : None. RADIO : QDM.

LANDMARKS DAY. : Farringdon Folly 317degrees magnetic.

LANDMARKS NIGHT : -

OBSTRUCTIONS : -

LANDING AREA SURFACE : Grass.

QDM	LENGTH X WIDTH	EXT. TO
NE-SW.	1150yds.	-
E-W.	1025yds.	-
NW-SE.	933yds.	-

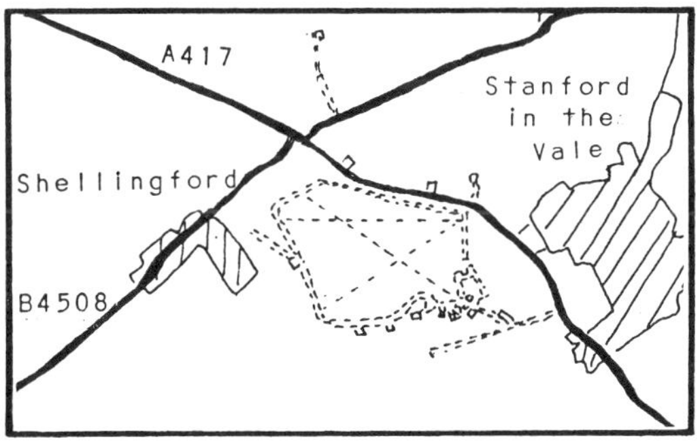

EXTENSIBILITY : None possible.

ACCOMMODATION : Temporary.
HANGARS : Bellman-4;Blister-11.

HARDSTANDINGS : -

	OFFICERS	S.N.C.O′s.	O.R′s.	TOTAL
R.A.F.	42.	39.	727.	808.
W.A.A.F.	-	-	-	-

AFFILIATED AIRFIELDS : -

PRESENT USE [1985] : Unspecified.

NO: 495.

AIRFIELD NAME: SHEPHERDS GROVE. OPENED : 1944.
COUNTY : Suffolk. CLOSED : 1963.
COMMAND : Bomber.
FORMATION : 3 Grp[Exning] GRID REF: M 445911[76]
FUNCTION : Care & Maintenance. O.S.REF.: TL 990728/144.
:
LOCALITY : 9miles NE of Bury St. Edmunds.
RAILWAY STN. : Thetford 6miles[LNER]

LATITUDE : 52 19 00N. HEIGHT ASL : 200′ LIGHTING : Mk2.
LONGITUDE : 00 55 15E. FLYING CONTROL : Yes. RADIO : QDM.

LANDMARKS DAY. : Large lake 6miles W of A/F.

LANDMARKS NIGHT : As day.

OBSTRUCTIONS : -

LANDING AREA SURFACE : Concrete.

QDM	LENGTH X WIDTH	EXT. TO
010.	2000 x 50yds.	-
080.	1400 x 50yds.	3000yds.
140.	1400 x 50yds.	2000yds.

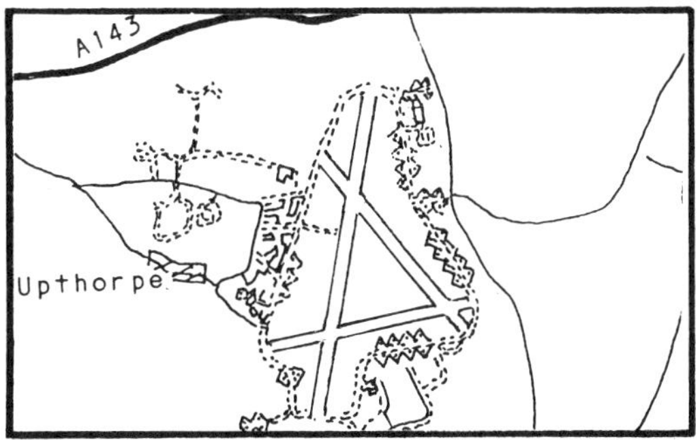

EXTENSIBILITY : Entails demolition of farm buildings

ACCOMMODATION : Temporary.
HANGARS : T2-2.

HARDSTANDINGS : Pan-1;spectacle-49.

	OFFICERS	S.N.C.O′s.	O.R′s.	TOTAL
R.A.F.	172.	368.	1676.	2216.
W.A.A.F.	12.	25.	507.	544.

AFFILIATED AIRFIELDS : -

PRESENT USE [1985] : Unspecified.

NO: 496.

AIRFIELD NAME: SHERBURN-in-ELMET. OPENED : 1917.
COUNTY : Yorkshire. CLOSED : 1945.
COMMAND : Flying Training.
FORMATION : 21 Grp[Spittlegate] GRID REF: E 984527[32]
FUNCTION : Experimental Station. O.S.REF.: SE 520330/105.
:
LOCALITY : 12.5miles E of Leeds.
RAILWAY STN. : Sherburn-in-Elmet .5miles[LNER]

LATITUDE : 53 47 15N. HEIGHT ASL : 26′ LIGHTING : Mk2.
LONGITUDE : 01 13 15W. FLYING CONTROL : Yes. RADIO : QDM.

LANDMARKS DAY. : LNER York-Sheffield & loop to Gascoigne Wood. Goods assembly yard on 2 sides of A/F.

LANDMARKS NIGHT : -

OBSTRUCTIONS : A/C factories on NE & SW corner of A/F.

LANDING AREA : Concrete.
SURFACE : [+240yd.extension in square mesh track]
QDM: 050. LENGTH X WIDTH: 2000 x 50yds.EXT. TO: 3500yds.
: : : 2050yds.
: : :
: : :

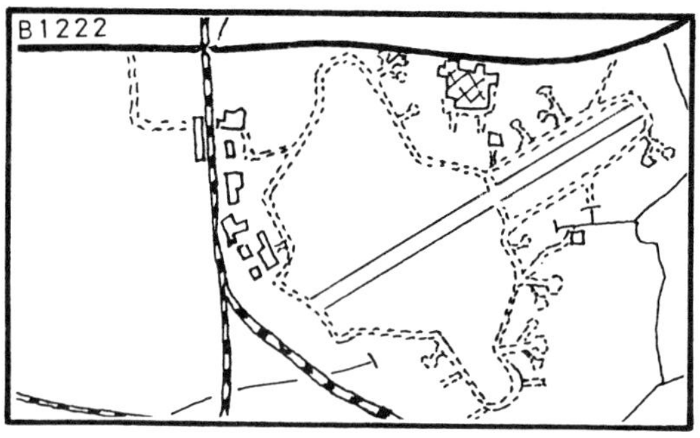

EXTENSIBILITY : Entails diversion of main road & demolition demolition of a farm.
ACCOMMODATION : Temporary.
HANGARS : 300x150′-2;400x200′-1;250x150′-1; 200x150′-1;200x100′-1;65′Blister-5.
HARDSTANDINGS : Circular-19.

R.A.F. : OFFICERS: 44.S.N.C.O′s.: 105.O.R′s.: 835.TOTAL: 984.
W.A.A.F.: " : 4. " : 4. " : 230. " : 238.

AFFILIATED AIRFIELDS : -

PRESENT USE [1985] : Industry.

NO: 497.

AIRFIELD NAME: SHIPDHAM. OPENED : 1942.
COUNTY : Norfolk. CLOSED : 1945.
COMMAND : 8th USAAF.
FORMATION : 44th Bomb Grp. GRID REF: G 440255[66]
FUNCTION : Operational. O.S.REF.: TF 982075/144.
:
LOCALITY : 3.5miles S of East Dereham.
RAILWAY STN. : Thuxton 3miles[LNER]

LATITUDE : 52 37 38N. HEIGHT ASL : 215′ LIGHTING : Mk2.
LONGITUDE : 00 56 00E. FLYING CONTROL : Yes. RADIO : QDM.

LANDMARKS DAY. : -

LANDMARKS NIGHT : -

OBSTRUCTIONS : -

LANDING AREA : Tarmac.
SURFACE :
QDM: 090. LENGTH X WIDTH: 2000 x 50yds.EXT. TO: 3000yds.
: 210. : 1400 x 50yds. : 1900yds.
: 030. : 1400 x 50yds. : 2000yds.
: : :

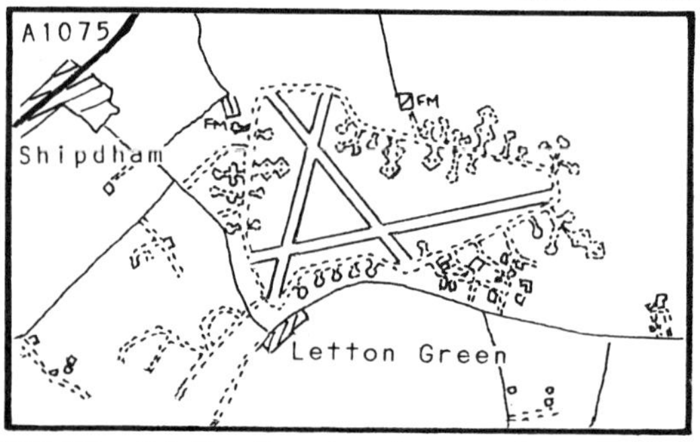

EXTENSIBILITY : Entails diversion of a secondary road, & demolition of a farm.
ACCOMMODATION : Temporary.
HANGARS : T2-3.

HARDSTANDINGS : Concrete-50.

USAAF. : OFFICERS: 443. Enlisted Men. : 2529.TOTAL: 2972.

AFFILIATED AIRFIELDS : -

PRESENT USE [1985] : Private flying.

NO: 498.

AIRFIELD NAME: SHOBDON. OPENED : 1940.
COUNTY : Herefordshire. CLOSED : 1946.
COMMAND : Flying Training.
FORMATION : 23 Grp[South Cerney] GRID REF: O 853820[80]
FUNCTION : Glider Training School. O.S.REF.: SO 390603/149.
:
LOCALITY : 6miles W of Leominster.
RAILWAY STN. : Pembridge .75miles[GWR]

LATITUDE : 52 14 08N. HEIGHT ASL : 300′ LIGHTING : None.
LONGITUDE : 02 53 00W. FLYING CONTROL : Yes. RADIO : QDM.

LANDMARKS DAY. : R Arrow E & W through Pembridge 1mile S of A/F.

LANDMARKS NIGHT : GWR[NE-SW]. Range of hills to N & NW.

OBSTRUCTIONS :Hills on NNW & SE.

LANDING AREA : Concrete & tarmac.
SURFACE : With 350yd. grass extension.
QDM: 275. LENGTH X WIDTH: 1600 x 50yds.EXT. TO: 3500yds.
: : : 1700yds.
: : : 1400yds.
: : :

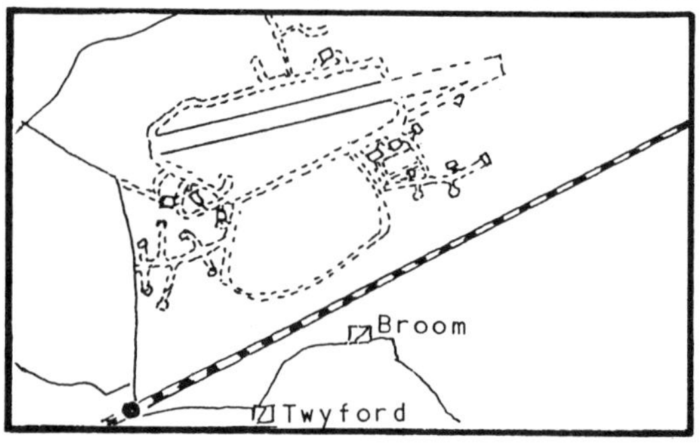

EXTENSIBILITY : Entails diversion of 2 secondary roads.

ACCOMMODATION : Temporary.
HANGARS : T2-6;Blister-6.

HARDSTANDINGS : Circular.

R.A.F. : OFFICERS: 91.S.N.C.O′s.: 395.O.R′s.: 864.TOTAL: 1350.
W.A.A.F.: " : 6. " : 12. " : 198. " : 216.

AFFILIATED AIRFIELDS : -

PRESENT USE [1985] : Private flying.

NO: 499.

AIRFIELD NAME: SHOREHAM.	OPENED : 1911.
COUNTY : Sussex.	CLOSED :
COMMAND : Fighter.
FORMATION : 11 Grp[Uxbridge]	GRID REF: Q 640248[133]
FUNCTION : Operational[satellite]	O.S.REF.: TQ 202055/198.
:
LOCALITY : 1mile N of Shoreham.
RAILWAY STN. : Shoreham on Sea[SR]

LATITUDE : 50 50 12N. HEIGHT ASL : 10′ LIGHTING : None.
LONGITUDE : 00 17 23W. FLYING CONTROL : None.RADIO : QDM.

LANDMARKS DAY. : Lancing College & R Adur.

LANDMARKS NIGHT : R Adur.

OBSTRUCTIONS : Richardo rail bridge. Lancing village.

LANDING AREA SURFACE : Grass.

QDM	LENGTH X WIDTH	EXT. TO
NW-SE.	1200yds.	-
NE-SW.	1150yds.	-

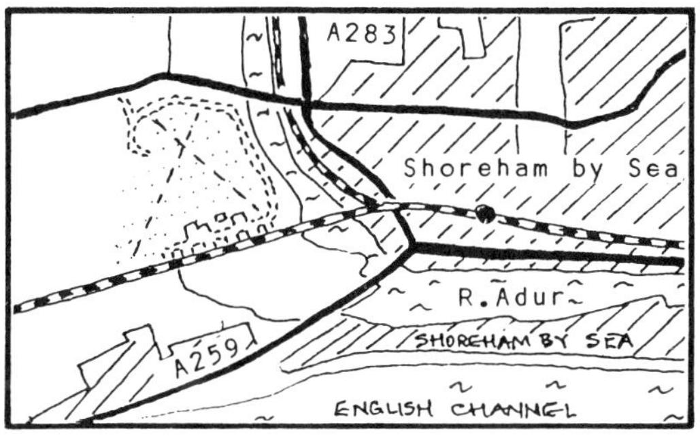

EXTENSIBILITY : None possible.

ACCOMMODATION : Temporary[except for civil airport buildings]
HANGARS : 0 Blister-4.

HARDSTANDINGS : TE-2;SE-4.

R.A.F. : OFFICERS: - S.N.C.O′s.: 84.O.R′s.: 530.TOTAL: 614.
W.A.A.F.: " : - " : - " : - " : -

AFFILIATED AIRFIELDS : Tangmere[Sector]

PRESENT USE [1985] : Civil Airport[Shoreham]

NO: 500.

AIRFIELD NAME: SHREWTON.	OPENED : 1940.
COUNTY : Wiltshire.	CLOSED : 1946.
COMMAND : Fighter.
FORMATION : 38 Grp[Marks Hall]	GRID REF: U 515665[122]
FUNCTION : Relief Landing Ground.	O.S.REF.: SU 076460/184.
:
LOCALITY : 11miles NNW of Salisbury.
RAILWAY STN. : Salisbury[SR]

LATITUDE : 51 12 45N. HEIGHT ASL : 350′ LIGHTING : None.
LONGITUDE : 01 53 30W. FLYING CONTROL : None.RADIO : QDM.

LANDMARKS DAY. : Stonehenge 3.5miles SW.

LANDMARKS NIGHT : -

OBSTRUCTIONS : -

LANDING AREA SURFACE : Grass.

QDM	LENGTH X WIDTH	EXT. TO
N-S.	1200yds.	-
NE-SW.	1200yds.	-
E-W.	1000yds.	-
NW-SE.	1100yds.	-

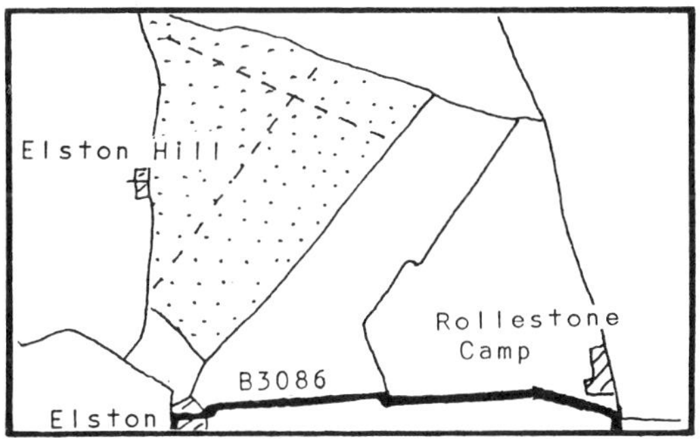

EXTENSIBILITY : -

ACCOMMODATION : Temporary.
HANGARS : Blister-3.

HARDSTANDINGS : -

R.A.F. : OFFICERS: 8.S.N.C.O′s.: 7.O.R′s.: 151.TOTAL: 166.
W.A.A.F.: " : - " : - " : - " : -

AFFILIATED AIRFIELDS : Netheravon[Parent]

PRESENT USE [1985] : Disused.

NO: 501.

AIRFIELD NAME: SIBSON.	OPENED : 1940.
COUNTY : Leicestershire.	CLOSED : 1946.
COMMAND : Flying Training.
FORMATION : 21 Grp[Spittlegate]	GRID REF: F 550150[74]
FUNCTION : Advanced Flying Unit	O.S.REF.: TL 095966/142.
: Pilots[satellite]
LOCALITY : 6miles WSW of Peterborough.
RAILWAY STN. : Stamford 5miles[LMS & LNER]

LATITUDE : 52 32 53N. HEIGHT ASL : 115′ LIGHTING : None.
LONGITUDE : 00 23 00W. FLYING CONTROL : None.RADIO : QDM.

LANDMARKS DAY. : Bend in river,N. Railway line with tunnel.

LANDMARKS NIGHT : -

OBSTRUCTIONS : -

LANDING AREA SURFACE : Grass.

QDM	LENGTH X WIDTH	EXT. TO
NE-SW.	1100yds.	-
N-S.	900yds.	-

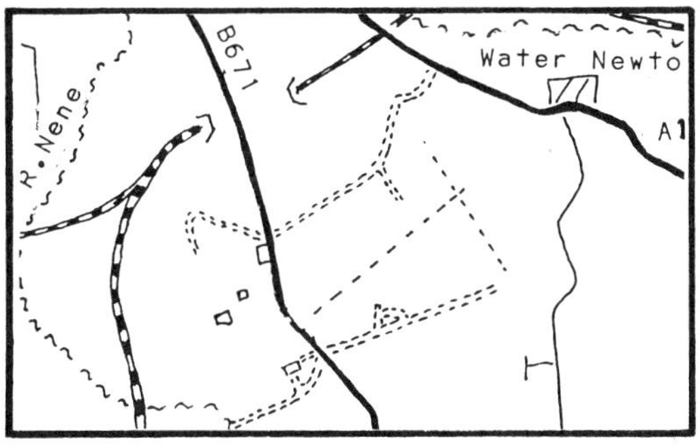

EXTENSIBILITY : To SE only by 500yds.

ACCOMMODATION : Temporary.
HANGARS : Blisters:single 65′-3;double 65′-1.

HARDSTANDINGS : -

R.A.F. : OFFICERS: 53.S.N.C.O′s.: 104.O.R′s.: 446.TOTAL: 603.
W.A.A.F.: " : 2. " : - " : 35. " : 37.

AFFILIATED AIRFIELDS : Peterborough[Parent]

PRESENT USE [1985] : Private flying.

NO: 502.

AIRFIELD NAME: SILLOTH. OPENED : 1939.
COUNTY : Cumberland. CLOSED : 1960.
COMMAND : Coastal.
FORMATION : 17 Grp[Edinburgh] GRID REF: Y 610755[8]
FUNCTION : Operational Training O.S.REF.: NY 124436/85.
: Unit.
LOCALITY : .75miles E of Silloth.
RAILWAY STN. : Silloth[LNER]

LATITUDE : 54 52 15N. HEIGHT ASL : 25′ LIGHTING : Mk1.
LONGITUDE : 03 21 30W. FLYING CONTROL : Yes. RADIO : QDM.

LANDMARKS DAY. : Solway Firth, Silloth town & docks.

LANDMARKS NIGHT : -

OBSTRUCTIONS : Church spire[lit at night] 1000yds. W of W-E R/W.

LANDING AREA SURFACE : Concrete.
QDM: 053. LENGTH X WIDTH: 1580 x 50yds.EXT. TO: 2180yds.
: 103. : 1090 x 50yds. : 1480yds.
: 013. : 1130 x 50yds. : 1400yds.

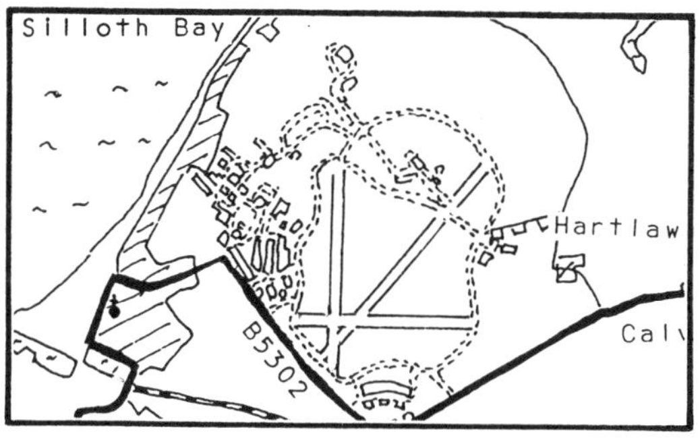

EXTENSIBILITY : -

ACCOMMODATION : Permanent[part]
HANGARS : Types:C-3;D-4;E-6;L-4;A1-1;Bellman-1; Robin-13;Super Robin-5.
HARDSTANDINGS : 100′dia-38;small MAP-13;40x120′-6;30x70′-24.

R.A.F. : OFFICERS: 91.S.N.C.O′s.: 260.O.R′s.: 1269.TOTAL: 1620.
W.A.A.F.: " : - " : - " : - " : -

AFFILIATED AIRFIELDS : Great Orton[Satellite]

PRESENT USE [1985] : Private flying.

NO: 503.

AIRFIELD NAME: SILVERSTONE. OPENED : 1943.
COUNTY : Northamptonshire. CLOSED : 1946.
COMMAND : Bomber.
FORMATION : 92 Grp[Winslow] GRID REF: L 125617[83]
FUNCTION : Operational Training O.S.REF.: SP 676418/152.
: Unit.
LOCALITY : 4miles S of Towcester.
RAILWAY STN. : Towcester[LMS]

LATITUDE : 52 04 15N. HEIGHT ASL : 506′ LIGHTING : Mk2.
LONGITUDE : 01 00 45W. FLYING CONTROL : Yes. RADIO : QDM.

LANDMARKS DAY. : Wolfe′s Obelisk 2miles S. Stowe Park with long avenue of trees.

LANDMARKS NIGHT : -

OBSTRUCTIONS : -

LANDING AREA SURFACE : Concrete & wood chippings.
QDM: 026. LENGTH X WIDTH: 2000 x 50yds.EXT. TO: 2300yds.
: 068. : 1400 x 50yds. : 1500yds.
: 144. : 1300 x 50yds. : 1500yds.
: : :

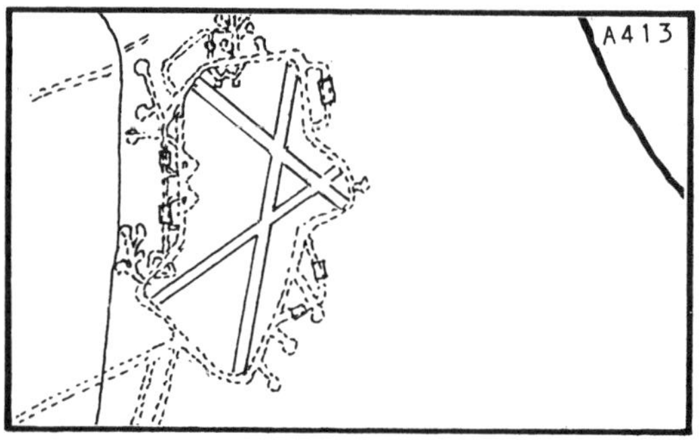

EXTENSIBILITY : -

ACCOMMODATION : Temporary.
HANGARS : T2-4;B1-1.

HARDSTANDINGS : Heavy bomber-30.

R.A.F. : OFFICERS: 174.S.N.C.O′s.: 553.O.R′s.: 865.TOTAL: 1592.
W.A.A.F.: " : 10. " : 13. " : 392. " : 415.

AFFILIATED AIRFIELDS : Turweston[Satellite]

PRESENT USE [1985] : Race track.

NO: 504.

AIRFIELD NAME: SKEABRAE. OPENED : 1940.
COUNTY : Orkneys. CLOSED : 1945.
COMMAND : Fighter.
FORMATION : 13 Grp[Inverness] GRID REF: Y 810420[6Scot]
FUNCTION : Forward Airfield. O.S.REF.: HY 269207/6.
:
LOCALITY : 12miles NW of Kirkwall.
RAILWAY STN. : Thurso[LMS]

LATITUDE : 59 03 53N. HEIGHT ASL : 60′ LIGHTING : None.
LONGITUDE : 03 16 00W. FLYING CONTROL : Yes. RADIO : QDM.

LANDMARKS DAY. : Brough Head 5.5miles N. Bay of Skaill 2.5miles W. Loch Harray 1mile S.

LANDMARKS NIGHT : -

OBSTRUCTIONS : W/T masts 80′high 210degrees 1.25miles.

LANDING AREA SURFACE : Tarmac.
QDM: 204. LENGTH X WIDTH: 1000 x 50yds.EXT. TO: -
: 334. : 1000 x 50yds. : -
: 294. : 1000 x 50yds. : -
: 064. : 1000 x 50yds. : -

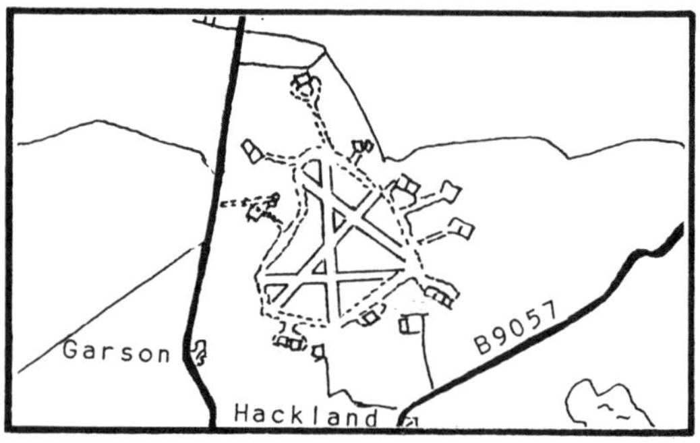

EXTENSIBILITY : -

ACCOMMODATION : Temporary.
HANGARS : Teesside-12;Callendar Hamilton-1.

HARDSTANDINGS : -

R.A.F. : OFFICERS: 94.S.N.C.O′s.: 110.O.R′s.: 1406.TOTAL: 1610.
W.A.A.F.: " : 6. " : 14. " : 154. " : 174.

AFFILIATED AIRFIELDS : Kirkwall Operations Room[Sector]

PRESENT USE [1985] : Disused.

NO: 505.

AIRFIELD NAME: SKELLINGTHORPE. OPENED : 1941.
COUNTY : Lincolnshire. CLOSED : 1952.
COMMAND : Bomber.
FORMATION : 5 Grp[Morton Hall] GRID REF: F 394890[47]
FUNCTION : Operational. O.S.REF.: SK 925688/121.

LOCALITY : 3miles W of Lincoln.
RAILWAY STN. : Skellingthorpe 2miles[LNER]

LATITUDE : 53 12 45N. HEIGHT ASL : 60' LIGHTING : Mk1.
LONGITUDE : 00 36 00W. FLYING CONTROL : Yes. RADIO : QDM.

LANDMARKS DAY. : Lake on E boundary. Railway 1mile E [Nottingham-Lincoln]

LANDMARKS NIGHT : -

OBSTRUCTIONS : -

LANDING AREA SURFACE : Concrete & tarmac.

QDM	LENGTH X WIDTH	EXT. TO
200.	1400 x 50yds.	3000yds.
286.	1400 x 50yds.	2000yds.
246.	2100 x 50yds.	2200yds.

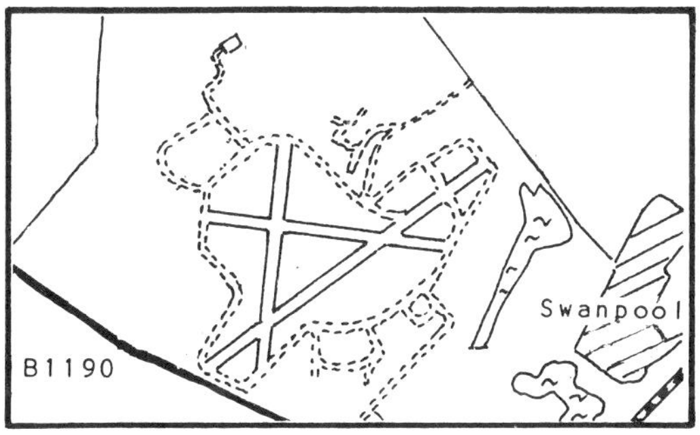

EXTENSIBILITY : Entails diversion of 2nd.class road.

ACCOMMODATION : Temporary.
HANGARS : T2-2;B1-1.

HARDSTANDINGS : Heavy bomber-36.

	OFFICERS	S.N.C.O's.	O.R's.	TOTAL
R.A.F.	157.	394.	1020.	1571.
W.A.A.F.	4.	5.	270.	279.

AFFILIATED AIRFIELDS : Waddington[53 Base]

PRESENT USE [1985] : Housing.

NO: 506.

AIRFIELD NAME: SKIPTON-on-SWALE. OPENED : 1942.
COUNTY : Yorkshire. CLOSED : 1945.
COMMAND : Bomber.
FORMATION : 6 RCAF Grp[Allerton Pk] GRID REF: Z 846012[21]
FUNCTION : Operational. O.S.REF.: SE 373812/99.

LOCALITY : 4miles W of Thirsk.
RAILWAY STN. : Topcliffe 1.5miles[LNER]

LATITUDE : 54 13 30N. HEIGHT ASL : 90' LIGHTING : Mk2.
LONGITUDE : 01 25 45W. FLYING CONTROL : Yes. RADIO : QDM.

LANDMARKS DAY. : R Swale W. Gt.North Road 1.5miles W. LNER main line 2.5miles E.

LANDMARKS NIGHT : R Swale.

OBSTRUCTIONS : Water tower on communal site; safety height stated to be 150'

LANDING AREA SURFACE : Tarmac.

QDM	LENGTH X WIDTH	EXT. TO
222.	2000 x 50yds.	3000yds.
273.	1400 x 50yds.	2000yds.
338.	1400 x 50yds.	2000yds.

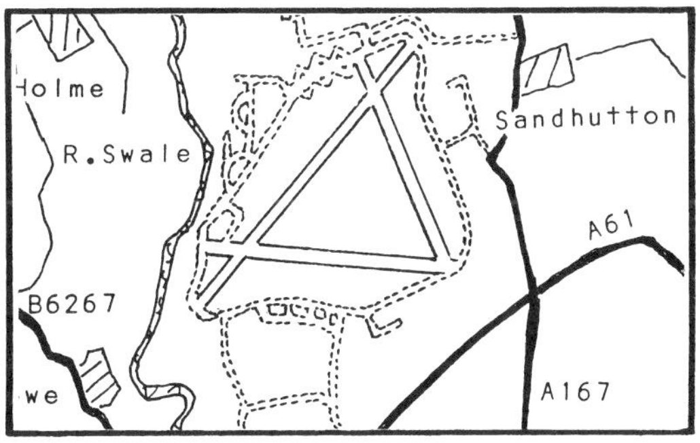

EXTENSIBILITY : Entaild diversaion of a short length of main road.
ACCOMMODATION : Temporary.
HANGARS : T2-2;B1-1.

HARDSTANDINGS : Heavy bomber.

	OFFICERS	S.N.C.O's.	O.R's.	TOTAL
R.C.A.F.	225.	457.	1242.	1924.
W.A.A.F.	4.	8.	154.	166.

AFFILIATED AIRFIELDS : Leeming[63 RCAF Base]

PRESENT USE [1985] : Agriculture.

NO: 507.

AIRFIELD NAME: SKITTON. OPENED : 1940.
COUNTY : Caithness. CLOSED : 1945.
COMMAND : Coastal.
FORMATION : 18 Grp[Pitreavie Castle] GRID REF: D 855785[12Scot]
FUNCTION : Operational[satellite] O.S.REF.: ND 327571/12.

LOCALITY : 4miles NNW of Wick.
RAILWAY STN. : Wick[LMS]

LATITUDE : 58 29 43N. HEIGHT ASL : 65' LIGHTING : Mk2.
LONGITUDE : 03 09 45W. FLYING CONTROL : Yes. RADIO : QDM.

LANDMARKS DAY. : Noss Head lighthouse. Wick. Duncansby Head.

LANDMARKS NIGHT : -

OBSTRUCTIONS : -

LANDING AREA SURFACE : Tarmac.

QDM	LENGTH X WIDTH	EXT. TO
188.	1590 x 50yds.	2000yds.
245.	1120 x 50yds.	1600yds.
306.	1350 x 50yds.	1600yds.

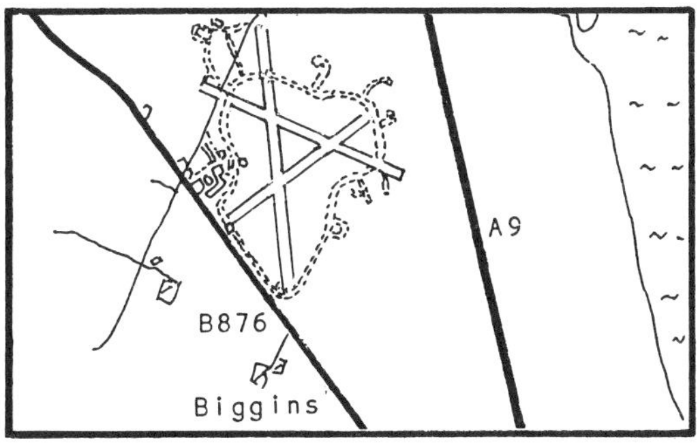

EXTENSIBILITY : Entails diversion of Wick-Thurso road.

ACCOMMODATION : Temporary.
HANGARS : Bellman-1;Blisters:double EO-6;standard-3.

HARDSTANDINGS : -

	OFFICERS	S.N.C.O's.	O.R's.	TOTAL
R.A.F.	32.	79.	1239.	1350.
W.A.A.F.	2.	8.	70.	80.

AFFILIATED AIRFIELDS : Wick[Parent]

PRESENT USE [1985] : Disused.

NO: 508.

AIRFIELD NAME: SLEAP. OPENED : 1943.
COUNTY : Shropshire. CLOSED : 1964.
COMMAND : Fighter.
FORMATION : 38 Grp[Marks Hall] GRID REF: J 940478[51&60]
FUNCTION : Operational Training O.S.REF.: SJ 482268/126.
: Unit[satellite]
LOCALITY : 9miles N of Shrewsbury.
RAILWAY STN. : Yorton 3.25miles[LMS]

LATITUDE : 52 50 00N. HEIGHT ASL : 272′ LIGHTING : Mk2.
LONGITUDE : 02 46 15W. FLYING CONTROL : Yes. RADIO : QDM.

LANDMARKS DAY. : Town of Wem.

LANDMARKS NIGHT : -

OBSTRUCTIONS : Grinshill 2.5miles SE of A/F 250′ AFL.
Red light on summit.

LANDING AREA SURFACE : Concrete.

QDM	LENGTH X WIDTH	EXT. TO
192.	1400 x 50yds.	1600yds.
282.	1400 x 50yds.	-
237.	2000 x 50yds.	2300yds.

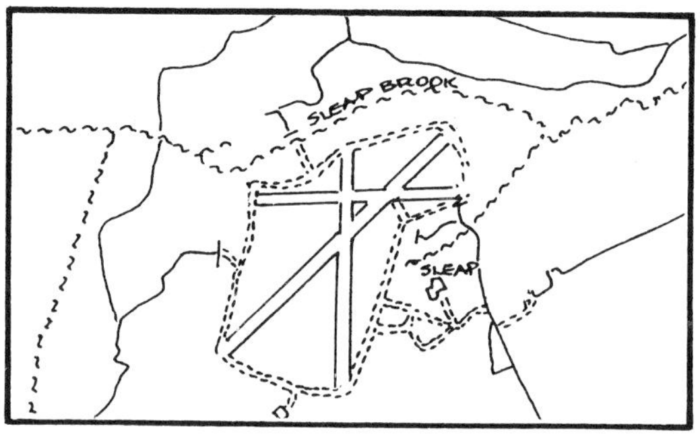

EXTENSIBILITY : -

ACCOMMODATION : Temporary.
HANGARS : B1-1;T2-1.

HARDSTANDINGS : Concrete-27.

R.A.F. : OFFICERS: 66.S.N.C.O′s.: 148.O.R′s.: 840.TOTAL: 1054.
W.A.A.F.: " : 2. " : 8. " : 135. " : 145.

AFFILIATED AIRFIELDS : Tilstock[Parent]

PRESENT USE [1985] : Private flying.

NO: 509.

AIRFIELD NAME: SEIGHFORD. OPENED : 1943.
COUNTY : Staffordshire. CLOSED : 1966.
COMMAND : Flying Training.
FORMATION : 23 Grp[South Cerney] GRID REF: K 325459[61]
FUNCTION : Heavy Glider Conversion O.S.REF.: SJ 865255/127.
: Unit[satellite]
LOCALITY : 4miles WNW of Stafford.
RAILWAY STN. : Stafford[LMS]

LATITUDE : 52 49 30N. HEIGHT ASL : 310′ LIGHTING : Mk2.
LONGITUDE : 02 12 00W. FLYING CONTROL : Yes. RADIO : QDM.

LANDMARKS DAY. : Stafford Castle.

LANDMARKS NIGHT : -

OBSTRUCTIONS : Stafford Castle 2.5miles 15degrees off main R/W.

LANDING AREA SURFACE : Concrete.

QDM	LENGTH X WIDTH	EXT. TO
181.	1400 x 50yds.	1600yds.
226.	1400 x 50yds.	1600yds.
309.	2000 x 50yds.	3200yds.

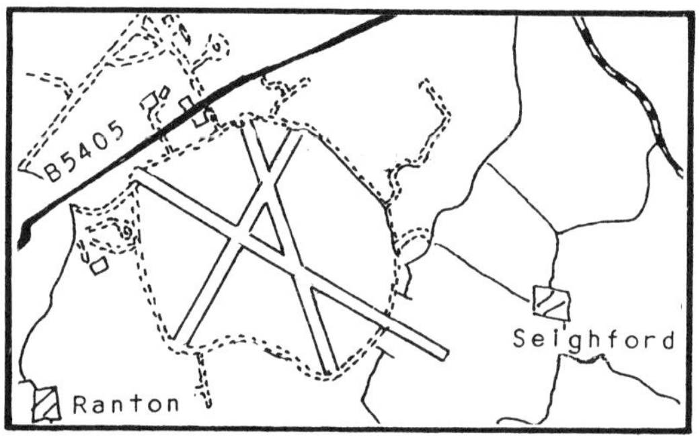

EXTENSIBILITY : Entails road diversion & demolition of 5 cottages.
ACCOMMODATION : Temporary.
HANGARS : T2-2;B1-1.

HARDSTANDINGS : Heavy bomber-27.

R.A.F. : OFFICERS: 72.S.N.C.O′s.: 279.O.R′s.: 926.TOTAL: 1277.
W.A.A.F.: " : 4. " : - " : 135. " : 139.

AFFILIATED AIRFIELDS : Peplow[Parent]

PRESENT USE [1985] : Agriculture.

NO: 510.

AIRFIELD NAME: SMITHS LAWN. OPENED : 1941.
COUNTY : Berkshire. CLOSED : 1945.
COMMAND : Flying Training.
FORMATION : 50 Grp[Reading] GRID REF: Q 405910[114]
FUNCTION : Elementary Flying O.S.REF.: SU 973698/176.
: Training School[RLG]
LOCALITY : Windsor Great Park.
RAILWAY STN. : Sunningdale 2.5miles[SR]

LATITUDE : 51 24 53N. HEIGHT ASL : 200′ LIGHTING : None.
LONGITUDE : 00 36 15W. FLYING CONTROL : None. RADIO : QDM.

LANDMARKS DAY. : Virginia Water immediately S. Windsor Castle 4miles W.

LANDMARKS NIGHT : Virgina Water.

OBSTRUCTIONS : Trees almost all round. Flying gaps situated on E boundary, also W &N boundaries.

LANDING AREA SURFACE : Grass.

QDM	LENGTH X WIDTH	EXT. TO
NNE-SSW.	916yds.	1700yds.
E-W.	860yds.	1000yds.
		1100yds.

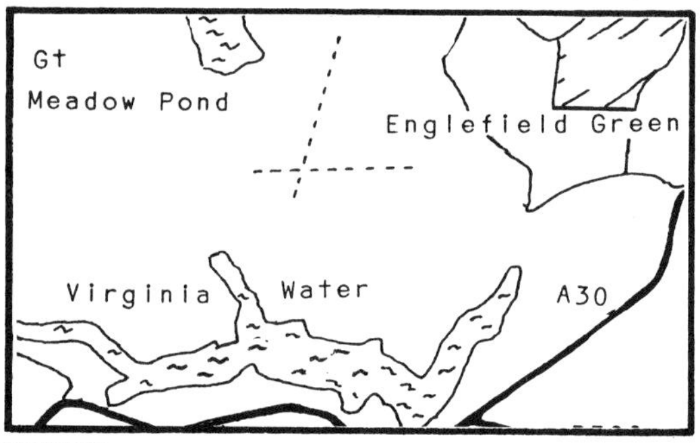

EXTENSIBILITY : -

ACCOMMODATION : Temporary.
HANGARS : EO Blisters[USAAF type]-2.

HARDSTANDINGS : -

R.A.F. : OFFICERS: 2.S.N.C.O′s.: 6.O.R′s.: 77.TOTAL: 85.
W.A.A.F.: " : - " : - " : - " : -

AFFILIATED AIRFIELDS : Fairoaks[Parent]

PRESENT USE [1985] : Parkland.

NO: 511.

AIRFIELD NAME: SNAILWELL. OPENED : 1941.
COUNTY : Suffolk. CLOSED : 1946.
COMMAND : Technical Training.
FORMATION : 28 Grp[17-19 Queen's Sq]GRID REF: M 105849[85]
FUNCTION : Belgium Training School.O.S.REF.: TL 656665/154.
:
LOCALITY : 2miles N of Newmarket.
RAILWAY STN. : Newmarket 3miles[LNER]

LATITUDE : 52 16 08N. HEIGHT ASL : 70' LIGHTING : Mk2.
LONGITUDE : 00 25 15E. FLYING CONTROL : Yes. RADIO : QDM.

LANDMARKS DAY. : Bounded on S by railway.

LANDMARKS NIGHT : -

OBSTRUCTIONS : -

LANDING AREA SURFACE : Grass.

QDM	LENGTH X WIDTH	EXT. TO
NNE-SSW.	1430yds.	3000yds.
ENE-WSW.	1680yds.	-
ESE-WNW.	1420yds.	-

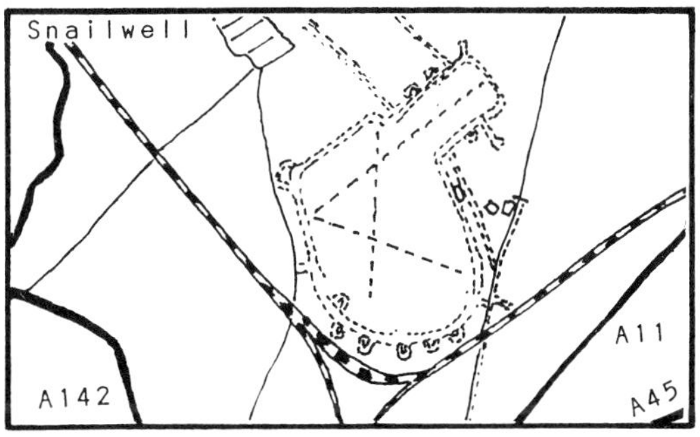

EXTENSIBILITY : -

ACCOMMODATION : Temporary.
HANGARS : Bellman-1;Blister-10.

HARDSTANDINGS : Blenheim-12;frying pan 50'-2.

	OFFICERS	S.N.C.O's.	O.R's.	TOTAL
R.A.F.	68.	90.	940.	1098.
W.A.A.F.	-	-	-	-

AFFILIATED AIRFIELDS : Westley[Satellite]

PRESENT USE [1985] : Agriculture.

NO: 512.

AIRFIELD NAME: SNAITH. OPENED : 1941.
COUNTY : Yorkshire. CLOSED : 1946.
COMMAND : Bomber.
FORMATION : 4 Grp[York] GRID REF: A 075409[32]
FUNCTION : Operational. O.S.REF.: SE 605210/105.
:
LOCALITY : 7miles W of Goole.
RAILWAY STN. : Heck .5miles[LNER]

LATITUDE : 53 40 53N. HEIGHT ASL : 33' LIGHTING : Mk2.
LONGITUDE : 01 05 00W. FLYING CONTROL : Yes. RADIO : QDM.

LANDMARKS DAY. : Southfields reservoir & Knottingley Hull canal & railways.

LANDMARKS NIGHT : Southfields reservoir.

OBSTRUCTIONS : 2 chimneys 100'high SE of A/F.

LANDING AREA SURFACE : Tarmac.

QDM	LENGTH X WIDTH	EXT. TO
231.	1400 x 50yds.	-
273.	1100 x 50yds.	1600yds.
319.	2000 x 50yds.	-

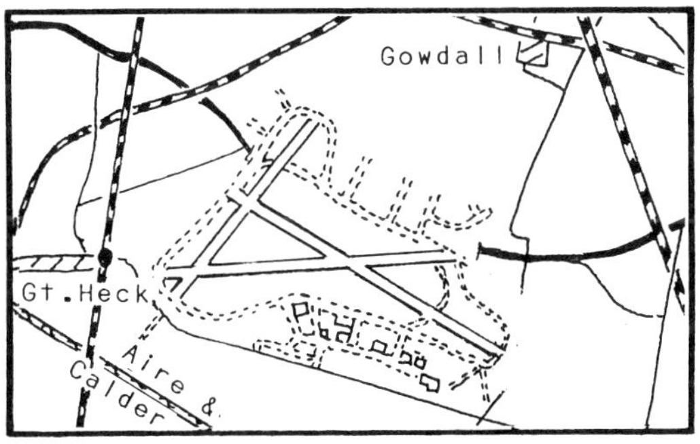

EXTENSIBILITY : Not recommended.

ACCOMMODATION : Temporary.
HANGARS : Type J-1;T2-2.

HARDSTANDINGS : Heavy bomber-36.

	OFFICERS	S.N.C.O's.	O.R's.	TOTAL
R.A.F.	164.	375.	1477.	2016.
W.A.A.F.	8.	8.	378.	394.

AFFILIATED AIRFIELDS : -

PRESENT USE [1985] : Agriculture.

NO: 513.

AIRFIELD NAME: SNETTERTON HEATH. OPENED : 1943.
COUNTY : Norfolk. CLOSED : 1948.
COMMAND : 8th USAAF.
FORMATION : 96th Bomb Grp. GRID REF: G 458078[76]
FUNCTION : Operational. O.S.REF.: TM 005895/144.
:
LOCALITY : 6miles SW of Attleborough.
RAILWAY STN. : Eccles Road 2.5miles[LNER]

LATITUDE : 52 28 00N. HEIGHT ASL : 150' LIGHTING : Mk2.
LONGITUDE : 00 57 15E. FLYING CONTROL : Yes. RADIO : QDM.

LANDMARKS DAY. : Factory chimney at Attleborough 6miles.

LANDMARKS NIGHT : -

OBSTRUCTIONS : -

LANDING AREA SURFACE : Concrete & wood chippings.

QDM	LENGTH X WIDTH	EXT. TO
230.	2000 x 50yds.	-
180.	1400 x 50yds.	1750yds.
270.	1400 x 50yds.	1950yds.

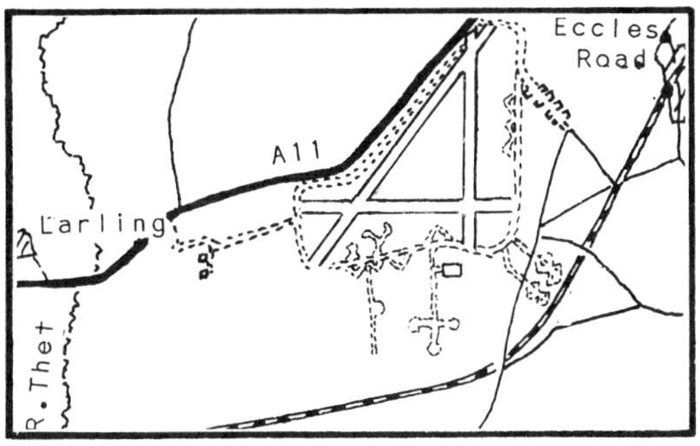

EXTENSIBILITY : Entails diversion of main Thetford-Norwich road.
ACCOMMODATION : Temporary.
HANGARS : T2-2.

HARDSTANDINGS : Loop-50.

USAAF. : OFFICERS: 443. Enlisted Men. : 2529.TOTAL: 2972.

AFFILIATED AIRFIELDS : -

PRESENT USE [1985] : Race track.

NO: 514.

AIRFIELD NAME: SNITTERFIELD. OPENED : 1943.
COUNTY : Warwickshire. CLOSED : 1946.
COMMAND : Flying Training.
FORMATION : 23 Grp[South Cerney] GRID REF: P 645802[82]
FUNCTION : Advanced Flying Unit O.S.REF.: SP 193598/151.
: Pilots[satellite]
LOCALITY : 3miles N of Stratford on Avon.
RAILWAY STN. : Bearley 1mile[GWR]

LATITUDE : 52 14 15N. HEIGHT ASL : 375′ LIGHTING : Mk2.
LONGITUDE : 01 42 45W. FLYING CONTROL : Yes. RADIO : QDM.

LANDMARKS DAY. : Obelisk 2miles SSE of A/F.

LANDMARKS NIGHT : Small reservoir 1mile S.

OBSTRUCTIONS : -

LANDING AREA SURFACE : Concrete covered with tarmac.

QDM	LENGTH X WIDTH	EXT. TO
040.	2000 x 50yds.	-
340.	1350 x 50yds.	-
270.	1250 x 50yds.	-

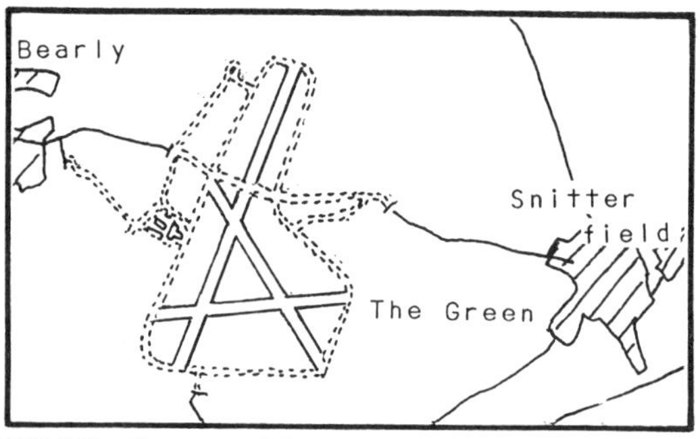

EXTENSIBILITY : None possible.

ACCOMMODATION : Temporary.
HANGARS : T2-4.

HARDSTANDINGS : Circular-30.

	OFFICERS	S.N.C.O's.	O.R's.	TOTAL
R.A.F.	175.	243.	1004.	1422.
W.A.A.F.	10.	10.	410.	430.

AFFILIATED AIRFIELDS : Church Lawford[Parent]

PRESENT USE [1985] : Industry.

NO: 515.

AIRFIELD NAME: SOUTH CERNEY. OPENED : 1937.
COUNTY : Gloucestershire. CLOSED :
COMMAND : Flying Training.
FORMATION : 23 Grp[South Cerney] GRID REF: P 498197[104]
FUNCTION : Advanced Flying Unit O.S.REF.: SU 056986/163.
: [Pilots]
LOCALITY : 4miles SE of Cirencester.
RAILWAY STN. : Cirencester Town 3.5miles[GWR]

LATITUDE : 51 41 20N. HEIGHT ASL : 350′ LIGHTING : Mk2.
LONGITUDE : 01 55 15W. FLYING CONTROL : Yes. RADIO : QDM.

LANDMARKS DAY. : Flooded gravel pits 1mile S. Cirencester town & large wood 3-5miles N-NW.

LANDMARKS NIGHT : -

OBSTRUCTIONS : Wind pumps 350yds. N of peritrack 40′. One obstruction light 10′ from ground level.

LANDING AREA SURFACE : Steel Matting[Sommerfeld track]

QDM	LENGTH X WIDTH	EXT. TO
190.	975yds.	1600yds.
270.	1075yds.	1850yds.

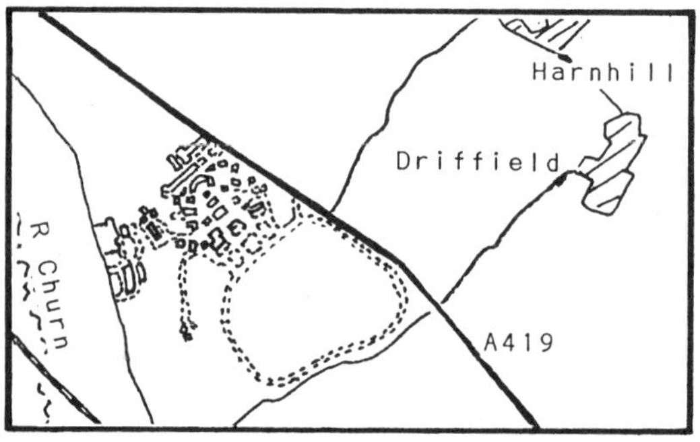

EXTENSIBILITY : Entails diversion of a road & demolition of a farm.
ACCOMMODATION : Permanent.
HANGARS : Type C-3;ARS-1;Bellman-2; Blisters:65′-3;Double 69′-8.
HARDSTANDINGS : -

	OFFICERS	S.N.C.O's.	O.R's.	TOTAL
R.A.F.	212.	112.	1640.	1964.
W.A.A.F.	13.	8.	382.	403.

AFFILIATED AIRFIELDS : Charmy Down & Southrop[Satellites]

PRESENT USE [1985] : Army.

NO: 516.

AIRFIELD NAME: SOUTHAM. OPENED : 1940.
COUNTY : Warwickshire. CLOSED : 1945.
COMMAND : Flying Training.
FORMATION : Miscellaneous A/F. GRID REF: P 881815[83]
FUNCTION : Care & Maintenance. O.S.REF.: SP 430620/163.
:
LOCALITY : 9miles SE of Warwick.
RAILWAY STN. : Long Itchington 2miles[LMS]

LATITUDE : 52 14 57N. HEIGHT ASL : 300′ LIGHTING : None.
LONGITUDE : 01 22 23W. FLYING CONTROL : None.RADIO : QDM.

LANDMARKS DAY. : Cement wks. 2.5miles E. Windmill 2miles E. Cement wks. 1.5miles N.

LANDMARKS NIGHT : Canal, reservoir 2miles N. Canal bends S towards Banbury.

OBSTRUCTIONS : Telephone wires S side, & water tower.

LANDING AREA SURFACE : Grass.

QDM	LENGTH X WIDTH	EXT. TO
ENE-WSW.	800yds.	-
NW-SE.	600yds.	-

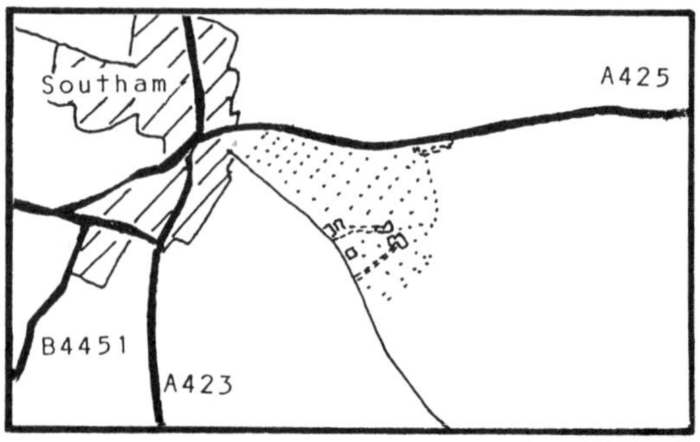

EXTENSIBILITY : None possible.

ACCOMMODATION : Temporary.
HANGARS : Blisters:Standard-4;EO-2.

HARDSTANDINGS : -

	OFFICERS	S.N.C.O's.	O.R's.	TOTAL
R.A.F.	-	-	69.	69.
W.A.A.F.	-	-	-	-

AFFILIATED AIRFIELDS : -

PRESENT USE [1985] : Unspecified.

AIRFIELD NAME: SOUTHEND. OPENED : 1916.
COUNTY : Essex. CLOSED :
COMMAND : Balloon.
FORMATION : 24 Balloon Centre. GRID REF: M 315078[108]
FUNCTION : Storage. O.S.REF.: TQ 872895/178.
:
LOCALITY : 2.5miles N of Southend.
RAILWAY STN. : Southend on Sea[LMS]

LATITUDE : 51 34 15N. HEIGHT ASL : 25' LIGHTING : None.
LONGITUDE : 00 42 08E. FLYING CONTROL : None.RADIO : QDM.

LANDMARKS DAY : R Roach estuary.

LANDMARKS NIGHT : Southend pier.

OBSTRUCTIONS : Hospital chimney N side 600yds. .
Church N side 200yds.

LANDING AREA SURFACE : Grass.

QDM: NE-SW. LENGTH X WIDTH: 1300yds. EXT. TO: -
: E-W. : 1100yds. :
: : :
: : :

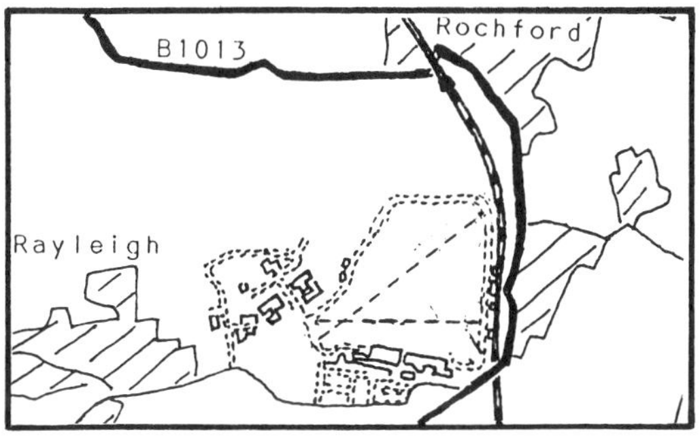

EXTENSIBILITY : Could be extended to 3 strips each 1000x150yds.
Entails demolition of RAF huts & a blister.
ACCOMMODATION : Temporary.
HANGARS : Bellman-2;O Blister-4.

HARDSTANDINGS : TE-36.

R.A.F. : OFFICERS: 89.S.N.C.O's.: 106.O.R's.: 1363.TOTAL: 1558.
W.A.A.F.: " : 4. " : 6. " : 163. " : 173.

AFFILIATED AIRFIELDS : -

PRESENT USE [1985] : Civil Airport[Southend]

NO: 518.

AIRFIELD NAME: SOUTHROP. OPENED : 1940.
COUNTY : Gloucestershire. CLOSED : 1945.
COMMAND : Flying Training.
FORMATION : 23 Grp[South Cerney] GRID REF: P 626239[104]
FUNCTION : Advanced Flying Unit O.S.REF.: TQ 872895/178.
: Pilots[satellite]
LOCALITY : 3miles NW of Lechlade.
RAILWAY STN. : Fairford 2.5miles[GWR]

LATITUDE : 51 43 38N. HEIGHT ASL : 350' LIGHTING : None.
LONGITUDE : 01 44 15W. FLYING CONTROL : None.RADIO : QDM.

LANDMARKS DAY : Fairford church.

LANDMARKS NIGHT : -

OBSTRUCTIONS : -

LANDING AREA SURFACE : Steel Matting[Army track]Grass E-W

QDM: 230. LENGTH X WIDTH: 1020yds. EXT. TO: 1300yds.
: 330. : 930yds. : 1400yds.
: E-W. : 1150yds. : 1100yds.
: : :

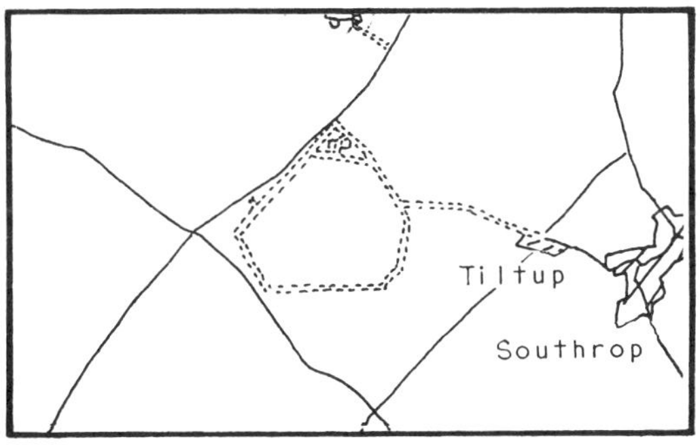

EXTENSIBILITY : Entails closure of 2 minor roads.

ACCOMMODATION : Temporary.
HANGARS : T1-1;Blister 69'-9.

HARDSTANDINGS : -

R.A.F. : OFFICERS: 70.S.N.C.O's.: 180.O.R's.: 570.TOTAL: 820.
W.A.A.F.: " : 4. " : 5. " : 117. " : 126.

AFFILIATED AIRFIELDS : South Cerney[Parent]

PRESENT USE [1985] : Agriculture.

NO: 519.

AIRFIELD NAME: SPANHOE. OPENED : 1943.
COUNTY : Northamptonshire. CLOSED : 1947.
COMMAND : 9th USAAF.
FORMATION : 315th Troop Carrier Grp. GRID REF: F 400170[64]
FUNCTION : Operational. O.S.REF.: SP 935970/141.
:
LOCALITY : 4.5miles E of Uppingham.
RAILWAY STN. : Harringworth[LMS]

LATITUDE : 52 34 00N. HEIGHT ASL : 340' LIGHTING : Mk2.
LONGITUDE : 00 37 00W. FLYING CONTROL : Yes. RADIO : QDM.

LANDMARKS DAY : Corby steel works 4miles SW.

LANDMARKS NIGHT : -

OBSTRUCTIONS : -

LANDING AREA SURFACE : Concrete & tarmac.

QDM: 078. LENGTH X WIDTH: 2000 x 50yds.EXT. TO: 2750yds.
: 205. : 1400 x 50yds. : -
: 141. : 1400 x 50yds. : -
: : :

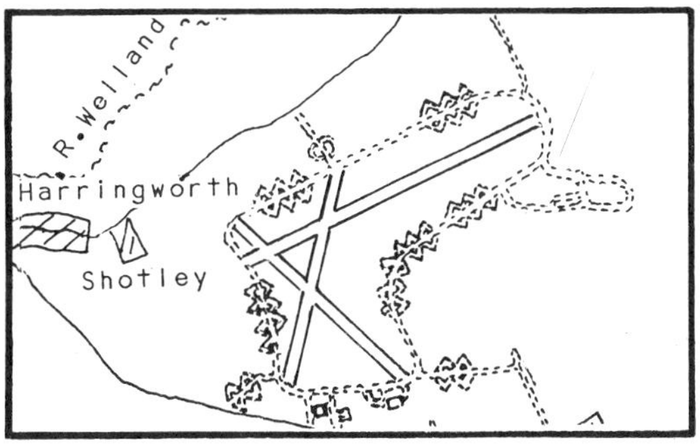

EXTENSIBILITY : -

ACCOMMODATION : Temporary.
HANGARS : T2-2.

HARDSTANDINGS : Eye glass-50.

USAAF. : OFFICERS: Enlisted Men. : TOTAL:

AFFILIATED AIRFIELDS : -

PRESENT USE [1985] : Agriculture.

NO: 520.

AIRFIELD NAME: SPEKE. OPENED : 1930.
COUNTY : Lancashire. CLOSED :
COMMAND : Dept. of Civil Aviation.
FORMATION : - GRID REF: D 876045[43]
FUNCTION : Civil Airport. O.S.REF.: SJ 414833/108.

LOCALITY : 5miles SE of Liverpool.
RAILWAY STN. : Liverpool: Exchange[LMS]Central[CLC]

LATITUDE : 53 20 38N. HEIGHT ASL : 65′ LIGHTING : Mk2.
LONGITUDE : 02 52 45W. FLYING CONTROL : Yes. RADIO : QDM.

LANDMARKS DAY. : R Mersey WNW. Chimneys 180′ 900yds. from A/F.

LANDMARKS NIGHT : R Mersey.

OBSTRUCTIONS : Chimneys 180′ high.

LANDING AREA SURFACE : Tarmac.

QDM	LENGTH X WIDTH	EXT. TO
261.	1660 x 50yds.	-
170.	1030yds.	-
221.	1400 x 50yds.	-

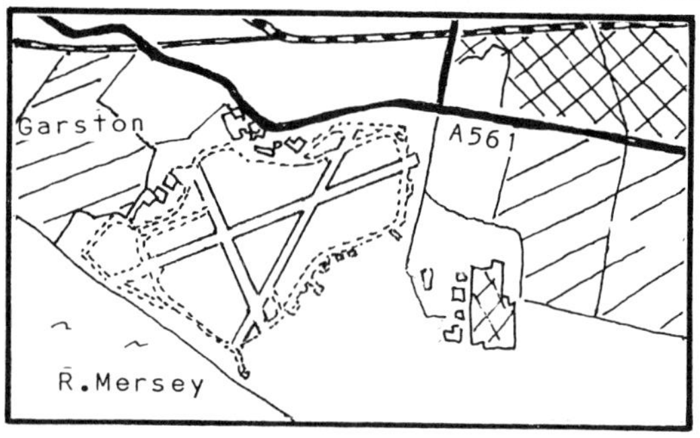

EXTENSIBILITY : -

ACCOMMODATION : Temporary.
HANGARS : Bellman-2;O Blister-6.

HARDSTANDINGS : -

	OFFICERS	S.N.C.O's.	O.R's.	TOTAL
R.A.F.	52.	25.	651.	728.
W.A.A.F.	"	6.	4.	176.	186.

AFFILIATED AIRFIELDS : -

PRESENT USE [1985] : Civil Airport[Liverpool]

NO: 521.

AIRFIELD NAME: SPILSBY. OPENED : 1943.
COUNTY : Lincolnshire. CLOSED : 1958.
COMMAND : Bomber.
FORMATION : 5 Grp[Morton Hall] GRID REF: F 915840[48]
FUNCTION : Operational. O.S.REF.: TF 450645/122.

LOCALITY : 3miles E of Spilsby.
RAILWAY STN. : Firsby Junction 1mile[LNER]

LATITUDE : 53 09 45N. HEIGHT ASL : 33′ LIGHTING : Mk2.
LONGITUDE : 00 10 15E. FLYING CONTROL : Yes. RADIO : QDM.

LANDMARKS DAY. : Firsby Junction[LNER]

LANDMARKS NIGHT : Red obstruction light on Gunby Hall when "outer circuit" is on.

OBSTRUCTIONS : Gunby Hall. CHL masts 240′ high. church at Halton Holegate 85′

LANDING AREA SURFACE : Concrete.

QDM	LENGTH X WIDTH	EXT. TO
050.	1400 x 50yds.	1900yds.
110.	2000 x 50yds.	3000yds.
205.	2000 x 50yds.	-

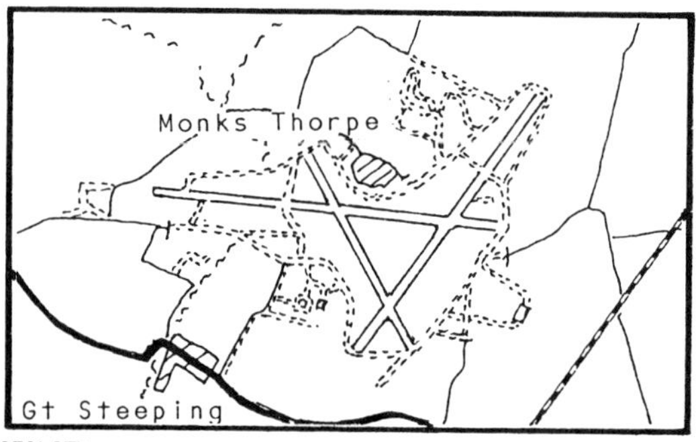

EXTENSIBILITY : -

ACCOMMODATION : Temporary.
HANGARS : T2-2;B1-1.

HARDSTANDINGS : Frying pan-15;Loop-19.

	OFFICERS	S.N.C.O's.	O.R's.	TOTAL
R.A.F.	112.	372.	1026.	1510.
W.A.A.F.	12.	20.	140.	172.

AFFILIATED AIRFIELDS : East Kirkby[55 Base]

PRESENT USE [1985] : Disused.

NO: 522.

AIRFIELD NAME: SPITTLEGATE. OPENED : 1916.
COUNTY : Lincolnshire. CLOSED :
COMMAND : Flying Training.
FORMATION : 21 Grp[Spittlegate] GRID REF: F 406543[55]
FUNCTION : Advanced Flying Unit Pilots. O.S.REF.: SK 935342/130.
LOCALITY : 1.75miles E of Grantham.
RAILWAY STN. : Grantham[LNER]

LATITUDE : 52 54 00N. HEIGHT ASL : 415′ LIGHTING : None.
LONGITUDE : 00 36 00W. FLYING CONTROL : Yes. RADIO : QDM.

LANDMARKS DAY. : Belvoir Castle 7miles W.

LANDMARKS NIGHT : Grantham station & marshalling yards, LNER.

OBSTRUCTIONS : -

LANDING AREA SURFACE : Steel Matting[Sommerfeld track]NE-SW Grass.

QDM	LENGTH X WIDTH	EXT. TO
290.	1160yds.	3000yds.
230.	1300yds.	2000yds.
NE-SW.	1500yds.	2000yds.

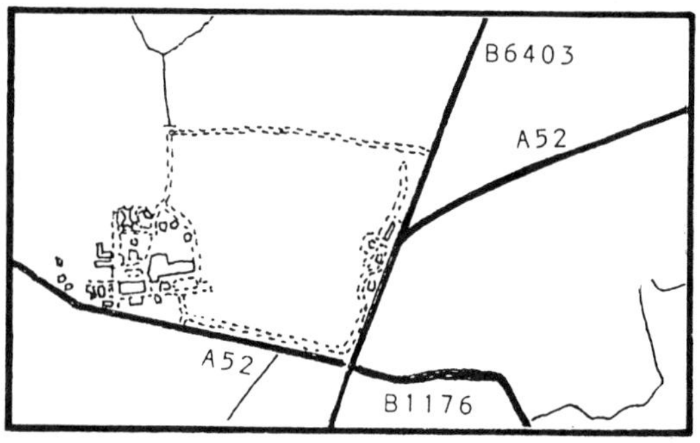

EXTENSIBILITY : Entails diversion of a road & demolition of a number of land settlement cottages.
ACCOMMODATION : Permanent.
HANGARS : Bellman-5;172x84x22′-5;177x102x28′-1; Blister:69′-7;65′-1.
HARDSTANDINGS : -

	OFFICERS	S.N.C.O's.	O.R's.	TOTAL
R.A.F.	255.	318.	939.	1512.
W.A.A.F.	15.	6.	448.	469.

AFFILIATED AIRFIELDS : Harlaxton[RLG]

PRESENT USE [1985] : Army.

NO: 523.

AIRFIELD NAME: SQUIRES GATE. OPENED : 1909.
COUNTY : Lancashire. CLOSED :
COMMAND : Coastal.
FORMATION : 17 Grp[Edinburgh] GRID REF: D 790527[29]
FUNCTION : General Reconnaisance O.S.REF.: SD 317311/102.
: School.
LOCALITY : 1mile SSE of Blackpool.
RAILWAY STN. : Squires Gate[LMS]

LATITUDE : 53 46 15N. HEIGHT ASL : 33′ LIGHTING : Mk2.
LONGITUDE : 03 02 00W. FLYING CONTROL : Yes. RADIO : QDM.

LANDMARKS DAY. : Blackpool Tower. Coastline. R Ribble.

LANDMARKS NIGHT : Coastline.

OBSTRUCTIONS : Blackpool Tower 520′.Smoke stack SW 625yds. Vickers factory NE boundary. House NNE 45yds. Houses NE 190yds.,E 350yds.

LANDING AREA SURFACE : Sand bitumen mix.
QDM: 080. LENGTH X WIDTH: 1400 x 50yds.EXT. TO: 1600yds.
: 140. : 1150 x 50yds. : 1200yds.
: 020. : 1100 x 50yds. : 1500yds.

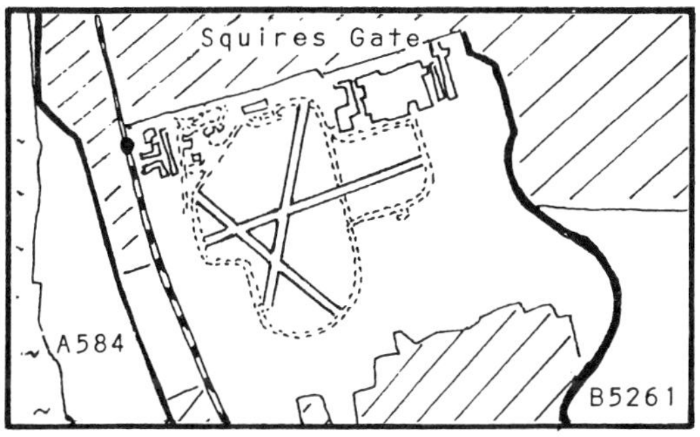

EXTENSIBILITY : Entails very heavy demolition to clear approaches.
ACCOMMODATION : Temporary.
HANGARS : Bellman-4;Boulton Paul[semi-permanent]-2;

HARDSTANDINGS : 100′dia.-16.

R.A.F. : OFFICERS: 58.S.N.C.O′s.: 23.O.R′s.: 357.TOTAL: 438.
W.A.A.F.: " : - " : - " : - " : -

AFFILIATED AIRFIELDS : -

PRESENT USE [1985] : Civil Airport[Blackpool]

NO: 524.

AIRFIELD NAME: ST.ANGELO. OPENED : 1941.
COUNTY : Fermanagh NI. CLOSED : 1947.
COMMAND : Coastal.
FORMATION : 17 Grp[Edinburgh] GRID REF: H 225504[318NI]
FUNCTION : Satellite. O.S.REF.: H 230500.
:
LOCALITY : 4miles S of Enniskillen.
RAILWAY STN. : Eniskillen 4miles[GNI/SL&NC]

LATITUDE : 54 24 00N. HEIGHT ASL : 165′ LIGHTING : None.
LONGITUDE : 07 39 07W. FLYING CONTROL : Yes. RADIO : QDM.

LANDMARKS DAY. : Lough Erne W.

LANDMARKS NIGHT : As day.

OBSTRUCTIONS : Church 250′, 250yds. from end of No.1 R/W. Hills 200′ 200yds. either side of No.1 R/W & 100yds. S of No.2 R/W.

LANDING AREA SURFACE : Concrete.
QDM: 336. LENGTH X WIDTH: 1460 x 50yds.EXT. TO: -
: 058. : 1860 x 50yds. : -

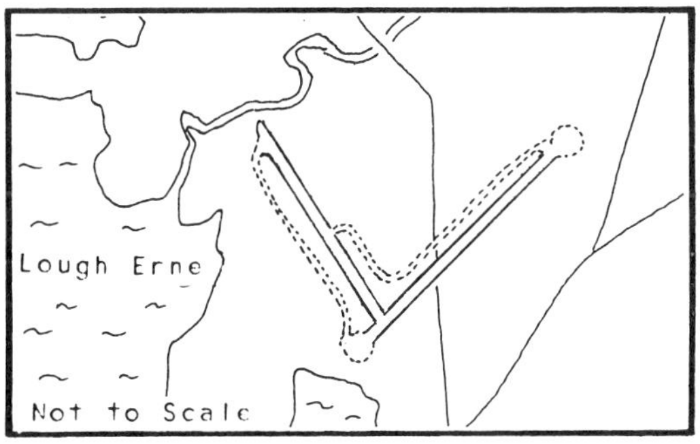

EXTENSIBILITY : None possible.

ACCOMMODATION : Temporary.
HANGARS : T1-3;Blister-8.

HARDSTANDINGS : 60′ dia-26.

R.A.F. : OFFICERS: 288.S.N.C.O′s.: 360.O.R′s.: 2496.TOTAL: 3144.
W.A.A.F.: " : - " : - " : - " :

AFFILIATED AIRFIELDS : Killadeas[Flyingboat base]

PRESENT USE [1985] : Disused.

NO: 525.

AIRFIELD NAME: ST. ATHAN. OPENED : 1939.
COUNTY : Glamorganshire. CLOSED :
COMMAND : Technical Training.
FORMATION : 24 Grp[Hereford] GRID REF: T 445903[109]
FUNCTION : Radio School. O.S.REF.: ST 005685/170.
:
LOCALITY : 3.5miles S of Cowbridge.
RAILWAY STN. : Gileston 2miles[GWR]

LATITUDE : 51 24 30N. HEIGHT ASL : 50′ LIGHTING : None.
LONGITUDE : 03 26 00W. FLYING CONTROL : Yes. RADIO : QDM.

LANDMARKS DAY. : Cement wks. Aberthaw chimneys 40000yds. SW. Water tower 800yds. from centre of A/F.

LANDMARKS NIGHT : -

OBSTRUCTIONS : Water tower on E side 78′.Surrounded by Bellman & other type hangars[not on approaches] Also large workshops.

LANDING AREA SURFACE : Tarmac, concrete & Sommerfeld track. : All 200yds. wide.
QDM: 260. LENGTH X WIDTH: 1200yds. EXT. TO: -
: 350. : 1100yds. : 2000yds.
: 330. : 1000yds. : 1400yds.
: : : 1500yds.

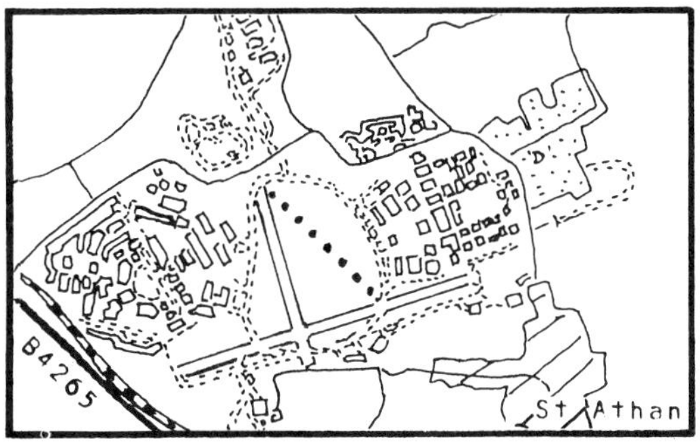

EXTENSIBILITY : Entails road diversion & demolition of 4 WD buildings.
ACCOMMODATION : Permanent.
HANGARS : Bellman-20;Types:D-2;E-6;C-4; Large workshops-4.
HARDSTANDINGS : Access-1;Sommerfeld track-1.

R.A.F. : OFFICERS: 359.S.N.C.O′s.: 775.O.R′s.: 11460TOTAL: 12594.
W.A.A.F.: " : 36. " : 41. " : 1299. " : 1376.

AFFILIATED AIRFIELDS : -

PRESENT USE [1985] : RAF.

NO: 526.

AIRFIELD NAME: ST.DAVIDS. OPENED : 1943.
COUNTY : Pembrokeshire. CLOSED :
COMMAND : Coastal.
FORMATION : 19 Grp[Plymouth] GRID REF: N 236486[88]
FUNCTION : Operational[parent] O.S.REF.: SM 790256/157.
:
LOCALITY : 12miles NW of Haverfordwest.
RAILWAY STN. : Haverfordwest[GWR]

LATITUDE : 51 53 10N. HEIGHT ASL : 250' LIGHTING : Mk2.
LONGITUDE : 05 12 45W. FLYING CONTROL : Yes. RADIO : QDM.

LANDMARKS DAY. : Carn Middi. Carnffard, Pen Berry Hills 3-4miles NW.

LANDMARKS NIGHT : -

OBSTRUCTIONS : Carn Middi 595'ASL. Carnffard 464'ASL. Pen Berry Hills 573' 3-4miles NW.

LANDING AREA SURFACE : Concrete & wood chippings.
QDM: 094. LENGTH X WIDTH: 2000 x 50yds.EXT. TO: -
: 049. : 1400 x 50yds. : 1400yds.
: 140. : 1200 x 50yds. : 1400yds.
: : :

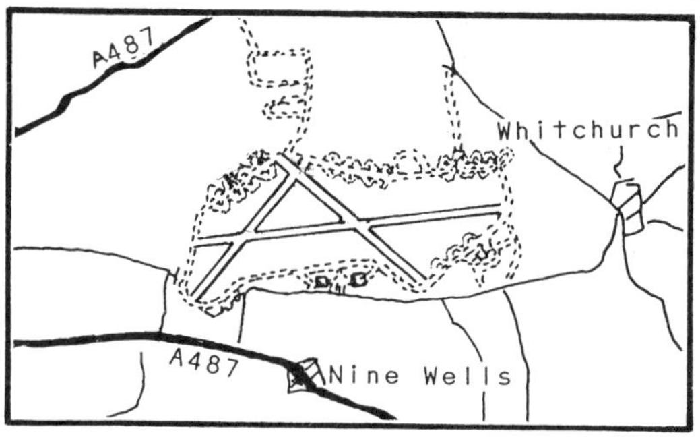

EXTENSIBILITY : Entails considerable work & possible road diversion.
ACCOMMODATION : Temporary.
HANGARS : T2[240x120']-3.

HARDSTANDINGS : Spectacle-30.

R.A.F. : OFFICERS: 195.S.N.C.O's.: 385.O.R's.: 1670.TOTAL: 2250.
W.A.A.F.: " : 10. " : 5. " : 270. " : 285.

AFFILIATED AIRFIELDS : -

PRESENT USE [1985] : RAF.

NO: 527.

AIRFIELD NAME: ST.EVAL. OPENED : 1939.
COUNTY : Cornwall. CLOSED : 1959.
COMMAND : Coastal.
FORMATION : 19 Grp[Plymouth] GRID REF: X 304914[136]
FUNCTION : Operational[parent] O.S.REF.: SW 875685/200.
:
LOCALITY : 6miles NE of Newquay.
RAILWAY STN. : Newquay[GWR]

LATITUDE : 50 28 38N. HEIGHT ASL : 340' LIGHTING : Mk2.
LONGITUDE : 04 59 45W. FLYING CONTROL : Yes. RADIO : QDM.

LANDMARKS DAY. : Church tower N boundary. Trevose Head & light-house 5miles NW. R Camal 6miles N.

LANDMARKS NIGHT : -

OBSTRUCTIONS : Church tower N side 100'high.

LANDING AREA SURFACE : Concrete & tarmac.
QDM: 261. LENGTH X WIDTH: 1980 x 50yds.EXT. TO: 2700yds.
: 201. : 1970 x 50yds. : 2200yds.
: 320. : 1600 x 50yds. : -
: : :

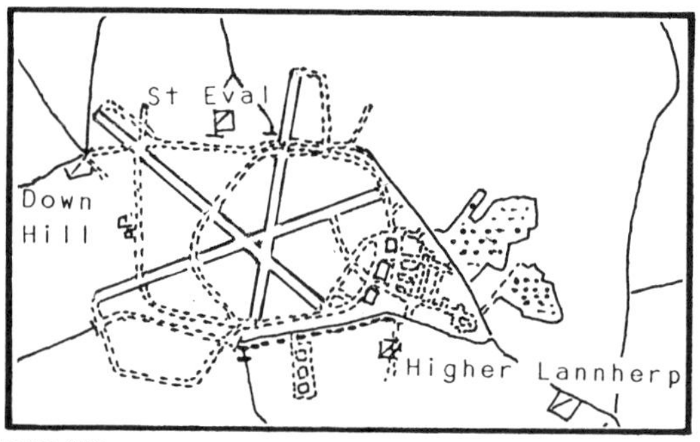

EXTENSIBILITY : -

ACCOMMODATION : Permanent[part]
HANGARS : Type C-3;Bellman-1;T2-2; Blister:45'-2;69'-5.
HARDSTANDINGS : Spectacle-48;circular-18.

R.A.F. : OFFICERS: 18.S.N.C.O's.: 168.O.R's.: 1116.TOTAL: 1302.
W.A.A.F.: " : - " : - " : - " : -

AFFILIATED AIRFIELDS : -

PRESENT USE [1985] : Disused.

NO: 528.

AIRFIELD NAME: ST.MARYS. OPENED : 1939.
COUNTY : Cornwall. CLOSED :
COMMAND : Fighter.
FORMATION : 10 Grp[Rudloe Manor] GRID REF: W 348348.
FUNCTION : Operational[satellite] O.S.REF.: SV 922104/203.
:
LOCALITY : Scillies,.75miles E of Hugh Town.
RAILWAY STN. : Penzance[GWR]

LATITUDE : 49 54 45N. HEIGHT ASL : 100' LIGHTING : None.
LONGITUDE : 06 17 28W. FLYING CONTROL : None.RADIO : QDM.

LANDMARKS DAY. : Largest Isle in Scillies Group.

LANDMARKS NIGHT : -

OBSTRUCTIONS : -

LANDING AREA SURFACE : Grass.
QDM: NE-SW. LENGTH X WIDTH: 666yds. EXT. TO: -
: N-S. : 600yds. : -
: NW-SE. : 593yds. : -
: : :

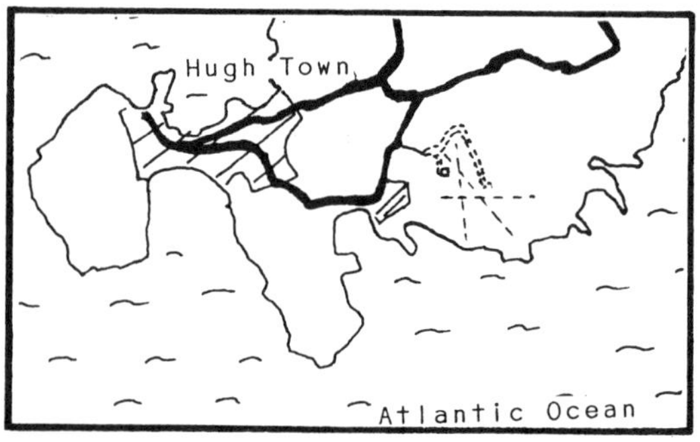

EXTENSIBILITY : None possible.

ACCOMMODATION : Temporary.
HANGARS : -

HARDSTANDINGS : 2.

R.A.F. : OFFICERS: 5.S.N.C.O's.: - O.R's.: 73.TOTAL: 78.
W.A.A.F.: " : - " : - " : - " : -

AFFILIATED AIRFIELDS : -

PRESENT USE [1985] : Civil Airport[Isles of Scilly]

NO: 529.

AIRFIELD NAME: ST.MAWGAN. OPENED : 1943.
COUNTY : Cornwall. CLOSED :
COMMAND : Transport.
FORMATION : 44 Grp[Gloucester] GRID REF: X 302873[143]
FUNCTION : Airport. O.S.REF.: SW 870646/200.
:
LOCALITY : 3.5miles NE of Newquay.
RAILWAY STN. : Newquay[GWR]

LATITUDE : 50 26 25N. HEIGHT ASL : 330′ LIGHTING : Mk2.
LONGITUDE : 05 00 30W. FLYING CONTROL : Yes. RADIO : QDM.

LANDMARKS DAY. : China clay refuse heaps showing white SE 4.5miles. Newquay SW 3miles. St.Eval to N.

LANDMARKS NIGHT : 4 illuminated radio masts in the form of a square with red obstruction lights 1500yds.S.

OBSTRUCTIONS : 4 radio masts & water tower 390′high S.

LANDING AREA SURFACE : Concrete.

QDM	LENGTH X WIDTH	EXT. TO
080.	2000 x 50yds.	3000yds.
140.	3000 x 100yds.	3400yds.
010.	1400 x 50yds.	-

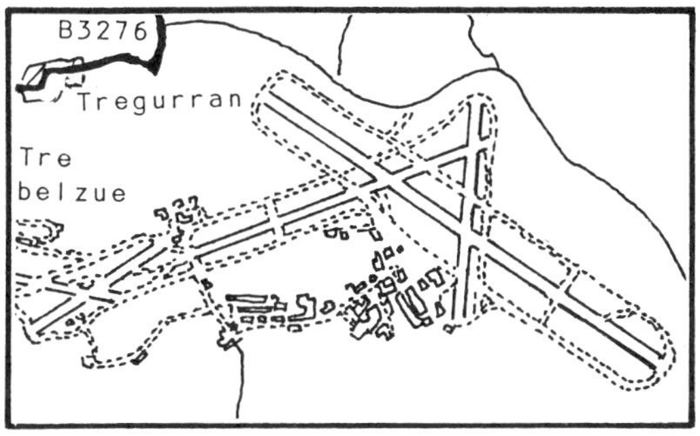

EXTENSIBILITY : -

ACCOMMODATION : Temporary.
HANGARS : T2-2;B1-2.

HARDSTANDINGS : Loop-60.

	OFFICERS	S.N.C.O′s.	O.R′s.	TOTAL
R.A.F.	132.	98.	1915.	2145.
W.A.A.F.	12.	8.	360.	380.

AFFILIATED AIRFIELDS : -

PRESENT USE [1985] : RAF.

NO: 530.

AIRFIELD NAME: ST.MERRYN. OPENED : 1940.
COUNTY : Cornwall. CLOSED : 1956.
COMMAND : RN.
FORMATION : HMS Vulture. GRID REF: X 320950[136]
FUNCTION : Operational Training School. O.S.REF.: SW 888715/200.
LOCALITY : 2.5miles SSW of Padstow.
RAILWAY STN. : Padstow[SR]

LATITUDE : 50 30 20N. HEIGHT ASL : 260′ LIGHTING : None.
LONGITUDE : 04 58 35W. FLYING CONTROL : Yes. RADIO : QDM.

LANDMARKS DAY. : Padstow Bay & mouth of R Camel.

LANDMARKS NIGHT : -

OBSTRUCTIONS : Ground 420′ 3.5miles ESE, 345′ 2miles SSE.

LANDING AREA SURFACE : Tarmac.

QDM	LENGTH X WIDTH	EXT. TO
014-194.	1000 x 30yds.	-
056-236.	1000 x 50yds.	-
105-285.	1030 x 30yds.	-
147-327.	1270 x 30yds.	-

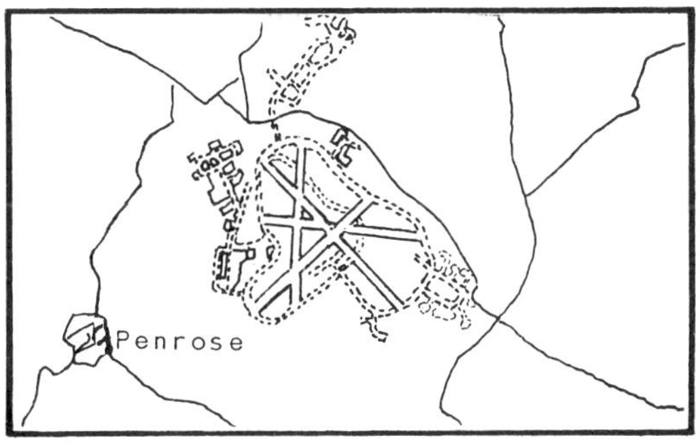

EXTENSIBILITY : -

ACCOMMODATION : Temporary.
HANGARS : Sqdn:60x70′-9;60x84′-6;185x105′-1; Storage:60x70′-9;60x84′-6.

HARDSTANDINGS : 7.

	OFFICERS	Chiefs/POs/Ratings.	TOTAL
R.N.	181.	1196.	1377.
W.R.N.S.	13.	502.	515.

AFFILIATED AIRFIELDS : -

PRESENT USE [1985] : Private flying.

NO: 531.

AIRFIELD NAME: STANSTEAD. OPENED : 1943.
COUNTY : Essex. CLOSED :
COMMAND : USSTAFE.
FORMATION : Air Service Command. GRID REF: L 983418[96]
FUNCTION : Air Depot. O.S.REF.: TL 538228/167.
:
LOCALITY : 3miles NE of Bishop Stortford.
RAILWAY STN. : Stanstead[LNER]

LATITUDE : 51 52 53N. HEIGHT ASL : 328′ LIGHTING : Mk2.
LONGITUDE : 00 13 45E. FLYING CONTROL : Yes. RADIO : QDM.

LANDMARKS DAY. : Glass greenhouses 2miles NW of A/F at Stanstead. Bishop Stortford 3miles W.

LANDMARKS NIGHT : -

OBSTRUCTIONS : -

LANDING AREA SURFACE : Concrete & tarmac.

QDM	LENGTH X WIDTH	EXT. TO
243.	2000 x 50yds.	3000yds.
190.	1400 x 50yds.	2550yds.
134.	1400 x 50yds.	2300yds.

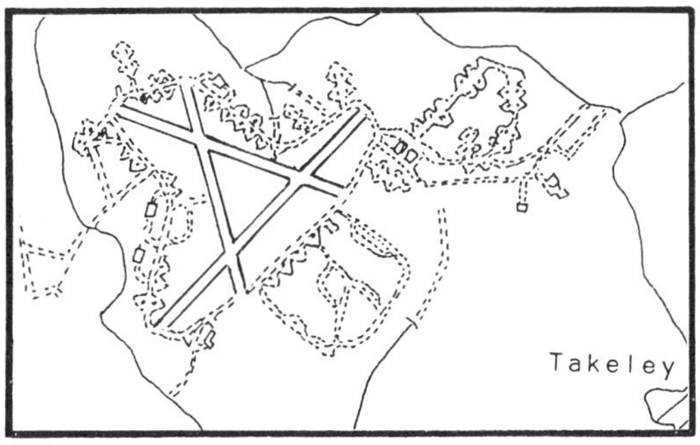

EXTENSIBILITY : Entails minor road diversion only.

ACCOMMODATION : Yemporary.
HANGARS : T2-4.

HARDSTANDINGS : Circular-56.

	OFFICERS	Enlisted Men.	TOTAL
USAAF.	417.	2241.	2658.

AFFILIATED AIRFIELDS : -

PRESENT USE [1985] : Civil Airport[London Stansted]

AIRFIELD NAME: STANTON HARCOURT. OPENED : 1940.
COUNTY : Oxfordshire. CLOSED : 1946.
COMMAND : Bomber.
FORMATION : 91 Grp[Abingdon] GRID REF: P 853250[105]
FUNCTION : Operational Training O.S.REF.: SP 410040/164.
: Unit[satellite]
LOCALITY : 5.5miles W of Oxford.
RAILWAY STN. : Eynsham 3miles[GWR]

LATITUDE : 51 44 30N. HEIGHT ASL : 230′ LIGHTING : Mk2.
LONGITUDE : 01 24 30W. FLYING CONTROL : Yes. RADIO : QDM.

LANDMARKS DAY. : Oxford 264degrees 7miles.

LANDMARKS NIGHT : -

OBSTRUCTIONS : Wytham Hill 539′ 3miles NE.

LANDING AREA SURFACE : Tarmac.
QDM: 056. LENGTH X WIDTH: 1600 x 50yds.EXT. TO: 2500yds.
: 177. : 1100 x 50yds. : 1400yds.
: 117. : 1100 x 50yds. : 1300yds.

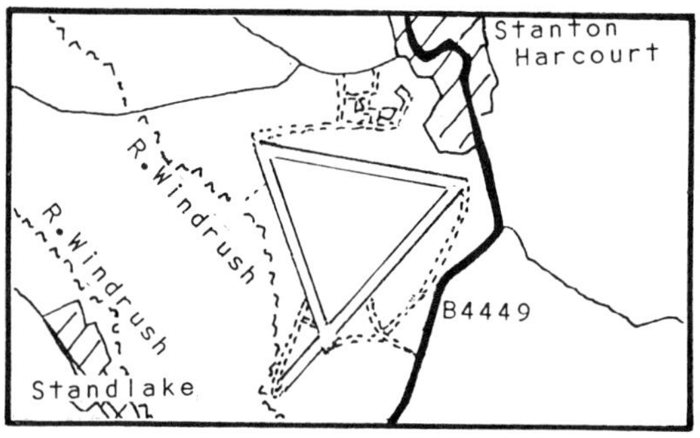

EXTENSIBILITY : Entails diversion of a minor road & demo-lition of 2 houses with outbuildings.
ACCOMMODATION : Temporary.
HANGARS : T2-1;B1-1.

HARDSTANDINGS : Heavy bomber-27.

R.A.F. : OFFICERS: 46.S.N.C.O′s.: 164.O.R′s.: 509.TOTAL: 719.
W.A.A.F.: " : 3. " : - " : 98. " : 101.

AFFILIATED AIRFIELDS : Abingdon[Parent]

PRESENT USE [1985] : Gravel extraction.

AIRFIELD NAME: STAPLEFORD TAWNEY. OPENED : 1934.
COUNTY : Essex. CLOSED :
COMMAND : Fighter.
FORMATION : 11 Grp[Uxbridge] GRID REF: L 930160[107]
FUNCTION : Forward Airfield. O.S.REF.: TL 493972/177.
:
LOCALITY : 5miles N of Romford.
RAILWAY STN. : Theydon Bois .25miles[LNER]

LATITUDE : 51 39 00N. HEIGHT ASL : 103′ LIGHTING : None.
LONGITUDE : 00 08 30E. FLYING CONTROL : None.RADIO : QDM.

LANDMARKS DAY. : W/T masts at North Weald 5miles N.

LANDMARKS NIGHT : -

OBSTRUCTIONS : -

LANDING AREA SURFACE : Grass.
QDM: E-W. LENGTH X WIDTH: 800yds. EXT. TO: -
: NE-SW. : 1133yds. : -

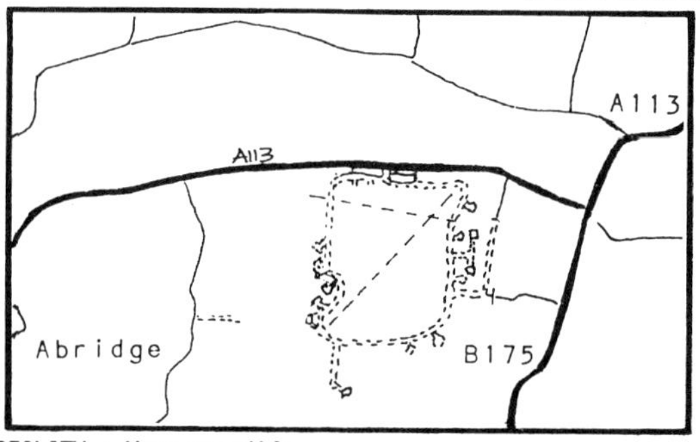

EXTENSIBILITY : None possible.

ACCOMMODATION : Temporary.
HANGARS : Civil-1;EO Blister-4.

HARDSTANDINGS : 6.

R.A.F. : OFFICERS: 33.S.N.C.O′s.: 68.O.R′s.: 731.TOTAL: 832.
W.A.A.F.: " : 2. " : 4. " : 40. " : 46.

AFFILIATED AIRFIELDS : North Weald[Sector]

PRESENT USE [1985] : Private flying.

AIRFIELD NAME: STAPLEHURST. OPENED : 1943.
COUNTY : Kent. CLOSED : 1944.
COMMAND : Fighter.
FORMATION : 11 Grp[Uxbridge] GRID REF: R 248620[126]
FUNCTION : Advanced Landing Ground.O.S.REF.: TQ 808433/188.
: [De-requisitioned]
LOCALITY : 8miles SSE of Maidstone.
RAILWAY STN. : Staplehurst[SR]

LATITUDE : 51 09 38N. HEIGHT ASL : 100′ LIGHTING : None.
LONGITUDE : 00 35 00E. FLYING CONTROL : None.RADIO : QDM.

LANDMARKS DAY. : -

LANDMARKS NIGHT : -

OBSTRUCTIONS : -

LANDING AREA SURFACE : Steel Matting[Sommerfeld track]
QDM: 100. LENGTH X WIDTH: 1400yds. EXT. TO: -
: 010. : 1100yds. : -

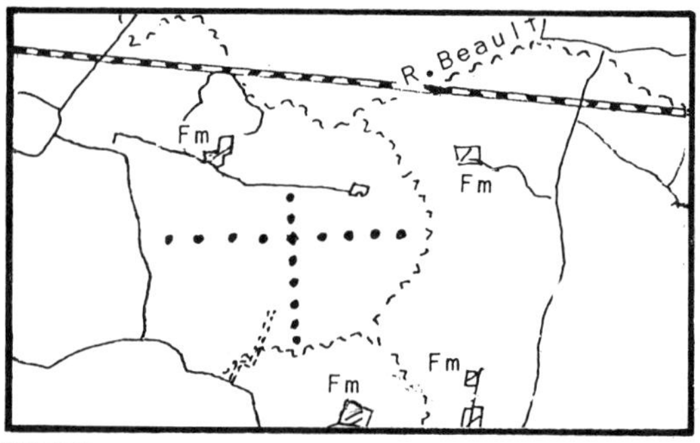

EXTENSIBILITY : -

ACCOMMODATION : Tented camp.
HANGARS : -

HARDSTANDINGS : Sommerfeld Track-70.

R.A.F. : OFFICERS: - S.N.C.O′s.: - O.R′s.: - TOTAL: -
W.A.A.F.: " : - " : - " : - " : -

AFFILIATED AIRFIELDS : -

PRESENT USE [1985] : Unspecified.

NO: 535.

AIRFIELD NAME: STAVERTON. OPENED : 1936.
COUNTY : Gloucestershire. CLOSED :
COMMAND : Flying Training.
FORMATION : 25 Grp[Market Drayton] GRID REF: P 334424[92]
FUNCTION : Advanced Flying Unit O.S.REF.: SO 887218/162-3.
: Observers.
LOCALITY : 4miles W of Cheltenham.
RAILWAY STN. : Gloucester or Cheltenham[GWR & LMS]

LATITUDE : 51 53 38N. HEIGHT ASL : 85′ LIGHTING : None.
LONGITUDE : 02 10 00W. FLYING CONTROL : Yes. RADIO : QDM.

LANDMARKS DAY. : Churchdown Hill 600′ 2miles SW. RSevern 4miles NW.

LANDMARKS NIGHT : Lights of Gloucester & Cheltenham.

OBSTRUCTIONS : Rising ground immediately on E boundary.

LANDING AREA SURFACE : Concrete & tarmac.
QDM: 210. LENGTH X WIDTH: 1000 x 50yds.EXT. TO: 1200yds.
: 270. : 1000 x 50yds. : -
: 170. : 1000 x 50yds. : -
: : :

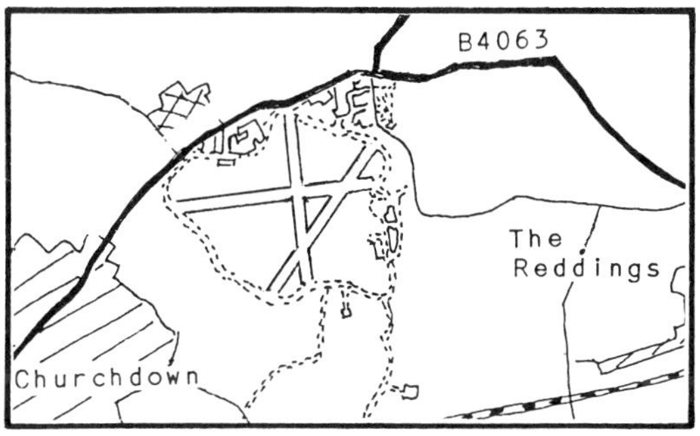

EXTENSIBILITY : Approaches would be improved by demolition of 4 houses & buildings.
ACCOMMODATION : Temporary.
HANGARS : Bellman-6;MAP Bellman-1;EO Blister-1.

HARDSTANDINGS : Hangar apron 300x80′;hardfloors of EO Blisters-12.

R.A.F. : OFFICERS: 36.S.N.C.O′s.: 122.O.R′s.: 421.TOTAL: 579.
W.A.A.F.: " : 4. " : 4. " : 315. " : 323.

AFFILIATED AIRFIELDS : Moreton Valence[Satellite]

PRESENT USE [1985] : Civil Airport[Gloucester/Cheltenham]

NO: 536.

AIRFIELD NAME: STEEPLE MORDEN. OPENED : 1940.
COUNTY : Cambridgeshire. CLOSED : 1946.
COMMAND : 8th USAAF.
FORMATION : 355th Fighter Grp. GRID REF: L 750605[85]
FUNCTION : Operational. O.S.REF.: TL 300420.
:
LOCALITY : 3.5miles W of Royston.
RAILWAY STN. : Ashwell & Morden 2.5miles[LNER]

LATITUDE : 52 03 34N. HEIGHT ASL : 168′ LIGHTING : Mk2.
LONGITUDE : 00 06 00W. FLYING CONTROL : Yes. RADIO : QDM.

LANDMARKS DAY. : Morden Grange plantation 1mile S of A/F.

LANDMARKS NIGHT : Railway running NE-SW 2miles S of A/F.

OBSTRUCTIONS : -

LANDING AREA SURFACE : Concrete & wood chippings.
QDM: 220. LENGTH X WIDTH: 1600 x 50yds.EXT. TO: -
: 160. : 1100 x 50yds. : 2000yds.
: 280. : 1075 x 50yds. : 4000yds.
: : :

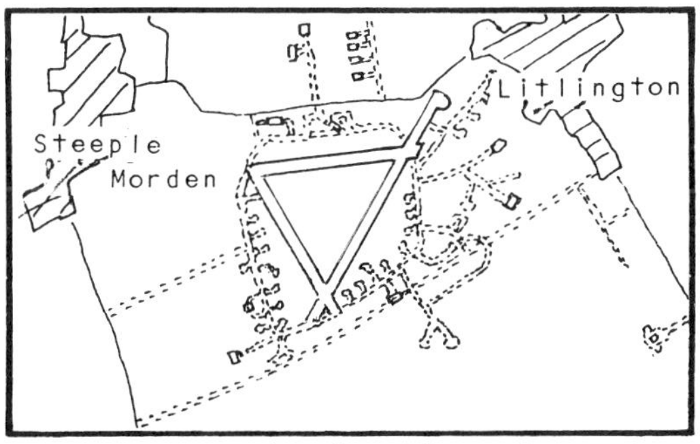

EXTENSIBILITY : Entails diversion of 2 secondary roads & demolition of a large block of houses.
ACCOMMODATION : Temporary.
HANGARS : T2-1;Blister-9.

HARDSTANDINGS : Concrete-80.

USAAF. : OFFICERS: 210. Enlisted Men. : 1749.TOTAL: 1959.
:

AFFILIATED AIRFIELDS : -

PRESENT USE [1985] : Agriculture.

NO: 537.

AIRFIELD NAME: STOKE ORCHARD. OPENED : 1941.
COUNTY : Gloucestershire. CLOSED : 1945.
COMMAND : Flying Training.
FORMATION : 23 Grp[South Cerney] GRID REF: P 376482[92]
FUNCTION : Glider Training Unit. O.S.REF.: SO 928275.
:
LOCALITY : 3.5miles NNW of Gloucester.
RAILWAY STN. : Cleeve.25miles[LMS]

LATITUDE : 51 56 45N. HEIGHT ASL : 100′ LIGHTING : None.
LONGITUDE : 02 06 15W. FLYING CONTROL : None.RADIO : QDM.

LANDMARKS DAY. : Cheltenham-Worcester railway W side. Cheltenham 3.5miles 160degrees.

LANDMARKS NIGHT : -

OBSTRUCTIONS : -

LANDING AREA SURFACE : Grass.
QDM: NW-SE. LENGTH X WIDTH: 1200yds. EXT. TO: -
: N-S. : 1100yds. : -
: : :
: : :

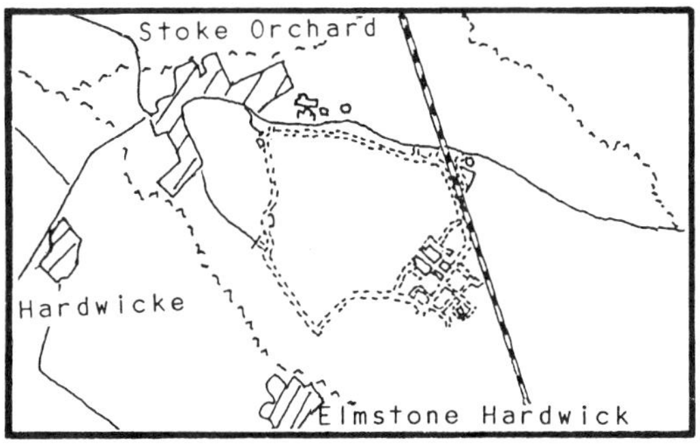

EXTENSIBILITY : Not suitable owing to bad approaches, but one strip of 1700yds. possible.
ACCOMMODATION : Temporary.
HANGARS : Bellman-4;Double 69′-7;Treble 69′-1.

HARDSTANDINGS : -

R.A.F. : OFFICERS: 46.S.N.C.O′s.: 116.O.R′s.: 483.TOTAL: 645.
W.A.A.F.: " : 4. " : 8. " : 189. " : 201.

AFFILIATED AIRFIELDS : Northleach[Satellite]

PRESENT USE [1985] : Unspecified.

NO: 538.

AIRFIELD NAME: STONEY CROSS. OPENED : 1942.
COUNTY : Hampshire. CLOSED : 1948.
COMMAND : Transport.
FORMATION : 116 Wing[Hendon] GRID REF: U 680328[131]
FUNCTION : Parent. O.S.REF.: SU 248121/195.

LOCALITY : 11miles W of Southampton.
RAILWAY STN. : Southampton[SR]

LATITUDE : 50 54 45N. HEIGHT ASL : 373′ LIGHTING : Mk2.
LONGITUDE : 01 39 08W. FLYING CONTROL : Yes. RADIO : QDM.

LANDMARKS DAY. : Jasmine pond.

LANDMARKS NIGHT : -

OBSTRUCTIONS : -

LANDING AREA SURFACE : Concrete & wood chippings.

QDM	LENGTH X WIDTH	EXT. TO
250.	2000 x 50yds.	-
328.	1520 x 50yds.	2230yds.
188.	1400 x 50yds.	-

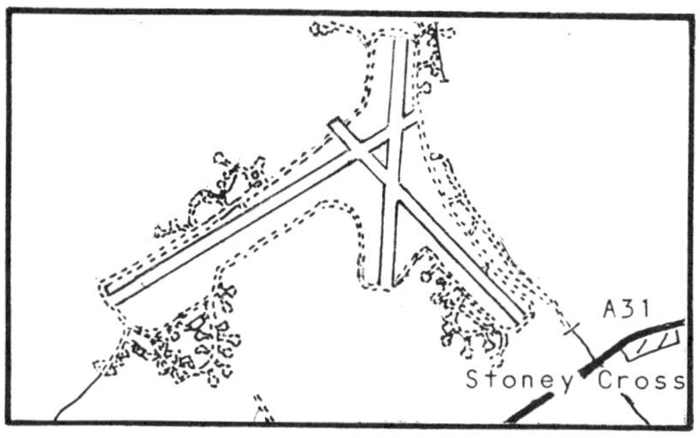

EXTENSIBILITY : Not recommended. Entails diversion of Ringwood-Romsey road.
ACCOMMODATION : Temporary.
HANGARS : T2-1;T2[14 bay]-1;Gliding T2-2;Blister-6.

HARDSTANDINGS : Frying pan:100′-21;125′-30; special loop-11.

	OFFICERS	S.N.C.O′s.	O.R′s.	TOTAL
R.A.F.	164.	450.	1437.	2051.
W.A.A.F.	12.	8.	375.	395.

AFFILIATED AIRFIELDS : -

PRESENT USE [1985] : Forestry Commission.

NO: 539.

AIRFIELD NAME: STORMY DOWN. OPENED : 1940.
COUNTY : Glamorganshire. CLOSED : 1945.
COMMAND : Flying Training.
FORMATION : 54 Grp[Sunningdale] GRID REF: O 285014[109]
FUNCTION : Initial Training Wing [Pilot] O.S.REF.: SS 842794/170.
LOCALITY : 5.75miles W of Bridgend.
RAILWAY STN. : Pyle[GWR]

LATITUDE : 51 30 08N. HEIGHT ASL : 350′ LIGHTING : None.
LONGITUDE : 03 40 00W. FLYING CONTROL : None. RADIO : QDM.

LANDMARKS DAY. : Kenfig Pool 2.5miles NW of A/F. Portcawl town 1.75miles SW of A/F.

LANDMARKS NIGHT : Kenfig Pool 2.5miles NW of A/F. Portcawl Point 2miles SW.

OBSTRUCTIONS : High ground[average 50′] with trees about .5miles from SE boundary.

LANDING AREA SURFACE : Grass.

QDM	LENGTH X WIDTH	EXT. TO
N-W.	980yds.	-
N-S.	1010yds.	-
NE-SW.	1000yds.	-
SE-NW.	1000yds.	-
E-W.	880yds.	-

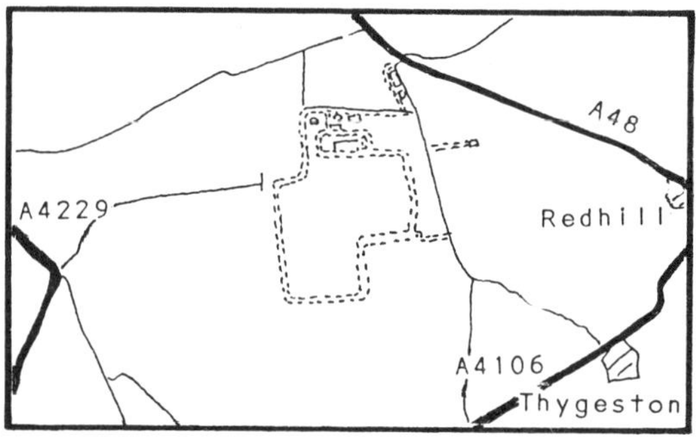

EXTENSIBILITY : None possible.

ACCOMMODATION : Temporary.
HANGARS : Bellman-4;SP-1;Type F-1; Bessoneau-1;EO Blister-5.
HARDSTANDINGS : Hangar apron:200x100′& 600x90′ approx.

	OFFICERS	S.N.C.O′s.	O.R′s.	TOTAL
R.A.F.	65.	204.	1375.	1644.
W.A.A.F.	6.	30.	497.	533.

AFFILIATED AIRFIELDS : -

PRESENT USE [1985] : Gliding.

NO: 540.

AIRFIELD NAME: STORNOWAY. OPENED : 1941.
COUNTY : Hebrides. CLOSED :
COMMAND : Coastal.
FORMATION : 18 Grp[Pitreavie Castle] GRID REF: B 987575[14Scot]
FUNCTION : Parent. O.S.REF.: NB 459932/8.

LOCALITY : 2.5miles NE of Stornoway.
RAILWAY STN. : Kyle of Lochalsh[LMS]

LATITUDE : 58 13 06N. HEIGHT ASL : 13′ LIGHTING : Mk2.
LONGITUDE : 06 20 00W. FLYING CONTROL : Yes. RADIO : QDM.

LANDMARKS DAY. : Isthmus to Eye Peninsula .5miles E. Town of Stornoway 2miles M. Memorial tower 2miles WNW.

LANDMARKS NIGHT : As day.

OBSTRUCTIONS : Hill 55′ ASL at E end of E-W runway. Radar masts 5miles NE 500′; MF/DF station masts.

LANDING AREA SURFACE : Tarmac.

QDM	LENGTH X WIDTH	EXT. TO
189.	2000 x 50yds.	3700yds.
254.	1350 x 50yds.	1800yds.
306.	1290 x 50yds.	1700yds.
238.	870 x 50yds.	890yds.

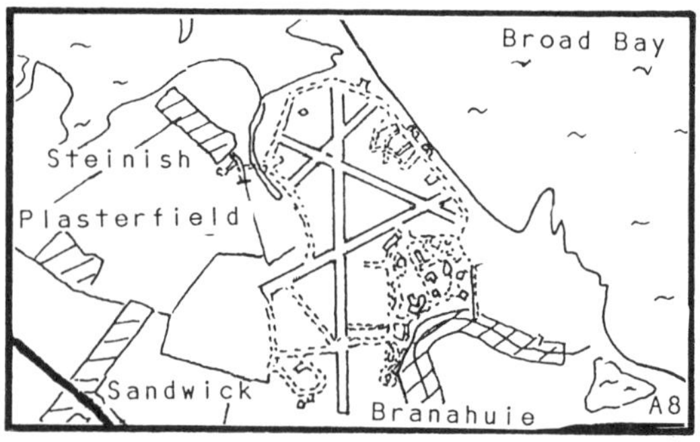

EXTENSIBILITY : -

ACCOMMODATION : Temporary.
HANGARS : T2-10.

HARDSTANDINGS : Circular 100′-5;R/W 238 used for parking A/C only.

	OFFICERS	S.N.C.O′s.	O.R′s.	TOTAL
R.A.F.	150.	190.	1653.	1993.
W.A.A.F.	16.	-	225.	241.

AFFILIATED AIRFIELDS : -

PRESENT USE [1985] : RAF.

NO: 541.

AIRFIELD NAME: STRACATHRO. OPENED : 1941.
COUNTY : Angus. CLOSED : 1946.
COMMAND : Flying Training.
FORMATION : 21 Grp[Spittlegate] GRID REF: P 154850[51Scot]
FUNCTION : Flying Instructor School O.S.REF.: NO 644635/45.
: [satellite]
LOCALITY : 3.25miles NE of Brechin.
RAILWAY STN. : Brechin[LMS]

LATITUDE : 56 45 53N. HEIGHT ASL : 300′ LIGHTING : None.
LONGITUDE : 02 35 00W. FLYING CONTROL : None. RADIO : QDM.

LANDMARKS DAY. : Dums Dish[lake].5miles S. R North Esk 1.25miles N. Brechin 3.5miles SW.

LANDMARKS NIGHT : As day.

OBSTRUCTIONS : Belt of pine trees on NE boundary. Water tower on site .25miles S.

LANDING AREA SURFACE : Grass.
QDM: NE-SW. LENGTH X WIDTH: 1300yds. EXT. TO: -

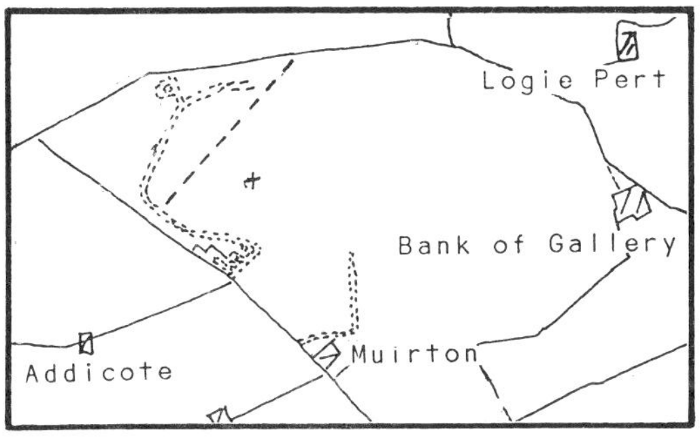

EXTENSIBILITY : -

ACCOMMODATION : Temporary.
HANGARS : Blister 69′-8.

HARDSTANDINGS : -

R.A.F. : OFFICERS: 26. S.N.C.O′s.: 60. O.R′s.: 237. TOTAL: 323.
W.A.A.F.: " : " : " : " :

AFFILIATED AIRFIELDS : Montrose[parent]

PRESENT USE [1985] : Disused.

NO: 542.

AIRFIELD NAME: STRADISHALL. OPENED : 1938.
COUNTY : Suffolk. CLOSED : 1970.
COMMAND : Bomber.
FORMATION : 3 Grp[Exning] GRID REF: M 172700[86]
FUNCTION : Operational[31 Base] O.S.REF.: TL 724512/154.
LOCALITY : 5miles NE Haverhill.
RAILWAY STN. : Haverhill[LNER]

LATITUDE : 52 08 00N. HEIGHT ASL : 382′ LIGHTING : Mk1.
LONGITUDE : 00 30 45E. FLYING CONTROL : Yes. RADIO : QDM.

LANDMARKS DAY. : -

LANDMARKS NIGHT : -

OBSTRUCTIONS : -

LANDING AREA SURFACE : Concrete.

QDM	LENGTH X WIDTH	EXT. TO
250.	2000 X 50yds.	-
320.	1400 X 50yds.	-
040.	1400 X 50yds.	2000yds.

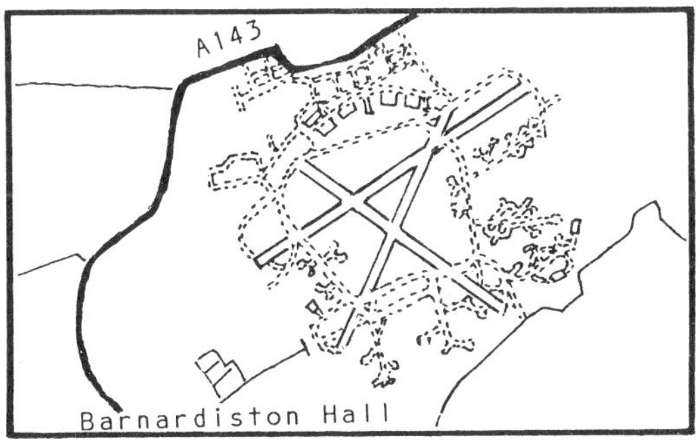

EXTENSIBILITY : -

ACCOMMODATION : Permanent.
HANGARS : Type C-5;T2-3.

HARDSTANDINGS : Heavy bomber-36.

R.A.F. : OFFICERS: 184. S.N.C.O′s.: 659. O.R′s.: 1367. TOTAL: 2210.
W.A.A.F.: " : 10. " : 26. " : 498. " : 534.

AFFILIATED AIRFIELDS : Chedburgh & Wratting Common[Sub-stations]

PRESENT USE [1985] : HM Prison.

NO: 543.

AIRFIELD NAME: STRATFORD. OPENED : 1941.
COUNTY : Warwickshire. CLOSED : 1945.
COMMAND : Bomber.
FORMATION : 91 Grp[Abingdon] GRID REF: P 667720[82]
FUNCTION : Operational Training O.S.REF.: SP 215515/151.
: Unit[satellite]
LOCALITY : 2.75miles SSE of Stratford on Avon.
RAILWAY STN. : Stratford on Avon[GWR & LMS]

LATITUDE : 52 09 38N. HEIGHT ASL : 185′ LIGHTING : Mk2.
LONGITUDE : 01 41 00W. FLYING CONTROL : Yes. RADIO : QDM.

LANDMARKS DAY. : Town of Stratford with R Avon 2.75miles N. R Stour 400yds.W.

LANDMARKS NIGHT : -

OBSTRUCTIONS : Meon Hill 630′ 4.5miles SW; railway E boundary. Water tower 800yds. from runway 320.

LANDING AREA SURFACE : Tarmac.

QDM	LENGTH X WIDTH	EXT. TO
192.	1600 x 50yds.	-
254.	1350 x 50yds.	-
320.	1210 x 50yds.	-

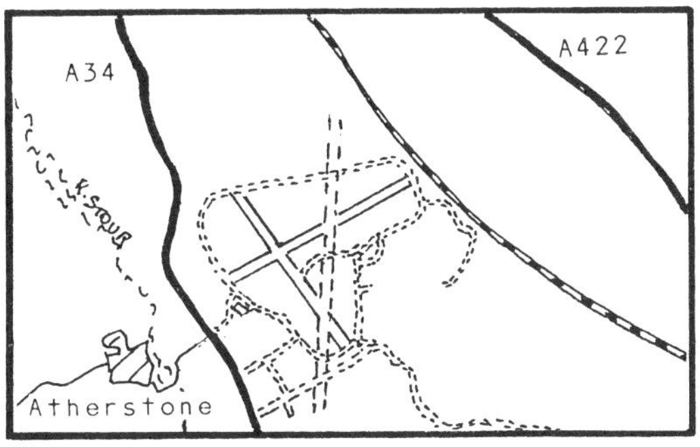

EXTENSIBILITY : None possible.

ACCOMMODATION : Temporary.
HANGARS : T2-1;B1-1.

HARDSTANDINGS : Heavy bomber-27.

R.A.F. : OFFICERS: 47. S.N.C.O′s.: 126. O.R′s.: 1308. TOTAL: 1481.
W.A.A.F.: " : 2. " : 5. " : 147. " : 154.

AFFILIATED AIRFIELDS : Wellesbourne Mountford[Parent]

PRESENT USE [1985] : Unspecified.

NO: 544.

AIRFIELD NAME: STRETTON. OPENED : 1942.
COUNTY : Lancashire. CLOSED : 1958.
COMMAND : RN.
FORMATION : HMS Blackcap. GRID REF: E 108046[44]
FUNCTION : A/C Maintenance Yard. O.S.REF.: SJ 652825/109.

LOCALITY : 3miles SE of Warrington.
RAILWAY STN. : Warrington[LMS]

LATITUDE : 53 20 45N. HEIGHT ASL : 220′ LIGHTING : Naval.
LONGITUDE : 02 31 45W. FLYING CONTROL : Yes. RADIO : QDM.

LANDMARKS DAY. : R Mersey. Warrington-Manchester railway 2.5miles NNW & then E to W. ICI factory at Northwich.

LANDMARKS NIGHT : -

OBSTRUCTIONS : -

LANDING AREA SURFACE : Tarmac.

QDM	LENGTH X WIDTH	EXT. TO
027-207.	1120 x 50yds.	-
097-277.	1600 x 50yds.	-
157-337.	1120 x 50yds.	-

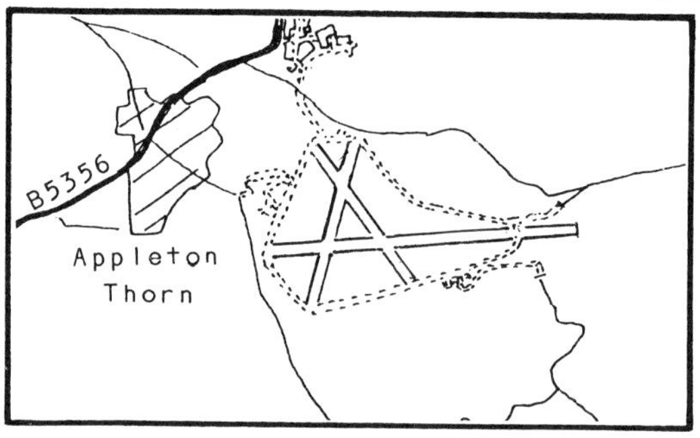

EXTENSIBILITY : -

ACCOMMODATION : Temporary.
HANGARS : 60x70′:Sqdn-4;storage-4.

HARDSTANDINGS : Pens-6;hardstandings-10.

R.N. : OFFICERS: 329. Chiefs/POs/Ratings. : 1016.TOTAL: 1345.
W.R.N.S.: " : 13. " : " : 104. " : 117.

AFFILIATED AIRFIELDS : -

PRESENT USE [1985] : Motorway.

NO: 545.

AIRFIELD NAME: STRUBBY. OPENED : 1944.
COUNTY : Lincolnshire. CLOSED : 1972.
COMMAND : Bomber.
FORMATION : 5 Grp[Morton Hall] GRID REF: A 915003[48]
FUNCTION : Operational. O.S.REF.: TF 450810/122.

LOCALITY : 3.5miles N of Alford.
RAILWAY STN. : Alford Town[LNER]

LATITUDE : 53 18 15N. HEIGHT ASL : 35′ LIGHTING : Mk2.
LONGITUDE : 00 10 45E. FLYING CONTROL : Yes. RADIO : QDM.

LANDMARKS DAY. : Water tower. Maplethorpe 050degrees 4.5miles.

LANDMARKS NIGHT : -

OBSTRUCTIONS : Maltby church tower situated in funnel of runway QDM. 226.

LANDING AREA SURFACE : Concrete & tarmac.

QDM	LENGTH X WIDTH	EXT. TO
086.	2000 x 50yds.	3000yds.
026.	1470 x 50yds.	2000yds.
146.	1576 x 50yds.	2000yds.

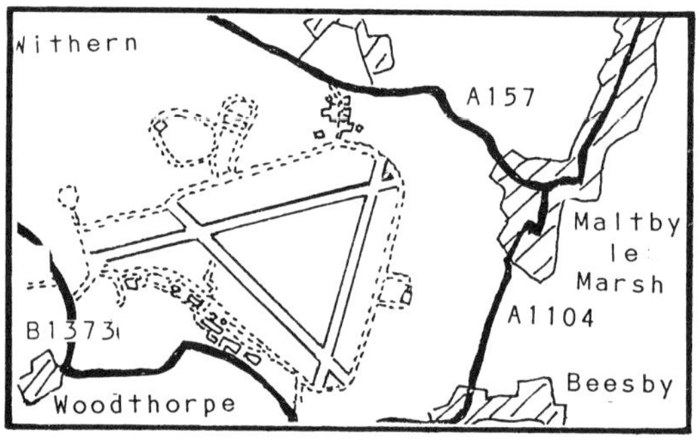

EXTENSIBILITY : Entails road diversion.

ACCOMMODATION : Temporary.
HANGARS : T2-2;B1-1.

HARDSTANDINGS : Loop-36.

R.A.F. : OFFICERS: 112.S.N.C.O′s.: 370.O.R′s.: 1261.TOTAL: 1743.
W.A.A.F.: " : 10. " : 20. " : 339. " : 369.

AFFILIATED AIRFIELDS : East Kirkby[55 Base]

PRESENT USE [1985] : Helicopters.

NO: 546.

AIRFIELD NAME: STURGATE. OPENED : 1944.
COUNTY : Lincolnshire. CLOSED : 1964.
COMMAND : Bomber.
FORMATION : 1 Grp[Bawtry] GRID REF: A 345074[39]
FUNCTION : Operational. O.S.REF.: SK 879878/121.

LOCALITY : 4miles ESE of Gainsborough.
RAILWAY STN. : Gainsborough Central[LNER]

LATITUDE : 53 22 45N. HEIGHT ASL : 55′ LIGHTING : Mk2.
LONGITUDE : 00 40 45W. FLYING CONTROL : Yes. RADIO : QDM.

LANDMARKS DAY. : Fillingham Lake 3miles ESE.

LANDMARKS NIGHT : -

OBSTRUCTIONS : -

LANDING AREA SURFACE : Concrete covered with asphalt.

QDM	LENGTH X WIDTH	EXT. TO
078.	2000 x 50yds.	3200yds.
205.	1400 x 50yds.	2100yds.
141.	1400 x 50yds.	2000yds.

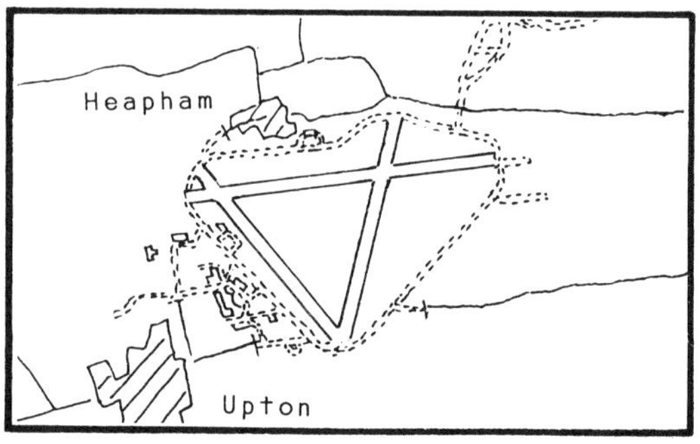

EXTENSIBILITY : Subsoil of clay & it is doubtful if it would stand up to heavy work.
ACCOMMODATION : Temporary.
HANGARS : T2-2;B1-1.

HARDSTANDINGS : Heavy bomber-36.

R.A.F. : OFFICERS: 75.S.N.C.O′s.: 190.O.R′s.: 420.TOTAL: 685.
W.A.A.F.: " : 10. " : 21. " : 255. " : 286.

AFFILIATED AIRFIELDS : Hemswell.

PRESENT USE [1985] : Private flying.

NO: 547.

AIRFIELD NAME: SUDBURY. OPENED : 1944.
COUNTY : Suffolk. CLOSED : 1945.
COMMAND : 8th USAAF.
FORMATION : 486th Bomb Grp. GRID REF: M 344625[86]
FUNCTION : Operational. O.S.REF.: TL 893435/155.
:
LOCALITY : 2miles N of Sudbury.
RAILWAY STN. : Sudbury[LNER]

LATITUDE : 52 03 26N. HEIGHT ASL : 220′ LIGHTING : Mk2.
LONGITUDE : 00 45 45E. FLYING CONTROL : Yes. RADIO : QDM.

LANDMARKS DAY : Large concrete water tower 2.5miles SE.

LANDMARKS NIGHT : -

OBSTRUCTIONS : -

LANDING AREA SURFACE : Concrete & tarmac.

QDM	LENGTH X WIDTH	EXT. TO
250.	2000 x 50yds.	3000yds.
190.	1400 x 50yds.	2000yds.
150.	1400 x 50yds.	1800yds.

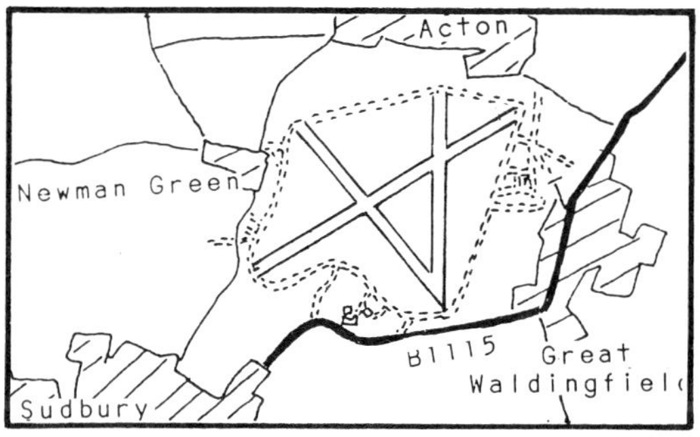

EXTENSIBILITY : Not recommended owing to very heavy demolition & also diversion of moderate importance.
ACCOMMODATION : Temporary.
HANGARS : T2-2.

HARDSTANDINGS : Spectacle-50.

USAAF. : OFFICERS: 443. Enlisted Men. : 2529.TOTAL: 2972.

AFFILIATED AIRFIELDS : -

PRESENT USE [1985] : Agriculture.

NO: 548.

AIRFIELD NAME: SUMBURGH. OPENED : 1936.
COUNTY : Shetlands. CLOSED :
COMMAND : Coastal.
FORMATION : 18 Grp[Pitreavie Castle]GRID REF: U 943309[4Scot]
FUNCTION : Operational parent. O.S.REF.: HU 395105/4.
:
LOCALITY : 1.25miles NNW of Sumburgh Head.
RAILWAY STN. : Aberdeen[LMS & LNER]

LATITUDE : 59 52 45N. HEIGHT ASL : 2′-4″LIGHTING : Mk2.
LONGITUDE : 01 17 13W. FLYING CONTROL : Yes. RADIO : QDM.

LANDMARKS DAY : Fitful & Compass Heads. Sumburgh lighthouse.

LANDMARKS NIGHT : As day.

OBSTRUCTIONS : Hills up to 928′.Pylons 1160′.
Masts up to 685′

LANDING AREA SURFACE : Tarmac.

QDM	LENGTH X WIDTH	EXT. TO
155.	1330 x 50yds.	1830yds.
045.	980 x 50yds.	-
100.	1120 x 50yds.	-

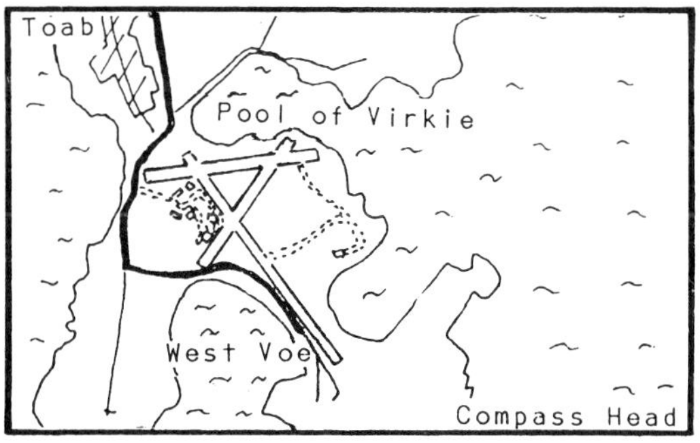

EXTENSIBILITY : -

ACCOMMODATION : Temporary.
HANGARS : Bellman-3.

HARDSTANDINGS : Area of 500x130′ approx.

R.A.F. : OFFICERS: 77.S.N.C.O′s.: 153.O.R′s.: 1091.TOTAL: 1321.
W.A.A.F.: " : - " : - " : - " : -

AFFILIATED AIRFIELDS : -

PRESENT USE [1985] : Civil airport[Shetlands]

NO: 549.

AIRFIELD NAME: SUTTON BRIDGE. OPENED : 1926.
COUNTY : Lincolnshire. CLOSED : 1958.
COMMAND : Flying Training.
FORMATION : 21 Grp[Spittlegate] GRID REF: F 944389[65]
FUNCTION : Advanced Flying Unit O.S.REF.: TF 476194/131.
: Pilots[satellite]
LOCALITY : 7miles NNE of Wisbech.
RAILWAY STN. : Sutton Bridge 1.25miles[LNER]

LATITUDE : 52 45 30N. HEIGHT ASL : 9′ LIGHTING : None.
LONGITUDE : 00 12 00E. FLYING CONTROL : None.RADIO : QDM.

LANDMARKS DAY : Wireless masts 2miles S.

LANDMARKS NIGHT : R Nene along W boundary.

OBSTRUCTIONS : Bank with telephone wires along N boundary.
W/T masts 90′ 2miles S.

LANDING AREA : Steel Matting[NE-SW grass]
SURFACE : 080-American steel planking,130-Sommerfeld Track.

QDM	LENGTH X WIDTH	EXT. TO
080.	1150yds.	2500yds.
130.	800yds.	1400yds.
NE-SW.	1400yds.	-

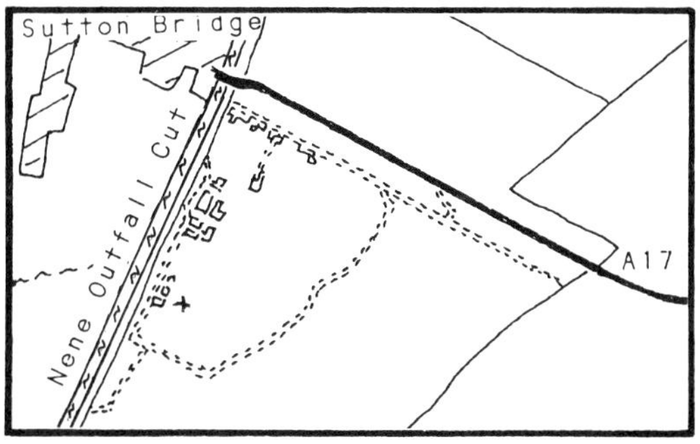

EXTENSIBILITY : Not recommended: entails demolition of 2 bungalows,, 3 cottages, a farm & numerous RAF buildings.
ACCOMMODATION : Permanent[part]
HANGARS : Bellman-2;ARS-1;Blister 69′-12.

HARDSTANDINGS : Tarmac on hardcore-14.

R.A.F. : OFFICERS: 109.S.N.C.O′s.: 110.O.R′s.: 1266.TOTAL: 1485.
W.A.A.F.: " : 6. " : 12. " : 361. " : 379.

AFFILIATED AIRFIELDS : Peterborough[Parent]

PRESENT USE [1985] : Agriculture.

NO: 550.

AIRFIELD NAME: SWANNINGTON. OPENED : 1944.
COUNTY : Norfolk. CLOSED : 1947.
COMMAND : Bomber.
FORMATION : 100 Grp[Bylaugh Hall] GRID REF: G 600390[67]
FUNCTION : Operational. O.S.REF.: TG 140206/133.

LOCALITY : 3miles SE of Reepham.
RAILWAY STN. : Reepham or Cawston[LNER]

LATITUDE : 52 44 30N. HEIGHT ASL : 135' LIGHTING : Mk2.
LONGITUDE : 01 10 15E. FLYING CONTROL : Yes. RADIO : QDM.

LANDMARKS DAY : Lake [15 acres of water] 750yds. 275degrees.

LANDMARKS NIGHT : -

OBSTRUCTIONS : -

LANDING AREA SURFACE : Concrete.

QDM	LENGTH X WIDTH	EXT. TO
277.	2000 x 50yds.	2500yds.
320.	1400 x 50yds.	2000yds.
230.	1400 x 50yds.	2000yds.

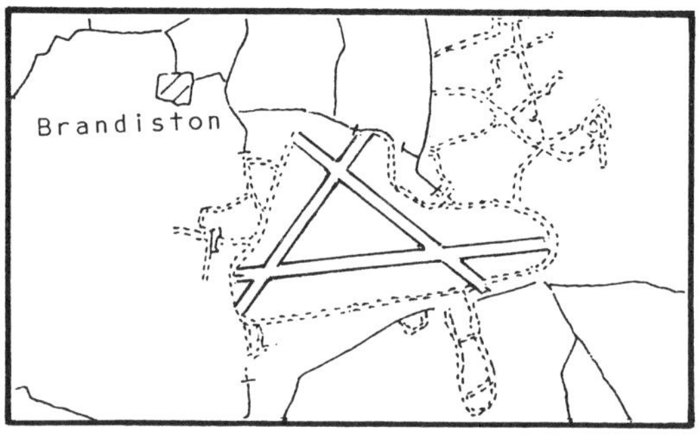

EXTENSIBILITY : Entails extensive demolition of farm buildings, 2 lodges,a pair of cottages, & a small school.
ACCOMMODATION : Temporary.
HANGARS : T2-2;B1-1.

HARDSTANDINGS : Spectacle-36.

	OFFICERS	S.N.C.O's.	O.R's.	TOTAL
R.A.F.	154.	161.	1065.	1380.
W.A.A.F.	10.	21.	248.	279.

AFFILIATED AIRFIELDS : -

PRESENT USE [1985] : Disused.

NO: 551.

AIRFIELD NAME: SWANTON MORLEY. OPENED : 1940.
COUNTY : Norfolk. CLOSED :
COMMAND : Fighter.
FORMATION : 12 Grp[Watnall] GRID REF: G 460367[66]
FUNCTION : Operational. O.S.REF.: TG 002187/132-3.

LOCALITY : 3.5miles N of East Dereham.
RAILWAY STN. : Dereham[LNER]

LATITUDE : 52 43 38N. HEIGHT ASL : 150' LIGHTING : Mk2.
LONGITUDE : 00 58 00E. FLYING CONTROL : Yes. RADIO : QDM.

LANDMARKS DAY : R Wensum W,N & E almost circles A/F. Railway Dereham-Fakenham on W. East Dereham 4miles S.

LANDMARKS NIGHT : As day.

OBSTRUCTIONS : -

LANDING AREA SURFACE : Grass.

QDM	LENGTH X WIDTH	EXT. TO
NE-SW.	1650yds.	2000yds.
NNW-SSE.	1600yds.	-
NW-SE.	1350yds.	1400yds.

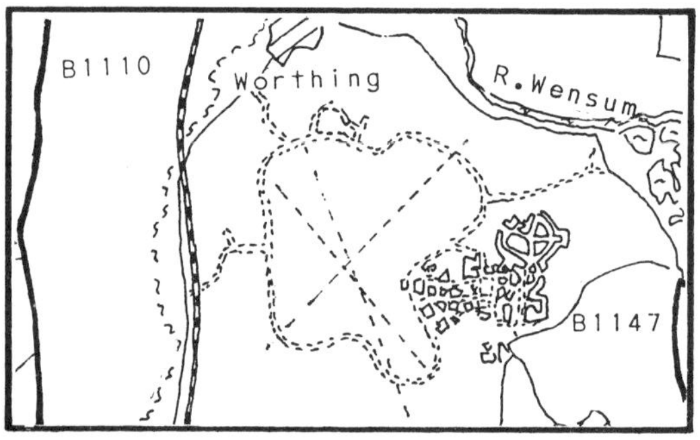

EXTENSIBILITY : -

ACCOMMODATION : Permanent.
HANGARS : Type J-1;T2-4;Blister-4.

HARDSTANDINGS : Frying pan-31.

	OFFICERS	S.N.C.O's.	O.R's.	TOTAL
R.A.F.	157.	422.	1389.	1968.
W.A.A.F.	4.	17.	369.	390.

AFFILIATED AIRFIELDS : -

PRESENT USE [1985] : RAF.

NO: 552.

AIRFIELD NAME: SWINDERBY. OPENED : 1940.
COUNTY : Lincolnshire. CLOSED :
COMMAND : Bomber.
FORMATION : 7 Grp[St.Vincents] GRID REF: F 348816[47]
FUNCTION : Operational[75 Base] O.S.REF.: SK 873616/121.

LOCALITY : 9miles SW of Lincoln.
RAILWAY STN. : Swinderby 2miles[LMS]

LATITUDE : 53 08 45N. HEIGHT ASL : 53' LIGHTING : Mk2.
LONGITUDE : 00 40 30W. FLYING CONTROL : Yes. RADIO : QDM.

LANDMARKS DAY : Lincoln cathedral 8miles NE.

LANDMARKS NIGHT : -

OBSTRUCTIONS : -

LANDING AREA SURFACE : Concrete.

QDM	LENGTH X WIDTH	EXT. TO
246.	2000 x 50yds.	2700yds.
201.	1400 x 50yds.	2150yds.
294.	1400 x 50yds.	2200yds.

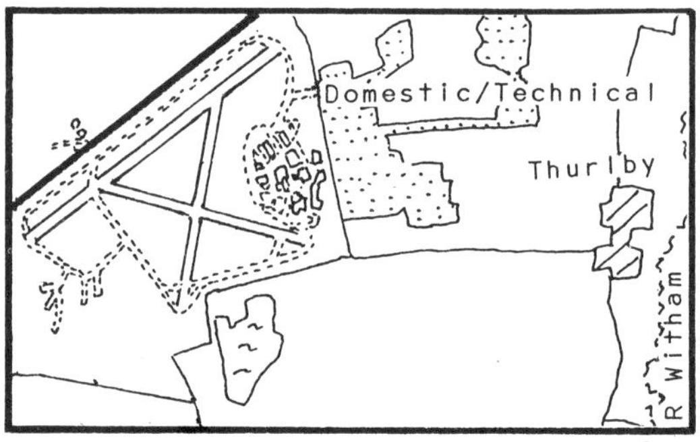

EXTENSIBILITY : Entails demolition of a cottage, farm & buildings, & a garage.
ACCOMMODATION : Permanent.
HANGARS : Type J-3;T2-3.

HARDSTANDINGS : Heavy bomber-36.

	OFFICERS	S.N.C.O's.	O.R's.	TOTAL
R.A.F.	194.	612.	1321.	2127.
W.A.A.F.	11.	16.	322.	349.

AFFILIATED AIRFIELDS : Wigsley & Winthorpe[Sub-stations]

PRESENT USE [1985] : RAF.

NO: 553.

AIRFIELD NAME: SWINGFIELD. OPENED : 1943.
COUNTY : Kent. CLOSED : 1945.
COMMAND : Fighter.
FORMATION : 11 Grp[Uxbridge] GRID REF: R 680630[117]
FUNCTION : Advanced Landing Ground. O.S.REF.: TR 240449/189.
: [Disused]
LOCALITY : 5miles NW of Dover.
RAILWAY STN. : Kearsney[SR]

LATITUDE : 51 09 45N. HEIGHT ASL : 460' LIGHTING : None.
LONGITUDE : 01 12 15E. FLYING CONTROL : None. RADIO : QDM.

LANDMARKS DAY. : Swingfield church SW. St.John's farm SW. Swanton farmhouse[main entrance]SE.

LANDMARKS NIGHT : -

OBSTRUCTIONS : -

LANDING AREA SURFACE : Steel Matting[Sommerfeld Track]

QDM	LENGTH X WIDTH	EXT. TO
N-S.	1400 X 52yds.	2100yds.
NE-SW.	1600 X 52yds.	2600yds.
:	:	2200yds.
:	:	:

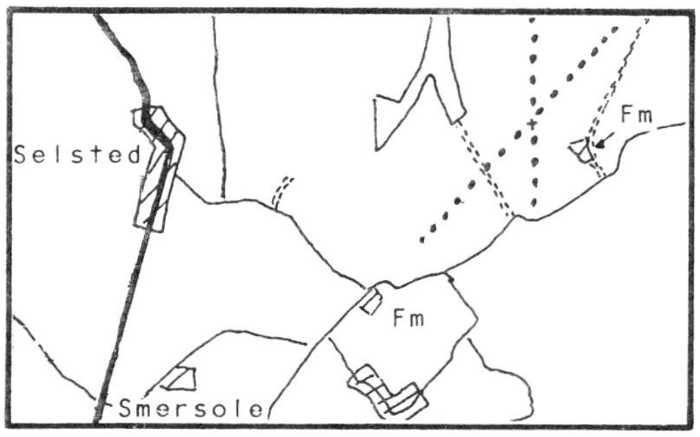

EXTENSIBILITY : Entails demolition of a cottage, farm & buildings, & a garage.
ACCOMMODATION : Tented camp.
HANGARS : Blister-4.

HARDSTANDINGS : Hardcore & gravel-50.

	OFFICERS	S.N.C.O's.	O.R's.	TOTAL
R.A.F.	-	-	-	-
W.A.A.F.	-	-	-	-

AFFILIATED AIRFIELDS : -

PRESENT USE [1985] : Agriculture.

NO: 554.

AIRFIELD NAME: SYERSTON. OPENED : 1940.
COUNTY : Nottinghamshire. CLOSED :
COMMAND : Bomber.
FORMATION : 5 Grp[Morton Hall] GRID REF: F 195677[54]
FUNCTION : Operational[56 Base] O.S.REF.: SK 730480/129.
:
LOCALITY : 5.5miles SW of Newark on Trent.
RAILWAY STN. : Newark on Trent[LMS]

LATITUDE : 53 01 15N. HEIGHT ASL : 211' LIGHTING : MK2.
LONGITUDE : 00 54 45W. FLYING CONTROL : Yes. RADIO : QDM.

LANDMARKS DAY. : R Trent to W and Fosse Way to E of A/F.

LANDMARKS NIGHT : As day.

OBSTRUCTIONS : NNW bomb dump gantries[4]

LANDING AREA SURFACE : Concrete.

QDM	LENGTH X WIDTH	EXT. TO
073.	1950 x 50yds.	-
120.	1400 x 50yds.	2000yds.
163.	1400 x 50yds.	2000yds.
:	:	:

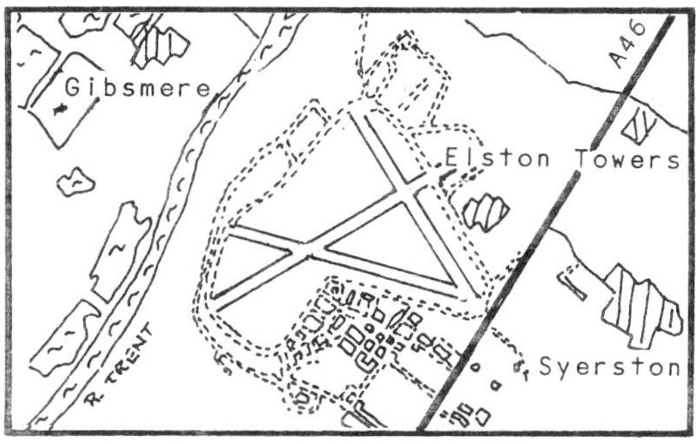

EXTENSIBILITY : Entaild diversion of main Newark-Leicester road.

ACCOMMODATION : Permanent.
HANGARS : Type J-2;T2-3;Glider[T2]-3;B1-1.

HARDSTANDINGS : Heavy bomber-36.

	OFFICERS	S.N.C.O's.	O.R's.	TOTAL
R.A.F.	190.	380.	2026.	2596.
W.A.A.F.	10.	27.	377.	414.

AFFILIATED AIRFIELDS : Balderton & Fulbeck[Sub-stations]

PRESENT USE [1985] : RAF.

NO: 555.

AIRFIELD NAME: SYWELL. OPENED : 1928.
COUNTY : Northamptonshire. CLOSED : 1953.
COMMAND : Flying Training.
FORMATION : 50 Grp[Reading] GRID REF: L 275870[73&74]
FUNCTION : Elementary Flying Training School. O.S.REF.: SP 823682/152.
LOCALITY : 6miles NE of Northampton.
RAILWAY STN. : Northampton Castle[LMS]

LATITUDE : 52 18 15N. HEIGHT ASL : 365' LIGHTING : None.
LONGITUDE : 00 47 30W. FLYING CONTROL : None. RADIO : QDM.

LANDMARKS DAY. : Reservoir SE of A/F.

LANDMARKS NIGHT : -

OBSTRUCTIONS : -

LANDING AREA SURFACE : Grass.

QDM	LENGTH X WIDTH	EXT. TO
N-S.	1020yds.	2000yds.
NE-SW.	1070yds.	1400yds.
E-W.	1260yds.	-
NW-SE.	1025yds.	-

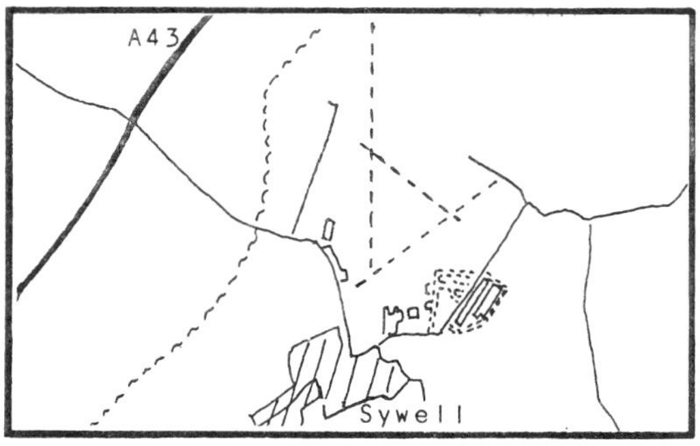

EXTENSIBILITY : On different alignments & breaking new ground but entails medium to light demolition.
ACCOMMODATION : Temporary[Hangars & club buildings permanent]
HANGARS : RAF-civil 200x140'-1;Blisters:standard-8; double-3;EO-4.MAP:300x115'-1;110x90'-1.
HARDSTANDINGS : - Factory buildings:300x100',200x60'& 300x120'

	OFFICERS	S.N.C.O's.	O.R's.	TOTAL
R.A.F.	73.	43.	273.	389.
W.A.A.F.	-	-	-	-

AFFILIATED AIRFIELDS : Denton[RLG]

PRESENT USE [1985] : Private flying.

NO: 556.

AIRFIELD NAME: TAIN. OPENED : 1941.
COUNTY : Ross-shire. CLOSED : 1946.
COMMAND : Coastal.
FORMATION : 18 Grp[Pitreavie Castle] GRID REF: D 352042[21Scot]
FUNCTION : Operational parent. O.S.REF.: NH 828818/21.
:
LOCALITY : 3.5miles E of Tain.
RAILWAY STN. : Tain[LMS]

LATITUDE : 57 48 30N. HEIGHT ASL : 0' LIGHTING : Mk2.
LONGITUDE : 03 58 30W. FLYING CONTROL : Yes. RADIO : QDM.

LANDMARKS DAY. : Dornoch Firth N of A/F. Loch Eye S.

LANDMARKS NIGHT : -

OBSTRUCTIONS : Escarpment 70' high 800yds. S of A/F[approx]

LANDING AREA SURFACE : Concrete.

QDM	LENGTH X WIDTH	EXT. TO
256.	2000 x 50yds.	-
316.	2000 x 50yds.	3000yds.
199.	1462 x 50yds.	3000yds.

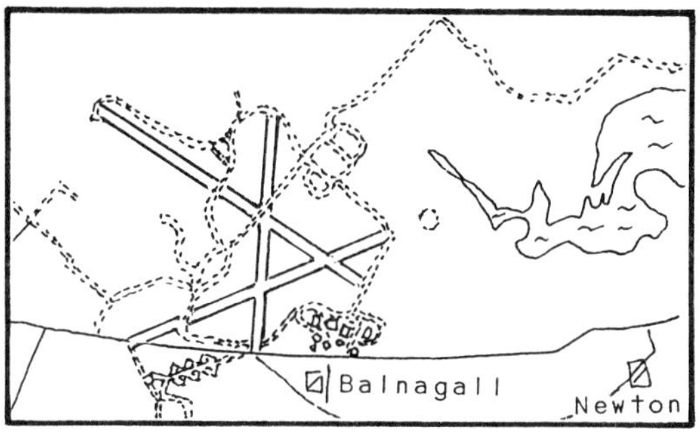

EXTENSIBILITY : -

ACCOMMODATION : Temporary.
HANGARS : T2-2;Bellman-3;EO Blister-8.

HARDSTANDINGS : Loop-17;frying pan-3;fighter standing-11.

R.A.F. : OFFICERS: 128.S.N.C.O's.: 323.O.R's.: 1400.TOTAL: 1851.
W.A.A.F.: " : 8. " : 15. " : 358. " : 381.

AFFILIATED AIRFIELDS : -

PRESENT USE [1985] : Disused.

NO: 557.

AIRFIELD NAME: TALBENNY. OPENED : 1942.
COUNTY : Pembrokeshire. CLOSED : 1946.
COMMAND : Transport.
FORMATION : 44 Grp[Gloucester] GRID REF: N 276344[99]
FUNCTION : Parent Station. O.S.REF.: SM 834113/157.
:
LOCALITY : 5.75miles NW of Milford Haven.
RAILWAY STN. : Haverfordwest 7miles[GWR]

LATITUDE : 51 45 23N. HEIGHT ASL : 230' LIGHTING : Mk2.
LONGITUDE : 05 08 30W. FLYING CONTROL : Yes. RADIO : QDM.

LANDMARKS DAY. : Milford Haven & distinctive nature of coast.

LANDMARKS NIGHT : -

OBSTRUCTIONS : Rising ground from N end of N-S runway[approx 60' above A/F level].Bad to take off S-N, & landing N-S.

LANDING AREA SURFACE : Concrete & tarmac.

QDM	LENGTH X WIDTH	EXT. TO
034.	1600 x 50yds.	2000yds.
272.	1100 x 50yds.	1300yds.
350.	1100 x 50yds.	-

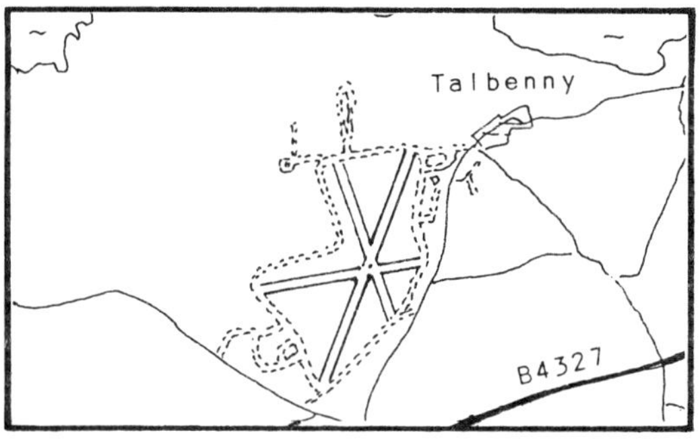

EXTENSIBILITY : Entails diversion of secondary road.

ACCOMMODATION : Temporary.
HANGARS : T2-2.

HARDSTANDINGS : Frying pan-36;concrete aprons to accomodate additional 22 A/C.

R.A.F. : OFFICERS: 145.S.N.C.O's.: 491.O.R's.: 1820.TOTAL: 2456.
W.A.A.F.: " : 8. " : 8. " : 300. " : 316.

AFFILIATED AIRFIELDS : -

PRESENT USE [1985] : Disused.

NO: 558.

AIRFIELD NAME: TANGMERE. OPENED : 1918.
COUNTY : Sussex. CLOSED : 1970.
COMMAND : Fighter.
FORMATION : 11 Grp[Uxbridge] GRID REF: Q 345257[133]
FUNCTION : Sector[night fighter] O.S.REF.: SU 913061/197.
:
LOCALITY : 2.5miles E of Chichester.
RAILWAY STN. : Chichester[SR]

LATITUDE : 50 50 48N. HEIGHT ASL : 50' LIGHTING : Mk2.
LONGITUDE : 00 42 23W. FLYING CONTROL : Yes. RADIO : QDM.

LANDMARKS DAY. : Chichester cathedral & harbour. Goodwood race course, railway.

LANDMARKS NIGHT : As above when visible in moonlight.

OBSTRUCTIONS : -

LANDING AREA SURFACE : Concrete.

QDM	LENGTH X WIDTH	EXT. TO
255.	2000 x 50yds.	3300yds.
170.	1600 x 50yds.	1850yds.

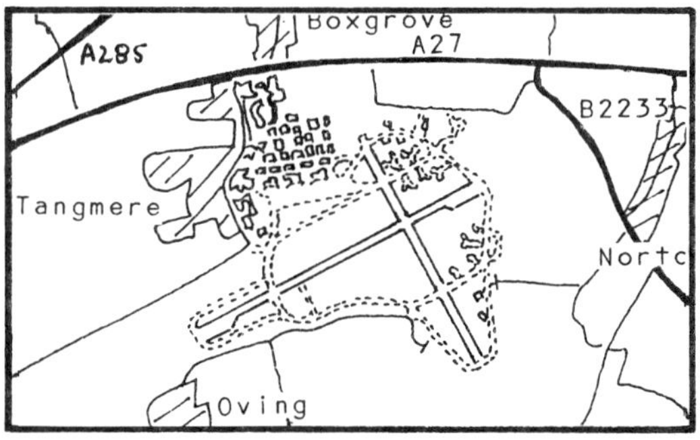

EXTENSIBILITY : Entails demolition of 4 houses.

ACCOMMODATION : Permanent[hangars temporary]
HANGARS : T2-1;Bessoneau-2;Blisters:O-10;EO-6. Civil-2.
HARDSTANDINGS : SE-14.

R.A.F. : OFFICERS: 225.S.N.C.O's.: 238.O.R's.: 3170.TOTAL: 3633.
W.A.A.F.: " : 17. " : 16. " : 732. " : 765.

AFFILIATED AIRFIELDS : Blackbushe, Ford[NF-FA];Odiham,Lasham etc.

PRESENT USE [1985] : Industry.

NO: 559.

AIRFIELD NAME: TARRANT RUSHTON. OPENED : 1943.
COUNTY : Dorsetshire. CLOSED : 1980.
COMMAND : Fighter.
FORMATION : 38 Grp[Marks Hall] GRID REF: U 380264[131]
FUNCTION : Parent Station. O.S.REF.: ST 946058/195.
:
LOCALITY : 4miles E of Blandford.
RAILWAY STN. : Blandford[LMS]

LATITUDE : 50 51 00N. HEIGHT ASL : 255′ LIGHTING : Mk2.
LONGITUDE : 02 04 30W. FLYING CONTROL : Yes. RADIO : QDM.

LANDMARKS DAY : Badbury Rings[Tumuli 327′ ASL]

LANDMARKS NIGHT : -

OBSTRUCTIONS : -

LANDING AREA SURFACE : Concrete & wood chippings.080 grass overshoot each end.010 grass overshoot 200yds.N&400yds S.
QDM: 010. LENGTH X WIDTH: 2000 x 50yds.EXT. TO: 2500yds.
: 080. : 1400 x 50yds. : -
: 130. : 1400 x 50yds. : -
: : :

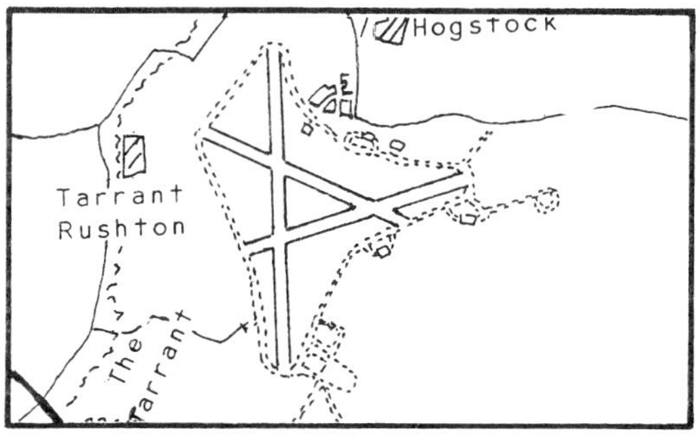

EXTENSIBILITY : -

ACCOMMODATION : Temporary.
HANGARS : T2-4.

HARDSTANDINGS : Spectacle loop-50.

R.A.F. : OFFICERS: 190.S.N.C.O′s.: 530.O.R′s.: 1605.TOTAL: 2325.
W.A.A.F.: " : 10. " : 25. " : 351. " : 386.

AFFILIATED AIRFIELDS : -

PRESENT USE [1985] : Disused.

NO: 560.

AIRFIELD NAME: TATENHILL. OPENED : 1941.
COUNTY : Staffordshire. CLOSED : 1947.
COMMAND : Flying Training.
FORMATION : 21 Grp[Spittlegate] GRID REF: K 620445[62]
FUNCTION : Advanced Flying Unit O.S.REF.: SK 158241.
: Pilots[satellite]
LOCALITY : 5miles W of Burton-on-Trent.
RAILWAY STN. : Burton-on-Trent[LMS]

LATITUDE : 52 48 45N. HEIGHT ASL : 450′ LIGHTING : Mk2.
LONGITUDE : 01 45 45W. FLYING CONTROL : Yes. RADIO : QDM.

LANDMARKS DAY : -

LANDMARKS NIGHT : -

OBSTRUCTIONS : -

LANDING AREA SURFACE : Concrete & wood chippings.
QDM: 090. LENGTH X WIDTH: 1600 x 50yds.EXT. TO: 1850yds.
: 040. : 1000 x 50yds. : -
: 180. : 1100 x 50yds. : -
: : :

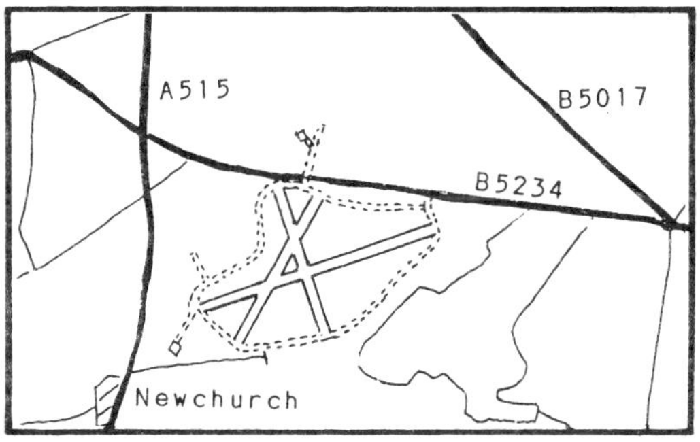

EXTENSIBILITY : -

ACCOMMODATION : Temporary.
HANGARS : T2-1;double 65′ Blister-2.

HARDSTANDINGS : Circular concrete-19.

R.A.F. : OFFICERS: 62.S.N.C.O′s.: 236.O.R′s.: 726.TOTAL: 1024.
W.A.A.F.: " : 4. " : 3. " : 128. " : 135.

AFFILIATED AIRFIELDS : Wheaton Aston[Parent]

PRESENT USE [1985] : Agriculture.

NO: 561.

AIRFIELD NAME: TATTON PARK. OPENED : 1940.
COUNTY : Cheshire. CLOSED : 1946.
COMMAND : Fighter.
FORMATION : 38 Grp[Marks Hall] GRID REF: E 218023[44]
FUNCTION : Relief Landing Ground. O.S.REF.: SJ 750815/109.
:
LOCALITY : 1.5miles N of Knutsford.
RAILWAY STN. : Knutsford[CLC]

LATITUDE : 53 19 38N. HEIGHT ASL : 200′ LIGHTING : None.
LONGITUDE : 02 22 30W. FLYING CONTROL : None.RADIO : QDM.

LANDMARKS DAY : Tatton Mere.

LANDMARKS NIGHT : As day.

OBSTRUCTIONS : Landing area surrounded by trees.Parachute descents. Tatton Park & area 3miles radius restricted to parachute training only.

LANDING AREA SURFACE : Grass.
QDM: N-S. LENGTH X WIDTH: 1000yds. EXT. TO: -
: : :
: : :

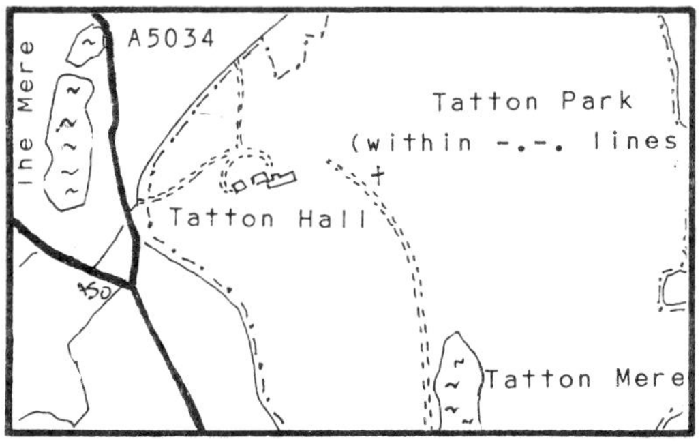

EXTENSIBILITY : None possible.

ACCOMMODATION : -
HANGARS : Pre-war wooden type-1.

HARDSTANDINGS : -

R.A.F. : OFFICERS: - S.N.C.O′s.: - O.R′s.: - TOTAL: -
W.A.A.F.: " : - " : - " : - " : -

AFFILIATED AIRFIELDS : Ringway[Parent]

PRESENT USE [1985] : Parkland.

NO: 562.

AIRFIELD NAME: TEALING.
COUNTY : Angus.
COMMAND : Flying Training.
FORMATION : 21 Grp[Spittlegate]
FUNCTION : Advanced Flying Unit
: Pilots[satellite]
LOCALITY : 4miles N of Dundee.
RAILWAY STN. : Dundee[LMS & LNER]

OPENED : 1942.
CLOSED : 1945.

GRID REF: O 910579[58Scot]
O.S.REF.: NO 405370/54.

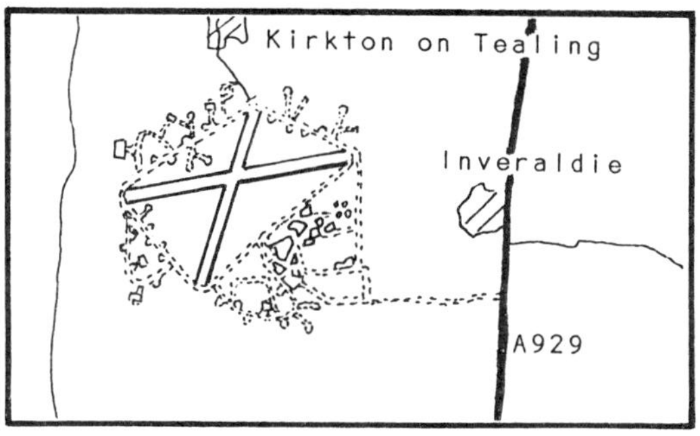

LATITUDE : 56 31 15N. HEIGHT ASL : 400′ LIGHTING : None.
LONGITUDE : 02 58 15W. FLYING CONTROL : Yes. RADIO : QDM.

LANDMARKS DAY : A/F situated just S of Sidlow Hills.

LANDMARKS NIGHT : -

OBSTRUCTIONS : -

LANDING AREA SURFACE : Concrete & wood chippings.

QDM	LENGTH X WIDTH	EXT. TO
272.	1500 x 50yds.	2500yds.
212.	1100 x 50yds.	-
:	:	:
:	:	:

EXTENSIBILITY : -

ACCOMMODATION : Temporary.
HANGARS : T1-3;O Blister-8.

HARDSTANDINGS : 52.

	OFFICERS	S.N.C.O's.	O.R's.	TOTAL
R.A.F.	72.	120.	1320.	1512.
W.A.A.F.	8.	15.	357.	380.

AFFILIATED AIRFIELDS : Errol[Parent]

PRESENT USE [1985] : Disused.

NO: 563.

AIRFIELD NAME: TEMPLETON.
COUNTY : Pembrokeshire.
COMMAND : Coastal.
FORMATION : 17 Grp[Edinburgh]
FUNCTION : Operational Training
: Unit[satellite]
LOCALITY : 7miles NNW of Tenby.
RAILWAY STN. : Templeton 1.5miles[GWR]

OPENED : 1943.
CLOSED : 1945.

GRID REF: N 546337[99]
O.S.REF.: SN 101112/158.

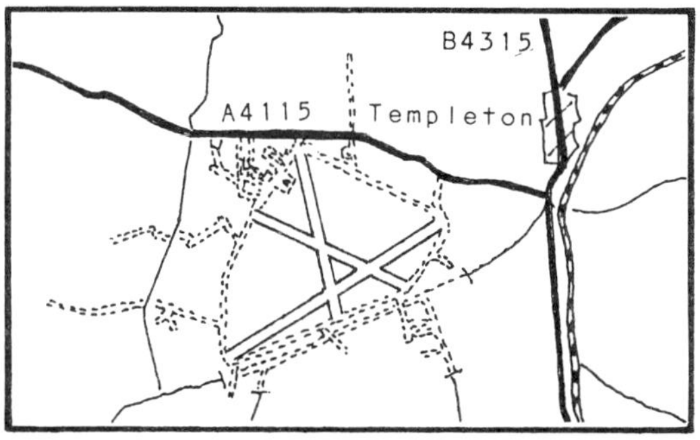

LATITUDE : 51 45 53N. HEIGHT ASL : 350′ LIGHTING : Mk2.
LONGITUDE : 04 45 15W. FLYING CONTROL : Yes. RADIO : QDM.

LANDMARKS DAY : Main GWR line, Cleathan-Canastan Wood.

LANDMARKS NIGHT : -

OBSTRUCTIONS : Hill 150-175′ from A/F, QDM 176degrees.

LANDING AREA SURFACE : Concrete & wood chippings.

QDM	LENGTH X WIDTH	EXT. TO
246.	1600 x 50yds.	2000yds.
304.	1100 x 50yds.	1700yds.
176.	1100 x 50yds.	-
:	:	:

EXTENSIBILITY : Entails diversion of 2 secondary roads.

ACCOMMODATION : Temporary.
HANGARS : T2-1.

HARDSTANDINGS : 125′ dia.-27.

	OFFICERS	S.N.C.O's.	O.R's.	TOTAL
R.A.F.	66.	140.	630.	836.
W.A.A.F.	2.	-	132.	134.

AFFILIATED AIRFIELDS : Haverfordwest[Parent]

PRESENT USE [1985] : Unspecified.

NO: 564.

AIRFIELD NAME: TEMPSFORD.
COUNTY : Bedfordshire.
COMMAND : Bomber.
FORMATION : 3 Grp[Exning]
FUNCTION : Operational.
:
LOCALITY : 9miles ENE of Bedford.
RAILWAY STN. : Sandy[LNER]

OPENED : 1941.
CLOSED : 1947.

GRID REF: L 638718[84]
O.S.REF.: TL 188525/153.

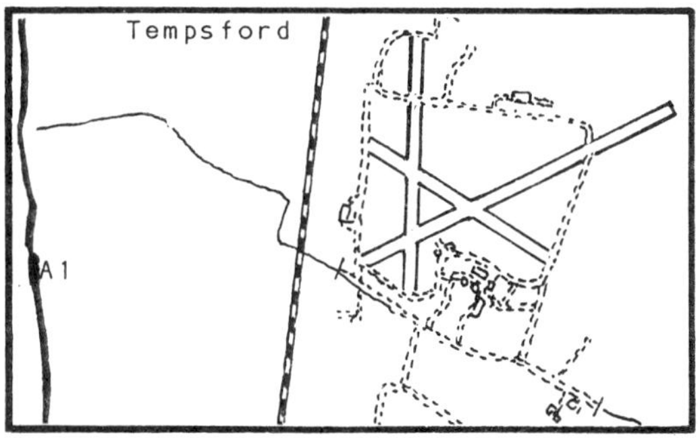

LATITUDE : 52 09 30N. HEIGHT ASL : 63′ LIGHTING : Mk1*.
LONGITUDE : 00 15 45W. FLYING CONTROL : Yes. RADIO : QDM.

LANDMARKS DAY : Main railway line adjacent to A/F. Chimney stack 285′ 3.5miles N.Cooler 175′ 3.5miles N.

LANDMARKS NIGHT : -
*Modified.

OBSTRUCTIONS : Church tower & hills SSE 275′

LANDING AREA SURFACE : Concrete.

QDM	LENGTH X WIDTH	EXT. TO
010.	1600 x 50yds.	-
251.	2000 x 50yds.	-
309.	1383 x 50yds.	-
:	:	:

EXTENSIBILITY : None possible.

ACCOMMODATION : Temporary.
HANGARS : T2-6;B1-1.

HARDSTANDINGS : Heavy bomber-36.

	OFFICERS	S.N.C.O's.	O.R's.	TOTAL
R.A.F.	262.	429.	1126.	1817.
W.A.A.F.	10.	15.	250.	275.

AFFILIATED AIRFIELDS : -

PRESENT USE [1985] : Unspecified.

NO: 565.

AIRFIELD NAME: TERNHILL. OPENED : 1916.
COUNTY : Shropshire. CLOSED : 1976.
COMMAND : Flying Training.
FORMATION : 21 Grp[Spittlegate] GRID REF: K 102520[52]
FUNCTION : Advanced Flying Unit O.S.REF.: SJ 642308/127.
: Pilots.
LOCALITY : 4miles SW of Market Drayton.
RAILWAY STN. : Ternhill 1miles[GWR]

LATITUDE : 52 52 23N. HEIGHT ASL : 280′ LIGHTING : MK2.
LONGITUDE : 02 32 00W. FLYING CONTROL : Yes. RADIO : QDM.

LANDMARKS DAY. : The Wrekin 180degrees 14miles. Hodnet Hill 255degrees 682′ 4miles.

LANDMARKS NIGHT : -

OBSTRUCTIONS : Tern Hill adjacent to NW of A/F 350′ approx ASL. Hodnet Hill W by S of A/F 4miles.

LANDING AREA SURFACE : Concrete covered with tarmac.

QDM:	LENGTH X WIDTH:	EXT. TO:
290.	1000 x 50yds.	1900yds.
230.	1000 x 50yds.	2350yds.
		1800yds.

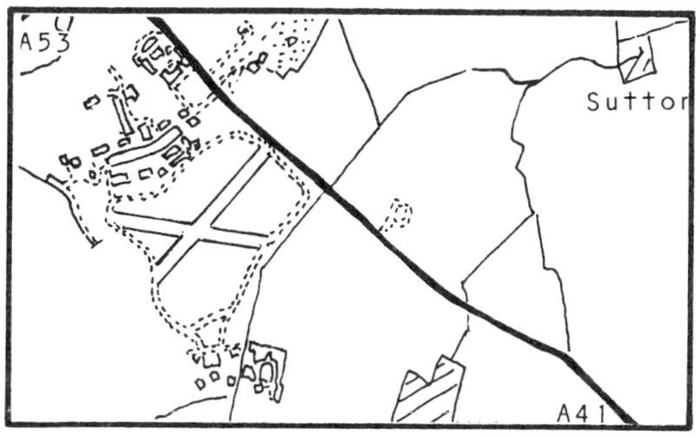

EXTENSIBILITY : Entails slight demolition.

ACCOMMODATION : Permanent.
HANGARS : Type C-4;Bellman-1;ARS-1;Lamella[MU]-6; Type D[MU]-2;Blister 65′-9.
HARDSTANDINGS : -

R.A.F. : OFFICERS: 197.S.N.C.O′s.: 255.O.R′s.: 1418.TOTAL: 1870.
W.A.A.F.: " : 24. " : 10. " : 376. " : 410.

AFFILIATED AIRFIELDS : Chetwynd & Bratton[RLG]Condover[satellite]

PRESENT USE [1985] : Disused.

NO: 566.

AIRFIELD NAME: THEALE. OPENED : 1941.
COUNTY : Berkshire. CLOSED : 1948.
COMMAND : Flying Training.
FORMATION : 50 Grp[Reading] GRID REF: Q 095903[113]
FUNCTION : Elementary Flying O.S.REF.: SU 654700/175.
: Training School.
LOCALITY : 5miles W of Reading.
RAILWAY STN. : Theale .5miles[GWR]

LATITUDE : 51 25 30N. HEIGHT ASL : 150′ LIGHTING : None.
LONGITUDE : 01 03 38W. FLYING CONTROL : None.RADIO : QDM.

LANDMARKS DAY. : Ordnance factory near NW corner. White horse SW on hill.

LANDMARKS NIGHT : Canal along N boundary.

OBSTRUCTIONS : Ridge, also S boundary.

LANDING AREA SURFACE : Grass.

QDM:	LENGTH X WIDTH:	EXT. TO:
N-S.	840yds.	-
NE-SW.	840yds.	-
E-W.	800yds.	-
NW-SE.	900yds.	-

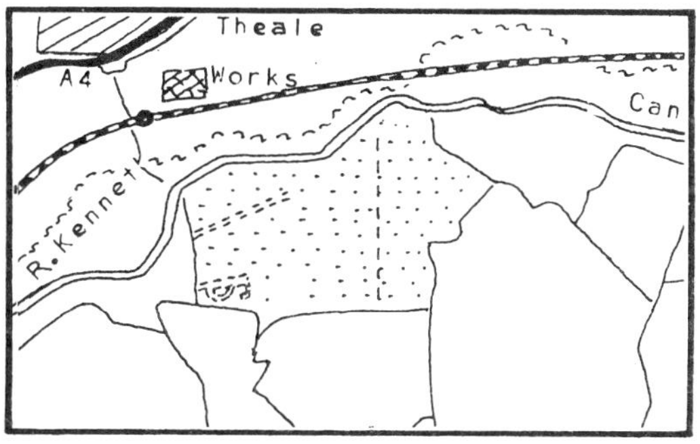

EXTENSIBILITY : 1600x900yds.

ACCOMMODATION : Temporary.
HANGARS : T1-1;Blisters:0-2;double standard-3.

HARDSTANDINGS : -

R.A.F. : OFFICERS: 23.S.N.C.O′s.: 52.O.R′s.: 134.TOTAL: 209.
W.A.A.F.: " : - " : - " : - " : -

AFFILIATED AIRFIELDS : -

PRESENT USE [1985] : Gravel extraction.

NO: 567.

AIRFIELD NAME: THOLTHORPE. OPENED : 1940.
COUNTY : Yorkshire. CLOSED : 1945.
COMMAND : Bomber.
FORMATION : 6 RCAF Grp[Allerton Pk] GRID REF: E 956877[27]
FUNCTION : Operational. O.S.REF.: SE 485678/100.
:
LOCALITY : 12miles NW of York.
RAILWAY STN. : Raskelf 1.75miles[LNER]

LATITUDE : 54 06 15N. HEIGHT ASL : 60′ LIGHTING : MK2.
LONGITUDE : 01 15 30W. FLYING CONTROL : Yes. RADIO : QDM.

LANDMARKS DAY. : Mainline LNER line York-Darlington 2miles due E. R Ure 1mile W.

LANDMARKS NIGHT : R Ure 1mile W.

OBSTRUCTIONS : Telegraph wires on railway E-W approach.

LANDING AREA SURFACE : Concrete & tarmac.

QDM:	LENGTH X WIDTH:	EXT. TO:
281.	2000 x 50yds.	2800yds.
056.	1400 x 50yds.	1800yds.
340.	1400 x 50yds.	3000yds.

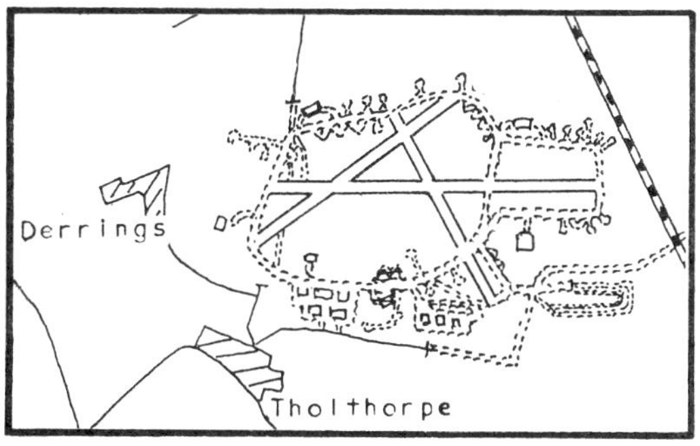

EXTENSIBILITY : -

ACCOMMODATION : Temporary.
HANGARS : T2-2;B1-1.

HARDSTANDINGS : Heavy bomber-36.

R.C.A.F.: OFFICERS: 131.S.N.C.O′s.: 468.O.R′s.: 902.TOTAL: 1501.
W.A.A.F.: " : 5. " : 8. " : 220. " : 233.

AFFILIATED AIRFIELDS : Linton-on-Ouse[62 RCAF Base]

PRESENT USE [1985] : Agriculture.

AIRFIELD NAME: THORNABY. OPENED : 1928.
COUNTY : Yorkshire. CLOSED : 1958.
COMMAND : Coastal.
FORMATION : 18 Grp[Pitreavie Castle] GRID REF: Z 936357[15]
FUNCTION : Operational parent. O.S.REF.: NZ 455163/93.
:
LOCALITY : 2miles SW of Middlesborough.
RAILWAY STN. : Thornaby[LNER]

LATITUDE : 54 32 00N. HEIGHT ASL : 60′ LIGHTING : Mk2.
LONGITUDE : 01 17 30W. FLYING CONTROL : Yes. RADIO : QDM.

LANDMARKS DAY. : R Tess. Road Maske-Yarn.

LANDMARKS NIGHT : -

OBSTRUCTIONS : -

LANDING AREA SURFACE : Concrete.

QDM	LENGTH X WIDTH	EXT. TO
227.	1980 x 50yds.	2500yds.
178.	1400 x 50yds.	2500yds.
287.	1410 x 50yds.	1000yds.

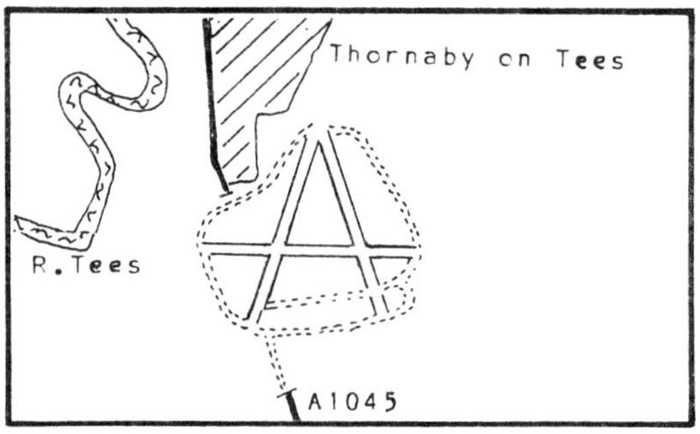

EXTENSIBILITY : Entails demolition of a farm.

ACCOMMODATION : Permanent[part]
HANGARS : Type C-2;Bellman-1;Aeroplane-2; Blisters-3.
HARDSTANDINGS : 33.

	OFFICERS	S.N.C.O's.	O.R's.	TOTAL
R.A.F.	130.	350.	1153.	1633.
W.A.A.F.	8.	5.	346.	359.

AFFILIATED AIRFIELDS : -

PRESENT USE [1985] : Housing.

AIRFIELD NAME: THORNEY ISLAND. OPENED : 1938.
COUNTY : Hampshire. CLOSED :
COMMAND : Coastal.
FORMATION : 16 Grp[Gillingham] GRID REF: Q 195228[132]
FUNCTION : Operational parent. O.S.REF.: SU 762025/197.
:
LOCALITY : 2miles S of Emsworth.
RAILWAY STN. : Emsworth[SR]

LATITUDE : 50 49 08N. HEIGHT ASL : 0′ LIGHTING : Mk1.
LONGITUDE : 00 55 08W. FLYING CONTROL : Yes. RADIO : QDM.

LANDMARKS DAY. : Waterways:a]Emsworth Channel to W;b]Thorney Island to E;c]Channel to N joining a]&b].

LANDMARKS NIGHT : As day.

OBSTRUCTIONS : Camp water tower 100′.

LANDING AREA SURFACE : Concrete.

QDM	LENGTH X WIDTH	EXT. TO
015.	1630 x 50yds.	-
057.	1700 x 50yds.	-
120.	1350 x 50yds.	-

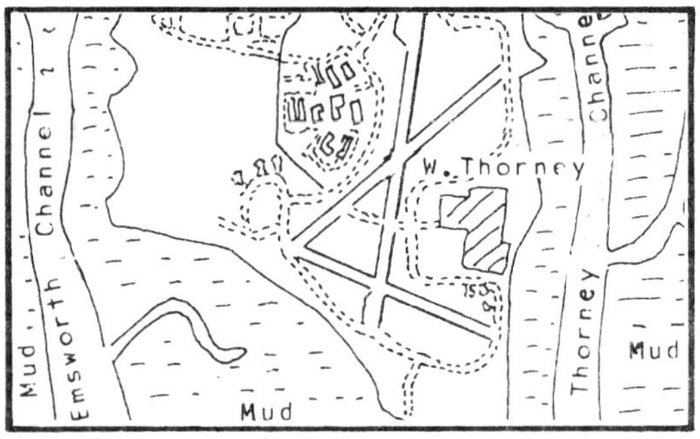

EXTENSIBILITY : -

ACCOMMODATION : Permanent.
HANGARS : Type C-6;EO Blister-16.

HARDSTANDINGS : 120′-42.

	OFFICERS	S.N.C.O's.	O.R's.	TOTAL
R.A.F.	330.	276.	3030.	3636.
W.A.A.F.	19.	-	489.	508.

AFFILIATED AIRFIELDS : -

PRESENT USE [1985] : Army.

AIRFIELD NAME: THORPE ABBOTS. OPENED : 1943.
COUNTY : Norfolk. CLOSED : 1956.
COMMAND : 8th USAAF.
FORMATION : 100th Bomb Grp. GRID REF: M 640990[77]
FUNCTION : Operational. O.S.REF.: TM 188809/156.
:
LOCALITY : 4.5miles E of Diss.
RAILWAY STN. : Diss[LNER]

LATITUDE : 52 22 53N. HEIGHT ASL : 165′ LIGHTING : Mk2.
LONGITUDE : 01 12 45E. FLYING CONTROL : Yes. RADIO : QDM.

LANDMARKS DAY. : Pulham airship shed.

LANDMARKS NIGHT : As day.

OBSTRUCTIONS : -

LANDING AREA SURFACE : Concrete & wood chippings.

QDM	LENGTH X WIDTH	EXT. TO
099.	2100 x 50yds.	3000yds.
350.	1400 x 50yds.	2000yds.
043.	1400 x 50yds.	2000yds.

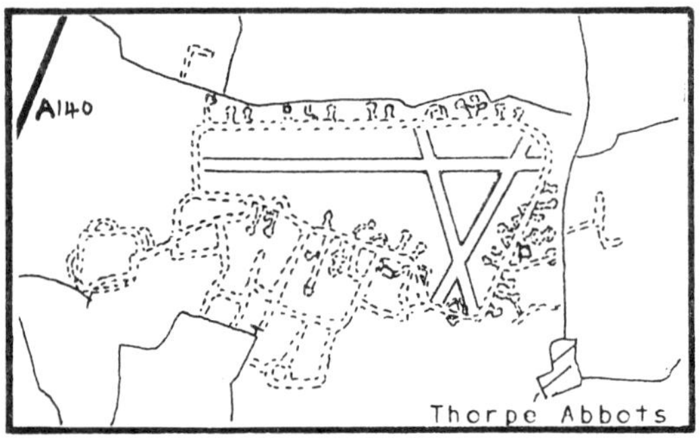

EXTENSIBILITY : By pivoting 2nd.R/W it can be extended to 2400x 400yds. Entails demolition of a farm & road div.
ACCOMMODATION : Temporary.
HANGARS : T2-2.

HARDSTANDINGS : Special concrete loop-50.

USAAF. : OFFICERS: 421. Enlisted Men. : 2473. TOTAL: 2894.

AFFILIATED AIRFIELDS : -

PRESENT USE [1985] : Agriculture.

NO: 571.

AIRFIELD NAME: THRUXTON.
COUNTY : Hampshire.
COMMAND : Fighter.
FORMATION : 38 Grp[Marks Hall]
FUNCTION : Operational.

OPENED : 1941.
CLOSED : 1946.
GRID REF: U 718658[122]
O.S.REF.: SU 280457/186.

LOCALITY : 5miles W of Andover.
RAILWAY STN. : Andover Junction[SR]

LATITUDE : 51 12 30N. HEIGHT ASL : 320′ LIGHTING : Mk2.
LONGITUDE : 01 36 00W. FLYING CONTROL : Yes. RADIO : QDM.

LANDMARKS DAY. : Andover town. Tidworth barracks. Railway S of A/F 2.5miles.

LANDMARKS NIGHT : -

OBSTRUCTIONS : London Hill 359′ .25miles S.

LANDING AREA SURFACE : Concrete & wood chippings.

QDM	LENGTH X WIDTH	EXT. TO
257.	1560 x 50yds.	-
315.	1150 x 50yds.	1400yds.
024.	1000 x 50yds.	1200yds.

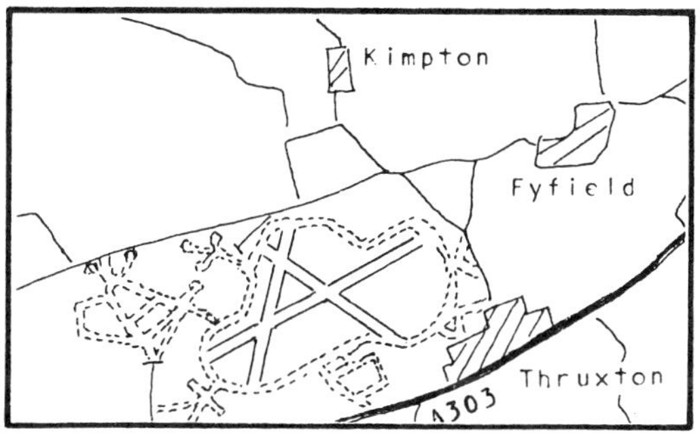

EXTENSIBILITY : -

ACCOMMODATION : Temporary.
HANGARS : T2-1;Blister-9;Bessoneau-1.

HARDSTANDINGS : Blenheim-6;frying pan-23.

R.A.F. : OFFICERS: 56.S.N.C.O′s.: 122.O.R′s.: 946.TOTAL: 1124.
W.A.A.F.: " : - " : - " : - " : -

AFFILIATED AIRFIELDS : -

PRESENT USE [1985] : Private flying.

NO: 572.

AIRFIELD NAME: THURLEIGH.
COUNTY : Bedfordshire.
COMMAND : 8th USAAF.
FORMATION : 306th Bomb Grp.
FUNCTION : Operational.

OPENED : 1941.
CLOSED :
GRID REF: L 493798[84]
O.S.REF.: TL 044063/153.

LOCALITY : 6.5miles N of Bedford.
RAILWAY STN. : Sharnbrook 5miles[LMS]

LATITUDE : 53 13 45N. HEIGHT ASL : 285′ LIGHTING : Mk2.
LONGITUDE : 00 28 30W. FLYING CONTROL : Yes. RADIO : QDM.

LANDMARKS DAY. : Windmill 1mile due N of A/F.Water tower 200′ 2 miles from A/F.Railway viaduct 2miles W of A/F, running for 3miles due S down Ouse valley. R Ouse running N-S.

LANDMARKS NIGHT : R Ouse running N-S. Ox bends 2miles SW of A/F.

OBSTRUCTIONS : -

LANDING AREA SURFACE : Concrete covered with asphalt.

QDM	LENGTH X WIDTH	EXT. TO
054.	2000 x 50yds.	-
172.	1400 x 50yds.	1800yds.
288.	1400 x 50yds.	1700yds.

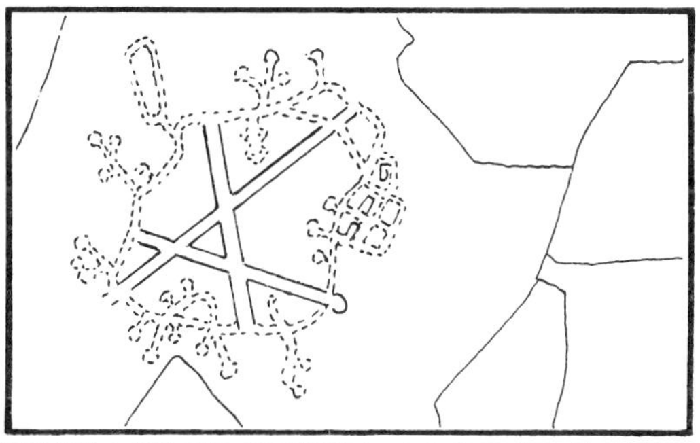

EXTENSIBILITY : Entails demolition of 1 farm & outbuildings.

ACCOMMODATION : Temporary.
HANGARS : T2-4.

HARDSTANDINGS : Frying pan & loop-51.

USAAF. : OFFICERS: 443. Enlisted Men. : 2529.TOTAL: 2972.

AFFILIATED AIRFIELDS : -

PRESENT USE [1985] : Royal Aircraft Establishment.

NO: 573.

AIRFIELD NAME: TIBENHAM.
COUNTY : Norfolk.
COMMAND : 8th USAAF.
FORMATION : 455th Bomb Grp.
FUNCTION : Operational.

OPENED : 1942.
CLOSED : 1959.
GRID REF: G 595068[77]
O.S.REF.: TM 145888/144.

LOCALITY : 13.5miles SSW of Norwich.
RAILWAY STN. : Tivetshall 2miles[LNER]

LATITUDE : 52 27 23N. HEIGHT ASL : 178′ LIGHTING : Mk2.
LONGITUDE : 01 09 15E. FLYING CONTROL : Yes. RADIO : QDM.

LANDMARKS DAY. : Tibenham church. Tivetshall railway station.

LANDMARKS NIGHT : Railway.

OBSTRUCTIONS : -

LANDING AREA SURFACE : Concrete & tarmac.

QDM	LENGTH X WIDTH	EXT. TO
211.	2000 x 50yds.	3000yds.
268.	1400 x 50yds.	2000yds.
332.	1400 x 50yds.	2000yds.

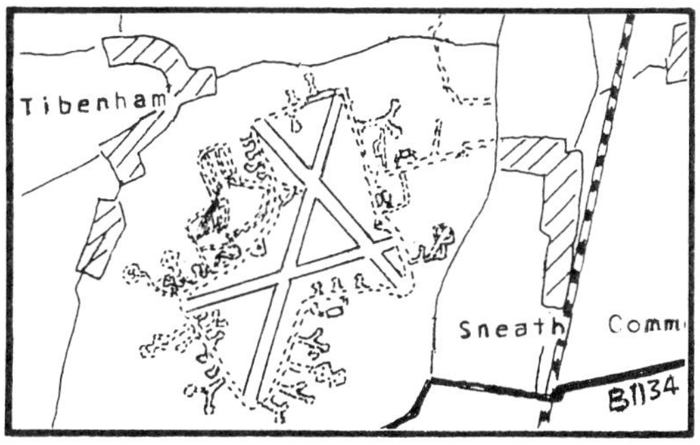

EXTENSIBILITY : Entails diversion of a minor road.

ACCOMMODATION : Temporary.
HANGARS : T2-2.

HARDSTANDINGS : Loop-50.

USAAF. : OFFICERS: 421. Enlisted Men. : 2473.TOTAL: 2894.

AFFILIATED AIRFIELDS : -

PRESENT USE [1985] : Gliding.

NO: 574.

AIRFIELD NAME: TILSTOCK. OPENED : 1942.
COUNTY : Shropshire. CLOSED : 1946.
COMMAND : Fighter.
FORMATION : 38 Grp[Marks Hall] GRID REF: K 022583[52]
FUNCTION : Operational Training O.S.REF.: SJ 562378/126.
: Unit.
LOCALITY : 3miles SSE of Whitchurch.
RAILWAY STN. : Whitchurch[LMS&LNER]

LATITUDE : 52 55 45N. HEIGHT ASL : 307′ LIGHTING : Mk2.
LONGITUDE : 02 39 00W. FLYING CONTROL : Yes. RADIO : QDM.

LANDMARKS DAY. : Whitchurch-Shrewsbury railway & road pass close to W side of A/F.

LANDMARKS NIGHT : Comber Mere 030degrees 5miles [crescent shaped lake]

OBSTRUCTIONS : Ash Hill 030degrees 1.25miles 170′ AFL.

LANDING AREA SURFACE : Concrete.

QDM	LENGTH X WIDTH	EXT. TO
030.	2000 x 50yds.	-
072.	1400 x 50yds.	15550yds.
154.	1400 x 50yds.	1650yds.

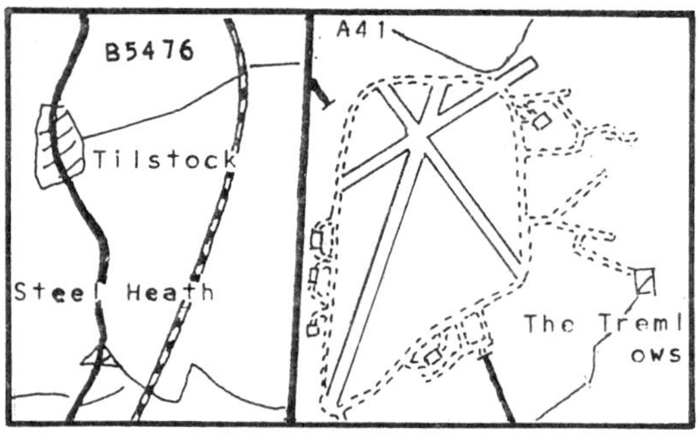

EXTENSIBILITY : Entails slight demolition.

ACCOMMODATION : Temporary.
HANGARS : T2-4.

HARDSTANDINGS : Pan-30.

R.A.F. : OFFICERS: 150.S.N.C.O′s.: 442.O.R′s.: 1359.TOTAL: 1951.
W.A.A.F.: " : 10. " : 27. " : 385. " : 422.

AFFILIATED AIRFIELDS : Sleap[Satellite]

PRESENT USE [1985] : Disused.

NO: 575.

AIRFIELD NAME: TIREE. OPENED : 1937.
COUNTY : Argyllshire. CLOSED :
COMMAND : Coastal.
FORMATION : 15 Grp[Liverpool] GRID REF: M 510686[52Scot]
FUNCTION : Operational Parent. O.S.REF.: NM 003449/46.
:
LOCALITY : Isle of Tiree.
RAILWAY STN. : Oban[LMS]

LATITUDE : 56 29 53N. HEIGHT ASL : 25′ LIGHTING : Mk2.
LONGITUDE : 06 52 15W. FLYING CONTROL : Yes. RADIO : QDM.

LANDMARKS DAY. : Ben Hynish 480′ 4miles SSW.

LANDMARKS NIGHT : Scarinsh lighthouse,every 30 seconds. Sken Yion lighthouse 2.5miles W.

OBSTRUCTIONS : VHF arials 1000yds. 107degrees.

LANDING AREA SURFACE : Concrete.

QDM	LENGTH X WIDTH	EXT. TO
062.	1840 x 50yds	2400yds.
122.	1400 x 50yds.	3300yds.
181.	2000 x 50yds.	2400yds.

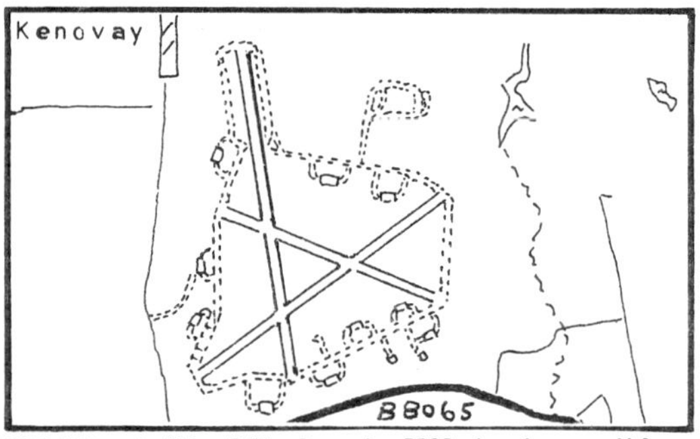

EXTENSIBILITY : A 4th. R/W of up to 3000yds. is possible.

ACCOMMODATION : Temporary.
HANGARS : 1/2 of T2-10.

HARDSTANDINGS : -

R.A.F. : OFFICERS: 69.S.N.C.O′s.: 52.O.R′s.: 1128.TOTAL: 1249.
W.A.A.F.: " : 10. " : 56. " : 96. " : 162.

AFFILIATED AIRFIELDS : -

PRESENT USE [1985] : Civil Airport[Tiree]

NO: 576.

AIRFIELD NAME: TOLLERTON. OPENED : 1930.
COUNTY : Nottinghamshire. CLOSED : 1956.
COMMAND : Flying Training.
FORMATION : 21 Grp[Spittlegate] GRID REF: F 080560[54]
FUNCTION : Service Flying Training O.S.REF.: SK 620360/129.
: School[satellite]
LOCALITY : 3miles SE of Nottingham.
RAILWAY STN. : Plumtree 2.5miles[LMS]

LATITUDE : 52 55 00N. HEIGHT ASL : 127′ LIGHTING : None.
LONGITUDE : 01 04 30W. FLYING CONTROL : Yes. RADIO : QDM.

LANDMARKS DAY. : Nottingham 3miles SE.

LANDMARKS NIGHT : Grantham canal.

OBSTRUCTIONS : Technical buildings. Tall buildings 3000yds. to N & 1.25miles NE. Cotgrave church 1.25miles SE. Tollerton church .75miles S.

LANDING AREA SURFACE : Concrete & wood chippings.

QDM	LENGTH X WIDTH	EXT. TO
040.	1119 x 50yds.	1200yds.
100.	1146 x 50yds.	1950yds.
160.	1035 x 50yds.	1150yds.

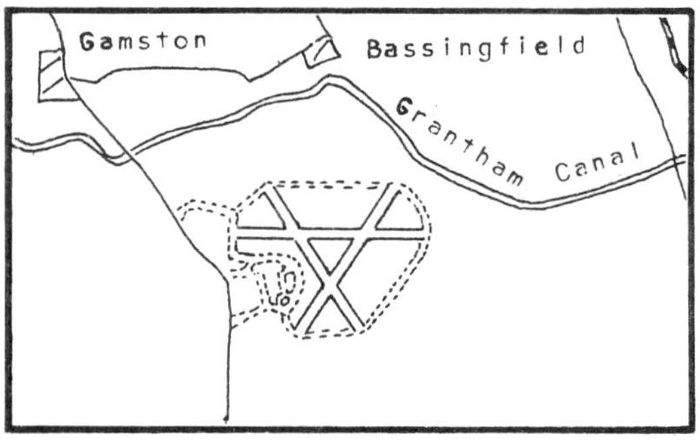

EXTENSIBILITY : Entails diversion of Tollerton-Nottingham road & demolition of a bungalow.
ACCOMMODATION : Temporary.
HANGARS : Bellman-1;O Blister-4.

HARDSTANDINGS : Circular-20[50% used by MAP]; Somerfeld track-33[for use by light A/C only]
R.A.F. : OFFICERS: 4.S.N.C.O′s.: 6.O.R′s.: 132.TOTAL: 142.
W.A.A.F.: " : - " : - " : - " : -

AFFILIATED AIRFIELDS : Newton[Parent]

PRESENT USE [1985] : Private flying.

NO: 577.

AIRFIELD NAME: TOOME. OPENED : 1943.
COUNTY : Antrim NI. CLOSED : 1954.
COMMAND : RAF NI.
FORMATION : Stormont[Belfast] GRID REF: 970908[308NI]
FUNCTION : Care & Maintenance. O.S.REF.: H 970908.
:
LOCALITY : 1.5miles NW of Toomebridge.
RAILWAY STN. : Castle Dawson 2miles[NCC]

LATITUDE : 54 45 12N. HEIGHT ASL : 56' LIGHTING : Mk2.
LONGITUDE : 06 29 30W. FLYING CONTROL : Yes. RADIO : QDM.

LANDMARKS DAY. : Lough Neagh. R Moyola.

LANDMARKS NIGHT : Railway runs approx parallel to No.2 R/W, & at an average distance of 1200' from it.

OBSTRUCTIONS : -

LANDING AREA SURFACE : Concrete & wood chippings.

QDM:	LENGTH X WIDTH:	EXT. TO:
270.	1920 x 50yds.	2470yds.
330.	1400 x 50yds.	1700yds.
220.	1400 x 50yds.	1600yds.

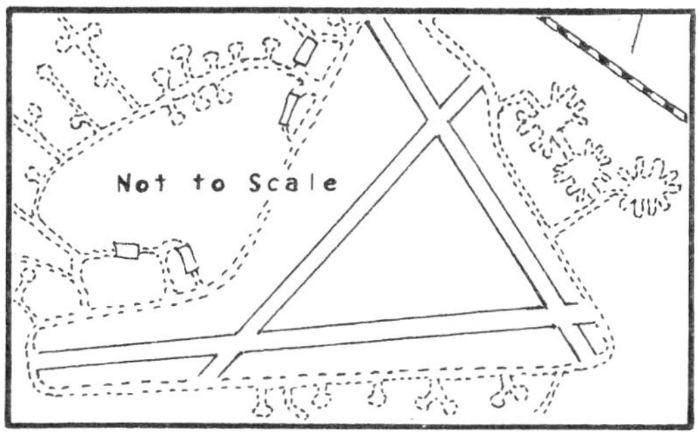

EXTENSIBILITY : -

ACCOMMODATION : Temporary.
HANGARS : T2-4.

HARDSTANDINGS : Loop-31.

R.A.F. : OFFICERS: S.N.C.O's.: O.R's.: TOTAL:
W.A.A.F.: " : " : " : " :

AFFILIATED AIRFIELDS : -

PRESENT USE [1985] : Disused.

NO: 578.

AIRFIELD NAME: TOPCLIFFE. OPENED : 1940.
COUNTY : Yorkshire. CLOSED :
COMMAND : Bomber.
FORMATION : 7 Grp[St.Vincents] GRID REF: E 880994[21]
FUNCTION : Operational. O.S.REF.: SE 405790/99.
: [76 RCAF Base]
LOCALITY : 2.5miles SW of Thirsk.
RAILWAY STN. : Thirsk[LNER]

LATITUDE : 54 12 30N. HEIGHT ASL : 81' LIGHTING : Mk2.
LONGITUDE : 01 23 00W. FLYING CONTROL : Yes. RADIO : QDM.

LANDMARKS DAY. : Church 2miles SW of A/F.

LANDMARKS NIGHT : -

OBSTRUCTIONS : Wood at SW end of R/W 314degrees.

LANDING AREA SURFACE : Concrete.

QDM:	LENGTH X WIDTH:	EXT. TO:
314.	2000 x 50yds.	3000yds.
266.	1400 x 50yds.	2000yds.
318.	1400 x 50yds.	2000yds.

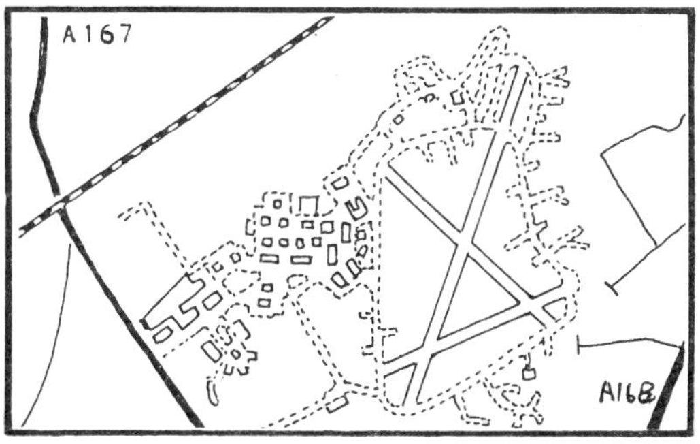

EXTENSIBILITY : Could be extended further but limited by hills to E.
ACCOMMODATION : Permanent.
HANGARS : Type C-5.

HARDSTANDINGS : Heavy bomber-36.

R.C.A.F.: OFFICERS: 242.S.N.C.O's.: 537.O.R's.: 1260.TOTAL: 2039.
W.A.A.F.: " : 8. " : 16. " : 396. " : 420.

AFFILIATED AIRFIELDS : Dalton,Disforth & Wombleton[Sub-stations]

PRESENT USE [1985] : Army.

NO: 579.

AIRFIELD NAME: TOWYN. OPENED : 1940.
COUNTY : Merioneth. CLOSED : 1945.
COMMAND : Fighter.
FORMATION : 70 Grp[Farnborough] GRID REF: J 039239[68]
FUNCTION : A/A Co-Operation Unit. O.S.REF.: JO 580018/135.
:
LOCALITY : .5miles NWN of Towyn.
RAILWAY STN. : Towyn on Sea[GWR]

LATITUDE : 52 35 38N. HEIGHT ASL : 9' LIGHTING : None.
LONGITUDE : 04 05 53W. FLYING CONTROL : None.RADIO : QDM.

LANDMARKS DAY. : Sea & railway on W side. Lake on N side 1mile. Towyn village SE.

LANDMARKS NIGHT : As day.

OBSTRUCTIONS : Hills to N & E. 2 W/T masts S side.

LANDING AREA SURFACE : Grass.

QDM:	LENGTH X WIDTH:	EXT. TO:
E-W.	700yds.	-
NE-SW.	1100yds.	-
NW-SE.	1200yds.	-

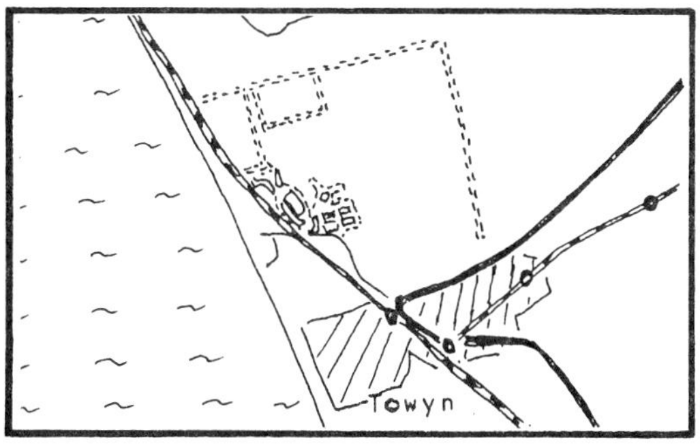

EXTENSIBILITY : None possible.

ACCOMMODATION : Temporary.
HANGARS : Bellman-2;Blister-2;Bessoneau-2.

HARDSTANDINGS : -

R.A.F. : OFFICERS: 13.S.N.C.O's.: 29.O.R's.: 393.TOTAL: 435.
W.A.A.F.: " : 2. " : 8. " : 92. " : 102.

AFFILIATED AIRFIELDS : -

PRESENT USE [1985] : Recreation.

NO: 580.

AIRFIELD NAME: TRELIGGA. OPENED : 1940.
COUNTY : Cornwall. CLOSED : 1955.
COMMAND : RN.
FORMATION : On books of HMS Vulture. GRID REF: S 475055[136]
FUNCTION : Emergency Landing Ground. O.S.REF.: SX 047848/200.
:
LOCALITY : 1.5miles WNW of Delabole.
RAILWAY STN. : Delabole[SR]

LATITUDE : 50 37 45N. HEIGHT ASL : 350' LIGHTING : None.
LONGITUDE : 04 45 40W. FLYING CONTROL : None. RADIO : None.

LANDMARKS DAY. : R Camel 7miles WSW.
Tintagel Head.

LANDMARKS NIGHT : As day.

OBSTRUCTIONS : Land rises to 660' 2.25miles NE.
Land rises to 200' 500yds. E.

LANDING AREA SURFACE : Grass.
QDM: 045-225. LENGTH X WIDTH: 700x100yds. EXT. TO: -
: 105-285. : 730x100yds. : -
: 165-345. : 800x100yds. : -
: : :

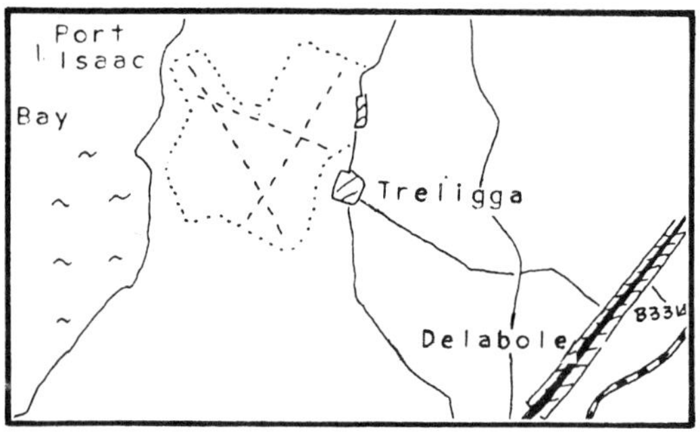

EXTENSIBILITY : -

ACCOMMODATION : No facilities.
HANGARS : None.

HARDSTANDINGS : -

R.N. : OFFICERS: - Chiefs/POs/Ratings. : - TOTAL: -
W.R.N.S. : " : - " : " : - " : -

AFFILIATED AIRFIELDS : St.Merryn[Parent]

PRESENT USE [1985] : Agriculture.

NO: 581.

AIRFIELD NAME: TUDDENHAM. OPENED : 1943.
COUNTY : Suffolk. CLOSED : 1963.
COMMAND : Bomber.
FORMATION : 3 Grp[Exning] GRID REF: M 210903[76]
FUNCTION : Operational. O.S.REF.: TL 754713/144.
:
LOCALITY : 7.5miles NW of Bury St. Edmunds.
RAILWAY STN. : Higham 3.5miles[LNER]

LATITUDE : 52 18 45N. HEIGHT ASL : 65' LIGHTING : Mk2.
LONGITUDE : 00 34 30E. FLYING CONTROL : Yes. RADIO : QDM.

LANDMARKS DAY. : -

LANDMARKS NIGHT : -

OBSTRUCTIONS : -

LANDING AREA SURFACE : Concrete.
QDM: 067. LENGTH X WIDTH: 1400 x 50yds. EXT. TO: 3000yds.
: 186. : 1400 x 50yds. : 2000yds.
: 300. : 2000 x 50yds. : -
: : :

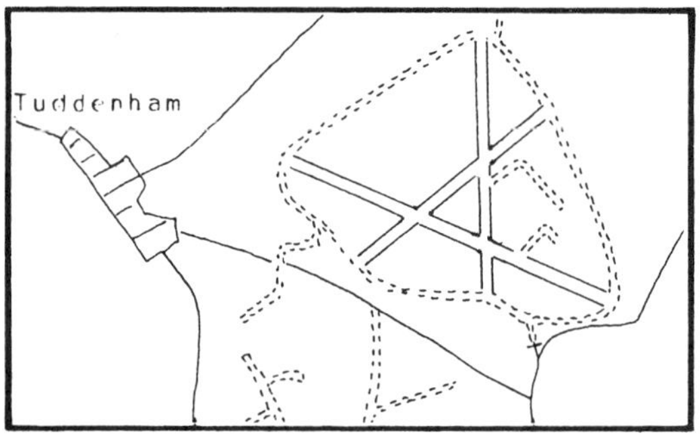

EXTENSIBILITY : Entails demolition of a house.

ACCOMMODATION : Temporary.
HANGARS : T2-2;B1-1.

HARDSTANDINGS : Loop-38.

R.A.F. : OFFICERS: 116. S.N.C.O's.: 290. O.R's.: 960. TOTAL: 1366.
W.A.A.F.: " : 8. " : 16. " : 260. " : 284.

AFFILIATED AIRFIELDS : Mildenhall[32 Base]

PRESENT USE [1985] : Agriculture.

NO: 582.

AIRFIELD NAME: TURNBERRY. OPENED : 1917.
COUNTY : Ayrshire. CLOSED : 1945.
COMMAND : Coastal.
FORMATION : 17 Grp[Edinburgh] GRID REF: S 697298[82Scot]
FUNCTION : Operational Training Unit. O.S.REF.: NS 208075/76.
LOCALITY : 7miles N of Girvan.
RAILWAY STN. : Girvan[[LMS]

LATITUDE : 55 19 30N. HEIGHT ASL : 35' LIGHTING : Mk2.
LONGITUDE : 04 49 45W. FLYING CONTROL : Yes. RADIO : QDM.

LANDMARKS DAY. : Ailsa Craig 1115' 246degreesT 12miles.
Lighthouse on W side of A/F.

LANDMARKS NIGHT : Lighthouse.

OBSTRUCTIONS : Hills 600' within 2miles.
Hills 900' within 5miles.

LANDING AREA SURFACE : Concrete covered with tarmac.
QDM: 222. LENGTH X WIDTH: 2010 x 50yds. EXT. TO: 2210yds.
: 181. : 1400 x 50yds. : -
: 275. : 1250 x 50yds. : -
: : :

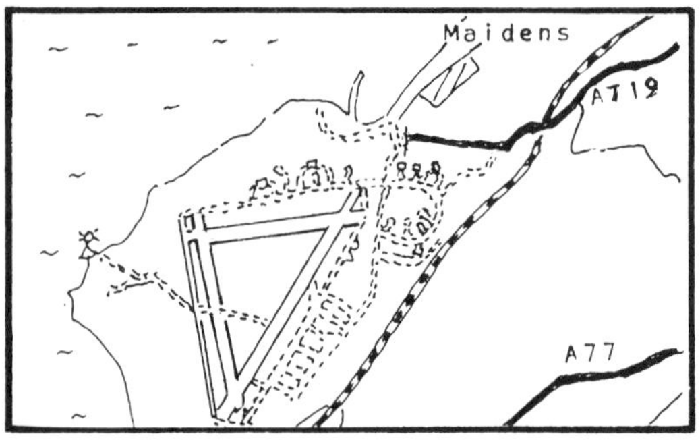

EXTENSIBILITY : R/Ws could be made 200yds. wide.

ACCOMMODATION : Temporary.
HANGARS : T2-2;half T2-2;EO Blister-24.

HARDSTANDINGS : 100' dia-31;fighter HS-3.

R.A.F. : OFFICERS: 195. S.N.C.O's.: 296. O.R's.: 1854. TOTAL: 2345.
W.A.A.F.: " : 15. " : 14. " : 408. " : 437.

AFFILIATED AIRFIELDS : -

PRESENT USE [1985] : Disused.

AIRFIELD NAME: TURNHOUSE. OPENED : 1916.
COUNTY : Midlothian. CLOSED :
COMMAND : Fighter.
FORMATION : 13 Grp[Inverness] GRID REF: T 657954[74Scot]
FUNCTION : Sector Station. O.S.REF.: NT 156734/65.
:
LOCALITY : 5miles W of Edinburgh.
RAILWAY STN. : Edinburgh Waverley & Princes St[NB]

LATITUDE : 55 56 57N. HEIGHT ASL : 100′ LIGHTING : None.
LONGITUDE : 03 20 53W. FLYING CONTROL : Yes. RADIO : QDM.

LANDMARKS DAY. : Forth Bridge 2.5miles N.

LANDMARKS NIGHT : Firth of Fourth.

OBSTRUCTIONS : Hills 200′ ASL QDM255degrees on approach to R/W 260. Torpichen Hill 1017′ ASL 11miles W of base.

LANDING AREA SURFACE : Concrete.
:
QDM: 260. LENGTH X WIDTH: 1133 x 50yds.EXT. TO: 2000yds.
: 310. : 1156 x 50yds. : 1900yds.
: 220. : 716 x 50yds. : -

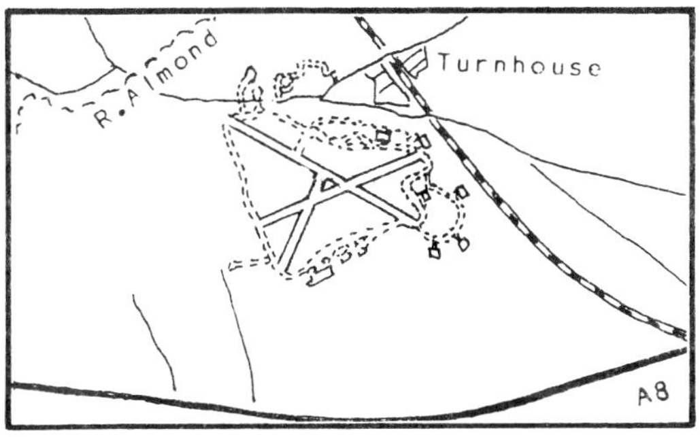

EXTENSIBILITY : Entails diversion of 2 roads & fairly heavy demolition.
ACCOMMODATION : Permanent.
HANGARS : Type C[225′]-1;Blister-6.

HARDSTANDINGS : Frying pan-4;Pens,double SE-12.

R.A.F. : OFFICERS: 112.S.N.C.O′s.: 110.O.R′s.: 1118.TOTAL: 1340.
W.A.A.F.: " : 12. " : 36. " : 595. " : 643.

AFFILIATED AIRFIELDS : Peterhead & Drem[NF-FA] Macmerry.

PRESENT USE [1985] : Civil Airport[Edinburgh]

NO: 584.

AIRFIELD NAME: TURWESTON. OPENED : 1942.
COUNTY : Buckinghamshire. CLOSED : 1945.
COMMAND : Bomber.
FORMATION : 92 Grp[Winslow] GRID REF: L 060583[94]
FUNCTION : Operational Training O.S.REF.: SP 615383/152.
: Unit[satellite]
LOCALITY : 9.5miles E of Aylesbury.
RAILWAY STN. : Brackley[LNER]

LATITUDE : 52 02 15N. HEIGHT ASL : 448′ LIGHTING : MK2.
LONGITUDE : 01 06 00W. FLYING CONTROL : Yes. RADIO : QDM.

LANDMARKS DAY. : -

LANDMARKS NIGHT : -

OBSTRUCTIONS : -

LANDING AREA SURFACE : Concrete.
:
QDM: 100. LENGTH X WIDTH: 2000 x 50yds.EXT. TO: -
: 040. : 1400 x 50yds. : 1750yds.
: 160. : 1100 x 50yds. : -
: : :

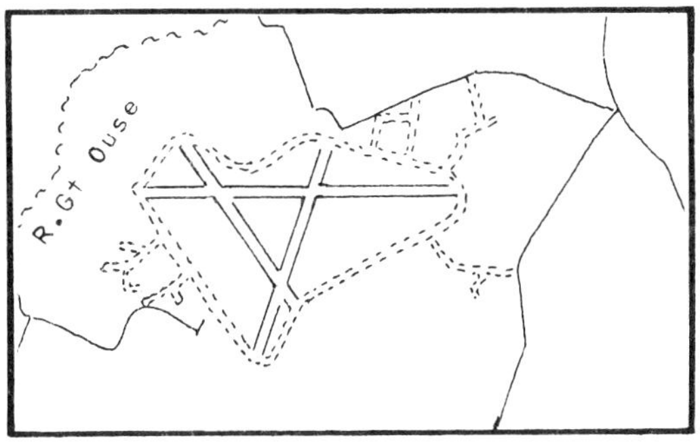

EXTENSIBILITY : -

ACCOMMODATION : Temporary.
HANGARS : T2-1.

HARDSTANDINGS : Heavy bomber-27.

R.A.F. : OFFICERS: 93.S.N.C.O′s.: 312.O.R′s.: 622.TOTAL: 1027.
W.A.A.F.: " : 3. " : 8. " : 171. " : 182.

AFFILIATED AIRFIELDS : Silverstone[Parent]

PRESENT USE [1985] : Agriculture.

NO: 585.

AIRFIELD NAME: TWATT. OPENED : 1941.
COUNTY : Orkneys. CLOSED : 1949.
COMMAND : RN.
FORMATION : HMS Tern. GRID REF: Y 803448[Scot]
FUNCTION : Fleet Requirements Unit.O.S.REF.: HY 265230/6.
:
LOCALITY : 12miles ESE of Kirkwall.
RAILWAY STN. : Thurso[LMS]

LATITUDE : 59 05 15N. HEIGHT ASL : 65′ LIGHTING : Naval.
LONGITUDE : 03 17 10W. FLYING CONTROL : Yes. RADIO : QDM.

LANDMARKS DAY. : Brough Head & Lock of Isbister.

LANDMARKS NIGHT : -

OBSTRUCTIONS : -

LANDING AREA SURFACE : Tarmac.
:
QDM: 013-193. LENGTH X WIDTH: 1000 x 30yds.EXT. TO: -
: 058-238. : 1000 x 30yds. : -
: 113-293. : 1030 x 30yds. : -
: 153-333. : 1200 x 30yds. : -

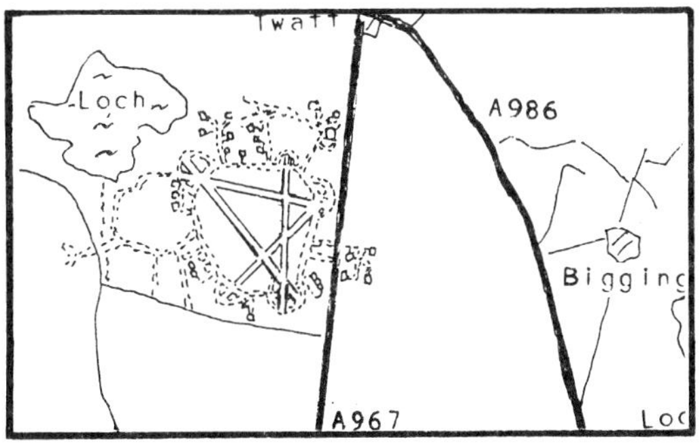

EXTENSIBILITY : -

ACCOMMODATION : Temporary.
HANGARS : Sqdn:60x50′-12;60x70′-9; Storage:60x70′-7;W/Shop-185x105′-1.
HARDSTANDINGS : -

R.N. : OFFICERS: 111. Chiefs/POs/Ratings. : 1008.TOTAL: 1119.
W.R.N.S.: " : 6. " : " : 176. " : 182.

AFFILIATED AIRFIELDS : -

PRESENT USE [1985] : Disused.

NO: 586.

AIRFIELD NAME: TWINWOOD FARM. OPENED : 1941.
COUNTY : Bedfordshire. CLOSED : 1945.
COMMAND : Fighter.
FORMATION : 12 Grp[Watnall] GRID REF: L 485744[84]
FUNCTION : Operational Training O.S.REF.: TL 035550/153.
: Unit[satellite]
LOCALITY : 4miles N of Bedford.
RAILWAY STN. : Oakley 1.5miles[LMS]

LATITUDE : 52 10 53N. HEIGHT ASL : 275′ LIGHTING : Mk2.
LONGITUDE : 00 29 08W. FLYING CONTROL : Yes. RADIO : QDM.

LANDMARKS DAY. : R Ouse 2miles W.

LANDMARKS NIGHT : As day.

OBSTRUCTIONS : Woods N-S.

LANDING AREA SURFACE : Concrete, wood & rubber chippings.

QDM	LENGTH X WIDTH	EXT. TO
330.	1600 x 50yds.	2600yds.
242.	1400 x 50yds.	-
278.	1100 x 50yds.	1450yds.

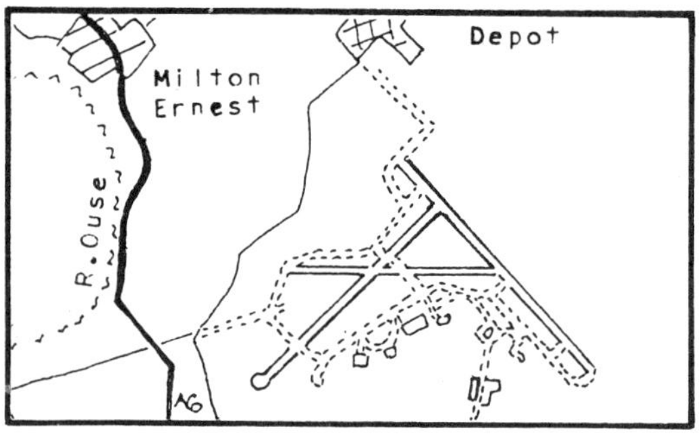

EXTENSIBILITY : -

ACCOMMODATION : Temporary.
HANGARS : Blister-6.

HARDSTANDINGS : 22.

	OFFICERS	S.N.C.O's.	O.R's.	TOTAL
R.A.F.	70.	118.	740.	928.
W.A.A.F.	1.	3.	146.	150.

AFFILIATED AIRFIELDS : Cranfield[Parent]

PRESENT USE [1985] : Disused.

NO: 587.

AIRFIELD NAME: UPAVON. OPENED : 1912.
COUNTY : Wiltshire. CLOSED :
COMMAND : Flying Training.
FORMATION : 23 Grp[South Cerney] GRID REF: U 605752[112]
FUNCTION : Flying Instructors O.S.REF.: SU 152542/173.
: School.
LOCALITY : 9miles S of Marlborough.
RAILWAY STN. : Pewsey 7miles[GWR]

LATITUDE : 51 17 23N. HEIGHT ASL : 570′ LIGHTING : None.
LONGITUDE : 01 46 00W. FLYING CONTROL : Yes. RADIO : QDM.

LANDMARKS DAY. : Kennet & Avon canal, & R Avon.

LANDMARKS NIGHT : As day.

OBSTRUCTIONS : -

LANDING AREA SURFACE : Grass[240-Sommerfeld track]

QDM	LENGTH X WIDTH	EXT. TO
240.	1250yds.	-
E-W.	1130yds.	-
N-S.	625yds.	-
NE-SW.	1300yds.	-

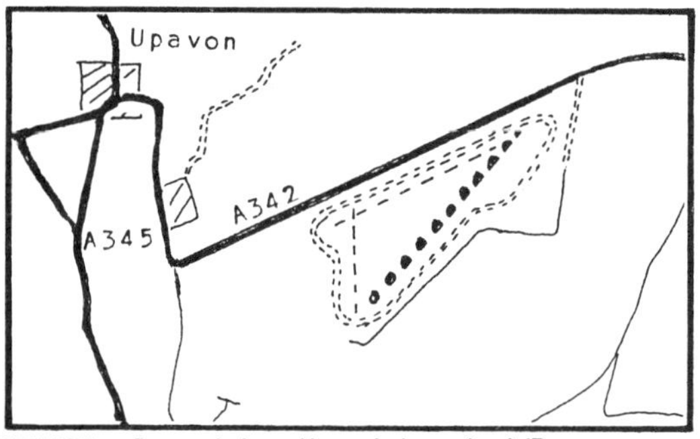

EXTENSIBILITY : Beam strip adjacent to main A/F. Grass 1300yds. QDM 035.
ACCOMMODATION : Permanent[part]
HANGARS : Types:A-2;C-1;L-1;Tunell-1;Blister-10.

HARDSTANDINGS : -

	OFFICERS	S.N.C.O's.	O.R's.	TOTAL
R.A.F.	142.	216.	529.	887.
W.A.A.F.	6.	8.	344.	358.

AFFILIATED AIRFIELDS : Overton Heath[RLG]

PRESENT USE [1985] : RAF.

NO: 588.

AIRFIELD NAME: UPOTTERY. OPENED : 1944.
COUNTY : Devon. CLOSED : 1948.
COMMAND : Fighter.
FORMATION : 70 Grp[Farnborough] GRID REF: T 618320[129]
FUNCTION : Operational[satellite] O.S.REF.: ST 184104/180.
:
LOCALITY : 6miles N of Honiton.
RAILWAY STN. : Honiton[SR]

LATITUDE : 50 53 08N. HEIGHT ASL : 825′ LIGHTING : Mk2.
LONGITUDE : 03 09 30W. FLYING CONTROL : Yes. RADIO : QDM.

LANDMARKS DAY. : Wellington monument 5miles NW.

LANDMARKS NIGHT : -

OBSTRUCTIONS : -

LANDING AREA SURFACE : Concrete & tarmac.

QDM	LENGTH X WIDTH	EXT. TO
270.	2000 x 50yds.	2400yds.
210.	1400 x 50yds.	2000yds.
330.	1400 x 50yds.	-

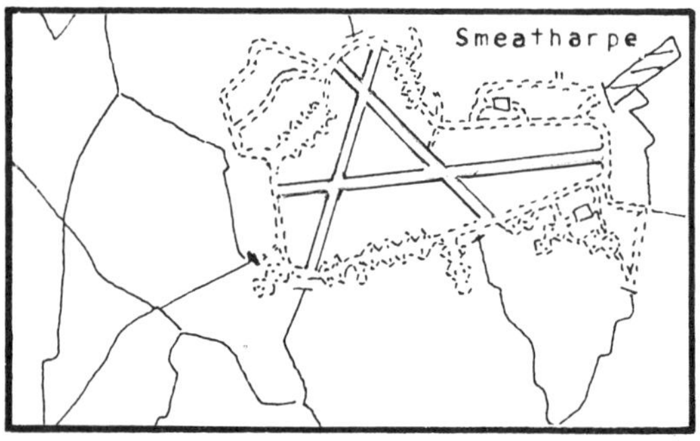

EXTENSIBILITY : -

ACCOMMODATION : Temporary.
HANGARS : T2-2.

HARDSTANDINGS : Spectacle-50.

	OFFICERS	S.N.C.O's.	O.R's.	TOTAL
R.A.F.	124.	660.	1396.	2180.
W.A.A.F.	6.	18.	300.	324.

AFFILIATED AIRFIELDS : Weston Zoyland[Parent]

PRESENT USE [1985] : Agriculture.

NO: 589.

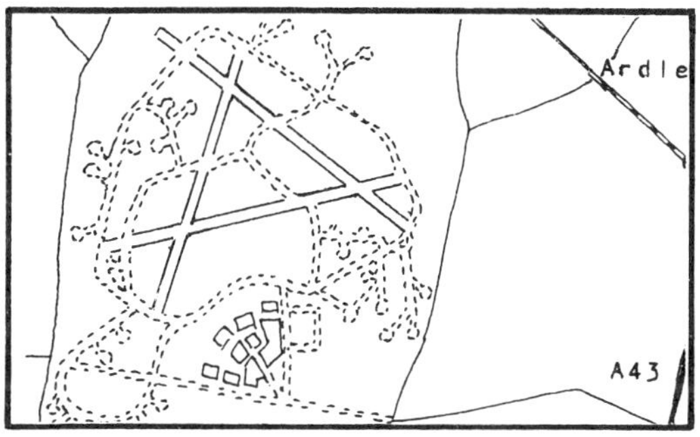

AIRFIELD NAME: UPPER HEYFORD. OPENED : 1917.
COUNTY : Oxfordshire. CLOSED :
COMMAND : Bomber.
FORMATION : 92 Grp[Winslow] GRID REF: P 958464[94]
FUNCTION : Operational Training Unit. O.S.REF.: SP 515268/164.
LOCALITY : 5miles NW of Bicester.
RAILWAY STN. : Heyford 3miles[GWR]

LATITUDE : 51 56 00N. HEIGHT ASL : 420' LIGHTING : Mk2.
LONGITUDE : 01 15 15W. FLYING CONTROL : Yes. RADIO : QDM.

LANDMARKS DAY. : R Cherwell & railway 2miles W.

LANDMARKS NIGHT : -

OBSTRUCTIONS : -

LANDING AREA SURFACE : Concrete.

QDM	LENGTH X WIDTH	EXT. TO
217.	2000 x 50yds.	3000yds.
264.	1700 x 50yds.	2000yds.
311.	1550 x 50yds.	2300yds.

EXTENSIBILITY : Entails slight demolition.

ACCOMMODATION : Permanent.
HANGARS : Type A-6.

HARDSTANDINGS : Loop-7;frying pan-23.

	OFFICERS	S.N.C.O's.	O.R's.	TOTAL
R.A.F.	202.	632.	1184.	2018.
W.A.A.F.	12.	9.	379.	400.

AFFILIATED AIRFIELDS : Barford St. John[Satellite]

PRESENT USE [1985] : USAFE.

NO: 590.

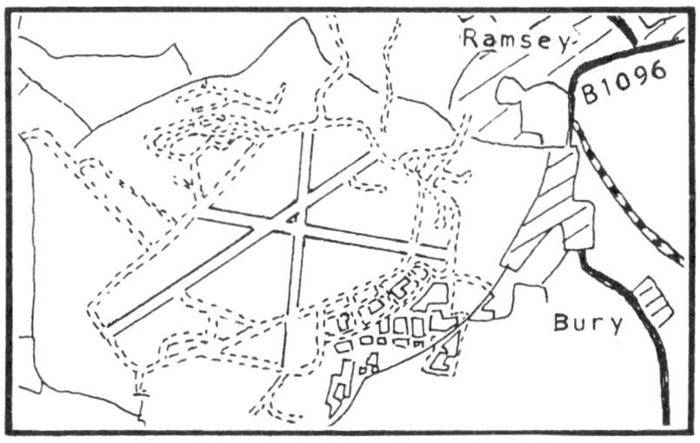

AIRFIELD NAME: UPWOOD. OPENED : 1937.
COUNTY : Huntingdonshire. CLOSED :
COMMAND : Bomber.
FORMATION : 8 Grp[Huntingdon] GRID REF: F 724029[75]
FUNCTION : Operational. O.S.REF.: TL 269842/142.
LOCALITY : 1.75miles SW of Ramsey.
RAILWAY STN. : Holme[LNER]

LATITUDE : 52 26 15N. HEIGHT ASL : 50' LIGHTING : MK2.
LONGITUDE : 00 08 00W. FLYING CONTROL : Yes. RADIO : QDM.

LANDMARKS DAY. : Ramsey 030degrees 1miles. Main LNER line running approx N & S 3.5miles to W. Warboys Wood 135 degrees 1.5miles. Wennington Wood 215degrees 3miles.

LANDMARKS NIGHT : -

OBSTRUCTIONS : -

LANDING AREA SURFACE : Concrete & tarmac.

QDM	LENGTH X WIDTH	EXT. TO
058.	2000 x 50yds.	2750yds.
288.	1600 x 50yds.	1660yds.
194.	1400 x 50yds.	-

EXTENSIBILITY : Entails demolition of a ruined house.

ACCOMMODATION : Permanent.
HANGARS : Type C-4.

HARDSTANDINGS : Heavy bomber-36.

	OFFICERS	S.N.C.O's.	O.R's.	TOTAL
R.A.F.	201.	510.	1374.	2085.
W.A.A.F.	5.	11.	320.	336.

AFFILIATED AIRFIELDS : -

PRESENT USE [1985] : USAFE.

NO: 591.

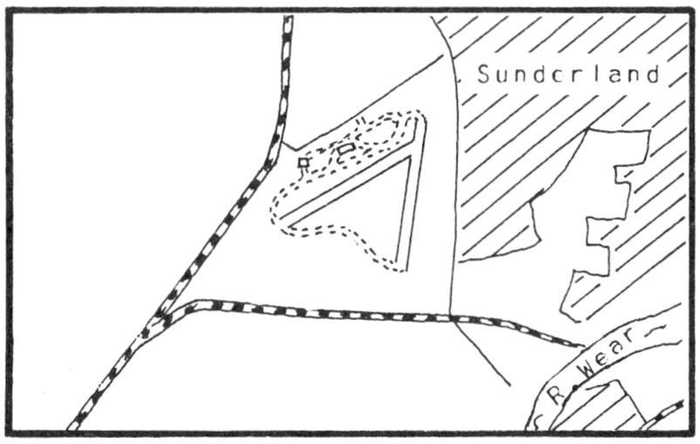

AIRFIELD NAME: USWORTH. OPENED : 1916.
COUNTY : Durham. CLOSED :
COMMAND : Maintenance.
FORMATION : 56 Wing[Carlisle] GRID REF: Z 826787[7]
FUNCTION : Storage Unit. O.S.REF.: NZ 340585/88.
LOCALITY : 3.75miles W of Sunderland.
RAILWAY STN. : Usworth 1.5miles[LNER]

LATITUDE : 54 55 15N. HEIGHT ASL : 120' LIGHTING : None.
LONGITUDE : 01 28 00W. FLYING CONTROL : None. RADIO : QDM.

LANDMARKS DAY. : Coast. R Tyne & R Wear. Memorial on hill 2.5miles S.

LANDMARKS NIGHT : Coast. R Tyne & R Wear.

OBSTRUCTIONS : Hill 307' 1mile NNE.

LANDING AREA SURFACE : Concrete covered with tarmac.

QDM	LENGTH X WIDTH	EXT. TO
236.	800 x 50yds.	2000yds.
192.	800 x 50yds.	2000yds.

EXTENSIBILITY : Entails cutting of important road.

ACCOMMODATION : Permanent.
HANGARS : Lemella-1;Calendar-1;O Blister-2; Standard Blister-1.
HARDSTANDINGS : Square pens-16;circular-14.

	OFFICERS	S.N.C.O's.	O.R's.	TOTAL
R.A.F.	39.	44.	940.	1023.
W.A.A.F.	3.	3.	109.	115.

AFFILIATED AIRFIELDS : -

PRESENT USE [1985] : Civil Airport[Sunderland]

NO: 592.

AIRFIELD NAME: VALLEY. OPENED : 1941.
COUNTY : Anglesey. CLOSED :
COMMAND : Transport.
FORMATION : 44 Grp[Gloucester] GRID REF: H 776977[41]
FUNCTION : Airport. O.S.REF.: SH 305758/114.

LOCALITY : 6miles SE of Holyhead.
RAILWAY STN. : Valley 2miles[LMS]

LATITUDE : 53 15 00N. HEIGHT ASL : 26′ LIGHTING : Mk2.
LONGITUDE : 04 32 15W. FLYING CONTROL : Yes. RADIO : QDM.

LANDMARKS DAY. : Bounded on N by Holyhead-Chester railway, & 3 lakes N of A/F.

LANDMARKS NIGHT : Holyhead mountain to NW.

OBSTRUCTIONS : Holyhead mountain 6.5miles 310degrees T.

LANDING AREA SURFACE : Tarmac.

QDM	LENGTH X WIDTH	EXT. TO
188.	1785 x 50yds.	2300yds.
251.	1400 x 50yds.	-
132.	2000 x 50yds.	-

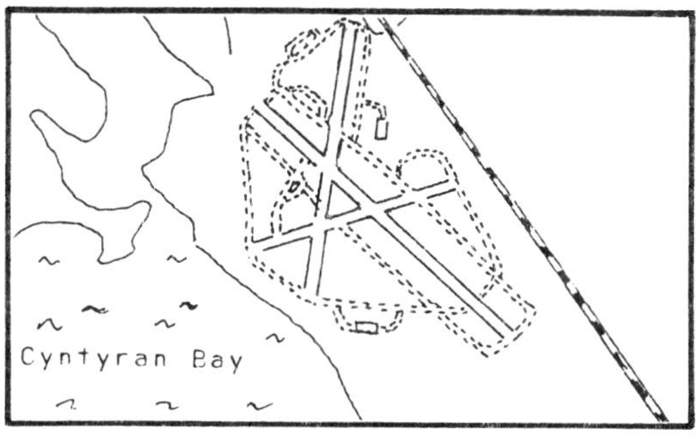

EXTENSIBILITY : With major engineering works could be extended to 3000-3100 & 2580yds. respectively.
ACCOMMODATION : Temporary.
HANGARS : Bellman-3;T2-3.

HARDSTANDINGS : TE-29;SE-22.

	OFFICERS	S.N.C.O′s.	O.R′s.	TOTAL
R.A.F.	98.	84.	1302.	1484.
W.A.A.F.	16.	8.	580.	604.

AFFILIATED AIRFIELDS : -

PRESENT USE [1985] : RAF.

NO: 593.

AIRFIELD NAME: WADDINGTON. OPENED : 1916.
COUNTY : Lincolnshire. CLOSED :
COMMAND : Bomber.
FORMATION : 5 Grp[Morton Hall] GRID REF: F 453843[47]
FUNCTION : Operational[53 Base] O.S.REF.: SK 982630/121.

LOCALITY : 4miles S of Lincoln.
RAILWAY STN. : Lincoln[LNER]

LATITUDE : 53 10 15N. HEIGHT ASL : 235′ LIGHTING : Mk2.
LONGITUDE : 00 31 15W. FLYING CONTROL : Yes. RADIO : QDM.

LANDMARKS DAY. : Hospital 1.5miles N. Lincoln-Grantham railway 1mile W.

LANDMARKS NIGHT : Lincoln cathedral 1.5miles N.

OBSTRUCTIONS : Water tower 90′

LANDING AREA SURFACE : Concrete & tarmac.

QDM	LENGTH X WIDTH	EXT. TO
212.	2000 x 50yds.	2750yds.
073.	1400 x 50yds.	2000yds.
256.	1400 x 50yds.	2000yds.

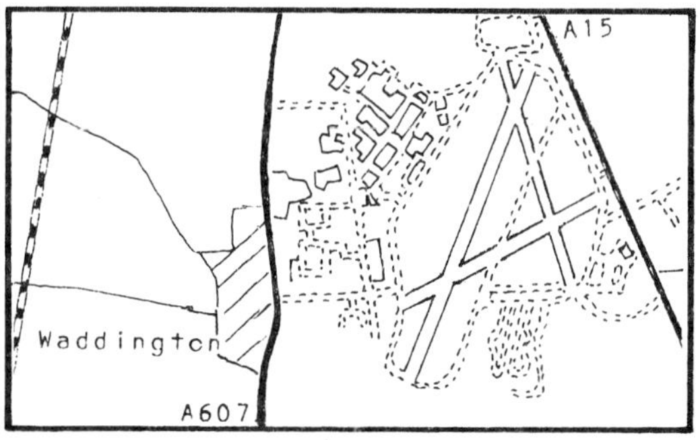

EXTENSIBILITY : Entails continued diversion of main Lincoln-Sleaford road for 1.75miles.
ACCOMMODATION : Permanent.
HANGARS : Type C-5.

HARDSTANDINGS : Heavy bomber-36.

	OFFICERS	S.N.C.O′s.	O.R′s.	TOTAL
R.A.F.	212.	466.	1407.	2085.
W.A.A.F.	13.	15.	362.	390.

AFFILIATED AIRFIELDS : Bardney & Skellingthorpe[Sub-stations]

PRESENT USE [1985] : RAF.

NO: 594.

AIRFIELD NAME: WANBOROUGH. OPENED : 1941.
COUNTY : Wiltshire. CLOSED : 1946.
COMMAND : Flying Training.
FORMATION : 50 Grp[Reading] GRID REF: P 662025[104]
FUNCTION : Beam Approach School [RLG] O.S.REF.: SU 218828/173.
LOCALITY : 5miles SE of Swindon.
RAILWAY STN. : Swindon 3miles[GWR]

LATITUDE : 51 32 08N. HEIGHT ASL : 650′ LIGHTING : None.
LONGITUDE : 01 41 00W. FLYING CONTROL : None. RADIO : QDM.

LANDMARKS DAY. : Liddington Hill S.

LANDMARKS NIGHT : -

OBSTRUCTIONS : Hill to S.

LANDING AREA SURFACE : Grass.

QDM	LENGTH X WIDTH	EXT. TO
N-S.	900yds.	-
NE-SW.	750yds.	-

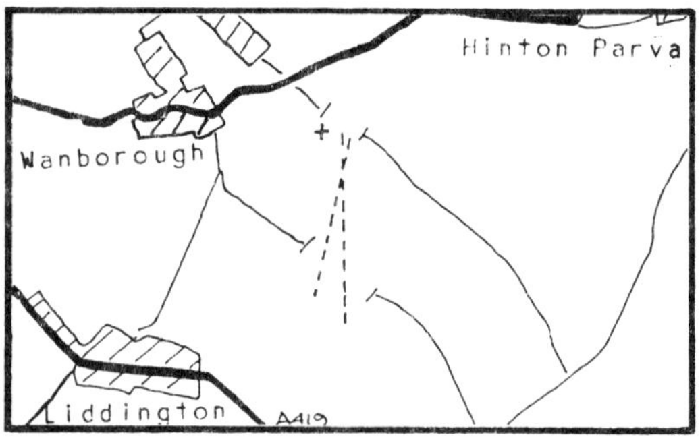

EXTENSIBILITY : None possible.

ACCOMMODATION : Temporary.
HANGARS : EO Blister-2.

HARDSTANDINGS : -

	OFFICERS	S.N.C.O′s.	O.R′s.	TOTAL
R.A.F.	8.	-	117.	125.
W.A.A.F.	-	-	-	-

AFFILIATED AIRFIELDS : Watchfield[Parent]

PRESENT USE [1985] : Recreation.

NO: 595.

AIRFIELD NAME: WARBOYS. OPENED : 1941.
COUNTY : Huntingdonshire. CLOSED : 1963.
COMMAND : Bomber.
FORMATION : 8 Grp[Huntingdon] GRID REF: L 752982[75]
FUNCTION : Operational. O.S.REF.: TL 290795/142.
:
LOCALITY : 5.75miles NE of Huntingdon.
RAILWAY STN. : Huntingdon North[LNER]

LATITUDE : 52 23 38N. HEIGHT ASL : 100' LIGHTING : Mk2.
LONGITUDE : 00 05 45W. FLYING CONTROL : Yes. RADIO : QDM.

LANDMARKS DAY. : Main LNER line Peterborough-Huntington 3.5miles W. Ramsey 350degrees 4miles. St.Ives 170degrees 5miles. Huntington 212degrees 6miles. 1 Large wood[Wennington Wood]260degrees 2miles.
LANDMARKS NIGHT : Warboys Wood 014degrees 1mile.

OBSTRUCTIONS : -

LANDING AREA SURFACE : Tarmac.
:

QDM	LENGTH X WIDTH	EXT. TO
122.	2000 x 50yds.	3300yds.
179.	1350 x 50yds.	-
069.	1400 x 50yds.	2000yds.

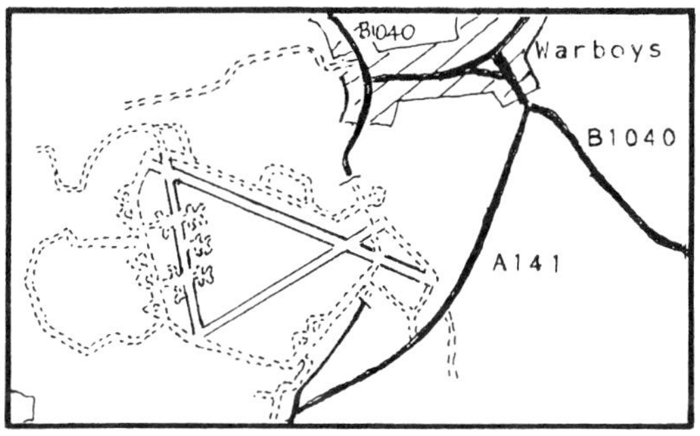

EXTENSIBILITY : Entails diversion of a new road & heavy demolition.
ACCOMMODATION : Temporary.
HANGARS : T2-2;B1-1.

HARDSTANDINGS : Heavy bomber-36.

	OFFICERS	S.N.C.O's.	O.R's.	TOTAL
R.A.F.	256.	245.	1458.	1959.
W.A.A.F.	4.	10.	277.	291.

AFFILIATED AIRFIELDS : -

PRESENT USE [1985] : Agriculture.

NO: 596.

AIRFIELD NAME: WARMWELL. OPENED : 1937.
COUNTY : Dorsetshire. CLOSED : 1945.
COMMAND : Fighter.
FORMATION : 11 Grp[Uxbridge] GRID REF: U 193092[140]
FUNCTION : Forward Airfield. O.S.REF.: SY 765885/194.
:
LOCALITY : 4miles E of Dorchester.
RAILWAY STN. : Moreton 1.25miles[SR]

LATITUDE : 50 41 40N. HEIGHT ASL : 203' LIGHTING : Mk2.
LONGITUDE : 02 20 30W. FLYING CONTROL : Yes. RADIO : QDM.

LANDMARKS DAY. : -

LANDMARKS NIGHT : -

OBSTRUCTIONS : -

LANDING AREA SURFACE : Grass.
:

QDM	LENGTH X WIDTH	EXT. TO
NE-SW.	900yds.	2500yds.
WNW-ESE.	1680yds.	2800yds.
NW-SE.	900yds.	-

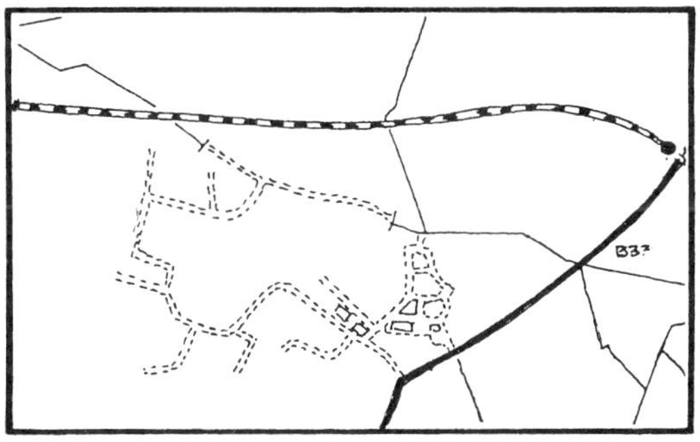

EXTENSIBILITY : Re-stripped could be 5000-1400 & 1000yds., but with diversion of main road & demolition.
ACCOMMODATION : Temporary.
HANGARS : Bellman-2;BNlister-8.

HARDSTANDINGS : SE-6;TE-12.

	OFFICERS	S.N.C.O's.	O.R's.	TOTAL
R.A.F.	144.	160.	1934.	2238.
W.A.A.F.	8.	10.	284.	302.

AFFILIATED AIRFIELDS : Middle Wallop[sector]

PRESENT USE [1985] : Housing.

NO: 597.

AIRFIELD NAME: WARTON. OPENED : 1942.
COUNTY : Lancashire. CLOSED :
COMMAND : USSTAFE.
FORMATION : Air Service Command. GRID REF: D 882492[29]
FUNCTION : No.2 Base Air Depot. O.S.REF.: SD 413278/102.
:
LOCALITY : 7.5miles W of Preston.
RAILWAY STN. : Lytham[LMS]

LATITUDE : 53 44 30N. HEIGHT ASL : 30' LIGHTING : None.
LONGITUDE : 02 53 15W. FLYING CONTROL : Yes. RADIO : QDM.

LANDMARKS DAY. : -

LANDMARKS NIGHT : -

OBSTRUCTIONS : -

LANDING AREA SURFACE : Concrete & tarmac.
:

QDM	LENGTH X WIDTH	EXT. TO
080.	1877 x 50yds.	2570yds.
200.	1394 x 50yds.	1690yds.
300.	1320 x 50yds.	1620yds.

EXTENSIBILITY : Entails very heavy demolition.

ACCOMMODATION : Temporary.
HANGARS : Storage-137363 sq.ft; Repair -623005 sq.ft.
HARDSTANDINGS : loop-50.

USAAF. : OFFICERS: 660. Enlisted Men .: 15242. TOTAL: 15902.

AFFILIATED AIRFIELDS : -

PRESENT USE [1985] : Aircraft Industry[British Aerospace]

NO: 598.

AIRFIELD NAME: WARWICK. OPENED : 1941.
COUNTY : Warwickshire. CLOSED : 1945.
COMMAND : Flying Training.
FORMATION : 23 Grp[South Cerney] GRID REF: P 722834[28]
FUNCTION : Advanced Flying Unit O.S.REF.: SP 268635/151.
: Pilots[RLG]
LOCALITY : 1mile SSW of Warwick.
RAILWAY STN. : Warwick[LMS]

LATITUDE : 52 16 00N. HEIGHT ASL : 160′ LIGHTING : None.
LONGITUDE : 01 36 15W. FLYING CONTROL : None. RADIO : QDM.

LANDMARKS DAY. : Warwick Castle.

LANDMARKS NIGHT : -

OBSTRUCTIONS : High ground on E & NE of airfield.

LANDING AREA : Grass.
SURFACE :

QDM	LENGTH X WIDTH	EXT. TO
NE-SW.	1050yds.	2000yds.
N-S.	1050yds.	1500yds.

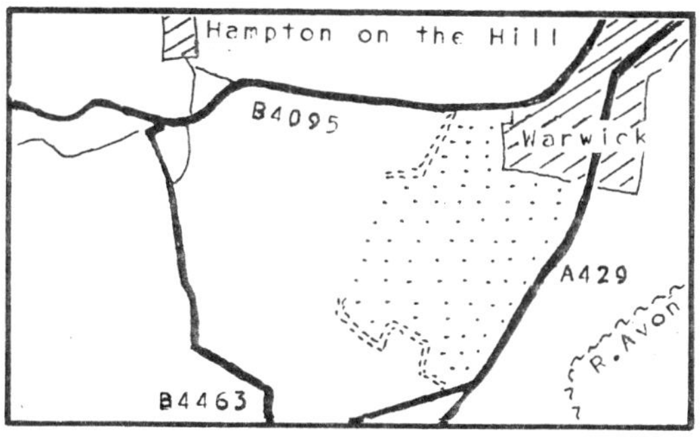

EXTENSIBILITY : Possible in 2 directions, but not recommended.

ACCOMMODATION : Temporary.
HANGARS : 69′ Blister-4.

HARDSTANDINGS : -

	OFFICERS	S.N.C.O's.	O.R's.	TOTAL
R.A.F.	2.	4.	88.	94.
W.A.A.F.	-	-	-	-

AFFILIATED AIRFIELDS : Church Lawford[Parent]

PRESENT USE [1985] : Parkland.

NO: 599.

AIRFIELD NAME: WATCHFIELD. OPENED : 1940.
COUNTY : Berkshire. CLOSED : 1950.
COMMAND : Flying Training.
FORMATION : 50 Grp[Reading] GRID REF: P 686115[104]
FUNCTION : Beam Approach School. O.S.REF.: SU 245912/173.
:
LOCALITY : 7miles NE of Swindon.
RAILWAY STN. : Shrivenham 3miles[GWR]

LATITUDE : 51 37 08N. HEIGHT ASL : 331′ LIGHTING : None.
LONGITUDE : 01 39 00W. FLYING CONTROL : Yes. RADIO : QDM.

LANDMARKS DAY. : Shrivenham barracks 1mile SSE. Highworth GWR 2miles S. Church tower 200′ 3miles E.

LANDMARKS NIGHT : -

OBSTRUCTIONS : Beechy copse NE 300yds from boundary 100′ above A/F level. Water tower 50′ above A/F level.

LANDING AREA : Grass.
SURFACE :

QDM	LENGTH X WIDTH	EXT. TO
NW-SE.	1400yds.	-
NNW-SSE.	1700yds.	-
N-S.	900yds.	

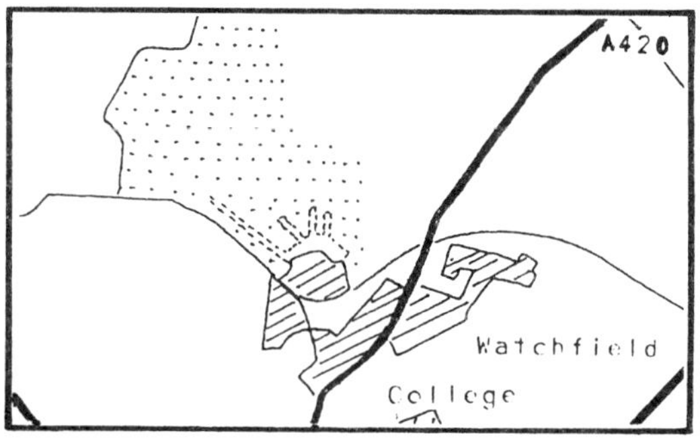

EXTENSIBILITY : None possible.

ACCOMMODATION : Temporary.
HANGARS : Bellman-5;O Blister-5.

HARDSTANDINGS : Concrete & terminal roads-11.

	OFFICERS	S.N.C.O's.	O.R's.	TOTAL
R.A.F.	130.	168.	391.	689.
W.A.A.F.	-	-	-	-

AFFILIATED AIRFIELDS : Kelmscott & Wanborough[RLG]

PRESENT USE [1985] : Unspecified.

NO: 600.

AIRFIELD NAME: WATERBEACH. OPENED : 1941.
COUNTY : Cambridgeshire. CLOSED :
COMMAND : Bomber.
FORMATION : 3 Grp[Exning] GRID REF: L 940860[85]
FUNCTION : Operational[33 Base] O.S.REF.: TL 486670/154.
:
LOCALITY : 5miles N of Cambridge.
RAILWAY STN. : Waterbeach 1mile[LNER]

LATITUDE : 52 16 45N. HEIGHT ASL : 17′ LIGHTING : Mk2.
LONGITUDE : 00 11 00E. FLYING CONTROL : Yes. RADIO : QDM.

LANDMARKS DAY. : Ely Cathedral 020degrees 8.5miles. Cambridge 205degrees 5.5miles.

LANDMARKS NIGHT : R Cam[passes SE at 1.5miles distance] Cambridge.

OBSTRUCTIONS : Nil[except normal height water tower]

LANDING AREA : Concrete covered with tarmac.
SURFACE :

QDM	LENGTH X WIDTH	EXT. TO
227.	2000 x 50yds.	4000yds.
099.	1400 x 50yds.	2000yds.
158.	1300 x 50yds.	2000yds.

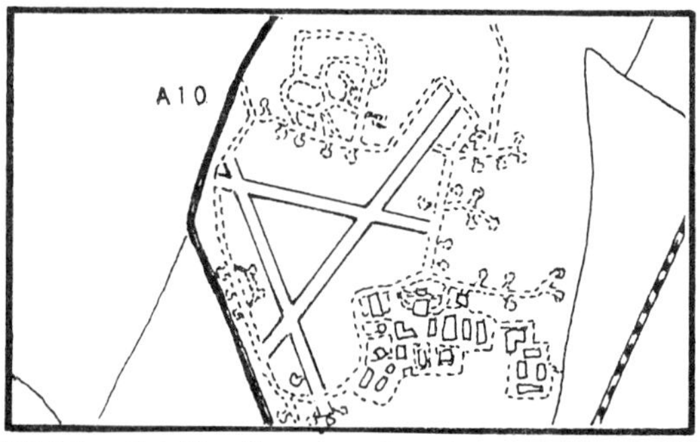

EXTENSIBILITY : Entails diversion of a minor road & demolition of a cottage, & re-siting of wireless masts.
ACCOMMODATION : Permanent.
HANGARS : Type J-2;T2-3;B1-1.

HARDSTANDINGS : Heavy bomber-36.

	OFFICERS	S.N.C.O's.	O.R's.	TOTAL
R.A.F.	138.	463.	1773.	2374.
W.A.A.F.	15.	16.	392.	423.

AFFILIATED AIRFIELDS : Mepal & Witchford[Sub-stations]

PRESENT USE [1985] : Army.

NO: 601.

AIRFIELD NAME: WATTISHAM. OPENED : 1939.
COUNTY : Suffolk. CLOSED :
COMMAND : 8th USAAF.
FORMATION : 479th Fighter Grp. GRID REF: M 475700[86]
FUNCTION : Operational. O.S.REF.: TM 024518/145.
:
LOCALITY : 9miles NW of Ipswich.
RAILWAY STN. : Needham 5.5miles[LNER]

LATITUDE : 52 07 30N. HEIGHT ASL : 290′ LIGHTING : Mk2.
LONGITUDE : 00 57 30E. FLYING CONTROL : Yes. RADIO : QDM.

LANDMARKS : -
DAY.

LANDMARKS : -
NIGHT

OBSTRUCTIONS : 4 hangars & watch office 55′ on E side of A/F.

LANDING AREA : Concrete & tarmac.
SURFACE :
QDM: 060. LENGTH X WIDTH: 2000 x 50yds.EXT. TO: -
: 110. : 1400 x 50yds. : 2000yds.
: 350. : 1400 x 50yds. : 2600yds.
: : :

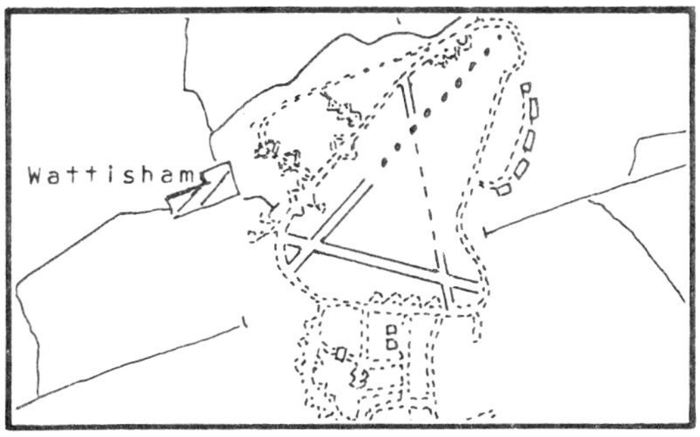

EXTENSIBILITY : -

ACCOMMODATION : Permanent.
HANGARS : Type L-4;T2-4.

HARDSTANDINGS : Spectacle-52;Frying pan-19.

USAAF. : OFFICERS: 190. Enlisted Men. : 1519.TOTAL: 1709.

AFFILIATED AIRFIELDS : -

PRESENT USE [1985] : RAF.

NO: 602.

AIRFIELD NAME: WATTON. OPENED : 1939.
COUNTY : Norfolk. CLOSED : 1978.
COMMAND : 8th USAAF.
FORMATION : 25th Bomb Grp[R] GRID REF: G 395186[66]
FUNCTION : Photo Reconnaissance. O.S.REF.: TF 940000/144.
:
LOCALITY : 11.5miles NE of Thetford.
RAILWAY STN. : Watton 1mile[LNER]

LATITUDE : 52 33 53N. HEIGHT ASL : 190′ LIGHTING : Mk2.
LONGITUDE : 00 51 45E. FLYING CONTROL : Yes. RADIO : QDM.

LANDMARKS : Scoulton Mere 3miles W. Woods in the vicinity
DAY. of Thetford. Griston church E side of A/F.

LANDMARKS : -
NIGHT

OBSTRUCTIONS : Water tower, hangars, Griston church & wood.

LANDING AREA : Concrete.
SURFACE :
QDM: 110. LENGTH X WIDTH: 2000 x 50yds.EXT. TO: 3500yds.
: : : 1400yds.
: : : 1600yds.
: : :

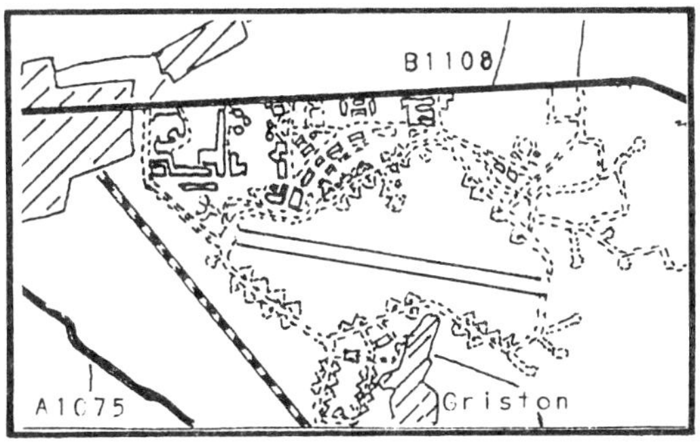

EXTENSIBILITY : Entails demolition of a small farm.

ACCOMMODATION : Permanent.
HANGARS : Type C4-4;B1-2;T2-3;Blister-3.

HARDSTANDINGS : Eye glass-41;Frying pan[concrete]-12.

USAAF. : OFFICERS: 190. Enlisted Men. : 1519.TOTAL: 1709.

AFFILIATED AIRFIELDS : -

PRESENT USE [1985] : HM Prison.

NO: 603.

AIRFIELD NAME: WELFORD. OPENED : 1943.
COUNTY : Berkshire. CLOSED :
COMMAND : 9th USAAF.
FORMATION : 435th Troop Carrier Grp. GRID REF: U 857945[113]
FUNCTION : Operational. O.S.REF.: SU 415745/175.
:
LOCALITY : 7miles NW of Newbury.
RAILWAY STN. : Welford Park 2miles[GWR]

LATITUDE : 51 28 03N. HEIGHT ASL : 450′ LIGHTING : Mk2.
LONGITUDE : 01 24 00W. FLYING CONTROL : Yes. RADIO : QDM.

LANDMARKS : -
DAY.

LANDMARKS : -
NIGHT

OBSTRUCTIONS : -

LANDING AREA : Concrete & wood chippings.
SURFACE :
QDM: 330. LENGTH X WIDTH: 2000 x 50yds.EXT. TO: 2500yds.
: 020. : 1400 x 50yds. : -
: 370. : 1400 x 50yds. : -
: : :

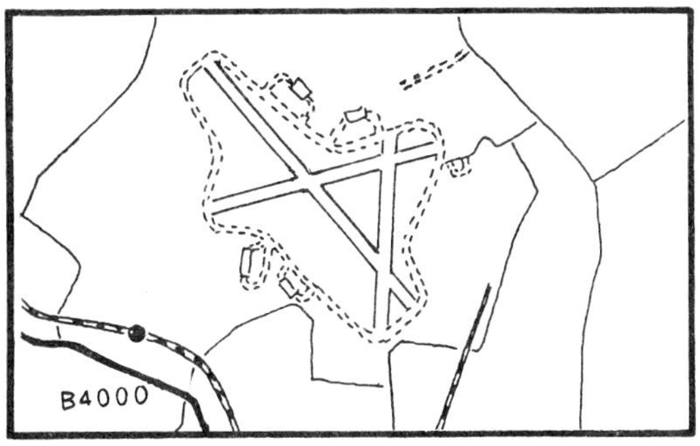

EXTENSIBILITY : -

ACCOMMODATION : Temporary.
HANGARS : T2-2.

HARDSTANDINGS : Frying pan-4;loop-46.

USAAF. : OFFICERS: 470. Enlisted Men. : 1898.TOTAL: 2368.

AFFILIATED AIRFIELDS : -

PRESENT USE [1985] : USAFE.

NO: 604.

AIRFIELD NAME: WELLESBOURNE MOUNTFORD. OPENED : 1941.
COUNTY : Warwickshire. CLOSED : 1964.
COMMAND : Bomber.
FORMATION : 91 Grp[Abingdon] GRID REF: P 718750[82]
FUNCTION : Operational Training O.S.REF.: SP 264549/151.
: Unit.
LOCALITY : 5miles E of Stratford on Avon.
RAILWAY STN. : Stratford on Avon[GWR & LMS]

LATITUDE : 52 11 23N. HEIGHT ASL : 154′ LIGHTING : Mk2.
LONGITUDE : 01 36 30W. FLYING CONTROL : Yes. RADIO : QDM.

LANDMARKS DAY : Stratford on Avon. Sickle shaped wood.

LANDMARKS NIGHT : Junction of R Avon & R Dene.
Compton Verney lake.

OBSTRUCTIONS : Wellesbourne Hill at S end of N-S R/W.
Wellesbourne House at E end of E-W R/W.

LANDING AREA SURFACE : Concrete & tarmac.

QDM: 187. LENGTH X WIDTH: 1100 x 50yds.EXT. TO: 2800yds.
: 236. : 1400 x 50yds. : -
: 294. : 1100 x 50yds. : 1300yds.
: : :

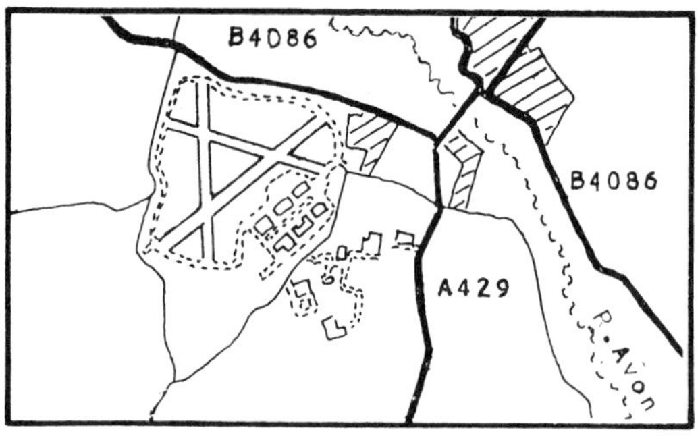

EXTENSIBILITY : -

ACCOMMODATION : Temporary[except Type J hangar]
HANGARS : T2-4.

HARDSTANDINGS : Heavy bomber-39.

R.A.F. : OFFICERS: 168.S.N.C.O′s.: 419.O.R′s.: 1735.TOTAL: 2322.
W.A.A.F.: " : 8. " : 20. " : 281. " : 309.

AFFILIATED AIRFIELDS : Gaydon & Stratford[Satellites]

PRESENT USE [1985] : Private flying.

NO: 605.

AIRFIELD NAME: WELLINGORE. OPENED : 1935.
COUNTY : Lincolnshire. CLOSED : 1945.
COMMAND : Technical Training.
FORMATION : 27 Grp[Cirencester] GRID REF: F 450740[47]
FUNCTION : Radio School[satellite] O.S.REF.: SK 988545/121.
:
LOCALITY : 10.5miles S of Lincoln.
RAILWAY STN. : Leadenham 3.5miles[LNER]

LATITUDE : 53 04 30N. HEIGHT ASL : 260′ LIGHTING : None.
LONGITUDE : 00 31 30W. FLYING CONTROL : None.RADIO : QDM.

LANDMARKS DAY : Central tower of Cranwell.

LANDMARKS NIGHT : -

OBSTRUCTIONS : -

LANDING AREA SURFACE : Grass.

QDM: NE-SW. LENGTH X WIDTH: 1100yds. EXT. TO: 2000yds.
: WNW-ESE. : 1050yds. : 1400yds.
: : :
: : :

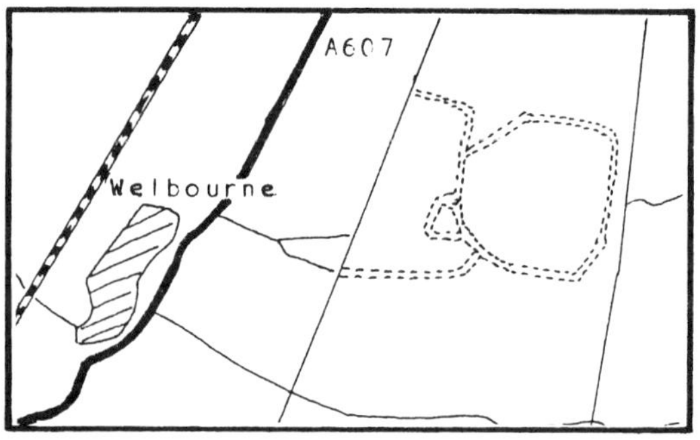

EXTENSIBILITY : -

ACCOMMODATION : Temporary.
HANGARS : Blisters:O-7;EO-1.

HARDSTANDINGS : TE-6.

R.A.F. : OFFICERS: 28.S.N.C.O′s.: 50.O.R′s.: 561.TOTAL: 639.
W.A.A.F.: " : - " : - " : - " : -

AFFILIATED AIRFIELDS : Cranwell[Parent]

PRESENT USE [1985] : Disused.

NO: 606.

AIRFIELD NAME: WENDLING. OPENED : 1942.
COUNTY : Norfolk. CLOSED : 1961.
COMMAND : 8th USAAF.
FORMATION : 392nd Bomb Grp. GRID REF: G 382333[66]
FUNCTION : Operational. O.S.REF.: TF 924151/132.
:
LOCALITY : 4miles WNW of East Dereham.
RAILWAY STN. : Wendling 1.5miles[LNER]

LATITUDE : 52 41 53N. HEIGHT ASL : 250′ LIGHTING : Mk2.
LONGITUDE : 00 50 45E. FLYING CONTROL : Yes. RADIO : QDM.

LANDMARKS DAY : Wood in E corner of A/F.

LANDMARKS NIGHT : -

OBSTRUCTIONS : -

LANDING AREA SURFACE : Concrete & wood chippings.

QDM: 260. LENGTH X WIDTH: 1400 x 50yds.EXT. TO: 3000yds.
: 010. : 2000 x 50yds. : -
: 130. : 1400 x 50yds. : 2000yds.
: : :

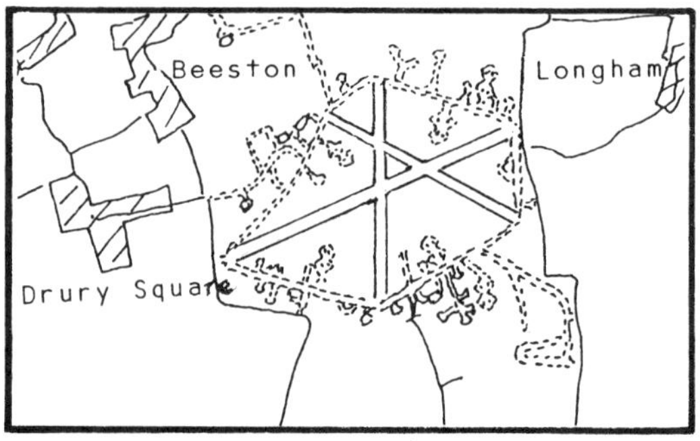

EXTENSIBILITY : Entails diversion of chief access road.

ACCOMMODATION : Temporary.
HANGARS : T2-2.

HARDSTANDINGS : Concrete-50.

USAAF. : OFFICERS: 421. Enlisted Men. : 2473.TOTAL: 2894.
:

AFFILIATED AIRFIELDS : -

PRESENT USE [1985] : Agriculture.

NO: 607.

AIRFIELD NAME: WEST FREUGH. OPENED : 1936.
COUNTY : Wigtownshire. CLOSED :
COMMAND : Flying Training.
FORMATION : 29 Grp[Dumfries] GRID REF: X 591774[90Scot]
FUNCTION : Advanced Flying Unit O.S.REF.: NX 110545/83.
: [Observer]
LOCALITY : 5.5miles SE of Stranraer.
RAILWAY STN. : Stranraer[LMS]

LATITUDE : 54 51 00N. HEIGHT ASL : 55′ LIGHTING : Mk2.
LONGITUDE : 04 56 38W. FLYING CONTROL : Yes. RADIO : QDM.

LANDMARKS DAY. : Mull of Galloway, Luce Bay & Loch Ryan.

LANDMARKS NIGHT : As day.

OBSTRUCTIONS : -

LANDING AREA SURFACE : Tarmac.
QDM: 070. LENGTH X WIDTH: 1500 x 50yds.EXT. TO: 1730yds
: 120. : 965 x 50yds. : -
: : :
: : :

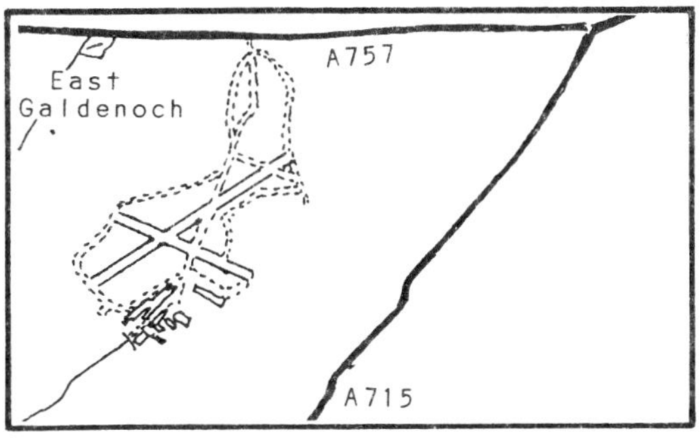

EXTENSIBILITY : -

ACCOMMODATION : Temporary[except for Type F hangar & MQs]
HANGARS : Type F-1;Bellman-7;Bessoneau-1;EO Blister-8.

HARDSTANDINGS : Twin fighter pens-3;tarmac area 200x120′

R.A.F. : OFFICERS: 195.S.N.C.O′s.: 500.O.R′s.: 681.TOTAL: 1376.
W.A.A.F.: " : 5. " : 4. " : 419. " : 428.

AFFILIATED AIRFIELDS : -

PRESENT USE [1985] : Royal Aircraft Establishment.

NO: 608.

AIRFIELD NAME: WEST HARTLEPOOL. OPENED : 1935.
COUNTY : Durham. CLOSED : 1945.
COMMAND : Coastal.
FORMATION : On loan to War Dept. GRID REF: Z 985484[15]
FUNCTION : On loan to War Dept. O.S.REF.: NZ 505285/93.
:
LOCALITY : 5miles N of Middlesborough.
RAILWAY STN. : West Hartlepool[LNER]

LATITUDE : 54 38 40N. HEIGHT ASL : 50′ LIGHTING : None.
LONGITUDE : 01 13 20W. FLYING CONTROL : None.RADIO : QDM.

LANDMARKS DAY. : Tees Bay. West Hartlepool.

LANDMARKS NIGHT : -

OBSTRUCTIONS : Mill 500yds. W of A/F marked by obstruction light. Factory chimney 1100yds. S marked by obstruction lights.

LANDING AREA SURFACE : Grass.
QDM: N-S. LENGTH X WIDTH: 1000yds. EXT. TO: 2000yds.
: NE-SW. : 1400yds. : 1600yds.
: E-W. : 1400yds. : 1600yds.
: SE-NW. : 1000yds. : -

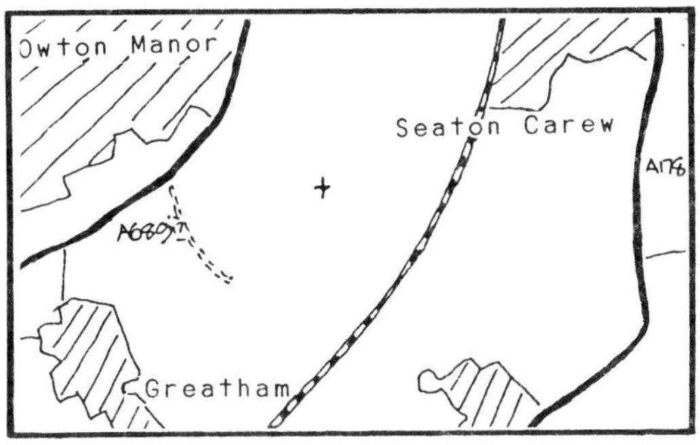

EXTENSIBILITY : -

ACCOMMODATION : Temporary.
HANGARS : -

HARDSTANDINGS : Hardcore-10.

R.A.F. : OFFICERS: 36.S.N.C.O′s.: 182.O.R′s.: 446.TOTAL: 664.
W.A.A.F.: " : - " : - " : - " : -

AFFILIATED AIRFIELDS : -

PRESENT USE [1985] : Industry.

NO: 609.

AIRFIELD NAME: WEST MALLING. OPENED : 1930.
COUNTY : Kent. CLOSED : 1969.
COMMAND : Fighter.
FORMATION : 11 Grp[Uxbridge] GRID REF: R 119740[115]
FUNCTION : Forward Airfield O.S.REF.: TQ 680555/188.
: [night fighter]
LOCALITY : 5miles W of Maidstone.
RAILWAY STN. : Malling[SR]

LATITUDE : 51 16 15N. HEIGHT ASL : 280′ LIGHTING : Mk2.
LONGITUDE : 00 24 23E. FLYING CONTROL : Yes. RADIO : QDM.

LANDMARKS DAY. : North Downs 4miles NNW & 6miles NE. R Medway.

LANDMARKS NIGHT : R Medway 1mile SW.

OBSTRUCTIONS : Hills 600′ ASL 4miles NNW & 6miles NE.

LANDING AREA SURFACE : Steel Matting[Sommerfeld Track] : 264-concrete[under construction]
QDM: 264. LENGTH X WIDTH: 2000 x 50yds.EXT. TO: 2600yds.
: : : 1800yds.
: 004. : 1600yds. : 2500yds.
: : :

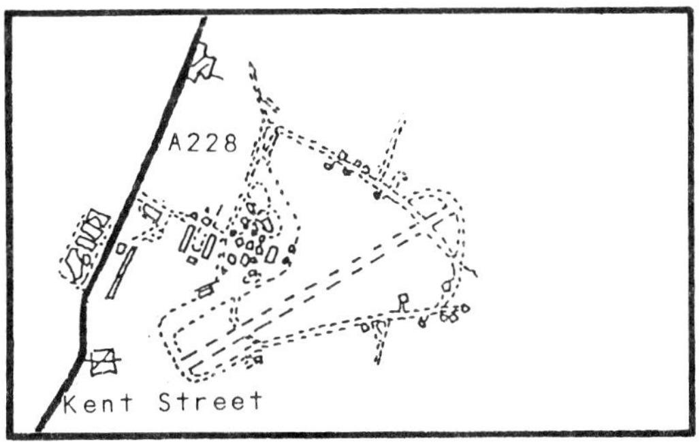

EXTENSIBILITY : On different alignments from existing tracks. Involves medium demolition.
ACCOMMODATION : Permanent.
HANGARS : Type J-1;Blister-16.

HARDSTANDINGS : Fry pan-13;Spitfire-3;Blenheim-4;Tempest-12.

R.A.F. : OFFICERS: 68.S.N.C.O′s.: 144.O.R′s.: 1200.TOTAL: 1412.
W.A.A.F.: " : - " : - " : - " : -

AFFILIATED AIRFIELDS : Biggin Hill[Sector]

PRESENT USE [1985] : Disused.

NO: 610.

AIRFIELD NAME: WEST RAYNHAM. OPENED : 1939.
COUNTY : Norfolk. CLOSED :
COMMAND : Bomber.
FORMATION : 100 Grp[Bylaugh Hall] GRID REF: G 308428[57]
FUNCTION : Operational. O.S.REF.: TF 850245/132.
:
LOCALITY : 5.5miles SW of Fakenham.
RAILWAY STN. : East Rudham 1mile[LNER]

LATITUDE : 52 47 00N. HEIGHT ASL : 241′ LIGHTING : Mk2.
LONGITUDE : 00 44 30E. FLYING CONTROL : Yes. RADIO : QDM.

LANDMARKS DAY. : -

LANDMARKS NIGHT : -

OBSTRUCTIONS : -

LANDING AREA SURFACE : Concrete & tarmac.

QDM	LENGTH X WIDTH	EXT. TO
040.	2000 x 50yds.	3000yds.
100.	1400 x 50yds.	3000yds.
:	:	2000yds.
:	:	:

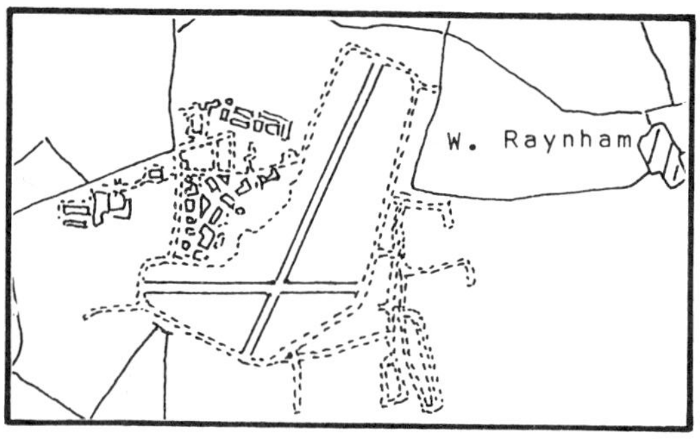

EXTENSIBILITY : Entails demolition of a farm & cottage.

ACCOMMODATION : Permanent.
HANGARS : Type C-4[half of Type C allocated to MAP]

HARDSTANDINGS : Heavy bomber-36.

	OFFICERS	S.N.C.O's.	O.R's.	TOTAL
R.A.F.	156.	144.	1364.	1664.
W.A.A.F.	12.	24.	324.	360.

AFFILIATED AIRFIELDS : -

PRESENT USE [1985] : RAF.

NO: 611.

AIRFIELD NAME: WESTCOTT. OPENED : 1942.
COUNTY : Buckinghamshire. CLOSED : 1945.
COMMAND : Bomber.
FORMATION : 92 Grp[Winslow] GRID REF: L 156368[94]
FUNCTION : Operational Training Unit. O.S.REF.: SP 710170/165.
LOCALITY : 7miles NW of Aylesbury.
RAILWAY STN. : Wootton[LNER]

LATITUDE : 51 50 45N. HEIGHT ASL : 262′ LIGHTING : Mk2.
LONGITUDE : 00 58 15W. FLYING CONTROL : Yes. RADIO : QDM.

LANDMARKS DAY. : Railway line adjoining A/F on W. Waddesdon Manor on top of 500′hill on E,1.25miles from centre of A/F. Two areas of water known as"The Lake" & "The Warrells" 2miles SW of A/F.

LANDMARKS NIGHT : Two areas of water 2miles SW of A/F.

OBSTRUCTIONS : Waddesdon Hill 3000yds. from centre of A/F. Chimney 1000yds. from end of NO.6 R/W. Ashenden Hill 1000yds. from end of No.3 R/W.

LANDING AREA SURFACE : Concrete.

QDM	LENGTH X WIDTH	EXT. TO
250.	1700 x 50yds.	2150yds.
311.	1400 x 50yds.	-
004.	1400 x 50yds.	-

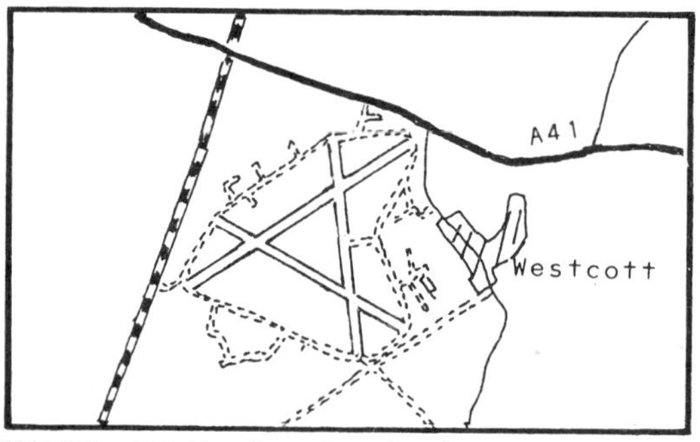

EXTENSIBILITY : Entails diversion of main road.

ACCOMMODATION : Temporary.
HANGARS : T2-4;B1-1.

HARDSTANDINGS : Heavy bomber-30.

	OFFICERS	S.N.C.O's.	O.R's.	TOTAL
R.A.F.	181.	488.	962.	1631.
W.A.A.F.	10.	9.	339.	358.

AFFILIATED AIRFIELDS : Oakley[Satellite]

PRESENT USE [1985] : Rocket Propulsion Establishment.

NO: 612.

AIRFIELD NAME: WESTHAMPNETT. OPENED : 1940.
COUNTY : Sussex. CLOSED :
COMMAND : Fighter.
FORMATION : 11 Grp[Uxbridge] GRID REF: Q 308269[133]
FUNCTION : Operational satellite. O.S.REF.: SU 875075/197.
:
LOCALITY : 1.5miles NNE of Chichester.
RAILWAY STN. : Chichester[SR]

LATITUDE : 50 51 38N. HEIGHT ASL : 110′ LIGHTING : None.
LONGITUDE : 00 45 30W. FLYING CONTROL : Yes. RADIO : QDM.

LANDMARKS DAY. : Mental hospital. Valdoe Wood 300yds. N. Goodwood racecourse N.

LANDMARKS NIGHT : -

OBSTRUCTIONS : Tower approx 150′high 1000yds. SSW of SW corner of peri track.

LANDING AREA SURFACE : Grass.

QDM	LENGTH X WIDTH	EXT. TO
WNW-ESE.	1100yds.	1800yds.
NE-SW.	1000ysa.	1700yds.
NW-SE.	1400yds.	-
:	:	:

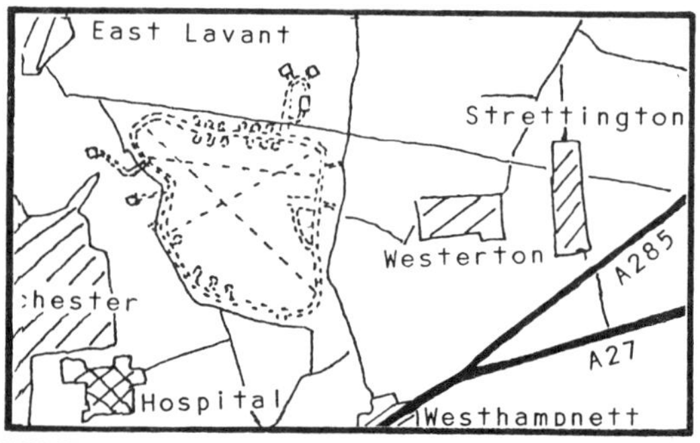

EXTENSIBILITY : -

ACCOMMODATION : Temporary.
HANGARS : Blisters:O-7;EO-1;T1-1.

HARDSTANDINGS : TE-19;SE-32.

	OFFICERS	S.N.C.O's.	O.R's.	TOTAL
R.A.F.	91.	100.	1171.	1362.
W.A.A.F.	-	-	51.	51.

AFFILIATED AIRFIELDS : Tangmere[sector]

PRESENT USE [1985] : Civil Airport[Chichester/Goodwood]

NO: 613.

AIRFIELD NAME: WESTLEY. OPENED : 1938.
COUNTY : Suffolk. CLOSED : 1945.
COMMAND : Technical Training.
FORMATION : 28 Grp[17-19 Queen's Sq] GRID REF: M 287830[86]
FUNCTION : Belgium Training School O.S.REF.: TM 825645/155.
: [satellite]
LOCALITY : West outskirts of Bury St. Edmunds.
RAILWAY STN. : Bury St. Edmunds 2miles[LNER]

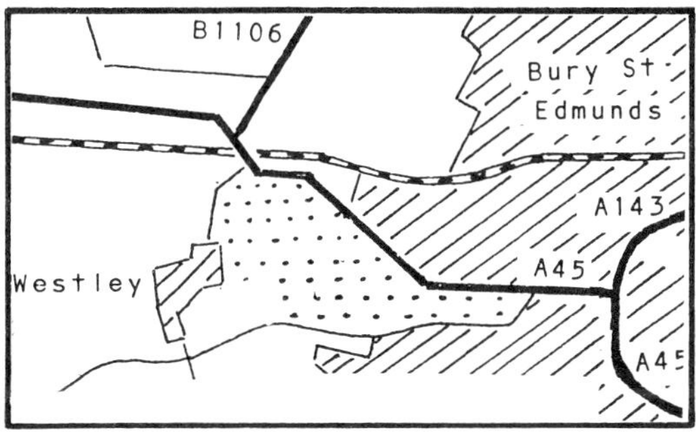

LATITUDE : 52 14 56N. HEIGHT ASL : 200' LIGHTING : None.
LONGITUDE : 00 41 10E. FLYING CONTROL : None.RADIO : QDM.

LANDMARKS DAY. : -

EXTENSIBILITY : None possible.

LANDMARKS NIGHT : -

ACCOMMODATION : Temporary.
HANGARS : 37x42'-1.

OBSTRUCTIONS : -

HARDSTANDINGS : -

LANDING AREA SURFACE : Grass.

QDM	LENGTH X WIDTH	EXT. TO
NE-SW.	700yds.	-
E-W.	550yds.	-
NW-SE.	500yds.	-
N-S.	670yds.	-

	OFFICERS	S.N.C.O's.	O.R's.	TOTAL
R.A.F.	-	-	93.	93.
W.A.A.F.	-	-	-	-

AFFILIATED AIRFIELDS : Snailwell[Parent]

PRESENT USE [1985] : Housing.

NO: 614.

AIRFIELD NAME: WESTON SUPER MARE. OPENED : 1936.
COUNTY : Somersetshire. CLOSED :
COMMAND : Technical Training.
FORMATION : 24 Grp[Hereford] GRID REF: T 787815[110]
FUNCTION : Satellite. O.S.REF.: ST 345602/182.
:
LOCALITY : 2.5miles SE of Weston super Mare.
RAILWAY STN. : Weston super Mare[GWR]

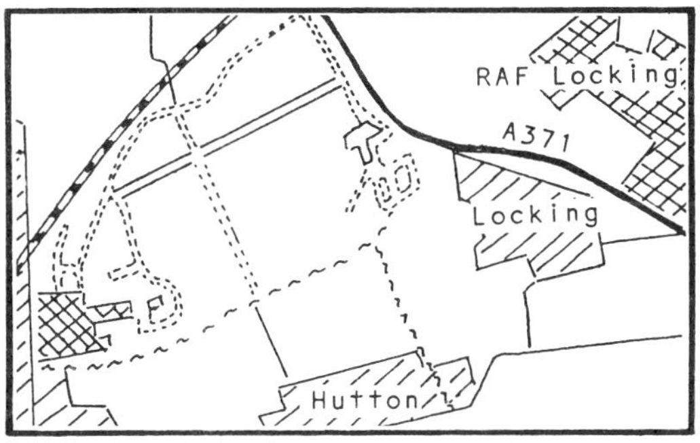

LATITUDE : 51 20 08N. HEIGHT ASL : 17' LIGHTING : None.
LONGITUDE : 02 56 15W. FLYING CONTROL : None.RADIO : QDM.

LANDMARKS DAY. : 550' hills to S, 350' hills to N. Bristol Channel to W.

EXTENSIBILITY : New R/W of 3000yds., but involves diversion of a road & slight demolition.

LANDMARKS NIGHT : English & Welsh Grounds lightship.

ACCOMMODATION : Temporary.
HANGARS : 0 blister-2;MAP-4.

OBSTRUCTIONS : 500' hill to S.

HARDSTANDINGS : -

LANDING AREA SURFACE : Tarmac.

QDM	LENGTH X WIDTH	EXT. TO
254.	1000 x 50yds.	1400yds.
		1400yds.

	OFFICERS	S.N.C.O's.	O.R's.	TOTAL
R.A.F.	-	20.	100.	120.
W.A.A.F.	-	-	-	-

AFFILIATED AIRFIELDS : Locking[Parent-ground station]

PRESENT USE [1985] : Civil Airport[Weston]

NO: 615.

AIRFIELD NAME: WESTON ZOYLAND. OPENED : 1926.
COUNTY : Somersetshire. CLOSED : 1969.
COMMAND : Fighter.
FORMATION : 70 Grp[Farnborough] GRID REF: T 803556[120]
FUNCTION : A.A. Co-operation Unit. O.S.REF.: ST 365345/182.
:
LOCALITY : 4.5miles SE of Bridgewater.
RAILWAY STN. : Bridgewater[GWR]

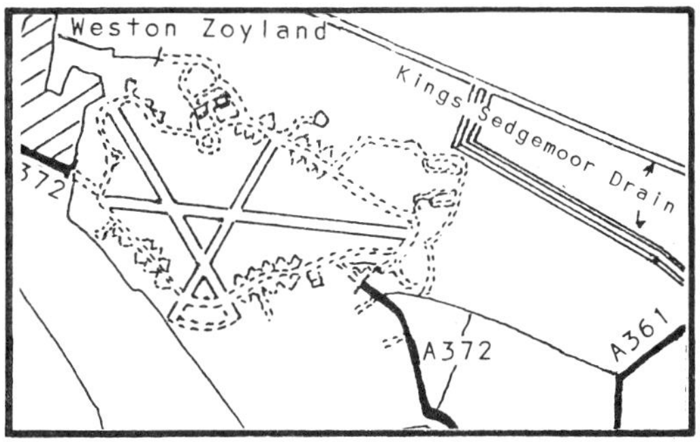

LATITUDE : 51 06 15N. HEIGHT ASL : 30' LIGHTING : Mk2.
LONGITUDE : 02 54 15W. FLYING CONTROL : Yes. RADIO : QDM.

LANDMARKS DAY. : 225degrees10minutes from Glastonbury Tor, approaching from Bristol Channel, follows R Parret to Bridgewater 4.5miles NW. Durleigh Beacon 51 07 15N & 03 02 30W.

EXTENSIBILITY : Entails demolition of a farm.

LANDMARKS NIGHT : -

ACCOMMODATION : Temporary.
HANGARS : T2[14 bay]-1;T2[13 bay]-2;Bellman-1; Bessoneau-1.

OBSTRUCTIONS : HT cables running SE-NW pass within .25miles of A/F.

HARDSTANDINGS : Frying pan 150'-2;Special loop-33.

LANDING AREA SURFACE : Concrete & wood chippings.

QDM	LENGTH X WIDTH	EXT. TO
285.	1925 x 50yds.	-
048.	1188 x 50yds.	1400yds.
343.	1367 x 50yds.	-

	OFFICERS	S.N.C.O's.	O.R's.	TOTAL
R.A.F.	107.	162.	618.	887.
W.A.A.F.	6.	10.	182.	198.

AFFILIATED AIRFIELDS : Merryfield & Upottery[Satellites]

PRESENT USE [1985] : Agriculture.

NO: 616.

AIRFIELD NAME: WESTON-on-the-GREEN. OPENED : 1918.
COUNTY : Oxfordshire. CLOSED :
COMMAND : Flying Training.
FORMATION : 23 Grp[South Cerney] GRID REF: P 985405[94]
FUNCTION : Advanced Flying Unit O.S.REF.: SP 535205/164.
: Pilots [satellite]
LOCALITY : 3.5miles SW of Bicester.
RAILWAY STN. : Bicester[GWR & LMS]

LATITUDE : 51 52 45N. HEIGHT ASL : 260′ LIGHTING : None.
LONGITUDE : 01 13 15W. FLYING CONTROL : None.RADIO : QDM.

LANDMARKS DAY. : Oxford-Bicester railway 1.5miles SE.

LANDMARKS NIGHT : Lake 200x50yds. 1mile WSW.

OBSTRUCTIONS : Trees 30′ on S boundary.

LANDING AREA SURFACE : Steel Matting[Sommerfeld Track]

QDM	LENGTH X WIDTH	EXT. TO
265.	1500yds.	3000yds.
210.	1200yds.	3000yds.
		2000yds.

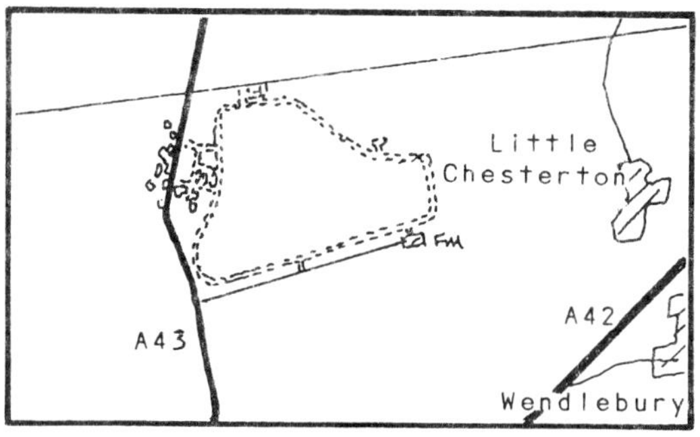

EXTENSIBILITY : Entails diversion of main road from Brackley to Oxford & demolition of a stone barn.
ACCOMMODATION : Temporary.
HANGARS : Bessoneau:9bays-2;12bays-2;T2-1; Blisters:Double 69′-4;Single 69′-6.
HARDSTANDINGS : -

R.A.F. : OFFICERS: 47.S.N.C.O′s.: 216.O.R′s.: 434.TOTAL: 697.
W.A.A.F.: " : 8. " : - " : 126. " : 134.

AFFILIATED AIRFIELDS : Kidlington.

PRESENT USE [1985] : Private flying.

NO: 617.

AIRFIELD NAME: WETHERSFIELD. OPENED : 1941.
COUNTY : Essex. CLOSED :
COMMAND : Fighter.
FORMATION : 38 Grp[Marks Hall] GRID REF: M 160520[97]
FUNCTION : Operational. O.S.REF.: TL 725335/167.
:
LOCALITY : 7miles NNW of Braintree.
RAILWAY STN. : Sible & Castle Hedington 4miles[LNER]

LATITUDE : 51 58 23N. HEIGHT ASL : 315′ LIGHTING : Mk2.
LONGITUDE : 00 30 38E. FLYING CONTROL : Yes. RADIO : QDM.

LANDMARKS DAY. : Military barracks in line with R/W 330. Concrete water tower SW of control tower.

LANDMARKS NIGHT : -

OBSTRUCTIONS : -

LANDING AREA SURFACE : Concrete.

QDM	LENGTH X WIDTH	EXT. TO
290.	2000 x 50yds.	3000yds.
330.	1400 x 50yds.	2400yds.
040.	1400 x 50yds.	2000yds.

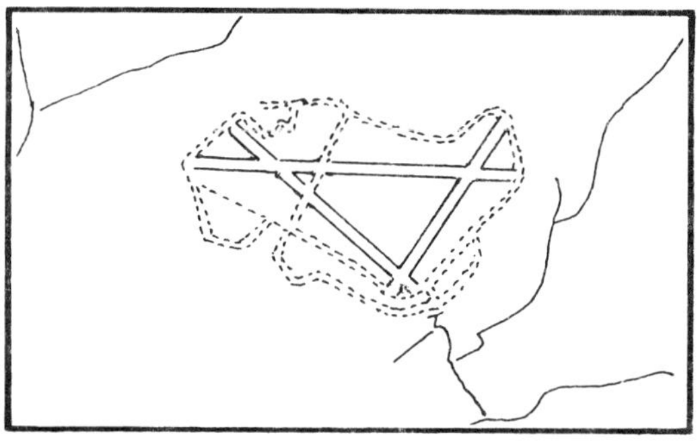

EXTENSIBILITY : -

ACCOMMODATION : Temporary.
HANGARS : T2-2.

HARDSTANDINGS :

R.A.F. : OFFICERS: 207.S.N.C.O′s.: 473.O.R′s.: 1360.TOTAL: 2040.
W.A.A.F.: " : 10. " : 7. " : 371. " : 388.

AFFILIATED AIRFIELDS : -

PRESENT USE [1985] : USAFE.

NO: 618.

AIRFIELD NAME: WHEATON ASTON. OPENED : 1941.
COUNTY : Staffordshire. CLOSED : 1947.
COMMAND : Flying Training.
FORMATION : 21 Grp[Spittlegate] GRID REF: K 299355[53]
FUNCTION : Advanced Flying Unit O.S.REF.: SJ 842150/127.
: [Pilots]
LOCALITY : 7miles SW of Sealand.
RAILWAY STN. : Gnosdall 5miles[LMS]

LATITUDE : 52 43 53N. HEIGHT ASL : 350′ LIGHTING : Mk2.
LONGITUDE : 02 14 00W. FLYING CONTROL : Yes. RADIO : QDM.

LANDMARKS DAY. : Shropshire Union canal E of A/F.

LANDMARKS NIGHT : Belvise reservoir.

OBSTRUCTIONS : -

LANDING AREA SURFACE : Concrete covered with tarmac.

QDM	LENGTH X WIDTH	EXT. TO
220.	1310 x 50yds.	-
280.	1100 x 50yds.	-
340.	1100 x 50yds.	-

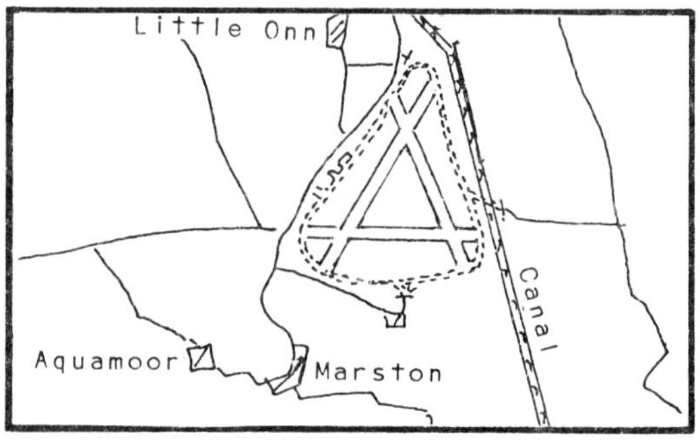

EXTENSIBILITY : None but new parallel R/W to No.1 of 1200yds. Entails demolition of a lodge & canal bridge.
ACCOMMODATION : Temporary.
HANGARS : T1-3;EO Blister-8.

HARDSTANDINGS : Concrete,round-4;fighter pen-1.

R.A.F. : OFFICERS: 143.S.N.C.O′s.: 338.O.R′s.: 975.TOTAL: 1456.
W.A.A.F.: " : 20. " : 42. " : 378. " : 440.

AFFILIATED AIRFIELDS : Perton & Tatenhill[Satellites]

PRESENT USE [1985] : Agriculture.

NO: 619.

AIRFIELD NAME: WHITEFIELD.
COUNTY : Perthshire.
COMMAND : Flying Training.
FORMATION : 51 Grp[Leeds]
FUNCTION : Elementary Flying
: Training School[RLG]
LOCALITY : 7.75miles NNE of Perth.
RAILWAY STN. : Burrelton 4miles[LMS]

OPENED : 1939.
CLOSED : 1945.

GRID REF: 0 675561[57Scot]
O.S.REF.: NO 175353/54.

LATITUDE : 56 20 45W. HEIGHT ASL : 395′ LIGHTING : None.
LONGITUDE : 03 20 45W. FLYING CONTROL : None.RADIO : QDM.

LANDMARKS DAY : R Isla 2.25miles NW.

LANDMARKS NIGHT : As day.

OBSTRUCTIONS : -

LANDING AREA SURFACE : Grass.

QDM: NE-SW. LENGTH X WIDTH: 900yds. EXT. TO: 1400yds.
: : : 1100yds.
: : :
: : :

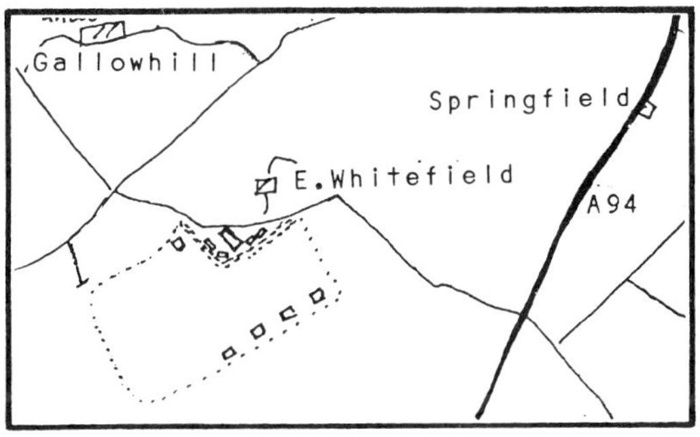

EXTENSIBILITY : -

ACCOMMODATION : Temporary.
HANGARS : EO Blister-8.

HARDSTANDINGS : -

R.A.F. : OFFICERS: - S.N.C.O′s.: - O.R′s.: 36.TOTAL: 36.
W.A.A.F.: " : - " : - " : - " : -

AFFILIATED AIRFIELDS : Perth[Parent]

PRESENT USE [1985] : Agriculture.

NO: 620.

AIRFIELD NAME: WICK.
COUNTY : Caithness.
COMMAND : Coastal.
FORMATION : 18 Grp[Pitreavie Castle]
FUNCTION : Operational.
:
LOCALITY : 1mile N of Wick.
RAILWAY STN. : Wick[LMS]

OPENED : 1939.
CLOSED : 1978.

GRID REF: D 899738[30Scot]
O.S.REF.: ND 363527/12.

LATITUDE : 58 27 23N. HEIGHT ASL : 120′ LIGHTING : Mk2.
LONGITUDE : 03 05 30W. FLYING CONTROL : Yes. RADIO : QDM.

LANDMARKS DAY : Moss lighthouse.

LANDMARKS NIGHT : As day.

OBSTRUCTIONS : -

LANDING AREA SURFACE : Tarmac.

QDM: 193. LENGTH X WIDTH: 1110 x 50yds.EXT. TO: 1400yds.
: 268. : 1150 x 50yds. : 1500yds.
: 326. : 1570 x 50yds. : 3500yds.
: : :

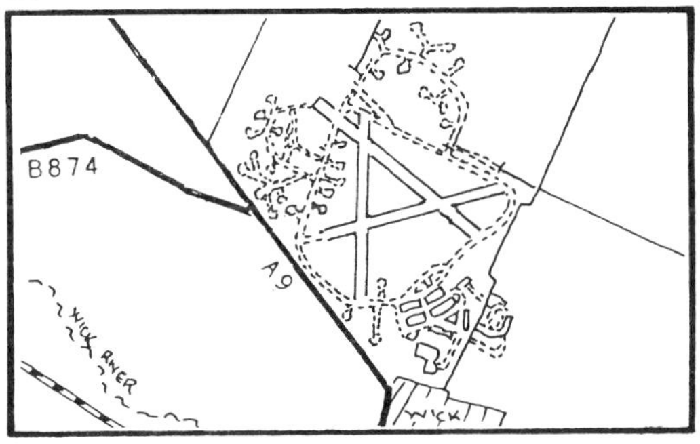

EXTENSIBILITY : Entails demolition of an important farm building.

ACCOMMODATION : Temporary[except type C hangars & MQ]
HANGARS : Type C-4;Bellman-2.

HARDSTANDINGS : 100′ dia-43.

R.A.F. : OFFICERS: 116.S.N.C.O′s.: 278.O.R′s.: 2668.TOTAL: 3062.
W.A.A.F.: " : 20. " : 14. " : 510. " : 544.

AFFILIATED AIRFIELDS : Skitton[Satellite]

PRESENT USE [1985] : Disused.

NO: 621.

AIRFIELD NAME: WICKENBY.
COUNTY : Lincolnshire.
COMMAND : Bomber.
FORMATION : 1 Grp[Bawtry]
FUNCTION : Operational.
:
LOCALITY : 9.5miles NE of Lincoln.
RAILWAY STN. : Snelland 3miles[LNER]

OPENED : 1942.
CLOSED : 1956.

GRID REF: A-F 56500[47]
O.S.REF.: TF 088803/121.

LATITUDE : 53 18 45N. HEIGHT ASL : 84′ LIGHTING : Mk2.
LONGITUDE : 00 21 00W. FLYING CONTROL : Yes. RADIO : QDM.

LANDMARKS DAY : -

LANDMARKS NIGHT : -

OBSTRUCTIONS : -

LANDING AREA SURFACE : Concrete & wood chippings.

QDM: 273. LENGTH X WIDTH: 2000 x 50yds.EXT. TO: 3500yds.
: 217. : 1400 x 50yds. : 1800yds.
: 162. : 1400 x 50yds. : 2000yds.
: : :

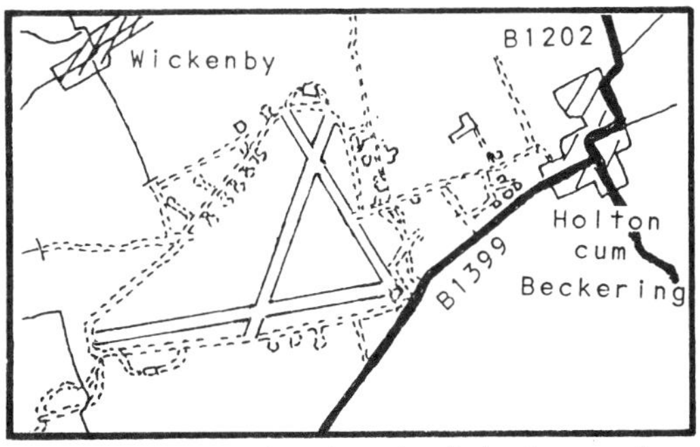

EXTENSIBILITY : Entails diversion of a 2nd. class road.

ACCOMMODATION : Temporary.
HANGARS : T2-2;B1-1.

HARDSTANDINGS : Heavy bomber-36.

R.A.F. : OFFICERS: 131.S.N.C.O′s.: 412.O.R′s.: 1245.TOTAL: 1788.
W.A.A.F.: " : 6. " : 8. " : 273. " : 287.

AFFILIATED AIRFIELDS : Ludford Magna[14 Base]

PRESENT USE [1985] : Agriculture.

NO: 622.

AIRFIELD NAME: WIGSLEY. OPENED : 1942.
COUNTY : Nottinghamshire. CLOSED : 1958.
COMMAND : Bomber.
FORMATION : 7 Grp[St.Vincents] GRID REF: F 315890[47]
FUNCTION : Operational. O.S.REF.: SK 855695/121.
:
LOCALITY : 7.5miles W of Lincoln.
RAILWAY STN. : Doddington & Harby 2miles[LNER]

LATITUDE : 53 13 00N. HEIGHT ASL : 33′ LIGHTING : Mk2.
LONGITUDE : 00 43 30W. FLYING CONTROL : Yes. RADIO : QDM.

LANDMARKS DAY. : R Trent, Lincoln-Tuxford railway. Lincoln cathedral.

LANDMARKS NIGHT : R Trent, Wigsley Woods.

OBSTRUCTIONS : -

LANDING AREA SURFACE : Concrete.

QDM	LENGTH X WIDTH	EXT. TO
207.	1400 x 50yds.	3400yds.
268.	2000 x 50yds.	3600yds.
325.	1400 x 50yds.	2300yds.

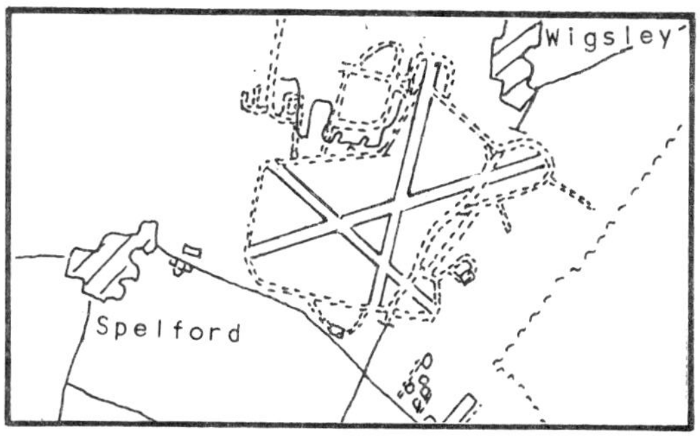

EXTENSIBILITY : -

ACCOMMODATION : Temporary.
HANGARS : T2-2;B1-1.

HARDSTANDINGS : Heavy bomber-36.

	OFFICERS	S.N.C.O's.	O.R's.	TOTAL
R.A.F.	55.	488.	1201.	1744.
W.A.A.F.	2.	8.	340.	350.

AFFILIATED AIRFIELDS : Swinderby[75 Base]

PRESENT USE [1985] : Agriculture.

NO: 623.

AIRFIELD NAME: WIGTOWN. OPENED : 1941.
COUNTY : Wigtownshire. CLOSED : 1948.
COMMAND : Flying Training.
FORMATION : 29 Grp[Dumfries] GRID REF: X 918750[91Scot]
FUNCTION : Advanced Flying Unit [Observer] O.S.REF.: NX 433536/83.
LOCALITY : 1mile S of Wigtown.
RAILWAY STN. : Kirkinner[LMS]

LATITUDE : 54 51 00N. HEIGHT ASL : 20′ LIGHTING : Mk2.
LONGITUDE : 04 26 30W. FLYING CONTROL : Yes. RADIO : QDM.

LANDMARKS DAY. : Barrow Head to S. Wigtown Bay to SE.

LANDMARKS NIGHT : As day.

OBSTRUCTIONS : Cannsmore 2329′ NNE. Knocheans Hill NE 969′

LANDING AREA SURFACE : Concrete.

QDM	LENGTH X WIDTH	EXT. TO
070.	1750 x 50yds.	1900yds.
160.	1380 x 50yds.	1900yds.

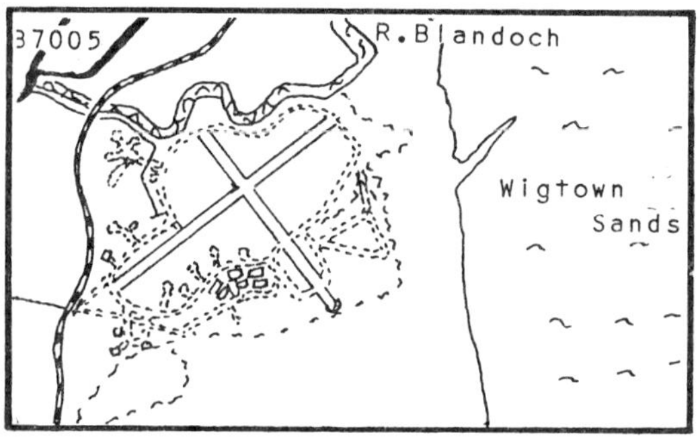

EXTENSIBILITY : -

ACCOMMODATION : Temporary.
HANGARS : Bellman-7;EO Blister-14.

HARDSTANDINGS : Circular-30.

	OFFICERS	S.N.C.O's.	O.R's.	TOTAL
R.A.F.	244.	491.	1240.	1975.
W.A.A.F.	12.	12.	468.	492.

AFFILIATED AIRFIELDS : -

PRESENT USE [1985] : Disused.

NO: 624.

AIRFIELD NAME: WINDRUSH. OPENED : 1940.
COUNTY : Gloucestershire. CLOSED : 1945.
COMMAND : Flying Training.
FORMATION : 23 Grp[South Cerney] GRID REF: P 625322[93]
FUNCTION : Advanced Flying Unit Pilots[satellite] O.S.REF.: SP 185115/163.
LOCALITY : 4.5miles W of Burford.
RAILWAY STN. : Bourton on the Water 9miles[GWR]

LATITUDE : 51 48 08N. HEIGHT ASL : 560. LIGHTING : None.
LONGITUDE : 01 43 53W. FLYING CONTROL : None. RADIO : QDM.

LANDMARKS DAY. : R Windrush 1.5miles NE. Pylon cables 1mile S.Burford 4.5miles E. Main Oxford-Cheltenham road .25miles N.

LANDMARKS NIGHT : R Windrush 1.5miles NE.

OBSTRUCTIONS : Trees .5miles NE. Pylon cables 1mile S.

LANDING AREA SURFACE : Steel Matting[Sommerfeld Track]

QDM	LENGTH X WIDTH	EXT. TO
011.	1000yds.	2000yds.
071.	1083yds.	1400yds.
		1750yds.

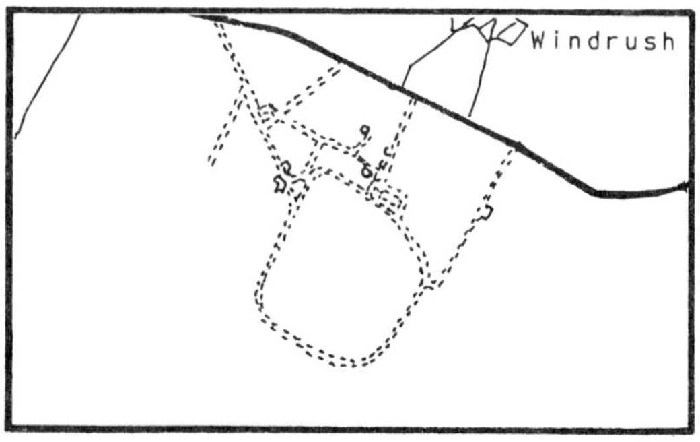

EXTENSIBILITY : -

ACCOMMODATION : Temporary.
HANGARS : T1-1;69′ Blisters:single-4;double-5.

HARDSTANDINGS : -

	OFFICERS	S.N.C.O's.	O.R's.	TOTAL
R.A.F.	132.	142.	519.	793.
W.A.A.F.	4.	2.	100.	106.

AFFILIATED AIRFIELDS : Little Rissington[Parent]

PRESENT USE [1985] : Disused.

NO: 625.

AIRFIELD NAME: WINFIELD.
COUNTY : Berwickshire.
COMMAND : Fighter.
FORMATION : 12 Grp[Watnall]
FUNCTION : Operational Training
: Unit[satellite]
LOCALITY : 6miles WSW of Berwick on Tweed.
RAILWAY STN. : Norham 4.5miles[LNER]

OPENED : 1942.
CLOSED : 1945.

GRID REF: U 394715[1]
O.S.REF.: NT 898505/74.

LATITUDE : 55 45 00N. HEIGHT ASL : 170′ LIGHTING : Mk2.
LONGITUDE : 02 10 00W. FLYING CONTROL : Yes. RADIO : QDM.

LANDMARKS DAY. : Ladykirk church. Longridge Towers.

LANDMARKS NIGHT : R Tweed & estuary.

OBSTRUCTIONS : -

LANDING AREA SURFACE : Tarmac.

QDM	LENGTH X WIDTH	EXT. TO
064.	1600 x 50yds.	3000yds.
127.	1160 x 50yds.	3000yds.

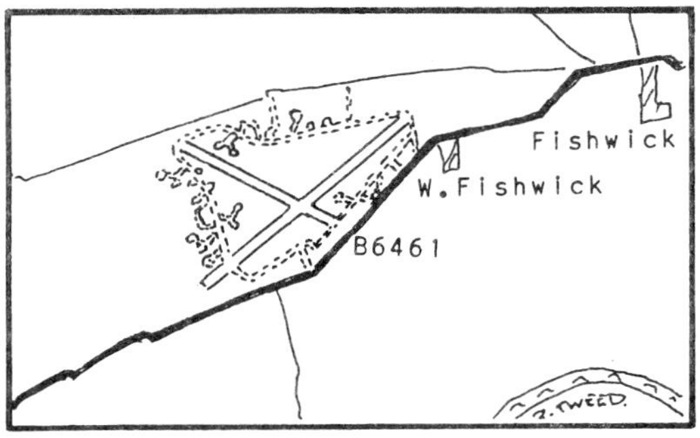

EXTENSIBILITY : Entails cutting of Berwick-Kelso road & light demolition.
ACCOMMODATION : Temporary.
HANGARS : EO Blister-4.

HARDSTANDINGS : 37.

	OFFICERS	S.N.C.O's.	O.R's.	TOTAL
R.A.F.	64.	64.	558.	686.
W.A.A.F.	2.	4.	50.	56.

AFFILIATED AIRFIELDS : Charter Hall[Parent]

PRESENT USE [1985] : Private flying.

NO: 626.

AIRFIELD NAME: WING.
COUNTY : Buckinghamshire.
COMMAND : Bomber.
FORMATION : 92 Grp[Winslow]
FUNCTION : Operational Training
: Unit.
LOCALITY : 4miles W of Leighton Buzzard.
RAILWAY STN. : Leighton Buzzard[LMS]

OPENED : 1941.
CLOSED : 1958.

GRID REF: L 307430[95]
O.S.REF.: SU 912726/175.

LATITUDE : 51 54 00N. HEIGHT ASL : 450′ LIGHTING : Mk2.
LONGITUDE : 00 45 15W. FLYING CONTROL : Yes. RADIO : QDM.

LANDMARKS DAY. : River & canal 3.5miles E running side by side N-S. Mentmore Towers[4] 3.5miles SE.

LANDMARKS NIGHT : River & canal.

OBSTRUCTIONS : -

LANDING AREA SURFACE : Concrete.

QDM	LENGTH X WIDTH	EXT. TO
170.	1400 x 50yds.	-
258.	2000 x 50yds.	-
302.	1160 x 50yds.	-

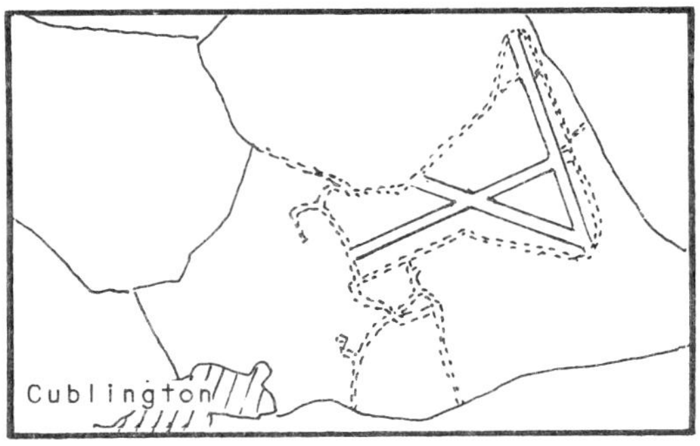

EXTENSIBILITY : None possible.

ACCOMMODATION : Temporary.
HANGARS : T2-4;B1-1.

HARDSTANDINGS : Heavy bomber-30.

	OFFICERS	S.N.C.O's.	O.R's.	TOTAL
R.A.F.	158.	526.	1292.	1976.
W.A.A.F.	10.	-	501.	511.

AFFILIATED AIRFIELDS : Little Horwood[Satellite]

PRESENT USE [1985] : Agriculture.

NO: 627.

AIRFIELD NAME: WINKFIELD.
COUNTY : Berkshire.
COMMAND : Flying Training.
FORMATION : 50 Grp[Reading]
FUNCTION : Elementary Flying
: Training School[RLG]
LOCALITY : 4miles SW of Windsor.
RAILWAY STN. : Ascot 4miles[SR]

OPENED : 1941.
CLOSED : 1945.

GRID REF: Q 354925[114]
O.S.REF.: SU 912726/175.

LATITUDE : 51 26 45N. HEIGHT ASL : 230′ LIGHTING : None.
LONGITUDE : 00 41 45W. FLYING CONTROL : None. RADIO : QDM.

LANDMARKS DAY. : Winkfield church just off S boundary.

LANDMARKS NIGHT : -

OBSTRUCTIONS : Winkfield church.

LANDING AREA SURFACE : Grass.

QDM	LENGTH X WIDTH	EXT. TO
N-S.	665yds.	2000yds.
NE-SW.	980yds.	1400yds.
E-W.	630yds.	1400yds.
NW-SE.	770yds.	-

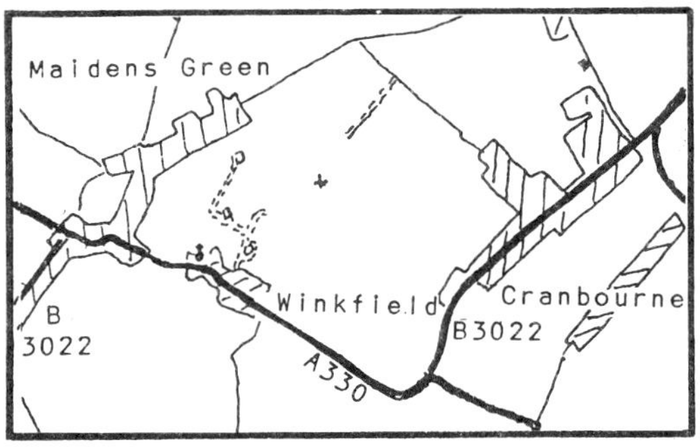

EXTENSIBILITY : Entails closure of 2 minor roads & some demolition. E-W recommended to 1400yds. only.
ACCOMMODATION : Temporary.
HANGARS : Blisters:standard-3;double-1;EO-1.

HARDSTANDINGS : Rectangular-1.

	OFFICERS	S.N.C.O's.	O.R's.	TOTAL
R.A.F.	3.	3.	60.	66.
W.A.A.F.	-	-	-	-

AFFILIATED AIRFIELDS : Fairoaks[parent]

PRESENT USE [1985] : Disused.

AIRFIELD NAME: WINKLEIGH. OPENED : 1943.
COUNTY : Devon. CLOSED : 1958.
COMMAND : Fighter.
FORMATION : 10 Grp[Rudloe Manor] GRID REF: T 057315[127]
FUNCTION : Operational. O.S.REF.: SS 620095/191.
:
LOCALITY : 9miles N of Okehampton.
RAILWAY STN. : Eggesford[GWR]

LATITUDE : 50 52 00N. HEIGHT ASL : 540′ LIGHTING : Mk2.
LONGITUDE : 03 57 30W. FLYING CONTROL : Yes. RADIO : QDM.

LANDMARKS DAY : -

LANDMARKS NIGHT : -

OBSTRUCTIONS : -

LANDING AREA SURFACE : Concrete & tarmac.

QDM	LENGTH X WIDTH	EXT. TO
270.	1550 x 50yds.	-
003.	1500 x 50yds.	-

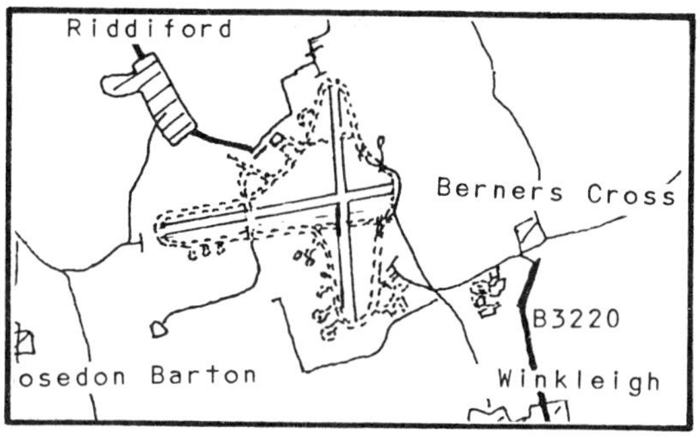

EXTENSIBILITY : None possible, but 2 new strips of 1560 & 1200 yds.can be added with no serious road diversion.
ACCOMMODATION : Temporary.
HANGARS : T2-1;0 Blister-8.

HARDSTANDINGS : Pens-6;open-9.

	OFFICERS	S.N.C.O's.	O.R's.	TOTAL
R.A.F.	82.	86.	894.	1062.
W.A.A.F.	10.	10.	180.	200.

AFFILIATED AIRFIELDS : Exeter[sector]

PRESENT USE [1985] : Industry.

AIRFIELD NAME: WINKTON. OPENED : 1944.
COUNTY : Hampshire. CLOSED : 1945.
COMMAND : Fighter.
FORMATION : 11 Grp[Uxbridge] GRID REF: U 605177[141]
FUNCTION : Advanced Landing Ground. O.S.REF.: SZ 165975/195.
: [De-requsitioned]
LOCALITY : 3miles NNE of Christchurch.
RAILWAY STN. : Christchurch[SR]

LATITUDE : 50 46 30N. HEIGHT ASL : 40′ LIGHTING : None.
LONGITUDE : 01 45 45W. FLYING CONTROL : None. RADIO : QDM.

LANDMARKS DAY : -

LANDMARKS NIGHT : -

OBSTRUCTIONS : -

LANDING AREA SURFACE : Steel Matting[Pierced planking & Sommerfeld track]

QDM	LENGTH X WIDTH	EXT. TO
N-S.	1600 x 50yds.	-
E-W.	1500 x 50yds.	-

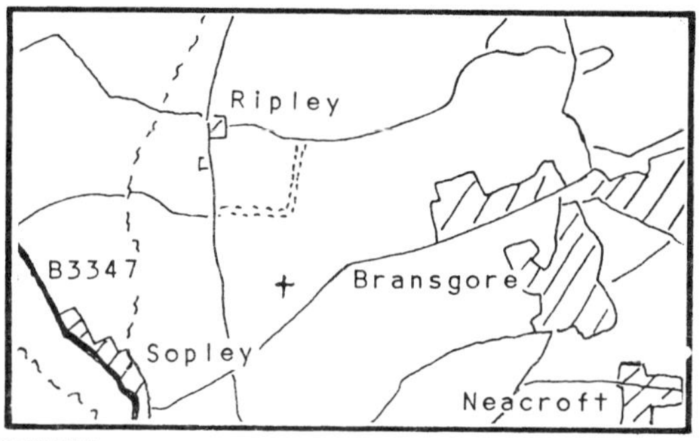

EXTENSIBILITY : -

ACCOMMODATION : Tented camp.
HANGARS : Blister-4.

HARDSTANDINGS : Sommerfeld Track-80.

	OFFICERS	S.N.C.O's.	O.R's.	TOTAL
R.A.F.	-	-	-	-
W.A.A.F.	-	-	-	-

AFFILIATED AIRFIELDS : -

PRESENT USE [1985] : Agriculture.

AIRFIELD NAME: WINTHORPE. OPENED : 1940.
COUNTY : Nottinghamshire. CLOSED : 1959.
COMMAND : Bomber.
FORMATION : 7 Grp[St.Vincents] GRID REF: F 286758[46]
FUNCTION : Operational. O.S.REF.: SK 825565/121.
:
LOCALITY : 1.5miles NE of Newark on Trent.
RAILWAY STN. : Newark on Trent[LNER]

LATITUDE : 53 05 45N. HEIGHT ASL : 54′ LIGHTING : Mk2.
LONGITUDE : 00 46 15W. FLYING CONTROL : Yes. RADIO : QDM.

LANDMARKS DAY : 3 chimney stacks & Newark church.

LANDMARKS NIGHT : -

OBSTRUCTIONS : -

LANDING AREA SURFACE : Concrete.

QDM	LENGTH X WIDTH	EXT. TO
042.	2000 x 50yds.	3000yds.
093.	1400 x 50yds.	1700yds.
151.	1400 x 50yds.	2000yds.

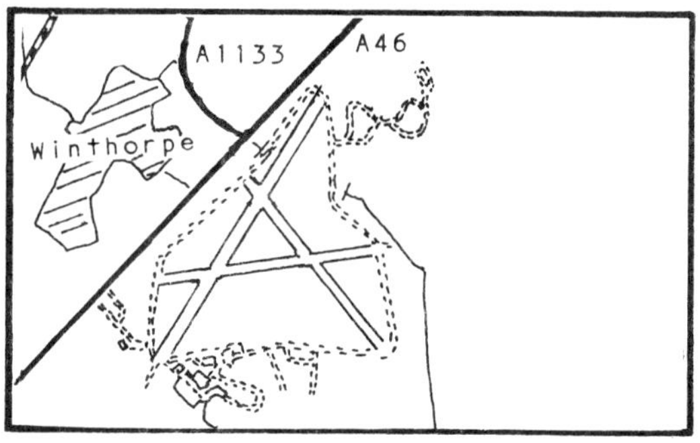

EXTENSIBILITY : Not recommended-entails diversion of Fosse Way.

ACCOMMODATION : Temporary.
HANGARS : T2-2;B1-1.

HARDSTANDINGS : Heavy bomber-36.

	OFFICERS	S.N.C.O's.	O.R's.	TOTAL
R.A.F.	137.	653.	872.	1662.
W.A.A.F.	4.	14.	252.	270.

AFFILIATED AIRFIELDS : Swinderby[75 Base]

PRESENT USE [1985] : Recreation.

NO: 631.

AIRFIELD NAME: WITCHFORD. OPENED : 1943.
COUNTY : Cambridgeshire. CLOSED : 1946.
COMMAND : Bomber.
FORMATION : 3 Grp[Exning] GRID REF: L 972970[75]
FUNCTION : Operational. O.S.REF.: TL 519785/143.
:
LOCALITY : 2miles SW of Ely.
RAILWAY STN. : Ely[LNER]

LATITUDE : 52 22 45N. HEIGHT ASL : 45′ LIGHTING : Mk2.
LONGITUDE : 00 14 00E. FLYING CONTROL : Yes. RADIO : QDM.

LANDMARKS DAY. : Ely cathedral & water towers. R Ouse & railway.

LANDMARKS NIGHT : R Ouse & Bedford rivers. Lights in railway goods yard.

OBSTRUCTIONS : -

LANDING AREA : Concrete.
SURFACE :

QDM	LENGTH X WIDTH	EXT. TO
100.	2000 x 50yds.	2400yds.
160.	1400 x 50yds.	2800yds.
220.	1400 x 50yds.	2650yds.

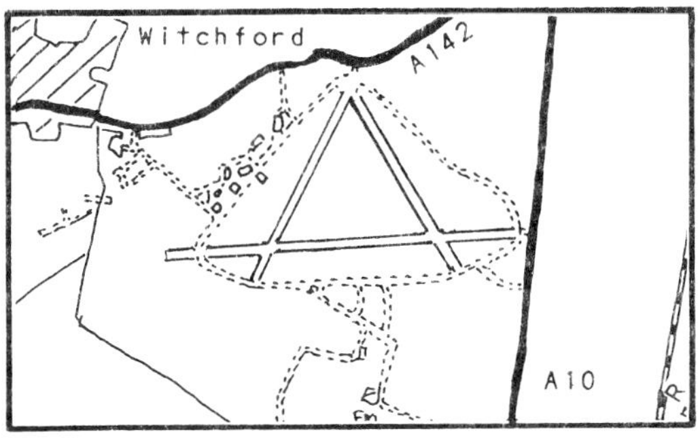

EXTENSIBILITY : Entails diversion of a road to N of A/F.

ACCOMMODATION : Temporary.
HANGARS : T2-2;B1-1.

HARDSTANDINGS : Heavy bomber-36.

	OFFICERS	S.N.C.O′s.	O.R′s.	TOTAL
R.A.F.	125.	345.	1032.	1502.
W.A.A.F.	2.	6.	222.	230.

AFFILIATED AIRFIELDS : Waterbeach[33 Base]

PRESENT USE [1985] : Agriculture.

NO: 632.

AIRFIELD NAME: WITTERING. OPENED : 1916.
COUNTY : Northamptonshire. CLOSED :
COMMAND : Fighter.
FORMATION : 12 Grp[Watnall] GRID REF: F 504225[64]
FUNCTION : Forward Airfield O.S.REF.: TF 028025/141.
: [Night fighter]
LOCALITY : 3miles SSE of Stamford.
RAILWAY STN. : Stamford[LMS & LNER]

LATITUDE : 52 36 45N. HEIGHT ASL : 250′ LIGHTING : Mk2.
LONGITUDE : 00 27 30W. FLYING CONTROL : Yes. RADIO : QDM.

LANDMARKS DAY. : Ketton chimney.

LANDMARKS NIGHT : As day.

OBSTRUCTIONS : -

LANDING AREA : Grass.
SURFACE :

QDM	LENGTH X WIDTH	EXT. TO
E-W.	4500yds.	5020yds.
NE-SW.	1450yds.	2600yds.
		2500yds.

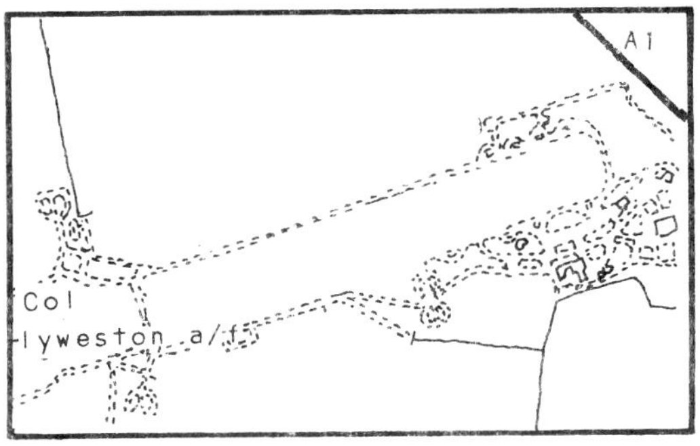

EXTENSIBILITY : -

ACCOMMODATION : Permanent.
HANGARS : EO Blister-1;Type C[225′]-2;GS-1.

HARDSTANDINGS : 16.

	OFFICERS	S.N.C.O′s.	O.R′s.	TOTAL
R.A.F.	186.	185.	2524.	2895.
W.A.A.F.	20.	28.	470.	518.

AFFILIATED AIRFIELDS : Digby[Sector]

PRESENT USE [1985] : RAF.

NO: 633.

AIRFIELD NAME: WOLVERHAMPTON. OPENED : 1938.
COUNTY : Staffordshire. CLOSED : 1971.
COMMAND : Flying Training.
FORMATION : 51 Grp[Leeds] GRID REF: K 355236[61]
FUNCTION : Elementary Flying O.S.REF.: SJ 900030/139.
: Training School.
LOCALITY : 2.5miles N of Wolverhampton.
RAILWAY STN. : Wolverhampton[LMS & GWR]

LATITUDE : 52 37 23N. HEIGHT ASL : 340′ LIGHTING : None.
LONGITUDE : 02 08 45W. FLYING CONTROL : None. RADIO : QDM.

LANDMARKS DAY. : Factory chimneys on S side.

LANDMARKS NIGHT : -

OBSTRUCTIONS : Factory chimneys 2miles S.

LANDING AREA : Grass.
SURFACE :

QDM	LENGTH X WIDTH	EXT. TO
E-W.	1050yds.	1400yds.
		1200yds.
		1000yds.

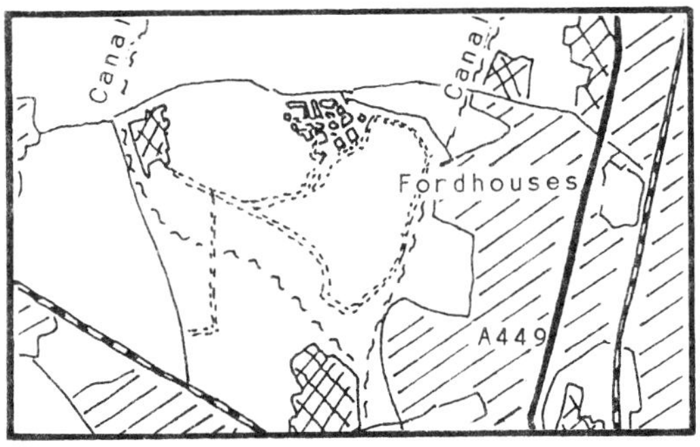

EXTENSIBILITY : Entails slight demolition & new strips would be 200yds. wide only.
ACCOMMODATION : Temporary[RAF buildings]
HANGARS : Bellman-4;Civil-1; Blisters:EO-3;double standard-3;standard-1.
HARDSTANDINGS : -

	OFFICERS	S.N.C.O′s.	O.R′s.	TOTAL
R.A.F.	55.	121.	630.	806.
W.A.A.F.	-	-	-	-

AFFILIATED AIRFIELDS : Penkridge[Satellite]

PRESENT USE [1985] : Housing.

NO: 634.

AIRFIELD NAME: WOMBLETON. OPENED : 1943.
COUNTY : Yorkshire. CLOSED : 1949.
COMMAND : Bomber.
FORMATION : 7 Grp[St.Vincents] GRID REF: V 147020[22]
FUNCTION : Operational. O.S.REF.: SE 673825/100.
:
LOCALITY : 3miles E of Helmsley.
RAILWAY STN. : Newton 1.5miles[LNER]

LATITUDE : 54 13 45N. HEIGHT ASL : 120' LIGHTING : Mk2.
LONGITUDE : 00 58 00W. FLYING CONTROL : Yes. RADIO : QDM.

LANDMARKS DAY. : Rievaulx Abbey 5miles WNW. Holmsley-Scarborough single line railway curving round A/F on W & N side.

LANDMARKS NIGHT : -

OBSTRUCTIONS : High ground 900' 5miles WSW-ENE.

LANDING AREA SURFACE : Concrete.

QDM:	LENGTH X WIDTH:	EXT. TO:
104.	2000 x 50yds.	3000yds.
046.	1400 x 50yds.	2000yds.
167.	1400 x 50yds.	2000yds.
:	:	:

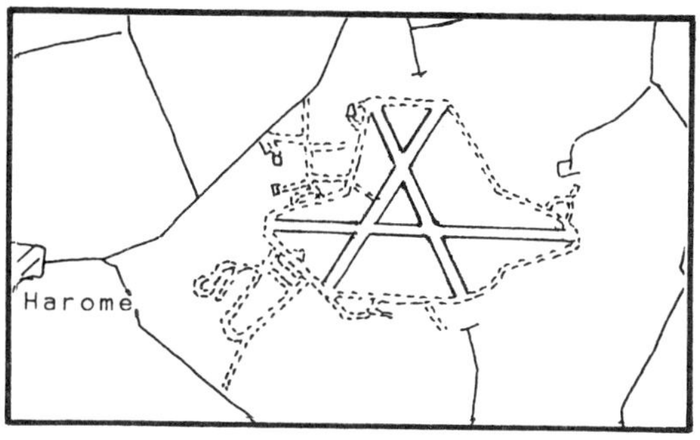

EXTENSIBILITY : Entails slight demolition.

ACCOMMODATION : Temporary.
HANGARS : T2-2;B1-1.

HARDSTANDINGS : Spectacle-36.

	OFFICERS:	S.N.C.O's.:	O.R's.:	TOTAL:
R.C.A.F.:	285.	466.	910.	1661.
W.A.A.F.:	11.	16.	177.	204.

AFFILIATED AIRFIELDS : Topcliffe[76 RCAF Base]

PRESENT USE [1985] : Disused.

NO: 635.

AIRFIELD NAME: WOODBRIDGE. OPENED : 1943.
COUNTY : Suffolk. CLOSED :
COMMAND : Bomber.
FORMATION : 3 Grp[Exning] GRID REF: M 767667[87]*
FUNCTION : Emergency runway. O.S.REF.: TM 334490/169.
: * runs to K 804673.
LOCALITY : 11miles ENE of Ipswich.
RAILWAY STN. : Melton 2.5miles[LNER]

LATITUDE : 52 05 20N. HEIGHT ASL : 70' LIGHTING : MK2.
LONGITUDE : 01 24 30E. FLYING CONTROL : Yes. RADIO : QDM.

LANDMARKS DAY. : R Debden & Tangham Forast.

LANDMARKS NIGHT : -

OBSTRUCTIONS : -

LANDING AREA : Bitumen & sand.
SURFACE : 500yd. grass extenion at each end.

QDM:	LENGTH X WIDTH:	EXT. TO:
270.	3000 x 250yds	5000yds.
:	:	3000yds.
:	:	3000yds.
:	:	:

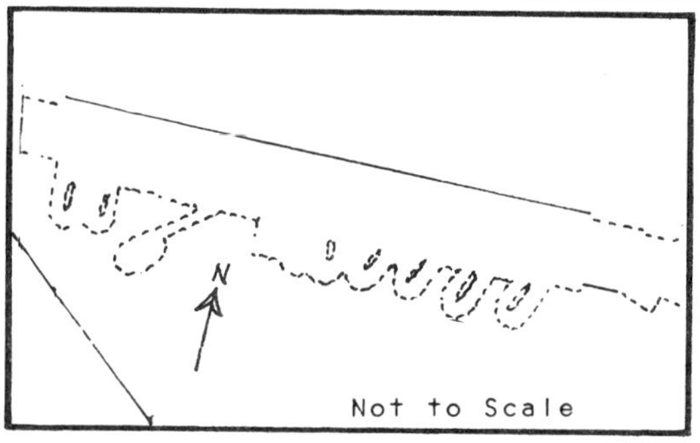

EXTENSIBILITY : Entails diversion of a minor road & demolition of 2 cottages.
ACCOMMODATION : Temporary.
HANGARS : B1-1;Blister-1.

HARDSTANDINGS : Loop for 15 heavy A/C.

	OFFICERS:	S.N.C.O's.:	O.R's.:	TOTAL:
R.A.F. :	18.	47.	520.	585.
W.A.A.F.:	-	-	-	-

AFFILIATED AIRFIELDS : -

PRESENT USE [1985] : USAFE.

NO: 636.

AIRFIELD NAME: WOODCHURCH. OPENED : 1943.
COUNTY : Kent. CLOSED : 1945.
COMMAND : Fighter.
FORMATION : 11 Grp[Uxbridge] GRID REF: R 386546[126]
FUNCTION : Advanced Landing Ground. O.S.REF.: TQ 948362/189.
: [De-requisitioned]
LOCALITY : 5.5miles SW of Ashford.
RAILWAY STN. : Ashford[SR]

LATITUDE : 51 05 30N. HEIGHT ASL : 150' LIGHTING : None.
LONGITUDE : 00 46 45E. FLYING CONTROL : None. RADIO : QDM.

LANDMARKS DAY. : -

LANDMARKS NIGHT : -

OBSTRUCTIONS : -

LANDING AREA : Steel Matting[Pierced planking & Sommerfeld track]
SURFACE :

QDM:	LENGTH X WIDTH:	EXT. TO:
010.	1600yds.	-
110.	1667yds.	-
:	:	:
:	:	:

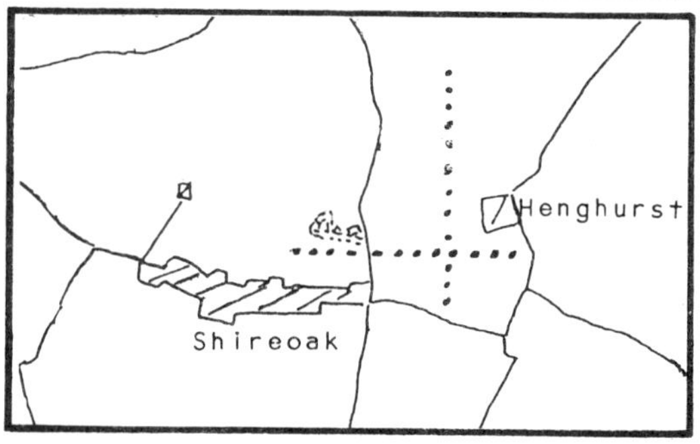

EXTENSIBILITY : -

ACCOMMODATION : Tented camp.
HANGARS : -

HARDSTANDINGS : Sommerfeld Track-70.

	OFFICERS:	S.N.C.O's.:	O.R's.:	TOTAL:
R.A.F. :	-	-	-	-
W.A.A.F.:	-	-	-	-

AFFILIATED AIRFIELDS : -

PRESENT USE [1985] : Disused.

AIRFIELD NAME: WOODHALL SPA. OPENED : 1942.
COUNTY : Lincolnshire. CLOSED : 1964.
COMMAND : Bomber.
FORMATION : 5 Grp[Morton Hall] GRID REF: F 675803[47]
FUNCTION : Operational. O.S.REF.: TF 204610/122.
LOCALITY : 6miles SW of Horncastle.
RAILWAY STN. : Coningsby 3miles[LNER]

LATITUDE : 53 08 00N. HEIGHT ASL : 45' LIGHTING : Mk2.
LONGITUDE : 00 11 30W. FLYING CONTROL : Yes. RADIO : QDM

LANDMARKS DAY : Tattershall Castle & woods, rivers & railway.

LANDMARKS NIGHT : Rivers & railway within 2miles Of A/F.

OBSTRUCTIONS : Tattershall Castle 180', lit by obstruction light.

LANDING AREA SURFACE : Concrete.

QDM	LENGTH X WIDTH	EXT. TO
180.	1400 x 50yds.	2000yds.
240.	2000 x 50yds.	2150yds.
300.	1400 x 50yds.	2000yds.

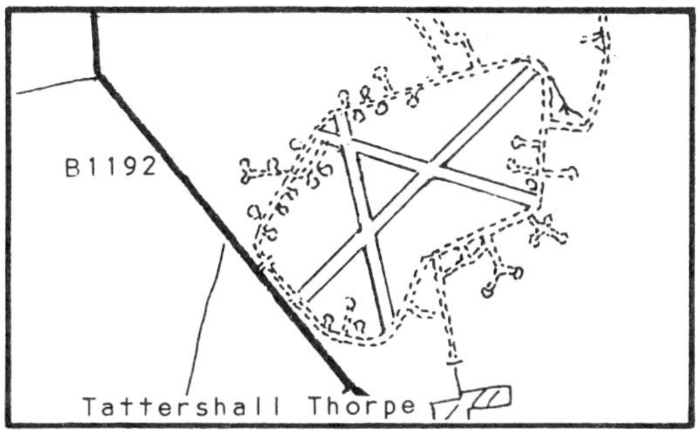

EXTENSIBILITY : Entails demolition of a farm.

ACCOMMODATION : Temporary.
HANGARS : T2-2;B1-1.

HARDSTANDINGS : Heavy bomber-36.

	OFFICERS	S.N.C.O's.	O.R's.	TOTAL
R.A.F.	167.	205.	681.	1053.
W.A.A.F.	-	-	-	-

AFFILIATED AIRFIELDS : Coningsby[54 Base]

PRESENT USE [1985] : Unspecified.

NO: 638.

AIRFIELD NAME: WOODLEY. OPENED : 1935.
COUNTY : Berkshire. CLOSED : 1953.
COMMAND : Flying Training.
FORMATION : 50 Grp[Reading] GRID REF: Q 214930[113]
FUNCTION : Flying Instructor's School. O.S.REF.: SU 780732/175.
LOCALITY : 3miles E of Reading.
RAILWAY STN. : Reading[SR & GWR]

LATITUDE : 51 27 08N. HEIGHT ASL : 150' LIGHTING : None.
LONGITUDE : 00 53 08W. FLYING CONTROL : None. RADIO : QDM.

LANDMARKS DAY : -

LANDMARKS NIGHT : -

OBSTRUCTIONS : Factory & school buildings.

LANDING AREA SURFACE : Grass.

QDM	LENGTH X WIDTH	EXT. TO
SW-NE.	800-1000yds.	-

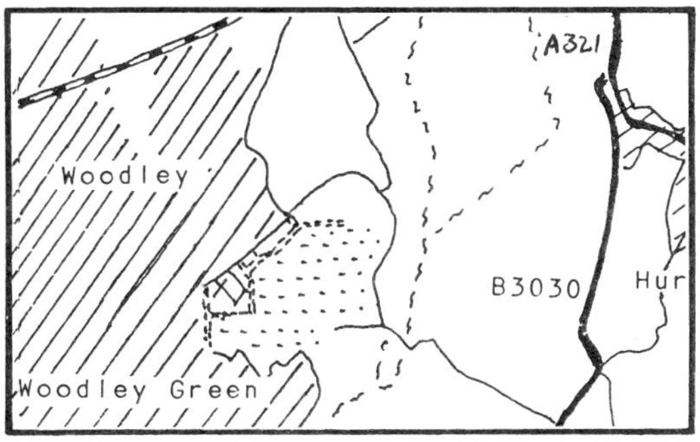

EXTENSIBILITY : -

ACCOMMODATION : Temporary[RAF]
HANGARS : Bellman-1;Standard Robin-1;Civil 420x200'-1; Blister:double EO-4;EO-1.

HARDSTANDINGS : -

	OFFICERS	S.N.C.O's.	O.R's.	TOTAL
R.A.F.	79.	208.	214.	501.
W.A.A.F.	-	-	-	-

AFFILIATED AIRFIELDS : Henley[RLG]

PRESENT USE [1985] : Housing.

NO: 639.

AIRFIELD NAME: WOODVALE. OPENED : 1941.
COUNTY : Lancashire. CLOSED :
COMMAND : Fighter.
FORMATION : 12 Grp[Watnall] GRID REF: D 768310[35]
FUNCTION : Forward Airfield Night Fighter. O.S.REF.: SD 302098/108.
LOCALITY : 12miles NNW of Liverpool.
RAILWAY STN. : Ainsdale 2miles[LMS]

LATITUDE : 53 34 53N. HEIGHT ASL : 35' LIGHTING : Mk2.
LONGITUDE : 03 03 15W. FLYING CONTROL : Yes. RADIO : QDM.

LANDMARKS DAY : Southport pier.

LANDMARKS NIGHT : -

OBSTRUCTIONS : -

LANDING AREA SURFACE : Asphalt.

QDM	LENGTH X WIDTH	EXT. TO
223.	1600 x 50yds.	2000yds.
351.	1100 x 50yds.	1700yds.
273.	1150 x 50yds.	-
		1700yds.

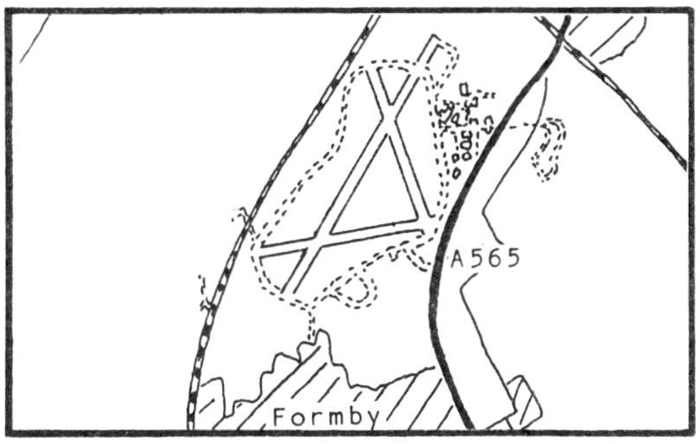

EXTENSIBILITY : Possible: 351-2700yds. & 273-2100yds., but entails serious road diversions & demolitions.
ACCOMMODATION : Temporary.
HANGARS : Bellman-3;EO Blister-9.

HARDSTANDINGS : TE-6;SE-6.

	OFFICERS	S.N.C.O's.	O.R's.	TOTAL
R.A.F.	122.	100.	776.	998.
W.A.A.F.	10.	11.	617.	638.

AFFILIATED AIRFIELDS : Church Fenton[Sector]

PRESENT USE [1985] : RAF.

NO: 640.

AIRFIELD NAME: WOOLFOX LODGE. OPENED : 1940.
COUNTY : Rutland. CLOSED : 1964.
COMMAND : Bomber.
FORMATION : 7 Grp[St.Vincents] GRID REF: F 420325[64]
FUNCTION : Operational. O.S.REF.: SK 962132/130.
:
LOCALITY : 6miles NW of Stamford.
RAILWAY STN. : Stamford[LMS & LNER]

LATITUDE : 52 42 30N. HEIGHT ASL : 345′ LIGHTING : Mk2.
LONGITUDE : 00 34 30W. FLYING CONTROL : Yes. RADIO : QDM.

LANDMARKS DAY. : Great North Road on W boundary.

LANDMARKS NIGHT : -

OBSTRUCTIONS : Ketton chimney 350′

LANDING AREA SURFACE : Tarmac.

QDM: 035. LENGTH X WIDTH: 1400 x 50yds.EXT. TO: 1600yds.
: 086. : 1400 x 50yds. : -
: 149. : 1850 x 50yds. : -
: : :

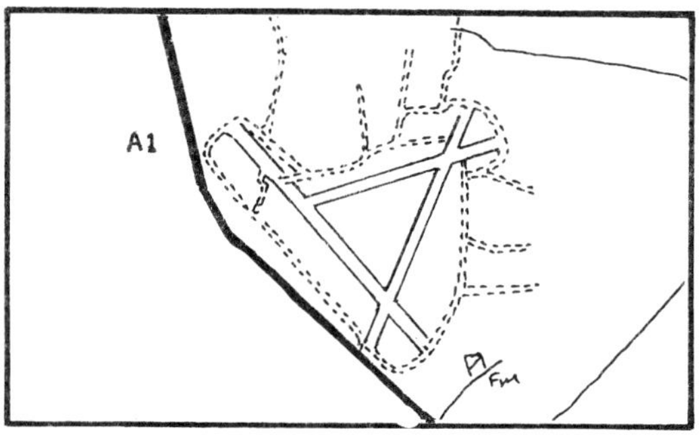

EXTENSIBILITY : -

ACCOMMODATION : Temporary.
HANGARS : T2-4;B1-1.

HARDSTANDINGS : Heavy bomber-50.

R.A.F. : OFFICERS: 108.S.N.C.O′s.: 262.O.R′s.: 779.TOTAL: 1149.
W.A.A.F.: " : 7. " : 6. " : 239. " : 252.

AFFILIATED AIRFIELDS : North Luffenham[73 Base]

PRESENT USE [1985] : Disused.

NO: 641.

AIRFIELD NAME: WOOLSINGTON. OPENED : 1935.
COUNTY : Northumberland. CLOSED :
COMMAND : Maintenance.
FORMATION : 43 Grp[Oxford] GRID REF: Z 680918[7]
FUNCTION : Storage Unit. O.S.REF.: NZ 195713/88.
:
LOCALITY : 5.75miles NW of Newcastle.
RAILWAY STN. : Newcastle Central[LNER]

LATITUDE : 55 02 00N. HEIGHT ASL : 273′ LIGHTING : None.
LONGITUDE : 01 42 00W. FLYING CONTROL : None.RADIO : QDM.

LANDMARKS DAY. : Single track railway SSW.

LANDMARKS NIGHT : As day.

OBSTRUCTIONS : Overhead colliery railway W-N.

LANDING AREA SURFACE : Grass.

QDM: N-S. LENGTH X WIDTH: 1150yds. EXT. TO: 1350yds.
: NE-SW. : 1350yds : 1550yds.
: E-W. : 1150yds. : -
: NW-SE. : 1050yds. : -

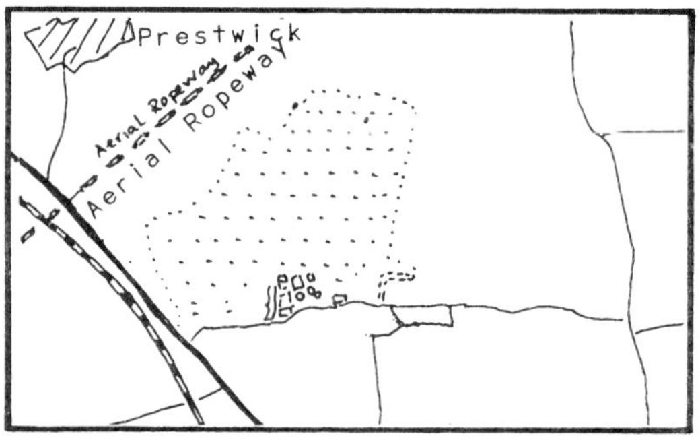

EXTENSIBILITY : -

ACCOMMODATION : Temporary.
HANGARS : Bellman-1;Blister-4;Civil-2.

HARDSTANDINGS : 1.

R.A.F. : OFFICERS: 24.S.N.C.O′s.: 60.O.R′s.: 517.TOTAL: 601.
W.A.A.F.: " : 2. " : 6. " : 84. " : 92.

AFFILIATED AIRFIELDS : -

PRESENT USE [1985] : Civil Airport[Newcastle]

NO: 642.

AIRFIELD NAME: WORCESTER. OPENED : 1936.
COUNTY : Worcestershire. CLOSED : 1946.
COMMAND : Flying Training.
FORMATION : 50 Grp[Reading] GRID REF: P 309783[81]
FUNCTION : Elementary Flying O.S.REF.: SO 855575/150.
: Training School.
LOCALITY : 1.75miles N of Worcester.
RAILWAY STN. : Worcester[LMS & GWR]

LATITUDE : 52 12 53N. HEIGHT ASL : 100′ LIGHTING : None.
LONGITUDE : 02 12 30W. FLYING CONTROL : None.RADIO : QDM.

LANDMARKS DAY. : Small lake outside W boundary. Canal E boundary.

LANDMARKS NIGHT : -

OBSTRUCTIONS : Factory chimney situated close to NE corner.

LANDING AREA SURFACE : Grass.

QDM: NE-SW. LENGTH X WIDTH: 800yds. EXT. TO: -
: E-W. : 620yds. : -
: : :
: : :

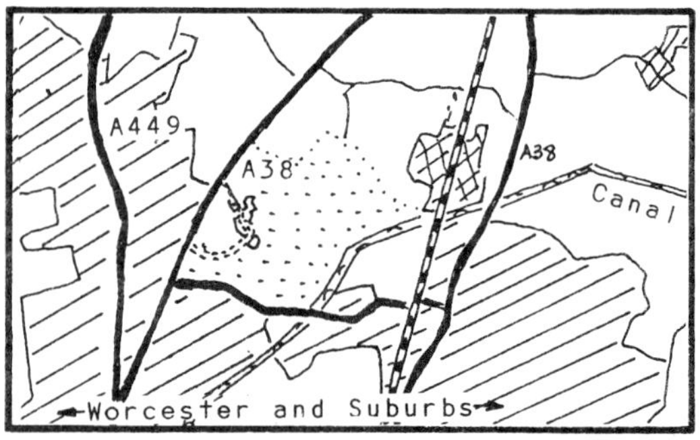

EXTENSIBILITY : None possible except with very heavy preparation.

ACCOMMODATION : Temporary[RAF]
HANGARS : Civil-60x60′-1;Ovens-3;Blister:Standard-1; double standard-1;triple standard-2.
HARDSTANDINGS : -

R.A.F. : OFFICERS: 18.S.N.C.O′s.: 48.O.R′s.: 80.TOTAL: 146.
W.A.A.F.: " : - " : - " : - " : -

AFFILIATED AIRFIELDS : -

PRESENT USE [1985] : Recreation.

NO: 643.

AIRFIELD NAME: WORKSOP. OPENED : 1943.
COUNTY : Nottinghamshire. CLOSED : 1960.
COMMAND : Bomber.
FORMATION : 91 Grp[Abingdon] GRID REF: A 092013[46]
FUNCTION : Operational Training O.S.REF.: SK 625815/120.
: Unit[satellite]
LOCALITY : 4.5miles W of East Retford.
RAILWAY STN. : Worksop 4miles[LNER]

LATITUDE : 53 19 45N. HEIGHT ASL : 195′ LIGHTING : Mk2.
LONGITUDE : 01 03 30W. FLYING CONTROL : Yes. RADIO : QDM.

LANDMARKS DAY. : 1]Manton colliery chimney 3miles W of S.
2]Worksop town 4miles W of S.
3]Welbeck Abbey 8miles SW.

LANDMARKS NIGHT : Manchester Union canal E-W boundary of A/F.

OBSTRUCTIONS : Colliery chimney 20degrees07minutes W of S 207.5′ high.

LANDING AREA SURFACE : Concrete.

QDM	LENGTH X WIDTH	EXT. TO
220.	1400 x 50yds.	2000yds.
280.	2000 x 50yds.	-
340.	1180 x 50yds.	1166yds.

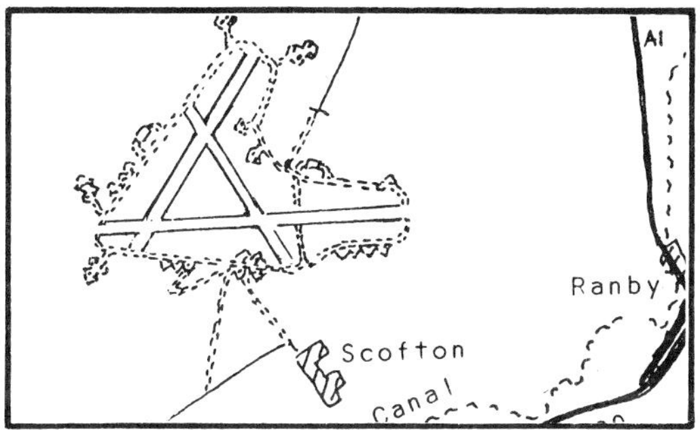

EXTENSIBILITY : -

ACCOMMODATION : Temporary.
HANGARS : T2-2.

HARDSTANDINGS : Spectacle-36.

	OFFICERS	S.N.C.O's.	O.R's.	TOTAL
R.A.F.	102.	296.	1340.	1738.
W.A.A.F.	10.	16.	304.	330.

AFFILIATED AIRFIELDS : Finningley[parent]

PRESENT USE [1985] : Disused.

NO: 644.

AIRFIELD NAME: WORMINGFORD. OPENED : 1943.
COUNTY : Essex. CLOSED : 1947.
COMMAND : 8th USAAF.
FORMATION : 55th Fighter Grp. GRID REF: M 365487[97]
FUNCTION : Operational. O.S.REF.: TL 918306/168.

LOCALITY : 6miles NW of Colchester.
RAILWAY STN. : Bures 3miles[LNER]

LATITUDE : 51 56 20N. HEIGHT ASL : 220′ LIGHTING : Mk2.
LONGITUDE : 00 47 38E. FLYING CONTROL : Yes. RADIO : QDM.

LANDMARKS DAY. : Large reservoir 8.5miles SSE. White water tank approx 1mile W of A/F.

LANDMARKS NIGHT : -

OBSTRUCTIONS : -

LANDING AREA SURFACE : Concrete & tarmac.

QDM	LENGTH X WIDTH	EXT. TO
270.	2000 x 50yds.	2400yds.
230.	1400 x 50yds.	2100yds.
330.	1400 x 50yds.	2000yds.

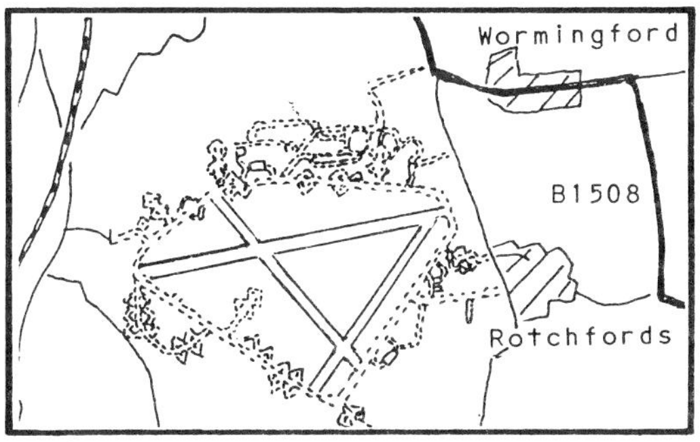

EXTENSIBILITY : Entails road diversion & demolition of 3 cottages.
ACCOMMODATION : Temporary.
HANGARS : T2-2.

HARDSTANDINGS : Loop-50.

USAAF. : OFFICERS: 421. Enlisted Men. : 2473. TOTAL: 2894.

AFFILIATED AIRFIELDS : -

PRESENT USE [1985] : Agriculture.

NO: 645.

AIRFIELD NAME: WORTHY DOWN. OPENED : 1918.
COUNTY : Hampshire. CLOSED :
COMMAND : RN.
FORMATION : HMS Kestrel. GRID REF: U 901500[123]
FUNCTION : School of Aircraft O.S.REF.: SU 468353/185.
: Maintenance.
LOCALITY : 2.5miles N of Winchester.
RAILWAY STN. : Winchester[SR]

LATITUDE : 51 06 45N. HEIGHT ASL : 345′ LIGHTING : None.
LONGITUDE : 01 19 10W. FLYING CONTROL : None. RADIO : QDM.

LANDMARKS DAY. : Southampton Water & City of Southampton.

LANDMARKS NIGHT : Winchester on R Itchen.

OBSTRUCTIONS : -

LANDING AREA SURFACE : Grass.

QDM	LENGTH X WIDTH	EXT. TO
N-S.	770yds.	-
E-W.	1400yds.	-

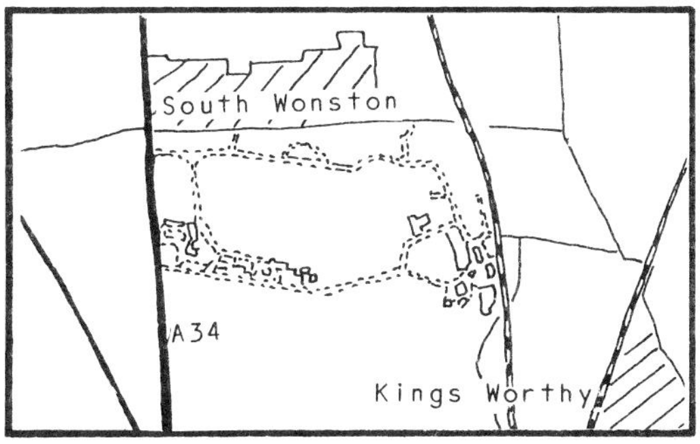

EXTENSIBILITY : -

ACCOMMODATION : Permanent.
HANGARS : 170x100′-2;Bellman-2;Bessoneau-2;Fromson-1.

HARDSTANDINGS : -

	OFFICERS	Chiefs/POs/Ratings.	TOTAL
R.N.	148.	1740.	1888.
W.R.N.S.	4.	352.	356.

AFFILIATED AIRFIELDS : -

PRESENT USE [1985] : Army.

NO: 646.

AIRFIELD NAME: WRATTING COMMON. OPENED : 1943.
COUNTY : Cambridgeshire. CLOSED : 1946.
COMMAND : Bomber.
FORMATION : 3 Grp[Exning] GRID REF: L 093692[85]
FUNCTION : Operational. O.S.REF.: TL 645500/154.

LOCALITY : 3.75miles NNW of Haverhill.
RAILWAY STN. : Haverhill[LNER]

LATITUDE : 52 07 38N. HEIGHT ASL : 398′ LIGHTING : Mk2.
LONGITUDE : 00 24 00E. FLYING CONTROL : Yes. RADIO : QDM.

LANDMARKS DAY. : -

LANDMARKS NIGHT : -

OBSTRUCTIONS : -

LANDING AREA SURFACE : Concrete & wood chippings.

QDM	LENGTH X WIDTH	EXT. TO
308.	2000 x 50yds.	-
252.	1400 x 50yds.	3000yds.
197.	1400 x 50yds.	2000yds.

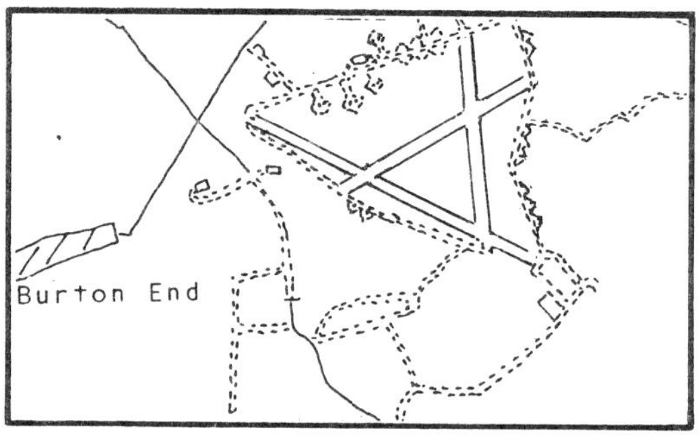

EXTENSIBILITY : Entails demolition of 8 cottages, & a farm would be isolated by peri track.
ACCOMMODATION : Temporary.
HANGARS : T2-4;B1-1.

HARDSTANDINGS : Spectacle-36.

	OFFICERS	S.N.C.O's.	O.R's.	TOTAL
R.A.F.	164.	609.	1352.	2125.
W.A.A.F.	6.	12.	330.	348.

AFFILIATED AIRFIELDS : Stradishall[31 Base]

PRESENT USE [1985] : Disused.

NO: 647.

AIRFIELD NAME: WREXHAM. OPENED : 1941.
COUNTY : Denbighshire. CLOSED : 1945.
COMMAND : Flying Training.
FORMATION : 21 Grp[Spittlegate] GRID REF: J 826737[51]
FUNCTION : Advanced Flying Unit Pilots[satellite] O.S.REF.: SJ 363526/117.
LOCALITY : 9miles SSW of Chester.
RAILWAY STN. : Wrexham[GWR]

LATITUDE : 53 04 00N. HEIGHT ASL : 250′ LIGHTING : Mk2.
LONGITUDE : 02 57 00W. FLYING CONTROL : Yes. RADIO : QDM.

LANDMARKS DAY. : Gresford colliery slag heap.

LANDMARKS NIGHT : -

OBSTRUCTIONS : Hills up to 2000′ from N to SW 4miles.

LANDING AREA SURFACE : Concrete.

QDM	LENGTH X WIDTH	EXT. TO
350.	1350 x 50yds.	2000yds.
050.	1100 x 50yds.	1600yds.
110.	1560 x 50yds.	1600yds.

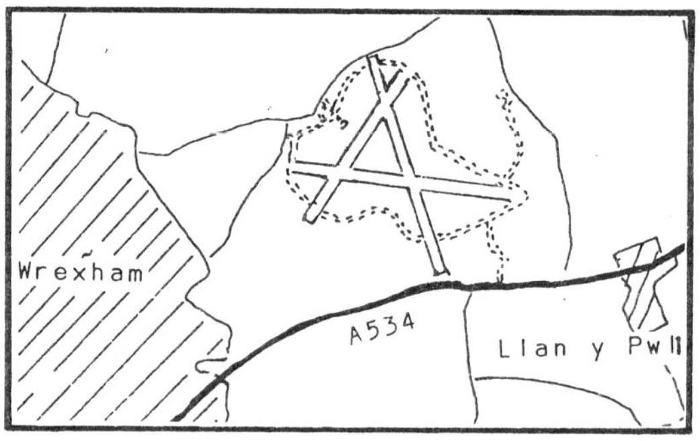

EXTENSIBILITY : R/W 350 & 050 recommended only to 1560 & 1350yds. respectively as it entails only slight demolition.
ACCOMMODATION : Temporary.
HANGARS : Bellman-1;Blister 69′-11.

HARDSTANDINGS : -

	OFFICERS	S.N.C.O's.	O.R's.	TOTAL
R.A.F.	90.	202.	612.	904.
W.A.A.F.	8.	8.	240.	256.

AFFILIATED AIRFIELDS : Calveley[Parent]

PRESENT USE [1985] : Private flying.

NO: 648.

AIRFIELD NAME: WROUGHTON. OPENED : 1940.
COUNTY : Wiltshire. CLOSED :
COMMAND : Maintenance.
FORMATION : 41 Grp[Andover] GRID REF: U 584996[112]
FUNCTION : Parent Station. O.S.REF.: SU 139786/173.

LOCALITY : 4miles S of Swindon.
RAILWAY STN. : Swindon[GWR]

LATITUDE : 51 30 15N. HEIGHT ASL : 600′ LIGHTING : None.
LONGITUDE : 01 48 00W. FLYING CONTROL : * RADIO : QDM.

LANDMARKS DAY. : 3 clumps of trees on top of ridge.
* Modified control during daylight only.

LANDMARKS NIGHT : Coate reservoir 3miles bearing 40degrees N of A/F.

OBSTRUCTIONS : Water tower 100′ 600yds. E. Ridge 200′ high .5mile S of S boundary.

LANDING AREA SURFACE : Concrete.

QDM	LENGTH X WIDTH	EXT. TO
220.	1630 x 50yds.	-
180.	1376 x 50yds.	2500yds.
270.	1333 x 50yds.	-

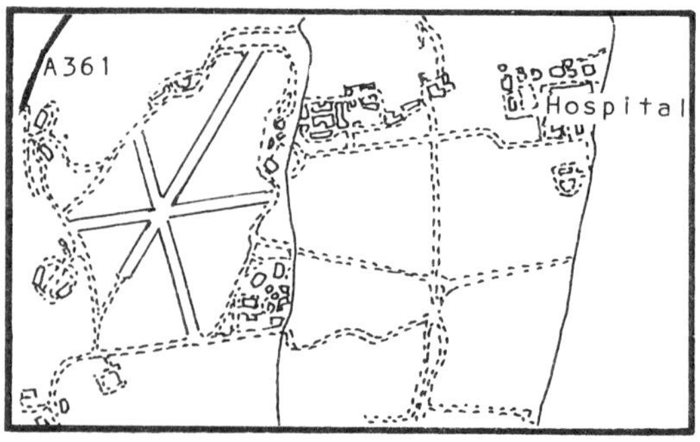

EXTENSIBILITY : Entails diversion of access road.

ACCOMMODATION : Permanent[part]
HANGARS : Types:B-2;C-3;D-4;L-7;Robin-27.

HARDSTANDINGS : Hardcore & asphalt roads-66.

	OFFICERS	S.N.C.O's.	O.R's.	TOTAL
R.A.F.	44.	49.	112.	205.
W.A.A.F.	1.	1.	15.	17.

AFFILIATED AIRFIELDS : -

PRESENT USE [1985] : RN.

NO: 649.

AIRFIELD NAME: WYMESWOLD. OPENED : 1942.
COUNTY : Leicestershire. CLOSED : 1957.
COMMAND : Transport.
FORMATION : 44 Grp[Gloucester] GRID REF: F 044420[63]
FUNCTION : Operational Training O.S.REF.: SK 586224/129.
: Unit.
LOCALITY : 3.75miles ENE of Loughborough.
RAILWAY STN. : Loughborough[LMS & LNER]

LATITUDE : 52 47 38N. HEIGHT ASL : 272′ LIGHTING : Mk2.
LONGITUDE : 01 07 45W. FLYING CONTROL : Yes. RADIO : QDM.

LANDMARKS DAY. : Brush electrical works, Loughborough.

LANDMARKS NIGHT : Town of Loughborough.

OBSTRUCTIONS : Woods.

LANDING AREA SURFACE : Concrete.

QDM	LENGTH X WIDTH	EXT. TO
198.	1250 x 50yds.	1300yds.
254.	2000 x 50yds.	-
312.	1250 x 50yds.	1400yds.

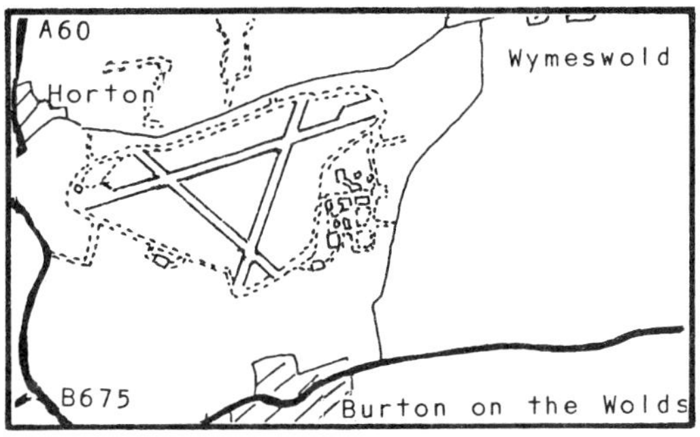

EXTENSIBILITY : Entails demolition in approaches of 2 houses & 4 huts.
ACCOMMODATION : Temporary.
HANGARS : T2-4;B1-1.

HARDSTANDINGS : Heavy Bomber-30.

	OFFICERS	S.N.C.O′s.	O.R′s.	TOTAL
R.A.F.	190.	520.	1226.	1936.
W.A.A.F.	10.	14.	411.	435.

AFFILIATED AIRFIELDS : Castle Donnington[Satellite]

PRESENT USE [1985] : Disused.

NO: 650.

AIRFIELD NAME: WYTON. OPENED : 1937.
COUNTY : Huntingdonshire. CLOSED :
COMMAND : Bomber.
FORMATION : 8 Grp[Huntingdon] GRID REF: L 740935[75]
FUNCTION : Operational. O.S.REF.: TL 288750/142.
:
LOCALITY : 3.5miles NE of Huntingdon.
RAILWAY STN. : Huntingdon North[LNER]

LATITUDE : 52 21 23N. HEIGHT ASL : 132′ LIGHTING : Mk1.
LONGITUDE : 00 06 53W. FLYING CONTROL : Yes. RADIO : QDM.

LANDMARKS DAY. : Huntingdon 4miles SW. R Ouse 2miles S.

LANDMARKS NIGHT : -

OBSTRUCTIONS : Rifle range E side of A/F.

LANDING AREA SURFACE : Concrete.

QDM	LENGTH X WIDTH	EXT. TO
093.	2000 x 50yds.	2800yds.
057.	1400 x 50yds.	2200yds.
340.	1400 x 50yds.	3600yds.

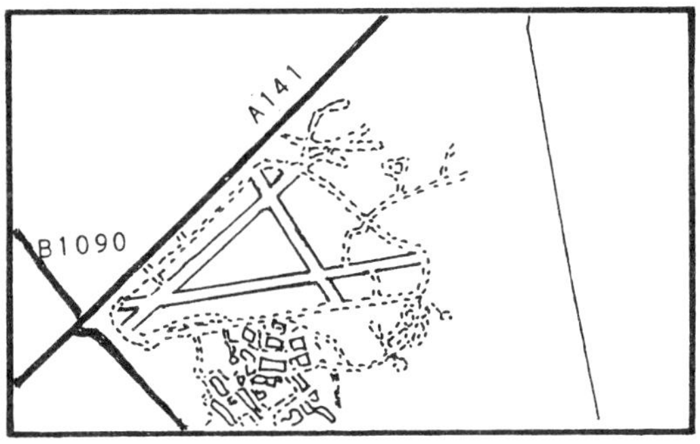

EXTENSIBILITY : Entails diversion of 2 stone cottages & a derelict house.
ACCOMMODATION : Permanent.
HANGARS : Type C-4.

HARDSTANDINGS : Heavy bomber-36.

	OFFICERS	S.N.C.O′s.	O.R′s.	TOTAL
R.A.F.	252.	301.	1740.	2293.
W.A.A.F.	8.	14.	406.	428.

AFFILIATED AIRFIELDS : -

PRESENT USE [1985] : RAF.

NO: 651.

AIRFIELD NAME: YATESBURY. OPENED : 1917.
COUNTY : Wiltshire. CLOSED : 1969.
COMMAND : Technical Training.
FORMATION : 27 Grp[Cirencester] GRID REF: U 495913[112]
FUNCTION : Radio School. O.S.REF.: SU 060710/173.
:
LOCALITY : 4.5miles E of Calne.
RAILWAY STN. : Calne[GWR]

LATITUDE : 51 25 54N. HEIGHT ASL : 570′ LIGHTING : None.
LONGITUDE : 01 54 00W. FLYING CONTROL : Yes. RADIO : QDM.

LANDMARKS DAY. : Landsdown monument;Cheshill;Copse;Oldbury Down.

LANDMARKS NIGHT : -

OBSTRUCTIONS : Hill & monument 400′ .5miles S.

LANDING AREA SURFACE : Steel Matting[Sommerfeld track]

QDM	LENGTH X WIDTH	EXT. TO
310.	972yds.	1400yds.
210.	946yds.	1070yds.
		-

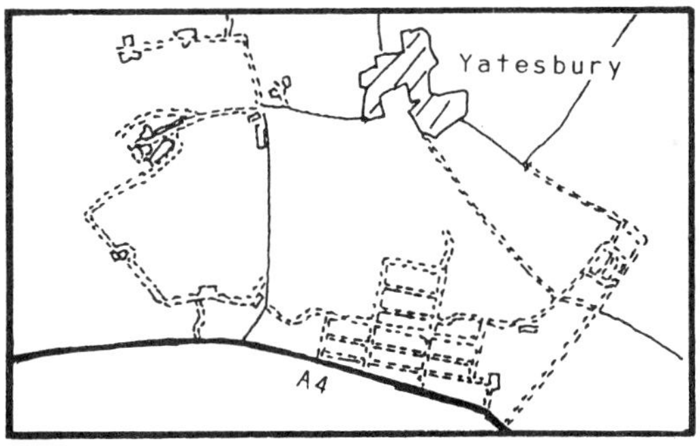

EXTENSIBILITY : -

ACCOMMODATION : Temporary.
HANGARS : Northern Light-1;Single span-3 Bellman-1;Blister-11.
HARDSTANDINGS : Concrete aprons only:250x60yds-1 200x75yds-1;200x50yds.-1.

	OFFICERS	S.N.C.O′s.	O.R′s.	TOTAL
R.A.F.	209.	1479.	5491.	7179.
W.A.A.F.	16.	15.	650.	681.

AFFILIATED AIRFIELDS : -

PRESENT USE [1985] : Agriculture.

NO: 652.

AIRFIELD NAME: YEOVILTON. OPENED : 1940.
COUNTY : Somersetshire. CLOSED :
COMMAND : RN.
FORMATION : HMS Heron. GRID REF: T 875350[129]
FUNCTION : Fighter School. O.S.REF.: ST 554234/183.
:
LOCALITY : 4miles N of Yeovil.
RAILWAY STN. : Sparkford 3miles[GWR]

LATITUDE : 51 00 40N. HEIGHT ASL : 60′ LIGHTING : Naval
LONGITUDE : 02 38 25W. FLYING CONTROL : Yes. RADIO : QDM.

LANDMARKS DAY. : Railway junction at Yeovil.

LANDMARKS NIGHT : -

OBSTRUCTIONS : Corton Hill 646′ 4miles E.

LANDING AREA : Tarmac.
SURFACE :
QDM: 006-186. LENGTH X WIDTH: 1060 x 33yds.EXT. TO: -
: 048-228. : 1215 x 50yds. : -
: 096-276. : 1160 x 33yds. : -
: 141-321. : 1070 x 33yds. : -

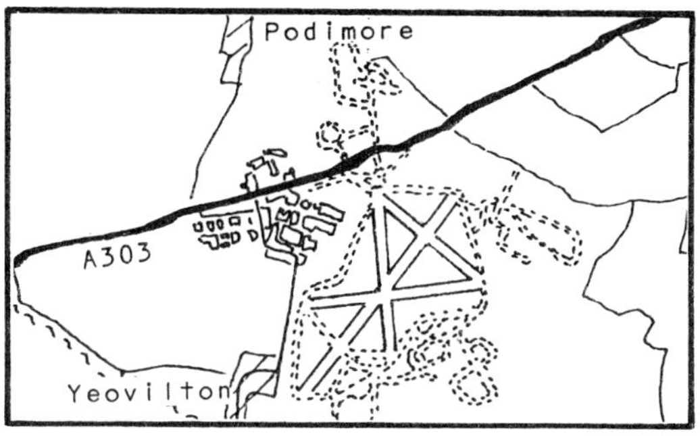

EXTENSIBILITY : -

ACCOMMODATION : Temporary.
HANGARS : 187.5x106′-8;60x70′-2;250x110′-1.

HARDSTANDINGS : -

R.N. : OFFICERS: 294. Chiefs/POs/Ratings.: 1502.TOTAL: 1796.
W.R.N.S.: " : 27. " " : 607. " : 634.

AFFILIATED AIRFIELDS : -

PRESENT USE [1985] : RN.

NO: 653.

AIRFIELD NAME: YORK. OPENED : 1936.
COUNTY : Yorkshire. CLOSED : 1952.
COMMAND : Fighter.
FORMATION : 12 Grp[Watnall] GRID REF: A 064748[27]
FUNCTION : Forward Airfield. O.S.REF.: SE 590550/105.
:
LOCALITY : 2miles NNW of York.
RAILWAY STN. : York[LNER]

LATITUDE : 53 59 15N. HEIGHT ASL : 30′ LIGHTING : Mk2.
LONGITUDE : 01 05 45W. FLYING CONTROL : Yes. RADIO : QDM.

LANDMARKS DAY. : York Minster.

LANDMARKS NIGHT : -

OBSTRUCTIONS : -

LANDING AREA : Concrete & tarmac.
SURFACE :
QDM: 245. LENGTH X WIDTH: 1600 x 50yds.EXT. TO: 2400yds.
: 353. : 1400 x 50yds. : 2400yds.
: 308. : 1400 x 50yds. : 2200yds.
: : :

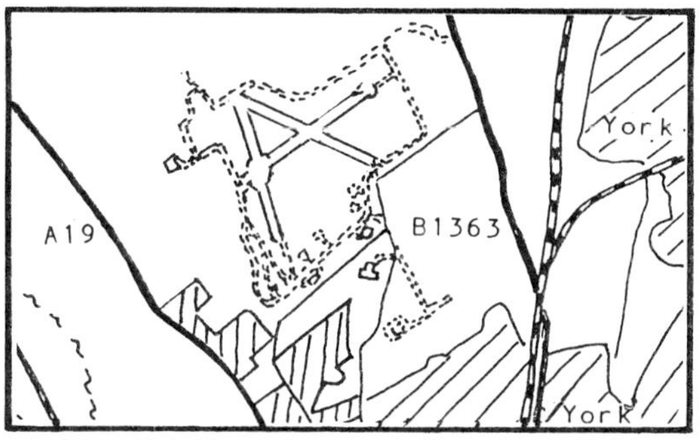

EXTENSIBILITY : Entails serious road diversion & light demolition.
ACCOMMODATION : Temporary[RAF]
HANGARS : T1-1;Blister-12;Robin-1.

HARDSTANDINGS : Blenheim-12;frypan 50′-3.

R.A.F. : OFFICERS: 39.S.N.C.O′s.: 59.O.R′s.: 286.TOTAL: 384.
W.A.A.F.: " : 4. " : 10. " : 105. " : 119.

AFFILIATED AIRFIELDS : Church Fenton[Sector]

PRESENT USE [1985] : Housing.

NO: 654.

AIRFIELD NAME: ZEALS. OPENED : 1942.
COUNTY : Wiltshire. CLOSED : 1946.
COMMAND : Balloon.
FORMATION : 32 Grp[Bath] GRID REF: U 216535[121]
FUNCTION : Storage. O.S.REF.: ST 777325/183.
:
LOCALITY : 4miles NNW of Gillingham.
RAILWAY STN. : Gillingham 2miles[SR]

LATITUDE : 51 05 30N. HEIGHT ASL : 550′ LIGHTING : Mk2.
LONGITUDE : 02 18 45W. FLYING CONTROL : Yes. RADIO : QDM.

LANDMARKS DAY. : Alfred Tower 2miles NW.

LANDMARKS NIGHT : 3 lakes .5miles NW.

OBSTRUCTIONS : Range of hills[750-899′] 2miles E.

LANDING AREA : Grass.
SURFACE :
QDM: N-S. LENGTH X WIDTH: 1600yds. EXT. TO: 2000yds.
: E-W. : 1417yds. : -
: SE-NW. : 1417yds. : -
: : :

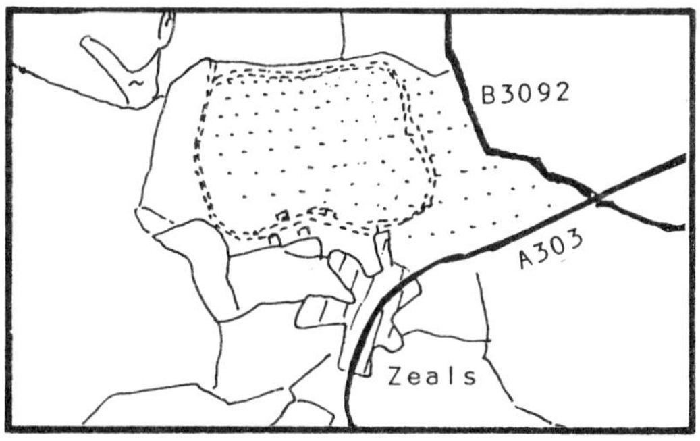

EXTENSIBILITY : -

ACCOMMODATION : Temporary.
HANGARS : O Blister-8;T1-1.

HARDSTANDINGS : TE-30;Sommerfeld Track-12.

R.A.F. : OFFICERS: 20.S.N.C.O′s.: 180.O.R′s.: 1684.TOTAL: 1884.
W.A.A.F.: " : 6. " : 6. " : 230. " : 242.

AFFILIATED AIRFIELDS : -

PRESENT USE [1985] : Agriculture.

APPENDIX 'A'. ORDER OF BATTLE OF R.A.F., DOMINION & ALLIED UNITS. 1/12/44.

ROYAL AIR FORCE HOME COMMAND ORGANISATION DECEMBER 1944.

AIR MINISTRY. KINGSWAY, LONDON W.C.2.

BOMBER COMMAND. WALTERS ASH, HIGH WYCOMBE, BUCKS.

NO. 1 BOMBER GROUP BAWTRY.

STATION		UNIT	EQUIPMENT.	AIRFIELD NO.
BINBROOK.	[No.12 Base]	No 460[R.A.A.F] Sqdn.	Lancaster 1/111	49.
		No. 1 G.G. School		
Grimsby.		No. 100 Sqdn.	Lancaster 1/111	264.
		No. 2722 Regiment A.A. Sqdn.	Bofors	
Kelstern.		No. 625 Sqdn.	Lancaster 1/111	321.
ELSHAM WOLDS.	[No.13 Base]	No. 103 Sqdn.	Lancaster 1/111	210.
		No. 2835 Regiment A.A. Sqdn.	Bofors	
Kirmington.		No. 166 Sqdn.	Lancaster 1/111	336.
North Killingholme.		No. 550 Sqdn.	Lancaster 1/111	426.
Hemswell.		Night Bomber Tactical School		284.
Cammeringham.		No. 1687[B]Defence Training Flt.	Spitfire/Hurricane.	97.
Sturgate.		No. 1481[B]Gunnery Flt	Hurricane.	546.
		No. 1520 BAT Flt[23 Grp]	Oxford.	
LUDFORD MAGNA.	[No.14 Base]	No. 101 Sqdn.	Lancaster 1/111	371.
Wickenby.		No. 12 Sqdn.	Lancaster 1/111	621.
		No. 626 Sqdn.	Lancaster 1/111	
Faldingworth.		No. 300[Polish]Sqdn	Lancaster 1/111	222.
		No. 1533 BAT Flt[23 Grp]	Oxford.	
		No. 1546 BAT Flt[23 Grp]	Oxford.	
SCAMPTON.	[No.15 Base]	No. 153 Sqdn.	Lancaster 1/111	486.
Dunholme Lodge.		No. 170 Sqdn.	Lancaster 1/111	191.
		No. 2799 Regiment A.A. Sqdn.	Bofors	
Fiskerton.		No. 150 Sqdn.	Lancaster 1/111	232.
		No. 576 Sqdn.	Lancaster 1/111	
		No. 1515 BAT Flt[21 Grp]	Oxford.	

NO 3 BOMBER GROUP. EXNING, NEWMARKET.

STATION		UNIT	EQUIPMENT.	AIRFIELD NO.
STRADISHALL.	[No. 31 Base]	No.1657 H.C.U.	Stirling/Lanc/Oxford.	542.
Chedburgh.		No.1653 H.C.U.	Stirling.	118.
Gosfield.		Care & Maintenance		249.
Matching.		" " "		389.
Shepherds Grove.		" " "		495.
Wratting Common.		No. 195 Sqdn.	Lancaster 1/111	646.
Tempsford.		No. 138[S.D.]Sqdn.	Stirling 1V S.D.	564.
		No. 161[S.D.]Sqdn.	Hudson 1/111	
			-Stirling 1V S.D.	
Feltwell.		No. 3 Lancaster Finishing School.	Lancaster 1/111	225.
		No. 2807 Regiment AA Sqdn.	Bofors.	
		No. 1519 BAT Flt.[23 Grp]	Oxford.	
		No. 6219 Bomb Disposal Flt.		
Methwold.		No. 149[East Indies]Sqdn.	Lancaster 1/111	401.
		No. 218[Gold Coast]Sqdn.	Lancaster 1/111	
MILDENHALL.	[No.32 Base]	No. 15 Sqdn.	Lancaster 1/111	404.
		No. 622 Sqdn.	Lancaster 1/111	
Newmarket.		No. 3 Grp. Comms. Flt.	Various	421.
		Bombing Development unit.	Various	
		No. 1688[B]Defence Training Flt.	Spitfire/Hurricane.	
Tuddenham.		No. 90 Sqdn.	Lancaster 1/111	581.
		No. 186 Sqdn.	Lancaster 1/111	
WATERBEACH.	[No. 33 Base]	No. 514 Sqdn.	Lancaster 11	600.
		No. 5133 Bomb Disposal Sqdn.		
Mepal.		No. 75[N.Z.]Sqdn.	Lancaster 1/111	396.
Witchford.		No. 115 Sqdn.	Lancaster 1/111	631.
Woodbridge.		Emergency Runway.		635.
		Bomb Ballistic Unit[M.A.P.Unit]	Halifax/Mosquito	

NO 4 BOMBER GROUP . YORK.

Carnaby.		Emergency Runway.		103.
POCKLINGTON.	[No. 42 Base]	No. 102[Ceylon]Sqdn.	Halifax 111	461.
Elvington.		No. 346[Free French]Sqdn.	Halifax 111	211.
		No. 347[Free French]Sqdn.	Halifax 111	
Full Sutton.		No. 77 Sqdn.	Halifax 111	243.
		No. 3 Grp. Comms. Flt.	Various	
Snaith.		No. 51 Sqdn.	Halifax 111	512.
		No. 5131 Bomb Disposal Sqdn.		
		No. 6204 Bomb Disposal Flt.		
		No. 2955 Regiment A.A.Sqdn.	Bofors.	
Burn.		No. 578 Sqdn.	Halifax 111	88.
		No. 2890 Regiment A.A.Sqdn.	Bofors.	
DRIFFIELD.	[No. 43 Base]	No. 462[R.A.A.F]Sqdn.	Halifax 11/111	188.
		No. 466[R.A.A.F]Sqdn.	Halifax 11/111	
Leconfield.		No. 640 Sqdn.	Halifax 111	346.
Lissett.		No. 158 Sqdn.	Halifax 111	356.
HOLME.	[No. 44 Base]	No. 76 Sqdn.	Halifax 111	298.
		No. 1689[B]Defence Training Flt.	Spitfire.	
Breighton.		No. 78 Sqdn.	Halifax 111	79.
Melbourne.		No. 10 Sqdn.	Halifax 111	392.

NO 5 BOMBER GROUP. MORTON HALL,SWINDERBY.

WADDINGTON.	[No. 53 Base]	No. 463[R.A.A.F]Sqdn.	Lancaster 1/111	593.
		No. 467[R.A.A.F]Sqdn.	Lancaster 1/111	
Skellingthorpe.		No. 50 Sqdn.	Lancaster 1/11	505.
		No. 61 Sqdn.	Lancaster 1/111	
Bardney.		No. 9 Sqdn.	Lancaster 1/111'	33.
CONINGSBY.	[No. 54 Base]	No. 83 Sqdn.	Lancaster 1/111	140.
		No. 97[Straits Settlements]Sqdn.	Lancaster 1/111	
Woodhall Spa.		No. 617 Sqdn.	Lancaster 1/111	637.
		No. 627 Sqdn.	Mosquito V/XX	
Metheringham.		No. 106 Sqdn.	Lancaster 1/111	400.
		No. 1690[B]Defence Training Flt.	Spitfire.	
		No. 2763 Regiment A.A. Sqdn.	Bofors.	
EAST KIRKBY.	[No. 55 Base]	No. 57 Sqdn.	Lancaster 1/111	200.
Spilsby.		No. 44[Rhodesia]Sqdn.	Lancaster 1/111	521.
		No. 207 Sqdn.	Lancaster 1/111	
Strubby.		No. 619 Sqdn.	Lancaster 1/111	545.
		No. 630 Sqdn.	Lancaster 1/111	
		No.2735 Regiment A.A. Sqdn.	Bofors.	
SYERSTON.	[No. 56 Base]	No. 5 Lancaster Finishing School.	Lancaster 1/111	554.
Balderton.		No. 227 Sqdn.	Lancaster 1/111	29.
		No. 5 Aircrew School.		
Fulbeck.		No. 49 Sqdn.	Lancaster 1/111	242.
		No. 189 Sqdn.	Lancaster 1/111	

NO. 6 BOMBER[R.C.A.F.]GROUP. ALLERTON PARK, KNARESBOROUGH

LINTON-ON-OUSE .	[No.62 Base]	No. 408[R.C.A.F]Sqdn.	Halifax V11	355.
		No. 426[R.C.A.F]Sqdn.	Halifax 111	
Tholthorpe.		No. 420[R.C.A.F]Sqdn.	Halifax V11	567.
East Moor.		No. 415[R.C.A.F]Sqdn.	Halifax 111	201.
		No. 425[R.C.A.F]Sqdn.	Halifax 111	
		No. 432[R.C.A.F]Sqdn.	Halifax V11	
LEEMING.	[No. 63 Base]	No. 427[R.C.A.F]Sqdn.	Halifax 111	348.
		No. 429[R.C.A.F]Sqdn	Halifax 111	
Skipton-on-Swale.		No. 424[R.C.A.F]Sqdn	Halifax 111	506.
		No. 433[R.C.A.F]Sqdn.	Halifax 111	
MIDDLETON-ST-GEORGE.	[No. 64 Base]	No. 419[R.C.A.F]Sqdn.	Lancaster X	403.
		No. 428[R.C.A.F]Sqdn.	Lancaster X	
Croft.		No. 431[R.C.A.F]Sqdn.	Halifax 111	153.
		No. 434[R.C.A.F]Sqdn.	Halifax X	

NO. 7 BOMBER[H.C.U.]GROUP. ST.VINCENTS. GRANTHAM.

LINDHOLME.	[No.71 Base]	No. 1656 H.C.U.	Hali. 11/V, Lanc 1/111	354.
Blyton.		No. 1662 H.C.U.	Hali. 11/V, Lanc 1/111	58.
Sandtoft.		No. 1667 H.C.U.	Hali. 11/V, Lanc 1/111	484.
BOTTESFORD.	[No.72 Base]	No. 1668 H.C.U.	Lancaster 1/11/111	66.
		No. 7 Group Comms. Flt.	Various.	
Langar.		No. 1669 H.C.U.	Lancaster 1/111	340.
NORTH LUFFENHAM.	[No. 73 Base]	Glider Erection Unit[M.A.P.]		427.
Woolfox Lodge.		No. 1651 H.C.U.	Lancaster 1/111C	640.
MARSTON MOOR.	[No.74 Base]	No. 1652 H.C.U.	Halifax 111	387.
Rufforth.		No. 1663 H.C.U.	Halifax 111	482.
Riccall.		No. 1658 H.C.U.	Halifax 111	476.
Acaster Malbis.		No. 4 Aircrew School.		5.
SWINDERBY.	[No. 75 Base]	No. 1660 H.C.U.	Stirling.	552.
		No. 5 Grp. Comms. Flt.	Various.	
Wigsley.		No. 1654 H.C.U.	Stirling.	622.
Winthorpe.		No. 1661 H.C.U.	Stirling	630.
TOPCLIFFE.	[No. 76 RCAF Base]	No. 1659 H.C.U.	Halifax 111	578.
Disforth.		No. 1664 H.C.U.	Halifax V	179.
		No. 6[R.C.A.F]Grp. Comms. Flt.	Various	
Wombleton.		No. 1666 H.C.U.	Halifax 111	634.
Dalton.		No. 1695[B]Defence Training Flt.	Spitfire/Hurricane,	163.
		No. 4 Aircrew School.		
Gamston.		No. 3 Aircrew School.		245.
		Wellington Disposal Centre.	Wellington.	

NO 8 [P.F.F.] GROUP. CASTLE HILL HOUSE, HUNTINGDON.

Bourn.	No. 105 Sqdn.	Mosquito 1X/XV1	69.
	No. 9 Instructors School[E.V.T.]		
	No. 1696[B]Defence Training Flt.	Spitfire/Hurricane.	
Downham Market.	No. 608 Sqdn.	Mosquito 1V/XX	186.
	No. 635 Sqdn.	Lancaster 1/111	
Gransden Lodge.	No. 405[R.C.A.F]Sqdn.	Lancaster 1/111	254.
	No. 142 Sqdn.	Mosquito XXV	
	No. 2784 Regiment A.A. Sqdn.	Bofors.	
Graveley.	No. 35[Madras Presidency]Sqdn.	Lancaster 1/111	255.
	No. 692 Sqdn.	Mosquito 1V/XX	
Little Staughton.	No. 109 Sqdn.	Mosquito 1X/XV1	360.
	No. 582 Sqdn.	Lancaster 1/111	
Oakington.	No. 7 Sqdn.	Lancaster 1/111	436.
	No. 571 Sqdn.	Mosquito 1X/XV1	
Upwood.	No. 139[Jamaica]Sqdn.	Mosquito V1/XX	590.
	No. 156 Sqdn.	Lancaster 1/111	
	Mosquito Major Servicing Section.		
Warboys.	Pathfinder Nav. Training Unit.	Lancaster 1/111	595.
	No.1655 Mosquito Training Unit.	Mosquito/Oxford	
	F.N.Training Unit[M.A.P.]		
Wyton.	No. 8[P.F.F.]Grp. Comms. Flt.	Various.	650.
	No. 1409[Met]Flt.	Mosquito 1X/XV1	
	Lancaster Major Servicing Section.		
	No. 128 Sqdn.	Mosquito 1X/XV1	
	No. 2844 Regiment A.A.	Bofors.	

NO. 26 BOMBER[SIGNALS]GROUP. LANGLEY HALL, BUCKS.

HINTON-in-the-HEDGES.	R.V.S.U.	Radio Storage Unit.	295.
HONILEY.	Signals Development Wing.	Wellington/Anson.	301.
Baginton.			27.

NO.91 BOMBER[O.T.U.]GROUP. ABINGDON.

ABINGDON.	No. 91 Grp. Comms. Flt.	Various.	4.
	No. 10 O.T.U.	Wellington 111/X.	
Stanton Harcourt.			532.
FINNINGLEY.	No. 18 O.T.U.	Wellington 111/X.	230.
	No. 2898 Regiment A.A. Sqdn.	Bofors.	
Worksop.			643.
HONEYBOURNE.	No. 24 O.T.U.	Wellington 1/111.	300.
Long Marston.			
KINLOSS.	No.19 O.T.U.	Wellington 111/X.	330.
LOSSIEMOUTH.	No. 20 O.T.U.	Wellington 111/X.	370.
Elgin.			208.
MORTON-in-MARSH.	No. 21 O.T.U.	Wellington 111/ X.	412.
Enstone.			212.
WELLESBOURNE MOUNTFORD.	No. 22 O.T.U.	Wellington 111/X.	604.
Gaydon.			247.
Stratford.			543.

NO. 92 BOMBER[O.T.U.]GROUP. WINSLOW.

BRUNTINGTHORPE.	No. 29 O.T.U.	Wellington 111/X.	85.
	Bombing Analysis School.		
CHIPPING WARDEN.	No. 12 O.T.U.	Wellington 111/X.	126.
	No. 1517 B.A.T. Flt[23 Grp]	Oxford.	205.
Edgehill.			
DESBOROUGH.	No. 84 O.T.U.	Wellington 111/X.	175.
HUSBANDS BOSWORTH.	No. 85 O.T.U.	Wellington 111/X.	312.
MARKET HARBOROUGH.	No. 14 O.T.U.	Wellington 111/X.	386.
SILVERSTONE.	No. 17 O.T.U.	Wellington 111/X.	503.
Turweston.			584.
UPPER HEYFORD.	No. 16 O.T.U.	Wellington 111/X.	589.
Barford St. John.			34.
WING.	No. 28 O.T.U.	Wellington 111/X.	626.
		Hurricane.	
	No. 92 Grp.Comms. Flt.	Various.	
Little Horwood.			357.
WESTCOTT.	No. 11 O.T.U.	Wellington X.	611.
	Engine Control Demonstration Unit.	Wellington 111.	
Oakley.			437.

NO. 93 BOMBER[O.T.U.]GROUP. EGGINTON.

HIXON.	No. 30 O.T.U.	Wellington 111/X.	296.
LICHFIELD.	No. 27 O.T.U.	Wellington 111/X.	352.
	No. 93 Grp.Comms. Flt.	Various.	
	No. 51 M.U.[41 Grp]	A/C Storage & Packing Unit.	
Church Broughton.			129.
OSSINGTON.	No. 82 O.T.U.	Wellington 111/X.	444.
		Hurricane.	

NO. 100[SPECIAL DUTIES]GROUP. BYLAUGH HALL, EAST DEREHAM, NORFOLK.

FOULSHAM	No. 192[BS]Sqdn.	Halifax 111, Wellingt. X,Mosq. 1V, Anson,Tiger Moth.	237.
	The Development Unit.	Various.	
GREAT MASSINGHAM.	No. 169[BS]Sqdn.	Mosquito V1.	259.
	No. 1694[B]Defence Training Flt.	Spitfire.	
	No. 1692[BS]Training Unit.	Anson, Mosquito.	
LITTLE SNORING.	No. 23[BS] Sqdn.	Mosquito V1.	359.
	No. 515[BS]Sqdn.	Mosquito V1.	
NORTH CREAKE.	No. 199[BS]Sqdn.	Stirling.	425.
	No. 171[BS]Sqdn.	Halifax 111.	
OULTON.	No. 214[BS]Federated Malay States Sqdn.	Fortress 11.	445.
	No. 223[BS]Sqdn.	Liberator.	
	No.1699 Training Flt.	Fortress/Liberator.	
SWANNINGTON	No. 85[BS]Sqdn.	Mosquito XXX.	550.
	No. 157[BS]Sqdn.	Mosquito X1X.	
WEST RAYNHAM.	No. 239[BS]Sqdn.	Mosquito V1.	610.
	No. 141[BS]Sqdn.	Mosquito V1.	

MISCELLANEOUS AIRFIELDS.

LAKENHEATH.	Under Re-construction.	339.
MARHAM.	Under Re-construction.	385
SCULTHORPE.	Under Re-construction.	489.

Note 1. Bases & Stations are shown in capitals. Sub-stations & satellites are in small letters.

Note 2. All O.T.U.s have Ansons in addition to their operational type.

FIGHTER COMMAND. BENTLEY PRIORY,STANMORE,MIDDLESEX.

NO 10 FIGHTER GROUP. RUDLOE MANOR, BOX, WILTS.

COLERNE.	No. 10 Group Comms. Flt.	Various.	136.
	No. 406[R.C.A.F]Sqdn.	Mosquito XXX	
	No. 1026 Servicing Wing H.Q		
	No. 39 M.U.[41 Grp]	Aircraft Storage Unit.	
	No. 218 M.U.[43 Grp]	Secret Installation Fitting Unit.	
	No. 6203 Bomb Disposal Flt. [44 Grp]		
Defford.	Telecommunications Flying Unit.	Various.	170.
Fairwood Common.	No. 11 Armament Practice Camp	Master,Lysander,Martinet	221.
	No. 18 Armament Practice Camp	Master,Lysander,Martinet.	
	No. 1013 Servicing Wing H.Q.		
EXETER.	No. 6229 Bomb Disposal Flt [44 Grp]		216.
Bolt Head.*	No. 275[A.S.R.]Sqdn.	Spitfire,Walrus,Sea Otter.	62.
Culmhead.*	Care & Maintenance Party.		159.
Harrowbeer*	Care & Maintenance Party.		275.
Winkleigh.*	Care & Maintenance Party.		628.
PORTREATH.	No. 276[A.S.R.]Sqdn.	Spitfire,Walrus,Sea Otter.	465.
	No.1 Overseas Aircraft Despatch Unit[44 Grp]		
Predannack.	No. 604 Sqdn.	Mosquito X111	467.
	No. 264 Sqdn.	Mosquito X111	
	No. 1024 Servicing Wing H.Q.		
St. Marys.*	Care & Maintenance Party.		528.

NO 11 FIGHTER GROUP. UXBRIDGE,MIDDLESEX.

BIGGIN HILL	No. 154 Sqdn.	Spitfire V11	48.
	No. 1020 Servicing Wing H.Q.		
Detling.	No. 1 Sqdn.	Spitfire 1XB	177.
	No. 165 Sqdn.	Spitfire 1X	
	No. 2753 Regiment A.A. Sqdn.	Bofors.	
	No. 2769 Regiment A.A. Sqdn.	Bofors.	
	No. 1025 Servicing Wing H.Q.		
Friston.	No. 2706 Regiment A.A. Sqdn.	Bofors.	241.
	No. 2803 Regiment A.A. Sqdn.	Bofors.	
Gatwick.	No. 1028 Servicing Wing H.Q.		246.
	No. 2702 Regiment A.A. Sqdn.	Bofors.	
	No. 2792 Regiment A.A. Sqdn.	Bofors.	
	No. 287[A.A.C.]Sqdn. 70 Grp.	Tempest,Spitfire,Oxford	
Redhill.*	No. 116[Calibration]Sqdn.	Oxford 1	473.
	No. 1 Aircraft Delivery Flt.		
Hawkinge.	No. 441[R.C.A.F.]Sqdn.	Spitfire 1X	281.
	No. 277[A.S.R.]Sqdn.	Various.	
	No. 1009 Servicing Wing H.Q.		
	No. 1 Refuelling & Rearming Party.		
	No. 2740 Regiment A.A. Sqdn.	Bofors.	
	No. 2741 Regiment A.A. Sqdn.	Bofors.	
	No. 2767 Regiment A.A. Sqdn.	Bofors.	
Lympne.*	No. 1015 Servicing Wing H.Q.		376.
	No. 2823 Regiment A.A. Sqdn	Bofors.	
	No. 2847 Regiment A.A. Sqgn.	Bofors.	
Kenley.	No. 6201 Bomb Disposal Flt.[44 Grp]		323.
Penshurst.*			453.
Manston.	No. 118 Sqdn.	Spitfire 1Xc	384.
	No. 124 Sqdn.	Spitfire 1X	
	No. 91 Sqdn.	Spitfire 1Xb	
	No. 504 Sqdn.	Spitfire 1X	
	No. 605 Sqdn.	Mosquito FB V1	
	No. 616 Sqdn.	Meteor 1	
	No.1401 Met. Flt.	Spitfire.	
	No. 1001 Servicing Wing H.Q.		
	No. 1027 Servicing Wing H.Q.		
	No. 2720 Regiment A.A. Sqdn.	Bofors.	
	No. 2838 Regiment A.A. Sqdn.	Bofors.	
West Malling.	No. 5134 Bomb Disposal Sqdn.[44 Grp]		609.
	No. 6223 Bomb Disposal Flt[44 Grp]		
	No. 2707 Regiment A.A. Sqdn.	Bofors.	
	No. 2731 Regiment A.A. Sqdn	Bofors.	
	No. 2766 Regiment A.A. Sqdn.	Bofors.	
	No. 2797 Regiment A.A. Sqdn.	Bofors.	
	No. 5134 Bomb Disposal Sqdn[44 Grp]		
	No. 6223 Bomb Disposal Flt [44 Grp]		
Gravesend.*	Care & Maintenance		256.
MIDDLE WALLOP.	No. 1006 Servicing Wing H.Q.		402.
	No. 3501 Servicing Unit.		
	No. 371 Repair & Salvage Unit.		
Beaulieu.	No. 2762 Regiment A.A. Sqdn.	Bofors.	39.
	No. 2892 Regiment A.A. Sqdn.	Bofors.	
Ibsley.			314.
Christchurch.*			128.
Warmwell.	No. 14 Armament Practice Camp.	Master,Lysander,Martinet.	596.
	No. 17 Armament Practice Camp.	Master,Lysander,Martinet.	
	No. 1010 Servicing Wing H.Q.		
	No. 2954 Regiment A.A. Sqdn.	Bofors.	
Chilbolton.*	Care & Maintenance.		123.
NORTH WEALD.	NO.234[Madras Presidency]Sqdn.	Mustang 111	429.
	No. 310[Czech]Sqdn.	Spitfire 1X	
	No. 313[Czech]Sqdn.	Spitfire 1X	
	No. 63 Sqdn.	Spitfire Vb	
	No. 1007 Servicing Wing H.Q.		
	No. 5133 Bomb Disposal Sqdn.		
	No. 6207 Bomb Disposal Flt.		
Andrews Field.	No 150 Wing H.Q.		14.
	No. 19 Sqdn.	Mustang 111	
	No. 65 Sqdn.	Mustang 111	
	No 122 Sqdn.	Mustang 111	
	No. 133[Polish]Wing H.Q.		
	No. 129 Sqdn.	Mustang 111	
	No. 306[Polish]Sqdn.	Mustang 111	
	No. 316[Polish]Sqdn.	Mustang 111	
	No. 1002 Servicing Wing H.Q.		
Bentwaters.			45.
Bottisham.	Care & Maintenance Party.		67.

NO 11 FIGHTER GROUP. [Continued]

Bradwell Bay.	No. 64 Sqdn.	Spitfire 1X	73.
	No. 126 Sqdn.	Spitfire 1X	
	No. 501 Sqdn.	Tempest V	
	No. 312[Czech]Sqdn.	Spitfire 1X	
	No. 1011 Servicing Wing H.Q.		
	No. 2840 Regiment A.A. Sqdn.	Bofors	
Castle Camps.	No. 25 Sqdn.	Mosquito XXX	105.
	No. 1008 Servicing Wing H.Q.		
	No. 1020 Servicing Wing H.Q.		
			123.
Hornchurch.	No. 55 Repair Unit[Buildings]		305.
	No. 6221 Bomb Disposal Flt[44 Grp]		
	No. 567[A.A.C.]Sqdn. 70 Grp.	Hurricane,Martinet, Vengeance T.T.	
Hunsdon.	No. 418[R.C.A.F]Sqdn.	Mosquito V1	310.
	No. 488[R.N.Z.A.F]Sqdn.	Mosquito XXX	
	No. 29 Sqdn.	Mosquito X111	
	No. 1018 Servicing Wing H.Q.		
Stapleford Tawney.	Care & Maintenance Party.		533.
	No. 2727 Regiment AA. Sqdn.	Bofors.	
	No. 2839 Regiment A.A. Sqdn.	Bofors.	
TANGMERE.	No. 26 Sqdn.	Mustang 1	558.
	No. 6222 Bomb Disposal Flt [44 Grp]		
	No. 2704 Regiment A.A. Sqdn.	Bofors.	
	No. 2709 Regiment A.A. Sqdn.	Bofors.	
	No. 2803 Regiment A.A. Sqdn.	Bofors.	
	No. 1005 Servicing Wing H.Q.		
Merston.*	No. 2723 Regiment A.A. Sqdn.	Bofors.	398.
	No. 2761 Regiment A.A. Sqdn.	Bofors.	
	No. 2832 Regiment A.A. Sqdn.	Bofors.	
Westhampnett.*			612.
Ford.	No. 456[R.A.A.F.]Sqdn.	Mosquito XV11	234.
	No. 1003 Servicing Wing H.Q.		
	No. 2758 Regiment A.A. Sqdn.	Bofors.	
	No. 2828 Regiment A.A. Sqdn.	Bofors.	
Shoreham.	Care & Maintenance Party.		499.
Northolt.	Fighter Command Comms. Sqdn.	Various.	432.
	No. 1017 Servicing Wing H.Q.		
	No. 1322[A.D.L.S]Flt 46 Grp.		
	No. 1697[A.D.L.S]Flt. 46 Grp.		
Heston.			289.
Odiham.	No. 96 Sqdn.	Mosquito X11	439
	No. 1019 Servicing Wing H.Q.		
Dunsfold.			194.
Blackbushe.			56.
Lasham.	84 Grp. Support Unit.	Spitfire,Typhoon,Mustang Auster.	343.
Appledram.	Advanced Landing Ground.		18.
Bognor.	" " "		61.
Bisterne.	" " "		54.
Brenzett.	" " "		80.
Chailey.	" " "		113.
Coolham.	" " "		142.
Deanland.	" " "		166.
Funtington.	" " "		244.
Headcorn.	" " "		282.
Horne.	" " "		306.
High Haldon.	" " "		293.
Kingsnorth.	" " "		328.
Lashenden.	" " "		344.
Lydd.	" " "		374.
Lymington.	" " "		375.
Needs Ore Point.	" " "		417.
Newchurch.	" " "		420.
New Romney.	" " "		419.
Selsey.	" " "		492.
Staplehurst.	" " "		534.
Swingfield.	" " "		553.
Winkton.	" " "		629.
Woodchurch.	" " "		636.

NO 12 FIGHTER GROUP. WATNALL.

CHURCH FENTON	No. 307[Polish]Sqdn.	Mosquito X11	130.
	No.1022 Servicing Wing H.Q.		
Hutton Cranswick	No. 291[A.A.C]Sqdn.[70 Grp]	Martinet, Vengeance T.T.	313.
	No. 2746 Regiment A.A. Sqdn.	Bofors.	
	No. 2805 Regiment A.A. Sqdn.	Bofors.	
Woodvale	No. 1021 Servicing Wing H.Q.		639.
	No. 285[A.A.C]Sqdn. [70 Grp]	Oxford, Hurricane.	
York	No. 4 Aircraft Delivery Unit.		653.
	No. 87 M.U. [56 Wing]	Equipment Park.	
	No. 60 M.U. [43 Grp]	Repair & Salvage Unit.	
	No. 13 Mobile Dental Surgery.	Tender Type.	
COLTISHALL	No. 303 [Polish] Sqdn.	Spitfire 1X	138.
	No. 125 Sqdn.	Mosquito XV11	
	No. 68 Sqdn.	Mosquito XV11	
	No. 1004 Servicing Wing H.Q.		
	No. 1016 Servicing Wing H.Q.		
	No. 6218 Bomb Disposal Flt.		
Matlask*	No. 453[R.A.A.F]Sqdn.	Spitfire XV1	390.
	No. 229 Sqdn.	Spitfire 1X	
Swanton Morley	No. 100[B.S.]Grp. Comms. Flt	Various.	551.
DIGBY	No. 1023 Servicing Wing H.Q.		178.
	No. 6212 Bomb Disposal Flt[44 Grp]		
	No. 6215 Bomb Disposal Flt[44 Grp]		
Wittering.	No. 1020 Servicing Wing H.Q.		632.
	Central Fighter Establishment.		
	No. 6208 Bomb Disposal Flt[44 Grp]		
Collyweston.*	Gunnery Research Unit.		137.
Acklington.	No. 2718 Regiment A.A. Sqdn.	Bofors.	6.
	No. 2738 Regiment A.A. Sqdn.	Bofors.	
	No. 2820 Regiment A.A. Sqdn.	Bofors.	
Catterick.			111.
Aston Down.	No. 3 Tactical Exercise Unit.	Hurricane.	22.
	No. 20 M.U.[41 Grp]	Aircraft Storage Unit.	
Chedworth*			120.
Charter Hall.	No. 54 O.T.U.	Beaufort/Beaufighter.	117.
Winfield*			625.
Cranfield.	No. 51 O.T.U.	Beaufighter/Mosquito Havoc.	149.
Twinwood Farm*	No. 371 Repair & Salvage Unit		586.
	A.I. Conversion Flt.		
Eshott.	No. 57 O.T.U.	Spitfire.	214.
Boulmer*			
Harwell.	No. 13 O.T.U.	Various.	276.
	No. 5135 Bomb Disposal Sqdn[44 Grp]		
	No. 6226 Bomb Disposal Flt.[44 Grp]		
Bicester*			47.
Finmere*			229.
Hampstead Norris*			
Kingston Bagpuize*	No. 2747 Regiment A.A. Sqdn.	Bofors.	329.
	No. 2786 Regiment A.A. Sqdn.	Bofors.	
	No. 2796 Regiment A.A. Sqdn.	Bofors.	
	No. 2753 Regiment A.A. Sqdn.	Bofors.	
	No. 2883 Regiment A.A. Sqdn.	Bofors.	
	No. 2889 Regiment A.A. Sqdn.	Bofors.	
Harwarden.	No. 41 O.T.U.	Mustang/Harvard.	280.
	No. 48 M.U[41 Grp]	Aircraft Storage Unit.	
Poulton*	No. 1515 BAT Flt[21 Grp]		466.
High Ercall.	No. 60 O.T.U.	Mosquito.	292.
	No. 222 M.U[53 Wing]	Packing Depot.	
	No. 29 M.U[41 Grp]	Aircraft Storage Unit.	
Kirton-in-Lindsey.	No. 53 O.T.U.	Spitfire.	337.
	No. 2733 Regiment A.A. Sqdn.	Bofors.	
	No. 2774 Regiment A.A. Sqdn	Bofors	
	No. 2886 Regiment A.A. Sqdn	Bofors	
Hibaldstow*			291.
Llanbedr.	No. 12 Armament Practice Camp.		
	No. 13 Armament Practice Camp.		
	No. 2778 Regiment A.A. Sqdn.	Bofors.	
	No. 2793 Regiment A.A. Sqdn.	Bofors.	
Milfield.			405.
Brunton*			86.
Ouston.	No. 62 O.T.U.	Anson.	446.
Rednal.	No. 61 O.T.U.	Spitfire.	474.
Montford Bridge*			410.

NO 13 FIGHTER GROUP. INVERNESS

Castletown.			109.
Skeabrae	No. 611 Sqdn.	Spitfire V11	504.
	No 1029 Servicing Wing H.Q.		
Inverness.	No. 13 Grp. Comms.Flt.	Various.	316.
	No. 79 M.U[56 Wing]	Equipment Park.	
	42 Group Depot.	Aviation Fuel & Oil.	
	No. 56 M.U[43 Grp]	Repair & Salvage Unit.	
	No. 17 M.D.S[43 Grp]	Tender Type.	
	No. 23 M.D.S[43 Grp]	Tender Type.	
TURNHOUSE	No. 1012 Servicing Wing H.Q.		583.
	No. 289[A.A.C.]Sqdn.[70 Grp]	Oxford/Hurricane.	
	No. 290[A.A.C]Sqdn.[70 Grp]	T.T./Oxford/Hurricane.	
	No. 17 Grp. Comms. Flt.	Various.	
Macmerry*	No. 5130 Bomb Disposal Sqdn[44 Grp]		379.
	No. 6202 Bomb Disposal Flt.[44 Grp]		
Drem	No. 309[Polish]Sqdn.	Mustang 111	187.
	No. 1030 Servicing Wing H.Q.		
Peterhead	No. 315[Polish]Sqdn.	Mustang 111	460.
	No. 598[A.A.C]Sqdn.[70 Grp]	Oxford/T.T.	
	No. 1014 Servicing Wing H.Q.		
	No. 15 Armament Practice Camp		

NO. 38 [AIRBORNE FORCES]GROUP. MARKS HALL, EARLS COLNE, ESSEX.

Ashbourne.	No. 42 O.T.U.	Blenheim/Whitley/Anson	20.
Darley Moor*			164.
Earls Colne.	No. 38 Grp. Comms. Flt.	Oxford.	197.
	No. 296 Sqdn.	Halifax V	
	No. 297 Sqdn.	Halifax V	
	No. 7 Glider Servicing Echelon.	Horsa.	
	No. 8 Glider Servicing Echelon.	Horsa.	
Great. Dunmow.	No. 190 Sqdn.	Stirling 1V	258.
	No. 620 Sqdn.	Stirling 1V	
	No. 3 Glider Servicing Echelon.	Horsa.	
	No. 4 Glider Servicing Echelon.	Horsa.	
	Operational & Refresher Training Unit.	Albermarle/Horsa/T.Moth	
	No. 1526[B.A.T]Flt.	Oxford.	
Netheravon.	No. 1 Heavy Glider Servicing Unit.	Horsa/Hamilcar.	418.
	No. 12 Glider Servicing Echelon.	Horsa.	
	No. 13 Glider Servicing Echelon.	Horsa.	
	No. 38 Grp Parachute Maintenance & Servicing Unit.		
	No. 1 Mobile Parachute Servicing Unit.		
	No. 4 " " " "		
	No. 6 " " " "		
	No. 7 " " " "		
	Air Transport Tactical Development Unit[46 Grp]		
	R.A.F. School of Air Transport[46 Grp]		
Shrewton*			500.
Thruxton*			571.
Ringway.	No. 1 Parachute Traini ng School	Various.	478.
	No. 14 F.P.P.[41 Grp]	Various.	
Tatton Park*			561.
Rivenhall.	No. 295 Sqdn.	Stirling 1V	479.
	No. 570 Sqdn.	Stirling 1V	
	No. 1677 Target Towing Flt.	Martinet.	
	No. 5 Glider Servicing Echelon.	Horsa.	
	No. 6 Glider Servicing Echelon.	Horsa.	
Tarrant Rushton.	No. 298 Sqdn.	Halifax 111	559.
	No. 644 Sqdn.	Halifax 111A	
	No. 14 Glider Servicing Echelon.	Hamilcar.	
	No. 15 Glider Servicing Echelon.	Hamilcar.	
Tilstock.	No. 1665 H.C.U.	Stirling.	574.
	No. 81 O.T.U.	Whitley.	
Sleap*			508.
Wethersfield.	No. 196 Sqdn.	Stirling 1V	617.
	No. 299 Sqdn.	Stirling 1V	
	No. 1 Glider Servicing Echelon.	Horsa.	
	No. 2 Glider Servicing Echelon.	Horsa.	

NO 70 [TRAINING]GROUP. FARNBOROUGH.

Aberporth.	No. 595 Sqdn.	Martinet/Vengeance T.T./ Hurricane/Spitfire.	3.
Andover.	No. 43 O.T.U. H.Q.Maintenance Command H.Q., No. 53 Wing. No. 41 Grp.Misc. A/C Supply Centre.	Auster.	12.
Bodorgan.	No. 1606 Flt. No. 3506 Servicing Unit	Various.	60.
Castle Bromwich.	No. 577 Sqdn.	Hurricane/Oxford.	104.
Cleave.	No. 639 Sqdn.	Martinet/Vengeance T.T./ Hurricane.	132.
Ipswich.	No. 679 Sqdn	Martinet/Vengeance T.T./ Hurricane.	317.
Manorbier.	Pilotless Aircraft Unit.	Queen Bee.	383.
Old Sarum.	The R.A.F. School of Army Co-operation.		442.
Oaklands Hill*	Care & Maintenance Party.		438.
Towyn.	No. 631 Sqdn.	Martinet/Vengeance T.T./ Hurricane.	579.
	No. 4 R.A.F. Regiment A.A. Practice Camp[22 Grp]	Bofors.	
Weston Zoyland.	No. 286 Sqdn.	Oxford/Hurricane.	615.
	No. 587 Sqdn.	Martinet/Vengeance T.T./ Hurricane.	
	No. 2 Cylinder Block Servicing Unit.		
Merryfield*	Care & Maintenance Party.		397.
Upottery*	Care & maintenance Party.		588.

Note 1. Sector Stations are shown in capitals. Forward Airfields Are shown in small letters.

Note 2. Satellites are indicated thus *

COASTAL COMMAND-NORTHWOOD.

NO. 15 [G.R.]GROUP. LIVERPOOL.

Ballykelly.	No. 59 Sqdn. No. 120 Sqdn.	Liberator V Liberator V	31.
Benbecula.	No. 304[Polish]Sqdn. 42 Grp. Depot	Wellington X1/X11 Aviation Fuel & Oil.	43.
Limavady.	No. 612 Sqdn. No. 172 Sqdn.	Wellington X11/X1V Wellington X11/X1V	353.
Mullaghmore.	No. 36 Sqdn. Loran Training Unit.	Wellington X1V Wellington X111	416.
Port Ellen.	No. 67 Air/Sea Rescue Marine Craft Unit. No. 30 Embarkation Unit[home]		464.
Tiree.	No. 518 Sqdn. No. 281 Sqdn. 42 Grp. Depot. No. 31 Embarkation Unit[home]	Halifax V Warwick 11/Sea Otter. Aviation Fuel & Oil.	575.

NO 16 [G.R.]GROUP. GILLINGHAM

Beccles.	No. 280 Sqdn.	Warwick 1/Hurricane 11c	40.
	No. 618 Sqdn.	Mosquitio 1V	
Bircham Newton.	No. 119 Sqdn.	Albacore 1	51.
	No. 10 Instructors School[E.V.T.]		
	No. 157 G.R. Wing.		
Docking*	No. 1525 B.A.T. Flt.[23 Grp]		180.
Gosport.	Air Torpedo Development Unit.	Various.	250.
	No. 667 Sqdn.[70 Grp]	Various.	
	No. 2837 Regiment A.A. Sqdn.	Bofors.	
	No. 2954 Regiment A.A. Sqdn.	Bofors.	
Langham.	No. 521 Sqdn.	Hudson/Hurricane 11	342.
	No. 524 Sqdn.	Wellington X111	
	No. 2 Armament Practice Camp.		
	No. 2 Regiment A.A. Practice Camp[22 Grp]		
North Coates.	No. 254 Sqdn.	Beaufighter V1C	424.
	No. 236 Sqdn.	Beaufighter X	
	No. 22 Mobile Servicing Unit[Torpedo]		
Donna Nook.*	No. 2854 Regiment A.A. Sqdn.	Bofors.	183.
Thorney Island.	No. 2772 Regiment A.A. Sqdn.	Bofors.	569.

NO 17 TRAINING GROUP. EDINBURGH

Aldergrove.	No. 1674 H.C.U.	Liberator 111/V	9.
	No. 1402 Met. Flt[15 Grp]	Hurricane/Spitfire V1	
	No. 1 Armament Practice Camp.	Lysander/Martinet	
	No. 23 M.U.[41 Grp]	Aircraft Storage Unit.	
East Fortune.	No. 132 O.T.U.	Beaufighter/Beaufort/ Mosquito 11 & V1	198.
Haverfordwest.	Care & Maintenance Party.		279
Templeton*			563.
St. Angelo*	No. 12[Operational]Flying Instructors School.	Various.	524.
Connel*			141.
Silloth.	No. 6 O.T.U.	Wellington.	502.
	No. 22 M.U.[41 Grp]	Aircraft Storage Unit	
Great Orton.*			260.
Squires Gate.	No. 3 School of G.R.	Anson.	523.
	No. 1510 Flt.	Anson.	
Turnberry.	No. 5 O.T.U.	Warwick 1/Beaufighter V1c/Ventura/Hudson	582.
	No. 24 Mobile Servicing Unit[Torpedo]		

NO. 18 [G.R.]GROUP. PITREAVIE CASTLE,DUMFERMLINE.

Banff.	No. 143 Sqdn.	Mosquito V1	32.
	No. 235 Sqdn.	Mosquito V1	
	No. 248 Sqdn.	Mosquito V1/XV111	
	No. 23 Mobile Servicing Unit[Torpedo]		
Fraserburgh.*			240.
Dallachy.	No. 144 Sqdn.	Beaufighter X	162.
	No. 404[R.C.A.F.]Sqdn.	Beaufighter X1	
	No. 455[R.A.A.F]Sqdn.	Beaufighter X	
	No. 489[R.N.Z.A.F]Sqdn.	Beaufighter X	
	No. 21 Mobile Servicing Unit[Torpedo]		
Leuchars.	No. 18 Grp. Comms. Flt.	Various.	351.
	No. 206 Sqdn.	Liberator V/V1	
	No. 547 Sqdn.	Wellington X1/X111	
	No. 3 Armament Practice Camp.	Lysander.	
	No. 333[Norwegian]Sqdn.	Catalina/Mosquito.	
Milltown.	No. 224 Sqdn.	Liberator V	407.
	No. 502 Sqdn.	Halifax 11	
Stornoway.	No. 58 Sqdn.	Halifax 11	540.
	No. 66[15 Grp]Air Sea Rescue Marine Craft Unit		
	No. 42 Grp. Depot.	Aviation Fuel & Oil.	
	No. 36 Embarkation Unit[Home]		
Scatsta*			487.

Sumburgh.	No. 1693 Flt.	Anson.	548.
	No. 42 Grp. Depot.	Aviation Fuel &Oil.	
Tain.	No. 86 Sqdn.	Liberator V	556.
	No. 311[Czech]Sqdn.	Liberator V	
Thornaby.	No. 279 Sqdn.	Warwick 1	568.
	No. 42 Grp. Depot.	Aviation Fuel & Oil.	
	No. 6209 Domb Disposal Flt[44 Grp]		
Wick.	No. 519 Sqdn.	Hudson 111/Spitfire V 1	620.
	No. 4 Air Sea Rescue Marine Craft Unit.		
	No. 6 D.F. Station[26 Grp]		
Skitton*			507.

NO 19 [G.R.]GROUP. PLYMOUTH.

Chivenor.	No. 14 Sqdn.	Wellington X1V	127.
	No. 407 Sqdn.	Wellington X11/X1V	
Davidstow Moor.	No. 2708 Regiment A.A. Sqdn.	Bofors.	165.
	No. 2743 Regiment A.A. Sqdn.	Bofors.	
	No. 2802 Regiment A.A. Sqdn.	Bofors.	
	No. 2810 Regiment A.A. Sqdn.	Bofors.	
	No. 2821 Regiment A.A. Sqdn.	Bofors.	
	No. 2846 Regiment A.A. Sqdn.	Bofors.	
	No. 2852 Regiment A.A. Sqdn.	Bofors.	
	No. 2896 Regiment A.A. Sqdn.	Bofors.	
Roborough.*	No. 19 Grp. Comm. Flt.	Various.	480.
	No. 691 Sqdn[70 Grp]	Martinet/Vengeance T.T. /Hurricane.	
Angle.*			15.
St. Davids.	No. 517 Sqdn.	Halifax V	526.
Brawdy*			77.
St. Eval.	No. 179 Sqdn.	Warwick V	527.
	No. 282 Sqdn.	Warwick 1	
	L.R.C.R. D/F Station[26 grp]		
	No. 2782 Regiment A.A. Sqdn.	Bofors.	

NO. 106[P.R.] GROUP. FIFIELD HOUSE, BENSON.

Benson.	P.R.D.U.		44.
	No. 540 Sqdn.	Mosquito 1X/XV1	
	No. 541 Sqdn.	Spitfire X/X1/X1X	
	No. 542 Sqdn.	Spitfire X/X1/X1X	
	No. 544 Sqdn.	Mosquito 1X/XV1/ Spitfire X1	
	No. 309 Ferry Training & Aircraft Despatch Unit.	Master.	
Dyce.	No. 8 O.T.U.	Mosquito/Spitfire.	196.
	No. 1509[B.A.T]Flt.	Wellington/Spitfire.	
	L.R.C.R. D/F Station[26 Grp]		

Note 1. Satellite airfields are shown thus *

Note 2. From time to time various squadrons of the Fleet Air Arm are attached to Coastal Command for operations and are located at Coastal Command stations.

Note 3. Coastal Command has the following overseas formations:-
No. 247 Group. Angra, Terceira, Azores.
H.Q., R.A.F. Iceland.
H.Q. R.A.F. Gibraltar.

TRANSPORT COMMAND-HARROW.

NO. 44 GROUP. GLOUCESTER.

BRAMCOTE.	No. 105 [Transport]O.T.U.	Wellington.	74.
Nuneaton.	No. 1513 B.A.T.Flt.	Oxford.	433.
Bitteswell.	No. 5132 Bomb Disposal Sqdn.		55.
	No. 6211 Bomb Disposal Flt.		
CROSBY-on-EDEN.	No. 109[Transport]O.T.U.	Dakota.	154.
Longtown.			369.
DONCASTER.	No.1&18 Aviation Candidates Selection Boards[54 Grp]		181.
	Bomb Disposal School.		
DUNDONALD.	516 Sqdn.	Various.	190.
FILTON.	No. 2 Aircraft Preparation Unit.	Various.	227.
	Centaurus Test Flt.		
LLANDOW.	No.3 Aircraft Preparation Unit.	Various.	364.
	Transport Command Central Night Vision Training School.		
	No. 38 M.U.[41Grp]	Aircraft Storage Unit.	
	No. 93 Forward Staging Post[46Grp]		
	No. 94 Forward Staging Post[46Grp]		
MELTON MOWBRAY.	No. 12 Ferry Unit.	Various.	393.
NUTTS CORNER.	Units in European Wing,A.T.C.		435.
	No. 1332 Heavy Conversion Unit.	Liberator/Stirling/York.	
PERSHORE.	No. 1 Ferry Unit.	Various.	456.
	No. 15 Air Transportable Signals Unit.		
PRESTWICK.	Transatlantic Aircraft Control.		468.
	No. 1527 B.A.T.Flt.	Oxford.	
	No. 1680[Transport]Flt[116Wing]		
	No. 4 F.P.P.[41Grp]	Ferrying.	
ST. MAWGAN.	No. 2 Overseas Aircraft Despatch Unit.		529.
	Units in European Wing A.T.C.		
	Traffic Control School.		
TALBENNY.	No. 11 Ferry Unit.		557.
	No. 3 Overseas Aircraft Despatch Unit.		
	No. 4 Armament Practice Camp[19Grp]	Lysander.	
VALLEY.	Units in European Wing A.T.C.		592.
	No. 1528 B.A.T. Flt.	Oxford.	
WYMESWOLD	No. 108[Transport]O.T.U.	Dakota 111.	649.
	No. 1523 B.A.T. Flt[23Grp]	Oxford.	
Castle Donnington.			107.

NO.46 GROUP. HARROW WEALD.

BLAKEHILL FARM.	No. 233 Sqdn.	Dakota 111.	57.
	No. 437[R.C.A.F] Sqdn.	Dakota 111.	
	No. 123 Staging Post.		
	No. 11 & 16 Glider Servicing Echelons[38 Grp]	Horsa.	
BROADWELL.	No. 512 Sqdn.	Dakota 111.	83.
	No. 575 Sqdn.	Dakota 111.	
DOWN AMPNEY.	No. 48 Sqdn.	Dakota 111.	185.
	No. 271 Sqdn.	Dakota 111.	
	No. 120 Staging Post.		
	No. 122 Staging Post.		
LEICESTER EAST.	No. 107 O.T.U.	Dakota 111.	349.
PERRANPORTH.	Transport Command Staging Post.		455.

NO. 110 WING. CROYDON.

CROYDON.	No. 147 Sqdn.	Warwick/Dakota.	156.

NO. 116[TRANSPORT] WING. HENDON.

HENDON.	No. 24 Sqdn. RAF Intelligence School. RAF School of Discussion Method. No.107 Wing HQ[46 Grp] Book Production & Distribution Centre[26 Grp] No. 6224 Bomb Disposal Flt[44 Grp]	Dakota 111.	285.
HOLMSLEY SOUTH.	No. 167 Sqdn[110 Wing]	Warwick.	299.
KEMBLE.	Transport Aircraft Modification Section. No. 5 M.U[41 Grp] HQ Service Ferry Pool.	 Aircraft Storage Unit.	322.
LYNEHAM.	No. 246 Sqdn. No. 511 Sqdn. No. 525 Sqdn. No. 7 M.U. Site[57 Wing Southern] No. 33 M.U[41 Grp]	Liberator 11/111/V11. Liberator V11/York C1. Dakota 111/1V. Aircraft Storage Unit.	377.
STONEY CROSS.	No. 232 Sqdn. No. 242 Sqdn	Wellington XV1. Wellington XV1.	538.

MISCELLANEOUS AIRFIELDS.

HEATHROW.	Under construction.	283.

Note. Transport Command has the following overseas formations :-
No. 114 Wing. Accra, West Africa.
No. 216 Group. Heliopolis.
No. 229 Group. Delhi.

FLYING TRAINING COMMAND-READING.

NO 21 TRAINING GROUP. SPITTLEGATE.

CALVELEY. Wrexham. Cranage.	No. 11[Pilot]Advanced Flying Unit.	Oxford.	95. 647. 148.
ERROL. Tealing.	No. 9[Pilot]Advanced Flying Unit.	Harvard 11	213. 562.
HUCKNALL. Firbeck.	No. 25[Polish]Elementary Flying Training School.	Tiger Moth.	308. 231.
Papplewick Moor.	12 Grp Comms Flt. Aircrew Training Centre[Polish]	Various.	449.
MONTROSE. Stracathro. Kinnell.	No. 2 Flying Instructors School[A]	Various.	411 541. 331.
NEWTON. Orston. Tollerton.	No. 16[Polish]Service Flying Training School. No. 1524 B.A.T. Flt.	Harvard 11b. Oxford.	422. 443. 576.
PETERBOROUGH. Sibson. Sutton Bridge.	No. 7[Pilot]Advanced Flying Unit.	Hurricane/Spitfire Oxford.	459. 501. 549.
SHERBURN-in-ELMET.	Airborne Forces Experimental Establishment. No. 7 A.T.A. Ferry Pool[41 Grp]	Various.	496.
SPITTLEGATE. Harlaxton.	No. 12[Pilot]Advanced Flying Unit. No. 1536 B.A.T. Flt. No. 21Grp.Comms. Flt.	Blenheim/Oxford. Oxford. Various.	522. 273.
TERNHILL. Chetwynd. Condover.	No. 5[Pilots]Advanced Flying Unit. No. 25 Grp.Comms.Flt. No. 24 M.U.[43Grp]	Hurricane/Master. Various. Repair Depot.	565. 122. 139.
WHEATON ASTON. Perton. Tatenhill.	No. 21[Pilot]Advanced Flying Unit. No. 1511 B.A.T.Flt.	Oxford. Oxford.	618. 458. 560.

NO. 23 TRAINING GROUP. SOUTH CERNEY.

BABDOWN FARM.	No. 15[Pilot]Advanced Flying Unit.	Oxford/Anson.	26.
	No. 1532 B.A.T. Flt.	Oxford.	
Long Newnton.			368.
Castle Combe.			106.
BOSCOMBE DOWN.	A.&A.E.E.	Various.	65.
	Intensive Flying[Development]Flt.		
	Aircraft Gun Mounting Establishment.		
	Empire Test Pilots School.		
BRIZE NORTON.	No. 21 Heavy Glider Conversion Unit.	Whitley/Horsa.	82.
	FT Command Instructors School.	Various.	
	No. 6 M.U.[41Grp]	Aircraft Storage Unit.	
CHURCH LAWFORD.	No. 18[Pilot]Advanced Flying Unit.	Oxford.	131.
	N0. 5 Instructors School[EVT]		
	No. 1533 B.A.T. Flt.	Oxford.	
Snitterfield.			514.
Warwick.			598.
HULLAVINGTON.	Empire Central Flying School.	Various.	309.
	E.C.F.S. Handling Sqdn.		
	No. 10 M.U.[41Grp]	Aircraft Storage Unit.	
KEEVIL.	No. 22 Heavy Glider Conversion/ Refresher Training Unit.	Albermarle/Horsa/ Hadrian.	319.
Fairford.			218.
KIDLINGTON.	No. 20[Pilot]Advanced Flying Unit.	Oxford.	325.
	Polish Initial Training Wing.		
Croughton.			155.
Weston-on-the-Green.			616.
Kiddington.			324.
LITTLE RISSINGTON.	No. 6[Pilot]Advanced Flying Unit.	Oxford.	358.
	No. 8 M.U.[41 Grp]	Aircraft Storage Unit.	
	No. 1523 B.A.T. Flt.	Oxford.	
Chipping Norton.			124.
Windrush.			624.
Akeman Street.			7.
LULSGATE BOTTOM.	No. 3 Flying Instructor's School[A]	Oxford/Master.	373.
	No. 1540 B.A.T. Flt.	Oxford.	
PEPLOW.	No.23 Heavy Glider Conversion Unit/ Refresher Training Unit.	Albermarle/Horsa/ Hadrian.	454.
Seighford.			509.
SHOBDON.	No.5 Glider Training School.	Master/Hotspur.	498.
	Glider Instructor's Flt.		
SOUTH CERNEY.	No.3[Pilot]Advanced Flying Unit.	Anson.	515.
Charmy Down.			116.
Southrop.			518.
STOKE ORCHARD.	No.3 Glider Training School.	Master/Oxford/Hotspur.	537.
North leach.			431.
UPAVON.	No.7 Flying Instructor's School.	Oxford.	587.
	No.1537 B.A.T.Flt.	Oxford.	
Overton Heath.			447.

NO.25 ARMAMENT GROUP. MARKET DRAYTON.

BARROW.	No.10 Air Gunners School.	Anson/Martinet.	36.
CARK.	Staff Pilots Training Unit.	Various.	101.
CATFOSS.	Central Gunnery School.	Various.	110.
HALFPENNY GREEN.	No.3[Observer]Advanced Flying Unit.	Anson/Lysander/ Martinet.	269.
	No.1545 B.A.T.Flt.	Oxford.	
MANBY.	Empire Air Armament School.	Wellington/Martinet/ Hurricane.	382.
MILLOM.	No.2[Observer]Advanced Flying Unit.	Battle/Blenheim/Anson.	406.
MONA.	No.8[Observer]Advanced Flying Unit.	Anson.	409.
PEMBREY.	No.1 Air Gunner's School.	Anson/Wellington/ Spitfire/Martinet.	450.

PENRHOS.	No.9[Observer]Advanced Flying Unit.	Anson.	452.
Llandwrog.			365.
SHAWBURY.	Central Navigation School.	Various.	493.
	No.1534 B.A.T. Flt.	Oxford.	
	No.27 M.U.[41Grp]	Aircraft Storage Unit.	
Bratton.			75.
STAVERTON.	No.6[Observer]Advanced Flying Unit.	Anson.	535.
	No.44 Grp.Comms.Flt.	Various.	
Morton Valence.			413.

NO.29 TRAINING GROUP. DUMFRIES.

ANDREAS.	No.11 Air Gunners School.	Anson/Martinet.	13.
BISHOPS COURT.	No.7[Observer]Advanced Flying Unit.	Anson.	53.
	No.12 Air Gunner's School.	Anson/Martinet.	
BRACKLA.	Aircrew Allocation Centre.		72.
CASTLE KENNEDY.	No.3 Air Gunner's School.	Anson/Martinet.	108.
DALCROSS.	No.2 Air Gunner's School	Anson/Martinet.	160.
DUMFRIES.	No.10[Observer]Advanced Flying Unit.	Anson.	189.
	No.29 Grp.Comms.Flt.	Various.	
	No.18 M.U.[41 Grp]	Aircraft Storage Unit.	
	No.215 M.U.[53 Wing]	Packing Depot.	
	No.220 M.U.[40 Grp]	Barrack & Clothing Depot.	
JURBY.	Air Navigation & Bombing School.	Anson/Wellington.	318.
MORPETH.	No.4 Air Gunners' School.	Anson/Martinet.	414.
WEST FREUGH.	No.4[Observer]Advanced Flying Unit.	Anson.	607.
WIGTOWN.	No.1[Observer]Advanced Flying Unit.	Anson.	623.

NO 50 TRAINING GROUP. READING.

BOOKER.	No.21 E.F.T.S	Tiger Moth.	63.
Denham.			171.
CAMBRIDGE.	No.22 E.F.T.S.	Tiger Moth.	96.
Caxton Gibbet.			112.
CLYFFE PYPARD.	No.29 E.F.T.S.	Tiger Moth.	134.
Alton Barnes.			11.
FAIR OAKS.	No.18 E.F.T.S.	Tiger Moth.	220.
Winkfield.			627.
Smiths Lawn.			510.
Bray.			78.
PANSHANGAR.	No.1 E.F.T.S.	Tiger Moth.	448.
Hatfield.			277.
SHELLINGFORD.	No.3 E.F.TS.	Tiger Moth.	494.
SYWELL.	No.6 E.F.T.S.	Tiger Moth.	555.
Denton.			172.
THEALE.	No.26 E.F.T.S.	Tiger Moth.	566.
WATCHFIELD.	Airfield Controllers School.		599.
	School of Flying Control.		
	No.1 Beam Approach School.	Oxford.	
Kelmscott.			320.
Wanborough.			594.
WOODLEY.	No.10 Flying Instructors School[E]	Tiger Moth.	638.
Henley.			286.
WORCESTER.	No.2 E.F.T.S.	Tiger Moth.	642.

NO. 51 TRAINING GROUP. LEEDS.

BROUGH.	No.4 E.F.T.S.	Tiger Moth.	84.
Bellasize.			42.
CARLISLE.	No.15 E.F.T.S.	Tiger Moth.	102.
Burnfoot.			89.
Kirkpatrick.			335.
DERBY.	No.16 E.F.T.S.	Tiger Moth.	174.
Abbots Bromley.			1.
Battlestead Hill.			38.
DESFORD.	No.7 E.F.T.S.	Tiger Moth.	176.
Braunstone.			76.
ELMDON.	No.14 E.F.T.S.	Tiger Moth.	209.
Hockley Heath.			297.
PERTH.	No.11 E.F.T.S.	Tiger Moth.	457.
Whitefield.			619.
WOLVERHAMPTON.	No.28 E.F.T.S. Pupil Pilots' Pool.	Tiger Moth.	633.
Penkridge.			451.

NO. 54 GROUP. SUNNINGDALE.

EASTCHURCH.	Combined Re-selection Centre.	203.
STORMY DOWN.	No. 40 Initial Training Wing[Pilots]	539.

MISCELLANEOUS AIRFIELDS.

Southam.	Care & Maintenance.	516.

TECHNICAL TRAINING COMMAND-READING.

NO 24 TRAINING GROUP. HEREFORD.

COSFORD.	No. 2 School of Tech Training. No. 1 Instructor's School[EVT] No. 6 Instructor's School[EVT] R.A.F. Czechoslovak Depot. R.A.F. Officer's School[22 Grp] No. 15 Radio School[27 Grp] R.A.F. School of Physical Training. No. 9 M.U.[41 Grp]	 A/C Storage & Packing Unit.	143.
FARNBOROUGH.	No. 1 School of Photography.		223.
HALTON.	No.1 School of Tech Training. Princess Mary's Hospital. Bomber Command Comms. Flt. Air Training Corps Flt. School of Hygiene[28 Grp] Institute of Pathology & Tropical Medicine[28 Grp]	 Various. Various.	270.
Weston-super-Mare.	Air Torpedo Development Unit Det[16 Grp]	Various.	614.
ST.ATHAN	No.4 School of Tech Training. RAF Hospital. RCAF Flt.Engineer's Training Unit. No.14 Radio School[27 Grp] No. 19 M.U[41 Grp] No. 32 M.U[43 Grp] No. 4 R.E.U[43 Grp]	 Aircraft Storage Unit. Repair Depot. Repairable Equip. Depot.	525.

NO. 27 TRAINING GROUP. ROYAL AGRICULTURAL COLLEGE. CIRENCESTER.

CRANWELL	No. 1 Officer's Advanced Training School. No.17 Service Flying Training School[21 Grp] No. 8 Radio School. No. 1 Radio School.	150.
Caister.*		94.
Coleby Grange.*		135.
Wellingore.*	Supplies Depot.	605.
CAREW CHERITON.	No. 10 Radio School.	100.
MADLEY.	No. 4 Radio School.	380.
YATESBURY.	No. 9 Radio School.	651.

NO. 28 TRAINING GROUP. 17-19 QUEEN'S SQUARE, LONDON, WC2.

SNAILWELL.	Belgian Training School.		511.
Westley.*	Belgian Training School.		613.

MAINTENANCE COMMAND. ANDOVER.

NO. 41 MAINTENANCE GROUP. ANDOVER [OPERATIONALLY CONTROLLED BY M.A.P]

EDZELL.	No. 44 M.U.	A/C Storage Unit.	206.
KIRKBRIDE.	No. 12 M.U.	A/C storage Unit.	332.
WROUGHTON.	No. 15 M.U. RAF Hospital[28 Grp] No. 76 M.U[53 Wing]	A/C Storage Unit. Packing Depot.	648.

NO. 42 MAINTENANCE GROUP. BURGHFIELD COMMON, READING.

ASHFORD		Packed fuel storage unit.	21.
BRIDLEWAY GATE.	No. 245 M.U.	Packed fuel storage Unit.	81.
COTTAM.	No. 244 M.U.	Air Ammunition Park.	144.
KIRKNEWTON.	No. 243 M.U.	Air Ammunition Park.	334.

NO. 43 MAINTENANCE GROUP. OXFORD. [OPERATIONALLY CONTROLLED BY M.A.P]

HENLOW.	No. 13 M.U. No. 6 R.E.U. Nos. 4, 21 & 22 M.D.S School of Aeronautical Engineering [Officers] [24 Grp]	Repair Depot. Repairable Equipment Depot. Mobile Dental Surgeries [tender type]	287.
SEALAND.	No. 30 M.U. No. 5 R.E.U. No. 12 M.D.S. No. 24 E.F.T.S[51 Grp] No. 47 M.U[53 Wing] No. 6204 Bomb Disposal Flt[Det]	Repair Depot. Repairable Equipment Depot. Mobile Dental Surgery. Tiger Moth. Packing Depot.	490.
Little Sutton.			361.
WOOLSINGTON.	No. 83 M.U. Nos. 14 & 24 M.D.S.	Repair & Salvage Unit. Mobile Dental Surgeries. [tender type]	641.

NO. 53 WING. ANDOVER.

CARDIFF.	No. 52 M.U.	Packing Depot.	99.

NO. 56 WING[NORTHERN]. CARLISLE.

ANNAN.	Site of No. 14 M.U. Carlisle.	A/C Equipment Depot.	16.
GRANGEMOUTH.	Site of No. 14 M.U. Carlisle.	A/C Equipment Depot.	253.
HOOTON PARK.	Site of No. 35 M.U. Heywood.	A/C Equipment Depot.	303.
USWORTH.	Site of No. 14 M.U. Carlisle.	A/C Equipment Depot.	591.

NO. 57 WING[SOUTHERN]. MILTON.

BIBURY.	Site of No. 7 M.U. Quedgeley. No.1539 B.A.T.Flt[23 Grp]	A/C Equipment Depot. Oxford.	46.
OKEHAMPTON.	No. 73 M.U.	Equipment Park.	440.
RHOOSE.	Site of No. 214 M.U. Newport.	Barrack & Clothing Depot.	475.

MISCELLANEOUS AIRFIELDS.

BIRCOTES.		Storage Unit.	52.
SAWBRIDGEWORTH.		Storage Unit.	485.

APPENDIX 'B'. ORDER OF BATTLE OF U.S.A.A.F. UNITS 1/12/44.

U.S. STRATEGIC AIR FORCES EUROPE. BUSHY PARK, HERTS.

8th.U.S.A.A.F. DAWS HILL LODGE, HIGH WYCOMBE, BUCKS.

1st. BOMBARDMENT DIVISION. BRAMPTON GRANGE, HUNTINGTON.

1st BOMBARDMENT WING. BASSINGBOURN, CAMBS.

BASSINGBOURN.	91st. Bomb Group. 322-323-324 & 401 Sqdns.	B 17.	37.
RIDGEWELL.	381st. Bomb Group. 532-533-534 & 535 Sqdns.	B 17.	477.
NUTHAMPSTEAD.	398th. Bomb Group. 600-601-602 & 603 Sqdns.	B 17.	434.

40th. BOMBARDMENT WING. THURLEIGH, BEDS.

PODINGTON.	92nd. Bomb Group. 325-326-327 & 407 Sqdns.	B 17.	462.
CHELVESTON.	305th. Bomb Group. 364-365-366 & 422 Sqdns.	B 17.	121.
THURLEIGH.	306th. Bomb Group. 367-368-369 & 423 Sqdns.	B 17.	572.

41st BOMBARDMENT WING. MOLESWORTH, NORTHANTS.

MOLESWORTH.	303rd. Bomb Group. 358-359-360 & 427 Sqdns.	B 17.	408.
KIMBOLTON.	379th. Bomb Group. 524-525-526 & 527 Sqdns.	B 17.	326.
GRAFTON UNDERWOOD.	384th. Bomb Group. 544-545-546 & 547 Sqdns.	B 17.	252.

94th. BOMBARDMENT WING. POLEBROOK, NORTHANTS.

POLEBROOK.	351st. Bomb Group. 408-409-410 & 411 Sqdns.	B 17.	463.
DEENETHORPE.	401st. Bomb Group. 612-613-614 & 615 Sqdn.	B 17.	169.
GLATTON.	457th. Bomb Group. 748-749-750 & 751 Sqdns.	B 17.	248.

67th. FIGHTER WING. WALCOTT HALL, SHROPSHIRE.

KINGS CLIFFE.	20th. Fighter Group. 55-77 & 79 Sqdns.	P 51.	327.
BODNEY.	352nd. Fighter Group. 328-486 & 487 Sqdns.	P 51.	59.
EAST WRETHAM.	359th. Fighter Group. 368-369 & 370 Sqdns. 3rd. Gunnery & Tow Target Flt.	P 51. A-35B.	202.
LITTLE WALDEN.	361st. Fighter Group. 374-375 & 376 Sqdns. 1st. Gunnery & Tow Target Flt.	P 51. A-35B.	362.
HONINGTON.	364th. Fighter Group. 383-384 & 385 Sqdn.	P 51.	302.
ATCHAM.	495th. Fighter Training Group. 551 & 552 Sqdns.	P 47.	23.

2nd BOMBARDMENT DIVISION. KETTERINGHAM HALL. NORFOLK.

2nd. BOMBARDMENT WING. HETHEL. NORFOLK.

HETHEL.	389th Bomb Group. 564-565-566 & 567 Sqdns.	B 24.	290.
TIBENHAM.	445th.Bomb Group. 700-701-702 & 703 Sqdns.	B 24.	573.
OLD BUCKENHAM.	453rd. Bomb Group. 732-733-734 & 735 Sqdns.	B 24.	441.

14th. BOMBARDMENT WING. BURY ST. EDMUNDS. SUFFOLK.

SHIPDHAM.	44th. Bomb Group. 66-67-68 & 506 Sqdns.	B 24.	497.
WENDLING.	392nd. Bomb Group. 576-577-578 & 579 Sqdns.	B 24.	606.
HARRINGTON.	492nd. Bomb Group. 856-857-858 & 859 Sqdns	B 24.	274.

20th. BOMBARDMENT WING. HARDWICK. NORFOLK.

HARDWICK.	93rd. Bomb Group. 328-329-330 & 409 Sqdns.	B 24.	272.
BUNGAY.	446th. Bomb Group. 704-705-706 & 707 Sqdns.	B 24.	87.
SEETHING.	448th. Bomb Group. 712-713-714 & 715 Sqdns.	B 24.	491.

95th. BOMBARDMENT WING. KETTERINGHAM HALL. NORFOLK.

NORTH PICKENHAM.	491st. Bomb Group. 852-853-854 & 855 Sqdns.	B 24.	428.
HALESWORTH.	De-activated.		268.

96th. BOMBARDMENT WING. HORSHAM ST. FAITH. SUFFOLK.

HORSHAM ST. FAITH.	458th. Bomb Group. 752-753-754 & 755 Sqdns.	B 24.	307.
ATTLEBRIDGE.	466th. Bomb Group. 784-785-786 & 787 Sqdns.	B 24.	24.
RACKHEATH.	467th. Bomb Grp. 788-789-790 & 791 Sqdns.	B 24.	469.

65th. FIGHTER WING. SAFFRON WALDEN. ESSEX.

DEBDEN.	4th. Fighter Group. 334-335 & 336 Sqdns.	P 51.	168.
BOXTED.	56th. Fighter Group. 61-62 & 63 Sqdns. 5th. Emergency Rescue Sqdn.	P 47. P 47.	71.
STEEPLE MORDEN.	355th. Fighter Group. 354-357 & 358 Sqdns.	P 51.	536.
MARTLESHAM HEATH.	356th. Fighter Grp. 359-360 & 361 Sqdns. No. 278[ASR]Sqdn. R.A.F.	P 51. Spitfire/Walrus/ Sea Otter.	388.
WATTISHAM.	479th. Fighter Group. 434-435 & 436 Sqdns.	P 51.	601.
GOXHILL.	496th. Fighter Training Group. 554 & 555 Sqdns.	P 51.	251.

3rd BOMBARDMENT DIVISION. ELVEDON HALL, SUFFOLK.

4th. BOMBARDMENT WING. BURY ST. EDMUNDS, SUFFOLK.

BURY ST EDMUNDS.	94th. Bomb Group. 331-332-333 & 410 Sqdns.	B 17.	92.
GREAT ASHFIELD.	385th.Bomb Group. 548-549-550 & 551 Sqdns.	B 17.	257.
RATTLESDEN.	447th.Bomb Group. 708-709-710 & 711 Sqdns.	B 17.	471.

13th. BOMBARDMENT WING. HORHAM, SUFFOLK.

HORHAM.	95th.Bomb Group. 334-335-336 & 412 Sqdns.	B 17.	304.
THORPE ABBOTS.	100th. Bomb Group. 349-350-351 & 418 Sqdns.	B 17.	570.
FRAMLINGHAM.	390th. Bomb Group. 568-569-570 & 571 Sqdns.	B 17.	239.

45th. BOMBARDMENT WING. SNETTERTON HEATH, NORFOLK.

SNETTERTON HEATH.	96th. Bomb Group. 337-338-339 & 413 Sqdns. 1st. Combat Crew Gunnery School.	B 17.	513.
KNETTISHALL.	388th. Bomb Group. 560-561-562 & 563 Sqdns.	B 17.	338.
DEOPHAM GREEN.	452nd. Bomb Group. 728-729-730 & 731 Sqdns.	B 17.	173.

92nd. BOMBARDMENT WING. BURY ST. EDMUNDS, SUFFOLK.

SUDBURY.	486th. Bomb Group. 832-833-834 & 835 Sqdns.	B 17.	547.
LAVENHAM.	487th.Bomb Group. 836-837-838 & 839 Sqdns.	B 17.	345.

93rd. BOMBARDMENT WING. MENDLESHAM, SUFFOLK.

MENDLESHAM.	34th. Bomb Group. 4-7-18 & 391 Sqdns.	B 17.	395.
EYE.	490th Bomb Group. 848-849-850 & 851 Sqdns.	B 17.	217.
DEBACH.	493rd. Bomb Group. 860-861-862 & 863 Sqdns.	B 17.	167.

66th. FIGHTER WING. SAWSTON, CAMBS.

WORMINGFORD.	55th. Fighter Group. 38-338 & 343 Sqdns.	P 51.	644.
DUXFORD.	78th. Fighter Group. 82-84 & 84 Sqdns.	P 47.	195.
FOWLMERE.	339th. Fighter Group. 503-504 & 505 Sqdns.	P 51.	238.
RAYDON.	353rd. Fighter Group. 350-351 & 352 Sqdns.	P 51.	472.
LEISTON.	357th. Fighter Group. 362-363 & 367 Sqdns. 2nd. Gunnery & Tow Target Flt.	P 51. A-35B.	350.

325th PHOTOGRAPHIC WING[R] WATTON, NORFOLK.

WATTON.	25th Bomb Group[R] 652-653 & 654 Sqdns.	B 17.	602.
MOUNT FARM.	7th. Photographic Group. 13-14- 22 & 27 Sqdns.	Spitfire 1X.	415.

MISCELLANEOUS AIRFIELDS.

ALCONBURY.	482nd Bomb Grp[Pathfinder] 812-813 & 814 Sqdns.	B 17 & B 24.	8.
CHEDDINGTON.	36th. Bomb Sqdn[RCM] 406th. Bomb Sqdn[Night leaflet Sqdn]	B 24. B 24.	119.
FERSFIELD.	Aphrodite & Batty projects. [Radio & TV controlled bombs]	B 17 & B 24.	226.
BIRCH.	Reserve Airfield.		50.

9th U.S.A.A.F. SUNNINGHILL PARK, BERKS

1X TROOP CARRIER COMMAND.ASCOT, BERKS.

52nd. TROOP CARRIER WING. COTTESMORE, RUTLAND.

BARKSTON HEATH.	61st. Troop Carrier Grp. 14-15-53 & 59th. Sqdns.	C 47 & C 53.	35.
FOLKINGHAM.	313rd. Troop Carrier Grp. 29-47-48 & 49th. Sqdns.	C 47 & C 53.	233.
SALTBY.	314th. Troop Carrier Grp. 32-50-61&62nd. Sqdns.	C 47 & C 53.	483.
SPANHOE.	315th. Troop Carrier Grp. 34-43-309 & 310th. Sqdns.	C 47 & C 53.	519.
COTTESMORE.	316th. Troop Carrier Grp. 36-37-44-45-75 & 77th Sqdns.	C 47 & C 53.	145.

53rd. TROOP CARRIER WING. GREENHAM COMMON, BERKS.

ALDERMASTON.	434th. Troop Carrier Grp. 71-72-73 & 74 Sqdns.	C 47.	10.
WELFORD.	435th. Troop carrier Grp. 74-76-77 & 78th. Sqdns.	C 46 & C 47.	603.
MEMBURY.	436th. Troop Carrier Grp. 79 -80-81 & 82nd. Sqdns.	C 47.	394.
RAMSBURY.	437th. Troop Carrier Grp. 83-84-85- & 86th. Sqdns.	C 46 & C 47.	470.
GREENHAM COMMON.	438th. Troop Carrier Grp. 87-88-89 & 90th. Sqdns.	C 47.	263.
CHALGROVE.	De-activated.		114.

AIR SERVICE COMMAND. BUSHY PARK, HERTS.

BURTONWOOD.	No. 1 Base Air Depot.		91.
LANGFORD LODGE.	No. 3 Base Air Depot. No. 311-312 & 321 Air Transport Sqdns.	C 47.	341.
GREENCASTLE.	Air Depot.		262.
WARTON.	No. 2 Base Air Depot. No. 310 Air Transport Sqdn.	C 47.	597.
STANSTE A D.	Air Depot.		
GROVE.	3rd. Tactical Air Depot. 302nd.Air Transport Wing. 31st. Air Transport Grp.	C 47.	266.
NORTH WITHAM.	1st. Tactical Air Depot.		430.

AIR DISARMAMENT COMMAND.

BOREHAM.	64.
CHIPPING ONGAR.	125.

AIR TRANSPORT COMMAND. EUROPEAN DIVISION.

BOVINGDON.	70.
METFIELD.	399.

U.S. NAVY.

FLEET AIR WING 7. PLYMOUTH, DEVON.

DUNKESWELL.	VP 103-105 & 107.	PB4Y-1.	193.

APPENDIX 'C'. ROYAL NAVAL AIR STATIONS IN THE U.K.

HEADQUARTERS, FLAG OFFICER, NAVAL AIR SERVICE. LEE-ON-SOLENT, HANTS.

ABBOTSINCH.	Reserve A/C Storage & Maintenance Yard.	HMS Sanderling.	2.
ANTHORN.	No. 1 A/C Receipt & Despatch Unit.	HMS Nuthatch.	17.
ARBROATH.	Observers, Deck Landing & Air Signals Schools.	HMS Condor.	19.
AYR.	Disembarked Sqdns.	HMS Wagtail.	25.
BELFAST.	Disembarked Sqdns.	HMS Gadwall.	41.
BURSCOUGH.	Disembarked Sqdns.	HMS Ringtail.	90.
BUSH BARN.	Care & Maintenance.	Books of Kestrel.	93.
CAMPBELTOWN.	Disembarked Sqdns.	Books of Landrail.	98.
CHARLTON HORETHORNE.	Fighter Direction School.	Books of Heron.	115.
COWDRAY PARK.	Care & Maintenance.	Books of Daedalus.	146.
CRAIL.	Training of Torpedo Sqdns.	HMS Jackdaw.	147.
CRIMOND.	Training of Torpedo Sqdns.	HMS Merganser.	152.
CULDROSE.	-	Not Commissioned.	157.
CULHAM.	No.2 A/C Receipt & Despatch Unit.	HMS Hornbill.	158.
DALE.	Twin A/C Conversion Unit.	HMS Goldcrest.	161.
DONIBRISTLE.	A/C Repair Yard & Comms Sqdns.	HMS Merlin.	182.
DOUNREAY.	-	Not Commissioned.	184.
DUNINO.	Reserve A/C Storage.	Books of Jackdaw.	192.
EAST HAVEN.	Deck Landing Training School.	HMS Peewit.	199.
EASTLEIGH.	Safety Equipment & Air Medicine Schools.	HMS Raven.	204.
EGLINTON.	Working up of 1st. & 2nd. Line Sqdns.	HMS Gannet.	207.
EVANTON.	A/C Maintenance Yard.	HMS Fieldfare.	215.
FEARN.	Working up of 1st. Line Sqdns.	HMS Owl.	224.
GRIMSETTER.	Disembarked Sqdns	HMS Robin.	265.
HALDON.	Glider Training for ATC.	Books of Heron.	267.
HATSTON.	Disembarked Sqdns.	HMS Sparrowhawk.	278.
HENSTRIDGE.	No. 2 Air Fighter School.	HMS Dipper.	288.
HINSTOCK.	Naval Advanced Instrument Flying School.	HMS Godwit.	294.
INSKIP.	Operational Training Unit.	HMS Nightjar.	315.
LEE-on-SOLENT.	General Training Facilities.	Books of Daedalus.	347.
LUDHAM.	H.Q. Mobile Naval Airfield Organisation.	HMS Flycatcher.	372.
MACHRIHANISH.	Disembarked Sqdns.	HMS Landrail.	378.
MAYDOWN.	Anti U Boat School.	HMS Shrike.	391.
RONALDSWAY.	Training of Torpedo Sqdns.	HMS Urley.	481.
ST. MERRYN.	Naval Air Warfare School.	HMS Vulture.	530.
STRETTON.	A/C Maintenance Yard & Reserve A/C Storage.	HMS Blackcap.	544.
TRELIGGA.	Emergency Landing Ground.	Books of Vulture.	580.
TWATT.	Disembarked Sqdns.	HMS Tern.	585.
WORTHY DOWN.	A/C Maintenance & Air Gunners Schools.	HMS Kestrel.	645.
YEOVILTON.	No. 1 Naval Air Fighting School & A/C Direction Centre.	HMS Heron.	652.

APPENDIX 'D'. MISCELLANEOUS AIRFIELDS.

R.A.F. IN NORTHERN IRELAND. STORMONT,BELFAST.

BALLYHALBERT.	N.I. Training School.		30.
CLUNTOE.	Care & Maintenance.		133.
KIRKISTOWN.	Care & Maintenance.		333.
LONG KESH.	No. 22 Recruits Centre[22 Grp]		366.
MAGHABERRY.	Care & Maintenance.		381.
NEWTOWNARDS.	Care & Maintenance.		423.
TOOME.	Care & Maintenance.		577.

BALLOON COMMAND-STANMORE.

FAIRLOP.	No. 24 Balloon Centre.		219.
GREAT SAMPFORD.	No. 945 & 947 Balloon Sqdns.	Non-operational.	261.
SCORTON.	Storage.		488.
SOUTHEND.	Storage.		517.
ZEALS.	Storage.		654.

R.A.F.AIRFIELDS ON LOAN TO WAR DEPT.

Balado Bridge.	Fighter Command.	28.
Findo Gask.	Flying Training Command.	228.
Fordoun.	Flying Training Command.	235.
Forres.	Bomber Command.	236.
West Hartlepool.	Coastal Command.	608.

R.A.F. AIRFIELDS ON LOAN TO DIRECTOR GENERAL OF CIVIL AVIATION.

HURN.	Fighter Command.	311.

DIRECTOR GENERAL OF CIVIL AVIATION.

SPEKE.	Civil Airport. 15 Grp. Coms. Flt.	Various.	520.

APPENDIX 'E'. R.A.F. & R.N. SEAPLANE STATIONS.

ROYAL AIR FORCE FLYING BOAT BASES & EMERGENCY ALIGHTING AREAS.

ALNESS.	Scotland.	R.A.F. Flying Boat Station.
BOWMORE.	Scotland.	" " " "
CALSHOT.	Hampshire.	" Station.
CASTLE ARCHDALE.	Northern Ireland.	" Flying Boat Station.
FALMOUTH.	Cornwall.	Seaplane Harbour.
FELIXSTOWE.	Suffolk.	R.A.F. Station.
GREENOCK.	Scotland.	" "
HELENSBURGH.	Scotland.	" Flying Boat Base.
KILLADEAS.	Northern Ireland.	" " " Station.
LAARGS CHANNEL.	Scotland.	Advanced Base.
MOUNT BATT EN.	Devon.	R.A.F. Flying Boat Station.
OBAN.	Scotland.	" " " "
PEMBROKE DOCK.	Wales.	" Operational Station.
SULLOM VOE.	Shetlands.	" Flying Boat Station.
WOODHAVEN.	Scotland.	" Station.

ROYAL NAVAL AIR STATIONS.

DUNDEE.	Scotland.	Seaplane Base.
LAWRENNY FERRY.	Pembrokeshire.	" "
PORTLAND.	Dorsetshire.	" "
SANDBANKS.	"	" "

APPENDIX 'F'. GEOGRAPHICAL LOCATION OF AIRFIELDS BY COUNTIES.

COUNTY	AIRFIELD NAME	LOCALITY	LATITUDE	LONGITUDE	O.S.REF.	NO
Aberdeenshire.						
	CRIMOND.	6miles SE of Fraserburgh.	57 36 35N	01 53 20W.	NK 065580.	152.
	DYCE.	5miles NNW of Aberdeen.	57 12 15N.	02 12 15W.	NO 879126.	196.
	FRASERBURGH.	17.5miles NW of Peterhead.	57 40 08N.	01 56 00W.	NK 040645.	240.
	PETERHEAD.	3miles W of Peterhead.	57 30 53N.	01 52 15W.	NK 079473.	460.
Anglesey.						
	BODORGAN.	12miles SE of Holyhead.	53 11 07N.	04 25 30W	SH 375688.	060.
	MONA.	3miles W of Llangefni.	53 15 30N.	04 22 38W.	SH 415760.	409.
	VALLEY.	6miles SE of Holyhead.	53 15 00N.	04 32 15W.	SH 305758.	592.
Angus.						
	ARBROATH.	1.5miles NW of Arbroath.	56 34 55N.	02 37 10W.	NO 623433.	019.
	EAST HAVEN.	3miles SW of Arbroath.	56 31 45N.	02 39 55W.	NO 595375.	199.
	KINNELL.	5.5miles S of Brechin.	56 39 00N.	02 38 15W.	NO 610510.	331.
	MONTROSE.	1mile N of Montrose.	56 43 40N.	02 27 15W.	NO 725598.	411.
	STRACATHRO.	3.25miles NE of Brechin.	56 45 53N.	02 35 00W.	NO 644635.	541.
	TEALING.	4miles N of Dundee.	56 31 15N.	02 58 15W.	NO 405370.	562.
Antrim NI.						
	ALDERGROVE.	13miles NW of Belfast.	54 39 08N.	06 13 30W.	J 150800.	009.
	LANGFORD LODGE.	4miles W of Crumlin.	54 37 23N.	06 18 00W.	J 100760.	341.
	MAGHABERRY.	5miles W of Lisburn.	54 30 53N.	06 10 38W.	J 180645.	381.
	NUTTS CORNER.	2.5miles ENE of Crumlin.	54 37 45N.	06 09 00W.	J 190775.	435.
	TOOME.	1.5miles NW of Toomebridge.	54 45 12N.	06 29 30W.	H 970905.	577.
Argyllshire.						
	CAMPBELTOWN.	2miles W of Campbeltown.	55 25 10N.	05 40 05W.	NR 690210.	098.
	CONNEL.	5miles NE of Oban.	56 28 00N.	05 23 58W.	NM 905351.	141.
	MACHRIHANISH.	3.25miles WNW of Campbeltown.	55 26 30N.	05 41 55W.	NR 660233.	378.
	PORT ELLEN.	Isle of Islay.	55 40 58N.	06 15 03W.	NR 325515.	464.
	TIREE.	Isle of Tiree.	56 29 53N.	06 52 15W.	NM 003449.	575.
Ayrshire.						
	AYR.	4miles SSE of Troon.	55 28 55N.	04 35 45W.	NS 358425.	025.
	DUNDONALD.	4.5miles SW of Kilmarnock.	55 35 00N.	04 36 30W.	NS 370362.	190.
	PRESTWICK.	3miles NNE of Ayr.	55 30 30N.	04 35 30W.	NS 365268.	468.
	TURNBERRY.	7miles N of Girvan.	55 19 30N.	04 49 45W.	NS 208075.	582.
Banffshire.						
	BANFF.	4.5miles W of Banff.	57 40 00N.	02 38 00W.	NJ 619643.	032.
Bedfordshire.						
	CRANFIELD.	8miles SW of Bedford.	52 04 08W.	00 37 15W.	SP 946421.	149.
	GRANSDEN LODGE.	10miles W of Cambridge.	52 10 45N.	00 07 00W.	TL 290555.	254.
	HENLOW.	5.5miles N of Hitchin.	52 01 00N.	00 18 15W.	TL 165370.	287.
	PODINGTON.	6miles SE of Wellingborough.	52 13 53N.	00 36 10W.	SP 953603.	462.
	TEMPSFORD.	9miles ENE of Bedford.	52 09 30N.	00 15 45W.	TL 188525.	564.
	THURLEIGH.	6.5miles N of Bedford.	53 13 45N.	00 28 30W.	TL 044063.	572.
	TWINWOOD FARM.	4miles N of Bedford.	52 10 53N.	00 29 08W.	TL 035550.	586.
Berkshire.						
	ABINGDON.	NW of Abingdon.	51 41 30N.	01 19 00W.	SU 475992	004.
	ALDERMASTON.	10miles SW of Reading.	51 21 53N.	01 08 45W.	SU 598635.	010.
	BRAY.	3.75miles WNW of Windsor.	51 29 37N.	00 41 39W.	SP 905777.	078.
	BUSH BARN.	10miles SW of Oxford.	51 39 40N.	01 28 46W.	SU 360962.	093.
	GREENHAM COMMON.	2miles SE of Newbury.	51 22 38N.	01 17 15W.	SU 502646.	263.
	GROVE.	1.5miles NW of Wantage.	51 36 08N.	01 26 15W.	SU 389898.	266.
	HAMPSTEAD NORRIS.	11miles WNW of Reading.	51 46 53N.	00 43 30W.	SU 545773.	271.
	HARWELL.	6miles S of Abingdon.	51 34 30N.	01 18 30W.	SU 475865.	276.
	HENLEY.	6miles NNE of Reading.	51 31 45N.	00 51 15W.	SU 795824.	286.
	KINGSTON BAGPUIZE.	5miles W of Abingdon.	51 40 15N.	01 24 30W.	SU 410974.	329.
	MEMBURY.	3miles SE of Lambourn.	51 28 38N.	01 33 23W.	SU 308754.	394.
	SHELLINGFORD.	2.75miles SE of Farringdon.	51 38 15N.	01 31 30W.	SU 328925.	494.
	SMITHS LAWN.	Windsor Great Park.	51 24 53N.	00 36 15W.	SU 973698.	510.
	THEALE.	5miles W of Reading.	51 25 30N.	01 03 38W.	SU 654700.	566.
	WATCHFIELD.	7miles NE of Swindon.	51 37 08N.	01 39 00W.	SU 245912.	599.
	WELFORD.	7miles NW of Newbury.	51 28 03N.	01 24 00W.	SU 415745.	603.
	WINKFIELD.	4miles SW of Windsor.	51 26 45N.	00 41 45W.	SU 912726.	627.
	WOODLEY.	3miles E of Reading.	51 27 08N.	00 53 08W.	SU 780732.	638.
Berwickshire.						
	CHARTER HALL.	15miles WSW of Berwick on Tweed.	55 42 38N.	02 22 30W.	NT 765463.	117.
	WINFIELD.	6miles WSW of Berwick on Tweed.	55 45 00N.	02 10 00W.	NT 898505.	625.
Buckinghamshire.						
	BOOKER.	3miles SW of High Wycombe.	51 36 30N.	00 48 30W.	SU 828910.	063.
	CHEDDINGTON.	6.75miles ENE of Aylesbury.	51 50 00N.	00 40 45W.	SP 910160.	119.
	DENHAM.	2miles NW of Uxbridge.	51 35 15N.	00 30 45W.	TQ 030886.	171.
	FINMERE.	3.5miles W of Buckingham.	51 58 46N.	01 03 45W.	SP 642322.	229.
	HALTON.	4miles SE of Aylesbury.	51 46 53N.	00 43 30W.	SP 870112.	270.
	LITTLE HORWOOD.	2.5miles NE of Winslow.	51 57 38N.	00 52 00W.	SP 777298.	357.
	OAKLEY.	11.5miles WSW of Aylesbury.	51 47 00N.	01 04 30W.	SP 638103.	437.
	TURWESTON.	9.5miles E of Aylesbury.	52 02 15N.	01 06 00W.	SP 615383.	584.
	WESTCOTT.	7miles NW of Aylesbury.	51 50 45N.	00 58 15W.	SP 710170.	611.
	WING.	4miles W of Leighton Buzzard.	51 54 00N.	00 45 15W.	SU 912726.	626.
Caernarvonshire.						
	LLANDWROG.	4miles SE of Caernarvon.	53 06 15N.	04 20 00W.	SH 434590.	365.
	PENRHOS.	2.5miles SW of Pwllheli.	52 52 23N.	04 28 23W.	SO 975495.	452.
Caithness.						
	CASTLETOWN.	5.5miles E of Thurso.	58 35 00N.	03 20 30W.	ND 215669.	109.
	DOUNREAY.	1.5miles NE of Reay.	58 34 45N.	03 43 35W.	NC 993670.	184.
	SKITTON.	4miles NNW of Wick.	58 29 43N.	03 09 45W.	ND 327571.	507.
	WICK.	1mile N of Wick.	58 27 23N.	03 05 30W.	ND 363527.	620.
Cambridgeshire.						
	BASSINGBOURN.	3.5miles NNW of Royston.	52 05 53N.	00 03 00W.	TL 330462.	037.
	BOTTISHAM.	5.5miles E of Cambridge.	52 12 45N.	00 15 23E.	TL 540592.	067.
	BOURN.	7miles W of Cambridge.	52 12 45N.	00 02 15W.	TL 341595.	069.
	CAMBRIDGE.	2miles E of Cambridge.	52 12 30N.	00 10 45E.	TL 486584.	096.
	CAXTON GIBBET.	9miles W of Cambridge.	52 13 15N.	00 05 15W.	TL 754793.	112.
	DUXFORD.	8miles S of Cambridge.	52 05 27N.	00 08 00W.	TL 464558.	195.
	FOWLMERE.	3.5miles NE of Royston.	52 04 30N.	00 03 45E.	TL 415446.	238.
	MEPAL.	6miles W of Ely.	52 23 38N.	00 07 30E.	TL 445796.	396.
	OAKINGTON.	5miles NW of Cambridge.	52 16 08N.	00 04 00E.	TL 412654.	436.
	STEEPLE MORDEN.	3.5miles W of Royston.	52 03 34N.	00 06 00W.	TL 300420	536.
	WATERBEACH.	5miles N of Cambridge.	52 16 45N.	00 11 00E.	TL 486670.	600.
	WITCHFORD.	2miles SW of Ely.	52 22 45N.	00 14 00E.	TL 519785.	631.
	WRATTING COMMON.	3.75miles NNW of Haverhill.	52 07 38N.	00 24 00E.	TL 645500.	646.
Cardiganshire.						
	ABERPORTH.	5.5miles NE of Cardigan.	52 07 00N.	04 33 15W.	SN 250494.	003.

Carmarthenshire.						
	PEMBREY.	5miles W of Llanelly.	51 42 30N.	04 18 45W.	SN 401035.	450.
Cheshire.						
	CALVELEY.	5miles NW of Nantwich.	53 06 45N.	02 36 15W.	SJ 595575.	095.
	CRANAGE.	2.75miles NNE of Middlewich.	53 13 23N.	02 24 00W.	SJ 730697.	148.
	HOOTON PARK.	7miles SE of Birkenhead.	53 18 15N.	02 56 15W.	SJ 375792.	303.
	LITTLE SUTTON.	6miles NW of Chester.	53 16 42N.	02 56 57W.	SJ 358774.	361.
	RINGWAY.	3.5miles SE of Altrincham.	53 21 15N.	02 16 30W.	SJ 816843.	478.
	TATTON PARK.	1.5miles N of Knutsford.	53 19 38N.	02 22 30W.	SJ 750815.	561.
Cornwall.						
	CLEAVE.	4.5miles N of Bude.	50 53 08N.	04 33 00W.	SS 205128.	132.
	CULDROSE.	1mile SE of Helston.	50 04 50N.	05 14 50W.	SW 675258.	157.
	DAVIDSTOW MOOR.	11miles W of Launceston.	50 38 00N.	04 37 15W.	SX 150850.	165.
	PERRANPORTH.	7miles SSW of Newquay.	50 19 40N.	05 10 45W.	SW 740528.	455.
	PORTREATH.	3.5miles N of Redruth.	50 16 00N.	05 16 00W.	SW 672465.	465.
	PREDANNACK.	7.5miles S of Helston.	50 00 00N.	05 13 45W.	SW 468164.	467.
	ST.EVAL.	6miles NE of Newquay.	50 28 38N.	04 59 45W.	SW 875685.	527.
	ST.MARYS.	Scillies,.75miles E of Hugh Town.	49 54 45N.	06 17 28W.	SV 922104.	528.
	ST.MAWGAN.	3.5miles NE of Newquay.	50 26 25N.	05 00 30W.	SW 870646.	529.
	ST.MERRYN.	2.5miles SSW of Padstow.	50 30 20N.	04 58 35W.	SW 888715.	530.
	TRELIGGA.	1.5miles WNW of Delabole.	50 37 45N.	04 45 40W.	SX 047848.	580.
Cumberland.						
	ANTHORN.	11miles W of Carlisle.	54 54 35N.	03 16 30W.	NY 182581.	017.
	BURNFOOT.	7miles NNW of Carlisle.	54 59 15N.	02 59 00W.	NY 368665.	089.
	CARLISLE.	2miles N of Carlisle.	54 55 23N.	02 58 00W.	NY 390595.	102.
	CROSBY-on-EDEN.	6miles NE of Carlisle.	54 56 14N.	02 48 30W.	NY 482606.	154.
	GREAT ORTON.	1.25miles S of Kirkbampton.	54 52 30N.	03 04 30W.	NY 310538.	260.
	KIRKBRIDE.	12miles W of Carlisle.	54 52 45N.	03 12 15W.	NY 229548.	332.
	LONGTOWN.	8miles N of Carlisle.	55 00 15N.	02 55 30W.	NY 411681.	369.
	MILLOM.	2miles WSW of Millom.	54 12 00N.	03 19 00W.	SD 138790.	406.
	SILLOTH.	.75miles E of Silloth.	54 52 15N.	03 21 30W.	NY 124436.	502.
Denbighshire.						
	POULTON.	4.5miles S of Chester.	53 07 38N.	02 53 45W.	SJ 402595.	466.
	WREXHAM.	9miles SSW of Chester.	53 04 00N.	02 57 00W.	SJ 363526.	647.
Derbyshire.						
	ASHBOURNE.	9miles NW of Derby.	53 00 23N.	01 42 15W.	SK 198455.	020.
	CHURCH BROUGHTON.	9miles W of Derby.	52 53 08N.	01 41 45W.	SK 205325.	129.
	DARLEY MOOR.	3miles S of Ashbourne.	52 58 30N.	01 44 30W.	SK 175425.	164.
	DERBY.	5miles SW of Derby.	52 52 15N.	01 34 00W.	SK 290303.	174.
Devonshire.						
	BOLT HEAD.	4.5miles SSW of Kingsbridge.	50 30 00N.	03 48 00W.	SX 710373.	062.
	CHIVENOR.	4.5miles W of Barnstaple.	51 05 18N.	04 09 00W.	SS 492344.	127.
	DUNKESWELL.	5miles NNW of Honiton.	50 51 45N.	03 14 00W.	ST 132079.	193.
	EXETER.	4miles E Exeter.	50 44 00N.	03 24 45W.	SY 002938.	216.
	HALDON.	2miles NW of Teignmouth.	50 34 40N.	03 31 50W.	SX 884812.	267.
	HARROWBEER.	9miles NNE of Plymouth.	50 29 30N.	04 05 45W.	SX 513680.	275.
	OKEHAMPTON.	1mile N of Okehampton.	50 45 08N.	04 01 08W.	SX 575974.	440.
	ROBOROUGH.	4miles NNE of Plymouth.	50 26 00N.	04 07 00W.	SX 503605.	480.
	UPOTTERY.	6miles N of Honiton.	50 53 08N.	03 09 30W.	ST 184104.	588.
	WINKLEIGH.	9miles N of Okehampton.	50 52 00N.	03 57 30W.	SS 620095.	628.
Dorsetshire.						
	CHARLTON HORETHORNE.	1mile WNW of Charlton Horethorne.	51 01 05N.	02 30 30W.	ST 642244.	115.
	TARRANT RUSHTON.	4miles E of Blandford.	50 51 00N.	02 04 30W.	ST 946058.	559.
	WARMWELL.	4miles E of Dorchester.	50 41 40N.	02 20 30W.	SY 765885.	596.
Down NI.						
	BALLYHALBERT.	11miles SE of Newtownards.	54 29 45N.	05 28 00W.	J 635635.	030.
	BELFAST.	E side of Belfast Docks.	54 36 45N.	05 52 26W.	J 375765.	041.
	BISHOPS COURT.	4miles NNE of Ardglass.	54 18 27N.	05 34 30W.	J 580425.	053.
	GREENCASTLE.	2miles SW of Kinkeel.	54 02 15N.	06 02 08W.	J 285115.	262.
	KIRKISTOWN.	2.5miles S of Ballyhalbert.	54 27 03N.	05 27 53W.	J 645595.	333.
	LONG KESH.	2.5miles SW of Lisburn.	54 29 15N.	06 06 00W.	J 230615.	366.
	NEWTOWNARDS.	10miles E of Belfast.	54 35 00N.	05 41 30W.	J 495725.	423.
Dumfriesshire.						
	ANNAN.	2.75miles NE of Annan.	55 01 00N.	03 13 45W.	NY 218700.	016.
	DUMFRIES.	2miles NNE of Dumfries.	55 05 38N.	03 34 15W.	NX 998788.	189.
	KIRKPATRICK.	13miles NW of Carlisle.	55 01 15N.	03 10 15W.	NY 255702.	335.
Durham.						
	MIDDLETON-St-GEORGE.	5miles E of Darlington.	54 30 45N.	01 25 30W.	NZ 375131.	403.
	USWORTH.	3.75miles W of Sunderland.	54 55 15N.	01 28 00W.	NZ 340585.	591.
	WEST HARTLEPOOL.	5miles N of Middlesborough.	54 38 40N.	01 13 20W.	NZ 505285.	608.
East Lothian.						
	DREM.	4miles NNW Haddington.	56 01 07N.	02 48 00W.	NT 505810.	187.
	EAST FORTUNE.	4miles NNE of Haddington.	56 00 00N.	02 42 45W.	NT 555786.	198.
	MACMERRY.	14miles E of Edinburgh.	55 57 00N.	02 53 45W.	NT 445734.	379.
Essex	ANDREWS FIELD.	5miles W of Braintree.	51 63 45N.	00 27 30E.	TL 693250.	014.
	BIRCH.	5miles SW of Colchester.	51 50 30N.	00 47 00E.	TL 918915.	050.
	BOREHAM.	3.5miles NE of Chelmsford.	51 46 45N.	00 31 30E.	TL 743120.	064.
	BOXTED.	3miles N of Colchester.	51 56 58N.	00 56 00E.	TM 015305.	071.
	BRADWELL BAY.	6miles NNE of Southminster.	51 44 04N.	00 54 15E.	TM 005082.	073.
	CASTLE CAMPS.	6miles NE Saffron Walden.	52 03 00N.	00 23 00E.	TL 633420.	105.
	CHIPPING ONGAR.	2 miles NE of Chipping Ongar.	51 43 48N.	00 17 40E.	TL 582055.	125.
	DEBDEN.	2miles SSE of Saffron Walden.	51 59 15N.	00 16 45E.	TL 562351.	168.
	EARLS COLNE.	3miles SW of Halstead.	51 54 30N.	00 41 15E.	TL 848270.	197.
	FAIRLOP.	3miles NE of Ilford.	51 35 30N.	00 06 08E.	TQ 460905.	219.
	GOSFIELD.	2miles W of Halstead.	51 57 00N.	00 35 00E.	TL 778312.	249.
	GREAT DUNMOW.	6.5miles E of Bishops Stortford.	51 53 00N.	00 18 45E.	TL 592235.	258.
	GREAT SAMPFORD.	7miles SE of Saffron Walden.	51 59 23N.	00 21 15E.	TL 616350.	261.
	HORNCHURCH.	2miles SE of Romford.	51 32 15N.	00 12 45E.	TQ 530845.	305.
	LITTLE WALDEN.	3.5miles NNE of Saffron Walden.	52 04 00N.	00 16 15E.	TL 558435.	362.
	MATCHING.	5miles E of Harlow.	51 46 53N.	00 14 45E.	TL 550120.	389.
	NORTH WEALD.	2.5miles NE of Epping.	51 43 00N.	00 09 15E.	TL 488044.	429.
	RIDGEWELL.	7.5miles NNW of Halstead.	52 02 38N.	00 33 30E.	TL 756416.	477.
	RIVENHALL.	1.75miles N of Witham.	51 51 15N.	00 38 30E.	TL 820206.	479.
	SOUTHEND.	2.5miles N of Southend.	51 34 15N.	00 42 08E.	TQ 872895.	517.
	STANSTEAD.	3miles NE of Bishop Stortford.	51 52 53N.	00 13 45E.	TL 538228.	531.
	STAPLEFORD TAWNEY.	5miles N of Romford.	51 39 00N.	00 08 30E.	TL 493972.	534.
	WETHERSFIELD.	7miles NNW of Braintree.	51 58 23N.	00 30 38E.	TL 725335.	617.
	WORMINGFORD.	6miles NW of Colchester.	51 56 20N.	00 47 38E.	TL 918306.	644.
Fermanagh NI.						
	ST.ANGELO.	4miles S of Enniskillen.	54 24 00N.	07 39 07W.	H 230500.	524.

Fifeshire.						
	CRAIL.	7.5miles SE of St Andrews.	56 61 20N.	02 36 15W.	NO 625085.	147.
	DONIBRISTLE.	2.5miles NE of Queensferry.	56 02 25N.	03 21 00W.	NT 155834.	182.
	DUNINO.	4miles SE of St Andrews.	56 17 25N.	02 42 20W.	NO 565115.	192.
	LEUCHARS.	4miles NW of St Andrews.	56 22 23N.	02 52 15W.	NO 467205.	351.
Flintshire.						
	HAWARDEN.	4.5miles WSW of Chester.	53 10 45N.	02 58 45W.	SJ 345651.	280.
	SEALAND.	5miles NW of Chester.	53 13 30N.	03 00 15W.	SJ 331709.	490.
Forfarshire.						
	EDZELL.	6.5miles N of Brechin.	56 48 38N.	02 36 23W.	NO 632691.	206.
Glamorganshire.						
	CARDIFF.	West outskirts of Cardiff.	51 29 08N.	03 07 56W.	ST 215770.	099.
	FAIRWOOD COMMON.	5miles W of Swansea.	51 36 08N.	04 04 08W.	SS 568912.	221.
	LLANDOW.	14miles WSW of Cardiff.	51 26 00N.	03 29 45W.	SS 959716.	364.
	RHOOSE.	3miles W of Barry.	51 23 45N.	03 20 45W.	ST 064675.	475.
	ST. ATHAN.	3.5miles S of Cowbridge.	51 24 30N.	03 26 00W.	ST 005685.	525.
	STORMY DOWN.	5.75miles W of Bridgend.	51 30 08N.	03 40 00W.	SS 842794.	539.
Gloucestershire.						
	ASTON DOWN.	4.5miles S of Stroud.	51 42 30N.	02 07 45W.	SO 912010.	022.
	BABDOWN FARM.	14miles S of Gloucester.	51 38 34N.	02 13 27W.	ST 845936.	026.
	BIBURY.	6.5miles NE of Cirencester.	51 46 38N.	01 50 00W.	SP 115092.	046.
	CHEDWORTH.	8miles SE of Cheltenham.	51 48 53N.	01 56 23W.	SP 042131.	120.
	FAIRFORD.	9miles N of Swindon.	51 40 53N.	01 46 30W.	SU 154982.	218.
	FILTON.	4.75miles NW of Bristol.	51 31 11N.	02 34 40W.	ST 600804.	227.
	KEMBLE.	4.5miles SW of Cirencester.	51 40 00N.	02 03 15W.	ST 960965.	322.
	LITTLE RISSINGTON.	4.5miles NE of Burford.	51 52 00N.	01 41 45W.	SP 210188.	358.
	LONG MARSTON.	3.5miles SSW of Stratford on Avon.	52 08 08N.	01 45 15W.	TL 170490.	367.
	MORETON VALENCE.	6miles SSE of Gloucester.	51 47 23N.	02 17 38W.	SO 796100.	413.
	MORETON-in-MARSH.	14miles S of Stratford on Avon.	51 59 38N.	01 41 00W.	SP 218329.	412.
	NORTHLEACH.	12miles E of Cheltenham.	51 50 19N.	01 50 30W.	SP 103148.	431.
	SOUTH CERNEY.	4miles SE of Cirencester.	51 41 20N.	01 55 15W.	SU 056986.	515.
	SOUTHROP.	3miles NW of Lechlade.	51 43 38N.	01 44 15W.	TQ 872895.	518.
	STAVERTON.	4miles W of Cheltenham.	51 53 38N.	02 10 00W.	SO 887218.	535.
	STOKE ORCHARD.	3.5miles NNW of Gloucester.	51 56 45N.	02 06 15W.	SO 928275.	537.
	WINDRUSH.	4.5miles W of Burford.	51 48 08N.	01 43 53W.	SP 185115.	624.
Hampshire.						
	ANDOVER.	2.5miles W of Andover.	51 12 30N.	01 31 30W.	SU 329459.	012.
	BEAULIEU.	3.5miles NNE of Lymington.	50 48 15N.	01 30 15W.	SU 350008.	039.
	BISTERNE.	2miles S of Ringwood.	50 49 00N.	01 46 45W.	SU 148015.	054.
	BLACKBUSHE.	10miles SSE of Reading.	51 19 30N.	00 50 30W.	SU 806595.	056.
	CHILBOLTON.	4miles SE of Andover.	51 08 38N.	01 26 08W.	SU 393385.	123.
	CHRISTCHURCH.	1.5miles E of Christchurch.	50 44 03N.	01 44 53W.	SZ 186933.	128.
	EASTLEIGH.	NE outskirts of Southampton.	50 57 00N.	01 21 35W.	SU 452168.	204.
	FARNBOROUGH.	1.5miles NNE of Aldershot.	51 16 45N.	00 45 53W.	SU 856538.	223.
	GOSPORT.	4miles W of Portsmouth.	51 57 00N.	00 35 00E.	SU 586010.	250.
	HOLMSLEY SOUTH.	6miles NE of Christchurch.	50 47 15N.	01 42 00W.	SZ 215988.	299.
	HURN.	4miles NE of Christchurch.	50 47 00N.	01 50 18W.	SU 115980.	311.
	IBSLEY.	3miles N of Ringwood.	50 52 30N.	01 46 53W.	SU 153087.	314.
	LASHAM.	6miles SSE of Basingstoke.	51 11 00N.	01 01 45W.	SU 675435.	343.
	LEE-on-SOLENT.	4miles WNW of Portsmouth.	50 48 35N.	01 12 25W.	SU 562020.	347.
	LYMINGTON.	1mile E of Lymington.	50 45 40N.	01 30 15W.	SZ 343960.	375.
	MIDDLE WALLOP.	6miles SW of Andover.	51 08 45N.	01 34 07W.	SU 303385.	402.
	NEEDS OAR POINT.	5miles E of Lymington.	50 46 23N.	01 23 53W.	SZ 410975.	417.
	ODIHAM.	6.5miles ESE of Basingstoke.	51 14 00N.	00 56 45W.	SU 738492.	439.
	STONEY CROSS.	11miles W of Southampton.	50 54 45N.	01 39 08W.	SU 248121.	538.
	THORNEY ISLAND.	2miles S of Emsworth.	50 49 08N.	00 55 08W.	SU 762025.	569.
	THRUXTON.	5miles W of Andover.	51 12 30N.	01 36 00W.	SU 280457.	571.
	WINKTON.	3miles NNE of Christchurch.	50 46 30N.	01 45 45W.	SZ 165975.	629.
	WORTHY DOWN.	2.5miles N of Winchester.	51 06 45N.	01 19 10W.	SU 468353.	645.
Hebrides.						
	BENBECULA.	Isle of Benbecula.	57 29 00N.	07 21 30W.	NF 787562.	043.
	STORNOWAY.	2.5miles NE of Stornoway.	58 13 06N.	06 20 00W.	NB 459932.	540.
Herefordshire.						
	MADLEY.	6.5miles W of Hereford.	52 01 50N.	02 51 00W.	SO 418374.	380.
	SHOBDON.	6miles W of Leominster.	52 14 08N.	02 53 00W.	SO 390603.	498.
Hertfordshire.						
	BOVINGDON.	7miles W of Watford.	51 43 30N.	00 32 30W	TL 005045.	070.
	HATFIELD.	6miles SSW of Hertford.	51 45 53N.	00 14 45W.	TL 206090.	277.
	HUNSDON.	4miles ESE of Ware.	51 48 00N.	00 03 00E.	TL 426138.	310.
	NUTHAMPSTEAD.	5.5miles SE of Royston.	51 59 30N.	00 04 00E.	TL 420346.	434.
	PANSHANGAR.	3.5miles N of Hitchin.	51 48 04N.	00 09 45W.	TL 266128.	448.
	SAWBRIDGEWORTH.	3miles SW of Bishops Stortford.	51 50 08N.	00 07 15E.	TL 464178.	485.
Huntingdonshire.						
	ALCONBURY.	4miles NW of Huntingdon.	52 22 23N.	00 13 45W.	TL 205768.	008.
	GLATTON.	10miles N of Huntingdon.	52 27 53N.	00 15 00W.	TL 186868.	248.
	GRAVELEY.	5miles S of Huntingdon.	52 15 45N.	00 11 00W.	TL 290555.	255.
	KIMBOLTON.	8miles W of Huntingdon.	52 19 00N.	00 23 00W.	TL 102701.	326.
	LITTLE STAUGHTON.	8.5miles NNE of Bedford.	52 14 27N.	00 21 45W.	TL 116615.	360.
	MOLESWORTH.	10.5miles WNW of Huntingdon.	52 23 06N.	00 25 15W.	TL 078774.	408.
	UPWOOD.	1.75miles SW of Ramsey.	52 26 15N.	00 08 00W.	TL 269842.	590.
	WARBOYS.	5.75miles NE of Huntingdon.	52 23 38N.	00 05 45W.	TL 290795.	595.
	WYTON.	3.5miles NE of Huntingdon.	52 21 23N.	00 06 53W.	TL 288750.	650.
Inverness-shire.						
	DALCROSS.	6.75miles NE of Inverness.	57 32 32N.	04 03 08W.	NH 775521.	160.
	INVERNESS.	.75miles N of Inverness.	57 28 00N.	01 14 00W.	NH 670465.	316.
Isle of Man.						
	ANDREAS.	4miles NW of Ramsey.	54 22 15N.	04 25 15W.	SC 426000.	013.
	JURBY.	6miles WNW of Ramsey.	54 21 15N.	04 31 15W.	SC 361983.	318.
	RONALDSWAY.	7miles SW of Douglas.	54 05 10N.	04 37 50W.	SC 285685.	481.
Kent.						
	ASHFORD.	2.5miles SW of Ashford.	51 07 15N.	00 49 00E.	TM 972405.	021.
	BIGGIN HILL.	5.5miles SSE of Bromley.	51 19 30N.	00 02 00E.	TQ 415606.	048.
	BRENZETT.	3miles NW of New Romney.	51 01 00N.	00 52 30E.	TR 014281.	080.
	DETLING.	3.5miles NE of Maidstone.	51 18 20N.	00 36 00E.	TQ 812595.	177.
	EASTCHURCH.	4.5miles SE of Sheppey.	51 23 30N.	00 51 00E.	TQ 988698.	203.
	GRAVESEND.	2 miles SE of Gravesend.	51 25 00N.	00 23 47E.	TQ 675720.	256.
	HAWKINGE.	2miles N of Folkestone.	51 06 40N.	01 09 30E.	TR 211395.	281.
	HEADCORN.	8miles WSW of Ashford.	51 10 53N.	00 41 23E.	TQ 878460.	282.
	HIGH HALDON.	6.5miles WSW of Ashford.	51 07 19N.	00 42 15E.	TQ 893391.	293.
	KINGSNORTH.	2miles S of Ashford.	51 06 12N.	00 53 30E	TR 025381.	328.
	LASHENDEN.	9miles SE of Maidstone.	51 09 15N.	00 39 00E.	TQ 855429.	344.
	LYDD.	5.5miles NW of Dungeness.	50 58 17N.	00 51 53E.	TR 011033.	374.
	LYMPNE.	2.5miles W of Hythe.	51 04 38N.	01 01 00E.	TR 110355.	376.
	MANSTON.	2.75miles WNW of Ramsgate.	51 20 45N.	01 21 00E.	TR 332599.	384.
	NEW ROMNEY.	1.5miles N of New Romney.	51 00 15N.	00 56 15E.	TR 061269.	419.
	NEWCHURCH.	7miles SSE of Ashford.	51 02 45N.	00 55 15E.	TR 048314.	420.
	PENSHURST.	4miles SW of Tonbridge.	51 12 00N.	00 10 53E.	TQ 518468.	453.
	STAPLEHURST.	8miles SSE of Maidstone.	51 09 38N.	00 35 00E.	TQ 808433.	533.
	SWINGFIELD.	5miles NW of Dover.	51 09 45N.	01 12 15E.	TR 240449.	553.
	WEST MALLING.	5miles W of Maidstone.	51 16 15N.	00 24 23E.	TQ 680555.	609.
	WOODCHURCH.	5.5miles SW of Ashford.	51 05 30N.	00 46 45E.	TQ 948362.	636.

Kincardineshire.						
	FORDOUN.	9miles SW of Stonehaven.	56 53 08N.	02 24 15W.	NH 755774.	235.
Kinross-shire.						
	BALADO BRIDGE.	2miles W of Kinross.	56 12 53N.	03 27 30W.	NO 095035.	028.
Lancashire.						
	BARROW.	Walney Island.	54 07 45N.	03 16 00W.	SD 175712.	036.
	BURSCOUGH.	1mile NE of Ormskirk.	53 35 35N.	02 51 35W.	SD 425114.	090.
	BURTONWOOD.	3miles NW of Warrington.	53 24 34N.	02 39 15W.	SJ 568910.	091.
	CARK.	1.75miles S of Cartmel.	54 09 45N.	02 57 30W.	SD 374745.	101.
	INSKIP.	7.5miles E of Blackpool.	53 49 35N.	02 49 40W.	SD 451371.	315.
	SPEKE.	5miles SE of Liverpool.	53 20 38N.	02 52 45W.	SJ 414833.	520.
	SQUIRES GATE.	1mile SSE of Blackpool.	53 46 15N.	03 02 00W.	SD 317311.	523.
	STRETTON.	3miles SE of Warrington.	53 20 45N.	02 31 45W.	SJ 652825.	544.
	WARTON.	7.5miles W of Preston.	53 44 30N.	02 53 15W.	SD 413278.	597.
	WOODVALE.	12miles NNW of Liverpool.	53 34 53N.	03 03 15W.	SD 302098.	639.
Leicestershire.						
	BITTESWELL.	6.5miles N or Rugby.	52 27 30N.	01 14 30W.	SP 514846.	055.
	BOTTESFORD.	7miles NW of Grantham.	52 58 00N.	00 46 45W.	SK 819415.	066.
	BRAUNSTONE.	2.5miles W of Leicester.	52 38 00N.	01 12 15W.	SK 538048.	076.
	BRUNTINGTHORPE.	10miles S of Leicester.	52 29 30N.	01 07 15W.	SP 590885.	085.
	CASTLE DONNINGTON.	9miles SE of Derby.	52 49 45N.	01 19 30W	SK 454262.	107.
	DESFORD.	6.5miles WSW of Leicester.	52 36 45N.	01 17 30W.	SK 478020.	176.
	HUSBANDS BOSWORTH.	10miles NE of Rugby.	52 26 00N.	01 02 30W.	SP 653825.	312.
	LEICESTER EAST.	4miles SE of Leicester.	52 36 23N.	01 02 00W.	SK 656015.	349.
	MARKET HARBOROUGH.	2miles NW of Market Harborough.	52 29 30N.	00 57 00W.	SP 712887.	386.
	MELTON MOWBRAY.	2miles S of Melton Mowbray.	52 44 00N.	00 53 30W.	SK 750158.	393.
	NUNEATON.	4.5miles NNE of Nuneaton.	52 33 45N.	01 26 45W.	SP 375963.	433.
	SALTBY.	8miles NE of Melton Mowbray.	52 49 45N.	00 42 30W.	SK 868265.	483.
	SIBSON.	6miles WSW of Peterborough.	52 32 53N.	00 23 00W.	TL 095966.	501.
	WYMESWOLD.	3.75miles ENE of Loughborough.	52 47 38N.	01 07 45W.	SK 586224.	649.
Lincolnshire.						
	BARDNEY.	10miles E of Lincoln.	53 13 30N.	00 17 30W.	TF 140712.	033.
	BARKSTON HEATH.	5miles NNE of Grantham.	52 57 30N.	00 33 30W.	SK 970415.	035.
	BINBROOK.	9miles SW of Grimsby.	53 26 45N.	00 12 00W.	TF 189959.	049.
	BLYTON.	16miles NNW of Lincoln.	53 27 15N.	00 41 30W.	SK 868958.	058.
	CAISTER.	5.5miles SE of Brigg.	53 30 15N.	00 21 38W.	TA 086021.	094.
	CAMMERINGHAM.	8miles NNW of Lincoln.	52 20 30N.	00 33 15W.	SK 965838.	097.
	COLEBY GRANGE.	6miles S of Lincoln.	53 07 53N.	00 29 53W.	TF 005605.	135.
	CONINGSBY.	7.5miles SSW of Horncastle.	53 05 30N.	00 10 15W.	TF 225565.	140.
	CRANWELL.	4miles NW of Sleaford.	53 02 15N.	00 29 30W.	TF 025515.	150.
	DIGBY.	10miles SSE of Lincoln.	53 05 53N.	00 26 30W.	TF 042570.	178.
	DONNA NOOK.	12.5miles SE of Grimsby.	53 27 30N.	00 09 30E.	TF 430980.	183.
	DUNHOLME LODGE.	5miles NE of Lincoln.	53 17 30N.	00 30 15W.	SK 995784.	191.
	EAST KIRKBY.	4miles SW of Spilsby.	53 08 00N.	00 00 15E.	TF 342618.	200.
	ELSHAM WOLDS.	5miles NNE of Brigg.	53 36 30N.	00 25 15W.	TA 042135.	210.
	FALDINGWORTH.	5.25miles SW of Market Rasen.	53 21 15N.	00 26 30W.	TF 037849.	222.
	FISKERTON.	4.5miles E of Lincoln.	53 14 30N.	00 25 45W.	TF 045730.	232.
	FOLKINGHAM.	8miles ESE of Grantham.	52 51 30N.	00 26 30W.	TF 049301.	233.
	FULBECK.	6.5miles ESE of Newark on Trent.	53 03 00N.	00 39 30W.	SK 900510.	242.
	GOXHILL.	5miles E of Barrow on Humber.	53 40 38N.	00 18 53W.	TA 115218.	251.
	GRIMSBY.	9miles S of Grimsby.	53 30 15N.	00 04 23W.	TA 279025.	264.
	HARLAXTON.	2miles S of Grantham.	52 53 00N.	00 39 15W.	SX 902325.	273.
	HEMSWELL.	7miles E of Gainsborough.	53 24 08N.	00 34 53W.	SK 941908.	284.
	HIBALDSTOW.	3miles SW of Brigg.	53 29 45N.	00 31 00W.	SE 982010.	291.
	KELSTERN.	5miles NW of Lough.	53 24 38N.	00 06 00W.	TF 262922.	321.
	KIRMINGTON.	6miles NE of Brigg.	53 34 45N.	00 20 45W.	TA 095103.	336.
	KIRTON-in-LINDSEY.	16miles N of Lincoln.	53 27 45N.	00 34 30W.	SK 945972.	337.
	LUDFORD MAGNA.	6miles E of Market Rasen.	53 22 30N.	00 11 30W.	TF 201879.	371.
	MANBY.	4miles E of Louth.	52 21 30N.	00 05 15E.	TF 385866.	382.
	METHERINGHAM.	10miles SE of Lincoln.	53 08 00N.	00 20 45W.	TF 105610.	400.
	NORTH COATES.	5miles SE of Grimsby.	53 30 15N.	00 04 00E.	TA 372028.	424.
	NORTH KILLINGHOLME.	10miles NW of Grimsby.	53 38 15N.	00 17 15W.	TA 131169.	426.
	NORTH WITHAM.	8.5miles S of Grantham.	52 47 15N.	00 36 00W.	SK 946225.	430.
	SANDTOFT.	11.75miles NE of Doncaster.	52 49 45N.	00 42 30W.	SK 750075.	484.
	SCAMPTON.	5.5miles N of Lincoln.	53 18 15N.	00 33 00W.	SK 965798.	486.
	SKELLINGTHORPE.	3miles W of Lincoln.	53 12 45N.	00 36 00W.	SK 925688.	505.
	SPILSBY.	3miles E of Spilsby.	53 09 45N.	00 10 15E.	TF 450645.	521.
	SPITTLEGATE.	1.75miles E of Grantham.	52 54 00N.	00 36 00W.	SK 935342.	522.
	STRUBBY.	3.5miles N of Alford.	53 18 15N.	00 10 45E.	TF 450810.	545.
	STURGATE.	4miles ESE of Gainsborough.	53 22 45N.	00 40 45W.	SK 879878.	546.
	SUTTON BRIDGE.	7miles NNE of Wisbech.	52 45 30N.	00 12 00E.	TF 476194.	549.
	SWINDERBY.	9miles SW of Lincoln.	53 08 45N.	00 40 30W.	SK 873616.	552.
	WADDINGTON.	4miles S of Lincoln.	53 10 15N.	00 31 15W.	SK 982630.	593.
	WELLINGORE.	10.5miles S of Lincoln.	53 04 30N.	00 31 30W.	SK 988545.	605.
	WICKENBY.	9.5miles NE of Lincoln.	53 18 45N.	00 21 00W.	TF 088803.	621.
	WOODHALL SPA.	6miles SW of Horncastle.	53 08 00N.	00 11 30W.	TF 204610.	637.
Londonderry NI.						
	BALLYKELLY.	3miles W of Limavady.	55 03 45N.	07 00 31W.	C 630240.	031.
	EGLINTON.	7miles NE of Londonderry.	55 02 30N.	07 09 30W.	C 540220.	207.
	LIMAVADY.	2miles N of Limavady.	55 04 23N.	06 56 15W.	C 675255.	353.
	MAYDOWN.	3miles NE of Londonderry.	55 02 00N.	07 14 25W.	C 487208.	391.
	MULLAGHMORE.	4miles SW of Ballymorey.	55 01 53N.	06 35 38W.	C 900210.	416.
Merioneth.						
	LLANBEDR.	3miles SSW of Harlech	52 48 45N.	04 07 15W.	SH 569258.	363.
	TOWYN.	.5miles NWN of Towyn.	52 35 38N.	04 05 53W.	JO 580018.	579.
Middlesex.						
	HEATHROW.	3.25miles NE of Staines.	51 28 15N.	00 27 00W.	TQ 075755.	283.
	HENDON.	8miles NW of St.Pauls.	51 36 00N.	00 14 42W.	TQ 215905.	285.
	HESTON.	1.25miles SSW of Southall.	51 29 15N.	00 23 52W.	TQ 118781.	289.
	NORTHOLT.	3miles E of Uxbridge.	51 33 15N.	00 24 38W.	TQ 098850.	432.
Midlothian.						
	KIRKNEWTON.	9miles SW of Edinburgh.	55 52 27N.	03 24 00W.	NT 125655.	334.
	TURNHOUSE.	5miles W of Edinburgh.	55 56 57N.	03 20 53W.	NT 156734.	583.
Morayshire.						
	DALLACHY.	9miles E of Elgin.	57 39 23N.	03 04 00W.	NJ 365635.	162.
	ELGIN.	1.75miles SW of Elgin.	57 37 30N.	03 20 15W.	NJ 200600.	208.
	FORRES.	13miles WSW of Elgin.	57 35 53N.	03 38 30W.	NJ 019578.	236.
	KINLOSS.	9miles W of Elgin.	57 38 45N.	03 33 45N.	NJ 065536.	330.
	LOSSIEMOUTH.	4.5miles N of Elgin.	57 42 38N.	03 19 30W.	NJ 210695.	370.
	MILLTOWN.	4miles NE of Elgin.	57 40 38N.	03 13 38W.	NJ 265655.	407.
Nairnshire.						
	BRACKLA.	12miles NE Inverness.	57 32 30N	03 54 38W.	NH 858519.	072.

Norfolk.						
	ATTLEBRIDGE.	8miles NW of Norwich.	52 41 30N.	01 06 45E.	TG 105150.	024.
	BIRCHAM NEWTON.	8miles WNW of Fakenham.	52 52 23N.	00 39 15E.	TF 785345.	051.
	BODNEY.	4.5miles W of Watton.	52 33 38N.	00 42 45E.	TL 840995.	059.
	COLTISHALL.	8miles NNE of Norwich.	52 45 15N.	01 21 30E.	TG 262225.	138.
	DEOPHAM GREEN.	1.75miles N of Attleborough.	53 33 08N.	00 59 38W.	TM 030990.	173.
	DOCKING.	10miles NW of Fakenham.	52 55 15N.	00 39 45E.	TF 788393.	180.
	DOWNHAM MARKET.	10miles S of Kings Lynn.	52 36 30N.	00 24 30E.	TF 630042.	186.
	EAST WRETHAM.	6miles NE of Thetford.	52 28 08N.	00 48 15E.	TL 905895.	202.
	FELTWELL.	5miles NW of Brandon.	52 28 45N.	00 31 00E.	TL 712898.	225.
	FERSFIELD.	16miles SW of Norwich.	52 25 23N.	01 03 15E.	TM 080850.	226.
	FOULSHAM.	8.5miles NNE of Dereham.	52 48 00N.	01 00 30E.	TG 028269.	237.
	GREAT MASSINGHAM.	7.5miles WSW of Fakenham.	52 46 53N.	00 40 45E.	TF 805236.	259.
	HARDWICK.	5.5miles W of Bungay.	52 28 08N.	01 18 45E.	TM 248906.	272.
	HETHEL.	5miles SW of Norwich.	52 33 38N.	01 10 30E.	TG 155008.	290.
	HORSHAM-St-FAITH.	4miles N of Norwich.	52 40 23N.	01 17 00E.	TG 221137.	307.
	LANGHAM.	5.5miles NW of Holt.	52 56 23N.	00 58 00E.	TF 988420.	342.
	LITTLE SNORING.	3.5miles NE of Fakenham.	52 51 38N.	00 54 45E.	TF 963334.	359.
	LUDHAM.	11miles NE of Norwich.	52 43 15N.	01 32 50E.	TG 400195.	372.
	MARHAM.	10miles SE of Kings Lynn.	52 39 08N.	00 33 00E.	TF 725084.	385.
	MATLASK.	5.5miles SE of Holt.	52 51 38N.	01 11 30E.	TG 145340.	390.
	METHWOLD.	5miles NW of Brandon.	52 30 45N.	00 33 00E.	TL 730935.	401.
	NORTH CREAKE.	2miles NW of Little Walsingham.	52 54 38N.	00 49 15E.	TA 131169.	425.
	NORTH PICKENHAM.	2.5miles SE of Swaffham.	52 37 30N.	00 44 00E.	TF 849068.	428.
	OLD BUCKENHAM.	2miles SE of Attleborough.	52 30 00N.	01 03 45E.	TM 078936.	441.
	OULTON.	3miles W of Aylsham.	52 48 00N.	01 11 00E.	TG 145275.	445.
	RACKHEATH.	5miles NE of Norwich.	52 40 30N.	01 23 00E.	SU 270703.	469.
	SCULTHORPE.	4miles WNW of Fakenham.	52 50 45N.	00 45 45W.	TF 862313.	489.
	SEETHING.	9.5miles SE of Norwich.	52 30 30N.	01 24 45E.	TM 315955.	491.
	SHIPDHAM.	3.5miles S of East Dereham.	52 37 38N.	00 56 00E.	TF 982075.	497.
	SNETTERTON HEATH.	6miles SW of Attleborough.	52 28 00N.	00 57 15E.	TM 005895.	513.
	SWANNINGTON.	3miles SE of Reepham.	52 44 30N.	01 10 15E.	TG 140206.	550.
	SWANTON MORLEY.	3.5miles N of East Dereham.	52 43 38N.	00 58 00E.	TG 002187.	551.
	THORPE ABBOTS.	4.5miles E of Diss.	52 22 53N.	01 12 45E.	TM 188809.	570.
	TIBENHAM.	13.5miles SSW of Norwich.	52 27 23N.	01 09 15E.	TM 145888.	573.
	WATTON.	11.5miles NE of Thetford.	52 33 53N.	00 51 45E.	TF 940000.	602.
	WENDLING.	4miles WNW of East Dereham.	52 41 53N.	00 50 45E.	TF 924151.	606.
	WEST RAYNHAM.	5.5miles SW of Fakenham.	52 47 00N.	00 44 30E.	TF 850245.	610.
Northamptonshire.						
	CHELVESTON.	6.5miles S of Thrapston.	52 18 15N.	00 31 23W.	TL 006685.	121.
	COLLYWESTON.	3miles SSW of Stamford.	52 36 00N.	00 30 00W.	TF 015023.	137.
	CROUGHTON.	3miles SSW of Brackley.	51 59 15N.	01 11 00W.	SP 563225.	155.
	DEENTHORPE.	9miles NNE of Kettering.	52 30 15N.	00 35 15W.	SP 958902.	169.
	DENTON.	5miles SE of Northampton.	52 12 23N.	00 47 15W.	SP 835578.	172.
	DESBOROUGH.	6miles NNW of Kettering.	52 28 00N.	00 48 00W.	SP 817865.	175.
	GRAFTON UNDERWOOD.	3.75miles ENE of Kettering.	52 25 15N.	00 38 45W.	SP 923813.	252.
	HARRINGTON.	5miles W of Kettering.	52 23 30N.	00 51 30W.	SP 775778.	274.
	HINTON-in-the-HEDGES.	6miles ESE of Banbury.	52 01 38N.	01 12 30W.	SP 545371.	295.
	KINGSCLIFFE.	12miles W of Peterborough.	52 34 00N.	00 29 15W.	TL 028978.	327.
	PETERBOROUGH.	1.5miles NNW of Peterborough.	52 35 15N.	00 16 00W.	TF 174005.	459.
	POLEBROOK.	3.5miles ESE of Oundle.	52 27 57N.	00 23 30W.	TL 093863.	463.
	SILVERSTONE.	4miles S of Towcester.	52 04 15N.	01 00 45W.	SP 676418.	503.
	SPANHOE.	4.5miles E of Uppingham.	52 34 00N.	00 37 00W.	SP 935970.	519.
	SYWELL.	6miles NE of Northampton.	52 18 15N.	00 47 30W.	SP 823682.	555.
	WITTERING.	3miles SSE of Stamford.	52 36 45N.	00 27 30W.	TF 028025.	632.
Northumberland.						
	ACKLINGTON.	3miles SW of Amble.	55 18 00N.	01 38 30W.	NU 230010.	006.
	BOULMER.	3.75miles E of Alnwick.	55 24 45N.	01 35 45W.	NU 259133.	068.
	BRUNTON.	9miles N of Alnwick.	55 31 30N.	01 40 30W.	NU 205257.	086.
	ESHOTT.	7.75miles NNW of Ashington.	55 16 45N.	01 42 45W.	NZ 183984.	214.
	MILFIELD.	4miles NW of Wooler.	55 35 30N.	02 05 00W.	NU 945330.	405.
	MORPETH.	3miles SW of Morpeth.	55 07 45N.	01 43 45W.	NZ 169818.	414.
	OUSTON.	1mile S of Stamfordham.	55 01 15N.	01 52 15W.	NZ 082700.	446.
	WOOLSINGTON.	5.75miles NW of Newcastle.	55 02 00N.	01 42 00W.	NZ 195713.	641.
Nottinghamshire.						
	BALDERTON.	2.75miles SSE of Newark on Trent.	53 02 08N.	00 46 50W.	SK 816498.	029.
	BIRCOTES.	1mile W of Bawtry.	53 26 15N.	01 02 15W.	SK 642940.	052.
	GAMSTON.	3miles S of East Retford.	53 16 45N.	00 57 30W.	SK 693762.	245.
	HUCKNALL.	8miles NW of Nottingham.	53 01 00N.	01 13 00W.	SK 526470.	308.
	LANGAR.	9miles SE of Nottingham.	52 53 30N.	00 54 00W.	SK 740335.	340.
	NEWTON.	7miles E of Nottingham.	52 57 38N.	00 59 15W.	SK 680415.	422.
	ORSTON.	4.5miles E of Bingham.	52 57 30N.	00 50 15W.	SK 780413.	443.
	OSSINGTON.	8miles NNW of Newark-on-Trent.	53 10 30N.	00 53 00W.	SK 780413.	444.
	PAPPLEWICK MOOR.	6miles N of Nottingham.	53 02 45N.	01 10 15W.	SK 550510.	449.
	SYERSTON.	5.5miles SW of Newark on Trent.	53 01 15N.	00 54 45W.	SK 730480.	554.
	TOLLERTON.	3miles SE of Nottingham.	52 55 00N.	01 04 30W.	SK 620360.	576.
	WIGSLEY.	7.5miles W of Lincoln.	53 13 00N.	00 43 30W.	SK 855695.	622.
	WINTHORPE.	1.5miles NE of Newark on Trent.	53 05 45N.	00 46 15W.	SK 825565.	630.
	WORKSOP.	4.5miles W of East Retford.	53 19 45N.	01 03 30W.	SK 625815.	643.
Orkneys.						
	GRIMSETTER.	SE portion of mainland Orkney.	58 57 15N.	02 54 00W.	HY 481083.	265.
	HATSTON.	N coast of mainland Orkney.	58 59 30W.	02 58 40W.	NY 435123.	278.
	SKEABRAE.	12miles NW of Kirkwall.	59 03 53N.	03 16 00W.	HY 269207.	504.
	TWATT.	12miles ESE of Kirkwall.	59 05 15N.	03 17 10W.	HY 265230.	585.
Oxfordshire.						
	AKEMAN STREET.	3miles NNW of Witney.	51 49 15N.	01 31 00W.	SP 332138.	007.
	BARFORD St. JOHN.	4.5miles SSE of Banbury.	52 00 08N.	01 21 15W.	SP 442341.	034.
	BENSON.	1.75miles NE of Wallingford.	51 37 00N.	01 05 15W.	SU 628914.	044.
	BICESTER.	1.75miles NNE of Bicester.	51 54 53N.	01 08 00W.	SP 598245.	047.
	BRIZE NORTON.	4miles SW of Witney.	51 45 08N.	01 34 30W.	SP 293058.	082.
	BROADWELL.	3miles S of Burford.	51 45 30N.	01 38 23W.	SP 248065.	083.
	CHALGROVE.	9miles SE of Oxford.	51 40 30N.	01 04 30W.	SU 635977.	114.
	CHIPPING NORTON.	1.5miles SSE of Chipping Norton.	51 55 23N.	01 31 30W.	SP 325253.	124.
	CHIPPING WARDEN.	6miles NNE of Banbury.	52 08 40N.	01 16 30W.	SP 495498.	126.
	CULHAM.	5miles S of Oxford.	51 39 35N.	01 13 40W.	SU 535958.	158.
	ENSTONE.	5miles E of Chipping Norton.	51 55 45N.	01 25 45W.	SP 390258.	212.
	KELMSCOTT.	2.5miles ENE of Lechlade.	51 41 53N.	01 39 00W.	SU 243998.	320.
	KIDDINGTON.	9miles NW of Oxford.	51 54 15N.	01 22 00W.	SP 424230.	324.
	KIDLINGTON.	5miles N of Oxford.	51 50 00N.	01 19 00W.	SP 468156.	325.
	MOUNT FARM.	8miles SE of Oxford.	51 39 50N.	01 09 30W.	SU 583965.	415.
	STANTON HARCOURT.	5.5miles W of Oxford.	51 44 30N.	01 24 30W.	SP 410040.	532.
	UPPER HEYFORD.	5miles NW of Bicester.	51 56 00N.	01 15 15W.	SP 515268.	589.
	WESTON-on-the-GREEN.	3.5miles SW of Bicester.	51 52 45N.	01 13 15W.	SP 535205.	616.
Pembrokeshire.						
	ANGLE.	8.75miles W. of Pembroke.	51 40 23N.	05 05 45W.	SM 858019.	015.
	BRAWDY.	9miles NW of Haverfordwest.	51 53 08N.	05 07 23W.	SM 852252.	077.
	CAREW CHERITON.	6miles W of Tenby.	51 41 15N.	04 48 45W.	SN 055026.	100.
	DALE.	7miles W of Milford Haven.	51 43 00N.	05 11 30W.	SM 795065.	161.
	HAVERFORDWEST.	2miles N of Haverfordwest.	51 49 53N.	04 57 45W.	SM 958192.	279.
	MANORBIER.	4miles SW of Tenby.	51 38 38N.	04 46 45W.	SS 075990.	383.
	ST.DAVIDS.	12miles NW of Haverfordwest.	51 53 10N.	05 12 45W.	SM 790256.	526.
	TALBENNY.	5.75miles NW of Milford Haven.	51 45 23N.	05 08 30W.	SM 834113.	557.
	TEMPLETON.	7miles NNW of Tenby.	51 45 53N.	04 45 15W.	SN 101112.	563.

Perthshire.						
	ERROL.	1mile NE of Errol.	56 24 10N.	03 11 00W.	NO 268242.	213.
	FINDO GASK.	7miles W of Perth.	56 22 30N.	03 36 23W.	NO 009215.	228.
	PERTH.	3.5miles NE of Perth.	56 26 23N.	03 22 08W.	NO 156285.	457.
	WHITEFIELD.	7.75miles NNE of Perth.	56 20 45W.	03 20 45W.	NO 175353.	619.
Renfrewshire.						
	ABBOTSINCH.	2.5 miles W of Girvan.	55 52 10N.	04 25 45W.	NS 479670	002.
Ross-shire.						
	EVANTON.	6.5miles NE of Dingwall.	57 40 08N.	04 18 38W.	NH 625664.	215.
	FEARN.	8.5miles NE of Invergordon.	57 45 35N.	03 56 10W.	NH 842758.	224.
	TAIN.	3.5miles E of Tain.	57 48 30N.	03 58 30W.	NH 828818.	556.
Rutland.						
	COTTESMORE.	5.5miles NNE of Oakham.	52 43 45N.	00 39 15W.	SK 910158.	145.
	NORTH LUFFENHAM.	6miles SW of Oakham.	52 37 53N.	00 36 15W.	SK 941098.	427.
	WOOLFOX LODGE.	6miles NW of Stamford.	52 42 30N.	00 34 30W.	SK 962132.	640.
Shetlands.						
	SCATSTA.	20miles N of Lerwick.	60 26 00N.	01 17 45W.	HU 388725.	487.
	SUMBURGH.	1.25miles NNW of Sumburgh Head.	59 52 45N.	01 17 13W.	HU 395105.	548.
Shropshire.						
	ATCHAM.	5miles E of Shrewsbury.	52 41 23N.	02 38 00W.	SJ 572104.	023.
	BRATTON.	2miles NNE of Wellington.	52 43 45N.	02 32 15W.	SJ 635145.	075.
	BRIDLEWAY GATE.	9miles NNE of Shrewsbury.	52 49 53N.	02 41 15W.	SJ 541258.	081.
	CHETWYND.	2.5miles NNW of Newport.	52 48 45N.	02 24 23W.	SJ 725254.	122.
	CONDOVER.	4.5miles S of Shrewsbury.	52 38 08N.	02 43 45W.	SJ 505045.	139.
	COSFORD.	8miles NW of Wolverhampton.	52 38 30N.	02 18 15W.	SJ 792046.	143.
	HIGH ERCALL.	5.25miles NNW of Wellington.	52 45 45W.	02 35 15W.	SJ 608186.	292.
	HINSTOCK.	4miles SW of Market Drayton.	52 50 05N.	02 30 20W.	SJ 660265.	294.
	MONTFORD BRIDGE.	4.5miles WNW of Shrewsbury.	52 44 52N.	02 51 45W.	SJ 430170.	410.
	PEPLOW.	7miles S of Market Drayton.	52 48 30N.	02 30 00W.	SJ 661233.	454.
	REDNAL.	12miles NW of Shrewsbury.	52 50 30N.	02 56 00W.	SJ 373275.	474.
	SHAWBURY.	6.5miles NE of Shrewsbury.	52 47 45N.	02 40 00W.	SJ 550220.	493.
	SLEAP.	9miles N of Shrewsbury.	52 50 00N.	02 46 15W.	SJ 482268.	508.
	TERNHILL.	4miles SW of Market Drayton.	52 52 23N.	02 32 00W.	SJ 642308.	565.
	TILSTOCK.	3miles SSE of Whitchurch.	52 55 45N.	02 39 00W.	SJ 562378.	574.
Somerset						
	CHARMY DOWN.	3.5miles N of Bath.	51 25 38N.	02 20 31W.	ST 764700.	116.
	CULMHEAD.	6miles S of Taunton.	50 55 45N.	03 07 45W.	ST 208154.	159.
	HENSTRIDGE.	10miles NE of Yeovil.	50 58 50N.	02 21 25W.	ST 752205.	288.
	LULSGATE BOTTOM.	7miles SW of Bristol.	52 43 23N.	01 33 15W.	ST 504651.	373.
	MERRYFIELD.	8miles SE of Taunton.	50 57 45N.	02 56 15W.	ST 342186.	397.
	WESTON SUPER MARE.	2.5miles SE of Weston super Mare.	51 20 08N.	02 56 15W.	ST 345602.	614.
	WESTON ZOYLAND.	4.5miles SE of Bridgewater.	51 06 15N.	02 54 15W.	ST 365345.	615.
	YEOVILTON.	4miles N of Yeovil.	51 00 40N.	02 38 25W.	ST 554234.	652.
Staffordshire.						
	ABBOTS BROMLEY.	5 miles S. of Uttoxeter.	52 48 38N.	01 53 30W.	SK 075253.	001.
	BATTLESTEAD HILL.	1.5miles W of Burton-on-Trent.	52 48 23N.	01 41 00W.	SK 212232.	038.
	HIXON.	7miles NE of Stafford.	52 50 08N.	02 00 23W.	SJ 993266.	296.
	LICHFIELD.	3miles NE of Lichfield.	52 42 45N.	01 47 00W.	SK 146131.	352.
	PENKRIDGE.	6miles S of Stafford.	52 42 30N.	02 05 30W.	SJ 935137.	451.
	PERTON.	3.5miles W of Wolverhampton.	52 35 45N.	02 12 15W.	SJ 865000.	458.
	SEIGHFORD.	4miles WNW of Stafford.	52 49 30N.	02 12 00W.	SJ 865255.	509.
	TATENHILL.	5miles W of Burton-on-Trent.	52 48 45N.	01 45 45W.	SK 158241.	560.
	WHEATON ASTON.	7miles SW of Sealand.	52 43 53N.	02 14 00W.	SJ 842150.	618.
	WOLVERHAMPTON.	2.5miles N of Wolverhampton.	52 37 23N.	02 08 45W.	SJ 900030.	633.
Stirlingshire.						
	GRANGEMOUTH.	3miles NE of Falkirk.	56 00 27N.	03 42 00W.	NS 946820.	253.
Suffolk.						
	BECCLES.	5.5miles SW of Lowestoft.	52 26 08N.	01 36 30E.	TM 453882.	040.
	BENTWATERS.	4.5miles NE of Woodbridge.	52 07 30N.	01 26 15E.	TM 353533.	045.
	BUNGAY.	6miles WSW of Beccles.	52 25 45N.	01 25 15E.	TM 323868.	087.
	BURY-St-EDMUNDS.	3miles E of Bury St. Edmunds.	52 14 38N.	00 46 00E.	TL 898644.	092.
	CHEDBURGH.	6miles SW of Bury St. Edmunds.	52 10 53N.	00 37 15E.	TL 790570.	118.
	DEBACH.	3miles NW of Woodbridge.	52 08 08N.	01 16 23E.	TM 240540.	167.
	EYE.	11miles NNE of Stowmarket.	52 20 00N.	01 08 00E.	TM 130750.	217.
	FRAMLINGHAM.	3miles SE of Framlingham.	52 11 38N.	01 24 30E.	TM 330608.	239.
	GREAT ASHFIELD.	10miles E of Bury St. Edmunds.	52 15 15N.	00 56 45E.	TM 010663.	257.
	HALESWORTH.	7.5miles W of Southwold.	52 21 45N.	01 32 00E.	TM 402798.	268.
	HONINGTON.	7miles NNE of Bury St. Edmunds.	52 20 38N.	00 46 30E.	TL 891754.	302.
	HORHAM.	4miles ESE of Eye.	52 18 35N.	01 14 00E.	TM 205735.	304.
	IPSWICH.	SE boundary of Ipswich.	52 01 38N.	01 11 45E.	TM 190410.	317.
	KNETTISHALL.	6miles SE of Thetford.	52 22 30N.	00 53 30E.	TL 968795.	338.
	LAKENHEATH.	4.5miles SW of Brandon.	52 24 15N.	00 33 15E.	TL 740820.	339.
	LAVENHAM.	7miles N of Sudbury.	52 08 04N.	00 46 15E.	TL 895524.	345.
	LEISTON.	3miles E of Saxmundham.	52 13 23N.	01 33 38E.	TM 430645.	350.
	MARTLESHAM HEATH.	1.5miles SW of Woodbridge.	52 03 30N.	01 16 30E.	TM 242454.	388.
	MENDLESHAM.	5.5miles NE of Stowmarket.	52 13 53N.	01 07 15E.	TM 130638.	395.
	METFIELD.	5miles SE of Harleston.	52 21 40N.	01 23 45E.	TM 311789.	399.
	MILDENHALL.	12miles NW of Bury St. Edmunds.	52 21 45N.	00 28 45E.	TL 690767.	404.
	NEWMARKET.	1.25miles W of Newmarket.	52 14 30N.	00 22 00E.	TL 620630.	421.
	RATTLESDEN.	9miles SE of Bury St. Edmunds.	52 10 00N.	00 52 15E.	TL 961560.	471.
	RAYDON.	3miles SE of Hadleigh.	52 00 45N.	01 00 15E.	TM 060390.	472.
	SHEPHERDS GROVE.	9miles NE of Bury St. Edmunds.	52 19 00N.	00 55 15E.	TL 990728.	495.
	SNAILWELL.	2miles N of Newmarket.	52 16 08N.	00 25 15E.	TL 656665.	511.
	STRADISHALL.	5miles NE Haverhill.	52 08 00N.	00 30 45E.	TL 724512.	542.
	SUDBURY.	2miles N of Sudbury.	52 03 26N.	00 45 45E.	TL 893435.	547.
	TUDDENHAM.	7.5miles NW of Bury St. Edmunds.	52 18 45N.	00 34 30E.	TL 754713.	581.
	WATTISHAM.	9miles NW of Ipswich.	52 07 30N.	00 57 30E.	TM 024518.	601.
	WESTLEY.	West outskirts of Bury St. Edmunds.	52 14 56N.	00 41 10E.	TM 825645.	613.
	WOODBRIDGE.	11miles ENE of Ipswich.	52 05 20N.	01 24 30E.	TM 334490.	635.
Surrey.						
	CROYDON.	2.5miles SW of Croydon.	51 21 15N.	00 07 30W.	TQ 306635.	156.
	DUNSFOLD.	8.5miles SSE of Guildford.	51 06 53N.	00 31 53W.	TQ 025363.	194.
	FAIROAKS.	2miles N of Woking.	51 20 53N.	00 33 30W.	TQ 005623.	220.
	GATWICK.	6miles SSE of Reigate.	51 09 00N.	00 10 00W.	TQ 270404.	246.
	HORNE.	6.5miles SE of Redhill.	51 10 23N.	00 04 38W.	TQ 332435.	306.
	KENLEY.	4miles S of Croydon.	51 18 15N.	00 05 18W.	TQ 328580.	323.
	REDHILL.	2miles SE of Redhill.	51 12 53N.	00 08 15W.	TQ 298476.	473.

Sussex.						
	APPLEDRAM.	1.5miles S of Chichester.	50 48 38N.	00 48 45W.	SU 842023.	018.
	BOGNOR.	2miles NW of Bognor.	50 47 15N.	00 42 30W.	SU 912006.	061.
	CHAILEY.	9miles NNW of Brighton.	50 57 15N.	00 02 45W.	TQ 378205.	113.
	COOLHAM.	6miles SSW of Horsham.	50 59 15N	00 23 45W.	TQ 125224.	142.
	COWDRAY PARK.	2miles E of Midhurst.	50 58 30N.	00 41 15W.	SU 902218.	146.
	DEANLAND.	4miles WNW of Hailsham.	50 53 00N.	00 10 00E.	TQ 518115.	166.
	FORD.	2.25miles NW of Littlehampton.	50 48 53N.	00 35 00W.	SU 995029.	234.
	FRISTON.	5miles WSW of Eastbourne.	50 45 43N.	00 10 15E.	TV 555989.	241.
	FUNTINGTON.	5miles W of Chichester.	50 52 00N.	00 52 45W.	SU 790083.	244.
	MERSTON.	2.5miles SE of Chichester.	50 49 08N.	00 44 30W.	SU 885031.	398
	SELSEY.	5miles S of Chichester.	50 45 15N.	00 46 30W.	SZ 865985.	492.
	SHOREHAM.	1mile N of Shoreham.	50 50 12N.	00 17 23W.	TQ 202055.	499.
	TANGMERE.	2.5miles E of Chichester.	50 50 48N.	00 42 23W.	SU 913061.	558.
	WESTHAMPNETT.	1.5miles NNE of Chichester.	50 51 38N.	00 45 30W.	SU 875075.	612.
Tyrone NI.						
	CLUNTOE.	10miles SE of Cookstown.	54 37 10N.	06 32 15W.	H 945755.	133.
Warwickshire.						
	BAGINTON.	3miles SE of Coventry.	52 21 30N.	01 28 50W.	SP 346748.	027.
	BRAMCOTE.	4miles SE of Nuneaton.	52 29 15N.	01 23 45W.	SP 406883.	074.
	CASTLE BROMWICH.	5miles N of Birmingham.	52 31 08N.	01 47 15W.	SP 145915.	104.
	CHURCH LAWFORD.	3.5miles WSW of Rugby.	52 21 23N.	01 20 15W.	SP 448736.	131.
	EDGE HILL.	3miles SE of Kineton.	52 05 08N.	01 28 15W.	SP 363433.	205.
	ELMDON.	6.5miles SE of Birmingham.	52 07 00N.	01 44 45W.	SP 172840.	209.
	GAYDON.	7.5miles SSE of Leamington.	52 11 15N.	01 29 00W.	SP 353458.	247.
	HOCKLEY HEATH.	9miles SW of Birmingham.	52 21 38N.	01 47 08W.	SK 147743.	297.
	HONILEY.	7miles SW of Coventry.	52 21 30N.	01 39 30W.	SP 233736.	301.
	SNITTERFIELD.	3miles N of Stratford on Avon.	52 14 15N.	01 42 45W.	SP 193598.	514.
	SOUTHAM.	9miles SE of Warwick.	52 14 57N.	01 22 23W.	SP 430620.	516.
	STRATFORD.	2.75miles SSE of Stratford on Avon.	52 09 38N.	01 41 00W.	SP 215515.	543.
	WARWICK.	1mile SSW of Warwick.	52 16 00N.	01 36 15W.	SP 268635.	598.
	WELLESBOURNE MOUNTFORD.	5miles E of Stratford on Avon.	52 11 23N.	01 36 30W.	SP 264549.	604.
Wigtownshire.						
	CASTLE KENNEDY.	3.5miles E of Stranraer.	54 54 40N.	04 56 05W.	NX 119598.	108.
	WEST FREUGH.	5.5miles SE of Stranraer.	54 51 00N.	04 56 38W.	NX 110545.	607.
	WIGTOWN.	1mile S of Wigtown.	54 51 00N.	04 26 30W.	NX 433536.	623.
Wiltshire.						
	ALTON BARNES.	6miles E of Devizes.	51 21 23N.	01 51 23W.	SU 114618.	011.
	BLAKEHILL FARM.	2miles SW of Cricklade.	51 37 23N.	01 53 15W.	SU 078915.	057.
	BOSCOMBE DOWN.	1.5miles E of Amesbury.	51 09 38N.	01 44 30W.	SU 182398.	065.
	CASTLE COMBE.	5.5miles NW of Chippenham.	51 29 20N.	02 12 45W.	ST 854767.	106.
	CLYFFE PYPARD.	3.5miles S of Wootton Bassett.	51 28 45N.	01 54 00W.	SU 070756.	134.
	COLERNE.	6miles NNE of Bath.	51 26 45N.	02 16 45W.	ST 803715.	136.
	DOWN AMPNEY.	7miles NNW of Swindon.	51 40 00N.	01 50 15W.	SU 112965.	185.
	HULLAVINGTON.	5miles N of Chippenham.	51 31 30N.	02 08 00W.	ST 900810.	309.
	KEEVIL.	4.5miles E of Trowbridge.	51 18 45N.	02 06 45W.	ST 922571.	319.
	LONG NEWNTON.	2miles SE of Tetbury.	51 37 30N.	02 06 00W.	ST 929920.	368.
	LYNEHAM.	6.5miles NE of Chippenham.	51 30 23N.	01 59 30W.	SU 004788.	377.
	NETHERAVON.	6miles N of Amesbury.	51 14 23N.	01 46 00W.	SU 165490.	418.
	OATLANDS HILL.	7miles NNW of Salisbury.	51 09 53N.	01 52 00W.	SU 090405.	438.
	OLD SARUM.	1.5miles N of Salisbury.	51 05 53N.	01 47 00W.	SU 155355.	442.
	OVERTON HEATH.	1.5miles S of Marlborough.	51 23 19N.	01 44 40W.	SU 168655.	447.
	RAMSBURY.	4.5miles E of Marlborough.	51 25 45N.	01 36 53W.	SU 270703.	470.
	SHREWTON.	11miles NNW of Salisbury.	51 12 45N.	01 53 30W.	SU 076460.	500.
	UPAVON.	9miles S of Marlborough.	51 17 23N.	01 46 00W.	SU 152542.	587.
	WANBOROUGH.	5miles SE of Swindon.	51 32 08N.	01 41 00W.	SU 218828.	594.
	WROUGHTON.	4miles S of Swindon.	51 30 15N.	01 48 00W.	SU 139786.	648.
	YATESBURY.	4.5miles E of Calne.	51 25 54N.	01 54 00W.	SU 060710.	651.
	ZEALS.	4miles NNW of Gillingham.	51 05 30N.	02 18 45W.	ST 777325.	654.
Worcestershire.						
	DEFFORD.	7.5miles SSE of Worcester.	52 05 45N.	02 08 30W.	SO 903443.	170.
	HALFPENNY GREEN.	7miles SW of Wolverhampton.	53 30 53N.	02 15 38W.	SO 824912.	269.
	HONEYBOURNE.	4.75miles E of Evesham.	52 04 45N.	01 50 00W.	SP 112426.	300.
	PERSHORE.	8miles ESE of Worcester.	52 08 30N.	02 02 15W.	SO 975495.	456.
	WORCESTER.	1.75miles N of Worcester.	52 12 53N.	02 12 30W.	SO 855575.	642.
Yorkshire.						
	ACASTER MALBIS.	6miles S of York.	53 52 45N.	01 06 45W.	SE 578430.	005.
	BELLASIZE.	4.5miles E of Howden.	53 44 08N.	00 45 38W.	SE 818278.	042.
	BREIGHTON.	13miles SE of York.	53 48 15N.	00 54 30W.	SE 721350.	079.
	BROUGH.	7miles W of Hull.	53 43 00N.	00 33 45W.	SE 948255.	084.
	BURN.	2.5miles S of Selby.	53 44 53N.	01 05 08W.	SE 604285.	088.
	CARNABY.	1.75miles SW of Bridlington.	54 03 45N.	00 15 30W.	TA 140640.	103.
	CATFOSS.	4 miles W of Hornsea.	53 55 15N.	00 16 30W.	TA 135485.	110.
	CATTERICK.	4.5miles SE of Richmond.	54 22 00N.	01 37 00W.	SE 250968.	111.
	CHURCH FENTON.	4miles SE of Tadcaster.	53 50 00N.	01 12 00W.	SE 531378.	130.
	COTTAM.	5.5miles N of Driffield.	54 03 45N.	00 28 45W.	SE 995644.	144.
	CROFT.	4.5miles S of Darlington.	54 27 15N.	01 33 45W.	NZ 285068.	153.
	DALTON.	4miles S of Thirsk.	54 10 30N.	01 21 30W.	SE 420760.	163.
	DISHFORTH.	4miles E of Rippon.	54 08 15N.	01 25 00W.	SE 381719.	179.
	DONCASTER.	1.25miles SE of Doncaster.	53 30 30N.	01 06 15W.	SE 595020.	181.
	DRIFFIELD.	2miles WSW of Great Driffield.	53 59 45N.	00 28 15W.	SE 995565.	188.
	EAST MOOR.	7.75miles N of York.	54 04 00N.	01 05 00W.	SE 600640.	201.
	ELVINGTON.	5miles ESE of York.	53 55 30N.	00 58 30W.	SE 665480.	211.
	FINNINGLEY.	7.5miles SE of Doncaster.	53 29 00N.	01 00 15W.	SK 663985.	230.
	FIRBECK.	6miles NNW of Worksop.	53 23 15N.	01 09 45W.	SK 555892.	231.
	FULL SUTTON.	8miles E of York.	53 58 45N.	00 52 00W.	SE 745545.	243.
	HOLME.	5miles SW of Market Weighton.	53 48 23N.	00 44 23W.	SE 829351.	298.
	HUTTON CRANSWICK.	4miles SSW of Driffield.	53 57 00N.	00 27 30W.	TA 008514.	313.
	LECONFIELD.	2.75miles N of Beverley.	53 52 45N.	00 26 00W.	TA 030435.	346.
	LEEMING.	7miles SW of Northallerton.	54 18 00N.	01 32 00W.	SE 305892.	348.
	LINDHOLME.	7miles ENE of Doncaster.	53 33 00N.	00 58 00W.	SK 685065.	354.
	LINTON-on-OUSE.	8.75miles NW of York.	54 02 45N.	01 15 00W.	SE 490618.	355.
	LISSETT.	6miles SSW of Bridlington.	54 00 15N.	00 16 30W.	TA 135582.	356.
	MARSTON MOOR.	8.5miles W of York.	53 57 45N.	01 18 00W.	SE 460520.	387.
	MELBOURNE.	12miles SE of York.	53 52 15N.	00 50 15W.	SE 766421.	392.
	POCKLINGTON.	12miles ESE of York.	53 55 45N.	00 48 00W.	SE 790485.	461.
	RICCALL.	10miles S of York.	53 49 08N.	01 01 45W.	SE 636365.	476.
	RUFFORTH.	3.5miles W of York.	53 56 45N.	01 11 00W.	SE 535505.	482.
	SCORTON.	9miles SSW of Darlington.	54 23 45N.	01 37 45W.	NZ 240003.	488.
	SHERBURN-in-ELMET.	12.5miles E of Leeds.	53 47 15N.	01 13 15W.	SE 520330.	496.
	SKIPTON-on-SWALE.	4miles W of Thirsk.	54 13 30N.	01 25 45W.	SE 373812.	506.
	SNAITH.	7miles W of Goole.	53 40 53N.	01 05 00W.	SE 605210.	512.
	THOLTHORPE.	12miles NW of York.	54 06 15N.	01 15 30W.	SE 485678.	567.
	THORNABY.	2miles SW of Middlesborough.	54 32 00N.	01 17 30W.	NZ 455163.	568.
	TOPCLIFFE.	2.5miles SW of Thirsk.	54 12 30N.	01 23 00W.	SE 405790.	578.
	WOMBLETON.	3miles E of Helmsley.	54 13 45N.	00 58 00W.	SE 673825.	634.
	YORK.	2miles NNW of York.	53 59 15N.	01 05 45W.	SE 590550.	653.

APPENDIX 'G'. WARTIME USE OF AIRFIELD SITES.

FUNCTION.	AIRFIELD NAME.	COMMAND.
A.A. Co-operation Units.	Aberporth.	Fighter.
	Bodorgan.	"
	Castle Bromwich.	"
	Cleave.	"
	Ipswich.	"
	Manorbier.	"
	Towyn.	"
	Weston Zoyland.	"
Advanced Flying Units. [Observor]	Bishops Court.	Flying Training.
	Crimond.	R.N.
	Dumfries.	Flying Training.
	Halfpenny Green.	" "
	Millom.	" "
	Mona.	" "
	Moreton Valence.	" "
	Penrhos.	" "
	Staverton.	" "
	West Freugh.	" "
	Wigtown.	" "
Advanced Flying Units. [Pilot]	Akeman Street.	Flying Training.
	Babdown Farm.	" "
	Bratton.	" "
	Calveley.	" "
	Castle Combe.	" "
	Charlton Horethorn.	R.N.
	Chetwynd.	Flying Training.
	Church Lawford.	" "
	Condover.	" "
	Cranage.	" "
	Croughton.	" "
	Dale.	R.N.
	Errol.	Flying Training.
	Harlaxton.	" "
	Henstridge.	R.N.
	Kiddington.	Flying Training.
	Kidlington.	" "
	Little Rissington.	" "
	Long Newnton.	" "
	Perton.	" "
	Peterborough.	" "
	Sibson.	" "
	Snitterfield.	" "
	South Cerney.	" "
	Southrop.	" "
	Spittlegate.	" "
	Sutton Bridge.	" "
	Tatenhill.	" "
	Tealing.	" "
	Ternhill.	" "
	Warwick.	" "
	Weston-on-the-Green.	" "
	Wheaton Aston.	" "
	Windrush.	" "
	Wrexham.	" "
Advanced Landing Grounds.	Appledram.	Fighter.
	Bisterne.	"
	Bognor.	"
	Brenzett.	"
	Chailey.	"
	Coolham.	"
	Deanland.	"
	Funtington.	"
	Headcorn.	"
	High Haldon.	"
	Horne.	"
	Kingsnorth.	"
	Lashenden.	"
	Lydd.	"
	Lymington.	"
	Needs Oar Point.	"
	New Romney.	"
	Newchurch.	"
	Penshurst.	"
	Selsey.	"
	Staplehurst.	"
	Swingfield.	"
	Winkton.	"
	Woodchurch.	"
Advanced Training Units.	Charmy Down.	Flying training.
	Chipping Norton.	" "
	Llandwrog.	" "
Air Depots.	Burtonwood.	USSTAFE.
	Greencastle.	"
	Grove.	"
Air Depots[continued]	Langford Lodge.	USSTAFE.
	North Witham.	"
	Stanstead.	"
	Warton.	"
Air Gunnery Schools.	Andreas.	Flying Training.
	Barrow.	" "
	Castle Kennedy.	" "
	Catfoss.	" "
	Dalcross.	" "
	Morpeth.	" "
	Pembrey.	" "
Aircrew Allocation Units.	Atcham	8th. USAAF.
	Brackla.	Flying Training.
	Eastchurch.	" "
	Goxhill.	8th. USAAF.
Airports.	Bovingdon.	USATC.
	Hendon.	Transport.
	Lyneham.	"
	Metfield.	USATC.
	Nutts Corner.	Transport.
	Prestwick.	"
	St. Morgan.	"
	Valley.	"
Armament Practice Camp.	Fairwood Common.	Fighter.
Beam Approach Schools.	Hinstock.	R.N.
	Kelmscott.	Flying Training.
	Wanborough.	" "
	Watchfield.	" "
Care & Mainenance.	Birch.	8th. USAAF.
	Bottisham.	Fighter.
	Chalgrove.	9th. USAAF.
	Cluntoe.	R.A.F. NI.
	Doncaster.	Transport.
	Gosfield.	Bomber.
	Halesworth.	8th. USAAF.
	Harrowbeer.	Fighter.
	Haverfordwest.	Coastal.
	Kirkistown.	R.A.F. NI.
	Matching.	Bomber.
	Merryfield.	Fighter.
	Shepherds Grove.	Bomber.
	Southam.	Flying training.
	Toome.	R.A.F. NI.
Civil Airports.	Croydon.	Dept. of Civil Aviation.
	Hurn.	On loan from Fighter.
	Speke.	Dept. of Civil Aviation.
Elementary Flying Training Schools.	Abbots Bromley.	Flying Training.
	Alton Barnes.	" "
	Battlestead Hill.	" "
	Bellasize.	" "
	Booker.	" "
	Braunstone.	" "
	Bray.	" "
	Brough.	" "
	Burnfoot.	" "
	Cambridge.	" "
	Carlisle.	" "
	Caxton Gibbet.	" "
	Clyffe Pypard.	" "
	Denham.	" "
	Denton.	" "
	Derby.	" "
	Desford.	" "
	Elmdon.	" "
	Fairoaks.	" "
	Firbeck.	" "
	Hatfield.	" "
	Henley.	" "
	Hockley Heath.	" "
	Hucknall.	" "
	Kirkpatrick.	" "
	Panshangar.	" "
	Papplewick Moor.	" "
	Penkridge.	" "
	Perth.	" "
	Shellingford.	" "
	Smiths Lawn.	" "
	Sywell.	" "
	Theale.	" "
	Whitefield.	" "
	Winkfield.	" "
	Wolverhampton.	" "
	Worcester.	" "

Emergency Runways.	Carnaby.	Bomber.
	Woodbridge.	"
Empire Air Schools.	Hullavington.	Flying Training.
	Manby.	" "
	Shawbury.	" "
Experimental Stations.	Boscombe Down.	Flying Training.
	Fersfield.	8th USAAF.
	Gosport.	Coastal.
	Sherburn-in-Elmet.	Flying Training.
Flying Instructor Schools.	Kinnell.	Flying Training.
	Lulsgate Bottom.	" "
	Montrose.	" "
	Overton Heath.	" "
	Stracathro.	" "
	Upavon.	" "
	Woodley.	" "
Flying Training Schools.	Cark.	Flying Training.
	Jurby.	" "
	Squires Gate.	Coastal.
Forward Airfields.	Acklington.	Fighter.
	Andrews Field.	"
	Beaulieu.	"
	Bentwaters.	"
	Blackbushe.	"
	Castle Camps.	"
	Castletown.	"
	Catterick.	"
	Defford.	"
	Detling.	"
	Drem.	"
	Dunsfold.	"
	Ford.	"
	Gatwick.	"
	Hawkinge.	"
	Hornchurch.	"
	Hunsdon.	"
	Ibsley.	"
	Kenley.	"
	Lasham.	"
	Manston.	"
	Northolt.	"
	Odiham.	"
	Peterhead.	"
	Predannack.	"
	Skeabrae.	"
	Stapleford Tawney.	"
	Warmwell.	"
	West Malling.	"
	Wittering.	"
	Woodvale.	"
	York.	"
Glider Training Units.	Brize Norton.	Flying Training.
	Fairford.	" "
	Haldon.	R.N.
	Keevil.	Flying training.
	North Leach.	" "
	Peplow.	Flying Training.
	Seighford.	" "
	Shobdon.	" "
	Stoke Orchard.	" "
Naval Disembarked Sqdns.	Ayr.	R.N.
	Grimsetter.	"
	Hatston.	"
	Machrihanish.	"
	Twatt.	"
Naval H.Q. Units.	Donibristle.	R.N.
	Lee-on-Solent.	"
	Ludham.	"
Non-operational.	Fairlop.	Balloon.
	Inverness.	Fighter.
	Llanbedr.	"
Operational Training Units.	Abingdon.	Bomber.
	Aldergrove.	Coastal.
	Andover.	Fighter.
	Ashbourne.	"
	Barford St. John.	Bomber.
	Bicester.	Fighter.
	Bitteswell.	Transport.
	Boulmer.	Fighter.
	Bramcote.	Transport.
	Bruntingthorpe.	Bomber.
	Brunton.	Fighter.
	Burscough.	R.N.
	Castle Donnington.	Transport.
	Charter Hall.	Fighter.
	Chipping Warden	Bomber.
	Church Broughton.	"
	Crail.	R.N.
	Cranfield.	Fighter.
	Crosby-on-Eden.	Transport.
	Darley Moor.	Fighter.
	Desborough.	Bomber.
	Dundonald.	Transport.
	East Fortune.	Coastal.
	East Haven.	R.N.
	Edge Hill.	Bomber.
	Eglington.	R.N.
	Elgin.	Bomber.
	Enstone.	"
	Eshott.	Fighter.
	Finmere.	"
	Finningley.	Bomber.
	Gaydon.	"
	Great Orton.	Coastal.
	Hampstead Norris.	Fighter.
	Harwell.	"
	Hawarden.	"
	Hibaldstow.	"
	High Ercall.	"
	Hixon.	Bomber.
	Honeybourne.	"
	Husbands Bosworth.	"
	Inskip.	R.N.
	Kingston Bagpuize.	Fighter.
	Kinloss.	Bomber.
	Kirton-in-Lindsey.	Fighter.
	Leicester East.	Transport.
	Lichfield.	Bomber.
	Little Horwood.	"
	Long Marston.	"
	Longtown.	Transport.
	Lossiemouth.	Bomber.
	Market Harborough.	"
	Maydown.	R.N.
	Milfield.	Fighter.
	Montford Bridge.	"
	Moreton-in-Marsh.	Bomber.
	Nuneaton.	Transport.
	Oakley.	Bomber.
	Old Sarum.	Fighter.
	Ossington.	Bomber.
	Ouston.	Fighter.
	Poulton.	Flying training.
	Rednal.	Fighter.
	Ronaldsway.	R.N.
	Silloth.	Coastal.
	Silverstone.	Bomber.
	Sleap.	Fighter.
	St. Merryn.	R.N.
	Stanton Harcourt.	Bomber.
	Stratford.	"
	Templeton.	Coastal.
	Tilstock.	Fighter.
	Turnberry.	Coastal.
	Turweston.	Bomber.
	Twinwood Farm.	Fighter.
	Upper Heyford.	Bomber.
	Wellesbourne Mountford.	"
	Westcott.	"
	Winfield.	Fighter.
	Wing.	Bomber.
	Worksop.	"
	Wymeswold.	Transport.
	Yeovilton.	R.N.

Operational.	Acaster Malbis.	Bomber.
	Alconbury.	8th USAAF.
	Aldermaston.	9th USAAF.
	Angle.	Coastal.
	Attlebridge.	8th USAAF.
	Baginton.	Bomber.
	Balderton.	"
	Ballykelly.	Coastal.
	Banff.	"
	Bardney.	Bomber.
	Barkston Heath.	9th USAAF.
	Bassingbourn.	8th USAAF.
	Beccles.	Coastal.
	Benbecula.	"
	Bircham Newton.	"
	Blakehill Farm.	Transport.
	Blyton.	Bomber.
	Bodney.	8th USAAF.
	Bolt Head.	Fighter.
	Boreham.	USSTAFE.
	Bourn.	Bomber.
	Boxted.	8th USAAF.
	Bradwell Bay.	Fighter.
	Brawdy.	Coastal.
	Breighton.	Bomber.
	Bungay.	8th USAAF.
	Burn.	Bomber.
	Bury-St-Edmunds.	8th USAAF.
	Cammeringham.	Bomber.
	Chedburgh.	"
	Cheddington.	8th USAAF.
	Chelveston.	" "
	Chilbolton.	Fighter.
	Chipping Ongar.	USSTAFE.
	Chivenor.	Coastal.
	Christchurch.	Fighter.
	Collyweston.	"
	Cottesmore.	9th USAAF.
	Croft.	Bomber.
	Culmhead.	Fighter.
	Dallachy.	Coastal.
	Dalton.	Bomber.
	Davidstow Moor.	Coastal.
	Debach.	8th USAAF.
	Debden.	" "
	Deenethorpe.	" "
	Deopham Green.	" "
	Disforth.	Bomber.
	Docking.	Coastal.
	Donna Nook.	"
	Down Ampney.	Transport.
	Downham Market.	Bomber.
	Dunholme Lodge.	"
	Dunkeswell.	USNAC.
	Duxford.	8th USAAF.
	Earls Colne.	Fighter
	East Moor.	Bomber.
	East Wretham.	8th USAAF.
	Elvington.	Bomber.
	Eye.	8th USAAF.
	Faldingworth.	Bomber.
	Fiskerton.	"
	Folkingham.	9th USAAF.
	Foulsham.	Bomber.
	Fowlmere.	8th USAAF.
	Framlingham.	" "
	Fraserburgh.	Coastal.
	Friston.	Fighter.
	Fulbeck.	Bomber.
	Full Sutton.	Bomber.
	Gamston.	"
	Glatton.	8th USAAF.
	Grafton Underwood.	" "
	Gransden Lodge.	Bomber.
	Graveley.	"
	Gravesend.	Fighter.
	Great Ashfield.	8th USAAF.
	Great Dunmow.	Fighter.
	Great Massingham.	Bomber.
	Greenham Common.	9th USAAF.
	Grimsby.	Bomber.
	Hardwick.	8th USAAF.
	Harrington.	" "
	Hemswell.	Bomber.
	Heston.	Fighter.
	Hethel.	8th USAAF.
	Honington.	" "
	Horham.	" "
	Horsham-St-Faith.	" "
	Hutton Cranswick.	Fighter.
	Kelstern.	Bomber.
Operational[continued]	Kimbolton.	8th USAAF.
	Kingscliffe.	" "
	Kirmington.	Bomber.
	Knettishall.	8th USAAF.
	Langar.	Bomber.
	Langham.	Coastal.
	Lavenham.	8th USAAF.
	Leconfield.	Bomber.
	Leiston.	8th USAAF.
	Leuchars.	Coastal.
	Limavady.	Coastal.
	Lissett.	Bomber.
	Little Snoring.	"
	Little Staughton.	"
	Little Walden.	8th USAAF.
	Macmerry.	Fighter.
	Martlesham Heath.	8th USAAF.
	Matlast.	Fighter.
	Melbourne.	Bomber.
	Membury.	9th USAAF.
	Mendlesham.	8th USAAF.
	Mepal.	Bomber.
	Metheringham.	"
	Methwold.	"
	Milltown.	Coastal.
	Molesworth.	8th USAAF.
	Newmarket.	Bomber.
	North Coates.	Coastal.
	North Creake.	Bomber.
	North Killingholme.	"
	North Pickenham.	8th USAAF.
	Nuthampstead.	" "
	Oakington.	Bomber.
	Old Buckenham.	8th USAAF.
	Oulton.	Bomber.
	Podington.	8th USAAF.
	Polebrook.	" "
	Port Ellen.	Coastal.
	Rackheath.	8th USAAF.
	Ramsbury.	9th USAAF.
	Rattlesden.	8th USAAF.
	Raydon.	" "
	Redhill.	Fighter.
	Riccall.	Bomber.
	Ridgewell.	8th USAAF.
	Rivenhall.	Fighter.
	Rufforth.	Bomber.
	Saltby.	9th USAAF.
	Sandtoft.	Bomber.
	Seething.	8th USAAF.
	Shipdham.	" "
	Skellingthorpe.	Bomber.
	Skipton-on-Swale.	"
	Snaith.	"
	Snetterton Heath.	8th USAAF.
	Spanhoe.	9th USAAF.
	Spilsby.	Bomber.
	St. Davids.	Coastal.
	St. Eval.	"
	Steeple Morden.	8th USAAF.
	Strubby.	Bomber.
	Sturgate.	"
	Sudbury.	8th USAAF.
	Swannington.	Bomber.
	Swanton Morley.	Fighter.
	Tempsford.	Bomber.
	Tholthorpe.	"
	Thorpe Abbots.	8th USAAF.
	Thruxton.	Fighter.
	Thurleigh.	8th USAAF.
	Tibenham.	" "
	Tuddenham.	Bomber.
	Upward.	"
	Warboys.	"
	Wattisham.	8th USAAF.
	Welford.	9th USAAF.
	Wendling.	8th USAAF.
	West Raynham.	Bomber.
	Wethersfield.	Fighter.
	Wick.	Coastal.
	Wickenby.	Bomber.
	Wigsley.	"
	Winkleigh.	Fighter.
	Winthorpe.	Bomber.
	Witchford.	"
	Wombleton.	"
	Woodhall Spa.	"
	Woolfox Lodge.	"
	Wormingford.	8th USAAF.
	Wratting Common.	Bomber.
	Wyton.	"

Operational[Base]	Binbrook.	Bomber.
	Bottisford.	"
	Coningsby.	"
	Driffield.	"
	East Kirkby.	"
	Elsham Wolds.	"
	Holme.	"
	Leeming.	"
	Lindholme.	"
	Linton-on-Ouse.	"
	Ludford Magna.	"
	Marston Moor.	"
	Middleton-St-George.	"
	Mildenhall.	"
	North Luffenham.	"
	Pocklington.	"
	Scampton.	"
	Stradishall.	"
	Swinderby.	"
	Syerston.	"
	Topcliffe.	"
	Waddington.	"
	Waterbeach.	"
Operational[Parent]	Netheravon.	Fighter.
	Sumburgh.	"
	Tain.	"
	Thornaby.	"
	Thorney Island.	"
	Tiree.	
Operational[satellite]	Lympne.	Fighter.
	Merston.	"
	Shoreham.	"
	Skitton.	"
	St. Marys.	"
	Upottery.	"
	Westhampnett.	"
Parachute Training.	Ringway.	Fighter.
Parent Stations.	Broardwell.	Transport.
	Filton.	"
	Holmsley South.	"
	Honily.	Bomber.
	Kemble.	Transport.
	Kirkbride.	Maintenance.
	Llandow.	Transport.
	Long Kesh.	R.A.F. NI.
	Machaberry.	" "
	Melton Mowbray.	Transport.
	Mullagmore.	Coastal.
	Newtownards.	R.A.F. NI.
	Perranporth.	Transport.
	Pershore.	"
	Sealand.	Maintenance.
	Stoney Cross.	Transport.
	Stornoway.	Coastal.
	Talbenny.	Transport.
	Tarrant Rushton.	Fighter.
	Wroughton.	Maintenance.
Photographic Reconnaissance Units.	Benson.	Coastal.
	Dyce.	"
	Mount Farm.	8th USAAF.
	Watton.	" "
Relief landing Grounds.	Bridleway Gate.	Maintenance.
	Shrewton.	Fighter.
	Tatton park.	"
	Treligga.	R.N.
Repair Depot.	Henlow.	Maintenance.
Satellites.	Connel.	Coastal.
	Little Sutton.	Maintenance.
	Oatlands Hill.	Fighter.
	Roborough.	Coastal.
	Scatsta.	"
	St. Angelo.	"
	Weston Super Mare.	Technical Traini

Sector Stations.	Biggin Hill.	Fighter.
	Church Fenton.	"
	Colerne.	"
	Coltishall.	"
	Digby.	"
	Exeter.	"
	Middle Wallop.	"
	North Weald.	"
	Portreath.	"
	Tangmere.	"
	Turnhouse.	"
Service Flying Training Schools.	Newton.	Flying Training.
	Orston.	" "
	Tollerton.	" "
Storage Units.	Annan.	Maintenance.
	Anthorn.	R.N.
	Ashford.	Maintenance.
	Bibury.	"
	Bircotes.	"
	Bush Barn.	R.N.
	Campbeltown.	"
	Cardiff.	Maintenance.
	Cottam.	"
	Cowdray Park.	R.N.
	Culham.	"
	Dunino.	"
	Edzell.	Maintenance.
	Evanton.	R.N.
	Grangemouth.	Maintenance.
	Great Sampford.	Balloon.
	Hinton-in-the-Hedges.	Bomber.
	Hooton Park.	Maintenance.
	Kirknewton.	"
	Okehampton.	"
	Rhoose.	"
	Sawbridgeworth.	"
	Scorton.	Balloon.
	Southend.	"
	Usworth.	Maintenance.
	Woolsington.	"
	Zeals.	Balloon.
Tactical Exercise Units.	Aston Down.	Fighter.
	Chedworth.	"
Training Schools.	Arbroath.	R.N.
	Ballyhalbert.	R.A.F. NI.
	Caister.	Technical Training.
	Carew Cheriton.	" "
	Coleby Grange.	" "
	Cosford.	" "
	Cranwell.	" "
	Eastleigh.	R.N.
	Farnborough.	Technical Training.
	Fearn.	R.N.
	Feltwell.	Bomber.
	Halton.	Technical Training.
	Madley.	" "
	Snailwell.	" "
	St. Athan.	" "
	Stormy Down.	Flying Training.
	Wellingore.	Technical Training.
	Westley.	" "
	Worthy Down.	R.N.
	Yatesbury.	Technical Training.
Under construction.	Culdrose.	R.N.
	Dounray.	"
	Heathrow.	Transport.
Under re-construction.	Abbotsinch.	R.N.
	Lakenheath.	Bomber.
	Marham.	"
	Sculthorpe.	"
War Department.	Balado Bridge.	On loan from Fighter.
	Findo Gask.	" " " Flying Training.
	Fordoun.	" " " " "
	Forres.	" " " Bomber.
	West Hartlepool.	" " " Coastal.

APPENDIX 'H'. 1985 USE OF AIRFIELD SITES.

Agriculture.

Abbots Bromley.
Alton Barnes.
Andreas.
Andrews Field.
Appledram.
Ashford.
Atcham.
Attlebridge.
Bisterne.
Blyton.
Bodney.
Bodorgan.
Bognor.
Bolt Head.
Bourn.
Bovingdon.
Boxted.
Brenzett.
Burnfoot.
Cammeringham.
Castle Camps.
Caxton Gibbet.
Chailey.
Charleton Horethorne.
Chedworth.
Chipping Norton.
Chipping Ongar.
Clyffe Pypard.
Coleby Grange.
Coolham.
Dale.
Deanland.
Denton.
Desborough.
Detling.
Donna Nook.
Driffield.
Dundonald.
Dunholme Lodge.
Dunino.
East Kirkby.
East Moor.
Elgin.
Eye.
Fearn.
Fiskerton.
Folkingham.
Fowlmere.
Framlingham.
Fraserburgh.
Friston.
Funtington.
Gransden Lodge.
Graveley.
Great Ashfield.
Great Dunmow.
Great Massingham.
Halesworth.
Hardwick.
Harrington.
Headcorn.
Hibaldstow.
Hinton-in-the-Hedges
Hixon.
Kelmscott.
Kelstern.
Kimbolton.
Kingscliffe.
Kingsnorth.
Kinnell.
Langham.
Lavenham.
Leiston.
Lissett.
Little Horwood
Long Newnton.
Ludham.
Lydd.
Lymington.
Macmerry.
Madley.
Mepal.
Merston.
Methwold.
Mount Farm.
Needs Oar Point.
New Romney.
Newchurch.
North Creake.
Nuthampstead.
Oatlands Hill.
Orston.
Ossington.
Overton Heath.
Papplewick Moor.
Peplow.
Perton.
Pocklington.
Polebrook.
Ramsbury.
Riccall.
Ridgewell.
Rufforth.
Saltby.
Scorton.
Seighford.
Selsey.
Skipton-on-Swale.
Snailwell.
Snaith.
Southrop.
Spanhoe.
Steeple Morden.
Sudbury.
Sutton Bridge.
Swingfield.
Tatenhill.
Tholthorpe.
Thorpe Abbots.
Treligga.
Tuddenham.
Turweston.
Upottery.
Warboys.
Wendling.
Weston Zoyland.
Wheaton Aston.
Whitefield.
Wickenby.
Wigsley.
Wing.
Winkton.
Whichfield.
Wormingford.
Yatesbury.
Zeals.

Aircraft Industry

[Airwork]	Perth.
[British Aerospace]	Bitteswell. Brough. Dunsfold. Filton. Hatfield. Hawarden. Holme. Hurn. Warton.
[Edgley Aircraft]	Old Sarum.
[Marshalls]	Cambridge.
[Martin Baker]	Chalgrove.

Army.

Andover.
Ballykelly.
Bassingbourn.
Bramcote.
Cheddington.
Kenley.
Kirton-in-Lindsey.
Middle Wallop.
Netheravon.
Oakington.
Ouston.
South Cerney.
Spittlegate.
Thorney Island.
Topcliffe.
Waterbeach.
Worthy Down.

Atomic Energy Commission.

Culham.
Harwell.

Atomic Weapons Research Establishment.

Aldermaston.

Motor Industry

[Ford]	Boreham.
[General Motors]	Hooton Park.
[Lotus]	Hethel.
[Research Association]	Nuneaton.

Caravan Sites.

Ballyhalbert.
Penrhos.

Civil Airports

[Aberdeen]	Dyce.
[Aldergrove]	Aldergrove.
[Belfast]	Belfast.
[Birmingham]	Elmdon.
[Blackpool]	Squires Gate.
[Bristol]	Luisgate Bottom.
[Cardiff]	Rhoose.
[Carlisle]	Crosby-on-Eden.
[Chichester/Goodwood]	Westhampnett.
[Coventry]	Baginton.
[East Midlands]	Castle Donnington.
[Edinburgh]	Turnhouse.
[Exeter]	Exeter.
[Glasgow]	Abbotsinch.
[Gloucester/Cheltenham]	Staverton.
[Humberside]	Kirmington.
[Inverness]	Dalcross.
[Ipswich]	Ipswich.
[Isle of Man]	Ronaldsway.
[Isles of Scilly]	St. Marys.
[Kirkwall]	Grimsetter.
[Leicester]	Leicester East.
[Liverpool]	Speke.
[London Gatwick]	Gatwick.
[" Heathrow]	Heathrow.
[" Stansted]	Stanstead.
[Manchester]	Ringway.
[Newcastle]	Woolsington.
[Norwich]	Horsham St. Faith.
[Oxford]	Kidlington.
[Plymouth]	Roborough.
[Prestwick]	Prestwick.
[Shetlands]	Sumburgh.
[Shoreham]	Shoreham.
[Southampton]	Eastleigh.
[Southend]	Southend.
[Sunderland]	Usworth.
[Swansea]	Fairwood Common.
[Tees-Side]	Middleton St. George.
[Tiree]	Tiree.
[Western Isles]	Benbecula.
[Weston]	Weston super Mare.

Consumer's Association.

Gosfield.

Disused.

Broadwell.
Acaster Malbis.
Akeman Street.
Angle.
Ayr.
Babdown Farm.
Balderton.
Banff.
Bardney.
Bellasize.
Bibury.
Bircotes.
Bottesford.
Brackla.
Bratton.
Breighton.
Brunton.
Bungay.
Burn.
Burscough.
Caister.
Calveley.
Campbeltown.
Carew Cheriton.
Carlisle.
Castle Combe.
Castle Kennedy.
Castletown.
Catfoss.
Charmy Down.
Charter Hall.
Chedburgh.
Chipping Warden.
Church Broughton.
Church Lawford.
Cluntoe.
Condover.
Cottam.
Crail.
Cranage.
Croft.
Dallachy.
Darley Moor.
Davidstow Moor.
Debach.
Debden.
Deenthorpe.
Deopham Green.
Derby.
Docking.
Downham Market.
Drem.
Earls Colne.
East haven.
East Wretham.
Edge Hill.
Eglington.
Errol.
Eshott.
Fairlop.
Fersfield.
Findo Gask.
Firbeck.
Forres.
Foulsham.
Fulbeck.
Full Sutton.
Gamston.
Goxhill.
Grafton Underwood.
Great Sampford.
Grimsby.
Haldon.
Hampstead Norris.
Harlaxton.
Harrowbeer.
Hatston.
Hemswell.
Hinstock.
Hunsdon.
Jurby.
Keevil.
Kemble.
Kingston Bagpuize.
Kirkpatrick.
Knettishall.
Langar.
Lichfield.
Limavady.
Little Snoring.
Longtown.
Manby.
Manorbier.
Matlask.
Maydown.
Melbourne.
Metheringham.
Milfield.
Mullaghmore.
Nutts Corner.
Oakley.
Old Buckenham.
Oulton.
Perranporth.
Rattlesden.
Raydon.
Rednal.
Seething.
Shrewton.
Skeabrae.
Skitton.
Spilsby.
St. Angelo.
St. Eval.
Stracathro.
Swannington.
Tain.
Talbenny.
Tarrent Rushton.
Tealing.
Ternhill.
Tilstock.
Toome.
Turnberry.
Twatt.
Twinwood Farm.
Wellingore.
West Malling.
Wick.
Wigtown.
Windrush.
Winkfield.
Wombleton.
Woodchurch.
Woolfox Lodge.
Worksop.
Wratting Common.
Wymeswold.

Explosive Testing & Storage.

Faldingworth.

Forestry Commission.

Beaulieu.
Holmsley South.
Morpeth.
North Witham.
Okehampton.
Stoney Cross.

Gliding.

Husbands Bosworth.
Kirknewton.
Stormy Down.
Tibenham.

Gravel Extraction.

Bray.
Down Ampney.
Ibsley.
Stanton Harcourt.
Theale.

Helicopters.

Beccles.
Redhill.
Strubby.

H.M. Prisons.

Acklington.
Eastchurch.
Ford.
Lindholme.
Long Kesh.
Maghaberry.
Market Harborough.
Millom.
Stradishall.
Watton.

Home Office.

Aston Down.
Llandow.
Marston Moor.
Moreton-in-Marsh.

Housing.

Battlestead Hill.
Braunstone.
Castle Bromwich.
Croydon.
Donibristle.
Gosport.
Gravesend.
Grove.
Hawkinge.
Heston.
Hornchurch.
Newtownards.
Peterborough.
Skellingthorpe.
Thornaby.
Warmwell.
Westley.
Wolverhampton.
Woodley.
York.

Industry Training Board [Construction]

Bircham Newton.

[Road Transport]

High Ercall.

Industry.

Ashbourne.
Bruntingthorpe.
Bury St. Edmunds.
Cardiff.
Carnaby.
Christchurch.
Dalton.
Desford.
Dumfries.
Dunkeswell.
Evanton.
Gaydon.
Grangemouth.
Greencastle.
Hucknall.
Hutton Cranswick.
Inverness.
Martlesham Heath.
Melton Mowbray.
Mendlesham.
Montrose.
Morton Valence.
North Killingholme.
North Pickenham.
Northweald.
Rackheath.
Rivenhall.
Sherburn-in-Elmet.
Snitterfield.
Tangmere.
West Hartlepool.
Winkleigh.

Institute of Technology.

Cranfield.

Motorways.

Bottisham.
Elsham Wolds.
Stretton.

Museums [Imperial War Museum]

Duxford.

[Royal Air Force]

Hendon.

[Scottish Museum of Flight]

East Fortune.

Nuclear Power Stations[Bradwell Bay]	Bradwell Bay.			
[Chapel Cross]	Annan.			
[Dounreay]	Dounreay.			
Parkland.	Cowdray Park.	Smiths Lawn.	Warwick	
	Kiddington.	Tatton Park.		
Private Flying.	Barrow.	Glatton.	Membury.	Sleap.
	Birch.	Halfpenny Green.	Montford Bridge.	St. Merryn.
	Blackbushe.	Haverfordwest.	Panshangar.	Stapleford Tawney.
	Booker.	Henstridge.	Peterhead.	Sturgate.
	Cark.	Kirkbride.	Port Ellen.	Sywell.
	Connel.	Lasham.	Sandtoft.	Thruxton.
	Denham.	Lashenden.	Scatsta.	Tollerton.
	Doncaster.	Little Staughton.	Shipdham.	Welesbourne Mountford.
	Enstone.	Llandwrog.	Shobdon.	Weston-on-the-Green.
	Fairoaks.	Long Marston.	Sibson.	Winfield.
	Finmere.	Lympne.	Silloth.	Wrexham.
	Fordoun.			
Race Course.	Newmarket.			
Race Tracks.	Podington.	Silverstone.	Snetterton Heath.	
Radio Research Stations.	Anthorn.	Chilbolton.	Croughton.	Inskip.
	Balado Bridge.	Cleave.	Culmhead.	Milltown.
	Barford St. John.	Crimond.	Edzell.	Pershore.
	Blakehill Farm.			
Royal Air Force.	Abingdon.	Coltishall.	Leuchars.	Shawbury.
	Barkston Heath.	Coningsby.	Linton-on-Ouse.	St. Athan
	Benson.	Cosford.	Lossiemouth.	St. Davids.
	Bicester.	Cottesmore.	Lyneham.	St. Mawgan.
	Biggin Hill.	Cranwell.	Manston.	Stornoway.
	Binbrook.	Digby.	Marham.	Swanton Morley.
	Bishops Court.	Dishforth.	Mona.	Swinderby.
	Boscombe Down.	Elvington.	Newton.	Syerston.
	Boulmer.	Finningley.	North Coates.	Upavon.
	Brawdy.	Halton.	North Luffenham.	Valley.
	Brize Norton.	Henlow.	Northolt.	Waddington.
	Catterick.	Honington.	Odiham.	Wattisham.
	Chivenor.	Hullavington.	Pembrey.	West Raynham.
	Church Fenton.	Kinloss.	Portreath.	Wittering.
	Colerne.	Leconfield.	Scampton.	Woodvale.
	Collyweston.	Leeming.	Sealand.	Wyton.
Recreation.	Kirkistown.	Wanborough.		
	Towyn.	Winthorpe.		
	Worcester.			
Royal Navy.	Arbroath.	Merryfield.	Wroughton.	
	Culdrose.	Predannack.	Yeovilton.	
	Lee-on-Solent.			
Rocket Propulsion Establishment.	Westcott.			
Royal Aircraft Establishments.	Aberporth.	Llanbedr.	West Freugh.	
	Farnborough.	Thurleigh.		
Royal Radar Establishment.	Defford.			
Unspecified.	Bridleway Gate.	Horam.	North Leach.	Staplehurst.
	Bush Barn.	Horne.	Penkridge.	Stoke Orchard.
	Chetwynd.	Langford Lodge.	Penshurst.	Stratford.
	Henley.	Little Sutton.	Sawbridgeworth.	Templeton.
	High Haldon.	Little Walden.	Shellingford.	Tempsford.
	Hockley Heath.	Matching.	Shepherds Grove.	Watchfield.
	Honeybourne.	Metfield.	Southam.	Woodhall Spa.
	Honiley.			
United States Airforces Europe.	Alconbury.	Feltwell.	Mildenhall.	Upwood.
	Bentwaters.	Greenham Common.	Molesworth.	Welford.
	Burtonwood.	Lakenheath.	Sculthorpe.	Wethersfield.
	Chelveston.	Little Rissington.	Upper Heyford.	Woodbridge.
	Fairford.			
United States Navy.	Machrihanish.			

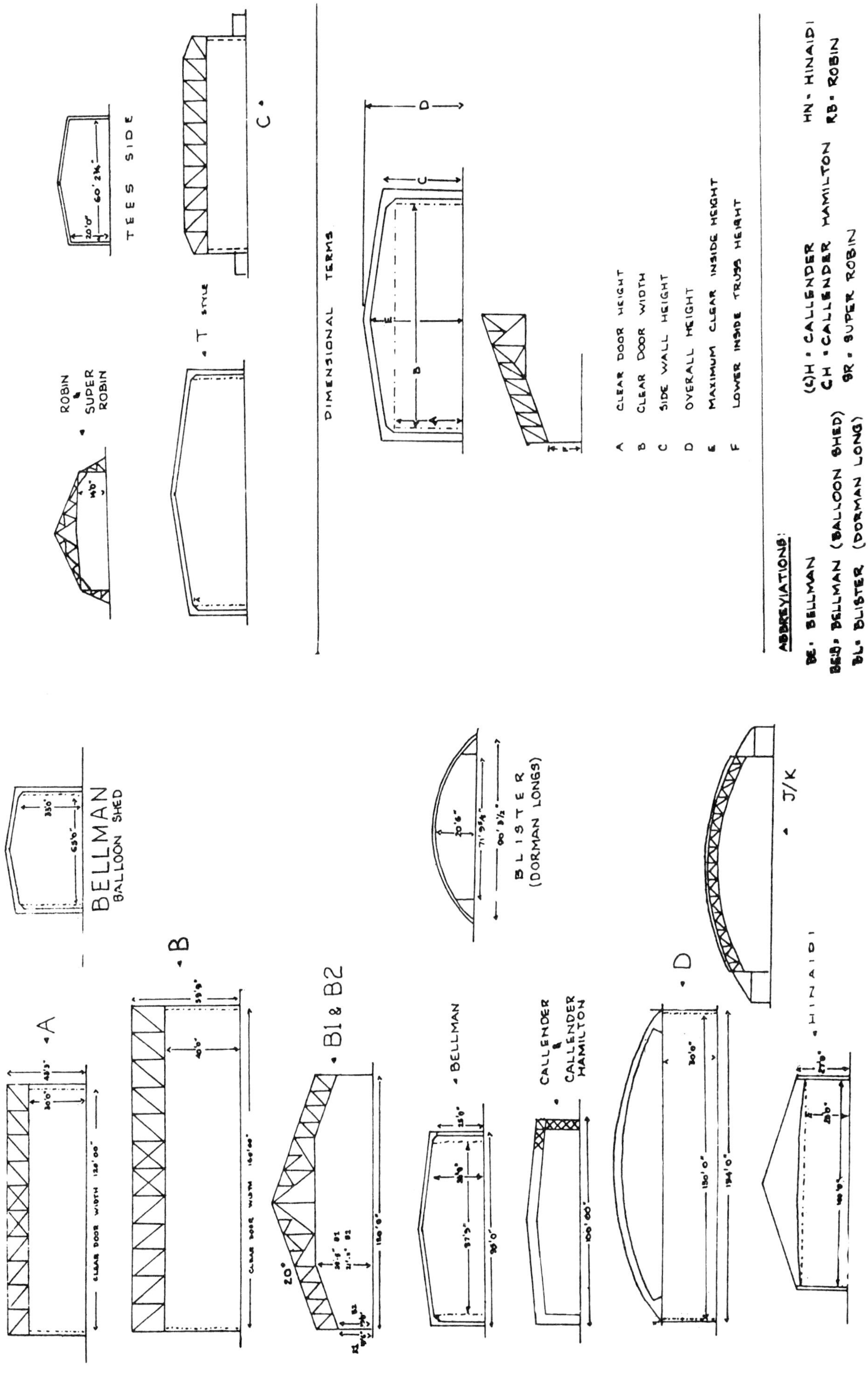
A
CLEAR DOOR WIDTH 120'00"
B
CLEAR DOOR WIDTH 150'00"
B1 & B2
20°
BELLMAN
CALLENDER
&
CALLENDER
HAMILTON
D
HINAIDI
BELLMAN
BALLOON SHED
BLISTER
(DORMAN LONGS)
J/K
ROBIN
&
SUPER
ROBIN
T STYLE
TEES SIDE
C
DIMENSIONAL TERMS
A CLEAR DOOR HEIGHT
B CLEAR DOOR WIDTH
C SIDE WALL HEIGHT
D OVERALL HEIGHT
E MAXIMUM CLEAR INSIDE HEIGHT
F LOWER INSIDE TRUSS HEIGHT
ABBREVIATIONS:
BE · BELLMAN
BE(S) · BELLMAN (BALLOON SHED)
BL · BLISTER (DORMAN LONG)
WK · WORKSHOP
(C)H · CALLENDER
CH · CALLENDER HAMILTON
SR · SUPER ROBIN
TS · TEES-SIDE
HN · HINAIDI
RB · ROBIN

HANGAR SPECIFICATIONS

HANGAR TYPE	ARRANGEMENT DRAWING No.	WEIGHT (TONS) with STEEL DOORS	WEIGHT (TONS) with CANVAS DOORS	HEIGHT OVERALL	CLEAR DOOR HEIGHT	SIDE WALL HEIGHT	MAXIMUM CLEAR INSIDE HEIGHT	LOWER INSIDE TRUSS HEIGHT	WIDTH OVERALL	CLEAR DOOR WIDTH	BAY WIDTH	No. OF BAYS	LENGTH OVERALL
A	19/24A	-	-	43'3"	30'0"	43'3"	30'0"	-	122'3"	120'0"	38'4"	-	250'0"
B	4714/41	-	-	53'9"	40'0"	53'9"	40'0"	-	162'7"	160'0"	30'4"	-	121'4"
B1	11776/42	163	-	52'1"	27'0"	28'5"	27'0"	19'6"	120'0"	114'6"	15'3"	15	227'6"
B2	11776/42	163	-	45'7"	20'6"	21'11"	20'6"	19'0"	120'0"	114'6"	15'2"	15	227'6"
* BE	8349/37	60	45	33'9"	25'0"	26'0"		-	95'0"	87'9"	12'6"	14	175'0"
* BE:B	7897/37	-	-	41'0"	33'0"	33'10"		-		63'0"			87'6"
* BL	4630/42	12¾	-	22'2"	20'6"	-	20'6"	9'2"	90'3½"	71'8⅝"	-	-	45'0"
C	2029/34	600		52'4"	30'0" / 35'0"	30'0"	30'0" / 35'0"		182'8"	180'0"	28'0"	variable	
* (C)H	6633/37	90	-	35'5¼"	25'0"	30'0"		-	100'0"	90'0"	20'0"	9	185'0"
* CH	17346/40	90	-	27'3½"	17'0"	22'7"		-	100'0"	90'0"	20'0"	9	185'0"
D	2312 / 2313 /36	205	-	52'3"	30'0"	30'0		-	154'0"	150'0"	20'0"	15	301'8"
* HN	1136 /27	220	-	45'3"	25'0"	27'0"				100'0"	13'4"	18	240'0"
J/K	3084/39			48'10"	30'0"	31'0"	30'0"	20'0"	151'2"	150'0"	16'8"	18	300'0"
* RB	2204/41			24'0"	14'0"	14'0"	14'0"	-	56'7"	44'0"	12'6"	5	62'6"
* SR	2243/41	24	-	25'0"	14'0"	14'0"	14'0"	-	72.7"	60'0"	12'0"	6	72'0"
T1	7541/41	105	-	31'1"	19'0"	23'0"		-	97'2"	90'0"	12'6"	14	175'0"
T1	7557/41	115	-	37'1"	25'0"	29'0"		-	97'2"	90'0"	12'6"	14	175'0"
T(FB)	11916/42	234½	-	45'5 9/32"	35'0"	35'5"	35'0"	-	120'10⅝"	114'0⅜"	10'0"	24	240'0"
T2	8254/40	178	-	39'0"	25'0"	29'0"		-	120'10"	113'0"	10'5"	23	239'7"
T2	6304/42	c.187	-	39'0 7/32"	25'0"	29'0"		-	120'10"	113'6"	10'5"	26	270'10"
T2	3653/42	178½	-	39'0 7/32"	25'0"	29'0"		-	120'10"	113'6"	10'5"	23	239'7"
T2	3669/42	124½	-	39'0 7/32"	25'0"	29'0"		-	120'10"	113'6"	10'5"	14	145'10"
T2	3670/42	110¼	-	39'0 7/32"	25'0"	29'0"		-	120'10"	113'6"	10'5"	15	155'8"
T3	3505/42	49¾	-	29'1½"	19'0"	23'0"		-	73'5⅞"	66'0"	12'6"	6	75'0"
* TS	12919/40	26½	-	26'3"	20'0"	21'2½"		-	62'4¾"	60'2¾"			50'0"
* TS	3621/41		-	26'3"	20'0"	21'2½"		-	62'4¾"	60'2¾"			70'0"
* WK	74/42		-		19'0"				"	113'6"	10.5'	23	240'0"

GUARD HOUSE

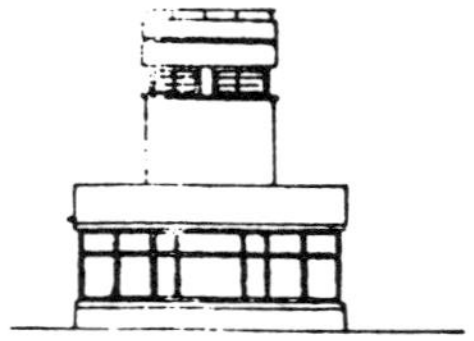
CONTROL TOWER

STATION HEADQUARTERS

AIRMEN'S MESS

MAYCRETE HUT

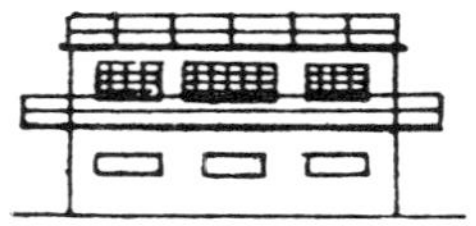
CONTROL TOWER

NISSEN HUT

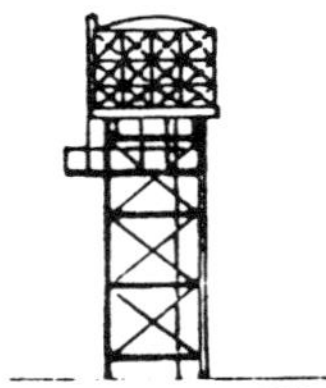
BRAITHWAITE WATER TOWER

APPENDIX 'J'. CHRONOLOGICAL CHART OF OPENING/CLOSING OF BRITISH AIRFIELDS.

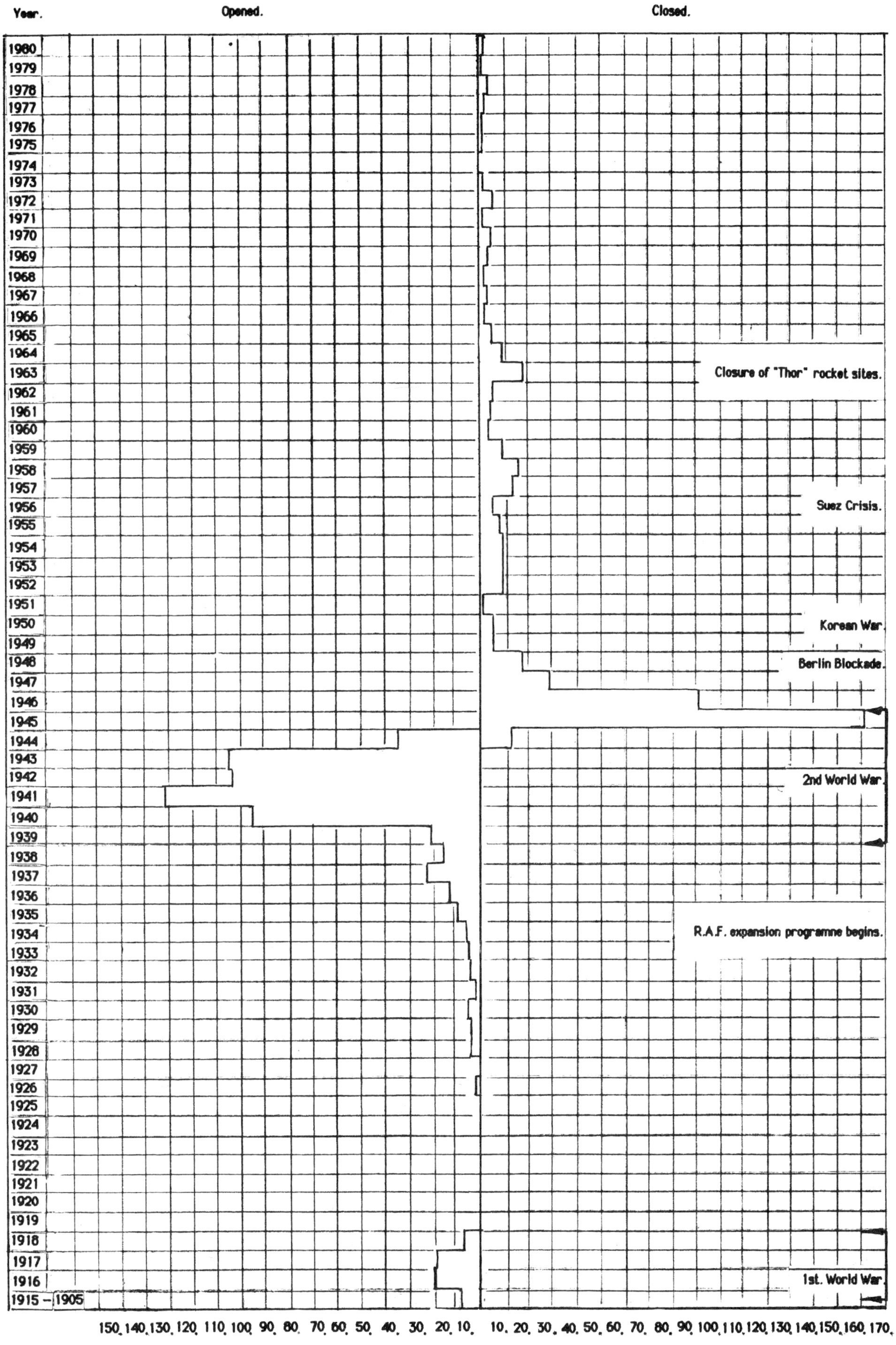

APPENDIX 'K'. AIRCRAFT ESTABLISHMENT OF COASTAL COMMAND-DECEMBER 1944.

UNIT	STATION.	AIRCRAFT.	NUMBER.
119 Sqdn.	Bircham Newton.	Albacore	15.
1693 Flt.	Sumburgh.	Anson.	6.
236 Sqdn.	North Coates.	Beaufighter X.	20.
254 Sqdn.	North Coates.	Beaufighter X.	20.
114 Sqdn.	Dallachy.	Beaufighter X.	20.
404 Sqdn.	Dallachy.	Beaufighter X.	20.
455 Sqdn.	Dallachy.	Beaufighter X.	20.
489 Sqdn.	Dallachy.	Beaufighter X.	20.
58 Sqdn.	Stornoway.	Halifax 11 SB.	15.
502 Sqdn.	Stornoway.	Halifax 11 SB.	15.
53 Sqdn.	Ballykelly.	Liberator 1V SG.	15.
59 Sqdn.	Ballykelly.	Liberator 1V SG.	15.
120 Sqdn.	Ballykelly.	Liberator V SG.	15.
86 Sqdn.	Tain.	Liberator 111 PA & V SG.	15.
311[Czech]Sqdn.	Tain.	Liberator V SF.	15.
206 Sqdn.	Leuchars.	Liberator V SG.	15.
547 Sqdn.	Leuchars.	Liberator V1 SG.	15.
547 Sqdn.	Leuchars.	Liberator V1 SG.	15.
220 Sqdn.	Lagens.	Liberator V1 SG.	8.
		Fortress 111.	7.
269 Sqdn.	Lagens.	Warwick ASR 1.	6.
224 Sqdn.	Milltown.	Liberator V1 SG.	15.
282 Sqdn.	St. Eval.	Warwick ASR 1.	10.
		Mosquito XV111.	8.
179 Sqdn.	St. Eval.	Warwick V.	15.
235 Sqdn.	Banff.	Mosquito V1.	20.
333[Norwegian]Sqdn.	Banff.	Mosquito V1.	20.
143 Sqdn.	Banff.	Mosquito V1.	16.
524 Sqdn.	Langham.	Wellington X1V.	20.
612 Sqdn.	Langham.	Wellington X1V.	15.
14 Sqdn.	Chivenor.	Wellington X1V.	15.
36 Sqdn.	Chivenor.	Wellington X1V.	15.
407 Sqdn.	Chivenor.	Wellington X1V.	15.
172 Sqdn.	Limavady.	Wellington X1V.	15.
304[Polish]Sqdn.	Benbecula.	Wellington X1V.	15.
10[RAAF]Sqdn.	Mount Batten.	Sunderland 111.	12.
162[RCAF]Sqdn.	Reykjavik.	Canso A.	15.
201 Sqdn.	Castle Archdale.	Sunderland 111.	12.
423 [RCAF]Sqdn.	Castle Archdale.	Sunderland 111.	12.
202 Sqdn.	Castle Archdale.	Catalina 1V.	16.
210 Sqdn.	Sullom Voe.	Catalina 1V.	12.
330[Norwegian]Sqdn.	Sullom Voe.	Sunderland 111.	9.
228 Sqdn.	Pembroke Dock.	Sunderland 111.	12.
461[RAAF]Sqdn.	Pembroke Dock.	Sunderland 111.	12.
333[Norwegian]Sqdn.	Leuchars.	Catalina 1B.	3.
279 Sqdn.	Thornaby.	Warwick ASR 1.	20.
		Hurricane 11C.	8.
280 Sqdn.	Beccles.	Warwick ASR 1.	24.
281 Sqdn.	Tiree.	Warwick ASR 1.	12.
		Sea Otter.	6.
540 Sqdn.	Benson.	Mosquito XV1.	20.
541 Sqdn.	Benson.	Spitfire X1.	20.
542 Sqdn.	Benson.	Spitfire X1.	20.
544 Sqdn.	Benson.	Mosquito XV1.	20.
103 [USNAC]Sqdn.	Dunkeswell.	PB4Y-1.	13.
105 [USNAC]Sqdn.	Dunkeswell.	PB4y-1.	20.
110 [USNAC]Sqdn.	Dunkeswell.	PB4Y-1.	15.
114 [USNAC]Sqdn.	Dunkeswell.	PB4Y-1.	13.
517 Sqdn.	Brawdy.	Halifax V.	13.
518 Sqdn.	Tiree.	Halifax V.	22.
519 Sqdn.	Wick.	Fortress 11.	12.
		Spitfire.	3.
521 Sqdn.	Langham.	Various.	9
1402 Met Flt.	Ballyhalbert.	Various.	9.
3 School of G.R.	Squires Gate.	Anson.	61.
School of A.S.R.	Squires Gate.	Anson.	4.
1674 H.C.U.	Aldergrove.	Liberator.	11.
		Halifax.	4.
		Various.	14.
4 OTU.	Alness.	Sunderland.	44.
5 OTU.	Turnberry.	Various.	52.
6 OTU.	Siloth.	Various.	42.
8 OTU.	Dyce.	Various.	47.
131 OTU.	Killadeas.	Various.	57.
132 OTU.	East Fortune.	Various.	86.
302 OTU.	Oban.	Various.	31.
			1373.

APPENDIX L. SELECTED BIBLIOGRAPHY.

Ashworth, C.	Action Stations 5 : Military Airfields of the South-West, Patrick Stephens, Cambridge, 1982.
Ashworth, C.	Action Stations 9 : Military Airfields of the Central South & South East, Patrick Stephens, Cambridge, 1985.
Blake, R.N.E.	Disused Airfields as a Planning Resource, Trent Papers in Planning No.78/8, Trent Polytechnic, Nottingham, 1978.
Blake, R.N.E., Hodgson, M., & Taylor, W.J.	The Airfields of Lincolnshire since 1912, Midland Counties Publications, Earl Shilton, 1984.
Bowyer, C.	Royal Air Force Handbook 1939-1945, Ian Allen , London 1984.
Bowyer, M.J.F.	Action Stations 1 : Military Airfields of East Anglia, Patrick Stephens, Cambridge, 1979.
Bowyer, M.J.F.	Action Stations 6 : Military Airfields of the Cotswolds & the Central Midlands Patrick Stephens, Cambridge, 1983
Butler, P.H.	British Isles Airfield Guide, Merseyside Aviation Society, Liverpool, 1978.
Ferguson, A.P.	A History of R.A.F. Woodvale, Merseyside Aviation Society Liverpool 1974.
Ferguson, A.P.	A History of R.A.F. Shawbury, Merseyside Aviation Society Liverpool 1974.
Freeman, R.A.	The Mighty Eighth. A History of the U.S. 8th. Army Air Force, MacDonald & Janes, London, 1970.
Freeman, R.A.	Airfields of the Eighth Then & Now, After the Battle Magazine, London, 1978.
Gibson, M.L.	Aviation in Northamptonshire, Northamptonshire Libraries, Northampton, 1982.
Halley, J.J.	The Squadrons of the R.A.F., Air Britain[Historians]Ltd., Tonbridge, 1980.
Halpenny, B.B.	Action Stations 2: Military Airfields of Lincolnshire & the East Midlands, Patrick Stephens, Cambridge, 1981.
Halpenny, B.B.	Action Stations 4: Military Airfields of Yorkshire, Patrick Stephens, Cambridge, 1982.
Halpenny, B.B.	Action Stations 8: Military Airfields of Greater London, Patrick Stephens, Cambridge, 1984.
Finn, S.	Lincolnshire Air War 1939-1945, Aero Litho Co[Lincoln]Ltd., Lincoln 1973.
Hancock, T.N.	Bomber County-A History of the Royal Air Force in Lincolnshire, Lincolnshire Library Service, Lincoln 1978.
Mercer, P.S.	British Military Airfields, Jackson Publications, Loughborough, 1981.
Osborne, M.B.	A Brief History of R.A.F. Peterborough[Westwood Farm], Peterborough Educational Development Centre, Peterborough, 1983.
Rapier, B.J.	White Rose Base, Aero Litho Co[Lincoln]Ltd., Lincoln, 1972.
Rennison, J.	Wings Over Rutland, Rutland Local History Society, Oakham, 1980.
Rhodes, E.	The Wash in Wartime, Enthusiasts Publications, Sherington, 1980.
Rust, K.C.	The 9th. Air Force in World War 11, Aero Publishers, Fallbrook, 1967.
Smith, D.J.	Action Stations 3 : Military Airfields of Wales & the North West, Patrick Stephens, Cambridge, 1981.
Smith, D.J.	Action Stations 7 : Military Airfields of Scotland, the North-East & Northern Ireland, Patrick Stephens, Cambridge, 1983.
Sturtivant, R.	The Squadrons of the Fleet Air Arm, Air Britain[Historians]Ltd., Tonbridge, 1984.
Teague, D.C.	Aviation in South West Britain1909-1979, Baron Jay, Plymouth, 1982.
Teague, D.C. & White, P.R.	A Guide to the Airfields of South Western England, Baron Jay, Plymouth, 1980.
Willard, R.H., S/Sgt.	Installations & U.S.A.A.F. Combat Units in the United Kingdom 1942-1945, H.Q. 3rd. U.S.A.F.E., Mildenhall, 1975.
Periodicals, the Files of.	After the Battle, Aeromilitaria, Aeroplane, Air International, Air Pictorial, Aviation News, Flypast.
Public Record Office Documents.	Air10/3836, Air10/3961, Air10/4039, Air15/737, Air20/2022 & Air20/2023.

APPENDIX 'M' ABBREVIATIONS.

AA.	Anti Aircraft.
AAC.	Anti Aircraft Co-Operation.
A&AEE.	Aircraft & Armament Experimental Establishment.
AFU.	Advanced Flying Unit. [P]=Pilot, [O]=Observer.
AI.	Air Interception.
ASL.	Above sea level.
ASR.	Air Sea Rescue.
ATA.	Air Transport Auxiliary.
ATC.	Air Transport Command.
BAT.	Blind Approach Training.
B&CD.	Belfast & County Down.
BNC.	Belfast & Northern Counties.
CLC.	Cheshire Lines Committee.
DAJT.	Dundee & Arbroath Joint.
EFTS.	Elementary Flying Training School.
EVT.	Extra Vocational Training.
FN.	Fraser Nash.
FPP.	Ferry Pilots' Pool.
GNI.	Great Nothern of Ireland.
GNS.	Great North of Scotland.
GE.	Great Eastern.
GR.	General Reconnaissance.
GWR.	Great Western Railway.
HCU.	Heavy Conversion Unit.
LMS.	London Midland Scottish Railway.
LNER.	London North Eastern Railway.
M&GN.	Midland & Great Northern Joint.
MAP.	Ministry of Aircraft Production.
MNCI.	Midland Northern Counties of Ireland.
MU.	Maintenance Unit.
NB.	North British.
OS.	Ordnance Survey.
OTU.	Operational Training Unit.
PFF.	Pathfinder Force.
PRDU.	Photographic Reconnaissance Development Unit.
QDM.	Q-code[Degrees Magnetic]
RAF.	Royal Air Force.
RCAF.	Royal Canadian Air Force.
RAAF.	Royal Australian Air Force.
RNZAF.	Royal New Zealand Air Force.
RN.	Royal Navy.
S&D.	Stockton & Darlington Joint.
SD.	Special Duties.
SE.	Single engine.
SE&C.	South Eastern & Chatham.
SL&NC.	Sligo, Leitrim & Northern Counties.
SR	Southern Railway.
TE.	Twin engine.
WRNS.	Womans Royal Navy Service.
USAAF.	United States Army Air Force.
USSATAF.	United States Strategic Air Force.
WAAF.	Womans Auxiliary Air Force.

LANDING AREA.	AIRFIELD NAME.		
Asphalt & wood chippings.	Grafton Underwood.		
Asphalt.	Biggin Hill.	Defford.	Hunsdon.
	Castletown.	Elvington.	Kinnel.
	Catterick.	Exeter.	Portreath.
	Cosford.	Harrowbeer.	Woodvale.
	Culmhead.		
Asphalt[308-Sommerfeld track]	Northalt.		
Bitumen & Sand.	Benbecula.	Squires Gate.	
	Port Ellen.	Woodbridge.	
Bitumen, special.	Carnaby.		
Concrete & asphalt.	Alconbury.	Fairford.	Pershore.
	Bovingdon.	Fairlop.	Riccall.
	Coningsby.		
Concrete & Tarmac with grass extension.	Manston.	Newtownards.	
Concrete & tarmac.	Binbrook.	Hardwick.	Ringway.
	Birch.	Haverfordwest.	Rivenhall.
	Boreham.	Hemswell.	Sandtoft.
	Burn.	Hinton in the Hedges.	Scampton.
	Chalgrove.	Hixon.	Shobdon.
	Chelveston.	Kelstern.	Skellingthorpe.
	Church Broughton.	Kinloss.	Spanhoe.
	Church Fenton.	Kirkbride.	St. Eval.
	Cluntoe.	Kirmington.	Stanstead.
	Debach.	Langar.	Staverton.
	Debden.	Leeming.	Strubby.
	Deopham Green.	Leiston.	Sudbury.
	Dishforth.	Limavady.	Talbenny.
	Dumfries.	Lindholme.	Tholthorpe.
	Dunholme Lodge.	Little Staughton.	Tibenham.
	Edge Hill.	Lossiemouth.	Upottery.
	Filton.	Market Harborough.	Upwood.
	Finningley.	Melbourne.	Waddington.
	Fiskerton.	Mendlesham.	Warton.
	Folkingham.	Milltown.	Wattisham.
	Fulbeck.	Moreton in Marsh.	Wellesbourne Mountford.
	Full Sutton.	North Pickenham.	West Raynham.
	Gamston.	Pocklington.	Winkleigh.
	Greenham Common.	Podington.	Wormingford.
	Grimsby.	Ramsbury.	York.
	Hampstead Norris.	Rattlesden.	
Concrete & wood chippings.	Aldermaston.	Gosfield.	Peplow.
	Ashbourne.	Great Ashfield.	Poulton.
	Barkston Heath.	Great Dunmow.	Ridgewell.
	Benson.	Greencastle.	Silverstone.
	Bitteswell.	Halesworth.	Snetterton Heath.
	Blackbushe.	Hawarden.	St. Davids.
	Brawdy.	Hethal.	Steeple Morden.
	Brize Norton.	Husbands Bosworth.	Stoney Cross.
	Broadwell.	Keevil.	Tarrant Rushton.
	Bruntingthorpe.	Knettishall.	Tatenhill.
	Cardiff.	Lasham.	Tealing.
	Catfoss.	Leuchars.	Templeton.
	Cheddington.	Little Walden.	Thorpe Abbots.
	Chipping Ongar.	Ludford Magna.	Thruxton.
	Condover.	Manby.	Tollerton.
	Cottam.	Matching.	Toome.
	Darley Moor.	Membury.	Welford.
	Deenthorpe.	Metfield.	Wendling.
	Dunsfold.	Milfield.	Weston Zoyland.
	Faldingworth.	Odiham.	Wickenby.
	Finmere.	Old Buckenham.	Wratting Common.
	Framlingham.		
Concrete covered with asphalt.	Attlebridge.	Dunkeswell.	Mullaghmore.
	Bassingbourn.	Kemble.	Sturgate.
	Burtonwood.	Kimbolton.	Thurleigh.
	Chivener.		
Concrete covered with bitumen.	Merryfield.		

Concrete covered with tarmac.
Brough.
Carew Cheriton.
Castle Kennedy.
Church Lawford.
Dyce.
Gaydon.
Great Orton.
Halfpenny Green.
Hullavington.
Langham.
Little Rissington.
Ludham.
Lyneham.
Nuthampstead.
Oakington.
Polebrook.
Snitterfield.
Ternhill.
Turnberry.
Usworth.
Waterbeach.
Wheaton Aston.

Concrete, tarmac & wood chippings.
Boxted.
Bungay.
Bury-St-Edmunds.
Chilbolton.
Earls Colne.
Pembrey.

Concrete, wood & rubber chippings.
Twinwood Farm.

Concrete.
Abingdon.
Acaster Malbis.
Aldergrove.
Ballykelly.
Banff.
Bardney.
Belfast.
Bentwaters.
Bishops Court.
Bottesford.
Bourn.
Calveley.
Castle Bromwich.
Castle Donnington.
Chedburgh.
Chipping Warden.
Cranfield.
Dalcross.
Dallachy.
Davidstow Moor.
Down Ampney.
Downham Market.
Driffield.
East Kirkby.
East Moor.
Edzell.
Elmdon.
Elsham Wolds.
Enstone.
Farnborough.
Fersfield.
Fordoun.
Gransden Lodge.
Graveley.
Great Massingham.
Grove.
Harrington.
Harwell.
High Ercall.
Honeybourne.
Horham.
Horsham-St-Faith.
Hurn.
Kenley.
Lavenham.
Leconfield.
Leicester East.
Linton-on-Ouse.
Lissett.
Little Horwood.
Little Snoring.
Llanbedr.
Longtown.
Maghaberry.
Marston Moor.
Maydown.
Melton Mowbray.
Mepal.
Metheringham.
Methwold.
Mildenhall.
Mona.
Moreton Valence.
Mount Farm.
North Creake.
North Killingholme.
North Luffenham.
North Witham.
Nuneaton.
Oakley.
Ossington.
Oulton.
Prestwick.
Rackheath.
Raydon.
Seething.
Seighford.
Shepherds Grove.
Sherburn-in-Elmet.
Silloth.
Sleap.
Spilsby.
St. Angelo.
St. Mawgan.
Stradishall.
Swannington.
Swinderby.
Syerston.
Tain.
Tangmere.
Tempsford.
Thornaby.
Thorney Island.
Tilstock.
Tiree.
Topcliffe.
Tuddenham.
Turnhouse.
Turweston.
Upper Heyford.
Watton.
Westcott.
Wethersfield.
Wigsley.
Wigtown.
Wing.
Winthorpe.
Witchford.
Wombleton.
Woodhall Spa.
Worksop.
Wrexham.
Wroughton.
Wymeswold.
Wyton.

Concrete[NW-SE grass]
North Coates.

Concrete[part]covered with tarmac.
Madley.

Grass.
Abbots Bromley.
Aberporth.
Akeman Street.
Alton Barnes.
Andover.
Baginton.
Battlestead Hill.
Bellasize.
Bicester.
Bircotes.
Bodney.
Bodorgan.
Booker.
Brackla.
Bratton.
Braunstone.
Bray.
Bridleway Gate.
Burnfoot.
Bush Barn.
Caister.
Cambridge.
Cammeringham.
Campbeltown.
Carlisle.
Caxton Gibbet.
Charlton Horethorne.
Chetwynd.
Cleave.
Clyffe Pypard.
Coleby Grange.
Collyweston.
Cowdray Park.
Croughton.
Croydon.
Denham.
Denton.
Derby.
Desford.
Detling.
Digby.
Docking.
Donna Nook.
Drem.
Duxford.
East Wretham.
Eastchurch.
Eastleigh.
Elgin.
Fairoaks.
Feltwell.
Firebeck.
Forres.
Friston.
Gravesend.
Haldon.
Halton.
Harlaxton.
Hatfield.
Hawkinge.
Henley.
Heston.
Hockley Heath.
Hornchurch.
Hucknall.
Inverness.
Ipswich.
Kelmscott.
Kiddington.
Kirkpatrick.
Kirton-in-Lindsey.
Little Sutton.
Lympne.
Macmerry.
Manorbier.
Matlask.
Netheravon.
Newmarket.
Newton.
Northleach.
Oaklands Hill.
Okehampton.
Old Sarum.
Orston.
Panshangar.
Papplewick Moor.
Penkridge.
Penrhos.
Penshurst.
Perth.
Peterborough.
Roborough.
Shellingford.
Shoreham.
Shrewton.
Sibson.
Smiths Lawn.
Snailwell.
Southam.
Southend.
St. Marys.
Stapleford Tawney.
Stoke Orchard.
Stormy Down.
Stracathro.
Swanton Morley.
Sywell.
Tatton Park.
Theale.
Towyn.
Treligga.
Wanborough.
Warmwell.
Warwick.
Watchfield.
Wellingore.
West Hartlepool.
Westhampnett.
Westley.
Whitefield.
Winkfield.
Wittering.
Wolverhampton.
Woodley.
Woolsington.
Worcester.
Worthy Down.
Zeals.

Grass[051-231 steel matting]	Dunino.		
Grass[1100yds. of E-W asphalt]	Cranwell.		
Grass[240-concrete]	Boscombe Down.		
Grass[240-Sommerfeld Track]	Upavon.		
Grass[280-steel matting]	Honington.		
Grass[310-tarmac]	Sealand.		
Grass[987yds. of No.3 strip Sommerfeld Track]	Doncaster.		
Grass[NNW-SSE & NE-SW tarmac]	Gosport.		
Hardcore & concrete.	Balado Bridge.		
Hardcore & tarmac	Charter Hall.	East Fortune.	Millom.
Hardcore tarmac & wood chippings.	Boulmer.		
Hardcore.	Eshott.		
Screeded finish.	Eye.		
Steel Matting[Army track]	Kidlington.	Redhill.	
Steel Matting[Army track] E-W grass.	Southrop.		
Steel matting[Army track] NW-SE grass.	Gatwick.		
Steel Matting[BRC netting track]	Bircham Newton.		
Steel Matting[BRC netting track] 245-concrete & grass.	Christchurch.		
Steel Matting[E-W=American S-N=British]	Lymington.		
Steel Matting[NE-SW grass]	Sutton Bridge.		
Steel Matting[Sommerfeld Track]	Appledram. Bibury. Bisterne. Bognor. Bolt Head. Bramcote. Brenzett. Chailey. Chipping Norton. Coltishall. Coolham. Deanland. Dundonald.	Findow Gask. Fowlmere. Funtington. Great Sampford. Henlow. Hinstock. Horne. Lashenden. Long Newnton. Lydd. Merston. Middle Wallop. Montrose.	Needs Oar Point. New Romney. Newchurch. Overton Heath. Sawbridgeworth. Selsey. South Cerney. Staplehurst. Swingfield. West Malling. Weston-on-the-Green. Windrush. Yatesbury.
Steel Matting[Sommerfeld Track] NE-SW grass.	Castle Combe.	Spittlegate.	
Steel Matting[Sommerfeld Track] NW-SE grass.	Babdown Farm.	Bottisham.	
Steel Matting[U.S.steel planking]	Cranage. Headcorn.	High Haldon. Kingston Bagpuize.	
Steel Matting[U.S. steel planking & Sommerfeld Track]	Ashford. Kingsnorth.	Winkton. Woodchurch.	
Tarmac & asphalt.	Acklington. Ayr.	Bradwell Bay. Langford Lodge.	
Tarmac & rubber chippings.	Angle. Atcham.	Montford Bridge.	
Tarmac & sealed coat.	Fairwood Common.		
Tarmac & wood chippings.	Ballyhalbert. Desborough. Errol.	Ford. Foulsham.	Glatton. North Weald.
Tarmac, concrete & Sommerfeld Track.	St. Athan.		

Tarmac.	Andreas. Andrews Field. Balderton. Barrow. Beaulieu. Blakehill Farm. Blyton. Breighton. Brunton. Burscough. Cark. Castle Camps. Charmy Down. Chedworth. Colerne. Connel. Cottesmore. Crail. Croft. Crosby-on-Eden. Dale. Dalton. Donibristle. East Haven. Eglington. Evanton. Fearn. Fraserborough. Goxhill.	Grangemouth. Hatston. Hendon. Henstridge. Hibaldstow. Holme. Holmsley South. Honiley. Hooton Park. Hutton Cranswick. Ibsley. Inskip. Jurby. Kirkistown. Kirknewton. Lichfield. Llandow. Llandwrog. Long Kesh. Long Marston. Lulsgate Bottom. Middleton St. George. Morepeth. Nutts Corner. Ouston. Perranporth. Perton. Peterhead. Predannack.	Rednal. Rhoose. Ronaldsway. Rufforth. Saltby. Scatsta. Scorton. Shawbury. Shipdham. Skeabrea. Skipton-on-Swale. Skitton. Snaith. Speke. St. Merryn. Stanton Harcourt. Stornoway. Stratford. Stretton. Sumburgh. Twatt. Valley. Warboys. West Freugh. Weston Super Mare. Wick. Winfield. Woolfox Lodge. Yeovilton.
Under construction.	Anthorn. Crimond. Culdrose. Culham.	Dounreay. Grimsetter. Heathrow.	
Under re-construction.	Abbotsinch. Lakenheath.	Marham. Sculthorpe.	
Unspecified hard surface.	Annan. Arbroath. Aston Down. Barford St. John. Beccles.	Kingscliffe. Lee-on-Solent. Machrihanish. Martlesham Heath. Molesworth.	

INDEX.

AIRFIELDS.

FORMATIONS.

R.A.F.

R.C.A.F.

AILWAY STATIONS.

G.W.R.

L.M.S.